SPEAKING
the TRUTH
in LOVE

SPEAKING THE TRUTH IN LOVE

THE THEOLOGY OF
JOHN M. FRAME

Edited by
JOHN J. HUGHES

PUBLISHING
P.O. BOX 817 • PHILLIPSBURG • NEW JERSEY 08865-0817

Typesetting by Bits & Bytes, Inc. and P&R Publishing

General Editor: John J. Hughes

Printed in the United States of America

Library of Congress Cataloging-in-Publication Data

Speaking the truth in love : the theology of John M. Frame / edited by John J. Hughes.
   p. cm.
 Includes bibliographical references and indexes.
 ISBN 978-1-59638-164-3 (cloth)
 1. Frame, John M., 1939- 2. Reformed Church--Doctrines. 3. Theology, Doctrinal. I. Hughes, John J., 1947-
 BX9419.F73S64 2009
 230'.42092--dc22

2009034141

In Memory of
Professor John Murray
1898–1975

CONTENTS

A Note to the Reader

John J. Hughes

THIS IS AN UNUSUAL festschrift for several reasons. As John Frame explains in the Preface, he and I have worked together to craft this book so that it will serve as an in-depth introduction to and exploration of all the major categories of his theology.[1] Therefore, we have added a number of features to make the festschrift more informative, user-friendly, and to provide greater access to John's writings. This "Note to the Reader" explains some of these features.

Abbreviations. To avoid endless repetition in footnotes and articles, and to conserve space, we created abbreviations for all of John's major works. These abbreviations are listed in the Abbreviations section below.

Appendices. John created two directory-like appendices. One correlates his major ideas with his key discussions of them; the other does the same thing for the major triads John uses.

Annotated Bibliography. This includes all the books, articles, written sermons, course materials, and audio and video materials John has produced to date. John arranged these publications by topic to make the Bib-

---

1. John suggested almost all the authors and topics for this festschrift and designed the book's basic structure, which is carried through in the Bibliography, Glossary, and Recommended Resources.

liography more useful, and he annotated many entries. Occasionally, one title will be included under more than one topical designation.[2]

Glossary. John created this to define terms he has invented, terms to which he has attached unusual definitions, and terms that have a special prominence in his writings. The Glossary uses the same topical headings used in the Bibliography, but omits topics for which there are no distinctive terms to be defined. The Glossary also includes references to places in John's books and articles where he discusses these concepts.

Index of Subjects. As we received contributions to the festschrift, John read each one and created a two-level Index of Subjects. This index will help readers locate discussions of all the major topics in this book.

Recommended Resources. This is a reading program designed for persons who wish to acquaint themselves with John's works. In it, John uses the same topical structure as found in the Bibliography, Glossary, and the festschrift itself. Titles are not listed alphabetically but in John's suggested order for study—most basic to more detailed.

---

2. For a year-by-year bibliography, see http://www.frame-poythress.org. Also see John's chapter "My Books: Their Genesis and Main Ideas" in this festschrift.

FOREWORD

J. I. PACKER

A THOUGHTFUL PERSON might well wonder whether I have enough in common with John Frame to make me a suitable introducer of this very elaborate celebration of his life's work.

For who am I? A Brit by extraction, tall, skinny, and quiet, drawn in midlife to cross the Atlantic and teach at Regent College, a newish, small, and at that time nonstandard evangelical school in western Canada. An Anglican clergyman who nurses both a headache and a heartache regarding his churchly heritage—one who has often looked over the fence to see how his Presbyterian buddies are getting along, yet has never jumped ship denominationally or let himself be drawn into the intensities of Reformed in-house debates. A friendly moth, flitting around the heady and somewhat explosive world of the two Westminsters, fiercely intellectualist, combatively confessional, and censorious in its apologetics as that world is. A five-point Calvinist who patently puts his generic evangelical identity ahead of both his specifically Anglican and his specifically Reformed commitment. A historically oriented pietist who seeks to map the flow of the Christian mainstream, who to that end talks to Roman Catholics and Orthodox, and who periodically ends up in hot water with other evangelicals for doing so. A theological generalist, with recognized expertise only in some fields of historical theology. (That was why Alister McGrath proposed calling him a *theologizer* rather than a *theologian*.) An adult catechist, who makes it his main business to teach, first, the truths by which Christians are to live and, second, how Christians are to live by them. A writer of texts not on dogmatics but on the Christian life, basic books for believers rather than broad-based graduate-level treatises for fellow clergy and academic peers. An embodiment of the dictum that inside a theologian there may well be a Bible teacher struggling to get out. An odd fellow altogether, then—that's me.

Furthermore, it has to be said that over the years John Frame and I have passed and re-passed each other like ships in the night. I can recall only one serious conversation with him, over an IHOP breakfast (and that was not really so very serious, as IHOP patrons will surely understand). Our orbits have not significantly intersected at all.

So anyone pondering my profile might reasonably conclude that it was an eccentric imprudence on the publisher's part to request this Foreword, and an egregious error of judgment on my part to consent to write it.

Yet the proverb that a cat may look at a king precisely illustrates what I am doing here. And I am doing it with more than ordinary delight, for there are few, past or present, whom I would place in the royal class ahead of Professor Frame. The most unassuming of men, he has never sought the limelight and is not at present widely known. But as this volume seems to me to show, he has been privileged to make a strategic and potentially huge contribution to the future well-being not just of the Reformed faith, but of the entire evangelical world. How so? Let me say it as I see it.

Before John Frame, Cornelius Van Til's landmark and surely correct insistence on the presuppositional, revelation-related character of all human reasoning about ultimate things was being maintained in so abstract, antithetical, and arcane a way as to sideline itself. And at the same time the cause of conservative gospel piety, which at surface level was prospering throughout the world, was growing increasingly shaky with regard to its own first principles and mental method: a spectrum of subjectivisms seemed to be jostling for dominance within it, and the outlook was, to say the least, unsettled and unsettling. It was within this double context—this "frame," if we may put it so—that the "Frame-work" of the past forty years has been carried through. (Forgive the puns; they were irresistible.)

John Frame has reaffirmed the essential Van Til positions, ontological, epistemological, methodological, and apologetic, with disarming simplicity, limpid lucidity, and luminous clarity. He has confirmed Van Til's contention that not to make clear at every point the fundamental antithesis between faithful, dependent Christian thinking and the would-be autonomy of its non-Christian counterpart is actually to obscure the gospel. With restraint, charity, wide learning, and much logical and analytical skill he has remapped the relativizing relationship of the Van Til body of thought to other systems; and he has conceptualized a way of theologizing about anything that combines all the angles of awareness that Van Til sought to bring out with all the space for dialogue and self-criticism that militancy had once excluded. This is the biblically shaped perspectival procedure that in substance always was and always will be the high road to wisdom (living by known truth) for sinful humans who are being reconstructed through the sovereign grace of the Father, the Son, and the Holy Spirit. Frame's is a spectacular achievement, from which the entire church on earth, in its own authentic transcultural life of obedience and doxology, stands and needs to benefit. I count it a privilege to be the first person in this book to say so.

Whether this benefit will be received, and evangelicalism around the world actually be strengthened and stabilized by it, is of course another matter. The world of the Westminsters, of the Reformed Seminary network, and of the smaller Presbyterian denominations is somewhat marginal in relation to the wider evangelical spread, and seems likely to remain so. And John Frame's books are anchored in that world; they were written to sort out, sustain, purge, and redirect aspects of its inner life. P&R Publishing has a fine catalogue, but is not one of the biggest or best known in its field. Globally speaking, communities and organizations of pneumatocentric Pentecostal types make the running these days, and one cannot be confident that a theological writer who will be seen as one of Cornelius Van Til's successors will be listened to as he should be. It is to be hoped, however, that readers of this book will discern John Frame as the forward-looking philosopher, apologist, dogmatician, ethicist, liturgist, and churchman that in fact he is. To his admirers he is already something of a legend; it has long been the case that, as with Oliver Goldsmith's schoolmaster, "still the wonder grew / That one small head could carry all he knew."

The range and breadth of the knowledge and the wisdom of John Frame are indeed remarkable. May the legacy that he is leaving to the evangelical cause and the church at large soon come to be appreciated as its true and abiding worth.

PREFACE

JOHN M. FRAME

THE FESTSCHRIFT IS a pleasant custom of the academic community. The idea is that when a scholar reaches a certain age and gains some recognition for his work, his colleagues and friends get together and present him with a book of essays. The essays are usually not *about* the honoree. The authors write essays in their own specialized fields, essays that they might have published elsewhere, such as in academic journals. But the authors donate their essays to the festschrift instead, believing that the honoree would enjoy reading them and would take these as an expression of his friends' respect and affection.

Usually the festschrift is a surprise to the honoree. They tell a story here at Reformed Theological Seminary about how theologian Roger Nicole, a bibliophile, once read a notice that InterVarsity Press was publishing a book of essays on the atonement, edited by Roger's colleagues Frank James and Charles (Chuck) Hill.[1] Roger approached his colleagues to ask why he had not been asked to contribute an essay to the collection. The atonement had, after all, been Roger's life work. Frank and Chuck hedged a bit. A little later, however, they invited Roger to lunch and informed him that this book of essays was to be a festschrift for Roger. Roger was appropriately surprised, amused, and grateful. But he did not forget what had originally been on his mind: he asked again to be allowed

---

1. The book was later published as *The Glory of the Atonement* (Downers Grove, IL: InterVarsity Press, 2004).

to include an essay of his own in the volume, a request the editors did not hesitate to grant.

Well, the present volume is different in several ways from the ones I have just described. For one thing, it is not a surprise to me. John Hughes, the editor of this volume, a dear former student and friend of many years, wrote me about his idea a year or so ago, not even trying to hide anything. The reason is that he wanted the volume not only to honor me, but also to be about me.[2] Because it was to be about me, I would have to be directly involved in its development, suggesting authors and topics, contributing materials,[3] and aiding in the publicity.

Now, I hesitated about that proposal. For one thing, I feared that this exercise would be a kind of ego trip, and I wasn't sure that would be spiritually good for me. (A book all about me? Yet I have been telling everybody that life is not about them, but about Jesus.) For another thing, I knew from the beginning it would be a lot of work, at a time when I already had too much to do. At seventy, one wishes to slow down, and one has automatic excuses for turning down assignments.

Nevertheless, I did agree to work with John on the project. The main reason is that I wanted my work to receive some serious scrutiny. God has blessed me in many ways through my career, but one blessing I've largely missed has been that of sympathetic, critical analysis. I have had my fill of the unsympathetic kind—mainly people who tell the world that I am not really Reformed, or really Van Tillian. These are people who seem to think I have never been right about even one thing, and they can't put forth the effort even to describe my positions without serious misrepresentation. But I have wished for someone to come along and give my work a professional going-over, a careful analysis and evaluation. I'm not sure why I haven't had much of that (aside from a very few longer reviews). Perhaps it is because I haven't done much networking; to be honest, I've been just a bit reclusive. Perhaps my views

2. In this respect, we are following somewhat the model of the two festschrifts given to my mentor, Cornelius Van Til: E. R. Geehan, ed., *Jerusalem and Athens* (Nutley, NJ: Presbyterian and Reformed, 1970) and Gary North, ed., *Foundations of Christian Scholarship* (Vallecito, CA: Ross House Books, 1976).

3. In addition to this Preface, I contributed "Reflections of a Lifetime Theologian" (with Andrew Sandlin as interviewer), "Backgrounds to My Thought," "My Major Books," "Recommended Resources," a Bibliography, a Glossary, Appendices, and suggestions for the Index of Subjects . I also wrote publicity material, and I will be participating in a session at the Evangelical Theological Society meeting in November 2009, when the volume will be released.

are too extreme in various areas for many to take them seriously.[4] Or, it has occurred to me, it may be that my work has not achieved sufficient excellence to be discussed by the most competent thinkers in my profession.

Anyhow, in this project we just went and asked some people I respect and admire to come and tell us what they really think. I find it remarkable that so many agreed to do it. So although my festschrift has not surprised me in the way that Roger Nicole's surprised him, it is in its sheer quantity and quality of writers a surprise that I will long remember.[5] John tells me this may be the biggest festschrift ever published. That may or may not be good for sales. But it will fulfill for years, maybe the rest of my life, my desire for thoughtful interaction.

So I offer thanks to God for bringing this project to pass, and to every writer who sacrificed his or her time to help us with it. I am especially thankful to our numerous editors, who put the book together with amazing speed and accuracy, to P&R for our continuing excellent working relationship, and to John Hughes, who devised this project, and who put a huge amount of good thought and effort into it. John never seemed to run out of good ideas, and he has promoted my work far more than I have deserved.

---

4. I'm thinking especially of my proposal, in *ER*, to abolish denominations, but of other things too. By the way, if any think my previous writing has been out of the mainstream, wait until they read my forthcoming *Doctrine of the Word of God*. For better or worse, the book will leave the academic mainstream far to one side.

5. The Personal Words in this volume, except for a few, will also be a surprise to me. I won't see them until the volume is released. But without seeing them, I am already very thankful to those who took the trouble to write.

ACKNOWLEDGMENTS

JOHN J. HUGHES

IN THE PREFACE, John Frame explains this festschrift's genesis, introduces its purpose, and sketches its development. For over a year, he and I have labored side by side, through many hundreds of e-mails, to shape and hone this volume. Without John's close involvement and hard work, this book would not exist. John never said "No" to a task I asked him to do, and his cheerful, upbeat e-mails encouraged me along the way. In effect, John has served as my coeditor in this undertaking. Thank you, John, for your many labors, creative ideas, and ongoing support as we created this tome.

We have been blessed by the large number of contributors who said "Yes" to our invitation to contribute an article or a personal word. To each one of you I say, "Thank you for honoring John with your contribution." I also wish to thank those several persons who worked on articles but were prevented from contributing them by circumstances beyond their control.

Every professionally published book is a team effort. Since May 2008, when I first suggested the idea for this festschrift to Bryce Craig, president of P&R Publishing, and to Marvin Padgett, P&R's vice president-editorial, I have received strong encouragement and outstanding support from the P&R Publishing team. Without their professional expertise, can-do attitude, and concrete help, this festschrift would not exist. So thank you, Aaron, Barb, Bryce, Charles, Dawn, Ian, Kristen, Marvin, and Thom. You are the best!

Much of the brunt of the work for a book of this magnitude rests in the hands of the copyeditors. I have been blessed with three world-class editors who have labored tirelessly, cheerfully, and professionally, under looming deadlines, and who have done a magnificent job. Thank you, Karen Magnuson, Brian W. Kinney, and Rick Matt. Only the four of us really know how exciting and exhausting it is to drive at 100 mph for weeks on end! Thanks also to Allan Sholes and Dana Adams, two fine editors who joined us at the tail end of the project and whose help proved invaluable. Thanks also to my son Ryan D. Hughes for his valuable preliminary help with the graphics.

Producing a useful subject index is a challenging task. John Frame carefully created the entries, and Jeffrey L. Brown, Kendall Cleveland, John Fulginiti III, Lucas Hillman, Jonathan Hutchison, Brian W. Kinney, Justin Richter, and Allen Stanton labored faithfully under a pressing deadline to correlate entries with page numbers. Thank you, one and all. A special thank-you to Brian Kinney, who edited, checked, and proofed the Scripture and subject indices. Without your help, Brian, these indices would not exist.

No one assisting me has devoted more time to making this book a reality than Karen Magnuson, a professional legal editor with an astounding number of books to her credit. In addition to editing a great many festschrift articles, Karen proofread the entire work at least once and some parts multiple times. She labored tirelessly and cheerfully, weekends included! I have constantly been amazed by her eagle-eyed ability to find inconsistencies and mistakes. Thanks also, Karen, for helping with the Index of Names—another do-or-die effort.

Dawn Premako's careful, cheerful, and professional proofing of my typesetting resulted in a much better product. Thank you, Dawn, for your timely help and sound advice. I learned a lot from you!

I also wish to thank Claire, my dear wife of forty years, for her deep enthusiasm and unceasing prayer support for this undertaking. Claire is a big fan of John Frame, having taken courses from him at Westminster Theological Seminary in the early 1970s and having helped me with the editing of John's *DKG* and *ME*.

Last, but not least, though they will never read these words, thanks to my two constant Golden Retriever companions, Charlie and Russell, whose sunny dispositions and ebullient personalities never cease to buoy my spirits. I'm sure they have no idea why I have been glued to the computer, rather than throwing their racquetball, for the past many months!

Along with all named or referenced here, I join you in giving thanks to our Lord, who has graciously raised up in the person of John Frame an extraordinary human being, teacher, theologian, and writer. May God continue to bless and strengthen you, John, and may he grant you many, many more fruitful years of ministry and writing.

ABBREVIATIONS

ANEP	*The Ancient Near East in Pictures Relating to the Old Testament*, ed. J. B. Pritchard (Princeton: Princeton University Press, 1954)
ANET	*Ancient Near Eastern Texts Relating to the Old Testament*, 3rd ed., ed. J. B. Pritchard (Princeton: Princeton University Press, 1969)
ASV	American Standard Version
BDB	F. Brown, S. R. Driver, and C. A. Briggs, *A Hebrew and English Lexicon of the Old Testament* (Oxford: Clarendon, 1907)
Bib	*Biblica*
CD	Karl Barth, *Church Dogmatics*, 13 vols., trans. and ed. G. W. Bromiley and T. F. Torrance (Edinburgh: T & T Clark, 1956–75)
CTJ	*Calvin Theological Journal*
ESV	English Standard Version
EVV	English Versions
HALOT	L. Koehler, W. Baumgartner, and J. J. Stamm, *The Hebrew and Aramaic Lexicon of the Old Testament*, 4 vols., trans. and ed. under supervision of M. E. J. Richardson (Leiden: Brill, 1994–99)

IBHS	B. K. Waltke and M. O'Connor, *Introduction to Biblical Hebrew Syntax* (Winona Lake, IN: Eisenbrauns, 1990)
JBL	*Journal of Biblical Literature*
JETS	*Journal of the Evangelical Theological Society*
KJV	King James Version
LXX	Septuagint
NASB	New American Standard Bible
NIBC	New International Biblical Commentary
NICNT	New International Commentary on the New Testament
NICOT	New International Commentary on the Old Testament
NIV	New International Version
NKJV	New King James Version
NT	New Testament
OT	Old Testament
TLOT	*Theological Lexicon of the Old Testament*, 3 vols., ed. Ernst Jenni with assistance from Claus Westermann, trans. Mark E. Biddle (Peabody, MA: Hendrickson, 1997)
TNIV	Today's New International Version
TWOT	*Theological Wordbook of the Old Testament*, 2 vols., ed. R. L. Harris, G. L. Archer, and B. K. Waltke (Chicago: Moody, 1980)
TynBul	*Tyndale Bulletin*
WBC	World Biblical Commentary
WCF	Westminster Confession of Faith
WLC	Westminster Larger Catechism
WSC	Westminster Shorter Catechism
WTJ	*Westminster Theological Journal*

JOHN FRAME'S WORKS[1]

AGG	*Apologetics to the Glory of God: An Introduction*
CVT	*Cornelius Van Til: An Analysis of His Thought*
CWM	*Contemporary Worship Music: A Biblical Defense*
CWT	*Collected Works of John M. Frame, Volume 1: Theology*
DCL	*Doctrine of the Christian Life*
DG	*Doctrine of God*
DKG	*Doctrine of the Knowledge of God*
DWG	*Doctrine of the Word of God* (forthcoming)
ER	*Evangelical Reunion*
IDSCB	"In Defense of Something Close to Biblicism"
IRF	*Introduction to the Reformed Faith*
ME	*Medical Ethics: Principles, Persons, and Problems*
MWC	"Machen's Warrior Children"
NOG	*No Other God: A Response to Open Theism*
PP	*A Primer on Perspectivalism*
PWG	*Perspectives on the Word of God: An Introduction to Christian Ethics*
RLT	"Reflections of a Lifetime Theologian"
SBL	*Salvation Belongs to the Lord: An Introduction to Systematic Theology*
TAM	*Theology at the Movies* (on http://www.frame-poythress.com site only)
TAP	*The Amsterdam Philosophy*
TRAD	"Traditionalism"
WST	*Worship in Spirit and Truth*

1. See Bibliography for complete bibliographical information.

A NOTE OF SPECIAL APPRECIATION

ROBERT C. (RIC) CANNADA JR.

THE FAMOUS GANGSTER "Baby Face" Nelson made an impression. On July 23, 1934, after John Dillinger had been killed the previous day, FBI Director J. Edgar Hoover named Nelson as Public Enemy No. 1. Nelson was elevated to the pinnacle of public awareness as an enemy of society.

"Baby Face" John Frame has made an impression, too. Although his name is not as well known in the public sphere of our society, John may well have been labeled by Satan over the years as Enemy No. 1 of Satan's kingdom of darkness because of John's defense of the gospel and his preparation of others to spread the gospel around the world. John has certainly been a force for good, as Nelson was a force for evil.

The first time I saw John Frame I noticed his baby face, as others have, but I was also impressed even then by his mature mind that has been so greatly used to bless the kingdom of Christ and by his gracious spirit. I was a senior in my undergraduate program at Vanderbilt University in February 1970 when I decided that the Lord was calling me to seminary. Along with my friend and college mate John Hughes, I decided to visit two well-known seminaries, Trinity Evangelical Divinity School in the Chicago area and Westminster Theological Seminary in the Philadelphia area. We left school for a week to drive to and visit Trinity for the first half of the week and Westminster for the second half. This Mississippi boy made the mistake of planning those visits in February; there seemed to be ten feet of snow piled up that week in each place. I later decided to enroll in Reformed Theological

Seminary, a fledgling seminary at the time in Jackson, Mississippi, of which my father was one of the founders. Johnny enrolled at Westminster.

I never forgot my visit to Westminster. The one professor in particular that I remember from that visit was John Frame. Perhaps that was because I was majoring in philosophy at Vanderbilt and John's teaching included an appreciation for philosophy, approaching it within a biblical framework. I thoroughly enjoyed John's class that week in Philadelphia.

While I was a student in those early years of RTS, we all were keenly aware that RTS in many ways was just the baby sister of Westminster Seminary. We owed so much to the faithfulness of the founders and professors at Westminster through the previous years, and we clearly understood that what we were being taught was the blessing of that Westminster heritage. Since I had visited Westminster, I had a clear vision of the campus and of John Frame, among others, holding forth the Reformed truth as our colaborers up north just as we were seeking to spread that truth in the Southeast.

My second encounter with John Frame came in the fall of 1973. I had graduated from RTS in May 1973 with an MDiv degree and had entered the pastoral ministry as the assistant pastor of the First Presbyterian Church in Clinton, South Carolina. I was ordained in the PCUS (the Southern Presbyterian Church). The PCA (Presbyterian Church in America) was formally established in December 1973, and the church where I served stayed in the PCUS. The members of FPC in Clinton included many fine conservative Christians; but the church also included a number of more liberal members, particularly from the local college, Presbyterian College. During my first summer in Clinton as I taught in an adult Bible school, I realized the challenges I would be facing, particularly on the issue of the inerrancy and authority of the Bible.

As I began to work with students from Presbyterian College in the fall of 1973, I realized even more the seriousness of the conflict. The Bible professors at the college and I were members of the same denomination, worshiping in the same congregation, working with the same college students, and teaching them exactly the opposite theology, especially regarding the nature of the Bible. Then I saw a tiny advertisement in *Christianity Today* about a conference on the inerrancy of Scripture at a place and by a group entirely new to me. It turned out that this was the very first Ligonier conference, organized by R. C. Sproul and held at a retreat center in Pennsylvania in October 1973. Every important conservative writer on the authority of

Scripture of whom I had ever heard was invited to speak at the conference that week. Although I had been at the church in Clinton only a few months, my senior pastor agreed to let me attend that conference. I believe I was the only person from the Southeast who was in attendance.

That conference was my first time to hear R. C. Sproul, whom I had not previously known and who was not well known yet, at least in the South. I learned to love and appreciate R. C. then and through the years have attended a number of other Ligonier conferences. I had previously heard other speakers who were there that fall, such as J. I. Packer, John Warwick Montgomery, John Gerstner, and Clark Pinnock, along with new ones I met then, such as Sproul and Peter Jones. As I remember it, there were seven speakers and fewer than a hundred people registered for the conference, so we had a good deal of personal time with the speakers.

One of the speakers at that first Ligonier conference was John Frame. Again I was thoroughly impressed and came away from that conference helped more by John than by anyone else. It was a very interesting conference because all the speakers were conservatives at the time (although one of them shifted greatly in later years) and all of them held to a high view of the authority and inerrancy of the Bible. A book edited by John Warwick Montgomery, *God's Inerrant Word: An International Symposium on the Trustworthiness of Scripture*,[1] was later published as a compilation of the lectures delivered at that conference. All the speakers were defending Scripture against the more liberal views that were prevalent at that time and are still present today. But since the presenters all agreed on the inerrancy of Scripture, the conference became more of a debate among themselves over *how* we should defend Scripture, a debate over apologetics. Some defended Scripture using a traditional evidentialist approach; others defended Scripture using a presuppositional approach. For a young minister like me, the differences in perspectives were fascinating.

Two things impressed me about John Frame at that Ligonier conference. Those same two traits had impressed me at Westminster several years earlier and have continued to impress me through the years. John was very strong in his defense of the authority and inerrancy of Scripture, which he clearly presented in the context of presuppositional apologetics. I still remember in particular his emphasis on the Holy Spirit. At a time when the charismatic movement was on the rise and many Reformed people were hesitant to talk

1. Calgary: Canadian Institute for Law, Theology, and Public Policy, 1974.

about the Holy Spirit, John emphasized that the Spirit is still actively at work today and pointed out from the Westminster Confession of Faith that only the current activity of the Holy Spirit in the hearts and minds of people will convince anyone of the truth of Scripture's inerrancy:

> We may be moved and induced by the testimony of the Church to an high and reverent esteem of the holy Scripture. And the heavenliness of the matter, the efficacy of the doctrine, the majesty of the style, the consent of all the parts, the scope of the whole (which is, to give all glory to God), the full discovery it makes of the only way of man's salvation, the many other incomparable excellencies, and the entire perfection thereof, are arguments whereby it does abundantly evidence itself to be the Word of God: yet notwithstanding, our full persuasion and assurance of the infallible truth and divine authority thereof, is from the inward work of the Holy Spirit bearing witness by and with the Word in our hearts.[2]

John was clear in his teaching, but he was also winsome in his spirit at the conference. Even when the discussions in the question/answer sessions or in the informal times around the tables became a little heated, John was always the calm one, pouring out kindness even as he presented his position. He was and is a careful scholar, a gracious mediator, a truly kind person, a humble listener, and one who is even able to receive correction with a good heart.

After twenty years as a pastor, in 1993 I was asked to join the staff of Reformed Theological Seminary in order to establish the third RTS campus, in Charlotte, North Carolina. At RTS my path would cross that of John Frame once more. In 2000, John Frame joined the faculty of the RTS Orlando campus. I was the executive vice president (chief operating officer) for RTS at the time and had the privilege of being involved in some of John's interviews, especially when he was interviewed by the board's executive committee. The same traits were evident: a clear presentation of his theology in a winsome and gentle manner. Since that time I have had the privilege of working with John in a variety of settings at RTS.

Although his scholarly output is impressive, perhaps even more impressive are some of John's less scholarly works aimed to help theological students and others with practical issues. Two such booklets are *Learning at Jesus'*

---

2. WCF 1.5.

Feet: A Case for Seminary Training and *Studying Theology as a Servant of Jesus*, both published by RTS for our students and prospective students. These simple but very helpful works make the same impression: clear truth winsomely presented.

Others are much better able than I to analyze and evaluate the depth of John's scholarly work and its impact on theologians around the world. I have seen his personal impact on students and young pastors like me through many years. John still has that baby face, although it has many more lines and wrinkles now. He also still has that mature mind and winsome spirit that drew me to him years ago, and he has made a good, lasting impression for the kingdom of Christ on many, many others as well. Thank you, John.

Personal Words

Jay Adams, PhD,
Dean, Institute for Nouthetic Studies,
Greenville, South Carolina

Doubtless, other contributors to this festschrift will justly praise John for his writing and teaching. Well and good. I want to tell a story about him. It's probably my most vivid remembrance of John at Westminster.

Way back in the Vietnam War days, in order to avoid the draft, a number of students enrolled in seminaries. We had our share in Philadelphia. Among them (many of the professors supposed) were those who adhered to the Dooyeweerdian philosophy of Sphere Sovereignty. They gave us a lot of trouble as a faculty. One once said in class that there was more revelation in the thermometer on the wall than in the Bible.

Eventually, they invited one of their champions to descend on the school from their "headquarters" in Canada. They were all ecstatic at the presence of such a big gun on the campus. He was to lecture and set us all straight.

Well, he gave his presentation, and you could see the elation on their faces. He then settled down to await a response. John got up to give the rebuttal. And what a rebuttal it was! Never before nor since have I ever heard anything to equal it. He thoroughly trounced the erroneous views of his opponent, cutting him off at the knees. Then, not satisfied with that, he systematically sliced and diced him verbally, logically, and scripturally. Thereupon, he buried the remains. When the bigwig was firmly interred, John jumped up and down on his grave to be certain the task was properly completed.

I'll never forget it. Nor will students who were present. The cause of the dissenting faction of the student body, along with their mentor (who shall remain unnamed), was permanently set back, and we had a large measure of peace again. When I remember the event, I can't help chuckling. Good work, John! Keep on burying the opposition!

JAMES C. BLAND III, DMIN,
COORDINATOR OF MISSION TO NORTH AMERICA (PCA)

In the teaching and writings of John Frame, orthodoxy and orthopraxis join together to reveal a scholar's mind and a pastor's heart. In particular, I am indebted to Dr. Frame for his study of the principles and practice of biblical worship. In the early part of this decade, I invited several colleagues together, including John Frame, to help me write a practical guideline for worship among church planters in the Presbyterian Church in America (PCA). John was keenly insightful and of significant help in this project that has served us well in establishing biblically healthy churches.

RICHARD BLEDSOE, DMIN,
PROFESSOR OF BIBLICAL STUDIES,
RIVENDELL COLLEGE, BOULDER

What to say about my friend John Frame? He was (and is) my friend, and is still my professor.

He was perhaps the principal reason I showed up at Westminster West in Escondido, California, in August of 1981. I wanted to study under him. To that time, I was an "autodidact," and I was already a preacher. I had read and studied a great deal, and among my theological books were also Herman Dooyeweerd and Cornelius Van Til. I had read Van Til until I was blue in the face. Not easy to understand. And some parts of him remained elusive, no matter how many times one pored over them. I even thought then, "If I were to be able to study under Van Til, I would not want to. It is obvious that Van Til is one of the worst commentators on Van Til that there is."

No, I wanted to study under John Frame, who had the knack and the gift of clarity. So I showed up in 1981 to study under John. And he did have that gift. He made the very profound but unclear Dutchman comprehensible. He "unpacked" him, as we now say. But clarity was not his only gift.

Human beings are fascinating, just by virtue of being human beings, the image of God. But when human beings are "gifts to the church," they are even more fascinating. John Frame is a package deal put together by God in most interesting ways.

I remember one day when Van Til's nemesis showed up at Westminster. That was Dr. John Gerstner, by then one of the great deans of the Calvinistic world. Dr. Gerstner had been known to and by John for years, all the way back to youth, and they were friends. Gerstner was a famous teacher, perhaps the greatest Socratic teacher of his generation, and was legendary in the classroom for his sparring and fencing with students. He was also one of the greatest debaters of his time. I used to say that the ultimate meeting of the unmovable and the unstoppable would be debate between John Gerstner and Greg Bahnsen that was moderated by John Warwick Montgomery. It would be an event that would rival the dropping of the first hydrogen bomb on Bikini.

A debate was staged in our classroom between John and Dr. Gerstner.

Now, John Frame in person is a rather timid man. He is sometimes not particularly comfortable in social settings and is not so good at small talk. And although an unfailingly cheerful man, he is in fact shy, quite shy. He is anything but a personally confrontational person. Except . . .

I would not want to meet John Gerstner in debate, especially public debate. It would be like standing in the street, holding your hand up to meet an oncoming bus. No, thank you. But John Frame stood in the street, and held his hand up, and the bus met an equal force. He not only fought back, and did combat, he was on the offensive and at the very least was the full equal in fearlessly meeting John Gerstner in the joust. He defended our champion, Cornelius Van Til, and his position, and perhaps won. That little story tells you something about John Frame.

He is a shy man in person, but the quality that I most admire in John Frame is his courage. If something is right, he will defend it, and defend it fearlessly. But what makes that quality so interesting, what makes it an "apple of gold in a setting of silver," is that John is not a combative man, or a warrior "by nature." He is in fact famously the man who sees the good in every person, in every position. But that is a temperate and a prudent quality in him, not an appeasing one. I do not know of anyone who has less appeasement in his soul than John Frame. And when that quality of boldness and even fearlessness is offset by a temperament that is in many ways the exact opposite, it is striking, remarkably striking. Like Moses, he will stammer out his disqualifications (I have heard him do so when nominated to be an elder—disqualifications the congregation rejected, I believe unanimously), and like Gideon, go forth to war, fearlessly.

Davids sometimes come in odd packages, and in this way one really does know it is a gift from God.

ROBERT J. CARA, PhD, PROFESSOR OF NEW TESTAMENT AND CHIEF ACADEMIC OFFICER, REFORMED THEOLOGICAL SEMINARY, CHARLOTTE

The Bible, Calvin's *Institutes*, and Frame's *The Doctrine of the Knowledge of God* (*DKG*)—these three are the most important books you will ever read. At least this is what an influential professor at Reformed Theological Seminary Jackson boldly proclaimed to my seminary class in 1987. The professor had us read *DKG* and tested us on its contents. Also, he "made" us each write a personal one-page note to John, commenting on the book's impact upon us. And yes, this professor was known for a bit of hyperbole. Therefore, the students were never completely sure whether he really thought that John's book was actually the third most important book ever written, or not.

What did I think of *DKG* as a seminary student? Since I was a convinced "Van Tillian" coming to seminary, I was predisposed to agree with much in the book. Well, I did love the book with its emphasis on considering the normative, situational, and existential perspectives, which significantly broadened my outlook. My love for the book was not dampened despite having some disagreement with it. In the end, I did not agree with (or understand?) John's multiperspectivalism of normative/situational/existential as a *philosophical* system. I was, however, and am still significantly impacted by these three perspectives *pragmatically*. That is, there are many situations in which I use the three perspectives as a grid to make sure I have covered all the bases, especially in ethics and hermeneutics.

As it turns out, I was the teaching assistant for the above professor who required us to read *DKG*. This professor allowed me to read John's personal correspondence to him related to John's reading of the students' notes. I recall being very impressed by John's humble response. Many years later, as currently John and I are colleagues at Reformed Theological Seminary, I am still impressed by his humbleness.

John, although I think *DKG* is very good, I am not yet willing to put it at number three all time!

D. A. CARSON, PhD,
RESEARCH PROFESSOR OF NEW TESTAMENT,
TRINITY EVANGELICAL DIVINITY SCHOOL

All of us in Christian ministry know that we stand on the shoulders of others. Many of these "others" are figures of the past: we know them through their literary remains, through biographies that cover their lives, through responsibly written history. We benefit from Ignatius, Irenaeus, John Chrysostom, Augustine, Bernard de Clairvaux, Wycliffe, Tyndale, Calvin, Turretin, Whitefield, and so on. (I am sure you will not try to infer anything from the myriads of names I have not mentioned!) But we also stand on the shoulders of contemporary "others," whether family and friends and colleagues or contemporary Christian thinkers whose works we read but whom we know (or knew) personally—F. F. Bruce, John Stott, Jim Packer, Doug Moo, John Piper, Dick Lucas, and countless others. They have helped to make us what we are.

But you belong on a shorter list that does not quite fit into either category—a list of major contemporary figures whose works have helped shape me but whom I do not really know. Only twice, I think, have we briefly chatted together. I think I was first impressed with the quality of your reviews. Eventually I became familiar with most of your *oeuvre*, with special thanks to God for particular essays (e.g., "Some Questions about the Regulative Principle," *WTJ* 59 [1992]: 357–66), polemics (e.g., *No Other God: A Response to Open Theism*), apologetics (e.g., *Apologetics to the Glory of God*), and works of constructive theology (e.g., *The Doctrine of the Knowledge of God*). If you write it, I read it, not because I always find myself in perfect agreement, but because you teach me.

So thanks for your shoulders. *Ad multos annos*!

Bryan Chapell, PhD, Professor of Homiletics and President, Covenant Theological Seminary

Any student, colleague, or friend of John Frame can tell you what a delightful combination of giftedness and humility he embodies. Even many of those who consider themselves John's opponents in the world of theological scholarship will attest to this, offering stories of the fair and charitable way he treats those who disagree with him. In this volume, writers, scholars, pastors, and others from a variety of backgrounds and traditions have all come together to pay tribute to a man whose work has inspired both great praise and occasional controversy, but whose winning personality, fine mind, and obvious love for the Lord have made him a popular teacher, speaker, and friend.

A recognized expert on the thought of his mentor, Cornelius Van Til, John has produced his own writings on multiperspectivalism, presuppositionalism, epistemology, apologetics, ethics, and worship that have been widely read and profoundly influential. Again, the contents of the present volume speak to the scope of his work, the depth of his thinking, and the range of his appeal. It is hard to imagine an area of theological study that has not been impacted by John's work in some way. I cherish this opportunity to celebrate the life and work of a man who has such a burning passion for the truth of God's Word, such a deep desire to communicate what that Word teaches, and such an abiding love for the Savior, whose redemptive work on our behalf is the subject of that Word's every chapter.

We praise God for the gift that the Bible is to all who believe. Let us also praise him for the gift that John Frame and his work have been to all who strive to understand and share the message of the Bible for the glory of our Lord.

Bryce H. Craig, ThM, President of P&R Publishing

As a publisher working with Dr. Frame over the years, I have found the experience to be both humbling and rewarding. It has been humbling in that he would choose to work with us, and rewarding as we have seen the wealth of material that has come forth from his pen and continues to minister to a people hungry for rich, sound biblical teaching. In addition, the honor of accepting a coveted Gold Medallion award for his book *The Doctrine of the Word of God* was one of the highlights of P&R's years of publishing. So on behalf of the staff of P&R, we are truly thankful for his long and faithful service to our Savior and Lord, and we pray for many more years of fruitful service together.

Daniel M. Doriani, PhD, Senior Pastor, Central Presbyterian Church, St. Louis

John Frame was my professor at Westminster Seminary during Westminster's season of primacy. In the days before Westminster divided east and west, the youngish Poythress and Godfrey were developing superb lectures with fountains of information. Dillard and Gaffin and Strimple were admirable men and assured lecturers; Strimple was avuncular and learned.

It wasn't obvious where to place Frame, nearing forty but seeming ageless somehow. He was not an enthusiastic lecturer. Some professors lean in as they lecture; Frame seemed to lean back, not out of indifference or timidity but, it seemed, from a desire to stay detached, the better to lead his dispassionate quest for truth.

His foundational courses in apologetics, ethics, and theology were marked by extraordinary depth and clarity. The massive outlines, the innumerable Scripture proofs, the timely, apt citations from great theologians and philosophers past shouted, "This must become a book someday."

We heard the big ideas that have been the cornerstone of his theological influence, but Frame the professor and lecturer offered lessons that Frame the writer couldn't teach. His humility and quest for the truth seemed to be sides of one coin. He never drew attention to himself. Personal comments were extremely rare (he stunned us one day by revealing that his dog had just died and he was grieving). If a student wrote an outstanding paper, he might soon have an invitation to deliver it as a lecture in class. Some students complained, but he noted that they had his full lecture outline, so nothing was lost and something was gained. Beyond the lecture outlines, he also provided—and insisted that we answer—what seemed like vast numbers of study questions. Some baffled us. No one could find the answer to one about Van Til and a black Buick. Someone gathered his nerve to break custom and ask the professor for the answer. He replied, "I don't know; I was hoping one of you might figure it out." Class readings were not burdensome; he explained that he would rather have us read fewer pages well than many poorly. The last two notes I read as keys, not to his *content* but to his approach: he wanted us to think hard, figure things out for ourselves, know a few sources well—above all, Scripture—to find God's truth and to know, love, and obey the Lord himself.

CHARLES DUNAHOO, DMIN, COORDINATOR OF CHRISTIAN EDUCATION AND PUBLICATIONS (PCA)

It has been my privilege and honor to know John Frame for a good number of years. Our mutual connection with Westminster Theological Seminary gave us more than simply Reformed theology and presuppositional apologetics in common. John's careful scholarship, Christian piety, and ability to open deep biblical truth have blessed not only me in my Christian life but so many others as well. I have referred to him many times as one of those few men who I believe is a must-read for anyone wanting to grow in the faith.

John Frame has one of the keenest minds of all the people I know. His gift of discernment and ability to teach and write have certainly contributed to the growth and expansion of God's kingdom. John is a master of taking complex issues and opening them up in a marvelous way. He can peel back the layers of complicated issues such as open theism, sanctification, apologetics, systematic theology, and epistemology, to name a few topics. I regularly refer to him in my own study, teaching, and writing. One example of his kingdom perspective illustrates my point: "I was amazed to find that the same Bible that presents the message of salvation also presents a distinctive philosophy, including metaphysics, epistemology, and ethics, one of which alone makes sense of human life. Van Til's work encouraged me to take an offensive, rather than a mere defensive, stance against non-Christian thought." He further writes, "In the biblical worldview, nothing makes sense apart from the presupposition of God's reality." That sums up John Frame's unique giftedness. God has given gifts and gifted people to his church, and John Frame is one of those special people.

It is my honor and privilege to express my appreciation to John Frame, especially for his desire to think God's thoughts after him and apply them to all of life, and his efforts to encourage us to do the same. I must admit I have been frustrated by John's writings. With each one I have said, this is the one you must read; then another is published and I say the same thing.

May God continue to bless and use you in the building up of his church and the expansion of his kingdom.

JOHN S. FEINBERG, PHD,
CHAIR, PROFESSOR OF BIBLICAL AND SYSTEMATIC
THEOLOGY, TRINITY EVANGELICAL DIVINITY SCHOOL

I have never met John Frame. Nor have we ever corresponded or talked by phone. Still, it would be hard to imagine an evangelical theologian working broadly in the Reformed tradition during the latter part of the twentieth century who didn't know of John Frame. I have been privileged to serve with faculty colleagues who were John's former students, and they uniformly and unequivocally speak highly of him in many regards.

First, he has served the cause of Christ with great distinction as a professor of systematic theology and apologetics. Former students speak highly of his skills as a teacher. But even more than his ability as a communicator, they mention two things repeatedly. One is that the content of his lectures, preaching, and everyday conversation is filled with Scripture. This involves not only constant reference to biblical passages as the basis of what he thinks and teaches, but also speech is filled with ideas that reflect the fundamental worldview of Scripture, even when Scripture isn't quoted. Every idea and act must be judged by whether it fits or contradicts biblical thinking. Invariably as well, those who know him emphasize that what he teaches is not just information he presents so as to make a living, but the foundation of his own life and ministry. John Frame teaches evangelical theology both by his lectures and writings, and also by his life!

Second, those who work in the fields of apologetics and philosophy of religion know John Frame as an able proponent of presuppositional apologetics. A student of Cornelius Van Til, another great Reformed theologian and apologist, John Frame is easily the most eloquent and able contemporary spokesman for this method of doing apologetics. Here, as with his theology, his commitment to this way of defending the faith stems from his belief that it best squares with biblical thinking and gives God greater glory than any other method of apologetics. Although arguably Frame's influence as a theologian is greater than his influence on apologetics, he is still a most important contributor to ongoing discussions about the best way to defend Christianity to nonbelievers.

Then, there are many people who never sat in John Frame's class or heard him preach, who have still been blessed by his ministry. That is so because he is a prolific writer. Not only has he written many pages, but the topics he addresses cover a broad spectrum of evangelical thinking in the fields of systematic theology and apologetics. As with his other ministries, his writings exhibit a careful thinker, grounded in the Word of God, who shows not only a wealth of knowledge but also a heart and mind devoted totally to God himself.

Former colleagues who had him as their teacher uniformly speak of his godly life, his devotion to his family, and his insistence in all things to conform his thinking and action to the Word of God and the God of the Word. For all of these reasons and more, it is right on this festive occasion to celebrate him and his service to the Lord! I am pleased to be among those given the opportunity in this more formal way to offer him my congratulations. May the Lord continue to bless you richly, John, and give you many more years of fruitful service to his glory!

MARK D. FUTATO SR., PhD,
PROFESSOR OF OLD TESTAMENT,
REFORMED THEOLOGICAL SEMINARY, ORLANDO

The Old Testament occasionally speaks of a "worthy man." We occasionally have the privilege of knowing a worthy man. If John Frame had been an Old Testament character, he would have been noted as a worthy man.

I have known John for quite some time. John was my professor at Westminster Theological Seminary in the late 1970s. We taught together at Westminster Theological Seminary in California from 1988 to 1999 and have been teaching together at Reformed Theological Seminary in Orlando since 2000. Throughout these years I have had the privilege of watching John live a life worthy of the high calling that he has received.

Several characteristics come to mind when I think of John as a worthy man. One is his rare combination of brilliance and humility. John is one of the brightest people and clearest thinkers that I know personally, and at the same time, he exhibits a humility that is not often found in the academy or in the church. A second, related to the first, is his phenomenal ability to listen. By that I mean his ability and willingness to understand another's position. I have read John's reviews and critiques of the thoughts and writings of others over the years. I doubt that many if any have responded to John by saying, "You misunderstood what I said." A third, related to the first and second, is John's graciousness. I cannot think of anyone that I know personally who is more gracious with people with whom he disagrees than John is. John's willingness to grant the benefit of the doubt and to learn from all sides of the argument makes him a man worthy of emulation.

It has been an honor and a delight to know John for some thirty years. I trust that God will bless him with many more fruitful years, until he hears his Master say, "Well done; you are a worthy man."

RICHARD B. GAFFIN JR., ThD, PROFESSOR EMERITUS, BIBLICAL AND SYSTEMATIC THEOLOGY, WESTMINSTER THEOLOGICAL SEMINARY

I first met John in the early 1960s when we were students, I a couple of years ahead of him, in the BD program at Westminster Seminary. Among the memories I have of him from that time, in addition to his already evident brilliance, was the way, with his background in philosophy, he did not hesitate to question Dr. Van Til rather aggressively on key aspects of the latter's understanding of philosophy and position on apologetics. An encouragement to me over the years has been to see him, along with criticisms (not all of which I share), embrace that position and emerge, through his teaching and writing, as a premier proponent in recent decades of presuppositional apologetics.

Later in that decade we both began teaching at Westminster, where a few years after me (1965) he replaced me (in 1968) as the "baby" on the faculty, which after several decades of remarkable stability was into a period of transition. John was certainly a key in effecting a transition that maintained the standard of godliness as well as academic and classroom excellence set by our teachers.

When John left around 1980 for the beginning of what is now Westminster Seminary California, I lost a valued colleague. Of so much that could be said here, I think of his stress that our use of language in theology be clear and careful, an emphasis that included having to observe occasionally, in the face of accents in my own teaching and, as I recall, with a degree of exasperation with certain student enthusiasts, that biblical theology and redemptive-historical are not magic wands that solve every theological problem with a wave!

John, despite the impression you may still have, I don't think biblical theology is more basic than or primary to systematic theology; as distinct disciplines the relationship between them is reciprocal, mutually enriching and correcting. But I do believe that attention to the redemptive-historical context is essential in a crucial and decisive way for sound biblical exegesis, which I'm sure we both believe is the lifeblood of sound systematic theology. Might we agree that biblical theology is the indispensable servant of systematic theology?

John, I thank God for you and your years of distinguished service. May he grant you health and strength for continuing productivity for the good of the church.

RICHARD C. GAMBLE, PhD,
PROFESSOR OF SYSTEMATIC THEOLOGY,
REFORMED PRESBYTERIAN THEOLOGICAL SEMINARY,
PITTSBURGH

I thank God that our lives have intertwined over the years. When I arrived at WTS Philadelphia, you had just moved to Escondido. The two faculties were about as far away from each other geographically as is possible, but we were united in mission.

Our relationship took a different turn when you joined us in Orlando. We are both early risers, and you were faithfully at work in your office each morning. Your life had a regularity and discipline that included faithfulness to your seminary responsibilities but also faithfulness to your wife, family, and church. That discipline made it possible for you to produce the enormous amount of significant theological research that carries your name.

In other words, you embodied a faithfulness that reminds me of different Old Testament figures. Noah labored day and night for a hundred years in faithfulness to the word that God spoke to him. God blessed that obedience. Abraham journeyed to an unknown country in faithfulness to God's promise. God blessed that obedience too.

You have modeled Christian faithfulness to our God as you have listened to his word and labored in a quiet way to advance his church and kingdom. May God continue to bless you!

Michael J. Glodo, ThM,
Associate Professor of Biblical Studies,
Dean of the Chapel,
Reformed Theological Seminary, Orlando

John Frame was my professor long before I ever met him. Those Christian minds that influenced me most and that I found most compelling turned out to share in common the mark of John Frame upon their own development. My delight at eventually becoming his colleague has only grown from that time. On the occasion of this festschrift, I am once again reminded of how his reflection of biblical epistemology has permeated so many areas in which I now teach. I pray God's grace to reflect as faithfully John's contribution to my life as he has faithfully reflected our Servant Lord.

R. J. Gore Jr., PhD,
Professor of Systematic Theology,
Erskine Theological Seminary,
Due West, South Carolina

I first came across John Frame's writings while at Westminster Seminary Philadelphia in the 1980s. His wide range of interests appealed to me, but it took a few years before it all "clicked." And what a deliciously clarifying moment that was! In an earlier moment of theological clarity I had become a Calvinist; later, the presuppositional apologetics light came on and I embraced Van Til. Then one day "Frame's triangle" clicked—and I began to understand the normative, situational, and existential perspectives in ethics. This simple yet profound approach to ethical issues has helped me and my students for more than a decade.

Let me mention four things I appreciate about John Frame. First, he is biblical. Some criticize him for being "biblicistic," or not sufficiently "confessional." However, John understands the meaning of "subordinate" standards and I celebrate his priorities: commitment, first, to Scripture, and then to confessional standards. Second, although some complain about his *sic et non* method, I commend his willingness to see the truth offered by other perspectives, to seek to understand opposing viewpoints. Third, although some are peeved that he occasionally thinks out loud, I applaud his transparent desire to find the best answers for the questions of our day, not just repeating answers that *once* were adequate (e.g., see his books on worship and worship music). Fourth, he graciously wrote the foreword to my book, *Covenantal Worship*, a kindness for which he has been much abused!

Like many others, I have never studied under John Frame, although I have been his student for two decades. He has never been my classroom teacher, although he has instructed me in apologetics, ethics, philosophy, theology, Scripture, pastoral ministry—and Christian charity. Once, while driving from the airport to Erskine Seminary for his lectures on "Christianity and Ethics," we chatted. In response to one question, he smiled, eyes twinkling, and said, "Well, we're Reformed, but we're not angry about it." Blessed are those who have been taught by John Frame—whether in the classroom or by the printed page. In our contentious day, may his irenic spirit—and his tribe—increase!

STEVE HAYS, MAR (CANDIDATE),
TEACHER'S ASSISTANT,
REFORMED THEOLOGICAL SEMINARY;
CHRISTIAN AUTHOR, BLOGGER (TRIABLOGUE)

Someone once said the difference between Richard Feynmann and Murray Gell-Mann is that Gell-Mann makes sure you know what an extraordinary person he is although Feynmann is not a person at all but a more advanced life-form pretending to be human to spare your feelings.

In terms of sheer intellect, we'd expect a man like Frame to be teaching at Harvard or Oxford. Beyond his intellectual endowments, Frame also came from a wealthy family, so he could afford to pursue any career he chose. But because of his sense of Christian vocation, he chose to train men for Christian ministry.

Frame is most associated with Cornelius Van Til, but in terms of theological method he was also influenced by the exegetical orientation of John Murray, his other mentor.

Van Til was a revolutionary of sorts in challenging traditional apologetics. As such he was somewhat prone to hyperbole. Frame has scaled back some of the rhetorical overkill. In addition, Frame, with his triperspectivalism, has always had his own way of conceptualizing the issues.

Frame is controversial in some circles. That's partly because, like Feynmann, he simply operates at a higher level than most of his critics. He sails over their heads.

It's also because Frame, like Murray, takes *sola Scriptura* quite seriously. For him, Scripture takes precedence over tradition. And he puts that into practice. It's a way of life, not a slogan on the wall.

Van Til had the kind of charismatic personality and divisive rhetoric that inspired passionate supporters and passionate opponents. Frame, with his more irenic style and temperament, hasn't had the same polarizing effect. At the same time, his influence is likely to be more enduring because it is less driven by personal dynamics—which inevitably fade over time with the demise of the principals.

Always the consummate Christian gentleman, Frame has been a wise, patient, and attentive mentor to many students over his long teaching career. A man of keen intellect with a pastor's heart, he sets an example, not merely of how to think, but how to speak and how to be.

Andrew Hoffecker, PhD,
Professor of Church History,
Reformed Theological Seminary, Jackson

John Frame has contributed masterfully to theological reflection in general and Reformed theology in particular for over forty years. Consistent with the greats who preceded him in mining the depths of Christian thought, John has gracefully and humbly added immeasurably to our rich heritage. Whether writing on theology, ethics, apologetics, or cultural themes, what is most notable is the breadth of his vision and the soundness of his insights. His Theology of Lordship series demonstrates his facility in restating in fresh ways the great biblical truths that have sustained Christians for almost five hundred years.

Repeatedly I have found that whether I went to his volumes to research a point about which I knew little or to recalibrate my thinking on matters I have held for years, I would inevitably realize how much time slipped by simply because I kept reading beyond my original intent. The clarity of his expression and the way that he led me to consider additional points seized my attention. Students who read John's books because they were assigned in my syllabi commented on how he made complex ideas accessible and articulated biblical themes with such striking illustrations.

Although John and I teach on separate campuses of Reformed Theological Seminary, we meet biannually at our faculty retreats. John unselfishly contributes to those gatherings by his musicianship. How many times I have walked into the meeting room to be greeted by his rendition of familiar hymns and choruses on the piano. He plays seamlessly from one favorite to another, thereby setting the tone for our corporate worship. How appropriate that I remember John in this way, for Reformed theology, which he expounds so profoundly, not only challenges our intellect but also drives us to worship.

John Calvin said that it is easier to reform theology than to reform piety. His struggles to achieve those goals in sixteenth-century Geneva are well documented. John's labors in theology and ethics in the twenty-first century have made that task clearer by his writings. May God continue to bless John's works to take minds and hearts captive to Christ.

Joel C. Hunter, DMin,
Senior Pastor, Northland, A Church Distributed, Orlando

As I delight in reading the voluminous works of John Frame, part of my pleasure comes from knowing that they are written "from the fields." John is not ordinarily hidden in the stacks of a library; he is with students or at churches available to serve.

When Paul wrote the Epistles, he wrote "from the fields." Whether in prison or on the way to encourage another group of struggling Christians, his presence in person shaped his needed message to the churches. It is no stretch for me to compare John to Paul.

Here is a superior intellect that is an unassuming congregant, usually sitting with his wife, sometimes with one of his sons, worshiping along with others. He is a regular part of our family at Northland Church, although a member of a PCA church (and who knows how many other ministries he serves). Whenever I see him, I know that he is not there to ask anything of me. He is there to worship, to serve when called upon, and to be a part of the extended body of Christ. He has no hidden agenda, other than to glorify God and support the saints in service.

As I speak a word to him, and Mary too, in the hallways, he is always gracious but conscious that a pastor has many to talk with during that time in addition to him. So he will say as much or as little as I like, answering my questions in cordial and personal terms but not presuming to conduct evaluations or counsel on the spot. Although I could use the latter, I am impressed with the former. His humility is so much a part of his personality that he would never notice it.

I am a great fan of John Frame, and I am a student of his also. He has taught me much about the Word written and in person and for that I am forever thankful.

FRANK A. JAMES III, DPHIL, PHD, PROVOST, PROFESSOR OF HISTORICAL THEOLOGY, GORDON-CONWELL THEOLOGICAL SEMINARY

I will never forget the day nearly thirty years ago when I walked into Professor Frame's class in Philadelphia and saw three marvelous words scrawled on the chalkboard—"Theology is life." Something clicked inside me; somehow I knew wisdom when I saw it. As soon as class was over, I sped home to tell Carolyn what Frame had said. I understood in my bones that true theology and life are so deeply intertwined that we can distinguish them only theoretically. I have embraced this wisdom, and it has become formative in my life both as a professor and as a follower of Jesus. For me this was revolutionary stuff. If I may say so, our Reformed heritage has inculcated the tendency to live in our heads, that is, to detach doctrine from life. But John Frame has always known that the founders of Reformed tradition (John Calvin, Peter Martyr Vermigli, Martin Bucer, and Heinrich Bullinger) never separated doctrine from piety or piety from doctrine. Bucer perhaps said it best when he defined *theology* as the "art of living a virtuous . . . life."

John Frame is not just an award-winning theologian; he walks the talk. Over dinner one evening, I recall being stunned to hear that he and his beloved Mary had ministered to the outcasts of society by inviting them to live in their home in California. "Were you not afraid?" I asked. John simply replied: "They needed help." I discovered that John actually believes in the power of the gospel.

From my vantage point, both as John's student at Westminster Seminary in Philadelphia and as his colleague and friend at Reformed Theological Seminary in Orlando, I view him as a quiet radical. Always unassuming, yet he was never afraid to speak the radical truth of Jesus Christ or to befriend a theological outcast. Of course he has been criticized for these associations, but the gospel compels John to be a friend even if he does not share someone's particular viewpoint. I guess John really believes what Jesus said when he called his followers to "love one another even as I have loved you" (John 13:34).

One of John's most famous articles is "Machen's Warrior Children," in which he recounts all the theological carnage that followed Machen's death in 1937. He asked me to read it before sending it to the publisher. When I put it down, I could not help but lament all the infighting among those who share the same fundamental theological commitments. I am pretty sure John intended that we, the theological descendants of Machen, stop and take stock; that we stop employing theology as a weapon; that we stop behaving as if "theology is death" and again turn to the gospel truth that theology is life.

JAMES B. (JIM) JORDAN, DLITT, DIRECTOR, BIBLICAL HORIZONS

It is with great pleasure that I write this note of congratulations to John Frame on the occasion of his seventieth birthday. Although I had read the occasional piece by John in the 1970s, it was not until I began finishing up my theological studies by moving to Westminster Theological Seminary in Philadelphia that I met him. Over the next year and a half I happily availed myself of every course he offered, and was privileged to serve as one of his teaching assistants. I also found myself singing in the classical music ensemble at which John was pianist and organist.

We became friends, and I recall when a few of us older students took John out to lunch on his fortieth birthday. At that time he lamented that he would probably never get married. It was only a couple of years later that the secretary at Westminster Theological Seminary in California informed me, when I called to speak with John, that he had just gotten married and was already the father of two children!

I was privileged to have John as my ThM adviser, and also to have him write the introduction to my first book, *The Law of the Covenant* (1984). Over the years from time to time we have glanced through one another's manuscripts. I don't believe, however, that John sent me a preview of *Contemporary Worship Music: A Biblical Defense*, although he did send me a signed copy inscribed "Dear Jim, Read it and weep!" Those who know my own liturgical labors will know that John and I differ over the best ways to reform liturgical music—although, perhaps oddly for Reformed/Presbyterian people, neither of us has felt the need to anathematize the other!

I was happy when director of Geneva Ministries to publish serially John's outline studies on ethics in the pages of *The Geneva Review*, and later on, before the days of Amazon.com, to sell John's books through my Biblical Horizons book catalogue.

Although I have learned much from John's work over the years, and hold him in high esteem as one of the best theologians of our time, I have also admired his combination of flexibility and boldness. John is a model for reading other thinkers on their own terms, and he is intolerant of intolerance. John paid a price for standing up for his beliefs in the face of increasing gnostic Klinean quackodoxy (my terms, not his) at what is now called Westminster Seminary. Our Lord was gracious, however, and John was immediately hired by Reformed Theological Seminary in Orlando, a place appreciative of his many gifts, and a friendly environment for him to complete his labors.

Finally, for a while John was present in an online discussion group where, in honor of his middle name, he became affectionately known as The Ancient MacElphatrick. Well, John, at the age of seventy, you are now TAM indeed!

BOB KAUFLIN, BA IN PIANO PERFORMANCE, DIRECTOR OF WORSHIP DEVELOPMENT, SOVEREIGN GRACE MINISTRIES, GAITHERSBURG, MARYLAND

I first came across John Frame's writings when I was studying the topic of worship. His book *Worship in Spirit and Truth* helped me realize that approaching worship in a biblically informed way helps us avoid the errors of passionless orthodoxy or mindless enthusiasm. His *Contemporary Worship Music: A Biblical Defense* strengthened my conviction that God can use music of all types to bring glory to his name. As I read more of John's writings, certain themes began to emerge. A commitment to biblical authority. An ability to make theologically complex concepts understandable. A humility and generosity toward those who disagree with him. A love for Scripture and the church. A passion for the gospel. A desire to serve others. As I've had the privilege of spending time with John, I've found his life to be the mirror image of his writings. He is a humble, gracious man who truly desires to help the church know and worship God more biblically and passionately. I thank God for the many years he has used John Frame to proclaim his Word and exalt the glories of Christ. I pray there are many more.

RICHARD P. KAUFMANN, MD,
ASSOCIATE PASTOR,
HARBOR PRESBYTERIAN CHURCH, SAN DIEGO

Congratulations! Happy Birthday! And especially, Thanks! Thanks for shaping the way I think. Each day I find myself walking around triangles as I study, problem-solve, and reflect on life. Our pastoral team often sits around playing "Triangle Frisbee," as we work on issues together. I am so grateful for the fourteen years we had together at New Life Presbyterian Church, in Escondido. Thanks for being my mentor, friend, and associate pastor.

One thing stands out during our time at New Life: you were a servant of Jesus' bride. You taught and modeled what it means to love and serve the local church. The apostle Paul evaluates churches not on the basis of size, programs, or facilities, but on the basis of faith, hope, and love. It follows that a servant of the church should give himself to growing the local church in faith, hope, and love. John, your teaching, writing, and life have done that in churches throughout the world. The impact is beyond anything I can get my mind around, so let me focus on one local church—New Life—1980–1994.

You grew us in our faith!

DOUGLAS F. KELLY, PhD,
RICHARD JORDAN PROFESSOR OF THEOLOGY,
REFORMED THEOLOGICAL SEMINARY, CHARLOTTE

I admired Professor John Frame long before I started teaching at RTS Jackson (in 1983); I appreciated his explanations of Van Til, and his engagement in an orthodox way with our contemporary culture. Once I got to RTS, I ordered his theology syllabi from Westminster West, and these were very helpful. John Frame beautifully holds together biblical fidelity and Reformed orthodoxy with a heart for our lost society, and a penetrating critique of it, a critique that is incisive, but never lacking in compassion and mercy. His classroom teaching has marked generations for the Lord, and his ever-increasing writings will continue to be a sound and uplifting guide for the Christian church for a long time to come. May this faithful servant of the Master be encouraged in every way; may his influence for the Risen Jesus increase!

You specifically grew us in our faith in the Lord Jesus (Eph. 1:15).

Of course, you did this in your teaching and preaching! But I am especially thinking of how you led us every Sunday in worship. You called us to worship with the gospel! For me it was always a highlight of the service. You drew us afresh and anew into the simple, unfathomable wonder of God's reckless love for us in Jesus! And it was not just what you said, but how you said it! It was clear that beneath your brilliance was a heart filled with love for our Savior. For those who knew you personally, it was especially meaningful because we knew that Jesus' love made a difference in how you lived each day. And as you played and sang, you enabled us not only to understand the content, but to experience the range of emotions expressed in the music. John, you taught me to love worship! You grew us in our faith in the Lord Jesus!

You grew us in our hope!

You specifically grew us in the hope that springs from two realities: our glorious inheritance in Jesus and his great power at work in us (Eph. 1:18–19)! John, you especially helped us understand God's power at work in us as the Spirit of God and the Word of God, for "where the Word is the Spirit is" (Eph. 5:18b; Col. 3:16)! This led to two results: hope in the world and hope for the world!

You grew us in our hope in the world! You enabled us to see that whatever suffering or struggles we face, there are no hopeless situations! With God's Word, God's Spirit, and God's people, we can respond to the most difficult hardships with wisdom, courage, and grace! We faced some very difficult issues during those fourteen years. The hardest were matters of life and death. The first one was Michael D., a young boy, who in a matter of one or two days went from vibrant health, to life support, to the unthinkable: when do we remove life support? John, you helped me and the parents think it through biblically, which enabled them to make the hardest decision they ever made, but with a sense that God's Word was giving them light in the darkest darkness.

There also were the criticisms we received for our worship style! Thanks for helping us process the input biblically. Thanks for being willing to answer those letters, especially the ones I never saw! And thank you for the two books on worship that flowed out of writing those letters. Those books are a blessing to the church at large and have quieted the worship wars! Thanks for growing us in our hope in the world.

You also grew us in our hope for the world! You lived a life that showed us that no matter how far from God people are, there are no hopeless people. You have a great heart for the lost and a great zeal for evangelism. So much so, that you willingly set aside your own preference in music and adopted a style that would more effectively resonate with the hearts of people in Escondido who did not know Jesus. And through Jesus' pursuing love, we had the joy of welcoming many into his family.

And you and Mary and your kids modeled your hope for the world, as you opened your hearts and your home to some very needy and in some cases some very difficult people! I vividly remember some late-night visits at your home from both the pastor and the police. And yet, the amazing thing is that lives were changed by the power of God's Spirit and Word. You grew us in our hope in and for the world.

You grew us in our love!

You specifically grew us in our love for all the saints (Eph. 1:15)!

Your love for Jesus' bride was especially evident in your teaching on the necessity of the visible unity of the church. When the New Life session struggled with the question whether we could/should leave the denomination in order to better fulfill our calling as a church, you led us to the Scriptures to draw out principles that would inform us as to when a church can leave a denomination. You focused us on God's Word, convinced that Scripture would lead us to do the right thing, in the right way, out of love for God's church. It was a hard process, and yet in the process you helped us grow in valuing the unity of the church and love for each of our brothers and sisters. And out of this experience came your book *Evangelical Reunion*, which is the clearest call to unity I have ever read.

You also grew us in our love for God's people by the way you debated. In the classroom, in session and presbytery meetings, and in personal discussions, you graciously expressed your appreciation for the other person's position. Most often you presented the argument for their position even more clearly than they had. You were able to do that with all sincerity, for you were convinced that even heresies were truths taken to a wrong extreme. But you didn't just do it out of an intellectual commitment, you did it out of love for your brother in the Lord. You did not want to win an argument at the expense of one who was purchased by the blood of Jesus. John, this is one of your greatest legacies to the church: you grew us in our love for one another.

John, I will forever be grateful for the impact you have had on my life, especially during those fourteen years at New Life, in Escondido. Your teaching, modeling, and friendship continue to grow me in faith, hope, and love. To whatever extent that I am a servant of Jesus' bride, it is to a large extent due to your gentle, powerful influence! And there is a great army of those who would say the same!

John, you asked me to exhort you as a pastor. Well, here it goes: Keep serving the bride of Christ! Keep teaching, writing, and modeling to us what it means to be a servant of the church, so together we will all grow in faith, hope, and love! And one day stand before Jesus and hear him say: "Well done, my good and faithful servant!"

SIMON J. KISTEMAKER, ThD, PROFESSOR EMERITUS OF NEW TESTAMENT, REFORMED THEOLOGICAL SEMINARY, ORLANDO

Characterized by quietness and unassuming discretion, John has served the church and kingdom of Jesus Christ in exemplary ways. He is a person who knows the Scriptures to such an extent that in his teaching and writing he is a veritable walking concordance. This knowledge of God's Word enables him to set forth sound doctrine, to expose teaching that conflicts with the Scriptures, and to be wise in the ways of the Lord. By way of his publications he has a proven record as a scholar who steadfastly promotes the truth of God.

In the classroom, John Frame has excelled as a teacher of the Reformed faith at the seminary campuses of Westminster and Reformed. At these schools he has devoted forty years in a teaching ministry that has drawn students from this country and all parts of the world. He has a personal interest in his students, knows their strengths and weaknesses, and meets with them to pass on counsel and advice. Students appreciate his teaching ministry and take his instruction into the churches they serve, so that Frame's effectiveness is passed on from the classroom to pulpits throughout the nation and abroad.

Frame has distinguished himself as an author of numerous volumes, among which his trilogy of *The Doctrine of God*, *The Doctrine of the Knowledge of God*, and *The Doctrine of the Christian Life* are outstanding examples. As a disciple of Cornelius Van Til, he demonstrates his expertise in theology and apologetics. He meets his opponents with gentleness, fairness, and grace, but he is unwilling to compromise the teachings of God's Word. He is a true defender of the faith.

John Frame's contributions to the church and to scholarship are many, which he shows in his publications by reaching out to elders and deacons, to the person in the pew, and to pastors and professors. His books address issues that relate to contemporary worship music, evangelical reunion, open theism, theonomy, the lordship of Christ, and the inerrancy of the Scriptures.

I express my personal thanks and appreciation to my friend, fellow teacher, and author who has served the Lord well in both church and kingdom.

PAUL D. KOOISTRA, PhD,
COORDINATOR OF MISSION TO THE WORLD (PCA)

What a privilege it is to be included with those who bring glory to our Savior by honoring his rich grace, which we have observed in the life and ministry of Dr. John Frame. John mentored me in ways that he has not even been aware of. When I was the president of Covenant Theological Seminary, I advocated holding the Reformed faith in a warm and winsome way. John taught me how to contend for the faith, in which we believe so strongly, but to do so in a way that also mirrors the gentleness and love of Christ. His way of practicing theology always seemed to reflect Paul's admonition to the church in Philippians chapter 2, "Have this mind in you which is also in Christ Jesus."

As a churchman, John has on a number of occasions encouraged me and others to embrace the Reformed church as a "larger tent," rather than a "small tent." He always seemed to believe that we need each other and that our church is far richer because of the diversity that we find within the Reformed faith and within the church that God has given us. This is no small matter, and I believe we need prophetic voices like his to continually call us away from our tendency toward sectarianism to a church that reflects the fact that they shall know us by our love for one another.

Most importantly, John's life and ministry have encouraged me to exercise the grace that I have received from Christ toward others—to avoid focusing on the foibles of others and to embrace the work of the Holy Spirit that I find within the body of Christ. I'm very thankful that Christ has given us examples such as John, who look like the Lord Jesus Christ.

Peter J. Leithart, PhD, Senior Fellow of Theology and Literature, New St. Andrews College, Moscow, Idaho

I still vividly remember John Frame's Van Til lectures delivered at Westminster, Philadelphia, when I was a student. It was the only time I regretted my decision to attend seminary in the east rather than the west. I have met John Frame a handful of times since, but in the main, I have known him through his books. I return to them often, and *The Doctrine of the Knowledge of God* is one of the anchors for a theology course I've taught to sophomore undergraduates for the past decade.

Why do I keep going back? Three reasons—of course, *three.*

First, Frame is a model of biblical faithfulness. A biblicist in the best sense, he doesn't let tradition, or trendiness, muzzle God's own words. Whatever the issue, he cuts through clutter and confusion and pushes me back to what the text of Scripture actually says. Second, Frame's "revisionist" presuppositionalism provides a way for theologians to absorb and build from the brilliant insights of Van Til's work without becoming ideologues or groupies. He has penetrated Van Til's potent creativity more deeply than anyone else, and in doing so has shown that creativity is a theological virtue. Finally, Frame is a model of academic clarity and, more importantly, of academic charity. Perspectivalism is Christian love made into theological method. I always insist that my students carefully study the appendices to

DKG about writing theological papers and critiquing others' work. I only wish I could demand the same of some of Frame's critics.

Peter A. Lillback, PhD,
President and Professor of Historical Theology,
Westminster Theological Seminary, Philadelphia

It is a joy and an honor to write a word of congratulations in celebration of the long and fruitful career of John Frame.

To my own disappointment, I've never had the privilege to have John as one of my classroom teachers. Nevertheless, his life and thought have made a deep impression on me.

I was a young, impressionable newcomer to the Reformed faith and its form of government when I met Dr. Frame, a distinguished teacher, elder, and leader in the courts of the church.

I first saw John in action as a presbyter when I was coming under care of presbytery at one of the meetings of the OPC's Philadelphia Presbytery. I can still remember John speaking on the floor with upraised arms. His words were persuasive, to be sure, but what I remember most was his blue shirt with both sleeves torn loose under his arms! This was, to be sure, a most remarkable first impression of a renowned theological leader. As I recall, John was still a bachelor at the time.

But the greatest impressions of Professor Frame have come through the years when I heard "Frame's views" reported by church leaders and seminary students in various contexts. His views of the OPC's and the PCA's joining and receiving, his views of worship, his views of the Old School/New School and Old Side/New Side debates, his engagement with Clark and Van Til, and on and on, always captured my interest and made me think more deeply.

Personally, I think I've most benefited from what was, in my time, his unpublished cogent syllabus on ethics, and his magisterial work on the knowledge of God.

So let me simply conclude—from shirtsleeves to sovereign grace, from apologetics to Presbyterian polity and politics, from churchman to seminary colleague—I thank God for the privilege of ministering in Christ's kingdom with John Frame, a theologian of the highest order.

May his writings—in print and on disk—ever enrich the people of God, even as they have enriched my labors for Christ and his church.

SAM T. LOGAN JR., PhD,
INTERNATIONAL DIRECTOR,
WORLD REFORMED FELLOWSHIP

I am a devoted follower of John Frame! I followed him to Princeton and I followed him to the Princeton Evangelical Fellowship and I followed him to Westminster!

And I continue following John Frame—what he writes is extraordinarily helpful to evangelical Reformed Christians who genuinely desire to engage the culture in which we live (both the Christian culture and the secular culture) from the perspective of Reformed orthodoxy. John demonstrates that it is not our exclusive task to be "safe" in our faith. It is, rather, our mission to interact with our world in ways that call the world, on the basis of the inerrant, infallible Word of God, into full obedience to and faithful worship of our sovereign Creator and Savior. John shows well all that it can mean to "invest" the "talents" that the Lord has given us in the work of extending his kingdom, even while some seek to bury their light lest it be endangered by the inevitable winds that blow when significant kingdom-extending activities are pursued.

Of all John's works, the most helpful to me has been his essay on "Machen's Warrior Children." It has been helpful because of the way in which it shows and chastises our/my frequent tendency (I would call it our/my "sinful" tendency) to treat as enemies precisely those who are closest to us theologically. Maintaining rigorous Reformed orthodoxy, even rigorously Reformed Van Tillian and Vosian orthodoxy, John has still reached out in winsome and effective ways to those who are not "orthodox" in those particular ways. This is the primary reason why I have followed John Frame and why I intend to continue to follow John Frame.

ROD MAYS, DMIN,
NATIONAL COORDINATOR, REFORMED UNIVERSITY MINISTRIES, VISITING PROFESSOR OF PRACTICAL THEOLOGY, REFORMED THEOLOGICAL SEMINARY, CHARLOTTE

Some people age with such grace and wit that they are forever young, both in their physical presence and in their writing. John Frame is such a person: a man who seems always able to provide a special gift for the church when it is needed most. Many would probably say he has been—

and continues to be—a progressive thinker, a man way ahead of his time. In an obvious wordplay, we could say that he has given the Reformed world an engaging new Frame-work for discerning the times, as well as a helpful thinking process for dealing with critical issues facing the church in postmodern culture. Whether challenging the church to rediscover "the knowledge of God when He is a stranger in the land," or calling her to affirm "the reason to believe in a pluralistic culture," or, perhaps, to get a grasp on "medical ethics in light of advancing medical technology and a low view of man," John has attempted to be a peacemaker. He has issued the plea, "let us reason together," in the worship wars and in denominational divisions. When many have called for evangelical separatism, John has advocated an "evangelical reunion." He has helped many campus ministers to grow in their formative years and to come to an understanding that the real aim of apologetics is to connect people with the truth and to love them, not to win arguments and crush the opposition. We all owe a great debt of gratitude to John Frame for his intellectual and academic gravitas. Many of us who do not speak or write with that kind of gifted authority and clarity have been able to reach to our bookshelves and find immediate help from John Frame. Thank you, John, for your timely responses to church controversies. Your measured words and wisdom have helped us to be better pastors and more thoughtful leaders as we have attempted to shepherd people wounded by the words and actions of those who hold strong opinions as to their own preferences. You have truly pastored pastors.

David K. Naugle, PhD,
Professor of Philosophy,
Dallas Baptist University

"Such is, each one, as is his love." So said St. Augustine, and John Frame's love—for the triune God and for his Word, world, and people—tells us all we need to know about this man. Frame is a man of God: a man of faith, of hope, and most of all a man of Christian love. Over the years, this greatest of the theological virtues has animated John Frame and his fruitful labors of which we are all beneficiaries. His life and work have been for the glory of God and our good. Praise God from whom all blessings flow, and one of those God-given blessings to the church and the world is John Frame. And we are grateful.

Thom Notaro, ThM,
P&R Publishing, 1978–2009

Authors distinguish themselves in many different ways. Some are voracious researchers. Others do incisive analysis or offer creative perspectives. A few capture bulky concepts in simple language. Some are marked by boldness while challenging flawed ideas. Winsomeness and an irenic spirit set others apart.

John Frame is among a small number of writers who combine all these traits. Yet what has long impressed me as much is his willingness to listen to people far less astute than he is and rework a paragraph in light of their concerns or questions. Usually that's a matter of heading off confusion, but John figures that if a reviewer or editor is struggling with a passage, others might struggle too.

Authors worthy of publication are authorities in their disciplines. John is an authority who, in an important sense, submits to his readers (plural, and at different places in their understandings) by listening to them and responding with care, although not compromise. Upholding biblical norms while uplifting people in their situations, he has been one of the most gracious, patient, and pleasant authors this former student has worked with through the years, and one most deserving of his readers' attention.

K. Scott Oliphint, PhD,
Professor of Apologetics and Systematic Theology,
Westminster Theological Seminary

In 1983–84, I was a ThM student at Westminster Seminary in Philadelphia. On the advice of my ThM thesis adviser, I decided to write my thesis on a comparison of Cornelius Van Til and Herman Dooyeweerd. Because Professor Frame was one of the few I knew who could evaluate such a thesis, I asked my adviser whether he would allow me to ask Professor Frame, who was then teaching at Westminster in California, if he would serve as the second reader on my thesis. I will never forget my adviser's response to that question: "You can ask him, but be aware that he is a very tough grader and you may regret your choice."

Professor Frame and I had never met. He had moved to California in 1980 and I had come to Westminster Philadelphia in 1981. So I called him—although neither of us knew the other—and asked whether he would agree to serve as the second reader on my thesis. His response was typically gracious. He did, however, inform me that this time in his life, for various reasons, was particularly intense and busy, and he expressed his hope that the thesis would not be too lengthy and would not take too much of his time.

As I moved through the thesis, it was apparent to me that Professor Frame's hope for a shorter piece was not going to materialize. It was going to be lengthy. Even worse, however, were the events that transpired soon after Professor Frame agreed to be my second reader.

I was asked by my thesis adviser to submit to him each chapter upon its completion. Chapter 1 was an overview of the methods of Van Til and Dooyeweerd, which, according to my adviser, was right on target. Chapter 2 was a provisional critique of some of Dooyeweerd's main tenets. As soon as my adviser received and read that chapter, he called me into his office. He told me, in no uncertain terms, that Chapter 2 was without merit, that it was of inferior quality for a ThM thesis, and that he had decided that he could not sign the thesis. This decision of his meant that I could not graduate from Westminster, and that I would have to return home without a ThM, having wasted a year of study.

After receiving my adviser's evaluation, I immediately called Professor Frame and told him what had happened. He responded by saying he would read the chapter as soon as it came in the mail and let me know his conclusions. I'll never forget the phone call I received one evening, and where I was when it came. My wife and I had just put our children to bed. I answered the phone: "Scott, this is John Frame. I'm willing to go to bat for you on this thesis." I was overwhelmed.

There is much more to tell but no space to tell it. Professor Frame did go to bat for me; I still have the letter that he sent (April 7, 1984), supporting my work. There were plenty of negative criticisms, but his bottom-line analysis was this: "Scott has wrestled with Dooyeweerdian concepts in great detail. The thesis (despite its great length) is enormously concise, so that there is a mountain of meaning on each page. Thus the sheer *quantity* of ideas is itself impressive. But the quantity is also qualitatively excellent."

Although he had never met me, although he was inundated with personal matters, although the thesis was much too long, although he had hoped that being second reader would not take up much of his time—Professor

Frame, in God's providence, is the reason that I was able to graduate with my ThM, and later to pursue further studies in apologetics.

I thanked him then, but I am not sure he has ever understood how centrally important his self-sacrifice to me in those days has been in my life. Humanly speaking, I never would have been able to pursue the discipline of apologetics had Professor Frame not taken the time—and it took much time—to defend my work. He took some personal "hits" because of that defense, but his evaluation was vindicated by others in the end, and thus my thesis adviser was constrained to sign the thesis. As it turned out, contrary to my adviser's warning, I did not in the least regret the choice I had made (although I am sure Professor Frame regretted it many times). The "tough grader" turned out to be the one who saw to it that my thesis was accepted.

Again, humanly speaking, I owe my calling as an apologist and a professor to John Frame, and to his selfless actions toward an unknown student in the mid-1980s. For that I will be forever grateful and thankful to the Lord.

Miller Peck, MS, Professor Emeritus, Mathematics and Computer Science, Westminster College, New Wilmington, Pennsylvania

John was a student at Princeton when we met. We attended sister Presbyterian churches in Mt. Lebanon (south hills of Pittsburgh). Sunday in his Virginia Manor home was a time for delightful conversations, often about Murray, Van Til, Gerstner, Leitch.

I lost contact with him during the years he was teaching at Westminster Seminary, and I at Westminster College. But now through e-mail we communicate often, especially when students and friends ask me hard questions. Like Francis Schaeffer, we try to give "honest answers to honest questions."

Recently our conversations turn on the loss of civility in our circles. Why can't we discuss our differences and questions like human beings? Is perfect doctrine the basis for friendship? Shibboleths test our loyalty, with brothers slaughtering brothers. Thankfully, John is a healing presence. We thank God for him and his ministry.

Andrew J. Peterson, PhD,
President, Reformed Theological Seminary,
Virtual Campus

Remembering the theme of his revival series in my local Methodist church, Dr. E. Stanley Jones would repeat the phrase, "Jesus is Lord." A commitment to Christ as a youngster was to respect this fact. Yet, years later, graduate training in social science and psychology would deny this fact and rephrase it as, if anything, "Jesus is Lord . . . in my opinion." Actually, the question might not even come up, since the education was lacking in a philosophy, let alone a theology, of science. A "theology of lordship" was desperately needed.

Fast-forward to the mid-1980s and a volume titled *The Doctrine of the Knowledge of God*. The proposition was that epistemology is a subarea of ethics . . . and "Jesus is Lord." With a lot of ink, John Frame provided a diagnosis and treatment for the myth of neutrality in the various modern disciplines of knowledge and learning. I remember the warning at the beginning of his course, The Christian Mind: "Seminary education can be very dangerous. With its regular teaching of the Bible, it can either soften or harden the heart." No neutrality personally, professionally, or academically.

Over the past few years, we have worked together on course development at the Virtual Campus. There is now a triad(!) of courses running 24/7 for online graduate students in the RTSV master's program, which hosts hundreds of students and runs at a significant profit for the seminary. Our students can listen to the lectures on Apple iTunes U, read the texts on DVD or Kindle e-book, and learn deeper with the interactive video social simulations written by the professor and our team with NexLearn. They also interact in online discussion forums with John, who writes e-notes, publication-ready! History of philosophy, Christian apologetics, and pastoral and social ethics make kingdom advances in the history of intellectual ideas . . . 24/7.

May God bless John and Mary Frame as they continue to assert the theology of lordship in all areas of life and culture. Love is the most important thing, but no neutrality, please.

ROBERT A. PETERSON, PhD,
PROFESSOR OF SYSTEMATIC THEOLOGY,
COVENANT THEOLOGICAL SEMINARY, ST. LOUIS

It is an honor to write a word of appreciation for your festschrift. Although I have never sat in your classroom, you have been one of my teachers for years. When I think of your books that have helped me, these immediately come to mind: *The Doctrine of the Knowledge of God, The Doctrine of God*, and *No Other God: A Response to Open Theism*. Because my training is exegetical and historical and not philosophical, I rely on theologians who are trained in philosophy. But I am frequently displeased with the place the Bible occupies in their work. You, however, please me, brother, because you seek to deliberately and consistently subordinate your own ideas to the Word of God. That places you in the company of a few philosophically competent theologians whose work I really trust. Your work is characterized by a capable handling of Holy Scripture, historical awareness, and astute theological thinking in the Reformed tradition. All in all, I give you this high commendation: your writings have helped me to love God with my mind.

JOHN PIPER, ThD,
PASTOR FOR PREACHING AND VISION,
BETHLEHEM BAPTIST CHURCH, MINNEAPOLIS;
CHANCELLOR/PROFESSOR OF PRACTICAL THEOLOGY,
BETHLEHEM COLLEGE/SEMINARY

John Frame loves the church and serves her well. From the power of great theological volumes, to the practicalities of denominational tensions, he is a helpful guide. From the rarefied air of Van Til, to the mists of rock music, to the morning light of creative theological education, Frame deals with us in a fatherly way. He is not bombastic. The imperfections of the church are his burden, not his whipping boy.

So when he takes up arms against doctrinal declination, as with feminism or open theism, we do not hear a strident voice. What is refreshing is his ability to model a firm stance on truth with a heartfelt affection for people. Razor-sharp reason is used to carve error away from truth, not skin off adversaries.

The witness of those who have taken classes with him is that he is personable, friendly, winsome, remarkably humble, and unassuming—the down-to-earth neighbor next door as much as the world-class theologian.

I thank God for raising up John Frame in our day. We are the wiser, the more biblical, and the healthier because of it. And because he has written so deeply and so well about such great truths about a great God, this will, I believe, be the testimony of generations to come.

Vernon E. Rainwater, MA, MSW, Pastor, Northland Church, Longwood, Florida

A biblically balanced view of worship must take into account both God's transcendence and his immanence, his exaltation and his nearness, his majestic holiness and his unmeasurable love. This balance is not always easy to maintain. Churches that focus on divine transcendence are in danger of making God appear distant, aloof, unfriendly, unloving, devoid of grace. Churches that focus on God's immanence sometimes lose sight of his majesty and purity, his hatred of sin, and the consequent seriousness of any divine-human encounter. To maintain this balance, we must go back again and again to the Scriptures themselves so that we may please God in worship rather than merely acting on our own intuitions.[1]

Reading the words above (in their context) was a formative moment in my work as a worship pastor. Having been in the role of a pastor, a "lead worshiper," a student of worship, I was caught up in the "worship wars" going on at the time. I longed to find the balance of sharing the heritage of the theologians, poets, preachers, and musicians the church has shared for millennia. But I believed the church should speak the language of the culture. Often these positions seemed in conflict. And then I read John Frame.

Through his writing and teaching, Dr. Frame has helped us find that balance of the transcendent and immanent God.

Furthermore, even when we think we get it "right" or balanced, Dr. Frame's work keeps my focus in the right direction. I offer this example:

1. *CWM*, 14.

It often surprises people to learn that God is not always pleased when people worship him. We might be inclined to think that God should be thankful for any attention we give him out of our busy schedules. But worship is not about God's thanking us; it is about our thanking him. And God is not pleased with just anything we choose to do in his presence. The mighty Lord of heaven and earth demands that our worship, indeed, all of life be governed by his word.[2]

Lastly, because Dr. Frame has written so widely and deeply on the nature and doctrine of God, he has helped me/us take God very seriously and ourselves . . . well, not so much. I love John Frame. He has changed how we worship God.

Harry L. Reeder, III, DD,
Senior Pastor, Briarwood Presbyterian Church, Birmingham

Festschrift is not a word that many of us encounter on a regular basis. This is because a festschrift is not a regular occurrence. Its etymology is Germanic, meaning "a book of celebration." A festschrift allows students as well as fellow scholars the opportunity to honor a mentor, colleague, and friend. It is my privilege to celebrate and honor Dr. John Frame in each of these relationships as one who epitomizes faithful biblical scholarship, passionate teaching, and a heart for the majesty of God as well as the expansion of the kingdom of God.

Dr. Frame's impact in my life was profound yet unexpected. I want to focus on three areas that I hope will encourage the readers of this book as well as John himself.

When I enrolled in Westminster Seminary I longed to benefit from the legacy of presuppositional apologetics established by Dr. Cornelius Van Til, but in God's providence he had retired. Subsequently, I would not only benefit from Dr. Van Til's legacy but be challenged by Dr. Frame in unexpected ways. Through his teaching, which was done with biblical precision and personal passion, my desire to make the majesty of God known through an effective apologetic was suddenly enlarged through a life-altering chal-

2. *WST*, 37.

lenge. A mighty God does mighty acts, and if I desired to make him known then I needed to know the mighty acts of God intimately.

Secondly this challenge was taken to another level when Dr. Frame's book *The Doctrine of the Knowledge of God*, appropriately subtitled *A Theology of Lordship*, was placed in my hands. This yet-unmatched treatment of evangelical epistemology was not only faithful but innovative. Its creativity was stimulating and staunchly orthodox without wavering or ambiguous uses of clichés so prevalent in many contemporary treatments of theological issues.

Thirdly the publications and personal ministry of Dr. John Frame in the arena of doxology (the praise of God "in Spirit and in truth") have manifested the motivation of his commitment to theological clarity and his passion for stretching the lives and ministries of his students and colleagues.

John's scholarship, penmanship, and leadership have been exposed as the simple yet profound manifestation of a heart that passionately embraces the worship of the triune God. In all of life "let every thing that hath breath praise the LORD" (Ps. 150:6 KJV). I gladly praise the Lord for the "breath of life" manifested through the life and ministry of Dr. John Frame—a friend, a teacher, and a fellow servant in the majesty and lordship of Jesus Christ.

ANDRÉE SEU,
SENIOR WRITER, *WORLD* MAGAZINE

Just as no two people in the world have the same mother, I'm quite sure I have a different John Frame from the rest of you. I knew him first as professor in the late 1970s, and was riveted by his ability to look at many sides of a question, but always with Scripture as the plumb line. A decade and a half later, in great distress of soul, I knew him as a counselor. Gradually, I knew him as a friend. That is to say, I know John Frame's story mainly as it intersects with mine. This is way too self-referential, but it's the same way I know God. There are whole continents of Frame's thought that are beyond my passport, but what I can understand continues to shine light on my walk with God. In a kind of de facto (and non remunerative) continuing-education course, I am one of legions who clutter his e-mail box daily with every kind of theological query. If this is tiresome for the professor, he doesn't show it, replying, as is his habit, with many pages of considerations where a lesser man might have offered a paragraph.

I confess a prejudice toward theologians who accord their opponents, even the vitriolic ones, respect and love. I have seen this over the years with John. And I have figured, with obstinate simplicity, that erudition must be accompanied by godliness to be genuine. John once told me, when I asked for advice on my own career, that we as followers of Christ should always be conscious of exhibiting the fruit of the Spirit in our writing. There is not a jotting I make that is not restrained from its worst impulses by the echo of these words in my brain.

John also told me that 1 Timothy 1:5 was his favorite verse about theology: "The goal of our instruction is love." Charity is often the casualty of theological debate. It is from John that I learned that love is theology at the point of perfection.

NORMAN SHEPHERD, THM, PASTOR, COTTAGE GROVE CHRISTIAN REFORMED CHURCH, SOUTH HOLLAND, ILLINOIS

I appreciate this opportunity to congratulate John M. Frame on completing seven decades of service in the kingdom of God. They have been enormously fruitful years, and my prayer is that his next two decades may be even more of a blessing to the church of Jesus Christ. He has performed valuable service mainly in the academic world, preparing men for ministry, but also in the organized church, and among the many who have sought his counsel on a personal and private level. The Lord did not give him the opportunity to serve as the pastor of a church, but his pastoral heart has been evident wherever he has gone. His understanding of issues under discussion, his wisdom and balance in their evaluation, and his deep desire "to live in peace with all men" (Heb. 12:14), even when the terms of debate called for sharp differences with others, has served as a model for a whole generation of students.

Our paths crossed for the first time in January 1963, on the second floor of Machen Hall at Westminster Seminary Philadelphia. It was my very first day as a teacher there. Meredith G. Kline was coming out of the classroom, and he offered encouragement by reminding me of Machen's words to his faculty colleagues: "Gentlemen, our strength lies in the ignorance of the students." One of the students in that class of seniors was John M. Frame. He was by no means ignorant, and I knew that because his reputation had preceded him. But he tolerated with characteristic grace this stand-in for Ned B. Stonehouse, who had died unexpectedly just a few months earlier.

I had the privilege a few years later of driving to New Haven, where he was studying at Yale University, to invite him to return to Westminster as a member of the faculty in my department. It would mean delaying his doctoral work, but when the call came he was willing to join with us in the great cause the seminary represented. Since that day he has done enough, and more than enough, to earn the doctorate he deserves.

Actually, we were related long before we met at Westminster because we both grew up in the old United Presbyterian Church of North America. The old UP Church was like *The Wonderful One-Hoss Shay* of Oliver Wendell Holmes in that "It ran a hundred years to a day [1858–1958], / And then, of a sudden it—" was gone, "All at once, and nothing first, / Just as bubbles do when they burst." The poet was, of course, beating on Calvinism as a marvelous machine with every proposition in place, and every proposition just as strong as every other one, so that nothing could go wrong at any one point without dooming the whole machine "all at once." There are people today who still think of Calvinism that way, but thankfully John Frame is not one of them. His first and ultimate commitment has always been to the truth of God's Word by which every theological and confessional proposition must be tested. That is why his work has been so constructive and so fruitful.

N. T. Wright wrote recently of telling his students that 20 percent of what he taught them was probably wrong, but he didn't know which 20 percent. I can hear John Frame making the same sort of confession because that is the humble kind of servant of Jesus Christ he is. Thank you, John, for all that you have taught us. May the Lord grant you many happy retirement years to enjoy your wife and children.

JOHN SOWELL, MDIV,
PRESIDENT, REFORMED THEOLOGICAL SEMINARY, ATLANTA

Too often, those whose ideas and writings are destined to outlive them unwittingly bequeath to subsequent generations an unintentional consequence. After these great thinkers impart the fruit of their fertile reflection upon those who will follow, intimate knowledge of their personalities becomes clouded. Although interest in their intellectual and spiritual contributions increases, perceptions of the individuals themselves either erode or else take on mythical proportions.

Knowing Professor Frame first as his student, and subsequently as a colleague for more than two decades in two seminaries, I have witnessed his character from his mid-years on to maturity, through exaltation and trials, from singleness, to his marriage, to fatherhood. In reflecting upon one who has been my friend for more than a quarter of a century, I hope a vibrant aspect of his persona will be preserved for those who will read about but will not have had the privilege of knowing this gifted man.

Generations who will ponder the giftedness of John Frame need to be introduced to the man whom his contemporaries know and love—a theological giant not only in intellect, but in Christlike example. One who displays a joyful countenance equally during seasons of adulation and of criticism. A pious gentleman whose writings, sermons, and musical performances consistently exalt the living God. A man whose passion, sincerity, and convictions lead to doxology, as he pauses his lectures to exclaim, "Our God is *so powerful!*"

Dr. Frame's legacy will be as a writer and teacher of lasting import and of unswerving faithfulness to the Holy Scriptures. Those who call this dear man their friend know him as a joyful, tenderhearted Christian with eyes that sharpen with intensity, yet twinkle with childlike joy when he speaks of his Lord and Savior.

The Scriptures teach that "the builder of a house has greater honor than the house itself." For generations, Dr. Frame's works will be edifying and provocative. Greater richness, however, will come from understanding that the author of those volumes is a man of humility and contagious joy, based on the confident conviction of a living faith.

R. C. Sproul, Drs, PhD
Founder and Chairman, Ligonier Ministries;
Senior Minister of Preaching and Teaching,
St. Andrew's Chapel, Sanford, Florida

For over four decades, John Frame has served the church both nationally and around the world as a teacher par excellence. John is something of a Renaissance man in that he has distinguished himself in the fields of

in that church when Mary was in high school. Pastor Calvin Cummings, Mary's dad, also had the distinction of serving on the board of trustees of Westminster in Philadelphia for some fifty years! And Mary's three brothers are all lifetime OPC ministers.

And not only was John himself so abundantly blessed during his twenty years at Westminster Seminary California, he was also such a rich blessing to so many others, both as a theologian and as a churchman. It would be hard to measure all he meant to New Life Church as elder, teacher, and worship leader. John has always been a professor who not only *talks about* the significance of the church as the body of Christ, but lives out that truth in terms of his own priorities and dedication. In that he has always been a most excellent model for his students.

As professor, John was one of the three full-time faculty members who taught classes in that very first year of Westminster Seminary California, along with Al Mawhinney and me. And through his teaching, and especially through his publications, he helped put our fledgling seminary on the Presbyterian and Reformed map. Our director of admissions told me several times that as he looked over the responses of new students to the question, "What attracted you to apply to WSC?" John Frame's name was mentioned more than any other. My own son, Steve, who graduated from WSC after studying at Gordon College and graduating cum laude from the University of California in San Diego, who has taught Bible for many years at Santa Fe Christian High School, and whom I consider to be an excellent judge of teaching talent, names Professor Frame as the best teacher he ever had (a rating that duly humbles me, since Steve had me as a teacher also). And my wife, Alice, who audited each of John's required courses at WSC, has him in her top five best teachers ever. (Happily, she has the good judgment to include me in her list.)

To my mind, what stands out in John's teaching is his ability to get students to actually *think*!—which is not as easy as it might sound. I've often said that what future ministers of the gospel so often seem to need is a course in Common Sense 101, or simply in the ability to think through an issue logically, reasonably, step by step. But the difficulty, of course, lies in knowing how one would teach such a course. It may be that John himself isn't always sure how much success he has had in teaching thinking, but I would put him at the first rank of teachers in this most important skill.

John's moving from Westminster Seminary California to Reformed Seminary in Orlando almost a decade ago now has been a great loss for WSC, but it has been a tremendous gain for RTS. And just as the move from Philadelphia to California proved to be such a blessing for John and Mary, so the move from California to Florida has proved to be such a joyous new chapter in their lives, and in the lives of all those touched by their faithful ministries. Thank you, John, for all you have meant to WSC, and to the Strimple family, by God's grace. We love you in the Lord.

Douglass E. Swagerty, MDiv, Senior Pastor, North Coast Presbyterian Church, Encinitas, California

What a privilege to be asked to share some personal words! You have blessed my life in several ways, and I will mention three of them briefly. First, I have been blessed to be one of your students and, as I go deeper and longer in ministry, I continue to be shaped by your insights. Your triperspectival approach to God's Word and world has profoundly affected how I perceive the gospel, my various ministry contexts, and my own gifts.

Second, you have excelled not only as a theologian, but also as a practitioner. It has been almost thirty years since we moved to Escondido the same summer, and the four years I spent with you as a fellow elder and pastor gave me the opportunity to benefit from your godly wisdom and careful shepherding of God's people. Lois also has wonderful memories of working together with you in the music ministry of the church.

Third, you have served as a wonderful model to me of how to treat those with whom you disagree. You once made a statement to the effect that a seminary can be a very "violent" atmosphere where words become weapons and fellow believers are treated as enemies. You certainly have the intellect to wage destructive theological warfare, but I have never met anyone who was more fair and loving to his critics. I remember going with you to Fuller Seminary in the early 1980s, at the height of the inerrancy debate, and observing you interact with Paul Jewett and Jack Rogers. And one of my greatest joys was bringing you and my college professor, Gordon Clark, into dialogue and seeing the two of you move beyond the unhelpful caricatures of past theological battles and come to a far more informed understanding of one another. John, whenever I read Paul's admonition to "speak the truth in love," I think of you.

Thank you for your friendship through all these years! When we taught together a few summers ago in Orlando, it was a joy to pick up our life stories where we had left them when you moved from California. I only wish those times were more frequent!

TIM TRACEY,
EXECUTIVE DIRECTOR WORSHIP,
NORTHLAND, A CHURCH DISTRIBUTED,
LONGWOOD, FLORIDA

John, I am grateful for the opportunity to honor God in his gift of you to the church. Northland Church is where God called me in 1992, and I'm fairly sure it's my first and last calling to a local church body. I came to my role at Northland with no experience and no idea what to do. I floundered. I had a clear calling, a hunger for God's Word, and an amazing community. But I had little understanding of a corporate worship theology or even the local ethos of worship in our community. And that, despite the reality that Saturdays came with amazing regularity! Further, "worship" was emerging as a "market" in contemporary Christian music, further exerting pressure on the local church to "get it right." I continued to flounder . . . and I was sobered by the reality that creativity would fail me and my mind would soon empty of any stored bank of "good ideas."

Then I read *Worship in Spirit and Truth*. My heart and mind were opened to my calling to the Northland body. In many ways, the Northland body was way ahead of me. Your words made concrete what was happening in our corporate worship gatherings. I began to understand the *Who* and the *why* more clearly. The work of the Spirit in sustaining me in my call was finally made clear through your words. I now had a blueprint that was centered on God's Word and built upon the person of Jesus Christ. As I read through your book and processed it in my community, I began to be set free from the tyranny of "creativity," "good ideas," and "relevance."

On the other side of our author/reader relationship, I now—and I consider it a great, great gift—know and experience the source of your great wisdom, a radically pervasive relationship with the person of Jesus Christ.

Each time I hear you speak, you speak only of Christ. Your relationship with him is prominent in all you are, all you speak, and all you write.

On this, the celebration of your seventieth birthday, I give thanks to God for you as a gift to the local church. I am so very glad you were born!

KEVIN J. VANHOOZER, PhD, BLANCHARD PROFESSOR OF THEOLOGY, WHEATON COLLEGE AND GRADUATE SCHOOL

Dear John,

Thirty years ago I sent out requests to various theology professors around the United States, asking them to recommend their seminaries to me, a prospective MDiv student. Some didn't understand my parody of the genre (viz., application forms) or the manner in which I had turned the tables. They informed me that it was usually the student, not the seminary, who provided letters of reference (duh!).

You, however, entered into the game with relish. To my question, "What are the strengths and weaknesses of the applicant?" you praised your faculty colleagues for their scholarship and saintliness, and then added, "Except me—I'm totally depraved." I knew then that I had found a kindred spirit, and my mentor.

You did not disappoint—well, at least not until you left for Westminster California at the end of my first year. Still, you went the extra mile by agreeing to supervise my MDiv honors thesis on "The Special Status of the Bible in James Barr, Brevard Childs, and David Kelsey" (and thanks, by the way, for introducing me to Kelsey; I still require his *Uses of Scripture in Recent Theology* for my theological method courses).

John, your example continues to represent the high bar for teaching that I am still trying to jump. Your lecture notes are the gold standard of the genre; no other professor I have had has even come close to rivaling them. But the most important thing I took away as a student was the conviction that it was possible to be both creative and faithful to Scripture and Reformed tradition, because you were.

I could mention many other things—for example, my indebtedness to you for introducing me to speech-act categories (and don't get me started about how multiperspectivalism anticipated what I later discovered in

Bakhtin)—but let me just say that neither a single letter, nor even a chapter in the present book, can suffice to express my gratitude. That is why I have instead dedicated my next book—*Remythologizing Theology: Divine Action, Passion, and Authorship* (Cambridge, forthcoming 2010)—to you:

> To John Frame: my first graduate-school theology professor, a master-pedagogue and triangulator extraordinaire, whose multiperspectival approach to the doctrine of God has been a source of continuing inspiration. As a scholar, he exemplifies sanctified erudition in engaging other positions with charitable criticism; as a saint, he personifies a compelling model of how to do theology with creative fidelity while remaining boldly yet humbly honest to God.

Happy birthday!

DOUGLAS WILSON, MA, MINISTER AT CHRIST CHURCH, FELLOW OF THEOLOGY, NEW ST. ANDREWS COLLEGE

John Frame and I have met only once, when we were speaking at a conference together, and we of course got along famously. This was only to be expected, because we got along quite well when we were not speaking at conferences together as well. John's attitude over the years, whether he has agreed or not, has always been consistently cordial, warm, appreciative, and unthreatened. Committed to the truths of Scripture and the Reformed faith, in that order, John has not been afraid to think creatively within those boundaries. He has also not been afraid to defend others who had the same priorities, whether he agreed with them or not. John has been a model for Reformed theologians in this profoundly secure demeanor.

When asked to write this personal word, I was glad to have the honor of saying something. John Frame has contributed enormously to the edification of the church today. He has excelled at winnowing various intellectual and theological contributions made in different sectors of the church, and having separated the wheat and chaff, bringing all the different kinds of wheat together. The result is fine flour, and really hearty bread.

Theology is meant to be lived, and one of the characteristics of John's contributions is that they are preeminently applicable. Sometimes the applications are made by him, as with his fine book on medical ethics, and other times he sets out the principles that others will get to apply—as with his work on apologetics. In a word, I am very grateful that John has been faithful in doing what the Lord has given him to do. He has been a man faithful in his generation.

JON ZENS, DMIN,
EDITOR, *SEARCHING TOGETHER*,
COPASTOR, WORD OF LIFE CHURCH,
TAYLORS FALLS, MINNESOTA

I began as a student at Westminster Philadelphia during John Frame's first year as a professor there. It was a privilege indeed to be in his classes. I was immediately struck by his humility and approachability, and the insights he gleaned from biblical texts. He stressed that our growing in the knowledge of the Lord was designed to impact our lives at a very practical level. I am thankful that the Lord allowed me to be influenced by Professor Frame's godly wisdom.

PART 1

INTRODUCTION

As I understand God's lordship, it includes God's control, authority, and presence. Reformed theology has been somewhat imbalanced in favor of the first two, liberal and broad evangelical theologies in favor of the latter. In Theology of Lordship, I try to bring these emphases together and provide a balance. Balance is essential because control, authority, and presence are *perspectives* on one another. An adequate understanding of each requires an adequate understanding of the others. That should bring a respite to unprofitable theological battles, which may turn out to be differences over emphasis and perspective rather than principle.

In the books of this series and all my other books, I seek to narrow the differences between factions and traditions within Christianity by suggesting that our differences are at least partly based on differences of emphasis and perspective. This study of God's lordship should also warn modern Christians and non-Christians to forsake their autonomous thinking and to see human thought as one area of service to God, since thought, like all the rest of human life, is subject to God's lordship. (The books try to bring together the concerns of theology with those of presuppositional apologetics.) It should also help us to see that Scripture, God's Word, is sufficient not only for "sacred" matters, but for all areas of human life, since God is Lord over all of life.

The Doctrine of the Knowledge of God (1987)

This work is my attempt to develop an epistemology, or theory of knowledge, based on the Bible. The main idea is that because of the nature of God's lordship, human thought cannot be autonomous. Thinking is one thing we do, and like all other human actions, it must be subject to God's authority. But because God's lordship also involves his presence with us, knowledge also has a subjective dimension.

I am especially concerned in this book with the concept of theology and its method. I develop the view that theology is the application of God's Word, by persons, to all areas of life—note the three perspectives. In theology we are not trying to find truth as such; that is already given to us in Scripture. Rather, theology is for us, to meet human needs from the Word. This excludes at the same time many imbalances commonly found in theology: absolutization of confessions and historical theology, the academic pride of many theological writings, speculative approaches, and subjectivist approaches.

Epistemology and theology can be approached from many perspectives because of the multiperspectival nature of God and of his creation.

The Doctrine of God (2002)

This book contains my most elaborate analysis of the concept of God's lordship in Scripture and my most extensive argument for the primacy of God's lordship therein. It also shows how the concept of lordship can illumine many other things that Scripture says about God. It provides antidotes to speculative, scholastic, and liberal approaches such as process theology and open theism. The structure of the book is intended to make the doctrine of God less philosophical and abstract and more focused on God's personal qualities in relationship with his people. And my multiperspectival approach tries to show how God can be understood from a variety of angles.

The Doctrine of the Christian Life (2008)

This book focuses on ethics and elaborates the case that all of human life (including our thought) is ethical, that is, subject to God's lordship. Half the book is metaethical, discussing what ethics is and how to do it, from the three lordship perspectives. Here I try to reconcile the concerns of Christian command ethics, narrative ethics, and virtue ethics, distinguishing these as equally ultimate perspectives. The other half is properly ethical, showing what Scripture says directly about ethical questions (using the Ten Commandments as a focal point). My ethic is based on *sola Scriptura* and contains frequent critique of natural-law approaches and the related notion that some ethical problems should be resolved by autonomous reasoning, rather than by Scripture.

The Doctrine of the Word of God (forthcoming)

This book urges that the Word of God is, first, God himself, and second, God's personal speech to us, creating obligations in its hearers: to believe, obey, and respond in many other ways. This Word comes to us today indirectly through a complicated process—copies, translations, editions, etc.—but God himself comes with it in the Spirit to illumine the Word and demonstrate its truth. God's Word is God himself speaking as Lord, and this Word manifests his lordship attributes of control, authority, and presence. So today the Word comes to us as the power of God, as his personal spoken word, and as the dwelling place of God himself with us. Since God always speaks truth to us, his Word is inerrant, but inerrancy is only one of the many qualities of God's personal speech.

Medical Ethics: Principles, Persons, and Problems (1988)

This book emerged from lectures I gave at a conference in the San Diego area. It briefly sets forth my triperspectival ethical methodology and then, in dialogue with secular and Roman Catholic ethical writers, takes up issues such as patient autonomy, informed consent, confidentiality, justice, clinical trials, and living wills. *The Doctrine of the Christian Life* presents a much fuller methodological analysis, and it overlaps *Medical Ethics* on some questions, such as the definition of death. But it does not cover the earlier list of issues I have mentioned here.

Perspectives on the Word of God (1990)

This book emerged from a series of lectures I gave at Trinity Evangelical Divinity School. It summarizes my approach to the doctrine of the Word of God, thus anticipating *The Doctrine of the Word of God*, and ethics, thus anticipating *The Doctrine of the Christian Life*.

Apologetics to the Glory of God: An Introduction (1994)

My apologetics text aims to resolve some matters of dispute among some presuppositional apologists and then to address actual problems of inquirers, something rarely done in the presuppositional literature. Cornelius Van Til had suggested that presuppositional apologetics can employ traditional arguments and uses of evidence. I try to show in general *how* that is possible: Evidences and psychological appeals represent the situational and existential perspectives within the broadly circular transcendental argument that represents the normative perspective.

Cornelius Van Til: An Analysis of His Thought (1995)

Written for the hundredth anniversary of Van Til's birth, this work analyzes Van Til's ideas—theological and apologetic. I have always thought of Van Til as more a theologian than an apologist, although his apologetic approach is very valuable. He put forth a remarkably creative approach to all theological questions, an approach that I have tried to utilize in my other books and that I explain here.

No Other God: A Response to Open Theism (2001)

In this book, I take a number of ideas from *The Doctrine of God* and add an analysis of open theism to show that the latter movement is a distortion of Scripture.

Salvation Belongs to the Lord: An Introduction to Systematic Theology (2006)

This book, taken from a taped lecture series, is as close as I will ever get to a complete systematic theology. It is a relatively brief survey of the topics of systematics, in popular style. Some of the chapters summarize parts of my longer books, particularly the Theology of Lordship series. Others treat subjects such as Christology and soteriology that I have never addressed elsewhere. One might well ask why I haven't written Lordship books on these topics. The answer is that I have never been asked to teach them on the seminary level, and therefore I haven't researched them to the degree that I have studied the subjects covered in the Lordship books. Blame the system of academic specialization! But certainly all the topics in *Salvation Belongs to the Lord* are important, and I'm happy that I have been able to address them, at least at a popular level. And you will find here, even on these subjects, some triperspectival distinctions that may be helpful.

Worship in Spirit and Truth: A Refreshing Study of the Principles and Practice of Biblical Worship (1996)

In this book, I try to show that Reformed theology allows more freedom in worship than is usually believed. I deal with basic biblical principles of worship, along with controversial matters such as the regulative principle, traditional worship models, contemporary music, dance, and drama. I distinguish between worship's narrow sense (Sunday services) and broad sense (our bodies as living sacrifices, Rom. 12:1–2), to show that in one sense all

duty theology; he later became a professor of New Testament at Pittsburgh Theological Seminary. Another professor there was Dr. John H. Gerstner, the same one who had such a deep influence on R. C. Sproul. Gerstner was a frequent speaker at our youth camps and rallies. He was a Socratic master teacher: I don't think I've completely forgotten anything I heard him say, or any of the thought processes he conjured up within me.

In high school years I also listened closely to a number of radio preachers, particularly Donald Grey Barnhouse of the *Bible Study Hour* and Peter Eldersveld of the *Back to God Hour*. Barnhouse was an evangelical pastor in the liberal Presbyterian denomination (PCUSA), rather dispensational in his theology. Eldersveld was a Dutch Calvinist from the Christian Reformed Church. Both had gifts for vivid language and persuasive argument. I hung on their every word.

Princeton University, 1957–61

At Princeton University, the main influences on me were my teachers on the one hand and the Princeton Evangelical Fellowship (PEF) on the other. The PEF was just about the only evangelical group on campus at the time. Through its ministry (and that of Westerly Road Church) I grew spiritually as at no other time in my life. My knowledge of the Bible went to a deeper level at PEF under the teaching of Dr. Donald Fullerton.[1] Both PEF and Beverly Heights encouraged me to memorize Scripture. I learned some seven hundred verses through the Navigators' Topical Memory System, and those are the verses that continue today to serve as landmarks for my theology.

PEF was dispensational in its viewpoint, as Barnhouse was, but Gerstner thought dispensationalism was an awful heresy. I never accepted the dispensational system, but neither could I accept Gerstner's harshly negative verdict about it. My friends at PEF were godly people who loved Jesus and the Word. We prayed together every day and visited dorm rooms to bring the gospel to fellow students. Princeton was a spiritual battleground, and the PEF folks were my fellow soldiers. Struggling together for Jesus against opposition tends to magnify the unity of believers and to decrease the importance of disagreement. Surely Jesus intended for his

---

1. For more reflections on this period in my life, see "Remembering Donald B. Fullerton," http://www.frame-poythress.org/frame_articles/Remembering_fullerton.htm.

people to wage this battle together, not separated into different denominations and theological factions. My experience with PEF (and earlier with Graham) prevented me from ever being anti-evangelical, as are many of my Reformed friends. At Princeton, I became an ecumenist.

I majored in philosophy and also took courses in religion, literature, and history. The religion courses, together with the denominational campus ministries, gave me my first introduction to theological liberalism. Although I had toyed with similar ideas during my high school years, I sharply rebelled against liberalism in college. Princeton liberalism was casual religion: no authoritative Bible, no passion for souls, no desire for holiness, no vitality. Indeed, the Christ of Scripture simply wasn't there. Later, I read J. Gresham Machen's *Christianity and Liberalism*,[2] which argued that liberalism was an entirely different religion from Christianity, and I found it entirely persuasive. Although liberalism has changed its face in the years since, I still see it as the opposite of the biblical gospel.

PEF taught me the importance of holding firmly to the supreme authority (including infallibility and inerrancy) of Scripture as God's Word, over against liberal religion. I have never abandoned that foundation, and it has played a major role in my teaching. In PEF, further, one could never argue a theological position without appealing directly to Scripture. Although this approach is sometimes derided as "proof-texting," I believe that rightly used, it constitutes the only sound theological method, and this has been a major emphasis in my work through my life. In this regard, see especially my article *IDSCB*.

My philosophy teachers, for the most part, did not profess to be Christians at all, liberal or otherwise. Walter Kaufmann, who had recently published his *Critique of Religion and Philosophy*,[3] was an expert on Friedrich Nietzsche and himself a very Nietzschean thinker, who did his best to destroy his students' Christian beliefs. His anti-Christian arguments didn't bother me much, by the grace of God. But I greatly enjoyed Kaufmann's brilliant intellect, clarity, and wit. His writings influenced my own writing style. (Over the years, I have had to temper the polemic edge of that style.) And like me, he had no sympathy with liberal theology. He attacked both conservative and liberal Christianity with equal zest, even presenting a persuasive critique

2. Grand Rapids: Eerdmans, 1923.
3. New York: Harper, 1958.

of the liberal "documentary hypothesis," which divided the Pentateuch into works of many different authors.

Other philosophy teachers gave me a good introduction to the history of philosophy, particularly Gregory Vlastos in Greek and medieval philosophy and George Pitcher in the modern period. I also studied with Ledger Wood, who revised and updated Frank Thilly's widely used *A History of Philosophy*.[4] But in general, the Princeton philosophers took a negative approach to their discipline's history. For them, the history of philosophy was largely a history of error. When we studied Plato, the important thing was to see all the mistakes Plato had made, not to value his vision. Same with other philosophers. This negativism can be understood partly from the fact that Princeton's philosophy department was one of the last to abandon logical positivism. Carl Hempel, the positivist of the Berlin school, taught logic and philosophy of science and, like other positivists, despised metaphysics, which had been such a central concern of the philosophic tradition.

Yet I did take a course in metaphysics at Princeton. It was the last one ever taught in that era: shortly afterward, the department voted to never again list a course with the word *metaphysics* in it. But the course I took from G. Dennis O'Brien had a large impact on my thinking. O'Brien was a young Roman Catholic (although Kaufmann said he could not vouch for O'Brien's orthodoxy). He had studied at the University of Chicago and valued the "classical realism" of Richard McKeon and John Wild.

In the metaphysics course, we studied Aristotle, Spinoza, and John Dewey, three philosophers of very different eras, with very different-looking metaphysical systems. O'Brien rejected the find-the-mistakes approach of his colleagues. When he taught Aristotle, one would have assumed that he was Aristotelian. But when he taught Spinoza, he seemed Spinozist, and when he taught Dewey, Deweyan. His general point was that if you started where Aristotle started, understanding his inheritance from his predecessors, understanding the questions he tried to answer, using the conceptual equipment available to him, thinking with the same intellectual gifts Aristotle enjoyed, you would probably come to the same conclusions he did. For O'Brien, the same could be said of Spinoza and of Dewey.

Aristotle described the world as a collection of things, Spinoza of facts, Dewey of processes; but these, to O'Brien, were not so much factual differences as differences in the philosopher's "way with the facts." Metaphysics in

4. New York: Henry Holt and Co., 1951.

general, he thought, was not a discovery of new facts, but rather it explored "ways with the facts."[5] Although O'Brien didn't use this terminology, what I took from his analysis was that Aristotle, Spinoza, and Dewey looked at the world from three "perspectives," as if viewing from three different angles.

I didn't entirely agree with this approach, and still do not. I think there are such things as "metaphysical facts," and I believe that many disagreements in metaphysics are precisely factual disagreements. But O'Brien's course was stimulating to me as few other courses have been. I was convinced that alongside other differences among philosophers (including factual differences), there were also "perspectival" differences. That is to say, not all the differences between thinkers are differences between truth and falsity, right and wrong; factual disagreements; or differences between clear thinking and "mistakes." Some are also differences in perspective, looking at the same truth from different angles. That was the beginning of my inclination to understand reality "perspectivally."

So when I graduated from Princeton, I was biblically oriented (almost biblicistic, but I think in a good way), antiliberal, ecumenical, and incipiently perspectivalist.

WESTMINSTER THEOLOGICAL SEMINARY (PHILADELPHIA), 1961–64

At Westminster, I studied largely with the "old faculty" that had taught there from the 1930s: Cornelius Van Til, John Murray, Ned Stonehouse, Paul Woolley, and Edward J. Young, plus some gifted younger men, such as Edmund Clowney and Meredith G. Kline.

I had begun to read Van Til in college, seeking help in dealing with the philosophical problems I encountered at Princeton. I had earlier read C. S. Lewis's *Mere Christianity*,[6] *The Problem of Pain*,[7] and *Miracles*.[8] Van Til was very critical of Lewis, but Lewis actually prepared me for Van Til. The *Miracles* book was especially helpful to me. There, Lewis showed that naturalism and Christianity were two distinct and incompatible worldviews, and that

---

5. One humorist in the class proposed the following essay question for the final exam: "Distinguish between 'a way with the facts' and 'away with the facts!' "

6. New York: Harper, 2001.

7. New York: Macmillan, 1957.

8. New York: Macmillan, 1947.

arguments against miracles typically assume that naturalism is true. Lewis seemed to me to be entirely right, and that readied me to believe Van Til's assertion that the Christian faith is a worldview unto itself, with its own distinctive metaphysics, epistemology, and ethics. Lewis also prepared me to accept Van Til's view that opposition to Christianity is not based fundamentally on factual discovery, but rather on presuppositions that rule out Christianity from the outset of the discussion.

Van Til became the greatest influence on my apologetics and theology. In my view, although I have been subjected to some derision for saying this, Van Til was the most important Christian thinker since John Calvin. His message is precisely what people of our time need most to hear: that the lordship of Jesus Christ must govern our thoughts (2 Cor. 10:5) as well as every other area of life. Every problem of theology, apologetics, biblical studies, science, and philosophy takes on a very different appearance when we reject non-Christian presuppositions and seek to think consistently according to Christian ones. Certainly, nobody who has not spent time with Van Til can understand well what I am about.[9]

I was interested in Van Til not only for his presuppositional epistemology and apologetic, but also for ideas of his that are less well known. In my *Van Til the Theologian*[10] booklet and in my larger book *CVT*, I discuss Van Til as a theologian, particularly his understanding of theological method. I took an interest, for example, in his threefold understanding of revelation in his *Introduction to Systematic Theology*:[11] revelation from God, nature, and man. He subdivided these, in turn, into various permutations: revelation from God about God, from God about nature, from God about man, from nature about God, etc. He also developed his ethics in accord with another threefold distinction found in the Westminster Confession of Faith: every ethical decision may be evaluated according to its goal, motive, and standard.[12] He denied that these topics must be taken up in any particular order, for he believed that each implied the others.

O'Brien had led me to think in terms of "perspectives." My Christian adaptation of O'Brien, under Van Til's tutelage, was that perspectivalism was

---

9. See especially the titles of Van Til on my "Recommended Resources" list in this volume.

10. Phillipsburg, NJ: Pilgrim Publishing, 1976; also available at http://www.frame-poythress.org/frame_articles/1976VanTil.htm.

11. Nutley, NJ: Presbyterian and Reformed, 1974, 64–109.

12. Cornelius Van Til, *Christian Theistic Ethics* (Nutley, NJ: Presbyterian and Reformed, 1971), 1–6. Cf. WCF 16.7.

necessary, since unlike God we are finite beings. We cannot see everything at once, as God does. So we must investigate things, first from this angle, then from that. But Van Til took me a step further: from a general perspectivalism to what would be called *tri*perspectivalism, to a set of threefold distinctions that are especially important for our reflection. Nature, man, and God; goal, motive, and standard.

Edmund Clowney reinforced this triadic perspective. In his course on the doctrine of the church, he produced an impressive pyramid diagram. The pyramid's base was divided into two intersecting triads, one listing the church's ministries, the other the church's leadership. The ministries were worship, edification, and witness. The offices of the church provided leadership in teaching, rule, and mercy. The diagram also distinguished "general" officers from "special," by bifurcating the triangle into an upper and a lower section. All Christians hold the "general" office as teachers, rulers, and givers of mercy. But there are also specially ordained people who have particular responsibilities in these areas: teaching elders, ruling elders, and deacons. Above the pyramid, with a space between him and the rest of the pyramid, was Jesus Christ, the head of the church, who embodies the ultimate in all the offices, the supreme Prophet, Priest, and King.[13]

My triperspectivalism began to bring together Van Til's triads, Clowney's triads, and some others into a general overview. When I later began teaching at Westminster, I taught the doctrine of God, organizing the material under the general headings of God's *transcendence* and *immanence*, following a common pattern in theology. But I became uneasy with this approach, coming to sense that *transcendence* was an ambiguous idea. Does it mean that God is so far from us as to be "wholly other" (Otto, Barth)? If so, how can he also be immanent? It occurred to me that biblically it would make more sense to define *transcendence* in terms of God's kingship or lordship: God is not infinitely removed from us in Scripture; rather, he *rules* us. My studies in divine lordship yielded an emphasis on God's *control, authority,* and *covenant presence,* which I came to call his *lordship attributes.* When Scripture talks about God's being "high" and "lifted up," it is not referring to some kind of wholly-otherness, but to God's kingly control and authority over his own domain. So why not define *transcendence* in those terms? And then *immanence* can refer to his covenant presence, his determination to be "with" his people, *Immanuel.*

13. See Edmund Clowney, *The Church* (Downers Grove, IL: InterVarsity Press, 1995).

Then (since I also taught ethics) I came to see that this threefold scheme correlated with Van Til's "goal, motive, standard." God's *control* was his lordship over nature and history, so that they conspired always to achieve the *goal* of God's glory. His *authority* was the *standard* for the behavior of his creatures. And his redemptive *presence*, in the hearts of his people, creates in them the *motives* necessary for good works.

This threefold understanding also applied to the doctrine of revelation and Scripture, which I also taught in my early years. As Van Til said, there is revelation from God, nature, and man *about* God, nature, and man. Nature is, of course, under God's *control*. But God also comes in person (and in his written Word) to speak to us with *authority*. Further, he reveals himself in human beings, his image, which is to say that God's revelation is *present* in us as well as outside us.

I came to believe that the ultimate root of these triads was the triune character of God. He is the Father, who develops an *authoritative* plan; the Son, who carries out that plan by his powerful *control* of all things; and the Spirit, who as the *presence* of God applies that plan to nature, history, and human beings.

This narrative has gone beyond my Westminster student years, but I need to return there to mention some other influences. One important influence was certainly Meredith G. Kline, who made exciting discoveries about the nature of biblical covenants. In my later teaching and writing, I made much use of Kline's idea that covenants were essentially *treaties* between the great King Yahweh and the "vassal" people that he has called to be his. As Kline showed, these treaties took written form, and their literary structure was somewhat constant: the name of the great King, the historical description of his past blessings to the vassal, the stipulations or laws of the covenant, and the sanctions: the blessings for obedience and the curses for disobedience. In the triad of history, law, sanctions, I found another application of my triperspectivalism. The history describes God's powerful *control* over nature and history; the law pronounces his *authoritative* requirements; the sanctions show that he is not an absentee Lord, but is *present* to show mercy to and discipline his people.

Kline identifies Scripture as God's treaty document in his *The Structure of Biblical Authority*,[14] a book that I have used again and again in my own teaching and writing. I think it is the first real theological breakthrough

---

14. Grand Rapids: Eerdmans, 1972.

since B. B. Warfield on the nature of the Bible. The treaty is authored by the great King, is holy (placed in the sanctuary), and has supreme authority for the vassal. In this study, Kline shows that God intends to rule his people by a book.

But I also received much help from other Westminster professors in maintaining a strong doctrine of Scripture. Edward J. Young's *Thy Word Is Truth*[15] was a great help in showing me the biblical rationale for the doctrine of inerrancy. Indeed, every course I took at Westminster in some way reinforced the truth of the authority of Scripture. Edmund Clowney showed us that the primacy of God's Word could be found on nearly every page of Scripture. Van Til, in *The Protestant Doctrine of Scripture*[16] and in *An Introduction to Systematic Theology*, presented biblical authority as inevitable, in terms of a Christian philosophy. And John Murray's wonderful article "The Attestation of Scripture"[17] and his *Calvin on Scripture and Divine Sovereignty*[18] summarized the issues masterfully.

I should say something more about John Murray. It was common in those days for students to say that they had come to Westminster for Van Til but that they stayed for Murray. Murray was not well known outside Reformed circles, but as a theologian he was peerless. Murray, Clowney, and Van Til are the authors I refer to most often today. Murray's *Collected Writings*[19] are a wonderful treasury of exegesis and theological reflection. The present-day criticism of Murray in Reformed circles is in my judgment unworthy of him.

What I learned best from Murray was his theological method. At Princeton, my PEF friends urged me not to study at Westminster. In their view, Reformed theology was more a celebration of its own tradition than a serious reading of Scripture. When I came to Westminster, I was armed by this criticism. If Westminster had defended its teaching mainly by referring to its confessions and past thinkers, I would not have been persuaded. But Murray focused on Scripture itself. His classes were almost entirely spent in exegeting the main biblical sources on each topic. In this, he was not afraid

15. Grand Rapids: Eerdmans, 1957.
16. Nutley, NJ: Presbyterian and Reformed, 1967.
17. In Ned Stonehouse and Paul Woolley, eds., *The Infallible Word* (Philadelphia: Presbyterian and Reformed, 1946), 1–54. This volume contains essays by many Westminster professors, which were and are very helpful.
18. Grand Rapids: Baker, 1960.
19. 4 vols. (Edinburgh: Banner of Truth, 1982).

to differ from Reformed tradition, even the confessions, when he believed the biblical text pointed in a different direction. He described his method in his essay "Systematic Theology,"[20] which I have read again and again, and on which every young theologian should deeply meditate. Here he condemns traditionalism and advocates a concentration on biblical exegesis.

My own theology is very unlike Murray's in style, diction, and emphasis. But in its method and most of its conclusions, my work is more like his than any other theological writer's.

I was more ambivalent to the large emphasis at Westminster on redemptive history or biblical theology. A number of the professors had been deeply influenced by Geerhardus Vos, professor of biblical theology at Princeton Seminary. Edmund Clowney, although he had not studied with Vos, was also enthusiastic about Vos's ideas and taught students to focus their sermons on the redemptive-historical significance of each text. This meant that biblical texts were intended to proclaim redemption in Christ (the Old Testament looking forward to him, the New Testament reflecting on his incarnation, atonement, resurrection, and ascension). Sermons, on this view, should also focus on redemption and not on, say, the moral successes or failures of biblical characters. Sermons that used biblical characters to illustrate spiritual or moral issues were called "exemplarist" or "moralistic."

I, too, was impressed by the importance of redemptive history, and to this day I benefit most from sermons that have that focus, which is, in the end, a focus on Christ. Clowney was one of my very favorite preachers. In some circles, however, this emphasis has become divisive and sectarian. Churches have been divided by extreme advocates of redemptive history who say that one must never, ever use a biblical character as a moral example, and who bend texts in bizarre ways to make them "point to Christ." I think this extreme form of the movement has been harmful. The extreme polemic against "exemplarism" is misplaced. Scripture does, in fact, point to characters in its narrative as positive and negative examples (Matt. 12:3–8; 1 Cor. 11:1; Heb. 11; 12:16), and Scripture strongly emphasizes godly examples as an aid to spiritual growth (1 Tim. 4:12; cf. 3:1–13). This is not opposed to the centrality of Christ. In the Bible, Christ is Redeemer, but he is also the supreme example of holy living (Phil. 2:1–11; 1 Peter 2:21; 4:1; 1 John 3:16). So Westminster's emphasis on redemptive history was a stimulus to my

20. *Collected Writings*, 4:1–21.

thinking, but my experience there led me to oppose redemptive-historical extremism.[21]

I should also mention another major influence on my thought from this period, although from one who was not on the Westminster faculty: Francis Schaeffer. I met Schaeffer only three or four times in my life. I spent a night at his chalet in Switzerland in 1960, but he was away in the States at the time. I hoped to spend more time there, but God never opened the door. Nevertheless, reports of God's work at L'Abri stirred my soul, and I sought any opportunity to read Schaeffer's letters and, when later available, his books.

Early in my study at Westminster, I read Schaeffer's article "A Review of a Review," published in *The Bible Today*.[22] Schaeffer had studied both with Van Til and with the editor of *The Bible Today*, J. Oliver Buswell. Buswell had been very critical of Van Til. Schaeffer's article sought to bring them closer together. Much of Schaeffer's argument made sense to me, and from then on I believed that the differences between Van Til's and the "traditional" apologetic were somewhat less than Van Til understood them to be.

Even more impressive to me, however, was Schaeffer's example as an evangelist. L'Abri sought both to give "honest answers to honest questions" to the people who visited and to show them an example of radical Christian love and hospitality, a "demonstration that God is real." I came to know many who had been converted through L'Abri, or had been deeply influenced by the ministry. Almost without exception, these believers were spiritually mature, balanced, passionate about both truth and holiness. Although I watched L'Abri from afar off, it influenced my own ministry more than many who were closer by.

I also thought much during my student years about the process of theological education itself. Westminster education was very academic. The seminary sought to draw a very sharp line between academy and church, to the point that many students (more radical than their professors, of course) thought it was inappropriate to have chapel exercises or prayer meetings on campus. I reacted sharply against this kind of thinking. It seemed to me that there was no biblical reason to think that training for the ministry should

21. See *DCL*, 271–97; also "Some Journal Entries on Preaching," http://www.frame-poythress.org/frame_articles/1999Journal.htm.

22. *The Bible Today* (October 1948): 7–9; also available at http://www.pcahistory.org/documents/schaefferreview.html.

be apart from the church, much reason to think that such training should be saturated with the means of grace. Many at Westminster said that it was wrong to "separate" the Christian life from Christian doctrine. But as I've often noted, *separate* is an ambiguous term. What this phrase sometimes meant at Westminster was that if you got the doctrines right, spiritual growth was the inevitable outcome. Yet both Scripture and my own experience invalidated that judgment.

So some years later (1972) I wrote "Proposal for a New Seminary,"[23] which argued that theological education should be first of all a practical field education within the church with academic supplements as needed (rather the opposite of the current model). This Proposal humbled me: I saw that I would not have been fit to be a teacher in such a seminary. Later, I argued that there was also benefit to be found in the traditional model (in which I have, in fact, participated through my life).[24] But my Proposal remains my ideal.

My student years at Westminster were deeply formative. Particularly, I emerged fully convinced of biblical authority and presuppositional epis-temology, modified a bit in Schaeffer's direction, ambivalent toward the redemptive-historical emphasis, somewhat biblicistic in my theological method, and inclined to a perspectival understanding of biblical concepts and theological issues. I believed that theological education was truly a ministry of the church, using all the means of God's grace. So I sought to speak the truth in love.

YALE UNIVERSITY, 1964–68

I went to Yale for graduate study in philosophical theology. I earned both an MA and an MPhil there, but, alas, I did not finish my dissertation for the PhD.

The program allowed me to take courses both in philosophy and in religion-theology. In philosophy, I took courses from Paul Weiss, who modi-fied Alfred North Whitehead's process philosophy; from William Christian, who tried to schematize the language of religion; and from H. D. Lewis, a defender of libertarian free will. I did not accept Lewis's arguments, but I still

23. *Journal of Pastoral Practice* 2, 1 (Winter 1978): 10–17; also available at http://www.frame-poythress.org/frame_articles/1978Proposal.htm.
24. "Learning at Jesus' Feet," http://www.frame-poythress.org/frame_articles/2003Learning.htm.

consider his philosophical formulations of libertarianism to be definitive.[25] I also served as a teaching assistant to John Wild, who by then had abandoned "classical realism" in favor of a form of existential philosophy.

In theology, I studied with the brilliant young David Kelsey (who raised the question of how Scripture should be *used* as an authority),[26] theologian of culture Julian Hartt, and George Lindbeck,[27] now known as the father of postliberalism.[28] I took courses from Lindbeck on Aquinas and Tillich, but the one that affected me most was a course I audited on comparative dogmatics. Here he urged a perspectival approach to the different confessional traditions. He described himself as "on the conservative wing of the avant-garde of the ecumenical movement." By "avant-garde" he meant that he was serious about breaking down barriers between different traditions. By "conservative" he meant that he took these differences themselves seriously: he wanted to reconcile the traditions, not dismantle them. As O'Brien had managed to reconcile Aristotle, Spinoza, and Dewey by analyzing their questions in their intellectual context, so in a similar way Lindbeck sought to reconcile the various theological traditions. He recommended to us, for example, Stephen Pfurtner's *Luther and Aquinas on Salvation*,[29] which presents even the deep divide over justification in a perspectival way. I was not convinced, yet I was challenged not to take the traditional interdenominational arguments at face value, but to see if I could find ways in which the parties could look at one another more sympathetically. My ecumenism and my perspectivalism were drawing together.

Another major influence on my thinking at Yale was Paul Holmer,[30] my thesis adviser. Holmer had been raised an evangelical and had come

25. See, for example, his *Our Experience of God* (London: Allen and Unwin, 1959), and *Freedom and History* (London: Allen and Unwin, 1962). For my view of libertarianism, see my *DG*, 135–45, and *NOG*, 119–31.

26. See my review of his *The Uses of Scripture in Recent Theology*, in *WTJ* 39, 2 (Spring 1977): 328–53; also available at http://www.frame-poythress.org.

27. See my review of his *The Nature of Theology* in *The Presbyterian Journal* 43 (February 27, 1985): 11–12; also Appendix H to my *DKG*.

28. Hans Frei, one of the main figures of "narrative theology," also taught at Yale at the time, but I did not take courses from him. His graduate courses at the time dealt with nineteenth-century German thinkers and required students to read them in German. Although I knew some German, I did not want to spend time in this type of course, even for the great benefit of studying with Frei.

29. New York: Sheed and Ward, 1964.

30. See my review of Holmer's *The Grammar of Faith*, in *WTJ* 42, 1 (Fall 1979): 219–31; also available at http://www.frame-poythress.org.

back to the evangelical faith after some time as what he called a "positivist." His theological heroes were Martin Luther and Søren Kierkegaard, and his philosophic hero Ludwig Wittgenstein. I had read both Kierkegaard and Wittgenstein at Princeton, but it was Holmer who got me excited about them. Although Kierkegaard still fascinates me, the scholarly debates on how to interpret him have left me frustrated, and I have not made much use of him in my own thinking. Wittgenstein, however, is a thinker I often turn back to. His view that meaning is, in most cases, its *use* in the language certainly influenced my own view that "theology is application," although I have been very careful to distinguish my general position from Wittgenstein's. For other uses of Wittgenstein in my work, see his entry in the name index of my *DKG*.

In brief, I left Yale thinking more deeply about Scripture and perspectivalism, strongly opposed to libertarianism, and persuaded that theology is the use of biblical language for the edification of people. My basic convictions about the authority of Scripture and the presuppositional nature of thought held firm, despite challenges by respected thinkers.

Back to Westminster, 1968–80

At Norman Shepherd's invitation, I returned to Westminster to teach systematic theology. Cornelius Van Til then asked me if I would also teach some courses in the apologetics department, and by 1976 the administration had added "apologetics" to my title. My required courses were in the doctrine of Scripture, the doctrine of God, apologetics, and ethics. All of these involved reflection on epistemology, so that field also consumed much of my study. With the later addition of worship, these were the subjects on which I have done most of my writing over the course of my life.

As a teacher at Westminster, I sought to formulate and communicate the thinking I had previously developed, but my theology did not remain static. I continued to be influenced by people and literature.

Sometimes I was influenced by my own students. When I arrived, many students at Westminster were disciples of the Dutch Calvinistic philosopher Herman Dooyeweerd. These students tended to be pretty arrogant, arguing that the traditional Reformed theology that Westminster represented was "dualist," "scholastic," and so on. Eventually I found myself at odds with them and their ideology. I was particularly concerned about their doctrine of revelation, in which the authority of Scripture was limited to the "realm of faith" and our main guidance for life was to be found, not in Scripture at all, but rather in the "word of creation," i.e., natural revelation understood through the lens of Dooyeweerd's philosophy. The Bibliography in this volume contains a number of titles arising out of this controversy, particularly my booklet *TAP*.

Although I opposed the Dooyeweerdian movement, it motivated me to rethink some things. Particularly, I had to learn how to give some account of the place of Scripture in relation to general revelation, Christ as the Word of God, and the various unwritten media by which the Word of God comes to us. I found help in Van Til's triads, nature, man, and God, which contributed to my own triperspectivalism.

Also contributing much to triperspectivalism was Vern Poythress, who studied at Westminster in the early 1970s. Poythress took a great interest in my work, and my student soon became my teacher. Poythress had studied with Kenneth Pike, the famous linguist who taught many of the Wycliffe Bible Translators. Pike had developed what Vern described as triperspectival distinctions within linguistics: particle, wave, and field. Poythress was and is very brilliant, and he stimulated me to see dimensions to my triperspectival ideas that I could not have thought of myself. His support convinced me that God had led us into some important insights, and Vern has ever since been a friend and theological partner. See especially his *Symphonic Theology*,[31] but his many other books also articulate our joint vision. For many books and articles he has written, see our joint Web site, http://www.frame-poythress.org.

In a different way, Norman Shepherd was influential in my thinking and life. Norman had graduated from Westminster by the time I arrived as a student, but even in his absence he was well known on campus. My fellow students often referred to him as the likely successor to John Murray. Both men were brilliant and were exclusive psalm singers. Shepherd lacked Murray's Scottish brogue, but his style of lecturing, his choice of words, and even his mannerisms were very similar to Murray's.

When Ned Stonehouse died in 1962, Shepherd was asked to teach Stonehouse's former course in New Testament biblical theology. Shepherd's major field was systematic theology, not New Testament, but we students were in awe of him. Given little advance notice in teaching the course, he

---

31. Grand Rapids: Zondervan, 1987; also available at http://www.frame-poythress.org.

worked hard to stay ahead of the class. We saw him every day, sitting at a library table, surrounded by books and notes. I put in a special effort to understand his material, out of respect for his hard work and excellent presentation. Perhaps I worked too hard, because my mind went blank during the final exam. I was given one of the lower grades that I received as a seminary student.

In the mid-1960s, Shepherd was called to work alongside Murray in systematics, and then, when Murray retired, Shepherd taught all the systematics courses for one year. He wrote to me at Yale to see whether I would be interested in helping him out, and of course I was, although I was surprised that he would call on one who had made a mere B+ in his New Testament biblical theology course. I got to know him fairly well in those days; we attended the same church as well as participating together in the seminary program. Even as a colleague, I was still in awe of him. His understanding of the Scriptures and the Reformed tradition far exceeded mine.

Shepherd was the last person that I (or anyone else) would have expected to create doctrinal controversy. He was so like Murray, and Murray had virtually defined Reformed orthodoxy for the rest of us. But in 1974 Shepherd was challenged on his view of justification and continues today to be a figure of controversy.[32] Today I don't think I can fairly be called a "Shepherdite" in terms of that controversy. But I learned a huge amount of theology from Shepherd. I audited two of his courses just for my own personal edification, and I continue to be edified by what I learned there. Shepherd remains for me a model of careful, precise, responsible theological scholarship and doctrinal formulation. Like Murray, he always puts Scripture ahead of tradition, and in that respect he remains a model for me.

Another colleague who influenced me profoundly was C. John Miller, who taught practical theology. Although "Jack," as we called him, was an able scholar, his heart was in evangelism and church planting. He founded New Life Church, which rapidly became a megachurch, the World Harvest Mission, and the Sonship ministry, a ministry of conferences and tapes that articulate Miller's vision of gospel-centered Christian living.[33] I greatly admired Jack's evangelistic boldness and humble spirit. On a number of occasions, he invited me to accompany him on evangelistic projects. I

32. For my response to his view of justification, see my *RLT* in this volume. For Shepherd's position, see his book *The Call of Grace* (Phillipsburg, NJ: P&R Publishing, 2000).

33. For my evaluation of Sonship, see my *RLT* in this volume.

declined, citing other business; but I regret now that I didn't make time to be with Jack at those times. I think that would have made me a better Christian and theologian.

I suppose that Jack's greatest influence on me was to make me willing to endure the scorn of traditionalists in the church. Jack's emphasis on evangelism led him to employ a style of worship at New Life that was far from the Presbyterian tradition. He used contemporary songs, guitars, cultivated informality. Many in our circles balked at this, even ridiculed it. But people came to Christ by God's grace, overcame besetting sins, became zealous for Christ. Eventually, many who had at first mocked New Life became enthusiastic members.

When I moved to California, we planted "New Life Presbyterian Church in Escondido," patterned in many ways after New Life in Philadelphia. The pastor was Dick Kaufmann, who had been a ruling elder at New Life in Philadelphia. We hoped to reach the unchurched, rather than merely to attract Reformed people. (Had we adopted the latter policy and succeeded, we would have added another division to a rather small Reformed community.) I was the elder in charge of worship, and I taught adults a class on worship, which led to my book *WST*. I was also asked to reply to letters we received that were critical of our worship, and that correspondence led to my book *CWM*. So I cite Jack Miller as a major inspiration for my work in this area. His books, especially *Outgrowing the Ingrown Church*,[34] defined for me what life in the church should be like, and Dick Kaufmann, my pastor for fourteen years, defined for me the model of a godly pastor. Miller and Kaufmann had a very broad influence on my thinking in many areas. Their attitude of love and grace to believer and unbeliever, friend and enemy alike rebuked my pride and spiritual complacency.

In my years of teaching in Philadelphia, I also had a good relationship with my colleague Jay E. Adams, who developed a new approach to pastoral counseling that was known as "nouthetic" or "biblical" counseling. Jay has been very supportive and encouraging to me over the years. Later we were also colleagues at Westminster in California.

He wrote many books on nouthetic counseling, but the basic exposition of his position was *Competent to Counsel*.[35] I have waxed hot and cold on this approach through the years. Since counseling is not my field, I have not

34. Grand Rapids: Zondervan, 1986.
35. Grand Rapids: Baker, 1970.

had to take a final position on it, and I'm glad of that. On the positive side, Adams's counseling method is presuppositional and semi-biblicistic in the way that I am. I love it when people search the Scriptures to find what the Bible says on a subject of importance. On the other hand, Adams has been criticized for not making sufficient use of general revelation, and therefore for his almost entirely negative view of secular psychology. That criticism rings a bell with me, too, because for all my biblicism I do believe it is important to understand extrabiblical truth, if only to accurately apply the Bible to a situation. (This is what I call the "situational perspective.") Practically, I've seen nouthetic counselors, by God's grace, help people solve many serious problems in their lives. But I've also seen some nouthetic counselors who have not listened hard enough to their counselees, who have ignored important situational factors, and who have therefore brought harm. I think the younger generation of nouthetic counselors, such as David Powlison and Ed Welch, have found a better balance here.

Another student during the Philadelphia years who led me to rethink some things was Greg Bahnsen. He was a disciple of Van Til and Rousas Rushdoony and became the leading formulator and defender of theonomy, the view that Old Testament civil law must be followed by modern civil governments, particularly that the penalties of crimes laid out in the Old Testament are norms for contemporary penology.[36] Bahnsen was a friend until his untimely death in 1995 from the complications of heart surgery, although our friendship did have some ups and downs. I never became a theonomist, but theonomy was a major motivation in my attempt to think through the implications of the law of Moses for today, as in my *DCL*. Vern Poythress's *The Shadow of Christ in the Law of Moses*,[37] in my view, gives the best answers to the questions raised by theonomy, and I consult it regularly.

WESTMINSTER IN CALIFORNIA, 1980–2000

I moved to California in 1980 to help establish a new campus for Westminster. Other founders and early teachers were Robert Strimple, Allen Mawhinney, Dennis Johnson, Jay Adams, Robert Godfrey, Derke Bergsma, and Meredith Kline. We went with a missionary vision, for California had

36. See his *Theonomy in Christian Ethics* (Nutley, NJ: Presbyterian and Reformed, 1977).
37. Brentwood, TN: Wolgemuth & Hyatt, 1991; also available at http://www.frame-poythress.org/Poythress_books/Shadow/bl0.html.

very few Reformed churches, and we were probably the only Reformed seminary west of the Mississippi. The excitement of those early years (along with the planting of New Life Church, as I described it earlier) stirred me. There was a wonderful collegiality among the early faculty and students, despite some theological diversity.

My ecumenical vision was tested in the mid-1980s, when the Orthodox Presbyterian Church (of which New Life was a congregation) declined to join the Presbyterian Church in America, in my opinion for quite inadequate reasons. In 1989, New Life, and I with the church, left the OP denomination for the PCA. Jack Miller and the New Life Church in Philadelphia made the same decision. My *ER* was motivated by these events and summarized my thinking about them. In this context I came to see that denominationalism itself was unbiblical, and the book dealt with that broader issue.

By the 1990s, things at the seminary had also deteriorated, from my point of view. Differences that had been tolerable in the 1980s became matters of contention and faction in the 1990s. Among these were redemptive history, worship style, the regulative principle of worship, and the place of confessions. Some new faculty made the situation worse, in my opinion. I came to see that factionalism itself as a major evil, both in the churches and in the seminary. This situation influenced my writing thereafter.

My colleague Meredith Kline also became something of a negative influence on me during this period. I mentioned that during my student years at Westminster Seminary, Kline was one of my heroes. He stood for the Bible against Reformed traditionalism and taught me how theology could be wonderfully creative within the bounds of orthodoxy. But in later years, Kline developed a degree of rigidity and dogmatism that surprised and disappointed me. Perhaps his conflicts with theonomy and with Norman Shepherd in the 1970s had marked the turning point. I thought his review of Bahnsen's *Theonomy*[38] was over the top, as we say. And in his response to Shepherd, Kline seemed to be saying that one could not be orthodox unless one adhered to Kline's distinctive (and sometimes innovative) positions on the covenant of works and the culture/cult distinction.

Even though I disagreed with Kline, I was happy that he was willing to join us at Westminster in California, for I thought he was still the most brilliant biblical theologian in the Reformed community, and he was the

---

38. "Comments on an Old-New Error," *WTJ* (1978–79): 172–89; also available at http://www.covopc.org/Kline/Kline_on_Theonomy.html.

one who, more than anyone else, could get students excited about biblical theology. In retrospect, however, I see Kline as a divisive figure at the California campus. In the mid-1980s, he wrote letters to colleagues, attacking my apologetics as insufficiently Van Tillian. Those letters raised issues that I had already answered a number of times, and they showed an inadequate grasp of what I was trying to say. I thought that perhaps he had turned against me because he thought I was too close to Bahnsen and to Shepherd. The administration and faculty treated Kline's letters with "benign neglect." But in later years, Kline pressed with students the argument that one must accept his distinctives to be truly Reformed. Whether explicitly or not, intentionally or not, he thereby condemned my thinking as non-Reformed, and many students drew that inference. I tried to counter this in ways consistent with my continuing deep respect for Kline. But Kline proved to be more persuasive to the students than I was, to the effect that I became increasingly isolated. That, and a great many other problems, led to my resignation from Westminster and joining the faculty of Reformed Theological Seminary (RTS) in Orlando in 2000.

I mention this now only to indicate that although I mourned Kline's death in 2007, his work is now to me both a positive and a negative influence. I still revere him as a brilliant and devoted servant of Christ, and I make liberal use of his early studies in suzerainty treaties and divine lordship. But I argue against much of his later work, particularly his distinction between cult and culture, which leads to sharp distinctions between sacred and secular and between church and culture—sort of like Luther's "two kingdoms." This is a fairly pervasive theme of my *DCL*. Not only do I believe this teaching is wrong, but, as maintained by Kline himself and by many of his followers, I consider it divisive to the church. Even if this teaching were true, it would not be suitable as a test of Reformed orthodoxy, if only because it is not required by the Reformed confessional standards.

Another major division at Westminster in California was between those who saw theology as primarily a republication of Reformed confessions and traditions and those who saw it, as I did, as an application of Scripture to human life in the present. The traditionalist emphasis seemed to me to encourage ministries to be inward-facing rather than outward, to deemphasize evangelism and social action, and to emphasize denominational distinctives. As I interpret the situation, traditionalism came to prevail at Westminster in California. And for questioning it, I myself was considered less than truly Reformed. So I had to move on. The separation between me and the seminary to which I had given twenty years was traumatic to me. I had seen not only the theological error of traditionalism (which John Murray had taught me) but also the practical effects of it in the Christian community. So this conflict (and a number of similar ones that occurred through my life) influenced me to see traditionalism as an error to be opposed. I refer to it often in my writings.[39]

Reformed Theological Seminary, 2000–Present

After the trouble at Westminster Seminary in California, my move to RTS Orlando was like dying and going to heaven. I received a warm welcome at RTS beyond my fondest dreams. Seven of my former students were on the Orlando faculty and two more at other RTS campuses. More important, many of my colleagues made use of my work and sought to build on it. Many of the writers featured in this volume, as well as others, have been part of that cooperative effort, and we have learned much together. I consider them now to be among the influences on my own thinking and writing.

Most of all, RTS has convinced me that it is possible to have a genuinely, unapologetically Reformed seminary in which believers cooperate peacefully and enthusiastically to prepare students for ministry, without partisanship or rancor. Here we have a slogan: we are not T.R. ("truly Reformed") or B.R. ("barely Reformed"), but W.R. ("winsomely Reformed"). The seminary has provided me with a vision of what seminary education can be, one that I honestly hope will be implemented elsewhere.

Historical

I would be remiss if I didn't list among the influences on my work people who wrote before my own lifetime. I am not primarily a historical theologian, and my reading has been more in recent and contemporary sources than in older writings. Yet to be Reformed at all is to be profoundly influenced by the Reformers, their predecessors, and their successors.

Among the church fathers, Athanasius is my favorite—a man persecuted for his faith, but courageous and steadfast, and right about so many things, so early.

39. See, for example, *TRAD.*

I arrived at Westminster as a six-year-old Christian who had majored in philosophy at Vanderbilt University, taken classes at Vanderbilt Divinity School for a semester, spent two wonderful months at L'Abri, and read voraciously among the works of Van Til, Machen, Warfield, Packer, Schaeffer, and other luminaries, but who had never received any serious, formal Bible teaching. I hit the ground in Philadelphia with an insatiable appetite to learn everything I could about the Bible, theology, and apologetics.

John provided five-course meal after five-course meal, which he elegantly served and over which he presided with kindness and patience! John's dishes were not to be gulped and swallowed unreflectively and then regurgitated at exam time. Instead, we were encouraged to analyze the food, inspect it, query its nutritional value, and raise all sorts of other pertinent questions. No question was out of bounds, save those absurd ones we formulated solely to see if we could stump John; we couldn't.[3] He good-naturedly took our frequently inane attempts for what they were—youthful yappings.[4]

Many meals appealed to all—Doctrine of God, Doctrine of the Word of God, and Ethics. Others, such as The Aseity of God, Christianity and Analytic Philosophy, and Wittgenstein, appealed to the more philosophically minded. Consider the last course. In a small seminar setting in the Stonehouse Room of the library, along with the Bible a handful of us read Wittgenstein's *Tractatus Logico-Philosophicus*,[5] *Lectures on Aesthetics, Psychology, and Religious Belief*,[6] and *Philosophical Investigations*,[7] learned which of his perspectives—especially "meaning as use"—are helpful within a Christian worldview, and discerned how to employ them to understand God's Word better, all the while acquiring a biblical appreciation of the wonder, depth, beauty, and majesty of God and his Word. Talk about

3. On one occasion, my fellow classmate the late Greg Bahnsen and I spent fifteen to twenty minutes formulating and editing the most obtuse pair of questions we could dream up. We were pretty good dreamers, and as fellow philosophy majors, we knew how to be obtuse. John and the class laughed when they heard our questions, which John easily answered, using a triperspectival approach, as I recall. That was the end of our "stump the professor" project.

4. If you are not familiar with John's terrific sense of humor, *CWT* contains over seventy hours of wonderfully restored MP3 lectures, many of which involve humorous interchanges with his students.

5. London: Routledge and Kegan Paul, 1961.

6. Oxford: Blackwell, 1966.

7. Oxford: Blackwell, 1953. This book was our main text.

taking jewels from the Egyptians to adorn the temple—Wittgenstein serving the Word![8]

This chapter examines the heart of John's theology.[9] With few exceptions, all the other chapters in this festschrift explore in depth various aspects of the key categories of John's thought (theology, apologetics, the church, worship, ethics, and culture), thus making this book the first large-scale, systematic analysis of John's distinctive approach to theology[10]—an introduction to his thinking. This chapter, which is divided into three parts—"Where to Start," "Five Seminal Works," and "The Heart of the Matter"—focuses on the defining ideas that shape John's theology as a whole.

WHERE TO START

When a scholar has continually published for forty years and no introduction to his work exists, it can be daunting to know what to read to gain an overview of the man and his thought. A beginner might read John's *DKG* and conclude that he is a Christian epistemologist. Someone else might read his *DG* and infer that he is a systematic theologian. Another person might read John's *DCL* and say that he is a Christian ethicist. Still another might read his *AGG* and *CVT* and deduce that he is a Christian apologist. One could read John's *WST* and *CWM* and surmise that he is a worship leader. And still another person could read his *ER* and construe John as an ecumenist. Like the three blind men examining the elephant, all six of our hypothetical

8. John kindly sent me the syllabus and exam questions we had used in this course. We met twelve times, for several hours per session, and were given a three-page, single-spaced bibliography! The course was auspiciously listed as "Apologetics 4931: Seminar on Wittgenstein." Among the nine exam questions, the following three reveal how John integrated philosophy and theology in this course in the service of Christian understanding: (1) "What, precisely, does Wittgenstein mean by 'use'? How does he defend the view that meaning is use? In what way and to what extent may a Christian make 'use' of this conception?" (2) "Discuss Wittgenstein's concepts of 'grammar' and 'form of life.' How are these related? How do 'pictures' and 'rules' function within a 'form of life'? May the 'laws' of Scripture properly be regarded as 'rules' in Wittgenstein's sense? Why or why not?" (3) "What is religious belief according to Wittgenstein's 'Lectures'? How do believers differ from unbelievers? How are religious *assertions* related to a religious 'form of life'? Evaluate from a Christian perspective."

9. In this chapter, I will use *theology* as a synonym for *thought* and *teaching*, as a catchall term to encompass all John has written. Unless noted otherwise, all quotations from the Bible are from the NIV translation.

10. Unlike most festschriften, the authors and topics in this one were selected by the honoree, so that the resulting book functions as an introduction to John's theology.

readers would be correct, but none would have the big picture—an overview of what makes John "tick" and what his major concerns are.

Realizing that, in the Bibliography to this festschrift, under the heading "The Gist of My Theological Approach," John lists five titles and says, "These titles present in summary form some of my more characteristic ideas. For people who are becoming acquainted with my work for the first time, I would recommend reading them in this order."[11]

FIVE SEMINAL WORKS

In this section we will look at the five titles John suggests—three articles, a long booklet, and one paperback book—in the order in which they are listed in "The Gist of My Theological Approach." We will examine "Reflections of a Lifetime Theologian" (2008), "A Primer on Perspectivalism" (2008), "Introduction to the Reformed Faith" (1999), *Perspectives on the Word of God* (1988), and *Salvation Belongs to the Lord: An Introduction to Systematic Theology* (2006). *RLT*, *PP*, and *SBL* are quite recent and so offer current insights into John's theology. Collectively, these five seminal works reveal the originality and power of John's theology and provide an excellent summary of its main themes.

Reflections of a Lifetime Theologian: An Extended Interview with John M. Frame

Appearing in 2008, *RLT* is the *longest published interview* John has given.[12] In this extended question-and-answer interview with P. Andrew Sandlin, John gives wide-ranging answers to twenty-five thoughtful questions that reveal much about him, his thought, and the major influences on his life and theology. For example, John's answer to Sandlin's second question—"In using the term *theologian* we sometimes take for granted that everybody knows what we mean. It seems we should be clear on this matter.

11. Also see "Appendix A: Directory of Frame's Main Ideas" in this festschrift for a listing of John's major ideas and the key discussions of them in his writings.

12. P. Andrew Sandlin and John M. Frame. This chapter was originally published in the April and May 2008 issues of *Christian Culture* (http://www.christianculture.com) and is included in this festschrift in a slightly edited form. I will quote from the festschrift version. John's article "Backgrounds to My Thought" in this festschrift complements and augments *RLT*.

What is a theologian, and what is the task of theology?"—is a heads-up to the observant reader that John is no ordinary theologian.

> I don't think definitions are matters of life and death. You can define *theology* in a number of ways as long as you don't mislead people. My own definition is a bit idiosyncratic: "The application of Scripture, by persons, to all areas of human life." *Application* is the only word I know that's broad enough to include all the legitimate ways we use Scripture, including translation, paraphrase, analysis, preaching, teaching, counseling, evangelism. In all these activities, we use Scripture to meet some human need. So the word *application* is appropriate.
>
> So everybody is a theologian, in a way. Everybody deals with Scripture in one way or another. Everybody applies it—rightly or wrongly. Even non-Christians are inevitably confronted with Scripture in their experience. Even to reject Scripture is a kind of application, a theological statement.
>
> The task of theology is to bring the good news of Scripture to everybody and to help them thereby to glorify God, in theory and practice, in private and in public, in worship and culture, in all that they think, speak, and do.

In his answer, John defines theology as application, shows that everyone is a theologian, and relates theology's task to evangelism and glorifying God in all we are and do. He takes theology out of the academy and into the streets, down from the tower and out to the people. All Christians should be and are, whether they realize it or not, *theologians*. Theology and theologizing are not the exclusive province of academicians. Ordinary believers should cultivate theology, for theology is, at its heart and in its expression, applying God's Word to all areas of human life—existential (me), personal (you), and cultural (them).[13] Theology is not merely something you know; it is something you do. Knowing and doing are reciprocal and correlative; you demonstrate that you know by your ability to do. If you can't do, you don't know. If you can't apply the Word correctly, you do not understand the Word properly.[14] Once you

13. This is not to diminish the role of gifted persons, such as John, whom God calls to train and equip themselves as, for lack of a better term, "professional theologians," and who then train others for ministry.

14. In *DKG*, 97–98, 219–20, John offers a fascinating analysis of Wittgenstein's "meaning as use," shows the strengths and weaknesses of this concept, and then explains how we can use a biblical understanding of this concept, "grounded in distinctively Christian norms," in the service of hermeneutics and Reformed theology. John's biblical understanding of "meaning as use" has strongly

courage of his convictions, and he is willing to endure with patience the fire and ire they draw.

A Primer on Perspectivalism

Written in 2008, *PP*[19] is John's first *article-length* introduction to perspectivalism and his most recent treatment of this fundamental aspect of his theology.[20] John's theology has several hallmarks. "Theology as application" (see above) surely is one, but he is most famous for his *triperspectivalism*. Many chapters in this festschrift do a wonderful job of presenting, explaining, and applying John's triperspectivalism in various ways. I will not repeat their detailed work here, but I will offer a synopsis of this seminal article.[21]

PP is divided into two parts, "Perspectivalism in General" and "Triperspectivalism." Regarding perspectivalism in general, John says:

19. *CWT* (2008) and http://www.frame-poythress.org/frame_articles/2008Primer.htm (hereafter cited as *PP*).

20. John's other main treatments of perspectivalism can be found in *PWG* and in *DCL*, chaps. 3 and 4, as it pertains to ethics. *DG*, chaps. 1–7, develops an exegetical argument for the biblical concept of divine lordship, which underlies perspectivalism. "Epistemological Perspectives and Evangelical Apologetics," a paper delivered before the Evangelical Theological Society in 1982, shows the relationship of perspectivalism to apologetics and is available at http://www.frame-poythress.org/frame_articles/1982Epistemological.html.

21. Regarding the root of his triperspectival thinking, in *SBL*, 317n3, John says, "Van Til's discussion [of the three necessary and sufficient conditions for good works: right motive, right standard, and right goal] was the seed thought behind all the triads in this book and in my Theology of Lordship series." John's comments in his article "Backgrounds" provide further clarification. As an undergraduate at Princeton University majoring in philosophy, John took a course in metaphysics from G. Dennis O'Brien. Observing how O'Brien analyzed philosophers such as Aristotle, Spinoza, and Dewey, John began to see the importance of "perspectives." He says, "I was convinced that alongside other differences among philosophers (including factual differences), there were also 'perspectival' differences. That is to say, not all the differences between thinkers are differences between truth and falsity, right and wrong; factual disagreements; or differences between clear thinking and 'mistakes.' Some are also differences in perspective, looking at the same truth from different angles. That was the beginning of my inclination to understand reality 'perspectivally.' " He goes on to say, "My Christian adaptation of O'Brien, under Van Til's tutelage, was that perspectivalism was necessary, since unlike God we are finite beings. We cannot see everything at once, as God does. So we must investigate things, first from this angle, then from that. But Van Til took me a step further: from a general perspectivalism to what would be called *tri*perspectivalism, to a set of threefold distinctions that are especially important for our reflection. Nature, man, and God; goal, motive, and standard." In "Backgrounds," John says, "Also contributing much to triperspectivalism was Vern Poythress, who studied at Westminster in the early 1970s. Poythress took a great interest in my work, and my student soon became my teacher." Also see John's remarks about Vern in *PP*. Many of Vern's and John's works are available at http://www.frame-poythress.org.

I employ perspectivalisms of two kinds, as a general concept, and as a more specific method. The general concept is simply that because we are not God, because we are finite, not infinite, we cannot know everything at a glance, and therefore our knowledge is limited to one perspective or another.

God knows absolutely everything, because he planned everything, made everything, and determines what happens in the world he made. So we describe him as omniscient. One interesting implication of God's omniscience is that he not only knows all the facts about himself and the world; he also knows how everything appears from every possible perspective.... Indeed, because God knows hypothetical situations as well as actualities, God knows exhaustively.... God's knowledge, then, is not only omniscient, but omniperspectival. He knows from his own infinite perspective; but that infinite perspective includes a knowledge of all created perspectives, possible and actual.[22]

Our knowledge and knowing are different from God's in two fundamental ways, both metaphysical.[23] First, because we are finite, our knowledge is finite. So, unlike God, our knowledge of the world is limited—restricted to our creaturely perspectives. Second, unlike God, to obtain knowledge my perspective needs to be modified by your perspective. So we need two things to arrive at certainty in knowledge: a divine Word that reveals a normative perspective on God, the world, and ourselves, and the ability to learn from other people—to understand and benefit from their perspectives. Thus, certainty in knowledge has a twofold, *communal* dimension—the divine and the human. God speaks inerrantly and infallibly in his living Word, the Bible, and this normative perspective informs and reforms our creaturely perspectives; we learn what is true from God's Word. The perspectives of other people have a semi-normative epistemic role; they also should inform and reform our own perspectives. We arrive at truth by learning from others. John says, "To see everything perfectly from my own perspective involves seeing everything from everyone else's perspective, and from God's. Finite perspectives are dependent on God's and interdependent on one another's."[24]

22. *PP.*
23. Our knowledge is also unlike God's in that we are sinful, and sin skews knowledge. Here I am focusing on the relationship of finitude and epistemology.
24. *PP.*

That abbreviated synopsis of what could be called "The General Theory of Perspectivalism" shows our need for God's absolute, infinite perspective, if we are to know anything with certainty, and our need for the perspectives of others, if we are to modify our own perspectives in understanding God's Word, the world, and ourselves. We cannot enter into God's absolute perspective and look at the world from his perspective, rather than our own—now or in the future—because of our metaphysical limitation; we are creatures, not the Creator. But we can listen to, learn from, embrace, and submit to God's absolute perspective as revealed in his Word. So God's absolute, exhaustive perspective—the perspective that includes all other perspectives, real or possible—guarantees certainty in human knowing, and this "knowledge can never be invalidated by any other perspective. It is true from any possible perspective."[25] And we can enter into one another's perspectives, thus enriching and modifying our perspectives and understanding. This is what we mean by *learning*—I reach outside of my perspective to listen to and see the world from another's perspective, and when I conclude that the new perspective offers a true insight, I make it part of my own perspective.[26] In this manner we advance toward truth, step by step.[27]

If there is a General Theory of Perspectivalism, there must be a Special Theory of Perspectivalism, what John calls *triperspectivalism*. Triperspectival-

---

25. This is a simplified presentation of John's position. Other factors enter into the argument that God's omniscience guarantees certainty in human knowledge. Consider at least seven main points: (1) God's holy character means that he does not lie (Num. 23:19; Titus 1:2); indeed, he *cannot* lie (Heb. 6:18). (2) Therefore, his Word is not just true; it is *truth* (John 1:14; 17:17). *All* his words are true (Ps. 119:160); it could not be otherwise. (3) Because God is holy, he does not and cannot mislead us; all his words are *trustworthy* (Pss. 19:7; 111:7; 119:86, 138); this also could not be otherwise. (4) Because our holy God is sovereign, he controls and superintends the inscripturation of his words (2 Tim. 3:14–17; 2 Peter 1:20–21; cf. John 16:12–15) and preserves their faithful transmission. God *could not* allow errors or untrustworthy statements to enter his Word through the hands of the human authors of Scripture, for then *his* Word would be neither true nor trustworthy. Thus, quoting Warfield, "What the Bible says, God says" (*The Works of Benjamin B. Warfield*, vol. 1, *Revelation and Inspiration* [New York: Oxford University Press, 1929], 92). (5) God created human beings with the capacity to understand his words. (6) God renews Christians so that we can know him and understand his Word (Col. 3:10; cf. Rom. 2:12). (7) God gifts and raises up pastor-teachers in the church to help us "all reach unity in the faith and in the knowledge of the Son of God and become mature, attaining to the whole measure of the fullness of Christ" (Eph. 4:13).

26. How we conclude that another's perspective offers a "true insight" is a related but different topic.

27. See the discussion on *interdependence* in the next section, *Triad Dynamics*.

ism refers to various sets of triads[28] that have great heuristic and pedagogical value and that, perhaps, reveal "a kind of deep structure of the universe and of Bible truth."[29] Of the six major triads[30] discussed in *PP*,[31] I will summarize three, after providing a brief introduction to "triad dynamics."[32]

Triad Dynamics. The perspectives in each triad (Trinitarian, lordship, epistemological, ethical, and others) are interdependent and inclusive—epistemological characteristics that we may call "triad dynamics."[33] The interdependence and inclusivity of each perspective within a triad are foundational concepts within triperspectivalism.

In *PP* John says:

> All finite perspectives are *interdependent*. God's perspective is independent in a way that ours are not, for God governs all perspectives. But even his knowledge, as we have seen, includes a knowledge of all finite perspectives.

28. See "Appendix B: Directory of Frame's Major Triads" in this festschrift for a listing of John's major triads and the key discussions of them in his writings.

29. *PP*. Triperspectivalism is an epistemological *tool* for analyzing God, man, and the world; a pedagogical *device* for teaching about God, man, and the world; and, perhaps, an ontological *insight* into the being of God and his creation. In *SBL*, 330, John says, "Sometimes, in a moment of overweening pride, I think that my three perspectives are an incredibly deep insight into the fundamental structure of biblical truth. But most of the time I just think they are a good pedagogical device, a set of hooks on which to hang the doctrines of the faith."

30. *Triads* in John's sense are not to be confused with the infamous "Hong Kong Triads"—highly organized criminal groups that specialize in counterfeiting, among other things (http://en.wikipedia.org/wiki/Triad_(underground_societies)#Recent_developments). "Reflections" mentions the creation of "Machen's Warrior Children" T-shirts as a direct response to and disagreement with the main point John makes in an article by the same name. Perhaps it's time for a more positive statement in the T-shirt wars: *Frame's Triads*. I suggest not wearing these in Hong Kong!

31. There are even triads within triads, much like Ezekiel's wheels within wheels (Ezek. 1:16). In *SBL*, 330, John says, "God's actions can be classified as redemption (existential), the acts by which he controls the world (situational), and his decrees (normative). Here we see triads within triads. The acts by which God controls the world are creation, providence, and miracle. I think of creation as normative, for it defines the nature of everything in the world. Providence is situational, because it includes everything that happens in the world. Miracle is existential, because it demonstrates in a vivid way the presence of God in his world. But each event in this whole group of divine acts, creation-providence-miracle, does three things: it reveals God's purpose and will (normative), expresses God's power (situational), and brings God near to us (presence). That is especially obvious with miracle, since the three major New Testament words for miracle are *sign* (normative revelation), *wonder* (evoking a personal, existential response), and *power* (situational efficacy)."

32. The six triads discussed in *PP* are Trinitarian, lordship, Christological, salvific, epistemological, and ethical.

33. *Triad dynamics* is my terminology. One of John's most helpful discussions of the interdependence of perspectives in triads is in *SBL*, 323–25.

And all finite perspectives must, to attain truth, "think God's thoughts after him." So in one sense, all perspectives coincide. Each, when fully informed, includes all the knowledge found in every other. There is one truth, and each perspective is merely an angle from which that truth can be viewed.[34]

For our purposes, we may define *interdependence* and *inclusivity* as follows. Two (or more) perspectives are *interdependent* if each is necessary for properly understanding the other.[35] No one has made this point more clearly than John Calvin in his opening statements in the *Institutes*. At the beginning of book 1, chapter 1, under the heading "The Knowledge of God and That of Ourselves Are Connected. How They Are Interrelated," Calvin's first and second points are: "1. Without knowledge of self there is no knowledge of God. . . . 2. Without knowledge of God there is no knowledge of self"; each is a necessary but not a sufficient condition for the other.[36] Immediately after making the first point, Calvin says, "Nearly all the wisdom we possess, that is to say, true and sound wisdom, consists of two parts: the knowledge of God and of ourselves. But, while joined by many bonds, which one precedes and brings forth the other is not easy to discern."[37]

The inclusivity of perspectives is a function of their interdependence. If two (or more) perspectives—knowledge of God and knowledge of man—are interdependent, they also are mutually inclusive, because studying one perspective *necessarily* requires studying the other to gain a full understanding of either perspective. I believe *brings forth* in Calvin's words—"which one precedes and brings forth the other is not easy to discern"—is a way of talking about the inclusiveness of interdependent perspectives. Studying one perspective—knowledge of God—"brings forth" a study of the other—knowledge of man, and vice versa. Inclusivity, then, presupposes interdependence, is a function of it, and addresses how

34. Also see *DKG*, 18–40; *CVT*, 97–113.

35. *Reciprocity* and *correlativity* are other terms sometimes used to describe the interdependence of perspectives in triperspectivalism.

36. John Calvin, *Calvin: Institutes of the Christian Religion*, ed. John T. McNeill, trans. Ford Lewis Battles (Philadelphia: Westminster, 1967), 1.1.1, 1.1.2. See 36n2, where McNeill and Battles note that prior to the 1559 edition of the *Institutes*, Calvin had separate chapters on "knowledge of God" and "knowledge of man." Beginning with the 1559 edition, Calvin combined these two topics to show more clearly their close interrelationship, "emphasizing, both in title and content, 'how they are interrelated.' "

37. Calvin, *Institutes*, 1.1.1.

studying one perspective in a set of interdependent perspectives brings forth a study of the other perspectives. Additionally, Calvin's acknowledgment that he could not discern which is more fundamental and which entails the other—knowledge of God or knowledge of self—shows that he believed either perspective to be equally valid as a starting point for investigating both perspectives, since both perspectives are interdependent and inclusive.

Because of the triad dynamics of interdependence and inclusivity, perspectives in any given triad are not *parts* of knowledge but different entrances into the *whole* object of knowledge. Each perspective represents a different emphasis, a different initial question. Thus, in the end, the three perspectives in each triad coincide so that "a true understanding of each will include true understandings of the others."[38] Therefore, the perspectives in a given triad "are ultimately identical."[39]

Trinitarian Triad. Scripture reveals that God eternally exists as Father, Son, and Holy Spirit. These are three distinct persons, yet one God—a mystery. Scripture has much to say about the distinctive roles of the Father, Son, and Holy Spirit—roles that are not arbitrary but fundamental to each member of the Trinity. After affirming the distinctiveness of the three persons in the Godhead, and thus denying Sabellianism, John says:

> But if the three persons are not *mere* perspectives on the Godhead, they nevertheless *are* perspectives. They are more than perspectives, but not less. For as I have indicated, each of the three persons bears the whole divine nature, with all the divine attributes. Each is *in* each of the others. So you cannot fully know the Son without knowing the Father and Spirit, and so on. Although the three persons are distinct, our knowledge of each involves knowledge of the others, so that for us knowledge of the Father coincides with knowledge of the Son and Spirit. . . . Although all three persons are active in every act of God, there seems to be a general division of labor among the persons in the work of redemption. The Father establishes the eternal plan of salvation; the Son executes it, and the Spirit applies it to people. It was the Father who sent the Son to redeem us, the Son who accomplished redemption, and the Spirit who applies the benefits of Christ's atonement to believers. . . . Generalizing, we gather that the Father is the

38. *SBL*, 324.
39. Ibid.

supreme *authority*, the Son the *executive power*, and the Spirit the divine *presence* who dwells in and with God's people.[40]

Thus, the Trinitarian triad focuses on God's redemptive activity.[41] The Father is the supreme *authority* who plans redemption; the Son is the executive *power* who carries out redemption; and the Spirit is the divine *presence* who applies redemption and dwells in and with God's people. John says:

> We cannot know any of these [members of the Trinity] adequately without knowing the others. Although the three are distinguishable, our knowledge of each is a perspective on the others and on the whole. To know the Spirit's work, we must see it as an application of the Son's work by the Father's plan. Similarly with knowing the work of the Father and Son. So our *knowledge* of the work of the three persons is perspectival. In a sense, these divine works are also perspectival in their *nature*.[42]

The Trinitarian triad can be summarized in three words: *authority, power, presence*. Understood properly, the Trinitarian triad has enormous significance for understanding God and the great drama of redemption.

Lordship Triad. Among John's many triads, the lordship triad may be seen as foundational to his epistemological and ethical triads;[43] it is certainly one of his best known.[44] Using Exodus 3:14–15 as his point of departure, John exegetes a host of biblical texts to show three things. First, the name *Lord* is central in both testaments. It is God's memorial name (Ex. 3:15), and God performs many mighty works so that people "will know that I am the LORD" (Ex. 14:4). Second, *Lord* is frequently applied to Jesus Christ, Yahweh incarnate, and this transference of *Lord* from the God of

---

40. *PP.*

41. This same triad also applies to God's creative activity: The Father created the universe (authority), through the Son (power), by means of the Spirit (presence). See Gen. 1:1; John 1:1–3; 1 Cor. 8:6; Col. 1:15–17; Heb. 1:1–3.

42. *PP.*

43. In *SBL*, 331, John says, "Perhaps the ultimate source of these triads is the doctrine of the Trinity."

44. John's most extensive exegetical account of divine lordship and the lordship triad can be found in the first seven chapters of *DG.* Also see *SBL*, chap. 1.

Abraham, Isaac, and Jacob to Jesus Christ is one of the most striking proofs of the New Testament's affirmation of his deity.[45] Third, "the fundamental confessions of faith in both testaments[46] . . . are confessions of lordship. One may say that the basic message of the OT is 'God is Lord,' and the basic message of the NT is 'Jesus Christ is Lord'. "[47] After reading John's detailed development of the divine lordship theme in *DG*, it is difficult to imagine anyone dissenting from the simple proposition that divine lordship is the central theme of the Bible.

The lordship triad consists of these three propositions, each derived from careful exegesis: The Lord *controls* all things by his mighty power; he speaks with absolute *authority*, requiring all to obey; and he gives himself to his people in covenant intimacy—he is present with his people. John calls this third aspect *presence*. Notice three things. First, the God of the Bible is sovereign and personal, transcendent and immanent. The heaven of heavens cannot contain him, yet he dwells among and in his people. He is the absolute-personal God. Second, he is the God who speaks. He speaks with absolute authority, and all his words are true and trustworthy. His words are not to be doubted; they are to be cherished and obeyed. They bring life and death, blessing and cursing, hope and judgment.[48] Third, he is the God who enters into covenant relationship with a people he calls to himself. He promises sinful people great blessing if they will obey his covenant, and when they fail, he sends his only Son to meet the demands of the covenant, that its blessings might come to us sinners. He is a merciful and compassionate God. These three aspects of God's lordship—extensions of the lordship triad—are unique to Christianity.

45. In *IRF*, John says, "As He [Christ] takes that name ['Lord,' *kurios*], he takes the *role* that Yahweh had in the Old Testament as the Lord, the head of the covenant. In my mind, that is one of the most powerful Scripture proofs of the deity of Christ."

46. Deut. 6:4–5; Rom. 10:9–10; 1 Cor. 12:3; Phil. 2:11.

47. *PP.*

48. John's article "Scripture Speaks for Itself," in John W. Montgomery, ed., *God's Inerrant Word* (Grand Rapids: Bethany Fellowship [a division of Baker Publishing Group], 1974), 178–200, expands this aspect of the lordship triad. John says, "God's demands are absolute in at least three senses: (1) They *cannot be questioned*. The Lord God has the right to demand unwavering, unflinching obedience. . . . (2) God's demand is absolute also in the sense that it *transcends all other loyalties*, all other demands. The Lord God will not tolerate competition; he demands *exclusive* loyalty. The servant must love his Lord with all his heart, soul and strength. One cannot serve two masters. . . . (3) God's demand is also absolute in that it *governs all areas of life*. . . . *Whatsoever* we do, even eating and drinking, must be done to the glory of God. We must never shut the Lord out of any compartment of our lives; there must be no areas kept to ourselves. God's lordship involves such *absolute demands*" (183).

Epistemological Triad. The epistemological triad and the ethical triad[49] are joined at the hip.[50] To understand John's position on the former is to understand his position on the latter, and vice versa. Epistemology— *biblical* epistemology—is the unifying topic of *DKG*, which is 437 pages long. *PP* offers a handy synopsis. John sets out the secular epistemological problem this way:

> Secular epistemologies have found it difficult to relate sense experience, reason, and feelings in their accounts of human knowledge. They have also been perplexed by the relation of the subject (the knower), the object (what the knower knows), and the norms or rules of knowledge (logic, reason, etc.).[51]

John addresses this epistemological quandary about the relationship of the subject, object, and norm of knowledge by using the *lordship triad*, thus underscoring his teaching that a Christian theory of knowledge (*epistemol-*

---

49. Secular ethical systems can be categorized as existential, teleological, or deontological, and these ethical perspectives correspond with John's existential, situational, and normative epistemological triad. Correspondingly, the three main types of Christian ethical systems are *command ethics* (normative), *narrative ethics* (situational), and *virtue ethics* (existential); see *SBL*, 319–20. I will discuss the ethical triad under *Perspectives on the Word of God*, below.

50. In *PWG*, John says, "Although I published my epistemology before my ethics, I developed the threefold scheme in ethics before applying it to epistemology. Ethics is its natural home, and I think the ethical applications of it are more easily understood than the applications to epistemological theory. Indeed the point of my epistemology is that epistemology can be fruitfully understood as a subdivision of ethics and thus can be fruitfully analyzed by the use of my meta-ethic [a general method for approaching ethical problems]." On July 4, 2009, I e-mailed John and asked him to comment on the logical relationship of the ethical and epistemological triads. He responded as follows. "Well, I think there is a perspectival relationship (surprise!) between ethics and epistemology. I've said in *DKG* that epistemology is an aspect of ethics, because epistemology deals with what we 'ought' to believe. But I could also say the reverse: ethics is an aspect of epistemology, because it describes the knowledge of a particular sphere, the area of right and wrong, good and bad. And metaphysics is the third perspective. Ethics and epistemology each presuppose all the facts, and of course we can't do metaphysics without knowing about knowing, and without knowing the values that knowing presupposes. So, the normative perspective of ethics is to look at everything as what we ought to believe and do. The normative perspective of epistemology is what we ought to believe. These coincide. The situational perspective of ethics is the world, considered as the facts to which ethical norms should be applied. The situational perspective of epistemology is the objects of knowledge, understood according to the laws of thought. These coincide. The existential perspective of ethics is our inner knowledge and experience of right and wrong (conscience, etc.—*DCL*). The existential perspective of epistemology is the inner experience of gaining knowledge (terminating in cognitive rest). These coincide. I'm not sure if I've discussed it just this way in any of my writings, but feel free to quote this note."

51. *PP*.

ogy) must be derived from a biblical *theology*.[52] Because this is our Father's world, we must approach our study of it as his children, fully submitted to his will and teaching.

The lordship triad addresses epistemology as follows. God created and *controls* the world—the object of knowledge. God speaks with *authority* in his Word about the world, thus providing a norm, an absolute standard for knowledge. As knowing subjects, we stand in God's *presence* in his world, surrounded not only by revelation about God (e.g., Psalms 19 and 139) but by God himself (e.g., Acts 17:28). Therefore, everyone (including non-Christians) *knows God* in a fundamentally *personal* way (Rom. 1:21).[53] This means that all human beings are without excuse for not exalting God as their *authority* (the normative perspective), for treating the world (the situational perspective) as something he does not *control*, and for imagining they can achieve knowledge (the existential perspective) apart from acknowledging and submitting to him—his *presence*. These three themes are powerfully woven together in Paul's indictment of the human race in Romans 1:18–32.

52. Here, I am not using *biblical theology* in its technical sense to mean something like "the study of progressive revelation in its redemptive-historical context." I am using it to refer to a theology that is derived from the Bible.

53. Regarding "knowing God" in Romans 1:21, Bill Edgar, in his article "Frame the Apologist" in this festschrift, says that "the aorist active participle, indicates the full and active knowledge of God possessed by unbelievers that makes them all the more without excuse for not honoring him as God." Douglas J. Moo, in his *The Epistle to the Romans* (Grand Rapids: Eerdmans, 1996), 106–7, says, "Such language ['knowing God' in Rom. 1:21] is normally confined to the intimate, personal relationship to God and Christ that is possible only for the believer. In light of the use to which this knowledge is put, this is plainly not the case here." Moo says that "knowing God" must be "given a strictly limited sense compatible with Paul's argument in this passage." After chastising Cranfield for greatly weakening the sense of "knowing God" in this verse, Moo continues, "But the elimination of any subjective perception from the meaning of the verb has no basis in Paul's usage. People do have some knowledge of God." Moo restricts this "knowledge" to "the narrow range of understanding of God available in nature" and paraphrases "They knew of God," approvingly citing J. B. Phillips's paraphrase, "They knew all the time that there is a God." Moo seems to be of two minds. On the one hand, the grammar of the verse pushes him toward acknowledging that unbelievers indeed *know God* in a real, profound, and *personal* (though nonsalvific) sense. They do not merely *know that* there is a God; they *know God himself*. On the other hand, Moo's theology seems to pull him away from a wholehearted embrace of this teaching. Edgar's position seems more in line with Paul's argument in Romans 1:18–23. God continually, actively, and personally reveals *himself* to creatures made in his image, and we continually, actively, and personally say "No" to *him*—we fail to glorify *him*, to give thanks to *him*. The notion of failing to glorify God or give thanks to him presupposes a *personal knowledge* of him. We stand in the very presence of our Creator and say "No" to the King of the universe.

God has created a world in which sense experience reveals truth, which is to be interpreted in terms of God's norms (verbal revelation), by knowers who do not resist the truth and are able to receive it. For this to work, we must submit our reason and logic—used to interpret sense experience (broadly understood)—to the norm of God's Word, which mediates between us and the objects of knowledge—the world.[54]

Thus, the lordship triad—authority, control, and presence—finds its analogue in the epistemological triad—normative, situational, and existential. We need a *norm* for knowledge, an absolute by which to measure all truth claims; otherwise, certainty is not possible. Because the Lord speaks with absolute *authority* in his Word about himself and his world, we have such a norm. We need assurance that the *object* of knowledge—the situational perspective—is knowable, stable, and not illusory; otherwise, knowledge is not possible. Because the Lord *controls* his world—he made it and he maintains it—it can be known. Finally, we need confidence that *we*—the existential perspective—are able to understand the world; otherwise, knowing is not possible. Because we stand in the *presence* of the Lord, bearing his image and likeness, we can understand God's world. As God's image-bearers, we have been created to rule and subdue his world for his glory and our good (Gen. 1:26–28). This task presupposes that God's words can be understood, that the world is intelligible to human beings, and that the world will "lend itself" to our investigations. In other words, the cultural mandate (Gen. 1:26–28) presupposes an epistemic "fit" between God's Word (the normative perspective), our minds (the existential perspective), and the world (the situational perspective). True knowledge of the world is attainable, and the human race has been tasked with obtaining it.[55]

---

54. For purposes of simplification, this discussion omits the essential epistemic role of the Holy Spirit in our Christian lives, including the Spirit's initial role of "opening our eyes" to the truth of the gospel. See Luke 24:30–32, 44–49; John 8:12; 12:46; Acts 16:14; 26:15–18; 2 Cor. 4:1–6; 6:14; Eph. 1:17–19b; 5:8; 1 Peter 2:9–10.

55. In *SBL*, 88–90, John discusses the meaning and significance of mankind's being the *image of God* as this relates to the lordship triad. This is not a technical, exegetical discussion, such as one finds in Bruce K. Waltke, *Genesis: A Commentary* (Grand Rapids: Zondervan, 2001), 65–66, 69–70, or in D. J. A. Clines, "The Image of God in Man," *TynBul* 19 (1968): 53–103, both of which I highly recommend. It is a theological discussion. John shows that being God's *image*—tasked with the covenantal, kingly, kingdom-building activity of ruling and subduing the world as God's vice-regents—involves having the derivative lordship attributes of authority, control, and presence. Several things John says in this discussion make me think that, with proper qualification, we could speak of God's being *virtually present* in all people. (Of course, I am not speaking here

In John's discussion of any triad, the interdependence and inclusiveness of the perspectives are paramount in his thinking. Thus, regarding the normative, situational, and existential epistemic perspectives, he says:

> These three aspects of knowledge are perspectival. You can't have one without the others, and with each, you will have the others. Every item of true human knowledge is the application of God's authoritative norm to a fact of creation, by a person in God's image. Take away one of those, and there is no knowledge at all.[56]

The Usefulness of Triads. John concludes his presentation of perspectivalism in *PP* with a brief discussion of the usefulness of this concept. He makes three main points: Perspectivalism resolves many traditional arguments;[57] it encourages balance in preaching;[58] and it encourages church unity.[59] Regarding the third point, John says, "*Sometimes* our divisions of theology and practice are differences of perspective, of balance, rather than differences over the essentials of faith. So perspectivalism will help us better to appreciate one another, and to appreciate the diversity of God's work among us."[60]

---

of God's indwelling presence, which is his gift to Christians only—it's what constitutes us as Christians—or of a saving presence of God.) Consider John's remarks: "But we image God far more profoundly [than a mirror reflects us]: we reflect everything in God, and everything in us reflects God in some way. Does this mean there is no difference between ourselves and God? No, because a reflection is both similar to and different from its source. . . . Now the image of God is much closer to reality than a mirror image" (*SBL*, 88).

56. *PP.*

57. For example, in *PP* John says, "For one thing, I think it resolves a lot of traditional theological arguments, such as whether redemptive history (the situation) is more important than the divine law (normative) or believing subjectivity. You need each to appreciate the others. That fact has implications for preaching, evangelism, and our personal appropriation of Scripture."

58. In *PP* John says, "Preaching that focuses all the time on law (normative) and not grace (situational) will be corrected by an understanding of the true relation between these. Same vice versa. People who emphasize the objective (normative and situational) while disparaging human experience and feelings (existential) can be corrected by a multiperspectival understanding. And vice versa. Perspectivalism is a way of checking ourselves. If a pastor develops a ministry that focuses on norms and situations, he may need to supplement it with something that does justice to the existential perspective, and so on. If a congregation has a lot of prophetic gifts, but few kingly or priestly, perhaps it needs to seek leadership in the last two areas."

59. Ibid.

60. Ibid. See the discussion below of *MWC* under "The Heart of the Matter."

Introduction to the Reformed Faith[61]

First posted on the Third Mill[62] Web site in 1999 while John was teaching at WTS, "Introduction to the Reformed Faith" is John's only *article-length* introduction to the basics of Reformed theology. Because more and more incoming WTS students were from non-Reformed backgrounds, John wrote this article for them. Although it focuses on the fundamentals of Reformed theology, it also discusses the whys and wherefores of Reformed confessions. In its own way, it is much like John R. W. Stott's *Basic Christianity*;[63] it is an essay for inquirers and beginners. As such, it offers a unique opportunity to hear what John thinks is important and what he believes is less important in matters Reformed. In this regard, it affords a clear view of John's demeanor, spirit, beliefs, and focus.

Realizing that the notion of a written confession (e.g., the WCF) may be new or problematic for incoming students, John begins here. His opening remarks are wise and winsome:

> In my heart, I wish there were no need for creeds or for the denominations that subscribe to them. Denominations are always to some extent the result of sin, of party spirit. I wish that when someone asked me my religious affiliation, I could simply say "Christian," and that when someone asked me my religious beliefs, I could simply say, "the Bible."
>
> Unfortunately, such simple answers are no longer sufficient. All sorts of people today claim to be Christians, and even Bible-believers, who are actually far from the kingdom of Christ. Liberals, cultists, and new-age syncretists abound. When you visit a neighbor, inviting him to church, he has a right to know what you believe. If you tell him you are a Christian and believe the Bible, he has a right to ask the further question, "what do you (and your church) think the Bible teaches?" That is the question which creeds and confessions are designed to answer. A creed is simply a summary of an individual's or church's beliefs as to the teachings of Scripture. And there can be no objection, surely, to placing such a summary in writing for the convenience of members and inquirers.[64]

61. *CWT* and http://www.frame-poythress.org/frame_articles/1999Introduction.htm (hereafter cited as *IRF*).

62. Third Millennium Ministries, http://www.thirdmill.org.

63. Grand Rapids: Eerdmans, 1981.

64. *IRF*. In *ER* John expounds 1 Corinthians 1–4 and its condemnation of a party spirit.

Confessions, John says, are not Scripture and "should not be treated as infallible or as ultimately normative."[65] In fact, churches should be able to dissent from and to revise creeds in the light of the Bible. Otherwise, creeds will "be elevated to a position of authority equivalent to Scripture."[66] Rather than protecting orthodoxy, "strict confessionalism," in which ministers are not permitted to teach contrary to any details of the creed, "is actually subversive of orthodoxy, because it is subversive of biblical authority and sufficiency. . . . Scripture is not given the freedom to reform the church according to God's will."[67]

I find John's remarks biblically sound, refreshing, and liberating. John is serious about the *sola* in *sola Scriptura*. Toward the end of his essay, John says:

> The Reformed faith, therefore, is not in essence "traditionalist," although some Reformed people have had, in my estimation, an unhealthy reverence for tradition. There is a Reformed slogan, "*semper reformanda*," "always reforming." Hence, "*fides reformata semper reformanda est*," "the Reformed faith is always reforming." There is some division in Reformed circles between some who emphasize *reformata* (Reformed) and others who emphasize *reformanda* (reforming). Both are important, and both should be kept in balance. Our faith should be "Reformed," that is in agreement with the fundamental principles of the Scriptures, as summarized in the Reformed confessions. However, it should also be "Reforming," seeking to bring our thought and practice *more* in line with Scripture, even if that process requires the elimination of some traditions. The Reformers were both: conservative in their adherence to biblical doctrine, radical in their critique of church tradition. We ought to do the same. Beware, therefore, of people who tell you that you must worship, or think, or behave, in accord with some historical tradition. Prove all things by God's word, 1 Thess. 5:21. Search the Scriptures daily to see if what you hear is really true, Acts 17:11.

After discussing the role of confessions in the lives of Christians, churches, and seminaries, John presents his understanding of the Reformed faith. In this discussion he argues three main points: "The Reformed faith

65. *IRF.*
66. Ibid.
67. Ibid.

is evangelical; the Reformed faith is predestinarian; and the Reformed faith teaches the comprehensive covenant lordship of God."[68] In the next three subsections, I will present the highlights of John's remarks.

The Reformed Faith Is Evangelical. What label should Bible-believing Protestant Christians use to describe themselves? After rejecting *Bible-believing Christian* (too vague), *orthodox* (sounds like beards!), *conservative* (sounds like politics), and *fundamentalist* (too pejorative, too anti-intellectual), John says, "I think the best term to describe all Bible-believing Protestant Christians is the term 'evangelical.' "[69] Beginning with the Lutheran reformers and ending in our day, John spends several paragraphs examining the historical use of *evangelical* and justifying his recommendation.

"The Reformed and the Evangelicals are united on many significant doctrinal points, arguably on the most important ones,"[70] John says, and this justifies subsuming the Reformed faith under *evangelical*. "An evangelical," according to John, "is one who professes historic Protestant theology." John then presents the gospel in six brief paragraphs, one each on God, man, Christ, salvation, Scripture, and prayer, and says that "Reformed people are united with all evangelicals"[71] in believing this gospel. John concludes this discussion by saying:

> It hurts me when I hear Reformed people saying that "we have nothing in common with Arminians." In fact, we have the biblical gospel in common with them, and that is a great deal. I would certainly argue that Arminian theology is not consistent with that gospel. But I cannot doubt that most of them believe that gospel from the heart.
>
> In this respect, Reformed people not only stand with their Arminian brothers and sisters in confessing biblical truth, but they also stand with them against common corruptions of the faith. We stand with all evangelicals against secular humanism, the cults, the New Age movements, and the liberal traditions in theology.[72]

68. Ibid.

69. Ibid. As John notes, in making this recommendation he differs from Van Til's *A Christian Theory of Knowledge* (Nutley, NJ: Presbyterian and Reformed, 1969), 194, which defined *evangelical* as "non-Reformed Protestant."

70. *IRF*.

71. Ibid.

72. Ibid.

I find these remarks biblically sound, balanced, and timely.

The Reformed Faith Is Predestinarian. John begins this section with a short statement about Jacob Arminius, the Synod of Dordt, and the "five points of Calvinism"—TULIP[73]—which summarize the Reformed faith's doctrine of predestination, its most controversial and distinctive teaching. John reminds us that at Dordt, the Arminians, in effect, set the agenda, to which the Calvinists replied with TULIP. Thus, TULIP is not a summary of the Reformed system of doctrine but a summary of "what Arminians don't like about Calvinism,"[74] namely, its predestinarianism. John says:

> Controversial points are not necessarily the most fundamental concerns of a system. In the case of the Reformed faith, the doctrinal system is far more than five points; it is a comprehensive understanding of Scripture, and thus a comprehensive world-and-life view.[75]

John then provides a concise summary of TULIP, clearly showing, with supporting biblical evidence, how the first point leads to the second point, which leads to the third point, and so forth. (T) *Total depravity* means that fallen people are incapable of doing anything that pleases God, who judges our hearts, which are evil. (U) Therefore, God does not choose (elect) us because he sees something good in us or sees that we will believe the gospel, which would be a truly good action. He chooses us "simply out of his totally unmerited favor—out of grace"—unconditionally.[76] (L) Christ's atonement does not make salvation possible; it actually saves; it is efficacious. Those for whom Christ died will be saved (e.g., 2 Cor. 5:15). "Thus he died only for those who are actually saved,"[77] and in that regard the atonement is limited not in its power but in its application to the elect. (I) Grace is God's sovereign expression of his divine *favor*; we cannot stop God from loving us and saving us. God draws those for whom Christ died irresistibly to himself. (P) Finally, God's grace extends to upholding us as members of his family, to enabling us to persevere.

---

73. Total depravity, Unconditional election, Limited atonement, Irresistible grace, Perseverance of the saints. The Synod of Dordt met from 1618 to 1619.

74. *IRF.*

75. Ibid.

76. Ibid.

77. Ibid.

Although that summary of TULIP is not new, by placing it in the context of his larger discussion of the Reformed faith, especially the next section of *IRF* ("3. The Reformed Faith Teaches the Comprehensive Covenant Lordship of God"), John makes it more likely that those who are new to the doctrine of predestination will give it a fairer hearing. There is wisdom in this approach.

The Reformed Faith Teaches the Comprehensive Covenant Lordship of God. Since I have covered John's teaching about lordship earlier in my discussion of his "A Primer on Perspectivalism" (under *Lordship Triad*), I will mention only a few highlights of John's treatment of this topic in *IRF*. John's discussion includes a substantial number of biblical references, thus making it easy for readers to look up the evidence that supports his points.

John's discussions of the "problem of evil" and God's causal relationship to sin are short but helpful, especially for those who are new to Reformed teaching, as are his discussions of law, theonomy, the regulative principle of worship, human freedom, contextualization, and the cultural mandate.

After summarizing the different "camps" within the Reformed family—piets, Kuyps, and docts[78]—John concludes his article on this irenic note:

It seems to me that there is room in the Reformed movement for all these different emphases. None of us can maintain a perfect balance of emphasis. And different situations require of us different emphases, as we "contextualize" our theology to bring God's word to bear on the situations we are in. Also, God gives different gifts to different people. Not all are gifted in the area of political action, or the formulation of doctrines with precision, or in personal evangelism. We all do what we can do, and we do what seems most to need doing in a situation. Within the boundaries of the Reformed faith sketched here, we should be thankful for the different emphases, not critical of them. The different emphases supplement one another and complete one another.[79]

78. "Wolterstorff and others have suggested a way of distinguishing various theological mentalities within the Reformed churches (especially those of Dutch background). They speak of 'piets, Kuyps and docts.' The piets, somewhat influenced by pietism, seek above all a deeper personal relation to Christ. The docts are concerned above all with maintaining theological orthodoxy. The Kuyps are concerned to bring great changes in society" (ibid.).
79. Ibid.

Perspectives on the Word of God[80]

Originally given at Trinity Evangelical Divinity School in 1988 as three lectures in honor of Kenneth Kantzer, *PWG* develops some of the ideas presented in *DKG* by "making some fresh applications"[81] of *DKG*'s basic perspective. In a 1999 introductory note to *PWG*, John says that *PWG* supplements *DKG* and (his then forthcoming) *DG*, while adumbrating the general approach he would take in *DCL* and (the forthcoming) *DWG*. Thus, this short, seventy-six-page book extends *DKG* and looks ahead to *DG*, *DCL*, and *DWG*. In this regard, it is John's only *single-item overview* of his Theology of Lordship[82] series.

The first lecture covers "The Nature of the Word of God." The central question John addresses is "What is the Word of God?" He answers by defining the Word as God's "self-expression," and then he specifies the three main forms of self-expression that Scripture describes as divine speech. "First, the Word of God is the *power* by which God brings all things to pass according to the counsel of his will (Eph. 1:11)."[83] John sketches how this works in creation, providence, and redemption. Second, "the Word of God is also God's *authoritative* speech. The difference between 'power' and 'authority' in my vocabulary (though not always in the English Bible) is that God's power determines what *will* happen, while God's authority determines what *ought to* happen."[84] Third, "the Word of God is also God's *personal presence* with his creatures. Even in human language, it is difficult in many circumstances to separate a speaker from his words."[85]

The second lecture covers "The Media of the Word of God." The central question John addresses is "How does God's Word get from him to us?" This is a question about media. There are three basic types of media—event, word, and person. By means of *event media*, "God reveals himself through what he *does* in our world. God's acts include: (a) nature and general history . . . , (b) redemptive history . . . , and (c) miracle."[86] By means of *word media*, God

80. Available in print and in *CWT* (hereafter cited as *PWG*). I will cite from the *CWT* version.
81. *PWG*.
82. The Theology of Lordship series consists of *DKG* (1987), *DG* (2002), *DCL* (2008), and *DWG* (forthcoming).
83. *PWG*.
84. "The distinction between power and authority is the same as the distinction in traditional theology between God's 'decretive' and 'preceptive' wills" (ibid.).
85. "If you are sitting out there thinking that my words are stupid, you are at the same time thinking that I am stupid. If you honor the words of Hemingway, to that extent you are honoring Hemingway" (ibid.).
86. Ibid.

"reveals himself by speaking in human words," for example, (a) the divine voice, (b) God's Word through the prophets and apostles, (c) God's written Word, and (d) preaching, properly qualified.[87] By means of *person media*, God reveals himself through persons. "This type of revelation, like the others, occurs in various forms: (a) the human constitution . . . , (b) the example of Christian leaders . . . , and (c) the presence of God himself."[88]

The third lecture covers "The Word of God and Christian Ethics." The central question John addresses is "How do humans use God's Word to make ethical decisions?" John addresses this question by discussing three basic metaethical tendencies[89]—existential ethics, teleological ethics,[90] and deontological ethics—and showing their fundamental inadequacies.[91] *Metaethics* is a "general *method* for approaching ethical problems," rather than a discussion of specific ethical issues.[92] John's discussion is illuminating. Each of these tendencies, or trajectories, tends toward absolutizing one of the three ethical perspectives—existential, situational, or normative.

Existential ethics focuses on the *role* of the decision maker in the ethical process. According to existential ethics, "ethical behavior is an expression of what a person is. One ought not to mask his nature; rather he should act it out. He should be what he is. There is no standard outside ourselves; what values there are in the world are the results of our decisions."[93] Thus, existential ethics results in skepticism and relativism, since, in effect, everyone is urged to "act authentically," to do what is right in his own eyes.

In his discussion of teleological ethics, John says that it could be used to justify genocide. The same is true with existential ethics. One person cannot

87. Ibid. Regarding word media, John says, "Notice that at this point I am beginning to speak of the 'Word of God' in a second sense. Originally, I defined 'Word of God' as the self-expression of God's lordship. In this sense, the Word of God is expressed in all media. Now we can use 'Word of God' also in a somewhat narrower sense: a self-expression of God's lordship delivered to us through a particular kind of medium, the medium of human words."

88. Ibid.

89. In *IRF* John says, "I say 'tendencies' rather than 'positions,' because most ethical writers reflect more than one; rarely does anyone seek to be a pure representative of one or another."

90. *Teleological* derives from the Greek word *telos*, which means "end" or "goal."

91. Deontological ethics corresponds to the normative perspective, existential ethics to the ethical perspective, and teleological ethics to the situational perspective. *Deontological* derives from the Greek word *deon*, "obligation" or "duty," and *logia*, which as an Anglicized suffix means "the study of."

92. *IRF* (emphasis mine).

93. Ibid. Representatives of this position include the Sophists, Socrates, Aristotle, Aquinas, Hegel, and Sartre.

commit genocide, but a society of genocidal maniacs could—and has. In his groundbreaking book *Hitler's Willing Executioners: Ordinary Germans and the Holocaust*,[94] Daniel Jonah Goldhagen meticulously demonstrates five terrifying truths about the Germans and the Holocaust. (1) Those who carried out the genocide of the Jews were not primarily SS men or Nazi party members; for the most part they were ordinary German men and women who represented most professions and came from all walks of life. (2) They were not coerced into killing Jews; they brutalized and killed Jews "willingly, approvingly, even zealously."[95] (3) They did so because ordinary Germans had absorbed a virulent "eliminationist" anti-Semitism that demonized the Jews and demanded their expulsion or extermination. (4) A large proportion of the killers were told by their commanders that they could refuse to kill Jews, but they slaughtered Jews anyway. (5) Hundreds of thousands of Germans were involved in the mass murder, and millions more knew about it. In other words, in the Third Reich millions of Germans had embraced an eliminationist anti-Semitism, and under Hitler's leadership they acted out who they were; they acted authentically; they did not mask their natures.[96]

Teleological ethics focuses on the *goal* of the decision maker in the ethical process, usually expressing the goal as "happiness" or "pleasure,"[97] and thus affirming an ethical standard external to the decision maker.[98]

94. New York: Vintage, 1997. This controversial and scholarly book is based on the author's Harvard doctoral dissertation, which won the American Political Science Association's 1994 Gabriel A. Almond Award for the best dissertation in the field of comparative politics.

95. *Publishers Weekly* (February 5, 1996): 72.

96. In "The Nazi Revolution," the epilogue to his book, Goldhagen says, "This study of the Holocaust and its perpetrators assigns to their beliefs paramount importance. It reverses the Marxist dictum, in holding that consciousness determined being. Its conclusion that the eliminationist antisemitic German political culture . . . was the prime mover of both the Nazi leadership and ordinary Germans in the persecution and extermination of the Jews, and therefore was the Holocaust's principal cause, may at once be hard to believe for many and commonsensical to others. The evidence that so many ordinary people did maintain at the center of their worldview palpably absurd beliefs about Jews like those Hitler articulated in *Mein Kampf* is overwhelming. . . . The revolution was primarily the transformation of consciousness—the inculcation in the Germans of a new ethos" (455–56).

97. *IRF.* Representatives of this position include Aristotle, the Epicureans, Jeremy Bentham, and John Stuart Mill.

98. "Indeed, one might say that democracy is biased in favor of teleological ethics; for the voting process (and to a great extent also the Gallup-type poll) gives people frequent means of expressing to their representatives their degree of happiness. Arguments about what is right, therefore, often get resolved into arguments about what will make people happy, and that question in turn becomes the question of what people will vote for, or what pollsters think the people want" (ibid.).

Yet teleological ethics also results in skepticism. Why should happiness or pleasure function as a normative goal?[99] And whose pleasure or happiness should be the goal—mine, yours, theirs? Teleological ethics also results in relativism; it is wide open to ends justifying means. For example, the principle of acting for "the greatest good for the greatest number" could be used to justify genocide. Hitler used this type of argument. The greatest good in Hitler's opinion was a purified German people, united on the basis of race.[100] According to Hitler, true Germans were "Aryans," and they constituted the vast majority of the population. Therefore, maximizing the greatest good—racial unity and purity—for the greatest number, "Aryans," meant purifying the German race by eliminating—exterminating—"non-Aryans," e.g., Jews,[101] Gypsies,[102] and so on.[103]

Deontological ethics focuses on the decision maker's *duty*. "A good person does his duty simply because it is his duty," *duty* being a self-attesting and supremely authoritative concept.[104] Like existential and teleological ethics, deontological ethics also results in skepticism and relativism. As John notes, "there is a major problem in deontologism as well, namely the problem of identifying the absolute, self-attesting moral principles."[105] Who defines *duty*; how can we discover it? As with teleological ethics, deontological ethics can be used to justify genocide.

99. Ibid. Nietzsche thought power, not pleasure, a more fundamental goal. Additionally, you cannot derive *ought* from *is* (the "naturalistic fallacy"); just because people seek happiness, pleasure, or power does not mean that they *should* do so.

100. In *Mein Kampf*, Hitler said, "Race . . . does not lie in the language, but exclusively in the blood" (http://www.hitler.org/writings/Mein_Kampf/mkv1ch11.html). Hitler's speech at the 1927 Nuremberg rally rings with the notion of the importance of the purity of German blood (http://www.calvin.edu/academic/cas/gpa/rpt27c.htm).

101. The number of Jews thought to have been exterminated ranges between five and seven million—two-thirds of European Jewry and one-third of world Jewry at the time (http://www.jewishvirtuallibrary.org/jsource/Holocaust/history.html).

102. Approximately 250,000 Gypsies were exterminated, even though they were "Aryans" (http://www.jewishvirtuallibrary.org/jsource/Holocaust/gypsies.html).

103. *IRF*. Along these lines, see Lucy S. Dawidowicz, *The War against the Jews, 1933–1945* (New York: Bantam, 1975), as well as Goldhagen's remarks quoted above. In her fascinating and penetrating book, Dawidowicz cogently argues that Hitler's primary war was a war against the *Jews*, that his war against the Jews was a pure expression of his *racial ideology*, and that his primary political goal was to *exterminate* the Jews. She says, "The mass murder of the Jews was the consummation of his [Hitler's] fundamental beliefs and ideological conviction" (3).

104. *IRF*. Representatives of this position include Plato, the Cynics and Stoics, David Hume, G. E. Moore, and above all, Immanuel Kant.

105. Ibid.

Consider once more the example of the Third Reich. The many hundreds of thousands of Germans who participated, one way or another, in the Holocaust were doing their duty, obeying orders.[106] As the supreme head of state, Hitler defined *duty* as unquestioning loyalty to *himself*—his plans and goals for Germany. Every soldier in the Wehrmacht (German Army) swore "by almighty God this sacred oath: I will render unconditional obedience to the Fuehrer of the German Reich and people, Adolf Hitler, Supreme Commander of the Wehrmacht."[107] Loyalty to Hitler was a *sacred duty*.[108] In the name of doing their duty, Germans followed Hitler to their doom and unleashed a continent-wide maelstrom of death and destruction.

John then examines mixed approaches—metaethical systems that combine the existential and deontological perspectives (Plato and Kant) or the teleological and deontological perspectives (Henry Sidgwick and G. E. Moore) in a sort of secular multiperspectivalism. John's quick examination of these mixed positions further reveals the bankruptcy of secular metaethics.

If each of the three secular metaethical systems can easily be used to justify genocide—and, indeed, have been—then clearly something is foundationally defective with these systems. Trees are recognized by their fruit (Matt. 7:20; 12:33b). Good trees bear good fruit; bad trees yield bad fruit (Matt. 7:17). More importantly, "A good tree *cannot* bear bad fruit, and a bad tree *cannot* bear good fruit" (Matt. 7:18). What, then, is the root problem with secular metaethics? It is that these systems are secular—anti-theistic—they deny the God of the Bible and his Word. By definition, these *secular* ethical approaches seek an absolute—an ethical standard—in creation, rather than seeking their absolute in the Creator and his true and trustworthy Word. These secular standards include human

106. If you desire that which is your duty, and if that which is your duty appeals to your desire, then acting from desire and acting from a sense of duty are not incompatible; instead, they reinforce one another. Therefore, Hitler's "willing executioners" could have been motivated by desire and by duty, by an existential and a deontological ethic, as well as by a teleological one. Perhaps *desire* (existential), *duty* (deontological), and *destination* (teleological) form another triad!

107. Jewish Virtual Library, http://www.jewishvirtuallibrary.org/jsource/Holocaust/oath.html. Tellingly, prior to August 2, 1934, the day President Paul von Hindenburg died and Hitler became Germany's sole leader, German soldiers swore "by almighty God this sacred oath: I will at all times loyally and honestly serve my people and country." Notice the switch between swearing a sacred oath to "serve . . . people and country" and swearing a sacred oath to "render unconditional obedience to . . . Adolf Hitler."

108. At the Nuremberg Trials (1945–46), the standard excuse or explanation given by the defendants was that they had only been "following orders"—doing their duty as loyal soldiers—and therefore were not morally culpable. The wording used was "Befehl ist Befehl"—"order is order," or more colloquially, "orders are orders." This ploy has become known as the "Nuremberg Defense."

subjectivity (existentialism), the world itself (teleologism), and logic or reason (deontologism); the secularist has no other options. You might think that is the end of it, but John says something very interesting:

> Seeking truth in those locations is not entirely wrong; as we shall see, one who looks *faithfully* in those places will find the Word of God which *is* an adequate ethical standard. And what truth exists in secular ethics exists because, despite its meta-ethic, it has encountered God's Word in the self, in the world, and in the realm of norms (Rom. 1:32). But the secularist is forced to reconcile what he finds in these three realms with his fundamental atheism, and herein the difficulties begin. For if God doesn't exist, what assurance do we have that self, world and law will tell us the same things? On a theistic basis, God creates the human self and the world to exist together in harmony; and he reveals his own law as the law by which self and world will find fulfillment. But on a non-theistic basis, there is no reason to suppose that self, world and law will peacefully coexist, or that ethical judgments derived from one source will necessarily cohere with ethical judgments derived from the other two. Indeed, on such a basis, there is every reason to suppose that these supposed sources of ethical knowledge will *not* be mutually consistent, and that therefore one must choose which of the three to accept unconditionally. Those who reject God, in other words, must find an alternate source of absolute truth, a substitute god, an idol. But different people prefer different idols. Hence all the confusion.[109]

A Christian metaethic "accepts as final only God's Word. That Word is found pre-eminently in Scripture, the covenant constitution of the people of God (Deut. 6:6–9; Matt. 5:17–20; 2 Tim. 3:15–17; 2 Peter 1:21), but is also revealed in the world (Ps. 19:1ff.; Rom. 1:18ff.) and in the self (Gen. 1:27ff.; 9:6, Eph. 4:24; Col. 3:10). A Christian will study these three realms presupposing their coherence and therefore seeking at each point to integrate each source of knowledge with the other two."[110]

Like existentialist ethicists, Christians seek a metaethic that will realize human nature and human freedom, *but only as these are revealed in Scripture* (the normative perspective). The Bible teaches that we are made in God's image and therefore unique in all creation, but that we are sinful, rebellious, proud, slaves to sin, and blinded by the devil to God's truth. We

109. *PWG.*
110. Ibid.

need forgiveness of sin, liberation from the devil, and transformation of our hearts, minds, and wills if we are to become the people God created us to be.[111] In short, we need Christ—crucified, risen, exalted, and indwelling us by means of his Spirit.

Like teleological ethicists, Christians seek a metaethic that will bring about the greatest good for the greatest number of people, *but only as this concept is defined in Scripture.* The Bible teaches us to extend God's "kingdom of . . . righteousness, peace and joy in the Holy Spirit" (Rom. 14:17) by loving our fellow man with Christlike love (Rom. 14:15), and it illustrates this doctrine concretely (e.g., in terms of what we eat and drink, Rom. 14:15).[112]

Like deontological ethicists, Christians seek a metaethic that will help us know our duty, *but only as this is defined in Scripture.* The Bible teaches that we are to love God with all our heart, mind, soul, and strength and to love our neighbors as ourselves (Matt. 22:37–40). In other words, we are to be perfect as our heavenly Father is perfect (Matt. 5:43–48). The Bible defines Christian love concretely in terms of attitudes, actions, and laws, illustrates this love clearly, and teaches that loving God and loving our neighbors are covenant obligations.

111. Our three enemies—the world, the flesh, and the devil—may be seen as an adversarial triad: World is situational; flesh is existential; and the devil is, in an evil way, normative—"the ruler of the kingdom of the air" (Eph. 2:2), "the prince of this world" (John 12:31; 14:30; 16:11). On "the world, the flesh, and the devil," see *The Book of Common Prayer,* "The Great Litany," which includes this petition: "From all inordinate and sinful affections; and from all the deceits of the world, the flesh, and the devil, *Good Lord, deliver us.*"

112. "Righteousness, peace, and joy" may be seen as a kingdom triad. Righteousness refers to right conduct and so is normative. Peace refers to the right relationships that result from treating one another righteously and so is situational. Joy refers to the heartfelt emotion of true delight in the peaceful state of affairs brought about by righteous behavior and so is existential. The righteousness, peace, and joy of which Paul speaks are possible only by means of the empowering presence of the Holy Spirit on the one hand and our decision to serve Christ "in this way" (Rom. 14:18) on the other. Paul's righteousness-peace-joy triad is a significant definition of what the kingdom of God *looks like,* both now and in the future. Romans 14:17 contains another triad, one that envelops the verse as a whole. The kingdom of God can be seen as normative; righteousness, peace, and joy as the situational; and the Holy Spirit as existential—God's presence with us. Interestingly, and importantly, Romans 14:17 is one of only three unambiguous references in Paul to the kingdom of God as a present reality. The other two references are 1 Corinthians 4:20 and Colossians 1:13. Of course, Paul can refer to kingdom realities without using the word *kingdom.* John Murray, in his *The Epistle to the Romans,* NICNT (Grand Rapids: Eerdmans, 1968), 2:193–94, does an excellent job of showing that "righteousness, peace, and joy" are to be understood ethically (in terms of horizontal relationships among believers), not forensically (in terms of our vertical relationship with God).

Unlike secular metaethical systems, a Christian metaethic must be unashamedly multiperspectival, always using the existential, situational, and normative perspectives to analyze and understand each ethical issue. Romans 14 is an excellent example of this principle.[113] We are to use our freedom in Christ (existential perspective) to extend God's kingdom (situational perspective) by loving people as Christ does (normative perspective). Although stronger Christians may eat anything (existential perspective), if doing so distresses a weaker brother (situational perspective), we should refrain from doing so out of love for that brother (normative perspective). Each perspective is a vantage point from which to view the issue at hand, and answering the questions raised by one perspective requires answering the questions raised by the other two perspectives.[114] Thus John says:

> Put in more practical terms, all of this means that when we face an ethical problem, or when we are counselling someone else, we need to ask three questions, (1) what is the problem? (situational perspective), (2) what does Scripture say about it? (normative perspective), and (3) what changes are needed in me (him, her), so that I (he, she) may do the right thing? (existential perspective). Each of those questions must be asked and answered seriously and carefully. And it should be evident that none of those three questions can be fully answered unless we have some answer to the others.[115]

113. In Romans 14, Paul is addressing Jewish Christians who were unclear about the relationship between old covenant laws that regulated Israel's diet and holy days and the regulations of the new covenant. Thus, in this chapter Paul is dealing with matters of conscience. What is entirely permissible—eating meat (Rom. 14:14)—may be considered impermissible by weaker Christians. For such a person, eating meat, or being subjected to the meat-eating behavior of stronger Christians, violates the weaker Christian's conscience, distresses him, and may tend to destroy his faith. Presumably, Paul would have no problem with stronger Christians' eating all the meat they wanted as long as they did so in such a way that they did not offend their weaker brothers, for example, by eating meat in private and not talking about it in front of the weaker brothers. In the church today, smoking and drinking are two issues that are functionally equivalent to meat-eating in Romans 14. For a detailed discussion of the root issue in Romans 14:1–15:13, see Moo, *Romans*, 828–33. After examining six different views regarding the identity of the "weak," Moo says, "These considerations suggest that the 'weak' were Jewish Christians . . . who believed that they were still bound by certain 'ritual' requirements of the Mosaic law" (831). For an interesting comment by J. Gresham Machen about the felicitous relationship of cigar smoking and Christian fellowship, friendship, and patience (!), see note 20 here: http://www.desiringgod.org/ResourceLibrary/Biographies/1464_J_Gresham_Machens_Response_to_Modernism/.

114. In our earlier discussion of *triad dynamics*, we saw that the perspectives in each triad are interdependent and include one another.

115. *PWG.*

In the Romans 14 example, the questions and answers would be these: (1) What is the problem (situational perspective)? Weaker Christians are stumbling in their faith and distressed in their hearts because of the meat-eating behavior of stronger Christians. (2) What does Scripture say about it (normative perspective)? Love leads to peace and mutual edification (Rom. 14:19); it does not distress a brother or destroy God's work (vv. 15, 19–20a); and it extends God's kingdom of righteousness, peace, and joy (v. 17). What changes are needed in the stronger Christian so that he can do the right thing (situational perspective)? It is better to stop eating meat than to cause a brother to stumble (vv. 2–21). Presumably, we could also argue that it would be a good thing for weaker brothers, by studying and understanding Scripture more fully, to grow stronger in their opinions about such matters, even if they choose not to become meat-eaters! In this manner, Christian metaethics avoids the rotten fruit of skepticism and relativity that result from seeking an absolute root in creation—human subjectivity (existentialism), the world (teleologism), and logic or reason (deontologism)—by being firmly rooted and grounded in the objective revelation of God's written Word, the Bible, and by viewing ethical issues triperspectivally.

Salvation Belongs to the Lord[116]

Published in 2006 and based on an edited series of lectures given in 2004 for the Institute of Theological Studies in Grand Rapids,[117] *SBL* is John's only *systematic theology*. Its recent date indicates that it reveals John's current thinking about the topics it covers, and it covers all the main theological loci, including several John has not taught at the seminary level (for example, the atonement, the *ordo salutis*, and eschatology). In *SBL*, John has enhanced most of the taped lectures and added notes and discussions of several additional topics. All of this makes *SBL* a unique overview of the major contours of John's theology. Eight of *SBL*'s twenty-five chapters are directly related to books in the Theology of Lordship series; in terms of John's published books, the other chapters cover new ground.

Parts of this introduction to systematic theology summarize the Lordship books. Chapters 1–3 and 10 and a few portions of other chapters summarize

116. Available in print and in *CWT* (hereafter cited as *SBL*). I will cite from the print version.
117. Available in MP3 CD, audio CD, and audio/MP3 CD formats as *Foundations of Systematic Theology* from http://store.itscourses.org.

sections of *Doctrine of God*. Chapters 4–5 anticipate the teaching of my forthcoming *Doctrine of the Word of God*. Chapter 6 recalls elements of *Doctrine of the Knowledge of God*. Chapter 24 summarizes *Doctrine of the Christian Life*, which I'm currently writing. And chapter 25 lists a catalog of lordship triads from all the loci in the manner of the Lordship volumes.

In my opinion, *SBL* is the single best publication to read to acquire a balanced and nuanced overview of John's theology. It is engaging, readable, almost conversational, yet carefully thought out, tightly organized, clear, and pastoral. If someone were to ask me, "What does John Frame believe?," I would hand the person a copy of *SBL* and say, "Read this carefully."[118]

It is not possible to summarize a 382-page book in a few paragraphs. Instead, I will focus on a few of the highlights of chapters 24 and 25. Before plunging into the 1,069 pages of *DCL*, I suggest first reading *SBL*'s chapter 24, "How Then Shall We Live?"[119] It begins with this definition of Christian ethics:

> Christian ethics is theology viewed as a means of determining what human persons, acts, and attitudes are acceptable to God and which are not. The Christian life is living under God's lordship. The heart of our obligation is love to him and to our neighbor, which Scripture summarizes in the Ten Commandments.[120]

The three main divisions of this chapter—"Lordship and Ethics," "The Ethical Life," and "The Lord's Commands"—and the discussions in each of those sections provide a firm foundation and sturdy framework that should help the beginning student of John's thought move more easily into *DCL*. Especially helpful are John's discussions of "Necessary and Sufficient Criteria of Good Works,"[121] "Biblical Reasons to Do Good Works,"[122] and "Interdependence of the [Ethical] Perspectives."[123]

Chapter 25, "Summary and Conclusions,"[124] offers a helpful, chapter-by-chapter summary of *SBL* that illuminates the flow of John's thought in the

---

118. *SBL* would make an ideal book for any Sunday school class from senior-high age up.
119. *SBL*, 314–27.
120. Ibid., 314.
121. Ibid., 315–17.
122. Ibid., 317–19.
123. Ibid., 323–25.
124. Ibid., 328–42.

book, as well as the triads he uses in preceding chapters. Because John uses triads throughout the preceding twenty-four chapters, chapter 25 contains the largest collection of Framean triads known to me and is worth reading for that fact alone.

It is not accidental that the last section of the last chapter in *SBL* is titled simply "Application."[125] John's writings consistently address how the specifics of theology address the particulars of our lives, how theology is the application of Scripture, by persons, to all areas of human life. John begins this section by asking, "How will you use your study from this book?"[126] and offers three suggestions—a triad, as mentioned earlier in this article. First, God wants us to know his Word—the normative perspective. Second, he wants us to preach it, teach it, and use it in evangelism, counseling, and child-rearing—the situational perspective. And third, God wants his Word written on our hearts—the existential perspective.

THE HEART OF THE MATTER

Having surveyed the five seminal works listed in "The Gist of My Theological Approach" and investigated the defining ideas that shape John's theology as a whole, we now turn in this last section to look at John's e-mail, counseling, Web site, preaching, and worship ministries, as well as to examine one final article, "Machen's Warrior Children." Collectively, these ministries and the article reveal a great deal about John's heart—not the heart of his theology, which we surveyed above, but the heart of the man himself.

E-mail Ministry

Some time ago, I learned that John has carried on an extensive e-mail ministry since 1993. Since 2000, he has replied to over eighteen thousand e-mails on an incredibly broad range of topics, for which he has developed over 150 categories for filing purposes. After I picked myself up off the floor and tried to digest the fact that in the midst of being a husband, father, professor, prolific author, worship leader, and frequent preacher John has taken time to respond to thousands of questions from students, friends, and strangers, I asked on P&R Publishing's behalf whether I could see these. I

125. Ibid., 341–42.
126. Ibid., 341.

thought most would be cursory, maybe even superficial; I was wrong. John's e-mails vary in length, depending on the complexity of the question or topic and the corresponding amount of detail he believes is warranted, but all the e-mails I have read make me think I am hearing John talking or lecturing. His responses are friendly, clear, analytical, helpful, thought-provoking, frequently pastoral, and often graced with humor.

The topics to which John responds in these e-mails include everything from soup to nuts—from *abortion, angels*, and *art* to *Barth, birth control*, and *Buddhism* to *cloning, cults*, and *culture* to *education, environment*, and *euthanasia*—and that was merely a selective sampling of categories listed under the letters *a, b, c*, and *e*. Almost every other imaginable theological, ethical, and epistemological topic is also included.

John's e-mail ministry is a daily one. He responds to ten or more e-mails each week. With John's permission, I am including the following e-mail I sent him and his reply, both slightly edited. I wrote and said:

> Good evening. I had a conversation today with a couple of Reformed brothers that troubled me. They indicated they found it difficult to believe that many Roman Catholics are saved. Their remarks arose in a context in which it was not appropriate for me to pursue the topic, but I was flabbergasted. I realize their remarks reflect something commonly found among Reformed folks. I am writing to ask if you have addressed this topic anywhere—e-mails, journaling, wherever. I have known a number of Roman Catholics—nominal churchgo-ers, those who seem to trust their membership in the RC church for their salvation, and a number who truly seem to love and trust Jesus for their salvation. I believe I could place all the Protestants I know in those same three categories—really trusting Jesus, trusting right doctrine/church membership, and nominal churchgoers. What are your thoughts?[127]

To which John replied:

> I have probably written on this issue both in my journals and in correspon-dence, but it would be difficult to find that now. Here are a few thoughts.
> 1. I, too, have known many Roman Catholics who are clearly trusting Christ alone for their salvation, and I would expect to see them in heaven.

127. E-mail from me to John dated July 7, 2009.

66

2. I've also known many Protestants and Catholics who are nominal or who seem to trust their doctrine or church membership rather than Jesus himself. God knows their hearts; I don't.

3. I do think that the official teaching of Protestantism puts the gospel more clearly than that of Roman Catholicism, which greatly obscures it. That gives an advantage to Protestantism, which could in some cases be a saving advantage. But in the open communication of our time, many Roman Catholics are deeply influenced by Protestant-originated formulations of the gospel.

4. Luther said, of course, that the doctrine of justification is the doctrine "on which the church stands or falls." But I could not affirm that. It's almost impossible to find in the period 100 AD to 1517 AD (or was it 1520?) any clear statement of justification by faith alone. Augustine was a great preacher of grace, but not specifically of justification. Of course, all the Medievals quoted Paul with approval, but few if any drew from him a teaching and emphasis like Luther's. Does that mean, then, that the church from 100–1517 was apostate? That doesn't square with the NT assurance that Jesus will not abandon his church.

5. In the end, faith is a matter of the heart, not of doctrinal understanding. The Lord saves infants (WCF 10.3) and people who cannot be "outwardly called by the ministry of the Word." Doubtless he also saves many who are very confused in doctrinal matters. But he has ways of knowing whether a person is inclined to trust in himself or in Christ. That will be the principle of judgment.

6. Doctrinal profession is an obligation of discipleship, not a definition of it. Once one is a disciple, he is obligated to search the Scripture, find the true doctrines, and profess them, as best he can. Normally that would mean in the present context that someone should profess Reformed doctrine! But God forgives mistakes.

7. Ecclesiastical membership is a tertiary matter—after heart-trust and doctrinal profession. Again, God forgives mistakes people make.

8. So, I could never say that someone is unsaved just because he is a member of the Roman Catholic Church. Nor could I say that someone is saved just because he is a member of a Protestant church.[128]

I did not write to John with the intention of including his answer in this article, nor did he reply thinking I would. His reply is indicative of how he responds to e-mails from "petitioners" with questions.

128. E-mail from John to me dated July 8, 2009.

Counseling Ministry

Having read many of John's e-mails, I asked whether he has a counseling ministry. It seemed to me that one could hardly carry on such an extensive e-mail correspondence without being asked to respond to many questions that would fall into the "counseling" category. John responded and said:

> On counseling. Well, yes, I guess a lot of my correspondence might be considered counseling. I didn't send you all of my correspondence, only the files that I thought were mostly theological questions. But I also have a file of "friends correspondence," one for "counseling," others that would fit that label. But though I've always answered letters asking for pastoral help of different kinds, I've always felt awkward about it. I usually tell correspondents that the more practical their question, the less likely I am to give a good answer to it. And I always try to avoid getting into long exchanges with people (which is typical in counseling situations), while at the same time trying to be gracious and encouraging. That balance has not been easy for me to manage.[129]

So there are more than 150 categories for John's e-mails. Some categories contain e-mails in which John addresses questions of a more personal nature, writing more as a counselor than as a theologian. But since theology is the application of the Bible to human needs, the line between theologizing and counseling is a thin one.

Web Site Ministry

John and Vern Poythress share a Web site (http://www.frame-poythress.org), where many of their articles and books are freely available. The site exists to make their writings accessible to a broad audience.

In addition to many dozens of articles and the full text of two books, John's side of the site also includes a fascinating, booklike section *Theology at the Movies*,[130] which contains reviews of approximately fifty movies, along with a preface, introduction, and articles on "Should Christians Go to Movies," "Film and Culture," and "Questions to Ask of Films." If you like movies,

---

129. E-mail from John to me dated July 5, 2009.
130. See http://www.frame-poythress.org/frame_books.htm.

as I do, I believe you will find this section of the Frame-Poythress site quite interesting. John describes his focus on film as follows:

> Perhaps because I am less knowledgeable than [others] . . . about matters of cinematic detail, I tend to focus more than they on the larger picture. I see the "messages" of the films less in the context of film as such than in the context of the general culture and of those great cultural debates which are at bottom theological. My approach is to stand back from each film and ask, what is it trying to tell me? What is its worldview, its law, its gospel? The worldview is the most important issue in film. That is the element that is most culturally influential (often in a destructive way), and it is often most central to the filmmaker's purpose.

John's comments remind me of Francis Schaeffer and Hans Rookmaaker, both of whom saw film as a reflection of culture and its worldviews.

Preaching Ministry

Having worked with John to create *CWT*, I realized that he has preached a good deal over the years. So I asked John about his preaching ministry. From the early 1970s until around 2005, John preached approximately ten times a year. In 2005, he decided to focus his energy and attention on writing, which he says is by far his greater gift and thus his more important ministry.

In the midst of our e-mail exchange about John's preaching ministry, he offered this interesting bit of information. Regarding preaching less since 2005, John said:

> This may also be related to some developments in my theological views about preaching. I used to follow the usual Reformed idea that preaching is a chief vehicle of the word—heralding and all that—and that in worship preaching should be "central." But in the last few years I have come to question that. . . . In short: The missionary preaching of the Book of Acts is indeed something glorious—heralding of the king. But preaching in Christian worship services need not emulate that. It may be something more humble—a "lesson" (*didache*).[131]

131. E-mail from John to me dated July 5, 2009.

John provided a link in his e-mail to some thoughts he wrote in 1999 that I find radical, commonsensical, and liberating and that if seriously taken to heart would upset many a homiletical apple cart. He said:

> Scripture never commands us to preach sermons in church . . . at least the kind of sermons we are accustomed to. 1 Cor. 14:26 does refer to a "lesson" (*didache*) taught in the worship service, but it says very little about the character of that teaching. In general, Scripture doesn't tell us anywhere to preach on a single text (even the inspired preaching of the apostles fails to do this), or to have just one sermon per service. It doesn't tell us that every sermon has to be by an ordained officer, and by only one. It doesn't forbid drama as a means of communication. It doesn't tell us we must always preach on the history of redemption as opposed to "moralistic" ethics. It doesn't appoint the preacher to be an official herald of the coming age. Indeed, it doesn't tell us much of anything. Thus it seems to me that we have great freedom. . . . There are many maxims in homiletical texts. But in my estimation, there are only four rules: (1) make it biblical, (2) make it clear, (3) apply it correctly to the congregation, (4) make it interesting. I wish we could focus on these rules in the teaching of homiletics. Perhaps some of our failure here stems from our pride, our wanting to be seen as preaching more profoundly than mere fundamentalists, and with much better scholarship. And as God's poetic justice would have it, the result is often less rich, less interesting, less penetrating, and less clear than many mere radio preachers. We should be able to do better, perhaps by setting our sights lower.[132]

To say that those comments contain food for thought would be a gross understatement! There is a book in those comments, waiting to be born.

Worship Ministry

In *WST* and *CWM*, John took radical stands on the regulative principle of worship and contemporary worship music. One of the questions and answers in *RLT* focuses on the "worship wars," the role of contemporary worship music in them, and John's modified support for the latter. In the *RLT* article, John says that as a young person his conversion to Christ came about through his church's youth and music ministries. The former taught him the gospel; the latter drove it into his heart.

132. Used with permission.

John has played piano and organ in church services for over fifty-five years. He loves traditional, classical hymns. But when he lived in Escondido and led worship at New Life PCA, he employed a contemporary style of worship. In his reflections about this in the *RLT* article, he says, "A number of people thought that our use of contemporary forms and songs placed us outside the Reformed camp. Part of this was debate over the Reformed Regulative Principle, which I discuss under the second commandment in my *Doctrine of the Christian Life*."[133] He goes on to say:

> In California we had a wonderful chance to try to reach unchurched folks, people who ordinarily would not darken the door of a Presbyterian church. For them, the traditional Presbyterian hymns did not clearly communicate God's grace. So I was carried kicking and screaming into the world of contemporary worship music, and we had to say no to the traditionalists. God blessed our ministry there, and I think we did exactly the right thing.

Because people have deep emotional ties to the worship music they grew up with, they will go to great lengths to try to justify their music as the only really worthy worship music. What amazes me about John in this regard is that not only was he able to step outside his skin in order to reach others for Christ (cf. 1 Cor. 9:19–23), but he also wrote *WST* and *CWM* to explain the biblical basis for doing so, knowing that these books would make him an easy target for staunch traditionalists—and they have.

Machen's Warrior Children[134]

Several years ago, I came across John's article "Machen's Warrior Children," while working on *CWT*. As I read this, I had a minor epiphany. A number of disparate events, attitudes, and arguments suddenly gelled into a coherent whole. I found myself saying, "That's right" out loud. So the first thing I did after finishing the article was to create a PDF and e-mail copies to many Reformed friends. In my opinion, *MWC* is the best available illustration of triperspectivalism's usefulness as an analytical tool for understanding theo-

133. *DCL*, 464–86, esp. 464–81.
134. Originally published in Sung Wook Chung, ed., *Alister E. McGrath and Evangelical Theology: A Dynamic Engagement* (Grand Rapids: Baker, 2003), 113–46. Also available in *CWT* and here: http://www.frame-poythress.org/frame_articles/2003Machen.htm. I will cite from *CWT*, which contains the version that appeared in *Alister E. McGrath*.

tianity needs a vision that encompasses not only doctrinal statements, but also our piety, evangelistic outreach and missions of mercy.[142]

CONCLUSION

I believe the most appropriate way to conclude this article is to quote "An Unrealistic Dream," the last section of *MWC*. Although labeled a dream, it reads like a prayer. John dreams and prays:

> That Reformed thinkers continue to have bright, fresh ideas, but that they present these ideas with humility and treat with grace and patience those who are not immediately convinced.
>
> That Reformed thinkers with bright ideas discourage the rapid formation of parties to contend for those ideas.
>
> That those initially opposed to those bright ideas allow some time for gentle, thoughtful discussion before declaring the bright ideas to be heresy.
>
> That these opponents also discourage the rapid formation of partisan groups.
>
> That those contending for various doctrinal positions accept the burden of proof, willing to bear the difficulty of serious biblical exegesis.
>
> That we try much harder to guard our tongues (James 3:1–12), saving the strongest language of condemnation (for example "denying the gospel") for those who have been declared heretics by the judicial processes of the church.
>
> That Reformed churches, ministries and institutions be open to a wider range of opinions than they are now—within limits, of course.
>
> That we honour one another as much for character and witness as we do for agreement with our theological positions.
>
> That occasionally we smile and jest about our relatively minor differences, while praying, worshipping and working together in the love of Christ.

May God "who calls things that are not as though they were" (Rom. 4:17) turn this "unrealistic dream" into a defining reality. May the dream become our prayer, and may we not lose heart as we await its fulfillment.

142. *MWC.* Earlier, in note 68, John says, "As Ulrich Zwingli eliminated music from the worship service, turning it into a teaching meeting, Reformed leaders through history have tended to value intellectual rigour at the expense of people's emotions. In my judgement, this intellectualism is a mistaken emphasis and needs to be overcome." See *DKG*, 319–46.

4

REFLECTIONS OF A LIFETIME THEOLOGIAN: AN EXTENDED INTERVIEW WITH JOHN M. FRAME

P. ANDREW SANDLIN AND JOHN M. FRAME

OUR GUEST IS John M. Frame (AB, BD, MA, MPhil, DD), professor of systematic theology and philosophy at Reformed Seminary in Orlando, Florida.[1] He held similar positions at Westminster Seminary Philadelphia and Westminster Seminary California, where he was a founding faculty member. He has written numerous books and hundreds of scholarly and popular articles, many of which appear at http://www.frame-poythress.org. His theological magnum opus is the Lordship Series, of which *The Doctrine of God* is the latest installment, with at least two more massive volumes to come. He is arguably among the greatest and most respected Reformed theologians in the world today.

In this interview, he reflects on a wide array of issues, often in an autobiographical and intimate way. This interview, in fact, although by no means comprehensive, may serve as a sort of reference guide to Professor Frame's thought on many of the leading theological topics of our time.

1. This chapter was originally published in the April and May 2008 issues of *Christian Culture* (www.christianculture.com). This version of the article has been slightly edited. Used with permission.

CCL: John, give us a little background on your theological education and the leading influences on your theology.

JMF: God led me to trust Christ as Savior and Lord when I was around 13 years old. Very shortly after that, I developed an intense interest in theology. I was particularly impressed by Dr. John H. Gerstner, who taught at Pittsburgh Theological Seminary. After majoring in philosophy at Princeton University, I went to Westminster Seminary in Philadelphia. When I entered there in 1961, the "old faculty" that had taught there since the 1930s was largely intact: Cornelius Van Til, Ned Stonehouse, Paul Woolley, John Murray, and Edward J. Young. I also studied with gifted younger professors: Meredith Kline and Edmund P. Clowney. These teachers were really superb. When I went on to grad study at Yale, I felt that I was thoroughly prepared.

At Yale I studied with theologian of culture Julian Hartt, with George Lindbeck, the father of postliberalism, and with the brilliant and insightful David Kelsey. I studied philosophy of religion with Whitehead disciple Paul Weiss, free-will defender H. D. Lewis, and meta-theologian William Christian. I heard lectures in the history of doctrine from both Robert Lowry Calhoun and his successor, Jaroslav Pelikan. My thesis adviser was Paul Holmer, a somewhat maverick evangelical, who loved Luther, Wittgenstein, Kierkegaard, and especially Jesus. Alas, I never finished my dissertation, which would have dealt with the doctrine of Scripture. But I have great admiration and affection for the Yale faculty.

Yet the thinkers I keep returning to are the Westminster men, especially John Murray and Cornelius Van Til. Nobody I have studied since that time has had a comparable influence, except Vern Poythress—a student of mine in the 1970s who has become my teacher.

CCL: In using the term *theologian* we sometimes take for granted that everybody knows what we mean. It seems we should be clear on this matter. What is a theologian, and what is the task of theology?

JMF: I don't think definitions are matters of life and death. You can define *theology* in a number of ways as long as you don't mislead people. My own definition is a bit idiosyncratic: "The application of Scripture, by persons, to all areas of human life." *Application* is the only word I know that's broad enough to include all the legitimate ways we use Scripture, including translation, paraphrase, analysis, preaching, teaching, counseling, evangelism. In all these activities, we use Scripture to meet some human need.

Theology should be equated with *teaching* in the New Testament, and this includes any use of Scripture to meet human needs. So the word *application* is appropriate.

So everybody is a theologian, in a way. Everybody deals with Scripture in one way or another. Everybody applies it—rightly or wrongly. Even non-Christians are inevitably confronted with Scripture in their experience. Even to reject Scripture is a kind of application, a theological statement.

The task of theology is to bring the good news of Scripture to everybody and to help them thereby to glorify God, in theory and practice, in private and in public, in worship and culture, in all that they think, speak, and do.

CCL: You mentioned Vern Poythress, whom you have elsewhere described as your alter ego. Talk a little about your friendship, as well your theological affinities, with him.

JMF: Vern took a PhD at Harvard in mathematics, taught for a while, and then came to WTS as a student around 1970, two years after I joined the faculty. Even before he arrived, he was a brilliant, creative, self-taught theologian. He had studied linguistics with Dr. Kenneth Pike of Wycliffe Bible Translators and had made some contributions to that field. WTS hardly knew what to do with him. What happened was that we invented an "experimental honors program," wherein the student did not have to take classes and was free to attend lectures or not, as he chose. He was tested, then, on five or six areas of theology and various writing assignments. Some later students also benefited from this program; others did not do well with it. But it seemed perfect for Vern.

He attended a number of my courses, and he and I developed a real friendship and theological affinity. Almost from the beginning, I regarded him more as a colleague than as a student. He took a great interest in my triperspectival theological approach, and he built on it, integrating it with Pike's linguistic triads: contrast, variation, distribution; particle, wave, field. He helped me out in my early critical conversations with the Dooyeweerdians. Much of this early interaction between us influenced his first book, *Philosophy, Science, and the Sovereignty of God*.

He then earned a second doctorate, this time in New Testament, from the University of Stellenbosch, after which he joined the WTS faculty. Although we were in different fields—he in New Testament and hermeneutics, I in apologetics and systematic theology, we tended often to finish one another's sentences. I can't list the number of times when

I thought I had developed an original idea and then learned that Vern had been thinking and teaching the same thing. After I left Philadelphia for California, I wrote *Doctrine of the Knowledge of God*, introducing my triperspectival approach. It was published in 1987. Lo and behold, that same year Vern published his *Symphonic Theology*, which told the same story more concisely and arguably more cogently. More recently I wrote an essay called "Copyright and the Responsible Use of Technology" that I thought was so far from the mainstream that people would dismiss it as utterly idiosyncratic. Vern wrote that he agreed with it, and he produced his own essay, arguing the same conclusions but far more knowledgeably and cogently. More recently, I started working on *Doctrine of the Word of God*, only to discover that Vern was working on a Christian theory of language.

Although we have not taught on the same faculty since 1980, I have kept in touch with him by e-mail and occasional visits, and I have read his writings with great profit. I think his books on the law (*The Shadow of Christ in the Law of Moses*), dispensationalism (*Understanding Dispensationalists*), hermeneutics (*God-Centered Biblical Interpretation*), the book of Revelation (*The Returning King*), gender-neutral translations (*The Gender-Neutral Bible Controversy*), science (*Redeeming Science*), and his forthcoming book on language are the very best things available on those subjects. He has a wonderful way of integrating Reformed theology with all the academic disciplines. Usually when Christians write about such things, they back away from their theological convictions, hoping to gain plaudits from the mainstream. Vern is absolutely fearless and forthright. Whatever he talks about, his Christian faith shows through clearly. He believes, as I do, that we really can't make progress on any of these subjects unless we appeal up front to the reality of the triune God of Scripture and the Christian-theistic worldview.

Vern also is a godly man, and his family is exemplary. See, for example, "How I Helped My Boys to Become Christian Men" at http://www.frame-poythress.org/poythress_articles/1999How.htm.

Several years ago, he arranged to set up a Web site to contain all his writings, and he invited me to join him, which I was very happy to do-www.frame-poythress.org. After all these years, we are still finishing one another's sentences.

78

CCL: As you survey the theological landscape today, what factors stand out as the most significant changes (both favorable and unfavorable) in your lifetime?

JMF: 1. Since the mid-1960s, there has been great confusion within the evangelical tradition about the inspiration, authority, inerrancy, and sufficiency of Scripture, similar to the confusion within the liberal and neo-orthodox traditions.

2. Postmodernism has challenged the primacy of reason, logic, and science in Western thought, promoting a needed epistemological humility but also threatening people's confidence in God's Word. In the "emergent churches," postmodernism has led to extremely sloppy theological thinking, often even to a distaste for theology itself.

3. In the last thirty years, a great many Christians have entered the field of philosophy, gaining the respect of non-Christians in that discipline. These have often been helpful to theology, but they have also raised some new challenges. The greatest weakness of the new Christian philosophers, in my judgment, is their failure to acknowledge Scripture as the cornerstone of any legitimate theory of knowledge.

4. Open theism has arisen to oppose the traditional (and to my mind biblical) view that God has exhaustive knowledge of the future.

5. Sharp divisions among evangelicals have emerged on the question of how Christians should relate to culture, especially to politics. Traditional Anabaptist, two-kingdom, and Kuyperian positions have been militantly espoused.

6. Battles have divided Reformed Christians over matters that in my judgment should not have been made tests of orthodoxy, particularly six-day creation, the "Federal Vision," and Norman Shepherd's and Meredith Kline's views of covenant and justification.

7. The "missional" concept of the church has been beneficial both to the theology and the practice of ministry.

8. New ideas of worship and new methods of communication have transformed evangelical churches, sometimes for the better, sometimes for the worse. But I am pleased with the general quality of the theological response to this development. I think (as well as hope) that the "worship wars" of the 1970s and 1980s are coming to an end, as churches learn the value of blending the new with the old.

9. Advances in medicine have raised new challenges for Christian ethics.

10. The discussion of the man-woman relationship has greatly intensified since the 1970s. Women's ordination and male headship in the home have become controversial issues in theology and the church. Although this development has led to healthy questioning of male oppression, in general I am appalled at how easily evangelicals have changed their exegesis under the pressure of these cultural movements.

11. Since 1995, the gay and lesbian movements have insisted on reconsideration of the very nature of the family and the Scripture's teachings on sex. As with #10, the theological response to these demands has been very disappointing to me.

12. Liberation theology was the dominant form of liberal theology from 1970 to about 2000. I think its attractive power is weakening somewhat.

13. Process theology also has been declining in its influence over this period. I guess I am amazed that it ever became prominent. But its strong advocacy of libertarian freedom and, indeed, of man's power over God still appeals to the worst instincts of theologians.

14. The New Perspective on Paul has been a major development of the last twenty years. It has shown us, I think, that Paul had important interests and concerns over and above individual forgiveness of sins. But I don't think it succeeds insofar as it tries to show individual forgiveness to be irrelevant to Paul. I tend to applaud this and other movements for what they affirm but not what they deny.

15. N. T. Wright has been a particularly impressive new voice, both in biblical scholarship and in theology generally. He is known as one of the developers and advocates of the "new perspective," but he is much more than that. He is a "theologian of lordship"—an emphasis that I have always recommended. I greatly appreciate his message that the gospel is focused on the lordship of Christ, as opposed to the lordship of Caesar, and therefore has many political implications. However, I don't appreciate (1) his denial of God's imputation to individuals of Christ's righteousness, (2) his formulation of the doctrine of Scripture, or (3) his substantive political platform, which is rather to the left of mine.

16. Many churches in the Reformed tradition have come to a fuller understanding of the primacy of grace in preaching and in the Christian life. There is some danger here of a drift toward antinomianism, and there

is need for more careful theological reflection on these matters. But for the most part I think the result has been increased spiritual vitality.

17. There has been a trend toward an overly strict confessionalism and traditionalism, a trend I consider a threat to *sola Scriptura*. In some circles, historical theology has come to have a primacy over biblical exegesis. In other circles (indeed some of the same ones) people have argued theological conclusions based on little more than their own distaste for this or that cultural movement.

18. In a related development, theologians have seemed to me to be less and less able to develop substantial arguments for their proposals. Often they simply express their preferences, quote people who agree with them, distort and caricature the positions of those who disagree, and then consider their case to be established. Many don't seem to have a clue as to how to make a cogent theological case.

19. It seems that as the years have gone by, theological debate has become shriller and nastier, contrary to the biblical standards for relationships between believers.

20. The Internet has made it possible for untrained and immature people to broadcast their theological ideas (and their attacks on others) far and wide. Evangelical churches have long neglected the discipline of their members, and they seem particularly impotent in governing the theological chatter on the Web. The result has been that many good names have been irreparably tarnished.

21. Another consequence of the Internet is that theological debate tends to move much faster than ever before, leading to formation of parties and condemnations of ideas and persons, without time for any substantial theological reflection.

22. The growing partisanship within the body of Christ has been terribly divisive. At the same time, large numbers of believers have tried to stand above these battles, planting new churches, evangelizing, teaching, nurturing. It is from this latter group that I would expect the most useful theology to come in future years.

CCL: Harold Lindsell's "Battle for the Bible" from the 1970s and 1980s has apparently died down, yet there does not appear to be a marked return to the older view of infallibility among many professed evangelicals—quite the opposite, in fact. Have evangelicals on the whole given up a dogged insistence on biblical infallibility as one of their distinctives?

JMF: There are a number of seminaries where the older view is still taught, and in the smaller Presbyterian denominations (OPC, PCA, RPNA, etc.), it is still true that no one can be ordained without upholding biblical infallibility—indeed, inerrancy. But in other denominations and independent churches, one looks very old-fashioned if he insists on infallibility in the traditional sense. Those who emphasize "story" or "narrative" often give the impression that, like a parable, redemptive history can function perfectly well as a story, whether or not it is true. I disagree with this, but I think that the defense of infallibility today will require some new formulations and arguments. For one thing, we need to emphasize in a fresh way that Scripture is a *presupposition* of Christian thought and that therefore we cannot look at Bible difficulties from a neutral standpoint.

CCL: One of your original contributions to theology (or "co-original" contributions, with Vern Poythress) is your multiperspectivalism. Can you summarize this approach and briefly describe how it serves your theology, citing a couple of examples where you employ it?

JMF: I speak of multiperspectivalism in two senses, broader and narrower. In the broad sense, multiperspectivalism simply means that because we are finite (unlike God) we must take pains to look at reality from many angles and to benefit as much as possible from the perspectives of others. Ultimately, we need to benefit from God's perspective, which includes all truth from all possible perspectives, as God reveals this in Scripture. Although some people charge multiperspectivalism with relativism, it is as far from that as can be imagined. Multiperspectivalism assumes that all our perspectives are perspectives *on something*, namely, on the objective truth of God. But it does insist that only God's perspective is exhaustive. So it requires humility on our part to be willing to correct our perspectives by the perspectives of others and of God.

In the narrower sense, I have developed a series of threefold perspectival distinctions that I think are helpful in understanding Scripture and God's world. These are ultimately based, I would say, in the Trinity: the Father, Son, and Spirit are all "in" one another (*circumincessio*), so that to know one is always to know the others. In general, the Father is the planner of redemption, the Son the accomplisher, and the Spirit the one who applies it to people's hearts. These three aspects come up again and again in biblical theology. To say that God is Lord, for example, is to say that he rules the world by his authority (parallel to the Father's authoritative plan), his powerful control (parallel to the Son's accomplishment), and his intimate presence with his creatures (parallel to the Spirit's application of redemption). I find it valuable to apply these triads to ethics (*Doctrine of the Christian Life*), epistemology (*Doctrine of the Knowledge of God*), and indeed the doctrine of God itself (*Doctrine of God*), and other theological doctrines (*Salvation Belongs to the Lord*).

For a somewhat longer introduction to this subject, see my "A Primer on Perspectivalism," http://www.frame-poythress.org/frame_articles/PrimerOnPerspectivalism.htm.

CCL: You mention the Emergent Movement (EM) as well as postmodernity. Although diverse, it seems fair to say that the EM was birthed in a conscious concession to postmodernity. Brian McLaren's recent book is titled (hyperbolically, one hopes) *Everything Must Change*. Certain strands of the EM question biblical infallibility, Christ's substitutionary atonement, and even Jesus as the exclusive way of humanity's salvation. As much as we deplore the rancor among evangelicals (as you have noted), it is hard to resist the conclusion that these EM distinctives look suspiciously like the older theological liberalism. Is this a fair assessment?

JMF: In those ways, EM coincides with the views of the older liberalism, though there are some forms of it that are more conservative. But the milieu of the more liberal EM writers is a little different from the older liberalism. Brian McLaren, one of the main EM writers, concedes, almost boasts, that he has had no formal theological training. Yet he spends a lot of time questioning traditional theology with arguments that would embarrass most any seminarian. The older liberalism at least had some genuine scholars and thinkers in its ranks. EM seems to disparage any kind of thoughtful formulation. The older liberalism took pride in uncovering the real objective truth about the Bible. The postmodern EM ignores or rejects the possibility of objective truth.

CCL: Although there is much diversity in the EM, there appears to be an almost unanimous inclination to support more liberal or at least interventionist economic policies. Ironically, nearly twenty years after the collapse of Communism on a worldwide scale, socialism of an evangelical stripe (such as we see in Jim Wallis's Sojourners and Ron Sider's Evangelicals for Social Action) appears to be gaining traction among a new generation of evangelicals, including the emergents. How do you view these trends?

JMF: The Wallis-Sider position puts a lot of weight on the biblical condemnation of those who oppress the poor. (You might be interested to know that I knew Ron Sider at Yale and attended a Bible study in which he held forth on these issues.) And Sider, at least, says that he's not in favor of socialism. But they seem to be convinced that government welfare (plus large voluntary sacrifices by individuals) is the answer. I agree that Scripture speaks very strongly against the oppression of the poor. In that respect, evangelical priorities need to become more like those of Sider and Wallis. We have not thought or done nearly enough in this area. However, distinctions have to be made. (1) Contrary to the evangelical left, Scripture does not tell us to eliminate the gap between rich and poor. Instead, it tells us to feed the hungry. (2) The polemic of the prophets is not against the existence of poverty as such but against those who *oppress* the poor, those who use their resources and the law to rob the poor. (3) Scripture does not endorse the idea that the government should control or manage the economy. Its remedies for poverty are family-centered and employment-centered (inheritance, gleaning, no-interest charitable loans, radical giving by believers). Our free-market economy has been one of the greatest means for bringing people out of poverty, and I have no doubt that for that reason and others it may claim a scriptural sanction. But some fall through the cracks of a free-market system, and for them special efforts and sacrifices are needed.

CCL: Open theism claims to be evangelical, but its view of God (for instance, His alleged ignorance of certain future events) appears outside the pale of orthodox belief. How elastic is the moniker *evangelical*?

JMF: Open theism is really an attempt to fix a problem in traditional Arminianism. Arminianism says that (1) we have a kind of free will that is "libertarian"—absolutely uncaused and unpredictable, and (2) God knows all the future in advance. Now, these two propositions are inconsistent. If we have that kind of freedom, nobody, not even God, can know in advance what a free person will do. On the other hand, if God knows in advance what we will do, then we can't do otherwise, and then we are not free in this sense. Calvinists reject (1) and affirm (2). But open theists are unwilling to reject (1), so they reject (2), contrary to a great deal of Scripture.

Now, we usually consider Arminians to be evangelical. I suppose someone might make a case that therefore open theism, the new, improved version of Arminianism, is evangelical also. Most of the Open Theists are from evangelical backgrounds. Still, one has to draw the line somewhere. Open theism rejects a divine attribute that the church has confessed universally—except for the Socinian heretics of the sixteenth century. So I really can't accept Open Theists as evangelicals. The Evangelical Theological Society a few years ago voted—rightly, I think—to reject open theism. To say this is not to question the salvation of the open theists; only God knows their hearts and mine.

CCL: Amid the burgeoning of Christian philosophy to which you refer, Alvin Plantinga's name stands out. Do you agree with the basic epistemic theses of his "Warranted Christian Belief"? Is his "soft foundationalism" a good antidote to an arrogant modernist epistemology on the one hand and to an excessively skeptical postmodern epistemology on the other hand?

JMF: Plantinga's epistemology is a great achievement in many ways, and it leads to important apologetic conclusions. He argues that beliefs are "innocent until proven guilty." That is, we have the right to believe many things without evidence or argument, and we do. There is no final rational proof that the future will be like the past, that other human beings have minds like mine, or that the world is older than five minutes. Yet we all believe these propositions without question. So Plantinga argues that belief in God, too, is not usually acquired by adding up evidence; it's a natural belief that we form in certain contexts (family, church, meditating on the creation). Of course, Plantinga says, such natural beliefs are not always right (e.g., as Linus's Great Pumpkin), and we should be open to arguments against them. At that point evidence plays a role—to rebut the rebuttals. But our initial belief is not based on a rationalistic survey of evidence or arguments, and that is perfectly OK. Nobody can accuse the Christian of holding such beliefs irrationally, because they are precisely on a par with other beliefs that everybody holds.

In Plantinga's view, "basic" beliefs, like the belief that the future will be like the past or belief in God, are "foundational." That is, they are not established by other beliefs, but they are the foundation on which other beliefs are built. This is the "soft foundationalism" you refer to. "Hard foundationalists" like Descartes thought they could logically deduce the whole of human knowledge from certain indubitable premises like "I think." Plantinga does not think a proposition must be indubitable to serve as a foundation for other beliefs. So even "God exists," to Plantinga, although foundational, is defeasible—capable of being rebutted.

I think Plantinga is correct in his demonstration that belief in God is not irrational. Of course, that's only a very small step in developing an apologetic.

He does not claim that his epistemology shows that God exists, only that belief in God can be rational. Plantinga does also argue for the existence of God, using some traditional arguments, some not so traditional.

I also think that Plantinga is right in a negative way: he is not persuaded by postmodern skepticism or by arrogant claims for human reason.

I do, however, have some disagreements with Plantinga. (1) Christian belief in God is not merely a "basic" belief in Plantinga's sense. It is a *presupposition* (as Van Til put it). Therefore, it *governs* our other beliefs, including what we accept as evidence and as valid arguments. Thus, it is not defeasible—not subject to rebuttal by evidence and argument unless another contrary presupposition is adopted. (2) Scripture must play a basic role in any Christian epistemology. Plantinga has very little to say about that. It is the clear revelation of God that most strongly challenges both the pretenses of human rationalism and the skepticism of postmodernism.

CCL: You mentioned the sharp divisions among Christians over political philosophy and engagement. Are you surprised by the resurgence of natural-law theory in the Reformed camp (Mike Horton and David VanDrunen, for example), a sector of evangelicalism that has tended in recent times to be more Bible-based in its social theory?

JMF: Very surprised. Westminster Seminary in Van Til's day sought to bring the Bible into every area of human life. Van Til saw "natural law" as a Roman Catholic theory in which culture and politics are governed by autonomous human reason rather than by Scripture. In that view, Scripture is limited to the realm of the "spiritual," or "redemption," or "the church." But now we see Westminster professors contradicting Van Til's position, something that twenty years ago would have been unthinkable at Westminster.

One major factor in this change, I think, has been the teaching of the late Meredith Kline, who taught at Westminster in California for many years. Kline claimed to be Van Tillian; indeed, he thought that I was not Van Tillian enough. But he developed a theory that made very sharp distinctions between sacred and secular, holy and common, special- and common-grace realms, and church and culture. He limited Scripture to one realm and left the other to natural law. In this area, he contradicted Van Til very sharply, and his enthusiastic disciples Horton and VanDrunen followed him without thinking much about the consequences. One thing that has brought me immense shame is that I taught Van Tillian apologetics and ethics at Westminster in California for twenty years, and now Van Til is barely known there.

Of course, there are other factors, too, that have influenced this development. Many evangelicals like J. Budziszewski have promoted natural-law approaches to ethics for years. Many evangelicals think of this as the most conservative position they can hold in the context of contemporary discussion. They don't want to accept the prevailing relativism, but they don't like either the idea of slinging Bible verses at opponents. It seems to them that a natural-law approach gives them an objective standard without having to appeal to religion. I think Horton and VanDrunen have bought into that.

There also have been arguments to the effect that Luther and Calvin accepted natural-law approaches. I am skeptical about this. Calvin said, for example, that the civil magistrate is responsible to enforce the whole Decalogue, including the first four commandments, although he did make some allowance for the differences between church and state. (Part of the problem here, I think, is that the larger Christ/culture issue is often confused with the issue of church/state. These need to be distinguished more carefully.) I am not, however, a good enough historian to adjudicate this issue. I think, however, that in this matter and others, writers have paid too much attention to the history of theology and too little attention to the teachings of Scripture itself.

I wouldn't say either that we should enter the public arena slinging Bible verses in every direction. But I do believe that God's entire revelation gives us the only objective truth available in any area of human life or thought. There is no room for autonomous human thought in any realm of life; such thought will inevitably fail. We need to take our standards from Scripture. And if it helps occasionally to actually quote Scripture, we should be unashamed to do that.

CCL: Before we discuss issues in the Reformed world more specifically, are you generally encouraged or discouraged by the quality, vigor, and output of Reformed theology in the United States over the last twenty years?

JMF: Discouraged, on the whole. As Jim Jordan recently wrote ("The Closing of the Calvinistic Mind," http://www.biblicalhorizons.com/biblical-horizons/no-177-the-closing-of-the-calvinistic-mind/), the quality has gone down significantly. Nobody writing today (except my friend Vern Poythress) compares with Warfield, Bavinck, Machen, Vos, Van Til, Dooyeweerd, or Murray in their clarity, cogency, profundity, or comprehensive scope. Some of the problems today include the following. (1) Many biblical and theological scholars try too hard to emulate and interact with liberal scholars, with little serious critique. (2) Much theology (as I believe I mentioned earlier) is too historical in its focus, thinking it has done its job when it has surveyed the history of a doctrine, even if it has not wrestled in a serious way with the biblical data. (3) The historical focus often inhibits the cogency of theological arguments; the writer thinks it sufficient to quote historical figures who agree with him and present in a distorted way the ideas of people who don't agree. (4) There is so much unfairness in theological polemics. One writer will critique another by placing the worst possible interpretation on the other's words. (5) I think many writers are too lazy, or perhaps not smart enough, to give really serious attention to issues. Too often they assume consensus opinions without really thinking them through. (6) Very few Reformed or evangelical writers today argue their theses from a comprehensive worldview orientation.

CCL: Several years back you wrote for the Alister McGrath festschrift an essay titled "Machen's Warrior Children," which described specific internecine controversies of twentieth century American Presbyterians and the Reformed subsequent to the justly revered Machen. Your essay has been widely read and discussed. Interestingly, some Calvinists have even donned the title "Machen's Warrior Children" (even producing T-shirts and such) as a proud description of their own combative theological style, which was the opposite of your intent. Since you have committed yourself to an "Evangelical Reunion" (one of your book titles), how do you assess the specific polemics in today's American Presbyterians and Reformed world?

JMF: Well, I have a pretty thick skin about the T-shirts and such. I'm even amused by them. Any publicity, as they say in Hollywood, is good publicity. Substantively, I'm actually happy that the partisan differences within the body are becoming more visible, though the existence of those differences and the combative style do grieve me. At least the T-shirts indicate that we are able to discuss these issues with a sense of humor now, and that is always an advance.

I don't think this particular flap either hurts or helps the cause of reunion. It just makes more visible the divisions that have always been there. In general, though, I think prospects for reunion have diminished during my lifetime. (It is my curse that whenever I take a position, sentiment seems to increase on the opposite side. The Greek myth of Cassandra comes to mind.) If we can't get the OPC and PCA together, what hope is there for larger unions? But the prospects for OPC and PCA union are worse than at any time in the past thirty years. And part of the cause of this is the general nastiness in theological debate that I referred to earlier.

CCL: You mentioned earlier the renewed commitment to God's grace in the Reformed world. Jack Miller's ministry has been central in that renewal. What is your view of his teaching and perspective?

JMF: Jack was a colleague of mine at Westminster in Philadelphia, and since then many of my closest friends and many of the Christian workers I most admire have been Miller disciples. His ministries, New Life Church, World Harvest Mission, and the Sonship movement, have been wonderful blessings to the church, as have his books.

Still, I have a few hesitations (I guess that's my job as a theologian). I think the Sonship movement makes too sharp a distinction between law and gospel and actually sometimes disparages meditation on the law (i.e., what the righteous man does in Psalm 1).

They rightly emphasize that grace is central both to justification and to sanctification. But in saying that sanctification, like justification, is "by grace alone through faith alone," like justification, they tend to minimize the New Testament's emphasis on effort, running a race, fighting a war.

I certainly appreciate their emphasis that all sin is of the heart and that we need to confront our heart-idolatries if we are to deal with our sins. But the Bible also puts an emphasis on making wise behavioral choices, whether or not we have the time to make an in-depth examination of our heart motives. Sometimes, indeed, for a regenerate person obedience is a pathway to a renewed heart.

As with other movements, I tend to agree with what Sonship affirms, not with what they deny (or seem to deny). I think their view of sanctification is often too one-sided—monoperspectival.

Still, I'd far rather be ministered to by Sonship folks than by traditional Calvinists. The Sonship people have wonderfully godly attitudes, especially in difficulty or controversy. Their priorities—church planting, evangelism, mission, and loving ministry to real people—are my priorities. Although I think their view of sanctification is somewhat monoperspectival, in other areas, such as church planting, they are very enthusiastic about my multi-perspectivalism, and I think my teaching has been helpful to them in that regard. They have no inclination at all to think they have the final truth and that everybody must agree with every detail of their thinking. They are the first to admit that they need repentance and renewal by God's grace. Although they probably know that I am not 100 percent with them on everything, they have loved me dearly, and I love them back.

CCL: You noted that Norman Shepherd first recruited you to teach at Westminster Seminary in Philadelphia. Many of our readers will know at least the basics of the controversy that led to his leaving WTS in the early 1980s. To this day his writings polarize the Reformed community. How do you view his theology, including his controversial thesis about "living faith"? How do you view the negative reactions to his theology?

JMF: Norman Shepherd is one of the theologians I most admire. Even apart from his kindnesses to me, I admire him as a godly man and a brilliant thinker. One of the sad consequences of his leaving WTS is that this event deprived the church of one who had great insights, even in areas other than those discussed in the "Shepherd controversy." I audited his lectures, for example, in the Doctrine of God, and no experience was more helpful in the writing of my own book on that subject.

I taught at Westminster in Philadelphia during most of the "Shepherd controversy," which began in 1974. I left in 1980—partly because of the polarization of the campus over that controversy. Shepherd was fired a year or two later. He then took a pastorate in the Christian Reformed Church, then another, and then he retired. In 2000 he published *The Call of Grace* and in 2009 *The Way of Righteousness*. He also has published a number of articles on covenants and justification. And the controversy has returned as well.

I have followed the discussion closely, but I have not, I confess, contributed much to it, for these reasons. (1) I have never taught covenants or justification on the seminary level. (2) I am not as knowledgeable on the history of confessions and theology as Shepherd and his critics are, and much of the discussion (too much, in my view) has focused on that. (3) I have, from time to time, sent out "trial balloons," suggesting ways of dealing with the controversy; but I've heard from both sides, in effect, that I really don't understand the issues very well. (That may indeed very well be the case.) (4) Finally, I have little respect for the quality of the debate so far, including the various denominational statements about it. It seems to me that positions have become hardened, so that even if I came up with a thoroughly adequate position, one that satisfied me, it probably wouldn't persuade anybody.

Given the controversy over this issue in American Presbyterianism and the hard feelings that have developed over it, I am reluctant to inject additional ideas into the debate that are likely to antagonize both sides, create even more division, and possibly endanger my own standing as a teacher in the church. If I were surer of my position, I might jump right into the debate, but for now I must stand in the shadows.

But here is the best (very tentative) account I can come up with at this time. The Shepherd controversy began in 1974 with Norman saying that either faith or works could be the "instrument" of justification, as long as we regard neither as the ground. My initial reaction was that this was an interesting theological proposal and that it would depend on analysis of words like *instrument* and *ground*. But that formulation raised a furor, because, of course, the WCF says that faith is the "only instrument." It seemed to me at the time that it was wrong to assume that the WCF could not be corrected and that we had to endorse forever, without further analysis, its choice of extra-biblical technical terms like *instrument*. But Norman backed down from that formulation, and so there was no further discussion.

The next phase of the controversy was a debate over James 2:14–26 and other passages in Scripture in which works are a condition of salvation. Norman read these as saying that good works were "necessary to" saving faith and therefore necessary to justification. The term *necessary* caused a storm, as had the word *instrument* before. It seemed obvious to me that Norman was right here. I had, after all, studied logic. If faith is necessary to justification and works are necessary to faith, then works are necessary to justification.

I still affirm what he said. But I questioned, and still question, his choice of words. Most people don't understand the logical meaning of *necessity*. When they hear it, they think of works as being some kind of efficient cause of justification—making it happen, earning it, etc. That's not what the word means; it only means, in this context, that whenever there is true faith, there are also good works. The one inevitably accompanies the other. Norman, I think, was not effective in making this distinction clear. If it had been me, I would have simply apologized for using a misleading word and shifted my vocabulary to talk about works as "inevitably accompanying" saving faith, etc. Reformed literature abounds with slogans like "It's faith alone that saves, but the faith that saves is never alone." Had Norman adopted such a formulation, I think it would not have been controversial.

But Norman had a kind of agenda. He thought that much Reformed theology was antinomian and "easy-believist." He thought that Lutheran theology and much American evangelicalism was like that, and he wanted a formulation that would directly confront that type of thinking. For him, then, *necessity* was indispensable, and he argued that anybody who rejected it must be, in effect, Lutheran, Baptist, quietist, or whatever. I didn't think so. I thought many rejected Norman's language out of honest misunderstanding. He should, I think, have tried harder to win over that group. But eventually the lines hardened between Norman and his critics, so that many read Norman's writings in the worst sense possible to make him sound like a legalist, a Roman Catholic, or worse. Once that hardening had taken place, no reconciliation was possible.

Another issue that emerged was Norman's rejection of the idea of "merit." As he sees it, merit is a kind of moral-spiritual wage. You do this, God gives you that as a quid pro quo. Norman points out that Roman Catholics have made much use of this concept: to have fellowship with God, you must earn a certain amount of merit. Jesus earned an especially large amount of it, which he shares with the saints, and they share it with one another. But Protestants also have made liberal use of the concept: Adam in the garden was required to merit divine rewards for good behavior. He failed, but Christ earned merits in behalf of his people, which they receive by faith. On both Catholic and Protestant views, you need merit in order to have fellowship with God.

Now, Norman rejects this whole concept, and with it the "covenant of works" (in which, he says, Adam had to earn merit in order to gain a special reward), and the "imputation of the active obedience of Christ" (which he sees as an imputation of the merits Christ earned while on earth).

Now, I don't think it is right to reject the concept of merit altogether. If I thought it necessarily connoted a moral-spiritual wage arrangement, I would reject it, too. Norman is right to say that God did not require Adam to "earn" his reward through accumulating points over a period of time. There is no biblical evidence of that. Adam's blessings, including the blessing of existence itself, were blessings he could never have paid for, even in his unfallen state. This was not in any sense a market transaction. It was really grace.

But the word *merit* doesn't necessarily suggest such a commercial arrangement. *Merit* can simply mean "desert." When my son mows the lawn, he deserves what I pay him, even though that payment may be much less—or much more—than market value. When a criminal is justly punished, he deserves his punishment, and we may say he "merited" it, without having in mind some kind of precise free-market value system. And had Adam maintained his integrity, he would have deserved (merited) God's reward, even if he had not "earned" it. Same for Jesus. Certainly he deserved the Father's approbation for the work of his earthly life as well as his death. But one cannot measure the value of this on any market scale. Yet I don't think it wrong to say that his work was meritorious. (*Meritorious* can be a general adjective of commendation, and of course Jesus' work is infinitely meritorious in that sense.)

Finally, Norman also denies the imputation to believers of Christ's "active righteousness," that is, the righteousness of his earthly life before his atoning death. Norman sees this idea as based on the notion that God charged Jesus with accumulating a certain amount of "merit" by his good works on earth, before his death—merit that then is transferred ("imputed") to believers. His opponents say that because of our sinful state, we need not only divine forgiveness (provided by the atonement) but also positive righteousness (provided by the imputation of Jesus' active righteousness).

Now, the exegetical data here are shaky, and a good case can be made that the NT never says specifically that Christ's active righteousness is imputed to believers. A good case can, I think, be made on the other side as well. However, I think that even if with Norman we reject the notion of a quasi-commercial "merit" transaction, there is a positive dimension to our salvation—not only forgiveness of sin but also a granting of a new, righteous status before God (as, e.g., in 2 Cor. 5:21). We can see this in the nature of the Old Testament sacrifices fulfilled in Christ: the lamb must be spotless if its sacrifice is to be valid. Essential to the sacrifice is not only the death of the animal, representing God's judgment for sin, but also the animal's (symbolically) perfect life. Similarly, the NT affirms the sinlessness of Jesus. That sinlessness is not incidental to the meaning of his atoning work. He takes our sins; we take his righteousness (2 Cor. 5:21).

Furthermore, we need to consider the nature of union with Christ. To be "in Christ" is to be united to his entire character, certainly including his righteousness. I see no difference between saying "I am united to Christ's righteousness" and saying "Christ's righteousness is imputed to me." This righteousness of Christ is certainly more than the "active righteousness" he performed for thirty years or so on the earth, but it is not less, either. So it is not wrong to say that his active righteousness is ours by grace. To say it is "imputed" is simply to say that God has declared it to be so. And he has.

Therefore, I think there are good biblical reasons for using the more traditional language here; I think Norman is too hesitant to affirm it. But I have not heard him say anything that contradicts the account of imputation I have presented here. He is concerned not to contradict that but to separate our doctrine from a theory of quasi-commercial merit. That is a legitimate thing to do, although I do not see that evangelical or Reformed theology is generally threatened by that kind of view. The argument, I think, hinges on different understandings of "merit" and "imputation," and I wish both sides were more open to the language of their opponents. Norman is too quick, I think, to read into his opponents' language a quasi-commercial view of merit. And they are too quick to read into his language the denial of salvation by alien righteousness. I think the answer is to deny the commercial idea and also to deny the notion that we are saved only by Jesus' death in abstraction from his perfect life that gives meaning to his death.

But the notion that Norman teaches another gospel, a charge often made in the debate, is absurd. People who teach "another gospel" bear the Pauline curse (Gal. 1:9). They are wolves in sheep's clothing, not believers at all, doomed to hell. Norman, on the contrary, preaches eloquently that Jesus died for our sins and that we are united to him in his death and his resurrection—entirely by the grace of God, not by anything we have earned. That is the gospel of Scripture, and Norman affirms that clearly and consistently.

Beyond this, the controversy has taught me again the dangers of strict confessionalism and traditionalism in theology. Even if Norman's position is out of accord with one or more of the Reformed confessions (although he argues that he agrees with at least the earlier confessions), that should not settle the question. When a respected Reformed thinker raises a question about the confession, we need to go back to the Bible and, if necessary, consider revising the confession. However, because Presbyterian churches are "confessional," they are often tempted to let the confession have the final word. In my judgment, we need to rethink confessionalism in this regard. It is absurd to think that documents as elaborate as the Westminster Confession of Faith, written four hundred years ago, should be treated as infallible in the modern church. But that is what often happens.

I also think the controversy has shown us the dangers of taking extrabiblical technical terms too seriously. Note that each stage of the Shepherd controversy dealt with one or more technical terms: *ground, instrument, necessity, merit, covenant of works, active righteousness,* and *imputation.* In my judgment, these are all capable of more than one interpretation. But both Norman and his critics have assumed that each term has a single, clear meaning, so that Norman clearly affirms what his opponents deny, and vice versa. I don't think that is the case. So I think that we need to regard these terms as problematic, to analyze them carefully, and to try to understand the meanings attributed to them by our opponents. In Reformed theological controversy, it is far too often the case that one party takes the other's words in the worst possible sense. We should rather be zealous to guard the reputation of a brother and to assume that he is doing good, unless a solid case ("two or three witnesses") can be made against him.

CCL: The most recent controversy to rend the Presbyterians and the Reformed in the United States has been the "Federal Vision," with its emphasis on a higher ecclesiology, sacramental efficacy, justification rooted in union with Christ at baptism, paedocommunion, and so on. What is your assessment of this theology, and what are your impressions of how this controversy has played out?

JMF: Insofar as "Federal Vision" (FV) agrees with Shepherd's teachings, see above. I am about 180 degrees removed from the general mentality of FV. They are opposed to revival; I'm for it. They want everything to be objective, formal, and institutional; I plead for a stronger emphasis in Reformed theology upon the subjective, the inner life. They want to focus on the corporate; I tend more to emphasize the individual aspects of salvation. These are of course differences of emphasis. I freely grant that Scripture contains some emphasis on the objective as well as the subjective. The problem is achieving balance.

I do think Reformed churches need to take the sacraments more seriously, and I think a good biblical case can be made for paedocommunion. Certainly, baptism does initiate a union with Christ as well as with the visible church: we are *baptized into* Christ, *into the name of* Christ. But I think the union between Christ and the believer in baptism, unless inward regeneration also exists, is entrance into a conditional covenant, which can lead to either blessings or cursings, not necessarily eternal life.

FV people have been quoted as saying that baptism gives a person title to all the blessings of salvation, but they deny that it gives him title to the blessing of perseverance. That exception I take to be a refutation of their overall scheme.

I also think that their distinctive views of worship are not supported by Scripture. Worship in the new covenant is celebration of Jesus' resurrection, not a recapitulation of tabernacle or temple worship.

At the same time, I think the FV folks, like Shepherd, are within the bounds of orthodoxy. Like Shepherd, they maintain that we are saved by grace alone, through faith in Jesus' shed blood. Beyond that, they follow a type of Reformed thought that has precedents in the Reformation and post-Reformation periods. At points, they are closer to the Reformed confessions than their opponents are.

I do commend their explorations, trying to develop a more positive view of the workings of God's grace in history through the institutions of the sacraments and the church. That has been a weak point in evangelical and Reformed theology. Of course, they also affirm (with the Reformed tradition) that God's grace operates before history, above time, in eternal election. So they do not deny the tradition; at most they are seeking to add to it.

I think they have been treated unfairly in the PCA, for example. The denominational committee appointed to study the movement had no members sympathetic to FV and did not give FV adherents a fair hearing. As with Shepherd, the dominant mentality has been all too confession-centered, history-centered, without much of a serious attempt to wrestle with the biblical data.

CCL: You mention the decline of liberation theology (LT). In the 1970s and 1980s, process theology (PT) was also at its zenith. PT seems, like LT, to have subsided. However, some critics have argued that open theism has assimilated many of PT's distinctives. Is this a fair criticism? Does the current "revisioning" of God (i.e., rethinking his traditional attributes) even in evangelical circles trouble you?

JMF: Yes, I think open theism (OT) has taken some of the steam out of process theology. It seems to many that OT gives us the same kind of freedom PT did, with a more credible affirmation of divine creation and biblical salvation. Of course, PT is far more sophisticated as an intellectual system. So it's hard to know how OT and PT will relate in years ahead.

You know, we can revision the divine attributes all we want, as long as we do it in submission to Scripture. The problem today is that people want to rethink God in order to meet some political agenda, as when feminists want a feminine God and oppose the concept of divine lordship, or when liberationists want a God who can suffer with the poor. When they do that, the reader has to wonder: When did God reveal himself to these people? What qualifications do they have to correct Scripture's teaching about the divine attributes? Why should they imagine that their political agenda is religiously insightful enough to determine the attributes of God?

CCL: This entire trend seems to reflect what we might call the balkanization or "diversification" of theology: PT, LT, feminist theology, postmodern theology, environmental theology, African theology, even "gay theology," and so forth. How do you account for such a plethora of "theologies"?

JMF: Well, for one thing there are no really great thinkers around today. I disagree with Barth on a lot of things, but his ideas were so powerful that they swept away most all his rivals (ultimately, they swept away even Bultmann).

But as Barth lost influence, the balkanization began: new hermeneutic, the liberation theologies, death-of-God theology, secular theology, narrative ("story") theology, etc., etc. By the way, there is now a strong Barth revival going on, but that doesn't seem to be reversing the balkanization.

We should not forget also that generations of theologians died on the battle fields of two world wars in the early twentieth century. Barth and his colleagues were among the few survivors. That may be another reason why the period from 1920–60 was dominated by a very few influential thinkers.

The larger picture is that once you abandon the supreme authority of the Bible, "everyone does what is right in his own eyes." Individuals develop whatever concepts of God appeal to them, usually according to their political agendas or personal tastes. Hence, *balkanization*.

CCL: One crucial factor in the "worship wars" has been the rise of contemporary worship music (CWM), a topic you have addressed fully in a book as well as in shorter venues. Your modified support of CWM has elicited some of the fieriest criticism of your views within the Reformed world, for instance, that you play fast and loose with the "Regulative Principle of Worship." Why do feelings run so strongly on this issue of music in (public) worship, and how do you see this issue resolving itself in the church, if at all?

JMF: Well, I have been playing piano and organ in church services for about fifty-five years. My conversion to Christ came about, humanly speaking, both through the youth ministry and through the music ministry of my home church. The youth ministry taught me the gospel; the music ministry drove it into my heart. So these issues are important to me, even though worship has not been one of my theological specialties.

When I was in California, I led worship at New Life PCA in Escondido, which employed a contemporary style of worship. My books on this subject arose in a fiercely polemical context. A number of people thought that our use of contemporary forms and songs placed us outside the Reformed camp. Part of this was debate over the Reformed Regulative Principle, which I discuss under the second commandment in my *Doctrine of the Christian Life*.

But the feelings about these matters are strong also, I think, because music is such a big part of our worship, a part of it that we really treasure. Most Christians love the songs they were brought up with, and they don't want those songs to be set aside. So they come up with various quasi-aesthetic, quasi-theological arguments to show that only *their* songs should be sung, and that other traditions are unworthy. I understand that attitude. I spent my first forty years in traditional churches, and emotionally I am still tied to that musical repertoire. But in California we had a wonderful chance to try to reach unchurched folks, people who ordinarily would not darken the door of a Presbyterian church. For them, the traditional Presbyterian hymns did not clearly communicate God's grace. So I was carried kicking and screaming into the world of contemporary worship music, and we had to say no to the traditionalists. God blessed our ministry there, and I think we did exactly the right thing.

Today, however, I'm happy to say that I think the worship wars are drawing to an end. Here in Florida, the watchword is *blending*. Most churches use some contemporary songs and some traditional hymns. We use some traditional hymns in contemporary arrangements, and some contemporary songs that sound suspiciously like hymns. Most worshipers understand this, and in some churches this blending worship is deeply moving.

The late Prof. Robert Webber of Wheaton became famous for urging evangelicals to go back to their "roots," to employ ancient liturgies. But in the end he promoted blended worship—the bringing together of the old and the new. He had a great influence, and the approach he and others recommended has become the new norm.

CCL: Women's ordination, as you have noted, has become a front-burner issue in evangelicalism. In reaction, certain Calvinists have reasserted "federal [male] headship" such that women may not speak at all in public worship. I recall you once telling me that you believe that a woman in the church may do anything an unordained man may do. Does there seem to be some biblical middle ground here that accommodates gifted women in the church without surrendering to a full ministerial egalitarianism? What about the argument that since only males could be priests in the OT, only men can represent God to the congregation in the NT and, therefore, women may not speak or pray in the assembly?

JMF: As usual, I find myself in an uncomfortable middle position here. I describe myself to folks as "on the left wing of the complementarian position." *Complementarian* means "not egalitarian": the sexes are not interchangeable. Men are to rule in the home and in the church. But I'm on the "left wing" of the complementarian movement, because I think Scripture does not forbid women to teach, even preach, in church.

First Corinthians 14:33 does not, I believe, require women to be silent during the entire worship service. First Corinthians 11:5 makes that clear. I think, with many scholars, that 1 Cor. 14:33 forbids women to speak during the "weighing of the prophets," an activity limited to men, because only men could be rulers in the church. There are problems with this exegesis, but I think there are worse problems with the alternatives.

First Timothy 2:12 speaks of the official teaching of the church, which is limited to elders. (I argue this in *Doctrine of the Christian Life*.) Women should not engage in that kind of teaching, because they may not be elders.

However, the New Testament also mentions a kind of teaching (sometimes called "general office" teaching) that is not limited to elders. In this sense, every believer is to be a teacher (Col. 3:16; Heb. 5:12). Paul says explicitly that older women should teach younger women (Titus 2:4). In this sense, women also teach men, as in Acts 18:26 where Priscilla joined her husband in teaching Apollos. Might this "general office" teaching take place in church services, Sunday school classes, and other church ministries? I see nothing in Scripture that excludes it.

So, yes, I believe that a woman in church can do anything that an unordained man can do: lead in prayer, teach, sing, and participate in the mercy ministries. I'm not campaigning for any kind of equal gender representation in these activities. People should serve in the church according to their gifts and other responsibilities. I think that married women, during their childbearing and child-raising years, are usually needed more at home than in church activities. But I do not think it is sinful for a church to call on a woman to pray or teach.

The analogy with priests in the Old Testament is simply this: the New Testament elder is the successor of the Old Testament priest. (Interestingly, the Latin *presbyter* can be translated either "elder" or "priest.") It is true that both offices are limited to men. So women should not be elders. (I do think there is a good biblical argument for women deacons.) But this leaves open many opportunities for the use of women's gifts in the church, including their gifts of teaching.

As for the argument that only men can "represent God," (1) there is no biblical support that a preacher or worship leader "represents God" in a way that other believers cannot do. (2) If this were used as an argument against women praying and prophesying in worship, it would contradict 1 Corinthians 11. I think 1 Corinthians 11 trumps arguments based on the symbolism of the priesthood.

CCL: James Dunn and N. T. Wright, leading advocates of the New Perspective on Paul (NPP), have argued that the Reformation has fundamentally misunderstood Paul's conception of the Judaism of his time, whose error, alleges the NPP, was not works-righteousness but a refusal to abandon the Torah for Jesus Christ. This turns on its head Paul's polemic about justification, as understood by the Reformation. With your own commitment to *sola Scriptura* and opposition to traditionalism, what are your thoughts about such attempts to overturn such long-revered Reformation interpretations?

JMF: I certainly have no objection in principle to questioning any Christian traditions on the basis of Scripture. This includes the distinctive doctrines of the Protestant Reformation. On the other hand, when somebody proposes as large a revision of those traditions as NPP does, we have to look at it very carefully. I'm not an expert on second-temple Judaism, but I suspect there were some legalists among the Jews of that time, as there have been in all religious alignments, including Protestantism. The question here is not whether the Jews believed in salvation by works alone but whether they believed that God's grace required supplementation by human merit. Jesus' encounters with the Pharisees (e.g., the parables in Luke 15:11–22 and 18:9–14) suggest that legalism was one issue at the time. I would be surprised if Paul did not also run into this.

Of course, one main point of tension between Paul and the Jews (and Judaizers) was over the "distinctives" of Judaism—circumcision, Sabbath, feast days, and such. These were the main controversies with the Judaizers in the churches to which Paul wrote. We have learned much about this from the NPP, and we should be grateful for this instruction. The question is whether these were the only points of contention or whether Paul saw them as symptoms of a wider problem—that of trusting in works for salvation to some extent.

I do think that some Pauline texts cannot be read as dealing only with Jewish distinctives. Instead, they oppose any notion that we can earn our salvation through moral effort. Romans 1–3 is important here. Paul's argument is that *nobody* is righteous without God's grace—neither Gentiles nor Jews. His argument here is not only about Jewish distinctives (2:25–29) but also about general morality: idolatry (1:23), sexual sin (1:24–27), stealing (2:21), adultery (2:22), indeed, "all manner of unrighteousness" (1:29; note the long list of sins following that). His summary quotes in 3:10–18 are also very broad in their ethical range. So "all have sinned" (3:23), and the remedy for all forms of sin is grace.

It is because Jesus atoned for all sin that the Jewish distinctives no longer matter and that believing Gentiles should be admitted to full fellowship in the kingdom of God. That's the teaching of Ephesians 2.

I think I said in another connection that with many of these movements I applaud what they affirm but not what they deny. I applaud NPP for affirming the centrality of the Jew-Gentile relation in Paul's thought. But I don't appreciate their suggestion that this invalidates the concern of Luther about individual justification. It's both-and.

CCL: Earlier you said, "Theologians have seemed to me to be less and less able to develop substantial arguments for their proposals. Often they simply express their preferences, quote people who agree with them, distort and caricature the positions of those who disagree, and then consider their case to be established. Many don't seem to have a clue as to how to make a cogent theological case." This is a searing indictment. What are the causes of this (what shall we call it?) "theological malpractice"? Is there a relationship between the increased stridency and divisiveness on the one hand and a decreased quality of theology on the other?

JMF: I have complained elsewhere about the prominence of historical, as opposed to exegetical, theology in modern evangelical and Reformed thought. When people are trained as historians (or as experts in contemporary thought and culture), they often make their theological decisions by comparing this movement with that, rather than by going directly to Scripture. Of course the result is that their evaluations are based on their own reaction to various movements, rather than on a close theological (exegetical and logical) analysis of the issues, and they are rarely credible to people who believe they have a biblical case for another position.

This is not entirely bad. Nobody can do everything. If a scholar is trained in history, he should narrate the history and then make whatever evaluation he thinks is warranted. But he should not claim any kind of finality to such evaluations. He should rather admit that the real issues need to be resolved by exegesis, and he should defer to those who are trained in theology, especially to those who are ordained as teaching officers in the church.

Unfortunately, what we have today is that people who are relatively untrained in exegesis are claiming a level of theological authority far beyond what they are entitled to. They don't seem to understand that to commend a doctrine because Calvin believed it (or even because it's in the Westminster Confession) or to oppose one because Finney believed it is a genetic fallacy. Worse, they don't understand that in the Christian church doctrines are to be determined by biblical exegesis, not by autonomous evaluations of the historical or contemporary scenes. And they lack the humility to consider their lack of qualifications to dictate the theology of the church.

Part of the problem (and I have discussed this and others in my articles "In Defense of Something Close to Biblicism" [http://www.frame-poythress. org/frame_articles/Biblicism.htm] and "Traditionalism" [http://www.frame-poythress.org/frame_articles/1999Traditionalism.htm]) is that there are so few places where a believer can study orthodox systematic theology (i.e., determining doctrines and Christian behavior through biblical exegesis) at a doctoral level. One can do it at Westminster Seminary in Philadelphia and a few other places, but even there, many, if not most, of the dissertations are historical in character, rather than attempts to establish doctrine from Scripture. Secular universities and liberal seminaries do not offer such programs, because they don't believe that traditional systematics, with its assumptions about the unity, authority, and sufficiency of Scripture, is a legitimate discipline. Therefore, if a student wants the prestige of studying at a first-class university, he cannot study systematics. Rather, he does his work in church history, philosophy of religion, contemporary theology, or some other ancillary discipline.

Then he may take a teaching job as a systematic theologian. But then his doctorate is largely, though not entirely, irrelevant to the work he is doing, whether he knows it or not. In that situation, it is tempting for him to take short cuts, and the most common shortcut is the substitution of historical or cultural studies for real systematics.

I do agree there is a connection between this and the increased stridency of our current dialogue. Of course, we have to remember that Luther and Calvin were pretty strident as well, and I would not question the fact that they were real theologians. And even Jesus and Paul (to say nothing of the prophets) spoke in ways we would today consider strident. So sometimes stridency is appropriate (though I don't think Calvin and Luther always employed this language appropriately).

But the problem today is that a lot of people in our circles argue theology without having an adequate case, and inwardly they know it. When you don't have good reasons for your position, but you are irrevocably committed to it, you tend to raise your voice. So in a lot of cases today, theology has become a shouting match. We need to get back to thoughtful exchanges and teachability. That includes respect for those who have done the serious work of theology and the standing aside of people whose expertise is only in ancillary disciplines.

CCL: With the emergence of cloning, nanotechnology, human engineering, and cyborgs, we seem to have entered an actual brave new world. What aspects of this world are most troubling to you? What should be the overarching Christian attitude toward such medical-technological breakthroughs?

JMF: Of course many of these technologies, both in research and in practice, require the destruction of human embryos, and I think that is contrary to the pro-life position of Scripture. Another problem is that some of these technologies aim at creating human beings who are doomed to a high risk of disease and early death (e.g., in cloning), or who are prevented from the outset from achieving their human potential (e.g., creating embryos for "spare parts").

However, I don't share the idea of many that to interfere with the human genome at all is "playing God" and is therefore forbidden. Scripture gives us a broad mandate to have dominion over the earth, and that certainly includes dominion (under God) of our own bodies. In a way, playing God is exactly what God tells us to do: to exercise a vassal kingship over the earth analogous to his ultimate lordship. We have never questioned that in our battles against disease and injury. We should not assume that there is one part of the human body, the genome, that is off limits.

So I oppose cloning research today for the reasons noted in the first paragraph. But realistically I assume this research will take place anyway. If it does get to the point where there is no greater risk in clonal reproduction than in natural reproduction, I would not oppose it. Similarly for the other technologies: if they can be used to enhance, rather than to detract from, the health and quality of human life, I think Christians should support them.

CCL: John, as we draw to a conclusion, I cannot resist asking: As you look back over your academic and professional career as a distinguished theologian, if you had to do it over again knowing what you know now, what significant changes would you make, if any?

JMF: When I was younger, it seemed that all sorts of paths were open to me. I made various choices and sometimes regretted them. But at seventy, as I look back over it all, the whole story seems almost inevitable. For example, my parents thought I should become a lawyer, and I once thought I had the gifts to do that. But as I look today at what lawyers do, and what I do, I can't begin to imagine myself in the legal profession. Theology really seems like the only alternative for me. To say that is to commend the hand of God in all the seemingly contingent events of my past: my choice of schooling, of employment, of a wife, of locations, of writing projects.

Some scientists say that at the subatomic level, the universe seems chaotic, unpredictable, indeterminist, and libertarian; but in the macro level where we live, it seems there really is a causal order, that the universe is predictable. So I would say that in the individual moments of my life, it has seemed that anything could happen, but the long haul reveals a divine plan and an inevitable pattern.

So as I look back on my life and work, to be honest, there is not much that I would change. I have had many regrets, but even then it seems that God has overruled my mistakes and sins. I have regretted, for example, the fact that I didn't speak up more forthrightly in the Shepherd controversy of the 1970s and in the events that led me to leave Westminster Seminary in California in 2000. But what difference would that have made? I recall that the few times I did speak up, few of my hearers took any interest. And perhaps my speaking would have introduced new divisions into the community, when there were too many already.

I regret not spending time at L'Abri during Francis Schaeffer's ministry there. I think it would have made me a better person. But there was always a reason not to do it. Certainly that was God's hand.

I regret not finishing my dissertation at Yale. But as I look back, I think that document was such a mess that it couldn't have been completed back then, no matter how much time I had spent on it. As a grad student and in my early teaching, I didn't have a systematic way to look at the doctrine of Scripture, the subject of my dissertation. In later years, I think God gave me such a system—my triperspectivalism. And as I write *Doctrine of the Word of God*, if God permits me to do that, ideas from my dissertation may be raised from the dead.

I regret not being a better leader in my home. I have been a pretty passive husband and father. There are reasons for this, but no excuses. But I see God overruling here, too—working through me and in spite of me.

I regret spending too little time on writing, too much time in speaking engagements and other things. I wish I had learned to say "no" more often, with less fear of offending friends and superiors. I cannot yet see this failure through the lens of God's providence, but perhaps God used the interruptions somehow to make me a better writer. Or maybe I'll never know his purpose, and that's OK.

I don't regret any of my main theological decisions: Reformed theology, modified presuppositionalism, multiperspectivalism, theology as application, anti-denominationalism, opposition to strict subscriptionism, advocacy of contemporary worship, theology of lordship, opposition to open theism, and *sola Scriptura* ethics and theology. Nor do I regret trying to find third alternatives between warring factions and rebuking factionalism itself. I have tried to be a peacemaker, rather than a militant, in debates that are not essential to the gospel. On all those matters, I wouldn't change a thing.

I do wish I had spent less effort fighting disciples of Dooyeweerd in the early 1970s, although others who were there can testify of the atmosphere of crisis that led to those battles. I still think my position was basically right, but I wish my own writings in these exchanges had been better informed, less strident, and less arrogant. Today, I hate it when smarty-pants kid-theologians come along to tell us all what to believe. But I was one of those smarty-pants kids.

I do regret, every day, the unkind ways I have treated people, the ill-chosen words, and the social faux pas. I fully recognize these as sins. There have been thousands of these over the years, and every day some of them come to mind, tormenting me. In some cases, I have sought forgiveness from those I offended, and in a fewer number of cases I have received forgiveness from them. But on the human level, complete reconciliation with all of these people, all of them precious images of God, is impossible. How thankful I am for Calvary that I trust in Christ alone to deal with my sins.

CCL: Finally, what advice would you offer to theological students and young theologians as they face a lifetime of theological work?

JMF: Well, here are some thoughts, in no particular order.

1. Consider that you might not really be called to theological work. James 3:1 tells us that not many of us should become teachers and that teachers will be judged more strictly. To whom much (biblical knowledge) is given, of them shall much be required.

2. Value your relationship with Christ, your family, and the church above your career ambitions. You will influence more people by your life than by your theology. And deficiencies in your life will negate the influence of your ideas, even if those ideas are true.

3. Remember that the fundamental work of theology is to understand the Bible, God's Word, and apply it to the needs of people. Everything else—historical and linguistic expertise, exegetical acuteness and subtlety, knowledge of contemporary culture, and philosophical sophistication—must be subordinated to that fundamental goal. If it is not, you may be acclaimed as a historian, linguist, philosopher, or critic of culture, but you will not be a theologian.

4. In doing the work of theology (the fundamental work, #3), you have an obligation to make a case for what you advocate. That should be obvious, but most theologians today haven't a clue as to how to do it. Theology is an argumentative discipline, and you need to know enough about logic and persuasion to construct arguments that are valid, sound, and persuasive. In theology, it's not enough to display knowledge of history, culture, or some other knowledge. Nor is it enough to quote people you agree with and reprobate people you don't agree with. You actually have to make a theological case for what you say.

5. Learn to write and speak clearly and cogently. The best theologians are able to take profound ideas and present them in simple language. Don't try to persuade people of your expertise by writing in opaque prose.

6. Cultivate an intense devotional life and ignore people who criticize this as pietistic. Pray without ceasing. Read the Bible, not just as an academic text. Treasure opportunities to worship in chapel services and prayer meetings, as well as on Sunday. Give attention to your "spiritual formation," however you understand that.

7. A theologian is essentially a preacher, though he typically deals with more arcane subjects than preachers do. But be a *good* preacher. Find some way to make your theology speak to the hearts of people. Find a way to present your teaching so that people hear God's voice in it.

8. Be generous with your resources. Spend time talking to students, prospective students, and inquirers. Give away books and articles. Don't be tightfisted when it comes to copyrighted materials; grant copy permission to anybody who asks for it. Ministry first, money second.

9. In criticizing other theologians, traditions, or movements, follow biblical ethics. Don't say that somebody is a heretic unless you have a very good case. Don't throw around terms like "another gospel." (People who teach another gospel are under God's curse.) Don't destroy people's reputations by misquoting them, quoting them out of context, or taking their words in the worst possible sense. Be gentle and gracious unless you have irrefutable reasons for being harsh.

10. When there is a controversy, don't get on one side right away. Do some analytical work first, on both positions. Consider these possibilities: (a) that the two parties may be looking at the same issue from different perspectives, so they don't really contradict; (b) that both parties are overlooking something that could have brought them together; (c) that they are talking past one another because they use terms in different ways; (d) that there is a third alternative that is better than either of the opposing views and that might bring them together; (e) that their differences, though genuine, ought both to be tolerated in the church, like the differences between vegetarians and meat-eaters in Romans 14.

11. If you get a bright idea, don't expect everybody to get it right away. Don't immediately start a faction to promote it. Don't revile those who haven't come to appreciate your thinking. Reason gently with them, recognizing that you could be wrong and arrogant to boot.

12. Don't be reflexively critical of everything that comes out of a different tradition. Be humble enough to consider that other traditions may have something to teach you. Be teachable before you start teaching them. Take the beam out of your own eye.

13. Be willing to reexamine your own tradition with a critical eye. It is unreasonable to think that any single tradition has all the truth or is always right. And unless theologians develop critical perspectives on their own denominations and traditions, the reunion of the body of Christ will never take place. Don't be one of those theologians who are known mainly for trying to make Arminians become Calvinists (or vice versa).

14. See confessional documents in proper perspective. It is the work of theology, among other things, to rethink the doctrines of the confessions and to reform them, when necessary, by the Word of God. Do not assume that everything in the confession is forever settled.

15. Don't let your polemics be governed by jealousy, as when a theologian feels bound to be entirely negative toward the success of a megachurch.

16. Don't become known as a theologian who constantly takes potshots at other theologians or other Christians. The enemy is Satan, the world, and the flesh.

17. Guard your sexual instincts. Stay away from Internet pornography and illicit relationships. Theologians are not immune from the sins that plague others in the church.

18. Be active in a good church. Theologians need the means of grace as much as other believers. This is especially important when you are studying at a secular university or liberal seminary. You need the support of other believers to maintain proper theological perspective.

19. Get your basic training at a seminary that teaches the Bible as the Word of God. Become well-grounded in the theology of Scripture before you go off (as you may, of course) to get firsthand exposure to nonbiblical thought.

20. Come to appreciate the wisdom, even theological wisdom, of relatively uneducated Christians. Don't be one of those theologians who always has something negative to say when a simple believer describes his walk with the Lord. Don't look down at people from what Helmut Thielicke called "the high horse of enlightenment." Often, simple believers know God better than you do, and you need to learn from them, as did Abraham Kuyper, for instance.

21. Don't be one of those theologians who get excited about every new trend in politics, culture, hermeneutics, and even theology and who think we have to reconstruct our theology to go along with each trend. Don't think you have to be a feminist, e.g., just because everybody else is. Most of the theologies that try to be culturally savvy are unbiblical.

22. Be suspicious of all trendiness in theology. When everybody jumps on some theological bandwagon, whether narrative, feminism, redemptive history, natural law, liturgy, liberation, postmodernism, or whatever, that's the time to awaken your critical faculties. Don't jump on the bandwagon unless you have done your own study. When a theological trend comes along, ask reflexively, "What's wrong with that?" There is always something wrong. It simply is not the case that the newest is the truest. Indeed, many new movements turn out to be false steps entirely.

23. Our system of doctoral-level education requires "original thought," but that can be hard to do, given that the church has been studying Scripture for thousands of years. You'll be tempted to come up with something that sounds new (possibly by writing a thesis that isn't properly theological at all in the sense of #3 above). Well, do it; get it out of the way, and then come back to do some real theology.

24. At the same time, don't reject innovation simply because it is innovative. Even more, don't reject an idea merely because it doesn't *sound* like what you're used to. Learn to distinguish the sound-look-feel of an idea from what it actually means.

25. Be critical of arguments that turn on metaphors or extrabiblical technical terms. Don't assume that each one has a perfectly clear meaning. Usually they do not.

26. Learn to be skeptical of the skeptics. Unbelieving and liberal scholars are as prone to error as anybody—in fact, more so.

27. Respect your elders. Nothing is so ill-becoming as a young theologian who despises those who have been working in the field for decades. Disagreement is fine, as long as you acknowledge the maturity and the contributions of those you disagree with. Take 1 Timothy 5:1 to heart.

28. Young theologians often imagine themselves as the next Luther, just as little boys imagine themselves as the next Peyton Manning or Kevin Garnett. When they're too old to play cowboys and Indians, they want to play Luther and the Pope. When the real Pope won't play with them, they pick on somebody else and say, "You're it." Look: most likely God has not chosen you

to be the leader of a new Reformation. If he has, don't take the exalted title "Reformer" upon yourself. Let others decide if that is really what you are.

29. Decide early in your career (after some experimenting) what to focus on and what not to. When considering opportunities, it's just as important (perhaps more so) to know when to say no as to know when to say yes.

30. Don't lose your sense of humor. We should take God seriously, not ourselves, and certainly not theology. To lose your sense of humor is to lose your sense of proportion. And nothing is more important in theology than a sense of proportion.

5

PERSPECTIVES ON MULTIPERSPECTIVALISM

JOSEPH EMMANUEL TORRES

JOHN FRAME'S *DKG* was published in 1987 and introduced the theological community to his theological methodology of multiperspectivalism. This methodology was later applied to apologetics in his *AGG*. In the latter work, multiperspectivalism helped Frame transcend aspects of the methodological debate between presuppositionalists and evidentialists. The emphasis on presuppositions stressed the normative dimension of thought, while evidences properly interpreted stressed the situational testimony to the faith. Perspectivalism appeared in seminal form in Cornelius Van Til's *An Introduction to Systematic Theology*. Although Frame typically speaks of three perspectives, Van Til began with three (revelation about nature, revelation about man himself, and revelation about God), and expanded it to nine.[1] I am inclined to agree with Frame that Van Til's multiplying of perspectives was, in part, tongue in cheek. The point was to highlight the multifaceted nature of divine revelation.

This chapter is divided into two parts. First, I provide the reader an introduction to perspectivalism, with responses to some common objec-

1. Revelation about nature (1) from nature, (2) self, and (3) God. Revelation about man himself from (4) nature, (5) self, and (6) God. And lastly, revelation about God from (7) nature, (8) self, and (9) God. See Van Til, *An Introduction to Systematic Theology* (Phillipsburg, NJ: P&R Publishing, 1974), chap. 6. See also *CVT*, 119–23.

tions to Frame's program. The second part brings perspectivalism into dialogue with postmodernism. My conclusion is that multiperspectivalism aids navigation through the murky waters of postmodern theory and is an invaluable tool for its appropriation by a presuppositional apologetic. This tool allows the astute user to see many of the same dots, but to connect them in ways that avoid reductionism, reactionary rhetoric, and naive acceptance.

What Is Multiperspectivalism?

As Van Til's former student, Frame harnessed Van Til's insight, expanding it into an entire theological program, one in which all theologizing is done with an eye toward self-consciously integrating the many facets of God's revelation. But before we continue, let us stop and ask: what is multiperspectivalism (hereafter MP)? We'll look at what MP is, then what it is not.

First, we should distinguish between what I call general perspectivalism and triperspectivalism. General perspectivalism acknowledges that people focus on different aspects of reality, even when looking at the same thing. Some emphasize the ethical aspects of Scripture; others devote more time to the didactic portions. The majority of this essay will focus on triperspectivalism.[2]

Triperspectivalism

According to Frame, "Human knowledge can be understood in three ways: as knowledge of God's norm, as knowledge of the situation, and as knowledge of ourselves. None can be achieved without the others. Each includes the others."[3] In every epistemic act we are in constant contact with these three perspectives. There is always the person doing the knowing (the knowing subject), the thing being known (the object of knowledge), and the standard or criteria by which knowledge is attained. These three are interrelated such that each is a perspective on the whole knowing process. The first is the normative perspective, the second the situational perspective, and the third the existential perspective.

2. Unless otherwise noted, I will be using the terms *multiperspectivalism*, *triperspectivalism*, and *perspectivalism* interchangeably.
3. *DKG*, 75.

God's knowledge is absolute, unmediated, all-inclusive, and determinative of the facts. Human knowledge of God and his world is partial. Instead of denying that truth is "out there" to be discovered, perspectivalism recognizes that our epistemic *access* to this truth is relative to the particularities of our gifts, nationality, gender, chronological location, etc. Vern Poythress makes this point with precision:

> Our knowledge of the truth is partial. We know truth, but not all of the truth. And someone else may know truths that we do not know. We are enabled to learn what others know, partly by seeing things from their perspective. Again, we may use the analogy of a precious jewel. The jewel has many facets, each one analogous to a perspective. The facets are all present objectively, as is the jewel as a whole. But not all facets of the jewel may be seen equally well through only one facet. Likewise, not all aspects of the truth can be seen equally well through one perspective.[4]

The emphasis in the *normative* perspective is on the rules, laws, and norms for belief and action. It is an expression of God's lordship attribute of authority. Examples range from supposedly impersonal laws (laws of logic, planetary motion, gravity, etc.) to personal authorities (parents, employers, government officials, church leaders). There is a hierarchy of norms, with Scripture as the highest. The majority of this article deals with Scripture as the *Noma Normans non Normata*, while recognizing the existence of various subordinate norms.

Scripture calls for our obedience and adoration (cf. Ps. 56:4, 10). We all seek answers to the big questions from trusted authorities. Some turn to gurus, modern science, philosophy, family, or even leading personalities in popular culture. Adherence to some ultimate principle dictates our allegiance and is prioritized over all rivals, regardless of our degree of epistemological self-consciousness. The book of Proverbs reminds us of this very principle: "The fear of the LORD [ultimate authority] is the beginning [starting point] of knowledge [in our understanding of the world, God, and ourselves]" (Prov. 1:7). The normative perspective asks: What does God have to say? How can we think God's thoughts after him on a given issue?

The *situational* perspective directs us to the facts of human experience, including history, science, and evidences for our convictions. This

---

4. Vern S. Poythress, *Symphonic Theology: The Validity of Multiple Perspectives in Theology* (Phillipsburg, NJ: P&R Publishing, 1987), 46.

perspective reminds us to avoid a strictly deductive, top-down system that ignores evidence for ideology. The facts of reality demand our submission. To deny water's chemical composition, a situational fact, is to ignore and rebel against the way God created the universe, a normative structure. Likewise, our creational constitution reveals God (Rom. 2:14–16), and to encourage revolt against God's cardiographic law is to deny that he has spoken with authority. Yet science, history, and our internal data are never to be interpreted in a fashion that ignores epistemological norms.

The *existential* perspective focuses on the person doing the knowing. We all bring spiritual dispositions, temperaments, biases, presuppositions, and memories to every act. Humanity was given stewardship over the earth (Gen. 2:15), implying the ability to understand and subdue the earth. But this is complicated by both our finitude and fallenness. Our knowledge grows with time, and in this lifetime we are never completely free from the temptation to use our knowledge in self-serving, manipulative ways. Ignoring this reality risks constructing a wooden and naive approach to knowing. The existential perspective provides us with our theological motives for epistemic humility.

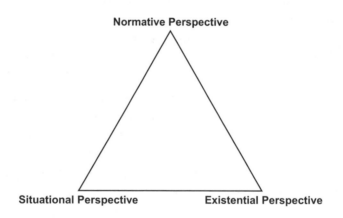

Fig. 5.1. Human Knowledge[5]

Triperspectivalism Applied

As a point of illustration, let us take something mundane. In coming to know my brother's dog, Smokey, I have come to the conclusion that he is a long-haired dog. How does this talk of "perspectives" relate to this

5. This diagram is taken from *DKG*, 75.

act of knowing? First, there is the subject of knowledge—me. Second, there is the object of knowledge—Smokey and his coat of fur. Third, there is the standard that I use to evaluate whether Smokey's hair is long or short. There is also my knowledge of what constitutes fur, what counts as a dog as opposed to a cat, and so on. There is interplay, or toggling, of perspectives.

As a more pressing example, let's look at the issue of abortion. A standard argument against abortion is the following: Murder is a wrong; abortion on demand is murder; therefore, abortion on demand is wrong.

Point one presents us an ethical imperative, providing an objective moral principle (Ex. 20:13). In order to arrive at point three we need to know several situational factors, such as whether abortion on demand takes the life of an innocent unborn person. Coming to grips with the facts of abortion helps us to apply point one. Our attention is drawn to the medical information on the nature of the unborn, the law of biogenesis, and the abortion procedure itself. This crucial information informs the application of God's command. "The interesting result of [this] line of reasoning is that we need to know the world to understand the meaning of Scripture."[6]

Biblical Foundations

Multiperspectivalism grows out of the recognition of three theological axioms. Here are the three pillars of MP:

(1) God's revelation is the absolute and ultimate authority over all human activity. Those who do not obey God's Word will ultimately give an account on the day of judgment (Matt. 7:24–27; Luke 12:3; 1 Peter 4:1–5).[7]

(2) The creator God directs history (Acts 17:26), including the individual actions and destinies of all people (Prov. 16:4; John 17:12; Rom. 9:6–24); controls even seemingly random occurrences (1 Kings 22:34; Prov. 16:33); and testifies to his own nature and character in all creation.[8]

6. Ibid., 67. In the original context, Frame is developing his notion that "meaning is application."
7. Frame has developed this in his *DWG*, forthcoming.
8. Cf. *DG*, chapts. 3–4, and *NOG*, chapt. 5.

(3) All human beings are created *imago Dei* (Gen. 1:26; 9:6; James 3:9).[9] Their creational constitution is revelational of God, and as such they are created to serve him. God is never far away from us, and is present with believer and unbeliever, either to bless or to judge.

These three pillars are summarized by what Frame calls God's *lordship attributes*: his (1) authority, (2) control, and (3) presence.

Clearing Up Confusion

Here we will cover several reservations with Frame's approach. Some of these objections I have come across in personal dialogue, read online, or seen in print. It is now beneficial to dig deeper into perspectivalism by the *via negativa*, by examining what it is not.

Multiperspectivalism Is Not Relativism

Some believe perspectivalism asserts that all positions are equally legitimate. Does this talk of perspectives not sound a lot like the story of the blind men feeling around an elephant? Each man thinks the part he is touching is the whole elephant. According to this objection, the "perceptive" perspectivalist sees the true problem: the "blind" theologians all think they see the "whole truth," when in fact they are simply looking at things from different angles. They are all correct, but in different ways. If this is true, perspectival thought flirts dangerously with theological pluralism. The fear is that with one wave of the perspectival wand all disagreements are swept under the rug. This is a particularly sad reading of Frame, considering that, in fact, perspectivalism actually assumes the opposite of relativism, that is, absolutism. Again, Poythress's comments are helpful: "Our opportunities, our intellectual ability, our interests, our teachers, and our presuppositions all influence which particular truths we come to know. Which particular facets of a jewel we see depends on where we are when we look at the jewel. Any particular bit of truth is always related to other bits. The exact relations we see and use depends on us."[10] Perspectivalism is ultimately the outworking

9. Cf. Frame, "Man and Woman in the Image of God," in *Recovering Biblical Manhood and Womanhood: A Response to Evangelical Feminism*, ed. John Piper and Wayne A. Grudem (Wheaton, IL: Crossway, 1991), chapt. 12.

10. Poythress, *Symphonic Theology*, 46.

of a chastened objectivism. It is a methodology rooted in an Augustinian ontology grounded in God's exhaustive sovereignty. It is a hermeneutics of finitude, not a denial of truth.

Not all disagreements are a matter of perspective.[11] MP does not reduce all differences to one of perspective. Take the debate between Calvinists and Arminians. Both sides do harbor perspectival differences. Arminians are usually fairly concerned to escape an unbiblical determinism and preserve human accountability, while the Reformed are concerned with the freedom of God in salvation and the human need of saving grace.[12]

These are perspectival differences, to say the least. But reducing the debate to mere differences of perspective, as if both sides were saying the same thing only using different theological language, is to overlook a crucial point. When looking at the same perspective—say, the spiritual abilities of man—Calvinism and Arminianism still disagree. Frame, for example, argues that the Reformed reading of passages such as John 6, Romans 1:18–32, Romans 8 and 9, and Ephesians 1–2 is more sensitive to the concerns of the text than the Arminian exegesis of the same passages.[13] The Reformed approach to God's justice, man's responsibility, and human sin avoids the excesses that Arminians fear, and preserves the integrity of their concerns. Perspectivalism has never been proposed as a sort of theological pluralism in which no one is wrong because we all see things our own way.

Multiperspectivalism Does Not Deny *Sola Scriptura*

A case has been made against perspectivalism based on a commitment to *sola Scriptura*. If the "knowledge of God's law, the world, and the self are interdependent and ultimately identical,"[14] do we not risk elevating our feelings and understanding of the world on par with the authority of God's Word? And if this is the case, does this not undermine the Bible as the sufficient guide for faith and life?

11. Here I am speaking of general perspectivalism, which is developed thoroughly in ibid., *passim*.

12. For how these concerns were developed in the theology of Pelagius as well as James Arminius, see R. C. Sproul's *Willing to Believe: The Controversy over Free Will* (Grand Rapids: Baker, 1997), chaps. 1, 6.

13. For more on these passages, see *Still Sovereign: Contemporary Perspectives on Election, Foreknowledge, and Grace*, ed. Bruce Ware and Thomas Schreiner (Grand Rapids: Baker, 2000).

14. *DKG*, 89.

117

The response to this charge is threefold. First, a perspectival approach does recognize the uniqueness of Scripture in its theological formulations. Only God's Word in Scripture provides us with infallible divine norms that cannot be challenged.[15] It is the covenant document of God's people.[16] This reservation is based on an oversimplified understanding of the perspectives. It confuses the normative perspective with the Bible itself, whereas Frame rejects such a mechanical identity between the two. He clarifies, "The normative perspective is not the Bible; it is my understanding of the Bible in its relations to me and all creation. . . . So understood, the normative perspective is certainly important, but it is not the Bible, and the primacy of Scripture does not of itself entail the primacy of the normative perspective."[17] The normative perspective is open to emendation; Scripture is not. We should recall that our understanding of one perspective grows as the others grow. They reflect a pluriform reality. They are interrelated and coterminous. Scripture in the normative role alone reduces the perspectives into separate parts and divides what God has united. But once we are settled in our understanding of a passage, we must submit unconditionally to what we believe God commands of us.

Second, there are normative, situational, and existential dimensions to everything. In the nature of this objection, let us take the Bible as our example. Normatively, the Bible presents us with God's verbal commands, given to direct all of life. Situationally, Scripture is a window to the redemptive-historical acts of God, and this inspired written record is a fact of human experience. Lastly, in the existential perspective we find that the Bible is God's address to his people, processed by our ears and eyes, understood by our intellect, and embraced or rejected by our hearts[18] as it reveals our spiritual condition.

Third, Frame himself is very vocal in his support of *sola Scriptura* and defends "something close to biblicism." It is ironic that while some charge Frame with looking too quickly to the Scripture apart from historical considerations,[19] others charge him with overlooking the supreme author-

15. Compare this with the definition of the sufficiency of Scripture in Wayne Grudem's *Systematic Theology* (Grand Rapids: Zondervan, 1994), 127, where he says that Scripture gives us all the words of God that we need.

16. Cf. *AGG*, 122–28.

17. *DKG*, 163.

18. For more on Scripture as a picture, window, and mirror, see ibid., 204–5.

19. This concern was expressed by Paul Helm in his overall positive review of *DG* in *Modern Reformation* 12, 2 (March/April 2003): 51–52.

ity of God's Word. Frame's "biblicist" pole is a reflection of his unflinching commitment to *sola Scriptura*,[20] while his perspectival pole is a reflection of his convictions on human finitude and sinfulness. Balancing both convictions is a daunting task. God's revelation is incredibly textured. Temptations persist to ignore or suppress the truth where it challenges and rebukes us. Likewise, we must overcome the myriad of hermeneutical difficulties that arise in our Bible reading. But God's voice cannot be muffled. We should recognize that not all biblical teachings are equally clear:

> Yet those things which are necessary to be known, believed, and observed for salvation are so clearly propounded, and opened in some place of Scripture or other, that not only the learned, but the unlearned, in a due use of the ordinary means, may attain unto a sufficient understanding of them.[21]

Despite interpretative difficulties, divine revelation is authoritative, necessary, perspicuous, and sufficient for its purposes.[22] To summarize, perspectivalism doesn't oppose *sola Scriptura*, but instead is a methodological application of the hermeneutical circle.

Multiperspectivalism Is Not an Unbiblical Theological Construct

This objection claims that since perspectivalism is not explicitly taught in Scripture, it has only the relative authority of a theological construct. Several points should be noted about this objection. First, it is true that Scripture does not teach perspectivalism directly. Frame's method is an extrapolation from the biblical data. But it is an extrapolation by "good and necessary consequence."[23] So, in this sense, perspectivalism is a theological construct. Second, we need not fear applying the term *construct* to this methodology. It is simply false to suppose that constructs are mutually exclusive with accurate teaching. One such example of this is the doctrine of the Trinity. No orthodox theologian would deny the exegetical support undergirding Trinitarianism, but neither would he believe that the Bible teaches it in all its pristine Athanasian creedal precision. While this is not

---

20. See Appendix 2 in *CWM*, "Sola Scripture in Theological Method."
21. WCF 1.7.
22. For more on this see *SBL*, chap. 5.
23. WCF 1.6.

to say that perspectivalism should be held up as a standard of Christian orthodoxy as Trinitarianism is, it is to show that *theological construct* is not a synonym for *false*.

Lastly, while perspectivalism is a construct of sorts, it is not optional for Christian analysis. One of the strong points of Frame's approach is that it is not completely novel. Theologians, philosophers, ethicists, and laypeople all employ a perspectival approach. As we noted earlier, in all decisions people (e) apply norms or laws (n) to situations (s).

ENGAGING POSTMODERNISM

Evangelical postures on postmodernism range from complete antagonism to the affirmation that any robust expression of Christianity will embrace postmodernism.[24] My conviction is that Christians can use the insights of many postmodern theorists positively for the benefit of Christ's kingdom. Here I briefly sketch out the beginnings of a fruitful dialogue between postmodern themes and Frame's perspectivalism. Without the necessary lenses of common grace and antithesis, such a dialogue is impossible.

Common Grace

Christians have much to learn from postmodernists, even though many of the latter are unbelievers. Unless we come to the grips with the fact that the line between truth and error runs down every human heart, we are prone to thinking that unbelieving postmodernists have nothing to

24. A sampling of titles from the last few years alone includes Heath White, *Postmodernism 101: A First Course for the Curious Christian* (Grand Rapids: Brazos, 2006); John D. Caputo, *What Would Jesus Deconstruct? The Good News of Postmodernism for the Church* (Grand Rapids: Baker Academic, 2007); Douglas Groothuis, *Truth Decay: Defending Christianity from the Challenge of Postmodernism* (Downers Grove, IL: InterVarsity Press, 2000); Bruce Ellis Benson, *Graven Ideologies: Nietzsche, Derrida & Marion on Modern Idolatry* (Downers Grove, IL: InterVarsity Press, 2002); Millard J. Erickson, Paul Kjoss Helseth, and Justin Taylor, eds., *Reclaiming the Center: Confronting Evangelical Accommodation in Postmodern Times* (Wheaton, IL: Crossway, 2004); Crystal Downing, *How Postmodernism Serves (My) Faith: Questioning Truth in Language, Philosophy and Art* (Downers Grove, IL: InterVarsity Press, 2006); Stanley J. Grenz, *A Primer on Postmodernism* (Grand Rapids: Eerdmans, 1996); James K. A. Smith, *Who's Afraid of Postmodernism? Taking Derrida, Lyotard, and Foucault to Church* (Grand Rapids: Baker Academic, 2006); Carl Raschke, *The Next Reformation: Why Evangelicals Must Embrace Postmodernism* (Grand Rapids: Baker Academic, 2004); Myron B. Penner, ed., *Christianity and the Postmodern Turn: Six Views* (Grand Rapids: Brazos, 2005); and Peter J. Leithart, *Solomon Among the Postmoderns* (Grand Rapids: Brazos, 2008).

offer us. But God can shine his light in the darkest recesses of the human heart. As Calvin observed:

> Whenever we come upon these matters in secular writers, let that admirable light of truth shining in them teach us that the mind of man, though fallen and perverted from its wholeness, is nevertheless clothed and ornamented with God's excellent gifts. If we regard the Spirit of God as the sole foundation of truth, we shall neither reject the truth itself, nor despise it wherever it shall appear, unless we wish to dishonor the Spirit of God.[25]

Sin has infected our every faculty. Nevertheless, God is gracious and has restrained it from doing its worst (Gen. 20:6). God also displays lovingkindness to both believers and nonbelievers in the unfolding of history (Matt. 5:45; Acts 14:16–17). God does use unbelievers to make true pronouncements (Num. 23:18–24; cf. Gen. 49:9), even when speaking God's truth was not their intention (John 11:47–51; Acts 5:34–39). Whether on the lips of faithful friend or fiercest foe, truth, Calvin notes, should be acknowledged as coming from the Spirit of God, the "sole foundation of truth."

Thus, we should heed Frame's suggestion to "use the prophets" of non-Christians in order to "bring to their attention the truth that they have been suppressing."[26] This leads us to our next point, the doctrine of antithesis.

Antithesis

Repeatedly, the various ways in which postmodernism has led, frankly speaking, to some silly conclusions has been pointed out. The most common critiques are the rampant relativism of postmodernity and the apparently self-referential incoherence of many postmodern denunciations of modernism. If it is said that "Western logic" is a mere social construct developed by old white men with an eye to muster power, we can always ask whether it is true that those who reject "Western logic" are also playing the power game.[27] The objector cannot have it both ways.

Postmodern sociology and anthropology argue that no culture is socially or morally superior to another. Postmodern ethicists often argue

---

25. John Calvin, *The Institutes of the Christian Religion*, 2.2.15.
26. *DKG*, 379, Maxim 61.
27. For all the various insights offered by Michel Foucault regarding the ways in which our sinful impulses to control others are manifested, this is the chief weakness of his power/knowledge thesis.

that any supposed ethic that applies to all people in all places at all times is an expression of Nietzsche's will to power. Postmodern literary theorists have argued that to insist on a single meaning to a text (one largely governed by the intent of the author) is an oppressive marginalization of heterogeneous readings. Should we accept *all* of this? Should we denounce *all* of this? Intuitively we recognize that neither of these is a viable alternative.

Is there any way in which aspects of postmodernism can serve Christ's kingdom? I believe so. Van Til's *In Defense of the Faith* may be read as two presentations of the same material.[28] The gospel message is presented in the language of traditional dogmatics and contemporary philosophy. In speaking the latter, Van Til did not thereby accept the conclusions of unbelieving philosophers. Rather, he used these concepts to highlight the fact that unbelief testifies against itself.

We benefit from being exposed to the language, questions, and concerns of postmodernism if for no other reason than to proclaim the gospel of Christ in our contemporary setting. Merold Westphal laid out the nature of a Christian reappropriation of postmodernism in these terms:

> Without forgetting the dual negativity of rejection and recontextualization, it is possible to think of such appropriation as an invitation to conversation. The appropriator, after listening carefully to the appropriatee, responds by saying, "I find these aspects of your presentation quite compelling and illuminating. But for me they work better when recontextualized as follows. Of course, that changes the project somewhat and involves the abandonment of this or that aspect of your original proposal. But don't you agree that those ideas of yours I find compelling work better in the context I propose, or at least, since they can be fruitfully put to work there, that they are not inherently wedded to the larger goals of your project?"[29]

My goal is to show that perspectivalists are in a unique position to recontextualize postmodernism because they can bring together under one roof all the tools of Christian analysis. Looking at the situational perspective, we see that our positionality or situatedness is not a hindrance to knowledge (as it is in Platonism) because we recognize that God's truth is instantiated in every

28. I owe this insight to Greg Bahnsen.

29. Merold Westphal, "Appropriating Postmodernism," in *Overcoming Onto-Theology: Toward a Postmodern Christian Faith* (New York: Fordham University Press, 2001), 76.

time, and in the particularities of every culture.[30] Looking to the existential, we find that our corrupted creaturehood is something that cannot be ignored in any of our thought. Yet in a Christian worldview, finitude and sin do not have the final say. God has not left us to our own devices. He has spoken a clear, normative, and penetrating Word that guides us epistemologically (telling us what truths we should embrace), ethically (building us up in holiness), and spiritually (feeding our hungry souls' need for divine fellowship).

PERSPECTIVALISM AND POSTMODERNISM

In the following section, we will briefly bring together common aspects in the discussion of postmodernism with perspectivalism. First, we will look at the issue of objectivity under the normative heading. Second, we will examine two writers whose works have become a standard part of postmodern theory. I will discuss Jacques Derrida's deconstruction and Jean Francois Lyotard's incredulity toward metanarratives as a resource for a situational critique of unbelief. Lastly, we will examine Foucault's doctrine of archaeology and power regimes as an exercise in existential critique of unbelief.

Theistic Objectivity and the Normative Perspective

When we claim the objective truth of the faith, do we violently privilege some, necessarily birthing oppressive regimes of "Truth"? "Postmodernists see a terrifying symmetry between modern theories, which suppress inconvenient facts, and modern colonial conquest, which suppress inconvenient peoples."[31] One of these "modern theories" is believed to be the importance of objectivity. Is the notion of objective truth an unbiblical artifact of modernity? Both the pros and the cons of "objectivity" must be evaluated. Many concerns with so-called objectivity are warranted. Objectivity is not a cover-all notion to which we can appeal when our witness fails. Neither is it necessary to do away with the concept altogether, as it has served the church well for many purposes.

30. Cf. Vern Poythress, *God-Centered Biblical Interpretation* (Phillipsburg, NJ: P&R Publishing, 1999), 66.
31. Leithart, *Solomon Among the Postmoderns*, 160.

First, emphasizing objectivity places the emphasis on God's extramental existence and the eschatological judgment. Such facts are true despite the skeptic's doubt. Judgment *is* still coming. *Every* knee will bow, both those who denied the truth of Scripture as well as those who lovingly submit to it. Moreover, the category of objectivity has rightly placed emphasis on the historicity of Christianity. Paradoxically, a Christian-theistic objectivity is the very thing that safeguards against a dehistoricizing of the redemptive message! Why is this? In order to avoiding approaching Scripture as ahistorical truths available to all people irrespective of background, we must firmly root our understanding of it in its original cultural and geographical setting. While God's eternal decrees are timeless, they unfold in the temporal order and could not be what they are without happening in the place, and occurring during the time, in which they did. The Son of Man precisely is the Son of Man, because in the fullness of time he was born of a woman, was born under the law (Gal. 4:4), suffered under Pontius Pilate, was crucified, died, was buried, was resurrected, and ascended into heaven. To ignore these contexts is to warp the message they present.

It is not objectivity but ahistorical systems that lead to unjust and oppressive "regimes." The modernist notion of objectivity as disembodied and unsituated must be rejected. It flies in the face of the Creator-creature distinction. It assumes that we can escape our creaturehood, since it is God who places us in our particular geographical and chronological contexts (Acts 17:26). Frame notes well:

> Sometimes we dream fondly of a "purely objective" knowledge of God [and of the world]—a knowledge of God freed from the limitations of our senses, minds, experiences, preparation, and so forth. But nothing of this sort is possible, and God does not demand that of us. Rather, he condescends to dwell in and with us, as in a temple. He identifies himself in and through our thoughts, ideas, and experiences. And that identification is clear; it is adequate for Christian certainty. A "purely objective" knowledge is precisely what we don't want! Such knowledge would presuppose a denial of our creaturehood and thus a denial of God and of all truth.[32]

If we allow Scripture to determine what is true, then we can possess objective knowledge but not the objectivity that modernists insist upon.

32. *DKG*, 65. Bracketed comment mine.

This objectivity is of the One who determines reality, and provides revelation. We maintain that *biblical objectivity is achieved in submission to God's authoritative interpretation.*

The Situational Critique of Unbelief

Jean Francois Lyotard's "incredulity toward metanarratives" is one of the most commonly cited examples of postmodern thought. Though perceived as antithetical to a robust Christianity, I believe Lyotard can serve presuppositional apologetics. First, let us examine Lyotard's meaning.

Lyotard confessed, "Simplifying to the extreme, I define postmodernism as incredulity toward metanarratives."[33] Many critics of postmodernism level an attack on such incredulity, taking Lyotard's comment as the rejection of *any* all-encompassing worldview. The original term, *grand recits*, means "big story." After all, is not Christianity a metanarrative? If so, such incredulity would rule out, a priori, its viability.

Upon closer inspection of Lyotard's work, it becomes clearer that he means something more subtle. In his own words, "I will use the term *modern* to designate any science that legitimates itself with reference to a metadiscourse of this kind making an explicit appeal to some grand narrative . . ."[34] Westphal observes, "Christianity is not Lyotard's target. Nor is it inherently the kind of story he criticizes."[35] Smith clarifies:

> What is at stake is not the *scope* of these narratives [i.e., that they seek to explain everything with reference to a world-and-life-view] but the *nature* of the claims they make. For Lyotard, metanarratives are a distinctly *modern* phenomenon: they are stories which not only tell a grand story (since even premodern and tribal stories do that), but also claim to be able to legitimate the story and its claims *by an appeal to universal reason.*[36]

Likewise, "the scientific stories told by modern rationalism (Kant), scientific naturalism, and sociobiology are metanarratives insofar as they

33. Jean-Francois Lyotard, *The Postmodern Condition: A Report on Knowledge*, trans. G. Bennington and B. Massumi (Minneapolis: University of Minnesota Press, 1984), xxiv.
34. Ibid.
35. Westphal, *Overcoming Onto-Theology*, xv.
36. James K. A. Smith, "A Little Story about Metanarratives," in *Christianity and the Postmodern Turn: Six Views*, ed. Penner, 125. Emphasis in original. Bracketed comment mine.

claim to be demonstrable by *reason alone.*"[37] So the *meta* in *metanarrative* can be understood in two senses; the first refers to its inclusivity (the "scope" of the story), and the other sense is "a second-order discourse designed to legitimize one or more first-order discourses."[38] It is this second sense that primarily concerns Lyotard.

Modernity sought to evade external authorities such as the Christian clergy. In time, the "scientific method" came to dominate all fields of inquiry. Shortly it trumped theology as the queen of the sciences. Lyotard reminds us that all authority claims are grounded in some narrative, a larger legitimizing framework. While renouncing authority-based legitimization, modernity sought to base beliefs upon concepts that were clear, distinct, and indubitable (as in continental rationalism), empirically verifiable (as in British empiricism and logical positivism), or a synthesis of the two (as in Kant). Procedures following this methodology were labeled "scientific," whereas alternative foundations for belief were denounced as superstition. Here the problem of an eternal regress rears its ugly head. How do we linearly justify belief in scientism? Premodern "myths" could in a sense legitimize themselves, but many modernists explicitly denied that this could be done.[39] This problem could be solved only by the construction of a metanarrative. Modernists began telling the story of progress, technology, and liberation to justify their faith in the scientific method. These attempts at justification are subject to postmodern incredulity. "Having overthrown various ancient regimes both of knowledge and social practice, modernity finds itself needing to legitimize its 'new authorities,' and it resorts to narrative to do so."[40]

Here Lyotard begins to sound like a presuppositionalist. Narrative is not the problem. The problem is the modernist denial of appealing to narrative. Appeals to "universal reason" are self-deceived by the myth of neutrality. Presuppositionalists have always insisted that all worldviews are grounded in presuppositions, a network of assumptions that form how we interpret the world. Smith comments, "one of the constructive engagements with

37. Smith, *Who's Afraid of Postmodernism?* 65. Emphasis added.
38. Merold Westphal, "Onto-theology, Metanarratives, Perspectivism, and the Gospel," in *Christianity and the Postmodern Turn: Six Views*, 148.
39. Here I use the term *myth* to refer to worldviews that are grounded in narratives, not mere fables or falsehoods. Likewise, *scientism* should be understood as the perspective on science that suffers from the reductionism of metaphysical and methodological naturalism.
40. Westphal, *Overcoming Onto-Theology*, xiii.

Lyotard would be to consider his discussion of language games and critique of metanarratives and its correlation with presuppositional discourses on worldviews and the critique of autonomous reason."[41] Such an engagement is sorely needed.

Derrida and Deconstruction

Of deconstruction, Kevin Vanhoozer has said, "Here we have what is in my opinion the single most helpful contribution of postmodernity to Christian thinkers: a thoroughgoing iconoclasm, a radical protest against oppressive systems of thought."[42] Can this be, considering that Derrida "rightly passes for an atheist"?[43] Perspectival apologists should note the similarities between Derrida's deconstruction and Frame's *Rationalism/Irrationalism Analysis* (hereafter RIA) of worldviews. This apologetic tool was introduced by Frame in *DKG* and further developed in *AGG*.[44]

RIAs are internal critiques, demonstrating how the principles of would-be autonomous (i.e., rationalistic) thought lead to irrational conclusions.[45] Similarly:

> Deconstruction attends to the competing trajectories within a text or corpus of writings, showing the way in which a text often "undoes" itself because of this internal tension . . . Texts deconstruct themselves. According to Derrida, this occurs when a text attempts to exclude what they assume. In other words, texts often feed off of what they exclude.[46]

Deconstruction shows the ambiguities and fragility of texts or systems of thought (such as Platonism) that define themselves in terms of binary opposites, pairs of antithetical concepts (such as us/them, faith/reason, natural/

41. Smith, *Who's Afraid of Postmodernism?* 68–69.

42. Kevin Vanhoozer, "Pilgrim's Digress: Christian Thinking On and About the Post/Modern Way," *Christianity and the Postmodern Turn: Six Views*, 80.

43. John Caputo, *The Prayers and Tears of Jacques Derrida: Religion without Religion*, The Indiana Series in the Philosophy of Religion (Bloomington and Indianapolis: University of Indiana Press, 1997), Introduction.

44. This was done under the headings of atheism and idolatry. See *AGG*, 193–202.

45. The careful reader will notice the strong family resemblances between Frame's analysis and Francis Schaeffer's upper-story/lower-story critiques.

46. "Deconstruction," "Postmodernism," in Kelly James Clark, Richard Lints, and James K. A. Smith, *101 Key Philosophical Terms in Philosophy and Their Importance for Theology* (Louisville: Westminster John Knox Press, 2004), 15.

unnatural, inside/outside, etc.).[47] By way of comparison, we'll look at how both Frame and Derrida apply their approaches to the work of Plato.

Perhaps the best example of Frame's application of RIAs is the recently published article "Greeks Bearing Gifts."[48] He examines thinkers from the pre-Socratic era to Plotinus. In Frame's analysis, Plato's genius is demonstrated by his synthesis of Pythagoras and Heraclitus. In doing so, Plato posits his two worlds. The first, and primary, is the world of the Forms, which are "quasi-mathematical formulae, recipes that can be used to construct trees, horses, virtue, and justice as the Pythagorean Theorem can be used to construct a triangle."[49] The second world is the material world, which is subject to flux, and is imperfectly patterned after the Forms. Frame's dismantling of Plato begins by his reading of the dialogue *Euthyphro*. In it, Socrates rejects the idea that goodness can be defined by specific acts. Why? Because "any time we try to define Goodness in terms of specific qualities (justice, prudence, temperance, etc.), we have descended to something less than the Form of Goodness."[50] Frame's diagnosis is that the Form of the Good in Plato's thought is utterly useless to guide moral behavior. Without particular instantiations of the Good, we are left without any idea of how we should live our lives.

Next, Frame moves to the *Timaeus*, Plato's creation account. Here the creator (the Demiurge) takes brute matter and patterns it after the Forms. This Form-shaped matter is then placed in the receptacle, which, due to some stubborn properties of matter, imperfectly "takes" to the imprint. A simple illustration is the following: A baker (the Demiurge) takes shapeless dough (raw matter) and orders and structures it by means of a cookie cutter (the Forms). The process is completed when the baker places the newly shaped dough into the oven (the receptacle).

According to Frame's analysis, the weaknesses with this narrative are twofold. First, Plato's story is intended to explain the creation of everything, but it fails to explain the origin of the four central figures: the Demiurge, raw matter, the Forms, and the receptacle! Second, Plato fails to account for the relationship between the unchanging perfect Forms and their mutable imperfect copies. He tries to do this in the *Timaeus* with the receptacle. But

47. See Downing, *How Postmodernism Serves (My) Faith*, 128–131, and Leithart, *Solomon Among the Postmoderns*, 30–33.

48. Frame, "Greeks Bearing Gifts," in *Revolutions in Worldview* (Phillipsburg, NJ: P&R Publishing, 2007), chapt. 1.

49. Ibid., 18.

50. Ibid., 19.

the Forms cannot model change. "So the imperfection and change of the experienced world has no rational explanation." Plato's goal is too high for him to achieve. Frame's conclusion?

> He is rationalistic about the Forms and irrationalistic about the sense-world. For him, reason is totally competent to understand the Forms but not competent to make sense of the changing world of experience. Yet he tries to analyze the changing world by means of changeless forms—an irrational world by a rationalistic principle.[51]

The things that Plato rejects as vital (transience and imperfection) are the very things he must account for if his project is to be successful.

In "Plato's Pharmacy"[52] Derrida examines Plato's discussion near the end of his dialogue *Phaedrus* on the origin of writing. Derrida points out two problems raised by the dialogue, one for interpreters and translators, and the other for Platonism itself. In the *Phaedrus* Plato recalls the story of the Egyptian god Theuth and the King Thamus. Theuth, the inventor-god, presents Thamus with his newest invention, writing, for the King's approval. Theuth refers to writing as a *pharmakon*, as does Thamus. But *pharmakon* has a semantic range from "cure" and "remedy" to its polar opposite, "poison."[53] Theuth calls writing a *pharmakon* for memory in the former sense(s), Thamus in the latter. Christopher Norris reflects on the interpretive difficulties raised by Derrida in this passage:

> *Pharmakon* is not just an "ambiguous" term, such that one could list its various meanings and appreciate the richness, subtlety or scope that it lends to Plato's text. For its two chief senses are "poison" on the one hand and "remedy" or "cure" on the other, meanings which one might think could hardly come together in any single utterance or context of usage.[54]

This is where Plato begins to auto-deconstruct. Derrida, contra Plato, points out that writing is *both* poison and cure. Derrida is not trying to

51. Ibid., 23.
52. See Jacques Derrida, *Dissemination*, trans. Barbara Johnson (Chicago: University of Chicago Press, 1983), sects, 1, 2.
53. *Pharmakon* is translated as "specific" in *The Dialogues of Plato*, Great Books of the Western World, vol. 7, trans. Benjamin Jowett (Chicago: Encyclopedia Britannica, 1952).
54. Christopher Norris, *Derrida* (Cambridge, MA: Harvard University Press, 1987), 37.

invert Plato's intention—making writing superior to speech—as is often supposed. "[This is] precisely Derrida's point: that these two antithetical senses of the word are everywhere copresent in Plato's text, defeating all attempts (on the part of tidy-minded scholars and translators) to choose one or the other according to context."[55]

Second, Derrida argues that the *Phaedrus* is constructed of a number of binary opposites that upon closer inspection do not hold up. Plato's speech/writing opposition is the clearest example. He denigrates writing as a second-rate mode of knowledge. While speech is one step removed from pure intellect, writing captures speech, adding an additional step away from thought. In their discussion, Thamus, reflecting Plato's view, condemns Theuth's invention. Writing is a poison because it will make people lazy, refusing to internalize knowledge. Yet Derrida notes the instability of the platonic hierarchy in the very method Plato adopts to communicate Socratic truth. In Plato's dialogues, Socrates is the master teacher, guiding his pupils via oral dialogue. He also never took a pen to paper. Plato is Socrates' literarily gifted student. He has both faithfully and unfaithfully preserved the tradition by committing it to an "inferior" mode. The deconstruction of the binary is complete; the superiority of speech is dependent upon writing! There lies the inherent instability and "undecidability" of Plato's epistemology.

Both in the case of deconstruction and in Frame's RIA the goal is to show instabilities within a system. Likewise, both, properly speaking, are what I call "passive analysis." They do not do anything to a text or system. Instead they detect weaknesses or systemic inconsistencies. Smith notes, "Deconstruction happens *in the middle voice* . . . it deconstructs itself." And "deconstruction happens within texts, from the inside, out of their own resources."[56] Yet while significant parallels exist between the two means of analysis, there is a crucial difference. RIAs are hammers while deconstruction is a chisel. Derrida methodically picks away at a text, occasionally smoothing off rough edges, and other times aggravating cracks. When his "reading" is complete, the edifice still stands, but its integrity is severely compromised. Frame's approach goes further than Derrida. The end product is radically more devastating. When executed well RIAs leave no doubt that their target is a hopelessly doomed project that simply *cannot* be true.

55. Ibid.
56. James K. A. Smith, *Jacques Derrida: Live Theory* (New York: Continuum, 2005), 9. Emphasis in original.

130

Derrida illustrates that rival systems of discourse built on autonomy will auto-deconstruct. Only God's revealed truth can handle the craggy features of life that defy tidy man-made systems. Deconstruction can also show that autonomous thought parasitically feeds off a concept that it ostensibly excludes as "other," namely, faith. Presuppositional apologetics has always opposed the bifurcation of faith and reason and sought its deconstruction. As with Caiaphas in the case of Jesus (John 11:50), Derrida has highlighted the need for divine provision without knowing it. Regardless of Derrida's personal ideology, deconstruction can be an extremely helpful tool. His concern was to open up a space for hearing the marginalized, the "other." Frame's RIA is geared toward clearing away intellectual obstacles to faith, razing fortresses erected to usurp the authority of the "Other," the Holy One of Israel.

The Existential Critique of Unbelief

The correlation between presuppositional apologetics and the archaeology of knowledge of Michel Foucault lies in the digging metaphor. Foucault sought to expose the modern notion that established "truths" are based purely on their intellectual credibility when in fact they are based on various discourses of power politics. The approved vision of "Reason" is propped up and displayed as being simply the "rational way people see the world." Smith defines the genealogy/archaeology of Michel Foucault as a method of "uncover[ing] the secret, submerged biases and prejudices that go into shaping what is called truth."[57] For Foucault (and Nietzsche before him), the goal is to demonstrate development for those things that are thought not to have a history.

Presuppositional apologetics has always been an existential and archaeological affair. Parallel to Foucault, presuppositionalism exposes the claim that skepticism is based on superior rationality, science, facts, or philosophical argumentation, but is the result of the purposeful work of suppression. When applied at the individual level, by patiently working through the layers (and levels) of unbelief, we can expose how supposed unbelieving a prioris are the result of various academic, cultural, and social developments.

The biblical foundation for a perspective appropriate of Foucault is Romans 1, where, according to the apostle Paul, the unbeliever is shown to have a personal knowledge of God, yet buries this knowledge by holding it

57. Smith, *Who's Afraid of Postmodernism?* 86

down in unrighteousness. The task of the apologist is to help bring out the buried knowledge within the unbeliever. He or she is to sift through the layers of suppression, exposing the fragile facades that mask the truth that lies hidden. Foucaultian "digs"[58] are helpful in this regard. Why does Sam affirm atheism? Is it because it relieves him of the moral accountability that comes with an extramarital affair? Richard may raise "scientific" objections to Christianity, but should we ignore the betrayal he suffered at the hands of believers? Little by little we peel back the layers of the unbeliever's espoused reasons and get to the heart of the matter—matters of the heart.

Now, admittedly, Foucault's approach is more subtle than this. Richard Kearney notes, "What Foucault is interested in discovering [in his archaeology of knowledge] are those theoretical archives which tell us how the 'facts' were interpreted in a specific epoch. Or to put it another way, he is less preoccupied with the 'things' of a particular cultural period than with the 'words' which were used to signify these things, that is, the ways in which these things were perceived, expressed and thereby *known*."[59]

Foucault's project might also be fruitfully employed in examining how the contemporary consensus in the biological sciences excludes any dissent from Darwinian evolution by defining science in naturalistic and positivistic terms. Such an examination is the outworking of the hermeneutics of suspicion. The hermeneutics of suspicion is not employed to determine the truth-value of a system, claim, or proposition. Instead, the question is one of *function*, how beliefs are put to use. Foucault reminds us that the current "absolute" of Darwinism is the outworking of various worldview-shaping discourses, namely, Enlightenment rationalism and deism. Scientific journals and universities have been accused of enforcing the "Truth" of origins established by Darwinism by refusing publication and tenure to those who openly express doubts about Darwinism.

PERSPECTIVAL PROBLEMS WITH POSTMODERNISM

Thus far, I have highlighted those aspects of postmodernism that can be reenlisted into Christian service. Now we turn to a perspectival critique of

58. Smith himself makes the connection between Foucault and presuppositionalism in ibid., 85n11.

59. Richard Kearney, *Modern Movements in European Philosophy: Phenomenology, Critical Theory, Structuralism*, 2nd ed. (Manchester, UK: Manchester University Press, 1994), 287.

postmodern excess. As above, I have organized my discussion perspectivally. Much more could be said, but perhaps the following comments will suffice.

Existential Problems

It is evident that non-Christian postmodernists—like Foucault, Lyotard, and Derrida—commit the same error that all autonomous thought makes: they suffer from the problem of borrowed capital. Presuppositionalism demands that the unbeliever justify his or her epistemological and moral claims. Given one's rejection of Christianity, how does the unbeliever explain his own belief in laws of logic and moral absolutes? In the same vein, we call non-Christian postmodernists to account for their cherished principles of justice, equality, and solidarity. Christians have a justification for these convictions (they are scriptural values); unbelieving postmoderns do not. We all are appalled at violence, oppression, and unjust marginalization because we have God's law written on our hearts. We intuitively know that certain things are wrong. How can postmodernists sustain their moral denunciations of marginalization, oppression, and violence without falling into the same ethnocentrism, chronocentrism, and logocentrism that they lay at the feet of their opponents?

Another existential problem that plagues postmodernism is in the artificial standard held up by postmodernists to the knowledge of the individual. All too often a false epistemological standard is erected: either we can know everything (in principle) or we can know nothing. The Bible teaches that one does not have to have exhaustive knowledge in order to have true knowledge. True knowledge as grounded in historical situatedness is not merely affirmed in Scripture; it is the heart of the biblical message (1 John 1:1–3).

Normative Problems

It is my conviction that behind the reactionary rhetoric of many evangelical responses to postmodernism is a genuine recognition that without a transcendent God who is not subject to the limitations of finitude—and without his verbal revelation to serve as our ultimate presupposition—there is no way to escape enslavement to something in creation, whether it be power structures or our own sinful passions. Relativity reigns when standards of truth, beauty, and goodness fluctuate from individual to individual.

The plurality of ideologies calls into question the very notion of epistemic certainty. Here we should be aware of a standard postmodern non-sequitur, moving from "we have absolute insight" to "there is no absolute insight."[60] It simply does not follow from our finitude and situatedness that no transcendent knowledge exists. In fact, Christopher Butler notes that the apprehension of postmoderns like Lyotard to master narratives is itself a reflection of a privileged minority.[61] A perspectiveless apprehension of reality is impossible, but as God condescends to provide us with revelation we must hold it firm, and never trade it for a mess of postmodern pottage.

Situational Problems

Although it may seem as if postmodernism collapses everything into the subjective or the existential, its idolatrous obsession with the situational is too often overlooked. Leithart gives this the name of *postmodern provisionalism*. He states, "For the postmodern, human knowledge is partial and provisional and has to be held loosely and tentatively. Postmoderns speak in modest 'it seems to me's': postmodernity does not thunder from pulpits."[62] The complexity of life is perceived as a nigh-impenetrable obstacle to true knowledge and final accountability. Too often accountability is paid merely to particular interest groups. Perspectivalists have also recognized these complexities, but deny that enculturation, finitude, and even sin can produce circumstances so great as to cloud out our duties before God and neighbor.

Ironically, the very thing that would put an end to the world's tyrannical cycle of oppression and marginalization of minority groups—a clear word from the creator God—is endlessly deferred. Derrida's notion of the "messianic" is, as noted by Peter Leithart, an anti-eschatology, denying a climactic conclusion to history.[63] It is always looking, but never finding; always open to "possibility," but closed to the possibility that God became flesh and dwelt among us. But if Jesus is God "with us," then his injunction to love your enemies and to pray for those who persecute you (Matt. 5:44)

60. Cf. Westphal, *Overcoming Onto-theology*, 86.

61. Christopher Butler, *Postmodernism: A Very Short Introduction* (New York: Oxford, 2002), 14–15. Leithart states it pointedly: "Perhaps postmodern theory is the ideology of rich and well-fed members of the knowledge class." *Solomon Among the Postmoderns*, 161.

62. Leithart, *Solomon Among the Postmoderns*, 70–71.

63. Ibid., 94. For Derrida's theme of the messianic, see Caputo, *The Prayers and Tears of Jacques Derrida*.

cannot be dismissed as sentimental hogwash. The living God has identified with the suffering of his people. The normative and the situational perspectives have embraced in Christ; therefore, his words have particular existential impact upon us.

In reducing worldviews to either narrative ("myth") or metanarrative (appealing to neutral Reason), Lyotard is hypersituational, sidestepping the normative perspective. He focuses more on how narrative is legitimized than on whether the narrative is true or not. Is the essence of Scripture a narrative? Redemptive history is a narrative that provides the interpretive backdrop for gospel kerygma, but it is more than mere narrative. The biblical worldview cannot be tamed by reductionistic categories of either myth or metanarrative. *It is the narratival-sapiential-propositional revelation of the triune God.*

Conclusion

In the first part of this article I have introduced John Frame's perspectival methodology. I have also clarified what multiperspectivalism is not. It is not relativism, does not reduce all differences to one of perspective, is not inconsistent with an affirmation of *sola Scriptura*, and is not an unbiblical construct. By addressing these misunderstandings I have hoped to shed light on the issues between perspectivalists and nonperspectivalists.

In the second section I have sketched out the benefits of a perspectival engagement with postmodernism. Positively, postmodernism has rocked the foundations of Enlightenment faith in autonomous reason, reevaluated language and social discourse, emphasized presuppositions, and attacked modernist individualism. Despite severe imbalances, this is a needed redirection after the last few centuries. Nevertheless, unqualified approval cannot be given to postmodernism. As previously noted, common grace is active in every era, but so is the principle of antithesis. While relativism is not something distinct to postmodernism—lest we forget the ancient sophists—never before has there been such a dominant and widespread ethos supporting and nourishing relativism in a variety of flavors.

But we can say both yes and no to postmodernism. I have organized a number of postmodern concerns by perspectival emphasis. Lyotard's discussion of metanarratives launches a powerful attack against the myth of neutrality. Jesus made the same point when he declared that no one can serve two masters (Matt. 6:24). Derrida aims to highlight that interpretation is never final, is never *adaequatio intellectus ad rei* (i.e., the perfect adequation between intellect and substance). Paul said this two millennia ago when he wrote that "we see in a mirror dimly" (1 Cor. 13:12). Postmodern insights may serve as excellent illustrations and reminders of what God has already told us in his Word. Between Van Til's example of a bilingual presentation of biblical content and Frame's methodology, perspectivalists are in an excellent position to speak the truth in love to postmoderns.

6

JOHN FRAME:
THE CLOSET RADICAL

STEPHEN W. BROWN

A NUMBER OF YEARS AGO, John Frame gave a lecture for the PCA Central Florida Presbytery, of which I'm a part. At the end of that lecture was a question-and-answer session, and someone asked a fairly controversial question. Dr. Frame prefaced his equally controversial answer with, "Oh, dear . . ."

After the meeting, I said to John: "John, you are a true revolutionary; but listen to me. Revolutionaries do not say, 'Oh, dear.' If you would like, I'll teach you to cuss."

When I was asked to write a chapter in this festschrift about John Frame as a closet radical, I thought about that incident. It captures some of the essence of John Frame as a closet radical: what appears to be true about John is often far different from the reality. The operative words in this essay are *closet* and *radical*.

Radicals rarely appear to be radical. They are like pool hustlers who appear to be inadequate to the game until one realizes that one's wallet is empty and the hustler is grinning. It is why evil radicals aren't stopped before great damage is done. It is also why God's radicals are often missed until one sees God glorified.

137

My first personal encounter with John Frame happened when he—at potentially great cost to his own reputation—defended a young man whom I loved and affirmed, but who didn't fit the "Reformed mold." Quietly and clearly, John stood with my young friend at a time when very few others did or would have. When my friend told me what had happened, I wrote to John and said that he didn't know who I was, but that I wanted him to know that a preacher in Florida was praying for him and rose up and called him "blessed."

John Frame is God's radical. He doesn't know it, and you may have missed it. John doesn't look, act, or sound like a radical and blushes when I say it. But he is!

Let me show you. You could miss it if you aren't careful.

Radicals are generally perceived as talkers. If you know John, you know that he isn't a talker. In fact, in my many years at Reformed Theological Seminary, I don't think I've ever heard John say a word at a faculty meeting unless he made a presentation or answered a direct question. I've been with John in a great variety of social situations, and he is an incredible and intense listener . . . but hardly ever a talker. Talkers just keep talking until something comes to mind.

That is not John Frame. In fact, there is a kind of humility and self-depreciation about him that is always surprising to those who don't know him. I have often heard, "No, you're kidding; that can't be *the* John Frame."

Although John isn't a talker, it doesn't mean that he doesn't say anything. It just means that when he does, people have a tendency to listen even though he speaks quite softly.

In Ephesians 6, Paul writes about how we should be strong and put on the "whole armor of God" (v. 11).[1] Then he asks for prayers for himself: "And also [pray] for me, that words may be given to me in opening my mouth boldly to proclaim the mystery of the gospel, for which I am an ambassador in chains, that I may declare it boldly, as I ought to speak" (vv. 19–20).

John Frame is one of the most gentle and quiet Christians I know, but he speaks truth to power and he doesn't shilly-shally. Whether he is talking about worship (he is a classically trained musician who defends contemporary worship and music), theology (he is quite clear on how "Machen's Warrior Children" have done great damage to the church), church splits (he says that any celebration of a church's or denomination's anniversary is a celebration of sin), the regulative principle (he says that the Puritans

---

1. All quotations from the Bible are from the ESV.

missed it and were minimalist)—whatever he is talking about—one never doubts where John Frame stands. There is always the recognition that he has a whole lot of insightful and strong convictions.

Pseudo-radicals are talkers. Real radicals are profound and clear, and don't cave in the face of controversy.

That reminds me of another way in which John Frame is a closet radical. One expects radicals to "divide and conquer," but when you look up *irenic* in the dictionary, you'll find John Frame's picture. I don't think I've ever met a man who is more considerate, kind, and irenic than John in dealing with his many critics.

Just take a cursory dip into the many Internet discussions of Reformed theology, and you will be shocked by the serial-killer nature of much of the theological discussion. It is, of course, all done in "love" and because of a "concern for truth," but occasionally one wonders. It often smacks instead of arrogance and self-righteousness.

Let me give you some quotations without names attached:

"Frame has spoken out of both sides of his mouth."

"Frame's position contradicts the clear teaching of Holy Scripture."

"Frame is putting forth views that are subtle and dangerous."

"Frame's views on worship are blatantly unconfessional and thus violate his claim to be Reformed."

"Frame's views are false and dangerous."

"Idolatry!"

"Heretical!"

When my longtime friend Tony Campolo (with whom I disagree about almost everything except Jesus) receives harsh criticism, he will often write to the critic, "I think someone used your name without your permission. I know that someone for whom Christ died would not write the kind of angry and hateful letter I got under your name. I would suggest that you find who is using your name and tell them to stop."

I get thousands of e-mails, letters, and phone calls at the ministry where I work, and a good many of them are highly critical of something I've done or said. Someone has said, "Bless those who curse you. Think what they would say if they knew the truth." Remembering that bit of wisdom makes me a bit "nicer" . . . but not much.

I used to write pages defending myself and my views, only to discover that there are those who will double my pages in response to my defense

139

and only add to the list of things about which they are "shocked," "puzzled," and "hurt." I have this day job, so I finally gave up and now generally answer criticism with a note: "Dear _____, You may be right, but you're probably wrong. Sincerely, Steve."

It drives the critics nuts! Talk about passive-aggressive!

Not John Frame. He never gives up, never backs down, never devalues or dismisses his critics, and never violates Ephesians 4:15. In every case of which I'm aware, John has spoken the truth in love.

Chaffer, Rushdoony, Miller, Van Til, Bahnsen, Shepherd, Lewis, Schaeffer, Adams, Crabb, Kline, Graham, Barnhouse, Gerstner, Machen, Aquinas, Luther, Calvin, Murray . . . and the list goes on and on. When I talk about God's servants or God's family and look at a list like that, there are some names that I would leave out or perhaps cover with a footnote. I suspect that you may feel constrained to add a "footnote," too.

Not John Frame. He doesn't compromise, but there is a supernatural love and respect that always amazes me. One might call that quality "radical."

And that brings me to one more thing. John Frame is a closet radical in his ability to speak softly and love deeply, but you'll still miss the radical side of John if you don't also get his passion for biblical truth and his gift of clearly defining and defending that truth.

One learns to suspect that radicals are spinning the truth they proclaim. In order to motivate their followers, they demonize the views of the enemy and are highly selective of the truth they speak to their followers. It's called manipulation, and it only appears to be radical. Real radicals speak truth even when it costs them—the whole truth and nothing but the truth.

When Barry Goldwater ran for the presidency of the United States, he was in constant trouble because he refused to spin his truth. When he was in Florida where retirees go to die, he was highly critical of Social Security. In Tennessee, he spoke against the TVA. And in Washington, he clearly pointed out the shallowness of politics.

One of Goldwater's Senate friends said to him, "Barry, there's a big bull in that field, and I know you have to go through the field. But you don't have to wave a red flag in his face every time you do."

That is what John Frame does. Because he waves the red flag without rancor or anger, though, you can miss it.

In John's "Backgrounds to My Thought," which appears elsewhere in this volume, he references the time he was a student at Princeton University and his involvement with the Princeton Evangelical Fellowship and Westerly Road Church. In that piece, John talks about his memorizing as many as seven hundred verses of Scripture through the Navigators memory system and then says, "Those are the verses that continue today to serve as landmarks for my theology." Later, he says that the Princeton Evangelical Fellowship taught him "the importance of holding firmly to the supreme authority (including infallibility and inerrancy) of Scripture as God's Word."

Paul's reference to himself in 2 Corinthians 13:8 can well be applied to John Frame: "For we cannot do anything against the truth, but only for the truth."

The late Grady Wilson, Billy Graham's longtime associate, was a great preacher but, in a wonderful act of humility and servanthood, set his own career aside in order to "hold up Mr. Graham's arms." For years, Grady was in the background and Mr. Graham's servant.

After hearing Grady preach, I invited him to come and preach at the church I was serving at the time. Our congregation loved Grady and his preaching. I don't have the space here to tell you some great stories about Grady, but one of the things I remember about him that is relevant here is this: When Grady said something controversial or irritating, he would hold up his Bible, smile, and say, "Don't be angry with me! I didn't say it. God said it!"

If you have read this chapter this far, you know that I'm not a scholar. I'm just an old, cynical preacher. It's insane that I've taught all these years in a theological seminary. I ran away from kindergarten, and it's been a struggle ever since.

Because that is true, John Frame has been a major gift to my ministry, my thought, and my preaching. Over and over, I've read what John wrote, listened to him teach, and watched how he took the time to make sure that his students understood. I have been his student for years (albeit an informal one), and the times I've found myself saying, "But of course" are countless.

When I read *AGG*, I found out that I had been "characterizing" presuppositional apologetics. I said, "But of course," and then I repented. When I read *NOG*, I said, "But of course," and joined the battle. When I read *WST* and *CWM*, I said, "But of course," and stopped making snide and arrogant jokes. When I "got" triperspectivalism, I said, "But of course," and used the tools I've been given in preaching. When I go to the Frame-Poythress Web site,[2] I find myself saying over and over again, "But of course."

Reading and being taught by John Frame is like going to a safe harbor after a major storm. It's truth—biblical, clear, and uncompromising. Churchill's oft-quoted statement about truth defines what John does as he teaches truth: "The truth is incontrovertible, malice may attack it, ignorance may deride it, but in the end; there it is."

You will remember the Hans Christian Andersen fairy tale *The Emperor's New Clothes*, in which the emperor has been conned into believing that he is dressed in fine new clothes when, in fact, he is as naked as a jaybird. Everybody, because of their fear, tells the emperor how good he looks in his "new clothes"—except for one little boy, who says, "He is buck naked!"

That is what John does. He doesn't spin it; he just speaks it. When it makes the "emperor" angry and defensive, John says, as it were, "I didn't say it. God said it!"

But the most surprising thing about John Frame is that he genuinely likes the emperor.

It's why John Frame is a radical.

2. http://www.frame-poythress.org.

PART 2

THEOLOGY

7

JOHN FRAME'S METHODOLOGY: A CASE STUDY IN CONSTRUCTIVE CALVINISM

TIM J. R. TRUMPER

"One of the most important functions of scholarship . . .
is to rethink conventional wisdom."
John Frame, *Contemporary Worship Music*

"I manage to offend both the traditionalists and the avant-garde."
John Frame, *The Doctrine of the Knowledge of God*

THE SINCERE JOY of honoring Professor Frame as a choice servant of the church, and leading Reformed theologian of our day, is a result, in part at least, of the stimulus provided by his theological method.[1] Possessing a hitherto undocumented historical significance, his method explains not only the theological and practical positions he has taken but also the diagnoses and remedies he offers our troubled Reformed tradition.

1. In the completion of this chapter, I am most grateful for the various kindnesses of Professor Frame and the editor; the Consistory of Seventh Reformed Church; congregants Dean Bekkering, Thad Lubbers, and especially Marilyn Van Dyke; and friends Henry and Connie Mast.

If theology is, in Frame's words, the "application of the Bible by persons to all areas of human life,"[2] theological method provides the route that leads us to it. Crucial to Frame's method is his commitment to Scripture—a commitment that drives the rigor of his thought and the evenhandedness of his reflections. What makes Frame's commitment stand out is his readiness to critique not only the avant-garde to the left but the unchallenged assumptions of traditionalism to the right.[3]

As Frame does not operate with a convenient label for his mediating center-right position—the words *Something Close to Biblicism* from his article's title being a little unwieldy for frequent reference—I have opted to analyze his method by means of my own paradigm. In its explanation of the current sociological trends in Reformed (specifically Presbyterian) thought, Frame's references to traditionalism coincide with what I call "orthodox Calvinism," and his allusions to the avant-garde equate to "revisionist Calvinism." The real advantage of the paradigm, however, lies in its use of the term *constructive Calvinism* to depict the identifiable ground situated between the traditionalists/orthodox Calvinists and the avant-garde/revisionist Calvinists. Certainly the term fits well with Frame's self-descriptions.[4]

The term *constructive Calvinism* has a number of benefits. First, it reveals differences of methodology and attitude among today's Westminster

2. *DKG*, 81–85; cf. "Systematic Theology and Apologetics at the Westminster Seminaries," in *The Pattern of Sound Doctrine: Systematic Theology at the Westminster Seminaries*, ed. David VanDrunen (Phillipsburg, NJ: P&R Publishing, 2004), 73; *RLT*. In this down-to-earth understanding of theology, as in so much else, Frame echoes the theological-pastoral concerns of Calvin (*DG*, 5).

3. Frame's cautions about the drawbacks of theological labels obviously do not preclude their careful use (*DKG*, 237–38).

4. On Frame's positioning see especially *MWC*. The paradigm used here to depict it first came to mind as a way of explaining the unmistakable methodological and attitudinal variations within the Calvinistic history of the doctrine of adoption (Tim J. R. Trumper, "An Historical Study of the Doctrine of Adoption in the Calvinistic Tradition" [PhD diss., University of Edinburgh, 2001], 29–34). I found it thereafter to have broader use in explaining the divisions within Scottish and North American Presbyterianism. For its general application, see "A Fresh Exposition of Adoption: II. Some Implications," *Scottish Bulletin of Evangelical Theology* 23, 2 (2005): 195. Its specific application is found in "Covenant Theology and Constructive Calvinism" (*WTJ* 64 [2002]: 387–404) and *When History Teaches Us Nothing: The Recent Reformed Sonship Debate in Context* (Eugene, OR: Wipf and Stock, 2008). Please note in this regard that, although published later, the chapter "Adoption: The Forgotten Doctrine of Westminster Soteriology" in *Reformed Theology in Contemporary Perspective* (Edinburgh: Rutherford House, 2006), 87–123, contains an earlier twofold version of the paradigm akin to Frame's talk of the traditionalists and the avant-garde. The use of these labels is not intended to be personal or divisive, but to give expression to differences already existing. Only by their open discussion can we hope for their resolution.

Calvinists (conservative Presbyterians). Whereas orthodox Calvinists are largely uncritical of their heritage and tend simply to regurgitate its theology, constructive Calvinists are sympathetic-critical (in that order!) and seek to renew it.[5] Furthermore, whereas orthodox Calvinists often adopt a hostile stance toward alternative points of view (even within Westminster Calvinism), constructive Calvinists look for the kernel of truth in other positions, applying it to our Reformed theology for its balance, enhancement, and overdue renewal.

Second, the term *constructive Calvinism* summarizes how fresh methodological and attitudinal approaches to the Reformed faith are encouraging the overhaul of the discipline of systematic theology and the biblical renewal of Westminster Calvinism. Andrew T. McGowan describes very well the beliefs firing constructive Calvinism:[6] (1) God still speaks today by his Spirit through his Word; (2) theologians make mistakes; (3) new issues require fresh thinking; (4) Scripture has priority over the confessions; (5) there is a right to private judgment (most relevant in the current climate). The sharing of these beliefs does not suggest, however, that constructive Calvinists agree on every detail. Modest variations of opinion exist. Nonetheless, they possess a mind-set clearly distinguishable from that of orthodox Calvinists.

Third, by allowing only sympathetic criticism of the Reformed tradition, the term *constructive Calvinism* cautions forward-thinking Westminster Calvinists from sliding into the revisionist-Calvinistic compromise or abandonment of Westminster Calvinism. Seeing the need for reform according to God's Word, constructive Calvinists are nevertheless one with their orthodox-Calvinistic counterparts in their concern for truth, but they believe there is a more effective way of defending and propagating it.

In what follows, I seek to demonstrate Frame's constructive Calvinism by summarizing the context, salient features, and advantages of his theological method.

5. The wording "sympathetic criticism" originates with Klaas Schilder and has entered the narration and discussion of constructive Calvinism via the influence of Richard B. Gaffin Jr. ("The Vitality of Reformed Systematic Theology," in *The Faith Once Delivered: Essays in Honor of Dr. Wayne R. Spear*, ed. Anthony T. Selvaggio [Phillipsburg, NJ: P&R Publishing, 2007], 29–32—a revised edition of an earlier chapter, "The Vitality of Reformed Dogmatics," in *The Vitality of Reformed Theology* [Kampen: Kok, 1994]).

6. Andrew T. B. McGowan, ed., introduction to *Always Reforming: Explorations in Systematic Theology* (Downers Grove, IL: IVP Academic, 2006), 13–17. The preface is by Frame.

CONTEXT

Constructive Calvinism has slowly, quietly, and almost imperceptibly been taking shape over the last century and more. Although the movement can be traced back to Princeton Seminary, its chief epicenter has been Westminster Seminary Philadelphia. Significantly, Frame has been connected to both institutions. Not only was he educated at Princeton and Westminster—later teaching at Westminster East and West[7]—his theological method has been influenced by the work of two well-known figures in the Princeton-Westminster narrative: Geerhardus Vos and John Murray.

Geerhardus Vos and John Murray

Although the twentieth-century renaissance in Calvin studies reveals the Genevan Reformer to have been, if you like, Vosian before Vos, it is Vos who has been described as "the father of a Reformed biblical theology."[8] His appointment to the newly created chair of biblical theology at Princeton in 1893 set in gradual motion a challenge to the traditional (specifically Puritan) method of teaching systematic theology. This challenge is only now coming into its own. At its heart lies Vos's emphasis on what Gaffin has called "the rich tradition of redemptive-historical exegesis we now possess."[9]

Were it not for Vos, Murray would likely have taught systematics at Westminster in the old Princeton manner, that is, by large reliance on Charles Hodge's three-volume *Systematic Theology*.[10] Hodge's method was governed by the goal of conservation, the core values of which were predictability and regularity.[11] Whereas Hodge's "unoriginal Calvinism"—to quote Darryl

---

7. Some but not all of Frame's biographical data has been gleaned from a prepublication viewing of his autobiographical chapter, "Backgrounds to My Thought," in this festschrift.

8. Gaffin, "The Vitality of Reformed Systematic Theology," 6.

9. Ibid. This exegesis observes what Vos calls the "principle of historical progression" or the "principle of periodicity"—Geerhardus Vos, *Biblical Theology: Old and New Testaments*, repr. (Edinburgh and Carlisle, PA: The Banner of Truth Trust, 1985), 3–18, esp. 16. This principle, however described, is found explicitly in the WCF only in 7.5–6.

10. Hodge's systematics were influenced in turn by Francis Turretin (Douglas F. Kelly, "Adoption: An Underdeveloped Heritage of the Westminster Standards," *Reformed Theological Review* 52 [1993]: 110–20). Thinking back on his student days at Westminster, Frame recalls the use of Hodge and Berkhof in the teaching of systematics, although students were graded for the most part on their understanding of Murray's lectures (*IDSCB*, 279; cf. "Backgrounds.")

11. D. G. Hart, "Systematic Theology at Old Princeton Seminary: Unoriginal Calvinism," in *The Pattern of Sound Doctrine*, 5.

Hart—was scientific in approach, focusing on facts and the exhibition of their internal relations,[12] Murray—who was equally concerned for conservation and methodological arrangement—made little if anything of systematics as a science, preferring under Vos's influence to ground his systematics in biblical-theological exegesis.[13]

Some, sensing the methodological differences between Murray and Hodge, claim that Murray was more interested in exegesis than in systematics.[14] It is more accurate to say that Murray began a process of reforming the discipline, essential to which is the redemptive-historical (progressive-revelational) contextualization of doctrine and the subjection of the traditional doctrinal formulae to increased exegetical scrutiny. Although it is unclear how much Murray was aware of the ramifications of his fresh approach, there is no doubt that he rendered impossible at Westminster the privileged position Hodge's method had enjoyed at Princeton. What Murray challenged was not the discipline of systematic theology *in se*, but the lopsidedness of the traditional approach. Strong on the divineness of Scripture, it was weak on its humanness; heavy in its propositional content, it was light in its attention to redemptive-historical exegesis; high in its view of Scripture, it was lower in its use of it; compelling in its content, it was alien to Scripture in its tone. Thus, Murray quietly but honestly introduced what we now call the sympathetic-critical approach to the theology and confessions of the Reformed tradition. Seemingly taken for granted during Murray's lifetime, this fresh approach has become foundational to the development of constructive Calvinism. Indeed, with hindsight we may describe Murray as the father of constructive Calvinism and Vos its grandfather.

12. Ibid., 7–9.

13. Ibid., 22. Cf. Murray's discussion of the discipline of systematic theology in "Systematic Theology," *The Collected Writings of John Murray* (Edinburgh and Carlisle, PA: The Banner of Truth Trust, 1976–82), 4:1–21. In contrasting the two theologians, I am not saying that Hodge was no exegete, for his commentaries amply demonstrate that he was, but that redemptive-historical exegesis did not impact his systematics as it did Murray's.

14. Interestingly, R. B. Kuiper, who taught systematics at Westminster the year prior to Murray's arrival from Princeton, does not seem to have dichotomized exegesis and systematics as do Murray's detractors today. Kuiper's biographer, Edward Heerema, writes: "Murray's teaching was strongly exegetical, so that his students were left in no doubt as to the thorough scripturalness of the Reformed faith. . . . R. B. did not hesitate to speak of John Murray as the best teacher of Systematic Theology in the world" (*R. B.: A Prophet in the Land* [Jordan Station, Ontario, Canada: Paideia Press, 1986], 117).

Richard Gaffin and John Frame

Murray's retirement in 1966 and the confused and confusing departure of Norman Shepherd from Westminster in 1981 would have brought to an abrupt end the development of constructive Calvinism at the seminary,[15] were it not for the work of two men. Overlapping as students at Westminster, both studying under Murray, Richard Gaffin and John Frame went on to join the faculty in 1965 and 1968, respectively. Whereas Gaffin began in the New Testament department, transitioning to systematics only after Shepherd's departure,[16] Frame began in the systematics department, later transitioning to apologetics.[17]

The affinity between Gaffin and Murray is unmistakable. Not only did Gaffin continue Murray's enthusiasm for Vos's biblical theology—becoming in the process the premier advocate of Vos in the English-speaking world—he sought to work through further the implications of biblical theology for systematic theology, especially as they pertain to the doctrinal profile of union with Christ and the arrangement of the *ordo salutis* (which he prefers to call the *applicatio salutis*).[18] In the process, Gaffin has been both a radical and a reactionary: "radical" in the sense of proposing the dropping of the

15. Frame's chapter "Backgrounds," assesses the similarities between Murray and Shepherd: "Like Murray, he always puts Scripture ahead of tradition" (cf. "Systematic Theology and Apologetics at the Westminster Seminaries," 94–95). This prioritization of Scripture is seen in Shepherd's sensitivity to the redemptive-historical unfolding of biblical doctrine, his understanding of the importance of union with Christ, and his recognition of the significance of the authorial diversity of the New Testament for doctrinal construction. However history judges the particularities of Shepherd's views (and surely he will get a fairer hearing there), the Reformed community can learn much from the example of Frame's careful and winsome treatment of Shepherd. See, for instance, his foreword to *Backbone of the Bible: Covenant in Contemporary Perspective*, ed. Andrew Sandlin (Nacogdoches, TX: Covenant Media Press, 2004), vii–xiii.

16. Gaffin was joined in the systematic department by Sinclair Ferguson. Notwithstanding his background in historical theology, Ferguson—"known," in Frame's words, "for his profound applications of the Reformed faith to the Christian life" ("Systematic Theology and Apologetics at the Westminster Seminaries," 96)—has been supportive of Murray and Gaffin, and of Frame, at least to a degree. His own creative orthodoxy is seen chiefly but not insignificantly in his early call for the recovery of the Fatherhood of God and of adoption (see Conclusion).

17. For these details, see Frame's piece, "Thanks for Dick Gaffin's Ministry"; "Systematic Theology and Apologetics at the Westminster Seminaries," 90–93. Frame continued to teach mostly systematic courses until 1975 (ibid., 93).

18. See especially Gaffin's seminal work, *Resurrection and Redemption: A Study in Paul's Soteriology*, 2nd ed. (Phillipsburg, NJ: Presbyterian and Reformed, 1987); also his more recent contributions: "Redemption and Resurrection: An Exercise in Biblical-Systematic Theology," in *A Confessing Theology for Postmodern Times*, ed. Michael S. Horton (Wheaton, IL: Crossway, 2000), and *By Faith, Not by Sight: Paul and the Order of Salvation* (Milton Keynes, UK: Paternoster Press, 2006).

nomenclature *systematic theology*, but "reactionary" of late in appearing to draw back from the implications of his work for the general development of the constructive-Calvinistic mind-set and the specific revision of the form and tone of the Westminster Standards.[19]

Frame, too, esteems Murray greatly, although this esteem cannot be spoken of in isolation from either the influence of Cornelius Van Til or his own transition from systematics to apologetics. "Van Til," Frame testifies, "became the greatest influence on [his] apologetics and theology."[20] Nowhere has this been more the case than in the development of his perspectivalism (see below).[21] Nonetheless, Murray's writings are right up there with Van Til's and Ed Clowney's as Frame's favorite sources.[22] "What I learned best from Murray," explains Frame, "was his theological method."[23] He continues: "My own theology is very unlike Murray's in style, diction, and emphasis. But in its method and most of its conclusions, my work is more like his than any other theological writer's." This may explain why Frame, a teacher of apologetics, sees himself first and foremost as a systematician, whose "main strengths have been the integration of the two disciplines [apologetics and systematics], in the spirit of Van Til and Murray."[24] Frame describes this integration as detailed exegesis with worldview consciousness.

19. I allude to Gaffin's final years at Westminster in which the exhibition of the confessional consistency of his views seems to have taken priority over their application to the biblical and spiritual renewal of Westminster Calvinism. It is for historians to ponder whether a bolder approach may have enhanced the seminary's contribution to the development of constructive Calvinism, thereby alleviating the concerns of some faculty members. If Peter Enns' *Inspiration and Incarnation* is representative, these faculty members have now pressed beyond constructive Calvinism toward revisionist Calvinism (a *critical-sympathetic* approach to Westminster Calvinism).

20. In "Backgrounds," Frame goes on to say, "Certainly, nobody who has not spent time with Van Til can understand well what I am about." Van Til, he explains, was "the chief intellectual influence of [his] seminary years and beyond" (*DKG*, xviii).

21. "Backgrounds."

22. In *SBL* (352), Frame states: "I turn to him [Murray] more than to any other writer."

23. "Backgrounds."

24. Significantly, Frame observes that "apologetics has probably never been related as closely to systematic theology as it was in the writings of Cornelius Van Til" ("Systematic Theology and Apologetics at the Westminster Seminaries," 74; cf. 97). This closeness may be explained not simply by the compatibility of presuppositional apologetics and Reformed systematics (ibid., 77), but by Van Til's deference to Murray's exegesis, and to the personal friendship between the two professors (ibid., 76; cf. Edmund P. Clowney, "Professor John Murray at Westminster Seminary," in *The Pattern of Sound Doctrine*, 28). Writes Frame: "The relation between Van Til and Murray established the pattern for later generations of Westminster apologists and systematic theo-

According to Frame, Van Til and Murray influenced not only his thought but Westminster's "high quality of theological creativity."[25] Although Van Til was, in Frame's view, more of an independent thinker than Murray, he is nevertheless enamored of "the independence of Murray's theology"— "its faithfulness to Scripture and . . . the independence and creativity of its formulations."[26] In particular, he observes the Scotsman's Calvin-like rejection of "stagnant traditionalism," "recogniz[ing] the importance of church history in the work of systematic theology, but . . . caution[ing] us not to remain content with even the best formulations of past theologians."[27] Observing Murray's prioritizing of biblical-theological and exegetical considerations in his systematics, Frame radically disagrees with those claiming, perhaps from the standpoint of an unwitting, dogmatic construal of Scripture, that Murray was no systematician. Murray, Frame astutely observes, was providing an answer to those fairly observing the tendency of Reformed thinkers to place Reformed traditions before Scripture.[28] In other words, he was shaping a constructive Calvinism that has over time begun to correct the drawbacks of Westminster Calvinism. Writes Frame: "We often associate orthodoxy with stagnancy and traditionalism. But at Westminster, the commitment to *sola Scriptura* propelled it in the opposite direction,"[29] thus making the orthodoxy creative.[30]

Frame's esteem for Murray is not simply theoretical. He, too, has broken from Hodge's scientific or objectivist approach to theology.[31] Frame believes Hodge: first, to have made too much of the parallel between

---

logians" ("Systematic Theology and Apologetics at the Westminster Seminaries," 88)—Frame regarding his role at Westminster as "a bridge between apologetics and systematics" (ibid., 90).

25. *CWM*, 183.

26. Ibid. Could it be that Murray was in fact more of an independent thinker than Van Til? I think not only of Murray's exegesis—arguably a weakness in Van Til—but of Van Til's reliance on Calvin. The heavy annotation of Book I of his personal copy of Calvin's *Institutes* (standing in striking contrast with his marginal notes on Books II–IV), helps explain an anecdote relating to Sinclair Ferguson's Westminster interview. When asked whether he had read Van Til, he is said to have replied: "I think so. I've read Calvin!" Whatever else historians conclude, we may say that Van Til was seeking to work out a consistent theocentricity for the post-Enlightenment context as Calvin had sought to do during the Reformation.

27. *IDSCB*, 276.

28. Ibid., 277.

29. Ibid.

30. This creative orthodoxy is not to be confused with the emergent church's generous orthodoxy, as is clear from Frame's review of Brian McLaren's *Generous Orthodoxy*.

31. In what follows, I summarize and at times quote from *DKG*, 77–81—a significant discussion overlooked by Hart in his support of Princeton's science-influenced unoriginal Calvinism.

theology and the natural sciences, failing in the process to acknowledge sufficiently that facts are not brute facts (devoid of intelligence); second, to have defined theology in a manner too intellectualistic, forgetting that theology is more than theory construction or a description of facts. Scripture, observes Frame,

> is full of other kinds of language: imperatives, interrogatives, promises, vows, poetry, proverbs, emotive language, and so forth. The purpose of Scripture is not merely to give us an authoritative list of things we must believe but also to exhort us, command us, inspire our imaginations, put songs in our hearts, question us, sanctify us, and so on. Surely the work of teaching in the church is not only to list what people must believe but also to communicate to them all the other content of Scripture.

Third, Frame objects to Hodge's implicit claim that theology does what Scripture has not done, which is to exhibit the facts of Scripture "in their *proper* order and relation" (Frame's emphasis). Theology is "a *secondary* description, a reinterpretation, and reproclamation of Scripture, both of its propositional and of its nonpropositional content." Its purpose is to meet human needs, because, despite the perspicuity of Scripture, people still fail to understand.

It is to Frame's credit that he, like Murray, has been able to distance himself from Hodge's method without simply exchanging its objectivism for the Schleiermacherian subjectivism against which Hodge was reacting.[32] Rejecting the Princetonian's science-based approach, Frame has shared Murray's preference for the injection of biblical-theological considerations into the systematization of Scripture's content. In this approach he is in line with Vos, Herman Ridderbos, Gaffin, and Meredith Kline.[33] "It is especially important for systematic theologians today," Frame writes, "to be aware of the developments in biblical theology, a discipline in which new discoveries are being made almost daily."[34] Although Frame has some druthers about the current interest in redemptive history (see below), he nevertheless lauds

---

32. Writes Frame: "Hodge was certainly closer to the truth than Schleiermacher, since Hodge was concerned to distinguish true and false in theology and to determine truth on the basis of Scripture" (ibid., 78).

33. Kline's biblical-theological approach to Scripture's covenant motif is not without dogmatic construal, which raises questions about his inclusion with Vos, Ridderbos, and Gaffin (cf. Frame's comments on Kline in "Backgrounds").

34. *DKG*, 212.

biblical theology as "an exciting discipline."[35] Yet, additional to affirming the emphases of Murray and Gaffin, Frame offers the development of constructive Calvinism a distinctive contribution in the form of perspectivalism. As we will see, perspectivalism contains elements that cannot but enhance the methodological and attitudinal renewal of systematic theology, and the Puritan tradition of theology we call Westminster Calvinism.

SALIENT FEATURES

We may summarize the countless features of Frame's method by focusing in turn on his biblicism, his understanding of the relationship between biblical and systematic theology, and his triperspectivalism.

Biblicism

Operating from a classical understanding of the doctrine of Scripture, we need not detain ourselves with Frame's views of the nature of Scripture. Rather, we consider his transparent, even courageous "Defense of Something Close to Biblicism."

At the heart of Frame's quasi-biblicism is the scriptural and Reformation doctrine of *sola Scriptura*: "the doctrine that Scripture, and only Scripture, has the final word on everything, all our doctrine, and all our life . . . even our interpretation of Scripture, even in our theological method."[36] Determining his focus on *sola Scriptura* is not only the belief that the Word of God is the objective basis of theology,[37] but also the concern that the primacy of the Word is under threat in evangelical and Reformed theology.

Notwithstanding Frame's language of "biblicism," he keenly disassociates himself from the tendencies the word brings to mind, namely, (1) the lack of appreciation for extrabiblical truth in theology (natural or general revelation); (2) the suggestion that Scripture is a textbook for science, philosophy, politics, economics, etc.; (3) the rejection of the role of confessional or catechetical standards; and (4) a "proof-texting" approach eschewing historical, cultural, logical, and literary contexts.

---

35. For Frame's thought on redemptive history, see *DG*, 207–9; "Systematic Theology and Apologetics at the Westminster Seminaries," 96.

36. *IDSCB*, 272. What follows in the next paragraph is taken from 272–75.

37. *DKG*, 88, 98.

All the same, Frame acknowledges that, rightly understood and utilized, *sola Scriptura* comes close to biblicism. The Bible surely testifies to the value of general revelation (within bounds), notwithstanding the fact that "all knowledge is knowledge of what Scripture requires of us." Scripture may not be a textbook, and yet "every thought must be answerable to God's word in Scripture." The catechisms and confessions of the church have their important place, but we must read our doctrinal standards through Scripture (and not vice versa). We eschew a "proof-texting" approach to Scripture; nonetheless, the verbal and plenary nature of inspiration reminds us to value each verse of Scripture. "It is not enough," says Frame, "for theologians to claim that an idea is biblical; they must be prepared to show in Scripture where that idea can be found."[38]

Denying, therefore, that Protestants are biblicistic, Frame nevertheless remarks that true Protestants (adherents and practitioners of *sola Scriptura*) should expect to be accused of biblicism from time to time. "Indeed, if we are not occasionally accused . . . , we should be concerned about the accuracy of our teaching in this area."

Of specific concern to Frame in the current climate of Reformed discussion and debate is the prominence given to historical theology. Admiring the fact that historical theologians "have typically mastered far more data and organized it more impressively than most of those . . . in the fields of systematics and apologetics,"[39] and understanding the importance of their work—which is to "apply the Word to the church's past for the sake of the church's present edification"—Frame nevertheless observes that "history-oriented theologies have sometimes been snares and delusions for the Church." Mentioning those whose subjective sense of history has replaced the authority of Scripture as the church's theological norm (e.g., Ritschl, Troeltsch, Barth, Cullman, Pannenberg, and Moltmann), Frame airs most concern about trends closer to home.

One example he cites is the evangelical swing that took place in the twentieth century from the anti-intellectualism following the Scopes trial (1925) to the uncritical intellectualism of the postwar "new" evangelicalism:

> For many evangelicals in the 1960s, a serious commitment to rationality demanded acceptance of the norms of critical biblical scholarship. Few

---

38. For more on proof-texting, see ibid., 197.
39. Unless otherwise stated, the following quotations are taken from *IDSCB*, 269–90.

even asked the question whether Scripture itself contained its own norms for scholarship, different from and opposed to those of the negative critics. So the sometimes sharp difference between evangelical and liberal scholarship has since the 1960s become a blur.

Lauding the likes of Francis Schaeffer and David Wells for resisting the evangelical compromise of the inerrancy of Scripture, Frame nevertheless takes issue with their use of the Word. Whereas Schaeffer, he claims, treated objective truth as an abstraction rather than the distinctive truth of the divine Word identical with Jesus Christ, in *No Place for Truth* and *God in the Wasteland*, Wells indicts evangelicalism for its subjectivism (prioritizing human experience over objective truth), therapy, consumerism (the power of marketing), and pragmatism (the vindication of results), but does so more along the lines of history and sociology than of theology. Pointing as evidence to the "recognizably Wellsian" Cambridge Declaration of the Alliance of Confessing Evangelicals, Frame offers a view of it clearly resonant of the method, balance, and attitude of constructive Calvinism:

> The document, like Wells's books, calls us back to a nostalgia for a past age. That, in my view, is a frail reed. It also calls us back to a greater fidelity to Scripture. That is a strong element of the document. But it needs to be spelled out in detail: what does Scripture say about missions, church growth, marketing, as opposed to the notions prevalent in our culture today? We need a document that gives us positive guidance, rather than merely negating present trends.

The problem, as Frame sees it, is not simply evangelical but specifically Reformed. He identifies it as "tradition in theology"[40]—an emphasis not only of the Alliance of Confessing Evangelicals but of individual scholars of some note. Acknowledging that "this emphasis has done some good by revitalizing interest in the Reformed heritage,"[41] Frame nevertheless describes the drawbacks of the orthodox Calvinism underlying it:

> The Reformed tradition consists [ideally], not in merely repeating previous Reformed traditions, but, as with Calvin, in using the Scriptures to criticize tradition. The history-oriented theologians tend to be uncritical of

40. *MWC*, 25.
41. Ibid.

traditions and critical of the contemporary church. But their arguments are often based on their preferences rather than biblical principle and therefore fail to persuade. The Reformed community, in my judgment, needs to return to an explicitly exegetical model of theology, following the example of John Murray. The exegetical approach is also (perhaps paradoxically) the most contemporary approach, for it applies Scripture directly to our lives today. The question is, of course, one of emphasis. We should never ignore our past. But my view is that the pendulum has swung too far in the direction of a historical emphasis.[42]

Frame perceives this traditionalism to impact many areas of current Reformed thought, including the following.

Uncritical acceptance of foundationalism. Not to be confused with the role Scripture plays as the foundation of all human knowledge, foundationalism is "the view that knowledge begins with a body of propositions that are known with absolute certainty and from which all the rest of our knowledge can be derived by logical deduction (or, perhaps, induction)."[43]

Defensive approach to scholasticism.[44] Frame also defends scholasticism, noting in his typically balanced manner how the criticisms of it have been vastly overstated. He notes that while the Reformers endeavored to purge theology of the pervasive use of Greek philosophical language, the later Protestant scholastics understood certain technical distinctions to be helpful to the theological task. This is because the Reformers saw their task as pastoral and polemical, the Protestant scholastics as academic and focused on the development of rigorous theological systems. All the same, Frame believes the Protestant scholastics were insufficiently critical of the Greek philosophers and the medieval scholastics. By borrowing their philosophical language, the Protestant scholastics impeded the church's use and understanding of Scripture.[45] Accordingly, Frame's emphases on *sola Scriptura* (i.e., something close to biblicism) and the shortcomings of the Protestant scholastics combine to ensure that his defense of scholasti-

---

42. Ibid., 25–26.
43. *DKG*, 128–29. Frame's description of foundationalism is not too far removed from the abuses of systematic-theological method, bringing the discipline into disrepute.
44. *DG*, 5–15.
45. Ibid., 3.

cism remains free of the defensiveness of the historical theologians, some of whom made their names defending Protestant scholasticism.

Preoccupation with confessionalism. Given that we will return to this subject below, we simply note here Frame's rightful objection to: (1) the placing of confessions and traditions *en par* with Scripture; (2) the equating of *sola Scriptura* with our confessional traditions; (3) the suspicion of ideas coming from outside our chosen tradition; (4) the preoccupation with historical polemics rather than the dangers of the present day; (5) the emphasizing of differences with other theological traditions to the exclusion of our commonalities; and (6) the failure to encourage self-criticism.

Obviously, much more could be said of Frame's biblicism and its shaping of his response to foundationalism, scholasticism, and confessionalism. Nevertheless, the main point is clear. Frame seeks to preserve the biblical substance of Reformed orthodoxy, while challenging its methodological and attitudinal liabilities. Such a give-and-take approach is vintage constructive Calvinism, and the only kind of reflection on Reformed orthodoxy that affirms without idolizing and critiques without derision.

Biblical and Systematic Theology

If Frame's discussion of *sola Scriptura* highlights the differences present within conservative Presbyterianism between orthodox and constructive Calvinists, his understanding of the relationship between biblical and systematic theology reminds us of the distance constructive Calvinists have to go in deciding issues germane to the biblical reform of Westminster Calvinism.[46]

Operating from an appreciation of biblical theology, Frame nevertheless cautions our community against obsessing with redemptive history.[47]

46. In what follows, we are chiefly concerned with the methodological variations within constructive Calvinism. Perhaps the most controversial of Frame's specific variations of opinion is his positive assessment of contemporary worship music. In this he openly and markedly differs from Murray's appropriation of the Regulative Principle. See *WST*, esp. 159; cf. *RLT*; *MWC*, 19–20; *IRF*, 11; *SBL*, 352.

47. See *RLT*. Although our tradition focuses almost exclusively on the redemptive-historical model of biblical theology, theological students should at least be aware of the array of the biblical-theological models espoused in the church. See, for instance, Brevard Childs's list in *Biblical Theology of the Old and New Testaments: Theological Reflection on the Christian Bible* (London: SCM Press, 1992). When Frame sometimes equates biblical theology and redemptive history, he probably does so because of the constituency for which he writes (e.g., *PWG*, 55).

His general concern is that biblical theology is not so much a division or department of theology as a perspective on it.[48] More specifically, Frame fears:[49] (1) the impression sometimes created that Scripture contains only redemptive history, when it also contains law, song, proverbs, letters, and evangelistic gospels, given not simply as history but with a view to eliciting faith and the submission of our lives; (2) the control of theology by redemptive history rather than by everything in Scripture (law, wisdom, poetry, and gospel);[50] (3) the belief that biblical theology, with its closeness to the text and vocabulary of Scripture, is more biblical than systematic theology—the theologian's task is not to mimic Scripture but to apply it; (4) the fanatical assumption that biblical theology requires "applicationless" redemptive-historical preaching;[51] (5) the need preaching has of an awareness of the redemptive-historical *and* systematic-theological context of any individual text of Scripture; and (6) the danger of pride and anti-abstractionism in an unbalanced attachment to any theological perspective, not least that which is biblical-theological.

So extensively has Frame qualified the growing enthusiasm for biblical theology that Richard Gamble wonders whether he relates orthodox biblical theology too closely to theological liberalism. This Frame denies.[52] Nonetheless, it is clear that differences of opinion exist among constructive Calvinists as to how biblical theology should impact systematics.[53] Headway may be made in time to come by defining the questions constructive Calvinists have yet to resolve. For example: (1) How do we understand biblical theology—is it a division or department of theology, or a perspec-

---

48. *DKG*, 206. In what follows, I am drawing fundamentally on ibid.,207–11.

49. Here I have compressed the eight concerns Frame offers in ibid., 209–11. Cf. the objections listed by Richard Gamble in "Biblical Theology and Systematic Theology" in *Always Reforming*, 228–32.

50. Cf. *DG*, 7–8, 197. Frame differs from Gaffin at this juncture. Looking back on their student and faculty interactions, he writes: Gaffin "thought, and still does evidently, that biblical theology should control systematics. I have always thought that no theological discipline is primary but that all should provide checks and balances for one another" ("Thanks for Dick Gaffin's Ministry," http://www.frame-poythress.org/frame_articles/2008Gaffin.htm).

51. Cf. *MWC*, 22.

52. Preface to *Always Reforming*, 10n1.

53. Gaffin now suggests the abolition of the nomenclature "systematic theology," although I suggest the biblical-theological overhaul of systematic theology, issuing in a revised discipline of biblical dogmatics (combining biblical-theological insights with the traditional systemic concerns for the coherence and unity of truth). Frame appears to offer a third option: the equal ultimacy of biblical and systematic theology as parallel perspectives on the theological task.

tive on it?; (2) How do we understand history when referring to redemptive history—is it an overarching umbrella under which is subsumed law, song, wisdom, etc., or one aspect of Scripture alongside others? (3) How do we understand systematic theology—as a broad discipline including not only logical consistency and the orderly structure of the explicitly didactic parts of Scripture, but also other scriptural elements such as poetry, drama, music, dialogue, exhortation, preaching?

Although the jury is out considering these questions, we can at least agree that there is more to Scripture than the redemptive-historical narrative, and that the redemptive-historical model does not require what has become known as redemptive-historical preaching.[54]

Triperspectivalism

Perspectivalism is what Frame calls in short "an exegetically based epistemology."[55] Although he states that perspectivalism is simply generic Calvinism—taking seriously both Scripture (special revelation) and nature (general revelation)—Frame's introduction and articulation of it constitutes a significant landmark in the development of constructive Calvinism.[56]

The nomenclature of perspectivalism can be used in a broader and a narrower sense.[57] When used broadly it reflects the fact that although God in his omniscience sees everything at once, we finite creatures see but one perspective at a time. Perspectivalism, therefore, cautions us against a know-it-all attitude. It calls us instead to understand and to appropriate as best we can those perspectives competing with our own. Although not all perspectives are right, Frame notes in constructive-Calvinistic fashion how even the kernel of truth in other perspectives can balance our own, and draw

54. Although agreed in our concerns about redemptive-historical preaching, especially the assumption that it is the true homiletical heir of biblical theology (cf. Tim J. R. Trumper, *Preaching and Politics: Engagement without Compromise* [Eugene, OR: Wipf and Stock, 2009], 21–22), Frame and I differ a little concerning the degree to which expository preaching is the normative alternative.

55. "Systematic Theology and Apologetics at the Westminster Seminaries," 92. For Frame's perspectivalism, go to *PP*; *DKG*, 165–346 (especially); *DCL*, 131–382; cf. Vern Poythress, *Symphonic Theology: The Validity of Multiple Perspectives in Theology* (Grand Rapids: Academie Books [Zondervan], 1987).

56. I am not saying by this that agreement with Frame's perspectivalism, and specifically his triperspectivalism, is a requirement for constructive Calvinism, but that the constructive Calvinist, in his/her creative orthodoxy, will at least give it a serious and sympathetic hearing.

57. *RLT*; *PP*, 1. Frame now questions the appropriateness of the term *perspectivalism*, not least because its spelling is so close to Nietzsche's relativistic *perspectivism* (*PP*, 1n7).

us nearer the harmonious multiperspectival content of Scripture. Scripture, being supreme, prevents our perspectivalism from degenerating into relativism.[58] This it does by testifying to the absolutism of God's perspective, and by attesting our human perspectives by contrast, correcting and balancing them as necessary. Thus, mortifying our often culturally and/or theologically driven dogmatism, perspectivalism helps shape the fresh attitude of constructive Calvinism by enabling us to hear the concerns outside conservative Presbyterianism, not least those avant-garde/revisionist-Calvinist protests against Westminster Calvinism.

Perspectivalism, narrowly considered, recognizes the fact that, in Scripture's multiple perspectives on any one theme, "there is a pervasive pattern of threefold distinctions which, though, mysterious, provide us with considerable illumination."[59] Frame and Poythress see this pattern in the Trinity—the oneness of God ensuring the harmony of the triadic perspectives, the three persons in their distinct but interrelated character.[60] Although all three persons are involved in every divine act, there is a certain division of labor in the economy of redemption—the Father functioning as the supreme authority, the Son as the executive power, and the Spirit as the divine presence. All three are necessary to our redemption, and provide different perspectives on it.

If the Trinity is the archetypal triad, there are many others that are ectypal: divine lordship (control, absolute authority, presence), revelation (general, special, existential [illumination]), the offices of Christ (King [control], Prophet [authority], Priest [presence]), aspects of salvation (redemption accomplished, law of God, redemption applied), human knowledge of God (object [world as God's control], norm [God's authority], subject [the knower standing in God's presence]), ethics or the knowledge of right and wrong (norm [obedience to God's Word], situation [application of the Word], existential [inner satisfaction]).[61]

From these triads, Frame draws the three terms so critical to his triperspectivalism: the *normative* (i.e., the use of Scripture); the *situational* (i.e., the

58. *DKG*, 194.

59. *PP*, 4.

60. Frame is understandably keen to point out that although the triadic perspectives find their origin in the triune nature of the Godhead, the persons of the Trinity are not mere perspectives, as in Sabellianism. They are "really persons" who "are more than perspectives, but not less" (ibid., 5).

61. Frame's list of triads is endless (ibid., 10, where he points readers to *SBL* and Appendix A of *DG*).

application of Scripture to the world of our experience); and the *existential* (i.e., our faculties and skills for use in knowing and applying Scripture).[62] Denying there is any such thing as a theological method "in the sense of a series of definite steps by which all theological problems can be solved," Frame regards these three perspectives as overlapping and intersecting in the affording of knowledge.

Although a thorough consideration of (tri)perspectivalism is beyond the scope of this chapter, and is the domain of other contributors (Vern Poythress, especially), our study of Frame's method must at least offer some points of evaluation.

First, perspectivalism enables Westminster Calvinists to shed what has too often become an unsanctified dogmatism—a small-minded arrogance and intolerance equating personal perspective with the full truth of God's Word.[63] Second, it promotes a sympathetic-critical approach to our own theology—a refreshing alternative to the congratulatory approach of orthodox Calvinism and the derisory approach of revisionist Calvinism. Third, perspectivalism comports with the authorial diversity of the New Testament—a matter hugely ignored in Puritan dogmatics, wherein the divineness (oneness) of Scripture regularly absorbs its humanness. Fourth, perspectivalism questions the legitimacy of many of our Reformed debates by challenging the predominance of the normative, situational, or existential perspectives and by urging tolerance when faced with multidimensional issues.[64] Fifth, by encouraging balance, perspectivalism promotes the unity of our tradition and of the church at large, yet without surrendering the importance of truth and the normativity of God's Word.

Soteriology is one area in which perspectivalism can be fruitfully applied. I think especially of how Gaffin's focus on union with Christ and Frame's perspectivalism could be brought together in the reworking of the *ordo* or *applicatio salutis*. Whereas Gaffin's emphasis restructures the doctrine of salvation, transforming it, diagrammatically speaking, from a line into a

---

62. *DKG*, 167–346.

63. This is implied in Frame's *MWC*. Writing of the twenty-one occasions of division among Machen's "warrior children," Frame notes, "With many, though not all, of the issues . . . it is possible to see the positions as complementary rather than as contradictory" (ibid., 30).

64. Ibid., 27–28; *PP*, 11. That said, "Not all 'perspectives' are equally prominent in Scripture or equally useful to the theologian. It is quite right for a theologian to prefer one perspective to another. He errs only when he gives to that perspective the kind of authority due only to the biblical canon as a whole or when he seeks to exclude other perspectives that also have some validity" (*DG*, 194).

circle (like a wheel with union with Christ as the hub and the blessings of the union as the spokes), Frame's perspectivalism encourages us to regard the various elements of soteriology as perspectives (slices of the circle?) rather than as consecutive elements.[65] Although Frame disavows the influence of his Westminster professor Edwin H. Palmer on his perspectivalism, Palmer's dissertation titled "Scheeben's Doctrine of Adoption" articulates very well my meaning. The application of salvation, he says,

> is not a question of either temporal or logical priority, but of a definition or description of another facet of the same object. Justification and redemption do not precede adoption, but are, as it were, alongside, parallel to, it. They are simply terms or descriptions that Paul uses to clarify for us the significance and varied richness of our salvation; but in reality, with God, whose thinking and actions are not to be compared with ours, it is impossible to speak of a logical priority, let alone a temporal one.[66]

Obviously, there is huge mileage in this discussion, a fact testifying to the pluses perspectivalism brings to the discussion of Reformed dogmatics. That said, we may wonder whether perspectivalism requires a specific triperspectivalism. No doubt the normative, situational, and existential categories are useful when exegetically justifiable in the study of any given text or passage, but Scripture does not always speak in terms of triads. Note, for instance, Scripture's mention of the twelve tribes, its special emphasis on the number

65. Writes Frame: "The Ordo Salutis has always seemed to me to be a confused idea, because the various items are not related to one another in the same sense of 'order.' Regeneration is the efficient cause of faith, but faith is not the efficient cause of justification. It is the 'instrumental cause,' as we say; but justification is neither the efficient nor the instrumental cause of adoption. So on we go . . . Such inadequacies of the traditional scholastic approaches were another factor in leading me to seek another way of teaching systematics, which, for better or for worse, is the method of the Theology of Lordship" (e-mail message to the author on May 2, 2003).

66. Edwin H. Palmer, *Scheeben's Doctrine of Divine Adoption* (Kampen: J. H. Kok N. V., 1953), 182–83. Similarly, Palmer comments: "This apparent overlapping of functions [between justification and adoption] is to be explained simply by the fact that both terms are descriptions of our whole salvation from different angles or aspects. The elect sinner enjoys one, great, indivisible salvation from God. In order to portray that in all of its fullness and richness, the Bible uses different descriptions. One aspect concerns God's holiness, which has been offended and violated by sin. . . . But this describes salvation from only one point of view, even though a glorious one. Another aspect, which is not, and cannot, be included in the idea of justification is the fact that in salvation the sinner does not only come to stand in a correct and proper relation to God's holiness and justice, but that he becomes the object of a tender, fatherly love. This side of redemption is expressed by the illustration of adoption" (ibid., 168; cf. 172).

seven, and its inclusion of four Gospels, etc. We need, therefore, to resist a perspectival construal of Scripture as much as we do a dogmatic construal. This resistance prevents the triperspectival paradigm from skewing the biblical data.

For instance, there is a general benefit in regarding justification, adoption, and sanctification as a triad (*triplex gratia Dei*). They are clearly biblical terms relating to three distinctive doctrines of Scripture, as is reflected in the Westminster Standards.[67] Yet to categorize justification as the normative, adoption as the situational, and sanctification as the existential perspective on salvation is to overlook the rich, complex nuances of these doctrines.[68] We are not necessarily helped by remembering that these three perspectives "overlap" and "interact." If, therefore, we can speak of triperspectivalism at all, and I believe we can, we are best doing so in the broadest of terms that spare us the temptation of coercing the biblical data or of creating the doctrinal confusion our paradigms seek to clarify. Unsurprisingly, Frame's sharply creative mind is alert to the danger of coercion:

> Sometimes in a moment of overweening pride, I think that my three perspectives are an incredibly deep insight into the fundamental structure of biblical truth. But most of the time I just think they are a good pedagogical device, a set of hooks on which to hang the doctrines of the faith.[69]

Advantages

Briefly stated, Frame's method, with its reassertion of the supremacy and balance of the Word, takes us a long way toward the overdue renewal of Westminster Calvinism.

The Supremacy of God's Word

Perhaps nowhere does Frame perceive more the compromise of our community's belief in the supremacy of God's Word than in the stagnant traditionalism of today's confessionalism. "Confessions are not Scripture,"

67. WCF 11–13; WLC 70–75; WSC 33–36.
68. It may be nearer to the truth to say that justification, adoption, and sanctification contain individually and inherently normative, situational, and existential elements.
69. *SBL*, 330; cf. *PP*, 10.

writes Frame, "and they should not be treated as infallible or as ultimately normative"[70] as they are in strict subscriptionism:

> A "strict" view of subscription in which ministers are never permitted to teach contrary to any detail of the creed might be seen as a way to protect the orthodoxy of the church. However, in my view, such a view is actually subversive of orthodoxy, because it is subversive of biblical authority and sufficiency. Under such a form of subscription, Scripture is not given the freedom to reform the church according to God's will.[71]

What Frame suggests is not the jettisoning of confessions, resulting in certain anarchy, but a revised understanding of them.

> A reaffirmation of confessionalism for our time ought to repudiate the commonly understood equation between confessionalism and traditionalism. It should rather reiterate a doctrine of *sola Scriptura* like that of Westminster at its best: one which will encourage careful thinking about the movements of our time rather than overstated condemnations and which will discourage romantic notions about past ages. A doctrine of *sola Scriptura* must actually, practically, point us to Scripture itself, rather than generalizations about historical trends, for our standards.[72]

Consistent with this, Frame argues for what Gaffin calls "flexible-full subscription":

> I believe it is important that in a church fellowship it be possible to revise the creeds, and for that purpose, it must be possible for members and officers to dissent from the creed within some limits. Otherwise, the creed will, practically speaking, be elevated to a position of authority equivalent to Scripture.

Although we may ask whether Frame's viewpoint, acted upon widely, would lead to creedal or confessional instability, there is no doubting that history permits his talk of confessional revision:

70. *IRF*, 2.
71. Ibid.
72. *IDSCB*, 290.

Calvinism has been a very "progressive" kind of theology. Reformed theology, typically, has not simply reiterated the statements of Calvin and the confessions. It has gone on to develop new applications of Scripture and Reformed doctrine. In the seventeenth century, there was a significant development in Reformed thinking about God's covenants. In the eighteenth-century thinker Jonathan Edwards, there is new teaching on the subjective dimensions of the Christian life. In the nineteenth and early twentieth centuries, there was the remarkable development, under Vos and others, of "biblical theology," the analysis of Scripture as a history of redemption. In the twentieth century there was Van Til's apologetics and Meredith Kline's *Structure of Biblical Authority*.[73]

Interestingly, although Frame makes more didactic use of the Westminster Standards than did his teachers at Westminster,[74] he insists, as they did, on the supreme authority of God's Word in theology and *praxis*. Not only does this authority comport with the Reformed principle of *sola Scriptura*, it: counters the traditionalism within Westminster Calvinism, which decides issues of doctrine, worship, evangelism, and church life by history more than by Scripture; encourages the searching of Scripture and the proving of doctrine by careful biblical exegesis (thereby increasing the weight of the doctrinal positions we adopt); shows deference to the church historians, whose responsibility it is to teach the church's confessions; and legitimizes talk of new or revised confessions based on Scripture, informed by confessions of the past, but relevant to the present.[75]

The Balance of God's Word

Frame understands that the renewal of conservative Presbyterianism requires not only the reassertion of the supremacy of God's Word, but also the balance it offers our theology and community. The importance of balance is found throughout Frame's works but is especially relevant to the basis, shape, and feel of our theology.

First, Frame challenges the Puritan practice of allowing the divineness of Scripture to absorb its humanness. Later encouraged by the Enlightenment

---

73. *IRF*, 12. Frame's sentiments here are reminiscent of R. B. Kuiper's *The Glorious Body of Christ: A Scriptural Appreciation of the One Holy Catholic Church*, repr. ed. (Edinburgh and Carlisle, PA: The Banner of Truth Trust, 2006), 83–85).

74. *IDSCB*, 279; "My Use of the Reformed Confessions," 2.

75. Ibid., 2–3. Cf. Frame's brief comments in *DG*, 10.

and more recent liberal threats to the unity of Scripture, this practice is now so entrenched as to have become a hallmark of orthodoxy. In reasserting the "double-authorship of Scripture,"[76] Frame seeks not the equal ultimacy of Scripture's divineness and humanness, for the Bible is in the final analysis God's Word and not that of man. Indeed, the denial of God's ultimate authorship of Scripture would render senseless Frame's talk of *sola Scriptura*. Nonetheless, by according the Bible's humanness fresh recognition, he shows sensitivity to its diversity yet without losing sight of its overall unity. Accordingly, he speaks more freely of issues of genre and the nature of religious language than those still basically following a traditional approach to systematics. In this, Frame's method resembles Calvin's biblical dogmatics, although in both cases more could be said of the authorial diversity of the New Testament without compromising the oneness of either Scripture or its message.[77]

Second, Frame balances wonderfully the objective and subjective sides of the faith. In doing so he proffers a fresh evangelical and specifically conservative Presbyterian response to the nineteenth-century liberal challenge to orthodoxy's inordinate emphasis on the objective propositions of the faith. Although it is too late in the day to stem the tide of that subjectivist revolt—orchestrated famously by Schleiermacher in Germany and in Scotland by the likes of Thomas Erskine of Linlathen and John McLeod Campbell—Frame's balancing of the gospel's objectivist and subjectivist elements at least ensures that Westminster Calvinism reaps some benefit from the kernel of truth discernible in Victorian liberalism. Although it would be inappropriate to underestimate the stands of Hodge and Gresham Machen in defense of the gospel's objectivity,[78] Frame rightly warns of the pitfalls of an exclusively objectivist approach to the faith, as if our belief has to do with propositions and little else. "I am fully aware that the Bible and theology, rightly done, are more than merely propositional. Theology is the whole theodrama, in which we participate."[79]

76. *DKG*, 199.

77. A reliable test case of a systematician's allowance for the authorial diversity of the New Testament is the discussion of the doctrine of adoption—the language (*huiothesia*) and metaphorical structure of which is uniquely Pauline. It is quintessential orthodox Calvinism to overlook the doctrine or to read it into the writings of biblical authors other than Paul (notably John—John 1:12 and Rev. 21:7, containing but possible hints of adoption). For Frame on adoption, see *SBL*, 205–10.

78. See especially Machen's volume *Christianity and Liberalism* (Grand Rapids: Eerdmans, 1923), wherein he argues that orthodox Christianity and theological liberalism are two different religions.

79. Preface to *Always Reforming*, 11.

Indeed, Frame sees practical dangers in the near-absolutist objectivism of traditionalism:

> It is all too easy for us to imagine that we have a higher task than merely that of helping people. Our pride constantly opposes the servant model. And it is all too easy for us to think of theological formulations as something more than truth-for-people, as a kind of special insight into God himself (which the biblical writers would have written about, had they known as much as we). But no, theology is not "purely objective truth" ... Our theologies are not even the best formulation of truth-for-people for all times and places; Scripture is that. Our theologies are merely attempts to help people, generally and in specific times and places, to use Scripture better.[80]

Third, Frame seeks to balance grace and truth in both the content and discussion of theology (John 1:14). Speaking to graduating students of Westminster West in 1999, Frame warned:

> There are many in our churches who haven't heard clearly the message of grace. The do's and don'ts of our preaching have so overshadowed the gospel, that many still labor under mountains of guilt, with no sense of forgiveness. This can happen even under pastors who know and believe the gospel, and who preach it regularly. Working the gospel into sermons is not enough. We need to show people what it means in daily life, how to maintain a grace perspective on everything.[81]

Frame is aware, however, that free grace in Christ must not be treated cheaply. "Many churches in the Reformed tradition have come to a fuller understanding of the primacy of grace in preaching and in the Christian life. There is some danger here of a drift toward antinomianism, and there is need for more careful theological reflection on these matters. But for the most part I think the result has been increased spiritual vitality."[82] Writing of World Harvest Mission's Sonship Discipleship course, for instance, Frame notes with characteristic fairness and balance:

---

80. *DKG*, 80.
81. John Frame, "Lessons on Ministry from the Pharisees: Charge to Westminster Theological Seminary Graduates, May, 1999."
82. *RLT*.

Those who have taken the course often emerge with a far more vital relationship with Christ. Nevertheless, advocates and opponents of Sonship have fought the typical Reformed battles. . . . I tend to agree with what Sonship affirms (the benefit of preaching the Gospel to ourselves) but not with what it denies (that reflecting on God's law and striving to obey are somehow harmful to our sanctification).[83]

Yet Frame is concerned not just about the place of grace in the theology of Westminster Calvinism, but about the importance of graciousness in our dialoguing. Noting that "in Reformed circles there is great need for pastors and theologians to cultivate the virtue of gentleness,"[84] Frame calls for fewer pastors like kings and generals and more like shepherds and nursing mothers. The source of the trouble, he surmises, may be our seminaries, wherein "even at its best, the atmosphere of academic debate falls far short of what God wants for his church." "It seems," he notes most relevantly, "that as years have gone by, theological debate has become more shrill, nastier, contrary to the Biblical standards of relationships between believers."[85] This "increased stridency of our current dialogue" Frame attributes to "the substitution of historical or cultural studies for real systematic."[86] Although the work of Calvin and Luther reminds us that stridency does not of itself deny theological status,

today . . . a lot of people in our circles argue theology without having an adequate case, and inwardly they know it. When you don't have good reasons for your position, but you are irrevocably committed to it, you tend to raise your voice. So in a lot of cases today, theology has become a shouting match. We need to get back to thoughtful exchanges and teachability. That includes respect for those who have done the serious work of theology, and the standing aside of people whose expertise is only in ancillary disciplines.[87]

83. *MWC*, 26; cf. *RLT*.

84. *DCL*, 938–42.

85. *RLT*. This Frame blames in part on the Internet, which "has made it possible for untrained and immature people to broadcast their theological ideas (and their attacks on others) far and wide" (ibid.). For Frame's concerns about the quality, vigor, and output of the Reformed faith in the United States, see *RLT*.

86. Ibid.

87. Ibid. Advising young theologians, Frame writes: "In criticizing other theologians, traditions, or movements, follow Biblical ethics. Don't say that somebody is a heretic unless you have a very good case. Don't throw around terms like 'another gospel.' . . . Don't destroy people's reputa-

Frame most generously and humbly confesses he has not always evaded the pitfalls he indicts. Who has? Nevertheless, he is a genuine role model of grace as well as courage and conviction.[88] We do well, then, to heed his advice not to enter controversy immediately, but to analyze first both sides of a debate:

> Consider these possibilities: (a) that the two parties may be looking at the same issue from different perspectives, so they don't really contradict; (b) that both parties are overlooking something that could have brought them together; (c) that they are talking past one another because they use terms in different ways; (d) that there is a third alternative that is better than either of the opposing views and that might bring them together; (e) that their differences, though genuine, ought both to be tolerated in the church, like the differences between vegetarians and meat-eaters in Rom. 14.[89]

Elsewhere, he explains the prevailing trigger-happiness in terms of the additional failure to discern the difference between primary and secondary concerns. "Battles have divided Reformed Christians over matters that in my judgment should not have been made tests of orthodoxy: particularly six-day creation, the 'federal vision,' Norman Shepherd's and Meredith Kline's views of covenant and justification."[90]

Conclusion

Professor Frame's seventieth birthday comes at an interesting time. On the one hand, recent years have testified to the success of Westminster Seminary Philadelphia in exporting constructive Calvinism (alias "Westminsterness") to other seminaries such as Reformed Seminary (perhaps especially its Orlando campus) and the new Redeemer Seminary in Dal-

---

tions by misquoting them, or quoting them out of context, or taking their words in the worst possible sense. Be gentle and gracious unless you have irrefutable reasons for being harsh" (ibid.).

88. Ibid. See, for example, Frame's reviews of Marva Dawn's *Reaching Out without Dumbing Down* (*CWM*, 155–74.) and Brian McLaren's *Generous Orthodoxy*. We also see it in his treatment of Norman Shepherd and his assessment of the debate between Van Til and Gordon Clark (*DKG*, 38–40). His reviews of the work of Mark Karlberg, although stronger, are fitting.

89. *RLT*.

90. Ibid. Of the advocates of the New Perspective, Frame states: "I applaud what they affirm, but not what they deny. I applaud NPP for affirming the centrality of the Jew-Gentile relation in Paul's thought. But I don't appreciate their suggestion that this invalidates the concern of Luther about individual justification. It's both-and" (ibid.).

las, Texas (a former campus of Westminster).[91] On the other hand, Gaffin's recent retirement from Westminster, coinciding but not connected with the present difficulties there, raises the real possibility that Westminster's days as the epicenter of constructive Calvinism are over. Only time will tell whether the minority lurch to the right in response to a commensurate drift to the left has made shipwreck of the seminary's balanced and innovative, constructive Calvinism.[92]

Regardless, a better understanding of the emergence of constructive Calvinism at its epicenter and of the issues yet requiring resolution—not least the interrelationship between biblical and systematic theology and the utilitarian value of perspectivalism (whether multi- or specifically triperspectivalism)—helps constructive Calvinists keep focused on the reform of systematic method and the biblical renewal of Westminster Calvinism. It seems to me that the realization of this exciting vision of the future of conservative Presbyterianism requires not only the resolution of the aforementioned issues, but at least one other thematic development. I mention here the recovery of the Fatherhood of God and the adoption of sons because of the role it could play in the tying together of the various thematic strands running through the development of constructive Calvinism.

Although the earliest appeals for the recovery of the familial elements of New Testament teaching predate the development of constructive Calvinism, more recent appeals have coincided with it.[93] Over the last fifteen years or so, the attempt has been made, in listening to these voices, to build from Scripture and from history (in that order!) a biblically revised understanding of adoption. The remarkable dovetailing of the emerging constructive Calvinism and the developing biblical-theological understanding of adoption is seen in the shared realization of (1) the importance of the redemptive-historical trajectory of Scripture, encompassing the first to the last things (in the case of adoption: Rom. 8:15–16, 22–23; 9:4; Gal. 4:4–5; Eph. 1:4–5); (2) the value of perspectives, underlined by the uniqueness of Paul's adoption

91. Writes Frame, "Reformed Theological Seminary, founded in Jackson[,] Mississippi[,] in 1966, . . . readily acknowledges a large debt to Westminster, in curriculum, theological emphasis, and faculty" (*MWC*, 5).

92. Constructive Calvinists such as Poythress remain, but it is uncertain how far they can steady the ship, let alone in the direction of constructive Calvinism.

93. I refer to the nineteenth-century appeals of Scottish Presbyterians Robert Candlish and Thomas Crawford and Southern Presbyterians John Girardeau and Robert Webb, and to the late twentieth-century appeals of James Packer (Anglican), Sinclair Ferguson, Errol Hulse (Baptist), and Douglas Kelly.

motif; (3) the centrality of union with Christ (adoption either figuring in Paul as a rich metaphorical expression of union with Christ or as a major benefit of it); and (4) the balancing of the multiple emphases of Scripture (in this case the legal and relational [familial and filial], the "now" but "not yet," the individual and corporate dimensions of the gospel, and grace and truth, etc.).

Such is the compatibility between the emerging constructive Calvinism and the maturing understanding of the fatherhood of God and adoption that it seems the two developments are now merging—the latter providing the next phase of the Scripture-based constructive-Calvinistic renewal of our systematics and Westminster Calvinism. Although Frame has said little in the area of soteriology,[94] everything he has written and the correspondence we have had lead me to suspect he would at least be sympathetic. After all, "in the present theological situation," he writes, "our main problem is not that of exegeting obscure texts, but rather the strange inability or reluctance of many to see what is big and bold and obvious."[95]

I end, then, hopeful for the future, praising God for the substantial content and stimulus of Professor Frame's work: his courage in following Scripture, his strength of character in rejecting traditionalism without aping the avant-garde, and his example in balancing grace and truth. Although the maladies of our Reformed tradition remain, Frame has added significantly to a path that heads through Scripture, via the cross, over the shoulders of our forebears, to a brighter and healthier future.

Accordingly, it remains just to say, "Thank you, brother, thank you so very much. May God spare you to lead us still further, and may he give us the courage and foresight to follow you back to Scripture!"

94. This is not a criticism so much as a recognizing that in the larger American seminaries the teaching of theology is divided among the various members of the department. Hence, there is/ are no volume(s) on Christology and soteriology in Frame's lordship series. Frame does provide, however, a popular treatment of these themes in *SBL*.

95. *DG*, 11.

8

MULTIPERSPECTIVALISM AND THE REFORMED FAITH

VERN SHERIDAN POYTHRESS

WHAT IS MULTIPERSPECTIVALISM? Multiperspectivalism appears as a characteristic aspect in virtually all the writings of John M. Frame. Recently, Frame himself has written a short piece, "A Primer on Perspectivalism," which summarizes its main features.[1] Let us focus on Frame's multiperspectivalism, but with a glance at the larger context.

FEATURES OF MULTIPERSPECTIVALISM

Human knowledge arises in the context of human finiteness. Any particular human being always knows and experiences truth from the standpoint of who he is.[2] He has a *perspective*. He can learn from others by listening sympathetically to what they understand from their differing backgrounds or

---

1. *PP.* A longer exposition, focusing specifically on ethics, is found in *PWG.* See also Vern S. Poythress, *Symphonic Theology: The Validity of Multiple Perspectives in Theology* (Phillipsburg, NJ: P&R Publishing, 2001). For the development of Frame's multiperspectivalism, see John Frame, "Backgrounds to My Thought," in this festschrift.

2. *PP.* "Because we are not God, because we are finite, not infinite, we cannot know everything at a glance, and therefore our knowledge is limited to one perspective or another."

perspectives. The diversity of human beings leads to a diversity in perspectives. John Frame affirms both the limitations of any finite human perspective and the absoluteness of God's knowledge. "It [perspectivalism] presupposes absolutism [the absoluteness of God's viewpoint]."[3] The presence of God implies that truth is accessible to human beings, and that there is a difference between truth and falsehood. In this way, Frame is an "absolutist" rather than a relativist. But he invites us to take seriously the insights and the differences in emphasis that arise from viewing a particular subject matter from more than one point of view.

Besides showing a wider interest in diverse human perspectives,[4] Frame introduces the use of perspectival triads and affirms their relation to the Trinitarian character of God.[5]

Frame primarily uses two triads. To discuss God's lordship, he uses the triad of authority, control, and presence. As Lord, God has authority over us, exerts control over us, and is present to us. Each of these three aspects of God's lordship can serve as a perspective on who God is and how he relates to us. These three perspectives are involved in one another, and each helps to define and deepen our understanding of the other two. All three aspects of lordship are involved in *all* God's relations to his creatures.[6]

To discuss ethics, Frame uses another triad of perspectives, namely the normative, situational, and existential perspectives.[7] The normative perspective focuses on the *norms*, God's law and his expressions of his ethical standards for human beings. The situational perspective focuses on the situation in which a human being must act, and endeavors to discern what attitudes and actions promote the glory of God within that situation. The existential perspective focuses on persons and their motives, particularly the central motive of love.

Again, these three are involved in one another. God's norms tell us to pay attention to the situation—in particular, the needs of others around us. The norms also tell us to pay attention to our attitudes (existential). Simi-

---

3. Ibid. See also Frame, "Backgrounds."
4. In *DCL* Frame argues that each of the Ten Commandments has its own distinctive focus, but each can also be used as a perspective on the whole range of our ethical obligations. This argument illustrates that Frame is aware of the possibility of other perspectives beyond the perspectival triads that are most characteristic of his writings. See also *PP*.
5. *PP*.
6. See the extensive discussion of this triad in *DKG* and *DG*.
7. The triad is introduced in *PWG*, and its use is developed extensively in *DCL*. The triad for ethics is closely related to the triad for lordship (Frame, "Backgrounds").

larly, the situation pushes us to pay attention to the norms, because God is the most important person in our situation, and what he desires matters supremely. The situation also pushes us to pay attention to the persons in the situation. Our own attitudes must be inspected for their potential to change the situation for good or ill.

Because God is Lord of all, these perspectives harmonize in principle. God promulgates the norms; God controls the situation; God created the human persons in his image. But in a fallen situation of sin, human beings have distortions in their ethical knowledge, and the use of one perspective can help in straightening out distortions that people have introduced in the context of another perspective.

The multiperspectivalism practiced by John Frame differs decisively from relativistic views that are sometimes called *perspectivism*.[8] Frame does his work self-consciously within the framework of a Christian commitment. He is a follower of Christ, and is committed to "take every thought captive to obey Christ" (2 Cor. 10:5).[9] The Bible has a central role in his multiperspectivalism, because he believes that it is the infallible Word of God,[10] and that God specifically designed it as a means to instruct us and free us from sin, including intellectual sin. The Bible is the infallible guide for sorting through and separating truth from error in the process of using different perspectives.

MULTIPERSPECTIVALISM IN RELATION TO THE REFORMED FAITH

How does multiperspectivalism relate to the Reformed faith? John Frame is Reformed in his theology, and has spent his career teaching at Reformed seminaries.[11] How does Frame's multiperspectivalism fit his commitment to the truths embodied in the Reformed confessions? In the early

8. Friedrich Nietzsche emphasized the centrality of the variety of human perspectives in the process of attaining knowledge, and for that reason his epistemological approach has been called *perspectivism*. Werner Krieglstein has built a viewpoint called *transcendental perspectivism* that endeavors to combine an acknowledgment of limited human perspectives with striving toward combining viewpoints in a search for higher truth. His approach is explicitly spiritualistic, in that it sees consciousness as universal. But his is a non-Christian form of spiritualism.

9. Second Corinthians 10:5 became an important principle in the apologetics of Cornelius Van Til, a tradition continued in Frame's apologetics.

10. See WCF 1.4–5.

11. Frame has taught at Westminster Theological Seminary in Philadelphia, Westminster Seminary in California, and Reformed Theological Seminary in Orlando, Florida. See Frame, "Backgrounds."

days, some people worried about whether multiperspectivalism would lead to relativism and whether it was compatible with traditional Reformed theology. Over time, the growing body of John Frame's writings has made it clear that Frame is building on Reformed orthodoxy and vigorously defending it, rather than flirting with the spirit of the age. Frame is indeed committed to the absolutism of God and not the relativism of non-Christian thinking.

But in theological style Frame's approach seems subtly different from some of the theological writing of past centuries. What is the relation? Do multiperspectivalism and the Reformed faith simply exist side by side, with no direct relationship? Is one dependent on the other? Do they aid one another?

We can try to answer these questions in two ways, either by looking at the origins of multiperspectivalism or by looking at its contemporary shape. Let us first look at the origins.

Origins of Multiperspectivalism

Frame's Multiperspectivalism

From an early point in his classroom teaching at Westminster Theological Seminary, John Frame deployed his key perspectival triads. When I became at student at Westminster in 1971, Frame was already using as a major pedagogical tool both the triad for lordship (authority, control, and presence) and the triad for ethics (normative, situational, and existential).[12] Both of these triads had obvious affinities with doctrines from classic Reformed theology.

The triad for lordship obviously linked itself to the long-standing Calvinist emphasis on the sovereignty of God. But the triad was also designed to express aspects of the way that God relates to human beings, both in his words and in his deeds. The classical Reformed tradition was accustomed to speaking about God's relation to human beings as a covenant.[13] *Authority* comes into covenant because God is the authoritative maker of covenant,

12. In 1971 Frame taught introduction to theology (including theology of the Word of God), the doctrine of God, and ethics. His lectures have led to his books: *DKG*, *DG*, *DCL*, and *DWG*. Frame also mentions the influence of G. Dennis O'Brien, a Catholic philosophy teacher at Princeton, who had some elements reminiscent of perspectival thinking (Frame, "Backgrounds") and George Lindbeck (ibid.).

13. See WCF 7; WLC 30–36.

and we as human beings are to submit to his authority. God *controls* the covenant relation both by protecting his people and by punishing and disciplining covenant violations. God is *present* in covenant in inaugurating and sustaining a relation of personal intimacy between God and man. Thus, Frame's triad for lordship can be seen as re-expressing some of the classic themes in covenant theology in the Reformed tradition.[14]

The Influence of Cornelius Van Til

Frame's triad for ethics derives directly from Cornelius Van Til's work, *Christian Theistic Ethics*.[15] In all his books Van Til made clear his own vigorous commitment to Reformed theology as the foundation for his whole enterprise. In his book on ethics, he emphasized the unique character of Christian ethics in contrast to all forms of non-Christian ethics. According to Van Til, Christians, with regenerate hearts and with a commitment to follow Christ, have an approach innately *antithetical* to all kinds of autonomous thinking and autonomous ethics.[16] Autonomous thinking derives from an unregenerate heart and is unwilling to submit to God's ways. In Van Til's view, Christian ethics is distinctive in its goal, in its standard, and in its motive. Van Til showed how these three—goal, standard, and motive—fit coherently together within a Christian approach.

This work by Van Til laid the foundation for Frame's perspectivalism. Van Til himself did not take the step of saying that the three aspects—goal, standard, and motive—could serve as perspectives on one another. But he came close to perspectivalism by stressing their coherence and mutual reinforcement. It remained for Frame, as a disciple of Van Til, to develop Van Til's insights into a fully articulate perspectivalism. The goal, when used as a perspective on the whole of ethics, became Frame's situational perspective. The standard, viewed as a perspective, became the normative perspective.

14. Frame, "Backgrounds." Frame also indicates a connection between this triad and Van Til's treatment of the correlation of God, man, and nature in Cornelius Van Til, *An Introduction to Systematic Theology: Prolegomena and the Doctrines of Revelation, Scripture, and God*, ed. William Edgar (Phillipsburg, NJ: P&R Publishing, 2007).

15. Cornelius Van Til, *Christian Theistic Ethics*, In Defense of Biblical Christianity, 2 (Philadelphia: den Dulk Christian Foundation, 1971). According to Frame, Van Til's triad can be traced back to WCF 16.7 (Frame, "Backgrounds").

16. See especially Cornelius Van Til, *The Defense of the Faith*, 2nd ed. (Philadelphia: Presbyterian and Reformed, 1963); Cornelius Van Til, *A Survey of Christian Epistemology* (Philadelphia: den Dulk Christian Foundation, 1969); *AGG*; *CVT*. Van Til built on the earlier thinking of Herman Bavinck, Abraham Kuyper, John Calvin, and St. Augustine.

And the motive became the existential perspective. The existential perspective has sometimes also been called the "personal" perspective to distinguish it pointedly from French existentialism. Frame's perspectivalism thus grew up within the soil of Reformed theology and the Reformed apologetics of Cornelius Van Til.

I would suggest that Van Til's apologetics contributed in another, less direct way. Van Til's emphasis on the antithesis between Christian and non-Christian thinking emboldened Van Til's followers to be willing to break fresh ground in their thinking. The antithesis implies that they should not merely adopt secondhand some non-Christian system of philosophical ethics and then make minor adjustments to try to use it within a Christian framework.

We can illustrate more specifically the distinctiveness of Christian thinking in the area of ethics. Frame has pointed out that non-Christian ethics has tended to take one of three major forms.[17] *De-ontological* ethical systems start with absolute norms and base everything else on them. These systems owe their plausibility to prioritizing the normative perspective. *Existentialist* ethical systems start with the primacy of the individual, his will, and his personal decisions. These prioritize the existential perspective. Finally, *teleological* and *utilitarian* ethical systems start with the goal of maximizing human pleasure and well-being. These prioritize the situational perspective. All three kinds of approaches refuse to recognize the Christian God, and so all three end up exalting one perspective as a kind of substitute for God and his authority. This one perspective is forced to become the monolithic source for everything else. By contrast, Christians can acknowledge the true God as the author of the norms (through his Word), the creator of the persons, and the governor over the situation.

Hence a Christian approach can affirm an intrinsic harmony among the three perspectives. It does not need to artificially create an autonomous, humanly generated source of ethics by making one perspective superior and giving it a godlike role. Instead, a Christian approach affirms that God alone is God. This affirmation, basic to the Christian faith, enables Christians to refuse to make God substitutes in the form of favored philosophical sources for ethical thinking. And it enables them to affirm that because of God's sovereign authority and control, normative, existential, and situational perspectives cohere in harmony.

17. See "Non-Christian Ethics" in *DCL*, 39–125.

The Influence of Biblical Theology in the Tradition of Geerhardus Vos

John Frame also acknowledges the influence of biblical theology on the development of his theological thinking and his program:

> Recall my emphasis in Part One [of *DKG*] on covenant lordship; that was biblical theology. The biblical theological method is prominent in my *Doctrine of the Word of God* and *Doctrine of God*, both as yet unpublished.[18]

That is to say, the whole structure of Frame's thinking about "covenant lordship," including his triad of perspectives—authority, control, and presence—is "biblical theology." By "biblical theology" Frame means biblical theology in the tradition of Geerhardus Vos, the study of "the *history* of God's dealings with creation."[19] Frame cites both Geerhardus Vos and his successors, such as Edmund P. Clowney, Meredith G. Kline, and Richard B. Gaffin Jr., all of whom developed their thinking within the framework of Reformed theology.[20] Frame writes as a systematic theologian, but acknowledges the need for systematic theology to be sensitive to dimensions of Scripture highlighted in biblical theology.[21]

How does Frame's thinking about covenant lordship reflect biblical theology? In discussing covenant lordship, he intends to point to the rich material in the Bible itself concerning God's covenantal relations to mankind and to Israel and to the church, in both the Old and New Testaments. Frame's

18. *DKG*, 209n35. Frame makes this remark in the context of a longer discussion of both the contributions of biblical theology and the dangers of prideful or immature use of it. See also his references in "Backgrounds."

19. *DKG*, 207. See Geerhardus Vos, *Biblical Theology: Old and New Testaments* (Grand Rapids: Eerdmans, 1966), 13. Vos expresses a preference for the label "History of Special Revelation" (ibid., 23); Frame prefers "history of the covenant" (*DKG*, 211). Both settle for "biblical theology" only because it is a more traditional expression.

20. See *DKG*, 207n33. At an early period in their careers, Clowney, Kline, Gaffin, and Frame were students at Westminster Theological Seminary, and all later taught at Westminster for a time. Vos stayed at Princeton Theological Seminary after the founding of Westminster Theological Seminary as a split-off of Princeton in 1929. But Vos's affinities with Westminster are still profound. So the developments of Frame's perspectivalism are closely tied to Westminster.

21. "It is especially important for systematic theologians today to be aware of the developments in biblical theology, a discipline in which new discoveries are being made almost daily. Too frequently, systematic theologians (including this one!) lag far behind biblical theologians in the sophistication of their exegesis." Frame also notes that some advocates of biblical theology have gone to excess (209–12; Frame, "Backgrounds,"). See also Vern S. Poythress, "Kinds of Biblical Theology," *WTJ* 70, 1 (2008): 129–42.

categories of authority, control, and presence, as well as the master term *Lord*, are meant to evoke the richness of the history of special revelation. Authority, control, and presence are manifest in God's creation of the world in Genesis 1, in his interaction with Adam and Eve in Genesis 2–3, in his relations to Noah, Abraham, Moses, and so on. Frame's categories have a flexibility that allows us to see how they are at work in all manifestations of God's lordship and in all the richness of covenantal relationships throughout the Old Testament.

The flexibility of categories is next door to their ability to function as perspectives. A tightly circumscribed, technical category like *burnt offering* has great specificity in meaning and in use. If we use it outside its narrow sphere, we use it only playfully or metaphorically. By contrast, Frame's triad of lordship has the flexibility built in. Such flexibility in many cases is more characteristic of biblical theology than it is of traditional systematic theology. The built-in flexibility permits an easy extension of the categories into perspectives. For example, *everything* that God does, whether or not we explicitly label it as a display of his presence, inevitably involves his presence. Presence becomes a perspective, in that it is characteristic of all passages in the Bible that involve God at all.

Wider Uses of Multiple Perspectives

In sum, Reformed theology as a whole, the Reformed apologetics of Cornelius Van Til, and the biblical theology of Geerhardus Vos had important influence and offered important encouragement for the development of Frame's multiperspectivalism. But was the Reformed background *necessary* for the development? My account up to this point might suggest that it was. But within multiperspectivalism we find also a concern to listen sympathetically to other perspectives. Logically this concern embraces perspectives from people who occupy other streams of Christian tradition. Could other Christian traditions develop multiperspectivalism?[22]

Here also Van Til's apologetics has a positive contribution. Van Til has an emphasis not only on *antithesis* but also on *common grace*.[23] The doctrine

22. More broadly still, could multiperspectivalism develop even outside of Christianity? Some forms of "perspectivism" crop up here and there (see footnote 8); but Frame's multiperspectivalism is grounded ultimately in the Trinity and therefore is possible only within the circle of Christian Trinitarian theology.

23. See, for example, Cornelius Van Til, *Common Grace and the Gospel* (Philadelphia: Presbyterian and Reformed, 1973).

of common grace says that God shows mercy and gives blessings even to rebels, and the blessings that God gives can include various human insights into truth. These insights come to non-Christians. How much more may we expect that God may give blessings and insights to Christians, including Christians in other traditions besides the Reformed tradition? God gives blessings not because our theology is already absolutely perfect but out of his grace, which he gives on the basis of Christ's perfection.

All genuine Christians have been regenerated through the work of the Holy Spirit, and have become a "new creation" (2 Cor. 5:17; see John 3:1–8; Eph. 4:22–24). The Lord has renewed their minds and set them on the path of righteousness, including righteous *thinking*. But all of us are inconsistent and still retain remnants of sinful ways of thinking. We need to help one another out of each other's sins. And God continues to bless us in ways we do not deserve. Hence, in principle, if multiperspectivalism is indeed a valid approach, any Christian anywhere can receive insights from the Lord leading him into a multiperspectival approach.

In fact, the commandment to "love your neighbor as yourself" (Matt. 22:39) leads in this very direction. If you love your neighbor, you are willing to listen to him sympathetically. And if you listen, you begin to understand his perspective. Maybe you find some erroneous thinking. But you also find some positive insights. When you find insights, you incorporate your neighbor's perspective into your own thinking, and then you have two perspectives instead of one. At a basic level, people are doing sympathetic listening all the time, whether in marriage and family, at work, or in education. Multiperspectivalism can be seen as little more than a self-conscious description and codification of some of the processes that are innate in loving your neighbor.

In particular, Christian cross-cultural missions have always involved multiple perspectives. A Christian crossing from American to Chinese culture has an American perspective with which he begins. As he learns more about Chinese culture, he learns about how things look from a Chinese as well as an American point of view. So he has two perspectives.

Similarly, biblically based Christian counseling involves multiple perspectives. The counselor has his perspective, which should be based on a mature knowledge of Scripture. He listens to the counselee sympathetically and tries to understand the counselee's thinking, feeling, and "perspective." The counselor gradually develops an understanding of a second perspective, the perspective of the counselee, and then endeavors to bridge between God's truth in Scripture and the counselee's situation.

God is the ultimate source for whatever insights we receive concerning multiple perspectives. God can give us insight suddenly, in a moment, in a flash. But frequently God uses means. Scripture itself is, of course, a primary means. But God also uses the skills and insights of others within the body of Christ. For example, John Frame learned from Van Til, rather than developing his multiperspectivalism completely from scratch. The Christian counselor learns from the example of more mature counselors, as well as from those who may undertake to instruct him in the art. The missionary intern learns from the missionary veteran. He sees how to move from one perspective to another both through instruction in general principles and through observing examples that embody the principles.

Thus, although it is possible in principle for people to develop a multiperspectival approach from scratch, it is certainly easier to do it when they build on the work of others.

My Own Growth in Multiperspectivalism

I may use my own growth in multiperspectivalism as a further example of how one person learns from another. In 1971 I became a student at Westminster Theological Seminary in Philadelphia, where John Frame was teaching. I was attracted to his teaching, including its multiperspectival dimensions, and adopted it as my own.

Frame's thinking was explicitly multiperspectival. But I also learned multiperspectival thinking from Edmund P. Clowney, who taught practical theology at Westminster. Clowney did not talk explicitly about perspectives. But his approach was nascently multiperspectival. How so?

Clowney's thinking used biblical theology. He followed the metaphorical and analogical aspects of Scripture as he showed how the Old Testament pointed forward to Christ. The Old Testament pointed forward partly through types and shadows that analogically pointed to Christ.[24]

---

24. This analogical connection was already propounded in the Westminster Standards: "This covenant [of grace] was differently administered in the time of the law, and in the time of the gospel: under the law it was administered by promises, prophecies, sacrifices, circumcision, the paschal lamb, and other types and ordinances delivered to the people of the Jews, all foresignifying Christ to come; which were, for that time, sufficient and efficacious, through the operation of the Spirit, to instruct and build up the elect in faith in the promised Messiah, by whom they had full remission of sins, and eternal salvation; and is called the Old Testament" (WCF 7.5; see WLC

Thus Clowney helped me adjust to using some key categories like *sacrifice*, *temple*, and *kingship* in a flexible way, as I saw relations between Old Testament institutions and Christ. This flexibility, as we have observed, is next door to perspectival practice.

Clowney also adopted an insight already found in the Westminster Standards, the insight that Christ is our final Prophet, King, and Priest.[25] Christ's teaching ministry showed his prophetic work. His working of miracles showed the exercise of power and therefore his kingship. His sacrifice on the cross showed his priestly work.

But as I thought about these truths, and combined them with Clowney's use of analogy and typology in the Old Testament, it seemed to me that these three aspects of Christ's work could not be neatly isolated. When Christ taught, he taught with *authority*. His teaching manifested a kingly claim. So his teaching was not only prophetic but kingly as well.

When Christ cast out demons with miraculous power, that was a kingly work. But he characteristically drove out the demons using verbal commands, which were prophetic utterances (Luke 4:36). Moreover, the very character of his miracles revealed the character of Christ. The miracles indirectly revealed something about who he was and the character of his kingdom. For example, his healing of the paralytic in Matthew 9:2–8 showed that Christ had power to forgive sins. The miracle taught something. And if it *taught*, it was indirectly *prophetic*, as well as directly kingly.

We can also look at the promise to forgive sins. The promise pronounced by Jesus is a pronouncement involving Jesus' exercise of his prophetic function. But we can also observe that forgiveness comes on the basis of substitution and sacrifice—ultimately, Christ's sacrifice. Forgiveness involves a priestly dimension. So a miracle that proclaims forgiveness also has a priestly dimension. Thus, the labels *prophet, king,* and *priest* can be used not merely in a more literal sense but as *perspectives* on the whole

---

34). Clowney developed these confessional themes further in books such as *Preaching and Biblical Theology* (Grand Rapids: Eerdmans, 1961) and *Preaching Christ in All of Scripture* (Wheaton, IL: Crossway, 2003). See also Vern S. Poythress, *The Shadow of Christ in the Law of Moses* (Phillipsburg, NJ: P&R Publishing, 1995).

25. "It pleased God, in His eternal purpose, to choose and ordain the Lord Jesus, His only begotten Son, to be the Mediator between God and man, the Prophet, Priest, and King . . ." (WCF 8.1). See WLC 43–45. Frame also mentions the influence of Clowney's thinking on his triperspectivalism (Frame, "Backgrounds").

of Christ's work. All of Christ's work is prophetic; it teaches things about him. All is kingly, because he is always acting with kingly authority. All is priestly; his work is part of the total program for reconciling his people to God through his sacrifice.

So from Edmund Clowney I had a perspectival triad—prophet, king, and priest. This triad came in addition to the triads I was learning from Frame. Of course, Clowney's triad also belonged to the Westminster Standards, but Clowney's use of biblical theology and its analogical structures encouraged me to use these older categories in an extended, analogical way, and it was but a step to use them perspectivally.

Having come this far, it was a small step to consider the possibility of taking almost any category from biblical theology and expanding it into a perspective.[26] For example, start with the theme of the temple. Stretch it out into a perspective. See it as a particular embodiment of the theme of "God with us," which is fulfilled in Christ (Matt. 1:23). In fact, John indicates that the temple theme is fulfilled in Christ, whose body is the temple (John 2:21). The temple is closely related to the theme of God's presence, one of the categories in Frame's covenant lordship triad. When the idea of *temple* is stretched out in this way, it becomes a perspective on all of God's dealings with us.

When I came to Westminster in 1971, Frame was already doing things of a similar sort. In ethics, Frame argued that each of the Ten Commandments has its own distinctive focus and that any one of the commandments could also be used as a perspective on the *whole* of our ethical responsibility.[27]

In his course on the Doctrine of God, Frame argued that the great miracles in the Bible could be used to provide a perspective on God's providence and on God's character. Pedagogically, Frame could start his theological discussion with miracles and go from there to look at providence, creation, and then the attributes of God.

This approach implies that miracles like the plagues in Egypt, the crossing of the Red Sea, the miracles of Elijah and Elisha, the miracles of Christ's earthly life, and the resurrection of Christ show in particularly intensive

---

26. The idea of using biblical themes as perspectives is further developed in Poythress, *Symphonic Theology*. I intended the title *Symphonic Theology* to be another label for Frame's multiperspectivalism. My title was, I think, prettier and more colorful than *multiperspectivalism*, and I hoped that it would stick. But the term *multiperspectivalism* is more precisely descriptive, and so it has remained the more conventional label.

27. See *DCL*.

form God's authority, power, and presence. Miracles also provide pictures of redemptive power that can encourage us as we confront hardships, each in our own circumstances. Any one miracle can therefore become a perspective onto the larger plan of God for our redemption.

Multiple Perspectives in the Work of Kenneth L. Pike

In many respects, Frame's multiperspectivalism developed under the influence of the theology and teaching at Westminster Theological Seminary.[28] But in my life I received another influence. Beginning in the summer of 1971, I studied for several summers at the Summer Institute of Linguistics in Norman, Oklahoma, where Kenneth L. Pike taught "tagmemics," a linguistic approach with multiperspectival characteristics. It is worthwhile for me to tell part of that story, because Pike developed his multiperspectivalism earlier than Frame and independent of the influence of Westminster Theological Seminary.[29] And yet at bottom the two kinds of multiperspectivalism are virtually identical in spirit.

Pike was a Christian linguist who taught linguistics at the University of Michigan and who spent a good deal of his career in the task of Bible translation with Wycliffe Bible Translators and its academic sister institution, the Summer Institute of Linguistics.[30] The challenge of translating a rich book like the Bible, and the challenge of analyzing a spectrum of exotic languages with no discernible relation to Indo-European languages, contributed to Pike's endeavor to build a linguistic approach that was both practical and rich. Over a period of decades, Pike built an approach called *tagmemic theory* that explicitly incorporated multiple perspectives.[31]

In retrospect we can find tentative steps toward multiple perspectives as early as 1947, when Pike wrote a book codifying his work on

28. See Frame, "Backgrounds."

29. Pike mentioned to me in a personal conversation that he had read some of Cornelius Van Til's writings. But I am not aware of any direct connection between Westminster Seminary and Pike's perspectivalism.

30. See the biographical information on Kenneth L. Pike at http://www.sil.org/klp/klp-bio.htm.

31. Pike tells the story himself in Kenneth L. Pike, "Toward the Development of Tagmemic Postulates," in *Theoretical Discussion*, vol. 2 of Ruth M. Brend and Kenneth L. Pike, eds., *Tagmemics* (The Hague/Paris: Mouton, 1976), 91–127. Others also contributed to the development, including Robert E. Longacre, Evelyn Pike (Kenneth's wife), and Kenneth's sister Eunice. Pike's article acknowledges contributions from many others.

sound systems of language ("phonemics").32 To account robustly for the complexity of sound patterns over a multitude of languages of the world, Pike had to balance a number of dimensions in these patterns. In his analysis we can see the early stages of what later developed into a perspectival triad: contrast, variation, and distribution.33 He also devoted attention to what later came to be known as particle, wave, and field phenomena. The phenomena were there and were acknowledged, but Pike had not yet fully organized them by generalization beyond the area of phonemics (sound).

In 1949 Pike began to concentrate on phenomena in the area of grammar, after thirteen years of concentration on sound patterns.[34] Comparisons between patterns in sound and in grammar led him to summarize the patterns in terms of three characteristic aspects of analysis of a linguistic unit: contrast, variation, and distribution.[35] These formed a perspectival triad, the first that Pike developed. The three aspects are interdependent and interlocked with one another. In actual phenomena in language use, they are not strictly isolatable but are copresent dimensions in the total function of the language.

In 1959 Pike wrote an article entitled "Language as Particle, Wave, and Field."[36] Here for the first time he introduced three "views" of language. Pike explained that linguistics could look at language as consisting of particles (a static approach oriented to distinguishable pieces), waves (a dynamic approach, looking at flow and mutual influence), and fields (a relational approach, focusing on systematic patterning of relations in multiple dimensions). In principle, each of these approaches can be applied to the same piece

32. Kenneth L. Pike, *Phonemics: A Technique for Reducing Languages to Writing* (Ann Arbor: University of Michigan Press, 1947).

33. Technically, *contrast* is more specifically *contrastive-identificational features* and includes features that help to establish the identity of a particular unit as well as features that bring that unit into contrast with other, similar units. See the exposition in Kenneth L. Pike, *Linguistic Concepts: An Introduction to Tagmemics* (Lincoln, NE/London: University of Nebraska Press, 1982), 42–51.

34. Pike, "Toward the Development," 94.

35. Ibid., 96. See the fully developed explanation of these concepts in Pike, *Linguistic Concepts*, 42–65.

36. Kenneth L. Pike, "Language as Particle, Wave, and Field," *Texas Quarterly* 2, 2 (1959): 37–54; reprinted in Ruth M. Brend, ed., *Kenneth L. Pike: Selected Writings to Commemorate the 60th Birthday of Kenneth Lee Pike* (The Hague/Paris: Mouton, 1972), 117–28. More mature explanation of the three perspectives can be found in Pike, *Linguistic Concepts*, 19–38.

of language, and people notice different patterns by using each approach. These views are three perspectives.[37]

By this time Pike was a self-conscious perspectivalist, but of what kind? His thinking continued to develop. By 1967 he was analyzing not only language but human behavior in general as "trimodal."[38] The three "modes" were the feature mode (identity and contrast), the manifestation mode (variation), and the distribution mode (distribution). These three interlock. His modal approach encompassed the earlier triads and uncovered further manifestations of them.[39]

In 1971 when I met him, Pike confided that he thought these modes reflected within language the Trinitarian character of God. The triadic modes were three-in-one modes, each distinct but each deeply interlocked with and presupposing the others, each also belonging to the unified whole, which was a linguistic unit. Each was a perspective on the whole.

Perspectives in Dorothy Sayers

Dorothy Sayers gives us an instance of perspectival thinking from a point even earlier in time than Pike or Frame. In 1941 Sayers published the book *The Mind of the Maker*.[40] She began with her own experience as a creative writer (she primarily wrote detective stories). Sayers finds in the process of artistic creation an analogy to the Trinitarian character of God. She observes that any act of human creation has three "coinherent" aspects, which she names *Idea*, *Energy*, and *Power*. The Creative Idea is the idea of the creative work as a whole, even before it comes to expression. "This is the image of the Father."[41] *The Creative Energy* or *Activity* is the process of

37. "His experience [the experience of an observer of language] of the factness around him is affected by his perspectives" (Pike, *Linguistic Concepts*, 12). On the relation of linguistic theories to human perspectives, see ibid., 5–13.

38. Kenneth L. Pike, *Language in Relation to a Unified Theory of the Structure of Human Behavior*, 2nd ed. (The Hague/Paris: Mouton, 1967).

39. The entire structure for a tagmemic framework for discourse can be derived analogically, starting with a single perspectival triad—particle, wave, and field. See Vern S. Poythress, "A Framework for Discourse Analysis: The Components of a Discourse, from a Tagmemic Viewpoint," *Semiotica* 38, 3/4 (1982): 277–98; Vern S. Poythress, "Hierarchy in Discourse Analysis: A Revision of Tagmemics," *Semiotica* 40, 1/2 (1982): 107–37.

40. Dorothy L. Sayers, *The Mind of the Maker* (New York: Harcourt, Brace and Company, 1941). Sayers's thinking about the Trinity is visible at an even earlier point in Dorothy Sayers, *Zeal of Thy House* (New York: Harcourt, Brace and World, 1937).

41. Ibid., 37.

working out the idea, both mentally and on paper. Sayers describes it as "working in time from the beginning to the end, with sweat and passion. . . . this is the image of the Word."[42] Third is *The Creative Power*, "the meaning of the work and its response in the lively soul . . . This is the image of the indwelling Spirit."[43]

Sayers also observes that each of three aspects, Idea, Activity, and Power, is intelligible only in the context of the others. She affirms the coinherence or indwelling of each in the others.[44]

THE PRESENT SHAPE OF MULTIPERSPECTIVALISM

Perspectivalism as an Implication of General Revelation

Now that we have looked briefly at some of the historical developments of perspectivalism, it is time to consider the character of the product. What is the distinctive character of multiperspectivalism?

Our survey of the historical developments is still pertinent. A form of perspectivalism related to the Trinitarian character of God appeared independently in at least three different places, in the work of John Frame, in the work of Kenneth Pike, and in the work of Dorothy Sayers. The independence of these three works suggests that God, as the archetype, has impressed ectypal images of his Trinitarian nature on the order of the created world.[45]

Sayers and Pike derived much of their reflection from general revelation in human artistic creativity and in language, respectively. At the same time, as Christians Sayers and Pike had the benefit of special revelation in the Bible, which articulated the Trinitarian character of God. Sayers and Pike undoubtedly deepened their reflections through the interaction that they discovered between special revelational knowledge of the Trinity and patterns of perspectival interlocking they observed from general revelation.[46] At the same time, both

---

42. Ibid.
43. Ibid., 37–38.
44. I have taken the liberty of reproducing here two paragraphs that are also to appear in Vern S. Poythress, *In the Beginning Was the Word: Language—A God-Centered Approach* (Wheaton, IL: Crossway, 2009).
45. See the argument for the Trinitarian basis for scientific law in Vern S. Poythress, *Redeeming Science: A God-Centered Approach* (Wheaton, IL: Crossway, 2006), 24–26; and the Trinitarian basis for language in Poythress, *In the Beginning*.
46. On the close correlation and interaction between general and special revelation, see Van Til, *Introduction to Systematic Theology*, chaps. 6–11.

authors directed their primary focus toward subject matter coming from general revelation. Pike's published work in professional linguistics seldom explicitly mentions his Christian commitment, let alone his Trinitarian thinking. Yet his work shows clear Trinitarian patterns in its use of perspectival triads.

The Key Role of Persons

We may also note the important role played by the study of persons and by the God-man relation in all the historical instances of Trinitarian perspectivalism.

Consider first Dorothy Sayers. At an early point she explicitly indicates that she is working with the concept of man as the image of God.[47] She undertakes to understand God's activity as Creator by analogy with human artistic creativity. In the process she uncovers a coinherent perspectival triad, namely, Idea, Energy, and Power. Creativity, as a characteristic of persons, becomes the key entry point for reflecting on the image of God, which has to do with man as personal. And man is in the image of God, who is personal and creative.

Next, consider Kenneth Pike. He is dealing with language, which is innately associated with persons. As a Bible translator, he is repeatedly confronted with the fact that God speaks in the Bible and that God's speech is analogous to human speech. Thus, he has before him a natural bridge between the Trinitarian character of God and the nature of human language. Pike uncovered the key triad of particle, wave, and field by interacting with what was going on in elementary particle physics.[48] But at the same time he was aware of the potential for persons, by choice, to take a stance in which they direct their awareness toward some one aspect of their situation. Personal choice introduces the possibility of multiple perspectives. Persons are central in his reckoning: "The observer standpoint is relevant to finding data: no 'thing-in-itself' (i.e., apart from an observer) is discussed in the theory [Pike's tagmemic theory]."[49]

John Frame obtained his fundamental triads in the context of persons. Frame's triad for covenant lordship comes, of course, in the context of cov-

---

47. Sayers, *Mind of the Maker*, 19–31.
48. Pike, "Toward the Development," 99.
49. Ibid., 91. Pike's inclusion of the observer is all the more striking when it is contrasted with the tendency of much linguistic theory of the time to construct a formal system, dropping the persons out of the picture.

enant, which is a *personal* relation between God and man. The triad for ethics comes in the context of ethical responsibility, which must be fully *personal* responsibility. Edmund Clowney's triad of prophet, king, and priest comes in the context of considering the work of Christ, who is a person. Christ's work fulfills the pattern of the various persons in the Old Testament who served in the personal roles of prophet, king, and priest.

The Trinitarian Root of Perspectivalism

In retrospect, we may guess that the role of persons in perspectivalism is no accident. Perspectivalism of a Trinitarian kind has its ultimate roots in the Trinitarian character of God. God is one God, and he is also three persons. The doctrine of the Trinity is itself fundamentally and deeply personal. We are forcefully confronted with the necessity for Trinitarian thinking, especially when we see the personalism in the Gospel of John. The Son relates personally to the Father, and the Spirit is introduced as "another Helper" who will function toward the disciples like the Son (John 14:16; also in John 16).

The three persons are distinct from one another. The Bible describes their interactions. The Father sends the Son, and the Son obeys the Father (John 6:38–39; 12:49; 14:31). The Father glorifies the Son and the Son glorifies the Father (John 13:31–32; 17:1–5). The Spirit speaks what he hears from the Father and the Son (John 16:13–14).

At the same time, all the persons of the Trinity are involved in all the acts of God. The Father created the world through the Word (that is, the Son) in the power of the Spirit (John 1:1–3; Gen. 1:2; Ps. 33:6; Ps. 104:30). So each Trinitarian person offers us a "perspective" on the acts of God. In fact, then, each person of the Trinity offers a "perspective" on God himself. Through the Son, that is, through the perspective that the Son gives us, we know the Father: "All things have been handed over to me by my Father, and no one knows the Son except the Father, and no one knows the Father except the Son and anyone to whom the Son chooses to reveal him" (Matt. 11:27–28).

The revelation of the Father through the Son is possible because the Father dwells in the Son to do his works:

> Whoever has seen me has seen the Father. How can you say, "Show us the Father"? Do you not believe that I am in the Father and the Father is

190

in me? The words that I say to you I do not speak on my own authority, but the Father who dwells in me does his works. Believe me that I am in the Father and the Father is in me, or else believe on account of the works themselves. (John 14:9–11)

The mutual indwelling of persons in the Trinity, called *coinherence* or *perichoresis*, is the ultimate background for how we know the Father through the Son. This knowledge is *perspectival*. We know the Father *through* the perspective offered in the Son.

Human experience of perspectives derives from an ultimate archetype, namely, the plurality of persons in the Trinity and their coinherence. This plurality of persons implies a plurality of perspectives. The indwelling of Trinitarian persons in coinherence implies the harmony and compatibility of distinct perspectives, as well as the fact that one starting point in one person opens the door to all three persons. Each of the three divine persons offers us a perspective on the whole of God.

Hence, the archetype for perspectives is the Trinity. The persons of the Trinity know one another (Matt. 11:27–28). Such knowledge is personal. The Son knows the Father as a person, as well as knowing all facts about the person. The Son knows the Father as Father from his standpoint as the Son. Hence, there are three archetypal perspectives on knowledge, the perspectives of the Father, the Son, and the Holy Spirit. These three are one. There is only one God.

This unity in plurality and plurality in unity has implications for derivative knowledge—the knowledge by creatures. As creatures we have knowledge that is an ectype, a derivative knowledge, rather than the archetype, the original infinite knowledge of God. Ectypal knowledge must inevitably show the stamp of its Trinitarian archetype, because all knowledge, insofar as it is true knowledge at all, is knowledge of truth, and archetypal truth is God's truth, truth in his mind. His truth is manifest in the Word, who is the truth in the absolute sense (John 14:6). To know truth is to know truth from the one who is the truth, from the Son, and in knowing truth from the Son, we know the image of the truth in the mind of the Father.

Additionally, we know through the teaching of the Holy Spirit: "But it is the spirit in man, the *breath of the Almighty*, that makes him understand" (Job 32:8). A number of New Testament passages emphasize the role of the Holy Spirit in giving us saving knowledge of God in Christ: "When the Spirit of truth comes, he will guide you into all the truth" (John 16:13). This promise comes only to those who believe in the Son. The Spirit has a special redemptive role for believers.

At the same time, on the basis of broader statements like that in Job 32:8 (see also Ps. 94:10), we may infer that the special redemptive teaching by the Spirit has as its broader background a general creational activity of the Spirit in teaching human beings anything they know at all. What the Spirit teaches in this creational activity derives from the source of knowledge in the Son, who is the Word, the Wisdom of God (1 Cor. 1:30; Col. 2:3), and the Truth of God (John 14:6). Hence all human knowledge has a Trinitarian structure in its source.

The Role of Man and the Centrality of Christ

Since human beings are made in the image of God, and since they can enjoy personal fellowship with God, it should not be surprising that we find some of the most striking analogues to the Trinitarian mystery in human beings: their knowledge, their covenantal relation to God (covenant lordship), their ethical responsibility to God (triad of ethics), their language (Kenneth Pike), and their artistic creativity (Dorothy Sayers). At the heart of all these manifestations of God is the mediation of the Son of God. Consider first the theme of covenant lordship, as developed by John Frame. Isaiah predicts the coming of the Messianic servant to bring final salvation and identifies him as both the Lord of the covenant (Isa. 9:6–7) and as the covenant itself (Isa. 42:6; 49:8). Christ supremely and climactically manifests authority, control, and presence. He has the authority of God (Matt. 5:21–22; Luke 4:36; 5:21–24); he manifests the control of God in healing and in ruling the waters (Matt. 8); he is the presence of God, "God with us" (Matt. 1:23).

Christ also sums up in his person the various dimensions of our ethical responsibility. His righteousness is the ultimate norm, which is reflected in the particular normative pronouncements throughout the Bible. His person is the ultimate goal, because the goal of history is to display the glory of God in the glory of Christ (John 17:1–5; Rev. 21:22–24). His person is also the ultimate motive: Christlikeness is worked in us through the Spirit (2 Cor. 3:18).

Christ as the Word of God is the ultimate origin behind all manifestations of language (Pike). Christ the Creator is the ultimate origin behind all instances of human creativity (Sayers). Christ as Prophet, King, and Priest is the ultimate model for the Old Testament ectypal instances of prophets, kings, and priests (Clowney).

In affirming the centrality of Christ, we do not produce a Christo-monism that collapses the full Trinitarian character of God into one person or (worse) into the human nature of Christ. Rather, we retain the distinction of persons and the distinction of the two natures of Christ. At the same time, we affirm the epistemological insight that any one can be a perspectival starting point for meditation on the whole.

Imaging

According to Genesis 1:26–28, man is made in the image of God, but in the New Testament we discover something more: Christ is "the image of the invisible God" (Col. 1:15; see Heb. 1:3). The statement about Christ occurs in the context of Christ as mediator of creation, rather than merely in the context of redemption. So we can infer that in the original act of creation, Adam was created not simply in the image of God, but after the pattern of the archetypal divine image, namely the Son, the second person of the Trinity. Adam, be it noted, also fathers Seth "in his own likeness, after his image" (Gen. 5:3).

Meredith G. Kline has further reflected on this imaging structure and extended the idea metaphorically, in the manner of the flexible terminology in biblical theology.[50] Theophanies in the Old Testament display or "image" God in visible manifestations. Kline sees a close relation between theophany, especially the cloud of glory, and the Holy Spirit. But theophanies include manifestations of God in human form, as in Ezekiel 1:26–28 and in some of the appearances to Abraham (Gen. 18) and others (Judg. 13:6, 18, 22). These appearances in human form surely anticipate the incarnation of Christ, who is the final, permanent "theophany" in human form.[51] Thus theophany is intrinsically Trinitarian. It is a revelation of the Father in the Son through the Spirit. How else could it be? If we as sinners stand before God in his holiness, we will die (Ex. 33:20–23; Isa. 6:5–7). We need mediation. Specifically, we need the mediation of the Son in whom dwells the Spirit and who sends the Spirit to unite us to himself.

The central theophany is in the Son, in his incarnation. But Old Testament theophanies also include visible manifestations, in light, in cloud,

---

50. Meredith G. Kline, *Images of the Spirit* (Grand Rapids: Baker, 1980).
51. See John 12:41, which alludes to Isaiah 6.

in thunder, in fire, in a burning bush. These physical phenomena "image" God in a subordinate way by displaying something of his character. In Psalm 104:1–4, creation itself is described in a manner reminiscent of theophanic language. Hence creation itself displays the character of God, which is exactly what the apostle Paul says in Romans:

> For what can be known about God is plain to them, because God has shown it to them. For his invisible attributes, namely, his eternal power and divine nature, have been clearly perceived, ever since the creation of the world, in the things that have been made. So they are without excuse. For although they knew God, they did not honor him as God or give thanks to him, but they became futile in their thinking, and their foolish hearts were darkened. (Rom. 1:19–21)

Theophany, as we have seen, is innately Trinitarian and therefore perspectival. We see the Father in the Son. By implication, the creation itself displays the imprint of Trinitarian structure. Although man is the image of God in a unique sense, the created world "images" God in a great variety of ways. It images the Trinitarian God. Therefore, it is rich with the potential for perspectival investigation.[52] Yet the darkness of darkened hearts in idolatry throws up barriers to the clarity and depth of knowledge.

Reformed Theology as an Aid to Multiperspectivalism

The work of Dorothy Sayers and Kenneth Pike shows that a multiperspectival approach can develop directly from Trinitarian doctrine and general revelation. It need not have strong, direct dependence on the distinctives of Reformed theology. Nevertheless, multiperspectivalism enjoys affinities with some of the distinctives in Reformed theology. The affinities are most obvious with the particular form of Reformed theology that resided at Westminster Theological Seminary. We have already noted several.

(1) Van Til's emphasis on antithesis emboldens students to think in a distinctively Christian manner and to be willing to break with the bulk of Western thought.

Antithesis, of course, is not uniquely a Reformed idea. Many people nowadays are waking up to the distinctions between a Christian worldview and various non-Christian worldviews. But Reformed theology emphasizes

---

52. Such investigation is part of the point of Poythress, *Redeeming Science*.

the radicality of the depravity in fallen human beings. Depravity extends to the mind (Eph. 4:17–19) and not merely to the will or the habits of the body. It affects the depths of the mind. And the effects can be subtle as well as overt. Hence, Reformed tradition offers a fertile soil for taking seriously the distinctiveness of Christian thought.

Van Til also analyzes ways in which Christian thinkers of the past have fallen into compromises with unbelieving, non-Christian thinking. He thus emboldens Christians not merely to adopt uncritically a metaphysical or epistemological framework that owes more to Kant or to Aristotle or to Plato than to Christ.

(2) Van Til emphasizes the Creator-creature distinction. The distinction underlines the absoluteness and exclusiveness of the claims of God the Creator. This emphasis encourages Christians to make sure that God alone receives our allegiance. Monoperspectival reductions of the truth frequently make some one perspective into a godlike origin for everything else.

On one level, knowledge of the Creator-creature distinction is common to all Christians, not merely Reformed Christians. But Reformed theology has made a point of dwelling on the absoluteness of God and trying to make sure that all of theological reflection remains consistent with his absoluteness.

(3) The Creator-creature distinction also reminds Christians that in the arena of knowledge they do not have to be God or to aspire to be divine in their knowledge. Christians can thus be free to admit that what they have is only finite knowledge and that they have their knowledge only from the "perspective" of who they are with finite experience and a finite location. At the same time, because God reveals himself in general and special revelation, and supremely through Christ, Christians can be confident they have genuine knowledge—knowledge of God and knowledge concerning things around them.

Human perspectives are limited but valid, insofar as they are not distorted by sin. Any one Christian human perspective coheres with the infinitude of divine knowledge, because the perspective comes as a gift from God. Multiple perspectives are intrinsically all right rather than an embarrassment or a frustration. Therefore, admitting you are a creature leads naturally to multiperspectivalism.

Suppose, by contrast, that you abolish the Creator-creature distinction in your own thinking. If you think God is on the same level with you, then your knowledge must be God's knowledge if it is to be true at all. You must be God. Or you must bring God down to your level in order to have assurance that your knowledge is valid. In that case, your perspective *is* God's perspective, pure and simple, and there is only one valid perspective, namely, your own. That point of view is what Van Til and John Frame call "non-Christian rationalism." The human mind claims absolute autonomy and becomes the standard for truth. That approach has an intrinsic tendency toward monoperspectivalism. It exalts a single chosen perspective and ends up crushing all diversity in human perspectives.

When such godlike claims become implausible, as they inevitably do, the non-Christian moves to the opposite pole, "non-Christian irrationalism." He admits he is not God, that his knowledge is not infinite, but he does not give up his autonomy. He still clings to the ultimacy of his own perspective, and therefore he lapses into skepticism. He concludes that no one can know anything rightly, because no one can attain infinity. Multiple perspectives then become relativistic, as is characteristic of much postmodernist thinking.

Christian thinking affirms the accessibility of God. Christian thinking is not postmodernist; it does not irrationalistically exalt diversity and give up unity. At the same time, Christian thinking rejects the modernist confidence in autonomous human rationality as an ultimate foundation for truth. Neither modernism nor postmodernism acknowledges the Creator-creature distinction. Therefore, neither agrees with the Christian answer, which is that we can remain creatures, in submission to the Creator. God gives us real but not exhaustive knowledge of the truth.

(4) Reformed theology also emphasizes the comprehensive sovereignty of God. Comprehensive sovereignty encourages Christians to affirm the intrinsically harmonious relation between different perspectives, such as the normative, existential, and situational perspectives. God guarantees perfect harmony between the perspectives, because he completely controls them all and all their manifestations. By contrast, if we doubt the comprehensiveness of God's control, we are leaving room for a final irrationalism. If we think something is even a little out of control, we have no guarantee it will fit with thorough harmony into other dimensions of truth and patterning we find throughout the world of thought.

Especially when we multiply the number of dimensions that we inspect, the very multiplicity of insights can become threatening. If these are not united by the all-controlling God with an all-controlling, coherent plan, what will we do? The multiple insights need a single master perspective, a master key, if they are to be united at all. If we do not allow God to control every detail, we are likely to make ourselves substitute gods. These gods can take the form of a master perspective that will bring us rationalistic harmony on our own autonomous terms. Or they can take the form of skepticism that gives up on harmony because there may be chaos and irrationalism at the bottom of what we investigate (this is the "polytheistic" solution).

(5) Biblical theology in the tradition of Geerhardus Vos and his successors at Westminster Seminary introduced flexible categories and flexibility in thinking analogically. Such flexibility is next door to perspectivalism. At the same time, Vos affirmed the importance of believing in divine revelation and the harmonious character of God's plan for all of history. Hence, coherence among the perspectives is guaranteed beforehand.

This coherence in Vosian biblical theology contrasts with other, non-Vosian forms of "biblical theology": some deviant kinds of biblical theology may allow for contradictory points of view to crop up in different parts of Scripture. The contradictions are alleged to be there on account of the variety of human authors and circumstances. This kind of contradiction breaks up the unity of the perspectives and leads to denial of the accessibility of God's speech to us in the Bible (2 Tim. 3:16). God is seen as absent or as hiding in obscurity somewhere behind the contradictions in the variety of human perspectives. Perspectives then lose their ultimate Trinitarian unity.

(6) Van Til's teaching emphasizes the "equal ultimacy" of the one and the many in God. God is one God in three persons. In God "the one," that is, the oneness of God, is equally ultimate with "the many," that is, the three persons. This equal ultimacy of the one and the many is the final foundation for the one and the many that occur at the level of the creature.[53]

For example, there are many dogs, and there is one species "dog." What is the relation between the two? Philosophers have found insuperable difficulties with this type of question. If the one is prior, how did the many ever come about? Or if the many are prior, how did the many ever attain any subsequent unity? Van Til maintains that God's Trinitarian character is the final foundation answering this dilemma.

---

53. Van Til, *Defense of the Faith*, 25–26; Van Til, *A Survey of Christian Epistemology*, 96; Rousas J. Rushdoony, *The One and the Many: Studies in the Philosophy of Order and Ultimacy* (Nutley, NJ: Craig Press, 1971); Vern S. Poythress, "A Biblical View of Mathematics," in Gary North, ed., *Foundations for Christian Scholarship: Essays in the Van Til Perspective* (Vallecito, CA: Ross House, 1976), 161.

This picture of equal ultimacy is an encouragement for multiperspectival thinking on a human level. The diversity of human beings on earth is neither subordinate to nor prior to the unity of the one human race. (Adam was a single individual, but from the beginning God designed that he would bring into being a plurality of human beings.) The diversity in thinking among human beings, and the diversity in their perspectives, is neither prior to nor posterior to the unity in thinking that is common to all people made in the image of God. Therefore, multiperspectivalism has a natural affinity to Van Til's thesis of equal ultimacy.

I have formulated the theme of the one and the many at a high level of generality. Now I will illustrate it. The crossing of the Red Sea is an example of God's redemption, but it is a key example. God calls on Israel to look back on this example in order to take heart in the present (Ps. 78:2–4, 12–14), and he uses the exodus as an analogy for future redemption (Isa. 51:9–11). The one particular instance of redemption (one out of many) becomes a window or perspective through which we can view the general principle of redemption (the general pattern that unifies the instances). The instances are "the many." The general pattern is "the one." The general pattern is supremely manifested and embodied in the redemption accomplished by Christ. This one redemption leads to many "mini-redemptions" in the form of application of the benefits of redemption to each individual. The pattern of Christ's one redemption is also manifested typologically in the earlier "foreshadowing" of redemption in the exodus from Egypt.

(7) The absoluteness of God, the finiteness of human knowledge, and the multiplicity of human viewpoints, when taken together, lead in a fairly obvious way to affirming multiple human perspectives and to affirming an intrinsic harmonizability of human perspectives in God's absolute knowledge. But God's absoluteness leads us further. His absoluteness implies his ability to make himself accessible. As Frame observes, if God controls all things, including his relation to us, he can make himself present and available to us.[54] Within a Christian framework, transcendence (control) undergirds immanence (presence), rather than being in tension with it.

God's presence—his accessibility, together with his mercy displayed in Christ and the power of his Holy Spirit working in us—encourage us to seek him fervently. His absoluteness implies that we must conform our minds to him, rather than vice-versa. This process of seeking him and conforming our minds

54. *DKG*, 12–18.

to him leads naturally to appreciating the role of God in our epistemology. Our minds must be brought into conformity to him. We can never exhaustively understand the Trinity, but the Trinity is at the root of our epistemology. Together, these thoughts naturally lead to seeing the roots of multiple perspectives in the knowledge relations among the persons of the Trinity. These knowledge relations touch on the coinherence of the persons. The coinherence of the persons guarantees the coherence of perspectives at the deepest ontological level.[55]

There can be no other ultimate foundation for perspectives than God himself. God alone is absolute. Therefore, absoluteness, a key concept in Reformed theology of God, serves naturally as a key incentive for moving toward multiperspectival thinking in human practice, a multiperspectivalism that imitates the coinherence of the persons in the Trinity.

Reformed Theology as Reforming

What does multiperspectivalism imply for the future? The finiteness of human knowledge, together with human access to God in Christ, provides the basis for progress. We can grow. We can know more of God in Christ (Rom. 11:33–36). A multiplicity of perspectives aids growth, which includes the further refinement of human thinking, which in this world remains contaminated by sin and the corruption of non-Christian influences.

As a tradition, Reformed theology has not yet reached perfection.[56] Therefore, Frame is not afraid to enrich that tradition and to challenge it, when he believes he is following Scripture in so doing. Continuing to grow and critically inspecting our heritage from past generations are implications of the depth of God's truth revealed in Scripture.

In fact, multiperspectivalism offers a radical challenge for growth. God in the absoluteness of his Trinitarian being is the final ontological foundation for the created order. And that has implications for language as a whole and for the category systems of our human thinking, including theological thinking.[57]

---

55. Thus multiperspectivalism has come to serve many areas: pedagogy, discovery (heuristic), ecclesiology (diversity of members in one body), analysis of conceptual terms (potential for varying use of a term), and ontology.

56. The reality of fallibility is explicitly affirmed in Reformed tradition in WCF 31.4: "All synods and councils, since the Apostles' times, whether general or particular, may err; and many have erred."

57. See Vern S. Poythress, "Reforming Ontology and Logic in the Light of the Trinity: An Application of Van Til's Idea of Analogy," *WTJ* 57 (1995): 187–219; Poythress, *In the Beginning*.

In a postmodernist environment where the primary note is skepticism and antipathy to absolutist claims, we should be careful to strike a note in opposition to both modernism and postmodernism. Both commit themselves to human autonomy. The way of Christ is the way of discipleship, the way of firm reliance on his instruction, which is found in Scripture. That way does not despise the fruits of centuries of saints who have profited from Scripture. In particular, we profit from saints within the Reformed tradition, which has been a significant aid in the blossoming of multiperspectivalism.

Multiperspectivalism means appreciating all the perspectives offered by saints in past generations and enriching them, rather than discarding them for the sake of novelty or rebellion. It would be folly, as well as ingratitude, to cast off that tradition by accommodating modernity or postmodernity. In the process, we also may appropriate, in good multiperspectival fashion, insights that arise from common grace within both postmodernism and modernism. But we will do so in submission to Christ the Lord, the absolute God who is in unity with the Father and the Spirit.

9

THE PROLEGOMENA PRINCIPLE: FRAME AND BAVINCK

K. SCOTT OLIPHINT

WE PROPOSE, in this chapter, to suggest that it is John Frame's emphasis, rather than Herman Bavinck's, that more consistently aids the church in order to think biblically about epistemology and theological prolegomena.[1] Specifically, we will first want to make explicit (some of) the principles that Frame asserts in his own epistemology. We will then attempt to answer the question as to whether or not Bavinck's argument for an epistemological realism is consistent with the Reformed theology that Frame sets forth (and, we should note, that Bavinck clearly sets forth in his *Dogmatics*). We will also want to examine whether or not Bavinck's insistence on the Logos as both the subjective and objective ground of knowledge is itself consistent with his realistic epistemology.

Our study below will argue that there is in Herman Bavinck's otherwise most useful analysis of epistemology and theological prolegomena a viral infection—call it Bavinck's bug—that, if it spreads, will serve to undermine the basic foundation of his own Reformed theology. We will also note that Frame's central and clear emphasis on the Word of God as our only *principium*

---

1. For purposes here, I will use *epistemology* and *prolegomena* interchangeably. Differences between the two need not detain us here.

for knowledge will provide the cure for Bavinck's bug. First, however, we need to set out the crux of Frame's epistemology, especially as that epistemology implies a theological prolegomena.

FRAME ON PROLEGOMENA

The first thing on which both Frame and Bavinck would agree would be the universal nature of faith with respect to knowledge. "Faith carries its own evidence; indeed, all knowledge begins with non-demonstrable assumptions."[2] This is the case, in part, because of the nature of ultimate presuppositions:

> Ultimate presuppositions, in that sense, are known intuitively, though they are verified by circular arguments of various sorts. This is true not only of Christianity but of all systems of thought. The human mind is finite; it cannot present an infinitely long argument and give an exhaustive reason for anything. It must, at some point, begin with a faith commitment, *whether in the true God or in an idol.*[3]

This "intuitive" knowledge on which all people depend is knowledge that comes simply by virtue of one's living in the world (which includes living in the presence of God and his revelation). The faith with which we begin, we should note, is itself a subjective condition, inextricably bound up with our constitution as made in the image of God.[4] Important to note here, however, is that Frame delineates the content of the "faith commitment" covenantally—one trusts either the true God or an idol; there is no third way, no third object of faith.

The epistemological/prolegomena question, which will serve to distinguish Frame's approach from Bavinck's, and to cure Bavinck's bug by way of Frame's fix, is this: What principle is rooted in the objective side of our knowledge? A couple of points to note before pursuing Frame's answer to that question. First, we should not suppose that the lines between subjective and objective are drawn too thickly. There are real differences between

---

2. *CWT.*
3. *DKG*, 346.
4. For more on the notion of this faith, see K. Scott Oliphint, "Covenant Faith," in *Justified in Christ: God's Wonderful Plan for Us in Justification*, ed. K. Scott Oliphint (Fearn, Ross-shire, UK: Christian Focus Publications, 2007).

the two, but the two are mutually dependent in important ways.[5] Second, the way in which we articulate the acquisition of knowledge, as well as its essential character, has everything to do with the questions of theological prolegomena.[6]

With respect to our starting point for knowledge, "God's revelation alone is the *pou sto*, our ultimate presupposition, *not reason, sensation, imagination*, etc."[7] That is to say, we begin our thinking and living not, first of all, with reason, sensation, or imagination, but with the revelation of God. Thus, in describing his epistemology, Frame affirms that "it is, of course, an epistemology centered on God's word (in nature and Scripture) and on the illuminating work of the Spirit. In Scripture, God tells us what knowledge is: thinking his thoughts after him."[8] Entailed in this is that "God's word, then, is involved in everything that he does—in his decrees, creation, providence, redemption, and judgment, not only in revelation narrowly defined. He performs all his acts by his speech.[9]

In a review of Winfried Corduan's work on prolegomena, Frame speculates as to why issues of prolegomena are not routinely included in works on systematic theology:

> I have not studied the history of this procedure, but I am sure it bears some relation to the theory that one cannot discuss the basic principles of a discipline from within that discipline. Thus theology cannot describe its nature

5. They are not mutually dependent in every way, given that creation of the world preceded the creation of man. Even there, however, there was a relationship between the Subject—God— and the objective creation.

6. More specifically, according to Muller: "Despite their late appearance and academic origin, however, theological prolegomena address issues that are always present and must always have their effect on doctrinal statement. The production of any theological formula brings with it fundamental questions of the relationship of language to divine truth, of the capability of any human statement to bear the weight of revelation, and of the relationship of statements concerning God to grammatically identical statements concerning the world of sense and experience. . . . Prolegomena merely makes these issues explicit. What is theology? What is the relationship of theology to God's own truth? Where does theology stand among the ways of human knowing? How can a knowledge or wisdom concerning divine things draw on the resources of human reason and human language? What are the necessary and irreducible foundations of theological statement?" Richard A. Muller, *Post-Reformation Reformed Dogmatics: The Rise and Development of Reformed Orthodoxy, ca. 1520 to ca. 1725: Prolegomena to Theology*, 4 vols. (Grand Rapids.: Baker, 2003), 1:86.

7. Frame, "Shorter Writings," in *CWT*.

8. Ibid.

9. *DG*, 471.

and basis. To describe those, we need a higher discipline—philosophy or metatheology or introduction or "prolegomena." Why is such a discipline thought to be necessary? I have never understood this argument. I suspect it relies on metaphors. Some, e.g., say that one cannot survey a field to best advantage from ground level; to do that one must ascend a tower. But intellectual disciplines are not fields and meta-disciplines are not towers. The fact is that the doctrine of Scripture is as much a theological doctrine as is the doctrine of the divine attributes. Same is the doctrine of how we come to know and teach about God, the doctrine of theology. We reach conclusions in these areas by studying Scripture, just as we reach any other theological conclusions. *The idea that some radically different method is needed for "introductory" matters is unwarranted and dangerous; dangerous because the only alternative to exegetical method is autonomous speculation.* And if we allow such speculation at the "introductory" level, where very fundamental matters are discussed, that speculation will infect our entire system.[10]

The insight offered here is helpful with respect to our analysis (below) of the infection of Bavinck's bug. While it cannot perhaps be definitively shown that Bavinck held that issues of prolegomena required a radically different method from that of theology, there is little question that Bavinck affirmed such a thing. The cure for such a methodological infection is, as Frame says, that "we reach conclusions in these areas by studying Scripture, just as we reach any other theological conclusions." Not only so, but we should not allow a methodological separation such that method in theology, specifically, differs, at root, from method, more generally, in science. Where the foundations of method are concerned, what is true for one discipline should be true for them all. So, says Frame, God's presence and revelation permeate all of creation:

> God's word, then, is involved in everything that he does—in his decrees, creation, providence, redemption, and judgment, not only in revelation narrowly defined. He performs all his acts by his speech. Further, God and his word are always present together. Where God is, his word is, and vice versa. Note the many biblical correlations between God's word and his Spirit: Genesis 1:2–3; Psalm 33:6 (cf. 104:30); Isaiah 34:16; 59:21; John 6:63; 16:13; Acts 2:1–4 (the coming of the Spirit leads to Spirit-empowered words); 1 Thessalonians 1:5; 2 Thessalonians 2:2; 2 Timothy 3:16 (the

10. Frame, "Shorter Writings," in *CWT*.

scriptural word is *theopneustos*, coming from the divine breath or spirit); 2 Peter 1:21 (the breath or Spirit of God carries the biblical writers along). The nearness of God is the nearness of the word (Deut. 4:5–8; 30:11–14), and that nearness is the nearness of Christ (Rom. 10:6–8).[11]

Examples and quotations from Frame could be easily multiplied, but this should suffice to make the basic points needed. Those points are (1) that God's revelation provides the foundation for *all* our knowing and living and that (2) because God's revelation is the *principium* for all knowledge, it cannot be the case that some other methodological process can be affirmed as a ground for knowledge. This latter affirmation seems to be a part of the epistemology and prolegomena in Herman Bavinck's thought. If this is indeed the case in Bavinck, we should note, it is Frame's emphasis that will provide the only proper remedy for Bavinck's bug.

Bavinck's Realism

Pertinent to the question of Bavinck's epistemology, and a helpful place with which to begin, is a review, not of the latest translation, but of the original first volume of Bavinck's *Dogmatiek* by Geerhardus Vos. In that review, as Vos attempts to allow Bavinck to "speak in his own words,"[12] Vos says this concerning Bavinck's view of knowledge:

> The Reformed theologians in opposing the Cartesian form of the *ideae innatae*, and in speaking of the mind as *tabula rasa*, did not mean this in the sense of Locke's empiricism. The essence of their gnosiology was, that the human mind always receives the first impulse for acquiring knowledge from the external world. But the nature of the intellect is such, they held, that in thus being impelled to work, it forms of itself involuntarily the fundamental principles and conceptions which are certain *a priori*, and therefore deserve to be called *veritates aeternae*. This, it will be observed, is the same theory of knowledge that has been set forth in this country by the late Dr. McCosh.[13]

---

11. *DG*, 471.

12. Geerhardus Vos, "Book Review, *Gereformeerde Dogmatiek*, Vol. 1," in *Redemptive History and Biblical Interpretation: The Shorter Writings of Geerhardus Vos*, ed. Richard B. Gaffin Jr. (Phillipsburg, NJ: Presbyterian and Reformed, 1980), 484.

13. Ibid., 478.

In other words, to summarize Vos here, the theory of knowledge that Bavinck sets forth in his prolegomena as a Reformed epistemology is "the same theory . . . that has been set forth in this country by the late Dr. McCosh," i.e., Scottish Common Sense Realism.[14]

From a more critical standpoint, Cornelius Van Til, who himself claims Bavinck as one of his primary spiritual and intellectual influences, nevertheless diagnoses the bug in Bavinck's epistemology.

> We note again the failure to distinguish carefully a Christian from the non-Christian epistemology. When he gives the distinguishing marks of the realism he is setting forth, he says no more than that against empiricism it maintains a certain independence of the intellect, while over against rationalism it maintains that the intellect depends to an extent on sensation. Bavinck does to an extent wish to correct Scholasticism, but this correction does not involve a rejection of its principle of commingling Aristotelianism with Christian principles. "The fault of Scholasticism," says Bavinck, "both Protestant and Catholic, lay only in this, that they had done too quickly with observation, and that it thought almost exclusively of the confession as taken up into the books of Euclid, Aristotle, and the Church fathers." Against this position Bavinck once again reiterates the doctrine that all knowledge must begin from observation. The net result of Bavinck's investigation is a moderate realism[15] which seeks on the one hand to avoid the extremes of realism, but on the other hand to avoid the extremes of idealism. It is not a specifically Christian position based upon the presupposition of the existence of the God of Scripture that we have before us in the moderate realism of Bavinck. Yet he himself has told us again and again that dogmatics must live by one *principium* only. It is difficult to see how dogmatics is to live by one principle if it is not the same principle that is to guide our thinking both in theology and in other science. If we are to be true to Bavinck's requirement that there shall be only one principle of interpretation for us, then we shall have to apply that principle when we work out an epistemology no less than when we are engaged in dogmatics proper.[16]

14. For more on McCosh and Common Sense Realism, see, for example, George M. Marsden, *The Soul of the American University: From Protestant Establishment to Established Nonbelief* (New York: Oxford University Press, 1994), 196ff.

15. The difference between realism and moderate realism will be explained below.

16. Cornelius Van Til, *An Introduction to Systematic Theology*, ed. William Edgar (Phillipsburg, NJ: P&R Publishing, 2007), 94–95.

What Van Til says relative to epistemology is exactly what Frame teaches. It is also what Bavinck has affirmed. What, then, is the problem with Bavinck's epistemology? Is it, in fact, consistent with the theology that he himself explicates? Is it the case, we could ask, as both Vos and Van Til seem to indicate, that Bavinck's realism is itself grounded in "common sense" principles (Vos) or in some principle or principles that differ from the one *principium* of the Word of the God of Scripture (Van Til and Frame)?

In order to begin to address these questions, we should first attempt to get straight what Bavinck himself says with respect to his epistemology. The statements themselves can be confusing. There appear to be statements that affirm the necessity of God's revelation as the only *principium* in order for knowledge to be had; but there are also statements that seem not to allow for such necessity in that they affirm other starting points for knowledge. The latter is what provokes Van Til's criticism and what puts Bavinck at odds with Frame's consistently biblical method.

The first place to begin in seeking to put together Bavinck's epistemology is with those statements that more positively set forth the necessity of a revelational *principium*. First of all, with respect to dogmatic method, which includes Scripture, tradition, and consciousness, Bavinck is clear that the principle of *sola Scriptura* must be in place:

> But in the logical order Scripture is the sole foundation (*principium unicum*) of church and theology. . . . Not the church but Scripture is self-authenticating (αὐτόπιστος), the judge of controversies . . . , and its own interpreter (*sui ipsius interpres*). Nothing must be put on a level with Scripture. . . . Scripture alone is the norm and rule of faith and life.[17]

Any method, therefore, of dogmatic theology that seeks to place tradition, or consciousness in general, or anything else on a par with Scripture is forbidden in a Reformed approach to dogmatics. Whatever means other than Scripture dogmatics uses in its task are themselves subordinate to and governed by Scripture itself. This, for Bavinck, is basic, and it is the basic principle outlined by John Frame in numerous places.

There is also a clear articulation, more generally, that God's revelation provides the foundation for all thought and reasoning:

17. Herman Bavinck, *Reformed Dogmatics: Prolegomena*, ed. John Bolt, trans. John Vriend (Grand Rapids: Baker Academic, 2003), 1:86.

Thus, we have discovered three foundations (*principia*): First, God as the essential foundation (*principium essendi*), the source, of theology; next, the external cognitive foundation (*principium cognoscendi externum*), viz., the self-revelation of God, which, insofar as it is recorded in Holy Scripture, bears an instrumental and temporary character; and finally, the internal principle of knowing (*principium cognoscendi internum*), the illumination of human beings by God's Spirit. These three are one in the respect that they have God as author and have as their content one identical knowledge of God. The archetypal knowledge of God in the divine consciousness; the ectypal knowledge of God granted in revelation and recorded in Holy Scripture; and the knowledge of God in the human subject, insofar as it proceeds from revelation and enters into the human consciousness, are all three of them from God. It is God himself who discloses his self-knowledge, communicates it through revelation, and introduces it into human beings. And materially they are one as well, for it is one identical, pure, and genuine knowledge of God, which he has of himself, communicates in revelation, and introduces into the human consciousness.[18]

More specifically with respect to this external and internal foundation, Bavinck is clear that it is the Logos who, externally and internally, grounds any and every attempt to know the world:

> The Logos who shines in the world must also let his light shine in our consciousness. That is the light of reason, the intellect, which, itself originating in the Logos, discovers and recognizes the Logos in things. It is the internal foundation of knowledge (*principium cognoscendi internum*).[19]
>
> Further on, he says: "Construed religiously, it is the Logos himself who through our spirit bears witness to the Logos in the world."[20]

These affirmations are consistent with everything that Frame has himself wanted to assert. Why, then, would Van Til accuse Bavinck of being less than consistent? It may be that Van Til detected distinctions in Bavinck's own formulations that allowed for such an inconsistency. Remember Van Til's point, above: "If we are to be true to Bavinck's requirement that there shall be only one principle of interpretation for us, then we shall have to

18. Ibid., 213–14.
19. Ibid., 233. Bavinck has a very good, concise discussion of the notion and kinds of principia on 210–11.
20. Ibid., 587.

apply that principle when we work out an epistemology no less than when we are engaged in dogmatics proper." Could it be that there is another principle at work in Bavinck, when he sets out his own epistemology, than the one so clearly affirmed above? Could it be that the clear affirmations of a revelational epistemology are more explicit when discussing dogmatics, and less explicit when discussing epistemology more generally? It would appear so.

As noted above, it seems clear that Bavinck allows for no other foundation than revelation when the context is dogmatic theology. He is clear that Reformation theology marked a return to Holy Scripture as the sole foundation of theology.[21] Thus, the only purpose of dogmatics is to set forth the thoughts of God that he himself has spoken in Scripture.[22] And as noted above, even though dogmatic method includes Scripture, tradition, and consciousness, it is *with respect to dogmatic method* that Scripture alone is the ground and foundation.

With respect to knowledge generally, or knowledge that obtains in other theoretical fields, such as science, Bavinck seems to waver on his revelational commitment. To be clear, it is not the case that he sets up a dichotomy between what he says concerning dogmatics and what he says concerning science. But it is without question the case that his analysis of scientific foundations, generally speaking, could easily (and perhaps consistently, of which more below) be interpreted as an argument for a generic, universally recognized epistemological foundation.

For example, at one point Bavinck gives this analysis:

> All life and all knowledge is based on a kind of agreement between subject and object. Human beings are so richly endowed because they are linked with the objective world by a great many extremely divers connections. . . . Now Scripture leads us to view all these human connections with the world religiously and to explain them theistically. . . . But this operation of the Spirit of God assumes a higher form in the intellectual, ethical, and religious life of people. It then takes the form of reason, conscience, and the sense of divinity, which are not inactive abilities but *capacities* that, as a result of stimuli from related phenomena in the outside world, leap into action.[23]

21. Ibid., 78.
22. Ibid., 83.
23. Ibid., 586, my emphasis.

K. Scott Oliphint

Bavinck further maintains that, with respect to this knowledge, "It is the one selfsame Logos who made all things in and outside of human beings. He is before all things, and they still continue jointly to exist through him (John 1:3; Col. 1:15–17)."[24] Whenever we consider the knowledge situation, therefore, says Bavinck, we must give due credit to the reality of the Logos. "Construed religiously, it is the Logos himself who through our spirit bears witness to the Logos in the world."[25]

In speaking of the analogy of the Spirit's work in the hearts of believers and his work in the world more generally, Bavinck notes:

> The objects of human knowledge are all self-attested (αὐτόπιστα); they rest in themselves. Their existence can be recognized but not proven. . . . To prove a thing is to trace the unknown to the known, the uncertain to the certain. . . . "There is no point in arguing against a person who rejects the first principles" (*Contra principia negantem non est disputandum*).[26]

That is to say, there is an analogy between the self-attestation of Scripture and the self-attestation of the objects of human knowledge which, according to Bavinck, "are all self-attested." Our belief in Scripture as the foundation of knowledge is itself "mystical in nature—like the belief in the first principles of the various sciences."[27]

It is in his discussion of "scientific foundations" that Bavinck most clearly lays out his epistemology. As noted above, he affirms that knowledge must be grounded in revelation; the "three *principia*" are themselves rooted in the triune God. However, it is not clear that this "rooting" takes the *principium cognoscendi* as seriously as it should.

Bavinck's bug is explicit when, after a survey of both rationalism and empiricism, he commits himself to realism with respect to epistemology. In this, he follows many of the Reformed, as well as Aquinas.

> The intellect is bound to the body and thus to the cosmos and therefore cannot become active except by and on the basis of the senses. From the outset the intellect is pure potentiality, a blank page (*tabula rasa*) without any content, and is only activated, aroused to actuality, by the sensible

24. Ibid.
25. Ibid., 587.
26. Ibid., 589.
27. Ibid., 590.

210

world. The primary impetus therefore comes from the sensible world; it impinges upon the human mind, arouses it, urges it to action. But the moment the intellect is activated, it immediately and spontaneously works in its own way and according to its own nature. . . . Since these concepts that are certain are a priori and precede all reasoning and proof, they deserve to be called eternal truths (*veritates alternae*).[28]

Consistent with the Thomistic and (much of the) Reformed tradition, therefore, argues Bavinck, we should avoid the extremes of rationalism and empiricism, and opt for a middle way, a way that takes the best of both and combines them. Realism, then, differs from rationalism in that it has a special view of the intellect, and from empiricism in that it recognizes that it must abstract from the things perceived the "logical element naturally inherent in those things. . . . Hence the starting point of all human knowledge is perception."[29]

It seems Bavinck is content to establish an epistemology of realism, but a realism that is grounded and founded in the triune God. In an attempt further to explicate the "mechanism" of concept-formation in a realistic epistemology, Bavinck takes his cue, at least in large part, from Aquinas.

Realism . . . was doubtlessly correct in assuming the reality of universal concepts, not in a Platonic or ontological sense prior to the thing itself (*ante rem*), but in an Aristotelian sense in the thing itself (*in re*) and therefore also in the human subsequent to the thing itself (*in mente hominis post rem*). The universality we express in a concept does not exist as such, as a universal, apart from us. In every specimen of a genus, particularly individualized and specialized, however, it has its basis in things and is abstracted from it and expressed in a concept by the activity of the intellect. So, in entertaining concepts we are not distancing ourselves from reality but we increasingly approximate it.[30]

The question to be asked is: Given Bavinck's analysis, is this, indeed, in the end, a revelational epistemology, or is it the germ of a disease that could infect the entire body?

28. Ibid., 225.
29. Ibid., 226.
30. Ibid., 321.

In a fascinating and thoughtful attempt to argue against *sola Scriptura* as sufficient for an evangelical theological method,[31] John Bolt uses Bavinck's own theological method (incorporating Bavinck's bug) as an example.[32] Bolt wants to argue that "a full and proper Christian theology must have an explicit epistemology that attempts to explain universal human experience. That is to say, Christian theology must incorporate an explicit metaphysic."[33] In his attempt to incorporate what he sees as the best of Bavinck's epistemology, he does affirm, with Bavinck, that realism has its roots in the triune God and activity of the Logos. Specifically, as he concludes his article, and in response to what he calls the (insufficient) biblical-theological approach to theology, he notes:

> As an alternative, I appealed to Herman Bavinck's Christian realism, the epistemology that is rooted in the creation of all things, including the human logos by the divine Logos. All truth is from God; we participate in the truth to the degree that our intellects adequately form concepts that correspond to the things of this world including our experience of God. . . . Concretely this means that while the Bible is the final source and norm for Christian theology, the knowledge of God obtained by natural reason, reflected in

31. A significant point of clarification is needed, which cannot be pursued here, in Bolt's assertion of *sola Scriptura* as a theological method. Historically, *sola Scriptura* was thought to be a foundational principle of authority (i.e., the formal principle of the Reformation), which itself would ground methodology. "It is, thus, entirely anachronistic to view the *sola Scriptura* of Luther and his contemporaries as a declaration that all of theology ought to be constructed anew, without reference to the church's tradition of interpretation, by the lonely exegete confronting the naked text." Muller, *Post-Reformation Reformed Dogmatics*, 2:63. Recognizing different degrees of authority within the church, *sola Scriptura* was meant to highlight the fact that "Scripture alone is worthy of faith (αὐτόπιστος) and the rule of faith." Ibid., 104. This may not be pertinent to what Bolt intends to argue, but just how *sola Scriptura* is, historically, thought by him to be itself a methodology is not clearly articulated.

32. So, says, Bolt, "when one considers that our modern and so-called postmodern world is characterized by a radical questioning of the very idea of God as well as a growing epistemological relativism, it should be apparent that Christian theology which seeks to tell the truth about God cannot afford the luxury of biblicism. It must face the truth question about God head on. To see that this is not a lamentable concession but a richer, more thorough approach to theological work, let us consider the example of Herman Bavinck as one who explicitly rejects using *sola Scriptura* as a theological method." John Bolt, "*Sola Scriptura* as an Evangelical Theological Method?" in *Reforming or Conforming? Post-Conservative Evangelicals and the Emerging Church*, ed. Gary L. W. Johnson and Ron N. Gleason (Wheaton, IL: Crossway, 2008), 78.

33. Ibid. These two statements seem confused, but we need not pursue that here. To say that one must have an explicit epistemology does not entail that one must have an explicit metaphysic, at least not without making an explicit connection between the two.

the religions of the world, as well as legitimate, reasonable inferences from biblical truth, are all part of the theologian's thesaurus of truth.[34]

There is more that could and needs to be said with respect to Bavinck's approach, and a bit more will be said below. For the present, however, some critical questions loom large. Perhaps we can work our way from the more specific to the general, in terms of Bavinck's realism.

First, specifically, is it the case that a realistic approach to universals, guided by Aquinas, can move us in the direction of a Christian epistemology? Although Thomas's approach to epistemology can, in places, be a helpful guide through the morass of current-day discussions on the topic,[35] questions remain with respect to the role of universals in his epistemology.

As Aquinas is forced to wrestle with the problem of universals in chapter 3 of *On Being and Essence*, he adopts what has come to be called a "moderate realism." Unlike Plato, the realist, who affirmed the actual existence of all universals, or Roscelin (and following him and Aquinas, Ockham), who saw the universals as having no real foundation in reality, Aquinas sought to show that the universals did indeed exist in the mind. Unlike the nominalists, these universals had their foundation in the existence of the particulars. All of this Bavinck thus far affirms.

Aquinas further delineates three different methods of scientific inquiry, each of which was related to its particular task.[36] There was, first of all, the method of natural science (or physics). Herein, says Aquinas, the physical scientist is required to abstract the universal from the particular. Physical science deals with those things in reality that cannot be understood apart from "sensible matter." The first level of abstraction, which pertains to physical science, must deal exclusively with individuating matter. "For example, it is necessary to include flesh and bones in the definition of a man." The second degree of abstraction deals not with sensible matter, but with so-called intelligible matter and is the method of the mathematician. Mathematics deals, according to Aquinas, with quantity, which, although dependent on matter for its being, is not dependent on matter for its being understood, as is the case in physical science. "This is the case with lines and numbers."

---

34. Ibid., 89.
35. For one analysis of such help, see K. Scott Oliphint, *Reasons for Faith: Philosophy in the Service of Theology* (Phillipsburg, NJ: P&R Publishing, 2006), chaps, 7, 8.
36. What follows is taken from Thomas Aquinas, *The Division and Methods of the Sciences*, trans. Armand Mauer (Toronto: The Pontifical Institute of Medieval Studies, 1963), 8ff.

That which is abstracted in this science is not sensible matter but intelligible matter which can be understood conceptually, quite apart from its existence in reality, although it can never exist apart from the matter itself.

Third, and most important for our purposes, is the science of metaphysics. It was Aristotle who maintained that metaphysical science alone exists for its own sake. Like Aristotle, Aquinas seems to see the science of metaphysics, what Aquinas calls theology or divine science, as the first philosophy. In metaphysics we reach the third level of abstraction, which, unlike the previous two, is not dependent on sensible matter, either for its being or for being understood. This third level could be called separation. Herein the mind considers being itself or being as being, and (here is the crucial point) it can so exist in reality. "There are objects of speculative knowledge that do not depend upon matter for their being, because they can exist without matter." He then goes on to give examples of such things: God, angels, substance, potency, act, one, many, etc. Such things may, at times, exist in matter but need not do so. The science of metaphysics, therefore, is the science that deals specifically with being as being and consequently with the relation that obtains between being and things.

For Aquinas, being was act in distinction from essence, which was potential existence or potency. Being, by definition, was pure actuality. Thus, Aquinas saw existence as at the root of the real. It is the one attribute or characteristic that is common to all things and thus is, in Aquinas's system, a transcendental notion, i.e., it transcends the limitations and perfections of any and every thing. Aquinas's metaphysics, then, begins with the primacy of existence over essence. In this, it has been called an "existential," in distinction from an "essentialistic," metaphysic (the latter of which would be more in line with Aristotle). It is existence that confers on an essence its act of existing. Aquinas seeks to delineate this, very simply, by asserting that we can know what a thing is without asserting its actual existence. Because we can conceptualize, for example, a unicorn without asserting its actual existence, there must be a distinction between a thing's essence, in this case a unicorn, and its existence.

Given Aquinas's distinction between existence and essence, he seeks to show that every "thing" participates in its received act of "to be" to the extent that its respective essence permits. This is the Aristotelian potency-limiting-act principle in natural philosophy translated by Aquinas into the science of metaphysics. In Thomas's metaphysics, potentiality limits actuality.

214

This is to say, essence is potential existence. It is not in itself existence and therefore does not have existence in itself as essence. When the perfection of being, which is inherently unlimited, confers existence on an essence, that which is unlimited and transcendental becomes limited and actual only to the degree that a thing's essence will allow.

In the realm of metaphysics, Aquinas sought to consider being qua being. Yet as Maritain has said, it is not enough, in Thomistic metaphysics, simply to say "being." Rather, we must have the intellectual perception of the inexhaustible and incomprehensible reality of this being.[37] What Maritain, in his attempt to be true to Aquinas, is saying is that whereas one must begin with sense experience, and whereas our senses communicate to us imperfectly, it remains for the intellect to perfect and to organize, to "universalize" that which is diverse. Thus, as we perceive that all things present to sense exist, and as we understand that it is possible to know what a thing is without making judgment as to its existence, we come to see existence as a transcendental notion distinct from essence. Thus, according to Aquinas, a being exists to the degree that its essence permits.

Because Aquinas (and Bavinck following him) seeks to begin with sense experience alone, he is never able to "see" being except as diverse, interspersed throughout different things in which essence and existence come together. A truly transcendental notion must include a real totality such that one is able to allow for both unity and diversity in reality itself. Aquinas's transcendental notion of being allows only for unity (of being) in the intellect, and diversity (of being) in reality, in things. The problem that we come to, therefore, is the epistemology problem.

How does Aquinas claim to know a thing such that he can avoid the dilemma of both Parmenides and Heraclitus? For Aquinas, truth and knowledge are the adequation of the immanence in act of our thought with that which exists outside our thought.[38] Because Aquinas (again, we hear Bavinck echoing this) associated the intellect with unity and sense experience with diversity, he saw all knowledge as, by nature, abstract. Herein he follows Aristotle. Because, in knowledge, the intellect abstracts from sensible reality that which does not exist in that reality as such—i.e., as abstracted—we are left with the problem of how one can know that that which is abstracted is of the character of that from

---

37. Jacques Maritain, *Existence and the Existent*, new ed. (New York: Pantheon Books, 1964), 30.
38. Ibid., 11.

which it is abstracted. Aquinas's answer, following Aristotle, was to refer to the hylomorphic theory. Whereas Plato believed that the real was that which was universal—i.e., the forms—Aristotle sought to "bring the forms down" into the matter itself. When one wants to know an object, therefore, the form is abstracted from the matter and, though existing in the mind as immaterial and immobile, and in reality as material and mobile, the form itself was analogous to, though not identical with, that from which it was abstracted. The form, for Aquinas, was that in the real (*in re*) which makes knowledge of it possible. Yet in order to maintain his distinction, Aquinas had to maintain that that which is abstracted is not in reality as such. The problem is now coming to the fore and is summarized for us by Aquinas himself.

> Nevertheless, it cannot be said that the character universal belongs to nature so understood, because commonality and unity belong to the character universal. . . . For if commonality were included in the notion of man, commonality would be found whenever humanity was found. But this is false, because in Socrates no commonality is found. On the contrary, whatever is in him is individuated.[39]

This is the problem. That which is in the mind, i.e., the universal, is *not in* individuating matter. The universal, however, can indeed exist in things, but only as individualized. Individuating matter can exist in the mind only as "common matter," or universalized form. Wolterstorff has expressed the problem in this way:

> So also, humanity is individualized in the things and universal in the mind. Thus, when humanity is in the mind, there is something which is individualized which is in the mind. But it does not follow that humanity is universal in the things, or that there is something in the things which is universal in the things. And it does not follow that humanity is individualized in the mind, or that there is something in the mind which is individualized in the mind. To say that humanity is individualized, is incomplete; it is individualized in the things. And to say that humanity is universal, is incomplete; it is universal in the mind.[40]

39. Thomas Aquinas, "On Being and Essence," in *Selected Writings of St. Thomas Aquinas*, ed. Thomas Goodwin (New York: Bobbs-Merrill, 1965), 48.
40. Nicholas Wolterstorff, *On Universals: An Essay in Ontology* (Chicago and London: University of Chicago Press, 1970), 146.

Aquinas's epistemological problem as related to his metaphysics becomes acute at this point. How can that which is individualized in things be common in the mind and still be true to reality? We must keep in mind that Aquinas is not here affirming that, for example, human nature has many instances, but rather, that it can be many or zero. To have many instances of human nature is to have that nature in common.[41] Yet Aquinas affirms that "human nature itself exists in the intellect in abstraction from all individuating conditions."[42] Therefore, once that which is universal in the mind is "applied" to individuating matter, it loses its universality such that the nature of Socrates is entirely different from the nature of Plato.

We could summarize the above discussion by saying that Aquinas, though he sought for similarity in forms between that which is individuated in matter and that which is in the mind, nevertheless failed to go beyond pure univocism and pure equivocism. The result is a kind of rationalism/irrationalism. That which is in the mind is common, yet that which is common in the mind is different in things. In other words, the meaning of the term *human nature*, if spoken of in its universal mode, is univocal. The same term, however, if spoken of in its individuated mode, is diverse, equivocal, never univocal.

What might Bavinck say to all of this? How indeed does he affirm the connection between that which is universal (in the mind) and that which is diverse (in things)? Fortunately for us, we need not speculate. Bavinck seems to be, at least implicitly, aware of the problem and provides a counterpoint. First, he says:

> The universality we express in a concept does not exist as such, as a universal, apart from us. In every specimen of a genus, particularly individualized and specialized, however it has its basis in things and is abstracted from it and expressed in a concept by the activity of the intellect [and here he cites Aquinas]. It seems strange, even amazing, that, converting mental representations into concepts and processing these again in accordance with the laws of thought, we should obtain results that correspond to reality. Still, one who abandons this conviction is lost.[43]

41. Ibid., 148.
42. Aquinas, "On Being and Essence," 48.
43. Bavinck, *Reformed Dogmatics: Prolegomena*, 1:231.

Thus, there is a kind of "impossibility of the contrary" notion asserted. Unless we hold to this kind of construct of human thought and knowing, we are lost. But Bavinck goes further:

> But the conviction can, therefore, rest only in the belief that it is the same Logos who created both the reality outside of us and the laws of thought within us and who produced an organic connection and correspondence between the two. . . . But insofar as things also exist logically, have come forth from thought, and are based in thought (John 1:3; Col. 1:15), they are also apprehensible and conceivable by the human mind.[44]

So Bavinck is explicit where Thomas, as far as I can tell, is not. Bavinck affirms that the connection between the universal and the particular is produced by the Logos.

Consistent with the notion of universals and particulars with respect to knowledge is Thomas's principle of participation, which Bavinck seems content to adopt. So Bavinck explains his amenability to Thomas this way:

> Says Thomas: just as we look into the natural world, not by being in the sun ourselves, but by the light of the sun that shines on us, so neither do we see things in the divine being but by the light that, originating in God shines in our own intellect. Reason in us is that divine light; it is not itself the divine logos, but it participates in it. To be (*esse*), to live (*vivere*) and to understand (*intelligere*) is the prerogative of God in respect of his being (*per essentiam*), ours in respect of participation (*per participationem*).

In order to get straight what Bavinck, following Thomas, means by "participation," a word about Thomas's view should help clarify.

Thomas proposes two types of principles of participation, both of which relate themselves to his notion of analogy. Neither of these is defined as such by Thomas, but they clearly reside in his writings. The first type is what has been called the "analogy of proper proportionality." Aquinas seeks in the analogy of proper proportionality to distinguish between the same attributes in different things.[45] He denies univocal predication on the basis

---

44. Ibid. Note Bavinck's reference to John 1:3, more of which below.

45. Aquinas's doctrine of analogy is found, among other places, in Thomas Aquinas, *Summa Theologiae: Latin Text, English Translation, Introduction, Notes, Appendices & Glossary*, ed. Thomas Gilby, 60 vols. (London and New York: Eyre & Spottiswoode and McGraw-Hill Book Company,

of God's coterminous character.[46] Because that which is ascribed to creatures or creation is ascribed in a divided and particular way, and because the same ascription would be simple and universal in God (because God is what he thinks and thinks what he is), such ascription to both cannot be univocal. But Aquinas also must deny equivocal predication.[47] There is indeed a certain likeness of creation to its Creator, though such likeness, as was said, cannot be univocal. Equivocation would show us that even though one name is predicated of several things, we cannot infer from one of those things the knowledge of the other because there is, by definition, no point of reference. We could, therefore, understand nothing of God by creation, which for Aquinas is patently false.

Thus, Aquinas proposed his doctrine of analogy. That which is predicated of God and man actually exists in both to the extent that their respective essences permit. To say that "God is good" and that "man is good" is to say that God is good in proportion to his received act of "to be" (which in God is his essence, of which more below) and that man is good with respect to his potential existence. Or to use another example, God knows as deity, man knows as man. The proportion that obtains between being and essence determines the truth of that which is predicated of each thing.

At this point we can see something here of Aquinas's so-called scale of being. Every thing is limited in being according to its essence. Every characteristic of a thing is further limited as to the proportion that obtains between its being and its essence. Thus, potential existence limits the received act of "to be" (existence) and the combination of the two in some thing limits the attributes and perfections of that which is. We could say, then, that angels know as angels are, men know as men are, and there is a proportion (1) between knowledge in angels as they exist and (2) between knowledge in angels and knowledge in men.[48] Knowledge, therefore, cannot be predicated in the same identical way when speaking of an angel's knowledge and a man's knowledge, the existences of such being proportional to their respective essences.

1964), 1.13, and, for our purposes here, in Thomas Aquinas, *Summa Contra Gentiles*, trans. Charles J. O'Neil, 4 vols. (Notre Dame and London: Notre Dame University Press, 1957), 1.124.

46. See ibid., 1, chap. 32.

47. See ibid., 1, chap. 33.

48. G. B. Phelan, *Saint Thomas and Analogy* (Milwaukee: Marquette University Press, 1941), 24.

So far, however, the type of analogical "participation" of which Bavinck speaks does not obtain. There is a tension internal to this Thomistic doctrine that has caused some controversy among his interpreters but is, nevertheless, crucial to his metaphysics. Simply stated (and on this all seem to agree), the analogy of proper proportionality cannot apply to God and his relations to the world. The reason for this is that the analogy of proper proportionality derives its basis from the proportion that obtains between essence and existence. But in God no such proportion obtains. God is Pure Act. His essence is his existence. Unlike any other thing, it belongs to the very essence of God to exist. How, then, can a real analogy be predicated of, for example, men, in which every act of existence is limited by essence, and God, in which essence and existence are identical and completely exhaustive one of the other? It seems that there must be a second kind of analogy introduced that will account for One in whom essence and existence are identical.

Such an analogy has been called "analogy of intrinsic attribution" and can be seen, for example, in the following statement from Aquinas:

> Such words apply to God and creatures neither univocally nor equivocally but by what I call analogy (or proportion). This is the way a word like healthy applies to organisms (in a primary sense) and to diets (as causing health) or complexions (as displaying it). Whatever we say of God and of creatures we say in virtue of the relation creatures bear to God as to the source and cause in which all their creaturely perfections pre-exist in a more excellent way. In language, the equivocal presupposes the univocal. But in causation the univocal presupposes the non-univocal. Non-univocal causes cause entire species, in the way the sun helps generate the whole human race. Univocal causes cause individuals of the species (in the way men reproduce men). Causes of individuals presuppose causes of the species, which are not univocal yet not wholly equivocal either, since they are expressing themselves in their effects. We could call them analogical. In language too all univocal terms presuppose the non-univocal analogical use of the term being.[49]

Note the absence (conceptually, not terminologically) of any proportionality in the description above. Such is the case because Aquinas is now

49. Thomas Aquinas, *Summa Theologiae: A Concise Translation*, trans. Timothy McDermott (Westminster, MD: Christian Classics, 1989), 32.

attempting to do justice to analogical knowledge with respect to the creator. This analogy of intrinsic attribution, therefore, has as its basis not proportionality but *causality*. The relation of creature to God in the quote above is a causal relation, yet is proposed as an analogical relationship. Because the definition of potential existence is that which makes a thing what it is, what is of the essence of a thing must be possessed fully by that thing. For example, it is impossible for man to be partly human. It follows, then, for Aquinas, that existence is not intrinsic to created being and therefore must be caused by one in whom essence and existence are identical. The analogy of intrinsic attribution becomes, then, in one sense, the basis for analogy of proper proportionality. Analogy of intrinsic attribution, then, will assure us that between limited beings of our direct experience, in whom there is a real relation between essence and existence, and a conceivable being in whom there is no such real relation, but identity of essence and existence, there is still real similarity. By our analogy of proper proportionality we can then assert that this latter being is actually intrinsically possessed, in an unlimited way, of all those perfections that we found proportionately in finite beings of our actual experience, with an assurance that only an analogy of attribution can provide.[50]

All of this is simply to say that if Bavinck affirms the Thomistic notion of the relationship of knowing with respect to God and man, what he is in reality affirming is (to oversimplify) that God is the cause of it. Our "participation" in knowledge, therefore, between God and man is rooted in the fact that the God who knows also causes his human creatures to know as well. As Bavinck states it, again following Aquinas, our reason is the light that participates in the divine Logos; it participates by virtue of the causal relationship.

One final, critical point needs consideration. The more general point, highlighted by the review of Vos, with respect to Bavinck's realism, is that it "is the same theory of knowledge that has been set forth in this country by the late Dr. McCosh." That is, Bavinck's realism is, if not identical with, certainly within the same family of Common Sense Realism.

Without moving too far afield, we can perhaps summarize the tenets of such an approach by way of its founder, Thomas Reid. According to Reid, a philosophy of common sense has at least the following four characteristics.

50. Charles A. Hart, *Thomistic Metaphysics: An Inquiry into the Act of Existing* (Englewood Cliffs, NJ: Prentice-Hall, 1959), 42.

First, it is "purely the gift of heaven," not learned or acquired by education.[51] Second, it is not merely a practical gift, but has a theoretical or speculative focus as well—not only does it make us "capable of acting with common prudence in the conduct of life"; it makes us "capable of discovering what is true and what is false in matters that are self-evident" when they are "distinctly apprehended." Third, the possession of such common sense entitles us "to the denomination of reasonable creatures." Fourth, and most important, Reid argues that common sense, and common sense alone, judges self-evident truths.[52]

According to Reid,

> we ascribe to reason two offices, or two degrees. The first is to judge of things self-evident; the second to draw conclusions that are not self-evident from those that are. The first of these is the province, and the sole province of common sense; and therefore it coincides with reason in its whole extent, and is only another name for one branch or one degree of reason.[53]

It is important to notice here that what Reid describes is (at least a version of) what has come to be called classical foundationalism. Classical foundationalism asserts that there are two kinds of beliefs—those that are self-evident (and then some would include other kinds of beliefs such as evident to the senses, incorrigible, etc.), and those that are inferred from the former.[54]

If it is indeed the case that Bavinck's epistemology is a realism, which itself is in the neighborhood of Reid's approach, then there are serious questions that need to be asked.[55] Perhaps the best critique of a Reidian approach

51. Thomas Reid, *Essays on the Powers of the Human Mind; to Which Are Added, an Essay on Quantity, and an Analysis of Aristotle's Logic* (London: Printed for Thomas Tegg; R. Griffin and Co., 1827), 276.
52. Ibid., 289.
53. Ibid., 276.
54. This brings up an entire contemporary discourse that cannot be pursued here. Alvin Plantinga has developed an ingenious and fascinating epistemological method that has, at its root, a Reidian approach to knowledge. In its initial stages, Plantinga designated his approach as a "Reformed epistemology," and considered himself to be in the general territory of the approaches of Calvin, Kuyper, Bavinck, and Barth. For more on this, see K. Scott Oliphint, "Epistemology and Christian Belief," *WTJ* 63, 1 (Spring 2001): 151–82; K. Scott Oliphint, "The Old New Reformed Epistemology," in *Revelation and Reason: New Essays in Reformed Apologetics*, ed. K. Scott Oliphint and Lane G. Tipton (Phillipsburg, NJ: P&R Publishing, 2007).
55. The relationship of Aquinas's views, affirmed by Bavinck, and Reidianism need not detain us here. Suffice it to say that Thomas's notions of separation and participation delineate the more

to epistemology can be found not in a critique of epistemology per se, but rather in a critique of an apologetic approach that, it is argued, has its roots deeply embedded into Reid's common sense philosophy.

In his excellent article "The Collapse of American Evangelical Academia,"[56] George Marsden attempts to show the (partial) historical progression in which scholarship has divorced itself from Christianity, beginning in the eighteenth[57] and into the nineteenth centuries. One of the key elements in this progression was the adoption (as well as the consequent failure) in evangelical apologetics of Reid's Common Sense philosophy. The primary reason for this failure, according to Marsden, was that it was never able to provide a ground or foundation for its most basic principles; it was never able to account for its understanding of "common sense" itself.

As Marsden follows the historical progression up to the middle of the nineteenth century, he notes the inability of evangelical apologetics to deal with the destructive elements of Darwinism. Marsden's central question, given such an inability, is this: "What . . . about this midnineteenth-century American evangelical apologetic made it particularly vulnerable to onslaughts of the scientific revolution associated with Darwinism?"[58] Now, the "midnineteenth-century American evangelical apologetic" of which Marsden speaks is that promoted by, among others, Mark Hopkins, Archibald Alexander, Charles Hodge, and B. B. Warfield. With regard to the approaches of these men, says Marsden, "Common-Sense philosophy was the starting point."[59]

An apologetic with its roots in Reid's Common Sense philosophy means that one would begin (and there is significant affinity with Plantinga's views on the matter) with the "immediate, noninferential beliefs . . . as Reid proposed, such as the existence of the self, the existence of other personal and rational beings, the existence of the material world, the relationship of

---

objective side of knowledge (i.e., form/matter and causality), while Reidianism highlights the more subjective side (i.e., common sense).

56. Ironically, this article, which provides a substantial refutation to Plantinga's Reidianism, is found in George Marsden, "The Collapse of American Evangelical Academia," in *Faith and Rationality*, ed. Alvin Plantinga and Nicholas Wolterstorff (Notre Dame and London: University of Notre Dame Press, 1983).

57. It is interesting to note that Marsden sees Jonathan Edwards as the only one among the specified group who saw the necessity of grounding common sense beliefs in biblical revelation. See ibid., 247.

58. Ibid., 241.

59. Ibid., 235.

cause and effect, the continuity of past and present . . ." These were called, by Reid, "principles of common-sense."[60] In defending Christianity, those who adopted this philosophy began by attempting to show how the basic truths and principles of Christianity could fit within the already established truths of common sense. In other words, they would argue, belief in God can fit with other common sense beliefs that we all already have (which, we should note, is just another way to phrase Plantinga's argument for theistic belief as properly basic).

Without reproducing Marsden's penetrating article, we should note carefully his analysis of the failure of the Reidian (via Hopkins, et al.) approach. As Hodge (following Reid) remarked in stating his assumptions, common sense truths were "given in the constitution of our nature." Having been so purposely designed, they could be relied on with perfect security. This is because Reid himself argued that it is possible to establish once for all a universal code of agreed-upon common sense principles.[61] So, asserted Hodge, the design of nature was assumed to involve the creation of a single universal human nature. Hence the presumption made by Hodge and others was that common sense principles were universal and unalterable.

But there are serious problems with Reid's assumption. For example, when Darwinism came on the scene, one of its most serious challenges was that it could retain its evolutionary principle without recourse to theism. The problem was not so much that Darwinism needed atheism, which would have been easier (because more explicit) to deal with, but rather that Darwinism needed only agnosticism. In other words, it was not that Darwinism had to contend, "There is no God, but there is design," but only, "We see design in everything, though we are not sure whether or not God exists," which is far less radical (and thus more challenging) than blatant atheism. So Darwinism challenged Christian theism's contention of the certainty of God's existence by postulating agnosticism along with a thesis for design. Tragically, those who adopted Reid's philosophy could only respond by positing that Darwin's position excluded an intel-

60. Ibid.
61. Ibid., 243. Plantinga has not gone so far as Reid in assuming that there is a universal code of principles. Some, however, have seen that such is exactly what Plantinga must affirm with regard to theistic beliefs if he wants to include them in the so-called paradigm cases of properly basic beliefs. See Mark S. McLeod, "The Analogy Argument for the Proper Basicality of Belief in God," *International Journal for Philosophy of Religion* 21 (1987): 101–38.

ligent Designer, which was all too obvious even to need asserting.[62] As Marsden points out, all that Hodge (for example) could do in the face of Darwinism was assert that large parts of the population still believed in an intelligent Designer. What, then, would happen to this "defense" when the next generation would show belief in an intelligent Designer to be far from universal?

Most damaging to the philosophy of common sense, therefore, and, according to Marsden, the fatal blow to Reidianism, was the nineteenth-century apologetic responses to the introduction of Darwinism. Marsden summarized the fatal blow this way: "Common sense could not settle a dispute over what was a matter of common sense."[63]

Common sense philosophy, therefore, when tried in the fire of apologetic methodology, and thus also of epistemology, failed in its attempt to defend the truth of Christianity in the face of a hostile science. In other words, the problem with a strict Reidian approach to epistemology is that there is no way, no method or mode, by which one might be able to determine just what beliefs are common and what beliefs are not. One man's properly basic belief, therefore, could easily be another man's irrationality. How might we address this problem?

Given Bavinck's (good and proper) appeal to the Logos as the fundamental principle of knowledge, we need, at least initially, to attempt to discern what the Logos principle is biblically in order, further, to ascertain whether that principle is consistently applied in Bavinck. If we couple this truth with Paul's similar affirmations in Romans 1:18ff., we can begin to see

---

62. Marsden, "Collapse," 243–44.

63. Plantinga was not unaware of this problem. In assessing how we might find criteria sufficient to determine which beliefs are properly basic and which are not, Plantinga says: "And hence the proper way to arrive at such a criterion is, broadly speaking, inductive. We must assemble examples of beliefs and conditions such that the former are obviously properly basic on the latter, and examples of beliefs and conditions such that the former are obviously not properly basic in the latter. We must then frame hypotheses as to the necessary and sufficient conditions of proper basicality and test these hypotheses by reference to those examples." Alvin Plantinga, "Rationality and Religious Belief," in *Contemporary Philosophy of Religion*, ed. Stephen M. Cahn and David Shatz (New York: Oxford University Press, 1982), 276. At least one of the reasons for this is that common sense beliefs were thought to function as principia, i.e., basic and fundamental principles of knowledge itself. But it was "common" knowledge that common sense beliefs were only generally common and not absolutely so. Therefore, there was no criterion by which to determine which views were and which were not "common sense." Or, to say it another way, since these beliefs were thought to be on the level of principia, there was no way to give a rationale for such common sense beliefs.

why an epistemology of realism, even if a Christianized version of realism, is insufficient as an application of the Logos principle in epistemology.

Two points of relevance need to be stated here with respect to Paul's teaching in the opening section of Romans.[64] First, Paul is clear that what all people have by virtue of God's natural revelation is *knowledge of God*, even in the midst of a sin-darkened world (cf. Rom. 1:18, 20–21, 23). There is no hint in Paul's discussion that people simply have a *capacity* for such knowledge,[65] or that the knowledge of God is only for those who reason and extrapolate in a certain way. Second, this knowledge that we have is, by all accounts, a *universal* knowledge, and it is *knowledge*. That is to say, Paul is establishing the fact that, whatever else may be true about people who remain in their sins, they are not, nor have they ever been, ignorant of the One against whom they continue to sin (Rom. 1:32). As Frame says:

> Because God is Lord, He is not only knowable but known to all (Rom. 1:21). The "agnostic" who says that he does not know if God exists is deceiving himself and may be seeking to deceive others. God's covenantal presence is with all His works, and therefore it is inescapable (Ps. 139). Furthermore, all things are under God's control, and *all knowledge, as we will see, is a recognition of divine norms for truth; it is a recognition of God's authority. Therefore in knowing anything, we know God.* Even those without the Scriptures have this knowledge: they know God, they know their obligations to Him (Rom. 1:32), and they know the wrath that is on them because of their disobedience (Rom. 1:18).[66]

This knowledge that we all have, by virtue of God's activity of revealing himself, is of such a nature that, if we die in our sins, we are able to offer no defense[67] for our rejection of him. Thus, the knowledge we have of God is clear and is understood by all people (v. 20). This is the case, we should note, because we are all made in his image, and thus remain in a covenant

64. For more on Romans 1, see K. Scott Oliphint, "A Primal and Simple Knowledge," in *A Theological Guide to Calvin's Institutes: Essays and Analysis*, ed. David Hall and Peter A. Lillback (Phillipsburg, NJ: P&R Publishing, 2008); K. Scott Oliphint, "The Clear and Distinct Knowledge of God," previously published at http://www.ref21.org.; K. Scott Oliphint, "The Irrationality of Unbelief," in *Revelation and Reason: New Essays in Reformed Apologetics*, ed. K. Scott Oliphint and Lane G. Tipton (Phillipsburg, NJ: P&R Publishing, 2007), 59–73.

65. Note again Bavinck, *Reformed Dogmatics: Prolegomena*, 1:586, where he speaks of reason, conscience, and the sense of divinity as capacities that all of us have.

66. *DKG* 18, my emphasis.

67. The word Paul uses in verse 20, typically translated as "without excuse," is ἀναπολογήτους.

relationship with him (either as *covenant*-breakers, in Adam, or *covenant*-keepers, in Christ).

All of this, Bavinck seems to affirm in places. But the affirmation of this surely carries implications that would destroy Bavinck's bug; it would disallow a realistic epistemology for the following reasons. First, though Bavinck wants to maintain that anyone not accepting the "first principles" of knowledge cannot engage in a dialogue about such things (*Contra principia negantem non est disputandum*), surely even a negation, even if in theory, of common sense principles has meaning only against the background of the knowledge of God that itself can never be erased. There is, therefore, a principle *of knowledge* (not of a capacity for such) that is the epistemological bedrock of anything else that is either affirmed or denied. Second, if we follow the teaching of what Paul affirms in Romans 1:18ff., it must be the case that the knowledge of God that comes to us by way of activity of the second person of the Trinity, as creator and revealer, *alone* must be *principium cognoscendi internum* of every person. Bavinck affirms this as well, but note his language (in places):

> We need eyes in order to see. . . . The Logos who shines in the world must also let his light shine in our consciousness. That is the light of reason, the intellect, which, itself originating in the Logos, discovers and recognizes the Logos in things. It is the internal foundation of knowledge (*principium cognoscendi internum*).[68]

Here Bavinck seems to affirm that what the Logos gives with respect to his "light" is the intellect, more abstractly conceived, so that we are able to recognize the Logos in things.

The confusion in Bavinck may be this: it seems that in the majority of cases, Bavinck attributes to the Logos not specifically the *principium cognoscendi*, but the *principium essendi*, in much the same way as Thomas Reid did. That is, if what we say about the Logos is that he is the originator of the intellect and of reason, or that (as Reid says) our "first principles" of reasoning "are the gift of heaven," all we have said thus far is that God, or the Logos, is the *principium essendi* of knowledge. He is the one who is the essential foundation or source, the *cause* of the knowledge that we have.

68. Bavinck, *Reformed Dogmatics*, 1:233.

This, we can now see from our discussion above of Aquinas and his principle of participation (with which Bavinck seems to agree), is true enough. God controls "whatsoever comes to pass," and thus is the one who ordains all things. But this is not a sufficient epistemological principle. What we need for an epistemological principle is not simply a *causal* principle (though that is necessary), but rather principle *of knowledge*. And ideally, we need a principle of knowledge that has universal application regardless of circumstances, context, or conditions. That principle, we should now be able to see, is the *knowledge of God* that the Word of God—as Logos and as written—provides by virtue of his exhaustive activity in the world that he has made.

Conclusion

In conclusion, we should reiterate here that Bavinck has said much that moves, without question, in the direction we have moved above. He has the remedy to his problems within his own system. However, to be consistent, an epistemology of realism, we should see, cannot be sustained if one hopes for some kind of universal *principia* in which all must participate. Bavinck's bug, if allowed to run through the entire system, will infect it all.

On the other hand, we have seen a consistency in Frame's epistemological principles (especially as those principles relate to issues of prolegomena) that avoid the infection of Bavinck's bug. Frame is unwavering in his insistence on the principle of God's revelation *alone* being the only foundation for knowledge *in any discipline*.

> I've mentioned that our knowledge of God is under his control and under his authority; that means that we have to seek knowledge in God's way. . . . The same principles apply to knowing God's world. After all, the world is God's creation. So, knowing the world is knowing God. To know the world is to know God's intentions, his tastes, his desires, and in some cases his sense of humor (think of the camel and the okapi).[69]

Not only so, but if we take Bolt's article as a faithful representation of Bavinck's bug, then the infection will surely spread; the door has opened wide

---

69. *SBL*, 76–77.

for a number of false principles to be emended in the discussion. In this regard, note again, finally, Bolt's conclusion:

> a strictly biblical-doctrinal approach runs the risk of appearing to non-Christians as privileged communication; a kind of gnosticism that only communicates to the initiated. In short, this approach fails to make universal claims about the gospel of Jesus Christ and makes no argument about the universally true knowledge about God that is the church's mission to proclaim to the world. As an alternative, I appealed to Herman Bavinck's Christian realism, the epistemology that is rooted in the creation of all things, including the human logos by the divine Logos. All truth is from God [note the *principium essendi* emphasis here]; we participate in the truth to the degree that our intellects adequately form concepts that correspond to the things of this world including our experience of God. . . . Concretely this means that while the Bible is the final source and norm for Christian theology, the knowledge of God obtained by natural reason, reflected in the religions of the world, as well as legitimate, reasonable inferences from biblical truth, are all part of the theologian's thesaurus of truth.[70]

This paragraph seems to move in the wrong direction. It allows Bavinck's virus to spread to the whole system. First, the universal knowledge of God is *not*, in the first place, "the church's mission to proclaim." Rather, the church's mission is to proclaim the gospel of Jesus Christ to all people, *who themselves have the knowledge of God* by virtue of what the Logos does/is doing in and through them. There is, then, no "gnosticism" prevalent, since God ensures that all his human creatures are "initiated" into covenant relation with him.

Second, speaking of an epistemology that is "rooted in the creation of all things" is to speak of the *essendi,* that is, the *causal* principle with respect to that epistemology, not its *content.* The fact that God (by way of the Logos), by virtue of his creation and providence, is the "root" of all things is true enough, but it does not give us an adequate account of the knowledge situation itself.

Third, not only is it the case that "the Bible is the final source and norm for Christian theology," but the Bible is the *beginning* point for all discussions of theology, of knowledge of God obtained by natural reason, and for all things "reflected in the religions of the world." On this matter,

---

70. Bolt, "*Sola Scriptura,*" 89.

John Frame has been abundantly clear. These latter elements can be a part of "the theologian's thesaurus of truth" only to the extent that, with Frame, we begin with Scripture *alone* as our *principium cognoscendi* and measure all else by its truth. We are back, therefore, to the principle of *sola Scriptura* as the ground and foundation for our prolegomena and our epistemology. Thus, God's revelation alone and not a realistic epistemology is able to bring the gospel to bear on the church and on the world.

Bibliography

Aquinas, Thomas. *Summa Contra Gentiles*. Translated by Charles J. O'Neil. 4 vols. Notre Dame and London: Notre Dame University Press, 1957.

————. *The Division and Methods of the Sciences*. Translated by Armand Mauer. Toronto: The Pontifical Institute of Medieval Studies, 1963.

————. *Summa Theologiae: Latin Text, English Translation, Introduction, Notes, Appendices & Glossary*. Edited by Thomas Gilby. 60 vols. London and New York: Eyre & Spottiswoode and McGraw-Hill Book Company, 1964.

————. "On Being and Essence." In *Selected Writings of St. Thomas Aquinas*, edited by Thomas Goodwin, 162. New York: Bobbs, 1965.

————. *Summa Theologiae: A Concise Translation*. Translated by Timothy McDermott. Maryland: Christian Classics, 1989.

Bavinck, Herman. *Reformed Dogmatics: Prolegomena*. Vol. 1. Edited by John Bolt. Translated by John Vriend. Grand Rapids: Baker Academic, 2003.

Bolt, John. "Sola Scriptura as an Evangelical Theological Method?" In *Reforming Or Conforming? Post-Conservative Evangelicals and the Emerging Church*, edited by Gary L. W. Johnson and Ron N. Gleason, 62–92. Wheaton, IL: Crossway, 2008.

Frame, John M. *The Doctrine of the Knowledge of God*. Phillipsburg, NJ: Presbyterian and Reformed, 1987.

————. *The Doctrine of God*. Phillipsburg, NJ: P&R Publishing, 2002.

————. *Salvation Belongs to the Lord: An Introduction to Systematic Theology*. Phillipsburg, NJ: P&R Publishing, 2006.

———. *The Collected Shorter Theological Writings.* Vol. 1. CD. Phillipsburg, NJ: P&R Publishing, 2007.

Hart, Charles A. *Thomistic Metaphysics: An Inquiry into the Act of Existing.* Englewood Cliffs, NJ: Prentice-Hall, 1959.

Maritain, Jacques. *Existence and the Existent.* New ed. New York: Pantheon Books, 1964.

Marsden, George. "The Collapse of American Evangelical Academia." In *Faith and Rationality,* edited by Alvin Plantinga and Nicholas Wolterstorff, 219–64. Notre Dame and London: University of Notre Dame Press, 1983.

———. *The Soul of the American University: From Protestant Establishment to Established Nonbelief.* New York: Oxford University Press, 1994.

McLeod, Mark S. "The Analogy Argument for the Proper Basicality of Belief in God." *International Journal for Philosophy of Religion* 21 (1987): 3–20.

Muller, Richard A. *Post-Reformation Reformed Dogmatics: The Rise and Development of Reformed Orthodoxy, ca. 1520 to ca. 1725.* Vol. 1, *Prolegomena to Theology.* 2nd ed. Grand Rapids: Baker, 2003.

———. *Post-Reformation Reformed Dogmatics: The Rise and Development of Reformed Orthodoxy, ca. 1520 to ca. 1725.* Vol 2, *Holy Scripture.* 2nd ed. Grand Rapids: Baker, 2003.

Oliphint, K. Scott. "Epistemology and Christian Belief." *WTJ* 63, 1 (2001): 151–82.

———. *Reasons for Faith: Philosophy in the Service of Theology.* Phillipsburg, NJ: P&R Publishing, 2006.

———. "The Clear and Distinct Knowledge of God." *Reformation 21,* May 2006. Previously published at http://www.ref21.org.

———. "Covenant Faith." In *Justified in Christ: God's Wonderful Plan for Us in Justification,* edited by K. Scott Oliphint, 153–74. Fearn, Ross-shire, UK: Christian Focus Publications, 2007.

———. "The Irrationality of Unbelief." In *Revelation and Reason: New Essays in Reformed Apologetics,* edited by K. Scott Oliphint and Lane G. Tipton. Phillipsburg, NJ: P&R Publishing, 2007.

————. "The Old New Reformed Epistemology." In *Revelation and Reason: New Essays in Reformed Apologetics*, edited by K. Scott Oliphint and Lane G. Tipton, 207–19. Phillipsburg, NJ: P&R Publishing, 2007.

————. "A Primal and Simple Knowledge." In *A Theological Guide to Calvin's Institutes: Essays and Analysis*, edited by David Hall and Peter A. Lillback. Phillipsburg, NJ: P&R Publishing, 2008.

Phelan, G. B. *Saint Thomas and Analogy*. Milwaukee: Marquette University Press, 1941.

Plantinga, Alvin. "Rationality and Religious Belief." In *Contemporary Philosophy of Religion*, edited by Stephen M. Cahn and David Shatz. New York: Oxford University Press, 1982.

Reid, Thomas. *Essays on the Powers of the Human Mind; to Which Are Added, an Essay on Quantity, and an Analysis of Aristotle's Logic*. London: Printed for Thomas Tegg; R. Griffin and Co., 1827.

Van Til, Cornelius. *An Introduction to Systematic Theology*. Edited by William Edgar. Phillipsburg, NJ: P&R Publishing, 2007.

Vos, Geerhardus. "Book Review, *Gereformeerde Dogmatiek*, Vol. 1." In *Redemptive History and Biblical Interpretation: The Shorter Writings of Geerhardus Vos*, edited by Richard B. Gaffin Jr., 475–84. Phillipsburg, NJ: Presbyterian and Reformed Publishing Co, 1980.

Wolterstorff, Nicholas. *On Universals: An Essay in Ontology*. Chicago and London: University of Chicago Press, 1970.

10

THE WORD MADE APPLICABLE: FRAME ON BIBLICAL THEOLOGY AMONG THE DISCIPLINES

MARK A. GARCIA

PROFESSOR JOHN FRAME has spent much of his long career commending and developing his approach to the task of theology. His concept of theology as "application" has an eye to both theoretical and practical concerns. It is no surprise, then, that any consideration of Frame's work on the theological disciplines must account not only for the way he relates the various disciplines themselves but also for how he understands the very notion of application. Because much in this picture is treated in other essays in this volume, in what follows I focus attention on introducing the basic features of Frame's model and on raising a series of questions about the relationship of biblical theology to the execution of his principles.

The reason for approaching the topic this way is simple. One controlling concern in the present essay is to warn against the illegitimate separation of application, or ethics, and biblical theology. To understand biblical theology properly is to see it as a self-conscious commitment to read all of Scripture, including its explicitly applicatory or ethical material, in the light of what it says about its own nature. The biblical theologian begins with the Bible as inscripturated—divine revelation designed to serve concrete, covenantal purposes that are historically circumscribed and, at the same time, eschatologically oriented. Ultimately, then, the question regards what it looks like, practically speaking, to read Scripture's ethical material on its own terms, and this involves the question of how properly to understand the relationship between text and reader. The most profitable engagement with Frame's model develops this connection with a view to Frame's own deep commitment to the primacy of Scripture.

FRAME ON THE THEOLOGICAL DISCIPLINES

Theology as Application

Frame defines *theology* as "the application of the Word of God by persons to all areas of life."[1] He defines *application* as "teaching" or "the use of God's revelation to meet the spiritual needs of people, to promote godliness and spiritual health."[2] For this reason, theology as "teaching" is not merely a description of religious feelings or merely an effort to formulate objective truth. It is no bare intellectual or academic exercise but the "use" of revelation for ethical renewal. Such a concept, Frame suggests, fits nicely with his triad of perspectives. It coordinates them because theology is "based on the Word of God (normative), and it applies that Word to situations (situational) on a person-to-person basis (existential)."[3] Taking a cue from Frame's insistence that "all theology is practical," the most recent evaluation of Frame's theology has called it a version of "practical theology."[4] Because of the way Frame defines theology, all his work (not only his work on theological method per se) is highly relevant to understanding his theological program, particularly his work on ethics and the Christian life. Despite the clarity of discussion and frequent repetition in his works, one has to read rather widely in Frame's publications to gain the full picture of just how he understands theology to be application.

1. Frame gives the most direct attention to theology as application in *DKG*, 81–85.
2. Ibid., 81.
3. Ibid.
4. *DCL*, 9; Richard C. Gamble, *God's Mighty Acts in the Old Testament*, vol. 1 of *The Whole Counsel of God* (Phillipsburg, NJ: P&R Publishing, 2009), 31. As one of three prevailing approaches to theological organization, Gamble refers to the "school" of practical theology. With the exception of one reference to Vern Poythress as a "proponent" of this approach, however, this "school" seems to be made up, in Gamble's discussion at least, of Frame alone. The other schools identified by Gamble are the "biblical theology" and the "missiological theology" ones.

Key to Frame's argument that theology is application is his rejection of a distinction between "meaning" and "application."[5] Frame has sometimes been critiqued along lines showing that he has not been understood on this point.[6] His guiding concern appears to be simply that theology is never, at any point, the consideration or formulation of objective content wholly divorced from human needs, "removed from all human questions and concerns."[7] Whether the need is ignorance or inability, to ask for the meaning of Scripture is always to ask for a remedy of some kind. As Frame puts it, "the work of theology is not to discover some truth-in-itself in abstraction from all that is human; it is to take the truth of Scripture and humbly to serve God's people by teaching and preaching it and by counselling and evangelizing."[8]

As one considers Frame's argument, some immediate questions come to mind, such as how theology may be viewed as the ethical "use" of revelation. This suggests that there is something distinct from the "use" that is to be taken up in that "use," i.e., our understanding of God's revelation. If this is the case, then there remains an implicit distinction between "meaning" and "use" or "application" persisting within the model of theology Frame proposes. Further, if theology is the application of the Word of God, it is not clear that in fact meaning as application does "coordinate" Frame's three perspectives. Instead, it appears to be identifiable with one or two of them: the situational, which Frame refers to as the application of the Word to situations; and, presumably, the existential, in which that application is made to particular persons. If one or two of these perspectives are explicitly "application" but the first is not (the normative, the Word of God), this suggests that theology in Frame's model is a matter of applying something understood in terms of God's revelation. There is the Word (normative), and then there is the Word applied (situational and existential), in which case there is an understanding of the Word that, if it is a matter of application at all, is so in some way distinct from the others.

But perhaps at this point one needs to remember again that Frame considers "application" the meeting of some human need. If so, possibly only the need for understanding is met in the normative dimension—but this is not clear either. And then one is still left with a distinction between

---

5. *DKG*, 82–85.

6. See, as an example, Frame's response in *DG*, 751–58 (Appendix B), to a review of *DKG* by Mark Karlberg.

7. *DKG*, 83.

8. Ibid., 84.

that dimension and the other one(s) explicitly called "application(s)," which may ultimately require that Frame ascribe at least two meanings to the term or at least two senses in which it is intended. The more significant questions arise as one considers the way in which theology as application is intended by Frame to overcome a chasm between Scripture's text and the reader.

The Disciplines in Relationship to Each Other

Knowing now that for Frame theology is application, one is in a better position to understand how he relates the various theological disciplines. In light of Frame's commitment to perspectivalism, his position is fairly straightforward. For Frame, "while exegetical theology focuses on specific passages and biblical theology focuses on the historical features of Scripture, systematic theology seeks to bring all the aspects of Scripture together, to synthesize them. Systematics asks, What does it all add up to?"[9] Whereas B. B. Warfield, for instance, had placed systematic theology on the foundation of apologetics,[10] Frame argues strongly for a full balancing of the disciplines as various "perspectives."[11] For this reason he is unhappy with language of various "departments," since this suggests a measure of independency and even isolation. Frame prefers instead to speak of the various "programs," "methods," "strategies," or "agendas" in the pursuit of a single task. "They are, that is to say," he explains, "different ways of doing the same thing, not sciences with different subject matters."[12]

This concern for balance, or the avoidance of extremes, is a frequent theme of Frame's work in this context. Another of Frame's dominant concerns over the years has been the gradual ascendency of traditionalism within Reformed circles, in particular the practical or functional substitution of historical theology for systematic theology. In opposition to this trend, Frame has insisted on the indispensably foundational place of biblical exegesis, which must continue to stand in critical relationship to tradition as norming norm. Frame has referred to this insistence as a matter of consistent

---

9. Ibid., 212.

10. B. B. Warfield, "The Idea of Systematic Theology" (1896), in *Studies in Theology*, vol. 9 of *The Works of Benjamin B. Warfield* (New York: Oxford University Press, 1932), 74.

11. For discussion of the various fields in relationship, see *DKG*, 206–14; cf. John M. Frame, "Systematic Theology and Apologetics at Westminster Seminaries," in *The Pattern of Sound Doctrine: Systematic Theology at the Westminster Seminaries: Essays in Honor of Robert B. Strimple*, ed. David VanDrunen (Phillipsburg, NJ: P&R Publishing, 2004), 73–98.

12. *DKG*, 206.

"biblicism," and although in my view Frame's rhetoric on this point some-times goes too far, there is no question that his concern is not an illusion.[13] Indicative of a form of traditionalism that marginalizes the work of exegesis and biblical and systematic theology, debates at both the ecclesiastical and individual levels often do suggest that historical theology has quietly become the principal mode of theological discourse and analysis. This is a form of traditionalism parading under the name of systematic theology to which Frame has long been acutely sensitive, and for good reason.[14]

COVENANT HISTORY AND ETHICS: FRAME ON THE LIMITATIONS OF BIBLICAL THEOLOGY

On the role of biblical theology (defined already as a "historical" dis-cipline) among the theological disciplines, Frame appreciates much of what has been done in this field but is unconvinced that it must occupy the central role that others have claimed for it. What he means by this is clarified in the course of his introduction to biblical theology as a method or program.[15] "Biblical theology," Frame writes, "studies the *history* of God's dealings with creation. As a theological discipline, it is the application of that history to human need."[16]

Frame explains that biblical theology "traces the outworking of God's plan for creation from the historical perspective of God's people. It traces the history of the covenant, showing us at each point in history what God has done for the redemption of His people."[17] Its method is one of "historical

13. For Frame's most direct critiques of traditionalism, see *TRAD* and *IDSCB*. Note the responses by David Wells ("On Being Framed," *WTJ* 59 [1997]: 293–300) and Richard Muller ("Historiography in the Service of Theology and Worship: Toward Dialogue with John Frame," *WTJ* 59 [1997]: 301–10). Frame replies to both Wells and Muller in the same issue ("Reply to Richard Muller and David Wells," *WTJ* 59 [1997]: 311–18).

14. The most explicit example of this trend in recent years has been the work of D. G. Hart. See, e.g., his historical approach to answering theological questions in D. G. Hart, *Recovering Mother Kirk: The Case for Liturgy in the Reformed Tradition* (Grand Rapids: Baker, 2003); and his criticisms of a biblical-theological mode for systematic theological inquiry in D. G. Hart, "Systematic Theology at Old Princeton Seminary: Unoriginal Calvinism," in VanDrunen, *The Pattern of Sound Doctrine*, 3–26. Contrast, in the same volume, the sober remarks on this question by Dennis E. Johnson, who also refers explicitly to Hart's *Recovering Mother Kirk* as an example of the problem ("On Practical Theology as Systematic Theology," 110–13).

15. *DKG*, 207–12.

16. Ibid., 207 (emphasis Frame's).

17. Ibid.

analysis," but as theology cannot be divorced from application, so in this case even analysis of the history of redemption meets our needs. It does so as "we are enabled to put ourselves into the stories, to imagine what it must have been like to have lived as a believer in the time of Abraham, or Moses, or Paul, for example. We learn to think the way David, Isaiah, and Amos must have thought about God's dealings, thinking in their terms, in their language." One further, and perhaps chief, benefit of biblical theology, says Frame, is in its integrating effect on the diversity of biblical revelation, particularly as it focuses attention on Christ, who, in his person and work, is the culmination of the drama of that history.[18]

Biblical Theology and the Narrative-Historical Genre

Significantly, Frame also points out what he calls various "limitations" of biblical theology. On close examination, however, in my view Frame's "limitations" either misunderstand the nature of biblical theology (and the work of the biblical theologian) or have in view limitations belonging to certain practitioners of biblical theology and not to biblical theology itself. Frame is unquestionably familiar with the best and most relevant work that has been done in the areas he raises as matters of concern, yet his discussions do not reflect careful consideration of the arguments pursued there. For our purposes, we will have to content ourselves with noting how Frame's perception of biblical theology's limitations, although often valid concerns in general, are at least somewhat off the mark when it comes to biblical theology.

The first of these "limitations" is the most important one in Frame's analysis and so will be the primary focus here. Frame writes, "Scripture is a redemptive history but not *only* that. It does not belong to the historical *genre.* (A) It includes a law code, a song book, a collection of proverbs, a set of letters (and these not merely as historical sources). (B) The content of Scripture is intended not only to give us historical information but also to govern our lives here and now (Rom. 15:4; 2 Tim. 3:16ff.; etc.). This is not the usual purpose of a historical text."[19] Frame proposes, then, that "redemptive history" or biblical theology (terms used synonymously by Frame) is only one way of "characterizing" Scripture, alongside which others, such as law, gospel, wisdom, comfort, and admonition, should be placed.[20]

18. Ibid., 208.
19. Ibid., 210 (emphases Frame's).
20. Ibid.

One might think this displaces Christ from his central role, but Frame argues that the opposite is true: a more perspectival orientation may do "more justice to the centrality of Christ than a narrowly redemptive-historical approach," for Christ would thus be central not only historically but also as "eternal lawgiver (Word), as the wisdom of God, as prophet, priest, and king."[21] He adds, "Furthermore, the death, resurrection, and ascension of Christ and the Pentecostal outpouring of the Spirit are important not merely as historical happenings . . . but also for their present impact on us, not least in their normative function (Rom. 12:1ff.; Eph. 4:1ff.)." Frame discusses redemptive history as narrative in *DCL*, and there again it appears to be confused with the narrative genre. On Frame's perspectivalism, the normative perspective gives us a Christian "command ethic," the existential perspective gives us a "virtue ethic," and the situational perspective gives us a "narrative" ethic. From the outset, then, the redemptive (or covenant) historical, as narrational, is but one of several possible perspectives.[22]

We must pause over Frame's comments here, for his discussion of this perceived limitation is the most puzzling feature of his work on this question. There is clear evidence here of confusion over the nature of biblical theology as a focus on *genre* or *subject matter*.[23] Frame frequently discusses biblical theology as though it is identifiable with the narrative or historical *genre* of Scripture. For this reason, he points to the other genres in Scripture, such as poetry, commands, and wisdom literature, as though the very existence of these genres somehow militates against seeing biblical theology as truly comprehensive of biblical revelation. Perhaps this is due to seeing biblical theology as "redemptive history" and thus, in some way, misunderstanding it as restricted to the historical genre. So Frame writes that Scripture is "not *only*" history and "does not belong to the historical genre."[24] As a further example that brings together genre and subject matter, in a paper titled "Ethics, Preaching, and Biblical Theology," Frame states that "although the two-age structure of Pauline ethics is important, it does not by any means exhaust the biblical teaching relevant to our ethical decisions. There are pages and pages of Scripture devoted to the details of God's law, to proverbs about the practical life of the believer, to the heart motivations of love and

21. Ibid.

22. *DCL*, 272.

23. See, among many other places, ibid., 272–73. See other references in this essay for further, selective documentation.

24. *DKG*, 209.

faith that should impel our passion for holiness." Similarly, he continues to note that although ethical preaching "should be redemptive-historical," "it should also expound God's laws and the new inner motivations to which we are called."[25]

The repeated use of "also" here is noteworthy, for in fact biblical theology is not identifiable with the historical or narrative genre; neither is its subject matter limited to history or any one single facet of biblical revelation. As a discipline, biblical theology is indeed the study of the organic development, in history, of God's revelation in Word and deed. It does have a historical rather than, say, topical interest.[26] But the biblical theologian is not for this reason preoccupied with history in contrast to other genres, for biblical theology is not a matter of genre. It is instead that study of Scripture in all its contents and genres, the "whole counsel of God," which takes into account from the start the way God, in his Word, has told us he has revealed himself. It is a matter of coming to any portion of Scripture with a self-conscious commitment to what it says about its own nature, to read and hear and preach and teach with the eschatological consciousness that Scripture itself requires of us. For this reason, perhaps it is better to speak of the biblical-theological mode of the study and communication of Holy Scripture, rather than of historical or narrative genre, as the more relevant question to explore.

Further, the biblical theologian sees a choice between the "details of God's law," proverbs, and motivations on the one hand, and Paul's eschatological framework on the other hand, as a fundamentally false one—a contrast not of apples and oranges but of apples and, say, gorillas. The biblical theologian certainly does not regard the events of Scripture as mere "historical happenings" that should be studied as such. Instead, biblical theologians

25. Frame, "Ethics, Preaching, and Biblical Theology," at http://www.frame-poythress.org/frame_articles/1999Ethics.htm; cf. DCL, 271–97, esp. 272–79.

26. See Geerhardus Vos, Biblical Theology: Old and New Testaments (Grand Rapids: Eerdmans, 1948), 3–18; "Introduction" to Richard B. Gaffin Jr., ed., Redemptive History and Biblical Interpretation: The Shorter Writings of Geerhardus Vos (Phillipsburg, NJ: Presbyterian and Reformed, 1980), xiv–xxiii. Gaffin's various essays on the relationship of biblical to systematic theology are important to the questions that Frame engages here and have, to a great extent at least, set the scene for the ongoing discussion. See in particular Richard B. Gaffin Jr., "Systematic Theology and Biblical Theology," WTJ 38 (1976): 281–99; "Biblical Theology and the Westminster Standards," WTJ 65 (2003): 165–79; and what is, in my view, the most relevant material from Gaffin in his "The Vitality of Reformed Dogmatics," in J. M. Batteau, J. W. Maris, and K. Veling, eds., The Vitality of Reformed Dogmatics (Kampen, Netherlands: Uitgeverij Kok, 1994), 16–50.

regard ethical concerns as fully biblical but as incapable, within Scripture itself, of being divorced from or lifted out of the covenantal-historical settings in which they are given to us. Not only are such concerns far from sidelined by biblical theology, but the biblical theologian stresses how these concerns are situated, by Paul for instance, within a clear eschatological (and thus biblical-theological) context. The biblical theologian finds no real tension here. The question at issue is the extent of our submission to the biblical revelation regarding the way ethics is indeed situated in that eschatological context, not whether one may stress ethics or eschatology.[27]

Scripture and Covenant History

As these comments suggest, in my view part of Frame's first identification of a "limitation" in biblical theology concerns the nature of Scripture. In the same discussion referred to above, he states, "As is often pointed out, the Gospels are not biographies of Jesus; they are *Gospels*. Their purpose is not merely to inform but to elicit faith. Most histories do not have this purpose."[28] Frame goes on to note that if we interpret *history* so broadly as to include those functions, we remove *history* from its ordinary sense in normal language. He concludes his discussion of this first "limitation" by stating, "I am therefore willing to say that Scripture is a redemptive history, but I am reluctant to say that this is the only way or the most important way of characterizing Scripture."[29] Further, "to say that Scripture is *normative* history is to say that Scripture is not only history but also *law* and that 'history' and 'law' are at least equally ultimate ways of characterizing Scripture."[30] In addition to further evidence of genre confusion, then, at issue is the doctrine of Scripture and, in connection with this, the relationship of law (as ethics) and covenant history.

---

27. On this point Frame must interact with the exegetical and theological arguments in William D. Dennison, "Biblical Theology and the Issue of Application in Preaching," in *Reformed Spirituality: Communing with Our Glorious God*, ed. Joseph A. Pipa Jr. and J. Andrew Wortman (Taylors, SC: Southern Presbyterian Press and Greenville Presbyterian Theological Seminary, 2003), 119–51; and William D. Dennison, "Indicative and Imperative: The Basic Structure of Pauline Ethics," *CTJ* 14, 1 (1979): 55–78.

28. *DKG*, 209 (emphasis Frame's). For a contrary, and in my view compelling, treatment of the complex relationship of history to ethics, see Dennison, "Biblical Theology and the Issue of Application in Preaching." A fuller, more comprehensive response to Frame on this point than is possible in this essay would have to involve engaging the history-ethics question at length.

29. *DKG*, 209.

30. Ibid., 210 (emphases Frame's). Note the comment on Kline in footnote 32 below.

Frame's discussion of the second "limitation" of biblical theology provides more evidence along these lines. He expresses his concern as follows: "Since Scripture, then, is not merely or primarily a 'history,' I would resist the view of some who argue that theology ought to be 'controlled' by redemptive history." In short, Frame's argument follows on his earlier perception of biblical theology as a matter of historical analysis and subject matter. If "theology ought to be controlled by *everything* Scripture says," and Scripture includes material not of the historical and narrative genre, then clearly biblical theology cannot control theology.[31]

By way of brief response to Frame's points of concern, perhaps it would be useful to sketch a profile of the way biblical theologians see Scripture as text in relationship to the biblical-theological task. Doing so may bring the fuller range of Frame's concerns into view from a biblical-theological perspective. It is necessary, however, to depend throughout on fuller discussions elsewhere for the critical exegetical and theological analyses that give rise to this biblical-theological orientation.

The biblical theologian is one whose theological consciousness is attuned to Scripture's self-witness regarding its nature as the divinely inspired text that is at the same time *determinative, part,* and *product* of covenant history. It is *determinative* inasmuch as Scripture's narration of covenant history is normative for the people's covenantal-historical self-consciousness. Essential here is the role of Deuteronomy's persistent interest in developing a corporate memory of event and word among Israel, *remember* serving as a principal motif of that central old covenant document (e.g., Deut. 5–11, esp. 8; see also Deut. 32, etc.). Israel's covenantal fortunes of life or death are tied repeatedly in Deuteronomy to her development of an *active historical self-consciousness*, which involves identification with the words and deeds experienced by earlier generations. Scripture is also *part* of that history inasmuch as the story of Scripture's own formation is an elemental part of the history of the covenant. In view here is the deep-running relationship of progress in covenant history to canon formation. Again a careful study of Deuteronomy as covenantal-historical document would be critically important to this topic. Finally, it is a *product* of that history inasmuch as Scripture, as canonical norm, and particularly in its completion with the new covenant witness, presupposes the story's eschatological climax in the person and work of Christ and is the authoritative interpretation of that historical climax.

---

31. *DKG*, 210.

The history of canonical shaping is the history of text bearing authoritative witness to revelatory Word and deed of God.

Beginning with the covenant-constitutive role in the life of Israel of Deuteronomy as covenantal treaty document, Scripture unfolds in its organic progression. By divine design and purpose it expands and evolves in keeping with advances in time of covenantal administration, and does so precisely in order to serve as norm for God's people in those various covenantal moments of her life.[32] As such, Scripture situates *itself*, in *all* its "contents" and regardless of genre, *in that history*. Rather than posing problems for biblical theology, therefore, the biblical theologian (who, one remembers, is not preoccupied with history as history or the genre of historical narrative) sees law, proverbs, psalms, and songs as narrative "pauses" in this story that must be situated within that story if they are to be faithfully heard.[33]

At the center of this complex of eschatology, Scripture, and ethics is the person and work of Christ. But this complex is more than the historical and redemptive presupposition of Christian ethics in the way this is sometimes presented by some inappropriately narrow or simplistic constructions of the indicative-imperative relationship. In Christ the new creation of promise has

32. These points are developed in the most important biblical-theological studies of recent decades. For instance, for the canon of the New Testament the work by Herman N. Ridderbos, *Redemptive History and the New Testament Scriptures*, trans. H. De Jongse; rev. Richard B. Gaffin Jr. (Philadelphia: Presbyterian and Reformed, 1963; rev. Phillipsburg, NJ: Presbyterian and Reformed, 1988), remains valuable; cf., extending Ridderbos's work further with noteworthy results, Richard B. Gaffin Jr., "The New Testament as Canon," in Harvie M. Conn, ed., *Inerrancy and Hermeneutic: A Tradition, A Challenge, A Debate* (Grand Rapids: Baker, 1988), 165–83; and C. E. Hill, "God's Speech in These Last Days: The New Testament Canon as an Eschatological Phenomenon," in Lane G. Tipton and Jeffrey C. Waddington, eds., *Resurrection and Eschatology: Theology in Service to the Church: Essays in Honor of Richard B. Gaffin Jr.* (Phillipsburg, NJ: P&R Publishing, 2008), 203–54. In my view, the most compelling treatment on biblical, especially Old Testament, canonical theology in relation to covenant remains Meredith G. Kline, *The Structure of Biblical Authority*, 2nd ed. (Grand Rapids: Eerdmans, 1975). Cf. his brief commentary on Deuteronomy in Charles F. Pfeiffer and Everett F. Harrison, eds., *The Wycliffe Bible Commentary* (London: Oliphants, 1969), 155–204. Frame (*DKG*, 210n36) points to Kline's work on the suzerain treaty in *Treaty of the Great King* (Grand Rapids: Eerdmans, 1963) in support of his idea of law and covenant as fully correlative. Especially in the fuller discussion in *Structure*, however, Kline clearly defines and locates law within a covenantal setting rather than rendering law an equally ultimate principle alongside covenant, which is suggested at least by Frame's perspectival model.

33. This is the helpful language of Gerard Loughlin, *Telling God's Story: Bible, Church, and Narrative Theology* (Cambridge: Cambridge University Press, 1996), 62, cited in the insightful essay by Craig G. Bartholomew and Michael W. Goheen, "Story and Biblical Theology," in Craig G. Bartholomew, Mary Healy, Karl Möller, and Robin Parry, eds., *Out of Egypt: Biblical Theology and Biblical Interpretation*, vol. 5 of Scripture and Hermeneutics Series, ed. Craig G. Bartholomew and Anthony C. Thiselton (Grand Rapids: Zondervan, 2004), 160n64.

begun, an order of exhaustive glory and righteousness into which believers, by union with Christ, have been ushered. The church is called to live out of her real and present heavenly citizenship in him even as she makes her way through an order and age that has not yet fully passed away. But to do so, according to the New Testament, is much more than merely thinking in terms of two ages and a Day to come. The ethical impulse in the New Testament is undeniably strong and concrete, and the biblical theologian does not shy away from this. But that impulse has a context: the present life of the believer is bound up with the Christ of history. More particularly, Christ, as the embodiment and *telos* of Israel's long covenantal story, is both source (by his Spirit) and pattern (in his humiliation-to-exaltation story) for the church's call to holiness.[34]

This positions us to interact with Frame's insistence that the argument that biblical ethics must be situated in an eschatological or "two-age" schema works both ways. He says, "If the law and the proverbs are to be understood in the context of the already and not-yet, the opposite is also true: The semi-eschatological tension must be understood in terms of the law of God. It is the law which defines the sinfulness from which Christ redeemed us. And God saves us so that we may keep the law (Rom. 8:4). The law defines *how* we should express our gratitude for Jesus' redemption."[35] But it is not clear why Frame is convinced that "the opposite is also true." Why must it also be true? For the biblical theologian, unless the eschatology of covenant provides the setting for law, law becomes an ahistorical abstraction divorced from the covenantal nature of the relationship of God with his human creatures. The fact that the law defines sin and also has the positive use to which Frame points bears no relationship to the question whether eschatology provides the context for law.[36]

With these considerations in place, the remaining limitations perceived by Frame do not require as much sustained comment. Frame's third "limitation" in biblical theology is based on various popular misunderstandings of the discipline (perhaps as a result of the term **biblical** *theology*) that it somehow sees itself as more "biblical" than, say, systematic theology. Frame's

34. See further the brief comments under "An Assessment" below, including the note on Philippians, and Mark A. Garcia, "Christ and the Spirit: The Meaning and Promise of a Reformed Idea," in Tipton and Waddington, *Resurrection and Eschatology*, 424–42.

35. Frame, "Ethics, Preaching, and Biblical Theology" (emphasis Frame's).

36. For this complex of questions with a view to the subordination of law to covenant, see Kline, *Structure of Biblical Authority*.

response is that all theology is, again, *application*, and thus reshapes the biblical material to some extent. He adds that "theology may (indeed must) *depart* from the structure of Scripture itself, for otherwise it could only repeat the exact words of Scripture, from Genesis to Revelation."[37]

In reply to this concern one ought to affirm, with Frame, that biblical theology is not more "biblical" than systematic theology, the differences being more a matter of the questions being asked by the theologian.[38] Yet on the matter of departing from the "structure of Scripture itself" in order to "apply" it in theology, we note again the nature of biblical theology as an exegetical and theological self-consciousness about the eschatological nature of inscripturated revelation. In this respect, as Richard Gaffin has concisely put it, one captures the issue best when one sees biblical theology as a matter of *right exegesis*, nothing more and nothing less,[39] so that those who believe theology must be exegetically grounded in the Scriptures should not feel at liberty to think differently or more dispensably of it.

Frame's fourth "limitation" combines the second and third ones. He is concerned that those who stress biblical theology tend to do an injustice to the parts of Scripture that are not "narrowly historical." Limitations five through eight similarly have to do with imbalanced or "fanatical" tendencies among self-professed biblical theologians, with *possibilities* and not with ideas or approaches inherent to biblical theology *as such*. This is an important distinction that Frame's discussion does not always make clear. One gets the impression that Frame's various "limitations" more often reflect his concerns with various practitioners rather than critical engagement with ideas intrinsic to the discipline or program itself. This impression is strengthened as one finds a great deal of what might be called anecdotal argument in Frame's analysis. When Frame wishes to critically engage the idea that biblical theology or the redemptive-historical should exercise control in exegesis, theology, and preaching, he often points to the abuse of this position in the hands of poor preachers as though it is evidence against the position itself.[40]

---

37. *DKG*, 211 (emphasis Frame's).

38. See the comments in Vos, *Biblical Theology*, 23; and Gaffin, "Systematic Theology and Biblical Theology," 295.

39. Gaffin, "Systematic Theology and Biblical Theology," 294.

40. See especially his paper "Ethics, Preaching, and Biblical Theology," where this is a dominant feature.

An Assessment

In view of these general considerations, then, an exegetical and biblical-theological analysis of the biblical texts points, I believe, to a theological architecture for ethics that is different in significant respects from what Frame suggests. This theological architecture is a matter of covenant-historical eschatology. As such, it is focused on union with the Christ of history, the Christ of humiliation to exaltation, the One in whom God's "yes" and "amen" have been spoken (2 Cor. 1:20) and the One in whom the last days' (eschatological) word of God has been spoken (Heb. 1:1–2). Union with this Christ is the irreducible and controlling eschatological atmosphere for the Christian's ethical life. In Christ, the new creation has been inaugurated, and it is to that new order that the believer belongs.

Therefore, whereas Frame attempts to bridge the chasm of biblical text and reader through a redefinition of "meaning" as "application," the biblical theologian turns the assumption on its head: the chasm is false, and the direction for "meaning" is precisely the opposite. Instead of trying to get the text into the believer, the biblical theologian puts the believer into the text, which is to say, into the ongoing story given in and signaled by the text and into the order inaugurated by Christ in his resurrection and ascension, who ministers to his own by his Word in the Spirit. The biblical theologian (as biblical!) is indeed concerned with the ethical but *in biblical-theological (because biblical) fashion*, which is, to echo what was said of Deuteronomy above, in the form of developing the active eschatological and covenant-historical consciousness basic to our covenantal fortunes. It is, in short, the cultivation of the "mind of Christ," which is to be "in us" as Christ himself is in us and we are in him, a "mind" that is, as Paul makes clear, the effect of being in the Christ of covenant-historical particularity, of first humiliation and then exaltation. This Christ, and this concrete history of Christ as the *telos* of covenant history, is the present arena of the ethical life of the believer. Thus, for the biblical theologian, union with Christ in covenant-historical terms is the theological rationale for a proper conception of application.[41]

On a final and intentionally positive note, in my view Professor Frame's most important contributions to Reformed theology are two. First, one notes

---

41. I am clearly drawing from Paul's letter to the Philippians here. In my view, the way in which union with the Christ of Philippians 2:5–11 functions as the covenant-historical center to Paul's extensive series of ethical admonitions in this letter is not only relevant but in fact nothing less than decisive for the points raised in this essay.

the integrity with which Frame has carried out his work, particularly with a view to his appropriately high standards for theological argumentation and discourse and to his handling of his critics. Frame has experienced what far too many working in our day also experience: the near absence of criticism that reflects a careful, extensive reading of one's work as the necessary prelude to assessment, or, alternatively, the absence of reasonable charity in the handling of it. In addition, the standards of analysis frequently fall far short of what we as Christians should expect of one another, and Frame has had more than his fair share of incompetent critics.

Frame's second great contribution is his appropriately dogged commitment to the primacy of Scripture over against the various forms of traditionalism that continue to plague ongoing theological debates. Frame is justly frustrated with appeals to historical figures, such as Calvin or Hodge or Murray, which function as though they are ultimate in theological discourse. It is to this praiseworthy commitment to the ultimacy of Scripture's authority that I desire ultimately to appeal in the foregoing. Indeed, I commend my reflections to Professor Frame in terms of the critical, common ground we share in our commitment to the normative function of Holy Scripture and our unqualified allegiance to God speaking to us there, as well as our determination to be ever more consistent in our submission to his sovereign lordship exercised through it.

11

JOHN FRAME:
ORTHODOXY AND CREATIVITY

LUDER G. WHITLOCK JR.

JOHN FRAME ENROLLED at Westminster Theological Seminary in the fall of 1961. Unusually gifted, he excelled so far beyond his contemporaries that he was in a class by himself. A quiet, serious, and profound man, his intellectual contribution—it was apparent even then—would be significant. As an entering student during Frame's final year, I immediately developed high esteem for him, and so I remember him well. It was no surprise to those of us who knew him that Westminster soon tapped him for a faculty position in theology.

The fact that he was a student at Westminster, was offered a professorial post early in his career, and spent the overwhelming majority of his career as a professor at Westminster in Philadelphia and California amply attests to his staunch orthodoxy. Westminster has, since its founding, been the leading example of evangelical Reformed orthodoxy. Had there been any doubt about his orthodoxy, it would have been impossible for him to remain on the faculty all those years. Should anyone be inclined to question his orthodoxy, however, a cursory evaluation of his writings, beginning with the doctrine of Scripture, should dispel those questions. It becomes apparent that he stands on the shoulders of Cornelius Van Til, J. Gresham Machen, and their Princetonian heritage.

THE DOCTRINE OF SCRIPTURE

Frame's high view of Scripture clearly indicates where he stands in the theological spectrum, because for him there is no doubt that the Bible is the Word of God, the ultimate authority for faith and life. He repeats this many times in various articles and books. Standing firmly in the Reformation tradition of *sola Scriptura*, he says:

> As the stone tablets rested by the holy ark of the covenant, so the Bible brings to us the very voice of the holy God. When Deuteronomy tells us not to turn to the left or the right of God's commands, it is referring to the written Word. When the psalmist speaks about the perfections of God's word over and over again (Ps. 119), it is primarily to the written Word that he refers. The written Word is the covenant constitution of the people of God, and its authority is absolute, because the authority of its author is absolute.[1]

So, as might be expected, Frame's definition of orthodoxy is limited to "one who accepts the supreme authority of Scripture and who accepts one or more of the classic Protestant confessions as biblically sound."[2]

Frame, therefore, although showing high regard for the confessions, clearly and intentionally attributes a subordinate authority to them. Not satisfied with making that point, he warns about the danger of any confessional challenge to biblical authority. He raises this issue because he is concerned about the tendency of some evangelical theologians to rely more on tradition, confessional or otherwise, than on the Bible.[3] This tendency, he correctly notes, accords an authority or normativeness that is undeserved to confessions and traditions—such as those regarding biblical interpretation. By calling attention to this matter, he touches a sensitive spot for those Reformed evangelicals who hold the confessions in such high esteem that on occasion the confessions, in practice, may seem as authoritative as Scripture.

The pastor or theologian who elevates a confession or confessions unduly will usually be the first to deny that he does so, and will quickly affirm the Bible as the supreme authority. The confession, he will argue, is a faithful and authoritative interpretation of what the Bible teaches and has

1. *DG*, 91.
2. Ibid., 6.
3. Ibid., 10.

had many years of acceptance. Subscription to it also establishes its authority in the church. Because of this great tradition of acceptance and respect, it is easy to accord as equally authoritative its interpretation of what the Bible teaches. This also explains the continuing resistance to any revision of the confessions. Tampering with, much less replacing, such revered confessions by drafting new ones is unacceptable to people who think that way.

Although the results caused by such people may be unintentional, the damage done to biblical authority is real nonetheless. As a corrective, Frame suggests the desirability of revising the confessions as well as any other teachings of the church that may not be aligned with Scripture. However, it does not faze him that conservative traditionalists oppose such changes, not just because he respects them and would not disregard them, but because he is far more concerned to discover and confess what the Bible says. If that means writing new confessions or revising doctrinal understandings, so be it. Frame is refreshingly candid in his approach to such matters. This is not because he is inclined toward free-thinking; rather, it is precisely because his high view of Scripture leads him to think this way.

He certainly can claim the high ground of the Reformation, which is responsible for the statement that to be Reformed is always to be reforming in the light of Scripture. Referring to the Westminster Confession of Faith, Frame observes: "According to the Reformed faith itself, we must be able to reform all the traditions of the church (including the confessions) according to the Word of God."[4] Given the authority of the Bible, biblical interpretation quickly takes an important role, in that one must interpret the Bible accurately so that its meaning is clear. If hermeneutics is important, then so are its tools and methods. It is important not only to learn the original languages and the basic principles of biblical hermeneutics, but also to access and analyze a great deal of historical material, in order to grasp the historical context so that the meaning of the biblical text becomes clear. Ongoing research involving ancient, social, and historical data has been valuable to biblical scholars. Although acknowledging that value and the use made of it by colleagues such as Meredith G. Kline, Frame is concerned that it not be misused, emphasizing that it is helpful information, but no more than that, to be used carefully in order to help understand what the Bible says.

Given his education and background, Frame obviously has a high regard for scholarship and the valuable contribution made by all the disciplines.

4. Ibid., 9.

Good scholarship enables the person who makes use of it to understand and apply the Bible more effectively. But as noted above, Frame is critical of evangelical scholars who pay lip service to *sola Scriptura* and then proceed to deny the Bible its rightful role in formulating answers to contemporary issues. Wary of scholars who tend to equate the authority of the intellect with the authority of the Bible, he notes the capitulation of some modern evangelical scholars who attempt to find common ground with unbelief in order to be academically and intellectually respectable.[5] For philosophers, this is an easy mistake. His background certainly qualifies him, and may prompt him, to say that. Following in the footsteps of Van Til, he rejects the primacy of the intellect, yet appreciates its value. With Calvin, he insists that the intellect must operate subject to the norms of Scripture.

Frame also distinguishes between the Bible and the Word of God, acknowledging and explaining how the latter is a broader concept. Although the Bible is most definitively the Word of God, carrying all of God's authority, the Word of God also "describes the power by which God controls the forces of nature, and in some mysterious way it is also a name of God's eternal son."[6] The Word of God is the self-expression of God's lordship and his communication through specific words, some of which are permanently recorded in the Scriptures. So how does Frame evaluate preaching or the exposition and application of Scripture, especially in view of the statement in the Second Helvetic Confession (1.4), which says, "The preaching of the Word of God is the Word of God"?

> The Bible is inspired (Theopneustos, II Tim. 3:16) but today's sermons are not. In that sense, preaching is not the Word of God. On the other hand, authentic preaching always seeks to set forth not the preacher's ideas, but the Scriptures. Insofar as the preacher *succeeds* at presenting not his own ideas, but God's, then surely there is a sense in which his sermon is the Word of God. After all, God's Word does not lose its authority merely by being placed on the lips of a human preacher, any more than it loses by being set on paper. Indeed, we may say that preaching, when it is true preaching, when it is authentic preaching, is the Word of God, nothing less.[7]

5. *CWM*, 158.
6. *PWG*, 10.
7. Ibid., 29–30.

But is this correct? Isn't there a distinct difference between the Scriptures as the Word of God and authentic preaching as the explanation and application of God's Word, no matter how well communicated? Granted, the message of the Lord is communicated effectively, even powerfully, so that its meaning is clear, perhaps clearer to the one who is listening than the original text. But that is different from the message itself, isn't it? If not, isn't Frame a bit closer to Barth than he wishes to be? Not really, because his concern is to emphasize that biblical truth is just as authoritative when it comes from the mouth of the preacher as it is when read from the Bible, but he does not intend to equate the preaching of the Bible with the Bible.[8]

An overall assessment of Frame's view of Scripture, and the way its authority shapes theology and his writings, demonstrates that he is more concerned to understand what the Bible says and clearly explain its meaning and significance than he is to produce an academically impressive work. Without question, his intellectual capability to engage the most formidable writings of eminent philosophers and theologians is apparent from his wide range of familiarity with them and the development of their thought.[9] Rather than spewing turgid prose and abstract formulations that would be useful only to a small, elite readership, he writes in a straightforward, personal style. His piety permeates his books, revealing a humble, helpful person who, writing without ostentation because his principal concern is a pastoral one, wants to assist others spiritually by helping them understand what the Bible says and the difference it should make in how they think and live. At one point he refers to an earlier book as a sermon. Seldom do you encounter such a directly pastoral spirit when reading theology. Yet for him, this is the nature of good theology, which is never merely propositional, but also expresses love and praise.

> The purpose of these disciplines is not merely to construct valid and sound arguments but to persuade people, to edify. And the goal is not merely to bring them to intellectual assent but to help them embrace the truth from the heart in love and joy, to motivate them to live out its implications in all areas of life.[10]

8. *DG*, 756.

9. Wayne Grudem, in his formidable *Systematic Theology* (Grand Rapids: Zondervan, 1994), 21, 79, 355, recognizes Frame's influence on him in various ways, including a definition of systematic theology.

10. *DKG*, 322.

For this reason, his volumes should have enduring value and usefulness to pastors who want to understand the theology of the Bible so that they can equip their people. It is the kind of biblically grounded, spiritually sensitive theology that they can confidently teach and preach. To borrow from Frame's statement about preaching, this is authentic theology in which the voice of God is clearly heard. Frankly, if more theology were written like his, it would find a large, avid readership.

During the twentieth century, philosophy—especially secular philosophy—became more esoteric. Theology too felt the shaping influence of academia. Frame has broken free from these influences, although benefiting from their development, as is apparent from his reviews of theological books. The result is the kind of integration of knowledge that is so desired and needed in the church, especially in its pastors. John Frame has not been overcome by the atomization of Western education with its specializations, disciplines, and subdisciplines. Simon Chan says, "There should be no separation between dogmatic theology and spiritual theology." But since we live in a world in which all branches of theology are already separated, we need to emphasize spiritual theology, so he wrote a book for that purpose.[11] Frame provides the kind of integrated model that Chan espouses. Given the damage to the unity of knowledge done by fragmentation of the curriculum, and the consequent effects on culture, his integrative model is far more powerful than it may appear to the naive reader. For as Craig Gay cautions:

> It seems that the ideas with the most profound consequences are frequently taken for granted. They are the ideas that lie just behind conscious thought, providing a kind of foundation for the deliberations of everyday life. These are the ideas that define "the way things are" and demarcate the possibilities of life. Indeed, the more consequential an idea is, the more likely that it is deeply embedded in institutions and traditions and habits of thought.[12]

THE DOCTRINE OF GOD

When considering the doctrine of God, one of the primary "loci" of systematic theology, Frame continues to be unswervingly orthodox. Noth-

---

11. Simon Chan, *Spiritual Theology* (Downers Grove, IL: InterVarsity Press, 1998), 17.
12. Craig Gay, *The Way of the (Modern) World* (Grand Rapids: Eerdmans, 1998).

ing, to him, is more important than knowing God. With Calvin, Frame views this as a matter of the highest priority. All creation communicates some useful, perhaps extremely valuable, information about God, but the Bible explains God's acts and plans so that their meaning is clear. Without the Bible, the information about Christ that is absolutely necessary for salvation would be unavailable. Just as the Bible is necessary in order to understand the gospel, so it is necessary in order to understand the God who is both Creator and Redeemer. Frame emphasizes this because of his concern that, historically, the church has been heavily influenced by philosophy—especially Greek philosophy—so that the nature of reflection and writing about God bears its mark.[13] That influence is not always in accord with the Bible. The only way to escape this problem is to be more directly biblical, and less controlled by philosophical thought and thought forms. His theology aimed at countering that influence becomes A Theology of Lordship, not to be confused with the short-lived Lordship Salvation controversy.[14] The overarching theme of the Bible—its unifying theme—is lordship, because "God is Lord of the Covenant."[15] So, as Frame puts it, "The first thing, and in one sense the only thing, we need to know about God is that he is Lord."[16] As Frame says:

> The doctrine of God, therefore, is not only important for its own sake, as Scripture teaches us, but also particularly important in our own time, as people routinely neglect its vast implications. Our message to the world must emphasize that God is real, and that he will not be trifled with. He is the almighty, majestic Lord of heaven and earth, and he demands our most passionate love and obedience.[17]

Given our secular world in which most people live as if God does not exist—or if he does, he is essentially irrelevant to the realities of their daily lives—Frame's emphasis is highly relevant. God is Lord and everyone is accountable to him, whether one acknowledges it or not.

13. *DG*, 10.

14. This was the controversy between John MacArthur and Zane Hodges. See MacArthur's *Gospel According to Jesus* (Grand Rapids: Zondervan, 1998) and Hodges' *Absolutely Free!* (Grand Rapids: Zondervan, 1989).

15. *DG*, 12.

16. Ibid., 21.

17. Ibid., 2–3.

Influenced by Kline's research and writing on covenant, he distinguishes three major features: control, authority, and presence—a nontraditional, creative nomenclature.[18] As one example, control—as Frame uses it—usually would be referred to as sovereignty and would also be considered as election, providence, the problem of evil, etc. God transcendentally controls everything. He speaks and acts with absolute authority, and he enters his creation and engages his creatures in order to draw them into a covenantal relationship with him. Moreover, everyone is subject to this covenantal relationship. No one can escape, because God is the Lord of all creation. For some, it brings blessing by faith, although for others it delivers judgment and punishment.

IMMANENCE AND TRANSCENDENCE

An example of the care John Frame gives to thinking about and, when necessary, restating what the Bible says about God is illustrated in his discussion of immanence and transcendence, a traditional way of describing God's relationship to the world. These are not, he observes, biblical terms.[19] His preference is to speak of God's presence rather than his immanence, and of God's royal dignity or lordship rather than his transcendence expressed through control and authority.[20] In agreement with Bavinck, he points to the deleterious effect of Greek philosophy on theologians, beginning with the early church and continuing through the modern era. When Bavinck cites Plotinus to that effect, Frame agrees, also mentioning Xenophonus, Lucretius, and the Gnostics.[21] The God of Greek philosophy seems so different and so far above human experience that whatever is known about him must be inadequate and impersonal. If so, what can be said about God with any assurance that it is accurate? Nothing, because he is too distant and different. Skepticism is the inevitable outcome.[22] Immanence poses a problem too, because God becomes virtually indistinguishable from the world. On the one hand, immanence may lead to pantheism, in which the whole world is God. On the other hand, reason or natural law may take on the authority of the divine.[23]

18. Ibid., 42.
19. Ibid., 103. See also *DKG*, 13–18.
20. *DG.*, 105. But he is not opposed to using these words, as he does in *CWM*, 12–15.
21. *DG.*, 107–9.
22. Ibid., 110.
23. Ibid., 111.

In modern philosophy and theology, this influence appears often. It is seen in Kant, Barth, and others. When Kant speaks of the "noumenal," he refers to that which is beyond or above human experience and is therefore unknowable. The "phenomenal," by contrast, may be known by experience. The problem with this, Frame warns, is that in various ways "man replaces God as both the ultimate source and the ultimate interpreter of reality."[24] And as he notes for Barth, God is "wholly other" and "wholly revealed." If Barth is right, then the only way anyone can understand God is by interpreting God's actions, not "through the definite words and sentences of the Bible."[25]

But the point Frame is determined to make is that the concept of lordship or kingship is far more important to understanding God's transcendence than is the idea of someone's being far beyond or above the earth: "It is God's control, not his absence from the world, that keeps us from controlling him."[26] So Barth's concerns about God's transcendence or "hiddenness" were misplaced. The real problem, Frame says, is not

> that theologians have differed over the *degree of emphasis* to be placed on transcendence or immanence. It is rather that modern theologians have adapted *views* of both transcendence and immanence that are sharply opposed to those of the Bible.[27]

These nonbiblical views of transcendence and immanence also imply a non-Christian epistemology. If so, "we are not talking about mere differences of opinion, but about spiritual warfare. These two opposite worldviews are contending today for the hearts of all people."[28] What appeared on the surface to be a matter of definition or emphasis plainly has greater implications as he dissects it. In doing so, Frame plants himself squarely in the tradition of Machen and Van Til.

THE ASEITY OF GOD

In general, theological treatments of the aseity of God are relatively uninspiring and touch on little more than the basic independence and

24. Ibid., 112.
25. Ibid.
26. Ibid.
27. Ibid., 114.
28. Ibid., 115.

self-sufficiency of God. Frame, to his credit and consistent with his methodology, offers practical assistance in understanding the meaning and value of God's aseity, showing that "it is essential to a credible doctrine of God, not a mere bit of abstract theorizing."[29] In fact, Frame desires to demonstrate that although all of God's attributes are absolute, they are personal, not abstract.[30] Reformed theologians, although they may have agreed on the importance of God's aseity, have in general failed to offer convincing biblical support for it. In order to compensate for this deficiency, he addresses numerous texts.[31] One of the benefits of referring to the biblical texts is that it enables Frame to show how this affects the believer's response, particularly for worship. Although most theologians relate aseity to the metaphysical, he suggests that it applies equally to epistemology and ethics, meaning that God is self-attesting and self-justifying, as well as self-existent.

> He not only exists without receiving existence from something else, but also gains his knowledge only from himself (his nature and his plan) and serves as his own criterion of truth. And his righteousness is self-justifying, based on the righteousness of his own nature and on his status as the ultimate criterion of rightness.[32]

What is the importance of God's aseity apart from demonstrating his self-sufficiency and worthiness as the object of our worship? In Frame's opinion, it is extremely important because it makes it possible for God to enter human history without any confusion of his being with that of the world. Because he has no needs, he is not dependent on the world or anything in it, so assuring the clear distinction between Creator and creature that is so necessary to our salvation.

He goes even further by raising the issue of emotions or feelings because not only is it related to aseity, but "without emotions, God would lack intellectual capacity, and he would be unable to speak the full truth about himself and the world."[33] In Scripture, God expresses emotion regularly. God is love, is he not? He becomes angry and is grieved. How can we

---

29. Ibid., 608.
30. Ibid., 602.
31. Ibid., 603–7.
32. Ibid., 602.
33. Ibid., 611.

fail to acknowledge the suffering of Jesus? Or his compassion? And so we have a God whom we can love and trust.

PERSPECTIVALISM

Perspectivalism is a new way of describing the interrelatedness of knowledge and the inescapability of that interrelatedness, or the unity of knowledge and experience. It is another way of saying that you do not understand something well unless you see how it fits into its greater context. The big picture is essential in order to understand the specific. It is also saying that if you walk around a house, it will look different from various angles, and from the outside and inside it looks quite different too. Yet it is one and the same house. So theology must take perspectivalism into account.[34] Frame may not be different from his Reformed heritage, but he certainly states it in a fresh way and is persistent in applying it to his own theological writings. In reflecting on my past, I realize how much more I know now than I did during my early years of study. My perspective on the Bible has changed beneficially as a result. Although this may sound strange to some readers, there are days when I think I am finally beginning to understand how to read the Bible. I now see and understand things that escaped me for years. Then I encounter other people who come from different theological persuasions or cultural backgrounds and notice that they bring a different perspective to reading the Bible and to their understanding of doctrine. They remind me that experience, knowledge, gifts, and interests affect one's view of a specific event or idea. Different perspectives have validity, yet are incomplete. This is one way to explain the occurrence of disagreements about differing accounts of what happened or what was said.

Knowledge is of three kinds for Frame: the world, the self, and the love of God. In one sense they are identical knowledge, but that knowledge comes from different perspectives. So the more one understands the world and himself, the more he can understand the Bible. Does this inadvertently erode the authority of Scripture? Does Frame's perspectivalism yield too much ground here? Frame explains:

34. Vern Poythress, author of *Symphonic Theology* (Phillipsburg, NJ: P&R Publishing, 2001), and John Frame have collaborated to explain perspectivalism. See also: http://www.frame-poythress.org.

Certainly Scripture does have a privileged position: What Scripture says must govern our thinking about the world and the self, and about Scripture too. The reciprocity works this way. We come to know Scripture through our senses and minds (self) and through Scripture's relation with the rest of the world. But then what we read in Scripture must be allowed to correct the ideas we have formed about these other areas. Then as we understand the other areas better, we understand Scripture better. There is a kind of circularity here, a "hermeneutical circle," if you will, but that does not prevent Scripture from ruling our thoughts; it merely describes the process by which that rule takes place.[35]

When explaining the lordship attributes, Frame does so with the triad of authority, control, and presence. These then correlate with the normative, situational, and existential. The triads continue to multiply. For example, the attributes are presented as power, knowledge, and goodness. Then we encounter the triad of accountability, liability, and responsibility, or duty, goal, and motivation, etc. This perspectival perspective appears to be a methodological proclivity that keeps reappearing, but is generally effective in stimulating the reader to think about what is being said in a new and fresh way. The underlying pattern is clear regarding the unity of knowledge. All knowledge is related, so if you discover something from one perspective you will also discover it from the other two. Moreover, you need the other two to understand the first, according to Frame.

CURRENT CHURCH ISSUES

An acquaintance with Frame's writings reveals more than a prolific theological pen and reverent attention to the Scriptures. Given his training and heritage, one might expect a more buttoned-down approach to theology, in the style of post-Reformation theologians. Not so for him. Although Frame respectfully acknowledges the contributions of those who have gone before, he is comfortable with his carefully researched conclusions once he is convinced that the Bible teaches them, regardless of other positions. He is also willing to address some of the current concerns and needs of the church, although it would be easy for him to ignore them and comfortably

35. *DKG*, 89.

write about other matters. Taking on the kinds of current issues that he does requires a certain amount of courage as well as a wholesome desire to contribute to the health of the church.

This is nowhere more apparent than in his writings on worship and church unity. Although his training was in classical music and it remains his preference, he defends contemporary worship music in spite of its deficiencies and problems, because of the good he sees in it. And he is well aware of the disapproval and rejection of much contemporary music by many evangelical Reformed leaders. He has also experienced their disapproval of him for defending contemporary worship music. His response is one of disappointment in his peers who criticize contemporary worship music for what he considers to be wrong reasons, including "aesthetic snobbery, idolatry of the intellect, romanticizing of past history, denominational and theological chauvinism and indifference to biblical principle."[36] Frame, far from being locked into the theological formulas and mind-sets of his tradition, demonstrates a remarkable ability to break from them when he is concerned that they lack adequate scriptural support for their positions. He is willing to reexamine and rethink conventional wisdom and traditional concepts, claiming merely to follow the example of Luther and Calvin.[37] In doing so, he certainly provides a much-needed model for the church.

Although he exposes deficiencies in contemporary worship music that cry for remedy, he finds much that is praiseworthy, too. He discovers much of this music to be strikingly scriptural and "profoundly God-centered and therefore Christ-centered."[38] So he asks, Is contemporary worship music authentically Christian? Does it edify? Does it dumb down worship? He concludes:

> I have often wondered why the theological establishment is so up in arms against contemporary worship music. As we have seen, contemporary worship music is the testimony of young Christians to God's grace in their lives. These songs are very close to the biblical text, focus on the praise of God, and communicate well with people of our time. It is hard to imagine why any knowledgeable Christian thinker would reject such music. But as we have seen, many do so out of ignorance of the songs and because of

36. *CWM*, 52. See also *WST*.
37. *CWM*, 4.
38. Ibid., 31–32.

broader theological agendas wrongly applied to the contemporary worship music songs.[39]

As one who has been an ordained minister in two denominations and seminaries that were the result of separation from mainline Presbyterianism, he is sensitive to the fragmentation of American Protestantism. He approaches the unity of the church, or rather its current disunity, with a candid spirit based on his experience in the church as well as his understanding of the Bible. Both convinced him that there is a need to "overcome the curse of denominationalism that I believe defames our Lord and so often enfeebles our witness."[40] Many denominations and sinful attitudes and behaviors have stained the witness of the church. Denominations are "contrary to God's will," and there are good reasons to seek the abolition of denominationalism, he contends.[41] He is forced to this conclusion by the fact that the unity of the church is a major theme of Scripture.[42] So he suggests steps that can be taken toward reunion. But he is realistic in recognizing some of the reasons for resistance to any suggestion of reunion. As might have been expected, his book received little attention and seems to have made no difference among evangelical Reformed churches other than to arouse criticism. True enough, it would have been well served by at least one more rewrite, but the outcome likely would have been the same.

What is striking, however, is Frame's willingness to address such important needs. Even more helpful is his ability to make it seem as if he is talking directly to you about this subject. In doing so, he has established a wholesome model for the church toward maturing and becoming what God intends it to be. Perhaps he will yet stir the uneasy conscience of evangelicals so that we can focus on these issues constructively in the unity of the Spirit.

We should be grateful for theologians such as John Frame who love the Lord and honor the Bible as his authoritative Word, not merely with lip service but consistently with their lives. He has reaped the harvest of historical scholarship and produced an appetizing, edifying body of work that will stimulate the church to think, pray, and live so that God will be pleased.

39. Ibid., 129.
40. *ER*. Posted at http://www.reformedperspectives.org and http://www.frame-poythress.org.
41. Ibid., 45.
42. Ibid., 70.

12

John Frame and Evangelicalism

James H. Grant Jr. and Justin Taylor

A Personal Introduction

It is a distinct and humbling honor for us to be part of the writing of this volume dedicated to our teacher and friend John Frame. In contrast with many of the contributors in this volume, we are members of a younger generation of students taught by Professor Frame (in twenty-first-century Orlando instead of twentieth-century Philadelphia or Escondido). As nontraditional students at Reformed Theological Seminary Orlando (laboring at that time in full-time ministry positions in Minneapolis and Chattanooga), we made several trips to Florida to take intensive classes—each of which consisted of forty hours of lectures in one week. The first class we took was Frame's Pastoral and Social Ethics, which was his popular class on the Doctrine of the Christian Life, a course he had been teaching and revising for nearly four decades (first at Westminster Theological Seminary in Philadelphia, then at Westminster Seminary California, and later at RTS Orlando). We chose the class for the opportunity to sit under the teaching of a man who already had significantly shaped our thinking through his writings.

As we sat under Frame's teaching that week, it slowly dawned on us that we were not only participating with our fellow students in that classroom, but were also being connected with hundreds of students from years past, many of them now influential teachers and preachers (e.g., Kevin Vanhoozer, Wayne Grudem, Richard Pratt, and almost all the faculty at RTS in Orlando). We also recognized that as a student himself, Frame had studied under some of the most gifted Reformed teachers of the twentieth century, including Cornelius Van Til, John Murray, and E. J. Young. They, in turn, were connected to the likes of J. Gresham Machen, B. B. Warfield, and Geerhardus Vos. We felt the privilege of sitting under the teaching of one who was connected to and continuing in the lineage of a faithful tradition of biblically rigorous teachers promoting and transferring sound doctrine.

Frame frequently spoke in his classes about the tradition of Reformed theology, and the confessions were mandatory reading.[1] Following that tradition, Frame's methodology in teaching ethics was to expound the Ten Commandments using the Westminster Larger Catechism,[2] but in each class was a particular influence from John Murray. Frame explains, "Though I'm a philosopher by background, I agree with John Murray that exegesis is the heart of the systematic theologian's work."[3] Elsewhere he writes, "Murray's actual theological writing consists almost entirely of the exegesis of particular texts: the proof texts of the doctrines under consideration. . . . Murray showed me that the Reformed faith was purely and simply the teaching of Scripture."[4] In this volume, Frame makes a similar point: "What I learned best from Murray was his theological method. . . . His classes were almost entirely spent in exegeting the main biblical sources on each topic."[5]

Following Murray's example, the class on ethics was largely an examination of what the whole Bible has to say today about ethical goals, motives, and standards with regard to various vexing issues. We probably examined more biblical texts in that ethics class than many classes devoted to biblical studies! Frame taught us the importance of interacting with tradition within the classroom, and demonstrated the central role that the Bible must play for any theologian.

Despite the fact that Frame was spending nearly eight hours a day teaching and answering questions—even during the breaks—he graciously agreed to go to lunch with us at the local Subway (where of course he would answer even

1. Frame assigned the relevant sections in the Belgic Confession, Heidelberg Catechism, Westminster Confession of Faith, Westminster Larger Catechism, and Westminster Shorter Catechism.
2. See *DCL*, 385–850.
3. John Frame, "Becoming a Theology Professor," http://www.frame-poythress.org/frame_articles/Professor.htm.
4. *IDSCB*, 277 (also published as an appendix to *CWM*).
5. John Frame, "Backgrounds to My Thought," in this festschrift.

more questions about theology, ethics, and a wide range of other topics). These discussions would be the first of many outside-the-class conversations, and included e-mails. This willingness to continue the conversation demonstrated for us something of his own multiperspectival theology and life.

We have a great deal of respect and affection for John Frame, and we are thankful for his work in theology, apologetics, philosophy, and ethics—as well as his personal investment in our lives.

AN OVERVIEW OF THIS ESSAY

Our assigned topic concerns John Frame's engagement with evangelicalism, in terms of both his influence on evangelicalism and its possible influence on him. Two or three caveats are important to mention at the outset. First, measuring influence is usually a difficult and subjective task. There are some clear-cut examples of teachers and their work directly and decisively changing the intellectual landscape and course of study for a particular field.[6] But by and large, influence works more subtly and indirectly, in ways that elude precision and definitive conclusions. The result is that humility requires any analyst to make judgments provisionally.

Second, as good Van Tillian/Framean presuppositionalists we readily acknowledge our lack of neutrality in this discussion. We are both products of, and ministers in, the broader evangelical world. We were not raised in a confessionally Reformed/Presbyterian environment. Although we have Reformational inclinations and instincts,[7] this is not properly an insider's account. Rather, we intend to offer an exploratory evaluation from an evangelical perspective regarding Frame's engagement with evangelicalism.

Finally, when we speak of "evangelicalism" we are referring to a broad movement that is difficult to define, with doctrinal parameters that continue

6. E. P. Sanders, *Paul and Palestinian Judaism* (Philadelphia: Fortress Press, 1977), comes to mind as an example for the way that it fundamentally altered the conversation among NT scholars, especially in Pauline studies.

7. This is an admittedly clumsy way of describing ourselves so as not to offend those who dislike Baptists calling themselves "Reformed," but we are being careful here because the definition of being Reformed is part of the controversy discussed in this essay. Our Reformational inclinations would include a desire to be "confessional" evangelicals, and although other writers make a distinction between *confessional* and *confessionalism*, giving a negative connotation to the latter, we are not drawing that type of distinction in this essay.

to be debated.[8] Obviously, we cannot enter into the debate for purposes of this essay, but we would point to something like Timothy George's summary as a working definition of evangelicalism at its best:

> At its heart [evangelicalism] is a theological core shaped by the Trinitarian and Christological consensus of the early church, the formal and material principles of the Reformation, the missionary movement that grew out of the Great Awakening and the new movements of the Spirit that indicate "surprising works of God" are still happening today.[9]

This not only helps us define evangelicalism, but provides us a particular picture of the world in which we are situating John Frame.

How has Frame engaged and interacted with evangelicalism—this movement born from but broader than the Reformation? At least two perspectives should be considered when discussing Frame and evangelicalism. The first is Frame's concern that the Reformed world truly believe what it confesses with regard to *sola Scriptura*, which in turn lessens the functionally authoritative role of tradition. In doing so, the intended effect can be seen as a broadening of today's Reformed world, infusing it with a more evangelical spirit. The second perspective is Frame's direct engagement with evangelicals and influence on them. Putting the two together, perhaps we could label these as Frame's evangelical influence in the Reformed world, and his Reformed influence on the evangelical world.

FRAME'S EVANGELICAL INFLUENCE IN THE REFORMED WORLD

John Frame has spent his ministerial life—his church involvement, teaching, lecturing, writing, etc.—largely within the Reformed/Presbyterian

8. For a helpful survey and informed proposal, see D. A. Carson, *Evangelicalism: What Is It and Is It Worth Keeping?* (Wheaton, IL: Crossway, forthcoming). For historical studies, see David W. Bebbington, *Evangelicals in Modern Britain: A History from the 1730s to the 1980s* (Grand Rapids: Baker, 1992), and D. G. Hart, ed., *Reckoning with the Past: Historical Essays on American Evangelicalism from the Institute for the Study of American Evangelicals* (Grand Rapids: Baker, 1995). For an alternative perspective on evangelicalism that is relevant to this essay, see also D. G. Hart, *Deconstructing Evangelicalism: Conservative Protestantism in the Age of Billy Graham* (Grand Rapids: Baker, 2003).

9. Timothy George, "Foreword," in *The Advent of Evangelicalism*, ed. Michael A. G. Haykin and Kenneth J. Steward (Nashville: B&H Academic, 2008), 14–15.

world. Although some have resisted his ideas, there seems little doubt that he has been a voice of influence.

Throughout his teaching career, Frame assigned the confessions as supplemental reading material in his various classes, interacting with the confessional tradition.[10] Although respecting this tradition, Frame has never treated it as sacrosanct. A strict and narrow confessional approach to Reformed theology, he argues, is in tension with the very confessions, not to mention Scripture itself. He is a *sola Scriptura* man, even describing his approach as "something close to biblicism." He explains: "We should expect that those who hold an authentic view of *sola Scriptura* will sometimes be confused with biblicists. Indeed, if we are not occasionally accused of biblicism, we should be concerned about the accuracy of our teaching in this area."[11]

Frame's multiperspectival approach to theology and tradition allows him to see different types of contributions to a theological problem, thus appreciating different traditions outside his own. From one perspective, Frame's work and engagement within the Reformed tradition was an attempt to move the church from a more narrow approach (which Frame often calls the "truly Reformed" view) to a broader "catholic" or "evangelical" perspective. Frame's approach here is both theological and attitudinal. As he says in his essay in this volume about the approach at RTS Orlando: "Here we have a slogan: we are not T.R. ('truly Reformed') or B.R. ('barely Reformed'), but W.R. ('winsomely Reformed')."[12]

This broadly evangelical/catholic push by John Frame brought about several controversies in the Reformed world, with two issues dominating the debate: the nature of Reformed worship and the nature of Reformed confessionalism.[13] In each of these cases, those disagreeing with Frame argued that he was not being consistently Reformed, which means he was not following

10. In "My Use of the Reformed Confessions," http://www.frame-poythress.org/frame_articles/MyUse.htm, Frame writes: "I make much use of the confessions, asking the students to read relevant portions of them and sometimes including material from the confessions in my lectures and exams. I do more of this, I believe, than my own teachers did at Westminster/Phila. in the early 1960s. At the same time, my courses are not catechism courses. The confessions and catechisms are not the focus of my teaching, although I do mention them and make substantial use of them. Rather the focus of my teaching is our primary standard, the Word of God itself."

11. *IDSCB*, 275.

12. Frame, "Backgrounds."

13. Certainly the case can be made for a third controversy, namely, Frame's view of the church as articulated in *ER*. In that book, Frame argues that denominationalism is a sin, and he encourages the Reformed church to adopt a more broadly "catholic" posture toward other denominations instead of narrowly defining itself, and urges Reformed ministers and churches to par-

the Reformed confessions (or, more particularly, the Westminster Standards). The implication, it seems, is that Frame claims to be Reformed but often sounds like and functions like an evangelical biblicist. We will consider the issues of worship and confessionalism in turn.

The Worship Debate

Frame's concentrated work on the theology and practice of worship came about in a ministerial context. Frame moved to California in 1980 to start the West Coast outpost of Westminster Seminary and help plant New Life Presbyterian Church in Escondido. Frame explains that the leadership had a specific goal with this church plant: "We hoped to reach the unchurched, rather than merely to attract Reformed people."[14] One of the ways that they reached out to the unchurched was through a more contemporary form of worship. Frame, as the elder in charge of worship, taught an adult Sunday school class on this topic in order to think and teach biblically through issues related to worship style and the Reformed tradition.[15]

It was over a decade later that Frame took some of his conclusions to the broader Reformed world, publishing "Some Questions about the Regulative Principle" in 1992.[16] The Westminster Confession of Faith 21.1 explains the regulative principle of worship (hereafter RPW)[17] as follows:

---

ticipate in the evangelical world. The issues of worship and confessionalism are specific cases of Frame's view of the church, and hence they provide examples of a more evangelical outlook.

14. Frame, "Backgrounds."

15. This eventually led to *WST*.

16. John Frame, "Some Questions about the Regulative Principle," *WTJ* 54, 2 (Fall 1992): 357–66.

17. The debate over the RPW is also beyond the scope of our paper. Frame's position is evident in his articles as well as *WST* and *CWM*. One should also consult R. J. Gore Jr., *Covenantal Worship: Reconsidering the Puritan Regulative Principle* (Phillipsburg, NJ: P&R Publishing, 2002). For variations on the traditional view, see Hughes Oliphant Old, *Worship That Is Reformed According to Scriptures* (Atlanta: John Knox Press, 1984); Frank J. Smith and David C. Lachman, eds., *Worship in the Presence of God* (Greenville, SC: Greenville Seminary Press, 1992); Philip Graham Ryken, Derek W. H. Thomas, and J. Ligon Duncan III, eds., *Give Praise to God: A Vision for Reforming Worship: Celebrating the Legacy of James Montgomery Boice* (Phillipsburg, NJ: P&R Publishing, 2003). Frame had not only traditional critics, but also liturgical critics in the Presbyterian world. The liturgical critics, however, agreed with Frame's arguments against a narrow interpretation of the RPW. They simply disagreed with his acceptance of more contemporary forms of worship. As an example, see Jeffrey J. Meyers, *The Lord's Service: The Grace of Covenant Renewal Worship* (Moscow, ID: Canon Press, 2003), 408.

But the acceptable way of worshiping the true God is instituted by himself, and so limited by his own revealed will, that he may not be worshiped according to the imaginations and devices of men, or the suggestions of Satan, under any visible representation, or any other way not prescribed in the Holy Scripture.

Frame happily assents to this teaching, understanding it to mean that we may do in worship only what Scripture *prescribes* (in distinction from the Lutheran-Anglican view that our worship is acceptable as long as Scripture does not *prohibit* it). The rub comes in the application of this principle. For Frame, the RPW applies not only to worship in a church service but to all of life.[18] For those in the Scottish and Puritan tradition, however, the RPW as applied to ecclesiastical worship has a more narrow and specific intention.[19]

In 1993, T. David Gordon, then a professor at Gordon-Conwell Theological Seminary, responded to Frame's questions with an article appropriately titled, "Some Answers about the Regulative Principle."[20] Gordon appealed to the historical development of the RPW, insisting that it must be understood first of all as an ecclesiastical doctrine that applies Presbyterian theology to both the scope of church power and the liberty of conscience. Gordon's basic argument against Frame is one that critics continue to make: Frame has reinterpreted the RPW to the point that it no longer reflects what the Reformed tradition and confessions articulated.

18. Frame states: "But when you think about it, the regulative principle is not limited to worship services. It is God's regulative principle for all areas of human life. It is not only in our Sunday worship services that we seek to please God rather than ourselves (1 Thess. 4:1, 2; 2 Tim. 2:3–4). Indeed, says Paul, 'whether you eat or drink or whatever you do, do it all for the glory of God' (1 Cor. 10:31). How do we find out how to glorify God in all of life? The same way we find out how to glorify God in worship: we consult His Word. So the sufficiency of Scripture is for all of life, not merely for one segment of it. The passages listed in the previous paragraph deal with all of life; they are not limited to the governance of worship meetings" ("A Fresh Look at the Regulative Principle," http://www.frame-poythress.org/frame_articles/RegulativePrinciple.htm).

19. See Edmund P. Clowney, "Distinctive Emphases in Presbyterian Church Polity," in *Pressing Toward the Mark: Essays Commemorating Fifty Years of the Orthodox Presbyterian Church*, ed. C. G. Dennison and R. Gamble (Philadelphia: Committee for the Historian of the Orthodox Presbyterian Church, 1986), 99–110. Clowney explains that historically the RPW addresses the scope of church power and the liberty of conscience concerning the Puritan struggle against state-imposed forms of worship.

20. T. David Gordon, "Some Answers about the Regulative Principle," *WTJ* 55, 2 (Fall 1993): 321–33. Gordon also provides a comprehensive bibliography regarding the historical development of the RPW.

Frame responded[21] to Gordon the following year by reiterating his concern with being biblical, and arguing that Reformed theology is often too "historical" in its approach. Frame argued that by focusing on the historical perspective of the RPW, Reformed theologians have lost the significance of the biblical perspective of the RPW.

Although the debate continued in various ways,[22] our interest in this story regards Frame's influence on the Reformed world. In the past twenty years, numerous Reformed churches have adopted contemporary forms of worship. Certainly this was not solely because of Frame's arguments and influence—but at the same time we should not underestimate the effective power of the case he set forth. Frame provided an interpretation of the RPW that allows a minister in a Reformed church to practice a more "evangelical" and contemporary form of worship without denying the RPW (or his own subscription to the Westminster Standards). The result is that worship in many Reformed churches looks much closer to certain types of evangelical worship than it does to what took place within the tradition.

The Confessional Debate

The debate on worship soon turned into a debate on confessionalism.[23] This was implicit in the exchange between Frame and Gordon in the *WTJ*,

21. John Frame, "Reply to T. David Gordon," *WTJ* 56, 1 (Spring 1994): 181–83. In the article, Frame references his paper "The Lordship of Christ and the Regulative Principle of Worship." Frame wrote this for the Worship Task Force of the Committee on Mission to North America, Presbyterian Church in America. It is an early draft of *WST*. What happened in the course of these events was that others in the Reformed tradition were critical of the worship approach adopted by New Life Presbyterian in Escondido and articulated in *WST*. *CWM* is the result of his arguments against those who opposed the style of worship articulated in *WST* and demonstrated at New Life Escondido.

22. For the arguments against Frame, see D. G. Hart, "It May Be Refreshing, But Is It Reformed?" *Calvin Theological Journal* 32 (1997): 423–31; Derek Thomas, "The Regulative Principle: Responding to Recent Criticism," in *Give Praise to God*, 74–93; Frank J. Smith and David C. Lachman, "Reframing Presbyterian Worship: A Critical Survey of the Worship Views of John M. Frame and R. J. Gore," *The Confessional Presbyterian* 1 (2005): 116–50; D. G. Hart and John Muether, *With Reverence and Awe: Returning to the Basics of Reformed Worship* (Phillipsburg, NJ: P&R Publishing, 2002); Terry L. Johnson, *Reformed Worship: Worship That Is According to Scripture* (Greenville, SC: Reformed Academic Press, 2002); R. Scott Clark, *Recovering the Reformed Confession: Our Theology, Piety, and Practice* (Phillipsburg, NJ: P&R Publishing, 2008), chap. 7: "Recovering Reformed Worship," 227–91. In response, one should consult Frame's unpublished essay "A Fresh Look at the Regulative Principle," http://www.frame-poythress.org/frame_articles/RegulativePrinciple.htm. For Frame's most recent work on the RPW, see *DCL*, 451–86, which covers the second commandment.

23. Our purpose is to observe this debate in relation to Frame, not to sketch out the nature of confessionalism (whether strict or system). On this topic, see Charles Hodge, *Discussions in*

but it became explicit in a 1998 debate on the Warfield e-mail list between Darryl Hart and John Frame on "The Regulative Principle: Scripture, Tradition, and Culture."[24] In this debate, the issue of what "Reformed" worship looks like comes up for discussion, especially concerning the confessions and traditions of the Reformed church. Early in the debate, Hart even says, "One of the reasons I was ambivalent about a debate on the RPW was that it would not really be about worship, but rather about hermeneutics, theological method, and ecclesiology." Hart argues that Frame's view on worship is not in line with the confession and is therefore not Presbyterian or Reformed, and Frame counters by arguing that Hart depends too much on history and does not have a healthy perspective on *sola Scriptura* in his understanding of the confession.

A similar debate took place in Frame's 1997 exchange with David Wells and Richard Muller in the *WTJ*.[25] It was in the midst of this that Frame wrote his article on *sola Scriptura* and biblicism (*IDSCB*), which he considers one of his most important articles. As he articulates his view of *sola Scriptura*, Frame expresses concern over the trend in both the evangelical and Reformed worlds to argue from a historical and/or contemporary basis, instead of grounding arguments in Scripture. He sees this demonstrated in the writings of David Wells and Richard Muller.[26]

As Frame develops the argument, his concern with historical and sociological analysis leads to an explanation of the dangers of confessionalism:

> I certainly favor a renewed confessionalism if it means a better appreciation for the teaching of the Reformation *solas*, indeed for the distinctive teach-

---

Church Polity, repr. ed. (New York: Westminster, 2001); Samuel Miller, *Doctrinal Integrity: The Utility and Importance of Creeds and Confessions and Adherence to Our Doctrinal Standards* (Dallas: Presbyterian Heritage Publications, 1989); John Skilton, ed., *Scripture and Confession: A Book about Confessions Old and New* (Nutley, NJ: Presbyterian and Reformed, 1973); David W. Hall, ed., *The Practice of Confessional Subscription* (Oak Ridge, TN: Covenant Foundation, 1997); and Clark, *Recovering the Reformed Confession*, 153–91.

24. Available online at http://www.frame-poythress.org/frame_articles/1998HartDebate.htm.

25. Along with *IDSCB*, see David Wells, "On Being Framed," *WTJ* 59, 2 (Fall 1997): 293–300; Richard Muller, "Historiography in the Service of Theology and Worship: Toward Dialogue with John Frame," *WTJ* 59, 2 (Fall 1997): 301–10; and Frame, "Reply to Richard Muller and David Wells," *WTJ* 59, 2 (Fall 1997): 311–18.

26. In *IDSCB* (282–88), Frame targets David Wells's two books *No Place for Truth* (Grand Rapids: Eerdmans, 1993) and *God in the Wasteland* (Grand Rapids: Eerdmans, 1994). For some background to *IDSCB*, see Frame, "Muller on Theology," *WTJ* 56, 1 (Spring 1994): 133–51; and Richard Muller, "The Study of Theology Revisited: A Response to John Frame," *WTJ* 56, 2 (Fall 1994): 409–17. *IDSCB* is a response to this last article from Muller. See also Frame's more recent essay, *TRAD*.

ings of the Reformed faith. The argument of this paper, however, should help us to guard against certain abuses of the confessionalist position, such as (1) emphasizing Confessions and traditions as if they were equal to Scripture in authority, (2) equating *sola Scriptura* with acceptance of confessional traditions, (3) automatic suspicion of any ideas which come from sources outside the tradition, (4) focusing on historical polemics rather than the dangers of the present day, (5) emphasizing differences with other confessional traditions to the virtual exclusion of recognizing commonalities, (6) failing to encourage self-criticism within our particular denominational, theological, and confessional communities.[27]

Frame's perspective on confessionalism is controlled by his concern regarding what he perceives as the abuse of the confessionalist position and his overall commitment to *sola Scriptura*.

Although few theologically oriented evangelicals would disagree with Frame's concerns regarding these abuses, he is clearly at odds with many in the Reformed tradition. Hart registered his objections in the debate on the RPW, and W. Robert Godfrey, president of Westminster Seminary California, offers a perspective similar to that of Hart:

> While fully recognizing that our confessions are human writings and may need to be changed in light of clearer understandings of the Word of God, our attitude to them in the first place is not critical, not even "sympathetic-critical." Our attitude in the first place is one of confidence because we have subscribed to them as our confession of faith.[28]

Frame would certainly be included among those who approach the confession in a "sympathetic-critical" manner.[29]

---

27. *IDSCB*, 290.

28. W. Robert Godfrey, "Westminster Seminary, the Doctrine of Justification, and the Reformed Confessions," in *The Pattern of Sound Doctrine: Systematic Theology at the Westminster Seminaries: Essays in Honor of Robert B. Strimple*, ed. David VanDrunen (Phillipsburg, NJ: P&R Publishing, 2004), 142. John R. Muether makes a similar point in the same volume: "The Whole Counsel of God: Westminster Seminary and the Orthodox Presbyterian Church," 223–54. See also Clark, *Recovering the Reformed Confession*, 17–27.

29. The term comes from Klaas Schilder and is used approvingly by Richard B. Gaffin Jr., "The Vitality of Reformed Dogmatics," in *The Vitality of Reformed Dogmatics*, ed. J. M. Batteau et al. (Kampen: Kok, 1994), 21; and Tim J. R. Trumper, "Covenant Theology and Constructive Theology," *WTJ* 64, 2 (Fall 2002): 388. Godfrey is arguing against them, but he also references Frame's interest in "improving upon" the confession from *IDSCB*, 279.

Why would we include these controversies in our chapter? We cannot engage these debates or even evaluate them in detail, but we do want to make an observation. From an evangelical perspective, it is often hard to wrap our minds around the form of confessionalism that Hart and Godfrey articulate. Even evangelicals who rightly resist *nuda Scriptura* (an understanding of Scripture supposedly abstracted from tradition) still tend to view strict subscription (at the level of detail of the Westminster Standards) as a functional threat to *sola Scriptura*. In that regard, Frame's position seems to take the biblical high ground, and hence is convincing to the average evangelical. The world in which Hart "situates" himself is one with which we are not completely familiar, and is in some ways a world difficult for evangelicals to understand. That seems to be precisely Hart's point: Reformed confessionalists are neither evangelical nor liberal.[30] So in both of these situations, evangelicals feel very comfortable with John Frame's arguments.[31]

Frame's influence on the Reformed church has been very broad, but our goal has been to demonstrate that Frame's particular influence on the Reformed church, as it relates to evangelicalism, was to encourage Reformed ministers and churches to follow the Scriptures and embrace a more "catholic" or evangelical Christianity, which brings the Reformed world closer to the evangelical world.

Frame's Reformed Influence on the Evangelical World

The second perspective concerns Frame's influence on evangelicals. Although Frame was pushing the Reformed world back to *sola Scriptura* and hence toward a more broadly evangelical position on certain issues, was he also pushing evangelicals toward a more robust Calvinism, a more God-centered approach to church life and theology? This is harder to gauge because Frame's influence on evangelicals has largely been indirect.

Frame began his theological reputation while a student of Cornelius Van Til at Westminster Theological Seminary. That reputation continued as he taught first at Westminster Theological Seminary in Philadelphia, then at Westminster Seminary California, and later at RTS Orlando. All these

---

30. See D. G. Hart, *Lost Soul of American Protestantism* (Lanham, MD: Rowman & Littlefield Publishers, 2002).

31. See below for further confirmation of Frame's influence on evangelical worship.

institutions are within the tradition that flows from the original Westminster Theological Seminary and the Presbyterian and Reformed world.

Although Frame is well known within the Presbyterian and Reformed world, he is relatively unknown in the broader evangelical world outside "Reformed confessionalism." In some ways this almost seems to have been by design. Although Frame lectures and writes *about* the wider worlds of evangelicalism and Christendom, his personal engagement has by and large been confined to Reformed and Presbyterian churches, institutions, ministries, journals, publishers, speaking venues, dialogue partners, etc.

Each of us has a unique calling from God, and each person must determine where best to utilize his or her gifts—cognizant of both strengths and weaknesses. It is not finally for others to judge, but at the same time we do not think Professor Frame would mind if we at least raised a few questions as we try to apply the theology from *ER*.

First, we stand in admiration of Frame's self-described homebody nature with regard to his local church. In the original preface to *ER* he wrote:

> All of what I know about God and about Jesus, I have learned, directly or indirectly, from the church. Most of my spiritual encouragement, challenge, comfort, has been through the church. Most of my friendships have been within the church. (I do admire Christians who are able to develop deep friendships with non-Christians, but I don't seem to have that gift.) Most of the love I have known has been in the church. I found my wife in the church, and now my children are growing up in the church. My home away from home is always the church. My favorite music is the music of the church. My favorite people are the people of the church. Many of my favorite times have been times spent in the worship of the church.
>
> I am probably even more "churchy" in my lifestyle than most theology professors. A theologian can justify a certain amount of "church hopping": spending his Sundays preaching and teaching in one church after another, never putting down roots in a single fellowship. For various reasons of temperament and gifts, I have never felt that God has called me to such an itinerant ministry, although I have no quarrel with my colleagues who do sense such a call. I am a "stay at home" type. I serve on the session of my local Presbyterian church. Every Sunday I play the piano and lead the congregation in worship. Often I will teach Sunday School as well.

273

You will find only admiration from us for a theologian of Frame's stature who week in and week out is happy to serve and to teach and to play piano and organ in his local church. But as a vocational writer and speaker, could Frame have done more to step outside his ecclesiastical circles in order to teach and engage evangelicals at large?

In an online appendix to *ER*, posted in 2000, Frame takes issue with the "village green" model of evangelicalism,[32] wherein evangelicals gather occasionally on the green but then retreat to their various dwelling places for worship and fellowship. Frame writes:

> Does Scripture give us [the] right to regard denominations as our true homes, our true family, and [the] rest of the world-wide body of Christ as a group of people outside the family with whom we may occasionally mingle? In my view, Scripture teaches that our true family is the whole body of Christ, not one segment of it. And if the whole body of Christ is our family, then it should live in one house, not just mingle occasionally on the village green.[33]

This issue of intentionally ministering, living, and fellowshipping with evangelicals is significant. Might some of the debates within evangelicalism have been well served by the more active "mingling" of a John Frame?[34] Would not evangelicals have been helped by reading his work and hearing him debate within the pages of *Christianity Today*? Would his ideas be better known if he had consistently presented papers at the

---

32. See, e.g., Michael Scott Horton, "Reflection: Is Evangelicalism Reformed or Wesleyan? Reopening the Marsden-Dayton Debate," *Christian Scholar's Review* 31 (2001): 131–55.

33. John Frame, "Appendix 2: Reunion, 2000," *ER*, 2nd ed., Web site version only, http://www.frame-poythress.org/frame_books/Evangelical_Reunion/Appendix2.html.

34. Lest we overstate our case, Frame has contributed to some important volumes, wherein he advances arguments for his position alongside members of the wider Christian community. For example, see Frame's essay "Men and Women in the Image of God," in *Recovering Biblical Manhood and Womanhood*, ed. John Piper and Wayne Grudem (Wheaton, IL: Crossway, 2006), 225–32. This book brought together men and women, Calvinists and Arminians, Baptists and Presbyterians, to make the case for a complementarian understanding of gender roles. Frame defended presuppositionalism and interacted with other approaches in the book *Five Views on Apologetics*, ed. Steve Cowan (Grand Rapids: Zondervan, 2000). He also participated in symposia on the doctrine of Scripture that resulted in the following essays: "Scripture Speaks for Itself," in *God's Inerrant Word*, ed. John W. Montgomery (Minneapolis: Bethany Fellowship, 1974), 178–200; and "The Spirit and the Scriptures," in *Hermeneutics, Authority and Canon*, ed. D. A. Carson and John Woodbridge (Grand Rapids: Zondervan, 1986), 217–35.

Evangelical Theological Society, or published essays advancing his arguments in *JETS*?[35] We, of course, are not privy to all of John Frame's relationships and actions in his decades of teaching and ministerial life, but we agree with Frame's call in *ER* to "Get involved in situations . . . where you are forced to share fellowship and/or ministry with Christians from other traditions."[36]

How precisely do we gauge the influence on evangelicalism of a theologian and churchman who lived most of his life within the confines of a confessionally Presbyterian environment and did not directly participate in evangelical institutions? We described Frame earlier as "relatively unknown" within evangelicalism, but that is different from saying that he is "completely unknown."[37] Frame's influence has levels of significance despite some of the challenges that we have identified.

Evangelicals in the Classroom

Although Frame has taught at specifically Reformed institutions throughout his career, his teaching in the classroom should be considered as part of his evangelical influence. Many students from broader evangelical backgrounds attended the seminaries in which Frame taught. RTS Orlando has workers and students from institutions such as Campus Crusade and Wycliffe, both of which are in Orlando. For more objective evidence, a brief examination of this present volume will allow the reader to see Frame's influence on evangelicalism. In each section there are individuals who represent broader evangelicalism, and this is part of the story of John Frame's legacy. Despite the fact that he did not directly engage evangelicalism through its most significant institutions and outlets, he continues to have an influence that only seems to be growing.

35. For example, Frame's book *NOG* is a direct engagement with the evangelical compromise concerning open theism, and many evangelicals have appreciated *NOG* as a significant rebuttal of this error. This is another good example of Frame's engaging in a debate that was a controversy outside the Reformed world. Perhaps it would have been helpful to the broader evangelical world to read something of those arguments in the pages of *CT* or *JETS*, or hear those arguments at ETS during the controversy.

36. *ER*, 165–66.

37. In 2003, *DG* won the Gold Medallion Award for Theology and Doctrine—an honor bestowed each year by the Evangelical Christian Publishing Association in honor of the best theology book of the year. Frame's work is solidly Calvinistic, providing evangelicals with a Reformed understanding of God's control, authority, and presence through the perspective of his lordship.

Frame on the Web

One of the advantages of the Internet is that influencing new pockets of Christendom is not limited by place. Beginning in 2006, Andrew Dionne helped John Frame and his former student and colleague and now theological partner, Vern Poythress, start the Frame-Poythress Web site. This provides access to a majority of Frame's articles, essays, class notes, and books. It has provided many avenues of influence in the evangelical world, as other popular evangelical Web sites such as http://www.monergism.com link to various articles. Monergism lists Frame in its Hall of Contemporary Reformers, alongside John Piper, R. C. Sproul, Tim Keller, John MacArthur, D. A. Carson, and others.

The rise of evangelical blogging has also contributed to Frame's newly found influence in the evangelical world. Two popular evangelical blogs, Challies.com and Between Two Worlds (http://theologica.blogspot.com), occasionally reference Frame's work.[38] In turn, other blogs connected to individuals and ministries now occasionally mention John Frame and cite his work.[39] This has resulted in YouTube videos and interviews for Frame,[40] which again have broadened his evangelical influence.

With the rise of the Internet and the popularity of online MP3s, more ministries offer their audio and video resources online, and Reformed Theological Seminary made a strategic move by putting many of its lectures on iTunes for free. This includes courses taught by John Frame, allowing people to discover the rich content of his work. To provide but one anecdotal example: Dan Phillips, a well-known contributor to the popular blog "PyroManiacs," posted an entry at his personal blog "Biblical Christianity" about his new appreciation for Frame's teaching. He had heard Frame's name, but had never read anything by him. When he downloaded the lectures, he found them to be "thoroughly enjoyable, stimulating, informative, and thought-provoking. Frame sounds like a wonderful teacher—and now his books are on my ever lengthening (never-shortening) list."[41] Here is someone who had never met Frame, never taken a

38. Third Millennium Ministries hosts several of John Frame's writings as well, http://www.thirdmill.org.

39. For example, see Pyromaniacs, http://teampyro.blogspot.com; Desiring God, http://www.desiringgod.org/Blog; The Resurgence, http://theresurgence.com; and Sovereign Grace, http://www.sovereigngraceministries.org/Blog.

40. Going to Seminary, http://www.goingtoseminary.com/frame/.

41. Dan Phillips, "New Appreciation: John Frame," posted on the Biblical Christianity blog on February 12, 2008, http://www.bibchr.blogspot.com/2008/02/new-appreciation-john-frame.

class from him in person, never even read a book by him—who in this digital age is being influenced by Frame's teaching and is suggesting it to others.

This pattern is repeated countless times as a new generation is introduced to Frame. They may vaguely recall his name—knowing perhaps that he has written books, or remembering that Wayne Grudem dedicated his best-selling *Systematic Theology* to Frame (along with several others). Then they see his name on blogs, read an article online, or are sent an iTunes link with a relevant lecture. The result is that Frame continues to have a slowly growing, but steady and increasingly significant, presence in the evangelical world.

Modified Van Tillian Presuppositional Apologetics

Thus far, our suggestions regarding his influence on evangelicals have been broad and anecdotal, but it may be instructive to examine the various areas of contribution that have influenced evangelicals. One example is apologetics. In some ways, John Frame is the theologian who introduced evangelicals to Cornelius Van Til. One way that he did this was by writing introductory essays on Van Til for publications aimed at evangelicals: the *Handbook of Evangelical Theologians*,[42] the *Biographical Dictionary of Evangelicals*,[43] the *New Dictionary of Apologetics*,[44] and the *Apologetics Study Bible*.[45] In 2000 Frame participated with other scholars—from different denominations and philosophical perspectives—in a book called *Five Views on Apologetics*.[46] Since these essays were published by mainstream evangelical presses, they not only introduced evangelicals to Van Til, but also directed readers to additional books on apologetics and Van Til's thought.[47]

---

html (accessed July 3, 2009).

42. John Frame, "Cornelius Van Til," in *Handbook of Evangelical Theologians*, ed. Walter A. Elwell (Grand Rapids: Baker, 1993), 156–67.

43. John Frame, "Cornelius Van Til," in *Biographical Dictionary of Evangelicals*, ed. Timothy T. Larsen, David W. Bebbington, and Mark A. Noll (Downers Grove, IL: InterVarsity Press, 2003), 682–84.

44. John Frame, "Van Til, Cornelius," in *New Dictionary of Christian Apologetics*, ed. W. C. Campbell-Jack, Gavin J. McGrath, and C. Stephen Evans (Downers Grove, IL: IVP Academic, 2006), 739–40.

45. John Frame, "Cornelius Van Til, Apologist," in *Apologetics Study Bible*, ed. Ted Cabal et al. (Nashville: Broadman and Holman, 2007), 1690.

46. John Frame, "Presuppositional Apologetics," in *Five Views on Apologetics*, 207–31. In this book, Frame also has four replies to the other positions as well as a concluding article.

47. *AGG* and *CVT*.

Contemporary Worship

Although the issue of worship has caused some of the heated controversies regarding Frame's influence within the Reformed world (see above), his views, when known, have been embraced by the evangelical world. His two books on worship, *WST* and *CWM*, were both read widely outside the Presbyterian and Reformed world. For example, in 2004 Frame gave the lectures at Southern Baptist Theological Seminary for the Institute for Christian Worship. Over the years, these lectures have included evangelicals such as Michael Card, Harold Best, Keith and Kristyn Getty, and Bob Kauflin. Frame's arguments in these two books have been utilized by worship leaders across the evangelical world and have contributed to his influence in shaping contemporary worship.[48]

The area of worship demonstrates the dual influences we have emphasized in this chapter. Although some Reformed theologians and churchmen lament the implications of Frame's broad understanding of the RPW, Frame is part of the influence on evangelicals developing a more God-centered perspective on worship. In the foreword to Paxson Jeancake's *The Art of Worship*, Frame says:

> One of the happiest developments in recent evangelical theologies of worship is the emphasis on gospel-centeredness. If the Great Commission is the distinctive task of the church, then the gospel must suffuse all aspects of the church's life and ministry, including worship. In our services, we need to hear and speak much more about how far we have fallen and how great has been God's grace to us in Jesus Christ. Traditions and contemporary practices that hinder the centrality of grace must be rooted out, and we need to do more careful thought on how each element of the service can proclaim the good news.[49]

This is precisely the influence that John Frame has had on the contemporary evangelical world concerning worship. Although Reformed confes-

---

48. See Paxson H. Jeancake, "Rethinking, Reforming: Frame's Contributions to Contemporary Worship," in this volume. Further evidence of this influence comes from the megachurch Northland: A Church Distributed, located in Lakewood, Florida. Frame lectured on worship at the Northland Worship School in 2002, 2003, and 2008. Vernon Rainwater is a pastor at Northland who leads the church in worship, and he has contributed a personal word in this volume about Frame's contribution to Northland's worship.

49. John Frame, "Foreword," in Paxson Jeancake, *The Art of Worship* (Eugene, OR: Wipf and Stock, 2006); http://www.frame-poythress.org/frame_articles/2006Foreword.htm.

sionalists would argue that Frame has lowered Reformed worship, a significant case can be made that he has actually pushed evangelical worship toward a more gospel-centered approach.

Missional Church Plants

Finally, John Frame's teaching on multiperspectivalism has found a surprising home in the missional-church planting movement. Drew Goodmanson, an elder at Kaleo Church in San Diego and an entrepreneur within the missional movement, has several extensive notes and articles at his Web site regarding the influence of multiperspectivalism as an effective framework for church ministry.[50] He explains that there are Acts 29 churches that are using this framework, and that his own church was influenced by Dick Kaufmann and Doug Swagerty from Harbor Presbyterian Church in San Diego. The influence of Kaufmann leads to the next section, in which we examine the way that Frame has served to influence some of the key leaders in evangelicalism today.

Tim Keller

When Frame moved to California to teach at the new campus of Westminster Seminary, he was part of the church plant called New Life Presbyterian Church in Escondido (as we mentioned above). The pastor of New Life Escondido was Kaufmann, who would remain Frame's pastor for fourteen years. In the 1990s, Kaufmann went on to become the executive pastor of Redeemer Presbyterian Church in New York for approximately five years. That connection introduced Tim Keller to John Frame on a more personal level.

Keller earned a DMin at Westminster from 1979–82. By that time, Frame was already in California, but Frame's influence at Philadelphia was still considerably strong. Keller discovered that although Frame had published very little, his syllabi were constantly used and referenced. Keller explained to us that Frame's influence is very significant in the area of theology and application. Frame took Meredith Kline's understanding of the Bible as a covenant document and applied it to the area of epistemology.[51] In other words, one of Frame's central contribu-

---

50. Drew Goodmanson, "Triperspectivalism and Church Ecclesiology," http://www.good manson.com/category/church/triperspectivalism/ (accessed on July 3, 2009).

51. Personal correspondence from Tim Keller (January 27, 2009).

tions to pastoral ministry is that you cannot really understand Scripture until you are obedient and apply it.[52] Keller, of course, is a leading evangelical influencer today, and his theology has Frame's fingerprints all over it.

Wayne Grudem

Wayne Grudem is research professor of theology and biblical studies at Phoenix Seminary, and prior to accepting that position he was chairman of the Department of Biblical and Systematic Theology at Trinity Evangelical Divinity School for twenty years. Grudem has served as president of the Evangelical Theological Society, and he is one of the people through whom John Frame's theology has influenced evangelicalism. Grudem studied at Westminster Theological Seminary from 1971–73 and took all his theology courses from Frame, as well as the ethics course, Doctrine of the Christian Life, that formed the basis for Frame's book of the same name. Grudem explained to us Frame's influence: "It was Frame's amazing knowledge of Scripture and deep, profound commitment to Scripture that profoundly affected me. You could just sense that he treated it and thought of it as a priceless, inexhaustible treasure from which we could learn from God's infinite store of wisdom."[53] Grudem eventually dedicated his popular *Systematic Theology* in part to John Frame (as well as Edmund P. Clowney and Poythress).[54] He is a contributor to this present volume, writing on Frame's influence in terms of ethics.

Kevin Vanhoozer

Kevin Vanhoozer is Blanchard Professor of Theology at Wheaton College Graduate School and was previously research professor of system-

52. For Frame's comprehensive discussion of "theology as application," see *DKG*, 1–100. Frame articulates a view of the Christian life that correlates doctrine to life and obedience to knowledge. This forms such a significant structure for the church-planting movement that it would be hard to overestimate. In terms of social ministry, many wonder whether we can really understand the Bible if we are not actively engaged in feeding the hungry and sheltering the homeless and clothing the poor. Although the direct connection is not there, the implication should be clear: theology is application, even if that means a type of social ministry that is not always considered "truly Reformed." See also Tim Keller, *Ministries of Mercy: The Call of the Jericho Road* (Phillipsburg, NJ: P&R Publishing, 1997).

53. Personal correspondence from Wayne Grudem (February 8, 2009).

54. There have been over 300,000 copies of Grudem's *Systematic Theology* printed in English, and it has been published in Portuguese, Korean, Romanian, Russian, Spanish, and Arabic, with plans for other languages.

atic theology at Trinity Evangelical Divinity School, where he taught from 1998–2009. Vanhoozer studied under Frame at Westminster Theological Seminary in Philadelphia for one year before Frame left the Philadelphia campus to help start the California campus. Vanhoozer recalls that he chose WTS for three reasons: (1) its Reformed heritage, (2) the honors program (a way of getting the MDiv largely through independent study), and (3) John Frame. Vanhoozer took every class that Frame offered that year since Frame was leaving for California, and he obtained notes from other students for the courses he wasn't able to take with Frame. Nearly thirty years later, Vanhoozer still has all the syllabi and lecture notes for his seven classes. In his letter included in this volume, he writes: "John, your example continues to represent the high bar for teaching that I am still trying to jump. Your lecture notes are the gold standard of the genre; no other professor I have had has even come close to rivaling them."

Frame's most significant influence on Vanhoozer was concerning the doctrine of Scripture, which was the subject of his MDiv thesis.[55] Frame taught him the "importance of the multi-faceted nature of biblical authority where each book had the authority peculiar to its literary form."[56] This was but one application of Frame's multiperspectival approach. In Vanhoozer's book *The Drama of Doctrine*,[57] he sought to defend the *sola Scriptura* principle that he learned from Frame.

In addition to these specific issues, Frame's primary influence on Vanhoozer was on the necessity of being biblical, and on being charitable before being critical. "John Frame," Vanhoozer writes, "set the bar high as far as what it means to be a theology professor. I have tried to be fair to other positions, which means really understanding them, before I criticize them. I have also tried to see things from different perspectives. Ultimately, however, I have tried to be biblical."[58] Frame also modeled for Vanhoozer the ability to be "both faithful and creative" in theology. Vanhoozer sees most evangelicals as being better at "reacting than constructing," and Frame pointed toward

55. Although Vanhoozer's time with Frame was limited, Frame was still able to supervise his 200-page MDiv thesis, "The Special Status of the Bible in Recent Theology: A Critical Comparison and Analysis of James Barr, Brevard Childs, and David Kelsey" (master's thesis, Westminster Theological Seminary, 1982), a topic he says served him well over the years, given that these three scholars were dominant figures into the twenty-first century.

56. Personal correspondence from Kevin Vanhoozer (January 27, 2009).

57. Kevin J. Vanhoozer, *The Drama of Doctrine: A Canonical-Linguistic Approach to Christian Theology* (Louisville: Westminster John Knox, 2005).

58. Personal correspondence from Vanhoozer.

a more faithful, biblical path. This is reflected in Vanhoozer's most recent book, which he dedicates to John Frame as follows:

> To John Frame: my first graduate-school theology professor, a master-pedagogue and triangulator extraordinaire, whose multiperspectival approach to the doctrine of God has been a source of continuing inspiration. As a scholar, he exemplifies sanctified erudition in engaging other positions with charitable criticism; as a saint, he personifies a compelling model of how to do theology with creative fidelity while remaining boldly yet humbly honest to God.[59]

Frame's influence will continue on to future generations, in part through the teaching and writing ministry of Kevin Vanhoozer.

Returning to our puzzle of precisely how to measure influence within evangelicalism—especially by one who operates outside the typical evangelical structures—we can clearly see Frame's influence among three of evangelicalism's key influencers: its most popular theologian (Grudem), its most academically respected theologian (Vanhoozer), and one of its most important pastor-theologians (Keller).

Multiperspectivalism as a Way of Life

The irony of our chapter—although it should not be surprising—is that Frame's influence on evangelicalism comes through multiple perspectives! Although Frame often chose not to interact with evangelicalism through some of its significant outlets, he has nevertheless influenced evangelicalism in a way that reflects his own theological perspective.

We began our essay with the story of our first class with John Frame, because in some ways it is a parable of his influence. In that class, Frame demonstrated to us the importance of scriptural authority, and he continually backed up his arguments with scriptural evidence. He also reminded us of the importance of tradition, and how we must interact with our tradition, seeking to understand it as well as critique it. And not to be ignored, Frame reminded us of the importance of personal involvement

---

59. Kevin J. Vanhoozer, *Remythologizing Theology: Divine Action, Passion, and Authorship*, Cambridge Studies in Christian Doctrine (Cambridge: Cambridge University Press, forthcoming 2010).

in the Christian life, taking time to talk with students—an activity that is sadly becoming less common within seminary environments. A natural introvert, Frame was nevertheless willing to engage and interact instead of withdrawing and relaxing.

What we see in Frame's own life is precisely that kind of influence. He has influenced people by teaching and writing, by engaging his tradition, and by taking time to sit down and talk with students and other followers of Christ, thus demonstrating that Frame's theology is a way of life. Given this multiperspectival approach to life and ministry, it should not be surprising to find that Frame's influence within the evangelical world will take time to see, because that influence takes place through multiple perspectives.

283

13

FRAME'S DOCTRINE OF GOD

PAUL HELM

SHORTLY AFTER STARTING to teach at the University of Liverpool, I was intrigued to read a piece by John Frame written for *Christianity Today* (I seem to remember). In it I learned that he had received an education in analytic philosophy at Yale, and by the time I read the piece he was teaching at Westminster Theological Seminary Philadelphia. So here was a Reformed theologian and apologete whose philosophical wavelength I might be able to tune in without taking a full immersion course in the philosophy of Josiah Royce or F. H. Bradley. He graciously replied (and replied graciously) to the letter I sent, and since then we have kept in touch in various ways, seen each other at conferences, that sort of thing. One of these points of contact has been the practice of occasionally reviewing each other's books.

In 1994, John wrote a generous review in the *Westminster Theological Journal* of my book *The Providence of God*,[1] and he has reprinted the review (along with others) as an appendix to *The Doctrine of God*. In the review, he says that there are parts of my book that could have done with expansion. So I thought that, after these many moons, I'd try to meet this point and say more about at least some of these things, as a modest gift to John.[2] The

---

1. Paul Helm, *The Providence of God* (Leicester: InterVarsity Press, 1993).
2. Thanks to Daniel Hill for suggesting this idea, and for help with a draft of this paper.

issues noted by John, as it happens, all fall within the scope of the doctrine of God, and most have to do with the relationship between God's immaculate holiness and the occurrence of evil in his creation.

So I will attempt, after all these years, to do more on some if not all of these points, without (to begin with) making any reference to John's *The Doctrine of God*. Then toward the end of the piece, I will remove the blindfold and look again at the text of his book to see how we compare. In that way I'll have the opportunity to say more about God's providence, and get to read some of *The Doctrine of God* again, and John will, at last, get a positive response to his request for another helping. Or he will have a response to at least some of his requests. He made several of them in the review, so it's possible to pick and choose among them. How self-indulgent can you get?

Among the things John mentions are levels of causation, evil as privation, the divine permission of evil, and divine weakness. I certainly don't want this essay, which is after all written in John's honor, to be a self-serving defense of Helm. So I'll try to exercise some discretion, and also take the liberty of thinking aloud concerning a couple of things about which (I realize) I could be accused of having said more than enough already. Then, as I said, it is back to John.

MORE OF HELM

Privation

I begin with privation. And given that what follows forms part of a discussion between Calvinists, John Calvin seems a good place to begin. Since I have been paying quite a bit of attention to Calvin recently, he'll make a number of appearances in this piece.

At one point in his work *Concerning the Eternal Predestination of God*, Calvin says, "I will not repeat here with Augustine what yet I willingly accept from him as true: There is nothing positive in sin and evil: for this subtlety does not satisfy many. For myself, I take another principle: Whatever things are done wrongly and unjustly by man, these very things are right and just works of God."[3] Here Calvin says that although he approves of Augustine's view that evil is a privation, yet because it is, or contains, a subtlety and does not satisfy many, for the most part he prefers another approach to

---

3. *Concerning the Eternal Predestination of God* (1552), trans. J. K. S. Reid (London: James Clarke and Co., 1961), 169.

evil, one that relies on the distinction between the evil intentions of his creatures and the immaculate intentions of God. So the Reformer provides not only a convenient point of departure, but also a warrant for moving in our discussion from evil as privation to evil as a product of the creaturely mind and will.

It is widely held that Augustine was in thrall to platonic philosophy, and some argue that this, and the patristic position more generally, represents a fall from grace in the development of Christian theology, replacing the biblical conceptuality with one that is alien to Scripture and imposed on it. Like the growth of a cataract over the eye, this is said to have obscured the vision of a truly biblical theology.

There is no question that Augustine was influenced by neoplatonism, but I think that estimating the extent of this influence can easily be overdone in the prosecution of an agenda of pure biblicism. When, in that dramatic section in *The Confessions*, Augustine is lent a bundle of parchment rolls of the "books of the platonists," he believed, he tells us, that the words he read in the Platonist literature were equivalent in meaning to some of the words from the prologue of John's Gospel.[4] Not to all the words, however. For Augustine insists that in the Platonist literature there was nothing equivalent to the idea that the Word of God was made flesh, or that it was possible for men and women to receive him. Did the Platonists teach some form of the eternal generation of the Son? Perhaps. What about the incarnation of the Son? Did they teach that? Certainly not. Augustine thought that the "light" occurring in the prologue to John's Gospel had the same reference as Platonic light, although with the added bonus, never to be derived from the Platonists, of the revelation of the incarnation of the Logos and his self-offering as Mediator.[5] Here is a case where the Platonist writings took him so far, but not into distinctively Christian territory. Their writings were a prologue to the prologue of John's Gospel, not a substitute for it.

In the case of privation, Augustine makes another positive judgment about the value of the Platonists' writings and their conceptuality. The language of privation is undoubtedly neoplatonic. It is a consequence of the neoplatonists' view that goodness is an aspect of being, or a description of being in other terms. We find this a strange idea, probably because of the prevalence in the culture of a scientific account of existence, or being, and

4. Augustine, *Confessions*, VII.9.14.
5. Ibid., VII.18.24.

of the widespread acceptance of Hume's point of not being able to deduce an *ought* from an *is*. Platonism would find both viewpoints strange. And perhaps the author of the book of Genesis would also find them strange. For in the early verses of his book, he provides us with an account of the formedness of the creation, and along with it he relays divine pronouncements of the goodness of the creation on account of its formedness. In other words, there is a strong linkage at this point in Scripture between the true existence of something, as it was intended by the Creator at the creation, and the goodness of that thing; likewise and by implication, we are presented with an account of evil as a departure, a lack, a falling short. This is not only an implication: "It is not good that the man should be alone" (Gen. 2:18; all Scripture quotations are from the ESV). So, I suggest, the platonic language linking being and goodness and evil and privation is not a thousand miles away from the biblical account of evil as a lack and of sin as a falling short of the glory of God.

This seems sufficient warrant for a Christian thinker to take seriously the idea of evil as a privation or lack. Why then does Calvin think that it is a "subtlety"? It is not immediately clear. Perhaps because evil and sin are so obviously manifest and active; how could what is so manifestly powerful be a deficiency? Perhaps it is because, according to Scripture, God himself may bring good out of evil; and how could he bring something not out of nothing, but what is nonetheless a departure, a fall? Perhaps Calvin thought that this bit of theory distracts us from the plain texts of Scripture that speak of God bringing about evil even while, at the same time, he is not its "author."

What is an undoubted advantage of the privation view of evil is that it provides a clear and distinct answer to this perennial challenge when we think about God's relation to moral evil, namely, how can God decree and create and uphold and govern everything and yet not be the author of sin? It is axiomatic, part of the "grammar" of Christian theism, that God cannot be the author of evil in the sense that he cannot, in the case of the evil he decrees, be motivated by whatever is hateful or malevolent, even though he is Lord of all, even of evil. How can this be? The idea of privation provides a neat metaphysical response to this ethical question. God, who is fullness of being and so is immaculate in holiness, cannot, metaphysically cannot, be the author of what is a deficiency, a lack. It provides an underscoring of what James says, that God cannot be tempted with evil, and he himself tempts no one (James 1:13), and of the prophet's assertion that he is of purer eyes than to behold evil (Hab. 1:13). And if God cannot be the author of evil, metaphysically cannot, then there must be a relationship between God and evil that is consistent and that does not make him its author in the sense already given. Perhaps at this point the privative notion of evil can help.

Calvin, who as we have seen does not favor this subtle approach, although he does not deny its validity, prefers another, the principle: "Whatever things are done wrongly and unjustly by man, these very things are right and just works of God." The basis of this view has less to do with the immaculate character of God per se (although it presupposes it) as with the warrant provided by the language of biblical history. In this history we find evil characters, or characters who do evil, whose evil actions are nonetheless decreed and upheld and governed by God, who even calls evil men his servants. (In this connection Calvin is particularly fond of the book of Job, in which the Lord, Satan, the Chaldeans, and Job and his wife are all participants in bringing about or increasing Job's sufferings.) Noting Calvin's preferred approach brings us to a second item that John wanted me to say more about, the idea of levels of causation, or at least to one particular application of this idea.

Primary and Secondary Causation

The idea of levels of causation was anciently employed (by Augustine, for example) to articulate God's relationship to the creation. It is said that God, the Creator, is the primary cause of all that happens, although his creatures are (various different kinds of) secondary cause. God's primary causal activity is not merely restricted to his upholding and so concurring with what his creatures do—although that would certainly be a form of the working together of primary and secondary causes—but extends to the decreeing and governing of their actions. God could, in theory, be only the upholder of his creatures and their actions, not their decreer, but in Scripture he is also portrayed as the one who decreed the actions in the first place. And this idea of decreeing the actions and then governing them introduces us to another, more positive, set of factors. As the governor of his creatures, God has motives and intentions; his governance is not random or mindless, or merely mechanical. And as intelligent creatures with desires and wills, human beings also have motives and intentions. So the divine decreeing is an expression of God's intentions. Calvin notes this when, as we have seen, he refers to the respective motives and intentions of man and God.

We have many instances of different motives being mixed together in carrying out one human action: two men may cooperate in carrying out some plan. Let us suppose that their cooperation is causally necessary and sufficient for executing the plan. The motives and intentions of one of these men might be significantly different from those of the other. But in the case of divine and human agency, although each has different motives or intentions in the action in which both are engaged, there is a significant asymmetry, since the divine agent is also the Creator and upholder of the human agent.

One way of expressing this asymmetry might be as follows. Although it seems clear that causation between creatures is transitive, that (where A, B, and C are events brought about by creatures) if A causes B, and B causes C, then A causes C, the sense of "cause" is the same in each occurrence, and there is no necessary sameness in the case of the causal aspects or features of the divine willing permission. It is thus not the case that if God positively governs his creation by willingly permitting some action (and so in one sense causes that action), and that evil action is brought about by an evil human motive (which in another sense causes that action), then God is causing that action in the same sense as the human agent is causing it. Because of the absence of straightforward transitivity, God's willing permission is a case of nontransitive causation, and those who (in an effort to undermine the biblical idea that God works all things after the counsel of his own will) seek to assimilate God's willing permission of evil to the actions of someone manipulating a puppet, or to hypnotism, or to brainwashing or programming (all these are cases of creature-to-creature causation), have failed to recognize important features of the character of such divine permission. The Creator's relation to evil cannot be straightforwardly assimilated to cases of causation between creatures. So there is, in our language about the divine causation of evil, an element of equivocation or analogy.

Such equivocation might be expected. For one thing, causation is a very flexible and multivalent concept. That's one reason why philosophers cannot agree on the correct analysis of "cause"; proposals for such analyses invariably run up against counterexamples that render some particular analysis unsatisfactory. Second, within Christian theology, talk of divine causation reflects this flexibility. So we blithely say that God created the universe out of nothing. But this is a very weird kind of causation, for it lacks the element of what Aristotle called material causation. In the case of the potter, say, there is some stuff out of which the pot is made; according to Aristotle, the activity of the potter is the efficient cause, the clay the material cause, the shape of the pot the formal cause, and the idea of the completed object the final cause. But in the case of divine creation there is, of course, nothing out of which the universe is made, not even the formless matter that Plato, in *Timaeus*, claimed that the Demiurge gave form to and made beautiful. Yet we do not hesitate to say that when God by his word created the heavens and the earth out of nothing, he *caused* them to exist.

There is another, more positive reason to think that God's causal activity is often rather different in meaning from creaturely causal activity. To see this, let us reflect for a moment longer on primary and secondary causation. If divine causation and creaturely causation were necessary in the same sense, in order to bring about a physical action such as my lifting my left arm, then we would have the following rather peculiar state of affairs: for my arm to be raised, then causation at the creaturely level would be necessary; but causation at the divine level would, in exactly the same sense, be necessary as well. Thus there would, for any creaturely action, be two sets of necessary causal conditions—a classic case of overdetermination, like two people who (independently of each other) prepare a meal for the same guest. Even if one of them failed to cook the fish and chips, the other would have provided the leg of lamb.

Perhaps, in order to parry this objection, we could say that divine decreeing is necessary and sufficient, but that creaturely causation is not truly efficacious. But then this would tend in the direction of "occasionalism," the idea that the only real or significant causal agency is divine agency. This surely does not do justice to the reality of creaturely causation. On the other hand, to say that divine upholding is necessary only, not necessary and sufficient, would imply a form of "freewill theism." So given these two sets of causally necessary causes, there is good reason to think that the divine willing and upholding of all things must be different in its causal character from the creaturely causation of action. If so, this should not surprise us. Rather, it would be surprising if the causal powers of the Creator were *not* somewhat different from the causal powers of the creature.

In his review, John suggests that the model of primary and secondary causation might be supplemented by that of the author and the characters in the novel. I certainly believe that this analogy is useful for clarifying some things in this area—for example, the idea that the author's time is distinct from the time (or times) of the characters in her fiction (or nonfiction) helps us to get a handle on the idea that divine timeless eternity is distinct from the time-boundedness of his creatures. It also helps us to keep in mind that the Creator-creature distinction is asymmetrical, like that of the author to his fictional characters.

Also, the authorial model makes clear that, say, Scrooge's meanness is not Dickens's meanness; Scrooge said, "Christmas? Bah! Humbug!" but Dickens didn't. Nonetheless, Dickens's authorship is both causally necessary and sufficient for the words Scrooge utters, just as (in *A Christmas Carol*) Scrooge is both causally necessary and sufficient for those words. It's not just that without Dickens, no words, and without Scrooge, no words. But without Dickens, in fact, not these very words, and with Dickens, in fact, these very words; and without Scrooge (in the fiction), not these very words, and with Scrooge (in the fiction), these very words. So the problem of there being two sets of necessary conditions remains, one set real and one set fictional, with the additional problem that unlike the eternal God's creatures, Dickens's fictional creatures are paper thin.

Power and Weakness

The Augustinian and Reformed emphasis on divine power in decreeing, creating, upholding, and governing all that comes to pass might be thought to invite a Nietzschean critique, that belief in such an account is a case of power worship, the will to power. Is the God of the Christians a God of pure power? Reformed theologians, even when they have differed among themselves about the nature and range of divine sovereignty, have by and large avoided talk of God's "absolute power." Since John thought that *The Providence of God* was short on the discussion and promotion of the idea of divine weakness, I will now avail myself of the chance to say a little more about this side of things.

If we think of the incarnation and the cross, of the apostolic preaching of them, and of the character of the Christian church, Christ's body, they are all characterized by weakness and fear. This has at least two aspects. One is soteric, the other ethical; these are distinct, although inseparable, for the Christian ethic of preferring the other, of recognizing that true greatness consists in service, arises out of salvation won by the Suffering Servant who thought equality with God his Father not a thing to be grasped after. Docetism is a temptation for those who, like the Reformed, stress the full and undiminished deity of the Son, and who also stress that the course of divine providence is in the hands of this sovereign Logos. With these thoughts in our minds it becomes tempting to think that the Mediator's suffering is not true suffering, because God cannot suffer, and because God is all the while "in control."

Although it's not my purpose here to go into the niceties of Christology, even were I capable of it, it is worth saying something about how in my view we should attempt to counter the charges of Docetism and also Monothelitism, to which Reformed Christology seems prone. The sufferings of Christ were real sufferings of body and mind, his submission to his Father one in which the divine and the human wills of Christ concurred, although this is perhaps too weak an expression. Yet the Gospels are remarkably restrained about how the divine Logos participates in the saving sufferings of Christ. Although on one well-known occasion Jesus distinguished what the Son knows from what the Father knows, he conveys the point in the third person. This distinction may be of some help over the participation question—it certainly provides warrant for raising the issue in the first place, but we do not have an inkling what it was like to be the incarnate Son. We possess no descriptions of his stream of consciousness, but there is a strong emphasis on the unity of that consciousness, not a split-mindedness nor any evidence of an oscillation between the two. *Verstehen* seems impossible, the attempt impious.

Such a stress on the unity of Christ's two-natured person is sufficient to warrant our talking about the weakness of God, surely. It seems to me more preferable that we do so in a guarded way than (as Calvin would say) "rend Christ in pieces" by assigning first this to his divine nature, then that to his human nature. Did Christ suffer? Did he suffer only "as man" or "as a man"? Is suffering not also to be ascribed to his divine person who brought the Mediator to the point of agony and who was united to that nature in its sufferings and sustained it through their course? Such language may certainly be warranted by the *communicatio idiomatum*. Suppose we say that as the eternal God, although fully impassioned, Christ cannot suffer, but as man, even man united to God, he (manifestly) can. No doubt this is true. But it is tritely true. For how does this help us to understand Jesus at the tomb of Lazarus, and at Gethsemane? If we are sufficiently guarded and careful, there is warrant for talking of the weakness of God. What God gives us, in the supreme act of his love for us, is a Mediator who is characterized by weakness. The "so loved" of John 3:16 expresses itself in submission to the earthly authorities. This is what an incarnate God who loves us maximally is like.

According to Paul, besides the power that made the worlds and upholds them, God also possesses power that is discontinuous with such power. God has chosen what is low and despised in the world, even things that are not, to bring to nothing things that are. The gospel comes to us in fear and trembling, and it is "sown in weakness." The power that upholds the physical forces of the universe provides the setting, the necessary conditions, for the exercise of this other sort of power, Pauline power as we might call it, which is not more of the same, but is a flat repudiation of what this passing world rates as power. It is power to lay down a life, and to be the king of a kingdom that is not of this world. It is power to provide necessary conditions not only for its exercise, but also for its intelligibility, for Pauline power can be understood only as the repudiation of or forswearing of power as conventionally understood.

Is Pauline power a divine perfection? It is an essential property of God that is exercised freely, and so there are elements of contingency to it. This is part of the way in which God of manifold wisdom and grace has chosen to redeem in our world. No doubt in other possible worlds than ours, Pauline power is exercised in other ways than through a cross. But then this is also true of the exercise of any of God's essential properties. The exercise of God's wisdom, for example, is conditioned by the contingencies of the world he has created. A Christian account of divine power could hardly omit the Pauline emphasis; it is power that ranks as weakness, and in a sense *is* weakness.

Besides thinking of the personhood of God, the Christian thinker must also think of his personality. By the personhood of God I mean that set of properties that constitute his nature: properties such as goodness and justice, properties that persons other than God possess but that he possesses to a superior degree. But besides these properties God has a schedule of preferences, of purposes or intentions, a will. Although it is possible to reflect on the personhood of God in an a priori fashion—using, among other intellectual tools, the idea of perfection—it seems to me that it is not possible to reflect in the same way on God's personality. His personality can be known only a posteriori, by what it is known or reasonably believed that he has done or allowed to be done.

293

Pauline power is as literally a case of power as is natural power. It is not that the wisdom of the Greeks is literally wisdom, and the wisdom of the cross loosely or metaphorically or symbolically so. There may be a moral or spiritual refraction that prevents some men and women from seeing divine power and wisdom for what it is, but according to Paul, such it is. The disagreement between Paul and the Jews and Greeks is over what divine power and wisdom literally are. According to Paul, the cross is an expression of the wisdom of God and the power of God.

Perhaps we may say this, that Pauline power has its distinctive character precisely because it requires God to restrain or curb the exercise of his essential omnipotence. Legions of angels could have been summoned, but were not. There is a sense in which every exercise by God of natural power is a curbing of some other potential exercise of that power. Not even God can will both that a tree grows in a certain place and time and that it not grow, and if he has willed that it grows there, then ipso facto his possible will that it not grow there, or that two trees grow there, is unfulfilled. But Pauline power requires divine restraint of a different kind, namely, that God submit to the exercise of natural power by another: that Christ submit to the priests, to the mob, to the faithlessness of his own disciples, and to Pilate.

Compatibilism

When those who have a robust sense of divine sovereignty give accounts of the relationship between divine sovereignty and human agency, there is a temptation to underplay the human and the created. We have seen this, and tried to address it, or at least to caution against it, in the cases of privation, of primary and secondary causation, and of the reality of Christ's suffering, as these are expressive of the divine nature. In fact, it has been a common thread to our discussion so far. I wish to make a similar point about compatibilism, the philosophical view that human freedom is compatible with causal determinism. There is a temptation for Calvinists to transpose this into the view that the divine decree is *compatible* with such compatibilism. God's decreeing a set of events is certainly consistent with a compatibilistic account of such events. But the divine decreeing of a free human action isn't itself necessarily a *case* of compatibilism.[6] If Jones designs, makes, and runs

6. Bruce Ware seems less than fully clear on this point when he says, "But not only does the Bible's teaching on the nature of human volition need to be *consistent* with its teaching on divine sovereignty, our human volition must be manifested in a manner that is *compatible* with the

a piece of machinery, the parts of the machine are in a mechanical relation to each other, but Jones's relation to the machine is not itself mechanical. Consistency between the divine decree and some versions of the philosophical thesis that human freedom is compatible with causal determinism is not itself a case of compatibilism. Perhaps some would argue that the divine decree requires compatibilism in this sense, just as some argue that human responsibility requires compatibilism, but that's a different matter, requiring separate argument.

Compatibilism may have different senses. As it is used to express a thesis about human freedom and determinism, it is a claim about certain creaturely causes and effects. According to the compatibilist, there are sets of sufficient causes of an action that are compatible with human freedom, full agency, responsibility, and the like. But there is no such creaturely causal condition in the case of the divine decree itself, which is not a creaturely action, but wholly divine. Compatibilists should be wary of arguing that it is a logically necessary truth, as Edwards did, for this entails that it applies to God himself, that the actions of God are themselves the effects of anterior causes. So there is need for caution in the use of the language of compatibilism.

There is another reason to make us wary of accepting the label of compatibilism without proper qualification. Compatibilism is the view that freedom/responsibility is compatible with (i.e., logically consistent with) determinism. Is this right or accurate? It is only partly accurate. Compatibilists typically hold that freedom is compatible with *some* versions of determinism. For example, deterministic systems that issue in physical/neurological compulsion are not often thought to be consistent with freedom/responsibility. It's typically said that people are free when they are (at least) psychologically free, when they are doing what they want to do, and when their choices arise from competing desires and intentions. And considering compatibilism in the context of the divine decree is different again. For the divine decree is not a force, but a decreeing personal will. It is not an immanent deterministic force such as heat, or chemical composition, or genetic endowment, or personal endowment, although its effects are felt immanently within the created order, of course. The divine will is not indifferent to its

strong understanding of divine sovereignty. Human freedom, in a word, must be compatibilistic. That is, exhaustive and meticulous divine sovereignty must be compatible with the actual and real manner in which human freedom operates." *God's Greater Glory* (Wheaton, IL: Crossway, 2004), 78 (italics in the original).

moral outcomes, as mere physical agencies and some human agencies are to theirs, but takes up an asymmetrical stance toward good and evil outcomes, respectively. Hence the business over divine permission. For these reasons (which space does not allow us to develop here), perhaps the truth of the philosophical doctrine of compatibilism is a sufficient condition of God's accomplishing some of his decrees, but not a necessary condition. Rather, God has multiple ways of accomplishing his decrees, as must be the case if physical indeterminacy is true. So it would be misleading to suppose that the relationship between God and his creation is merely a case of standard determinism, even though his creation contains standard determinist elements. It is one thing to say that human actions are deterministic, another to say that divine actions are as well.

There is need for further caution. Compatibilism is an ancient doctrine, but it has characteristically modern forms. Its modern forms are strongly influenced by modern science, particularly the idea of uniform scientific laws operating in sets of initial conditions. In fact, this scientific approach is the source of the chief family of arguments for modern compatibilism. But that is not all: these arguments color the conclusion, the sort of account of freedom that is held to be compatible with such science-influenced determinism.

Because of its reliance on universal causal principles to establish deterministic conclusions, there is a strongly reductionist tendency to modern compatibilism. The deterministic mechanisms are physical or genetic in character, and the action of human beings is determined because human beings themselves are the product of these causal forces, the outcome of particular sets of such forces exerted on particular occasions. To use the biological variety of this approach, human beings are nothing but genes, and their environment insofar as it is organic is also nothing but genes.

But older, premodern versions of compatibilism are not in the same way the product of accounts of the necessity of universal laws of nature, or of libertarianism, that depend on the denial of the operation of such laws. Calvinists do well to be cautious about this, if only because the transposed version for them is, "There is nothing but the divine decree." Jonathan Edwards, a determinist who argues in truly modern, Lockean, Newtonian fashion, comes close to holding that view. Edwards the determinist quickly becomes Edwards the occasionalist.[7]

---

7. On this, see Oliver Crisp, "How Occasional Was Edwards' Occasionalism?" in *Jonathan Edwards, Philosophical Theologian*, ed. Paul Helm and Oliver D. Crisp (Aldershot, UK: Ashgate, 2003).

On an older view of compatibilism, that to be found in the Stoics, in Augustine, and (I believe) in Calvin, a person is an autonomous center. The use of that word *autonomous* may cause a Calvinistic eyebrow or two to be raised. But it is intended seriously, although not in the well-known Kantian fashion. Human beings are agents, not merely junctions at which sets of impersonal forces gather and are relayed. For a person to be such a node and nothing more would be for that person to be heteronomous, and freedom simply to be the housing of these forces. We cannot say, if Jones had been in Smith's situation, that he would necessarily have acted like Smith, for this is to deny both Smith's and Jones's individuality, their uniqueness. We certainly cannot say that when Jones is in these circumstances again he will do exactly the same as he did the first time. Jones is one unique individual, to which his DNA attests, perhaps which his DNA ensures, and Smith is another. The agent is thus a cause in his own right, and his action is not the mere consequence of sets of external causes.[8] Although such a view may or may not be consistent with libertarianism, it certainly does not entail it.

The internality requirement for responsible human action—that people are free and responsible only when they do what they want to—is thus the product of features some at least of which are distinctively human. The "doing what one wants to" is not simply a psychological epiphenomenon of a purely material causal base. To use Leibnizian language, a person is a distinctive and unique individual essence. The point here (at any rate if we are mind-body dualists) is that the things done by the human mind cannot be wholly the product of external physical forces, but what it does is partly the outcome of its own individual nature. If we forget or deny this, then we settle for an account in which it functions in a way characteristic of things that do not possess minds, such as trees and stones.

These various short discussions have a bearing on each other. For example, what we have now been discussing, the nature of human autonomy as against bovine or canine autonomy, say, throws a little more light on the distinction between primary and secondary causation, discussed earlier, a discussion that we left rather up in the air. For not only is there that distinction, there are various kinds of it, depending on the characteristics and powers of the secondary causes in question.

---

8. *Institutes of the Christian Religion* (1559), ed. John T. McNeill, trans. Ford Lewis Battles (London: S.C.M. Press, 1960), 1.18.2.

Removing the Blindfold

Having indulged myself by trying to fill in some of the holes in *The Providence of God*, as well as walking around their edges and peering into the darkness, now is the time to return to John's text where he himself looks at such things, *The Doctrine of God*. That work, published in 2002, is a big book, and so no doubt has fewer holes. It's also organized in a way that is helpful to the themes of our discussion. I will look at part two, "Some Problem Areas," in which John deals with human responsibility and freedom; chapter 8, on the problem of evil; and chapters 9 and 14, on providence.

John and I share the same general outlook about the difficult questions of providence, responsibility, and evil, and that's a great source of pleasure. In these areas Christians should think in terms of biblical parameters, and within those parameters recognize different ways of expressing basic scriptural convictions. I think John would agree. So in what follows, as my eyes become accustomed to the light, I am not conducting a search for differences or making an attempt to magnify small differences into larger ones. Instead, I will ruminate aloud about two or three things that occurred to me as I read again what John has written in the general area of providence and evil.

Autonomy and Integrity

I was pleased to see that John stresses, as I have just been doing, the place of creaturely integrity within a broadly compatibilistic outlook. "By integrity I mean the ability of things to exist and function on their own terms, to be distinct from other objects, to play their own distinct roles in history."[9] He even introduces the word *autonomy*. This approach signals that John thinks in a nonreductionist way about God's decree and what it decrees, a way that is under challenge today from naturalistic reductionism of various kinds. This in turn means that God's decree as it embraces human beings must be consistent with the individual natures of human beings, respecting these and working through them. This, I think, gives us a clue to the importance, in attempting to plot an outline to the vexed question of God and evil, of keeping divine and human intentions distinct. God works through evil human intentions, but to work through them means to work with the intentions of others

9. *DG*, 148.

in accordance with intentions of his own. Nothing but confusion can result from merging or ignoring the different intentions at these two levels. It is of further importance that one of these levels is divine, the other creaturely. So God works through evil intentions, using them to fulfill his own immaculate intentions. This is one reason why the writers of Scripture can be so confident that God raises up Pharaoh and the evil Cyrus and so on, and yet he himself is not an accessory to their crimes. Why? Because not only are these intentions at different levels, but insofar as an evil human intention is held within a good divine intention, the situation is outside our experience, and the normal lines of co-responsibility in human–human cases do not hold.

Foreknowledge and Middle Knowledge

What John says about foreknowledge is a bit puzzling. To see why, we must first note what he has to say about permission. He endorses the view that evil occurs by God's willing permission, not by a "bare" permission, that is, a permission that is discretionary with respect to libertarian choices. Given this, one might expect that, in a parallel way, he would allow only for a divine foreknowledge that is determinative, and find no place for a divine foreknowledge that is purely that of a spectator and not that of a willer. That is, on the face of things, the denial of mere permission should, in consistency, carry with it the denial of "mere" foreknowledge, and vice versa. But this is what John says:

> There is in God's mind a reciprocity between foreknowledge and foreordination. Neither is simply "prior" to the other. Both are eternal. And, logically God's knowledge is based upon what he foreordains. But his foreordination is not an ignorant foreordination. He does not foreordain at random a set of circumstances and then look upon these circumstances with surprise.[10]

Yes, indeed. And yes, too, that these purely logical orderings in an eternal divine mind are also tricky; it would be better if they could be avoided, but they cannot easily be, because logical ordering may carry significant consequences down the line. John's idea is that God ordains in a wise and informed way and then (logical "then") knows what he has done, as we may

10. *DG*, 150.

plan an event and then (temporal and logical "then"), having planned it, foreknow its occurrence. But this seems too cumbersome. Why is not God's eternal ordination a causative foreknowing, based upon his knowledge of alternative sets of possibilities each of which is within his meticulous control? For those whom he foreknew he also predestined. God has not rejected his people whom he foreknew. God knows what he wants to bring to pass, and his decree of predestination is the infallible means of his achieving what he wants. Certainly God knows hypotheticals, but this knowledge is not purely spectatorial either, since the hypotheticals are part of the contents of his mind, his necessary knowledge. In my view, Middle Knowledge, which John discusses in this section, should not be given an inch, lest we find ourselves promoting or endorsing a kind of Calvinistic Molinism, which must be confused, or true Molinism with a kind of Augustinian fringe.[11]

Evil, Privation, and the Liability to Fall

When I removed my blindfold and looked at what John has to say about privation, in chapter 9 of *The Doctrine of God*, I was surprised at the length of his discussion. I hadn't remembered this. It's not at all clear to me what he thinks is at stake. Privation is something that engages him as well as concerns him. His discussion is fairly minatory and negative: he negates the negation, so to speak. As I noted earlier, I think that there is more to be said in favor of privation *an sich*, but also it's worth noting how the idea of privation is embedded in Reformed theology, despite what we noted earlier of Calvin's suspicion of it. Let's glance at these two points in turn.

John gives a good bit of attention to explaining and dissenting from the views of Etienne Gilson.[12] Gilson has the view that all good, created things have a tendency to "lapse back into nothingness" (words of Gilson, I think). As Frame puts this over, it looks like the claim that all created beings have such a tendency so that, given enough time, left to themselves, everything that could slip back would slip back into nonbeing. They "lose their goodness as well as their being" and "tend to lose their perfections," as John explains, and rational beings are especially prone to this (according

---

11. For such attempts, see Ware, *God's Greater Glory*, and Terrance L. Tiessen, "Why Calvinists Should Believe in Divine Middle Knowledge, Although They Reject Molinism," *WTJ* 69,2 (2007): 345–66. See also Paul Helm and Terrance Tiessen, "Does Calvinism Have Room for Middle Knowledge?," *WTJ* (November 2009).

12. *DG*, 164.

to Gilson), since the avoidance of imperfection, of the slip into nonbeing, requires their self-control, which they may fail to exercise. John seems not to like this, perhaps because it is speculative, it is at odds with the goodness of the creation, and it leaves one with a form of the freewill defense against the incompatibility of the existence of moral evil with a world created good by God. A word about each of these in turn.

If this is speculative, it is so in a way that has been endorsed from the time of Augustine, if not before. Augustine held that the human and angelic beings were created mutable, that is, with a liability to fall and to depart from the standard or level of goodness with which they were originally endowed by God. Perhaps this means that given enough time, those possessing such a liability would in fact mutate, unless awarded a grant of the upholding power of God. Is this speculative? Surely it follows from the fact that angels and mankind fell that they were liable to fall, they possessed the capacity to fall. If A falls, then A has the capacity to fall, when (in words that are almost precisely those of the Westminster Confession) A is "left to the liberty of its own will." But it does not follow from this that given enough time, they would fall.

Is such an idea at odds with the goodness of creation? The creation was created good, but was it created as good as it could be? Some thinkers, such as John Hick, have made the objection that there is a fatal incoherence at the heart of any theodicy that also has the traditional doctrine of the creation.

> The creator is preserved from any responsibility for the existence of evil by the claim that He made men (or angels) as free and finitely perfect creatures, happy in the knowledge of Himself, and subject to no strains or temptations, but that they themselves inexplicably and inexcusably rebelled against Him. But this amounts to a sheer self-contradiction.[13]

Of course there would have been a sheer self-contradiction if God had made angels and men such that they were impeccable. For it is not consistent to suppose that creatures incapable of falling nevertheless fall. But if we suppose that God made mankind without sin, good but not as good as could be, and made the angels likewise, then there is no contradiction. It's not at odds with the goodness of the creation precisely because different grades of goodness, or different grades of being, are conceivable, as we are seeing.

13. John Hick, *Evil and the God of Love* (London: Macmillan, 1966), 285–86.

There is the degree of goodness that is indefectible, the goodness of God himself; and there is the degree of goodness that is defectible, that degree with which humankind was originally created. And if created beings, who are defectible, defect, then the sort of being (or) goodness that they then enjoy is lower still, just as the degree of goodness enjoyed by the beatified, whose goodness is now rendered indefectible, is greater than that. None of this is to speak of the degree of existence possessed by lower animals and the inanimate creation, which occupy lower rungs on the ladder.

Does it leave one with a form of the freewill defense? Well, yes, it does. Arminians and libertarians more generally have no monopoly on the use of this idea. As we have already noticed, the Westminster Confession states that men were created "under a possibility of transgressing, being left to the liberty of their own will, which is subject to change" (4.2). This is a form of a freewill defense, although it is not a freewill defense in the Plantingan sense.

This scheme of things, with the idea of degrees of being, and therefore of the privative notion of evil, is also embedded in Reformed theology. I'll briefly try to show this in the case of Calvin. Strangely enough, there are places in which it seems that Calvin deliberately downplays that degree of goodness in which God originally created humankind. In a work on providence, *The Secret Providence of God*, published in 1558, Calvin refers to the man who was originally created as *quae fluxa et caduca erat*, "weak and liable to fall." This corresponds with what he wrote in the *Institutes*: "Adam, therefore, might have stood if he chose, since it was only by his own will that he fell; but it was because his will was pliable in either direction, and he had not received constancy to persevere, that he so easily fell."[14] "For surely the Deity could not be tied down to this condition—to make man such, that he either could not or would not sin. Such a nature might have been more excellent."[15] So man "easily fell" because he was inconstant, and there is a "more or less" to excellence in natures; some natures are more excellent as natures than others, and so it is possible to arrange these in a hierarchy—God, angelic creatures, human creatures incapable of sinning, angelic creatures and human creatures capable of sinning, angelic and human creatures actually sinning, nonhuman animals, and so on.

14. *Institutes* 1.15.8.
15. Ibid.

Adam was left to the liberty of his own will, and so he sinned by an act of his will. But—and this is where the standard Christian account of the fall differs from the modern idea of a freewill defense—Adam could have been so endowed as to be impeccable. There is a world in which unfallen Adam does not suffer from the mutability he was created with; perhaps there is a time in the world to come when he does not suffer from such an incapacity.

So there is good reason to think that quite a bit of sense can be made of the idea of sin as privation, and of degrees of being, and even of a freewill defense, provided that such notions are properly qualified. So in the case of the freewill defense, as endorsed by the Westminster Confession, it claims that Adam's mutability meant that his nature was such that he could stand or he could fall; not that, as regards his nature, he must fall; or that, as regards his nature, he must stand. When thinking simply of the sort of nature Adam had, then the fall was not inevitable, any more than the fact that Christ possessed normal bones meant that they would be broken. Possessing such bones, they may be broken and they may not. Of course, in giving the fuller story of the fall, as in giving the fuller story of the fate of Christ's bones, we have to have in mind not only the nature of those who fell, but the relevant divine decree. In the case of Christ's bones, there is a divine prophecy that they will not be broken. They will not be broken not because they are supernatural, unbreakable bones, but because by divine providence Christ's ordinary bones are kept from being broken.

Similarly, in Adam's case: he falls not because, given his nature, the fall is inevitable, but because it was divinely decreed that his mutable nature should in fact mutate, and he should fail. This is why, in discussing the nature of Adam, Calvin in effect counsels us to take one issue at a time: the nature of Adam, and then his fate. "It were here unreasonable to introduce the question concerning the eternal predestination of God, because we are not considering what might or might not happen, but what the nature of man truly was. Adam, therefore, might have stood if he chose."[16]

A peccable Adam lacks one thing that an impeccable Adam possesses, a lack that has immediate moral and spiritual implications that being a one-eyed person as against a two-eyed person does not carry. Isn't this lack a privation, and isn't such privation at least a moral lack or loss, even if there are some privations that do not have such immediate moral or spiri-

16. Ibid.

tual consequences? So evil is a privation, but a privation is not necessarily personally evil, culpable and so on, unless the choice that such a privation makes possible, a choice of what is evil, actually occurs, as it did in the garden of Eden.

Where the choice to fail occurs, then mutability is its necessary condition. It is not that, as John suggests, the evil choice causes privation.[17] Were this so, then introducing privation would certainly be an unnecessary complication, as he puts it. So we must distinguish between a mutable good state—which is a state that, by comparison with an immutably good state, is deprived—and the use or abuse made of that mutable state. In such a state, freedom to depart from God is possible.

I've said more about privation than I thought was either possible or necessary, offering a defense of it in the form of a commentary on some of John's reservations or strictures, because he also has a good deal to say. It would not do, of course, to lift the idea of privation straight from Plato and impose it on Christian theology. But this may be one of those situations in which distinctions in Plato correspond to distinctions in Scripture. Plato may be the occasion for the distinctions to be made clearly, and his language may be employed to do so, but it is too quick to say that the privative view is "platonic," any more than to say that Paul's thought as expressed in Acts 17:28 is "Epimenidean." Finally, it has to be said that John's view that either everything exists or it does not, and if it does then it exists in precisely the same sense that everything else exists, is a peculiarly modern view. Surely he cannot be serious?

John's great tome, *The Doctrine of God*, has many virtues. One of these, as I hope is clear from this tribute to him, is its capacity to stir the reader to ruminations of his own. I hope, then, that sounding off in this theological and philosophical vein is a fitting tribute both to the book and to the man.

17. *DG*, 166.

14

FRAME AS A REFORMED THEOLOGIAN

HOWARD GRIFFITH

IN THIS ESSAY I have tried to honor John M. Frame by reflecting something of the continuity of his thought with Reformed theology. That has proved to be a big job. Not only has Frame written voluminously on Reformed theology,[1] but there are a number of Reformed traditions. Frame comments on many strands of them, contemporary[2] and historical, but does not believe theology or ethics can be proved by reference to them but by Holy Scripture alone.

In the purity of its conception, Reformed theology has God himself and his sovereign decree at its heart.[3] It is radically nonspeculative, which is to say, it draws its life from the exegesis of Holy Scripture.[4] In its full vigor,

1. He is far more than a theologian, as his title at Reformed Theological Seminary shows: J. D. Trimble Professor of Systematic Theology and Philosophy.

2. See *MWC* and *DCL*, where he evaluates many controversies and theologies within the conservative Reformed community.

3. Herman Bavinck profiled Calvinism as a theology and worldview: "The root and principle of this Calvinism is the confession of God's absolute sovereignty. Not one special attribute of God, for instance His love or justice, His holiness or equity, but God Himself as such in the unity of all his attributes and the perfection of His entire Being is the point of departure of the thinking and acting of the Calvinist." "The Future of Calvinism," *Presbyterian and Reformed Review* 5 (1894): 4.

4. Note the comment of Richard B. Gaffin Jr.: "The systematic theologian is a custodial interpreter, proximately of church dogma, but ultimately of Scripture. This means that in any given point in time, the basic stance that systematic theology is to adopt toward the doctrines and confessions of the church is, as Klaas Schilder neatly captured it, 'sympathetic-

305

it seeks to understand and live all of life in God's good creation in the light of his eschatological revelation of salvation in Christ, as that salvation has been documented in Holy Scripture. These characteristics are found in a rich form in the writings of John Frame.[5]

In 2003, Paul Helm favorably reviewed Frame's *DG*.[6] Nonetheless, he notes that the book seems "ahistorical" in flavor (no mention of the Puritan doctrine of God, almost nothing on Jonathan Edwards).[7] As he concludes, Helm raises a few constructively critical questions about disquieting formulations regarding space and time. He wonders what is meant by one of Frame's three aspects of God's lordship, "covenant presence":

> Frame says that God acts on and in the creation and evaluates all that happens (94), and so is present everywhere, covenantally so. At times this seems simply to be equivalent to the idea of divine immanence. At other times the author is clearly referring to what some have called the covenant of works and (of course) the covenant of grace. But then if God's covenant presence, the same covenant presence, is manifested in the creation and in its sustenance (102), clearly the idea becomes somewhat diluted. . . .
> In what sense does God covenant with inanimate creation? Are there not biblical uses of covenant language, which are metaphorical? . . . This disquiet connects with another. If covenant presence is another way of referring to divine immanence, then Frame also avers that besides transcending time and space God is "fully present," covenantally present, in them, and so immanently temporal and spatial, presumably (496–497). God experiences change, temporal (and spatial?) transition, though being himself changeless. But if God learns new things, even if such language

---

critical.' One of its most cherished ambitions is that the church formulate only what is 'either expressly set down in Scripture, or by good and necessary consequence may be deduced from Scripture.' " See "The Vitality of Reformed Systematic Theology," in *The Faith Once Delivered: Essays in Honor of Dr. Wayne R. Spear*, ed. Anthony T. Selvaggio (Phillipsburg, NJ: P&R Publishing, 2007), 5.

5. For Frame's treatment of the five points of Calvinism, see *SBL*, 110–12, 178–79, 151–55, 182–87, 222–28. His *IRF* details the relationship between evangelical theology and Reformed theology (versus liberal theology, notably placing Karl Barth's theology on the side of liberalism), http://www.frame-poythress.org/frame_articles/1999Introduction.htm (accessed July 15, 2008). Frame evaluates feminist theology in *DG* (378–86), as well as Jurgen Moltmann's critique of monotheism (627–31) and openness theology's rejection of omniscience.

6. Paul Helm, "A Good Big Book," review of *DG* in *Modern Reformation* (March–April 2003): 51–52.

7. See *DCL*, xxviii, for his reply regarding historical theology. Nevertheless, the book is replete with references to the Westminster Standards, with a few references also to the Heidelberg Catechism.

is "anthropomorphic, but not merely anthropomorphic" (497), how can he be omniscient? And if he experiences spatial presence and transition, does this mean, as it seems to, that he occupies space?

Helm goes on to suggest that the scholastic distinction between willing a change and changing a will would have served to prevent these disquiets, as well as a more vigorous appeal to Calvin's notion of divine accommodation.[8] He wonders whether Frame thinks of God's omnipresence in physical terms, like an atmosphere.

Helm's questions are a good path into the subject of Frame's continuity with Reformed theology. As he remarks, covenant is a central motif of Reformed theology, as is the relation of God as absolute person to the world. I will compare Frame's treatment of these issues with that of Herman Bavinck, arguably the dean of twentieth-century Reformed theologians. Frame is much like Bavinck in his views of covenant and omnipresence. He also advances our understanding of these doctrines.

FRAME'S "COVENANT PRESENCE"

As we seek to grasp Frame's notion of covenant presence, let's begin by noting that central to all of Frame's theology is the absolute distinction between Creator and creature. Frame rejects the notion of "the great chain of being" as the proper way of understanding the relation of God and the world.[9] Instead, God relates to his people and to the whole of creation by way of covenant. At this point Frame is working from the redemptive covenants revealed in Scripture (especially God's revelation of the name *Yahweh* or *Lord*[10] in Exodus 3:12–15, and Jesus' appropriation of this name and "role" in the New Testament) and extending the content he finds in them to the whole of the Creator/creature relationship (more on this below). This stance is meant to reflect the fact that as Christians, we must do all our thinking about God as obedient covenant servants ourselves.[11] God's relationship to the world is one of lordship. Frame writes[12]:

8. See Paul Helm, *John Calvin's Ideas* (Oxford: Oxford University Press, 2004), 184–208.
9. *DG*, 216–20.
10. *Lord* is a "relational term." *SBL*, 115.
11. *DG*, 34.
12. E-mail to the author, May 4, 2009.

"Covenant" can function as a model for the creator-creature distinction. Essentially, God is the Lord, and the world is his covenant vassal. Hence his Lordship attributes can be generalized into his control, authority, and presence over the whole creation.

God is distinct from the world. He cannot be identified with it, nor does it exist "in" him. Further, he is necessarily Lord of creation.

God is a person, because *Yahweh* is a personal name. Thus all theologies or philosophies that reduce God or the world to impersonality are unbiblical. Of such reductions "the Bible teaches the opposite. The impersonal reduces to the personal. Matter, motion, space, time and chance are, ultimately, tools used by one great Person to organize and run the universe he has made."[13] The world is not reducible to the impersonal, because God is its Lord. Yet God is absolute person.[14] By *absolute* Frame means God's aseity or "independence, self-sufficiency, self-containment."[15] He brings out this aspect of God toward the end of *DG*, because, importantly, he understands aseity as in no sense contrary to God's personality. Although non-Christian thought sees God's transcendence and immanence as opposites, Frame argues that in Scripture they are complementary. Setting them in opposition is ultimately a function of religious antithesis between God and Satan.[16] The exaltedness of God over the world, his control and authority over it, is in no sense opposed to his involvement with it and nearness to it. Biblical expressions such as "most High," "exalted," and "lifted up" are to be understood not primarily as spatial concepts, but as references to God's kingship.[17] Frame writes, "The God of the Bible is not a nameless, unknowable Absolute, removed from the course of human history. Nor is he one who gives his power and authority over to the world he has made. He dwells everywhere with us as the covenant Lord."[18]

Throughout his great work, *Reformed Dogmatics*,[19] Herman Bavinck follows much the same line of thought by contrasting biblical,

13. *SBL*, 7.
14. Compare the description of God in WCF 2.1–2 as both absolute and personal.
15. *DG*, 601.
16. Ibid., 115. Frame means that although they may be Christians, those who do so are thinking unbiblically.
17. Ibid., 105–6.
18. Ibid., 114.
19. Herman Bavinck, *Reformed Dogmatics*, ed. John Bolt, trans. John Vriend, 4 vols. (Grand Rapids: Baker Academic, 2003–2008). The work is both an exposition and a history of Christian

Christian doctrine with the impulses of pantheism and deism. He summarizes the biblical doctrine of God's relation to the world in several propositions:[20] God is a personal being, with life, consciousness, and will of his own, highly exalted above the creation. He appeared and revealed himself to various persons at various times. Old Testament revelation, which was preparatory to the "supreme and permanent revelation in the person of Christ and his ongoing indwelling in the church," is "more a revelation to than in people." Old Testament revelation does furnish true and reliable knowledge of God, but not a knowledge that exhaustively corresponds to his being. Thus, Old Testament revelations, even theophanies, were signs and pledges of his presence and did not confine and encompass God.

> Although the God of Israel dwells in the midst of his people in the house that Solomon built for him, he cannot even be contained by the heavens (1 Kings 8:27). He manifests himself in nature and sympathizes, as it were, with his people, but he is simultaneously the incomprehensible One . . . the incomparable One . . . the one who is infinitely exalted above time and space and every creature. . . . In a word, throughout the Old Testament, these two elements occur hand in hand: God is with those who are of a contrite and humble spirit, and nevertheless is the high and lofty One who inhabits eternity (Isa. 57:15).[21]

Notably, Bavinck employs this last text later in *Reformed Dogmatics* as a summary of the covenant relationship. The New Testament revelation brings the "same combination": he is above all change, time, space, and creatures.

> But God has caused his fullness to dwell in Christ bodily (Col. 2:9), resides in the church as his temple (1 Cor. 3:16), and makes his home in those who love Jesus and keep his word (John 14:23). Or to put it in modern theological language, in Scripture the personality and the absoluteness of God go hand in hand.[22]

---

doctrine. In *DG* Frame refers twenty-six times to Bavinck's *Doctrine of God* (an earlier translation and edition of *Reformed Dogmatics*, vol. 2), mostly positively.

20. I have shortened them.

21. Bavinck, *Reformed Dogmatics,* vol. 2: *God and Creation*, ed. John Bolt, trans. John Vriend (Grand Rapids: Baker Academic, 2004), 33–34.

22. Ibid., 34.

Like Frame, Bavinck summarizes the biblical doctrine of God as absolute personality. Like Frame, he says this unity of personality and absoluteness in God is immediately broken outside the domain of special revelation.

Frame's account of transcendence and immanence structures his treatment of all of God's attributes. In his exposition of God's transcendence, Frame sees two interrelated perspectives in Holy Scripture (both in summary statements and in specific descriptions), God's control and God's authority.[23] *Control* is God's supreme direction of all aspects of created reality (nature, history, free individual human decisions—including sin and salvation). Frame rejects all accounts of libertarian human freedom. Humans are true actors, but exercise their freedom compatibly with God's absolute control.[24] *Authority* is God's right over all creatures. Control and authority imply each other. Because God is Creator and controller, he is the world's supreme evaluator. His evaluations and commands are beyond question. His authority covers all areas of life. God's communication in command, promise, divine name, covenant, law, gospel, prophecy, song, history, etc., requires absolute belief and obedience.

God's presence is the third aspect of lordship. It is not a physical presence, because God is incorporeal. "What we mean, rather, is that he is able to act on and in the creation and to evaluate all that is happening in the creation. Since God controls and evaluates all things, he is therefore present everywhere—as present as an incorporeal being can be."[25] The force of the adjective *covenantal* is that God is present with his creatures to bless and to judge in accordance with the terms of his covenant.[26] Frame finds this presence in God's reply to Moses at the bush (Ex. 3:11–12), promising deliverance for his people. Frame identifies this as "the Immanuel principle," God's committing himself to his people, beginning with his covenant promise to Abraham (Frame refers especially to Gen. 17:7) and finding consummation in the new heaven and earth (Rev. 21:3–4). In the interim, God is present with Israel in tabernacle and temple, and supremely in Jesus, the tabernacle of God in the flesh (John 1:14). Now he dwells by the Spirit in the church as his temple (1 Cor. 6:19).[27] "Covenant presence, then, means that God com-

23. He does not disapprove of the twofold distinction, but prefers his threefold version. *DG*, 103.
24. Ibid., 61–79.
25. Ibid., 94.
26. Ibid.
27. Ibid., 96.

mits himself to us, to be our God and to make us his people. He delivers us by his grace and rules us by his law, and he rules not only from above, but also with us and in us."[28] For Frame this means that although God transcends time, God's repeated message to his people is that he is *with* them to save (Ex. 3:6–8; John 8:56–59). Thus he is "now." It also means that he is "here," although he also transcends space. There is a special "intensity" of presence in theophany, and a unique presence in the incarnation. But these can all be unified as forms of covenant presence. This presence "conveys the intimate fellowship of the covenant, that he is our God and we are his people."[29] At the same time, for Frame the covenant is two-sided. God is present with his faithful people to bless, but with the disobedient, God is present to judge.[30] More on this below.

Thus Helm is correct that for Frame covenant presence does refer broadly to divine immanence. It is this as an aspect of God's lordship (but not a "part" of it, somehow separable from his control or authority).

COVENANTS OF WORKS AND GRACE

Frame's understanding of all the biblical covenants depends heavily on the early work of Meredith G. Kline, who analyzed biblical covenants (especially the Sinai covenant) in terms of ancient suzerainty treaties that documented the relationship between a "great king" and his vassals.[31] Frame follows the treaty pattern of the covenant in his broad thinking about covenant lordship. God identifies himself as a person in the treaty preamble. He describes his activity in favor to the vassal in the historical prologue. This corresponds to the lordship attribute of *control*. He states the stipulations of the relationship in the commandments. This corresponds to Frame's *authority*. The sanctions—blessings and curses—follow the obedience or disobedience, respectively, of the vassals. These correspond to Frame's *presence* (God enforcing the blessing or curse). Frame notes that the grace of God is found in two places in the covenant structure, both in the historical prologue and

28. Ibid.

29. Ibid., 100.

30. Frame lists the following proof texts in *IRF*: Ex. 3:7–14; 6:1–8; 20:5, 7, 12; Ps. 135:13ff.; Isa. 26:4–8; Hos. 12:4–9; 13:4ff; Mal. 3:6; John 8:31–59.

31. Kline made a compelling case that the Ten Commandments and the entire book of Deuteronomy follow this form. See *The Structure of Biblical Authority* (Grand Rapids: Eerdmans, 1972).

in the sanctions. "God gives us blessings before we have done anything to please him; he gives us more as we live lives of obedience."[32]

Frame's presentation of the covenant of works is brief, but he follows a straightforward pattern in Reformed theology. (He is not opposed to calling this a covenant, although he takes this name as an inference from Scripture.) The parties are God and Adam representing the human race. The historical prologue is God's creation of Adam from dust. The law requirement is perfect obedience: the threat death, the promise life. Frame has agreed with Norman Shepherd that the covenant was not a matter of the strict earning of merit.[33] Nevertheless, Frame is clear that Adam was a representative head, and that his reward would have been "deserved" (if not strictly earned).[34] Adam's sin was imputed to humanity.

> Why is this covenant of works important for us today? First, we should see ourselves as covenant breakers in Adam (Isa. 24:5). In him we have failed the test of works, and we have no hope of ever saving ourselves by our works. But where we failed, in Adam, Christ gloriously succeeded. He obeyed God perfectly and laid down his life as a sacrifice to make up for our disobedience. In ourselves we are covenant breakers, but in Christ covenant keepers.[35]

As a foundation for the redemption accomplished by Christ, Frame teaches an eternal *pactum salutis* between Father and Son for the elect. Again, this may be called a covenant, but in this case the parties are equal divine persons.[36]

The redemptive covenants of Scripture (Adam, Noah, Abraham, Moses, new covenant) are appropriately described, by "theological generalization," as a covenant of grace.[37] Displaying the same structure, this covenant's parties are God and man with Christ as Mediator. Union with Christ grants the blessings of the covenant given to believers.[38] God grants life in Christ

32. *SBL*, 118.

33. E-mail to the author, May 4, 2009.

34. Foreword to A. Sandlin, ed., *Backbone of the Bible*, http://www.frame-poythress.org/frame_articles/2004SandlinForward.htm (accessed July 3, 2009).

35. *SBL*, 119.

36. Ibid., 120.

37. Ibid.

38. Compare WLC 69: "Q. What is the communion in grace which the members of the invisible church have with Christ? A. The communion in grace which the members of the

as "a free gift; but there is one condition, that of faith."[39] Here Frame closely follows the Westminster Confession of Faith 7.3:

> Man by his fall having made himself incapable of life by that covenant, the Lord was pleased to make a second, commonly called the Covenant of Grace: whereby he freely offereth unto sinners life and salvation by Jesus Christ, requiring of them faith in him, that they may be saved, and promising to give unto all those that are ordained unto life his Holy Spirit, to make them willing and able to believe.

Faith is not meritorious but receptive. Nevertheless, as true faith, it is living and working. Believers cannot fall from faith, but there are folk who only seem to believe but later fall away. Frame concludes from this that the sanctions for unbelief and disobedience are the same in both the covenant of works and the covenant of grace:

> So, as with the covenant of works, Scripture declares blessings to those who by faith obey God's commands (John 15:10; Rev. 22:2) and curses to those who do not (Heb. 6:4–6; 10:26–31). It warns us to examine ourselves, lest on the last day God finds us to be hypocrites (1 Cor. 11:28; 2 Cor. 13:5).[40]

This emphasis on blessings according to obedience, albeit graciously given obedience, makes a place for conditionality in the covenant relationship, not only before but also after the fall. Even the Mosaic covenant, with its stress on commands, Frame does not see as different in kind from the other covenants. It is a fulfillment of the Abrahamic covenant. "The Mosaic covenant is itself a covenant of promise (Eph. 3:12), and it is based on God's grace, his gracious deliverance of Israel from Egypt."[41]

Here, Frame departs significantly from Kline, who distinguishes the Mosaic covenant sharply from the Abrahamic covenant. For Kline, the Mosaic covenant was an administration of the larger covenant of grace, but on the level of national election, type, and corporate obedience, it functioned on the principle of works-inheritance. Kline argues that God's covenant with

---

invisible church have with Christ, is their partaking of the virtue of his mediation, in their justification, adoption, sanctification, and whatever else, in this life, manifests their union with him."

39. *SBL*, 121.
40. Ibid., 121.
41. Ibid., 125.

Abraham was of the unconditional, land-grant form. Hence inheritance was not a matter of the fulfillment of conditions on the part of the recipient.[42] Frame disagrees. He writes:[43]

In my judgment there is no sharp difference between unconditional and conditional covenants. Kline's assertion that the Abrahamic covenant was a "land grant" type of treaty, which was unconditional, is unpersuasive.... All biblical covenants have conditional elements. In the Abrahamic, note Genesis 17:9–14; 22:16–17. Abraham must obey God to receive the blessing. James 2:21–23 indicates that Abraham's faith was a living, working faith (as Shepherd would say) and that if it had been a dead faith he would not have been justified. So though the chief emphasis in the Abrahamic Covenant is grace and promise, there are also conditions.

Even the new covenant with its stress on grace (Jer. 31; Heb. 8, 10) has conditions, which are fulfilled by God's graciously working in the hearts of his people.

Frame applies the notion of conditionality in the covenant to the recent controversy over the Federal Vision.[44] Frame writes of this theology:

FV people have been quoted as saying that baptism gives one title to all the blessings of salvation; but they deny that it gives him title to the blessing of perseverance. That exception I take to be a refutation of their overall scheme.[45]

The covenant is conditioned. What makes the difference is God's inner work of regeneration. "the union between Christ and the believer in baptism, unless regeneration also exists, is entrance into a conditional covenant, which can lead either to blessings or cursings, not necessarily to eternal life."

This picture of the covenant of grace is colored also by Frame's distinction between historical election and eternal election. This is another way of

42. Meredith G. Kline, *Kingdom Prologue: Genesis Foundations for a Covenantal Worldview* (n.p.: Two Age Press, 2000) and *God, Heaven, and Har-Magedon: A Covenantal Tale of Cosmos and Telos* (Eugene, OR: Wipf and Stock, 2006), 96–97.

43. E-mail to the author, May 4, 2009.

44. See E. Calvin Beisner, ed., *The Auburn Avenue Theology, Pros & Cons: Debating the Federal Vision* (Fort Lauderdale, FL: Knox Theological Seminary, 2004).

45. *RLT*, 1.

describing the relationship between the covenant community, old and new,[46] and the eternally elect. Historical election is rooted in God's eternal decree, but is not election for eternal salvation. Instead, it has the performance of certain historical tasks in view. Judas, for example, was historically chosen, but not chosen for salvation.[47] The most important form of historical election was God's choice of Israel as a nation. This choice was by grace, as Scripture says, "It was not because you were more in number than any other people that the LORD set his love on you and chose you, for you were the fewest of all peoples, but it is because the LORD loves you and is keeping the oath that he swore to your fathers, that the LORD has brought you out with a mighty hand and redeemed you from the house of slavery, from the hand of Pharaoh king of Egypt" (Deut. 7:7–8; all Scriptures quoted by the author are from the ESV, unless otherwise noted). Yet, not all the Israelites were eternally saved.

Historical election is a form of covenant presence. It is an eternally decreed relationship between God and people,[48] as is its counterpart, eternal election. Historical election, in Israel and in the visible church,[49] is God's means of gathering those who will receive his eternal blessing. However, eternal election, also gracious, is unconditional and cannot be lost.[50] Eternal election too is a decreed relationship with the Lord, a form of covenant presence.[51]

Frame's dependence on the suzerainty structure outlined above means that he places tremendous emphasis on the law of God in the believer's life. In the covenant structure of the Decalogue, redemptive grace precedes obedience. That obedience is the obedience of faith.[52] Frame structures a large

---

46. For Frame, the new covenant community is the visible church. Those who actually receive the benefits of the new covenant, who are regenerate and united to Christ by faith, cannot lose them. They are part of the visible church, but their regeneration is not itself visible. See *DG*, 322–23.

47. *SBL*, 178.

48. *DG*, 317.

49. Frame notes that in the WCF is "the first clear confessional distinction between the visible and invisible church (XXV)." http://www.frame-poythress.org/frame_articles/1984WCF.html (accessed June 30, 2009).

50. *DG*, 329.

51. Notice the equivalence of covenant presence with "relationship with the Lord" at ibid., 317.

52. Compare: "In the Bible God makes different sorts of demands upon us: when he speaks to us indicatively, he tells us authoritatively what to believe. When he speaks imperatively, he tells us what to do. Then there are promises, which are not merely indicatives or statements of fact, although they are in the indicative grammatical mode. Rather in giving promises, God commits himself personally to bringing his purposes to bear in history. A promise demands not only belief

part of *DCL*, his major work on Christian ethics, around the Decalogue. His exposition is the most comprehensive known to the present author.[53]

An illuminating instance of God's exercise of covenant presence is found in Frame's exposition of the Old Testament word *hesed* or "covenant love." Frame finds this in "intensely covenantal" contexts, referring to God's love. However, it is usually to be distinguished from *'ahavah*, the sovereign love by which God initiates the covenant relationship. Frame writes,

> *Hesed* (as in [Deut.] 7:9) typically refers, not to the love of God that initiates a covenant, but to a divine love that presupposes a covenant's present existence. God's *'ahavah* creates the relationship; his *hesed* fulfills and completes it. But *hesed* does frequently presuppose human obedience to the covenant stipulations. Note in Deuteronomy 7:9 that God keeps his covenant of *hesed* "to a thousand generations of those who fear him and keep his commandments." *Hesed* can be God's response to repentance (Deut. 4:30–31; Ps. 51:1). . . . *Hesed*, then, is typically conditional, in a way that *'ahavah* is not. . . . Normally, then, God's *hesed* is given to those who obey him. This fact should not, however, be used to justify a doctrine that we are saved by works.[54]

Despite the fact that Bavinck's work on the covenants was at least eighty years prior to Frame's—prior to the suzerainty treaty findings of Kline and others—there is significant continuity between them. Unfortunately, I can only sketch that continuity here. For Bavinck, covenant, both before and after

---

but trust. . . . I made these distinctions initially on the impulse of some philosophical study of the various distinctions within language. Indeed, I considered myself somewhat insightful. But somewhat later I re-read Westminster Confession 14, 'Of Saving Faith,' section 2, which reads in part, 'By this faith, a Christian believeth to be true whatsoever is revealed in the Word, for the authority of God himself speaking therein; and acteth differently upon that which each particular passage thereof containeth; yielding obedience to the commands, trembling at the threatenings, and embracing the promises of God for this life, and that which is to come.' You see that all my bright ideas were already there in our confession." "My Use of the Reformed Confessions, A Presentation to the Trustees of Westminster Theological Seminary in California," http://www.frame-poythress.org/frame_articles/MyUse.htm (accessed July 15, 2008).

53. Exposition of the Decalogue is, of course, ancient Christian practice in presenting God's will for the Christian life. In the Reformed tradition, this impulse has come to rights. See Herman Bavinck, *Reformed Dogmatics* vol. 4, *Holy Spirit, Church and New Creation*, ed. John Bolt, trans. John Vriend (Grand Rapids: Baker Academic, 2008), 455. Frame refers to the Westminster Standards, including the Larger Catechism—the most extensive creedal exposition of the commandments in history—fifty-six times in *DCL*.

54. *DG*, 437–41. Compare Herman Bavinck, *Our Reasonable Faith*, trans. Henry Zylstra (Grand Rapids: Eerdmans, 1956), 445–47.

the fall, is "the essence of true religion."[55] This consists of several "beautiful thoughts."[56] Because God is Creator and man creature, no religion, or fellowship with God, would seem possible because of the distinctness between them. Fellowship is impossible unless God condescends to reveal and impart himself to his creatures. "He who inhabits eternity and dwells in a high and lofty place must also dwell with those who are of a humble spirit (Isa. 57:15 [paraphrase]). But this is nothing other than the description of a covenant."[57] A consequence of this distinction is that no creature can have rights before God—either before the fall or after—thus, there is no such thing as merit. However, God does, as it were, give creatures rights to expect good from him, but those rights are based solely on his condescending grace. "No merit, either of condignity or of congruity, is possible." Writing of Adam's expectation of eternal life in the way of obedience to the law of creation, he writes, "There *is* no natural connection here between work and reward."[58] There is a unity between the covenant of works and the covenant of grace on this basis.

> True religion, accordingly, cannot be anything other than a covenant: it has its origin in the condescending goodness and grace of God. It has that character before as well as after the fall. For religion, like the moral law and the destiny of man, is one. The covenant of works and the covenant of grace do not differ in their final goal, but only in the way that leads to it. In both there is one mediator: then, a mediator of union; now, a mediator of reconciliation. In both there is one faith: then, faith in God; now, faith in God through Christ; and in both covenants there is one hope, one love. . . . Religion is always the same in essence; it differs only in form.[59]

Because humans are God's image, he desires to be loved by them freely, and with gratitude. The covenant relationship of mutual love remains the same because neither God nor humanity changes in essence. Special grace must

55. Bavinck, *God and Creation*, 569. "In Scripture 'covenant' is the fixed form in which the relationship of God with his people is presented. And even where the word does not occur, we always see the two parties, as it were, in dialogue with each other, dealing with each other, with God calling people to conversion, reminding them of their obligations, and obligating himself to provide all that is good."
56. Ibid., 572.
57. Ibid., 569.
58. Ibid., 571.
59. Ibid., 570.

save from God's just wrath on sin, but it saves human beings who remain God's image despite their rebellion.

Nonetheless, there are differences between the covenants of works and grace. Grace after the fall freely gives *forfeited* benefits. And the covenant of grace does not depend on the changeable, and losable, freedom of Adam.[60] It was made with Christ the Mediator. After a lengthy section on the *pactum salutis*,[61] which Bavinck relates closely to the covenant of grace, he writes, "In him, who shares the divine nature and attributes, this covenant has an unwaveringly firm foundation. . . . It rests not in any work of humans but solely in the good pleasure of God, in the work of the Mediator, in the Holy Spirit who remains forever."[62] Moreover, a great difference is that through Christ, the covenant of grace brings (eternally) elect believers not to the place of Adam before the fall, but to the place of Christ in his exalted glory. This was the goal of the covenant of works, and Christ accomplishes this goal. Hence the covenant of grace is unchangeable, and cannot be broken.

This appears to be at odds with Frame's view of conditionality in the covenant of grace. Even more, Bavinck writes, "In the covenant of grace, that is, in the gospel, which is the proclamation of the covenant of grace, there are actually no demands and no conditions."[63] However, Bavinck qualifies this significantly. First, Bavinck writes that the covenant, although it must be unilateral in imposition and origin—because God is the Creator—still has obligations. *Consistent* with the gracious character of the covenant, these obligations are not conditions for entry into the covenant, but "the way the people who had by grace been incorporated into the covenant henceforth had to conduct themselves."[64] The very unilateral character of the covenant in fact was more clearly revealed over the history of divine revelation, because Israel continued to break the covenant. Thus the prophets with increasing clarity revealed God's unchangeable gracious purpose.[65] Second, the grace of God in the covenant by its very nature produces a reciprocal response in believers. What is unilateral becomes bilateral.

---

60. Herman Bavinck, *Reformed Dogmatics*, vol. 3, *Sin and Salvation in Christ*, ed. John Bolt, trans. John Vriend (Grand Rapids: Baker Academic, 2006), 225.

61. Ibid., 212–16. In the *pactum salutis*, Bavinck identifies Christ not as Mediator, but as Surety.

62. Ibid.

63. Ibid., 230.

64. Ibid., 204.

65. Ibid., 205.

> The covenant of grace . . . is a work of the triune God and is totally com-
> pleted among the three Persons themselves. But it is destined to become
> bilateral, to be consciously accepted and kept by humans in the power
> of God . . . that the work of grace may be clearly reflected in the human
> consciousness and arouse the human will to exert itself energetically and
> forcefully.[66]

God intends that promises and commands be received and enacted by his
grace. Finally, Bavinck is quite clear that the membership of the covenant
community is not identical with election. Rather, it is the way in which
God accomplishes the purpose of election.

> The covenant of grace will temporarily—in its earthly administration and
> dispensation—also include those who remain inwardly unbelieving and
> do not share in the covenant's benefits. . . . The internal and external sides
> of [the covenant of grace], although on earth they never fully coincide[,]
> may not be split apart and be placed side by side. Certainly, there are bad
> branches in the vine. . . . Though not *of* the covenant, they are *in* the cov-
> enant, and will someday be judged accordingly.[67]

Judgment in the covenant is a matter of cursing. "Just as God's blessing bestows
all kinds of well-being and life on a person, so a divine curse is the abandonment of a person to corruption, ruin, death, judgment, Satan. Human beings
can only wish another person blessing or curses, but God's blessing and cursing is always performative; it accomplishes what it wishes."[68]

To be sure, the form of expression differs from Frame. Bavinck does not
use the term *conditions* of the covenant. This term was problematic in the
relation of Reformed theology to Lutheranism and Roman Catholicism.[69] But
the gracious character of the covenant excludes neither human obligation,
nor the judgment of the covenant on those who do not believe and obey.
Indeed, for Bavinck—like Frame—the covenant curse is not bestowed as a
matter of a works-principle, even in the Mosaic covenant. Bavinck writes,
"The covenant on Mount Sinai is and remains a covenant of grace. 'I am the

---

66. Ibid., 230. Compare John Murray, *The Covenant of Grace: A Biblico-Theological Study*
(Phillipsburg, NJ: Presbyterian and Reformed, 1953/1988).
67. Ibid., 232.
68. Ibid., 172.
69. Ibid., 229.

LORD your God who brought you out of the land of Egypt, out of the house of slavery' (Ex. 20:2) is the opening statement of the law, the essence of the covenant of grace." Like Frame, Bavinck understands the Mosaic covenant as a heightening and a fulfillment of the covenant with Abraham:

> Just as Abraham, when God allied himself with him, was obligated to "walk before his face," so Israel as a people was similarly admonished by God's covenant to a new obedience. The entire law, which the covenant of grace at Mount Sinai took into its service, is intended to prompt Israel as a people to "walk" in the way of the covenant. It is but an explication of the one statement to Abraham, "Walk before me and be blameless" [Gen. 17:1], and therefore no more a cancellation of the covenant of grace and the foundation of a covenant of works than this word spoken to Abraham. The law of Moses, accordingly, is not antithetical to grace but subservient to it.[70]

Bavinck's concept of the functioning of the covenant is not identical, but it is congruent with Frame's notion of God's covenant presence, administering the blessings and judgments of the covenant, in both the old and new dispensations of the covenant of grace.

God's Covenantal Relation to the World

How does God relate covenantally to the non-image-bearing creation? Helm suspects that this dilutes the notion of covenant presence. He wonders how God relates covenantally to inanimate creation.

Frame's position is that God is intimately related to the entire created order. Genesis 1 presents his acts of creation as the preparation of a temple, even a deliverance from the darkness and deep.[71] God is not at odds with matter, or in a continuum of being with the creation. He

---

70. Ibid., 222. Although in a different context, Bavinck draws a sharp contrast between law and gospel; that contrast presupposes the fall and the resultant moral impotence of fallen man. It is not a contrast between covenants, but an expression of the antithesis between sinful works and free grace. "Strictly speaking, there are no conditions in the covenant of grace. Faith and repentance are as much benefits of the covenant of grace as justification (and so forth). But concretely, the gospel never comes in that form. In practice it is always united with law and is therefore always interwoven with the law throughout Scripture." Bavinck, *Holy Spirit, Church and New Creation*, 454; compare *DCL*, 182–92.

71. *DG*, 102. Frame follows Meredith G. Kline closely here. See Kline's *Images of the Spirit* (Grand Rapids: Baker, 1980).

deals with it directly. "He controls it, interprets it, and thereby enters into an intimate relationship with his world."[72] Further, all humanity has a covenant relationship to God, after the fall, the broken covenant of works (Rom. 5:12–21). Since the flood, all humanity is also related to him by his acts of maintaining the seasons and delaying final judgment, as God has promised in the Noachic covenant (Gen. 8:20–9:17). Frame follows Cornelius Van Til's thought here: the meaning of nature must be understood in relation to God and man as the covenant has defined their relation.[73] Fallen man is still the center of God's creational purpose, and the world serves that purpose. It both speaks to man of God's curse on his sin and provides the stage for his ultimate redemption. Frame indicates this relation by noting how Scripture presents God's redemption as new creation (cf. Isa. 43:1–7, 14–15). Although sometimes Scripture does speak in images, the creation itself will in fact be released from the curse (Rom. 8:19–21).[74]

Bavinck follows much the same tack. "At first, God's blessing rested on the creation (Gen. 1:22, 28; 2:3), but that blessing changed into a curse (Gen. 3:17). . . . There really is a divine curse resting on humanity and the world. It is impossible to interpret life in light of the love of God alone. At work throughout the creation is a principle of divine wrath that only a superficial person can deny."[75] "The fact that all of nature shares in humanity's fall is not only clear from Scripture, but follows naturally from the central place that humanity occupies in the creation."[76] However, this curse is not allowed to run free. The covenant with nature (Frame's Noachic covenant) limits the curse: "The whole of the irrational world of nature is subjected to ordinances that are anchored in God's covenant."[77]

Although Scripture is quite clear to the effect that God's presence is related covenantally to the creation, and although this should not be described as "diluted," it is fair to say that the relation of common grace to saving grace is very difficult to fathom. Bavinck says they are like two streams running in the same channel—not easy, or even possible, to distinguish, yet very

---

72. *DG*, 295.

73. Cornelius Van Til, *An Introduction to Systematic Theology*, 2nd ed., ed. William Edgar (Phillipsburg, NJ: P&R Publishing, 2007), 147.

74. *DG*, 296–97.

75. Bavinck, *Sin and Salvation*, 172.

76. Ibid., 180.

77. Ibid., 218.

closely related. However, Holy Scripture also reveals that God exhaustively interprets all of nature and history, as he has decreed it all.

Immanent Relations and Omniscience

Does God's covenant presence, with its transition in time, suggest that he is less than omniscient? Frame answers "no." God's knowledge in Scripture expresses his lordship. Isaiah 40:12–14 says:

> Who has measured the waters in the hollow of his hand
> and marked off the heavens with a span,
> enclosed the dust of the earth in a measure
> and weighed the mountains in scales
> and the hills in a balance?
> Who has measured the Spirit of the Lord,
> or what man shows him his counsel?
> Whom did he consult,
> and who made him understand?
> Who taught him the path of justice,
> and taught him knowledge,
> and showed him the way of understanding?

This indicates that God's knowledge is connected to his control of all things. Since God has created all things, he knows them all. "That knowledge is self-contained; he did not learn it from anyone."[78] Both God's control and his authority are found in his decrees and plans for the universe. Isaiah 46:9–10 says:

> I am God and there is none like me, declaring the end from the beginning, and from ancient times things not yet done, saying, "My counsel shall stand, and I will accomplish all my purpose. . . ."

"Since God will certainly accomplish his purpose, and since that purpose encompasses all of time, the end from the beginning, he is able to make known whatever will come to pass. Such revelation, of course, presup-

---

78. *DG*, 482. Compare WCF 2.2: "In His sight all things are open and manifest, His knowledge is infinite, infallible, and independent upon the creature, so as nothing is to Him contingent, or uncertain."

poses knowledge."[79] God knows the future in general,[80] as well as free human decisions.[81] These decisions are not free, in the libertarian sense, of God's control.

What then do passages of Scripture mean that seem to teach an increase of God's knowledge, such as Genesis 18:20–21? Numerous clear biblical texts that assert God's literal omniscience demand an anthropomorphic understanding of God's statement, "I will know."[82] This passage and others like it have a judicial focus, "God as prosecutor gathering evidence,"[83] another aspect of the anthropomorphism. Nevertheless, Frame suggests there may be more than anthropomorphism involved because theophany anticipates the incarnation—what he calls "the greater theophany"—of God in Jesus Christ, who as incarnate remained fully omniscient.[84] Old Testament theophany may anticipate the incarnation. Frame concludes that the larger principle of covenant presence—relation or involvement—requires that God experience newness analogous to human knowledge. This claim, though, does not diminish God's omniscience. The anthropomorphism reveals a genuine resemblance between human knowledge and God's knowledge in his immanence. It is grounded in the nature of his involvement in the temporal sequence.[85]

Frame is not able to answer Helm's question, "How can God remain omniscient?" We simply note that even at this most difficult point, although Frame asserts change in God's knowledge, he still maintains that this is a "genuine resemblance"—not an identity—between human knowledge and God's immanent knowing. The nature of theophany is too obscure, and I would add, so is the nature of Jesus' incarnate knowing. Would Frame do better to explain such texts in terms of accommodation alone? I am inclined to say so, but there may be a redemptive-historical importance to his observation. In the final analysis, Frame does takes accommodation a step further, rather than challenging God's omniscience. This is why, I think, Helm says he comes *unnecessarily* close to contradiction.

79. *DG*, 483.
80. Ibid., 486–88.
81. Ibid., 488–94.
82. Ibid., 496.
83. Ibid.
84. Ibid., 497. Frame means that divine omniscience was true of his person as a function of his divine nature.
85. Ibid., 498.

Bavinck will not go as far as Frame in terms of omniscience. In the contexts I have noted, he always includes an "as it were" when analyzing God's immanence. Further, he writes, "God knows nothing by observation, but from and of himself."[86] Yet he does say something like Frame. The incarnation—necessary only on account of God's free choice to redeem elect sinners[87]—was anticipated in the covenant relation.

> This incarnation does not stand by itself in history. Granted, it is essentially different from all other facts and occupies a place uniquely its own, yet it is intimately connected with everything that took place before, alongside, and after itself. . . . Its preparation and presupposition is generation [by the Father], creation [in the image of God], revelation, and inspiration. Now it must be added, finally, that it is also integrally connected with the essence of religion. Religion is communion with God. Without it humans cannot be truly and completely human . . . that communion with God is a mystical union. It far exceeds our understanding. It is a most intimate union with God by the Holy Spirit, a union of persons, an unbreakable and eternal covenant between God and ourselves, which cannot at all be adequately described by the word "ethical" and is therefore called "mystical." It is so close that it transforms humans in the divine image and makes them participants in the divine nature (2 Cor. 3:18; Gal. 2:20; 2 Pet. 1:4).[88]

In other words, God has accomplished through the redemption of Christ a union between himself and his people in which he truly communicates himself to them. The distance between this formulation and some form of heterodoxy is, to use John Murray's phrase, not a chasm but a razor's edge. Yet it must be asserted all the same. Frame and Bavinck seek to teach both God's aseity and his covenant union with his people.

Is God spatial, in Frame's view? No. God is Lord of space, neither contained in it nor excluded from it. "He is not in space as if space were a kind of box confining him."[89] Frame argues that God is "immense" in a number of ways: Scripture teaches it explicitly in 1 Kings 8:27. Then, as a (simple) person God is everywhere.[90]

86. Bavinck, *God and Creation*, 196.
87. Bavinck, *Sin and Salvation*, 305.
88. Ibid., 304.
89. *DG*, 579.
90. Ibid.

In developing the idea of "spatial omnipresence" Frame writes, "God can instantly act at every place; he knows everything that happens and he personally governs and directs everything in the universe (from above and from below . . .)."[91] Why then does Scripture say he is "far" from some people? Frame helps us by distinguishing Scripture's statements. God's presence can mean that God is present everywhere, omnipresence proper. It can mean his presence in holy places such as the tabernacle, the temple, Christ, believers. "This language does not mean that God's power, knowledge, and freedom to act are greater in the holy places than elsewhere on earth. But we might say that in these places his presence is more intense and more intimate, and the penalties for disobedience are more severe. When God makes his dwelling in a place, that place becomes his throne. We show special deference to him there, and we become more aware of his presence to bless or curse."[92] Further, there is an ethical focus to some presence statements. God is "with the righteous (those in Christ) to bless" as in Isaiah 57:15.[93] He is far from the rebellious. Isaiah says:

> Behold, the LORD's hand is not shortened, that it cannot save,
>   or his ear dull, that it cannot hear;
> but your iniquities have made a separation
>   between you and your God,
> and your sins have hidden his face from you
>   so that he does not hear. (Isa. 59:1–2)

God's sovereignty does not exclude him from time and space, but means that "he relates himself to physical reality as the Lord, transcending it and using it as he chooses."[94] One further aspect should be noted. Although God is essentially[95] invisible—which means he is sovereign over making himself visible, as he did in theophany, and did decisively in the incarnation (John 1:18)—Frame says God becomes more visible as redemptive history reaches its climax in Christ. In the consummation of all things, God will be profoundly visible in theophany and incarnation,[96] as Jesus said, "Blessed are the pure in heart, for they shall see God" (Matt. 5:8; cf. 1 Cor. 13:12).

91. Ibid., 580.
92. Ibid., 581.
93. Ibid., 583.
94. Ibid., 587.
95. Ibid., 590.
96. Ibid., 591.

Bavinck defines time and space as essential characteristics of created being. Hence all discussion of God's relation to his people is an image: "Even where Scripture speaks in human terms, and with a view to giving us an image of God's being—as it were, infinitely enlarges space (Isa. 66:1; Ps. 139:7; Amos 9:2; Acts 17:24), the underlying idea is that God transcends all spatial boundaries."[97] He distinguishes, however, between God's "physical and his ethical immanence."[98] Sin "does not distance us from God locally, but spiritually (Isa. 59:1)." He recognizes the same biblical phenomena, but will not say God experiences immanent spatiality. However, Bavinck writes that in the eternal Sabbath, at the consummation of God's plan:

> Time is charged with the eternity of God. Space is full of his presence. Eternal becoming is wed to immutable being. Even the contrast between heaven and earth is gone. For all the things that are in heaven and on earth have been gathered up in Christ as head (Eph. 1:10). All creatures will then live and move and have their being in God, who is all in all, who reflects all his attributes in the mirror of his works and glorifies himself in them.[99]

CONCLUSION: CONTINUITY AND ADVANCE

Frame's epistemology goes further than Bavinck's. Like Bavinck, Frame affirms the distinction between God's knowledge and human knowledge. God is truly incomprehensible. However, he also wants to say that we do have literal knowledge of God, given by revelation.[100] We are created for it, and we have

---

97. Bavinck, *God and Creation*, 166.

98. Ibid., 169.

99. Bavinck, *Holy Spirit, Church and New Creation*, 730.

100. "It is wiser, in my view, not to make general claims of ignorance about God, but rather to carefully restrict our dogmatic claims to the teaching of Scripture, and to be honest about those questions that Scripture does not resolve. God's transcendence is not a wholly otherness, but his control and authority over the creation. His immanence, therefore, as his covenant presence, does not confer his ultimate wisdom on the theologian, but provides a revelation that governs and limits our thinking and speech." *DG*, 206. Frame approves of Van Til's urging that theologians be "fearlessly anthropomorphic" in this sense: "He is telling us to affirm the non-literal teachings [of Scripture] with confidence, since they contain genuine (I am tempted to say 'literal') truth). . . . He is not trying to say that apparently literal expressions are really figurative, but that apparently figurative expressions contain some element of literal truth." *CVT*, 94–95. Frame also endorses John Murray's formulation, " 'Our knowledge of the truth is analogical, but what we know is not analogical; e.g., our knowledge of that Truth is analogical, but it is not an analogy of the truth that we know. What we know is the Truth.' Murray says, if what we know, the object of our knowledge, is a mere analogy, then we do not know the truth at all." "Systematic Theology

it as those who believe the God-breathed Scriptures. Hence he is willing to view biblical language at certain points as having a more literal significance, and leave the question of "how?" more open than Bavinck does.[101]

How successful is he? Frame is unwilling to use spatial categories to define God's transcendence—we should not think of transcendence as distance, but as kingship—but is he consistent in using spatial categories for God's immanence? Perhaps we need new words to describe the perspectives, or perhaps we have gone as far as Holy Scripture will allow. Frame's lordship attributes are sometimes not easy to distinguish from each other, as when he infers covenant presence from control and evaluation, and then seems to define covenant presence as control and evaluation.

Still, Frame provokes us to think more carefully about the covenantal character of providence. Is God's covenantal presence legitimately described as "intimate" in the case of the unregenerate? Does this not introduce an ambiguity—that intimate fellowship is true for all, apart from condition of covenant keeping?[102] But perhaps this is simply speaking as Holy Scripture itself does about the covenant people, without answering the question either way.

Frame advances our understanding of God's dealings with the church. Covenant presence is not an addition to God's aseity: it does not compromise it, or challenge it. It does not assert that God is spatial, or limited to or by his interaction with the world and people. It simply articulates something of the relatedness of God's *a se* self to this world, in terms of the nature of God's plan to sum up all things in Christ. That plan takes the form of a covenant realized in time. Salvation recovers the union between God and man;

---

and Apologetics at the Westminster Seminaries," in *The Pattern of Sound Doctrine: Systematic Theology at the Westminster Seminaries*, ed. David VanDrunen (Phillipsburg, NJ: P&R Publishing, 2004), 80. In an e-mail to the author on May 4, 2009, Frame wrote, "My goal is to take the [doctrinal] strands and leave them just as loose as they are in Scripture: no tighter, no looser."

101. Frame criticizes Bavinck for inconsistency—denying that we can know God's essence, and later affirming that we can know God as he is in himself insofar as God has revealed that in Scripture. *DG*, 204.

102. Compare the distinction made by J. van Genderen and W. H. Velema between covenant as "promissory bond" and covenant as "vital communion." "This is not a doctrine of a two-fold covenant, but a distinction between what the covenant is as such and what is accomplished within the covenant. Being within the covenant is not identical to being born again. The essence of the covenant is not communion of life but the relationship of promise. The goal is communion of life: the real personal, spiritual, active relationship of life between God and believers through Christ the Mediator of the covenant worked by the Holy Spirit." *Concise Reformed Dogmatics*, trans. Gerrit Bilkes and Ed van der Maas (Phillipsburg, NJ: P&R Publishing, 2008), 565.

it removes the "distance" between God and man created by sin. In glory that distance will be no more. Nothing in the eternal consummation will alter or hinder the full glory of God. Instead, there will be the full revelation of God in all his ways, as creatures renewed in his image can know him. Covenant presence is rather a way of seeing his presence with the world in terms of the entire plan of salvation revealed in Christ—something well worth our attention in theology. Understanding the relation of God and the world in covenant categories is shared by Frame and Bavinck. It expresses a truth precious to Reformed theology.[103]

Frame's development of covenant presence can add a more biblical understanding of God's providence and of his shaping of the Christian life by his Word and Spirit, day by day, as it were. His response to open theism shows this—the covenant relation is the biblical way of relating God and human experience and history. In a word, God does respond to us and lead us.[104] However, this can function biblically only as long as we hold the biblical conception of God's absolute sovereignty (Frame's *control*), and reject libertarian free will. If we lose our grasp on this, the notion of covenant presence can devolve into hyper-Arminianism—or, worse, open theism or process theology.[105] However, if we can believe and communicate both—as Frame does—we can help provide the church the great comfort of God's absolute lordship and his precious nearness.

103. Spatial language for the covenantal acts of God appears in the WCF, as far as I can see, only in 5.5: "The most wise, righteous, and gracious God doth often-times leave, for a season, his own children to manifold temptations, and the corruption of their own hearts, to chastise them for their former sins, or to discover unto them the hidden strength of corruption and deceitfulness of their hearts, that they may be humbled; and, to raise them to a more close and constant dependence for their support upon himself, and to make them more watchful against all future occasions of sin, and for sundry other just and holy ends." See also 30.3: "Church censures are necessary . . . for preventing the wrath of God, which might justly fall upon the church, if they should suffer his covenant, and the seals thereof, to be profaned by notorious and obstinate offenders."

104. See *NOG*, 182: "God is not only transcendent beyond time and space, but also immanent in all times and spaces. From these immanent perspectives, God views each event from within history. As he does, he evaluates each event appropriately, when it happens. Such evaluations are, in the most obvious sense, responses. . . . Does such responsiveness imply passivity in God? To say so would be highly misleading. God responds (both transcendently and immanently) only to what he has himself ordained. He has chosen to create a world that will often grieve him. So ultimately, he is active rather than passive. Some may want to use the term *impassible* to indicate that fact."

105. Frame distances his views from a process understanding of God's relation to the world. The two bear only a "superficial resemblance." *DG*, 572–73.

I am deeply grateful for the many kindnesses John Frame has shown me as a junior colleague at Reformed Theological Seminary. *DG* was extremely welcome when I was assigned the task of teaching theology proper. I share William Edgar's assessment: Frame's theology is "at once vigorously orthodox and sweetly pastoral."[106]

---

106. From William Edgar's endorsement on the back of *SBL*.

15

A Living and Active Word:
Some Notes on Frame's View
of Holy Scripture

Roger Wagner

I HAVE BEEN INVITED to discuss John Frame's view of Holy Scripture. As one of his former students, I consider it a great privilege to do so. I have chosen to write a pastoral appreciation rather than a scholarly analysis of Frame's view of Scripture. I have a couple of reasons for that. Considered "perspectivally," one is "existential" and the other is "situational."[1]

First, the existential. I am not an academic theological scholar. I am, and have been for thirty-five years, a pastor and preacher. As such, I certainly must "do theology," but my theological reflection has always been done in the direct service of shepherding souls in the rough and tumble of their everyday lives. Theological analysis is never an end in and of itself.

John Frame is a pastor's theologian. His dictum "theology is application," although controversial for some, resonates in this pastor's heart. Frame was the first to teach me, when I was one of his students, to think of

---

1. I trust that I can safely assume that most of the readers of this volume are already familiar with Frame's triperspectival approach to everything theological (and a lot more besides), or will become so from reading other essays in this collection.

"application" not as an addendum to the work of systematic theology, but as its true *telos*. God's Word was given for the purpose of transforming human life—bringing men out of spiritual darkness into the light that is Christ Jesus, overcoming error and confusion in human thinking so that human beings may come to understand the being, character, and ways of the true and living God, and renewing within the human heart an ability and desire to will and to do God's good pleasure.

As I will show in a moment, Frame considers theology the servant of the Word of God, and thus it should serve Scripture's purpose. Academic investigation, analysis, and formulations are important, and can certainly be the life calling of some of God's servants. At the same time, many have recognized the danger that academic theology can become ivory-tower theology—too far removed from the actual shepherding of God's people. Seminaries can become theological think tanks, rather than places where pastors and preachers are equipped and trained. Some men who begin advanced theological training with a view to entering the pastoral ministry may, after two or three years in that rarefied atmosphere, find academic scholarship far more to their liking than pastoral work. Advanced degrees and scholarly publications are more appealing than pulpit ministry. Other men who actually enter the ministry never seem to manage to shake off the allure of the academic culture, and their preaching (and effectiveness) suffers because of it.

John Frame was explicit about his desire to train pastors. What set him apart from many of his colleagues was his approach to the teaching of theology. His organization of material and the way he presented it compellingly aided the accomplishment of his stated goal. He taught us to think about theology as pastors should—considering how biblical truth should impact and transform the lives of real people—and that made it much easier for us to bring the theological insights and skills he taught us into the service of both pulpit ministry and personal pastoral instruction and care.

So although festschrift collections often provide essayists with the opportunity to explore new scholarly territory, I'd prefer to reflect on some aspects of Frame's teaching about the doctrine of Scripture that have been especially helpful to me and others as pastors and preachers. I trust that my highly esteemed mentor will find in these few pages a suitable tribute from one who has been (and continues to be) profoundly shaped *as a pastor* by the instruction he received at his feet.

Now, a brief "situational" disclaimer. Although his teachings about the Bible are spread across all of Frame's lectures and writings, he has yet to publish his promised "big book" on the doctrine of Holy Scripture—a companion to his major studies of the doctrines of the knowledge of God, theology proper, and the Christian life.[2] Accordingly, a thorough scholarly treatment (analysis and critique) of his understanding of this doctrine is still somewhat premature. I can safely leave that task to others, in a different setting. I will stick with what I know and appreciate most about Frame's view of the Bible.

Frame as a Contemporary Orthodox Theologian

Let me begin with a word about the man who teaches the doctrine. Frame's view of Scripture is entirely in line with confessional Reformed orthodoxy. As an ordained minister of the Presbyterian Church in America, he has publicly committed himself to the statement regarding Holy Scripture contained in the first chapter of the Westminster Confession of Faith. Accordingly, he stands in a long line of faithful men who have taught and defended the doctrine of the divine authority of an inspired, infallible Bible.[3] Frame's genius has been to make use of that great tradition in fresh, sometimes innovative and challenging ways. Some of his ideas and the application of those ideas have been controversial, such as the debates over contemporary worship.[4] Nevertheless, his commitment to a high view of Scripture has remained unshaken.

In a day when many professional theologians spend their careers attempting to undermine their students' confidence in the Bible as the inerrant Word of God, the only infallible rule of faith and practice, Frame has been demonstrating the biblical cogency of that doctrine, and equipping pastors and laymen with compelling arguments with which to defend it.[5] This personal faithfulness must not be overlooked.

2. *DKG, DG,* and *DCL.*
3. Frame pays tribute to several of them in his essay "Backgrounds to My Thought," elsewhere in this volume.
4. For example, his online debate with Darryl Hart regarding the regulative principle of worship ("The Regulative Principle: Scripture, Tradition, and Culture," http://www.frame-poythress.org/frame_articles/1998HartDebate.htm).
5. For example, "God and Biblical Language: Transcendence and Immanence" and "Scripture Speaks for Itself," in John Warwick Montgomery, ed., *God's Inerrant Word* (Minneapolis: Bethany Fellowship, 1974), 159–200.

Paul wrote to Timothy, "What you have heard from me in the presence of many witnesses entrust to faithful men who will be able to teach others also" (2 Tim. 2:2).[6] I have learned over the years that doctrinal beliefs are more than a matter of merely embracing certain propositions intellectually. The personal element is very important. People choose beliefs, and cling to them, in part because of the people who bring those ideas into their lives (parents, teachers, celebrities, etc.). I and other students have been impressed from the first with the clarity, the reasonableness, and the depth of conviction that has characterized Frame's thought and teaching about the Bible.

Even within Reformed circles, where a rigorous commitment to the authority of Scripture is expected and required, Frame stands out as one for whom that commitment is no sterile statement of principle. Rather, he is a teacher who creates *passion* as well as respect for the Word of God in the hearts of his students. They in turn will be able to communicate that same zealous love for the Word of God to their congregations by means of their weekly ministry from the pulpit and the teaching and counseling of individuals.

Shaky pastors make for shaky Christians, and shaky pastors are made by weak and uncertain professors. The Bible has never been an embarrassment to Frame.[7] He finds in its pages "the words of eternal life" (John 6:68). He has formed in his students those same convictions. In teaching *about* Scripture, he has fed his students a rich diet of those very life-giving words. As a result, we can both preach and live out of the abundance of God's holy Word.

Paul, in speaking of his own ministry, declared, "It is required of stewards that they be found trustworthy" (1 Cor. 4:2). Frame in his own time has been trustworthy to his stewardship in the classroom. We who learned from him have been richly blessed as a result. He will one day hear the commendation of our Lord, "Well done, good and faithful servant" (Matt. 25:21).

---

6. All quotations from the Bible are from the ESV.

7. Frame says: "If God wants to tell us in his Word some things about the history of Israel that contradict a scholarly consensus, he has the right to do so, and we should stand with him against the scholars. . . . If God wants to tell us in Scripture that evolution is false, we should stand with him against the consensus of scientists. If God wants to tell us that abortion is wrong, we should stand with him and not with contemporary opinion makers." *DCL*, 153.

The Word, Theology, and Preaching

I have called Frame a "pastor's theologian." The way Frame does theology is very "user-friendly" for one engaged in weekly pulpit ministry. I'd like to explain that statement in a bit more detail.

Evangelical and Reformed theologians generally acknowledge the supreme authority of the Scriptures of the Old and New Testaments as the only infallible rule of faith and life.[8] The authority of God's written Word is primary; theological formulations (including creedal statements) are secondary. Theology and ethics must always be brought to the Bible and tested by that standard.[9] Frame, however, goes on to formulate his understanding of the relationship between Scripture and theology in a way that emphasizes the *functional* as well as the theoretical primacy of scriptural authority, and thereby provides help to the preacher as he fulfills his calling in the church.

Frame locates his definition of theology (as he puts it) within the "ball park" of the "study of, knowledge of, speaking of, teaching of, [and] learning about God."[10] He rejects the subjectivism of Friedrich Schleiermacher, who replaced the exposition of biblical doctrines as the *content* of theology with accounts of Christian religious *feelings*. While recognizing that there is a place within theology to describe such feelings, Frame objects to Schleiermacher's wholesale subjectivism as it displaces the theological authority of Scripture.[11]

At the same time, Frame is not satisfied with the objectivism of theologians in the Reformed tradition such as Charles Hodge. Perhaps in an overreaction to Schleiermacher, Hodge so stressed the objective ("scientific") character of theology that he ran the danger of portraying theology as somehow improving on the form (if not the content) of Scripture. Frame writes, "I am . . . disturbed by Hodge's statement that theology exhibits the facts of Scripture 'in their *proper* order and relation' (emphasis mine)."[12] Implicit in the normativity and perfection of

---

8. Cf. WCF 1.2.

9. "The Supreme Judge, by which all controversies of religion are to be determined, and all decrees of councils, opinions of ancient writers, doctrines of men, and private spirits, are to be examined, and in whose sentence we are to rest, can be no other but the Holy Spirit speaking in the Scripture." WCF 1.10.

10. *DKG*, 77.

11. Ibid.

12. Ibid., 79.

Scripture, Frame argues, is the idea that it has its Spirit-given order as well as its divine content. There is no need for the theologian to provide another, improved order.[13]

So what is the task of theology?

> Theology, then, must be a *secondary* description, a reinterpretation and reproclamation of Scripture, both of its propositional and of its non-propositional content. Why do we need such a reinterpretation? *To meet human needs.* The job of theology is to help people understand the Bible better . . . to teach people the truth of God. Although Scripture is clear, for various reasons people fail to understand and use it properly. Theology is justified . . . by the help it brings to people, by its success in helping people to use the truth.[14]

This places the task of the theologian as a servant of Scripture closely alongside that of the pastor/preacher, whose daily task it is to help the people understand the Bible and use it more effectively in their daily lives.

Frame cautions against a too-intellectualist concept of theology. Theology is not simply "an exercise in theory construction, in description of facts, in the accurate statement of 'principles' or 'general truths.' "[15] Although there is certainly a place for theoretical work in theology,[16] *theology must be attuned to the richness of Scripture itself.*

> Scripture is not merely a body of factual statements but is full of other kinds of language: imperatives, interrogatives, promises, vows, poetry, proverbs, emotive language, and so forth. The purpose of Scripture is not merely to give us an authoritative list of things we must believe but also to exhort us, command us, inspire our imaginations, put songs in our hearts, question us, sanctify us, and so on. Surely the work of teaching in the church is not only to list what people must believe but also to communicate to them all the other content of Scripture.[17]

13. We must "recognize that Scripture . . . has its own rational order, that it gives a perfect, normative, rational description and analysis of the facts of redemption." Ibid.

14. Ibid., 79–80 (emphasis in original).

15. Ibid., 78.

16. "By defining theology as application, I am not seeking to disparage the theoretical work of theologians. Theory is one kind of application. It answers certain kinds of questions and meets certain kinds of human needs." Ibid., 84–85.

17. Ibid., 78–79.

Accordingly, Frame proposes a "covenantal definition" of theology—"the application of the Word of God by persons to all areas of life."[18] And he defines "application" as "teaching" in the biblical sense—"the use of God's revelation to meet the spiritual needs of people, to promote godliness and spiritual health." Such teaching "is not a narrowly intellectualist or academic discipline."[19]

This definition, argues Frame, has strong advantages over either a narrowly "subjectivist" or "objectivist" definition. Theology so defined is not a reflection of any (imagined) "weakness" in Scripture itself, but rather is justified by its efforts to help Christians better understand and use Scripture. It obeys the biblical mandate to *teach*. It both takes account of human needs and supports the authority and sufficiency of Scripture. Such a view of the theologian's work protects it from any false intellectualism or academicism. And such theology can speak both theoretically, when necessary, and also "in nonacademic ways, as Scripture itself does—exhorting, questioning, telling parables, fashioning allegories and poems and proverbs and songs, expressing love, joy, patience . . ."[20]

In explaining why he prefers to speak in terms of "application" rather than "teaching," Frame writes, "I chose it to discourage a certain false distinction between 'meaning' and 'application' that I believe has resulted in much damage to God's people."[21] For example, in Frame's judgment, the *meaning* of the biblical text has too often been artificially distanced from its *usefulness* to the reader or hearer. Frame argues that this separation is unwarranted, and will not hold up under careful examination.[22]

> I understand the distinction between meaning and application as a remnant of objectivism, as an attempt to find somewhere a "bedrock" of pure facticity (meaning) on which all other uses of the text are to be based. But the true bedrock of the meaning of Scripture is Scripture itself, not some

---

18. Ibid., 81.
19. Ibid.
20. Ibid., 81–82.
21. Ibid., 82.
22. "Every request for 'meaning' is a request for an application because whenever we ask for the 'meaning' of a passage we are expressing a lack in ourselves, an ignorance, an inability to use the passage. Asking for "meaning" is asking for an application of Scripture to a need; we are asking Scripture to remedy that lack, that ignorance, that inability. Similarly, every request for an 'application' is a request for meaning; the one who asks doesn't understand the passage well enough to use it himself." Ibid., 83.

product of man's ingenuity . . . The work of theology is not to discover some truth-in-itself in abstraction from all that is human; it is to take the truth of Scripture and humbly to serve God's people by teaching and preaching it and by counseling and evangelizing.[23]

Such an understanding of the relationship between God's Word and our theological practices is of great help to the preacher. Too often, for pastors who are committed to preaching sound doctrine (Titus 2:1), "application" (if it is not neglected altogether) is little more than sermon illustration. The separation between "meaning" and "usefulness" can lead to an unhelpful division of labor between theologian and preacher—the former theorizes about meaning; the latter tries to make applications in real-life contexts. If the preacher sees application as simply an *addendum* to the "real work" of preaching (i.e., exegetical and theological exposition), he may not pay as careful attention to it as he should.

Paul urges Timothy to take pains with both his doctrine and his life (1 Tim. 4:16). Surely Paul is calling for more than simply "practicing what you preach" in the sense of avoiding hypocrisy. He is urging pastors to give careful thought to the way in which Scripture's teaching impacts their lives and, through them, the lives of their hearers. It is not enough to spend hours in sermon preparation developing the exegesis of a passage, and drawing out its redemptive-historical and theological implications, only to neglect similarly careful thought about how that teaching should transform the hearers' thinking, perspectives, and attitudes, as well as their outward behavior.[24]

Frame's consistent emphasis on the applicatory nature of theology helps remind the pastor that his engagement with the text of Scripture is not primarily theoretical, to which he may (or may not!) add some "practical applications." Rather, he understands that there is a *life-transforming purpose* to all of Scripture—to bring men and women into conformity with the image of God's Son (Rom. 8:29) by means of teaching, rebuke, correc-

---

23. Ibid., 83–84.

24. Over the years, I have frequently told pastoral interns that when they think they understand what a text is teaching, they have only "half the sermon." Next, they must begin again, this time with the person in the pew, and give prayerful thought not only to "application questions," but to those potential impediments in the hearer that might hinder the person's receiving the message given with faith and obedience (cf. Heb. 4:2). Good preachers will anticipate some of these barriers, and in the sermon itself help their audience to identify and begin to overcome them (e.g., Rom. 9:14, 19). Answers to these kinds of applicatory questions will provide the "other half of the sermon."

tion, and training in righteousness (2 Tim. 3:16–17)—and that purpose must be kept clearly in view throughout the process of preparing and delivering sermons.[25]

"Something Close to Biblicism"

Frame's commitment to the Reformation principle of *sola Scriptura* is deep and consistent. It arises from the Bible's own teaching concerning its self-attesting authority, absolute reliability, and supreme usefulness for the reshaping of human life and society.[26] This commitment has drawn Frame into discussions (and debates) with others within the Reformed community over the question of the relationship between Scripture and tradition as authorities for the doctrine and life of the church. Protestants denounce the way in which Roman Catholics place human tradition on a par with the authority of the Bible. They are sometimes less willing, in Frame's judgment, to be critical about the role that tradition (in the form of church-historical arguments[27]) plays within Reformed theology and ecclesiastical practice.[28] Much of Frame's writing in this vein has focused on the issue of "contemporary" worship practices, including styles of music, within Reformed and evangelical churches.[29]

It is not my purpose here to enter into this debate. Rather, I want to draw attention to another emphasis in Frame's teaching concerning the Holy Scriptures that provides special help to the thinking and practice of the pastor.

25. "You don't even *know* the Bible unless you can apply the Bible to questions that arise outside the Bible. You don't *know* the Bible unless you can *use* it rightly." John M. Frame, "A Theology of Opportunity: *Sola Scriptura* and the Great Commission," http://www.frame-poythress.org/frame_articles/1999ATheology.htm.

26. For an overview of Frame's doctrine of Holy Scripture, see the chapters on the Word of God and the authority of the Bible, chapters 4 and 5 in his *SBL*, 42–71.

27. That is, a line of argument for a theological conclusion that is based on the way in which the church has historically understood the Bible (e.g., as summarized in a confessional statement), rather than on direct exegetical and theological arguments based directly on Scripture. Frame, for example, contrasts the theological method of G. C. Berkouwer with that of John Murray along these lines. Although he admits that we can learn a great deal from Berkouwer's approach, he favors Murray's exegetical theology as more helpful in terms of *sola Scriptura* (cf. *CWM*, 182–83).

28. "As one committed heart and soul to the principle *sola Scriptura*, I find the trend toward traditionalism most unfortunate. It has, in my view, weakened the Evangelical witness in our time." *TRAD*.

29. Cf., e.g., *CWM*, and Frame's online debate with Darryl Hart on the regulative principle of worship (see footnote 4 above).

Ministers within the Reformed tradition usually share not only a high view of the authority of Scripture, but also a commitment to the confessional formulations that provide doctrinal consistency within their communions.[30] Thus the pastor carries out his ministry, if you will, *between Scripture and confession*. Scripture is foundational to the life and teaching of the church, but we agree that our confession of faith and catechisms give substantial expression to what we believe the Scriptures actually teach. Thus, in practical terms, the thought of the church is shaped in large measure by the confession. Doctrinal controversies, for example, are addressed from a confessional as well as a scriptural perspective, and sometimes the former is the more ecclesiastically decisive.

This practice has great value, but some danger also lurks. For the pastor, it often boils down to making good practically on his claim that, although the confession is a most helpful tool, it is Scripture (and Scripture *alone*) that bears supreme authority in the church. He must take advantage of the stability afforded by the confession, but at the same time seek to continually invigorate his preaching, pastoral care, and church leadership by direct contact with Scripture.

In *IDSCB*, which has appeared in more than one place,[31] Frame sets his view of *sola Scriptura* over against both evangelical traditionalism and what is sometimes called *biblicism*. The article is instructive both for what it says about Scripture and as an example of how Frame typically sets forth his theological case—defining terms, making careful distinctions, appreciating nuances. It also has some helpful implications for the pastor.

Frame sets out the common understanding of biblicism as follows:

> The term "biblicism" is usually derogatory. It is commonly applied to (1) someone who has no appreciation for the importance of extrabiblical truth in theology, who denies the value of general or natural revelation, (2) those suspected of believing that Scripture is a "textbook" of science, or philosophy, politics, ethics, economics, aesthetics, church government, etc., (3) those who have no respect for confessions, creeds, and past theo-

30. Confessions are frequently referred to as "secondary standards"—subject, of course, to the primary authority of Holy Scripture. Reformed ministers typically take ordination vows that include an explicit subscription to the confessional standards of the church as reflecting the teaching of Scripture.

31. It was first published in *WTJ* 59 (1997): 269–91, but also appeared as an appendix in Frame's *CWM* (see footnote 29 above). I will cite from that source.

logians, who insist on ignoring these and going back to the Bible to build up their doctrinal formulations from scratch, (4) those who employ a "proof texting" method, rather than trying to see Scripture texts in their historical, cultural, logical, and literary contexts.[32]

Frame disavows such biblicism, point by point. At the same time he acknowledges "how difficult it is to draw the line between these biblicisms and an authentic Reformation doctrine of *sola Scriptura*."[33]

> *Sola Scriptura* is the doctrine that Scripture, and only Scripture, has the final word on everything, all our doctrine, and all our life. Thus it has the final word even on our interpretation of Scripture, even in our theological method.[34]

Frame then proceeds to explain what is actually entailed in the idea of *sola Scriptura*.

Frame argues that unlike the "biblicist," who disparages the place of extrabiblical information in theology, we are guided by the principle of *sola Scriptura* to make rich use of extrabiblical *data* (which he distinguishes from extrabiblical *knowledge*), but always in accordance with "scriptural principles, scriptural norms, the permission of Scripture."[35] In this process, our understanding of the way in which Scripture addresses all of life is expanded. All our reflection becomes "scriptural," not because it is limited to the express statements of Scripture, but because (as Calvin said) Scripture becomes the "spectacles" through which we "read" and understand everything else. This means, as Frame goes on to explain, that "the range of subject matter to which [Scripture] may be applied, is unlimited." Echoing Cornelius Van Til, Frame declares, "Scripture speaks of everything."[36]

As a pastor seeks to bring the Word of God, in all its fullness, to bear upon the lives of his people, in all the richness of their experience and endeavor, this perspective is most helpful—and challenging. Too often

---

32. *CWM*, 176–77.

33. Ibid., 177.

34. Ibid.

35. Ibid., 178. For Frame, although it may seem somewhat paradoxical, extrabiblical *data* becomes scriptural *knowledge* once it is understood within the context of the normativity of Scripture itself. "In one sense, then, all our knowledge is scriptural knowledge. . . . All knowledge is knowledge of what Scripture requires of us." Ibid.

36. Ibid.

preachers portray the concerns of Scripture as very narrow. Applications are drawn predominantly from personal or domestic life. Wide areas of human concern (e.g., psychological, sociological, economic, political, and professional), many of which impact the lives of our people daily, are left largely unexamined.

I remember Francis Schaeffer telling a meeting of pastors I attended years ago that, in his opinion, the church was losing her young people (in part) because it gave them the impression that Christianity is very "poor" (i.e., shallow and narrow), when the world around them (especially as they were confronted with it in the university) seemed so "rich." They were unable to see the relevance of biblical faith to so many areas of life. But, Schaeffer argued, in reality it is Christianity that is very "rich," and the church should bring that rich message to bear upon her young people. A similar sentiment is consistently echoed by Frame. Inherent in our view of *sola Scriptura* is a concern for *all of life*.[37]

In Acts 20, Luke records Paul's speech to the elders of Ephesus. In it, the apostle reflects on his ministry among them. He uses several phrases to describe what he was doing as he brought the Word of God to them during his three-year ministry: He declared to them what was profitable (v. 20) and admonished them with tears (v. 31). He testified of repentance and faith (v. 21) and testified "to the gospel of the grace of God" (v. 24). He "did not shrink from declaring . . . the whole counsel of God" (v. 27).[38]

This last phrase has become a watchword among Reformed people— "the whole counsel of God" is equated with "Reformed theology" (in contrast to truncated messages, such as Arminianism). But it must be more than that. In that phrase Paul points us in the direction of

> [Abraham] Kuyper's claim that all areas of human thought and life must bow before the Word of God. . . . Scripture speaks of football games, atoms, cosmology, philosophy. . . . Every human thought must be answerable to God's Word in Scripture.[39]

---

37. Frame's teaching of ethics is an exploration of this broad range of human concerns under the rubric of *sola Scriptura* (cf. *DCL*).

38. For further discussion of these phrases, see Roger Wagner, *Tongues Aflame: Learning to Preach from the Apostles* (Fearn, Ross-shire, UK: Christian Focus Mentor, 2004), 288–92.

39. *CWM*, 179.

This is not to say that the Bible is a "textbook" for all these subjects. Rather, Scripture speaks to them indirectly. The Bible's message, while "centered" in Christ and his redemptive accomplishment for sinners, ultimately has a comprehensive vision for "new heavens and a new earth in which righteousness dwells" (2 Peter 3:13). Pastoral ministry—and the preaching of the Word—must have a vision that is equally broad.

Finally, Frame points out that *sola Scriptura* is methodologically determinative for our very work of interpreting Scripture. "Scripture interprets Scripture."

> *Sola Scriptura* also demands that theological proposals be accountable to Scripture in a specific way. It is not enough for theologians to claim that an idea is biblical; they must be prepared to show in Scripture where that idea can be found. The idea may be based on a general principle rather than a specific text; but a principle is not general unless it is first particular, unless that principle can be shown to be exemplified in particular texts. *So a theology worth its salt must always be prepared to show specifically where in Scripture its ideas come from.* And showing that always boils down in the final analysis to citations of particular texts. This is why, for all that can be said about the abuses of proof-texting, proof texts have played a large role in the history of Protestant thought. And there is something very right about that.[40]

As a pastor and preacher, I find these emphases (which are in no wise unique to Frame) immensely helpful. A confessional tradition is a great blessing, as Frame himself acknowledges.[41] Many of the confessional formulations superbly synthesize masses of biblical material and express the truth in a succinct and often memorable way. They can be of great usefulness to the preacher as he tries to help fix the truths of God's Word in the hearts and minds of his flock. What believer is not blessed by knowing (by heart) that "man's chief end is to glorify God, and to enjoy Him for ever"?[42]

At the same time, there are temptations that may draw us away from the biblical text. One of them is to rely too heavily on confessional formula-

---

40. Ibid., 180 (emphasis added).

41. "In my own theology courses, I always assign relevant portions of the confessions, and I try to make sure that every student understands the traditional formulations, even when I seek to improve upon them. Surely one important function of a seminary is to perpetuate and recommend the confessional traditions." Ibid., 185–86.

42. WSC 1.

tions.[43] It is important for the pastor to remember—especially as he ministers within a confessional ecclesiastical context—that he is, first and foremost, a servant of the words of Holy Scripture. Only so will he be able to provide consistently nourishing spiritual food to his flock. "Like newborn infants, long for the pure spiritual milk, that by it you may grow up into salvation—if indeed you have tasted that the Lord is good" (1 Peter 2:2–3). I am thankful for Frame's sustained emphasis on this important point.

PREACHING THE WORD OF THE LORD

Frame styles his theology A Theology of Lordship. This overarching theme unites his major studies of Christian epistemology, theology proper, and ethics. "God is the Lord" is the fundamental confession of the people of God in the Old Testament (cf. Deut. 6:4–5), and the confession "Jesus Christ is Lord" (Phil. 2:11; cf. 1 Cor. 12:3) is similarly central in the New Testament. Thus, in looking for a biblical basis for our theology, Frame believes "it would be hard to find any starting point more appropriate than that of lordship."[44]

Holy Scripture is, therefore, "the word of the LORD" (Gen. 15:1, and over 250 more times in the Bible). It speaks with divine power and absolute authority, and is indeed the communication of the very presence of God to his people and his creation.[45] By his Word, the Lord created all things and sustains all things, and through the Word of God incarnate, the Lord redeems his chosen people from their sins.[46]

I remember learning from Frame as a student that the Word of God is both *meaning* and *power*. He has since elaborated that distinction in terms of the three perspectives of control, authority, and presence.[47] These key ideas have been invaluable to my preparation and delivery of sermons over the years.

43. "*Sola Scriptura*, therefore, forbids us to absolutize tradition or to put the conclusions of historical scholarship on the same level as Scripture. As such, it is a charter of freedom for the Christian, though, to be sure, Scripture restricts our freedom in a number of ways. Jesus's yoke is easy, and as we take that yoke upon us, we lose the tyrannical yokes of those who would impose their traditions as law. May God enable us to understand and celebrate his gentle bonds and his wonderful liberty." *TRAD.*

44. *SBL*, 7.

45. Ibid., 44–50.

46. Ibid., 47.

47. This hardly needs footnoting, since these three perspectives form the skeleton of Frame's whole theology.

Preaching takes its authority from the self-attesting authority of the Holy Scriptures themselves. As the pastor proclaims the Word of God to the congregation, they must be called to believe and respond appropriately to it.

In describing "saving faith," the Westminster Confession of Faith declares that such faith accepts as true "whatsoever is revealed in the Word, for the authority of God Himself speaking therein," obeying its commands, trembling at its threatenings, and embracing its promises, and especially "accepting, receiving, and resting upon Christ alone for justification, sanctification, and eternal life, by virtue of the covenant of grace."[48] Frame echoes this understanding:

> The authority of Scripture takes various forms, varying with the different kinds of language and subject matter. That is to say, in the Bible God makes different sorts of demands upon us: when he speaks to us indicatively, he tells us authoritatively what to believe. When he speaks imperatively, he tells us what to do. Then there are promises, which are not mere indicatives or statements of fact, although they are in the indicative grammatical mode. Rather in giving promises, God commits himself personally to bringing his purposes to bear in history. A promise demands not only belief, but trust, expecting him to bring something to pass. Similarly a divine threat mandates fear, trembling, and repentance.[49]

The preacher must not only set out the commands, warnings, and promises from the texts of Scripture, but also exhort, persuade, and plead with his people to respond to God's Word in the appropriate ways. This pleading will be effective not (ultimately) because of the preacher's sincerity and communication skills,[50] but because the Word of God carries divine *power*. It not only informs; it *transforms*. As we minister the good news to men and women, "it is the power of God for salvation to everyone who believes" (Rom. 1:16). People are cut to the heart (Acts 2:37) and convicted because God's very *presence*—by the Holy Spirit—is at work in and with the Word (1 Thess. 1:5) to *bring about* the obeying, the trembling, and the receiving and resting that is *required* by the divine authority of the Word.

48. WCF 14.2.
49. "My Use of the Reformed Confessions," http://www.frame-poythress.org/frame_articles/MyUse.htm.
50. Even so, neither of these is to be minimized: cf. Acts 13:43; 2 Cor. 2:17.

Preachers sometimes get themselves into a bind trying to keep clear—in theory and in practice—the distinction between *human* action and *divine* action in the process of preaching. Some let reliance on communication skills and audience analysis all but eliminate conscious dependence on the power of the Word itself and the attending presence of the Spirit of God to teach and transform the lives of people. But others—fearful of somehow intruding on the sovereign work of the Spirit—shy away from "preaching for effect." They are sure that application is the Spirit's work and that the preacher should therefore limit himself to exposition alone—as if that were not equally the work of the Spirit!—and leave it to God to change hearts. Can there be a solution to this dilemma?

This is a place where Frame's threefold scheme proves so helpful to the pastor. The Bible is concerned with the power, authority, and presence of the Lord God at work and manifest through the Word. Therefore, as a servant of the Word, the preacher can give himself without hesitation to all aspects of his task in the pulpit—to exposition, explanation, exhortation (application), and persuasion—confident that the whole person of the hearer (intellect, will, attitudes, and emotions) will be confronted by *divine* authority and power. Indeed, the preacher can be confident that the hearer will encounter God himself, with life-transforming effect, through the preaching of the Word.[51]

ETHICS AND PREACHING

Much of pastoral ministry, including preaching, is concerned with applied ethics. In his study of the doctrine of the Christian life, Frame has much to say about the way in which Scripture explicates the true goal, motive, and standard of ethics.[52] Frame's study of biblical ethics not only helps us to understand "what duty God requires of man"[53] in terms of the ethical instructions of the Old and New Testaments, but also deals with the important questions of the inner ethical dispositions and motivations of the heart, as well as questions regarding the ethical significance of the consequences of human behavior. All of this is most helpful to the pastor as preacher and counselor.

51. See Wagner, *Tongues Aflame*, 77–86.
52. *DCL*, chaps. 9–13.
53. WSC 3.

A question has been raised by some, however, regarding the propriety of an ethical emphasis in preaching. Since the Bible is centered in the redemptive work of Christ, it is argued, preaching should find its proper focus in expounding and exalting what God has accomplished for our salvation through the death and resurrection of Christ. An emphasis in preaching on the believer's ethical obligation is warned against as a potentially dangerous "moralism." Frame has addressed this question in an important article entitled "Ethics, Preaching, and Biblical Theology."[54] It is another demonstration of how Frame draws out the implications of the doctrine of *sola Scriptura*, and is helpful for men whose calling is to minister God's Word to the church.

Frame is profoundly appreciative of the insights afforded by biblical theology, with its focus on redemptive history. It enables us to see clearly "how all of Scripture bears witness to Christ" and "opens up to us the wonderful vision of the eschatology of redemption: that in Christ the last days are here, and we are dwelling with him in the heavenly places."[55] Indeed, redemptive history must provide the "situational perspective" for Christian ethics.

> The [redemptive-historical] tension between the already and the not-yet is the setting of New Testament ethical reflection. God has justified us in Christ and has given us his Spirit; yet sin remains and will not be completely destroyed until the final day. Nevertheless, the "already," the definitive accomplishment of redemption in Christ is our motivation for obedience.
>
> In our preaching and teaching, we should clearly set forth this framework as the context of ethical decision making.[56]

We must be careful, however. The importance of this redemptive-historical perspective can be overemphasized. When that happens, it can lead to the neglect of other important biblical factors. Frame insists that we must also pay careful attention to what God reveals concerning the *standard* of holiness, righteousness, and justice. In addition, a great deal of the New Testament addresses the question of the new inner *motivations* of the heart that impel the believer to obedient living. Frame again tries to correct imbalances by resorting to the three interrelated biblical concerns: life context, standard of truth, and inward disposition.

---

54. http://www.frame-poythress.org/frame_articles/1999Ethics.htm.
55. Ibid.
56. Ibid.

To require that every sermon have a redemptive-historical emphasis is, in a sense, to *absolutize* the "situational perspective." The Bible itself does not warrant such myopia of purpose:

> There is nothing in the Bible itself that requires us to restrict preaching in this way. And there are many ethical passages in Scripture which do not explicitly focus on the eschatological ethical tension—such as Proverbs and some of the ethical passages of the New Testament. We should not demand that a preacher emphasize something that is not emphasized in his text.[57]

Inasmuch as the normative and existential perspectives are neglected—or, worse, suppressed—such imbalanced preaching can become detrimental to the spiritual health and service of God's people. As noticed earlier in this chapter, application itself may become suspect.

> Some redemptive-historical preachers seem to have an antipathy to the very idea of practical application. . . . They want [the sermon] to focus on gospel, not on law. So they want the sermon to evoke praise of Christ, not to demand concrete change in people's behavior. In their mind, Christocentricity excludes any sustained focus on specific practical matters. . . . I too think sermons should magnify Christ and evoke praise. But it is simply wrongheaded to deny the importance of concrete, practical, ethical application. Such application is the purpose of Scripture itself, according to 2 Tim. 3:16–17. And since Scripture contains many practical "how tos," our preaching should include those too. To say that this emphasis detracts from Christocentricity is unscriptural. . . . It is wrong to assume that an emphasis on Christ as Redeemer (redemptive history) excludes an emphasis on Christ as norm and motivator. When a preacher avoids concrete ethical applications in his sermons, he is not preaching the whole counsel of God, and he is not adequately edifying his people.[58]

What of the charge of moralism? In the name of guarding against any form of "works righteousness," some evangelicals have developed an antipathy to human action of virtually any sort in connection with our

57. Ibid.
58. Ibid.

salvation. To present God's people with any *obligation*—other than the obligation to *believe*—is considered "law" rather than "gospel." Although lip service is paid to the place of "good works" in the new life of the believer in Christ,[59] in practical terms, there is an awkwardness about urging Christians to their ethical duty. Such ethical preaching is considered "moralistic."

Frame argues that the charge of moralism is frequently unwarranted. If a preacher's sermons (taken as a whole[60]) are characterized by a substantial emphasis on salvation by grace alone, by an appreciation for forgiveness through the Savior's blood, by a recognition that we must engage in spiritual warfare and the pursuit of holiness, motivated by our experience of redemption, then that preaching may safely imitate the ethical exhortations and warnings of Scripture without danger of being moralistic.[61] Indeed, in Frame's judgment, "neglecting the redemptive-historical context is . . . no worse a sin than neglecting the normative or existential contexts of biblical ethics."[62]

There certainly is an ever-present danger that preaching *may* become moralistic. We may easily come to trust in the arm of the flesh, rather than in the grace of God. The solution, however, is not to avoid ethical application in preaching. That will endanger God's people from another direction—by allowing them to drift into lawlessness and hypocrisy.

Frame's solution is a better one: If the preacher, as he challenges believers with the ethical *norms* of Scripture,[63] also consistently keeps before his hearers the *situational* context of the redemptive accomplishment of Christ, and the Spirit-wrought *existential* transformation of their inner person, then he will be able to effectively lead them toward that goal of holiness and service to which they have been called in Christ Jesus (Phil. 3:14; cf. Eph. 4:1–4; 2 Tim. 1:9; Heb. 3:1).

---

59. That is, we were "created in Christ Jesus for good works, which God prepared beforehand, that we should walk in them" (Eph. 2:10).

60. Frame does not believe each and every sermon must focus on the death and resurrection of Jesus with their saving benefits. Rather, each text must dictate its distinctive emphasis.

61. "Ethics, Preaching, and Biblical Theology."

62. Ibid.

63. The norms themselves, as Frame points out, are often qualified (sometimes modified) by redemptive-historical factors (e.g., the changes from old to new covenant in the observance of dietary restrictions).

A LIVING AND ACTIVE WORD

When theologians who reverence the written Word of God set forth the doctrine of Holy Scripture, they rightly put before the church classic texts that convey Scripture's own view of itself. We are reminded that "all Scripture is breathed out by God and profitable for teaching, for reproof, for correction, and for training in righteousness" (2 Tim. 3:16); that "no prophecy was ever produced by the will of man, but men spoke from God as they were carried along by the Holy Spirit" (2 Peter 1:21); that "man does not live by bread alone, but man lives by every word that comes from the mouth of the LORD" (Deut. 8:3; Matt. 4:4).

When I consider John Frame's contribution to that rich body of theological reflection on the power and truthfulness of God's Word in Scripture, the text that comes most readily to mind is Hebrews 4:12–13:

> For the word of God is living and active, sharper than any two-edged sword, piercing to the division of soul and of spirit, of joints and of marrow, and discerning the thoughts and intentions of the heart. And no creature is hidden from his sight, but all are naked and exposed to the eyes of him to whom we must give account.

Here we are confronted by the dynamic, life-transforming power of God's true and authoritative Word. The Spirit alone "gives life" (John 6:63). Because Scripture is the Spirit-given Word, it is "living and active." No dead letter here, to be dissected and analyzed and systematized with clinical detachment.[64] This is a Word that will *read you* as much as ever you read it. It will wrestle your rebel heart into submission[65] and change your life, for it is the Word of the Lord.

---

64. "Many of you readers are seminary students or are enrolled in some other course of intensive study of God's Word. Don't ever look at the Word merely as an assignment. Say to the Lord from your heart, 'Speak, Lord, for your servant hears.' If you get into the habit of taking the Word for granted, it will harden you rather than bless you. Since the Word is powerful, it never leaves you the same. It will leave you either better off or worse off." *SBL*, 49–50.

65. The term used in verse 13, *trachelizein* (which occurs only here in the New Testament), comes from the world of wrestling or hand-to-hand combat, and means "to seize one by the throat and throw back the head." Cf. F. F. Bruce, *Commentary on the Epistle to the Hebrews* (Grand Rapids: Eerdmans, 1964), 83, and Philip Edgcumbe Hughes, *A Commentary on the Epistle to the Hebrews* (Grand Rapids: Eerdmans, 1977), 167. It seems to suggest more than mere exposure, but

This Word of the Lord *penetrates* to the very core of human personality—like a sharp "two-edged sword." It will divide what cannot be divided. And it will *expose* "the thoughts and intentions of the heart." Nothing can be hidden from it. By it all is laid open before God's sight. The Lord who searches, and thus understands, the human heart and tests the mind (Jer. 17:10) uses his Word to bring into his light not only your outward words and actions, but also your deepest thoughts, unexamined attitudes, and secret desires. In so doing, Scripture will help you discern the true character of your inner and outer life. It will move you to a conviction of conscience that will lead you meaningfully to the foot of the cross of Christ. God's Word will move you to cry out for more direction for life, and more of the life-transforming power of the Holy Spirit who is himself present with you in the Word.

It is this living, and *life-giving*, Word of the Lord that John Frame has loved, defended, explained, and applied throughout his long and fruitful ministry. To God be the glory!

---

also subduing an opponent. When you tangle with the Bible, you are (like Jacob) in a contest with the Lord himself (cf. Gen. 32:22–32). You will lose—and you will be transformed.

16

FRAME ON THE
ATTRIBUTES OF GOD

DEREK THOMAS

FEW SYSTEMATICIANS DESERVE to be in the same room as John Frame. His towering genius and unique formulations reveal lesser mortals for what they are. Dr. Frame is a valued colleague, and my critique of his theological contribution to the attributes of God is done from the perspective of deference.

My task is to write about John Frame's contribution to the understanding of God's so-called attributes. I am focusing chiefly on chapters 19–26 of *DG*.[1] As in so many other places in Frame's writings, one gets the impression of engaging in a personal conversation. At times, Frame can be amazingly self-deferential. In the topic in question, for example, he advocates a revision of the traditional discussion and classification of the attributes of God at the level of both classification and content.[2]

---

1. *DG*, 387–618.

2. For a traditional treatment, see Louis Berkhof, *Systematic Theology* (London: Banner of Truth, 1971), 52–81; Herman Bavinck, *God and Creation*, vol. 2 of *Reformed Dogmatics*, ed. John Bolt (Grand Rapids: Baker, 2004), 148–255; Charles Hodge, *Systematic Theology*, 3 vols. (London: James Clarke & Co. Ltd., 1960), 1:368–441. Berkhof and Bavinck adopt the communicable/incommunicable classification; Hodge follows the order of the Westminster Shorter Catechism. For the most comprehensive historical treatment, see Richard A. Muller, *The Divine Essence and Attributes*, vol. 3 of *Post-Reformation Reformed Dogmatics* (Grand Rapids: Baker Academic, 2003).

There is no avoiding it: John Frame thinks in terms of triads—here, as elsewhere. Recurring series of threes shower upon us. Thus, the attributes have three defining characteristics (*control, authority, presence*) and, within each one, another set of three groups (*goodness, knowledge,* and *power*). And just when we begin to suspect contrivance (a chart appears!), Frame anticipates our concern:

> I certainly am not dogmatic about the position of any attribute on this chart, or even about the usefulness of the chart itself. It is almost certainly too schematic to represent in more than a rough way the rich, complex interrelationships of the divine attributes. None of the attributes can really be contained in any single cell of the chart; they break out of the scheme with frustrating frequency. Nonetheless, the chart may be suggestive. It may help readers to see why I discuss the attributes in the order I do within the three major groupings, although I will not always follow the order indicated on the chart.[3]

Frame's suggestive and somewhat pragmatic approach makes evaluation something of a slippery eel to handle, and we can offer only a broad analysis in these few pages. But first, those triads. In an autobiographical account summarizing his approach to teaching in the Systematics department at Westminster Seminary in 1967, Frame writes:

> I was committed to Van Til's apologetic method and to Murray's exegetical emphasis. I sought to integrate these as much as possible: detailed exegesis with worldview consciousness. In Ethics, Van Til's distinction between goal, motive, and standard provided a course structure. In the Doctrine of the Word, I took special note of Van Til's emphasis on the interrelation of different forms of revelation: revelation from God, from the world, and from the self. In the Doctrine of God, I first structured the course using the traditional distinction between God's transcendence and immanence. But eventually I saw that "transcendence" is somewhat ambiguous . . . So I structured the Doctrine of God course in terms of God's control, authority (these constituting his transcendence), and presence (his immanence).
>
> Three Courses, three threefold distinctions: In Ethics, *goal, standard,* and *motive.* In Doctrine of the Word, revelation from *nature, God,* and *the self.* In Doctrine of God, *control, authority,* and *presence.*[4]

3. *DG,* 399.
4. "Systematic Theology and Apologetics at the Westminster Seminaries," in David Van-Drunen, ed., *The Pattern of Sound Doctrine: Systematic Theology at the Westminster Seminaries,*

And the triadic *control, authority, presence*—what Frame calls "lordship attributes"[5]—is further subjected to a triadic subdivision. Thus "Authoritative Descriptions of God" reveal *names, images,* and *attributes; attributes* further divide, as we have seen, into *love* (or *goodness*), *knowledge,* and *power;*[6] and the attributes themselves are "perspectivally related."[7] Thus, the entire discussion of this or any other aspect of the doctrine of God is viewed through a triperspectival lens.[8] Any assessment, therefore, of Frame's systematic theology is difficult to pinpoint, largely because of its novel grid lines. Analyses of Frame's triperspectivalism can be found elsewhere in this volume, so I will not rehearse them here.

In addition to triadic thought, Frame almost always avoids historical theology. To some, his approach is refreshingly "biblical" (just note the Bible references on any given page of, for example, *DG*)—or, to be more accurate, "biblical-theological." In avoiding historical trajectories and their consequent language, Frame invents categories and terms of his own with considerable flair. Of course, he opens himself up to all the criticisms of what is perceived to be ahistorical theology: that it is "novel" and therefore suspect. Of course, Frame knows his historical theology and when necessary employs traditional categories. But Frame is no slave to traditional theology either—choosing, where he sees dead ends and unhelpful paradigms, to ditch them altogether. Occasionally, this can create the suspicion that something is "new" to Frame (and therefore labeled as "Frame's doctrine of . . .") when it is in fact something that can be traced in complex and nuanced traditions of church history. But history is unfashionable today (ask any professor of church history or historical theology), and Frame's methodology speaks to young, restless, and Reformed types who view all theological discussion as equally valid—so long as they can type a blog entry, even if they could not hold a candle to Dr. Frame.

Essays in Honor of Robert B. Strimple (Phillipsburg, NJ: P&R Publishing, 2004), 91–92.

5. *DG*, 15–17.

6. In a self-deprecating comment, Frame shows some ambivalence in his own assessment of these triadic observations, ranging from "sometimes I think I have uncovered a deep layer of Trinitarian meaning in the Scriptures" to "there are times when I think even less of the scheme—as a kind of mental crutch, or at worst a procrustean bed for theological formulations." ibid., 15n31.

7. Ibid., 387.

8. *Perspectivalism* is a term also closely associated with the writings of Vern Poythress. See Vern Poythress, *Symphonic Theology* (Phillipsburg, NJ: Presbyterian and Reformed, 1987). Frame's former student Joe Torres has provided a fairly concise definition of Frame's understanding of perspectivalism in a Wikipedia article, http://en.wikipedia.org/wiki/John_Frame. See also *DG*, 767–68.

Frame's overall intention is to foster a biblical and theological discussion, and this aim sometimes forces him to override perceived theological axioms beloved of Reformed tradition. It can lead to rather sweeping statements: Post-Reformation scholasticism, Frame argues, has been speculative, philosophical, and irrelevant to the practical Christian life.[9] I pass this evaluation by with considerable reluctance.

IS ONE ATTRIBUTE MORE "FUNDAMENTAL" THAN ANOTHER?

Any discussion of the attributes of God raises the important question of priority: Is there a governing attribute around which all others are to be considered in subcategories? Frame answers, correctly in my view, in the negative. In his interactions with open theism, for example, Frame insists that the love of God cannot be considered as the central attribute. And the reason? The essential attributes of God are "perspectival." God's goodness, wisdom, eternity, love, and lordship each describe God from a different perspective. "In one sense," he writes, "any attribute may be taken as central, and the others seen in relation to it. But in that sense, the doctrine of God has many centers, not just one."[10]

Arguably, the structural prominence given to the lordship of God in Frame's *DG* suggests that lordship or sovereignty may well be considered a central attribute, but Frame denies it: "So instead of yielding to the temptation to make lordship fundamental, I yield to my other temptation, namely, to make all the attributes perspectival."[11] There's that word *perspectival* again!

If no single attribute can be considered as "fundamental" for Frame, this can lead to some rather odd conclusions: "Perhaps all of God's attributes can be derived from his holiness, aseity, love, jealousy, omnipotence, or any number of others. If all of the attributes describe God's simple essence from various perspectives, then any of them can be taken as fun-

---

9. *DG*, 5.

10. *NOG*, 52. Stephen N. Williams criticizes Frame (on structural grounds) for his treatment of the attribute of love: "We are well more than four-hundred pages into *The Doctrine of God* before the author touches on the fact that God's love involves humility." Williams's point is that Frame's structural treatment of the attributes necessarily leads to its being insufficiently Christological (Barthian?). Stephen N. Williams, "The Sovereignty of God," in Bruce L. McCormack, ed., *Engaging the Doctrine of God: Contemporary Protestant Perspectives* (Grand Rapids: Baker Academic/Rutherford House, 2008), 177–78.

11. *DG*, 393.

damental in a given context. All of them, after all, involve all the others. Ultimately, all of them, identical to God's simple essence, are identical also to each other."[12] What Frame means by the last sentence is unclear. Is he, perhaps, arguing against the view that the attributes of God are to be viewed as unrelated segments? Perhaps. And if so, he is stating what Reformed theology has always insisted on. But when he goes on to say that not all the attributes "are equally important," the meaning of the earlier statement is even less clear. What is clear is that Frame is insisting on the inseparability of the attributes of God from his essence. Some earlier theologies held otherwise, a view based on an Aristotelian distinction between substance and attribute.[13]

CLASSIFICATION OF THE ATTRIBUTES

Although Frame is, I think, wary of seventeenth-century categories, he reveals little of the biblical theologian's angst that classification must imply an imposition of foreign philosophical categories. Frame is refreshingly honest about the need for systematic classification of the attributes of God. In an age when rational thought and classification is immediately dubbed *Aristotelian* and *rationalistic* (both viewed as theological swearwords in our time), it is refreshing to find Frame outdoing the Ramists in theological categorizing. There are more labels in one of Frame's volumes than in a teenager's wardrobe! Thus he writes that God's attributes are "many" and "difficult to grasp individually or as a whole" unless "presented systematically."[14] Past presentations vary, and Frame lists close to a dozen examples of attempts to distinguish the attributes according to a natural division reflecting God's transcendence and immanence, only, of course, to dismiss them all.

We have already alluded to Frame's three-by-three classification: three groups of attributes (*goodness, knowledge,* and *power*) and three defining characteristics (*control, authority,* and *presence*). Whether they all possess intuitive meaning is debatable: it is not immediately clear why *mercy* is classified as an attribute of *control* or why *joy* is classified as an

12. Ibid.
13. See the discussion, for example, in W. G. T. Shedd, *Dogmatic Theology,* 3rd ed., ed. Alan W. Gomes (Phillipsburg, NJ: P&R Publishing, 2003), 274.
14. *DG,* 394.

attribute of *presence*, for example. Some of these distinctions are worthy of Thomas Aquinas!

Of equal interest (and concern) is the fact that Frame begins with ethical attributes (*goodness*) rather than those associated with transcendence (*infinity, eternality, unchangeability*). Frame argues that the traditional order has been encouraged by the "false assumption that the attributes of power or transcendence are more fundamental to God's nature than others" and that pedagogically he finds today's students less knowledgeable about (or interested in) the philosophical issues (metaphysics) that underlie it.[15] This is undoubtedly true.

Frame may well be on to something here, and perhaps it spells out the reason why his theology is so appealing. He points out that "those passages of Scripture that sound most like definitions of God tend to focus on his attributes of goodness, not his attributes of knowledge or power."[16] Yet this may not be altogether accurate. Exodus 3:12–15[17] and the prologue of the gospel of John come to mind, both of which highlight definitional attributes of transcendence. But in any case, what Frame does do here is to highlight the *covenantal* nature of our relationship with God. Adopting a relational primacy is a high-risk strategy: it could be viewed as anthropocentric and "from below." It does not appear to be the default setting of, say, Ephesians (theology followed by ethics); but equally, it has the advantage of appealing to the relational and more immediate benefits of God's covenantal dealings with us.

In readdressing theology for today's audience, we must purge several tendencies, including the predilection toward rationalism. Although the term *rationalism* is too frequently and too quickly employed as a battering ram against all theological formulations and expressions that refuse to dumb down for the sake of the poverty of today's intellectual understanding or against the suggestion of the priority of the intellect over the affections (according to a sixteenth- or seventeenth-century faculty psychology), the concern over what appears to be rationalism is a valid one. Reason may well be asleep in our churches and the zany elements of subjectivism very much alive, but Frame's appeal to the relational strikes a chord in the hearts of most of today's seminary students in a way that Francis Turretin

15. Ibid., 400.
16. Ibid.
17. Extensive assessments of both passages appear in ibid., 36–46, 664–66.

(alas!) does not. For my part, I still prefer Turretin; but I'm outnumbered and outflanked.

Turning now to some specific attributes, I regret that space will not allow for a detailed discussion of all that Frame writes. Instead I want to make some comments on a couple of issues of particular interest and relevance to our times raised by Frame's discussion of the attributes of omniscience and eternity (both, as it happens, emphasizing transcendence). In view, of course, are contemporary discussions within open theism. And here, Frame's genius has made significant inroads, clarifying the nature of the debate, highlighting fatal (unbiblical) errors, and pointing the way forward for further discussion where matters remain unclear.

OMNISCIENCE AND M & Ms (MIDDLE KNOWLEDGE AND MOLINISM)

It seems that some form of middle knowledge is in fashion among Reformed systematicians. Among them are Terrance Tiessen and Bruce Ware. The former has written a provocative *WTJ* article indicating not only his embracing of middle knowledge but also his belief that the rest of us should embrace it, too.[18] Ware's presentation differs slightly from Tiessen's and can be found in a variety of sources.[19]

The issue of middle knowledge, known in Calvin's time through the writings of the Spanish Jesuit Luis Molina (1535–1600), has arisen again in our time in the context of open theism. The discussion, then, is an old one, and the Reformed tradition is familiar enough with "Molinist" speculations. Chiefly, middle knowledge has been appealed to in order to prevent the allegation that God's sovereignty implicates him as the author of sin (a gossamer layer to Calvinism, for sure). Over the years, various attempts have been made to circumvent this allegation: sin is privation (given almost

18. "Why Calvinists Should Believe in Divine Middle Knowledge Although They Reject Molinism," *WTJ* 69, 2 (Fall 2007): 345–66.

19. See Ware's chapter, "A Modified Calvinist Doctrine of God," in *Perspectives on the Doctrine of God: 4 Views* (Nashville: B&H Academic, 2008), 76–120, and *God's Greater Glory* (Wheaton, IL: Crossway, 2008). Ware offers his view of middle knowledge as a consequence of his thoughts on God's asymmetrical attitude toward good and evil. God works everything according to his own will, in accord with a predetermined plan; but since God cannot be the author of sin, he cannot be placed in a position where he must imagine evil or wickedness that brings forth sin and evil. The way in which he works his will toward good is therefore necessarily different from the way he works his will toward evil.

creedal status in the Middle Ages by Aquinas), and since God has fullness of being, he cannot author evil; the Westminster divines chose the route of dual causation (primary and secondary—which also had a fine medieval pedigree); and then there is the language of "willing permission" without conferring causation or coercion (something that Calvin found deeply suspicious, suspecting that what lay behind the philosophical nuance was simply human autonomy in another guise).[20]

Frame introduces the idea of "middle knowledge" in his discussion of human responsibility and freedom. The discussion is brief (two pages), and in a footnote he clarifies that he disagrees with the idea as it is shaped by Molina, Arminius, and modern advocates such as William L. Craig and Alvin Plantinga.[21] It is in chapter 22, on "God's Knowledge," that Frame returns to the idea in a slightly lengthier discussion (just over five pages).[22]

What is *middle knowledge*? Frame cites Craig's definition, only to suggest that it would be "difficult to see at first why Reformed theologians have objected to the concept."[23] Craig defines the term this way: "God's knowledge of what every possible free creature would do under any possible set of circumstances and, hence, knowledge of those possible worlds which God can make actual. The content of this knowledge is not essential to God."[24] Frame's keen eye locks on to the use of the term *free* in Craig's definition and concludes that Craig is employing the term (as do "most all the defenders of middle knowledge") in a libertarian sense. And Frame is not a libertarian! If Craig is right about the nature of human freedom—that it really is libertarian—then this knowledge is not *necessary* knowledge. God is, in effect, blind to it. But Craig then does what all other advocates of middle knowledge do in some form or another: he tells us that God chooses *that* world in which *those free choices* were made. Yet this choice, too, is a form of predetermination and distinctly limits the nature of freedom. In fact, it kills the idea of libertarianism stone dead! Why choose *this* world and not another? It may bring some comfort to me for having made this choice of mine, but not to another whose choices he or she regrets. Thus Frame:

20. Bruce Ware offers the view that "compatibilist middle knowledge" is the way to address this thorny issue. "Modified Calvinist Doctrine of God," 109–20.
21. *DG*, 151, esp. n49.
22. Ibid., 501–5.
23. Ibid., 502.
24. Ibid., 501.

Craig would like to believe that middle knowledge reconciles divine sovereignty with libertarian freedom. In fact, it does not. If divine creation on the
basis of middle knowledge means anything, it means that libertarianism is
excluded. Craig is inconsistent to affirm libertarianism and the divine act of
actualizing a complete, possible world, including all creaturely choices.[25]

So Frame is no supporter of middle knowledge in Craig's sense, and his
critique is devastating. This is Frame at his best. But is his concession to
the "idea" of middle knowledge a step too far? Enter Paul Helm, who insists
that the very idea of middle knowledge is just a mirage on the horizon,
tempting the uninitiated into a Bunyanesque By-path Meadow of speculative theology. Speaking about Bruce Ware (not Frame), Helm asserts,
"Strictly speaking, there is no 'Molinist version' of middle knowledge."[26]
Helm's point is to dismiss not just Molinist middle knowledge, but middle
knowledge, period! And this seems at odds with Frame's more ameliorat-
ing attitude toward the idea of middle knowledge. Thus, at the close of
his discussion, Frame reminds us of his earlier reference to middle knowledge: "I suggested that this knowledge is indeed part of the rationale of
creation."[27] And again: "God does take human nature into account when
he formulates his plan for us," Frame argues in chapter 8.[28] Seemingly, this
provides Arminians and Calvinists with some common ground—but this
is only one perspective! "The other perspective is that God's knowledge of
our nature is itself dependent upon his plan to make us in a particular way."
The problem with the Arminian is his "monoperspectivalism."[29]

It isn't altogether clear what Frame wants us to grasp here, but I
remain unconvinced that a compatibilist view of middle knowledge
adds anything to the discussion on the nature of human freedom and
its relationship to divine foreordination in the classical Calvinist sense.
Whatever we say about the status of "counterfactuals," those possible

25. Ibid., 505. The language of "actualizing" states of affairs has entered the theological mainstream via the writings of Alvin Plantinga, *God, Freedom and Evil* (London: George Allen and
Unwin, 1975), 39 and *The Nature of Necessity* (Oxford: Clarendon Press, 1974). See Paul Helm,
"Classical Calvinist Doctrine of God," in *Perspectives on the Doctrine of God*, 35n93. Note Frame's
use of the term in *DG*, 153: "When God creates, he chooses to actualize one world among many
possible worlds, as contemporary modal logicians like to put it."
26. Helm, "Classical Calvinist Doctrine of God," 45.
27. *DG*, 505.
28. Ibid., 151.
29. Ibid., 152.

but nonactualized states of affairs—something clearly envisaged by such passages as 1 Samuel 23:7–13, where David asks the Lord whether or not Saul will kill him if he remains in Keilah, and Matthew 11:20–24, where Jesus says that if the gospel had been preached in Tyre and Sidon, rather than Bethsaida and Chorazin, they would have repented—they cannot provide the basis for resolving the "problem" of divine foreordination. In the end, everything that happens does so because God wills it to happen, wills it to happen in the way that it happens, and wills it to happen *before* it happens. Clearly, the Westminster divines sought refuge in primary and secondary causation as a starting point, but refused to accommodate to middle knowledge—chiefly because they viewed it as an essentially Arminian polemic.[30]

So here at least, we need Frame, the resolute Calvinist, to help us understand how any notion of middle knowledge resolves anything at all.

GOD AND TIME

Chapter 24 of *DG* finds Frame writing at length on (transcendent) aspects of God's infinity, eternity, and atemporality as well as (immanent) aspects of God's relationship within time itself, including unchangeability and the vexed issue of the seeming repentance of God in Scripture.[31] On the latter, Frame is at his very best; there are few more helpful treatments than Frame's on such statements as Moses' request of God in Exodus 32:9–12 that he change his mind and not destroy Israel as he has threatened.

Earlier in the chapter Frame tackles the issue whether we should speak of God as existing within a temporal frame of reference[32] as has become fashionable, particularly since Oscar Cullmann's *Christ and Time*, and more recently in the writings of Nicholas Wolterstorff and Richard Swinburne. In the classical Boethian-Augustinian camp is a contributor to this volume, Paul Helm, whose weighty volume *Eternal God*[33] makes the definitive case for God's atemporality.

---

30. See Richard Muller, *God, Creation, and Providence in the Thought of Jacob Arminius: Sources and Directions of Scholastic Protestantism in the Era of Early Orthodoxy* (Grand Rapids: Baker, 1991).

31. *DG*, 543–75.

32. Karl Barth spoke of the "infinite qualitative difference between time and eternity." *CD*, 2.1.635.

33. Paul Helm, *Eternal God* (Oxford: Clarendon Press, 1988).

Frame's conclusion is stated clearly enough: "I shall argue . . . that God is indeed temporal in his immanence, but that he is (most likely) atemporal in his transcendence. He exists in time as he exists throughout creation. But he also (I say with some reservations) exists beyond time, as he exists beyond creation."[34]

As Frame notes, Helm stands out as one of the few contemporary Christian philosophers to remain true to the classical position of God's timelessness. In addition to the challenges offered by Christian philosophers (Swinburne, Wolterstorff), challenges have also been raised by theologians. Among them is E. L. Mascall, in his work *The Openness of Being*,[35] who spoke of God as having two poles, an objective (eternal) pole and a subjective (temporal) pole. Frame himself makes the comment that "too little attention has been paid to God's temporal omnipresence in the discussion of his relationship to time."[36]

To begin with, Frame posits four axioms with respect to God's relationship to time. God is not subject to the following four limitations:[37]

- The limitation of beginning and end—God has no beginning in time, and he will have no end. "In the beginning was the Word . . ." (John 1:1).[38]
- The limitation of change—God is not subject to time in that it changes him in ways beyond his control. "For I am the LORD, I change not; therefore ye sons of Jacob are not consumed" (Mal. 3:6).
- The limitation of ignorance—God is fully aware of the past, the present, and the future. "Remember the former things of old: for I am God, and there is none else; I am God, and there is none like me, declaring the end from the beginning, and from ancient times the things that are not yet done, saying, My counsel shall stand, and I will do all my pleasure" (Isa. 46:9–10).

---

34. *DG*, 549.

35. E. L. Mascall, *The Openness of Being: Natural Theology Today*, The Gifford Lectures in the University of Edinburgh, 1970–71 (London: Darton, Longman & Todd, 1971).

36. *DG*, 558. Once again Frame appeals to the idea of covenant (relationally) and thinks that God's "temporal covenant presence" is the missing feature in these discussions.

37. Ibid., 554–57.

38. All quotations from the Bible are from the KJV.

- The limitation of temporal frustration—everything happens exactly according to God's timing. "But, beloved, be not ignorant of this one thing, that one day is with the Lord as a thousand years, and a thousand years as one day" (2 Peter 3:8).

We need to be clear about where Frame says he is going. His conclusions are that:

- Philosophical and scientific arguments "are insufficient to establish as doctrine either God's mere temporality or his atemporality";[39]
- A "watertight argument (from Scripture) for divine atemporality" cannot be made and "all the relevant considerations favor atemporality, and none favor temporality";[40]
- Just as we can speak of providence from above (government) and from below (concurrence), we may also speak of a covenantally present God, who can "feel with human beings the flow of time from one moment to the next . . . react to events in a significant sense . . . mourn one moment and rejoice the next . . . hear and respond to prayer in time."[41]

For Frame, then, the question of God's experience of time must be viewed with consideration of God's transcendence *and* immanence in creation (space and time). God is both the Lord *above* time and the Lord *in* time. Because God's redemptive actions in Scripture are temporally successive (worked out in salvation history), they testify not only to his sovereignty, but also to the importance of temporal relationships in the divinely ordained course of history. God is both inside and outside of the temporal box—a box that can neither confine him nor keep him out.[42]

Again, we are tantalized. God's transcendence places him outside of time, but his immanence places him in some kind of relationship to time. Frame seems to want to go beyond the language of Calvin's accommodation in these sentiments. God really does experience time in some way,

39. *DG*, 553.
40. Ibid., 557.
41. Ibid., 558–59.
42. Ibid., 159.

and it is more than just God's speaking to us in baby talk. The language of accommodation, as Calvin (for example) employed it, allows us to habitually think of God's accommodating himself to human, finite, time-bound, and space-bound modes of thought, thereby allowing us to "see" and "hear" him in what have been traditionally thought of as anthropomorphisms.[43] That God is "present" immanently in some form or fashion is not in question, but if this means that in his being he has become subject to constraints of space and time, then we have moved, in a fairly radical fashion, beyond the classical belief that God exists in an immutable, timelessly eternal fashion. For God, there can be no earlier and later; everything is immediately present to him. That he "appears" to be "near," listening in anticipation to our prayers, waiting for certain events to occur before he responds, is merely a human perspective, not a divine one; otherwise, God would be immutable in his transcendence but mutable in his immanence. I am persuaded that Calvin, for one, would not go here, and I am not persuaded that we should abandon Calvin's caution. Again, we are but musing on what are, to be sure, tantalizingly brief statements by Frame.

I said I would comment on a couple of Frame's observations, but now that I come to think of it, it might be more appropriate to employ a triad! Having commented a little on Frame's understanding of God's knowledge and his relationship to time, I want in the third place to say something about Frame's understanding of God's impassibility.[44]

IMPASSIBILITY

Frame begins his discussion by noting that "theological literature has sometimes ascribed to God the attribute of *impassibility*," but makes no mention of the fact that it received confessional status in the Westminster Confession of Faith: "There is but one only, living, and true God, who is infinite in being and perfection, a most pure spirit, invisible, without body, parts, or passions."[45] The notion has been used, Frame

43. See, for example, F. L. Battles, "God Was Accommodating Himself to Human Capacity," *Interpretation* (1977), republished in Robert Benedetto, ed., *Interpreting John Calvin* (Grand Rapids: Baker, 1996), 117–36. See also Paul Helm, "Divine Accommodation," in *John Calvin's Ideas* (Oxford and New York: Oxford University Press, 2004), 184–208.

44. Frame writes on this topic in *DG*, 608–16, even though, curiously, no entry for *impassibility* appears in the index.

45. WCF 2.1.

observes, "to deny that God has emotions or feelings and to deny that God suffers."[46] Put this way, it is unremarkable that today's theologians find trouble with it.

Clearly, we need some context, not least because the Westminster divines are following in a line of traditional thinking about God that goes back to the early fathers, who unanimously accepted passionlessness (*apatheia*[47]) as a controlling principle in their understanding of God. The Reformation and Puritan theologians left it entirely unaltered.[48]

Clearly, we are not the first generation to notice that the Bible speaks of God in emotional terms! The Westminster divines knew that the Bible speaks of God as experiencing anger, regret, even frustration, but were careful to affirm impassibility nevertheless. The range of emotions assigned to God in the Bible is not an insight gained merely from our overcommitment to psychotherapy in the twenty-first century. Indeed, Calvin's remarks here seem pertinent:

> What, therefore, does the word "repentance" mean? Surely its meaning is like that of all other modes of speaking that describe God for us in human terms. For because our weakness does not attain to his exalted state, the description of him that is given to us must be accommodated to our capacity so that we may understand it. Now the mode of accommodation is for him to represent himself to us not as he is in himself, but as he seems to us. Although he is beyond all disturbance of mind, yet he testifies that he is angry toward sinners. Therefore whenever we hear that God is angered, we ought not to imagine any emotion in him, but rather to consider that this expression has been taken from our own human experience; because God, whenever he is exercising judgment, exhibits the appearance of one kindled and angered. So we ought not to understand anything else under the word "repentance" than change of action, because men are wont by changing their action to testify that they are displeased with themselves. Therefore, since every change among men is a correction

---

46. *DG*, 608.

47. Arguably, *apatheia* is more closely aligned with *apathy*—a notion that cannot possibly be correct when applied to God.

48. For representative treatments of impassibility, see Donald MacLeod, "Can God Suffer?" in *Behold Your God* (Fearn, Ross-shire, UK: Christian Focus Publications, 1995), 31–37; Donald Bloesch, *God the Almighty: Power, Wisdom, Holiness, Love* (Downers Grove, IL: InterVarsity Press, 1995), 91–96; Gerald Bray, *The Doctrine of God*, Contours of Christian Theology (Downers Grove, IL: InterVarsity Press, 1993), 98–102; Richard Bauckham, " 'Only the Suffering God Can Help': Divine Passibility in Modern Theology," *Themelios* 9, 3 (1983–84): 6–12.

of what displeases them, but that correction arises out of repentance, then by the word "repentance" is meant the fact that God changes with respect to his actions. Meanwhile neither God's plan nor his will is reversed, nor his volition altered; but what he had from eternity foreseen, approved, and decreed, he pursues in uninterrupted tenor, however sudden the variation may appear in men's eyes.[49]

We also need to be careful in defining *impassibility*. The word is not to be confused with *impassability* or *impassivity*. God is not a blockage (*impassability*). Nor is he stoically disengaged from the world and its sufferings (*impassivity*). The term *impassibility* employs negative language, saying more about what is *not true* than about what *is true*.[50] Fascinatingly, David Bentley Hart puts it this way:

> I can at least offer a definition of divine *apatheia* as trinitarian love: God's impassibility is the utter fullness of an infinite dynamism, the absolutely complete and replete generation of the Son and procession of the Spirit from the Father, the infinite "drama" of God's joyous act of self-outpouring—which is his being as God. Within the plenitude of this motion, no contrary motion can fabricate an interval of negation, because it is the infinite possibility of every creaturely motion or act; no pathos is possible for God because pathos is, by definition, a finite instance of change visited upon a passive subject, actualising some potential, whereas God's love is pure positivity and pure activity.[51]

Apart from the question whether it is appropriate to speak of God as having "emotions"[52] rather than "affections," we need to ask what *impassibility* meant to theologians, say, of the sixteenth and seventeenth centuries. God has no body and therefore cannot possibly experience physical suffering. That Jesus is both God and man in hypostatic union *does* mean that suffering is something experienced by the theanthropic person; but it cannot

49. John Calvin, *Institutes of the Christian Religion*, 2 vols., ed. John T. McNeill, trans. Ford Lewis Battles (Philadelphia: Westminster, 1960), 1:227 (1.17.13).

50. Theology customarily employs similar negatives when speaking of God as infinite, incomprehensible, immutable, etc.

51. David Bentley Hart, *The Beauty of the Infinite: The Aesthetics of Christian Truth* (Grand Rapids: Eerdmans, 2003), 167.

52. *Emotion* is often understood in our time as conveying the loss of control and therefore poses a threat to God's aseity.

mean that in his divine nature, Jesus suffered the pain of crucifixion. Nor can God suffer stress, or mental conflict, or envy, or depression. Nor can he be a victim of emotions. He must always be in control.

True, significant problems arise in affirming impassibility, not least that it seriously jeopardizes the idea that God is personal. Donald MacLeod, who has himself challenged the classical doctrine of impassibility, points out, "This is exactly the process that led to the kind of death-of-God theology epitomized in the late John A. T. Robinson's *Honest to God*."[53] This leads MacLeod to conclude that "the more recent trend is closer to the Bible's teaching than the traditional."[54] MacLeod provides three reasons:

- Scripture (particularly the Old Testament) provides a rich tapestry of God's emotional life.
- Christ is the revelation of God. He is God's Word, form, image, glory, and exegesis. Did Christ merely suffer in his human nature (and not in his divine nature)? Whether this is true or not, the point is that *he* suffered, *in his person*.[55]
- For MacLeod, it is the doctrine of the atonement that effectively counters the notion of God's impassibility. "The moment we concede that the cross made a difference to God we are abandoning the whole notion of impassibility and *apatheia*. Here is an event in time which is absolutely decisive for God's attitude to man; an event of which we can even say that is the ground of the peace that fills the heart of God."[56] MacLeod concedes that it was Christ *in his human nature* who suffered and died, but "we cannot say that He did not suffer and we cannot say that He was not *homoousios* when He suffered. There is not one God who suffered—who bore the cost of our redemption—and another who did not. The cross is part of

53. MacLeod, "Can God Suffer?" 33.
54. Ibid., 32.
55. On this point, see Paul Helm, "B. B. Warfield on Divine Passion," *WTJ* (Spring 2007): 103: "How are we to understand the emotional life of our Lord? Are episodes in the life of our Lord—his reaction to the Temple money-changers, or to the death of Lazarus, for example—cases of God's emotion made flesh? In a way they are, but not (as Chalcedonian orthodoxy reminds us) in any way that involves the transmutation of the divine emotion into something else. It is God expressing his impassioned love (along with much else that he expresses) in the person of the Son in his assumed human nature."
56. MacLeod, "Can God Suffer?" 35.

the experience of God; otherwise He did not redeem us with His own blood."[57]

What drives the denial of impassibility is the notion of a God who seems distant and removed from our suffering. Some suggest that unless God suffers along with us, he can hardly be in a position to sympathize with us. He does not, in the colloquial language of our time, "feel our pain." But why apply this to God and not, say, to a doctor? As Gerald Bray points out, if we insisted that our doctor had to experience our pain along with us, "we would probably lose confidence in him"—especially, as Bray goes to suggest, if the doctor were to curl up beside us in the hospital bed![58] Frame conjectures that "emotional empathy can be called suffering,"[59] but it is unclear to me how helpful this is. One thing is for sure: the implications of a doctrine of divine passibility when applied to God (in his divine essence or nature) are catastrophic. We are left with a God who is crippled with pain and whose ability to engage in more than just empathy is severely curtailed as a consequence.

Frame does not wish to go anywhere near these conclusions. His instinct seems to be both pastoral and hermeneutical. Once again, he seems to approach theology instinctively "from below," and if I may offer a critique here, this may be his Achilles' heel. The need to run away from *apatheia* in its traditional sense of "apathy" is understandable, even laudable. Instead, the theanthropic line of thought—the suffering of the God-man at the heart of the Trinity—does provide a theologically sound avenue to explore. But we cannot impute suffering to the divine nature, at least any view of suffering implying that God changes in some way, for then we have raised yet another problem: that of mutability.

So I remain convinced by the traditional understanding of impassibility, even though I want to advocate a God who is impassioned (passionate?) about himself as three-in-one and one-in-three (*perichoresis/circumincessio*), about redeeming sinners, and about restoring a fallen cosmos to its former, created glory. Impassibility prevents me from advocating a God who is subject to fitful moods, an irritable God, liable to irrational outbursts of temper

---

57. Ibid. "He has redeemed the church by His own blood! He is Himself the propitiation for our sins! He is, in the blood language of Jürgen Moltmann, the Crucified God." Ibid. Frame's analysis of Moltmann in *DG*, 612–13 is typically thorough and astute.

58. Bray, *The Doctrine of God*, 100.

59. *DG*, 613.

and loss of control. And I am persuaded that Frame is entirely of the same mind, despite his equivocation over the traditional language.

Postscript

John Frame is one of the most outstanding theologians of the twentieth century. Like most other geniuses, his greatness may not be fully uncovered until long after his passing. This is God's way of keeping such men humble, I think. Frame's deferential tone, often admitting to uncertainty in expression and thought, here and there calling for his readers to help him to define something better, points to a servant spirit of humble demeanor. He loves the Bible, and his writings are suffused with biblical citations accompanied by careful exegesis. His philosophical-apologetic commitment to triads may sometimes get in the way of what he wants to say. But no one can mistake his impassioned concern for revealed truth, careful in areas where the Bible has spoken only a little and forthright in those areas where the text of Scripture is beyond dispute.

Frame's Calvinism has a gentle touch about it; it makes his theological musings all the more appealing and alluring. He has met and conversed with the greats of the mid- to late twentieth century, especially the giants of the Westminster seminaries (Gaffin, Murray, and Van Til). If I have ventured a criticism in these pages, think of it as a mouse in the presence of a giant. I am filled with admiration for John Frame's accomplishments, and as he (soon) begins the journey into semiretirement, I wish him many years of fruitful labor and writing. I am thankful to God for the honor of having served with him in the family that is Reformed Theological Seminary over the past decade and more. I could have wished that we had been on the same campus, but modern technology has made it possible for us to correspond about Van Til's doctrine of incomprehensibility and even his own take on the regulative principle of worship. Indeed, regarding the latter, he should consider it the highest form of flattery that we engage in an annual "Frame debate" in one of my classes in which I deliberately force Frame sympathizers to argue against him, and vice versa. I have often thought that had he been present on these occasions, he would have been thrilled at just how deeply another generation of gospel preachers have reflected on his writings.

17

Psalm 19: A Royal Sage Praises and Petitions I AM

Bruce K. Waltke

Introduction to This Essay

PROFESSOR FRAME'S REQUEST that I contribute an essay to his festschrift is a humbling honor. This essay, an exposition of Psalm 19, is dedicated to the honor of my esteemed colleague. I chose to exposit Psalm 19 because it is fraught with theological reflections to which Professor Frame addresses himself: God's person, revelation, and catechetical teaching and its relation to sin and salvation, and to piety and prayer. Moreover, Professor Frame is a lover of the arts, especially of music, and the psalmist packages his theological reflections in brilliant poetry.

Most modern academic expositors are apostate and so do not see the psalm so positively. My Regent colleague, Professor James M. Houston, notes:

> In science, the Heisenberg principle states that the outcome of a given experiment is very heavily influenced by the point of view of the observer. Likewise, the exegetical observer needs to be observed by what weight he is placing on what he interprets. For the word "interpretation" implies a reciprocal entry, both into the mind of the interpreter as well as into the text being penetrated. Expositors

369

who do not share the psalmist's faith, fail to celebrate its wonderful doctrines and tend to treat it as a non-revelatory scrap-book of ancient texts.[1]

In addition to failing to see the psalm's unity, and so its message, critical scholars also commonly fail to appreciate the psalm's poetry. In this respect, Bernard Duhm is an extreme example. Although he appreciates the poetic flair concerning God's glory in Nature in 19a (vv. 1–6), he depreciates 19b (vv. 7ff.).[2] Houston comments sarcastically on Duhm's evaluation: "It [Psalm 19 B] is at least better than its dreadful successor, Psalm 119! How narrow minded one must be to interpret all one's life within the compass of the Law. So the best one can say is that this is a good text for psychologists and historians of religion to examine, to see how narrow-minded primitive religious people have been."[3] By contrast, in his *Reflections on the Psalms*, C. S. Lewis wrote of Psalm 19, "I take this to be the greatest poem in the Psalter and one of the greatest lyrics in the world."

After this brief introduction, I will divide my essay into four parts: an original translation, an introduction to Psalm 19, an exegesis of it, and its contribution to Christian theology.

TRANSLATION

A psalm by David
[1]The heavens are telling the glory of God,
    And the firmament is declaring his handiwork.

1. Bruce K. Waltke and James M. Houston, *The Psalms in Christian Worship: Hearing the Voice of the Psalmist and of the Church in Response* (Grand Rapids: Eerdmans, forthcoming). Modern interpreters who see the psalm as consisting of two original psalms with little unity include Rabbi Martin Samuel Cohen, *Our Haven and Our Strength, The Psalms* (New York: Aviv Press, 2004); William P. Brown, *Seeing the Psalms: A Theology of Metaphor* (Louisville, London: Westminster John Knox Press, 2002); Georg Fohrer, *Psalmen* (Berlin and New York: de Gruyter, 1993); Mitchell Dahood, *Psalms*, Anchor Bible (New York: Doubleday, 1966–70); Hermann Gunkel, *Die Psalmnen* (Gottingen, 1929, 1968); R. Kittel, *Die Psalmen übersetzt und erklärt* (Leipzig, 1914, 1929). H. Spieckermann disparages even the twofold approach and divides the psalm into four parts (2–5a, 5b–7, 8–11, 12–15) with differing sources: Canaanite mediation, temple theology, later expansion, and anxious rigidity. He interprets anxiety, rather than praise and trust, as the tone of the psalm. These commentators do not aim to contribute to the apostolic doctrine. Tragically, critical scholars, who put their depraved reasoning above revelation, exclude from their conversation orthodox expositors who see the contribution of this psalm to Christian doctrine and devotion. And even more tragically, many evangelical scholars and publishers are trying to sit at their table, rather than with Christ and his apostles.
2. Bernard Duhm, *Die Psalmen* (Tübingen, 1899, 1922).
3. Waltke and Houston, *The Psalms in Christian Worship*.

²Day by day it pours forth words,

And night by night it proclaims knowledge.

³There is no speech, and there are no words;

Their⁴ voice is inaudible.

⁴The measuring cord [of their voice] stretches out to all the earth,

Even at the remotest point of the world are their words.

And he [God] has pitched⁵ a tent in them [the heavens] for the sun.

⁵ It is like a bridegroom who emerges from his chamber;

It rejoices like a strong man to run a course.

⁶It emerges from the edge of the earth,

And its orbit extends from one edge to another;

And nothing can be hidden from its glowing heat.

⁷The law of *I AM* is perfect, renewing vitality;

The stipulations of *I AM* are reliable, making wise the simple.

⁸The regulations of *I AM* are right, rejoicing the heart;

The commands⁶ of *I AM* are clean, causing the eyes to sparkle.

⁹The fear of *I AM* is pure, enduring forever;

The judgments of *I AM* are true; they are altogether righteous.

¹⁰They are more desirable than gold, even much fine gold;

And they are sweeter than honey, than virgin honey flowing from the comb.

¹¹Also, by them your slave is warned;

And in keeping them is great reward.

¹²As for errors, who can discern them?

As for hidden faults, declare me free from punishment.

¹³ Moreover, hold back your slave from insolent men,

let them not rule over me.

Then I will retain integrity,

and be free from the punishment for a great transgression.

¹⁴Let the words of my mouth and the mediation of heart find favor

before you,

I AM, my Rock and my Redeemer.

---

4. The addition of "where" or its equivalent in some EVV is grammatically unwarranted.

5. Šām is better construed as a perfect than a participle, for the poet more probably intends a tent God pitched at the creation of the world than a tent he is in process of setting up.

6. Construing the singular as a collective to designate the group. See B. K. Waltke, *Introduction to Biblical Hebrew Syntax* (Winona Lake, IN: Eisenbrauns, 1990), 113, 7.2.1b, hereafter *IBHS*.

Introduction to the Psalm

Author and Date

No empirical reason calls into question the superscription's claim that David authored Psalm 19.[7] Most scholars, however, think the firmament's hymn of praise (vv. 1–6) is older than the rest of the psalm. There may be some truth here. Perhaps David adopted and *adapted* an old hymn to the Canaanite god 'El (proper name).

Rhetoric and Content

Form and rhetorical critical analyses show that the psalm consists of a superscript, two stanzas of praise (1–6, 7–10), one stanza of petition (11–14), a dedicatory prayer (15), and a subscript.[8]

Superscript	Superscript [1]B
I. Firmament's Praise of God's Glory and Knowledge	vv. 1–6
A. Temporal and Spatial Universality of its Inaudible Praise	vv. 1–4
1. Temporal Universality of Firmament's Praise	vv. 1–2
2. Spatial Universality of the Heaven's Inaudible Praise	vv. 3–4
B. Sun's Universal Testimony	vv. 5–6
II. Psalmist's Praise of *I AM*'s Torah	vv. 7–10
A. Strophe 1: ab//a'b' structure	vv. 7–8
B. Strophe 2: ab structure	vv. 9–10
III. Psalmist's Petitions for Salvation	vv. 11–13
A. Pardon for Hidden Guilt	vv. 11–12
B. Preserve from Guilt of Apostasy	vv. 13–14
Epilogue: Dedicatory Prayer	v. 15
Subscript: To the chief musician	Psalm 20: superscript A [1A]

---

7. See Bruce K. Waltke with Charles Yu, *An Old Testament Theology: An Exegetical, Canonical, and Thematic Approach* (Grand Rapids: Zondervan, 2007), 872ff.

8. See Bruce K. Waltke, "Superscripts, Subscripts or Both," *JBL* 110 (1991): 583–96.

The three stanzas consist of seven quatrains (i.e., two bi-cola): 1–2, 3–4, 5–6, 7–8, 9–10, 11–12. The number seven signifies perfection, completeness, and so suggests that whatever the origin of stanzas, an author composed a unified poem.[9] The psalm is a conceptual unity, focusing on God's two books of revelation: the general revelation of creation and the special revelation of Scripture: "Both books magnify the Author's excellence."[10] Some find a unity in the movement of the stanzas. M. Fishbane observes the movement from the heavens speak (vv. 1–6), to *I AM* speaks (vv. 7–10), to the psalmist speaks (vv. 11–14);[11] A. Meinhold, from words about God, to words from God, to words to God;[12] C. Broyles, a contracting movement, from the vastness of God's skies, to *I AM*'s law, to the worshiper himself. "This threefold movement is also reflected in the divine names: 'God' (or 'El'), the LORD (Yahweh) and my rock and my Redeemer."[13] Are these movements the intended creations of the artist or the creations of ingenious interpreters? Are the stanzas related by the psychology of awe? "The starry sky above me," said Kant, "and the moral law in me . . . are the two things which fill the soul with ever new and increasing admiration and reverence."[14] R. Clifford sees a logical unity (see below).

The striking formal differences (i.e., subject matter, mood, language, and meter[15]) between the first two stanzas of hymns to God and to *I AM* and the abrupt way they are joined together, lacking any transition, suggest the author pieced together two originally independent poems. Ancient Near Eastern poets had no scruples about joining together pieces of literature (cf. Ps. 108).[16] Ancient Near Eastern evidence put forward by Schröder[17] and Dürr[18] also favors seeing the psalm as a unity. Whatever their origin, the

9. He uses the name *I AM* seven times, all in the last two stanzas.

10. Charles H. Spurgeon, *The Treasury of David: Spurgeon's Great Commentary on the Psalms*, updated Roy H. Clarke (Nashville: Thomas Nelson, 1997), 125.

11. M. A. Fishbane, *Text and Texture* (New York: Schocken, 1979), 86.

12. A. Meinhold, "Überlegungen zur Theologie des 19. Psalms," *ZTK* 80 (1983): 119–36.

13. C. Broyles, *Psalms*, NIBC (Grand Rapids: Zondervan, 1999), 109.

14. Wallace, *Kant*, 53, cited by A. F. Kirkpatrick, *The Book of Psalms*, CBSC (Cambridge: Cambridge University Press, 1916), 101.

15. The more extended verses—especially the two tri-cola in verses 5–6—match its theme of the heaven's expansive praise.

16. It can be said that Israel's authors are redactors. Put that way, it becomes apparent that a distinction between author and redactor is a false dichotomy.

17. O. Schröder, "Zu Psalm 19," *ZAW* 34 (1914): 69–70.

18. L. Dürr, "Zur Frage nach der Einheit von Ps. 19," in *Festschrift für E. Sellin*, BWANT 13 (Stuttgart, 1927), 37–48.

poet who composed the whole, as in so much of biblical literature, allows his audience to tease out the connection.

To understand the poet's images in his personifying the firmament's praise of God, one needs to understand his Ancient Near Eastern cosmology. In brief, the "firmament" is the phenomenal dome or vault that was thought to separate the supernal ocean above from the earth and water below.[19] Moreover, knowledge that Near Eastern religions associated the sun with righteousness and law,[20] reflected in many Old Testament passages (e.g., Job 38:12–15), provides an understanding of the immediate link between the celebration of the sun in the conclusion of the first stanza and of the law in the second, as Delitzsch recognized. The physical light of the sun that exposes the hideaways of the wicked corresponds to the spiritual light of the law that exposes hidden sins.

Form and Theology

Psalm 19 is obviously a poem, characterized as it is by parallelism, terseness, and heightened style, including manifold figures of speech (metaphors, metonymies, personification, etc.). It is not scientific literature.

More specifically it is a song, a hymn. The superscript labels its genre "a psalm" (*mizmôr*, a song sung to the pizzicato of a stringed instrument), and an inspired editor included it in Israel's hymn book. The Psalter's songs are mostly hymns of praise and petition. Psalm 19 is both. The first two stanzas resemble hymns of praise: praise to God, the Creator (vv. 1–6; cf. Pss. 104, 148), and praise of *I AM*, author of Torah (i.e., catechetical teaching, vv. 7–10; cf. Pss. 1, 119).[21] As for the first hymn, I say "resemble" because there is no call to the congregation to praise and no address to God, unlike typical praise hymns. The praise of Torah is a Janus. Below we reflect more fully on the connection in wisdom literature between the God of creation and the God of Israel's law. In the light of God's law, his slave is warned and offers his penitential petition in a third stanza. Like petition psalms, Psalm 19

19. For a fuller discussion see Waltke, *An Old Testament Theology*, 194–96.

20. The diorite stela on which is written the famous law-code of Hammurap/bi is topped "by a bas-relief showing Hammurabi in the act of receiving the commission to write the lawbook from the god of justice, the sun-god Shamash" (*ANET*, 163; see *ANEP*, 77, Fig. 246).

21. The two names of God, *El* (God as Creator) and *I AM* (God as Israel's covenant keeper), used in its two halves respectively, superficially seem to point to two unrelated psalms, but when it is recalled that descriptive praise psalms normally praise God both as Creator and as Israel's covenant keeper, the twofold names point to the psalm's unity.

typically includes the motifs of petition and praise, but atypically it reverses the movement; instead of moving from petition to praise, it escalates from praise to petition. In other words, praise is the basis, not the result, of petition. This atypical sequence leads to my classifying the psalm as both praise and penitential. The third stanza is a penitential petition for salvation: pardon and preservation (vv. 11–14).

More specifically, Psalm 19 is a wisdom psalm; it belongs to the genres of both hymnic and wisdom literatures. David expresses himself in the form of a praise psalm and a petition psalm, but he thinks as a sage.[22] That he thinks as a sage can be seen in his wisdom vocabulary: "knowledge," "simple," "wise," "fear of *I AM*," "warned." Second, in typical wisdom fashion he connects God's revelation in creation with his special revelation in Torah by using the former to buttress and/or illustrate the latter.[23] R. Clifford, as mentioned above, sees a logical unity holding the psalm together. "The poetic logic is clear: The divine wisdom (meaning ability to govern) discernible in the daily movements of the heavens (vv. 1–4b), especially in the sun's course (vv. 4c–6), is also visible in the teaching (vv. 7–9) to which human beings have access through humble prayer (vv. 10–14)." But his attempt to show analogies between the creation and the law are not all equally convincing.[24] Third and more specifically, the first hymn (vv. 1–6) celebrates God's creation that displays his knowledge (see v. 2), and the second stanza celebrates his Torah that gives humankind wisdom (v. 7). Fourth, and most importantly, because the Creator of all things knows comprehensively, he knows absolutely and certainly. The heavens declare that God's knowledge is vast. Implicitly, God's special revelation of Torah is based on his comprehensive knowledge as Creator. God alone sees "ontologically" (i.e., the whole of what actually is). To be wise, a person must transcend the relativity and depravity of human epistemology. Earthbound mortals cannot find transcendent wisdom apart from the transcendent knowledge of *I AM*. Real wisdom must find its starting point in the order of creation: in his light, we see light (Ps. 36:9 [10]).[25] Only the Creator knows what is true and false, what is right

---

22. Most recently Mark D. Futato, *Interpreting the Psalms: An Exegetical Handbook* (Grand Rapids: Kregel, 2007), 179, classified Psalm 19 as a wisdom psalm.

23. For the wisdom-like ethos of verses 1–4a, see O. H. Steck, "Bemerkungen zur thematischen Einheit von Psalm 19:2–7," in *Werden und Wirken des Alten Testament: Festschrift für Claus Westermann*, ed. Rainer Albertz et al. (Göttingen: Vandenhoeck & Ruprecht, 1980), 318–24.

24. R. Clifford, *Psalms 1–72*, AOTC (Nashville: Abingdon Press, 2002), 111–12.

25. B. K. Waltke, *The Book of Proverbs Chapters 15–31* (Grand Rapids: Eerdmans, 2006), 471.

and wrong; and only the humble, who are willing to live by faith, are wise; the unbeliever is a fool.

The subscript shows all Israel should join the king's praises and petitions. Without using direct address, the king implicitly addresses the nation in the first two stanzas, and although he explicitly addresses *I AM* by referring to himself as "your slave"[26] in the third stanza, he implicitly exemplifies for the nation a godly response to Torah and wisdom.[27] In sum, the psalm is a unified mixture of hymns praising the Creator and Torah, as well as a penitential psalm, both of which function to instruct the nation, and, as will be seen in the conclusion, a mystery that veils the Christian faith.

EXEGESIS

Superscript—s/s [1]

Superscripts of more than three words are numbered as separate verses in the Hebrew Bible; they are an integral part of the psalms. A *psalm* (Heb. *mizmôr*) refers to a song that is sung to the pizzicato of a stringed instrument. The traditions that Heb. *Ldwd* means "by David" and that Israel's greatest king authored the psalms credited to him are reliable interpretations.[28]

Firmament and Heavens Declare God's Glory—1–4 [2–5]

The first stanza consists of two strophes: the heavens' universal proclamation of God's glory and knowledge (1–4) and the sun's proclamation in particular (5–6). The first strophe consists of two quatrains that have an alternating pattern: a/a': the firmament and heavens are declaring God's glory (a, v. 1) in inaudible words (a', v. 3); b/b': the universality of their proclamation in time (b, v. 2) and in space (b', v. 4). The distinction between singular and plural *heavens* shows that the firmament is the subject of verse 2 and the heavens of verses 3–4. The heaven's vastness, splendor, order, and mystery should prompt rational creatures to celebrate the Creator's glory. Aristotle speculated: "Should a man live underground, and converse with the works of art and mechanism,

---

26. Cf. Psalm 18: superscript, where the epithet clearly refers to David.

27. Cf. L. C. Allen, "David as an Exemplar of Spirituality," *Bib* 67 (1986): 544–46.

28. B. K. Waltke, "Psalms: Theology of," in *New International Dictionary of Exegesis and Old Testament Theology*, ed. W. A. VanGemeren (Grand Rapids: Zondervan, 1997), 4:1100–1115.

and afterwards be brought up into the day to see the several glories of the heaven and earth, he would immediately pronounce them the work of such a Being as we define God to be."[29] Compare Addison's paraphrase:

> What though in solemn silence all[30] / Move round the dark terrestrial ball?
> What though nor real voice nor sound / Amid their radiant orbs be found?
> In reason's ear they all rejoice / And utter forth a glorious voice,
> For ever singing, as they shine, / "The hand that made us is divine."

A. Temporal universality of the firmament's praise—1-2 [2-3]

Verse 2 is linked to verse 1 by the subject of the firmament, by verbs of speaking, and by a chiasm of the verbs' stems: *Piel* and *Hiphil* // *Hiphil* and *Piel*.

1. The firmament praises God's glory—1 [2]

In the introductory summary statement of this stanza, the synonyms "heavens" and "firmament" constitute its outer frame (a/a'), "announcing" and "declaring" occupy the b/b' slot, and its inner core matches "glory of God," a metonymy of effect, with "work of his hands," a metonymy of cause (c/c').[31]

The firmament and heavens, personified as hymnists, proclaim that God's government over them shows his glory and knowledge. His skill and knowledge should encourage covenant people to submit to *I AM*'s government of society through Torah (i.e., catechetical teaching). Moreover, God's order of creation lays the firm foundation for his order of redemption through Torah. Pope John Paul II noted in his remarks to Roman Catholic bishops, "Grace never casts nature aside or cancels it out, but rather perfects it and ennobles it."[32]

"The heavens" (*haššāmāyim*) may refer to everything above the earth, the firmament (cf. Gen. 1:8) and/or the supernal waters held up by "the firmament" (*hārāqîaʿ*). The firmament is metonymy associated with the

---

29. James Barr, *The Concept of Biblical Theology: An Old Testament Perspective* (Minneapolis: Fortress Press, 1999), rightly restores the role of natural theology and of science and reason to overcome dialectical theology.

30. Aristotle (384 BC), cited by Spurgeon, *Treasury of David*, 125.

31. E. W. Bullinger, *Figures of Speech Used in the Bible* (Grand Rapids: Baker, 1968), 539, 560.

32. Richard John Neuhaus, "True Christian Feminism," *National Review* (November 25, 1988): 24.

sun, moon, and stars, which make their orbits within it (cf. Ps. 8:4). The Bible images the expansive firmament and the high heavens as inhabited by God and his angelic court to represent among other sublimities God's omniscience. In this metaphor, God sees the world holistically and clearly and so can "speak" absolutely and with certainty, unlike earthbound mortals, who apart from revelation must speak tentatively because of their limited vision (see Job 28:12–24).

Mᵉsappᵉrîm ("are telling") means "to count again," and/or "to enumerate (that is to relate or narrate in detail)."[33] Both senses are intended—the former because of the synonyms of speaking in this strophe and the latter because it repeats its proclamation day and night; "to count again" also may be intended. The grammatical form is a participle, signifying a durative (i.e., a continuous) situation.[34] This is also true of *maggîd* ("are declaring"), which signifies the process whereby a speaker communicates to the addressee a *vitally important* message, namely, the Creator's *handiwork* (*maʿᵃśēh ŷdāyw*, lit., "the work of his hands")—a metonymy of source for the effect *glory* (*kābôd*). Israel tells *I AM's* glory—his weight, dignity, importance, honor—among the nations (Ps. 96:3); the heavens tell God's glory to the whole earth. David speaks of *God* (*'ēl*), because *'ēl* represents his transcendence over the creation, whereas *I AM*, which he uses in his Torah praise, connotes his immanence with his covenant people. Recall Calvin's comment that "the heavens declaring" stirs up our senses and teaches more clearly and more profitably than simply "our beholding."

2. Temporal universality of their praise—2 [3]

The chiastic pattern of verse 1 is replaced with an alternating pattern: slot a ("day by day"), slot b ("pours forth"), and slot c (words) //a' ("night by night") b' ("declares") c' ("knowledge"). The note of the constancy of heaven's praise sounds quietly in the durative participles (v. 1), then intensifies in the merism of "day and night," i.e., "all the time" (see Ps. 1:2), and comes to a resounding climax in the distributives "day by day" and "night by night," i.e., every day and every night.[35] *Day* (*yôm*) refers to the cycle of daylight (cf. Prov. 4:18), not of twenty-four hours. The firmament proclaims God's

33. The *Piel* is used with verbs of speaking to express a "frequentative" situation (cf. *IBHS*, 414–15, 24.5).
34. Ibid., 626, 37.6e.
35. Ibid., 115–16, 7.2.3.

glory from the rising of the sun in the east to the fading sun in the west, whereupon it replaces that witness to God's glory with the heliacal orbit of the moon and stars at *night* (*lay*ᵉ*lâ*).

The personified firmament is the subject of "pours forth" (*yabbîaʿ*), because the predicate continues to be verbs of speaking. *Yabbîaʿ* denotes an uncontrollable or uncontrolled gushing forth of words, like that of the swollen waters of a gushing wadi. The metaphor derives from conceiving the mouth as a fountain (cf. Prov. 18:4; Matt. 12:34).[36] The firmament's uninterrupted proclamation of God's glory is copious, "extravagant," powerful, and inescapable. If the naked eye can "hear" the sight-language of the heaven's proclamation, how much more when its sight-hearing is amplified a billion-fold by the Hubble telescope. Stars, many times larger than our modest sun, thousands of light-years apart, are more numerous than the sand on earth's beaches. The synonym "declare" (*ḥawwâ*, "to make known," "to inform someone") is used only in poetry (Job 13:17; 15:17; 32:6, 10, 17; 36:2; Ps. 52:11; Hab. 3:2—*Qere*). Both verbs occur in the iterative imperfective conjugation in conformity with the distributive singulars of "day by day" and "night by night." *ʾŌmer* ("words," "sayings," "news") also occurs only in poetry (Job 22:18; Pss. 19:2 [3], 3 [4]; 68:12; 77:9; Hab. 3:9). "Word" refers to the expression; its parallel "knowledge" (*daʿat*) refers to the substance communicated. According to C. Kayatz, in the theological system of the Egyptian city of Heliopolis, the creator god, Re, is characterized by *sja*, "knowledge," and *hû*, "expression."[37] Knowledge signifies the fact or condition of knowing something, of understanding, of having information. God's apparent vast knowledge, as seen in his masterpiece, garners him glory. Unlike human knowledge that must be learned or acquired (Isa. 40:12–14), God's knowledge is inherent in his being.

B. Spatial universality of the heaven's inaudible praise—3–4 [4–5]

The second strophe is linked to the first by the rare catch-word *ʾōmer* ("words"); by shifting from the masculine singular pronoun ("it"), having "firmament" of verse 1b as its antecedent, to the third masculine plural pronoun ("their, them"), having "heavens" of verse 1a as its antecedent; by using

36. F. Delitzsch, *Biblical Commentary on the Proverbs of Solomon*, trans. M. G. Estong (Grand Rapids: Eerdmans, 1983), 71.

37. C. Kayatz, *Studizu Proverbien 1–9: Eine form- und motivgeschichtliche untersuchung unter Einbeziehung ägyptischen Vergleichsmaterials*, WMANT 22 (Neukirchen-Vluyn: Neukirchener, 1966), 11.

other synonyms of speaking; and by the alternating pattern of representing the notion of the heaven's witness followed by the universality of that witness.

1. Unspoken eloquence—3 [4]

Three negations emphasize that their "voice" is inaudible, twice repeating "there is no" (Heb. '*ên*, a predicator of non-existence) in construct with '*ōmer*, "words" (see v. 2), and its synonym "speech" (*dᵉbārîm*). Whereas the root '*mr* directs attention to the contents of the speech, *dbr* points to the activity of speaking.[38] The third negation is *bᵉlî* ("without"), which is replaced in late Hebrew by '*ênl*.[39] The oxymoron of a silent declaration can be felt more fully when it is understood that *qôl*, "voice," describes everything that can be perceived acoustically. But their voice "is inaudible" (*bᵉlî nišmā'*, lit., "without being able to hear"). *šm'*, like English "to hear," refers minimally to acoustic perception. The point of the oxymoron: Although the heavens are seen with the eye, like a portrait they "speak" the language of sight to the ear of reason and of the heart to generate the worship of God (cf. Rom. 10:17).[40]

2. Spatial universality of the heavens' witness—4 [5]

The second quatrain highlights the heavens' spatial universality. Its structure alternates ab/a'b': "In all the earth" (slot a) emphatically introduces the theme of this quatrain. By its contrast to the heavens, "earth" (*hā'āreṣ*) has its cosmological nuance, not its normal geographical sense of "land." "All" (*kôl*) is quantitative (= totality), not qualitative ("all sorts of"). "Even in the extremities of the world" (slot a') intensifies the spatial universality. Since slot /a'/ heightens slot /a/ and does not add a new thought, *waw* is ascensive "even," not conjunctive "and."[41] "Extremities" (*qāṣēh*, from the root *qṣh*, "to cut off") refers to earth's "farthest, most remote" places. "World" (*tēbel*) is a stock-in-trade parallel of "earth," but in contrast to the earth it

38. Cf. G. Gerleman, *TLOT*, 1:327, s.v. *dābār*.

39. *IBHS*, 603, 36.2.1g.

40. On a clipper ship tour of the Alaska Inside Passage, a geologist lectured on the rocks, and a naturalist discoursed on the flora and fauna, but neither one mentioned the Creator. I expressed my appreciation for their knowledge, likening the geologist's work to that of an art critic's comments on the pigment of the paint Michelangelo used in the Sistine Chapel, and I compared the naturalist's explanation to the art critic's exposition of his brushstrokes. But I noted that it was the landscape itself that attracts and that delights the tourists and that the Artist of such a masterpiece must be what we call God. They now include the analogy in their lectures.

41. See *IBHS*, 39.2.4b.

refers to the inhabited and cultivated areas of the mainland, what we would call continents.

In slot /b/ "their measuring cord" (*qaw*) denotes the ancient's tape measure. Israel's prophets use it as a metaphor for the extent of *I AM*'s judgment or salvation of a land. As a person's allotment of land is measured or marked off (2 Sam. 8:2), so land is marked off by God or some other agent for ruin or restoration (Isa. 34:11, 17). Here the metaphor refers to the extent of land reached by the heavens' message. "Their voice" is added to clarify the metaphor. *Qaw* commonly occurs with *ntḥ*, "to stretch out," but here, as in Jeremiah 31:39 (*Qere*), *qav* occurs with *yṣ'* "to go out," probably because no agent stretches it out. Nevertheless, for the sake of the English idiom, *yṣ'* is glossed "stretches out." The parallel in slot /b'/, "their words" (*millêhem*), validates this interpretation of the metaphor. *Millîm*, another synonym for "words," is borrowed from Aramaic and occurs exclusively in poetry.

C. Sun's universal testimony—4c-6 [5c-7]

Verse 4c is a Janus that links the universality of heaven's witness (v. 4a, b) to the particular universal witness of the sun (vv. 5–6). The Masoretic text combines "And God has pitched . . ." with verse 4. But it is better to combine it with verses 5 and 6, since their topic is the sun, which is introduced in 4c. Moreover, by emending the versification, verses 5a and b give two similes in two balanced tri-cola. Syntactically, the two strophes are linked by "in them," i.e., "the heavens." Rhetorically, the strophes are linked by three catchwords (*yṣ'*, "goes forth," vv. 4a and 5a, 6a; *qṣh*, "edge," vv. 4a, 6a; *'ên*, "there is no"/ "nothing," vv. 3a, 6a) and by the inclusio *haššāmayim* ("the heavens," vv. 1a, 6b). The sun implicitly testifies to God's knowledge and glory all the time (v. 5, cf. v. 2) and everywhere (v. 6, cf. v. 4 [5]). The strophe traces the course of the sun at night and in the morning, and its orbit from sunrise to sunset.

1. Sun's tent at night—4 [5]c

Although unseen at night, the sun is still present in the heavens, implying its universal presence in space as well as in time. At the earth's most remote horizon "God" (lit., "he") pitched a metaphorical "tent" (*'ōhel*, see Ps. 15:1) "for the sun" (*laššemeš*) to spend the night. The antecedent of "he" is ambiguous, but conceptually Israel's monotheism demands the clarifying gloss "God" (see v. 1). The sun becomes theologically significant in the Old Testament because of the importance it plays in the pantheon of ancient

Near Eastern gods. "Pitched" glosses *śām* (lit., "set," "set up"). In v. 5a the poet transforms the image of the tent into a marriage chamber from which the sun emerges in the morning.

2. Sun's morning radiance—5 [6]

Semantic pertinence demands interpreting *haššemeš* ("the sun") as the antecedent of *hû'* ("it"). The comparative *k*ᵉ ("like") has its qualitative sense, expressing resemblance in respect of some attribute, action, character, appearance of "a bridegroom" (*ḥātān*). In the seven occurrences of the bridegroom, reference is made to his adorning (Isa. 61:10) and to his rejoicing with exuberance over his bride (Isa. 62:5; Jer. 7:34; 16:9; 25:10; 33:11; cf. Joel 2:16). So the personification and simile connote the morning sun's glorious radiance, "who emerges" (lit. "going forth"—*yōṣē'*, see vv. 4, 6) "like a bridegroom" (*k*ᵉ*ḥātān*) "from his chamber" (*mēḥuppātô*).⁴² The simile connotes youthful freshness, beauty, vigor, and joy. *Ḥuppâ* occurs only three times in the Hebrew Bible and refers broadly to "shelter" (Isa. 4:5), a hyponym of "tent" in verse 4c. In Joel 2:16, the bride's chamber is distinguished from the bridegroom's room (Joel 2:16), and in Psalm 19:5 the "shelter" refers to bridegroom's chamber where presumably he takes his bride to consummate their marriage (Ps. 19:5).

The parallel simile in the B verset, "it rejoices" (*yāśîś*), supports the interpretation that the bridegroom simile images the rising sun as radiantly exulting. The simile marked by "like" (*k*ᵉ) supplements the joy of a bridegroom with the strength of "a strong man" (*gibbôr*). The strong man rejoices about "to run" (*lārûṣ*) "a [race] course" (*'ōraḥ*, a poetic word for "track") because none can compete with him for either speed or distance. The metaphorical track—he is no cross-country runner—refers to the sun's orbit in the firmament. The sun has the speed of a sprinter and the endurance and strength of a marathon runner.

3. Sun's universal heat throughout the day—6 [7]

"It emerges" glosses "its going forth" (*môṣā'ô*, the nominal form of *yṣ'* —see vv. 4a, 5a, and 6). This is the third occurrence of this catchword and shows that the verset opens with reference to the morning sun of verse 5. Conjunctive "and" (*û*) links the rising sun to "its orbit" (*t*ᵉ*qûpātô*), a gloss for this rare word that in its three other occurrences means "cycle" (Ex. 34:22; 1 Sam. 1:20;

---

42. Note the alliteration of *ḥtn* and *ḥpt*.

2 Chron. 24:23). That orbit extends from one edge of the earth to the other (*'al-q^eṣôtām*, lit., "upon[43] their edges"). Conjunctive "and" adds the further thought that the sun's heat is felt universally. "Nothing" (*'ên*, see its construct usc in v. 4) "can be hidden" (*nistār*), which here, like English "to hide" (with reference to sight), has both negative and positive nuances. It can mean to prevent a person or thing from being perceived by another or to protect them. "From its glowing heat" (*mēhammātô*) is appropriate with both notions: none can be prevented from feeling the sun's heat or be protected from it. *Hammâ* refers to glowing heat and so is used by poets as a metonymy for the sun in its five other occurrences: Job 30:28; Song 6:10; Isa. 24:23; 30:26 (twice).

Psalmist's Praise of I AM's Torah—7-10 [8-11]

David now shifts his praise of God's knowledge and glory through the mediated proclamation of the firmament to his own praise of the Torah of Israel's covenant-keeping God, *I AM*.[44] His praise of the Torah is unified by a steady beat of three words in the A versets and two words in their B versets of the first two quatrains (vv. 7-8), which is slowed down to two beats in each verset in verses 9-10, although in verse 9a there are still three words. Matching this cadence is a similar structure, using qualifying adjectives/nouns to praise the Torah and assertions of its beneficences to the covenant community. However, whereas in the A versets of verses 7-8 adjectives celebrate the Law's moral beauty and their B versets celebrate its social benefits, in verse 9 the whole quatrain uses only adjectives for its moral perfection, and verse 10 speaks of its beneficences. So there are two strophes of contrasting rhythms and structures: verses 7-8 and 9-10.

The A versets of verses 7-10 have an abc pattern. The /a/ slot features a hyponym for Torah: "Law," "statutes," "precepts," "commands," "fear of *I AM*," and "judgments" (i.e., court verdicts).[45] The /b/ slot cites the author: *I AM* (*yhwh*). The /c/ slot features the predicate adjectives: "perfect," "reliable," "right," "clean," "pure," "firm." The B verset of verses 7-8 praises the beneficences of Torah, using participles with the initial letter *m* and denoting a durative situation and a causing of the verbal notion: "renewing," "making wise," "rejoicing," "enlightening,"

---

43. Some mss. read *'ad*, not *'al*, but the correction is unnecessary; the preposition implies a verb of motion such as *extend* (*IBHS*, 224, 11.4.3d).

44. God's full name, a sentence, means "I am who I Am," that is to say, "I am eternal, incomparable, and self-defined." See Waltke, *Theology*, 364–67.

45. *Huqqîm* ("apodictic laws") is not used in Psalm 19.

with objects appropriate to them. The sustained cadence and the anaphora of structure have a rhetorical effect similar to that of Lincoln's Gettysburg address: "we cannot dedicate—we cannot consecrate—we cannot hallow." The manifold anaphora of verses 7–10 elevates step by step the moral sublimity of *I AM*'s Torah. Verse 11 crowns the whole: its judgments are more valuable than much pure gold and more delightful than virgin honey from the comb.

A. Strophe 1: Pattern ab//a'/b'—7–8 [8–9]

Verse 7 is the basic step in the elevation of Torah. Its A verset uses the most comprehensive term for the Law, *Torah*, and its B verset states its most basic benefit, renewing vitality.[46] "Law" (*tôrâ*, catechetical teaching) refers to the law of Moses elsewhere in the Psalter. Although mediated through Moses, its author is *I AM* (*yhwh*).[47] Its most comprehensive sublimity is its being "perfect" (*t°mîmâ*),[48] "being complete," and "having integrity" (see Pss. 15:2; 19:13). Spurgeon reflects: "It is a crime to add to it, treason to alter it, and felony to take from it."[49] The first cited and most essential benefit of the Torah is that of "renewing" (*m°šîbat*) "vitality" (*nepeš*, passionate vitality; trad. "soul," see Ps. 3 n2). *Šûb* ("renew") has the central meaning of having moved in a particular direction to move thereupon in the opposite direction. In a context pertaining to evil, it means "to convert [from evil]" (so some evv), but the beneficiaries of Torah's blessings are implicitly true covenant people. Better, then, to invest *šûb* with the nuance of "to restore," "to put back into order," as in the case of Jerusalem (Dan. 9:25), a territory (2 Kings 14:2), and people (Ps. 80:4, 8, 20). In connection with the human psyche and spirit, it is best glossed to "restore/renew/revive liveliness, vitality" (*joie de vivre*) to the sad and discouraged (Ruth 4:15; Ps. 19:8; Lam. 1:11).

The second step escalates reviving life to "making wise the simple." The hyponym "stipulations" (*ēdût*, "written expressions of *I AM*'s solemn will") were first written by God's own fingers and then mediated through

46. Verse 7 is united phonetically by a memorable sevenfold alliteration of *t* in its ten words: twice in the first and in the last constructions: *trt yhwh* and *mhkymt pty*.

47. In God's own mouth his sentence name means "I AM WHO I AM." His name entails his aseity—his incomprehensibility and his incomparability. Hilary of Poitiers (c. 320–367/8), the earliest recorded bishop of Poitiers in Gaul, was brought into the Christian life while meditating on Exodus 3:14, where Moses experienced the revelation of God as "I AM." That one single statement, God the Creator "testifying about himself" as I am who I am, penetrated more deeply into Hilary's soul than anything he had ever heard or read from any other philosopher.

48. Note also initial *t*.

49. Spurgeon, *Treasury of David*, 129.

Moses. As such, they are totally "reliable" (*ne'emānâ*). Its root *'mn* (cf. "amen") means "to be firm, secure, dependable." Inferentially, it is reliable because it is based on God's comprehensive knowledge (v. 2) and derives from his sublime character. Such a firm spiritual foundation has the benefit of "making wise" (*maḥkîmat*). The root *ḥkm* means generally "to have masterful understanding," "to be skillful," "become an expert"[50] (see "Form and Theology" above). That function is beneficial "to the simple" (*peṭî*, from the verb *pth*). *Pth* means "to be open." Its nominal derivative denotes a person who is open to teaching. This can be bad, as in the book of Proverbs, where "the simple" love to be open to everything, and so gullible, having never made a commitment to God and his wisdom (cf. Prov. 1:32).[51] In the Psalter, however, the simple are open to God's teaching, having made a faith commitment to God and his Word. Consequently, in the book of Proverbs the simple are categorized with fools; in the Psalter, with the wise.

The third step celebrates the Law's capacity to cause rejoicing by its artistic form. The gloss "regulations" (*piqqûdîm*) is uncertain because *piqqûdîm* occurs only as a parallel hyponym to Torah and has no definitive benchmarks, except that it occurs in contexts of divine commands (Pss. 103:18; 111:7; 119 [21 times]). Their sublimity is that they are "right" (*yešārîm*). *Yāšār* has the geometric notion of being straight, either horizontally or vertically, or, when a surface is involved, flat. This geometric use assumes a fixed order to which something can be compared. God's teachings/commands conform to a fixed order by which they can be judged. But that raises the question of truth; who decides something is right? Plato, in his Dialogue called *Euthyprho*, posed the moral problem in its classic form by placing his audience on the horns of a dilemma: "Is something good/right because God wills it?" or "Does God will it because it is good/upright?" If the former, God could be a diabolical tyrant, and we would be forced to turn the moral order upside-down. If the latter, God is not sovereign and bows to a higher order. The Bible cuts through the nonsense: *I AM* is inherently good/upright and from his character issues his teachings that by nature are right.

Their straight form is the cause of "rejoicing" (*mesammeḥê*). "*Śāmaḥ* denotes being glad or joyful with the whole disposition, as indicated by its association with the heart (cf. Ex. 4:14; Ps. 19:8 [9]; 104:15; 105:3), the soul

---

50. See Bruce K. Waltke, *Proverbs 1–15*, NICOT (Grand Rapids: Eerdmans, 2004), 76–77.
51. Ibid., 111.

(Ps. 86:4), and with the lighting up of the eyes (Prov. 15:30)."[52] The precepts are like a piece of art that includes both a formal and an informal aspect. The external form in art refers to the visible elements of a piece, independent of their meaning. For example, when viewing Leonardo's *Mona Lisa* the formal elements therein are color, dimension, lines, mass, shape, etc. But art also consists of the informal products of the viewer's imagination—in the case of the *Mona Lisa*, the feelings of mystery and intrigue. If the form of being upright rejoices the heart, then the heart brings to it an imagination of the righteous that delights in an upright moral order, unlike the wicked, who prefer no boundaries. "The heart" (*lēb*) combines the complex interplay of intellect, sensibility, and will.[53]

The fourth step, making "the eyes to sparkle" without, builds on the third step of "rejoicing the heart" within. The Torah's moral rightness carries moral imperatives that must be obeyed, that is to say, they are "commands"[54] of *I AM*. They "are radiant" (*bārâ*, lit., "clean") for they have been scoured from all moral impurity. No stain of sin defiles them. A derivative of *brr* is *bôr*, "lye" (a cleaning agent made out of the ashes of the soap plant). Daniel 11:35 combines "to cleanse" (*lᵉbārēr*) with "to make white" (*lalbēn*), and Song 6:10 speaks of the bright sun as clean. In Akkadian and Ugaritic, *brr* means to be "pure" of metal and to glitter. This shining cleanness may account for "enlightening" (*mᵉʾîrat*, lit., "causing to light up," "illuminate") and explains the gloss "radiant." The clean and radiant commands within a person's heart light up the "eyes" (*ʿênāyim*, see Ps. 15:4) without, visible for all to see. The light of the eyes in Proverbs 15:30 connotes the manifestation of the inward vitality and joy of a person. Scripture associates sparkling eyes with righteousness (Prov. 13:9; Matt. 6:22–23) ans with life and good fortune (Job 3:16; 33:23; Prov. 4:18; 6:23; 13:9; 16:15).

B. Strophe 2: Pattern of ab—9-10 [10-11]

The second flight of the praise of *I AM's* Torah does so by adjectives (v. 9 [10]) and then by its benefits (v. 10 [11]). Although the second flight, it is the first in the fifth step and builds on the fourth, for the Law's purity assumes it has been purged of any impurity. Moreover, it points to its eternal nature: it will never pass away (Matt. 5:17–18). The *fear of I AM* (*yirat yhwh*)

52. B. K. Waltke, *TWOT*, 2:879, s.v. *śāmaḥ*.

53. Waltke, *Proverbs 1–15*, 90–92.

54. See C. H. Dodd, *The Bible and the Greeks* (London: Hodder & Stoughton, 1954), 25ff., for crucial terms.

refers to *I AM*'s special revelation in the Bible, in contrast to the "fear of God," which according to the late R. N. Whybray refers "to a standard of moral conduct known and accepted by men in general."[55] The collocation "fear of *I AM*" refers to both the rational aspect of understanding the revelation and the nonrational, emotional aspect of responding to the revelation in fear, love, and trust.[56] The "fear of *I AM*" opens the door to wisdom (Job 28:28; Prov. 1:7; Eccl. 12:13)[57] and so probably associates this opening verse of the second strophe with that of the first, which speaks of "making wise" (v. 7b). It is "pure" (*tāhôr*), the opposite of being mixed. Pure incense has no wood mixed in; pure gold is without alloys; and pure animals are like our notions of a purebred dog or pedigreed horse.[58] So the "fear of *I AM*" is free of any mixture with moral impurity. Like being free of a disease, "they endure" (*'ômedet*, lit., "stand") "forever" (*lā'ad*). '*D* was probably chosen instead of the more frequent *le'ôlām* for its alliteration with '*md*. Perpetuity normally denotes the unforeseeable future, but when applied to God and his Word, it takes on the philosophical nuance of being eternal.

The sixth step assures us that the stairway is firm because the whole has been built according to righteousness. "The judgments of I AM" (*mišpe̜têyhwh*) refer to the judicial verdicts such as those found in Exodus 21–23. *I AM*'s case laws are "firm" ('*emet*, "true," "steady," "reliable," see v. 7), that is to say, they cannot be overturned, unlike human judgments. This is so because "they are righteous" (*sāde̜qû*); in conformity with God's rule, they serve the interest of the entire community, not the self in preference to others.[59] "Altogether" (*yahdaw*) adds that the verdicts in unison, without an exception, are righteous.

We have finally arrived at the top: the value and delight of God's judgments are breathtaking. Old people desire money; young people crave pleasure. The Word of God meets both needs. "They are . . . desirable" (*hanneḥe̜mādîm*) syntactically refers to "judgments," for both words are masculine plurals. The root *ḥāmad* designates the disposition of the self in the direction of appealing

55. R. N. Whybray, *Wisdom in Proverbs: The Concept of Wisdom in Proverbs 1–9* (London: SC, 1965), 96.

56. Bruce K. Waltke, "The Fear of the LORD," in J. I. Packer and L. Wilkinson, eds., *Alive to God* (Downers Grove, IL: InterVarsity Press, 1992), 17–33.

57. In Ecclesiastes 12:13 "fear of God" is a synonym for "fear of *I AM*" in other Scriptures.

58. Mary Douglas, *Purity and Danger: An Analysis of the Concepts of Pollution and Taboo* (London: Routledge and Kegan Paul, 1966), argues that the purity laws had the sociological purpose of helping Israel grasp the unity and perfection of God's creation, a worldview that set them apart from their neighbors.

59. Waltke, *Proverbs*, 97.

property, usually for its beauty and/or its power.[60] When the desired object belongs to a neighbor (i.e., "to covet," Ex. 20:17), it is a vice that must be renounced and not entertained because of love for God and neighbor (James 1:13–15); but when the desire is for the beauty and the power for life found in the morally perfect Law, it is a virtue. The comparative *min*, "than," indicates a positive comparison; both *I AM*'s judgments and gold are desirable for their value. "Gold" (*zāhāb*) may refer "to gold-ore, gold in a raw state, or gold dust" or to wealth in general.[61] Since it is further qualified as "than pure gold" (*mippaz*), which designates gold separated from its ore and from alloys, the first sense is intended. Money puts food on the table but not love around it; money builds a house but not a home; it bestows luxuries but not love. When the religio-ethical virtues of God's verdicts are delighted in, they give both material and spiritual benefits. As pure gold shows that the quality of gold makes no difference in this comparison, so "much" (*rab*) shows that the quantity of gold also does not matter.

Conjunctive "and" adds a second benefit: God's judgments are "sweeter" (*mᵉtûqîm*) "than honey" (*middᵉbaš*). The positive comparison is now between the allurement and delight of God's judgments and honey, finding that satisfying the palate with the most desirable food is less alluring and pleasant for the saint than the certainty that God's judgments will never be overturned or reversed. Once again, the notions of quantity and quality are excluded from compromising the comparison by intensifying honey to "virgin honey flowing from the comb" (i.e., the delicacy of bee's honey, not the more common date honey). Its overflowing quantity is indicated by endlessly "flowing" and its superior quality by its being virgin honey, not oxygenated by the air. Honey also has a medicinal, healing property (Prov. 16:24), but that property is not mentioned and so presumably is not in view. Adam and Eve found the

---

60. Marvin L. Chaney (" 'Coveting Your Neighbor's House' in Social Context," in *The Ten Commandments: The Reciprocity of Faithfulness*, ed. William P. Brown [Louisville: Westminster John Knox, 2004], 302–17) hopes to overthrow the ancient versions, Paul (Rom. 7:7; 13:9), Luther (Larger Catechism), Calvin (*Institutes* 2.8.49), and many moderns. He argues with Hermann and Alt that the verb entails the taking of property in addition to coveting it. His argument fails because he ignores that in the instances he cites a second verb of taking is added (e.g., Mic. 2:2), an addition lacking in the tenth commandment. The eighth commandment pertains to taking of property and entails "to covet it." If "to covet" entails "to take," then there is little difference between the two commandments, unless one restricts the eighth commandment to kidnapping. Most scholars, however, refer the eighth commandment to ordinary theft, e.g., B. S. Jackson, "Liability for Mere Intention in Early Jewish Law," in *Studies in Judaism in Late Antiquity*, vol. 10, *Essays in Jewish and Comparative Legal History* (Leiden: Brill, 1975), 206n12.

61. BDB, 262, s.v. *zāhāb*.

Tree of the Knowledge of Good and Evil, which offered them autonomy to make them wise, more desirable than God's Word, which offered them life (Gen. 3:6). But people who trust God and his covenant find the Law ranks higher than all earthly values and pleasures.

Psalmist's Petitions for Salvation—11–13 [12–14]

"Moreover" (*gam*) conceptually links the king's petitions to his praise of Torah, and "by them" (*bāhem*, masc. pl.) grammatically binds them. The stanza consists of two strophes, each having two quatrains (vv. 11 and 12, vv. 13a and b). The first petitions God to forgive the king's hidden sins and the second to restrain him from joining proud mockers. Each strophe is introduced by *gam* and by the metaphor of "your slave." *Gam* introduces a related new thought ("also"), not to emphasize a point ("yea"). The first *gam* unites the petition to the hymn of Torah praise, for it adds an additional benefit—this time personal—to be acquitted of *I AM*'s judgments. The second *gam* introduces a second petition: to be kept from apostates and that in turn will deliver him from guilt of the great transgression. His two petitions express his humility. By requesting to be acquitted of hidden sins and to be kept from apostates he implicitly confesses his own moral weakness.

A. Pardon for hidden guilt—11–12 [12–13]

The petition to be free from the guilt and punishment of hidden error is prompted by his teaching about God's judgments: sin is punished and righteousness is rewarded (v. 11). But what about unwitting sin? David's petition answers that nagging question (v. 12).

1. Judgments threaten punishment and promise reward—11

David speaks of himself "as your slave" (*'abdⁱkā*, cf. Ps. 18 superscript [1]). The nuances of *'ebed* range from an indentured slave contracted for a specific time as payment for a debt to a person in a position of trust of varying ranks. In other words, it is a metaphor for covenant keeping. (Kidnap slavery was a capital offense [Ex. 21:16], and so that kind of slave is not otherwise in view in the Old Testament legislation.) The metaphor of an indentured slave signifies: (1) responsible obedience to *I AM*'s direction; (2) faithful dependence on his care; (3) personal intimacy of trust of payment; and (4) humility. God's judgments caution the king to take heed. *Zāhar*, the root of "is warned" (*nizhār*), in *Hiphil* may mean "instruct" or "admonish" in

Exodus 18:20, but otherwise (in 2 Kings 6:10 [*Qere*] and in Ezekiel 3 and 33 [10 times]) it means "to caution," "to warn [of danger]," a meaning that agrees with the sense in *Niphal*, "to take heed to a warning/a threat." In short, *nizhār* means to be instructed about danger and to take heed. Moreover, "is warned" is a metonymy of effect, assuming the judgments exact punishments.

As for "by keeping them" (*b^ešomrām*), *šāmar* with objects in the semantic domain of concrete persons or things (e.g., a garden [Gen. 2:15], tree [Gen. 3:24], son [Prov. 2:8]) signifies to keep from danger so as to preserve; but with objects in the semantic domain of wisdom, commands, and judgments, it signifies to preserve them carefully by faithful obedience and compliance (Prov. 3:1, 21). By taking heed to the warnings entailed in the judgments, the king is kept from punishment by his carefully keeping the judgments "comes . . . reward" (*'ēqeb*). According to *HALOT*, *'ēqeb* originally meant "the very back," "the end" (Ps. 119:33, 122), leading to the derivative meaning of "wages" (Ps. 19:12).[62] The recompense is unstated but is certainly as great as the value of gold and honey (v. 9). The adjective *rab* ("great," "much"), the last Hebrew word of 10a and 13b, may signal the connection between "gold" and "reward." God's grace adds a hundredfold to the investment of complying with his judgments (Matt. 19:29; cf. Mark 9:41; Luke 6:23, 35; Rom. 2:6; 2 Cor. 4:17–18; 5:10).

2. Do not punish unwitting errors—12 [13]

The gloss "as for" emphasizes the topic; the question "who can discern" is the predicate. "Errors" (*š^enî'ot*, fem. pl.) occurs in the Bible only in this verse, making the gloss tentative. Nevertheless, its cognate in Mandean, *sĕugiana*, means "mistake," "oversight," "error." And when this meaning is combined with its parallel *nistārôt* ("hidden things"), the collocation yields the semantically pertinent notion "hidden faults." "Who" (*mî*) is a rhetorical question to negate with passion the notion of the verb "discern." This use of the personal interrogative pronoun involves self-abasement or insult, and "a generalized use of this pattern involves abasing all people, including the speaker, usually in implicit contrast to God."[63] The root of "can discern" (*bîn*) in *Hiphil* (*yābîn*) with a direct object denotes the act of giving heed and considering something with the senses (e.g., the eyes and ears) in such a way that understanding about the object takes place within oneself (i.e., one

62. *HALOT*, 92:873, s.v. *'ēqeb*.
63. *IBHS*, 322, 18.2.g.

acquires and possesses its object).[64] By definition, no person can discern his or her hidden errors. Semantic pertinence favors construing the preposition *min* in the phrase *minnistārôt* as causal ("of the situation"),[65] glossed "for" to serve the English idiom. "Hidden" (*nistārôt*, n 10) syntactically modifies "errors." "What is hidden" parallels "none can discern error." To facilitate the sense, "faults" is added. Freud may have been the first to have named the hidden abnormal psychological impulses that rule our lives as the "id," but David is well aware that none rules his own house and can free himself from errors. So he prays: "declare me free from punishment" (*naqqênî, Piel* of *nqh*). *HALOT* defines the verb "to declare to be free from punishment (with *min*, 'regarding') Ps. 19:13; Job 9:28; 10:14."[66] In his forbearance, kindness, and mercy, God will not judge us for sins of which we are unaware, and so cannot confess and renounce, because Christ made atonement for all sin.

B. Preserve from guilt of apostasy—13 [14]AB

The quatrain expressing the second petition consists of the petition to be restrained from joining mockers (13a) with the expectation that then he will not apostatize.

1. Hold back from rule of insolent men—13 [14]A

None is free from the danger of apostasy. Even King David recognizes that without God's gracious spiritual protection, mockers could rule him. So he prays: "hold back" (*ḥᵃsok*) your servant, like a horse with a bit, from their sway. The petition entails the work of the Holy Spirit on David's spirit (Rom. 8:2–4; Gal. 5:16). "Moreover" (*gam*, see v. 12) joins this second petition to the first. "From" (*min*) with "hold back" now has its ablative sense. The root of "insolent men" (*zēdîm*), *zēd*, occurs thirteen times, always in plural, apart from Proverbs 21:24. This masculine substantival adjective does not have as its antecedent the feminine noun "errors" (*šᵉnî'ot*). *Zēdîm* elsewhere refers to those who challenge God (Mal. 3:15), attack the psalmist (Ps. 86:15), mock the pious without restraint (Ps. 119:51), forge lies (Ps. 119:69), and dig pits (Ps. 119:85). The psalmist prays that God will put them to shame (Ps. 119:78) and not let them oppress him (Ps. 119:122). Jeremiah (43:2) uses it of those who reject his prophecy. *I AM* is said to rebuke them

---

64. Waltke, *Proverbs 1–15*, 176.
65. *IBHS*, 213, 11.2.11d.
66. *HALOT*, 2:720, s.v. *nqh*.

(Ps. 119:21), and he will cause their arrogance to cease (Isa. 13:11; cf. Mal. 4:1 [3:19]). In light of these eleven other occurrences of *zēdîm*, the conclusion may be drawn that *zedîm* refers to men who, because of their prideful, exaggerated opinion of their self-importance, disregard *I AM*, the wise, and revealed truth. "Mocker" is his name (Prov. 27). From joining such men David prays: "hold back" (*ḥªśōk*) "your servant" (*'abdᵉkā*, see v. 12). *Ḥśk* here means to "restrain," "keep back" your servant from joining them in their impiety and moral impudence.

David does not pray for salvation from within—the cachet that he is a member of the new covenant is the law written on his heart—but for salvation from satanic forces without that assail him. That is to say, "let them [insolent men] not rule over me" (*'al-yimšol bî*). *Māšal* means to govern the conduct of a subordinate. If insolent men rule over David, he too will disregard God, the godly, and Torah (cf. Matt. 6:11; John 17:1). Without God's help, the human spirit alone is no match for Satan, who energizes insolent men, as the failure of Adam and Eve to resist Satan's rule instructs us (cf. Eph. 6:12). This is probably what John means by "sin unto death" (1 John 5:16–17).

2. To be free from the guilt of apostasy—13[14]B

"Then" (*'az*) signifies a future consequence (with some emphasis intended) and with an accompanying logical force, implying the fulfillment of a condition: "*then = if* or *when this has been done* (with the impf.) ... Ps. 19:14."[67] "I will retain integrity" (*'êtām*, lit., "I will be complete, sound, unimpaired," see v. 7). "And I will be kept free from punishment" (*wᵉniqqêtî*) construes *Piel nqh* as resultative, not declarative. Whereas David could scarcely avoid committing hidden sins and so had to be declared innocent, now by being saved from insolent men, he is kept free from a justly deserved punishment. This punishment is just "because" (*min*, see v. 13) they are guilty of "great" (*rab*, see v. 10) "transgression" (*peša'*). *Peša'* denotes offenses against property and/or person. It may pertain to theft (Gen. 31:36) or killing (1 Sam. 24:10–14). Thus *pš'* designates a formal category encompassing the various types of material and personal crimes. R. Knierim calls it "a legal technical term for crimes that were subject to legal penalties." He also notes that "*peša'* is a theological term because the deeds it describes affect Yahweh or his sovereignty and consequently require his judgment or forgiveness." Furthermore, "Whoever commits *peša'* does not

67. BDB, 23, s.v. *'az*.

merely rebel or protest against Yahweh but breaks with him."[68] The singular could be collective, covering all kinds of crimes, but its specification by singular "great" suggests that a particularly serious crime is in view. According to the parallel verset, "to let insolent men rule over me," apostasy against God is meant. If God holds him back from such apostates, he will never be guilty of that great crime against God of breaking faith with him.

Epilogue: Dedicatory Prayer—14 [15]

The epilogue is united with the petitions by yet another petition: that his poem be accepted by *I AM*. Since it pertains not to personal pardon but to the "protocol of the royal court, asking for the favor of acceptance,"[69] his final petition is best construed as an epilogue to his poem—not just another in a sequence of petitions—and as a dedication of his song to *I AM*. Accordingly, ambiguous *yihyû* is best construed as a jussive, "let be," not as an imperfect, "it will be." The root meaning of *rāṣôn* in *lᵉrāṣôn*, "pleasing," according to N. Walker, "is two-sided, namely *will* and *pleasure*, whether oneself or another. Doing one's own will and pleasure involves one's desire, but doing the will and pleasure of another results in *acceptance, approval*, delight of another, and his returning *favor* and *blessing*"[70] (cf. Pss. 104:34; 119:108). In Malachi 2:13 the parallel to not finding favor is "he no longer looks at the gift." *I AM* looked with favor on David's psalm, for he included it in the canon of Holy Scripture. "The words of my mouth" (*'imrê-pî*, see v. 2) "and the meditation of my heart" (*wᵉhegyôm libbi*) are metonymies for his cognitive reflections on *I AM*'s firmament and on his Torah and his unique petitions of salvation. "Meditation" (*hegyon*) is the nominal derivate of *hgh* (etymologically "to utter inarticulate sounds"; see Ps. 1:2). David has pondered long and hard on what to say and how to say it (see Prov. 15:28). "Before you" (*lᵉpāneykā*) means "in your eyes, in your estimation, according to your viewpoint."[71]

I AM in verse 14 is the seventh occurrence of the divine name in this psalm (see the other six in vv. 7–9), who is first imaged as "My Rock" (*ṣûrî*), an image of God's protection and majestic strength: "The firm, unshakable rock images God's help (Ps. 18:47), saving activity (Ps. 19:15), protection (Isa. 17:10), faithfulness (Isa. 26:4), and his being a refuge (Ps. 18:3) to his

---

68. Knierim, *TLOT*, 2:1034–36, s.v. *pš'*.
69. Clifford, *Psalms 1–72*, 115.
70. N. Walker, "The Renderings of *Rāṣôn*," *JBL* 81 (1962): 184.
71. *TLOT*, 2:1012, s.v. *pnym*.

covenant partners who trust him and so find his approval." If "rock" images God's mighty power, then "and my Redeemer" (*wᵉgōʾᵃlî*) images *I AM* as the king's legal family protector from outside jurisdiction: Psalm 19:14 [15], like Proverbs 23:10ff. and Jeremiah 50:34, apply to Yahweh the status of the *gōēl* in a family as the helper of the relative fallen into distress, calling him *gōēl* as protector of the weak over against a mighty opponent. In sum, *I AM* both is able and has obliged himself to protect and to save the king.

Subscript—Psalm 20: superscript [1]A

"To the chief musician" in Psalm 20: superscript is a subscript to Psalm 19. Under the leadership of the chief musician, all Israel is to join their exemplary king in listening to the heaven's praise of God as Creator, to celebrate *I AM*'s Torah that enlightens and delights the godly, and in humility to petition God for their spiritual salvation. And let them seek *I AM*'s favor in singing this song, for he alone is their mighty Savior.

CONCLUSION

In the introduction to the psalm, I argued that it is a mixture of literary genres—praise, penitential petition, and instruction. Finally, within the canon of the Bible it is a mystery—that is to say, it contains hidden truth.

As for the first stanza, the firmament's universal hymn has intertextual links with the early church's universal testimony to the Jews. Paul asks, "Did they [all the Israelites] not hear [the word about Christ]?" Of course they did: "Their voice has gone out into all the earth, their words to the ends of the world" (Rom. 10:18). Here Paul uses the universal testimony of the sun to God's glory (v. 5) as an intertextual allusion, not a mystical fulfillment, that all the Israelites had heard—presumably through Christ himself and the apostles—the gospel that Christ died for sins, was buried, and was raised from the dead. Therefore, they are without excuse.

Second, as for the praise of Torah in the second stanza, David's praise of the Law's moral perfection, and so implicitly of God's holiness, points to Jesus Christ, God incarnate. Christ's life manifests God's perfect holiness and fulfills the Law's righteousness; his death provides atonement for many; and his resurrection demonstrates that he is Truth. Christians use David's praise of Torah to praise the sinless Lamb of God, who became righteousness for them, and who gives them his Spirit, enabling them to enjoy its value and delight.

Moreover, in every dispensation those who delight in the Law and find it reviving and enlightening are members of the new covenant and as such have the Law written on their hearts by the Holy Spirit (Jer. 31:31–34; Luke 22:20; 2 Cor. 3:1–3; Heb. 8, esp. vv. 7–12). For them it is the perfect law that gives freedom (James 1:5). The psalm is pregnant with these truths, but the New Testament births them.

David's humble penitential prayer in the third stanza (vv. 11–14) exemplifies another function of the Law: its commandments condemn sinners (Rom. 5:13; 1 Tim. 1:8–11). As noted, David thinks and teaches as a sage. Wisdom literature, otherwise, never gives voice to the student's response to the sage's catechetical teaching. The father's lecture in Proverbs 4:1–9 represents a son's passing on his father's teachings to the next generation, but it does not represent the son's spiritual response, other than that of acceptance. David's response exemplifies the appropriate response: prayer for salvation, not a resolve to obey, as one might expect. David's response is that of the tax collector: "God, be merciful to me, a sinner."

The Old Testament is a masterpiece of indirection. On the surface, the Old Testament Torah in its broadest sense misleads the proud into presumptuous resolutions to obey, but in fact the Torah proves humankind's inability to obey and so condemns them (cf. Deut. 30:6; Josh. 24:14–27). This is the error of Jews who boasted in themselves, the error against which Paul protects the church. In short, David, like Paul, uses the Law to condemn sin and in its light repents of his sin.

Finally, in his dedicatory prayer David addresses God as his Redeemer, the family Brother who saves the family from foreign jurisdiction. That faith is justified because Christ, by his death, provided redemption from the realm of sin and death. In other words, the psalm is pregnant with the gospel.

In sum, the righteous have always lived by faith in *I AM*, not by human resolve.

PART 3

APOLOGETICS

18

FRAME THE APOLOGIST

WILLIAM EDGAR

I FIRST MET JOHN in 1968 at a Sunday dinner at the home of Edmund and Jean Clowney. He had just been appointed to teach at Westminster Theological Seminary, which I was then attending as a student. I remember the moment well, first, because it was the beginning of a long friendship, one in which I was to be the chief beneficiary, and second, because of a particular conversation I observed between John and Ed (being a student, of course, I called them Mr. Frame and Dr. Clowney, respectively). Ed maintained that there was only one sermon in each passage of Scripture. It is a view he may not have held firmly all his life, but at that point he was arguing that the different pericopes of the written Word were fixed, and that a good sermon would uncover their unique structure and work from there toward the "right" sermon. Illustrations might vary, but not the basic outline. John, on the other hand, argued that there should be more flexibility than that, especially because the needs varied from congregation to congregation.

John's chief concern in that discussion was that we not forget the role of *application* in shaping our message. The outline of a sermon should strongly take into consideration the needs of the parishioners. Or, as he would later put it, the outline should take into account the *situation*. I mention this because his emphasis on context would be developed throughout his professional life and would become one of his major contributions to the fields of epistemology, ethics, and, our chief concern here, apologetics.

DEFINITIONAL ISSUES

Accordingly, one of John's earliest definitions of apologetics can be found in his first major work, *Doctrine of the Knowledge of God* (1987): "Apologetics may be defined as the application of Scripture to unbelief and as such may be seen as a subdivision of theology."[1] There it is up front: apologetics is application. If apologetics is a subdivision of theology, what, then, is theology? "I would suggest," as he tells us a few pages earlier, "that we define theology as 'the application of the Word of God by persons to all areas of life.' "[2] Both definitions are in the section "God and Our Studies" (which is the third chapter within part 1, "The Objects of Knowledge"). How broad and deep this approach to apologetics is can be confirmed by looking at a brief article written in 1990, describing apologetics at Westminster Seminary. Here, John says, "Apologetics at Westminster, therefore, is more than 'the defense of the faith.' It is also 'Christian theory of knowledge.' For in apologetics, we learn what God's word requires of us as we seek to know him, or indeed as we seek to know anything in his creation. We learn the primacy of Scripture for all human thought. We learn to use general revelation—God's witness in the world and in ourselves as his image—to better apply his word to specific problems."[3]

A further definition was given at the beginning of the later volume, *Apologetics to the Glory of God*. There, he works with 1 Peter 3:15 and defines apologetics as "the discipline that teaches Christians how to give a reason for their hope." Although this sounds different from what was said in *DKG*, adding the more personal element of persuasion to the mix, he explains in a footnote that this new definition is "logically equivalent" to the first because both defend the same norm of the Word of God.[4] Other definitions can be found. For example, in his entry on apologetics in the *Dictionary for the Theological Interpretation of the Bible*, the first sentence states, "Apologetics is the theological discipline that defends the truth of the Christian

---

1. *DKG*, 87. John Frame was widely published before this volume but almost always in book reviews, pamphlets, and, most significantly, extensive course syllabi.
2. Ibid., 81.
3. John M. Frame, "Apologetics at Westminster Seminary," *Update* 8, 2 (1990): 2.
4. *AGG*, 1.

message."[5] In the rest of the article John underscores the relation of apologetics to authority and the need to have one's defense always corrected by the hermeneutical circle.

These definitions reflect two major concerns. The first is to ensure both the distance and the complementarities between Scripture and theology. In order to do this, two extremes should be avoided, the "subjectivist" and the more "objectivist" views of doing theology.[6] For example, on the one hand, as he explains, Schleiermacher looks at doctrine as the account of Christian religious affections, a far too subjective view.[7] On the other hand, John understands Charles Hodge to argue for the necessity of theology's putting some kind of more logical order into the "facts" of Scripture, much in the way a scientist might gather facts from nature and then describe them as following certain laws. In doing so, Hodge believed he was discovering an objective order to be gleaned from the data of Scripture. Although appreciative of Hodge's respect for truth, something he does not find in Schleiermacher's more subjective approach to theology, John is nonetheless uncomfortable with seeing the Bible as a book of facts needing to be interpreted. Instead, he believes the Bible to be *language*, a text that comes to us already interpreted. As he puts it, "in the most important sense, [Scripture's self-interpretations and self-descriptions] cannot be improved upon."[8]

So if it should not set out to improve on the order of Scripture's propositions, what does theology do? John calls theology a secondary description, a reinterpretation, with a view to meeting human needs.[9] This emphasis is crucial for his method. At the heart of it, again, theology is doing application. Not just any application, of course, but for him, application is the sort of thing we do when "teaching," in the biblical sense of *didache* or *didaschalia*. And this in turn is quite close to what is meant by *doctrine*.[10] Here is the reason why many of the titles of John's most important volumes contain the word *doctrine* in the title.[11] For him, we are most able to respect the

---

5. Kevin Vanhoozer, ed., *Dictionary for the Theological Interpretation of the Bible* (Grand Rapids: Baker Academic, 2005), 57.

6. Here, we may follow his discussion in *DKG*, with occasional references to other writings.

7. *DKG*, 77.

8. Ibid., 78.

9. Ibid., 79.

10. Ibid., 81–85.

11. *DKG* (1987), *DG* (2002), *DCL* (2008). The three are united as the series A Theology of Lordship.

authority of Scripture when we apply it to every realm of life, not when we try to reorder it.

Of course, there is a proper order in the application, but what drives that order is two things. First, how does it lift up the gospel of salvation? So, for example, in his large volume *The Doctrine of God*, John affirms the need to relate the major loci of theology, and the major attributes of God, to salvation.[12] Take, for example, the traditional doctrine of the simplicity of God, which is discussed in the chapter on epistemology. John suggests that Thomas Aquinas sells the richness of God's attributes short by using a kind of neoplatonist approach to metaphysical simplicity. Instead, the more biblical approach is to link simplicity with "the unity of our covenant Lord, and the unity that he brings *into our lives* as we seek to honor him and him alone."[13]

And second, how does application serve the best pedagogical use? For example, John believes there can be progress in theology, such that it can be properly contextualized to fit the needs of different eras and different people groups.[14] Stated this way, it is not particularly controversial. But John's emphasis is that there may be important variants as we move through the centuries and from place to place. Thus, he takes the position that the historical creeds are highly valuable, yet cannot be taken as final, fixed systems for the ages. To do so is to invite traditionalism, or, worse, confusion between the authority of a creed and Scripture. To be sure, this has occasionally attracted criticism from those who fear the slippery slope of relativism.[15]

The second concern expressed in these definitions of apologetics and theology is rooted in John's philosophy of meaning. From the beginning, he has insisted that *meaning* comprises several components and should not be reduced to just one element. In an important appendix within *DKG* he describes his debt to William Alston, particularly his magnum opus, *Philosophy of Language*.[16] As Alston asserts, and as John develops it, there are three ways in which things may *mean*. First, the meaning of a word

12. It is notable that his recent volume on systematic theology is titled *Salvation Belongs to the Lord* (Phillipsburg, NJ: P&R Publishing, 2006).

13. *DG*, 230, italics mine.

14. *DKG*, chap. 9.

15. See, for example, Mark W. Karlberg, "John Frame and the Recasting of Van Tillian Apologetics: A Review Article," *Mid-America Journal of Theology* 9, 2 (1993): 285.

16. Appendix C, *DKG*, 93–98; William P. Alston, *Philosophy of Language* (Englewood Cliffs, NJ: Prentice Hall, 1964).

or phrase can be stated as a synonym. This is a syntactical approach. For example, although it doesn't get us very far, we can accurately define deafness as *inability to hear*. Second, the meaning of a word or phrase can be determined by a referent. This is a semantic approach. Thus, we could say "John Kennedy" and "president in 1960." Finally, and this is where we move to the most significant type of meaning, the word or phrase can be understood *pragmatically*. That is, how do we use it? What is the intention of the author? How can it be verified? Here, John engages in a brief discussion of Wittgenstein, who often tied meaning to use. In the case of biblical truth we should be asking, what is the God-ordained use of this word or phrase? In this case, a meaning is an application.

John argues for these in various ways. Reminiscent for me of our conversation in the Clowney home, he is anxious to avoid contextless, timeless, flat definitions, while at the same time denying any relativism. For example, he says, when someone asks for the meaning of something, the questioner is presenting a problem. At the moment the person in effect ignores the best way to use the language in question. To provide meaning is to relieve the questioner. So, for example, when someone wants to know the meaning of, say, *investment*, we must tell the person what it looks like: going to the bank, donating money for a cause, hoping for a profit, etc. Another argument is from biblical ethics. Scripture tells us to apply the Word, or risk hypocrisy. Again, John wards off anticipated criticism that he is slouching into subjectivism. So, in reference to proper biblical interpretation, he answers that the real danger is to imagine some entity called *the meaning*, which stands between the biblical text and its application. *Meaning*, thus understood, would only stand in the way of the text. Some of this is redolent of James Barr's critique of neoorthodoxy's word studies.[17]

An interesting aside: it would appear that the work of Kevin Vanhoozer bears a certain resemblance to John's. My guess, informed somewhat from John's own recollections, is that when Vanhoozer was a student at Westminster, he was influenced by John's way of thinking. Like John, Vanhoozer argues for the "theodrama" of Scripture, which includes the various ways it carries meaning. Vanhoozer argues that the propositional ("locutionary") content of Scripture, that is, what it teaches, points to, or argues, os often communicated in an "illocutionary" manner—a promise, a threat, etc.—or

17. *DKG*, 195. See James Barr, *The Semantics of Biblical Language* (London: Oxford University Press, 1961).

with a "perlocutionary" effect—actually scaring or reassuring the person, for example. Respecting this helps avoid seeing doctrine as a mere collection of data from the Bible, while safeguarding it from the various forms of subjectivism found in postliberalism.[18] This is surely why John calls the Scripture *language*, and why he expresses great concern to respect the different genres of biblical texts. Both theologians want to help the evangelical community get back to more solid doctrinal footing. Like John, Vanhoozer critiques Charles Hodge for his "biblical empiricism" and seeks a more canonical way to tell the whole story, rather than to amass data.[19] Intriguingly, too, Vanhoozer's view of "triangulation" somewhat resembles John's triperspectival approach. The two have, of course, gone in different directions. Vanhoozer has done a good deal of work on cultural analysis and John on ethics. I do suspect that John is not altogether comfortable with Vanhoozer's apparent underplaying of the primary exegetical work needed to get to the story, nor, perhaps, of the seeming neglect of the more normative aspects of the Bible's instructions. Indeed, in discussing his relationship with Vanhoozer and his high respect for him, John has nevertheless expressed doubts about the usefulness of largescale models and pleads for simply working more with Scripture—its teachings and implications.[20]

PERSPECTIVAL CONCERNS

Related to these two major concerns is a third entity, the whole background of perspectival thinking. The previous chapter in *DKG* to the one with our definitions, titled "God and the World," sets forth clearly for the first time in print John's triperspectival approach to knowledge, which is essential for the entire structure of his worldview. For those unfamiliar with this notion, there are three complementary aspects, three converging

18. Kevin J. Vanhoozer, *The Drama of Doctrine: A Canonical-Linguistic Approach to Christian Theology* (Louisville: Westminster-John Knox, 2005), 58ff. John has weighed in with a criticism of George Lindbeck that is similar to Vanhoozer's. See his review of *The Nature of Doctrine* in *The Presbyterian Journal* 43 (February 27, 1985): 11–12.

19. Kevin J. Vanhoozer, "On the Very Idea of a Theological System: An Essay in Aid of Triangulating Scripture, Church, and World," in A. T. B. McGowan, ed., *Always Reforming: Explorations in Systematic Theology* (Leicester: Apollos, 2006), 136. Yet, is it possible, according to the interesting suggestion of Everett Berry, that both have somewhat caricatured Hodge? See Everett Berry, "Theological vs. Methodological Postconservatism: Stanley Grenz and Kevin Vanhoozer as Test Cases," *WTJ* 69 (2007): 124.

20. John Frame, e-mail message to author, September 16, 2008.

angles to human knowledge. They are the normative, the situational, and the existential. (a) Knowledge engages the normative—the authoritative perspective. For Christians this is God's authority, his covenant law. (b) Knowledge engages the situational—the context or the world. For Christians this means to look at the creation, the place where we live. (c) Knowledge engages the existential—the subjective aspect, including motivation and faith. For Christians this includes knowing God by knowing ourselves, something Calvin was known to set forth.[21]

Naturally, John has spent considerable time defending this approach, although he is not as doctrinaire about it as some of his critics believe.[22] Although this is not the place to rehearse the many discussions that have surrounded such a creative idea, one of the more consistent charges against his views is relativism, which John vigorously denies. Indeed, he says although these perspectives are complementary, they are interdependent and "ultimately identical."[23] Another, related criticism is that centering on application is a kind of nominalism. *Nominalism* means that there is nothing really in common between individual things except the name. For example, although we have the term *chairs*, only individual pieces of furniture we sit on are real. Similar to *conceptualism*, the idea is that nothing is common to objects except our using terms to describe them. The accusation against perspectivalism is that calling the same thing by three different terms means that there can be no ultimate or universal truth about the thing. But John argues that different angles does not mean that there is no reality to the thing. The intention behind the multiperspectival approach is to be faithful to an important part of the Reformed tradition, which says we cannot exhaust the truth. John sees Cornelius Van Til doing the same thing, while he wants to develop this insight further.[24]

In keeping with this background, John further elucidates what he means by apologetics in *AGG*. It is (predictably!) triperspectival.[25] First, apologet-

---

21. Particularly in the *Institutes of the Christian Religion* 1.1.2.
22. *DG*, 15n31.
23. *DKG*, 89.
24. It can be noted, for example, that Van Til happily speaks of three dimensions in Christian ethics: the motive, the standard, and the purpose. See his *Christian Theistic Ethics* (Philadelphia: The Den Dulk Foundation, 1971), 1–3. See also John's discussion of *theological encyclopedia* in *DKG*, 91–92. K. Scott Oliphint suggested to me in a conversation that the discussion might significantly move forward if we could avoid the term *perspectivalism*, and stay with *multiperspectival*, or something of the sort. As John himself has somewhere remarked, often "isms" are bad because they polarize things, whereas "alities" are good because more complementary.
25. *AGG*, 2–3.

ics entails proving Christianity to be true, particularly in the face of doubt. Second, apologetics is defense. Here John alludes to Paul's mission to defend the gospel (Phil. 1:7). Third, apologetics, he says, is offense. Here he notes that we must go on the attack against falsehood. To put these in terms of the three perspectives, we have constructive apologetics as normative, offensive apologetics as situational, and defensive apologetics as existential.[26] This may seem rather involved to the casual reader. At the heart of what John is doing, though, there is the concern not to limit oneself just to defense, or merely to proof, etc., because this would do an injustice to the audience. In my own work, I have centered on two aspects of apologetics, *defending* and *commending* Christian faith. To *commend* has a more positive ring to it than to go on the *offensive*, for me, though I suspect we mean quite the same thing.

John would be the first to say that definitions are not all-important. What matters is what they communicate. One of the key emphases he wants to stress is that we cannot start from a neutral set of arguments in order to get people to believe the truth of revelation. Rather, the arguments themselves must derive from revelational norms.[27] This is a crucial discussion.

THE LARGER HISTORICAL SETTING

Defining apologetics as applying theology to unbelief, in the wider context of knowledge, may not be entirely original, but this particular formulation stands in an interesting relation to a number of perceptions. There are literally hundreds of definitions proposed by various theologians and philosophers. They tell us a good deal about the authors' commitments, as they should. For example, in his foundational book *The God Who Is There*, Francis Schaeffer defined apologetics this way: "There are two purposes of Christian apologetics. The first is defense. The second is to communicate Christianity in a way that any given generation can understand."[28] In a general way this fits Schaeffer's commitment to apologetics as evangelism, with the understanding that evangelism requires two postures: answering challenges and presenting cogent reasons for faith to a particular people in a particular age. For example, he says one of the reasons that he accepted

26. Ibid., 3n5.
27. *DKG*, 87.
28. Francis A. Schaeffer, *The God Who Is There* (Downers Grove, IL: InterVarsity Press, 1998), 171.

presuppositional apologetics is that it was more apt in the face of a post-Hegelian world than the older "evidentialist" method, which was effective only when there was more of a "Christian consensus."[29] Although he does not comment on Schaeffer's definition directly, as far as I know, John's own concerns are close to those of the founder of L'Abri Fellowship.

Of considerable interest for our purpose in situating John Frame's characterization of apologetics is briefly to examine the views of a few of his most significant predecessors. In his work on theological encyclopedia, F. D. E. Schleiermacher (1768–1834), mentioned earlier, famously placed apologetics alongside "polemics" as two branches of the prolegomena "philosophical theology." The purpose of apologetics, for him, is to compare Christianity with various religious communions in order to showcase the former's uniqueness. In contrast, polemics aims at looking into heresies and other variants of the faith. To be faithful to its task, then, apologetics must work toward "separating the conviction of truth from the mode of belief."[30] Put differently, Schleiermacher was anxious to minimize the role of rational proofs and to maximize the nature of faith in order to preserve the intellectual integrity of Christianity from the jaws of science. This, in turn, is in keeping with his overall view that the core of biblical religion is the feeling (*Gefühl*) of dependence.

This liberal Protestant initiative coincided with the birth of the modern discipline of apologetics in the academy. Other such theologians reinforced this innovation. Although at times he reverted to more traditional approaches, Schleiermacher's disciple Karl Heinrich Sacks (1789–1875) also contributed to defining this new discipline. In his *Christian Apologetics*, he sets forth the value of religion in general and then argues for the superiority of the Christian religion, particularly in its ability to contribute moral power and to lead to human progress.[31] This general direction was followed, albeit with considerable variation, in the thinkers of this and of the next genera-

29. Ibid., 27. There has been some debate among Schaeffer's commentators about the choice of Hegel rather than Kant as the watershed figure introducing the characteristic "nature/freedom" dichotomy of modernity. See, for example, Colin Duriez, *Francis Schaeffer: An Authentic Life* (Wheaton, IL: Crossway, 2008), 42, 170. Also, there has been considerable discussion of the particular form of presuppositionalism Schaeffer embraced. Although he trained under Van Til, he differed with him in various ways. See my "Two Christian Warriors: Cornelius Van Til and Francis A. Schaeffer Compared," *WTJ* 57 (Spring 1995): 57–80.

30. F. D. E. Schleiermacher, *Kurze Darstellung des theologischen Studiums zum Behuf einleitender Volesung* (Berlin, 1830), 31.

31. Karl Heinrich Sacks, *Christliche Apologetik* (Hambourg, 1829, rev. 1841).

tion, including Jacob Friedrich Fries (1773–1843), Wilhelm M. L. De Wette (1780–1849), Georg W. F. Hegel (1780–1849), something of a pantheist in the guise of a Christian theologian, and then various post-Hegelians, including the radical David Friedrich Strauss (1808–74).

Who would answer these more liberal thinkers? Two groups can be mentioned. The first is pietists of different stripes. Some of them, ironically, were influenced by Schleiermacher, and yet were most uncomfortable with the radical views of Hegel or Strauss. A number were products of the various early nineteenth-century awakenings. We may think of August Tholuck (1799–1877), of Louis Gaussen (1790–1863), and of Alexandre Vinet (1797–1847).[32] Many individuals rose to contribute various pieces to the apologetic enterprise, whether they made much use of the term or not. Of great significance for later generations is Søren Kierkegaard (1813–55), who rejected cold proofs in favor of the warm experience of Jesus Christ.

ABRAHAM KUYPER AND BENJAMIN B. WARFIELD

The second group, and of greater interest here, consists of the more orthodox Reformed thinkers, particularly Abraham Kuyper (1837–1920) and his interlocutors at Princeton, especially his slightly younger contemporary Benjamin B. Warfield (1851–1921). We know of Kuyper's resistance to apologetics, at least the way he understood it. In the first part of his opening lecture, "Calvinism a Life-System," after describing the fundamental opposition between the revolutionary worldview of modernity and the Christian life-system, which he describes as *the* struggle in Europe and America, he adds: "In this struggle Apologetics have advanced us not one single step. Apologists have invariably begun by abandoning the assailed breastwork, in order to entrench themselves cowardly in a ravelin[33] behind it."[34] His concern soon becomes obvious. Whereas apologetics deals with isolated proofs, true Calvinism deals with *principle*. There must be opposition to modern pantheism and Darwinism, he says, not by a Protestantism that has lost its moorings but by a life-system.[35]

32. See William Edgar, *La carte protestante* (Genève: Labor et Fides, 1997), 181ff.

33. A triangular fortification or detached outwork in front of the bastions of a fortress.

34. Abraham Kuyper, "Calvinism a Life-System," in *Lectures on Calvinism* (Grand Rapids: Eerdmans, 1931), 11.

35. Ibid., 18–19.

It might be asked what types of apologetics he encountered that made him think it was so ineffective. His opposition to apologetics is reminiscent of that of Karl Barth, who we can be sure was thinking of Schleiermacher. However, most of Kuyper's references to Schleiermacher are in reaction to his perceived pantheism and the reduction of Christian faith to ethics, rather than to his apologetics. Perhaps he was thinking of Bishop Joseph Butler, or his heirs, including the popular apologists of his day who looked to shore up their evangelism with various proofs and evidences. Perhaps he was thinking of Warfield himself. Neither here nor in the parallel section in the *Encyclopedia* does he tell us which apologists he has in mind that gave him such a bad taste. He did write about the post-Reformation orthodox Protestants, who might be the culprits. And he was profoundly aware of Thomas Aquinas, whose view of proving God's existence with unaided reason would have repelled him. My guess is that he simply lumped together any attempt to begin with reason or logical proofs and found them incompatible with faith, which, stemming from regeneration, is such a crucial component of his approach.

It is likely that we are indeed challenged with definitions in this matter. I am not convinced that Kuyper opposed apologetics in the most Reformed understanding. Here it is interesting to look at Warfield's own concerns about Kuyper. On the surface he takes an almost exactly opposite position. For example, in the article on "Apologetics," written by him for the Schaff-Herzog *Encyclopedia*, Warfield famously assigns this important role to the discipline: "Apologetics undertakes not the defense, not even the vindication, but the establishment, not, strictly speaking, of Christianity, but rather of that knowledge of God which Christianity professes to embody and seeks to make efficient in the world, and which it is the business of theology scientifically to explicate."[36] For Warfield, apologetics should have existed regardless of any "accidents," whether opposition or sin itself. We need it simply because we are human beings. Apologetics is needed in order to establish the possibility of theology. As he puts it, "It is, in other words, the function of apologetics to investigate, explicate, and establish the grounds on which a theology—a science, or systematized knowledge of God—is possible; and on the basis of which every science which has God for its object must rest, if it be a true science with claims to a place within the circle of the sciences."[37]

36. Samuel Macauley Jackson, ed., *The New Schaff-Herzog Encyclopedia of Religious Knowledge* (New York: Funk and Wagnalls, 1908), 1:232.
37. Ibid., 233.

Accordingly, Warfield complains that in Kuyper's system apologetics has been marginalized, "treated like a stepchild in the theological household." Why did Kuyper think this? Because faced with two apparently opposite tendencies, rationalism and mysticism, apologetics is patently ineffective. "To Rationalism, of course, Apologetics is an inanity; to Mysticism, an impertinence."[38] He accuses apologetics of failing adequately to respond to these extremes. Here, Warfield agrees about the failure of certain apologetics but doesn't want to throw out the baby with the bathwater. Thus he is puzzled by Kuyper's placing apologetics "hidden away in a subdivision of a subdivision" within his *Encyclopedia of Sacred Theology*.[39] Its sole purpose for Kuyper, as Warfield puts it, is the "narrow" one of defending Christianity against false philosophies. It does so alongside polemics and elenchtics, which fight against heterodoxy and paganism, respectively. Warfield notes that Kuyper in effect does a kind of apologetic, when he tells us where to begin. It is with regeneration, as we have seen, which enables a person to possess God's revelation in the Scriptures, and from there to do theology. The object of theology for Kuyper is the ectypal (copied, as opposed to archetypal, or original) knowledge of God. Thus, if we can "vindicate" the *sensus divinitatis*, we may move on to the knowledge of God. It is a sort of apologetics beginning from "the reality of a supernatural preparation of the heart of man to receive [revelation]."[40]

We may have a problem with some of Warfield's formulation. He takes issue with the apparent assumption that we may begin with Scripture, then historical theology, then systematics and practical theology, without any of them their being properly defended. Instead, he argues that if we are really going to work back to "first principles," we will need to begin with "apologetical theology," which must be first among all the others.[41] Warfield quite approves the fact that Kuyper wants to avoid placing us *above* the Scriptures, but rather keeping us *in* them. Still, he says, we must first *have* Scriptures, by way of authentication, before being within them. He also approves the position that maintains that we become believers not by so many demonstrations but by the new birth. Apologetics has no power

38. Benjamin B. Warfield, "Introduction to Francis R. Beattie's *Apologetics: or the Rational Vindication of Christianity*" (Richmond: Presbyterian Committee of Publication, 1903), reprinted in Benjamin B. Warfield, *Selected Shorter Writings*, ed. John E. Meeter (Nutley, NJ: Presbyterian and Reformed, 1973), 2:93–94.

39. Ibid., 95.

40. Ibid., 97.

41. Ibid., 98.

in itself to make a person Christian, let alone to conquer the world for Christ. Still, he says, that does not obviate the need for apologetic; quite the contrary. In opposition to fideism, he affirms, "For the Holy Spirit does not work a blind, an ungrounded faith in the heart." Rather, he works in us "a new ability of the heart to respond to the grounds of faith."[42]

Again, so much does he esteem Kuyper, Warfield is led to wonder why such an admirable thinker would make so little of apologetics. One answer, he suggests, is that he makes too much of the contrast between two kinds of science, the one produced by regenerate people, and the other not. It is true that Kuyper has a distinctive approach that could tend to exaggerate the difference, or to underestimate the commonality of human beings as human beings when it comes to producing theory or science. But his concern is to point out the difference of starting point.

THE HEART OF THE MATTER

Were they so very different? Probably not. Enter Cornelius Van Til. He appreciates Warfield, but he faults him for placing too much trust in reason. And although he, too, expresses a concern about Kuyper, actually he is more concerned that Kuyper has not gone far enough! One place Van Til explores is Kuyper's view that there are two kinds of science, one operated by regenerate people, the other not. Although Van Til recognizes what Kuyper means, he wants to make sure it is understood that both the unregenerate and the regenerate can operate in the same world. To be sure, it must be recognized that in principle they are coming from very different places. In addition, for example, Kuyper believes that "weighing and measuring" can be done by both believing and unbelieving people because sin has not affected their metaphysical setting. Van Til disagrees, because he says sin affects the subjective way in which the metaphysical data are interpreted.[43] So he has not gone far enough! Accordingly, Van Til faults Warfield for trying to reduce the distinction between the two kinds of science, based on the idea that "right reason," held by one and all, can accurately describe the natural world, be it the revealed truth of God's creation.[44]

42. Ibid., 99.
43. Cornelius Van Til, *The Defense of the Faith*, 4th ed. (Phillipsburg, NJ: P&R Publishing, 2008), 283–90 (henceforth *DF*).
44. Ibid., 350–51.

Enter John Frame. My sense is that John is profoundly committed to the deepest insights of both Kuyper and Warfield, although he will take great pains to define apologetics in a more Kuyperian way, and, of course, in a more Van Tillian way. Again, John's definition of apologetics is "the application of Scripture to unbelief and as such may be seen as a subdivision of theology."[45] John wants apologetics to admit its scriptural beginning point from the start. This puts him close to Van Til, who defines apologetics as "the vindication of the Christian philosophy of life against the various forms of the non-Christian philosophy of life."[46] He goes on to argue that because there has been defense at every point of the theological encyclopedia, it might be thought we do not need apologetics. To which he responds that apologetics is still needed. First, it is like a messenger boy in the army who informs one general of the plans of his allies across the disciplines of biblical exegesis, biblical theology, systematic theology, and practical theology. Second, it is like the scout who spies out the movements of the enemy. He adds that the military metaphor serves to remind us that apologetics cannot be very carefully defined![47] I believe John is at home with this approach, although he uses less military language than his mentor.

Back to definitions. John's concern, then, expressed in his definitions, is to begin from the Christian faith, not from neutral proofs or reasoning. Here he resembles Kuyper and Van Til. Like them, he is concerned to confront unbelief with "theology," rather than a piecemeal set of evidences. But he is also concerned to show that because of the kind of system it is, the Christian faith requires evidences and proofs, as in Warfield's view. In any case, in his work he will develop such proofs more than Van Til. And although definitions do not rank high on his list of priorities, the theological issues at stake are enormous. John is quite enthusiastic about the way these early discussions went, because they dealt with such important theological issues. Here is how he endorsed the fourth edition of Van Til's *Defense of the Faith*: "How stimulating it must have been to be part of that dialogue in the early days of Reformed apologetics! We need that stimulus now if we are to deal with unbelief in a God-honoring way."[48]

45. See footnote 1.
46. Cornelius Van Til, *Christian Apologetics*, 2nd ed. (Phillipsburg, NJ: P&R Publishing, 2003), 17 (henceforth *CA*).
47. Ibid., 22.
48. *DF*, back cover.

For John, perhaps more strongly than Kuyper and Van Til had ever put it, at the heart of the apologist's message is the gospel.[49] As he explains, the Christian faith is not simply an alternative to secularism, nor a better ethical system, but it is good news. Francis Schaeffer similarly told his audiences that the Christian worldview is not "a better dialectic" for winning points but is the truth of the gospel. To be fair, the same can be said for Cornelius Van Til, John's most important mentor. Indeed, it is impossible to separate Van Til the philosopher, or the apologist, from Van Til the gospel preacher. As John himself noted at the memorial service in May 1987, "Any account of Van Til's technical concepts, his *system* of apologetics, must take seriously his claim to be a gospel preacher. This fact is not only of biographical interest, but has a conceptual importance as well."[50] Accordingly, for John, apologetics that gets tangled up in arguments, proofs, defenses, and critiques but that does not center on evangelism is to deprive an unbeliever of what he needs most.[51]

Only when we recognize this gospel-centered intention can we do justice to John's various emphases within the realm of apologetics. What are those priorities? In one way, everything we may consider in relation to any part of the Christian worldview will have relevance for apologetics. Like Van Til, he believes every endeavor is subject to apologetic defense. Also, like his mentor, John believes one can begin a discussion anywhere at all. Thus, the details of John's understanding of the "regulative principle" of worship, even though not apparently related to Christian apologetics, do involve a defense of a biblical view against what John considers to be sub-biblical. This is because for him the regulative principle simply means "defensible on the basis of Scripture." Apologetics seen this way is a discipline that sharpens our discussions in order to find the fundamental opposition between truth and untruth within the issue, whatever the issue might be. But always, not far from the presentation issues, lies the challenge and the offer of the gospel.

PRESUPPOSITIONS

Having looked somewhat at length at definitions, it is appropriate to come to the central commitments we find in the content of John's apolo-

---

49. *AGG*, 53–54.
50. See http://www.frame-poythress.org/frame_articles/1987Message.htm.
51. *AGG*, 54.

getics. As can be surmised from many of his writings, and simply from the emphases he made over his entire career, John would place himself in the camp known as *presuppositionalism*. What is a presupposition, and how is the school that goes by this name different from others, say, *evidentialism*, or the *classical* position? At one level, things are straightforward. If Christ is Lord, there cannot be any way of knowing him truly other than by presupposing his lordship. In *DKG* John defines a presupposition primarily as a criterion, albeit one that is "religious" or a heart-commitment, not merely a norm or standard. It is a belief. To put it in a larger context, if knowledge is a covenant relationship, then knowing God is servant- knowledge, obedient knowledge, and so a true presupposition.[52] This is because there can be no deeper or more ultimate criteria for knowing Christ than those he himself establishes. Thus, as John puts it, "A presupposition is a belief that takes precedence over another and therefore serves as a criterion for another. An ultimate presupposition is a belief over which no other takes precedence." John assures the reader that in this matter of belief, we are not simply being intellectualistic, but beginning from the human heart.[53]

Furthermore, a presupposition may be false. Even so, a falsely held presupposition is not simply ignorant of the truth but an intentional distortion of the truth.[54] As such, then, it maintains its character as religious, even though disobediently religious.

Understandably, and helpfully, John wrestles with what this concept might mean in distinction from other neighboring possibilities. We should point out that although he accepts the term *presuppositional* as justified in Scripture as well as common sense, he does not particularly like it. One reason is that it conveys the notion that evidences and proofs are quite secondary. This may be true, for example, in Gordon Clark's thinking, but not for Van Til. The *pre* in *presuppositionalism* is not meant to be temporal. Nor is it meant to indicate a hypothesis. Rather, it indicates preeminence.[55] Another reason is that the history of the concept of presuppositions is tied to views that are quite foreign to what Van Til is trying to do. For example, the term is often synonymous with a priori reasoning, which is based on knowledge not derived from experience. From the ancient Greeks to Immanuel Kant and

52. *DKG*, 45ff.
53. Ibid., 45n43, 125.
54. *AGG*, 6.
55. Ibid., 12n16.

then later idealists, and even in their distinctive way, the existentialists, many philosophers have stated that we must begin somewhere outside of empirical facts. But although at points Van Til overlaps with a priori reasoning, his use of the concept of presuppositions is more inclusive, meant to convey that we begin with revelation, which can reach us both from outside and from experience and even empirical observation.[56] In expressing such caution, John is not alone. Most of us who stand in this tradition would rather find a different term, although few candidates are any better.

Many things could be said about the place of presuppositions in John's apologetics. In *AGG* he likens a Christian presupposition to a commitment to the lordship of Christ.[57] In keeping with the meaning of *Lord*, we begin (and end) everything with faith in Christ, the covenant head, the one who rules over all things. "Our Lord's demand upon us is comprehensive. In all that we do, we must seek to please him. No area of human life is neutral."[58] If this is right, who would not be a presuppositionalist? The problem is not the ultimate commitment, shared in one way or another by all Christians, but in the method of argumentation. Oftentimes opponents of presuppositionalism bring the charge of fideism, the idea that centering everything on Christ's lordship allows no reasoning, no proofs, no evidence, etc. They maintain that unless some degree of neutrality, or shared territory, be admitted, logic and proof are impossible. Although it's an old discussion, the last few decades have seen it come to more of a head.

Some of the possible misunderstandings of presuppositional apologetics may indeed be semantic. Thus, for various critics of the school, the term is said to be equivalent to a "supposition," or even an "assumption." As such it appears almost arbitrary or subjective. Perhaps in a postmodern setting that could be a good thing, some suggest. But such a view has little to do with mainstream presuppositional apologetics. Rather, a presupposition is a sort of *pre-judgment*, a scale of values that is ultimate, whether held by a believer or an unbeliever. As John puts it, a presupposition is a "basic heart commitment." For the Christian, it is "veridical knowledge," that is, looking upward to an ultimate, to use Mark Hanna's language. Again, we are not really talking of a "starting point" but of a faith-commitment.[59] Thus,

56. *CVT*, 131ff.
57. *AGG*, 3–9.
58. Ibid., 7.
59. Ibid., 125–26; see also *CVT*, 137–38.

for non-Christians, a presupposition is still a heart commitment but to the wrong thing—to an idol.[60] As such it is a substitute for believing the true God: "When people forsake the true God, they come under bondage to idols. When they reject the true standard, they adopt a false one."[61]

THE LIGONIER CONNECTION

In various writings, then, John spends considerable time defending presuppositionalism against the classical method, the so-called traditional approach, held by such stalwarts as Thomas Aquinas and (as he believes) by the majority of apologists in our own time. One debate that has framed the discussion is between John and the "Ligonier Apologetic," that is, the work of R. C. Sproul and his colleagues. In addition to various oral exchanges, a memorable twenty-page review of *Classical Apologetics* appeared in the *Westminster Theological Journal* in 1985. The book was meant to be a thoughtful critique of presuppositional apologetics, particularly Van Til's version of it, by three prominent theologians, R. C. Sproul, Art Lindsley, and John Gerstner. In a way, John's appraisal was much more than a review. It really was a manifesto for the presuppositionalist position, using this book as a kind of foil. Even if in retrospect it was something of a work in progress, as John has slightly nuanced his views since, still, as he says in the reprint in *AGG*, it speaks for him in his defense against rival approaches.[62]

At the heart of his critique of the three "Ligonier" authors is whether one must *think* about God before one can *know* him. The Ligonier authors assume we need some sort of objective standard for evaluating God's existence before we can truly know God, presumably a standard that does not begin blindly with God's authority. The three authors claim that Van Til abandons rational arguments, proofs, and evidences, and thus is guilty of the charge of fideism. They are particularly troubled by what appears to be his narrow circular argument: one cannot prove God without presupposing

---

60. *AGG*, 136.

61. Ibid., 195.

62. John M. Frame, "Van Til and the Ligonier Apologetic," *WTJ* 47, 2 (1985): 279–99; in the *AGG* reprint, to which I will refer in this article, he says, "Since writing this review, I have become a bit more favorable to the use of probability in apologetics [thus differing both with Van Til and with the Ligonier version of the tradition], and have become a bit more guarded in my defense of circularity" (219–43).

416

him. We have here, of course, one of the recurrent themes in the evaluation of presuppositional apologetics.

In the review and elsewhere, John explains that there is no other way to defend ultimate truth than appropriately to refer to it. First, because there is no one who is in any meaningful sense outside of the criteria by which they know that God is true (Romans 1 says unbelievers suppress that knowledge, but they possess it nevertheless). And second, because there is no alternative to a certain kind of circularity for anyone arguing for ultimate truth. Unbelievers, as anyone else, have some sort of ultimate standard by which they must judge all things. For example, if one believes money is everything, then there can be nothing to disprove that. Marriage? It is an investment. Love? It is a contract. But then John goes much deeper and shows that not all circles are the same. There are narrow, useless circles, such as, "He is deaf because of an impediment in his hearing." And there are broader, persuasive circles, such as, "The Bible is the Word of God based on its own self-witness, on Jesus' views, on its inspired claims, etc." Still circular, but not a *bare* circle. So, for example, in appealing to the many witnesses of the resurrection (1 Cor. 15:6), classical or evidentialist apologists will argue that we have facts and eyewitnesses proving on neutral grounds that Jesus rose from the dead. To which John replies, yes, but such a proof can work only according to biblical standards of attestation. Otherwise, as it was the case for David Hume, how do we know that for such a miracle we do not simply have a case of psychological associations on the mass level?[63]

I could wish a bit more had been said. Perhaps at least two areas could have been further explored. The first is that the reason logic, proofs, evidences, and the like can succeed, albeit within the circle, is because of the reality of creation. God made the world such that human beings are to live in it, make discoveries about it, verify certain views, all to the end of honoring God. Unlike Islam, which posits a constant authoritarian revelation in the Arabic language, the Christian faith requires exploration, trial and error, the testing of one view over against another. This is why so often we are told to "prove all things," or to discern God's will by "testing" it (1 Thess. 5:21; Rom. 12:2). An appeal to such discovery-by-trial is in no way a denial of ultimate circularity, but it takes away the intellectualism of "it is true because it is true"—the sort of tautology presuppositionalists are accused of believing.

63. *AGG*, 9–14; *DKG*, 130–33.

The second is to look more carefully at the difference between reasoning and argument. For example, when Van Til states that "all reasoning is, in the nature of the case, circular reasoning," he is not denying the need for careful argument.[64] In his felicitous notes to *The Defense of the Faith*, K. Scott Oliphint makes two clarifications. (1) Circular reasoning is not the same as circular argument. The fallacy known as *petitio principii* (begging the question) is a circular *argument* that assumes the conclusion within the premise. But proper circular *reasoning* is a necessity from the way things are. How else can one establish knowledge in one area without at the same time presupposing some knowledge in that area? We can never jump out of the world of revelation nor of our nature as God's image-bearers. (2) Van Til maintains that the best argument for the Christian faith is "indirect," rather than "direct."[65] That is, we can never go directly to the facts, because there must always be a context within which to place the facts. Whereas *petitio principii* is of necessity a direct argument, true circular reasoning is indirect, respecting the context of ultimate meaning, that is, being fully transcendental, for it to succeed.

At any rate, in his defense of Van Til over against the Ligonier apologetic, John asserts that Van Til's view is really quite simple, consisting of two themes: (1) everyone must presuppose God for their thinking, and (2) unbelievers resist such an obligation in their thought and life. This statement allows John both to agree and disagree with various portions of the Ligonier approach. For example, he finds substantial amounts of agreement between the two schools on the issue of the noetic effects of sin. The Ligonier authors insist that the ignorance of God taught in Romans 1 is not lack of information but a moral turning against clear evidence. Van Til agrees with this. Although the Ligonier authors believe Van Til thinks sin has destroyed any capacity to reason in the unbeliever, he holds no such position. Nor is he (and John, whom they cite) a *fideist*, thinking the way to arrive at faith is merely by the Holy Spirit's prompting, without the need for rational argument.[66]

One question this prompts, and John begins to deal with it, is "Why is Van Til so often misunderstood on this point?" In the book review, John suggests both the Ligonier folks and Van Til could have improved their arguments. Although Ligonier rightly insists that the kind of rebellion Romans 1

64. *DF*, 123.
65. Ibid., 123n8.
66. *AGG*, 230ff.

is teaching stems from a moral revolt, they appear to be unaware that our intellect itself can be affected by sin. By reducing any intellectual difficulty to "the moral problem," they do not sufficiently recognize that faulty reasoning is itself sinful. And they deny that all unbelievers are hostile to God, asserting that some are "seekers" who are merely dealing with the world around them. They accuse Van Til of denying any point of contact, which somehow ignores a large body of Van Til's distinctive contributions to apologetics.

The Paradox of Knowledge and Ignorance

At the same time, John wishes Van Til could have been clearer about how exactly sin affects the mind, as well as the moral self. Particularly, it would have been helpful if Van Til had said more about how exactly believers and unbelievers ("in spite of themselves") can hold areas of agreement, which he says they definitely do.[67] Of course, Van Til is not silent about the matter. Throughout his writings he stresses the difference between the regenerate and the unregenerate appropriation of reason. He argues that although metaphysically we have everything in common with unbelievers, *ethically* it is not so, and thus in its basic principle the unbeliever's view of reason is radically different from that of the Christian. His readers will remember the illustration of the buzz-saw. Meaning to cut fifty boards in order to build a floor, the carpenter sets the machine accordingly. But he leaves the room for a few minutes, and his son comes and changes the setting. The father returns, and starts the saw running. It cuts the wood perfectly, except that they are all slanted and useless because of the modified settings. Similarly, fallen creatures can and do use reason; their brains are quite capable of the mechanical operations involved. But because the "settings" are skewed through the fall, they get everything wrong. The brighter the person's intellect, the sharper will be his critique of the Christian position. The saw is as good as they get, but the numbers are wrong, and so the best the unbeliever can do is have a formal understanding of the way things are.[68]

John develops what might be the points of tension in the unbeliever's consciousness between true and false knowledge in a remarkable passage in *DKG*.[69] John compares the unbeliever's and the believer's knowledge in order

67. Ibid., 236.
68. *DF*, 97ff. See also 147, 290–94, 300–306.
69. *DKG*, 49–61.

to answer the questions, "How can the unbeliever know God at all? How can an unbeliever have both the knowledge and the ignorance portrayed in Scripture, and how does that affect his or her consciousness?" First, he looks at the similarities. They are such things as that God is knowable, though not exhaustively so. As such, it is covenant knowledge, in John's terms, involving all three perspectives: control, authority, and presence. He also insists the unbeliever's knowledge is not just *about* God but is knowledge of God himself (Rom. 1:21). This point is often missed or at least undervalued by critics of presuppositional apologetics. I dare say even certain presuppositionalists share a reticence to underscore the full measure of the unbeliever's knowledge. For example, Jim S. Halsey, in his *For Such a Time as This*, thinks the unbeliever's knowledge is only potential, that is, he ought to know but he is unable to know.[70] Romans 1:20 uses far stronger language. We may wonder with John whether Van Til himself did not shy away from the fullest sense of the knowledge by unbelievers in Paul's argument. Or perhaps he was satisfied simply to observe the dynamic of knowledge-and-suppression outlined in Romans 1. But could he not have gone further? For example, γνόντες τὸν θεὸν (Rom. 1:21), using the aorist active participle, indicates the full and active knowledge of God possessed by unbelievers that makes them all the more without excuse for not honoring him as God.[71]

Second, John looks at the differences between the unbeliever's and the believer's knowledge. Although in every instance there is true knowledge, ultimately this knowledge does not result in redemption. On the obvious level, then, it is knowledge without saving grace, disobedient knowledge that does not result in redemptive blessing. Or, to put it in John's preferred way, true understanding has friendship with God, unbelief does not. But can one say that it is merely psychological knowledge, not epistemological? Or merely formal and not functional knowledge? Or intellectual and not ethical?

John wants to deny such distinctions.[72] Why does the term *psychological knowledge* mean that it can exclude real knowledge? How can there be formal knowledge without some content? Here, too, John revisits the Clark controversy, on which he elaborates in other places.[73] Here he faults

70. Ibid., 51. See Jim S. Halsey, *For Such a Time as This* (Nutley, NJ: Presbyterian and Reformed, 1976), 63.

71. In Greek, the aorist, when combined with a participle, signifies something set in motion beforehand but with continuing effect in the present.

72. *DKG*, 51–54.

73. See especially *CVT*, 97–113.

Gordon Clark for limiting faith to assent, and minimizing the element of trust, in other words, not taking seriously enough the psychological element of belief. Accordingly, Clark seems to go little further than to equate belief with accepting propositional truths. The will is involved as well for him, so that when one accepts a proposition wholeheartedly, one then acts upon it. But John faults him for missing the possibility of conflicting beliefs, of self-deception, and the like. Basically, in the absence of this psychology of unbelief, it becomes difficult to take the biblical data about the unbeliever's knowledge of God as seriously as one ought.

John ends this section with his own formulation, which involves ten distinctions within the unbeliever's knowledge. They are items such as knowing enough to be without excuse, lack of friendship, stupidity(!), fighting the truth, and reaching for an impossible goal. This latter point has implications for apologetics, since one of the basic moves in the presuppositional approach is "the impossibility of the contrary." Furthermore, John wrestles with the paradox of belief and unbelief at the same time, and concludes that the question "remains a very mysterious one."[74] Here also John agrees with the general Reformed view of the structure, or the logic, of unbelief. Represented in Herman Dooyeweerd and Francis Schaeffer, and finding particular expression in Cornelius Van Til, the pattern found in unbelief is a dilemma, the alternative of irrationalism and rationalism at the same time. Such a diagnosis may be one of the most original contributions of the Reformed apologetic in its Amsterdam formulation.

In his *Roots of Western Culture*, based on a series of newspaper articles he wrote after the Second World War, Herman Dooyeweerd traces the struggle for the Christian influence on civilization and the shape of its decline in the modern period.[75] Not unlike his distant mentor Guillaume Groen Van Prinsterer, Dooyeweerd believes there is a spiritual root behind every manifestation of cultural power. As he traces it, in the West there have been four basic "ground motives" in history. For the more Christian motive, he argues there is a triad—creation/fall/redemption. For the unbelieving motive, we have a "religious dialectic"—a dual theme held in an unholy tension. In contrast to the biblical ground motive, these attempt, unsuccess-

---

74. *DKG*, 59.

75. Herman Dooyeweerd, *Roots of Western Culture: Pagan, Secular, and Christian Options*, trans. John Kraay (Toronto: Wedge Publishing, 1979), originally published in *Nieuw Nederland*, August 1945–May 1948.

fully, to hold together a transcendent and an immanent principle. They are, in order, form/matter (Greece and Rome), nature/grace (medieval), and nature/freedom (modern).[76] Of interest is the way Francis Schaeffer drew on these categories, with slight variations in terminology, in *Escape from Reason*, his first published book.[77]

The view that unbelief is dualistic is well-described by John, both in *Doctrine of the Knowledge of God* and in *Cornelius Van Til: An Analysis of His Thought*. In *DKG* discussion of rationalism and irrationalism appear in several places.[78] Putting them together as "the logic of unbelief" can be found in a couple of places. One is at the conclusion of the section mentioned above, from chapter 1.[79] There he equates the "irrationalist alternative" with the view that there is no god at all, but only chance. And he equates "a kind of rationalism" with the deification of something earthly. He then argues that not only are both self-refuting, but in an uncanny way they are identical. To claim irrationalism one must somehow trust in reason. Yet an irrational universe is incompatible with any use of reason. To maintain rationalism one must hold to some kind of foundation. But what can it be, if not pure thought? And that is meaningless. As he puts it, "Rationalism gives us a perfect knowledge—of nothing. Irrationalism leaves us ignorant—of everything."[80]

Another important consideration, besides the unholy interdependence of the two, is their parasitical attachment to the truth. Irrationalism, for example, draws on certain realities, such as human finitude and God's incomprehensibility. At one level, then, both irrationalism and rationalism are contradictory to revelation. At another level, they echo certain truths. John has illustrated these relationships with his famous "Frame's frame."

If we look at the left half of the square as the Christian view, and the right one as the non-Christian view, we then have the following relationships:

Getting these relationships right gives us important insights into the nature of unbelief. Non-Christians are not extraterrestrials. They must live in the real world and cope with its realities. Although they will resist the truth, they will do it in ways that resemble it at many levels.

76. Ibid., 15ff.
77. Francis A. Schaeffer, *Escape from Reason* (Leicester: InterVarsity, 1968).
78. *DKG*, 109, 111, 114, 120, passim.
79. Ibid., 60–61.
80. Ibid., 61.

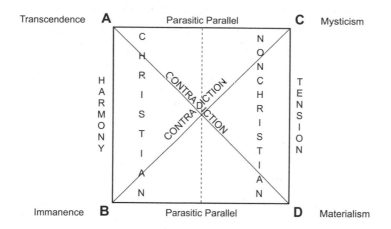

Fig. 18.1. The Square of Religious Opposition

- A-B True transcendence with true immanence.
- C-D Irrationalism and rationalism.
- A-D Contradiction: If God is transcendent, then rationalism cannot be true.
- B-C Contradiction: If God is immanent, then irrationalism cannot be true.
- A-C Parasitic parallel: Irrationalism is not utterly unlike transcendence.
- B-D Rationalism is not utterly unlike immanence.

Here I would like to refer the reader to a marvelous essay, "The Idol Factory," by L'Abri member Richard Keyes. This essay explores the relation between ancient and modern idolatries and argues they are quite similar.[81] He makes the same point John does: to speak of idolatry assumes there is a true God whom the idol counterfeits. Thus, "Idolatry may not involve explicit denials of God's existence or character. It may well come in the form of an over attachment to something that is, in itself, perfectly good."[82] Particularly, idols come in pairs. There is a principle that counterfeits *trust* and another that counterfeits *dominion*. Although we were meant to have proper dominion over God's creation, the idolater turns it into *domination*—an

81. Richard Keyes, "The Idol Factory," in Os Guinness and John Seel, eds., *No God But God: Breaking with the Idols of Our Age* (Chicago: Moody Press, 1992), 29–48.
82. Ibid., 33.

unhealthy attempt to control and manipulate people and surroundings, worshiping a nearby god. Although we were meant to engage in trusting God, we become instead *overdependent* on people or institutions, worshiping a faraway god. A perusal of Scripture shows how this was the case in the ancient world: Paul describes the little gods that had to be fed and the "Unknown God" of the people at the Areopagus (Acts 17:22–23). Today, we do the same. Think of the nearby idolatry of an obsessive collector or housecleaner. Think of the faraway idolatry of mysticism or the touting of vague love. This view is wonderfully complementary to John's (and the Reformed tradition's) understanding of how unbelief works. Keyes goes on to tell us what we may do in view of our idols. Repent, of course, but also come back to the true God, who can restore us to a healthy balance between dominion and trust.

As he describes unbelief, Keyes downplays the prevalence of atheism. It does exist but is rare, compared to various more blatant substitutes for God. Interestingly, in *Apologetics to the Glory of God*, John's description of unbelief centers on two types: atheism and idolatry.[83] I am not sure these categories cover the territory. Years ago in correspondence with John about this, he assured me that by *atheism* he meant something broader than militant denials of God, which, indeed, are somewhat rare. Atheism, though, is a major category for him. In *AGG* he credits Francis Schaeffer and the L'Abri group with critiquing atheistic relativism, as it works its way through art, music, philosophy, etc. Presumably he was weaker on idolatry. We may be dealing with shades here, rather than absolutes, but I am persuaded that Schaeffer, and his colleagues, particularly Hans Rookmaaker, were closer to identifying what Dick Keyes describes as the faraway and nearby gods than simply atheism leading to relativism. John argues that idolatry is less relativistic than atheism.[84] I wonder about this, too. In any case, for me idolatry is a more all-encompassing category, one that includes atheism. Pure atheism exists, but it is rare.

APOLOGETIC ARGUMENT

This brings us to perhaps the most important consideration of all. How does one actually proceed in an apologetic presentation? Here John makes

83. *AGG*, 193–202.
84. Ibid., 196.

a number of original contributions. He somewhat parts company with his mentor, Van Til, at least so it appears. In the chapters on "Apologetics as Proof" in *AGG*, John discusses the limits of a bare concept of proof, and voices a concern that although there is a certain manner in which to prove the Christian faith, one needs to hold that faith as a presupposition; if we are not careful, we will have airtight arguments that are not particularly persuasive. John considers the possibility of revising the concept of proof to include the unbeliever's response, but he does not finally go there, arguing that proofs for God abound but do not always persuade. So he then asks whether we should define proof as that which *ought* to persuade. This works better for him, but he worries about the inclusion in the definition of proof of a "narrowly circular type of argument," which is incompatible with biblically warranted reasoning.[85] There may be a semantic issue here. At the same time this discussion is critically important for those within Reformed apologetics who embrace the transcendental method.

Briefly stated, the transcendental argument says there must be more than sensory experience for something to be true. It states that unless a conclusion is true in itself, experience would be impossible. The argument owes its modern development to Immanuel Kant (1724–1804). Its opposite is realism. According to the realists, things in our experience are connected physically and send signals to the brain, which then proceeds to connect them correctly. But moving toward idealism, G. W. Leibniz (1646–1716) arrived at a radically different understanding of the universe, its contents, and the way we perceive things. According to his theory, known as Monadology, ordinary human perceptions of interactions between things in space and in time do not exist in the universe as such but originate in the mind of God. Kant, partly following Leibniz, but less overtly God-centered, developed the theory that our minds impose categories on experience. We do not perceive things-in-themselves. We recognize relations only because they have an ideal existence in our minds. He stressed that human knowledge is able to access the truth only because there are preconditions whereby anything has meaning. These preconditions are transcendental.

Cornelius Van Til studied the idealists at Princeton, during his doctoral work. Although he formulated arguments for absolutes in a vein similar to Kant, Van Til Christianized the procedure. Thus, unhappy with empiricism, he rejected evidentialist apologetics, without, of course, rejecting a proper

85. Ibid., 62–63.

presuppositional use of evidences, and adapted the form of the transcendental argument to use in defense of Christian theism. Without God, there can be no meaning, no grounds for predication. This is called "the impossibility of the contrary." Without presupposing the ontological Trinity, one has no basis for predication.

John is concerned with several matters. First, whether the transcendental argument is acceptable to unbelievers. As he puts it, "Although I agree that Van Til's premise that without God there is no meaning, I must grant that not everyone would immediately agree with that premise. How, then, is that premise to be proved?"[86] Second, it is not a given that traditional arguments for the existence of God, including the first cause, the intelligent designer, etc., do not point to the true God. John points out that God may be more than a first cause or a designer, but not less. A seeker may be quite persuaded by an argument for the first cause or an intelligent design. If so, why not stop there? If not, then a more fully transcendental approach might be needed.[87] According to John, the pure Van Tillian is committed to negative or indirect argument: without God, no meaning is possible. He thinks Van Til claimed that there is an absolutely certain argument for Christian theism. Accordingly, any argument that falls short of the circular, transcendental one is open to the charge of "blockhouse methodology," or the compromise of beginning with bare theism and only then moving on to something more biblical, such as the Trinity. John thinks such moves are not a necessary compromise with the gospel. As he puts it, the gospel may be more, but not less, than these assertions about God. He even believes that arguments from probability can be good ones, especially as they acknowledge mystery.[88] One of his major conclusions is that there is less distance between presuppositional argument and the traditional ones that apparently Van Til deplores.[89]

I do wonder whether, in part, we are dealing with semantics here. I am not sure that Van Til at his best did not agree that arguments beyond the circular one of "God exists because he exists" are not helpful. To be sure, there are occasions when he seemed to dismiss anyone short of a fully robust transcendentalism, and could sound as though he was in a shouting match. In a famous article by John Warwick Montgomery, he was accused of

86. Ibid., 71.
87. Ibid., 71–77.
88. Ibid., 80–82.
89. Ibid., 85–88.

simply engaging a nonbeliever in a series of claims and counterclaims. Van Til responds in an interesting way. He basically calls to mind neoorthodoxy and tells Montgomery he is glad neither of them are fideists![90] Still, it may be asked whether Van Til did not overreact to some of the broader kinds of arguments used by people basically in his camp.

I have always been a bit saddened by this tendency in Van Til. He consequently deprived himself of the insights and contributions of extraordinary cobelligerents, such as C. S. Lewis and Francis A. Schaeffer. He caught Schaeffer on some careless views of proof, of inconsistency, and the like, but he rather missed the overall thrust in the L'Abri approach, which was very close to his own, namely, getting on to the ground of the unbelieving position in order to demonstrate how, on its own terms, it is not possible to be consistent or to live successfully outside of acknowledging God's reality.[91] Van Til was not always skilled in actually applying this approach in conversations. I attended a meeting at Harvard where Van Til was the main speaker, and although he gave a marvelous lecture on the gospel, during the question-and-answer period he seemed awkward with students. To one of them he said, "I guess we will have to wait until the judgment to find out who is right."

But I do not think this is Van Til at his best. I believe he would fully admit that arguments of all kinds still fit under the rubric of the transcendental approach. His chief concern has always been to counter the non-Christian view that claims we have no basis to know in advance where our arguments may lead us. To that Van Til answers that we do know, because the gospel is true. But that does not mean that all arguments for Christian theism short of a sort of "repeat-after-me" narrow circle are ruled out. His fundamental burden is to show that a *consistent* use of non-Christian arguments can lead only to unbelief. But no one really is consistent. In anticipation of objections to his position, he raises the question: "Do you mean to assert that non-Christians do not discover truth by the methods they employ? The reply is that we mean nothing so absurd as that."[92] Non-Christians arrive at all kinds of true things. So do less-than-transcendental arguments. But it is all a question of context. Because we are in God's universe, lots of arguments

---

90. John Warwick Montgomery, "Once Upon an A Priori," in E. R. Geehan, ed., *Jerusalem and Athens* (Nutley, NJ: Presbyterian and Reformed, 1971), 380–92. Van Til's response is at 392–403.
91. See my article, "Two Christian Warriors," *WTJ* 57, 1 (Spring 1995): 57–80.
92. *DF*, 125.

work. Some work using borrowed capital; others work because there are so many different kinds of voices whereby the heavens declare the glory of God. Van Til's concern is to maintain that ultimately, without the presupposition of Christian theism, it is not possible to arrive at a basis for predication. But there are other concerns he did not voice as clearly. There is more caution than exploration in the master presuppositionalist.

So in fairness we may say that Van Til did not spend much time looking at various types of arguments for the gospel, at least in order to find in them valid ways to persuade people. He spent most of his time showing how, without the proper underlying framework, no account of meaning and value is possible. That is perfectly good in itself. John, on the other hand, does try to elaborate a number of actual arguments. He presents a dialogue with an unbelieving friend in order to show us how a conversation might be conducted.[93] I find this commendable. He even revisits the classical proofs—the teleological, cosmological, and ontological arguments—and finds much value in them. John would be the first to recognize the careless way some traditional apologists have failed to recognize presuppositions in their methods. However, John is somewhat "ecumenical"; he has opened a door for incorporating some of the marvelous insights of apologists who are not always strictly aware of the technicalities of a fully transcendental approach. And, to reiterate, it is my own conviction that the transcendental argument makes room for these "broader" approaches.

THE PROBLEM OF EVIL

Of particular interest for apologetics is John's work on the problem of evil. In addition to the two splendid chapters on the problem of evil in *AGG*, he has treated the question in a number of places. The fullest discussion, in view of defending the faith, is in *AGG*. The most robust doctrinal discussion is in *DG*. The most succinct formulation of his views is in *NOG*.[94]

To reminisce again, the very first course I took from John was titled "Aseity." The material included large numbers of scriptural references to God's immovability, his immensity, his omnipotence. Along the way, John discussed the issue of the origins and nature of evil. It was clear way back then that John was deeply sensitive to the questions of appar-

93. *AGG*, 203–17.
94. Ibid., 89–190; *DG*, 160–82; *NOG*, 134–41.

ent injustice. In addition to his theological astuteness, he showed what a pastoral heart he has.

John's sensitivity to the problem of evil is displayed in a fully mature way in the *AGG* chapters on this subject. Tellingly, he opens with a friendly critique of Jay Adams, whom he faults for having a neat, open-and-closed answer to the existence of evil: it is there to display the power of God.[95] Without denying this possibility, John pleads for more compassion and for the recognition of mystery. He cites horrendous cases of suffering children, the Holocaust, and above all the biblical authors who cry out, "Why, O Lord?"

Then, in somewhat typical fashion, he proceeds to describe succinctly yet clearly some of the representative answers to the problem. They include evil as unreal, God as weak, optimism (Leibniz), the free-will defense, character-building, stable-environment (C. S. Lewis), indirect cause, and several others. Of particular interest is his treatment of the free-will defense. From Augustine to Plantinga, and including a host of Arminian thinkers, this view may be the most popular today among evangelicals. In *AGG*, John reviews the basic grounds of the true nature of human freedom. He argues for his view more elaborately in *DG*,[96] where he describes freedom as non-compulsion or self-directed actions. When we choose, whether it be good or evil, we do so without the compulsion of an outside force. God himself does not *make* us do evil, even though in a sense he ordains everything, including our choices. Freedom means responsibility, not simply ability. In *DG*, John engages in a subtle and rich discussion of the question of ability. Although we cannot not sin (because of our evil nature), we still are accountable for wrong choices. Finally, John presents Jesus Christ as the answer for how God may be both good and all-powerful in the face of evil. Jesus comes to suffer and die in order that evil may be overcome.

Touchingly, John invites us to admire the heroes of the faith who are listed in Hebrews 11, because they suffered and endured, without the full revelation of the coming of Christ.[97] He also looks to the future and invites us to listen to the "Scripture songs" recorded in Revelation (15:3–4; 16:5–7; 19:1–2). In them, God is praised not only for his power but also for his justice. As John puts it, "At any rate, we may be assured that in the last day there will be no problem of evil. There will be no more doubt, no more

95. *AGG*, 151.
96. *DG*, 119–59.
97. *AGG*, 184.

complaint. If there is a residual theoretical problem, it will be one which we will be completely happy with. And if we believe now that that day will certainly come, can we not be content in the present?"[98] What strikes me, again, here, is that although John certainly knows much of the literature, he does not interact with it very much. Instead, he gives a strongly pastoral appeal, one that aims, with compassion, at the need for a heart of gratitude—a new heart that is willing to trust God.

Conclusions

No single person can do everything, even over a long and productive career. John has not engaged extensively in every area that apologetics is concerned about. He does very little with cultural critique, for example. He does, though, more than many presuppositionalists, explore various arguments that could be developed in conversations with real, live unbelievers. Having said that, he has delivered enormous contributions that will assure him a lasting influence.

The two most significant for me are his ability to translate large, complex issues into everyday theology. His style is lucid, personal, and almost conversational. This is quite unusual in theological circles. It is as though he made friends with you first and then took you down the path to rich theological considerations. Most of all, however, his accomplishments in apologetics have served as a wonderful reminder of how God has provided all we need to know in revelation. The Scripture is the basis for every endeavor. Believing as he does that apologetics is Scripture applied to unbelief, he has served the church immeasurably by providing a biblical framework for both the justification and the practice of Christian apologetics. Well done, John, and may you have many more years of fruitful ministry for the glory of God.

98. Ibid., 189.

19

PRESUPPOSITIONALISM AND FRAME'S EPISTEMOLOGY

JAMES N. ANDERSON

AS "LIGHT-BULB" MOMENTS GO, it was one of the more memorable in my life. I was standing in a Christian bookstore, perusing (as was my habit) the various items on the shelves labeled "Apologetics." One book suddenly caught my eye, not because of its cover design—eye-catching though it was—but because of its title: *Apologetics to the Glory of God*. Apologetics . . . *to the glory of God*? For several years I had taken a keen interest in Christian apologetics, devouring stacks of books on the subject. But until that moment I'd always thought of apologetics as having two purposes: first, to protect my personal faith against the hostile intellectual environment of a secular university, and second, to save me from looking like a credulous buffoon in the face of my unbelieving peers, in the hope that they might actually take the Christian faith seriously. Never before had I considered the idea that the overarching purpose of apologetics was to bring glory to almighty God. The very title of the book—never mind its contents, which I later digested with delight—had triggered a "Copernican Revolution" in my understanding not only of apologetics but of *every* intellectual pursuit. My modest hope is that this essay will serve as a fitting tribute to the author of that book, John M. Frame, who first roused me from my anthropocentric slumbers.

In what follows I will try to accomplish a number of things. First, I will describe the basic contours of Frame's epistemology, focusing on its two most distinctive elements: its emphasis on divine lordship and its triperspectival methodology. I will then explore the relevance of Frame's work to issues in "mainstream" analytical epistemology. Turning to matters of apologetics, I will discuss how Frame's epistemology undergirds his commitment to the Van Tillian school of presuppositionalism, before finally showing how Frame's triperspectivalism can be fruitfully applied in a presuppositional critique of one influential anti-Christian worldview.

AN EPISTEMOLOGY OF DIVINE LORDSHIP

The axis on which Frame's epistemology turns is undoubtedly the concept of divine lordship. One hardly need crack open the covers of *The Doctrine of the Knowledge of God* to detect this emphasis, since it is indicated both by the book's title (how many epistemology textbooks have the word *God* on their spines?) and by the name of the series of which *DKG* is the first volume: A Theology of Lordship. Significantly, what Frame presents to us is not so much a *theory* of knowledge as a *theology* of knowledge.[1]

One thus discovers immediately that Frame's epistemology isn't a theory of knowledge in the familiar sense. Traditional epistemology has focused on the concept of knowledge itself and a cluster of closely related concepts: belief, perception, justification, rationality, truth, and the like. Epistemologists typically ask questions such as: What do we mean when we speak about *knowledge*? What counts as knowledge? What is the structure of knowledge? What do we know, and what can we know? Do we in fact know anything at all? Questions such as these naturally arise for inquisitive human beings who take time to critically reflect on what they normally take for granted about themselves and the world they inhabit. The agenda for traditional epistemology is driven largely by human curiosity and self-reflection.

There's nothing intrinsically wrong with such an agenda, to be sure, but Frame's approach is self-consciously different. He approaches the topic of epistemology from the perspective of a Christian theologian already

---

1. "Though my book is, I trust, philosophically informed, it is probably more like theology than philosophy, as those terms are usually understood." *DKG*, 385. Indeed, *DKG* is not intended merely as a theological exposition, but "as a sermon." Ibid. Perhaps it would be more realistic to see *DKG* (over four hundred pages in length) as a sermon *series*!

committed to the ultimate authority and illuminating power of God's Word with respect to every aspect of human life, and thus his agenda is driven by this overarching question: What does God's Word teach us about our knowledge?[2] This is not to say that Frame is uninterested in the sorts of questions addressed by traditional epistemology, still less that he wants to evade them. On the contrary, *DKG* addresses many of these questions either directly or indirectly.[3] The point is simply this: Frame has his own priorities. *DKG* is an extended discussion of human knowledge for which the distinctive concerns and emphases of Scripture are to set the agenda.[4]

It isn't hard to see, viewed in this light, why the notion of divine lordship plays such a foundational and pervasive role in Frame's exposition. Beyond question, the primary subject matter of Scripture is *God*. And in Frame's studied judgment, the most prominent way in which Scripture presents God is as "the Lord."[5] It therefore follows that any discussion of human knowledge from a biblical perspective must be firmly tethered to a robust doctrine of divine lordship.

It comes as no surprise, then, to find the opening chapter of *DKG* laying the foundations with a discussion of the biblical concept of lordship. In the first place, lordship is a "covenantal concept."[6] God relates to human beings by way of covenants, and in every instance God is the covenant head.[7] God alone is the author, initiator, and governor of every divine-human covenant as to its participants, its conditions, and its consequences. God relates to us in this manner because he is at once absolutely sovereign and wholly gracious. At this point in the discussion, Frame spells out some implications for our understanding of *divine transcendence* and *divine immanence*.[8] The biblical notion of covenant lordship places certain constraints on our explication of

---

2. In contrasting *DKG* with the writings of the Reformed epistemologists (Alvin Plantinga, Nicholas Wolterstorff, William Alston, et al.), Frame declares, "I am expounding God's authoritative Word as I understand it to bear on epistemological questions." *DKG*, 384–85.

3. See, e.g., Frame's explanation of *DKG*'s structure and topics: ibid., 4–5.

4. This observation likely explains the dissatisfaction expressed by some Christian philosophers with Frame's writings on epistemology. The problem arises in part because of a failure to recognize that Frame's agenda doesn't coincide with theirs (although there is still considerable overlap, as we will see).

5. For the biblical arguments on this point, see *DKG*, 11–18, and at greater length, *DG*, 21–35.

6. *DKG*, 12.

7. Ibid., 13.

8. Ibid., 13–15.

these two doctrines, which if neglected inevitably lead to serious distortions in our knowledge of God—and thus in our knowledge of everything else.

The twin attributes of transcendence and immanence are staples of Christian theology, although they are less commonly placed in an explicitly covenantal context. The terms themselves, however, are the inventions (or rather adoptions) of theologians and bear no straightforward relation to the ways in which Scripture teaches, on the one hand, that the Creator is "over" and "beyond" his creation, and on the other, that the Creator is "with" and "in" his creation. These technical terms can therefore lead us astray if not firmly moored in the biblical picture of God. Recognizing this hazard—the casualties of which are strewn across the battlegrounds of twentieth-century theology—Frame has made an innovative contribution: to re-express these two traditional attributes as the triad of *control, authority,* and *presence*.

God's *control* is his creation and determination of all things other than God. Not only does the Lord possess the power to overcome any possible obstacle, he is also the initiator of every event in creation (not least his covenants) such that all things proceed according to his good and wise plans.[9] God's *authority* consists in his absolute rights over everything that is not God. In the simplest terms: what God says, goes. So the Lord rightly requires unqualified loyalty and obedience from his creatures, not merely to uphold his glory but also for their ultimate good.

Frame contends that the dual concepts of *control* and *authority* track the biblical vocabulary more closely than the classical notion of transcendence. Yet these two "lordship attributes" must be balanced with a third: God's *presence*, which consists in his nearness to the creation, his intimate involvement with his creatures, and, most of all, his person-to-person relationship with his people. Only in terms such as these—and not, say, the mutual dependence and influence posited by process theologians—does Scripture portray the Lord as "immanent."[10]

9. As the Westminster Confession of Faith puts it: "God from all eternity, did, by the most wise and holy counsel of His own will, freely, and unchangeably ordain whatsoever comes to pass; yet so, as thereby neither is God the author of sin, nor is violence offered to the will of the creatures; nor is the liberty or contingency of second causes taken away, but rather established." WCF 3.1.

10. For further discussion of the lordship attributes, with close reference to scriptural texts, see *DG,* 36–115. (See also "Backgrounds to My Thought," in the present volume.) The story of modern theology is in large measure a tragedy premised on the failure to explicate and balance the doctrines of divine transcendence and divine immanence in ways that closely track God's self-revelation in Scripture. Perhaps some of the damage might have been avoided if an

This triad of lordship attributes is not only evident throughout Scripture, argues Frame, but also reflected in the very Trinitarian nature of God. God the Father is the one who, by his authority, sends the Son and the Spirit. God the Son is the one who, by his sovereign power, carries out the Father's authoritative will. God the Spirit is the one who, by his dwelling in and with God's people, manifests God's presence in the world.[11]

To know God, then, is to know him first and foremost as the *covenant Lord*, which in turn means recognizing his control, authority, and presence.[12] Yet this God is not merely the primary *object* of our knowledge; he is also the primary *context* of our knowledge. Only "in him" do we live and move and have our being (Acts 17:28). This living and moving must surely include the *epistemic* dimensions of human existence. Without God, human knowledge would be impossible in principle—a point to which we will return.

As one might expect, the biblical doctrine that God is the covenant Lord has numerous ramifications for the way we approach and answer epistemological questions. The main burden of *DKG* is to identify those ramifications and draw out their application to our manifold intellectual endeavors as God's creatures. Frame asks: What does it mean in practice to know God, ourselves, and the world, recognizing that we are *within God's control, under God's authority*, and *in God's presence*?

My purpose in this opening section has been to locate the beating heart of Frame's epistemology so as to set the stage for what I say later on. But one particularly significant implication cannot pass without comment at this point. This is the principle—given great emphasis by Frame's mentor, Cornelius Van Til—that human thought is not autonomous; that is to say, it is not a law unto itself. The ultimate norms for human knowledge are found not in any human mind or minds, or anywhere else in creation, but in the mind of God. As creatures made in the image of God, and subject to his

---

understanding of God's "immanence" had been drawn more closely from a Hebrew etymology (*Immanuel*: "God with us") than from a Latin one (*in manere*: "to remain or dwell in").

11. This is not to say that each person of the Trinity reflects only one of the lordship attributes—a claim that would be anti-Trinitarian to the core. Frame's point, rather, is that distinctive roles of the persons, as revealed in redemptive history, broadly correspond in emphasis with the lordship triad. See *DG*, 727–28. See also *PP*, http://www.frame-poythress.org/frame_articles/2008Primer.htm (accessed May 14, 2009); "Backgrounds to My Thought."

12. I have often been tempted to think of Frame's lordship attributes as God's *might* (control), God's *right* (authority), and God's *light* (presence—cf. Pss. 18:28; 36:9; 56:13; 89:15; 90:8; 118:27; Rev. 22:5). Neat though it may be, it probably runs the risk of sacrificing conceptual precision at the altar of aesthetics!

lordship, we are obligated to pattern our own thinking after God's thinking—insofar as he has revealed it to us. As Van Tillians are fond of putting it, we are designed "to think God's thoughts after him." Indeed, to attempt to think in any other manner is not only sinful, but insanely self-destructive.[13] We must therefore strive in every area of knowledge to observe and conform ourselves to God's revelation, both in nature and in Scripture.[14]

Put this way, it's hard to see why any Christian would find this principle objectionable. It is a straightforward consequence of the biblical presentation of the Creator-creature relationship. Yet it's remarkable how rarely the principle is acknowledged and applied when Christians reflect on the various intellectual disciplines in which they participate: whether science, politics, economics, philosophy, history, arts, sociology, or psychology, to name but a handful. It isn't merely *theologians* (in the "professional" sense) who must seek the counsel of God in his Word and submit all their thoughts to it. Indeed, it isn't merely *Christians* who must do so; to say otherwise would be to reduce Yahweh to a provincial deity rather than the Lord of all creation. The fact that so many believers assume that Scripture has precious little to teach us about science, politics, economics, and all the rest reveals that we have failed to reflect in any depth on what Scripture has to say about human knowledge *in general*. A careful reading of *DKG* would be a first stride toward remedying that neglect.

A TRIPERSPECTIVAL EPISTEMOLOGY

If an overarching emphasis on divine lordship is the primary distinctive of Frame's epistemology, a close second must be its "triperspectival" approach to analysis. According to Frame, a balanced study of human knowledge requires that we consider it from three distinct yet complementary perspectives: the *normative*, the *situational*, and the *existential*. In order to understand the rationale for this claim, however, it will be important to first say a word or two about perspectivalism in general.

Framean perspectivalism is characterized by two core claims: (1) at any one time, each of us has only a partial and limited perspective on any subject

13. Cf. Rom. 1:18–32; 1 Cor. 2:14–16; Eph. 4:17–19.
14. This raises the question—which cannot be treated here—whether our understanding of Scripture should take priority over our understanding of nature (and in what respects). For Frame's thoughts on this, see *DKG*, 137–38; *AGG*, 23.

matter; and (2) in order to best understand any subject matter, we need to consider it from multiple perspectives. The first claim follows from the simple observation that we are not God. We are finite and not omniscient, and therefore our apprehension of any object of knowledge is inevitably "limited to one perspective or another."[15] The second claim is a natural extension of the first: given our perspectival limitations, it follows that our understanding of any subject matter can be developed and enhanced by considering it from alternative perspectives. This can be accomplished in a number of ways: for example, by shifting our point of view, either physically or conceptually; by reordering or reorganizing our data; by considering different emphases or "entry points"; and by consulting with others and allowing their insights to complement our own.[16]

Perhaps the most helpful analogy here is the geometrical one. Given that we are stereo-optical creatures restricted to one point of view in time and space, we lack the capacity to see every part of a three-dimensional object at once, particularly if it is large and complex. For example, suppose I visit a house to assess it as a potential purchase. Clearly, it is not possible for me to view the front, back, and sides of the house simultaneously. I need to change my vantage point—my *perspective*—to gain a fuller understanding of the house. Likewise, I cannot see the entire house all at once in fine detail. I can first stand back and take a wide view, but then I need to step up close and scrutinize individual features. Exterior and interior views give me further perspectives and enhance my knowledge. I may also decide to visit the property again in different weather or lighting conditions. Finally, it will be prudent of me to invite other people to view the house, so that I can benefit from their additional perspectives.

Our spatiotemporal limitations are but one aspect of our finitude. Frame's basic point is that what goes for geometrical perspectives goes for other kinds of conceptual perspectives too. The geometrical analogy also makes it clear that the charge of relativism, occasionally leveled at Framean perspectivalism by its critics, is quite misguided. It doesn't follow, from the fact that a house appears differently to five people standing in various loca-

15. *PP.*

16. One example of the fruitfulness of multiple perspectives can be found in Edward de Bono's best seller, *Six Thinking Hats* (Boston: Little, Brown and Co., 1985). This footnote seems as good a place as any to mention that in writing this essay I have benefited from the additional perspectives of Steve Hays, Paul Manata, Steve Scrivener, and John Frame, who were kind enough to send me critical comments on an earlier draft.

tions, that the house *as such* is different for each person or that there are no objective truths about the house. The critics thus conflate *relativism* and *relativity*; the former is self-defeating nonsense, whereas the latter ought to be self-evident common sense. In any case, Frame is careful to point out that the very *basis* for objectivity is the existence and self-revelation of an absolute God.[17] Since God's knowledge is comprehensive and determinative, it is *constitutive* of objectivity for humans. Our multiple, finite perspectives are like small windows onto God's unified, consistent, all-encompassing perspective on reality. This observation, we might say, is a further perspective on "thinking God's thoughts after him."[18] What's more, it suggests a distinctively Christian theistic alternative to the autonomous pretensions of both modernist epistemologies (which hold that pure objectivity is both attainable and desirable) and postmodernist epistemologies (which hold that no degree of objectivity is either attainable or desirable).

So much for perspectivalism as a general thesis. Frame, however, is convinced that many important perspectives occur in *triads*.[19] We have already considered his triperspectival analysis of divine lordship: control, authority, and presence. Throughout *DKG* we also find represented Frame's triperspectival analysis of human knowledge.[20] First, the *normative* perspective considers the norms for human intellectual activity: the standards, laws, principles, and criteria that apply to our truth-gathering and truth-utilizing. Second, the *situational* perspective considers the situation or circumstances in which the human knower is placed. In particular, it concerns the external objects or matters of fact toward which human thoughts are directed. Finally, as a necessary complement to these two outward-oriented perspectives, the *existential* perspective considers the subjective, internal, personal aspects of human knowledge. Note that the ordering of the perspectives here (as in Frame's own writings) is incidental. No one perspective is more important than any other or reducible to any other. Each perspective must be considered in conjunction with the other

17. See *PP*.
18. Thus Frame's "perspectival knowledge" roughly corresponds to what Van Til dubbed "analogical knowledge." See Cornelius Van Til, *An Introduction to Systematic Theology* (Nutley, NJ: Presbyterian and Reformed, 1974), 11–13; *The Defense of the Faith*, 3rd ed. (Philadelphia: Presbyterian and Reformed, 1967), 39–46; *CVT*, 89–95.
19. See, e.g., *DG*, 743–50; also *PP*.
20. *DKG*, 73–75. *DKG*'s entire structure is designed to reflect this triad. Ibid., 4–5, 107.

two; together they furnish us with a balanced and unified understanding (recall the earlier house-viewing analogy).[21]

On what basis does Frame identify and distinguish these three perspectives on knowledge? It turns out that Frame sees multiple lines of support for triperspectivalism in epistemology.[22] First, there is the classical distinction between the *subject* of knowledge (that which knows), the *object* of knowledge (that which is known), and the *relation* of knowledge (that by which the knower knows the known). These can be seen to correspond directly to the existential, situational, and normative perspectives.[23] Second, triperspectivalism is reflected in the distinctions between the three basic sources and objects of human knowledge: knowledge from and about *God* (the Creator), knowledge from and about *nature* (the created external world), and knowledge from and about *self* (the created internal world).[24]

As a further consideration, Frame points to parallels between epistemology and ethics; in fact, he argues that epistemology can be profitably viewed "as a subdivision of ethics, describing our obligations in the realm of knowledge."[25] His three perspectives arise in various places in ethics— for example, in the distinction between the *standard* (normative), the *goal*

---

21. At times Frame makes remarks about each perspective's "including" the other two that seem to erode their distinctiveness. One example, from his discussion of the role of the will in knowledge: "Which of our three perspectives does it fall under? Well, it doesn't much matter, since each perspective includes the others." *DKG*, 344; cf. ibid., 243. In another passage he makes the confusing claim that the knowledge gained through each perspective is "ultimately identical." Ibid., 89. Cf. *DG*, 213; *DCL*, 35. Perhaps this tension can be resolved by following Gottlob Frege's distinction between *sense* and *referent*. "Clark Kent," "Superman," and "the last survivor of the planet Krypton" have distinct senses but identical referents. Indeed, there is a sense (!) in which a sense is one perspective on a referent.

22. Frame does not appear to give any priority to these considerations, and none should be inferred from the order in which I discuss them.

23. The normativity of the knowledge relation is seen in the fact that the subject and the object must be related *in the right way* for there to be knowledge. Not just *any* subject-object relation will do. We will revisit this important point in the next section.

24. These distinctions give rise to nine different forms of source-object knowledge: knowledge from God about God; knowledge from God about nature; knowledge from God about self; knowledge from nature about God; and so on. As Frame explains in "Backgrounds to My Thought" and elsewhere, this particular triad is inspired by Van Til's treatment of revelation in *Introduction to Systematic Theology*, 64–74. In *DKG*, Frame cashes out the triad in terms of "the law," "the world," and "the self." *DKG*, 65–73. Concerning the first of these, Frame argues that since all ultimate normativity derives from God, we can identify God with God's law (broadly conceived). "To know God is to know His law. . . . God's law then is God himself; God himself is law to His creation." Ibid., 63.

25. *DKG*, 62–64, 73–75. Cf. *AGG*, 102–4; *DCL*, 178n5.

(situational), and the *motive* (existential) for human actions, each of which must be taken into account when determining whether or not a particular action is "moral" or "good."[26] The need to maintain a triperspectival balance in ethics is further suggested by the three-sided war in the history of modern ethics, between the deontological (rule-based) camp, the utilitarian (outcome-based) camp, and the subjectivist (feelings-based) camp.[27] Insofar as epistemology mirrors ethics, then, the three perspectives will prove as illuminating for the former as for the latter.

Finally, the three perspectives can be correlated with Frame's triad of lordship attributes. God's *authority* provides the standards for human knowledge (God's law). God's *control* accounts for the existence of the orderly, knowable world in which we are situated; the facts are what they are by the outworking of God's sovereign decree. God's *presence* is manifested in his *first-personal* covenantal immanence (God with *us*).[28]

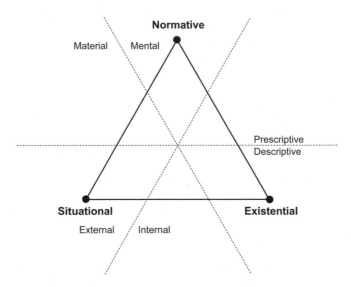

Fig. 19.1. Triperspectivalism and Common Philosophical Distinctions

It's hard to deny that Frame's triperspectival approach exhibits a certain appealing symmetry. In addition to the considerations above, we might note

26. *DCL*, 8. Cf. Cornelius Van Til, *Christian Theistic Ethics* (Nutley, NJ: Presbyterian and Reformed, 1971).

27. *DCL*, 49–53.

28. Cf. *PP*. I confess that I find this to be one of Frame's less evident correlations, but I have tried here to express it in the way that makes the best sense to me.

that the perspectives can be paired off (see Figure 1) in ways that correlate with some commonplace philosophical distinctions: between the prescriptive and the descriptive (cf. the fact-value distinction); between the "external world" and the "internal world"; and between the mental (or consciousness-dependent) and the material (or consciousness-independent). It seems, therefore, that Frame's triperspectivalism is a well-motivated analytical tool.

Triperspectivalism and "Mainstream" Epistemology

Frame's triperspectival methodology is certainly innovative and suggestive. But given that it was developed in an explicitly Christian context, we might wonder whether it has any relevance to "mainstream" epistemology. Can it illuminate any issues of concern to contemporary philosophers of knowledge? In this section, I want to highlight several areas that suggest further confirmation of the applicability and fruitfulness of triperspectival analysis.

Three Traditions in the History of Epistemology

In the first place, as Frame himself suggests, triperspectivalism offers a useful framework for understanding the history of epistemology and recognizing where many prominent theories of knowledge go wrong. One of the central questions asked by epistemologists is this: What serves as the basis or foundation for human knowledge? The history of answers to this question can be usefully divided into three traditions. The rationalist tradition answers in terms of *laws* and *criteria*: our knowledge is founded on certain indubitable first principles, such as the laws of logic and mathematics, and what can be rigorously deduced from them. The empiricist tradition, in contrast, puts emphasis on *facts* and *evidences*: our knowledge is founded on directly observable facts about the external world. The subjectivist tradition, a third contender, pitches its tent on the plain of *personal consciousness*: our knowledge is founded on what subjectively strikes each individual knower as true or credible. It isn't hard to see that each of these traditions takes one of Frame's three perspectives and absolutizes it at the expense of the others. But the ironic consequence is that all three traditions lead us into a dead end of debilitating skepticism. Rationalism furnishes us at best with abstract theoretical truths that are disconnected from our experience of the world. Empiricism undermines itself because it cannot justify its foundational assumption that our senses actually connect us to an external world of facts;

441

in the end, it reduces to solipsism. Subjectivism fares no better than its two competitors. In its purest form it collapses into relativism; thus the original question "What serves as the basis or foundation for human knowledge?" turns out to have no person-independent answer after all. The moral of the story is that any adequate account of knowledge must acknowledge and balance considerations from *all three perspectives*.[29]

The Tripartite Definition of *Knowledge*

A second confirmation of the relevance of Frame's triperspectivalism is suggested by the standard tripartite analysis of knowledge.[30] Until the 1960s, *knowledge* was commonly defined as "justified true belief," based on a surface analysis of the necessary and sufficient conditions for knowledge.[31] Consider first what is necessary for Sam to know some proposition—say, the proposition that the cat is on the mat. At a minimum, Sam must *believe* that the cat is on the mat, for it seems obvious that one cannot know what one doesn't even believe. Furthermore, Sam's belief that the cat is on the mat must be *true*; the cat must, as a matter of fact, be on the mat. It seems equally obvious that one can know only truths and not falsehoods. So already we can see that whatever knowledge is, it must involve *true belief*.

Yet surely not every true belief counts as knowledge. Suppose Sam has taken a hallucinogenic drug and experiences a vision of his cat, Felix, sitting on his front-door mat. Unable to distinguish between the vision and reality, he comes to *believe* that the cat is on the mat. At that very moment, however, it just so happens that Felix *is* sitting on the mat. Sam's belief would thus be *true*. But does Sam really *know* that his cat is on the mat? Our intuitive

29. Cf. *DKG*, 109–22. Frame is the first to acknowledge that no one figure in the history of philosophy represents any of these three traditions in an absolutely pure form. Even those who lean heavily toward one tradition (e.g., David Hume for the empiricist camp) typically end up tipping their hats to the other traditions in response to criticisms. But these concessions and qualifications only serve to confirm Frame's contention that we fall into problems when we privilege one perspective over the other two.

30. Here I focus on what is termed *propositional* knowledge: knowledge *that* such-and-such. It is distinguished from other kinds of knowledge, such as knowledge *of* such-and-such (immediate acquaintance) and "know-how." Contemporary epistemologists tend to focus most attention on propositional knowledge, mainly because the problem of refuting skepticism is typically expressed in terms of propositional knowledge.

31. This standard definition is sometimes traced back to remarks by Plato in the *Theaetetus* and the *Meno*. See, e.g., Paul K. Moser, "Tripartite Definition of Knowledge," in *A Companion to Epistemology*, ed. Jonathan Dancy and Ernest Sosa (Oxford: Blackwell Publishers, 1992), 509.

answer to the question is no. It follows that true belief is necessary but not sufficient for knowledge. Something else is needed: some third ingredient that bridges the gap between merely true belief and knowledge. What many epistemologists have wanted to say is that Sam's true belief must also be *justified*, where the justification in question is understood in terms of something like possession of sufficient evidential grounds. Put simply, Sam must also have good reasons or evidence to support his belief that the cat is on the mat. In this case, however, he lacks such reasons or evidence because his belief is held on the basis of a nonveridical hallucination.

Based on considerations such as these, the tripartite definition of *knowledge* as "justified true belief" has been widely endorsed. But note that each of the three components corresponds to one of Frame's three perspectives. *Justification* represents the normative component of knowledge. It shows that not just *any* true belief counts as knowledge; a true belief must meet certain standards or norms of reason before it can rise to the status of knowledge. *Truth* represents the situational component of knowledge. Knowledge necessarily involves a connection to the facts of the matter. We can't know what isn't factual; our knowledge must correspond to the way the world really is—to how it is situated. *Belief* represents the existential component of knowledge. Whereas truth is external and person-independent—postmodernist confusions notwithstanding—a belief is an internal mental state that constitutes a *personal* intellectual commitment on the part of the knower. So this standard analysis of knowledge consists of normative, situational, and existential components.

Readers familiar with contemporary epistemology will be aware, however, that the standard tripartite definition of *knowledge* has fallen on hard times. In 1963, a three-page journal article by Edmund Gettier sent shock waves through the philosophical community that still reverberate today.[32] Gettier offered several counterexamples to the standard definition: hypothetical scenarios in which a person has a justified true belief yet apparently lacks knowledge. It is widely conceded today (on the basis of a never-ending stream of "Gettier counterexamples") that justified true belief is *not* sufficient for knowledge after all.

Does this cast a shadow over Frame's triperspectival scheme? Actually, no. It remains relatively uncontroversial that knowledge requires both truth and belief and also that mere true belief is insufficient for knowledge. Knowledge must be true belief *plus* something else. Alvin Plantinga has proposed

32. Edmund L. Gettier, "Is Justified True Belief Knowledge?" *Analysis* 23 (1963): 121–23.

that the term *warrant* (rather than *justification*, which arguably carries too much prejudicial baggage) be used to refer to whatever it is that bridges the gap between mere true belief and knowledge. *Knowledge* can thus be generally defined as "warranted true belief," even while debate persists as to what constitutes warrant. Nevertheless, despite the continuing disagreement, it's reasonably clear that warrant must pertain to the normative dimension of knowledge. A true belief is warranted only if it is held in the right kind of way or on the right kind of grounds. *Warrant* is thus an evaluative category along with closely related terms such as *justification* and *rationality*. It is concerned with norms of belief-production, belief-retention, and belief-revision.

Knowledge and Proper Cognitive Function

In the aftermath of Gettier's controlled detonation, the focus in contemporary epistemology has largely shifted toward an analysis of epistemic warrant (as defined above). What are the necessary and sufficient conditions for warrant? Some epistemologists have argued that warrant is simply the classical notion of justification plus some additional (fourth) ingredient, such as "indefeasibility," crafted to plug the hole in the dike. Others have contended that justification is neither necessary nor sufficient for warrant; warrant is thus quite distinct from justification in the classical sense.

One of the most innovative and, in my judgment, persuasive accounts of warrant has been developed and defended by Plantinga. At the heart of his account is the notion of *proper cognitive function*: a belief is warranted only if it is produced by cognitive faculties that are functioning properly—that is, operating in the way they were designed to operate. Plantinga shows that most other recent accounts of warrant fall short because they overlook this aspect of proper cognitive function. For example, consider reliabilist accounts of warrant. According to reliabilism (in its simplest form), a belief is warranted only if it is formed through cognitive processes that are generally reliable, i.e., processes that produce predominantly true beliefs. The problem with such accounts, Plantinga argues, is that the cognitive processes in question could be reliable due to sheer dumb luck. If my beliefs happen to be true only by luck, by mere good fortune, then I cannot be said to *know* what I believe.[33]

---

33. Plantinga offers the hypothetical example of a man struck by a burst of cosmic rays that affect his cognitive function. After the incident, whenever the man hears the word *prime* he involuntarily forms a belief, with respect to a randomly selected natural number between 1 and 100,000, that it is not a prime number. Since most of the numbers in that range aren't primes, it

Plantinga summarizes his own proper-function account of warrant as follows:

> According to the central and paradigmatic core of our notion of warrant (so I say) a belief *B* has warrant for you if and only if (1) the cognitive faculties involved in the production of *B* are functioning properly (and this is to include the relevant defeater systems as well as those systems, if any, that provide *propositional* inputs to the system in question); (2) your cognitive environment is sufficiently similar to the one for which your cognitive faculties are designed; (3) the triple of the design plan governing the production of the belief in question involves, as purpose or function, the production of true beliefs (and the same goes for elements of the design plan governing the production of input beliefs to the system in question); and (4) the design plan is a good one: that is, there is a high statistical or objective probability that the belief produced in accordance with the relevant segment of the design plan in that sort of environment is true. Under the conditions, furthermore, the degree of warrant is given by some monotonically increasing function of the strength of S's belief that *B*. This account of warrant, therefore, depends essentially on the notion of proper function.[34]

The details of Plantinga's account, and the arguments by which he supports his analysis, need not concern us. All I wish to note here is that Plantinga's sophisticated post-Gettier analysis of warrant also reflects Frame's triperspectival scheme.[35] The normative perspective is found in the notion of *proper function*; a cognitive faculty can be said to function properly only if it proceeds according to certain design norms. The situational perspective is found in Plantinga's concept of a *cognitive environment*. Our cognitive faculties are designed to furnish us with true beliefs in specific environments (e.g., our perceptual faculties work optimally for medium-sized objects on the surface of this planet in adequate lighting conditions). This is just to say that we need to be situated in certain ways for our beliefs to be warranted.

---

turns out that the vast majority of these beliefs will be true, despite their strange provenance. So the cognitive process responsible for these beliefs is reliable, statistically speaking. But it ought to be evident that the true beliefs formed by such a process would not count as *knowledge*. Alvin Plantinga, *Warrant: The Current Debate* (Oxford: Oxford University Press, 1992), 210.

34. Alvin Plantinga, *Warrant and Proper Function* (Oxford: Oxford University Press, 1993), 194.

35. Since we have already identified warrant with the normative perspective on knowledge, it also illustrates Frame's contention that we often find triads within triads.

Finally, the existential perspective is found in Plantinga's suggestion that the *degree* to which a belief is warranted will depend (among other things) on the firmness or subjective confidence with which the belief is held.[36]

The fact that Frame's triad of normative, situational, and existential perspectives can be discerned here and elsewhere in "mainstream" epistemological discussions suggests that Frame is on to something important. In my view, triperspectivalism is rightly understood not as a theory of knowledge but rather as an analytical tool that can assist epistemologists in at least three ways: (1) as a guard against imbalance and omission in our analyses of knowledge and related concepts;[37] (2) as a means of obtaining greater insight into any topic under examination;[38] and (3) as a source of inspiration for new theories or methods.[39] Triperspectivalism should not be regarded as a competitor to contemporary epistemological theories (such as Plantinga's) but rather as one fruitful approach to developing, critiquing, and refining such theories.

DIVINE LORDSHIP: PRESUPPOSITIONALISM IN PRINCIPLE

Since I have been invited to write under the title "Presuppositionalism and Frame's Epistemology," it is time for me to shift gears and turn from Frame's epistemology to his work in apologetics. It comes as no surprise to find that there is a close relationship between the two; in what follows, I will try to explain how the former underwrites the latter.

Frame is commonly labeled a "presuppositionalist" because he endorses the apologetic vision of Cornelius Van Til.[40] Arguably, the term *presuppositionalist* is ill suited to capture what is distinctive about this

---

36. Ibid., 7–9, 194.

37. Many of the deficiencies found in theories of knowledge, both ancient and modern, can be understood as a failure to accommodate one or more of Frame's three perspectives. For example: naturalized epistemologies neglect the normative perspective; coherentist epistemologies, by severing the connection between justification and the external world, fail to accommodate the situational perspective; and some externalist epistemologies fall short under the existential perspective by not recognizing important internalist (subjective) constraints on epistemic warrant.

38. The idea here is that, as a general principle, adopting multiple perspectives promotes better understanding, and that Frame's normative, situational, and existential perspectives are particularly pervasive and illuminating in this regard.

39. Note that these three points apply not only to epistemology but also to ethics, theology, apologetics, psychology, and other fields.

40. "I believe that Van Til's approach is still the best foundation for Christian apologetics at the present time." *AGG*, xi.

apologetic tradition.[41] After all, few modern-day representatives of the different schools in Christian apologetics would deny that both Christians and non-Christians have philosophical presuppositions, that these presuppositions have a major bearing on how we evaluate arguments and evidences, and that any effective approach to apologetics must take such considerations into account. So the recognition of the importance of presuppositions is hardly distinctive to "presuppositionalists" such as Van Til and Frame. No more illuminating is the claim that disciples of this school insist that all apologetic arguments must "presuppose God" or "presuppose Christianity"—a highly ambiguous characterization that has led to the frequent misconception that presuppositionalists advocate question-begging arguments. Instead, I wish to suggest that the core of presuppositionalism can be encapsulated in two foundational principles: the *No-Neutrality Principle* and the *No-Autonomy Principle*.[42]

According to the No-Neutrality Principle, no one can approach any intellectual endeavor from a position of strict religious neutrality. Whenever we apply our minds to a particular subject matter, we inevitably bring with us a host of presuppositions—that is, tacit philosophical assumptions—about human nature, human origins, human reason, the constitution of reality, the laws of nature, the source of values, purpose, meaning, and ultimately God. These presuppositions may not be articulated or admitted—indeed, a person may not even be aware of them—but they are held nonetheless. Without such presuppositions, our thinking could not get off the ground in the first place, for they supply the necessary framework for meaningful thought, the scaffolding for every intellectual construction project from the majestic to the mundane. At the very least, a person's presuppositions will be implicit in the way he evaluates evidence and interprets his experiences, in how he makes judgments about what is possible or plausible or valuable, and in how he actually lives daily life. Significantly, many of these presuppositions concern religious matters, either directly or by implication. For example, how a person views human nature (that is, what kind of being he thinks he is) will inevitably impinge on such matters as the origins of the universe, the existence and nature of God, and the purpose of life. Thus, every single person exhibits *some* religious bias—the atheist no less than the Christian,

41. Cf. *AGG*, 12n16; Frame, "Presuppositional Apologetics," in *Five Views on Apologetics*, ed. Steven B. Cowan (Grand Rapids: Zondervan, 2000), 219n16.
42. Cf. *AGG*, 3–9, 42–43, 88.

the Muslim, and the Hindu.[43] Since religious neutrality is impossible in principle, it's misguided to speak and act as though it were possible or even preferable—as though we could simply "bracket out" our most significant and influential presuppositions when considering any subject matter.[44]

When placed in the context of a biblical worldview, the No-Neutrality Principle leads naturally to the No-Autonomy Principle. The first principle states that everyone has philosophical precommitments, many of which are religious in nature or have substantial religious implications. The second principle states that there are ultimately only two kinds of philosophical precommitments—those that are *for* God and those that are *against* God—and that only the former are acceptable. In short, either we are committed to the idea that God and his Word are our ultimate authority and standard in every area of life, including our intellectual endeavors, or we are committed (at least implicitly) to some *other* ultimate authority and standard—which amounts to a rejection of God and his Word. Either we acknowledge that we are creatures whose thoughts should be conformed to the mind of our Creator or we don't. And those who locate their ultimate authority and standard elsewhere than in the mind of God invariably try to locate it in the mind of man. (What other relevant mind is there?) Consequently, what is reasonable, plausible, possible, and so on turns out to be what conforms to our own "natural" patterns of thought. As noted earlier, the word *autonomy* literally means "self-law." An autonomous thinker is one whose mind has become a law unto itself: not subject to any higher authority or corrective standard. According to the No-Autonomy Principle, this understanding of human reason must be firmly rejected.

Taken together, these two presuppositionalist principles assert that everyone thinks with some kind of religious bias, and that the only acceptable religious bias is one submissive to the ultimate authority of God and his Word.

43. Not even the professing agnostic can escape such bias. First of all, in practice no one can suspend all belief, inference, and choice. Yet every belief, inference, and choice takes for granted some metaphysical framework that renders it intelligible. Furthermore, the central plea of the agnostic—"I honestly don't know"—presupposes certain ideas about man and God and divine revelation (e.g., that humans are not fallen in sin, suppressing the truth in unrighteousness; that God is hidden; that God's self-revelation is ambiguous and inefficacious).

44. For a penetrating defense of the No-Neutrality Principle, see Roy G. Clouser, *The Myth of Religious Neutrality* (Notre Dame, IN: University of Notre Dame Press, 1991).

It seems to me that Frame's "theology of knowledge," centered as it is on the doctrine of divine lordship, provides solid support for both the No-Neutrality Principle and the No-Autonomy Principle. Consider the three lordship attributes in turn. God's *authority* implies that God determines the standards and criteria for human thought and reason. Our pursuit of truth must submit to the authority of his revealed Word. If the human mind, along with the rest of creation, stands under the law of God, it cannot be a law unto itself. So there must be no autonomy. Furthermore, none of us can be indifferent toward God's authority. Failure to acknowledge and submit to God's authority is a de facto rejection of it. So there can be no neutrality.

God's *control* implies that the whole of creation lies under God's sovereign sway, subject to his comprehensive decree. Every contingent fact is as it is because of the will of God. This implies that every fact reveals God, objectively speaking, and that no fact can be properly interpreted without reference to God. All facts are God's facts. All truths are God's truths. There can be no God-neutral interpretations of the facts—which is to say that there can be no neutrality. In order to properly interpret the world, we must conform our patterns of thought to those of the Original Interpreter—which is to say that there must be no autonomy.

God's *presence* implies that we live and breathe in a God-pervaded universe.[45] Since all things are conditioned by God's immanence, there are no "neutral public spaces" in which studies and debates can be conducted without reference to him. Moreover, God's presence (as Frame expounds it) is bound up with the biblical theme that God relates to us primarily by way of covenant. Each of us is either a covenant-keeper or a covenant-breaker; there is no third option.[46] So we think either in covenant-keeping ways or in covenant-breaking ways.[47] There can be no neutrality. And since covenant-keeping thought is submissive to God's authoritative revelation and seeks to conform to the mind of the Creator, it is *antithetical* to autonomous thought. There must be no autonomy.

45. Jer. 23:23–24; Acts 17:24–28.
46. In terms of classical Reformed theology, our federal representative is either Adam (the covenant-breaker) or Christ (the covenant-keeper). If we are not under the terms and blessings of the covenant of grace, we are under the terms and curses of the covenant of works.
47. This is not to suggest, of course, that believers never think in God-dishonoring ways! Rather, it is a question of one's settled intellectual and spiritual orientation. Cf. Frame's remarks about a "presuppositionalism of the heart" in *AGG*, 87–88.

If Frame's conclusions about divine lordship and its implications for human thought have solid exegetical support, then, by the foregoing argument, so do the two foundational principles of presuppositional apologetics. Does this mean that the Van Tillian cause has been vindicated? We must be careful here. I suspect that most evangelical Christian apologists today, if asked whether they agree with the No-Neutrality Principle and the No-Autonomy Principle, would reply with an emphatic *Yes*. When the question is explicitly raised, there tends to be *formal* agreement across the board. So what really distinguishes presuppositionalists such as Frame from their classicalist and evidentialist colleagues? Just this: the latter rarely mention these principles in their discussions of apologetic method or allow them to have any impact on their apologetic practice. Yet the two principles are far from irrelevant. In the first place, they indicate that what is at stake between the believer and the unbeliever is *a clash of entire systems*. The two parties in the debate are committed to conflicting views of God, man, divine revelation, and human reason. Thus the ultimate criteria by which the unbeliever makes judgments about truth, evidence, possibility, probability, and so forth are fundamentally at odds with those of the believer. It's not merely that we have to persuade the unbeliever to add one more item (God) to his ontology or to add one more event (the resurrection) to his historiography, as though he merely needed the few missing pieces of a near-complete jigsaw puzzle. The problem is that the unbeliever wants to draw pieces from a different box altogether! This understanding of the apologetic challenge cannot but affect the tack one takes.

So how do our two presuppositionalist principles cash out in terms of apologetic method and practice? In my judgment, they do not rule out the use of traditional philosophical, scientific, or historical arguments for Christian theism, despite what some presuppositionalists have claimed. Even so, they do raise important questions about how we formulate and present those arguments, what we should expect of the unbelievers we engage with, and how we should respond when unbelievers resist those arguments. What should we take to be the common ground between Christians and non-Christians? What do *they* take to be the common ground—and should we address their misconceptions on that point? What forms of "natural theology" are possible and permissible? What message does it convey when an apologist invites unbelievers to treat divinely inspired Gospels "just like any other ancient historical documents"? How appropriate are minimalist defenses of the resurrection that appeal to "critical methods endorsed by most secular historians"? Is the project of theodicy biblically warranted—and if so, on what terms should it proceed? If the debate between the believer and the unbeliever boils down to a clash between ultimate epistemic authorities, how can a dialectical stalemate be avoided?[48] How should we address the objection that the Bible couldn't be divinely inspired because some of its core doctrines seem impossible to formulate in a logically consistent fashion?

I don't mean to suggest that there are obvious and straightforward answers to such questions. Quite the opposite. My point is simply that questions such as these are rarely asked in the first place by budding Christian apologists. Yet to overlook or ignore them is no more responsible than, say, to conduct infant baptisms without raising and answering questions about the purpose and significance of the sacraments, or to deliver a sermon without first reflecting carefully on what the Bible teaches about the goals and responsibilities of preaching. Scripture clearly has more to say about the defense of the faith than the bare exhortation to defend the faith.

TRIPERSPECTIVALISM: PRESUPPOSITIONALISM IN PRACTICE

Presuppositionalists are often criticized for being long on theory and short on practice.[49] A survey of the primary literature on presuppositional apologetics suggests that this charge has more than a grain of truth to it. I

48. The prospect of a "presuppositional standoff" between two competing systems of thought, in which each advances its own ultimate criteria for adjudicating between such systems, was one reason why Van Til advocated the use of transcendental argumentation. The idea is that such argumentation can resolve disputes at the system level without begging the question in favor of either system. For elaboration of this point, see my article "If Knowledge Then God: The Epistemological Theistic Arguments of Plantinga and Van Til," *Calvin Theological Journal* 40 (2005): 49–75, also available online at http://www.proginosko.com/docs/IfKnowledgeThenGod.pdf (accessed May 14, 2009). Although I cannot argue the point here, I believe Frame is mistaken in his suggestion (*AGG*, 73; "Presuppositional Apologetics," 220–21) that transcendental arguments are not substantially different from other forms of theistic argument. The former can be distinguished from the latter with respect to the scope, subject matter, and modality of their premises. For now, an analogy will have to substitute for an argument: traditional theistic arguments proceed from *what we see*, whereas transcendental arguments proceed from *the possibility of sight*.

49. See Frame's own admission in *AGG*, 203. Two notable exceptions are the late Greg Bahnsen, who conducted a number of public debates with atheists and other non-Christians, and Douglas Wilson, who has directly engaged with the anti-Christian polemics of two of the "New Atheists," Sam Harris and Christopher Hitchens. In fairness to Frame, we should not overlook his online debate with atheist philosopher Michael Martin (available at http://www.infidels.org and http://www.reformed.org), which represents a concrete application of his methodology.

hope that the final section of this essay will redress the balance somewhat by showing how Frame's triperspectival presuppositionalism can be applied toward a penetrating critique of one of the most prominent unbelieving worldviews of our day.[50]

Alvin Plantinga has suggested that the two most prominent worldviews in competition with Christian theism in the West today are "perennial naturalism" and "creative antirealism."[51] I believe he is right in this observation, although I will focus here only on the first of these. Naturalism, simply stated, is the view that nature is all there is. The universe is a causally closed spatiotemporal system—and that's it. Thus the only things that exist are *natural* things, that is, things that are spatiotemporal in nature, enter into causal relationships with one another, and can be studied by the natural sciences (all of which ultimately reduce to physics).[52] According to the naturalist, therefore, everything can be ultimately explained in terms of fundamental physical entities (such as particles, waves, and fields—whatever the current ontology of the empirical sciences happens to be) in conjunction with the natural laws that describe their behavior. Consequently, there exist no supernatural or nonnatural beings, such as souls, ghosts, angels, or—most importantly—God.

Naturalism thus construed is taken for granted by a large proportion of philosophers and scientists in the West today. It also holds considerable sway in other academic fields, such as psychology, medicine, law, and ethics. It is the basic worldview aggressively promoted by the so-called New

50. The critique takes the form of a series of negative transcendental arguments, which aim to show that certain anti-Christian metaphysical claims would, if true, render human reason and knowledge impossible in principle. In terms of Frame's three perspectives on apologetics, I am engaging in "apologetics as offense." *AGG*, 2–3.

51. Alvin Plantinga, "Augustinian Christian Philosophy," *The Monist* 75 (1992): 291–320; Plantinga, "Christian Philosophy at the End of the 20th Century," in *The Analytic Theist*, ed. James F. Sennett (Grand Rapids: Eerdmans, 1998), 328–52. Creative antirealism is the view that the world that each of us experiences and inhabits is ultimately a construction of our own minds. It is the worldview most commonly associated with postmodernist epistemology, although its origins go back at least as far as Immanuel Kant.

52. In one influential article, D. M. Armstrong defined *naturalism* as "the doctrine that reality consists of nothing but a single all-embracing spatio-temporal system." Armstrong, "Naturalism, Materialism and First Philosophy," *Philosophia* 8 (1978): 261–76. Bruce Aune expresses a similarly naturalistic outlook when he defines *existence* as "belong[ing] to the space-time-causal system that is our world." Aune, *Metaphysics: The Elements* (Minneapolis: University of Minnesota Press, 1985), 35.

Presuppositionalism and Frame's Epistemology

Atheists.[53] Advocates of naturalism are known to celebrate the rationality of their worldview: it is routinely presented as the most parsimonious, elegant, and homogenous view of reality, from which all objects of religious superstition have been shaved away by Occam's razor. But how rational is it when subjected to closer scrutiny? I will argue that if we subject this influential worldview to a triperspectival analysis, it quickly becomes apparent that *naturalism actually rules out the possibility of knowledge altogether.* Ironically, the antitheistic worldview that is praised in our day as the epitome of reason turns out to be one of the worst enemies of reason.

Take first the *normative* perspective on knowledge. I have already explained how any adequate analysis of human knowledge must account for its normative component (whether that component is labeled *justification, warrant,* or whatever). Roughly put, a meaningful distinction must be drawn between true beliefs that are formed "in the right way" or held "on good grounds" (and thus qualify as knowledge) and those that are formed "in the wrong way" or held "on poor grounds." Likewise, the very notion of rationality is irreducibly normative: to be rational means, at a minimum, to conform to certain norms of thought. Core epistemic concepts such as justification, warrant, and rationality pertain to how we *should* think rather than how we *do in fact* think.[54]

But the problem for metaphysical naturalism, as Plantinga (among others) has pointed out, is that it appears to leave no place for normativity:

> Naturalism, it seems to me, is eminently attackable. Its Achilles' heel (in addition to its deplorable falsehood) is that it has no room for *normativity.* There is no room, within naturalism, for right or wrong, or good or bad. . . . Naturalism also lacks room for the notion of *proper function* for non-artifacts, and hence lacks room for the notion of proper function for our

---

53. Richard Dawkins, *The God Delusion* (London: Bantam Press, 2006); Daniel Dennett, *Darwin's Dangerous Idea* (New York: Simon & Schuster, 1995); Dennett, *Breaking the Spell: Religion as a Natural Phenomenon* (London: Allen Lane, 2006); Sam Harris, *The End of Faith* (New York: W. W. Norton & Co., 2005); Christopher Hitchens, *God Is Not Great: How Religion Poisons Everything* (New York: Twelve, 2007); Victor J. Stenger, *God: The Failed Hypothesis* (Amherst, NY: Prometheus Books, 2007).

54. "[Epistemic] justification manifestly is normative. If a belief is justified for us, then it is *permissible* and *reasonable,* from the epistemic point of view, for us to hold it, and it would be *epistemically irresponsible* to hold beliefs that contradict it. . . . Epistemology is a normative discipline as much as, and in the same sense as, normative ethics." Jaegwon Kim, "What Is 'Naturalized Epistemology'?" in *Philosophical Perspectives 2,* ed. James E. Tomberlin (Atascadero, CA: Ridgeview Publishing, 1988), 383 (emphasis in original).

453

cognitive faculties. It therefore has no room for the notion of knowledge, at least if the account of warrant given in *Warrant and Proper Function* is anywhere near correct.[55]

Plantinga refers here to his own analysis of warrant, which is certainly incompatible with metaphysical naturalism, but one does not have to accept his particular analysis to grant the broader point. If the naturalist's view is correct, then there simply are no truths about the way the world *ought to be*. There are only truths about the way the world *actually is*. If the world is explicable entirely in terms of the physical sciences—in terms of paradigmatic physical properties such as mass, velocity, and electrical charge—then normative judgments are strictly meaningless. After all, physics is a descriptive science, not a prescriptive one. No purely physical account can tell us in principle how the world ought to be—including how a certain species of organism ought to think. But as we have seen, an examination of our commonsense notion of knowledge shows that it *must* have a normative component. The consequence is obvious: if naturalism were true, there could be no knowledge.[56]

It's worth noting that some naturalists have candidly conceded the point. Following the lead of W. V. Quine, advocates of "naturalized epistemology" have argued that traditional epistemology needs to be radically reconfigured (some would say replaced) in light of our modern commitment to the natural sciences—or, more precisely, in light of *their* ideological commitment to the exhaustive explanatory power of the natural sciences. This proposal boils down to the conviction that epistemology (how humans ought to think) must be reduced to psychology (how humans do in fact think). But this move is not so much a plausible defense of naturalism as an indication of just how high a price a thoroughgoing naturalism exacts. As a solution to naturalism's inhospitableness toward normativity, the suggestion that we should swap in psychology for epistemology amounts to little more than an attempt to change the subject. It is no more satisfactory than to replace applied ethics (how humans ought to behave) with empirical sociology (how humans do in fact behave). Modern-day antisupernaturalists are often aware

---

55. Alvin Plantinga, "Afterword," in *The Analytic Theist*, 356.
56. In fact, there could be no ignorance or irrationality either, for there would be no intelligible distinction between *warranted* and *unwarranted* or between *rational* and *irrational*. Any kind of normative epistemic judgment, whether positive or negative, is objectively meaningless in a naturalist ontology.

of the difficulty of accounting for objective *moral* norms within a naturalistic framework, but most are blissfully unaware of the parallel difficulty of accounting for objective *epistemic* norms.[57]

Let us turn now to the *situational* perspective on knowledge. This perspective invites us to consider the objects of knowledge. What exactly is it that we know? According to one view, what we know (or aspire to know) are *facts*. Philosophers often characterize facts as "states of affairs," such as *Bob's being six feet tall*, *Susan's purchasing of the chair*, and *Michael's washing of his car*.[58] But what sort of things are facts or states of affairs? A good argument can be made that they must be necessary, abstract entities, rather than contingent, concrete entities such as trees, tables, transistors, and other physical objects. Facts must certainly be distinguished from the objects to which those facts pertain: *Michael's washing of his car* is quite distinct from Michael and his car, not least because the latter could exist without the former (and vice versa, if there are such things as past facts and future facts). But if facts are abstract in nature, they are not spatiotemporal entities; thus they are not the sort of things that can be analyzed by the physical sciences. In short, there seems to be no clear place for facts (thus construed) in a strictly naturalistic ontology.[59]

A similar argument can be made with respect to *truths*, which would also be suitable candidates for the objects of our knowledge. When I claim to know *that* such-and-such, I'm claiming to know a *truth*—say, the truth that Bob is six feet tall, or that Susan is purchasing the chair, or that Michael is washing his car. But what exactly is a truth? A truth is a proposition; more precisely, it is a *true* proposition.[60] Propositions, simply put, are entities that

---

57. For further discussion of this point, see my online essay "The Theistic Preconditions of Knowledge: A Thumbnail Sketch," http://www.proginosko.com/docs/knowledge_and_theism. html (accessed May 14, 2009).

58. States of affairs are typically expressed with gerund verb forms. Thus, in speaking of our knowledge of states of affairs, we might say (somewhat awkwardly), "I know of Bob's being six feet tall," "I know of Susan's purchasing of the chair," and "I know of Michael's washing of his car." (Note the possessive use of the apostrophe in these examples.)

59. Couldn't a naturalist say that states of affairs *just are* physical objects configured in particular ways? There are a number of reasons why this won't do. One is that it's hard to see how modal facts (facts about possibilities and necessities) could be constituted by nothing more than how physical objects are actually configured. Modal facts about how nature *could be* and *must be* go beyond how the physical world *actually is*. But modal facts cannot be dismissed as irrelevant; they are ineradicable components of our understanding of the world.

60. This is why epistemologists describe knowledge *that* such-and-such as "propositional knowledge." In English, the word *that* picks out a proposition as the object of knowledge.

can possess a truth-value, i.e., they can be either true or false.[61] If propositions are the objects of knowledge, it follows that knowledge presupposes the existence of propositions. No propositions implies no knowledge. The problem for naturalists is that propositions don't appear to be physical entities or reducible to physical entities. In the first place, the properties most characteristic of propositions—the properties of *truth* and *falsity*—are nothing like physical properties, such as mass, velocity, and electrical charge. Furthermore, propositions have no location in space at all. (What sense does it make to say that the *truth* that Bob is taller than Jack resides at a particular address?) Second, it seems that propositions must exist independently of the physical universe. For example, if the physical universe had never existed—which is surely a possibility, since the universe has only contingent existence—there would still have been *truths*, such as the truth that no physical universe exists and the truth that a physical universe could have existed.

Recognizing that propositions are markedly unlike physical entities such as electrons and fields, some metaphysicians have tried to categorize them as *mental* entities. On this view, propositions reside in human minds and are the product of human mental activity. What should we make of this? It's true that propositions are more like mental objects than physical objects, but this is hardly a comfort for a metaphysical naturalist. Leaving aside the difficulty of accounting for *minds* on a naturalistic basis,[62] the second argument above shows that propositions cannot be dependent on human minds; for even if there were no human minds, there would still be truths (such as the truth that there are no human minds).

It thus appears that when naturalism is scrutinized from both the normative perspective and the situational perspective, its epistemological bankruptcy is exposed: first, in its inability to accommodate objective norms for human thought; and second, in its inability to accommodate facts and truths as real entities.

Consider finally the *existential* perspective on knowledge, which invites us to reflect on the subjective, personal component of human knowledge. Two particular problems for naturalism may be briefly highlighted here. First, let

61. Some philosophers would argue that propositions can also *lack* a truth-value, that is, they can be neither true nor false. Whether or not this view is correct has no bearing on my argument here. The important point is that only a proposition *could* be true or false.

62. See, e.g., Charles Talliaferro, "Naturalism and the Mind," in *Naturalism: A Critical Analysis*, ed. William Lane Craig and J. P. Moreland (New York: Routledge, 2000), 133–55; J. P. Moreland, *Consciousness and the Existence of God* (New York: Routledge, 2008).

us recall the obvious point that knowledge requires a *subject* of knowledge—a knower—as well as an object. A knower must have the capacity for conscious thought. He must have an awareness of the object of knowledge and the ability to direct his thoughts toward it.[63] The immediate problem here for naturalism is that there seems to be no place in a naturalist worldview for consciousness as a real property. Consciousness, like truth, is wholly dissimilar to the sorts of "natural" properties that physicists routinely trade in. Consciousness in particular appears to be irreducibly subjective: it presents us with a first-person perspective that cannot be reduced to a third-person perspective. Science, as a strictly objective discipline, purports to give us subject-independent third-person descriptions of the world. But such descriptions will necessarily omit (or rule out) any irreducibly subjective reality. Suppose for the sake of argument that a naturalist could obtain an utterly exhaustive scientific description of the human brain and sense organs, the atmosphere of our planet, the electromagnetic rays from the sun, and any other relevant physical reality. Such a description would tell us nothing about what it is like to experience a blue sky. Knowledge of our subjective experience of the world—in plain language, how it appears and feels to each of us—cannot in principle be reduced to scientific knowledge (empirical knowledge of particles, fields, etc.).

Another serious problem for naturalism arises from its difficulty in accounting for what philosophers call *intentionality*. We have already seen that having knowledge entails having beliefs. One distinctive feature of beliefs is that they are "about" other things. For example, my belief that Paris is the capital city of France is *about* something: the city of Paris. Our beliefs thus exhibit an external directedness: they refer to objects beyond themselves. The technical term for this "aboutness" is *intentionality*. One of the most interesting features of intentionality is that it appears to be a distinctively mental property. Purely physical things, such as puddles of water and rock formations, do not exhibit intentionality. They aren't "about" anything. (Just try asking such questions as these: "What is this puddle *about*?" "What does it *refer to*?")[64] Yet according to the natural-

---

63. Nonconscious physical objects, including computers, cannot be said to possess knowledge in anything but a derivative, analogical sense. Clearly, my Pocket PC does not literally *know* that I have a lunch appointment with a colleague next week, any more than a paper-based organizer would.

64. One might object that certain physical things, such as sentences written in ink on a page, can be "about" other things. But a moment's reflection should show that this is merely a derivative intentionality; physical inscriptions have meaning and reference only because of the prior

ist worldview, everything can be ultimately explained in purely physical terms, and what can't be so explained isn't real.[65] Naturalism thus appears unable to accommodate intentionality. Not only does it leave no room for the norms of knowledge and the objects of knowledge, it also leaves no room for the subjects of knowledge. In short, if the naturalist worldview were true, there could be no warranted true beliefs—there could be no knowledge.

I have argued that the application of Frame's triperspectivalism reveals a number of debilitating problems with one of the most prominent anti-Christian worldviews in the West today, problems that render it rationally untenable. Christian theism, with its more nourishing ontology, doesn't fall into the same difficulties. On the contrary, the reality of epistemic norms, objective truths, and finite consciousnesses make considerable sense in a worldview centered on the notion of an Absolute Person who delights to fashion creatures in his own image.[66]

In this essay I have tried to show (1) that Frame's epistemology of divine lordship is biblically warranted and has significant (yet frequently neglected) implications for all human intellectual endeavors; (2) that his triperspectival methodology is well motivated and can be an illuminating analytic tool in epistemology; (3) that his "theology of knowledge" provides ample support for the foundational principles of Van Tillian presuppositional apologetics; and (4) that triperspectivalism can be fruitfully applied in apologetics as the basis for exposing the serious philosophical shortcomings of one prominent anti-Christian worldview. Above all, I'm persuaded that Professor Frame has

---

interpretive activity of a (human) mind. So this only pushes the naturalist's problem back a step. The intentionality of written texts depends on the intentionality of human thoughts. But how can purely physical human brains exhibit intentionality?

65. Hence, as many commentators have noted, Daniel Dennett's books *The Intentional Stance* (Cambridge, MA: MIT Press, 1987) and *Consciousness Explained* (Boston: Little, Brown and Co., 1991) are not so much a naturalistic attempt to explain consciousness and intentionality as an attempt to explain them away.

66. Although space forbids elaboration, I believe similar critiques can be developed against other non-Christian worldviews, such as pantheism, panentheism, dualism, polytheism, and the more virulent strains of postmodernist thought. Insofar as post-modernism can be characterized as *hyper*-modernism—the modernist commitment to autonomy stripped of the remaining vestiges of Christian tradition and driven to its final destination—it actually serves to confirm our presuppositionalist critique of naturalism. The nominalism, antifoundationalism, antirealism, relativism, and nihilism propounded by postmodernists are arguably the "natural" fruit of a naturalist worldview, as Friedrich Nietzsche observed almost a century before Jacques Derrida and Richard Rorty arrived at the party.

rendered an invaluable service to the church and to Christian scholarship by his clarion call to shun autonomy in *every* intellectual endeavor—not least in Christian philosophy and apologetics—and to submit every thought to the revealed Word of our sovereign, authoritative, and ever-present Lord.

20

VAN TIL AND TRANSCENDENTAL
ARGUMENT REVISITED

DONALD COLLETT

THE PHRASE *COGNITIVE DISSONANCE* first fell upon my ears in the fall of 1994 while enrolled in Professor John Frame's course on the Christian Mind, the first in a series of three courses in Christian apologetics required for master of divinity students at Westminster Seminary in California.[1] According to conventional philosophical wisdom, when philosophers run headlong into this sort of dissonance in the course of constructing arguments, they typically seek to overcome it, either by making a distinction or by defining a new term. Following in the footsteps of his apologetics mentor, Cornelius Van Til, Professor Frame added yet a third option, namely, humbly acquiescing in the possibility that such dissonance may in fact constitute a philosophical testimony to the truth of the "Creator-creature distinction"

1. An earlier edition of this essay appeared in the Fall 2003 issue of *The Westminster Theological Journal*, and was followed by a substantially abbreviated version in *Revelation and Reason: New Essays in Reformed Apologetics*, ed. K. Scott Oliphint and Lane G. Tipton (Phillipsburg, NJ: P&R Publishing, 2007). For the purposes of this volume, I have introduced a number of clarifications and other changes. The essay thus appears here for the first time in a fully revised and expanded form. It is gratefully dedicated to Professor John M. Frame in appreciation for the model of Christian charity, graciousness, and scholarship he has embodied through many years of teaching.

and the Christian concept of mystery it entails. Not all forms of cognitive dissonance were to be regarded, therefore, as something analogous to a "charley horse between the ears" capable of being massaged away by the powers of reason and the tools of philosophical logic.[2]

It is crucial to keep this biblical wisdom in mind when it comes to assessing the debate over the distinctive character of transcendental argument in Van Til's apologetic approach. Although Frame and I continue to assess this debate differently, the passage of years and further reflection on this issue have led me to a greater appreciation for the semantically rich and complex character of the concept of presupposition in Van Til's apologetic. This should come as no surprise, especially since the theological reality to which the concept is linked in apologetic argument is nothing less than the triune God of Scripture. It is precisely because its semantic richness and complexity in apologetic argument ultimately derive from its subject matter, that is, God in his triune identity as Father, Son, and Spirit, that to some extent it will always resist linguistic appropriation in the form of artificially constructed languages. As far as the languages of formal logic are concerned, the concept of semantic presupposition will doubtless remain elusive, especially in the context of Christian-theistic apologetics.

In what follows, therefore, readers hoping to discover a comprehensive formal account of the concept of presupposition will find themselves disappointed. This is not to say, however, that it is impossible to give *formal* expression to certain semantic distinctions that obtain between the concept of presupposition, on the one hand, and the rules of inference in standard proposition logic, on the other, the latter of which often serve as vehicles for stating traditional apologetic arguments (e.g., *modus ponens* and *modus tollens*). Insofar as Van Til himself attempted to justify this distinction, he typically did so in terms of theological concerns rather than formal argument per se. Although I am far from suggesting that Van Til's theologically oriented approach to this issue lacks merit, ongoing debate over these matters attests to the fact that a formal basis for distinguishing his approach from traditional approaches is needed. The present essay seeks to address this issue by drawing on certain insights regarding the concept of "semantic presup-

2. Not that Frame himself resisted making distinctions or defining new terms. Anyone who has taken his courses or read his writings on apologetics will know that he is not averse to making distinctions at crucial junctures in philosophical and theological argument, or for that matter defining new terms when necessary (speaking more precisely, the latter usually amounted to redeploying ordinary language for specifically theological ends).

position" that have arisen within the tradition of analytic philosophy.[3] To that end I will begin with a survey of some important theological concerns underlying Van Til's commitment to the distinctive character of transcendental argument, then move on to briefly summarize what I will call "the reductionist objection" to transcendental arguments. Against this backdrop I will then attempt to provide a formal motivation for the distinctive character of Van Til's transcendental argument from predication while at the same time distinguishing it from the method of *reductio ad absurdum*.[4] This essay will then close with a discussion of possible objections in order to address potential misunderstandings and introduce further clarifications.

Van Til and Transcendental Argument

Central to the apologetic approach of Cornelius Van Til is the claim that a truly Christian apologetic and transcendental argument go hand in hand. Back of this claim lies the conviction, oft stated by Van Til, that the Christian theism disclosed in Scripture entails a distinctive apologetic method. For example, in the opening pages of *A Survey of Christian Epistemology*, Van Til writes that "every system of thought necessarily has a certain method of its own."[5] Thus Christian theism, considered as a coherent whole, requires an apologetic approach that is methodologically distinctive. For Van Til, this in turn *requires* the Christian apologist to employ a transcendental argument for God's existence, since "the only argument for an absolute God that holds water is a transcendental argument."[6]

3. See especially Peter Strawson, *An Introduction to Logical Theory* (London: Methuen, 1952), 174–79; Bas C. van Fraassen, "Presupposition, Implication, and Self-Reference," *Journal of Philosophy* (1968): 136–39. For a concise statement of the concept of semantic presupposition, see R. Bertolet, "Presupposition," The Cambridge Dictionary of Philosophy, Robert Audi ed., 2nd ed., (Cambridge: Cambridge University Press, 1999), 735.

4. Readers should note that my purpose in this paper is to defend the distinctiveness of transcendental arguments on a *formal* level. Such a defense, if successful, does not entail the conclusion that other argument types or forms have no place in a presuppositional apologetic. In general I agree, along with Bahnsen and Frame, that "there is no transcendental argument that 'rules out all other kinds of arguments' . . . either in general philosophy and scholarship or particularly in apologetics." Greg L. Bahnsen, *Van Til's Apologetic* (Phillipsburg, NJ: P&R Publishing, 1998), 502n64.

5. Cornelius Van Til, *A Survey of Christian Epistemology* (Nutley, NJ: Presbyterian and Reformed, 1969), 5 (hereafter *SCE*).

6. Ibid., 11.

Criticism of Van Til's stance on transcendental argument has not been lacking over the years, especially among Christian apologists who remain committed to inductive and deductive methods of argument, or who prefer to adopt a more integrative and methodologically diverse approach to the practice of apologetics.[7] In recent years the distinctive character of Van Til's transcendental approach has also generated critical debate within Van Tillian circles.[8] This debate is especially significant for apologists who share a basic commitment to Van Til's apologetic approach, inasmuch as it raises the question whether transcendental arguments can be distinguished from the traditional argument forms of natural theology, and if so, on what grounds.

Before turning to a discussion of the formal issues at stake, it is helpful to begin by surveying a few of the more prominent theological concerns that motivated Van Til's commitment to the distinctive character of transcendental argument in apologetic method and practice.[9] This should also help clarify some of the reasons why he found traditional approaches to apologetic argument inadequate. Foremost among these theological concerns are the two closely related doctrines of God's aseity and transcendence. For Van Til, safeguarding these doctrines in apologetic practice requires one to make use of a transcendental argument. To do otherwise is to fail to take seriously the *absolute* character of God's being when formulating an argument for Christian theism.[10] The problem with traditional approaches to inductive and deductive argument, argues Van Til, is that they typically begin with the assumption that certain axioms are more ultimate or epistemologically certain than God's existence (e.g., the principle of causality), then proceed

7. By way of qualification, one should note that Van Til's commitment to transcendental argument did not lead him to reject the use of inductive and deductive methods of argument per se. However, in keeping with his belief that Reformed theology entails an apologetic method that is distinctive, namely the transcendental method, Van Til called for the methodological reconstruction of deductive and inductive argument along transcendental lines (see *SCE*, 8–11, 201). It lies beyond the purview of this paper to enter into the question of why Van Til chose not to provide us with *formal* examples of such a reconstruction in his writings.

8. See *AGG*, 69–88; *CVT*, 317–20; "Presuppositional Apologetics," in *Five Views on Apologetics*, ed. Stanley N. Gundry and Steven B. Cowan (Grand Rapids: Zondervan, 2000), 220, 221n18; Bahnsen, *Van Til's Apologetic*, 499–502.

9. For a brief overview of these concerns, consult *SCE*, 4–13. It cannot be stressed enough that Van Til embedded the transcendental argument within a distinctly Christian worldview. Failure to reckon with the implications of this fact has led to a great deal of misunderstanding on the part of Van Til's critics over the years.

10. "It should be particularly noted, therefore, that only a system of philosophy that takes the concept of an absolute God seriously can really be said to be employing a transcendental method. A truly transcendent God and a transcendental method go hand-in-hand." Ibid., 11.

by means of "straight line" reasoning to derive or deduce God's existence from such principles.[11] In so doing they unwittingly assign to the concept of God's existence a logically derivative rather than logically primitive status,[12] thereby compromising both his aseity and his transcendence.

By way of contrast, a transcendental argument preserves the logically primitive and absolute character of God's existence by *starting* with the premise that God's existence is a necessary precondition for argument itself.[13] In this way argument is made to depend on God, rather than vice versa, since argument is possible if and only if God's existence is true from the outset of argument itself. Thus in contrast with both deductive and inductive forms of argument, a transcendental argument allows the concept of God to function as a logically primitive rather than logically derivative proposition, thereby bearing witness to the nonderivative character of God's existence on an argumentative level. To state matters another way, in Van Til's Christian-theistic construction of transcendental argument, the truth of God's existence is not a deductive consequence of the premises of the argument, but rather the ontological and logical ground for the very possibility of the premises themselves.[14] This is undoubtedly one of the reasons, if not the chief reason, why he believed that transcendental arguments were uniquely suited for the task of placing into sharp relief the nondeductive character of the truth of God's existence.

In the second place, it was Van Til's conviction that only a transcendental argument could do justice to the clarity of the objective evidence for God's existence, since its peculiar form is specially suited to the apologetic task of bearing witness to the *necessary* character of God's existence. That

11. Ibid., 8–11.

12. To my knowledge, Van Til never stated the matter in precisely these terms or categories (*logically derivative* vs. *logically primitive*). Their usage here I hope will clarify the point that Van Til is making when he contrasts the "straight line" reasoning inherent in deductive argument with the "presuppositional" reasoning inherent in transcendental argument.

13. "It is not as though we already know some facts and laws to begin with, irrespective of the existence of God, in order then to reason from such a beginning to further conclusions. It is certainly true that if God has any significance for any object of knowledge at all, the relation of God to that object of knowledge must be taken into consideration from the outset. It is this fact that the transcendental method seeks to recognize" (*SCE*, 201).

14. "The best, the only, the absolutely certain proof of the truth of Christianity is that unless its truth be presupposed there is no proof of anything. Christianity is proved as being the very foundation of the idea of proof itself." Cornelius Van Til, *The Defense of the Faith* (Philadelphia: Presbyterian and Reformed, 1955), 396. Subsequent references to *The Defense of the Faith* (hereafter *DOF*) are to the 1955 edition unless otherwise noted.

is to say, its formal character is such that it does not require the Christian apologist to implicitly grant the possibility that God's existence is falsifiable, and thereby "tone down the objective claims of God upon men."[15] Inasmuch as creation clearly testifies to the necessary character of God's existence, it follows that a Christian apologist cannot do justice to the objective evidence for Christian theism unless he or she affirms the noncontingent character of God's existence in apologetic argument. Van Til often buttressed this claim by means of an argument from predication, insisting that a transcendental argument, theistically constructed, begins all argument upon the premise that predication requires for its possibility the necessary truth of God's existence. In this manner the possibility of justifying predication is made to depend on God's existence from the outset of argument itself, thereby precluding any future possibility of using argument to falsify God's existence. Argument cannot proceed without predication, and predication requires for its possibility the necessary truth of God's existence.

At this juncture it is important to note that Van Til has in mind predication that affirms something is the case (e.g., *it is* the case that John is tall), *as well as* predication that *denies* something is the case (e.g., *it is not* the case that John is tall). In terms of assigning truth values to propositions, this amounts to the claim that it is ultimately impossible (logically speaking) to predicate truly *or* falsely about any proposition in the context of apologetic argument without *referentially* presupposing the truth of the proposition "God exists."[16]

VAN TIL AND TRADITIONAL ARGUMENT

In contradistinction to the logical semantics of transcendental argument, Van Til argued that traditional constructions of "theistic proofs" compromise the necessary character of God's existence. Responding to criticisms made by S. J. Ridderbos in this connection, Van Til reminds him that for an argument to serve as a witness to God, it cannot bear witness to any other god but the living and true God. Thus it must bear witness to God as he truly is,

15. Ibid., 197.
16. On the referential function of semantic presupposition, see John F. Post, "Referential Presupposition," *Australasian Journal of Philosophy* 50, 2 (1972): 160–67. On this account of the concept of "semantic presupposition," to argue that the concept X referentially presupposes the concept Y is logically equivalent to asserting that Y truly "refers" (i.e., that Y requires an existential, in this case the actual existence of God).

and this in turn requires that it bear witness to God as "the One who cannot but exist."[17] In other words, in order to be a *truthful* witness to the triune God disclosed in Scripture, the logical semantics of apologetic argument must be congruent with the identity of the subject matter it seeks to defend. Christian-theistic argument must therefore bear witness to the necessary character of God's self-existence, and this precludes it from embracing the contrary premise that God's existence, although true, *could be* otherwise. Thus in the context of apologetic argument, the concept of God's existence must not be allowed to function on the level of logical contingency, for to do so is to effectively grant the possibility that God's existence is falsifiable.

It is true, of course, that Van Til would sometimes argue the premise that God's existence is falsifiable in order to perform a *reductio ad absurdum* of the non-Christian position. His use of the *reductio*, however, was the second part of a two-phase apologetic strategy wherein he adopted the unbeliever's argument solely for the sake of argument. For this reason Van Til's "practical strategy"[18] of adopting the unbeliever's stance for the sake of refuting it should be distinguished from his transcendental argument per se.[19]

At this point, advocates of traditional apologetic methods might object that Van Til's endorsement of transcendental argument overlooks the fact that Anselm's version of the ontological argument also argues from the necessary character of God's being, and as such would be capable of addressing Van Til's concern. At least one apologist in the Reformed tradition has gone even further and expressed the opinion that Van Til's so-called transcendental argument is merely a sophisticated version of the ontological argument.[20] Despite formal resemblances between the two, however, transcendental and ontological arguments for God's existence are not merely two sides of the same coin. One must bear in mind that on Van Til's view of the matter, the ontological argument is ultimately incapable of doing justice to the uniquely *revelational* sense in which God's existence is necessary, since it

17. *DOF*, 197.

18. *CVT*, 320.

19. Frame suggests that Van Til's transcendental argument is "essentially a reductio" (ibid., 315, 319). For further discussion of the reasons why I regard this as misleading, consult the section of this essay on "Transcendental Argument and the *Reductio ad Absurdum*."

20. Cf. the debate over apologetic method between Greg L. Bahnsen and R. C. Sproul, titled "The Bahnsen/Sproul Debate over Apologetic Method," in which Sproul asserts that the differences between Van Til's transcendental argument and the ontological argument are nonsubstantive. Audio files of this debate are available from Covenant Media Foundation, 8784 FM 226, Nacogdoches, TX 75961 (http://www.cmfnow.com).

"proves" a God who exists "by the same necessity as does the universe," and thus a God who is no more than "an aspect of, or simply the whole of, the universe."[21] He was aware of the fact that advocates of the ontological argument, and Anselm in particular, make a distinction between two different senses of "necessity" in order to distinguish God's existence from that of the universe. For Van Til, however, this distinction is fatally undermined by the starting point of the argument. The ontological argument begins by defining God's being as that "than which nothing greater can be thought," thereby identifying God's being with humanity's highest thought. In other words, the ontological argument begins by identifying God's being with an order of thought and existence that is, on a biblical worldview, metaphysically contingent on the creative decree of God.

Moreover, even if a logical transfer into the realm of necessary being were possible by means of the ontological argument, such a transfer would not leave us with the biblical notion of God, a point often noted by Van Til himself: "If we take the highest being of which we can think, in the sense of have a concept of, and attribute to it actual existence, we do not have the biblical notion of God. God is not the reality that corresponds to the highest concept that man, considered as an independent being, can think."[22] In the practice of apologetics, therefore, one must distinguish the logical semantics of transcendental arguments from the semantics of arguments that are deductive in form, in this case the ontological argument. Those who equate the ontological argument with the transcendental argument implicitly assume that transcendental arguments are reducible to deductive arguments, yet typically fail to provide grounds for this assumption, thus begging the very point in dispute.

VAN TIL AND THE ARGUMENT FROM PREDICATION

There is yet a third reason why Van Til believed that transcendental arguments were uniquely suited for the task of Christian apologetics. Unfortunately, this aspect of Van Til's transcendental argument has not been given the weight it deserves, even though it is precisely this feature that

21. Cornelius Van Til, *The Reformed Pastor and Modern Thought* (Phillipsburg, NJ: Presbyterian and Reformed, 1980), 64–65.
22. Cornelius Van Til, *An Introduction to Systematic Theology* (Nutley, NJ: Presbyterian and Reformed, 1974), 206.

allows us to distinguish it on a formal level from traditional approaches to apologetic argument. At this point it is necessary to focus on a particular theological and apologetic concern of Van Til's, namely, the ontological basis for the possibility of predication. In his writings he frequently stressed the need for apologetic argument to engage this issue from a Christian-theistic point of view. Consider the following statement from *A Christian Theory of Knowledge*, which occurs in the context of Van Til's stated purpose "to indicate in a broad way the method of reasoning that is to be pursued" in the vindication of Christian theism:

> How then we ask is the Christian to challenge this non-Christian approach to the interpretation of human experience? He can do so only if he shows that man must presuppose God as the final reference point in predication. Otherwise, he would destroy experience itself. *He can do so only if he shows the non-Christian that even in his virtual negation of God, he is still really presupposing God.* He can do so only if he shows the non-Christian that he cannot deny God unless he first affirm him, and that his own approach throughout its history has been shown to be destructive of human experience itself.[23]

Here we are reminded that for Van Til, the ontological Trinity constitutes "the final reference point in predication," which is but another way of saying that the triune God of Scripture provides us with both the ontological and epistemological basis for the possibility of predication. We are also reminded that Van Til directly identified presuppositional (or transcendental) argument with the task of justifying this possibility on Christian-theistic grounds. In other words, by means of a transcendental argument from predication, Van Til sought to make definite the claim that *all* human predication, whether that of affirmation or negation, referentially presupposes the truth of God's existence:

> It is the firm conviction of every epistemologically self-conscious Christian that no human being can utter a single syllable, *whether in negation or affirmation*, unless it were for God's existence. Thus the transcendental argument seeks to discover what sort of foundations the house of human knowledge must have, in order to be what it is.[24]

23. Cornelius Van Til, *A Christian Theory of Knowledge* (Nutley, NJ: Presbyterian and Reformed, 1969), 13 (emphasis added).
24. *SCE*, 11 (emphasis added).

The last two quotes highlight the central position occupied by the transcendental argument from predication in Van Til's apologetic, and this prominence has been noted by John Frame as well.[25] Often overlooked, however, is Van Til's concern to emphasize that the argument from predication is not limited to cases of affirmation, but also extends to cases of negation. Might not this emphasis merit closer scrutiny, especially in light of the distinction he drew between his own approach and the methods of traditional argument?

Implicit in Van Til's argument is the criticism, albeit undeveloped on a formal level, that traditional methods of argument are inadequate because they proceed on the assumption that at least some types of predication are possible apart from the truth of God's existence. By way of contrast, Van Til sought to argue that predication itself is impossible, philosophically speaking, unless the proposition "God exists" is true in a referential sense. Christian-theistic arguments for God's existence must therefore make it clear that since his existence is the basis for *all* predication, one cannot predicate truly or falsely about anything in an apologetic context unless the assertion "God exists" actually obtains. In the words of the late Greg Bahnsen:

> Van Til's stunning application of this feature of transcendental argumentation to apologetics is that the truth of the Christian worldview is established not only by theistic premises and opinions, but also by antitheistic beliefs and opinions. As Van Til said, "Antitheism presupposes theism" (*SCE*, xii). Even if the unbeliever wants to start with the assertion that "God does not exist," a transcendental analysis of it would show that the possibility of its coherence and meaningfulness assumes the existence of the very God that it denies.[26]

Stated negatively, the argument utilized by a Christian apologist must not grant the non-Christian assumption that predication, either *in part* or *in toto*, can be justified independently of the truth of God's existence. Again,

---

25. Frame summarizes Van Til's approach to theistic proof as the belief that "all legitimate theistic proof reduces to the 'proof from the possibility of predication.' God exists, in other words, because without him it would not be possible to reason, to think, or even to attach a predicate to a subject." *AGG*, 70.

26. Cf. also the remarks of Greg Bahnsen in this regard. Bahnsen, *Van Til's Apologetic*, 502n63.

for Van Til, the peculiar form and logical semantics inherent in transcendental arguments are uniquely suited to address such concerns.

The question naturally arises as to whether Van Til was justified in thinking thus. Is it actually the case that the traditional arguments fail to do justice to the true character of the relation that obtains between God's existence and predication? On the other hand, what are we to make of his confidence in the ability of transcendental argument to succeed where traditional arguments have failed? Is his conviction in this regard something that can be justified, or is it merely a case of misdirected zeal on his part? In light of the preceding discussion, it would seem that the answers to these questions are to be found in a more precise clarification of the presuppositional nature of Van Til's transcendental argument from predication. Before entering into this project, however, it is necessary to briefly consider what I will call "the reductionist objection" to Van Til's belief in the distinctive character of transcendental argument.

JOHN FRAME AND THE LOGICAL SEMANTICS OF REDUCTION

Objections to the unique character of transcendental arguments are of some vintage in the history of philosophy, going back at least as far as Kant. The decade following the publication of Kant's *Critique* in 1781 witnessed a number of critical responses to the distinctive claims of Kant's transcendental program. Indeed, a number of Kant's German contemporaries insisted that insofar as Kant's transcendental program constituted an answer to Hume, it was merely restating arguments that had already been voiced by the rationalist philosopher Leibniz.[27] Such criticism paved the way for later, more sophisticated attempts to deny the distinctive character of transcendental argument. To take but one example, in a series of articles published during the latter third of the twentieth century, Moltke S. Gram mounted a sustained attack on the notion that transcendental arguments are

---

27. See Henry E. Allison, *The Kant-Eberhard Controversy* (Baltimore: The Johns Hopkins University Press, 1973). Eberhard was a contemporary critic of Kant who argued, according to Allison, "that whatever is true in Kant is already found in Leibniz, and that wherever Kant differs from Leibniz he is wrong." Ibid., 9. Kant's own response to Eberhard came in 1790 in the form of a short essay titled "On a Discovery According to Which Any New Critique of Pure Reason Has Been Made Superfluous by an Earlier One." Although Eberhard never argued that a formal equivalence obtains between transcendental and deductive arguments, he nevertheless opened the door to such criticism by questioning whether Kant's transcendental philosophy differed in substance from the deductive rationalism of Leibniz.

formally distinct from deductive arguments.[28] On Gram's view, statements of the form "p presupposes q" are *reducible* to statements of the form "p implies q."[29] Hence there is at least some justification for classifying arguments of this type under the title *the reductionist objection*. To be sure, the descriptive term *reductionist*, like the term *rationalist*, admits of a broad range of uses. However its application in this paper is somewhat restricted and refers primarily to someone who claims that a relationship of deductive equivalence obtains between the form of a transcendental argument and the argument forms of standard propositional logic (e.g., *modus ponens* and *modus tollens*).

Not surprisingly, the debate has also spilled over into Van Tillian circles. Greg Bahnsen and John Frame, arguably the two leading successors to Van Til in the twentieth century, have weighed in on different sides of the debate, with Frame arguing in favor of the reductionist objection in a number of articles and books.[30] Central to Frame's argument is the claim that "any indirect argument can be made into a direct argument with some creative rephrasing."[31] In support of this claim, Frame begins with an abbreviated statement of Van Til's transcendental argument, then goes on to argue that it translates into an argument that is basically deductive in form. Thus in the final analysis, argues Frame, "it doesn't make much difference whether you say 'Causality, therefore God' or 'Without God, no causality, therefore God.' "[32]

A closer look at Frame's program of reduction indicates that it turns on the deductive relationship that exists between two rules of inference in formal logic known as *modus ponens* and *modus tollens*. In order to see this more clearly, it is necessary to state Frame's argument more fully. Let us begin with Frame's abbreviated statement of the direct argument, namely, "Causality, therefore God." Spelled out more fully, this argument takes the form of *modus ponens*, or "the mode of affirmation":

---

28. See the helpful bibliography on Gram provided in Stephen Wentworth Arndt, "Transcendental Method and Transcendental Arguments," *International Philosophical Quarterly* 27 (1987): 43n1.

29. Moltke S. Gram, "Transcendental Arguments," *Nous* 5 (1971): 15–26.

30. Relevant bibliography is cited in footnote 8 above. It should be noted that in response to arguments advanced in the 2003 version of this essay, Frame has both clarified and qualified his position in some respects. See John M. Frame, "Reply to Don Collett on Transcendental Argument," *WTJ* 65 (2003): 307–9.

31. *AGG*, 76.

32. Ibid.

If causality, then God   (premise 1)
Causality   (premise 2)
Therefore God   (conclusion)

How does one get from this argument to Frame's abbreviated statement of the indirect or transcendental argument, namely, that "Without God, no causality"? By means of *modus tollens*, or "the mode of denial":

If causality, then God   (premise 1)
Not God   (premise 2)
Therefore not causality   (conclusion)

Here *modus tollens* functions as a *reductio ad absurdum* for God's existence. It assumes the proposition "not God" in order to refute it by deducing a conclusion from it that is obviously false (i.e., "not causality"). This refutation then serves to clear the way, as it were, for a positive affirmation of God's existence. As Frame puts it, "Since we are unwilling to accept the conclusion, we must negate the premise and say that God does exist."[33]

As noted earlier, Frame construes Van Til's transcendental argument as an "indirect argument" that essentially functions as a *reductio*.[34] On my view, this equation helps explain Frame's tendency to construe Van Til's transcendental argument in terms of *modus tollens*, a practice that in my opinion is misleading (see further below). The important thing to note here, however, especially with respect to Frame's program of reduction, is that the argument form *modus tollens* can be derived deductively from the common major premise it shares with the argument form *modus ponens*.[35] Using the rules of replacement for standard propositional logic, such a derivation might appear as follows:

1. $(p \supset q) \bullet \sim q$ (assumed premise)
2. $p \supset q$ (by simplification from 1)
3. $\sim q$ (by simplification from 1)

33. Ibid. By way of further clarification, one should also note that the conclusion "God exists" is not true unless premise 1 is true as well. In other words, Frame's reconstruction takes premise 1 as a given.

34. See footnote 19 above.

35. For a list of the rules of replacement commonly used in propositional logic, see Irving M. Copi, *Introduction to Logic*, 7th ed. (New York: MacMillan, 1986).

4. ~ p v q   (by material implication from 2)

5. ~ p   (by disjunctive syllogism from 3, 4)

6. $[(p \supset q) \bullet \sim q] \supset \sim p$ (completed proof from 1–5)

As the above derivation demonstrates, in a complete propositional logic where the form *modus ponens* is valid, the form *modus tollens* will be valid as well. Thus one can move inferentially, as it were, from the common major premise that *modus ponens* shares with *modus tollens* to the same conclusion one would have arrived at using the argument form *modus tollens*. As far as the semantics of standard propositional logic are concerned, therefore, Frame is essentially right in his claim that "most positive arguments can be put into negative form and vice versa, with some skill in phrasing."[36]

However, Frame goes even further. Having argued a case for the methodological equivalence of transcendental and traditional arguments, he goes on to suggest that Van Tillians should rest content with "a presuppositionalism of the heart" rather than continuing to insist on the distinctiveness of presuppositionalism on a formal or methodological level.[37] Although some Van Tillians may be uncomfortable with the conclusion that presuppositionalism's distinctiveness primarily consists in a subjective attitude rather than an objective method, such a conclusion is difficult to escape once the validity of Frame's reductionist program is granted. It should be noted, however, that a more conciliatory reading of Frame's argument is possible when one takes into account the following concession on his part: "I do not deny in principle that spiritual concerns can have specific methodological consequences. I am only saying that Van Til has not succeeded in proving that his spiritual concerns directly entail his methodological proposals."[38] Here Frame seems to be willing to grant *in principle* the possibility that Van Til's "spiritual concerns" may in fact translate into "specific methodological consequences," although he is clearly skeptical about the possibility of making a case for it. At the same time it is important to note that, despite his reservations on the matter, Frame never fully closes the door to the possibility of making a formal case for the distinctive character of transcendental arguments.[39]

36. *CVT*, 318.

37. Ibid., 320; *AGG*, 85–88.

38. *CVT*, 320.

39. Renewed awareness of this fact on my part, coupled with the reflections registered at the outset of this essay, has led me to the conclusion that when all is said and done, Frame and I are not that far apart in our understandings of the issues at hand.

Nevertheless, Christian apologists from both sides of the apologetic fence have questioned the validity of Frame's deductive reading of transcendental argument. In a recently published collection of apologetic essays, William Lane Craig asserts that Frame "confuses transcendental reasoning with what the medievals called *demonstratio quia*, proof that proceeds from consequence to ground."[40] This is but another way of saying that Frame confuses transcendental argument with a search for the premises in a deductive argument. Although I agree to some extent with Craig's observation, it should be noted that Craig does not interact with, much less refute, the case that Frame makes elsewhere in support of his particular reading of transcendental arguments.[41] Thus Craig's objection, although on the right track, fails to truly answer Frame.[42]

Criticism of Frame's program has also arisen from within the household of Van Til. In a series of lectures given at Westminster Seminary in California,[43] Bahnsen argues that Frame's denial of the distinctive character of transcendental argument rests upon equivocation with respect to the meaning of causality. Bahnsen points out that when a Thomist makes use of a causal premise in traditional argument, that premise speaks of nothing more than the mere function of causality (i.e., for every effect there is a cause). On the other hand, when a Van Tillian makes use of a causal premise in transcendental argument, that premise concerns not merely the function of causality, but the ground of its intelligibility. Hence Frame is allegedly guilty of confusing descriptive claims about causality (Aquinas) with normative or regulative claims about its possibility (Van Til), thus turning a premise about the mere function of causality into a premise about its intelligibility.

Bahnsen's reply, however, ultimately misses Frame's point. For Frame the problem is not whether Van Tillians and Thomists mean different things when they appeal to the concept of causality in apologetic argument, but

40. William Lane Craig, "A Classical Apologist's Response," in *Five Views on Apologetics*, 233.

41. Frame briefly references the case for his interpretation of transcendental argument in Frame, "Presuppositional Apologetics," in *Five Views on Apologetics*, 220n18.

42. Craig also attempts to identify Alvin Plantinga, rather than Van Til, as the true exponent of the transcendental argument for Christian theism in the twentieth century. Although Plantinga's arguments provide us with a devastating critique of naturalism on its own terms, to my knowledge he nowhere makes the transcendental claim, as did Van Til, that the very intelligibility of the naturalist's claims, whether true *or* false, *necessarily* presupposes the truth of Christian theism.

43. These lectures were taped and transcribed into a booklet titled *An Answer to Frame's Critique of Van Til: Profound Differences between the Traditional and Presuppositional Methods*. The booklet contains no publishing information, but apparently derives from a series of guest lectures Bahnsen delivered in 1993 at Westminster Seminary in California. The booklet is made available by the Westminster Campus Bookstore in Philadelphia.

whether these differences find expression on the level of apologetic method and formal argument as such. If they do not, then the sharp distinction Van Til posits between his method and the traditional method collapses, along with all attempts to distinguish, on methodological grounds alone, Van Tillian and Thomistic uses of the word *causality*.[44] The question that Bahnsen's objection leaves unanswered, at least as far as Frame is concerned, is how such equivocation is to be detected on the level of formal argument per se.[45] Thus Bahnsen's initial reply to Frame, although plausible in some respects, nevertheless fails to penetrate to the heart of Frame's argument.

Before proceeding to a concluding summary of Frame's arguments, it should be noted by way of anticipation that a more recent argument formulated by Bahnsen in *Van Til's Apologetic* comes much closer to addressing the precise issue raised by Frame.[46] To my knowledge Frame has not directly replied to this argument in print. An attempt to further clarify and extend Bahnsen's argument will be undertaken in the section of this essay on "Distinguishing Presupposition from Implication"; at the same time I will be adding a further argument of my own that attempts to exploit formal developments in the semantics of presupposition within the tradition of analytic philosophy.

Frame's argument, then, may be summarized in terms of two claims: First, that Van Til's *method* of apologetic argument *reduces* to the traditional method in view of the relationship of deductive equivalence that obtains between the two. Consequently, Van Til's attempt to draw a methodological distinction between his position and the argument forms of natural theology *fails*, since no such distinction exists. The second claim is closely related to the first, namely, that Van Til's presuppositionalism is best understood "as an appeal to the heart rather than as a straightforward apologetic method."[47]

One might be inclined to concede the case for "a presuppositionalism of the heart"[48] were it not for the fact that another interpretation of the con-

---

44. Although Frame is willing to grant that Van Til's understanding of causality differs at important points from that of Aquinas, he apparently believes that one must consult Aquinas' writings on nature and grace, rather than his apologetic method per se, to make a solid case for the claim that Aquinas defined the principle of causality in an "autonomous" fashion (e-mail correspondence from John Frame to the author).

45. "How do we know when an apologist is assuming that the universe is intelligible apart from God? Usually, not from the form of his argument as such." *CVT*, 319.

46. See Bahnsen, *Van Til's Apologetic*, 501–2.

47. *CVT*, 320.

48. The arguments that follow should not be construed as an attempt to deny that presuppositionalism involves a heart attitude as well as an objective method. I heartily concur with

cept of presupposition is available in the work of Peter Strawson, one that arguably makes more systematic sense of Van Til's transcendental argument, especially his argument from predication. Moreover, when this concept is used to clarify what is meant by the term *presupposition*, a plausible case can be made for the claim that transcendental arguments are *not* deductively equivalent with (or reducible to) the traditional argument forms of natural theology. Ironically, what Frame's program demonstrates is *not* that transcendental and traditional arguments are deductively equivalent, but that the logical semantics of traditional argument forms are inadequate when it comes to capturing the distinctive concerns of Van Til's apologetic.

Distinguishing Presupposition from Implication

By way of preface it should also be noted that although Van Til himself never provided a formal defense of the proposition that transcendental arguments are irreducible to either deductive or inductive arguments, it does not follow from this that he was unaware of the reductionist objection to his position. In *A Survey of Christian Epistemology*, a book that traces back to the earliest years of his teaching career, Van Til speaks of the distinction that exists between the transcendental method on the one hand, and the inductive and deductive method on the other:

> To us the only thing of great significance in this connection is that it is often found to be more difficult to distinguish our method from the deductive method than from the inductive method. But the favorite charge against us is that we are still bound to the past and are therefore employing the deductive method. Our opponents are thoughtlessly identifying our method with the Greek method of deduction. For this reason it is necessary for us to make the difference between these two methods as clear as we can.[49]

This passage serves as a reminder that the reductionist objection to transcendental argument is not new, nor was Van Til unaware of it. Nevertheless, there is truth in Frame's claim that Van Til never provided us with

---

Frame's insistence that presuppositionalism, rightly understood, requires a particular heart attitude. However, one need not concur with Frame's deductive reading of the transcendental argument in order to agree with him on this point.

49. *SCE*, 9. This work represents the second edition of a syllabus originally circulated by Van Til in 1932 under the title *The Metaphysics of Apologetics*.

an argument for its distinctiveness.[50] What follows is a tentative attempt to do so by making use of twentieth-century philosophical discussion of the concept of presupposition and the subsequent application of this discussion to transcendental argument. Admittedly, this will involve making use of ideas that, strictly speaking, do not appear in Van Til's writings. Nevertheless, I believe that the clarity they lend to the concept of presupposition in Van Til's approach to transcendental argument, and especially his argument from predication, will eventually justify their introduction. Perhaps not all Van Tillians will find my argument convincing. At the very least, however, it should serve to suggest a new avenue of approach to the question that others may perhaps build on.

The failure of traditional argument forms to capture what is meant by the concept of presupposition points up the need for a more precise way of construing the semantic relation between statements related by it. The most promising option that has emerged is arguably that of Peter Strawson. According to Strawson, a statement A may be said to *presuppose* a statement B if B is a necessary precondition of the truth or falsity of A.[51] Strawson's interpretation of the concept of presupposition has been restated in succinct fashion by Bas van Fraassen as follows: *A presupposes B if and only if A is neither true nor false unless B is true.*[52] This may also be stated as follows:[53]

(1) A presupposes B if and only if:
    a) A is true, then B is true.
    b) ~A is true, then B is true.

Van Fraassen's formulation is helpful for two reasons. First, it enables us to articulate more precisely Van Til's claim that "no human being can utter a

---

50. "The first thing to note is that in this discussion Van Til has not presented us with an actual argument. He has presented (1) a conclusion, (2) a logical model, and (3) a practical strategy. . . . I confess that I am not convinced that a transcendental argument for Christian theism must of necessity be indirect rather than direct. To my knowledge, Van Til never argues the point, but merely asserts it. But it is by no means obvious." *CVT*, 315, 317.

51. "A statement S presupposes a statement S' in the sense that the truth of S' is a precondition of the truth-or-falsity of S." Strawson, *Introduction to Logical Theory*, 175.

52. Van Fraassen, "Presupposition," 137. Cf. also the application of van Fraassen's work to Kant's transcendental argument in Gordon G. Brittan, *Kant's Theory of Science* (Princeton: Princeton University Press, 1978), 28–42.

53. Since A has no truth value (i.e., is neither true nor false) unless B is true, the truth of B must be presupposed whenever A has a truth value (i.e., whenever A is either true or false). Thus van Fraassen's definition may be restated in terms of the conjunction given in (1) above.

single syllable, *whether in negation or affirmation,* unless it were for God's existence."[54] Second, it provides us with more formal language by which to articulate the differences between transcendental and traditional argument forms. To illustrate this, let us begin by applying the semantic relation embodied in (1)(a) to the causal argument for God's existence. Letting C = causality, and G = God's existence, we translate as follows:

(2) C presupposes G   (premise 1)
    C   (premise 2)
    Therefore G   (conclusion)

A comparison of this argument form with *modus ponens* makes it clear, as van Fraassen has noted, "that an analogue of *modus ponens* holds also for presupposition."[55] Formal differences become apparent, however, when we negate the minor premise in (2) as follows:

(3) C presupposes G   (premise 1)
    ~C   (premise 2)
    Therefore G   (conclusion)

Note that in terms of the characterization provided by (1), the corollary principle (1)(b) shows that (3) is *valid,* whereas this argument would be *invalid* for implication. Moreover, although (2) may be legitimately construed as an "analogue" of *modus ponens,* (3) is neither an instance of *modus ponens* nor strictly speaking an analogue to it.[56] In other words, the argument form represented by (3) is apparently unique to arguments based on the semantic relation of presupposition.

We are now in a position to identify a distinguishing feature of arguments based on the concept of presupposition as we have formulated it here. That feature concerns what logicians refer to as "truth-functionality." In arguments (2) and (3), the truth value of the conclusion is *not* a function of the truth value of the antecedent minor premise (i.e., premise 2), since the conclusion remains true whether C or ~C obtains. By way of contrast, in the case of traditional arguments

54. *SCE,* 11 (emphasis added).
55. Van Fraassen, "Presupposition," 137.
56. Cf. the discussion of *modus ponens* in Copi, *Introduction to Logic,* 296.

formulated in terms of *modus ponens* or *modus tollens*, the truth value of the conclusion *is* a direct function of the truth value of the antecedent minor premise. In *Van Til's Apologetic*, Bahnsen calls attention to this peculiar feature of transcendental arguments. He summarizes the matter as follows:

> To put it simply, in the case of "direct" arguments (whether rational or empirical), the negation of one of their premises changes the truth or reliability of their conclusion. But this is not true of transcendental arguments, and that sets them off from the other kinds of proof or analysis. A transcendental argument begins with any item of experience or belief whatsoever and proceeds, by critical analysis, to ask what conditions (or what other beliefs) would need to be true in order for that original experience or belief to make sense, be meaningful, or be intelligible to us. Now then, if we should go back and negate the statement of that original belief (or consider a contrary experience), the transcendental analysis (if originally cogent or sound) would nevertheless reach the very same conclusion.[57]

Given the lack of a truth-functional relationship between the premises and conclusions of transcendental arguments, some may be inclined to question whether they should be regarded as actual instances of argument at all. However, it must be remembered that truth-functionality cannot be invoked as a normative criterion for defining what counts as "argument" and what does not, since arguments expressed in terms of first-order quantificational logic *also* lack a truth-functional character, although no one would deny their status as arguments for that reason.[58] Hence truth-functionality per se cannot serve as a decisive criterion by which to define what does or does not count as argument in apologetic discourse. On the other hand, as Bahnsen rightly recognized, this feature does serve to distinguish transcendental arguments from arguments expressed in terms of standard propositional logic (e.g., *modus ponens* and *modus tollens*).

Generally speaking, then, presuppositional or transcendental arguments may be distinguished from traditional arguments based on standard propositional logic, for instance *modus ponens* and *modus tollens*, in terms

57. Bahnsen, *Van Til's Apologetic*, 501–2.

58. Cf. the discussion of quantification in Mark Sainsbury, *Logical Forms: An Introduction to Philosophical Logic* (Cambridge, MA: Basil Blackwell, 1991), 182–85.

of "the truth-functional relation of their conclusions to their premises."[59] In view of this distinction, the claim that traditional forms of the causal argument yield "a transcendental conclusion"[60] becomes questionable. To qualify as a transcendental conclusion, the truth value of the conclusion in such arguments would have to be in some sense independent of the truth value of its antecedent premise (i.e., non truthfunctional). However, both *modus ponens* and *modus tollens*, two classic forms in which the causal argument has been traditionally expressed, fail to meet this criterion.[61] The same must be said with respect to the claim that we can reach a "transcendental conclusion by many kinds of specific arguments, including many of the traditional ones."[62] In the nature of the case, the truth of a transcendental conclusion does not depend on the truth value of its antecedent premise, regardless of whether this premise affirms causality or any other principle, since a transcendental conclusion constitutes the very ground for the proof of that premise.[63]

Formal differences between the concepts of presupposition and implication also emerge when we consider the analogue to *modus tollens* for presupposition:

(4) C presupposes G
    ~G
    Therefore ~C

Again, whereas this argument would be valid for implication as an instance of *modus tollens*, it is *not* valid when C and G are joined by the semantic relation of presupposition, since in the latter case C has no truth value unless G is true.[64] Thus the possibility of assigning a truth value to C depends on

---

59. Bahnsen, *Van Til's Apologetic*, 501.

60. Frame, "Presuppositional Apologetics," 220–21.

61. Noteworthy at this point is the fact that Frame construes the traditional causal argument for God's existence in terms of both *modus ponens* and *modus tollens*. AGG, 76.

62. Frame, "Presuppositional Apologetics," 220.

63. The classic definition of a transcendental principle in argument was given by Kant in his *Critique of Pure Reason*: "But though it needs proof, it should be entitled a *principle*, not a *theorem*, because it has the peculiar character that it makes possible the very experience which is its own ground of proof, and that in this experience it must always itself be presupposed." Immanuel Kant, *Critique of Pure Reason*, trans. Norman Kemp Smith (London: Macmillan, 1958), B765.

64. Recall that in terms of the way we have construed the presuppositional relation, the truth value of C (i.e., its truth or falsity) depends on the truth of G. Thus if G fails to obtain, then the possibility of predicating a truth value for C also fails to obtain.

the logically prior question of whether G truly "refers" or actually obtains.[65] Thus if ~G obtains, we have what Strawson refers to as "a failure of presupposition," in which case the possibility of assigning a truth value to C does not even arise.

John Frame has rightly noted that Van Til's apologetic method "seeks to show that *all* intelligibility depends on, or presupposes, Christian theism."[66] In light of the preceding arguments, however, there is reason to question whether traditional arguments expressed in terms of *modus tollens* meet this criterion. In argumentative instances where causality (C) and God's existence (G) are related by implication, ~C follows from ~G. In other words, an argument formulated in terms of *modus tollens* contains the implication, albeit subtle, that *at least some* types of predication are possible in cases where God's existence fails to obtain. By way of contrast, Van Til desired to argue that even cases of predicational negation presuppose the truth of God's existence. In light of this, *modus tollens* would seem to be incapable of sustaining the apologetically radical goal he was aiming at with his argument from predication.

To sum up, the problem with traditional argument forms is that they do not allow one to argue the proposition ~G *therefore neither C or ~C*, nor do they allow one to argue its corollary proposition ~C *therefore G*. The transcendental character of these propositions is evident from the fact that both of them depend on the assumption that G constitutes a necessary precondition for the very possibility of assigning a truth value to C. Since Van Til clearly sought to establish these propositions via apologetic argument, and since traditional argument forms do not allow one to do so—indeed, in at least two cases they actually invalidate these propositions—it follows that traditional argument forms simply cannot do justice to Van Til's apologetic goals. It also remains questionable whether there is any meaningful sense in which one may continue to say that traditional arguments yield transcendental conclusions. At best such a statement is highly ambiguous and ultimately misleading.

As noted in the section of this paper on "John Frame and the Logical Semantics of Reduction," the reductionist objection to the unique character of transcendental argument rests upon the assertion that "p implies q" and

65. On the referential function of the concept of semantic presupposition, at least as I'm construing it here, see footnote 16 above.

66. *CVT*, 314–15 (emphasis added).

"p presupposes q" are deductively equivalent propositions. However, if the arguments developed above are valid, as I am inclined to believe, then it follows that semantic differences between the concepts of presupposition and implication do in fact translate into differences on the level of formal argument and method. As such it is not possible to reduce "presuppositional" or transcendental arguments to arguments expressed in terms of standard propositional logic (e.g., *modus ponens* and *modus tollens*), all of which is to say that the reductionist objection to transcendental argument fails.

Transcendental Argument and the *Reductio ad Absurdum*

Strawson's concept of presupposition, as formulated by van Fraassen, also allows us to sharpen the distinction between the method of *reductio ad absurdum* and Van Til's transcendental argument from predication. In a *reductio*, a position is refuted by deducing a contradiction from its premises. In Van Til's transcendental argument from predication, the possibility of assigning a truth value—and thus by extension the very possibility of generating a contradiction—fails to obtain unless God's existence is already true (i.e., truly refers). In other words, Van Til's transcendental argument from predication makes a stronger claim than the claim generated by the *reductio*. The latter generates a contradiction from the non-Christian position, although Van Til's transcendental argument from predication makes the more radical claim that contradiction itself is impossible apart from the truth of God's existence. To state the contrast in slightly different terms, if God's existence is a necessary condition for the mere truth of causality, then denying God's existence while affirming causality results in contradiction. However, if God's existence is a necessary condition for both the truth or falsity of causality, then denying God's existence results in a failure to predicate anything at all.[67]

This points up an important reason why the transcendental argument should not be confused or equated with the method of *reductio ad absurdum*.

---

67. Strawson argues that the logical absurdity involved in self-contradiction should be distinguished from the logical absurdity involved in a failure of presupposition: "It is self-contradictory to conjoin S with the denial of S' if S' is a necessary condition of the truth, simply, of S. It is a different kind of logical absurdity to conjoin S with the denial of S' if S' is a necessary condition of the *truth or falsity* of S. The relation between S and S' in the first case is that S entails S'. We need a different name for the relation between S and S' in the second case; let us say . . . that S *presupposes* S'." Strawson, *An Introduction to Logical Theory*, 175.

For Van Til it was not enough to deduce a contradiction from the non-Christian's position and leave matters at that. Indeed, had Van Til stopped there, it is doubtful whether he would have ruffled as many apologetic feathers as he did. Rather, Van Til insisted on going further and making the *transcendental* claim that the very intelligibility of the non-Christian's claims, whether true *or* false, *necessarily* presupposes the truth of Christian theism. If there is an apologetic equivalent to the offense of the cross in Van Til's method, this would be it. To be sure, in the context of apologetic argument, the *reductio* helps clarify the nature of the presuppositional relation between God's existence and causality, and it does this by pointing out contradictions that arise in the non-Christian position when God's existence is denied. Strictly speaking, however, the *reductio* does not establish God's existence, since the possibility of argument itself *already* presupposes the truth of God's existence in a referential sense, and it is precisely the latter claim that Van Til's transcendental argument from predication seeks to demonstrate.

Van Til's transcendental argument from predication helps us to see that the most fundamental question in logic and argument turns out to be an ontological one, namely, that of God's existence.[68] For Van Til, God's existence is an ontological presupposition that grounds the very possibility of logic, and thus (by extension) argument itself. This is doubtless the reason why Van Til's apologetic method takes very seriously the essential character of the relation between God's existence and argument—so much so that on Van Til's view of things, the negation of God's existence renders argument impossible. How so? By rendering impossible the task of assigning truth values in argument (i.e., predication). In this way Van Til's transcendental argument from predication takes us beyond the analysis of particular arguments and raises the question of argument itself.

FURTHER OBJECTIONS

A few closing caveats in anticipation of possible objections.[69] First of all, one might object that although the preceding analysis serves to clarify

68. The primacy of ontology over epistemology in Van Til's apologetic traces back to his earliest writings, as evidenced by the title *The Metaphysics of Apologetics*, a work written by Van Til in 1932 (cf. footnote 49 above). Viewed from this perspective, Van Til's apologetic method is both thoroughly anti-Kantian and anti-modernist.

69. I would like to thank John Frame and James W. Allard (professor of philosophy at Montana State University) for reading over an earlier version of this essay and offering many

the concept of presupposition in Van Til's apologetic, it fails to provide an actual example of transcendental or "presuppositional" argument. By way of response, it may be helpful to examine more closely a few of the assumptions involved in asserting that the following *is* an argument:

(5) Causality implies God
   Not God
   Therefore not causality

while at the same time asserting that the following is *not* an argument:

(6) Causality presupposes God
   Not God
   Therefore neither causality or not causality (i.e., neither C nor ~C).[70]

Note that (6) constitutes a formally valid instance of argument, *given* the definition of presupposition stated in (1) in the section of this paper on "Distinguishing Presupposition from Implication." Hence the ground for privileging (5) while rejecting (6) as instances of argument appears to be motivated, at least in part, by a refusal to allow the introduction and integration of the concept of presupposition into one's definition of what counts as "argument."[71] Christian apologists should resist the rationalism lurking behind the Procrustean notion that the only arguments worthy of the name are those whose formal character can be articulated solely in terms of the semantic relations of propositional logic. Such a notion effectively forecloses the possibility of expanding the semantic domain of our concept of argument to include arguments similar in form to (6). Van Tillians in particular

---

helpful criticisms and suggestions. Their critical interaction provided the catalyst for many of the clarifications I have made throughout this essay.

70. The conclusion expressed by (6) should not be read as a denial of the existence of causality per se, but rather as a denial of the possibility of predicating truly or falsely about it. To state matters more generally, as an instance of transcendental argument, (6) concerns itself with those preconditions that secure the truth condition *under which* meaningful talk about the truth value of causality is possible. Again, the argument does not concern itself with establishing the ontological status of causality per se.

71. The most successful attempt to integrate the concept of "semantic presupposition" into formal logic is Bas van Fraassen's. See van Fraassen, "Presupposition," 136–52; cf. also the remarks of Post, "Referential Presupposition," 161n4.

should be wary of adopting a form of rationalist dogmatism that refuses to admit the limitations inherent in the argument forms of propositional logic.

Popular discussions of the discipline of logic often proceed as though it were a pure, objective science to be sharply distinguished from the more speculative and subjective character of other philosophical disciplines (e.g., metaphysics, epistemology, ethics, and aesthetics). If nothing else, continuing debates within the field of philosophical logic teach us that logic as a discipline is not immune from the influence of the ontological commitments of its practitioners, and thus should not be regarded as an independent and objective science, wholly isolated from the theological and philosophical outlook of scholarly communities and guilds. More importantly for the point at hand, such debates should also teach us that the semantics of standard propositional logic and its accompanying argument forms *do not* constitute an infallible canon that is above criticism and/or expansion. Controversies surrounding the concept of validity in propositional logic, or what Mark Sainsbury refers to as "P-validity," may be taken as a case in point. Reflecting on the adequacy of this concept, Sainsbury writes: "No one has ever supposed that P-validity *exhausts* the notion of validity, nor even that of formal validity. . . . What is at issue is whether P-validity gives a partial characterization of validity, or formal validity."[72]

One may nevertheless object that an argument such as (6) begs the question, inasmuch as it assumes that a certain semantic relation between God and causality obtains from the outset. However, other commonly accepted forms of argument, for instance arguments expressed in terms of propositional logic, also make use of semantic relations and concepts that inevitably involve certain assumptions, a number of which are notoriously controversial among philosophers of logic. Thus there appears to be no reason why, *prima facie*, an argument that begins with the premise "C presupposes G" should be assigned a lesser status than an argument that begins with the premise "C implies G." Indeed, one may go further and raise the question whether finite creatures can begin any argument without making assumptions of some sort or other. The real question is not whether initial assumptions can be avoided, but whether subsequent argument confirms their soundness.

The latter observation provides a convenient opportunity to address a possible misunderstanding of the nature of the claim being made here. In defending the right of (6) to lay claim to the title of "argument," the

---

72. Sainsbury, *Logical Forms*, 51 (emphasis added).

additional claim is *not* being made that (6) proves the whole of Christian theism in one argument. Although in my opinion (6) constitutes a legitimate instance of transcendental argument, it obviously does so in an abbreviated form. For this reason it is more accurate, and for apologetic purposes more useful, to regard (6) as an *abbreviated* transcendental argument. Other arguments may and in fact should be utilized in order to demonstrate the necessary character of the presuppositional relation between causality and God expressed in the major premise of (6). What (6) serves to illustrate is that an argument may be objectively valid from a formal point of view, yet insufficient from a practical point of view. In the concrete world of apologetic engagement one is certainly bound to make use of a variety of arguments. Admitting this does not entail the conclusion, however, that transcendental and traditional arguments cannot be distinguished from one another on formal grounds, or that they are somehow deductively equivalent to one another.

Finally, some might object that the arguments advanced in this paper entail the conclusion that Christian apologists, and Van Tillians in particular, are somehow obliged to stop using the argument forms of standard propositional logic. After all, if argument forms such as *modus tollens* are formally invalid when arguments such as (6) are operative, what place remains for the argument forms of standard propositional logic in a presuppositional apologetic? At this juncture it is helpful to keep in mind that in terms of the concept of presupposition set forth in this paper, both *modus ponens* and its presuppositional analogue represent valid forms of argument. This arises from the fact that semantic differences between the latter two argument forms, although clearly present, nevertheless do not register themselves on a formal level when the concept of presupposition is operative. Thus in the particular case of *modus ponens*, there is in fact *formal* overlap between an argument expressed in terms of propositional logic and its presuppositional analogue. Commenting on the nature of this overlap, van Fraassen writes: "Thus presupposition and implication are not the same, but they have something in common. What they have in common is that, if A either presupposes or implies B, the argument from A to B is valid."[73] Taken together, these considerations indicate that in argumentative contexts where *modus ponens* is operative, methodological differences between presuppositional and traditional approaches do not

73. Van Fraassen, "Presupposition," 138.

register themselves on a *formal* level. Thus it would appear that *modus ponens* is amenable to integration with the logical semantics of transcendental argument on a formal level, and as such places no stumbling block in the path leading to Van Til's apologetic.

Modus tollens, on the other hand, is obviously a more difficult case. Here we find ourselves bumping up against the issues mentioned at the outset of this essay, thus returning full circle to the place where we began. Alongside its traditional apologetic applications, *modus tollens* now functions as a useful index of the limitations inherent in the artificial languages of formal logic, thus warning us of the dangers inherent in the "rationalist dogmatism" mentioned above. From the fact that we have not been able to construct a logical language capable of *fully* reconciling these traditional applications with the logical semantics of presupposition, it does not follow that *modus tollens* should be immediately retired from the service of apologetic argument without further ado. To do so would be to fail to properly respond to the *partial* nature of the characterization of "validity" at work in the logical semantics of standard propositional logic. As an apologetic argument for God's existence, *modus tollens* clearly has limitations, and these limitations should be recognized as such. One must be careful at this point, however, not to throw out the philosophical baby with the bathwater. There are no compelling reasons for "presuppositionalists" to religiously abstain from making use of *modus tollens* in any and all apologetic contexts, provided that they have been properly sensitized to the limitations inherent in the languages of formal logic. It is entirely possible and permissible to make a fruitful use of *modus tollens* in the context of apologetic argument while at the same time recognizing that its logical form is simply not capable of accommodating an important feature of the inner relationship between God's existence and human predication. In this way the argument forms of standard propositional logic, properly qualified and thus circumscribed, find their true function and proper place under the larger umbrella provided by the semantics of presupposition and transcendental argument.

Conclusion

The philosophical journal *Nous* featured a symposium on transcendental arguments in 1971. Among the contributors to that symposium was Moltke S. Gram, who began his paper as follows: "The problem about transcendental arguments is whether there are any."[74] Obviously the passage of some forty years has not rendered this question moot by any means. Secular philosophers certainly have not reached anything like a consensus on this question. From this it does not follow, however, that Christian apologists are somehow bound to share in Gram's skepticism with respect to transcendental arguments. On the other hand, one must also grant that neither van Fraassen nor Strawson has said the last word on presupposition, and there may in fact be better ways to construe the relation of presupposition. There may also be different and even better ways of stating the case for the distinctive character of "presuppositional" or transcendental argument. At the very least, however, the arguments advanced in this paper call into question the assumption that the concept of presupposition lacks formal and methodological significance. A plausible case can be made for the distinctive character of Van Til's transcendental argument, provided one keeps an eye on the concept of presupposition and the distinctive way that it functions in his argument.

Glory be to the Father, and to the Son, and to the Holy Spirit, world without end. Amen.

74. Gram, "Transcendental Arguments," 15.

21

FRAME IN THE CONTEXT OF
RECENT APOLOGETICS

WILLIAM C. DAVIS

A FAN OF John Frame who performs an Internet search for *apologetics* to see Frame's place in the recent context is likely to be disappointed.[1] The list of sites offering help with apologetics is fantastically long, but Frame's name and works are not mentioned often. Over the past twenty years, apologetic resources have been multiplying like rabbits—or even faster. Books have appeared by the hundreds; apologetic training camps, seminars, and even an entire seminary have been formed.[2] The Internet has seen an amazing proliferation of Web sites, including lecture notes, lesson plans, podcast lessons, radio call-in shows, and live streaming training events. For most of the twentieth century, Frame's self-conscious efforts to maintain and extend Cornelius Van Til's apologetic methods had to contend with only a small handful of alternatives. But in the

1. I am indebted to Lauren Fritz for extensive research support and helpful suggestions in shaping this chapter and to my colleagues (John Wingard and Bill Tate) and students (Matthew Baddorf, Nathan Davis, Luke Granholm, Nathan Newman, Anna Phillips, and Jonathan Taylor) for critical comments on an early draft.
2. Southern Evangelical Seminary in Matthews, North Carolina, offers undergraduate and graduate programs that integrate "classical theology, philosophy, and apologetics for a comprehensive and coherent worldview" (http://www.ses.edu).

current context, it seems either that there are thousands of alternatives (one per Web site) or that there is only one, and that Frame's presuppositionalism has been eclipsed by an apologetic method focused on "evidences." Although Frame's presuppositionalism still gets attention among theologians trained in the classical systematic loci, the explosion of practical apologetic resources might seem to have settled on an unconscious evidentialism.[3]

In this chapter I will show that these appearances are misleading. Although Frame has never sought to be a brand name in apologetics, his central assertions about the biblical defense of the faith continue to be both important and influential. Indeed, with modernism widely abandoned and pluralism ascending, Frame's apologetics may be more worthy of close attention than ever before. I will defend these conclusions in four parts. In the first part, I will attempt to identify the heart of Frame's presupposition-alism and draw out some of the practical implications of his approach for apologetic efforts in a pluralist world. In the second part, I will consider the relationship between Frame's apologetic works and the explosion of popular resources for apologetic training. In the third part I will focus in detail on Frame and recent work on the Free Will Defense. Many other topics merit discussion, including Frame and Reformed epistemology,[4] Frame and recent

3. I use *evidentialism* to refer to the broad family of apologetic theories that make reasoning from *evidence* the heart of efforts to defend the faith *and* that explicitly or implicitly reject the need to presuppose anything that would be curious or offensive to someone doubting the claims of Christ. The classical apologetics of R. C. Sproul, John Gerstner, and Arthur Lindsley is thus self-conscious evidentialism as I will use the term, as is the natural theology of Thomas Aquinas, or the method advocated by William Lane Craig. See R. C. Sproul, John H. Gerstner, and Arthur W. Lindsley, *Classical Apologetics* (Grand Rapids: Zondervan, 1984); William Lane Craig, "Classical Apologetics," in Steven B. Cowan, ed., *Five Views on Apologetics* (Grand Rapids: Zondervan, 2000), 25–55, and replies to the other contributors. Apologetic methods that focus on reasoning from the evidence without stipulating Christian epistemological assumptions or questioning the adequacy of non-Christian assumptions or "worldview" in dealing with evidence are also included in *evidentialism*. See, for example, Gary Habermas, "Evidential Apologetics," in Cowan, *Five Views on Apologetics*, 91–121; J. P. Moreland, *Scaling the Secular City* (Ada, MI: Baker Academic, 1987); Josh McDowell, *Evidence That Demands a Verdict* (Carlisle, UK: Authentic Lifestyle, 2004); Sean McDowell, ed., *Apologetics for a New Generation* (Eugene, OR: Harvest House, 2009).

4. For a presuppositionalist treatment of Reformed epistemology, see Scott Oliphint, "The Old-New Reformed Epistemology," in Scott Oliphint and Lane G. Tipton, eds., *Revelation and Reason* (Phillipsburg, NJ: P&R Publishing, 2007), 207–19. The term *Reformed epistemology* is something of a joke. It was called "Reformed" *by others* because of Alvin Plantinga and Nicholas Wolterstorff's association with Calvin College and *not* because these two set out to give an episte-mology built on the commitments of historic Reformed Christianity. Their epistemology shared

critics of presuppositionalism,[5] Frame and New Age religion,[6] and Frame on Alvin Plantinga's *Warranted Christian Belief*.[7] But space is limited, and others have addressed these topics, so I will pass over these fruitful possibilities and close with a fourth part on Frame and the future of Reformed apologetics and on Tim Keller's version of presuppositionalism.

THE HEART OF FRAME'S APOLOGETIC APPROACH

John Frame's contribution to recent apologetics is easy to underestimate. Frame doesn't seek out public debates with atheists. He is slow to find fault with the work of other apologists, and he seems not to care whether he has followers. Although he does not shy away from insisting on the superiority of Van Til's apologetic methods, he acknowledges the value of the traditional evidence-based arguments used by other "schools."[8] Frame's apologetic recommendations are so practically focused and self-effacing that some have even suggested that Frame gives at best a partial apologetic theory.[9]

In this section I will show three things: first, that Frame's apologetic approach is not partial because its epistemological groundwork informs every aspect of the task of apologetics; second, that Frame's approach is more complete than many current alternatives because of his attention to the ethical dimension of defending the faith; and third, that Frame's emphasis on the ethical makes his approach particularly well suited to defending the faith in our current pluralist context. In keeping with Frame's analysis of the triperspectival nature of all ethical challenges, it is helpful to use the normative, situational, and existential perspectives to analyze Frame's central apologetic claims.

Calvin's conviction that knowledge of God's existence is universal and need not be based on any argument (but rather arises from awareness of creation).

5. Frame himself responds gently to some of his critics in Cowan, *Five Views on Apologetics*, 74–81, 132–37, 194–99, 307–12, 350–63.

6. Douglas Groothuis has helpful insights on New Age religion in *Confronting the New Age: How to Resist a Growing Religious Movement* (Downers Grove, IL: InterVarsity Press, 1988) and *Unmasking the New Age* (Downers Grove, IL: InterVarsity Press, 1986).

7. Although Plantinga is closely associated with Reformed epistemology, his work in *Warranted Christian Belief* (Oxford: Oxford University Press, 2000) goes well beyond the commitments common among advocates for Reformed epistemology. He extends his epistemology to acknowledge the crucial roles of the internal testimony of the Holy Spirit and the self-authenticating authority of the Word of God.

8. See, for example, Frame's sample apologetic method in his chapter in Cowan's *Five Views on Apologetics*, 223–31.

9. See Habermas, "Evidential Apologetics," 241, in response to Frame's exposition.

Lordship Epistemology: The Normative Perspective

At the very heart of Frame's apologetic works are epistemological recommendations rooted in the lordship of Jesus Christ. It is hard to imagine
a more fundamental normative consideration than the claim Jesus makes
on all that we do and say. Frame's lordship epistemology is developed in
detail in his works *DKG* and *DG*,[10] and the implications for apologetics are
profound. Indeed, the full "presupposition" that gives Frame's "presuppositional apologetics" its name is a lordship demand:

> The Presupposition: The God of the Bible is the Creator and Lord of all,
> and has been revealed in Jesus Christ and by the Word of God written.

Sometimes this presupposition is summarized as presupposing the God
of the Bible, or as presupposing the truth of the Word of God; but both of
these shorter versions assert the full presupposition that God is the Lord.

Frame's lordship epistemology is built on a vital biblical truth: every
epistemological claim—whether by a believer or nonbeliever—depends on
a lordship commitment. For Frame, this commitment is overt. He insists
that his heart is captive to the Word of God, and he aims to submit every
claim to the Word of God as the criterion or standard. The crucial concepts
in epistemology—*knowledge, rationality, truth, evidence*—are all constrained
by Scripture. Any discussion of what people *know*, whether reasoning is
rational, or whether *evidence* is sufficient must assume criteria for the use
of those concepts. Epistemological criteria are not chosen on the basis of
deeper criteria; they are accepted in an act of submission to a lordship claim.
Frame's apologetic method puts this act of submission on the table. Rather
than pretending to examine evidence or reasons from a lordship-neutral
standpoint, Frame calls on apologists to acknowledge the impossibility of
epistemological neutrality and the importance of "setting apart Jesus as
Lord" in their reason-giving.

Frame has been insisting on the importance of lordship epistemology
since his earliest works on Van Til, and the rest of the world is coming around
to his position. The impossibility of neutrality is increasingly accepted as
an obvious truth, both by philosophers and in popular discourse.[11] For the

10. *DKG*, 11–61, 124–25; *DG*, 21–102, 199–213, 469–512.
11. "Worldview" analyses trace back at least to Dutch statesman and philosopher Abraham
Kuyper and his *Lectures on Calvinism* (Grand Rapids: Eerdmans, 1947). James Sire's *The Uni-*

last fifty years, philosophers of science and "continental" philosophers have questioned the Enlightenment assumption that scientific practice provides or rests on a neutral, religion-free standard of reasoning.[12] Confidence that *evidence* can be assessed without serious metaphysical and axiological (i.e., religious) commitments has been declining in nearly every quarter. Some Christian apologists have lamented this decline, seeing it as a threat to our ability to defend the faith.[13] But the Bible never suggests that we should attempt to defend the faith from a position of neutrality. Continuing an emphasis found in Van Til, Frame insists that reasoning either submits to God's rule (presupposes Christ's lordship) or is a form of idolatry (submits to some other lord). Treating reason, or feeling, or sense experience as an authority apart from the lordship of Christ makes those capacities into idols. Apologetic arguments that utilize these capacities as ultimate standards encourage both the apologist and the doubter to believe the lie that they, mere creatures, have the authority to sit in judgment on God—in his existence, Christ's resurrection, or his Word.[14]

The very core of Frame's apologetic method is this concern for God's honor in everything we do. Even when an apologist adopts the doubter's presuppositions "for the sake of argument," the apologist should do it with the explicit qualification that the adoption is provisional.[15] Christ's lordship is not suspended. Rather, to make the goodness of Christ's rule more evident, the apologist shows the futility of the doubter's idolatry. Paul's reasoning with the Athenians in Acts 17 follows this line of argumentation. Paul does not point to the statue to an unknown god to praise the power of the Athe-

---

verse *Next Door* (Downers Grove, IL: InterVarsity Press, 1976) brought worldview thinking into the evangelical mainstream. For a careful treatment of the concept of worldview, see David K. Naugle, *Worldview: The History of a Concept* (Grand Rapids: Eerdmans, 2002).

12. See, for example, Thomas Kuhn, *The Structure of Scientific Revolutions* (Chicago: University of Chicago Press, 1996); Michel Foucault, "Structuralism and Poststructuralism," in *Ethics: Subjectivity and Truth: Aesthetics* (New York: The New Press, 2000); Julia Kristeva, "Women's Time," in Toril Moi, ed., *The Kristeva Reader* (Oxford: Blackwell, 1986); Alasdair MacIntyre, *Whose Justice? Which Rationality?* (Notre Dame, IN: University of Notre Dame Press, 1988).

13. See, for example, J. P. Moreland and Garrett DeWeese, "The Premature Report of Foundationalism's Demise," in Millard J. Erickson, Paul Kjoss Helseth, and Justin Taylor, eds., *Reclaiming the Center* (Wheaton: Crossway, 2004), 81–108.

14. I use *doubter* to refer to the person toward whom apologetic efforts are aimed. *Opponent* suggests that the encounter is a hostile contest, and Frame works hard to recast the challenge as personal and peaceful. See *AGG*, especially 203–17.

15. *AGG*, 75–77; also Cornelius Van Til, *The Defense of the Faith*, 3rd ed. (Philadelphia: Presbyterian and Reformed, 1967), 100–101.

nians' powers of reasoning. He shows the failure of that reasoning to get to the truth. Idolatrous, autonomous reasoning cannot deliver the true God as a conclusion. Unregenerate reason, without a change of lords, can at best produce an idolatrous projection of human excellence. Because we bear the image of God, this projection may well seem like a promising approximation of the true God, but it is still an idol.

Both Frame and his critics give careful attention to the threat that presuppositional apologetics engages in circular reasoning. The worry is that the barest reduction of a presuppositionalist argument is a tight circle: "God exists (presupposed premise), therefore God exists," or "The Bible is the Word of God and God cannot lie, therefore the Bible is the Word of God."[16] Frame argues that every system is ultimately circular if asked to justify its starting point (e.g., "Reason is infallible, therefore Reason is infallible"), and that because God is the source of all meaning and intelligibility, the Christian's circle is virtuous rather than vicious.[17] In this way, Frame pushes the problem of circularity back to a transcendental argument, according to which God's existence is the necessary precondition for all meaning or argumentation.[18]

But Frame's lordship epistemology suggests another response to the charge of circularity. The presupposition is never the mere proposition "God exists" or "The Bible is the Word of God." The presupposition is a heart commitment, an allegiance. The propositional content of this presupposition includes "God exists," but the problem of circularity arises only if the presupposition is reduced to a mere proposition! Stripped of the heart's submission to the Lord as the only rightful standard for reasoning, the mere assertion that "God exists" can be treated as any other premise in an autonomous logical calculus. Critics who treat "God exists" as a mere premise and (vacuous) conclusion in a thin circular argument have

16. An audio advertisement for Greg Koukl's *Stand to Reason* materials starts with "Tired of defending your faith with 'Because the Bible says so'?" The rhetorical weakness of the tight circle is undeniable, and Koukl is right that Christians can learn collateral reasons for their faith. But these collateral reasons will never have more genuine authority than the Word of God. Christians can be rightly embarrassed that their apologetic arguments are shallow, but they should never be embarrassed about their dependence on the Word of God as a source of confidence and hope. Happily, this advertisement does not represent Koukl's approach to the Scriptures in his own arguments. For more on Koukl, go to http://www.str.org.

17. *AGG*, 9–14; *DKG*, 130–33, 303–4; Cowan, *Five Views on Apologetics*, 354–57.

18. For more on Frame's treatment of transcendental arguments, see *AGG*, 69–75; "Transcendental Arguments," at http://www.frame-poythress.org/frame_articles/2005Transcendental.htm.

missed the point of Frame's epistemological discussion. In the context of Frame's lordship epistemology, the presupposition is much more than a mere proposition: it is an expression of submission to the Lord's right to rule every thought. Ultimately, the arguments involved are circular, but they are never small, tight circles.

Context-Sensitive Apologetics in a Pluralist World: The Situational Perspective

Frame's insistence that the apologist's approach is context-relative may not seem profound.[19] Nearly everyone writing on apologetic method today agrees with Frame, but it hasn't always been this way. From the beginning of his career Frame has been urging apologists to listen carefully and adapt their approach to the specific needs of doubters. Other apologists have disagreed, recommending instead that Christians learn a handful of powerful arguments and bring the conversation with a doubter around to those arguments.[20] In a cultural context characterized by widely shared styles of reasoning and a common memory of theism as reasonable, reliance on such a strategy of argument probably had some merit.[21] The Holy Spirit has often used these arguments as instruments in drawing scientifically minded people to himself. (The most enthusiastic defenders of the traditional theistic arguments that I have met are engineers and physicists.) Some worldview camps and Internet resources continue to teach apologetics as the development of a small set of devastating arguments against the major alternative worldviews. This approach also has some value: it provides young Christians with reasons they didn't have, and can allay the fear that their love for Christ is intellectually embarrassing. As Frame points out, comforting believers who doubt is an important part of the apologetic task.[22] So apologetics as a small set of big hammers has its place.

When apologists turn their attention from comforting believers to dealing with the unregenerate world, however, Frame's long-standing emphasis on cultural context and listening becomes crucial. The current

---

19. *DKG*, 352–54, 363–64; Cowan, *Five Views on Apologetics*, 222.

20. See esp. Sproul, Gerstner, and Lindsley, *Classical Apologetics*, 93–182.

21. For a brief history of the development of "cognitive styles" (or styles of reasoning) from the Enlightenment to today, see John Stackhouse, *Humble Apologetics* (Oxford: Oxford University Press, 2002), 13–37.

22. *AGG*, 2–3.

American context is no longer homogeneous regarding styles of reasoning or the rationality of theism. The truths of Christian theism are just as rational as they have ever been when measured against God's standard of rationality, but the very standards of rationality are under dispute today.[23] Here it is important to note with Frame that God's rationality is not identical with either Enlightenment rationality or even the older Aristotelian rationality. Some apologists continue to argue that it is sufficient to ask doubters to commit to being "fair-minded" or "objective" in assessing the arguments. Typically this means adopting a neutral, prejudice-free attitude that includes setting aside religious convictions. But this is simply a call to Enlightenment rationality, and not the rationality recommended in the Bible. When God says, "Come now, and let us reason together" (Isa. 1:18),[24] he calls wayward and doubting Israel to acknowledge both their sins (hardly a religiously neutral concept) and his lordly authority to forgive. The reasoning in Scripture never asks the doubter to bracket God's reality or the authority of his Word.

Calling doubters to a neutral fair-mindedness may have seemed sufficient in a modernist world. It may even have worked in a confused postmodern world, one in which most people were vaguely grieving over the loss of the orderly stability of modernity. But the apologetic context today is not even postmodern; it is now pluralist. Pluralism embraces a rich stew of styles of reasoning and a purposefully minimal conception of what is "rational." Fair-minded objectivity is no longer a requirement for serious discourse. Instead, it is increasingly expected that participants in a dialogue lay their commitments on the table. In other words, the wider culture is asking people to make their presuppositions explicit and to show how those presuppositions work themselves out in practice. Frame's presuppositional apologetics is particularly well suited to this context. Training young Christians to gently

---

23. MacIntyre, *Whose Justice? Which Rationality?* gives a particularly clear exposition of the ways in which concepts of rationality are culturally embedded. The "Intermission" section of Tim Keller, *The Reason for God* (New York: Dutton, 2008), 115–23, includes a section on "Which Rationality?" in which he questions the "strong rationality" of Enlightenment thought. The application of this problem to apologetics is discussed (with varying degrees of usefulness) by some of the contributors to Timothy R. Phillips and Dennis L. Okholm, *Christian Apologetics in the Postmodern World* (Downers Grove, IL: InterVarsity Press, 1995). See especially James W. Sire, "On Being a Fool for Christ and an Idiot for Nobody: Logocentricity and Postmodernity," 101–27; J. Richard Middleton and Brian J. Walsh, "Facing the Postmodern Scalpel: Can the Christian Faith Withstand Deconstruction?" 131–54.

24. All quotations from the Bible are from the KJV.

and respectfully articulate their full allegiance to Christ's lordship should be a central goal of any apologetic instruction.

It should not be surprising that the rise of pluralism has made the context-specificity of apologetics so clear. Frame was urging the importance of the situational perspective even when it was unpopular because he found it emphasized in the epistles of Peter and Paul, and in Paul's apologetic practice in the book of Acts.[25] The New Testament was written in a pluralist culture.[26] Instead of defending the faith by an appeal to objective, fair-minded reason, the first-century apologists placed allegiance to Christ's lordship at the start of their arguments and urged doubters to repent. They recognized that the problem was not merely—or even primarily—intellectual. The problem was spiritual blindness and rebellion.

One way to see the practical difference between Frame's context-sensitive apologetics and context-transcending (Enlightenment) apologetics is by looking at the ways in which persistent unbelief is explained. Why do unbelievers often continue in unbelief even after hearing a powerful presentation of a theistic argument or the evidence for Christ's resurrection? Enlightenment apologists might be tempted to say that the unbeliever is simply stupid, or illogical, or not working hard enough to consider the evidence. They might allow that the unbeliever is under a delusion, or in the grip of an ideology, or that the person's (animal) passions are overwhelming his reason. In short, the explanation will be that the unbeliever is irrational *in the sense that* the unbeliever is falling short of a well-known, universal standard of rationality. Frame's explanation is different. Unbelievers are irrational, but not in the Enlightenment sense. Unbelievers are irrational in that they are not reasoning as God would have them reason. Unbelievers are not reasoning in submission to God's lordship. Unbelievers may pay close attention, be undistracted by animal passions, and even be trying hard to be open-minded. The problem is spiritual blindness and unacknowledged rebellion, not a failure to think clearly, fairly, or hard enough.

---

25. *DKG*, 144–49; *AGG*, 149, 193.

26. Tim Keller's Veritas Forum address at the University of California at Berkeley highlights the similarities between first-century Rome and our times. The address is available at http://www.youtube.com/watch?v=C9fmKSwuoDE. See also Robert Webber, *Who Narrates the World? Contending for the Christian Story in an Age of Rivals* (Downers Grove, IL: InterVarsity Press, 2008). John Warwick Montgomery, on the other hand, contends that the pluralism of our times is unique in human history. See "Apologetics for the Twenty-first Century," in Norman L. Geisler and Chad V. Meister, eds., *Reasons for Faith* (Wheaton, IL: Crossway, 2007), 41.

Apologists who used to insist on the sufficiency of fair-mindedness have been gradually allowing for more context-specificity. This is commendable, since pluralism is likely to dominate our culture's imagination for the rest of our lives. This feature of the current apologetic context has at least three important implications. The most obvious implication is in the way apologetic discourse unfolds. In a world committed to scientific or legal standards of disputation, apologists can be openly argumentative without offending their doubting friends. In our pluralist context, argumentation is considered a form of assault. Uninvited arguments for controversial conclusions are often offensive precisely because they are rigorous, and especially when they are delivered forcefully. This reaction stems from the conviction that arguments are the standard tool used by those in power to intimidate and subdue their subjects. Gentle reasoning has its place, but it is welcome only in the context of a friendly relationship built on mutual respect. These relationships take time, and they are nurtured through testimony, shared narrative, and displays of sacrificial love.[27] Maybe there was a time—in a Paris salon, in 1765?—when it seemed that apologetics could be entirely a matter of objective argumentation without gentleness or respect; but that time is not now.

The second implication that our pluralist context has for apologetics is the role of Christian community in defending the faith. Both eighteenth-century Enlightenment and nineteenth-century Romantic rationality made individualism the ideal. Community was nice, but not essential to the progress of science or society. Whether by accident or design, Christian apologists in the twentieth century tended to treat apologetics as the science of equipping for solo combat. Effective apologetics was thought to depend on the power of the reasons given, and not on the life of the apologist or the Christian community. In a pluralist context, apologetics is unavoidably communal. As Lesslie Newbigin argues in *The Gospel in a Pluralist Society*, the visible church must take seriously its role as a "hermeneutic of the gospel."[28] Doubters must be able to make sense of apologetic reasons if the reasons are to be at all effective. In a post-Christian world, apologists cannot assume that common cultural assumptions will allow doubters to interpret their claims. Across this kind of cultural distance, the life of the apologist and the Christian community will be, for good or ill, the interpretive key—the hermeneutic—for understanding the gospel and its defense. This has always

27. Tim Keller argues for this in *The Reason for God*, ix–xxiii, 227–40.
28. Lesslie Newbigin, *The Gospel in a Pluralist Society* (Grand Rapids: Eerdmans, 1989), 222–33.

been true, and it is assumed in the careful attention that Peter gives to the witness of the Christian community in 1 Peter 3 and in John's admonitions in his first epistle. The practical homogeneity of modernist thought may have suggested otherwise, but in our current context apologists are increasingly aware of the role of the visible Christian community in providing an interpretive backdrop for giving reasons for the faith.[29]

The life of the church is not merely a backdrop for apologetics in a pluralist world. Pluralists are sure that the pursuit of absolute truth inevitably leads to strife and oppression. Christian churches publicly splintering over minor matters of doctrine confirm the pluralist conviction that truth destroys community. This conviction is given particularly clear expression in Richard Rorty's essay "Solidarity or Objectivity?" and Rorty's conclusions have sunk into the roots of our culture.[30] Rorty uses *Solidarity* to stand for the practice of committing first to community—to each other—and then defining *truth* as, roughly, "what the community affirms." He uses *Objectivity* to refer to the Enlightenment practice of making the pursuit of objective (absolute) truth the basis for communal life. Rorty's central claim is that we must pick between these strategies. If we organize our lives around the pursuit of objective truth, we will never achieve real community. The history of the West, he argues, is convincing proof that pursuing truth—which he believes is a myth—only results in divisions, wars, and oppression. Since we must choose, Rorty recommends that we embrace the pragmatist's strategy of Solidarity, forgoing absolute truth in order to pursue the peaceful, fulfilling life together that we so desire. Although Christians know that this won't be any more successful than other fallen attempts at utopia, our apologetics must take seriously the extent to which Rorty's analysis is widely believed. Merely arguing that he is wrong will play into the expectation that Christian convictions about truth are dangerous! Good arguments must be able to point to concrete examples of attractive community life built on the love of the truth. Frame's apologetic works were making this point long before pluralism became the dominant mind-set.[31]

29. See, for example, Dennis Hollinger, "The Church as Apologetic," in Phillips and Okholm, *Christian Apologetics in the Postmodern World*, 182–91; Stanley Grenz, *Created for Community* (Ada, MI: Baker Academic, 1998).

30. Richard Rorty, "Solidarity or Objectivity?" in *Objectivity, Relativism, and Truth* (Cambridge: Cambridge University Press, 1991), 21–34.

31. *AGG*, 17–18; *DKG*, 353–54; and he has continued to press the importance of the character of the Christian community; see *MWC*.

Genuine Spiritual Humility: The Existential Perspective

A third implication of the pluralist context is the necessity of genuine humility on the part of the apologist. In the twentieth century, apologists sometimes encouraged the picture of the bold champion of the faith striding into the arena, confident of his abilities. Apologetics training was training for combat; unflinching certainty was the proper attitude, not only about the truths being defended but about the likelihood of crushing the opponent. The appearance of humility might sometimes be necessary to set the opponent up, but real humility was not encouraged.[32] The defense of the faith was characterized as a battle, and humility in a warrior can be dangerous. Confidence rather than humility was recommended, both to defeat the enemy and to encourage fellow believers who might be watching the battle.

Contrary to this swashbuckling brand of apologetics, John Frame's approach to apologetic writing, debate, and image has recommended genuine spiritual humility. Whether in public debate, in private conversation, or in his writing, Frame treats doubters as hurting friends who need help rather than as enemies who need to be humiliated. He has never sought to carve out a niche for his private brand of apologetics, and has instead turned the attention of his audience to God's lordship and to God's Word. Genuine humility is spiritual, not rhetorical. It arises from a clear recognition of our utter dependence on God for everything. Every truth we see, every noble thing we do, and every delightful thing we enjoy comes from God. In our own strength, we would be as miserable and lost as the doubters we are called to serve with apologetic reasoning. Frame insists that apologists must be humble not because our reasons are lame, but because we apologists ourselves are lame; and the advantages we enjoy are not from our own brilliance or ingenuity. Christian apologists do not grasp the truths of the faith because Christians are smarter, more logical, or more honest about the evidence than those who are lost. Christian apologists apprehend the truth because God has graciously opened their spiritual eyes.

The humble acknowledgment of our own weakness and dependence on God is the first step in Frame's presuppositional apologetics. Here the interrelat-

---

32. It is tempting to refer to the appearance of humility as "tactical" humility, but that might suggest a criticism of Greg Koukl's recommendations about "tactical" apologetics in *Tactics* (Grand Rapids: Zondervan, 2009) and on his radio call-in show and podcast, *Stand to Reason*, available at http://www.str.org. Koukl's "tactics" typically exhibit not just the pretense of humility, but genuine, gracious questioning.

edness of the three perspectives is especially apparent. Frame's apologetics condemns arrogance, and calls on Christians not to claim more for their arguments than the arguments deserve. In an age more offended by arrogance than by any other social vice, Frame's approach is particularly well suited to the situational context. From the normative perspective, humility is the only appropriate stance for people submitting their reasoning to the lordship of Christ.

The point at which Frame's call for humility is most likely to offend fellow apologists is his insistence that we admit the limitations of our arguments. Following Van Til's lead, Frame is careful to expose the failure of the traditional arguments to move from neutral presuppositions to the truths that apologists are called to defend. The conclusion of Frame's analysis of the ontological argument is typical:

> The ontological argument proves the biblical God only if it presupposes distinctively Christian values and a Christian view of existence. Substitute other values and you change the conclusion . . . My conclusion is that either the ontological argument is a Christian presuppositional argument (and thus reducible to our earlier moral argument) or it is worth nothing.[33]

Given the amount of space Frame devotes to exposing these kinds of weaknesses, it is easy to understand why some apologists might find Frame's complaints about the traditional arguments counterproductive. If we suppose that the goal of apologetics is to supply young Christians with reasons they can bring forth to defend their faith, then it might seem that no one is helped when Frame points out that the traditional arguments fall short of silencing all doubt. Is Frame giving aid and comfort to the enemies of the truth? Is he depriving struggling Christians of weapons they ought to be confidently using in their battle with unbelief?

We would all love to have an argument guaranteed to leave unbelieving skeptics utterly speechless. Yet not even one has been found.[34] Many apologists still offer arguments while apparently expecting that if unbelievers would only allow themselves to consider the evidence fairly, they would have to admit that the evidence favors Christianity. But the problem is not primarily a lack of fairness or honesty. In themselves, the

---

33. *AGG*, 117–18.

34. In my chapter "Theistic Arguments," in Michael Murray, ed., *Reason for the Hope Within* (Grand Rapids: Eerdmans, 1999), 20–46, I summarize at least eight good arguments for God's existence. In each case, however, I note the argument's greatest weakness.

arguments all fail. There are two reasons for this. First, unless the truth and authority of the Word of God is acknowledged from the outset, then it is impossible to reason to the truth of *the gospel*. It may be possible to reason to the existence of a maximal being that has some properties in common with the divine being of Christianity, Judaism, and Islam. But *Christian* apologetics aims to defend our faith in the truth of the good news that Jesus saves sinners. This ultimate aim of apologetics can never be fulfilled without submitting to the authority of God's Word and its wonderful claims about God's grace in Christ. This kind of submission requires humility—not mere fair-mindedness—both in the apologist and in the doubter.

The second reason that the arguments in themselves cannot succeed is the ingenuity of unbelief. Some arguments seem airtight to believers. The premises look so obvious that no sane person could deny them, and the reasoning from those premises conforms to the most rigorous standards. But premises that are obvious to believers whose spiritual eyes have been opened are often far less obvious to unbelievers who are spiritually blind. This is one place where familiarity with non-Christian thought is particularly helpful. Even when they are trying their hardest to see reality clearly and to solve problems that bother them, non-Christian philosophers often insist on the truth of premises that are desperately false.[35] Moreover, such philosophers reach conclusions *about the premises* that clash with other beliefs they have, and with the conclusions of other non-Christians. The traditional arguments used by apologists are and should be tremendously encouraging *to believers* who see through the eyes of faith. But Christian apologists should have the humility to acknowledge that the arguments ultimately work for them because they see with spiritual eyes. Claiming that the arguments will work for anyone minimally fair-minded is ultimately a boast about the sufficiency of fallen human powers of reasoning.

Here an illustration may help. Craig Hazen opens his chapter on new apologetic methods with a story about a dramatic production that made a

---

35. Among many other examples, consider Albert Camus' confidently assumed premise that there is no God in *The Myth of Sisyphus* (New York: Random House, 1983), or David Hume's assertion in his *A Treatise of Human Nature* (Oxford: Clarendon Press, 1978), 1:1.1 that the only ideas arising from the data of sense are meaningful. Neither of these influential philosophers was trying to start from falsehoods.

deep impression on him.[36] The play depicts Jesus' disciples as developing plans to be persecuted and die for the message of Christ's resurrection *even though they know it to be false*. The actors decide to wrap their lives in this lie because it would be especially noble to live *for nothing*. "For what could be finer than to make both gods and men our enemies for no reason at all . . . ?" Hazen finds the implicit argument decisive:

> The reason the play stayed with me all these years is because it so effec-tively made a crucial apologetic point. Skeptics sometimes bring up the objection that the closest followers of Jesus probably made up the miracle stories and the account of the resurrection, but this dramatic production demonstrates in an unforgettable way just how ludicrous that idea is. Why would any of these "deceivers" face tremendous loss and death to maintain a lie that didn't benefit them, their families, or their friends whatsoever? Well, they wouldn't.[37]

Although no Christian would knowingly pursue such a pointless life, there are a depressing number of non-Christians who would. Hazen's description of the play did not indicate that it was written by a Christian. Before this was explained, I had concluded that Hazen was describing a play by Samuel Beckett or Jean-Paul Sartre, or maybe some lesser playwright, depicting an existentialist embrace of absurdity and large gestures aimed at asserting radical autonomy.[38]

Hazen notes that the play offered a version of an apologetic argument that goes back at least to Eusebius of Caesarea. It seems likely that any *regen-erate* person in any age watching the play would find the plan to die for a known lie wildly irrational. But it is illegitimate to say that any fair-minded *unregenerate* person would reach the same conclusion. It is true that any biblically rational person would reach that conclusion, but biblical rationality includes submission to God (the fear of the Lord). Frame's presuppositional apologetic method calls on believers to avoid suggesting—either to ourselves or to others—that there is a kind of rationality that is neutral about submit-

---

36. Craig Hazen, "Capturing the Imagination Before Engaging the Mind," in McDowell, *Apol-ogetics for a New Generation*, 97–108. The story appears on the first two pages of the chapter.

37. Ibid., 98.

38. For example, consider the hero of Sartre's *The Age of Reason* (New York: Vintage, 1992), or Samuel Beckett's play "Endgame" in *Samuel Beckett: Waiting for Godot, Endgame, Krapp's Last Tape* (London: Faber & Faber, 2001).

ting to God's standard of rationality. Humble apologists embrace submission to God's standards up front, and they are careful not to pretend that they have arguments that work without it.

The realization that our arguments may not be as convincing to non-Christians as they are to us should be liberating. It should also lead us to imagine the apologetic task differently. For at least the last century, an apologetic encounter with an unbeliever has been portrayed as a battle. Sometimes it was cast as a battle of intellects, but it was typically portrayed as a kill-or-be-killed death match. The doubter was to be destroyed, brought low, humiliated. It was important to listen carefully to the doubter's arguments, but only for the purpose of finding weaknesses and opportunities. If the doubter admitted confusion or pain, it was the longed-for admission of weaknesses that had to be exploited quickly and decisively.

This picture of the apologist as warrior and executioner is all but absent from the Bible.[39] Sadly, the Reformed tradition in apologetics has found this picture especially attractive, and it has produced its share of apologists who were outstanding at public debate. I grew up envying the ability of these champions to exploit tiny mistakes in their opponents' reasoning and to humiliate them in public. I also grew up wondering why I didn't have the skill or courage to do the same, and I shied away from opportunities to defend my faith out of shame at my inability.

The emphasis that John Frame puts on humility as internal to apologetics has been a profoundly encouraging, biblical corrective to this warrior picture. Both in his teaching about apologetics and in his encounters with doubters, Frame labors to put God's concerns above his own. Rather than working to build up his reputation as a debater, Frame seeks to minister to the needs of doubters. He consistently displays the recognition that every doubter is in pain, that the battle is the Lord's, and that he should put God's glory and the doubters' needs ahead of his own.[40] Because of this, he models genuine dialogue. He listens carefully not only to exploit mistaken ideas and reasoning, but also to affirm, clarify, and encourage. For a pluralist audience, this kind of honest dialogue could have been no more than a useful rhetorical strategy. But

39. "Answer a fool according to his folly" (Prov. 26:5) is hardly in itself a sufficient biblical support for the picture.

40. Hence K. Scott Oliphint's *The Battle Belongs to the Lord* (Phillipsburg, NJ: P&R Publishing, 2003).

Frame was recommending this kind of humility long before pluralism made honest dialogue hip and strategic.

FRAME AND THE EXPLOSION OF APOLOGETIC RESOURCES

This chapter opened by describing the rapid growth of apologetic resources being made available through a dizzying array of media. This explosion of resources deserves close attention for two reasons. First, the overwhelming majority of resources for apologetic training appear to reject Frame's admonition that apologists must presuppose the God of the Bible in defending the faith. These resources sometimes begin with or emphasize a claim to argue only "from the evidence" and to demand only "careful reasoning."[41] But despite this beginning, most of them follow presuppositionalist principles as soon as details matter. The second reason for a close look at the resources is the important effort they are making to encourage Christians to have reasons for what they believe. Although Frame has always stressed the need to give practical advice about defending the faith (apologetics proper), other Reformed apologists have focused mainly on theoretical perfection in *meta-apologetics*.[42] Too often this has meant giving clear directions about what should *not* be done when defending the faith (conceding a neutral common ground, allowing the existence of brute facts, arguing only for probabilities, etc.). The Christian who is given advice only about what to avoid may never be comfortable defending the faith at all. Frame's work in apologetics has sought to show Reformed apologists what might be said to real doubters, both Christian and non-Christian. All Christians need this kind of practical guidance, and this need is driving the rapid growth of apologetic resources.

One of the most obvious features of recent apologetic advice is intellectual confidence. Christians are urged to consider the many

41. The opening to the http://www.pleaseconvinceme.com podcasts makes this claim. See also the introduction to Paul Cowan, *When God Goes to Starbucks* (Grand Rapids: Baker, 2008), 10: "For those who are serious-minded seekers (rather than half-hearted dabblers), there are abundant indicators of God's existence."

42. *Meta-apologetics* is the science concerned with finding the most adequate account of what is happening in an apologetic encounter. It includes the epistemological, theological, and anthropological commitments that support a complete theory of how we should defend the faith. Only a fraction of the books on apologetics now being published deal with these issues. Maybe the last that attempted to place meta-apologetic theories side by side is Steven Cowan's *Five Views on Apologetics*, published in 2000.

ways that Christian beliefs provide the best explanation for the world that we know. Christians are urged not just to believe that Christianity should be accepted as one of many plausible interpretations of reality. Instead, young Christians—the typical audience for podcasts, Web sites, and summer camps—are given reasons for thinking that Christian beliefs and values are superior to alternative belief systems held by non-Christians. The reasons given for these conclusions are not always as powerful as advertised, but the conclusions are true; and Christian leaders have an obligation to help fellow believers learn reasons for what they believe. Christians *should* have intellectual confidence about what they believe, and the many resources working to build that confidence should be applauded for taking on the task even if they don't do everything perfectly.

Unlike the approach of some in Reformed circles, John Frame's approach to apologetics—in his writing, and even more in his teaching—aims to nurture *both* confidence in and awareness of the limitations of the traditional arguments used in defending the faith. To see the value of this balance, consider the moral argument for the existence of God. Suppose a new Christian can't see any convincing reason to believe there is a God, but continues to believe as a matter of grim determination. For such a believer, doubts are likely to arise often. It would strengthen the walk of this new believer if she were to consider the theological implications of the many moral judgments that she makes every day. Watching the news, she is appalled by stories of children being mistreated, financial corruption, and human-rights violations in other countries. These acts are not just sad or icky; they are evil. They violate universal standards that do not depend on any community's consensus. Even if everyone in the world accepted child molestation as permissible, it would still be objectively, absolutely wrong. The moral (or axiological) argument for God's existence aims to show this young believer that her moral convictions can be true only if the God of the Bible exists. Unless there is an absolute person who gives a universal law on his own authority, then no moral judgments can be absolute, universal, moral truths.

By means of the many Web sites, call-in shows, podcasts, camps, and books, more and more believers are encountering this moral argument for God's existence. This outcome is a very good thing. And it is still a good thing (although not quite *as* good) even when the power of the argument is exaggerated. Sometimes apologetics teachers suggest that this argument is irrefutable, or that non-Christians will be silenced by it. This suggestion is simply not true. Unbelievers always have the option of falling back on an idolatrous standard and digging in their heels. For example, non-Christians may give up the idea that there are universal human rights.[43] Americans are less and less comfortable with judging other cultures by American moral standards. They sense that norms of justice *should* be universal, but they feel guilty when they realize that it is *American* norms that they want to be universal. Praise, condemnation, and social activism all depend on an assumed standard of judgment, but Americans increasingly think it is enough for those standards to be local, constructed by communities.[44] In our pluralist culture, the moral argument for God's existence will succeed only if the doubter will renounce allegiance to our culture's pluralist moral ideals and submit to the truth that God's moral standards are absolute.

This "limitation" on the moral argument can be understood in two ways, and Frame gives both of them. On the one hand, the apologist can admit up front that our reasoning about morality (and the implications of our moral judgments) must acknowledge that God is the source of all absolute moral truth. That is, the apologist can insist that we begin by presupposing the God of the Bible. For Christians wrestling with doubts or lacking reasons for faith, this presupposition will be simple; and many of the current apologetic resources take this step implicitly. Their primary audience is believers, and they direct their audience to what the Bible says about God's holy will, the universal reach of the law, and God's right to rule as the Creator of all things. The authority of the Word of God is presupposed, with no hint that the Scriptures are only probably true, or that the Bible's authority depends on an argument from "the evidence."[45]

43. Richard Rorty includes universal human rights among the myths we should give up in order to move beyond the destructive pursuit of culturally transcendent truth. See his "Solidarity or Objectivity?"

44. The http://www.pleaseconvinceme.com podcast 51 (originally aired June 4, 2008) argues that all praise, condemnation, and activism depend on an absolute moral standard. It is true that these all depend on a standard, but only *absolute moral* praise and condemnation depend on an absolute moral standard. My praise for my five-year-old's finger painting is neither absolute nor moral. Similarly, not all social activism aims to correct absolute moral wrongs. A campaign to prohibit billboards on a freeway may depend on local aesthetic standards. Some non-Christians cling to the idea that all moral rules are local and aesthetic.

45. For examples of this implicit presuppositionalism, see http://www.str.org (Greg Koukl); http://www.bethinking.org (University and Colleges Christian Fellowship); http://www.always beready.com (Charlie Campbell); http://www.pleaseconvinceme.com (Jim Wallace).

The same pattern is followed when dealing with the other traditional arguments for God's existence: probabilities are turned into certainties by an appeal to the Word of God, making the Word of God the final authority for believers looking for reasons for their faith! And this is true even with the many resources that insist that they are reasoning merely from the evidence, for an audience committed only to being fair-minded. Good arguments are presented, the power of the argument is exaggerated, but the limitations in the arguments are remedied by an appeal to Scripture on the presupposition of God's existence and authority. Although the exaggeration in the middle of this approach is lamentable, it is not fatal. Modeling Christian charity, Frame is mindful of his audience when commenting on these arguments. For nonacademics (budding apologists) looking to defend their faith, he focuses on what is good (reason-giving, the dependence on Scripture) and highlights the way the arguments give reasons for intellectual confidence in the truth. For theoreticians (meta-apologists), he focuses on the weakness of the arguments apart from the presupposition of the God of the Bible.

For the meta-apologists, Frame offers a second way of dealing with the limitation on the moral argument. Instead of calling for God's existence to be presupposed, the argument can be recast as an "indirect" argument. On this approach, the doubter's assumptions are admitted "for the sake of argument." For example, the doubter may believe both that moral judgments are merely local standards of taste *and* that it is wrong for girls to be denied any education by Muslim extremists in southwest Asia. The apologist can then work to show that this pair of beliefs is incoherent, and can hope to eventually show that the doubter would much rather accept absolute morality (and the absolute, personal lawgiver required for that) than give up the ability to condemn human-rights violations. The Holy Spirit may use the argument to melt the heart of a non-Christian doubter. But apart from that melting, the argument will not work. Non-Christians who deny the rational force of the moral argument for God's existence need not be stupid, and they are not violating the standards of rationality that the world acknowledges. They are violating the standards of rationality revealed in God's Word; but until they acknowledge God's rule, they can refuse to accept that they are being "irrational" by any "neutral" standard.

Although the majority of the resources being offered in the recent explosion claim to be following methods developed by critics of presuppositionalism, the apologetic advice they give is more consistent with presuppositionalist principles than with any other meta-apologetic theory. The central focus of these resources is building up the faith of Christians. Their aim is to encourage Christians to know what they believe in greater detail, and to have reasons for what they believe. The audience is not asked to consider the evidence from a position of neutrality, or as brute facts; they are not encouraged to sit in judgment on the Bible's authority, or to sit in judgment on God's right to rule his creation. The Christian truth is defended *from Scripture*. When the questions and challenges from non-Christians are considered, they are answered *from Scripture*. When non-Christians are dealt with in person (as callers to a radio show, or as invited guests), an effort is made to discover how the non-Christians' assumptions (presuppositions!) differ from Christian assumptions. Often an attempt is made to show that the non-Christian assumptions are futile.[46] Sometimes the Christian host works to show that meaning, absolute value, or transcendent truth is impossible on the non-Christians' assumptions. These apologetic practices are not merely consistent with Frame's presuppositionalism. He recommends them. Moreover, these practices are often rejected by Frame's critics.

It is important for Reformed apologists to look beyond the surface meta-apologetic claims in the recent proliferation of apologetic resources. Although the protestations that they will do no more than follow the evidence imply that autonomous reasoning will rule the discussion, the actual practice typically looks to Scripture as the standard of truth and rationality. In two areas, however, autonomous reasoning is still encouraged: the existence of God and the historicity of the resurrection. The persistence of this reliance on autonomous reasoning is lamentable for three reasons. First, indulging autonomous reasoning in these areas concedes the right of the doubter to set the standard. Second, it forces some apologists to insist that none of their arguments depend on biblical assumptions. Third, proofs for God's existence and evidence for the resurrection are fully valuable to the Christian only if the proofs give good reasons for the Christian's hope. Proving the existence of a maximally great deity is valuable, but not enough. Giving the evidence for the historicity of the resurrection is important, but not enough. The hope for which we are to be ready to give a reason is not

46. This is especially true for resources connected to Ravi Zacharias International Ministries. In addition to the Web site http://www.rzim.org, see Amy Orr-Ewing, *Is Belief in God Irrational?* (Downers Grove, IL: InterVarsity Press, 2008).

merely that there is a maximally great being. He is the triune Lord who has acted in history to redeem us from our sin. Similarly, our hope is not merely that Jesus rising from the dead is the best explanation for some of the historical evidence. Our hope is that Jesus was raised *for our justification* (Rom. 4:25). Our hope is in what Jesus' resurrection accomplished, and that is known only by submitting to the Scriptures as the ultimate truth.

John Frame would be quick to add here that I need to be fair to those who offer evidence-based arguments for God's existence and Jesus' resurrection. First, the Scriptures themselves show that evidence can be used in giving reasons for believing these truths. Paul in Acts 17 is shown using the evidence of creation and the religious sensibilities of his audience to give reasons for his convictions, and both Paul and John use the evidence of eyewitness testimony to support their claims about Christ being raised. The problem is not in the use of evidence, which is a legitimate source of encouragement for believers. The problem is in overestimating what a rational examination of evidence *in itself* can accomplish. It is significant that even concerning the existence of God and the historicity of the resurrection, most of the recent resources I have consulted focus on the evidence as sources of comfort *for believers*, rather than as decisive ways to crush non-Christian doubts.[47]

At the risk of oversimplifying, I believe that most of the apologetic resources appearing on the Internet are worthy of attention, and that Christians should be encouraged to make use of them. I am confident that John Frame would agree, both on apologetic and broad church-unity grounds. Presuppositionalism should not be used to deepen divisions between Christians. "I am of Sproul" or "I am of Van Til" are no more justifiable today than were "I am of Apollos" or "I am of Peter" in first-century Corinth. Nearly any set of recommendations about defending the faith will have deficiencies. Those that would focus on the deficiencies in systems that are in fact building up the confidence and zeal of believers must meet a high burden of proof. They must show that the systems are leading believers *away* from the faith, not just that they are keeping believers from embracing the perfect systems held by the critics.

47. Lee Strobel, for example, at http://www.leestrobel.com aims primarily at a Christian audience, as does LeadershipU at http://www.leaderu.com, and Christian Apologetics & Research Ministry (CARM) at http://www.carm.org.

It can be difficult to determine whether a particular resource is leading people away from the faith. Frame's triperspectival approach to ethics suggests three kinds of questions that might be asked when evaluating a new book, Web site, or seminar on apologetics:

1. Does the resource honor the Word of God as the ultimate authority? The issue here is the normative perspective. Are Christian doubters encouraged to go to the Word for comfort, clarification, and confidence? Is the Word of God consulted extensively and handled faithfully?[48]

2. Is the central concern of the resource the building up of the body of Christ as it is understood in God's Word? The issue here is the situational perspective. The life of the church—as manifested in the godly lives of believers, in their submission to each other, and in their reasonable confidence in the truth—is the ultimate apologetic "argument." Insofar as apologetic resources pull users away from the life of the full body of Christ, the resources (unwittingly) compromise the power of the overall apologetic witness.

3. Does the resource exhibit genuine Christian humility? This is a concern from the existential perspective. No matter how convincing the arguments may seem, our dependence on God's grace for our confidence is absolute. Apologetic resources should acknowledge this dependence openly, and should not show disdain for unbelief. Doubters should not be mocked as stupid, or illogical, or deluded.

Humility may well be the most important characteristic to look for when assessing apologetic resources. Christian apologetics is the task of applying God's Word to unbelief. Apologists who are arrogant may be struggling to understand and apply the gospel to their own lives. Too often their arguments display their fear (that they are not right, or that they won't be intellectually respected) more than anything else. Even

48. It is hard to give an exhaustive set of guidelines for faithful handling of the Word. A good place to start, though, is to consider whether the resource handles the Word of God the way that approved preachers and teachers in your church handle it. For me, that means asking whether the resource interprets and uses the Bible the way the ordained teaching elders use it in the pulpit, in the classroom, and in their deliberations.

when they are not trusting their own reasoning most of all, their lack of gentleness reinforces the common worldly suspicion that Christianity is just another ideology looking for sheep to manipulate. It has probably always been true that fallen, rebellious people were quick to think that Christians were either fearful or controlling. In a post-Nietzschean pluralist world, it is even more likely that contempt and mocking will discredit the apologist's message. With suspicion like this so likely to arise, we have no alternative but to follow the scriptural command to love the lost more than we love our own reputations. We must show this love by asking questions and genuinely listening. *Arrogant apologist* is a biblical oxymoron.

FRAME AND THE FREE WILL DEFENSE

Recent apologetic work on the problem of evil has been dominated by variations on Alvin Plantinga's "Free Will Defense."[49] John Frame's analysis of this response to the problem of evil in *AGG* is typical of his general rejection of most of the standard apologetic treatments of the problem: brief, theologically incisive, and insistent on God's glory. If only a few things are going to be said about the Free Will Defense, Frame chooses the most important of them. In this section I will attempt to extend Frame's discussion of the Free Will Defense and to consider Plantinga's recent amplification of the defense in "Supralapsarianism, or 'O Felix Culpa.' "[50]

A careful look at Frame and Plantinga on this problem is valuable for at least three reasons. First, the Free Will Defense is exceptionally popular among Christian philosophers and apologists. Second, the argument makes use of a common and intuitively attractive definition of human free will.

---

49. The original formulation of the argument is in Alvin Plantinga, *God, Freedom, and Evil* (Grand Rapids: Eerdmans, 1974), which offers the same argument that Plantinga gives in one chapter of *The Nature of Necessity* (Oxford: Oxford University Press, 1974). Most secular philosophers encountered Plantinga's argument in the longer work. This is likely the principal reason that William Lane Craig cites Plantinga's *The Nature of Necessity* as one of the most influential apologetic works in the recent renaissance of Christian philosophy. See Craig's "Advice to Christian Apologists," at http://www.bethinking.org/resources/advice-to-christian-apologists.htm. For a more recent use of the Free Will Defense in dealing with the problem of evil, see Daniel Howard Snyder, "The Problem of Evil," in Murray, *Reason for the Hope Within*, 76–115.

50. Alvin Plantinga, "Supralapsarianism, or 'O Felix Culpa,' " in Peter van Inwagen, ed., *Christian Faith and the Problem of Evil* (Grand Rapids: Eerdmans, 2004), 1–25.

(It uses the "libertarian" or "incompatibilist" definition; Reformed schol-ars would call it Arminian—if not Pelagian.[51]) Third, Plantinga's recent amplification of the argument ends up being surprisingly compatible with Frame's presuppositionalist response to the problem of evil! Even though Plantinga's latest version does not renounce the difficulties that Frame rightly points out with the original version, those difficulties are not essential to it. Plantinga's "Felix Culpa" theodicy(!) does not depend either on a libertar-ian definition of free will or on the Molinist account of God's providence. Frame rightly rejects these positions because they compromise God's glory, but Plantinga need not have reaffirmed them. Moreover, Plantinga's recent argument employs a presuppositionalist methodology (although he calls it merely reasoning "according to Christian thought"). In order to understand these three reasons for a closer look, it is necessary to look at Plantinga's original argument in some detail.

The precise argument that Plantinga gives in his 1974 book *God, Free-dom, and Evil* transformed philosophical discussion of the topic. Before this argument appeared, most philosophers suspected that it was not logi-cally possible for all three of the following sentences to be compossible, that is, true at the same (logical) time:

(1) God is omnipotent;
(2) God is wholly good; and
(3) evil exists.

Although no one had demonstrated the impossibility, most felt sure that there must be a contradiction lurking in this set of claims. Plantinga argues that there is no contradiction in the set by offering a "model" that could be true, and under which all three of the sentences would be true. A model (in this sense) is a possibly true additional claim that makes the simultaneous possibility apparent.

51. Frame calls it Pelagian (*AGG*, 161n14), and coming from an author as charitable and patient as Frame, this is a very serious charge. For an explanation of the issues that is sympathetic with the libertarian position, see Scott Davison, "Divine Providence and Human Freedom," in Murray, *Reason for the Hope Within*, 217–37. For a philo-sophically sophisticated critique of the libertarian position, see Mark R. Talbot, "True Freedom: The Liberty That Scripture Portrays as Worth Having," in John Piper, Jus-tin Taylor, and Paul Kjoss Helseth, eds., *Beyond the Bounds* (Wheaton, IL: Crossway, 2003), 77–109.

Here a parallel example may help to show how a model can work. Consider this set of sentences:

(4) Figure ABC is a triangle;
(5) the interior angles of figure ABC are all congruent;
(6) all three of the interior angles of figure ABC are right angles.

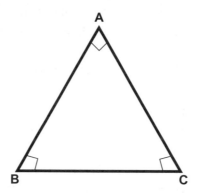

Fig. 21.1. ABC

A tenth-grade grasp of geometry screams that these can't all be true at the same time. Showing their compossibility by means of a model would mean showing that there is a further sentence that could be true, and in light of which all three of these sentences are true. Although it may not be immediately obvious, this can be done by adding:

(7) A, B, and C lie on the surface of a sphere.

(Consider a globe, a model of the earth, with point A at the North Pole and points B and C on the equator, 90 degrees of longitude apart. The figure formed by lines joining the points is a triangle; the interior angles are all equal; and all the angles are right angles. The seeming impossibility of all three sentences' being true arose because of an unnoticed presupposition: that the points all lay on a *plane*. In plane, Euclidean geometry, the three sentences are not compossible. A presupposition beyond the data created the perplexity.)

The point here has little to do with geometry. Instead, it is about the prospect of identifying a further sentence that is possibly true—probably presupposed to be false—on which the logical impossibility of the existence of both God and evil is removed. Is there something like (7) that might be added to (1), (2), and (3)? Plantinga's original Free Will Defense argues that the following sentence does the work:

(8) It was not within God's power to create a world containing moral good without creating one containing moral evil.

Before going further, it is important to note that Plantinga insists that (8) does not have to be actually true. It only has to be *possibly* true. Because he is not willing to claim that it *is* true, Plantinga concedes that he is offering only a "defense," not a "theodicy." A defense gives a possible reason that God included evil; a theodicy offers the reason that God in fact had for including evil in the world he made. This difference becomes especially important in the Felix Culpa argument. Plantinga is willing to call this later argument a theodicy.

Reformed intuitions will rightly recoil at the idea that there could be logically possible things that God is not able to bring about (as (8) claims). Plantinga's professed reasons for embracing (8) don't remove those worries. The complex argument that Plantinga gives for the truth of (8) has two steps, both of which are troubling. The first is the step of showing that there are logically possible worlds that God could not create, from which it would follow that some worlds are "feasible" for God and others are not.[52] This step turns on a Molinist account of God's knowledge of creaturely free acts. On this account, God's knowledge of what a creature will freely do in a given circumstance is part of God's "middle knowledge." The truths detailing all the ways that a creature would freely act in every possible circumstance are not made true by either God's nature (as with the moral law) or God's will (as with all the truths that God freely makes true by his decree). If, for example, it is a truth that

(9) Rachel would freely praise God if a tree fell on her car,[53]

then God can bring it about that Rachel freely praises him (in this particular way) by decreeing that the tree fall on her car. God thus knows that

---

52. Plantinga, *God, Freedom, and Evil*, 34–44.
53. Sentence (9) is an example of a "counterfactual of creaturely freedom." Such truths are pivotal to the Molinist account of God's providence. For a complete explanation of the Molinist position, see Thomas Flint, "Two Accounts of Providence," in Thomas V. Morris, ed., *Divine and Human Action* (Ithaca, NY: Cornell University Press, 1988), 147–81.

Rachel will praise him, but not (it is thought) in a way that violates Rachel's free will.[54] Although it is logically possible that Rachel would instead curse God when the tree fell, God would have to violate Rachel's free will in order to bring it about. For Plantinga, worlds possible only by violating Rachel's free will are not feasible worlds.

Clearly, there are problems here. But before I highlight them, consider how the rest of the argument for (8) goes. In addition to its being possible that there are infeasible worlds for God, Plantinga also argues that it is possible that every free creature suffers from "transworld depravity," that every free creature sins at least once in every possible world. If so, Plantinga argues, then it is possible that every world with moral good (from free choices) has at least one evil action in it. So it is possible that the world with moral good and no moral evil is not feasible. This is what (8) claims. And if (8) is possibly true, then Plantinga has provided a model that demonstrates that an all-powerful, wholly good God and evil are compossible. For many philosophers who thought that the heart of the problem of evil is the intellectual complaint that Christians must embrace a contradiction, this was thought to be a powerful, even a decisive, solution.

In its full philosophically complex form, this argument is hard to use in an ordinary discussion about the problem of evil. It is still very popular, however, in part because the complicated details are usually left out. The short version of the argument is much more compelling, and goes something like this:

> Human free will is a very great good. Surely it is possible that God couldn't have made a world with less evil than the world we know *without* violating human free will. In that case, God's perfect goodness would be vindicated because he brought about the great good of human freedom at the lowest cost possible.

This is what most people mean by the Free Will Defense. Yet Reformed thinkers, including John Frame, have never found this approach to the problem of

54. It is worth noting that the Westminster Confession of Faith rules out this way of thinking of God's foreknowledge. "Although God knows whatsoever may or can come to pass upon all supposed conditions; yet has He not decreed anything because He foresaw it as future, or as that which would come to pass upon such conditions" (WCF 3.2). For more on the biblical inadequacy of this view of God's foreknowledge, see Paul Helm, *The Providence of God* (Downers Grove, IL: InterVarsity Press, 1994), 55–61, and my brief article "Does God Know the Future?" *Modern Reformation* 8, 5 (September–October 1999): 20–25.

evil very attractive. Denying God's ability to do whatever is logically possible is simply too high a price to pay.

Frame's analysis of the Free Will Defense focuses on the role that human freedom plays in it.[55] He rightly points out that God never responds to complaints about evil by referring to human freedom as part of the explanation. He also correctly notes that the view of human freedom used in this defense is impossible to find in the Bible at all. For readers already convinced about Reformed theology, these reasons are sufficient. But there is another reason for rejecting the Free Will Defense that non-Reformed readers should consider. In the original version of Plantinga's Free Will Defense, God's choices are constrained by truths that are independent of God. Truths such as (9) about what Rachel would freely do are truths to which God must submit. They are true not because of God's nature or will, but because of Rachel's (radically independent) nature. This state of affairs would compromise God's independence.[56] Even fans of libertarian human freedom should find this troubling, since it means that some truths are not God's truths!

These difficulties may make it hard to see why the Free Will Defense deserves so much attention in a discussion of John Frame's apologetics. But there is more to the story. Although most apologists continue to lean on Plantinga's original formulation of the defense, Plantinga himself has recently added to it.[57] In this new response to the problem of evil, Plantinga aims to deal with the problem "according to Christian thought." That is, he will not limit himself to claims that non-Christians will readily accept. In relying on Scripture and specifically Christian teaching about God's redemptive work in Christ, Plantinga shifts the center of his argument. Instead of emphasizing human free will, Plantinga focuses on the incomparable goodness of Jesus' incarnation and his gracious giving of himself for us in the atonement.[58] Although Plantinga sets up the new argument by reiterating his claims about libertarian human freedom and a Molinist account of God's foreknowledge, neither of these commitments is essential to the new argument.

---

55. *AGG*, 159–63.

56. This is called the "grounding objection." See Richard H. Corrigan, "Could God Know What I Would Freely Do? Molinism and the Grounding Objection," *Philosophical Frontiers* 3, 1 (January–June 2008): 43–57.

57. Plantinga, "Supralapsarianism, or 'O Felix Culpa.' "

58. Whatever else Plantinga has said about the atonement in his other works, the claims he makes about the goodness of the atonement in this piece are consistent with a biblical understanding of it.

Plantinga's Felix Culpa version follows the same structure as the Free Will Defense, seeking to show that an all-powerful, wholly good God and evil are compossible by providing a further claim (the model) that is possibly true and, if true, removes the threat of contradiction. In the earlier version, libertarian human freedom and Molinism were needed in order to establish that (8) is possibly true. In place of (8), Plantinga uses this:

(10) God decrees evil in order to realize the incomparable good of the incarnation and the atonement.[59]

Most of Plantinga's new version focuses on establishing the truth of this claim by explaining what an "incomparable good" is, and by showing that the incarnation and atonement are this kind of good. As he explains it, incomparable goods are overwhelming; they are like infinite quantities. The incarnation and atonement are so very good that no matter how much evil and suffering a world contains, the presence of the incarnation and atonement in that world makes it "eligible" to be decreed by an all-powerful, wholly good God. Plantinga is aware that only Christians will see the goodness of the incarnation and atonement this way, and that their acceptance of (10) will depend on their confidence in what the Bible says. But he is reasoning "according to Christian thought."

With (10) established, the rest of the argument is simple. (10) provides the model that shows the logical compossibility of the existence of evil and the existence of an all-powerful, wholly good God. The mere possibility of the incomparable goodness of Christ's work removes the charge that evil is thought to bring against God's goodness and power. But as Plantinga is quick to point out, Christians know from Scripture that Christ's incarnation and atonement are not a mere possibility. They actually occurred! This is why Plantinga upgrades his argument from a "defense" to a "theodicy." He

59. My description of Plantinga's argument uses "decrees" where Plantinga uses "weakly actualizes" and uses "realize" where Plantinga uses "strongly actualize." This move is justified for two reasons. First, Plantinga explicitly draws the inference that this new version of the argument shows that supralapsarianism is superior to infralapsarianism ("Supralapsarianism, or 'O Felix Culpa,' " 14). He acknowledges that the issue in the supra-infra debate is the (something like) logical order of the divine decrees. Second, the difference between strong and weak actualization depends on the Molinist account of God's providence. With a compatibilist definition of human freedom, the need for Molinism drops away.

contends that he has identified a sufficient reason that God had for including evil in his choice (decree) of a world.

As may already be evident, Plantinga's Felix Culpa argument is surprisingly compatible with John Frame's analysis of the problem of evil. Although it starts out as a variant on the Free Will Defense, it ends up a version of what Frame calls the "Greater-Good Defense." Frame acknowledges that this approach is incomplete, but it has scriptural support.[60] In the course of reasoning "according to Christian thought," Plantinga (unwittingly?) renders unnecessary the biblically troubling features of the Free Will Defense: libertarian human freedom and Molinist providence. These troubling features are connected. Molinist providence is (thought to be) required to preserve God's omniscience about future events without violating libertarian human free will. If libertarian freedom is not needed for the Felix Culpa argument, then Molinism is not needed, either. Even from within Plantinga's analysis, however, it is evident that libertarian human freedom is not necessary. The incomparable goodness of the incarnation and atonement requires only that there be evils deserving God's wrath. The evil of betraying and crucifying Jesus deserves God's wrath even though it happened "according to the determinate counsel and foreknowledge of God" (Acts 2:23). Here free, culpable human evil and specific divine decree are manifestly compatible. So even on a compatibilist definition of human freedom, God's wrath is still deserved, and the incarnation and atonement are incomparably good.

For a generation it has been thought that libertarian human freedom had to be accepted in order to make use of Plantinga's philosophically powerful argument in *God, Freedom, and Evil*. Plantinga's recent work in "Supralapsarianism, or 'O Felix Culpa' " allows us to conclude otherwise. More than that, this work shows the apologetic power of presuppositionalist reasoning. Reasoning "according to Christian thought," Plantinga produces an answer to the problem of evil that echoes many of the principal conclusions reached in John Frame's treatment of the problem: the ultimate explanation concerns an incomparable good related to God's glory; Christ's incarnation and suffering are vital to any adequate consideration of God's goodness and our suffering; and confident reasoning from the perspective of God's Word is far more satisfying than reasoning from mere philosophical possibilities.[61] Plantinga's Felix Culpa version does not include every important aspect of

---

60. *AGG*, 184–85; *DG*, 160–89.
61. Compare these conclusions with Frame's summary statements in *AGG*, 175, 178.

Frame's analysis. In particular, Plantinga does not mention the crucial biblical theme that those who accuse God of injustice are themselves found guilty. But Plantinga's Felix Culpa development of his Free Will Defense is nonetheless a significant vindication of Frame's approach to the problem of evil.

FRAME AND THE FUTURE OF REFORMED APOLOGETICS

Although it may be hard to find Frame's impact through an Internet search, the legacy of his adaptation of Van Til's presuppositionalism is likely to be extensive in part because the cultural landscape has changed in a way that has brought his emphases on humility, listening, and worldview assumptions (presuppositions) into fashion. Even without these cultural developments, however, Frame's influence has been assured by the important work of his Van Tillian contemporaries and successors.

Lines of intellectual descent are tricky things. It is clear that Cornelius Van Til, C. S. Lewis, Francis Schaeffer, Ravi Zacharias, and John Frame shaped the thinking of Bill Edgar, Scott Oliphint, Michael Horton, Tim Keller, and many others; but it is not at all clear how to apportion credit and blame for the resulting approaches. To avoid having to deal with the precise debts and influences, I refer to this second group (Edgar, Oliphint, etc.) as Frame's apologetic "younger siblings." Regardless of the details of their connections to Frame, these younger siblings share with Frame a passion to defend the faith with open dependence on God's authority, grace, and revelation. They care more about the needs of doubters than they do about defending the perfection of their meta-apologetic theories. Although they are aware that presuppositionalism has critics, they prefer to spend their energy dealing with people wrestling with the truth of the gospel. They know that faithful apologetics must pay close attention both to biblical guidance and to the culture's shifting fascinations. In their writing and teaching, these fellow travelers with Frame display an apologetic approach that is both bold and humble. Christians and non-Christians in our pluralist world need both.

Humility is now widely recognized as important in apologetics.[62] But combining humility with biblical boldness is difficult. The approach on display in the work of Frame and his younger siblings achieves that difficult

---

62. One prominent advocate is Stackhouse, *Humble Apologetics*; but see also James W. Sire, *A Little Primer on Humble Apologetics* (Downers Grove, IL: InterVarsity Press, 2006); Sean McDowell, "Introduction," in McDowell, *Apologetics for a New Generation*, 24–25.

combination by making their dependence on the self-authenticating Word of God a starting point rather than the conclusion of some other argument. Starting from the authority of God's Word should result in true humility about our abilities and justified boldness about the perfectly certain hope offered in the gospel. Submission to God's Word produces the humility not to see ourselves as superior to the doubter, and to make us recoil at the prospect of turning the discussion into an intellectual contest with humiliation as the goal. Open dependence on God's Word enables the apologist to defend certainties rather than probabilities, and to provide doubters with the comfort that can come only by a word from the Lord.

Pluralism is attractive today in part because it allows people to believe that no one can legitimately question the way they are living their lives. Our culture cherishes the resulting sense of autonomy and immunity from criticism. The institutions that dominate contemporary American life—media, business, government, education—embody and exploit the myth that although facts are objective, every lifestyle choice is equally good and up to the individual.[63] Christian apologists have the socially offensive task of saying that this belief is false; but they also have something that everyone wants and pluralism denies: a word from the Lord. Recently, a successful twentysomething businessman told me that what he wanted most was a memo from God. He didn't care what it said; he would happily follow whatever directions God gave. As far as he could see, no one else was willing to give him clear directions about anything. His parents, his teachers, advertisers, and government officials all insisted that they would support whatever project he chose—but they would not impose their values on him. He found it frustrating.

The nearly limitless freedom that pluralism promises is ultimately disappointing. The immediate future of Christian apologetics lies in speaking to a culture that is desperate for the Word of the Lord, but that is reminded at every turn that autonomy is the greatest good. Although they don't see it, what they want is the gospel: freedom from slavery to sin and the glorious law of God as a lamp unto their feet. What they need is repentance, and apologists calling for repentance must be both humble and bold. They must be humble because they need grace as much as any doubter. They know firsthand that in their own strength—whether of good works or good arguments—they

---

63. See Stackhouse, *Humble Apologetics*, 3–11, on different forms of pluralism, including relativistic pluralism.

would be clinging to falsehoods, suppressing the truth in unrighteousness. Their boldness, on the other hand, rests on the power of the Word of God not to return void. They defend the faith with confidence because they have the Word of the Lord, the longed-for memo from God.

Among Frame's siblings, both older and younger, are a group of pre-suppositionalists doing "cultural" apologetics. They don't insist on the term *presupposition*, but their method turns on close attention to the presuppositions dominating a culture's mind-set. Apologists such as Francis Schaeffer, Ravi Zacharias, and Bill Edgar have invested the time necessary to learn the aspirations and anxieties of the culture in which they have been called to defend the faith.[64] Their apologetic arguments and strategies are adapted to the peculiar hopes and fears made manifest in the popular culture of their age. Loving attention to these presupposition-level hopes and fears enables them to follow Paul's example, in effect saying, "I see that you worship an unknown god. Let me tell you about this God. He is the maker of heaven and earth. He calls all men to repent. And he will judge all of us in the person of Jesus, whom he raised from the dead." Cultural apologetics is presuppositional apologetics. In a pluralist culture, the future of apologetics will lie in this direction.

At the heart of cultural/presuppositional apologetics is a new conception of the paradigm apologist, the kind that young Christians are encouraged to imitate. When the early church was facing legal prosecution and persecution, the paradigm apologists were lawyers. Justin Martyr and Tertullian, to name only two, defended the faith using legal reasoning. In the Middle Ages, the paradigm apologists were theologians. They defended the faith by constructing impressive demonstrations of the rational coherence of Christian claims. In the age of Enlightenment science, the paradigm apologists were analytic philosophers, experts at vindicating the truth of hypotheses by objective appeal to experimental data. They defended the faith by showing that Christianity holds the best explanation for the data of common human experience, often treating Christian beliefs about God's existence or Jesus' resurrection like scientific hypotheses. None of these paradigms is suited to a pluralist age, so the future of apologetics needs a

---

64. Francis Schaeffer, *The God Who Is There* (Downers Grove, IL: InterVarsity Press, 1998); Ravi Zacharias, *Can Man Live without God?* (Nashville: Thomas Nelson, 2004); William Edgar, *Reasons of the Heart: Recovering Christian Persuasion* (Phillipsburg, NJ: P&R Publishing, 2003).

new paradigm. John Frame's apologetics recommends a suitable replacement: the apologist as pastor.

Unlike lawyers and philosophers, pastors are gifted and trained as ministers of the Word. Unlike academic theologians, their calling is to apply the Word of God to the needs of ordinary people. Mindful of their own struggles and weakness, they apply the Word humbly. Aware of the authority and power of the Word, they apply it boldly. As John Frame insists, apologetics is the application of the Word of God to unbelief. The paradigm apologists ought to be pastors in every age. In a pluralist age, it is hard to justify any other ideal. And because pastoral apologetics can begin only with the Word of God, it will be presuppositionalist rather than evidentialist.

Apologists as pastors will focus more fully on loving the doubter than on gaining intellectual victory, so it may be difficult to see how their apologetic practice flows from the same commitments as Van Til's presuppositionalism. John Frame's development of Van Til's approach provides the bridge. One apologist standing on the other end of Frame's bridge is Tim Keller. His ministry applies the Word of God to the needs of young professionals in New York City. Among their needs is having their doubts addressed, and Keller's apologetic approach to those doubts is summarized in his book *The Reason for God*. Keller's primary concern is ministering to these doubts, whether from believers or unbelievers. He spends little time reflecting on meta-apologetic issues such as the possibility of a neutral common ground, the power of human reason, or even the possibility of considering evidence apart from presupposing the God of the Bible. As a result, some of the standard elements of a Van Tillian defense of the faith—heavy on these meta-apologetic matters—are hard to find in Keller's work.

Despite the absence of Van Tillian stipulations, however, Keller's apologetic approach is markedly in tune with the presuppositionalism of Van Til and Frame. His book deploys Frame's three kinds of apologetics. Part 1 does apologetics as "defense," answering the most common objections to the faith that Keller has heard from young people. The answers he gives never concede that the doubter has the right to sit in judgment of God, and he is open about his own dependence on God's Word. Because he is a pastor rather than a philosopher, his open submission to God's Word is acceptable! Part 2 does apologetics as "proof," building a rational case for the coherence and superiority not just of theism, but of the triune God's majesty and his mighty acts in history. Keller argues from "clues," from cultural aspirations, from the impossibility of meaning apart from God, and ultimately from Scripture. He argues that only the gospel can satisfy our longings for love, forgiveness, and community. The case he builds includes numerous instances of apologetics as "offense" as he exposes the futility of rival, idolatrous alternatives; and in places his arguments are careful transcendental arguments for the necessity of presupposing God in order to love or argue at all. His manner is patient, encouraging, and loving; but it is also unrelenting in its insistence that Jesus is the only way, that repentance is necessary, and that every other way is frustrating and harmful.[65]

Tim Keller never studied under John Frame, but in an interview he credits Frame with influencing his work.[66] Both in Keller's writing and in his public appearances, his apologetic practice and recommendations appear to be an especially promising example of what Frame is calling for. Frame's adaptations of Van Til's system are much more about apologetic manner and style than they are about meta-apologetic distinctives. Frame retains Van Til's adamant insistence on lordship epistemology and the apologist's obligation not to dishonor Christ by conceding the skeptic's right to autonomous reasoning. What Frame modifies is the paradigm for apologetic practice, replacing a warrior model with a pastoral model. This replacement has numerous implications for the apologist's role in the world. The most demanding implication is the need to love doubters enough to engage with them as individuals rather than as cartoonish "isms," to learn their specific aspirations and desires as well as their complaints, worries, and doubts. The pastoral model of apologetics demands a significant investment of time and energy, but the investment is necessary to discern the specific presuppositions that frustrate doubters. The investment is also crucial to making the satisfying presupposition of the God of the Bible clear and compelling.

As Frame's younger siblings demonstrate, Reformed apologists are already accepting the daunting task of making this investment. By encouraging this kind of apologetic ministry in the next generation of apologists, Frame is serving the future of Reformed apologetics especially well.

---

65. Keller explicitly claims to be doing presuppositional apologetics in his RTS lectures for the course "Preaching Christ in a Postmodern World" in the session titled "Adoring Christ: Getting Inside Their World Part Two." The audio for this lecture is available at http://www.itunes.com.

66. "Monergism Interview with Dr. Tim Keller," available at http://www.monergism.com/thethreshold/articles/onsite/kellerinterview.html.

22

FRAME'S AND VAN TIL'S APOLOGETIC

STEVE R. SCRIVENER

THIS ESSAY SEEKS to answer the following questions: (1) How have John Frame and Cornelius Van Til influenced each other in apologetics? That is the prelude to the main question: (2) assessing the constructive criticisms that Frame has made about Van Til's apologetic by asking what does the Bible say about Van Til's "transcendental method" and "traditional" apologetics? Then (3) how do we go forward in apologetics?

FRAME'S AND VAN TIL'S MUTUAL INFLUENCE

Cornelius Van Til taught systematic theology and apologetics at Westminster Theological Seminary Philadelphia from 1929 until he retired in 1972. Frame says that while a student at Westminster (1961–64), "Van Til became the greatest influence on my apologetics and theology"[1] and that "my own [presuppositional] approach [to apologetics] owes more to Van Til than to anyone else."[2]

After further study at Yale University, Frame returned to Westminster in 1968 to teach systematic theology. In 1975 Frame replaced

---

1. John Frame, "Backgrounds to My Thought," in this festschrift.
2. Steve B. Cowan and Stanley N. Gundry, eds., *Five Views on Apologetics* (Grand Rapids: Zondervan, 2000), 219n16 (hereinafter *FV*).

Van Til's successor, Harvie Conn, for the introductory apologetics course. Since then Frame has continued to teach and write on systematic theology, ethics, and apologetics (moving to Westminster California in 1980 and then Reformed Theological Seminary, Orlando, in 2000). Frame says:

> I was committed to Van Til's apologetic method and to [John] Murray's exegetical emphasis. I sought to integrate these even more intimately than Van Til and Murray had done: integrating detailed exegesis with worldview consciousness. . . .
>
> As I evaluate my own contributions, my chief strength in the area of apologetics has been my integration of the discipline with Reformed systematics, in the tri-perspectival framework ["situationally" (focusing on the nature of the created world), "normatively" (focusing on the authority of God's revelation) or "existentially" (focusing on God's presence with his people)]—see my *Apologetics to the Glory of God*.[3]

Frame and Van Til were not close friends,[4] and Frame did not have a direct influence on Van Til's teaching or writing about apologetics, since Van Til's apologetic had been long established before Frame began teaching. But Frame has had a real effect on Van Til's *legacy* in apologetics. For instance, in 1990 a lecture by James Grier stirred me to read Van Til and Frame.[5] First I read Van Til's *The Defense of the Faith* and I knew, under our sovereign Lord, that Grier had led me to a personal revolution in my apologetics and Christian life. I was captivated by Van Til's "bold exciting summaries, illustrations, and exhortation,"[6] but there was much in Van Til I did not understand. I then went on to read Frame's *DKG* and later *AGG*, and I felt that I was beginning to get a handle on presuppositional apologetics. Frame's *CVT* led me into reading and *understanding* various books

---

3. From an earlier version of John M. Frame, "Systematic Theology and Apologetics at the Westminster Seminaries," supplied by e-mail by Frame to me, with the text in square brackets inserted from the essay.

4. Frame, *CVT*, 17.

5. The lecture was later published as James Grier, "Is Evidence Really Necessary?" in the Metropolitan Tabernacle's *Sword and Trowel* (1992 No. 1): 8–12, to be posted at http://www.vantil.info.

6. *CVT*, 32. See further a collection of "Van Til's Illustrations, Focusing on Apologetics," available at http://www.vantil.info/articles/CVT_illustrations_v1.pdf.

of Van Til.[7] But without Frame as my guide, I would not have experienced the riches of Van Til.

Frame, along with the late Greg Bahnsen (1948–95), has been *the* sympathetic explainer, developer, and applier of Van Til's presuppositional apologetic. Unlike Bahnsen, Frame has also been a constructively *critical* disciple of Van Til, "evaluating his thought on the basis of Scripture, seeking to come to a position more fully scriptural than even his own"[8]—and who would argue against that? Frame adds, "I believe that Van Til's [Reformed apologetics] approach is still the best foundation for Christian apologetics at the present time. . . . I continue to follow, and occasionally depart from the Van Tillian model. . . . I think also that it needs some revision . . . lest its weaknesses obscure its tremendously important insights."[9] According to Frame, these revisions are that "my concept of transcendental argument differs somewhat from that of Van Til"[10] and that "contrary to Van Til I see considerable common ground between presuppositional apologetics and the schools of [apologetics]. . . . I do not automatically reject [traditional] theistic proofs and Christian evidences as non-transcendental."[11] He concludes: "It may no longer be possible to distinguish 'presuppositional' in distinction from 'traditional' apologetics merely by externals: by the form of argument, the explicit claim of certainty or probability, etc. Perhaps presuppositionalism is more an attitude of the heart."[12] Frame says that this "presuppositionalism of the heart" belongs to that special kind of Reformed apologetics developed by Cornelius Van Til but that some Van Tillians will describe Frame's work "as revisionist."[13]

7. I followed Frame's useful recommendations for reading Van Til's books at *CVT*, 26 and 446–50. I add these recommendations of my own: use the latest editions of Van Til's *Christian Apologetics*, *Defense of the Faith*, and *Introduction to Systematic Theology* (see endnote 2 in this essay), and read Greg Bahnsen's epic *Van Til's Apologetic: Readings & Analysis* (Phillipsburg, NJ: P&R Publishing, 1998) (hereinafter *VTARA*), since this organizes and explains the best of Van Til. In addition, see my own "Van Til's Presuppositional Apologetic in Practice" and "Classic Passages on Apologetics by Van Til Including His Main Themes," to be posted at http://www.vantil.info, and section 2, "Cornelius Van Til," under "Apologetics" in John Frame's Glossary in this volume.

8. *CVT*, 11. See ibid., 5–14 for Frame's explanation and justification of this position.

9. *AGG*, xi–xii.

10. *FV*, 20n18. Frame adds, "See my discussion in *AGG*, 69–88, and *CVT*, 241–297, 311–322."

11. *FV*, 357.

12. *AGG*, 87.

13. Ibid., xi. Here is a comment from one of the fairest comparisons of different apologetics schools: "Among Van Til interpreters, Frame alone has offered a critical, creative interpretation of presuppositionalism that makes room for many of the traditional kinds of apologetic argu-

Van Til "rarely offered his own judgment"[14] on Frame's approach. But in the presuppositional camp, Bahnsen "disagrees"[15] with Frame's revisions, whereas William Edgar's conviction is that "the transcendental argument makes room for [the] 'broader' approaches [to which Frame has opened the door]."[16] Who is right? How will we resolve this dilemma? What will this mean for actually doing apologetics? Well, I am going to take my cue from Frame: "that the most fundamental point of presuppositionalism is the application of *sola Scriptura* to apologetics, [that is,] the principle that only God, speaking in Scripture, has supreme authority over the human heart and mind."[17] Especially because, surprisingly, I think Frame's constructive criticisms are made on more pragmatic grounds. So let us see where a biblical assessment of Van Til's transcendental argument and traditional apologetics leads us.

A Biblical Assessment of Van Til's Transcendental Argument for God's Existence

Since we need to be clear on what Van Til's transcendental argument for God (VTAG) actually is, I will first describe it and highlight some of its features. I will use the following symbols: (1) ◊ means "it is possible (or intelligible) that"; (2) ⇐ means "presupposes" (my notation); (3) ~ means "not"; (4) ∴ means "therefore"; and (5) *TLAS* means "triune Lord and Savior."[18]

An Example of VTAG

And to put some flesh on the bones, here is an example of VTAG by Van Til that deals with the evolutionary worldview:

> The Christian presupposes the triune God and his redemptive plan for the universe as set forth once for all in Scripture.

---

ments criticized by Van Til." Kenneth D. Boa and Robert M. Bowman, *Faith Has Its Reasons: An Integrative Approach to Defending Christianity* (Colorado Springs: NavPress, 2001), 493. Additionally, the authors do not put Frame under "Reformed Apologetics" where Van Til is, but under "Apologists Who Favor Integration."

14. John R. Muether, *Cornelius Van Til: Reformed Apologist and Churchman* (Phillipsburg, NJ: P&R Publishing, 2008), 223.

15. *VTARA*, 674.

16. From William Edgar's essay "Frame the Apologist," in this festschrift. The remarks in Edgar's section "Apologetic Argument" supplement my own essay.

17. *FV*, 363, 362.

18. Notes to the three tables in this article appear at the end of the chapter.

Logical form	Description	Van Til references (classics in bold)
	***The twofold "for argument's sake" strategy* (indirect, reasoning by presupposition),** which:	* *DF4*, 122–24; *IW*, 38–39
	• appeals to unbelievers' suppressed knowledge; and	(From above: *DF4*, 124)
	• pleads with unbelievers to accept Christ as their Savior from the sin of autonomy.	*JA*, 426, 452; *DF3*, 4.
(1) $\Diamond x \Leftarrow ?$	**Introduction:** What presupposition is needed to affirm, or deny, the intelligibility of any human experience or object of knowledge (x)?	*SCE*, 10–11, 201, 204.
(2) $\sim\Diamond x \Leftarrow \sim$TLAS	**Procedure 1:** Show that the non-Christian's presupposition, if it were true for argument's sake, would make x unintelligible—that is, reasoning from the impossibility of the contrary position (if Christianity were not true, the unbeliever could not prove or understand anything). "Has not God made foolish the wisdom of the world?" (1 Cor. 1:20).[1] This can include pointing out:	* *GA*, 3–4; ***SCE***, xi, 204–6, 222–23.
	a) their knowledge from borrowed capital (presupposing the truth of the Christian position); and/or	*GH*, 243; ***JA***, 17–18, 91, 98.
	b) the irrationalist-rationalist dilemma.	*DF4*, 148; ***ICG***, 18.
(3) $\Diamond x \Leftarrow$ TLAS	**Procedure 2:** The Christian's presupposition, if it were true for argument's sake, is shown to be the foundation of making x intelligible.	*JA*, 302; see also * above.
(4) $\therefore$ TLAS	Conclusion: The triune Lord and Savior exists.	*IST2*, 180; cf. 178n6; *JA*, 452.[2][3]

Fig. 22.1. VTAG with Its Logical Form, in Symbolic Logic

The non-Christian presupposes a dialectic between "chance" and "regularity," the former accounting for the origin of matter and life, the latter accounting for the current success of the scientific enterprise. . . .

If the non-Christian attempts to account for the amenability of fact to logic in terms of the ultimate rationality of the cosmos, then he will be crippled when it comes to explaining the "evolution" of men and things. If he attempts to do so in terms of pure "chance" and ultimate "irrationality" as being the well out of which both rational man and a rationally amenable world sprang, then we shall point out that such an explanation is in fact no explanation at all and that it destroys predication.[19]

The Irrationalist-Rationalist Dilemma and Frame

Here Van Til uses the unbeliever's *irrationalist-rationalist dialectic* (or *dilemma*). Biblically, this dilemma has existed from the fall onward.[20] It is the tension and self-contradiction of being certain about uncertainty (irrationalism) and uncertain about certainty (rationalism). For example, postmodernism self-destructs with its slogans: "It's certain that there is no certainty"; "It's wrong to say others are wrong." Frame thinks Van Til's identification of the non-Christian's irrationalist-rationalist dilemma "is one of his best accomplishments. . . . Van Til's analysis provides a good perspective from which to understand the twists and turns of the history of thought . . . My only caveat is that we should avoid using this analysis in a wooden way, insensitive to the diversity among non-Christian thinkers. Nor should we assume that everything can be exhaustively explained by the rationalist-irrationalist dialectic. . . . Nevertheless, [Van Til] introduces a very helpful apologetic tool in showing that unbelief is inseparably linked to the dialectic of rationalism and irrationalism, which destroys all basis for intelligible predication."[21]

19. *JA*, 19, 20. The order of the two steps of procedures 1 and 2 is reversed. They can be done in any order—this is a *twofold strategy* comprising two "complementary moves." *CA2*, 7; cf. *VTARA*, 512n95.

20. *DF4*, 238–39.

21. *CVT*, 236, 238, 399. See also *CVT*, 232–38, 328–29; *DKG*, 60–61; *FV*, 212–13; *VTARA*, 316–17, 389–402. For Frame's application of this tool to actual people, including that the dilemma is in the unbeliever's logic *and life*, see *DKG*, 360–63; *AGG*, 201–2. He adds, "It is especially useful when we can show how the errors of non-Christian worldviews arise, not merely from logical mistakes or factual inaccuracy, but firm religious rebellion" (*FV*, 223).

The "For Argument's Sake" Strategy Explained

The VTAG example also shows that in reasoning by presupposition, "the Christian never really abandons his own presupposition, even for a moment. Even when accepting the unbeliever's principles 'for the sake of argument,' he still is thinking as a Christian. What really happens, then . . . is that the Christian is telling the unbeliever how the unbeliever's principles look to him as a Christian."[22] Van Til adds that otherwise, "we would drown with him. We use the figure of drowning in order to suggest what it is that we really do when we say that we are placing ourselves upon someone else's position. We may then compare ourselves to a lifesaver who goes out to save someone from drowning. Such a lifesaver must be bound to the shore to which he wants to rescue the other party. He may depend upon his power to swim, but this very power to swim is an invisible cord that connects him to the shore. Similarly, if we reason when we place ourselves upon our opponents' position, we cannot for a moment do more than argue thus for 'argument's sake.' "[23]

VTAG Is about the Unique (Triune) Lord and Savior

Before moving on to assessing VTAG, I want to highlight something very important: VTAG is about establishing the unique (triune) Lord and Savior of biblical Christianity; it is not about the god or gods of any other religion, cult, or "ism," such as Islam, Jehovah's Witnesses, Mormonism, or atheism (whose god is the self) and agnosticism (which is practical atheism; cf. Ps. 14:1–4).[24] In other words, that God is triune, and *the* Savior (by Christ, by grace alone, through faith alone), is only in Christianity.

As William Edgar says, "Van Til's apologetics is . . . profoundly gospel driven. . . . So many of the insights for which Van Til is justly famous fall flat if they are isolated from the great emphasis on redemption that pervades his work. . . . Apologetics for Van Til is simply a thoughtful form of evangelism."[25] For instance, Van Til says, "I [do] not . . . make any sharp distinction between

22. *DKG*, 359; cf. *CVT*, 319–21.
23. *SCE*, 205–6.
24. For Muslims and Jehovah's Witnesses, God is one but not three persons. Mormons have many gods, while atheists (and agnostics) have no gods other than themselves because the self is god. Essentially, all these religions believe in salvation by works—they want to try to climb up the mountain of religion to God. But in Christianity, God comes down the mountain to bring us to himself by Christ the Savior. Cf. *AGG*, 100, 92, 54. See also footnote 98 below.
25. *CA2*, 14.

witnessing to and defending the Christian faith. . . . My defense of the truth of Christianity is, as I think of it, always, at the same time, a witness to Christ as the Way, the Truth, and the Life."[26] Further:

> Protestant Christians ought therefore to celebrate the grace of God their Savior unto them by noting carefully from what they have been saved and to what they are called. Their method of apologetics should be in line with their theology. In both Christ should be taught and preached unto men who are lost in all their thinking and living without him. The natural man must be shown that on his presupposition or assumption of man's autonomy human predication has no meaning at all. But this negative task cannot be accomplished except on the presupposition that in Christ life does have meaning. Only when Protestant theology thus sees its apologetics to be an aspect of its theology of free grace can the glad tidings of the gospel ring out clearly and fully to men.[27]

Bahnsen's Biblical Basis for the Transcendental Argument Assessed

Now that VTAG is described, I will give and then examine (1) its biblical basis, and (2) its theological basis, which will naturally lead to answering these questions: How does Frame's transcendental (presuppositional) apologetics match up with the conclusions that I will draw regarding VTAG? What about his detailed criticisms of VTAG (in the light of Bahnsen's responses, on behalf of Van Til)?

In biblical support[28] of VTAG and believing that it is the way to do apologetics,[29] Van Til simply refers to only two Bible texts, Romans 1:18 and especially 1 Corinthians 1:20:[30] "reasoning . . . by way of presupposition . . . [is] following Paul's example when he asks, 'Hath not God made foolish the wisdom of this world' [1 Cor. 1:20b KJV]," and is appealing

26. *JA*, 452.

27. Cornelius Van Til, *The Defense of the Faith*, 3rd ed. (Philadelphia: Presbyterian and Reformed, 1967), 4—note the twofold strategy. See further K. Scott Oliphint, "Van Til the Evangelist," at http://www.opc.org/os.html?article_id=118; cf. *VTARA*, 43–44, 52–54, 70–71, 82–85; *AGG*, 16, 26–27, 54; *DKG*, 350, 355.

28. For the basis of the conclusions of this paragraph, see my "Van Til's Transcendental Argument Form and Theological and Biblical Basis," posted at http://www.vantil.info.

29. Including using proofs and evidences, which are related to VTAG. See *IST2*, 180, 242–43; cf. footnote 87 below.

30. Van Til likes and often quotes 1 Corinthians 1:20. See my "The Scriptures Van Til Quotes about Apologetics," at http://www.vantil.info.

to "the natural man['s] . . . knowledge of God [that] is suppressed"[31]—
Romans 1:18 confirms that it is right to appeal to suppressed knowledge,[32]
but it is not a proof text for VTAG. Bahnsen is the one who has argued
the biblical basis for the transcendental procedure.[33] He also views 1 Corinthians 1:20 as *the* Bible text basis for Van Til's method, for "Van Til's
presuppositional defense of the faith" is "following the inspired lead of
the apostle Paul, [as] it rhetorically asks: 'Where is the wise? Where is
the scribe? Where is the disputer of this world? Has not God made foolish the wisdom of the world?' (1 Cor. 1:20 [ASV])."[34] Bahnsen adds that
Proverbs 26:4–5 describes Van Til's twofold apologetic procedure: "Do
not answer a fool according to his folly, or you will be like him yourself.
Answer a fool according to his folly, or he will be wise in his own eyes."[35]
And Jesus' parable in Matthew 7:24–27 "substantiates [this] two-step
procedure and illustrates the difference between a wise man and a fool."
"It is foolish for [the unbeliever] to build his house on the ruinous sands
of human opinion, instead of the verbal rock of Christ."[36] He also mentions that Romans 1:22 (ASV), "Professing themselves to be wise, they
become fools," states Van Til's *reductio ad absurdum*,[37] and that doing
the presuppositional "internal examination" of other religions shows that
"their rock is not like our Rock" (Deut. 32:31a).[38]

31. *IW*, 38–39, reordered.

32. See also *DF4*, 90–91n2, 197–98n47.

33. See also my "Summary of Presuppositional Apologetic Method by *Greg Bahnsen* (from
Always Ready)—with Bahnsen's Bible References Added," at http://www.vantil.info/articles/
gb_spam.pdf.

34. *VTARA*, 5. See further ibid., 4–7, 484–89; Greg L. Bahnsen, *Always Ready: Directions
for Defending the Faith*, ed. Randy Booth (Atlanta: American Vision and Texarkana: Covenant
Media Foundation, 1996), 59–60 (hereinafter *AR*); Greg L. Bahnsen, *An Answer to John Frame's
Critique of Van Til: Profound Differences between the Traditional and Presuppositional Methods*
(Philadelphia: Westminster Seminary, n.d.), 48 (hereinafter *ATJF*). *ATJF* is a transcript of lectures that Bahnsen gave (in 1994?) at Westminster Theological Seminary, with responses by and
interaction with Frame.

35. *AR*, 59–64; Greg L. Bahnsen, *Pushing the Antithesis: The Apologetic Methodology of Greg
L. Bahnsen*, ed. Gary DeMar (Atlanta: American Vision, 2007), 140–44.

36. Bahnsen, *Pushing the Antithesis*, 143; *VTARA*, 5.

37. *VTARA*, 486; cf. ibid., 5.

38. Ibid., 524n126. I have just received Greg L. Bahnsen, *Presuppositional Apologetics: Stated
and Defended*, ed. Joel McDurmon (Powder Springs, GA: American Vision and Texas Covenant
Media Press, 2008). As far as I can tell, this work does not add further specific Bible texts supporting VTAG. Interestingly, Bahnsen's exposition of 1 Corinthians 1:18–21, at ibid., 48–49, is
similar to mine (which I turn to next), and in his book his main biblical thrust is to presuppose
and follow the Word of the Lord, which will be one of my main conclusions regarding VTAG.

Turning to the key text, 1 Corinthians 1:20, its immediate context is:

> For the message of the cross is foolishness to those who are perishing, but to us who are being saved it is the power of God. For it is written: "I will destroy the wisdom of the wise; the intelligence of the intelligent I will frustrate." [Isa. 29:14]
>
> Where is the wise man? Where is the scholar? Where is the philosopher of this age? Has not God made foolish the wisdom of the world? For since in the wisdom of God the world through its wisdom did not know him, God was pleased through the foolishness of what was preached to save those who believe. (vv. 18–21)

Now, the question is, does this rhetorical *reductio* in verse 20 teach Van Til's "general approach to apologetics—arguing for the impossibility of the contrary"?[39]

I do not think this passage is about "what presupposition is needed to affirm, or deny, the intelligibility of any human experience or object of knowledge (x)?" nor is it about "reasoning from the impossibility of the contrary position" (see Introduction and procedure 1 of VTAG above). Furthermore, it would be anachronistic to read the transcendental argument, which explicitly arose with Immanuel Kant in the eighteenth century,[40] back into 1 Corinthians 1:20. Paul is saying that *only* the message of the cross of Christ saves people from perishing and that this seems foolish to those who are perishing (vv. 18, 21), whereas wisdom from any other wise person of this world, including scholars and philosophers, is in fact foolishness. It is futile, and will be brought to nothing (frustrated). So where are these wise people now? They do not have the answers to life and on how to know God (v. 21). It seems to me that Paul is showing the futility and impossibility *of* the non-Christian position rather than arguing *from* the impossibility of the contrary position. Or we could say that Paul would show the unbeliever's need of salvation and that in this sense he is arguing from its impossibility—but that is not Van Til's arguing from "if Christianity were not true, the unbeliever could not prove or understand anything." VTAG, however, including "pleading to accept Christ as the Savior from the sin of autonomy," is *a* good way of following 1 Corinthians 1:20.

39. *ATJF*, 48.
40. *VTARA*, 496–99.

Regarding Bahnsen's other Bible texts, I think it would be overstretching them to say that they are about VTAG. So none of the texts used authorizes VTAG as *the* way to do apologetics.

The twofold strategy: show that their rock is not like our Rock. What is interesting for apologetics methodology is the thrust running through these texts. That thrust is *contrasting* the Christian's truth about the Lord and Savior with the non-Christian's beliefs, and showing that our Rock gives life, whereas the sandy wisdom of this world always leads to futility and judgment. So there is *a twofold procedure and strategy to show that their rock (presupposition) is not like our Rock.*[41] The strategy is to *explode* unbelievers' futile foundations by lovingly pushing non-Christians to the logical conclusion of their presuppositions, showing the impossibility of their position,[42] and to *expose* the related fault lines in their logic and life (the irrationalist-rationalist dilemma). All this is done to help them to realize their desperate need and bankruptcy and to turn to the Lord to save them from their lostness (cf. Deut. 32:39; Luke 5:31).

It is essential to add that Scripture teaches us to use this twofold apologetic procedure very flexibly. For instance, in John 3 Jesus tells religious Nicodemus that he must be born again by the Spirit of God as he believes in Jesus the Savior, or he will remain under God's wrath. In John 4,

41. Deut. 32:31a; cf. 1 Sam. 2:2; 2 Sam. 22:31–32/Ps. 18:30–31; Isa. 44:8. For an exposition of this strategy, see my "Show Their Rock Is Not Like Our Rock: The Apologetics of Deuteronomy 32," at http://www.vantil.info.

Now, to speak to another of John Frame's varied interests: Deuteronomy 32:31a is in Moses' swan song to Israel, which they are to sing as a witness from the Lord against them (31:19). Does the fact that Israel was to sing that their rock (idol) is not like our Rock (cf. 32:4–5, 15–21, 36–39) tell us that a way of doing apologetics is by singing such songs? The following are some hymns in this vein, whose memorable words and music can drive this healing sword into our hearts: Graham Kendrick's *All I Once Held Dear*; Michael Saward's *King of the Universe, Lord of the Ages*, to the tune in *Praise! Psalms, Hymns and Songs for Christian Worship: Music Edition* (Darlington, UK: Praise Trust, 2000), available at http://www.praise.org.uk, no. 249; August Toplady's *Rock of Ages, Cleft for Me* (also try Kendrick's new tune and chorus at http://www.grahamkendrick. co.uk/songs/sheetmusic/rock.pdf); Edwin Mote's *My Hope Is Built on Nothing Less*, with its presuppositional refrain "On Christ, the solid rock, I stand; all other ground is sinking sand" (which also has a new tune, in *Praise!*, no. 779). So let us sing *"apologetics to the glory of God"*!

42. This way of putting it is by Van Til's most famous student, Francis Schaeffer. See Francis A. Schaeffer, *A Christian View of Philosophy and Culture*, vol. 1 of *The Complete Works of Francis Schaeffer: A Christian Worldview*, 2nd ed. (Carlisle, UK: Paternoster Press, 1985), 138–42, which also includes his own version of the irrationalist-rationalist dilemma, which he calls "the point of tension" (ibid., 131–37; cf. ibid., 76–79; see also Schaeffer's *The God Who Is There*, sec. 4, chaps. 1 and 2, in *The Complete Works of Francis Schaeffer*, 131–42). See further Frame's "Some Thoughts on Schaeffer's Apologetics," to be posted at http://www.frame-poythress.org.

in contrast, Jesus converses with the semipagan Samaritan woman at the well about her need of living water because of her immoral lifestyle. Or look at Acts 17, where at the beginning of the chapter Paul is in a Jewish synagogue in Thessalonica and there "he reasoned with them from the Scriptures, explaining and proving that the Christ had to suffer and rise from the dead" (vv. 1–4; cf. Luke 24:46–47). But later to the pagan Athenians in Acts 17:22–31, Paul begins with who the Lord God is and who they are before God (they are in the darkness of idolatrous ignorance), and then commands them to repent because Jesus the Judge is coming.[43] Of course, if unbelievers are aware of their real need, then we go straight to the positive answer: Christ is the only Savior and foundation for life (see Acts 16:29–31).

Van Til's Theological Basis for the Transcendental Argument Assessed

Van Til also gives theological reasons for the transcendental argument, which rest on three doctrinal footings. He argues that the Reformed apologist must use the indirect, transcendental argument (reasoning by presupposition, including reasoning from the impossibility of the opposite/contrary position) because of:[44]

1. *The fallen nature of man* (total depravity)—Because believers and unbelievers do not agree on the transcendental basis (presupposition) needed to interpret any fact (they are not neutral), the indirect, transcendental argument must be used.[45]
2. *The transcendent (absolute*[46] *and self-sufficient) nature of God*— Van Til's slogan is "the only argument for a transcendent God that holds water is a transcendental argument":

43. It is fascinating to see the twofold "show that their rock is not like our Rock" strategy recur in the Old Testament. For instance, refer to the twofold appeals, often contrasting the unique Lord to idols and saying that the Lord is the only Savior: Deut. 30:19; 32:36–39; Isa. 43:10–13; 44:6–22; 45:17–25; 55:1–2; Jer. 2:11–13, 26–28; 10:1–16. Also, I once heard John Whitcomb say that "Psalm 115 is a presuppositional apologetic about idolatry."

44. See my "Van Til's Transcendental Argument Form and Theological and Biblical Basis," at http://www.vantil.info, for all the Van Til quotes that these conclusions are based on.

45. *IW*, 38–39; *DF4*, 122–24; Cornelius Van Til, *Christian Theory of Knowledge* (Nutley, NJ: Presbyterian and Reformed, 1969), 18 (hereinafter *CTK*).

46. "God is 'absolute' in the sense that he is the creator of all things and thus the ground of all reality. As such, he has no need of any other being (Acts 17:25) for his own existence. He is self-

a. Since God alone is *transcendent* (the absolute, self-contained God, that is, the ontological Trinity) and is the only *transcendental* basis (presupposition) of everything, there is not a *direct* straight-line argument to God from something within this universe; instead, the argument for him is *indirect* and *transcendental*, presupposing his existence.[47]

b. Since God alone is *transcendent* (self-sufficient with comprehensive knowledge of all things) and we are without comprehensive knowledge, we cannot prove and define God by mathematical demonstration; instead, the argument for him is a *transcendental* argument to show that we can find no meaning in our human experience unless there is a transcendent (self-sufficient) God—this is reasoning from the impossibility of the opposite/contrary.[48]

3. *The uniqueness of Christianity*, with its claims of "this or nothing" and that those who do not accept Christ are lost—our method of argumentation must show the same uniqueness by the method of the *impossibility of the contrary*.[49]

These are weighty reasons to use VTAG, and I think there are some significant points in them. Regarding (1), total depravity necessitating reasoning by presupposition, VTAG does ensure that you talk about presuppositions, which affect how any fact is interpreted, while remaining true to your presupposition by using the twofold, "for argument's sake" strategy.[50] And with regard to (2), a transcendent God and a transcendental argument for God going hand in hand, it is true that "the transcendental argument seeks to discover what sort of foundations the house of human knowledge must have, in order to be what it is. It does not seek to find *whether* the house has a foundation, but it presupposes that it has one."[51] So the Lord is presupposed.

But does total depravity and a transcendent God mean that only VTAG must be used with its spotlight on the basis of intelligibility or predication?

existent and self-sufficient" (*AGG*, 34).

47. *SCE*, 10–11; cf. *DF4*, 130–31; *JA*, 302.

48. Cornelius Van Til, *God and the Absolute* (unpublished diss., 1927), 3–4; cf. *DF4*, 197–98.

49. *SCE*, 222–23; cf. *CTK*, 18–19.

50. See *DKG*, 359; cf. *CVT*, 319–21; *SCE*, 205–6.

51. *SCE*, 11.

No, for we have seen that there are different approaches and arguments in the Bible and that bringing the answer of the gospel's wisdom is what is needed. We could say that the transcendental argument, with its search for an absolute basis of an object of knowledge, needs a transcendent, absolute God, but our apologetic method for our transcendent God is not limited to a transcendental *argument* (VTAG). Actually, Van Til himself sometimes says that we should not always be using VTAG: (a) "It is [the] works [of those who have made the Old and the New Testament their lifelong study] you must read for a detailed refutation of points of Biblical criticism. Others have specialized in physics and biology. To them I must refer you for a discussion of the many points connected with such matters as evolution."[52] Or (b) "I would . . . engage in historical apologetics."[53] Or (c) "we should notice that there are thousands who do not engage in intellectual consideration of the truth to any great extent, not so much because they are necessarily indifferent to such things by nature as because they are unsuited to it. With respect to these, it is obvious that it would be useless to present the intellectual argument for Christian theism in any subtle and detailed form. Nor is this necessary. A simple presentation of the truth in positive form, and once more largely by way of testimony, may be all that is required. Christianity is not for a few elite intellectualists. Its message is to the simple and to the learned. The argument must therefore be adapted to each one's mental capacity."[54] In other words, apologetics must be tailored to the individual (that is, person-variable), and VTAG is a good way to reason with "intellectuals,"[55] but with many people it would not be needed.[56] So as the Bible does, we can use a variety of arguments.

52. Cornelius Van Til, *Why I Believe in God*, 1st ed. (Philadelphia: Committee on Christian Education of the Orthodox Presbyterian Church, 1948), 8 (hereinafter *WIB1*), with the explanation in square brackets added from Van Til's previous sentence. *WIB1* is available at http://www.reformed.org/apologetics/index.html?mainframe=/apologetics/why_I_believe_cvt.html.

53. *DF4*, 257. See also *CVT*, 181–83; cf. *DKG*, 350, 353–54.

54. *SCE*, 211. See also *CVT*, 324–26 (and contrast *VTARA*, 477n23).

55. Why does Van Til usually give only VTAG as the way to reason? Could it be because his main apologetic mission was to "win" those who were "educated, . . . [with] some training in philosophy" (*DF4*, 45)? Cf. *JA*, 125–26. Consider also that *WIB1*, his one example of doing apologetics, is addressed to "a person of intelligence" who has looked "into, or at least been concerned about, what philosophers call your theory of reality" (*WIB1*, 1).

56. As Frame says, we do not have to bring up that "we can[not] reason, . . . etc., apart from God . . . explicitly in every apologetic encounter" and "the majority of inquirers," except "would-be intellectuals," "would not need to hear . . . specifically" about "the intellectual lordship of Christ" (*AGG*, 74) (I have reordered Frame's words after "and"). Bahnsen's response to that position was: "Frame and I are entirely in agreement" (*ATJF*, 36).

Surely the point of Van Til's footing (3) for VTAG is biblical and vital, that the method of argumentation must show that those who do not accept Christ are lost. VTAG is a good way of doing this but biblically not the only way. I reiterate that our apologetic method ought to *declare the unique (triune) Lord and Savior.*

Presupposing and personally knowing God. Although we have not found that a full VTAG is *theologically* required, we should add "we are to presuppose God" to the twofold strategy. This is because Van Til is right that the Bible does assume God's existence from its first words "In the beginning God" onward. This Lord is to be our beginning and reference point (cf. Prov. 1:7). So any apologetic argument must presuppose the transcendent, absolute Word of the Lord and the Lord of the Word, and proclaim the transcendent, absolute, self-contained, and self-sufficient God. This is the Lord that Paul proclaims to the Athenians (Acts 17:23–26). But Paul next says that the transcendent Lord was sovereign over all, so that people "would seek him and perhaps reach out [grope in the dark] for him" (v. 27). It is important to remind ourselves that not only do we need to know that there is a God and who he is, but we also need to personally know and relate to him in trust, love, and awe, through Jesus Christ, the Savior of the world.[57]

Exposing borrowed capital. Therefore, the Lord is the presupposition of anything and everything (Col. 1:15–17).[58] We were made to think God's thoughts after him.[59] It is only in the Lord's light that we see any light and truth (Ps. 36:9), and only in Christ are any and "all the treasures of wisdom and knowledge" deposited (Col. 2:3). This means that any truth anyone has, including unbelievers, ultimately presupposes the Lord, whether this is acknowledged or not.[60] More precisely, any knowledge is possible only

---

57. This is also what John Calvin stresses in his *Institutes of the Christian Religion*, 1.2, 1.5.9–10.

58. Therefore, I also think that biblically with regard to the form of VTAG (see above), it does not seem essential to include *intelligibility* (including the diamond ◊ symbol) throughout VTAG. Instead it can be considered as part of x (whatever) and "what is the foundation of x?"— this diamond is in the rich rock of the Lord, who is the presupposition of everything, including intelligibility and possibility. Interestingly enough, Collett's versions of VTAG in his essay in this festschrift do not have this either.

59. *CA2*, 77; *CTK*, 16; *JA*, 126; Cornelius Van Til, *Common Grace and the Gospel* (Nutley, NJ: Presbyterian and Reformed, 1972) 28 (hereinafter *CGG*).

60. This is often misunderstood as "Van Til's epistemological claims seem clearly to imply that non-Christians cannot know anything" (*FV*, 256). Van Til's answer is given in *DF4*, 125–26.

because we are made in God's image (James 3:9) and because this is God's world that he created, rules, and sustains. Unbelievers *possess* truth because they have the truth about God from general revelation (and common grace), which they *suppress*[61] (Rom. 1:18–20; cf. Acts 17:28). So we may *expose* unbelievers' borrowed and stolen capital.[62] They are presupposing the Lord whenever they claim to possess any knowledge, discern truth, use logic, etc. For instance, Van Til used to quip that non-Christians can count but cannot give an account for their counting[63] and that "the most compact and dramatic way of summarizing Van Til's apologetic"[64] is Van Til's three words "Antitheism presupposes theism,"[65] for to even think about denying theism assumes the meaningfulness of thinking, which presupposes Christian theism.

Apologetic Method Derived and
Frame's Transcendental Approach Compared

Thus, the method for apologetics that I have derived above is a somewhat modified VTAG, as given in Figure 22.2 below.

See also *FV*, 351–52; *AR*, 37–40; *VTARA*, 113–15; James Anderson, "Van Til FEM (Frequently Encountered Misconceptions)," A(I)(2), B(I)(2), at http://www.vantil.info/articles/vtfem.html; Richard L. Pratt Jr., "Common Misunderstandings of Van Til's Apologetics," Part 1 of 2, Misconception no. 2, at http://www.thirdmill.org/files/english/html/th/TH.h.Pratt.VanTil.1.html.

61. Cornelius Van Til, *The Reformed Pastor & Modern Thought* (Phillipsburg, NJ: Presbyterian and Reformed, 1980), 16–17.

62. Cornelius Van Til, *Christian Theistic Evidences* (Nutley, NJ: Presbyterian and Reformed, 1976), 64, 69 (hereinafter *CTEV*); *GH*, 240, 243; *IW*, 68; *JA*, 17–18, 91. (See also my "Van Til's Illustrations" for these quotes, under "Borrowed or Stolen Capital.") I have found only two instances of Frame's using the term *borrowed capital* in his apologetics books (*AGG*, 72; *CVT*, 42), and these refer more specifically to Van Til's position than Frame's. Frame adds in an e-mail to me on June 29, 2009, "I'm not sure why I haven't used the expression more. I do like it, but I think it is only the barest summary of a complicated matter, namely the way in which the unbeliever can be said to 'know God' or 'know the truth.' . . . I've tried to present a broader analysis in *DKG*, 49–61 and *CVT*, 187–238. . . . So perhaps I have avoided the phrase because I sense it is an oversimplification."

63. *VTARA*, 407; cf. ibid., 42n18. I have searched Eric H. Sigward, ed., *The Works of Cornelius Van Til, 1895–1987*, Logos CD-ROM (New York: Labels Army Co., 1997), and did not find this slogan in Van Til's writings, but one of his students advised me that Van Til said, "There are lots of people who can count. Einstein was a good mathematician; surely he could count. It's been said that there are only five people that can understand Einstein. Unfortunately, I'm not one of them! But Einstein, as smart as he was, could not account for why he could count."

64. *VTARA*, 113.

65. *SCE*, xii. As Van Til somewhat famously adds, "I believe that a Christian apologist must place himself for argument's sake upon the position of the non-believer and point out to him that he has to presuppose the truth of the Christian position even to oppose it. I saw a little girl one day on a train sitting on the lap of her 'daddy' slapping him in the face. If the 'daddy' had not held her on his lap she would not have been able to slap him" (*JA*, 98).

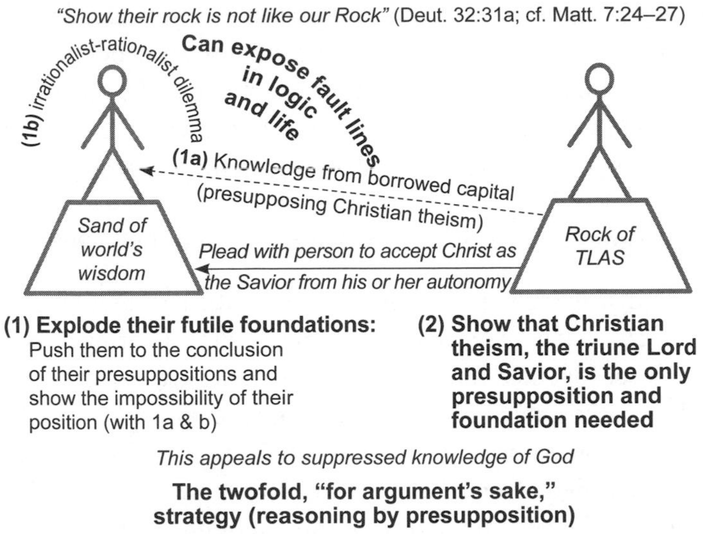

Fig. 22.2. Modified VTAG

Now, how does all this relate to Frame's revised version of VTAG, which he summarizes as follows?

3. Our apologetic should take special pains to present God as he really is: the sovereign Lord of heaven and earth, who alone saves his people from their sins.

4. As such, our argument should be *transcendental*. That is, it should present the biblical God, not merely as the conclusion to an argument, but as the one who makes argument possible.

5. We can reach this transcendental conclusion by many kinds of specific arguments . . .[66]

6. The actual arguments we use in apologetic witness will vary considerably, depending on who we are talking to. Apologetics is "person variable."[67]

Surely the biblical analysis I have given supports Frame's transcendental or presuppositional approach. Notice how Frame echoes that God is the Lord and Savior (see 3 above), who is the presupposition of everything (see 4), and

66. Frame goes on to say that the many kinds of specific arguments include "many of the traditional ones" (*FV*, 220), and we will look at that topic later.

67. Taken from *FV*, 220, 222, including the numbering. (See *FV*, 219–22 for Frame's most concise summary of his apologetic method.)

this is to be proclaimed by a variety of arguments person-variably (see 5 and 6). This can include but is not limited to using the transcendental argument (VTAG). So Frame's transcendental approach is biblically confirmed—that is, arguing on the basis of *presupposing* the Lord, with the transcendental "goal" or "thrust"[68] of leading the unbeliever to the transcendent Lord.

Assessing Frame's Criticisms of VTAG in the Light of Bahnsen's Responses

This still leaves us with Frame's detailed criticisms of VTAG, to which Bahnsen and Collett have replied. A la Frame, I will try to bring these brothers in Christ closer together. In doing so, the twofold strategy of showing that their rock is not like our Rock will be affirmed and further explained.

First, as I noted above,[69] Frame and Bahnsen agree that "we must *always* use the 'transcendental approach.' But that may be explicit or inexplicit . . . determined by the specific nature of the encounter."[70] Second, Bahnsen agrees that "it should be noted that there is no transcendental argument that 'rules out all other kinds of arguments,' as Frame puts it (*Apologetics to the Glory of God*, 73)—either in general philosophy and scholarship or particularly in apologetics."[71]

Next I would say that with regard to nearly all other differences about VTAG between Frame and Bahnsen, they are saying basically the same things, in practice,[72] from different perspectives. (Frame strikes again!) Frame says,[73] "[1 & 5] the transcendental argument requires supplementation by other arguments . . . [6] But certainly the overall goal of apologetics is transcendental. That is, the God we seek to prove is indeed the source of all meaning, the source of possibility, of actuality, and of predication"; while Bahnsen says, "These are simply 'illustrations' of the broader project laid out by the transcendental approach. The illustration that is used in a particular circumstance is 'person variable' (cf. Frame, [AGG] 72)." Frame states, "[4] I do not think that the whole of Christian theism can be established by a single argument"; whereas Bahnsen puts this as, "We cannot speak of everything simultaneously." Frame says, "[5] We must prove more than

---

68. *AGG*, 73; *CVT*, 317, 319.

69. See footnote 56.

70. John M. Frame, e-mail to me, October 2008; cf. *ATJF*, 36.

71. *VTARA*, 502n64.

72. Bahnsen makes the interesting observation that "debates over [apologetic] theory tend to divide, but I think you will find a greater harmony in the practice of apologetics" (*ATJF*, 25).

73. In what follows, Frame's statements, including the numbering, are taken from *AGG*, 71–73, and Bahnsen's words are taken from *VTARA*, 502n64.

that God is the author of meaning and rationality";[74] and Bahnsen describes this as, "We set forth for comparison the entire Biblical world view."

With respect to VTAG, this just leaves Bahnsen disagreeing[75] with Frame's position that "any indirect [or negative, *reductio ad absurdum*] argument . . . can be turned into a direct [or positive] argument by some creative phrasing. . . . It doesn't make much difference whether you say 'causality, therefore God,' or whether you say 'without God, no causality [which is absurd], therefore God.' . . . Indeed, if I say 'without God, no causality,' the argument is incomplete, unless I add the positive formulation, 'but there is causality, therefore God exists,' a formulation identical with the direct argument."[76]

Since Don Collett's essay in this festschrift addresses this area,[77] for now I will just say that it seems that the "Introduction" and procedure 1 of VTAG (see above) is a distinct indirect argument. Procedure 2, however, is a direct/positive formulation that is needed to complete VTAG.[78] The question remaining is "does VTAG need or can it be *traditional* arguments?" as Frame claims.[79] This is what we will examine as we now move on to assessing traditional apologetics.

A Biblical Assessment of Traditional Apologetics

I will begin here by explaining what traditional apologetics is and noting Frame's positive versus Bahnsen's (and Van Til's) negative response to traditional arguments.

74. Here Frame is referring to "Van Til's slogan 'Christian Theism is a unit' " (*AGG*, 72), and Bahnsen is saying that the transcendental argument is not (in Van Til's terminology) "an atomistic or 'blockhouse' apologetic" (*VTARA*, 502n64). For more on these two related aspects, see *CA2*, 18–19; *DF4*, 136–37; cf. ibid., 139; *IST2*, 12–13; *ATJF*, 31–32, 35–36; *VTARA*, 102–3, 708–9; John M. Frame, "Divine Aseity and Apologetics," in Lane Tipton and Scott Oliphint, eds., *Revelation and Reason* (Phillipsburg, NJ: P&R Publishing, 2007), 119.

75. *ATJF*, 37; cf. ibid., 32; *VTARA*, 501–2.

76. *AGG*, 76 (with words in square brackets added from ibid., 75); cf. *CVT*, 317–19.

77. Donald Collett, "Van Til and Transcendental Argument Revisited," in this festschrift; see also my "A Friendly Dialogue over Apologetics between Frame, Bahnsen, Collett and Scrivener," to be posted at http://www.vantil.info, for Frame's previous responses and my further comments. In addition, cf. James Anderson, "Presuppositionalism and Frame's Epistemology," n48, in this festschrift. Here I would like to take the opportunity of thanking James for giving me some very helpful comments on my essay.

78. So VTAG, or the indirect argument, is not just "a synonym for *reduction*," as Frame says in the festschrift Glossary; also cf. endnote 3 (D) at the end of this essay.

79. *AGG*, 71 (1); *FV*, 220 (5), 359–60.

Examples of Traditional Apologetics

The bread-and-butter arguments of traditional (or classical and evidential) apologetics are theistic proofs for God's (probable) existence and historical evidences that Jesus is (most probably) God. Here are two modern examples. William Craig uses this causal (*kalam* cosmological) theistic proof:

1. Whatever begins to exist has a cause;
2. The universe began to exist (as philosophy and science confirm);
3. Therefore, the universe has a cause, by something greater and beyond it—plausibly a personal being created the universe.[80]

And Josh McDowell has popularized the following noncircular evidential argument for Jesus' being God and the Bible's being God's Word:

1. Demonstrate the Bible is basically reliable and trustworthy, e.g., by number of copies, archaeology, etc.;
2. Then use this valid historical record to examine the evidence for Jesus' resurrection to overwhelmingly support that he has risen from the dead, and thus that he is the unique Son of God;
3. Then accept Jesus' authoritative teaching that the Bible is God's Word (Matt. 15:1–6 for the Old Testament and John 14:26 for the New Testament).[81]

Frame's Positive Use of Traditional Arguments and Bahnsen's Response[82]

According to Frame:

We can reach [the] transcendental conclusion[83] by many kinds of specific arguments, including many of the traditional ones. The traditional cosmo-

---

80. William Lane Craig, *Reasonable Faith: Christian Truth and Apologetics* (Wheaton, IL: Crossway, 1994), 116.

81. Josh McDowell, *The Best of Josh McDowell: A Ready Defense*, comp. Bill Wilson (Nashville: Thomas Nelson, 1993), 174–75.

82. See my "A Friendly Dialogue," where all of Frame's constructive criticisms of Van Til (about the transcendental argument and traditional apologetics) are given in the same order as in *AGG* and an appendix gives where all Frame's criticisms and Bahnsen's (and Collett's) responses can be found.

83. "That is, [presenting] the biblical God, not merely as the conclusion to an argument, but as the one who makes argument possible. We should present him as the source of all meaning-

logical argument, for example, argues that God must exist as the first cause of all the causes in the world. That conclusion is biblical and true, and if it can be drawn from true premises and valid logic, it may contribute to the goal of a transcendental conclusion. Certainly if God is the author of all meaning, he is the author of causality. And if God is the author of causality, the cause of all causes, then he is the cause of all meaning. Therefore the causal argument yields a transcendental conclusion.[84]

Now, Van Tillians might well consider this to be "revisionist." Indeed, Bahnsen, following the "master" presuppositionalist Van Til,[85] says that "there are great methodological differences . . . between the traditional and presuppositional approach."[86] "It is not simply a crack in the sidewalk that separates the two methods, but rather a discrepancy (in principle) as wide as the gap in the Grand Canyon." Plus, "Is it acceptable as apologists to use fallacious arguments?"[87] Bahnsen lists seven "profound epistemological differences," which "go beyond [Frame's differences of] heart attitudes and rhetorical order:"[88]

Traditional methodology (my summary)[4]	Problems in contrast to presuppositionalism (I have added these)
1. Autonomy and neutrality	not creator-creature dependence and suppression
2. Hypothetical presuppositions	not self-attesting presuppositions
3. Brute, uninterpreted facts	not facts understood within Christian worldview

---

ful communication, since he is the author of all order, truth, beauty, goodness, logical validity, empirical fact" (*FV*, 220 [4]).

84. Ibid., 220–21 (5).

85. See, e.g., *DF4*, 101, 255, 310–12, 340–41.

86. *ATJF*, 18.

87. VTARA, 546, and ATJF, 35. Positively, Van Til *is* in favor of *reformulating* the traditional proofs and evidences.

On proofs, see *VTARA*, 612–27; John M. Frame, "Cornelius Van Til," in Walter A. Elwell, ed., *Handbook of Evangelical Theologians* (Grand Rapids: Baker, 1993), 167–68, also available at http://www.frame-poythress.org/frame_articles/1993VanTil.htm.

On evidences, see *VTARA*, 634–48, 650–53; *CVT*, 178–84; cf. *DKG*, 142–49; Thom Notaro, *Van Til and the Use of Evidence* (Phillipsburg, NJ: Presbyterian and Reformed, 1980). See also my seed-form arguments at the end of this essay for examples of reformulated proofs and evidences.

88. *VTARA*, 536–37n11.

4. Unbelievers judge Christianity   not subject to God's authority
   by their standards

5. Unbeliever can reason across   not repentance
   antithesis into Christianity

6. Blockhouse methodology   not elements understood within
                                         Christian worldview

7. Christianity is very *probably* true not *certainly* true

But let us not label Frame as a "revisionist" until we see what hatches from his egg of presuppositionalism after additional biblical evaluation and analysis.

Evaluating the Examples of Traditional Apologetics, and Frame's Positiveness about Them, against Biblical Principles for Apologetics

I will now ask this: how do Craig's *kalam* and McDowell's traditional arguments, plus Frame's positiveness about the use of them, stack up against five biblical principles of apologetics that Frame and Van Til espouse? In each instance, I will simply give the principle and footnote where they can be found in Frame's and Van Til's works together with some supporting Bible references.[89]

Certainty: of God's truth, such as about God and the resurrection.[90] Both traditional arguments given above fall below "certainty," since Craig's conclusion is "*plausibly* a personal being created the universe,"[91] and McDowell says, "Demonstrate the Bible is *basically* reliable and trustworthy."[92] Craig also says, "I think that the evidence for the resurrection of Jesus is such that a well-informed investigator ought to agree

89. The wording of the principles is taken from my "Principles for Apologetics from Paul at Athens," at http://www.vantil.info.

90. *DF4*, 255 (b), 256–57 (d); *DKG*, 145; *AGG*, 78; "Presuppositional Apologetics: An Introduction: Part 2" (1999), at http://www.thirdmill.org/files/english/html/pt/PT.h.Frame.Presupp. Apol.2.html, 17, 18n7; "Certainty," in Campbell Campbell-Jack et al., eds., *New Dictionary of Apologetics* (Leicester, UK: IVP, 2006), 141–45, also available at http://www.frame-poythress.org/ frame_articles/2005Certainty.htm, 4–6 (and for the psychological aspects of certainty, see that article, which Frame is "particularly fond of," as he notes in the Bibliography in this festschrift). See Acts 17:22–23, 31; *VTARA*, 71.

91. Craig, *Reasonable Faith*, 116 (emphasis added).

92. McDowell, *The Best of Josh McDowell: A Ready Defense*, 174 (emphasis added).

that it is *more likely* than not to have occurred."[93] Frame in his response to Craig does not directly pick him up on this, and bearing in mind that elsewhere Frame affirms that probability can occur in human argument,[94] he seems to concur with allowing less than certainty here. But appearances can be deceptive; in a footnote to Craig he does say, "In presuppositionalism, evidence is *not a merely probable witness* to the truth of Christianity, *rather it is sure and certain*."[95] So Frame says what Van Til and Bahnsen mean, in that the *evidence* used in an argument *is certain*. But Frame makes a separate practical point that probability may arise in a human argument "because of . . . inadequate or incomplete presentation . . . of the evidence . . . or lack of understanding," for instance, concerning "the Second Law of Thermodynamics."[96]

Commentary. (a) Tell who God is—the (triune) Lord and Savior.[97] This principle does not mean that a complete description of who God is must be given in each encounter. The messages in Acts do not have a fixed template to follow. But at least some of the key characteristics of who the Lord God is, revealed in his words and deeds, must be given to distinguish the unique God of biblical Christianity. What especially distinguishes him from so-called other gods (Ps. 95:3–5; 1 Cor. 8:4–6) is that he is the (triune) Lord and only Savior.[98] Acts 17 teaches us that the Trinity can be implicit, not

93. *FV*, 53 (emphasis added). Craig also says that proofs are "probable" and that evidences are "probabilistically construed" (ibid., 48). Paul in 1 Corinthians 15:12–19 does use a "*what if* Jesus did not rise from the dead" argument, but this is for argument's sake, since it is framed (before and after) by the proclamation that Christ certainly is risen. Moreover, throughout there is a challenging commentary about the meaning of Christ's resurrection—it is part of the gospel message that we need to believe and hold on to in order to be saved, that is, *if* there is no resurrection, then we are still stuck in our sins and our faith is futile (v. 17). See also *DKG*, 146–47; *AGG*, 58; Notaro, *Van Til and the Use of Evidence*, 117–22.

94. *AGG*, 77–82; cf. *CVT*, 275–79; Frame, "Cornelius Van Til," 167.

95. *FV*, 78n6 (emphasis added); cf. footnote 90 above for how strong Frame actually is on this point.

96. *AGG*, 81.

97. According to Van Til, we are not only to say *that* God exists but also to proclaim *what* he is like and does. *DF4*, 30; *JA*, 427; cf. footnote 98; *FV*, 220 (3); *AGG*, 73 (1); cf. ibid., 34–55. See Acts 17:24–28.

98. For Van Til, what matters is not just bare theism (that just *a* God exists), but that it is the unique *Christian* God who is vindicated (*DF4*, 128). This is *the triune Lord and Savior*. As Van Til says, "I am interested in defending the metaphysics that comes from Scripture. This involves: (a) the doctrine of the self-contained God or ontological trinity, (b) the plan or counsel of this God pertaining to created reality, (c) the fact of temporal creation as the origin of all the facts of the

explicit, in our apologetic, which is why *triune* is in parentheses (here and elsewhere). But sharing that the Lord is the only Savior from sin, death, and God's wrath is not an optional extra.

There is a real danger, however, that traditional apologetics is low on the content of who God is. For instance, Craig's conclusion to his causal argument is that "a *personal being* created the universe."[99] Now, that is a very small part of who the God of the Bible is! To be fair to Craig, he does go on to deduce that this God is "uncaused," "changeless," "immaterial," "space-less," "enormously powerful, if not omnipotent," and "free and unimaginably intelligent, if not omniscient," and that "these properties constitute the central core of what theists mean by 'God.' "[100] This is better, although the hesitancy about God's being omnipotent and omniscient is not so good. All in all, it seems to me that Bahnsen is right when he says that "the God that is proved by most cosmological arguments doesn't have a whole lot to do with the Biblical God."[101] Now, Frame does in fact agree that "we must (or may in some cases) prove that God is personal, sovereign, transcendent, immanent and Trinitarian, not to mention infinite, eternal, wise, just, loving, omnipresent, etc."[102]

Nevertheless, I still have basic concern with Frame's saying, "I agree with Craig that the *Kalam* cosmological argument is a good argument."[103] The concern is that the *kalam* argument seems to prove theism and not *Christian* theism. Its roots in Muslim philosophy[104] betray the conclusion that it could apply to Allah as well. To resolve this, we must show, or link to our proof, that the God who causes all things is the (triune) Lord and only Savior.[105] This is a challenge to presuppositionalists too![106]

---

universe, (d) the fact of God's providential control over all created reality including the supernatural, and (e) the miraculous work of the redemption of the world through Christ" (*DF4*, 236). Here (a) = triune, (b) to (d) = Lord, and (e) = Savior. (See *CA2*, 29 for Van Til's explanation of the "ontological trinity.")

99. Craig, *Reasonable Faith*, 116 (emphasis added).

100. Ibid., 119.

101. Greg Bahnsen, MP3 GB1877:27, at http://www.cmfnow.com.

102. *AGG*, 73.

103. *FV*, 81.

104. William Lane Craig, *The Kalam Cosmological Argument* (New York: Barnes and Noble, 1979), 4.

105. Cf. my previous discussion above under "VTAG Is about the Unique (Triune) Lord and Savior."

106. Bahnsen has this to say to all presuppositionalists (are you listening?): "I would encourage many of you to think about this—it has concerned me for a number of years, not just looking at my own method, but wondering what my students might do. It's sometimes possible to present the transcendental argument, the precondition of intelligibility argu-

(b) Give facts with their meaning.[107] McDowell's evidential argument is that "the evidence for [Jesus Christ's] resurrection . . . overwhelmingly support[s] the contention that Christ has risen from the dead, [and thus that] he is the unique Son of God."[108] This is biblically true, but we are to pour more meaning into this fact. Frame agrees.[109]

Contrastingly: show that their rock is not like our Rock;[110] *and Challengingly: plead that they repent of autonomy.*[111] Neither Craig's causal proof nor McDowell's evidential argument for the Bible and Jesus shows that their rock is not like our Rock ("contrastingly"), neither do they cry "repent" ("challengingly"). I would not be hard on the missing element of contrast; some apologetic arguments will just seek to give positive proof. But the challenge to repent misses the fact that we must turn away with sorrow from our rebellion against the Judge of all the earth, while trusting that he is the only Savior from our sinful autonomy. Admittedly, this will not occur in every conversation, but the challenge to repent biblically must be part of our apologetic method. Frame agrees.[112] This is again where contrastingly showing that their rock is not like our Rock comes in, for it is showing that the gods of non-Christians do not save and that they are in the quicksand of futility and lostness, which will lead to the challenge to repent and be saved.

---

ment, in a way that seems to leave out the redemptive work of Christ. Ask yourselves, how do we more sufficiently and consistently incorporate that in the argument? . . . The reason I want to push that is because we want to make very clear that we have not done our work as apologists if we just get people to say, 'Well, you know, in order to be a good scientist, I'm going to have to admit there's a creator.' Because ultimately, the Bible says, being a scientist, you need to bow to Jesus Christ. He needs to be your Savior intellectually, morally, eschatologically. . . . I think we need to do a lot more work on the redemptive necessity of the Christian . . . view" (*ATJF*, 50).

107. *DF4*, 325; Cornelius Van Til, *Paul at Athens* (Philadelphia: Presbyterian and Reformed, 1954), 10–14 (hereinafter *PA*); *DKG*, 145–47, 352–53, 376 (maxim 22), 379 (maxim 60); *CVT*, 180–81, 183–84. Van Til's slogans here were "Uninterpreted things are uninterpretable. Brute facts are mute facts" (*GH*, 308), or as Bahnsen put it, "the facts don't speak for themselves" (e.g., MP3 GB1731, at http://www.cmfnow.com). See Acts 17:30–31; cf. Dan. 7:9–10, 13 and John 5:27–29; Acts 26:8, 22–23; cf. *AR*, 67–68; *VTARA*, 53.

108. McDowell, *The Best of Josh McDowell: A Ready Defense*, 175.

109. See footnote 107.

110. *DF4*, 88, 328; *AGG*, 53–55; also *DF4*, 121–23; cf. *VTARA*, 523–24n126. See Deut. 32:31a; Matt. 7:24–27; also refer to discussion under "The twofold strategy: show that their rock is not like our Rock" above.

111. *JA*, 7; *CTK*, 39; *AGG*, 16, 26–27, 54, 76; *DKG*, 142, 145, 355, 367; esp. *FV*, 219 (1); "Presuppositional Apologetics: An Introduction: Part 2," 18–20. See Acts 17:29–31; cf. 1 Thess. 1:9b.

112. See previous footnote.

Commonality: through the spectacles of special revelation,[113] *use general revelation*[114] *and unbelievers' twisted truths;*[115] *and Committedly: following the Lord and his Word (no neutrality or autonomy).*[116] Traditional and presuppositional apologists join hands in using general revelation and unbelievers' twisted truths. Yet here is the rub: the presuppositionalist adds that these must be viewed through the spectacles of Scripture. In other words, we are not to be neutral but to follow the Lord's Word—presupposing the Lord and his Word. Craig and McDowell object to this; they say it entails circular thinking. McDowell specifically wants to present a noncircular argument.[117] And Craig is committed to being a "natural theologian"[118] (that is, a neutral theologian, arguing for God's existence from what is naturally available, without using the Bible). Now, we have already noted that Frame thinks Craig's *kalam* causal argument "is a good argument." Yet he goes on to say, "But it is good only on the Christian presupposition that the world is a causal order and therefore a rational order."[119] Craig replies that this is "question-begging—that one's reason for believing the causal premise is that one believes in the existence of God."[120] So the claim is that the Achilles' heel of presuppositionalism is the question-begging of circular thinking.[121] But the Lord is the presupposition of everything, and from this foundation there will spiral out proofs and evidences.[122] So Frame's comment to Craig is

113. Cornelius Van Til, *The Protestant Doctrine of Scripture* (Philadelphia: Presbyterian and Reformed, 1967), 120; *AGG*, 22–26; *FV*, 216; cf. Calvin, *Institutes*, 1.5.14, 1.6.1.

114. *DF4*, 108–9, 4–5; *CVT*, 116–19; *DKG*, 145, 367. See Ps. 36:9; Acts 14:17; 17:22, 27–31; Rom. 1:18–21, 32; 2:14–15.

115. *IST2*, 208; *PA*, 11–12; cf. "borrowed capital" footnote 62 above; *DKG*, 367–68, 379 (maxim 61). See Acts 17:27–29; cf. *AR*, 259–63.

116. Neutrality is thinking one is free from presuppositions, bias, or an interpretive window on reality. Autonomy is living and thinking independently of God. Neither of these doors is open to Christians. *JA*, 7, 21 (3); *PA*, 1–2; *IST2*, 19; *DF4*, 130; *AGG*, 3–9, 43–44, 74–75, 86; *FV*, 197, 209, 221–22 (6). See Prov. 1:7; Matt. 12:30; Rom. 1:25; 2 Cor. 10:4–5; cf. Eph. 6:17b; Col. 2:8; 1 Peter 3:15; Bahnsen, *Presuppositional Apologetics*, 36–38 (in fact, the whole of chapter 2 of this work is a biblical study on this theme).

117. McDowell, *A Ready Defense*, 174–75: "Some Christians (and many non-Christians!) do argue for circles, but about the Bible they certainly don't need to." McDowell's own argument is in fact circular, however, because in premises 2 and 3 he assumes that the Bible gives the truth about Jesus and Jesus the truth about the Bible. Cf. *VTARA*, 72n69; *AGG*, 127–28; *FV*, 356–57.

118. *FV*, 51.

119. Ibid., 81; cf. ibid., 220–21 (5).

120. Ibid., 316.

121. Cf. ibid., 379–80.

122. This is an application of Van Til's "spiral reasoning." See *SCE*, 12, 201; *CVT*, 306–7; cf. Grier, "A Better Approach," in "Is Evidence Really Necessary?"

right, although he would add, "Do reason in a 'broad,' rather than a 'narrow' circle. Include in your arguments as many facts, as much data as you can."[123] Moreover, the need to presuppose the (triune) Lord and Savior, or be lost, can be illustrated by showing that their rock is not like our Rock.[124]

Frame has a related issue: "Certainly a presuppositional apologist will need to believe that 'Cause' is *not* intelligible apart from the biblical God. Perhaps it is desirable for him to say this explicitly during an apologetic dialogue. But if he doesn't say it explicitly, I cannot for that reason charge him with autonomy. And I cannot say that one *must* make this point explicit in order to be a bona fide presuppositionalist. The apologist may, for part of the discussion at least, want to hide his presupposition in his heart."[125] I think this is yet another way of saying, "We must *always* use the 'transcendental approach.' But that may be explicit or inexplicit . . . determined by the specific nature of the encounter."[126]

This leads to a final crucial issue: Do traditional arguments, like the causal argument, need reformulating, as Van Til says,[127] or can they be used, as Frame says, with a "presuppositionalism of the heart"?[128] Frame wants both![129] Is this not eating your cake and having it too? Frame wants the cake of traditional arguments without clearly mentioning that you need to use the fork of

123. See *DKG*, 376 (maxim 18). See also ibid., 130–33; *AGG*, 9–14; *FV*, 216–19; *CVT*, 301–8 (there, on 306–8, Frame answers, "(1) Does circular reasoning make it impossible for us to learn anything new? and (2) does circularity make communication with unbelievers impossible?"); *FV*, 209–10 (note Frame's "refinement" there: "The sequence is: God's rationality→human faith→human reasoning. The arrows may be read 'is rationally based on.' That sequence is linear, not circular."). Cf. *VTARA*, 518–20.

124. Cf. ibid., 621n152.

125. E-mail to me from John M. Frame, October 20, 2008; cf. footnote 56 above.

126. E-mail to me from Frame, October 20, 2008. Also, I think such presupposing of the Christian worldview, together with adding the other biblical principles, removes the fallacies that are in the traditional proofs, such as the causal argument. These are the fallacies in the causal argument: jumping from "some things have causes" to "everything has a cause"; from part of the universe to the whole universe; from many "natural" causes to one supernatural cause; and that infinite regress or chance can be given as the cause, or the unbeliever can ask, "But who caused God?" Frame himself critiques Craig's argument against infinite regress in John M. Frame, "Infinite Series," in Campbell-Jack et al., *New Dictionary of Apologetics*, 353–54, also available at http://www.frame-poythress.org/frame_articles/2005Infiniteseries.htm.

127. See footnote 87 above.

128. See *AGG*, 87 (whole section is 85–88); cf. *CVT*, 212, 319–20; Frame, "Cornelius Van Til," 166–67; "Presuppositional Apologetics: An Introduction: Part 2," 21.

129. Frame is in favor of reformulated arguments, as well as non-reformulated traditional arguments, for the examples he gives in *AGG*, 89–118 all have a "transcendental twist" (Frame, in this festschrift's Glossary, where he also summarizes his proofs).

"presuppositionalism [which] should not be seen as the *antithesis* of 'classical' or 'traditional' or 'evidential' apologetics, but as a Christian epistemology that seems to supplement, clarify, sharpen the traditional approaches with Biblical teachings that are at least sometimes overlooked, or even contradicted, in the tradition."[130] Notice the second part of that sentence.[131] I would add, yes, traditional apologetics needs reforming by the five-pronged fork of the biblical principles for apologetics given above. Also, these biblical teachings affirm Van Til's and Bahnsen's seven differences between traditional and presuppositional apologetics (see above). Now, here is a surprise. At Westminster Seminary, after Bahnsen had given the seven differences (see above) and his concerns over reducing them to a presuppositionalism of the heart, Frame said that his "statements are—very relative—it *may* no longer be possible, etc. to distinguish merely by externals. *Perhaps* presuppositionalism is more of an attitude at the heart, etc. So I'm not entirely ruling out what you're saying. And I think that there's a difference between us, here; in principle. *So far as your seven points are concerned, you know I agree substantially with everything you said.*"[132]

GOING FORWARD, BY *DOING* "FRAMILLIAN" APOLOGETICS

"Framillian" Apologetics

Now we can conclude that the bird that hatches from Frame's presuppositionalism belongs to the family of the mighty eagle of Van Til. Frame's presuppositionalism of the heart beats with the blood of Van Til. *Frame's work* gives a good biblical *framework* for apologetics. But I think I have shown that Frame needs a gentle dose of his own medicine—his formulations (as well as Van Til's) need *some* biblical improvements.

Combining the biblical strengths of Van Tillian and Framean apologetics into *Framillian* apologetics, together with the principles of apologet-

---

130. *FV*, 221n18.

131. Could it be that in Frame's good and godly desire "to try to bring warring parties closer together by looking for formulations that ease the differences somewhat" (*FV*, 358), he has not clearly spelled out in what biblical ways traditional arguments need sharpening?

132. *ATJF*, 19 (emphasis added and conversational style cosmetically edited). Later Frame clarified that "what people sometimes mean, when they talk about the traditional method of apologetics is simply the history of the uses of evidence, logic, and the kinds of arguments that have been actually brought to bear against unbelief. But I don't feel . . . that I have to distance myself from everything that sounds like that" (*ATJF*, 40; cf. *CVT*, 241–97, especially the conclusions on 296–97).

ics (which are already Framillian), we can sharpen Frame's ax of presuppositionalism of the heart (in his three perspectives)[133] as follows.[134]

Here presupposition is the basis of life, including thinking; it is what your heart is committed to. And the believer has as his or her presupposition the Word of the Lord and the Lord of the Word, namely, *the* (triune) God our Savior.

Perspective	*Presuppositionalism of the heart*
Normative	Reasoning *committed* to and **based on our presupposition**, including proclaiming the biblical God biblically with *certainty* and *commentary* (declaring who God is, and giving facts with their biblical meaning).
Existential (personal)	**Seeking to establish our presupposition** by *contrasting* that their rock is not like our Rock (including exposing their irrationalist-rationalist dilemma and borrowed capital, in logic and life), with the aim, by God's grace, of bringing about *the challenge* of **presuppositional change**. We humbly but boldly[5] proclaim the Lord as the only way to be saved. "Apologists, therefore, must resist temptations to contentiousness or arrogance. . . . First Peter 3:15–16 focuses, surprisingly, not on the brilliance, cogency or eloquence of apologists, but on their character: they must answer unbelievers with 'gentleness and respect, keeping a clear conscience.' Peter here tells us that a consistent Christian life plays a major role in the work of apologetics."[6]
Situational (contextual)	While speaking to the unbeliever's *context*, which includes using the *commonality* we share (general revelation and unbelievers' twisted truths); and **addressing non-Christians' specific expressions and the context of their presupposition** in appropriate ways.[7] In other words, "apologetics is 'person variable.' We must ask where the inquirer is coming from, his educational level, previous philosophical commitments, interests, seriousness, specific questions, etc."[8]

133. I got the idea for doing this in Frame's perspectives from the conclusion of Greg Welty, "Shall We Argue Transcendentally? A Perspectival Debate in Apologetic Methodology," at http://www.proginosko.com/welty/cvtframe.htm, an essay that complements mine. (Note: I am not sure whether the author still agrees with this online paper, since he wrote it as an MDiv student fourteen years ago.)

134. This adds the biblical principles of graciousness and godliness and applying God's truth to the unbeliever's situation and context—or, alliteratively, *Christianly* (see 2 Tim. 2:24–25; 1 Peter 3:15–16) and *Contextually* (see Acts 17:16–31; 1 Cor. 9:19–22), respectively.

Some Seed-Form Arguments

Frame concludes *CVT* thus: "It is also important for us to move beyond the traditional Van Tillian preoccupation with methodology.[135] Van Tillian courses in apologetics, including mine, have focused far too much on methods, especially upon distinguishing our methods from those of other schools of thought. More time should be spent on developing actual arguments."[136] So far I stand guilty of this too! Therefore, I want to give some suggestive seed-form arguments and indicate how a gospel link, of *turning* to the Lord and *trust* in Jesus the only Savior (Acts 20:21), could be made. I will try to give the sources of my seeds in the footnotes. I will concentrate on the areas I have addressed in this essay.[137] This will give my conclusions some feet to walk on.

1. Cosmological (causal) argument.
    a. Without our (triune) God, who is the all-wise and good Creator, Sustainer, and Lord, there would be no causal order, nor any possibility of causal argument. The non-Christian is, in fact, borrowing and presupposing the God of the Bible to even think about causality; *or* is left with irrationality and a self-defeating search for causes (the impossibility of the contrary position).[138]
    b. *A gospel link*: Our hearts will be restless until they rest[139] in the triune Lord and Savior. We were created to know, glorify, and enjoy the great and awesome Creator God, but we have lost this ability through our rebellion. The good news is that we can be reconciled to our Creator because the Father God gave his Son.
2. The sense of deity: awareness from general revelation that God exists.[140]

135. Frame: "Thanks to Greg Bahnsen who impressed this truth upon me in recent remarks." (My guess is that this is what is transcribed in *ATJF*, 25.)

136. *CVT*, 400.

137. I intend to give more seed-form arguments in my "Van Til's Presuppositional Apologetic in Practice," to be posted at http://www.vantil.info.

138. *FV*, 221; *AGG*, 114; cf. *CGG*, 190; *IST2*, 179–80, 183; cf. ibid., 178n6.

139. Augustine, *The Confessions of Saint Augustine* (AD 397), 1.1.1, available at http://www.leaderu.com/cyber/books/augconfessions/bk1.html.

140. Alvin Plantinga, *Warranted Christian Belief* (New York: Oxford University Press, 2000), 170–79, following Calvin, *Institutes*, 1.3–6 (including the mirror of *creation* at 1.5.1–3 and the worm of *conscience* at 1.3.2–3).

    a. At times, are you not aware from the wonders of *creation* and your guilty *conscience* that the almighty, all-knowing, Creator God is there and that he is your Judge whom you will have to face?

    b. This belief is *rational*. It is common sense, like believing that 2 + 2 = 4 (not 5) and that I have memories (they are basic beliefs made without inferring from them other beliefs or propositions).

    c. *A gospel link*: Flee from the wrath to come by coming to Christ, the Lord and Savior. Then the Creator will be your Father and friend.

3. Epistemological (rationality) argument.[141]

    a. The Lord is the I AM, therefore I think.[142] Rationality presupposes that we are made in the image of the God who is wise, self-consistent, rational, and relational in his triune being, a God of order, not disorder; *or* how do we get rationality from evolution's nonrationality?

    b. *A gospel link*: We were made to think God's thoughts after him, so we need to repent of our wrong thinking, and come to him in whom wisdom is found, and live by his wisdom.

4. The quintilemma: Jesus is God.[143]

    a. Jesus is *Lord* (e.g., Mark 2:1–10). He is not a *legend* (myth, made up), *lama* (spiritual guru, a great religious teacher), *liar*, or *lunatic* (or the last two leave us with the trilemma: Jesus is *bad, mad,* or *God*).[144]

    b. *A gospel link*: Receive his forgiveness and be freed to worship and serve him in all of life as your Lord and God.

5. Jesus' resurrection.

    a. Because Jesus has risen from the dead, this will mean that all alternative explanations will crumble. So knock down alternatives to the resurrection[145] and pour some of the biblical

---

141. *AGG*, 102–4.

142. *CTEV*, 42. This is turning Descartes' "I think, therefore I am" on its head.

143. See Boa and Bowman, *Faith Has Its Reasons*, 126–30.

144. C. S. Lewis, *Mere Christianity* (various editions), end of bk. 2, chap. 3; cf. Art Lindsley, *C. S. Lewis's Case for Christ: Insights from Reason, Imagination and Faith* (Downers Grove, IL: InterVarsity Press, 2005), 188–97.

145. E.g., Craig, *Reasonable Faith*, 272–93.

meaning into the fact of Jesus' resurrection. For instance, he "was appointed to be the Son of God with power [to save by the Holy Spirit] by his resurrection from the dead" (Rom. 1:4 NIV margin); "he was delivered over to death for our sins and was raised to life for our justification" (Rom. 4:25); "[God] has set a day when he will judge the world with justice by the man [Jesus] he has appointed. He has given proof of this to all men by raising him from the dead" (Acts 17:30–31); see also Rom. 6; 1 Cor. 15; etc.

  b. *A gospel link*: Follow some of the biblical meaning above to urge, believe, and confess that Jesus is the risen Lord and Savior in order to be saved (Rom. 10:9–10).

6. The Bible is God's Word.

  a. *Spiral out in evidences*: Because the Bible is God's Word, it has evidences for this, such as:[146] **H**armony; **H**istory (historical accuracy); **H**onesty (people's faults) **P**rophecy; **P**ower (in its speaking to you); **P**reservation (of text) **S**avingness; **S**ublimeness (contents sublime); **S**igns (miracles).

  b. *A gospel link*: believe the story of the Bible: **C**reation, **C**orruption, **C**hrist, and **C**onsummation.

  c. *Taste and see (testimony of the Holy Spirit), with built-in gospel link*: Read the Bible; hear its message (come to church). Then (those whom the Spirit inwardly teaches by giving proper taste buds) taste that Scripture has flowed to us from the very mouth of God by the ministry of men, bringing its life-changing message of salvation through faith in Christ. This is Scripture exhibiting self-authenticating evidence for its own truth, as sweet honey and bitter lemons do of their flavor (self-evidently). And if the Bible is tasteless to you, then you must be lacking taste buds.[147]

  d. *Show that their rock is not like our Rock*: The Word of the Lord and Lord of the Word testify to each other (John 5:39–40),

---

146. WCF 1.5; 1689 Baptist Confession 1.5; Calvin, *Institutes*, 1.8.

147. Calvin, *Institutes*, 1.7.1, 2, 4, 5, 1.8.1–2; cf. Randy Booth, "Of Taste Buds: Calvin's Apologetic," at http://www.cmfnow.com/articles/pa401.htm; Plantinga, *Warranted Christian Belief*, 259–63; *CTK*, 30, 33, 228–29; *DF4*, 374; *IW*, 36–37. This is not the same as the Mormon's believing despite the historical evidence against Mormonism, but the Spirit's enabling us to receive the Bible's truth and message (which does have historical evidences).

since there is no higher authority than the Lord speaking to us (he cannot swear outside of himself; Heb. 6:13). You have your own authority too, but where does that lead to? Without the Bible's being God's Word, we are completely lost at sea. Scripture presents itself as being the only light by which the truth about facts and their relations can be discovered.[148] The Bible is the spectacles we need so that we can see what this world and life are about.

e. *A gospel link*: Then lead them to the only Rock, our Savior, whom the Bible declares.

Come, let us sing for joy to the LORD; let us shout aloud to the Rock of our salvation. (Ps. 95:1)

NOTES IN TABLES

1. All quotations from the Bible are from the NIV, unless otherwise indicated.

2. The Van Til books referred to here, with their abbreviations, are as follows: Cornelius Van Til, *Christian Apologetics*, 2nd ed. (Phillipsburg, NJ: P&R Publishing, 2003) (hereinafter *CA2*)—lightly edited with an introduction and explanatory notes by William Edgar. Cornelius Van Til, *The Defense of the Faith*, 4th ed. (Phillipsburg, NJ: P&R Publishing, 2008) (hereinafter *DF4*)—the complete text of the original 1955 edition, with an introduction and explanatory notes by K. Scott Oliphint. Cornelius Van Til, *The God of Hope: Sermons and Addresses* (Phillipsburg, NJ: Presbyterian and Reformed, 1978) (hereinafter *GH*). Cornelius Van Til, *Intellectual Challenge of the Gospel* (London: Tyndale Press, 1950; repr., New York: Westminster Discount Books Service, 1980) (hereafter *ICG*). Cornelius Van Til, *An Introduction to Systematic Theology: Prolegomena and the Doctrines of Revelation, Scripture and God*, 2nd ed. (Phillipsburg, NJ: P&R Publishing, 2007) (hereinafter *IST2*)—lightly edited with an introduction and explanatory notes by William Edgar. Cornelius Van Til, "Introduction," in B. B. Warfield, *The Inspiration and Authority of the Bible*, ed. Samuel G. Craig (Philadelphia: Presbyterian and Reformed, 1948), 3–68 (hereinafter *IW*). E. R. Geehan, ed., *Jerusalem and Athens: Critical Discussions on the Theology and Apologetics of Cornelius Van Til* (Nutley, NJ: Presbyterian and Reformed, 1971) (hereinafter *JA*). Cornelius Van Til, *Survey of Christian Epistemology* (Nutley, NJ: Presbyterian and Reformed, 1969) (hereinafter *SCE*).

3. Following are various comments on VTAG's description. Van Til also calls the "transcendental argument" "indirect, reasoning by presupposition" (cf. *DF4*, 122–23 with *SCE*, 10, 205–6; see also *CVT*, 311–12). Here *presupposition* means not a mere personal preference or hypothesis to be verified but "the final or ultimate reference point" (*IST2*, 178n6); objective "state of affairs" or "foundation" (*JA*, 21 [5]); necessary "precondition" (Cornelius Van Til, *Christian Theistic Ethics* [Nutley, NJ: Presbyterian and Reformed, 1970], 245). Frame adds that this is "the belief that governs all other beliefs, or the most fundamental commitment of the heart" (Glossary [Van Til] in this festschrift).

148. See *DF4*, 130–31; *IST2*, 242–43.

For all the passages referenced and a version of VTAG in Van Til's own words from which I derived this summary, refer to my "Van Til's Transcendental Argument Form and Theological and Biblical Basis," at http://www.vantil.info. Although I have sought to base VTAG only on what Van Til actually said, my way of describing VTAG is somewhat different from that of others in the following ways:

A. Highlighting that it is about the *intelligibility* of something (including its *affirmation* or *negation*/denial; see *SCE*, 11)—for instance, "what is the basis of affirming or denying the *intelligibility* of causality?" In Van Til's writings about VTAG, however, "intelligibility" or "meaningfulness" is loosely interchangeable with "predication (affirmations or denials)" and "(truth) claims" (e.g., *SCE*, 10–11; *IST2*, 180; *SCE*, 222–23). I chose *intelligibility* for my description of VTAG because that is the word Van Til uses in three of the most important VTAG passages: *DF4*, 122–23; *SCE*, 10–11; *SCE*, 201, 204. But see footnote 58 above.

B. Including Van Til's "appeal to the unbeliever's suppressed knowledge of God" and clearly including "pointing out (a) [the unbeliever's] knowledge is from borrowed capital, and/or (b) the irrationalist-rationalist dilemma," can be part of "reasoning from the impossibility of the contrary position," cf. *CVT*, 315, 322.

C. Including "pleading with the unbeliever to accept Christ as their Savior from the sin of autonomy" and that the God we prove is "the triune Lord and Savior."

D. Van Til also says that procedure 1 is about reducing the non-Christian position to absurdity (a *reductio ad absurdum*) (e.g., *SCE*, xi, 204). I have not included this, however, because it could be misleading for these reasons: (1) strictly speaking, a *reductio ad absurdum* derives a logical contradiction in a person's beliefs, whereas VTAG shows that the person's presupposition cannot make x intelligible (this is not a *logical* inconsistency but a *performative* or operational inconsistency); and (2) "Van Til's transcendental argument from predication makes a stronger claim than the claim generated by the *reductio*. The latter generates a contradiction from the non-Christian position, although Van Til's transcendental argument from predication makes the more radical claim that contradiction itself is impossible apart from the truth of God's existence." Donald Collett, "Frame and Transcendental Argument Revisited," in this festschrift.

For Frame's description of VTAG, see *CVT*, 311–15 and *DKG*, 359–60; for Bahnsen's, see *VTARA*, 482–529; and for Edgar's, see *CA2*, 7–8.

The form (and even the validity) of transcendental arguments and VTAG is debated. See Michael R. Butler, "The Transcendental Argument for God's Existence," in Steven M. Schlissel, ed., *The Standard Bearer: A Festschrift for Greg L. Bahnsen* (Nacogdoches, TX: Covenant Media Press, 2002), also available at http://butler-harris.org/tag; Donald Collett, "Van Til and Transcendental Argument Revisited," in this festschrift; *VTARA*, 499, 500n60.

4. These are taken from *VTARA*, 537–46.

5. "Humbly but boldly" echoes Van Til. *CTK*, 21; *DF4*, 199; cf. *VTARA*, 114–15; *AR*, 33–36, 51–52 (1). This reflects Acts 4:29; 19:8; 1 Cor. 1:26–31; 2 Cor. 3:12; 10:1–2; Eph. 2:8–9.

6. *FV*, 220 (2). See also *DKG*, 357–58; *AGG*, 27–30.

7. Frame helpfully says: "Having come to some understanding of his audience, the apologist must, like all theologians, decide on the form in which to present his message. Here there are many possibilities; a good imagination will help the apologist to visualize them. Dialogue, lecture, fantasy tales, visual aids (see Jer. 27:1–7; Ezek. 4:1–3; Isa. 8:18), dramatic actions (Ezek. 4:4–17), various kinds of media presentations, letters to editors, books, many other approaches are legitimate vehicles of apologetic content. Flexibility here is important. The apostle became all things to all men that he might by all means save some (1 Cor. 9:22)" (*DKG*, 367). Do we just tend to think in terms of using "arguments"?

8. *FV*, 222 (7); cf. *DKG*, 365–68; *AGG*, 67–69; *CVT*, 182–83; cf. ibid., 296; *AR*, 64. Cf. footnote 134 above.

23

FRAME'S APOLOGETICS AND THE CHALLENGES OF OUR TIME

JOSHUA PEREZ

RECENT WORK in theological methodology among some evangelicals has tended toward questioning the validity or minimizing the importance of propositional theology. Questions are being raised regarding the legitimacy of doing systematic theology in this manner. The kind of systematic theology that is exemplified in the works of Charles Hodge, Louis Berkhof, Carl F. H. Henry, and Wayne Grudem, to name a few, is increasingly being criticized as the kind of systematic theology that ought not to be done.

Such concerns are, of course, nothing new within the history of theology. Charles Hodge, for example, writes of a viewpoint during his day that maintained that "Christianity consists not in propositions—it is life in the soul."[1] Along similar lines, B. B. Warfield makes reference to the tendency to exaggerate what he refers to as the "principle of the heart" and the minimizing of "rational thinking" in theology.[2] In general, theological liberalism views propositional theology as

---

1. Charles Hodge, "The Theology of the Intellect and That of the Feelings," in *Essays and Reviews* (New York: Robert Carter & Brothers, 1857), http://homepage.mac.com/shanerosenthal/reformationink/chfeelings.htm.
2. Benjamin B. Warfield, "Authority, Intellect, Heart," *The Presbyterian Messenger* (January 30, 1896), http://homepage.mac.com/shanerosenthal/reformationink/bbwaih.htm.

too intellectualist while at the same time failing to preserve the divine-human encounter.[3] Thus, suspicion toward propositional theology is nothing new.

Nevertheless, what is new about the current situation is a growing concern on the part of some evangelical theologians toward the role or function of propositions in "theological theorizing," to use an expression from John W. Montgomery.[4] Here are some representative examples: Stanley Grenz states that evangelicals need to rethink the function of theological propositions.[5] He argues that this concern with the organization of "facts" and "biblical summarization" is a result of the influence of early modernity on evangelical theologians.[6] Nancey Murphy is suspicious of what she calls the propositional theory of religious language because it is the outcome of the modernist referential theory of language, which she takes to be inadequate.[7] Furthermore, she maintains that this emphasis on propositions reflects the modernist tendency toward reductionism. The argument, in brief, is that applied to religious language, modernistic reductionism leads to a "bottom-up" approach in which the meaning of the whole is determined by the parts, which in turn leads to the "search for atomic propositions" as the key to determining meaning.[8] Joel Green, in a recent essay, states that if evangelicals are to do theological exegesis in a "post-critical world," they need to embrace the "promise" of narrative theology. He defines narrative theology as "a constellation of approaches to the theological task typically joined by their *antipathy towards forms of theology concerned with the systematic organization of propositions* grounded in ahistorical principles, and their attempt to discern an overall aim and ongoing plot in the ways of God as these are revealed in Scripture . . ."[9] Finally, in a recent essay in *Christianity Today* that reviewed

3. Peter Jensen, *The Revelation of God* (Downers Grove, IL: InterVarsity Press, 2002), 19–23. See also the work of Ronald H. Nash, *The Word of God and the Mind of Man* (Phillipsburg, NJ: Presbyterian and Reformed, 1982).

4. John W. Montgomery, *The Suicide of Christian Theology* (Minneapolis: Bethany Fellowship, 1970), 276–77.

5. Stanley J. Grenz, "Star Trek and the Next Generation: Postmodernism and the Future of Evangelical Theology," in *The Challenge of Postmodernism: An Evangelical Engagement*, 2nd ed., ed. David S. Dockery (Grand Rapids: Baker Academic, 2001), 85.

6. Stanley J. Grenz, *Revisioning Evangelical Theology* (Downers Grove, IL: InterVarsity Press, 1993), 65.

7. Nancey Murphy, *Beyond Liberalism and Fundamentalism: How Modern and Postmodern Philosophy Set the Theological Agenda* (Harrisburg, PA: Trinity Press, 1996), 42, 111.

8. Nancey Murphy, *Anglo-American Postmodernity: Philosophical Perspectives on Science, Religion, and Ethics* (Boulder, CO: Westview Press, 1997), 18.

9. Joel B. Green, "Practicing the Gospel in a Post-Critical World: The Promise of Theological Exegesis," *JETS* 47, 3 (September 2004): 393 (emphasis mine).

"five streams" of the emerging church, Scott McKnight observes that many in the emergent conversation "express nervousness about propositional truth."[10]

In light of such concerns, the aim of this paper is to analyze some of the most common arguments presented against propositional theology. I will classify such arguments by using John Frame's well-known three perspectives (normative, situational, and existential) as an organizing scheme. I will maintain that such arguments are not successful even though they may contain some legitimate insights that need to be recognized. I will then conclude by briefly stating some positive reasons in defense of propositional theology.

Four terms are used in theological discussions that incorporate in one way or another the term *proposition*. These are *propositional revelation*, *propositional theology*, *propositionalist theology*, and the term *proposition* itself. Clarifying these terms will be helpful at the outset.

Propositional revelation, as David K. Clark points out, emphasizes that the Bible is genuine divine revelation.[11] Along similar lines, Kevin Vanhoozer notes that the general thrust of propositional revelation is that "revelation discloses truth in a cognitive manner."[12] Such revelation is not reducible to a personal encounter, nor is it a mere witness to some revelatory experience.[13] We must clarify, though, as Ronald Nash points out, that the advocate of propositional revelation is not saying that written revelation must take a specific literary form.[14] In other words, propositional revelation is consistent with the viewpoint that emphasizes the importance for theological formulation of taking into account the diversity of literary genres in Scripture.

Closely related but conceptually distinct is the term *propositional theology*. This term, I believe, maintains that the revelation that God has given can be formulated in propositions, however imperfectly. Carl F. H. Henry emphasizes this point. He states that despite the diversity of literary

10. Scott McKnight, "Five Streams of the Emerging Church," *Christianity Today* 51, 2 (February 2007): 37.

11. David K. Clark, *To Know and Love God: Method for Theology*, Foundations of Evangelical Theology, ed. John S. Feinberg (Wheaton, IL: Crossway, 2003), 450n13.

12. Kevin Vanhoozer, "The Semantics of Biblical Literature: Truth and Scripture's Diverse Literary Forms," in *Hermeneutics, Authority, and Canon*, ed. D. A. Carson and John D. Woodbridge (Grand Rapids: Academie Books, 1986), 59.

13. Clark, *To Know and Love God*, 450n13.

14. Nash, *Word of God*, 50. For an analysis of the importance of recognizing the diversity of literary genres in Scripture, see Vanhoozer, "Semantics of Biblical Literature," 49–104.

genres, the content can be "propositionally formulated."[15] This presupposes that Scripture is propositional. However, in affirming the propositional nature of Scripture, one is not saying that Scripture is solely or exclusively propositional. As John Frame points out, Scripture is propositional, but "it is also much more."[16] The advocate of propositional theology recognizes the diversity of literary genres in the Scriptures and the value and importance of both descriptive and nondescriptive types of utterances.[17] In addition, a commitment to propositional theology recognizes, as Groothuis points out, that one of the main tasks of systematic theology is to "identify and articulate the revealed truths of Scripture in a logical, coherent and compelling manner."[18] This, of course, does not imply that such an intellectual task is the only task that systematic theology does.[19]

The third term that needs clarification is *propositionalist theology*. The term is employed by Vanhoozer to refer to an approach that maintains that the only thing of value in the Scriptures is the truth content or propositions contained in its various literary genres.[20] Setting aside the matter of who actually holds this position within evangelicalism,[21] it simply does not

15. Carl F. H. Henry, *God, Revelation and Authority*, 6 vols. (Wheaton, IL: Crossway, 1999), 3:453; Douglas Groothuis makes the same point. See his *Truth Decay: Defending Christianity against the Challenges of Postmodernism* (Downers Grove, IL: InterVarsity Press, 2000), 113–14.

16. Frame, *DKG*, 201. Vanhoozer makes the same point when he states that the truth of God's Word is "richly propositional," not "merely propositional." See his "Lost in Interpretation? Truth, Scripture, and Hermeneutics," *JETS* 48, 1 (March 2005): 110.

17. I borrow the terminology of descriptive and nondescriptive utterances from David K. Clark, "Beyond Inerrancy: Speech Acts and an Evangelical View of Scripture," in James Beilby, ed., *For Faith and Clarity: Philosophical Contributions to Christian Theology* (Grand Rapids: Baker Academic, 2006), 113–31.

18. Groothuis, *Truth Decay*, 112. Groothuis may have overstated his point here, for he says that such is "the task" of systematic theology. But I do not believe that he maintains that such a cognitive enterprise is all one does in theology. Later he writes that the "purpose of divine revelation is not merely the enunciation of a set of true propositions" (120).

19. J. I. Packer states that the rehabilitation of systematic theology within evangelicalism needs to include not only the recovery of theology as a spiritual task but also the demonstration of the "rationality and coherence of the parts of the system." Packer, "Is Systematic Theology a Mirage? An Introductory Discussion," in *Doing Theology in Today's World*, ed. John D. Woodbridge and Thomas E. McComiskey (Grand Rapids: Zondervan, 1991), 28.

20. Kevin Vanhoozer, "The Voice and the Actor: A Dramatic Proposal about the Ministry and Minstrelsy of Theology," in *Evangelical Futures: A Conversation on Theological Method*, ed. John G. Stackhouse Jr. (Grand Rapids: Baker, 2000), 75.

21. Some studies have raised questions as to whether some of the theologians accused of being "propositionalists" are as guilty of this charge as critics think. Rodney Decker, for instance, challenges Vanhoozer's reading of Henry and argues that both authors' positions are actually complementary to each other. See Decker's "May Evangelicals Dispense with Propositional Revelation?

follow that if one maintains the legitimacy of propositional theology, one is therefore advocating a *propositionalist* theology. This is similar to the distinction between legitimate science and scientism. The latter entails that the only means of obtaining truth about reality is using the methods of the natural sciences, which is a very different claim from saying that science is *a* legitimate means of obtaining knowledge about the world. Similarly, a commitment to propositional theology does not entail that the only thing of value are its propositions, although they are very important for the task of systematic theology .

The last term, *proposition*, is probably the most controversial and difficult to clarify. It is no secret that there is a conflict of interpretations among philosophers as to the ontological status of propositions. William Alston, for example, surveys five competing views on the nature of propositions in the literature.[22] Even among theologians there exists a plurality of views on their nature. Vanhoozer points to at least three different ways of understanding the nature of propositions among theologians committed to propositional revelation.[23] Nevertheless, while recognizing the importance of such debates, for purposes of my essay I will regard the term *propositions* in its more ordinary and basic sense. In such a view, a proposition refers to the "content of an assertion or a belief."[24] Similarly, Frame describes propositions as "assertions of fact."[25] Lest the reader think accepting this definition is a mere arbitrary move on my part, I believe there is good reason for it. According to Alston, "our most basic

Challenges to a Traditional Evangelical Doctrine" (paper presented at the 53rd annual meeting of the Evangelical Theological Society, Colorado Springs, CO, November 14, 2001). In addition, Paul K. Helseth criticizes the view that the Princeton Theologians were "scholastic rationalists" (which leads to propositionalism). See his "Are Postconservative Evangelicals Fundamentalists? Postconservative Evangelicalism, Old Princeton, and the Rise of Neo-Fundamentalism," in *Reclaiming the Center: Confronting Evangelical Accommodation in Postmodern Times*, ed. Millard J. Erickson, Paul K. Helseth, and Justin Taylor (Wheaton, IL: Crossway, 2004), 223–50.

22. William Alston, *A Realistic Conception of Truth* (Ithaca and London: Cornell University Press, 1996), 17–22.

23. See Vanhoozer, "Semantics of Biblical Literature," 56–59.

24. Alston, *Realistic Conception*, 15. Consistent with this approach, Moreland and Craig define propositions as "contents expressed in declarative sentences and contained in people's minds when they are thinking." J. P. Moreland and William L. Craig, *Philosophical Foundations for a Christian Worldview* (Downers Grove, IL: InterVarsity Press, 2003), 184. Some philosophers and/or theologians distinguish between propositions and sentences. For one theologian who does this, see Richard Swinburne, *Revelation: From Metaphor to Analogy*, 2nd ed. (Oxford: Oxford University Press, 2007), 8–12.

25. *DKG*, 26.

notion of a proposition is of what forms the content of assertions and other illocutionary acts, and what forms the content of beliefs and other (aptly named) 'propositional attitudes.'" Discussions about the nature of propositions, however interesting and complex, seem to be "responsible to this primary context."[26] Furthermore, propositions, so understood, are the "bearers of truth value."[27] As Plantinga points out, propositions, whatever their nature, are "the things" that can be believed or disbelieved and are capable of being true or false.[28]

What are the criticisms against propositional theology, and what can be said in its defense? I find it interesting that the most common arguments against propositional theology of which I am aware can be classified along the lines of Frame's three perspectives: the normative, situational, and existential. Using these perspectives as an organizing scheme, I will examine four common arguments against propositional theology. My aim here is not to be exhaustive but to describe and evaluate representative arguments in the literature.

QUESTIONING PROPOSITIONAL THEOLOGY

The first type of argument against propositional theology is concerned with the normative perspective. Arguments of this type tend to emphasize that the theologian who engages in propositional theology ends up misusing the norm of Christian theology, namely, the Scriptures.[29]

A good example of this kind of argument is the one maintained by Nancey Murphy. According to Murphy, conservative theology can be labeled *propositional* because it is based on the modernist referential theory of language.[30] This view of language can best be described as "atomistic and referential."[31] It is referential because Murphy maintains that the modernist

26. Alston, *Realistic Conception*, 15.

27. Ibid., 15–16. For an explanation and defense of the view that propositions are the bearers of truth value, see Clark, *To Know and Love God*, 357–60.

28. Alvin Plantinga, *Warrant and Proper Function* (New York and Oxford: Oxford University Press, 1993), 117.

29. I understand, of course, that the normative perspective as defined by Frame has to do with one's understanding of Scripture. See *DKG*, 163.

30. Murphy, *Beyond Liberalism and Fundamentalism*, 36–46.

31. Nancey Murphy, "Textual Relativism, Philosophy of Language, and the Baptist Vision," in *Theology without Foundations: Religious Practice & the Future of Theological Truth*, ed. Stanley Hauerwas, Nancey Murphy, and Mark Nation (Nashville: Abingdon Press, 1994), 246.

theory of language incorporates a predominant metaphor, namely, language as a picture or mirror of reality.[32] This entails that the primary function of religious language is to describe. Hence the emphasis on propositions as linguistic utterances that refer to and represent states of affairs in the world. It is "atomistic" because, according to Murphy, this view of language highlights the "sentence or proposition as the smallest unit of meaningful discourse."[33] As a consequence, you have the "search for atomic propositions."[34] How is this an argument against propositional theology? It is in the sense that it shows the reductionistic tendency of conservative theology (propositional) because the focus is on "atomic" propositions without consideration of the narrative context.[35]

Another theologian who is concerned about how propositional theology treats its norm is Kevin Vanhoozer.[36] One major worry that Vanhoozer has with traditional theology is that it reduces the richness of biblical truth, its diverse literary genres, to one single form: *"dedramatized propositions."*[37] In other words, propositional theology is reductionistic.[38] Using an analysis similar to Murphy's, Vanhoozer maintains that what has led to this unfortunate consequence is an inadequate view of language, namely, language as essentially "picturing states of affairs." This approach is positivistic because "it regards theology as nothing more than summaries of exegetical data or statements about extractable propositions."[39] His concern here is that such a "single voice" does not adequately articulate the whole truth of the text.

How should one respond to these criticisms? For the sake of clarity it is important first of all to recognize that despite the similarities in the conclusion of their respective arguments, Murphy and Vanhoozer are operating from very different theoretical concerns. Murphy's argu-

32. Murphy, *Beyond Liberalism and Fundamentalism*, 111.
33. Murphy, *Anglo-American Postmodernity*, 11.
34. Ibid., 18.
35. R. Scott Smith, "Should We Talk as Nancey Murphy Talks?" (paper presented at the Evangelical Philosophical Society National Meeting, Atlanta, GA, November 2003), 5.
36. In describing Murphy and Vanhoozer as two theologians who raise questions about propositional theology as it relates to the norm of theology, I am not suggesting that they agree on all points nor that they have a similar theological methodology.
37. Kevin J. Vanhoozer, *The Drama of Doctrine: A Canonical-Linguistic Approach to Christian Theology* (Louisville: Westminster John Knox Press, 2005), 269 (italics his).
38. Ibid., 268.
39. Ibid., 271.

ment against propositional theology is governed by a particular way of understanding the relationship of language to the world. I consider this aspect of her argument below. Vanhoozer's understanding of this matter is different, since he is a proponent of a critical realism that allows for an adequate yet genuine access to reality.[40] In light of this, I will focus on the basic criticisms that propositional theology is reductionistic because it overlooks the rich diversity of literary genres, it does not consider the narrative context, and it views the proposition as the only thing of value in the Scriptures.

In response to these criticisms, several things can be said. First, there is nothing about propositional theology per se that necessarily leads to the devaluing of other forms of discourse in Scripture. David K. Clark, for instance, observes that to value the importance of nondescriptive language and the importance of descriptive language is not an either/or situation.[41] As an example, John Frame presents several criticisms on the manner in which Charles Hodge conceives of theological methodology,[42] yet nevertheless emphasizes that "propositional language is important to theology" and that theology is never "*merely* propositional; it is simultaneously an expression of love and praise."[43] Second, one wonders if the suspicion toward propositional theology is itself reductionistic. Let me explain. Traditionally, systematic theology has been concerned with integrating the various truths taught in Scripture so as to present these truths in an orderly and unified manner and to apply such truths to all areas of life.[44] Thus, Geerhardus Vos notes that the difference between systematic theology and biblical theology is not that one is more bound to the Scriptures than the other; rather, it has to do with the basic principle that guides each approach. The principle of biblical theology is "historical," whereas for systematic theology it is "logical."[45] Along similar lines,

---

40. Kevin J. Vanhoozer, *Is There a Meaning in This Text? The Bible, the Reader, and the Morality of Literary Knowledge* (Grand Rapids: Zondervan, 1998), 322–23.

41. See his essay "Beyond Inerrancy."

42. See *DKG*, 77–81.

43. Ibid., 321 (italics his).

44. In emphasizing the last point I am taking into account John Frame's "covenantal" definition of theology, namely, that it involves the application of God's Word to all areas of life (see *DKG*, 81).

45. Geerhardus Vos, *Biblical Theology: Old and New Testaments* (Grand Rapids: Eerdmans, 1948), 15–16. I would also refer the reader to the online essay written by Paul Helm on this issue. See "Analysis 3—Systematic and Biblical," available at http://paulhelmsdeep.blogspot.com.

D. A. Carson notes that the ordering principles for systematic theology are "topical, logical, hierarchical, and as synchronic as possible," whereas those of biblical theology "trace out the history of redemption, and are (ideally) profoundly inductive, comparative and as diachronic as possible."[46] Thus, when Murphy claims that traditional theology does not take into account the "narrative context," is this not an attempt to reduce systematic theology to a biblical theology? As long as the theologian recognizes that systematic theology is not the only "voice" that attempts to articulate the truth of Scripture, I do not see why that should entail less of an emphasis on propositional theology.[47]

Some arguments against propositional theology correspond to the situational perspective. I consider two arguments under this category. The first argument claims that propositional theology aims at a theology that is timeless and culture-free. The argument maintains that the theologian committed to propositional theology has lost sight of the historical nature of theologizing. Perhaps the theologian has confused *à la* Hegel his own feeble attempt to construct a systematic theology with the absolute systematic theology. Vanhoozer refers to this approach as "doctrine as epic."[48] According to him, this theological "style" attempts to provide a "comprehensive account of how things are told from the perspective of a single 'voice.'"[49] The problem with such theologies is that they appear to be written by "impersonal and omniscient narrators who stand nowhere in particular."[50] Along these lines, McGrath, for example, accuses Grudem of taking this approach in his *Systematic Theology*.[51] McGrath maintains that Grudem treats Scripture passages as "timeless and culture-free statements that can be assembled to yield a timeless and culture-free theology that stands over and above the shifting sands of our postmodern culture."[52] Similarly, Grenz and Franke point out that because conservative theologians view the Bible as a "storehouse of theological facts," the goal becomes that

---

46. D. A. Carson, "Systematic Theology and Biblical Theology," in *New Dictionary of Biblical Theology* (Downers Grove, IL: InterVarsity Press, 2000), 102–3.

47. Vanhoozer recognizes this when he speaks of the "polyphonic truth" in Scripture and of a "canonical-linguistic plurality." See *Drama of Doctrine*, 276–85.

48. Ibid., 84.

49. Ibid., 85.

50. Ibid.

51. Wayne Grudem, *Systematic Theology* (Grand Rapids: Zondervan, 1994).

52. Alister McGrath, "Engaging the Great Tradition: Evangelical Theology and the Role of Tradition," in Stackhouse, ed. *Evangelical Futures*, 30.

of compiling the "timeless body of right doctrines."[53] They also point out that the danger of this approach, although they do not accuse anyone of this, is that once the true biblical system of doctrine is captured, it could make the Bible "superfluous."[54]

In response to this criticism, it is important first of all to note that it is not always clear what the objector is getting at in making such claims. Is it a matter of presenting a truth claim that purports to be always true? If this is the case, why is that a problem? When a theologian says, "The Bible teaches that God is just and merciful," and if that statement adequately captures what the Bible as a whole teaches on the issue in question, would it not be correct to say that such a statement expresses what is always true of God? Of course, the theologian would recognize that such a summary does not exhaustively capture what Scripture as a whole teaches about God. Nevertheless, a general truth claim that does not exhaustively describe the subject matter of discourse would still be a truth.

Perhaps the problem is formulating such statements in the first place. That is, there is a problem in attempting to "abstract" the cognitive content from a narrative or poetic discourse. If so, then the same basic response given to the first argument applies here as well.

A third possibility is that the critic is maintaining that theologians committed to propositional theology are tempted to view their own systematic formulations with the absolute and final system of theology. If such is the case, then the criticism seems to misconstrue what such theologians are saying. Consider some representative examples.

James Orr, in *The Progress of Dogma*, writes: "Existing systems are not final; as works of human understanding they are necessarily imperfect; there is none which is not in some degree affected by the nature of the intellectual environment, and the factors the mind had, at the time of formulation, to work with."[55] Likewise, Carl F. H. Henry, a strong proponent of propositional theology, states that there is a distinction between the "canonical content of revelation" and the "systems derived from it."[56] Furthermore, he maintains that we do not possess a "theology of glory" and that evangelical theology should

---

53. Stanley J. Grenz and John R. Franke, *Beyond Foundationalism: Shaping Theology in a Postmodern Context* (Louisville: Westminster John Knox Press, 2001), 62.

54. Ibid., 63.

55. James Orr, *The Progress of Dogma* (Grand Rapids: Eerdmans, 1952), 30–31, quoted in Peter Toon, *The Development of Doctrine in the Church* (Grand Rapids: Eerdmans, 1979), 68.

56. Henry, *God, Revelation, and Authority*, 1:240.

be characterized by the virtue of humility.[57] At its best, then, this argument reminds theologians of the fallible nature of theological construction, but it does not entail a rejection of propositional theology properly construed.

There is a second argument against propositional theology that can be classified as being concerned with the situational perspective. In brief, the argument maintains that the emphasis on propositional theology is based on a misunderstanding of the language-world relationship.[58] Grenz and Franke seem to move in this direction. On the one hand they claim that there is an "undeniable givenness to the universe apart from the human linguistic-constructive task," but on the other hand, they state that "we do not inhabit the 'world-in-itself'; instead, we live in a linguistic world of our own making."[59] Nancey Murphy makes a similar point. She observes that "we *live* in our traditions and can only think and perceive by means of the categories, images, stories they provide" and that "standards of rationality do not stand outside the history of traditions, but rather develop within them."[60] R. Scott Smith believes this argument is the central contention that drives postconservative postmodernism.[61]

The basic idea here seems to be the claim that we cannot access the world as it truly is because we cannot step outside language in order to know reality. A popular metaphor used to convey this idea is that of a lens. Our beliefs, traditions, worldviews, etc., are a kind of lens through which we see the world. Dallas Willard observes that this model of the language-world relationship is not merely one of mediation. In this model, the concepts that mediate the mind-world relationship turn that mediation into a making, a production.[62]

But how does the point above affect propositional theology? It does so, I believe, in the following manner. According to Murphy, a propositional view of language "*requires* an outside-in epistemology."[63] That is, proposi-

<hr>

57. Ibid., 212.

58. I borrow the terminology of "language-world" relationship from R. Scott Smith, "Language, Theological Knowledge," in *Reclaiming the Center*, 109–33.

59. Grenz and Franke, *Beyond Foundationalism*, 53.

60. Murphy, *Beyond Liberalism and Fundamentalism*, 105–6. Murphy correctly raises the issue of relativism at this point and attempts to give a response to the problem in 106–9. See also chapter 6 of her *Anglo-American Postmodernity*. But for an analysis and critique of her proposal, see Smith, "Language, Theological Knowledge," 109–33.

61. Smith, "Language, Theological Knowledge," 110.

62. Dallas Willard, "How Concepts Relate the Mind to Its Objects: The 'God's Eye View' Vindicated?" *Philosophia Christi* 1, 2 (Winter 1999): 5–20.

63. Murphy, *Beyond Liberalism*, 52 (italics hers).

tions describe or make reference to external states of affairs. Another way of making the same point is to say that religious language is referential. Once the view of language (the modern referential view) is shown to be inadequate, then a particular move associated with that view (the propositional approach) ends up being inadequate as well.

R. Scott Smith points out the problem with the "we are inside language and cannot know the world as it is in itself" kind of argument. On the one hand, proponents of this argument seem to be presenting their conclusion not simply as a description of their particular community but rather as a true description of the way reality is. But the problem is that "their methodology denies that we can go out into the world-in-itself and just observe things as they are, since all such observations are linguistically mediated."[64] On the other hand, if the argument above is presented as only a description of a particular community's view of the language-world relationship, then the conclusion of the argument is not normative for other communities.[65] Either way you go, the argument is inadequate.

Furthermore, Scripture is clear that despite the limitations of our knowledge brought about by our sinful condition, human beings know enough about the true God that they are rendered inexcusable before him (Rom. 1:19–20). Thus, as Frame points out, "everyone knows God," even though in a more profound sense only believers know him.[66] It is obvious that worldviews influence how people view reality. Nevertheless, the Scriptures affirm that because God is Lord and Creator, all human beings know enough of the "world-as-it-is-in-itself" so as to be accountable to the living God.

The fourth argument against propositional theology is concerned with the existential perspective. It is the claim that such theology leads to a lack of spiritual vitality or to a theology that tends to be impersonal. Vanhoozer points out that some modern theologians worry that propositional theology "depersonalizes revelation by rendering it abstract and lifeless."[67] In a later essay, he observes that the idea that propositional theology leads to a disconnect between theory and practice is probably "the

---

64. R. Scott Smith, "Christian Postmodernism and the Linguistic Turn," in *Christianity and the Postmodern Turn*, ed. Myron B. Penner (Grand Rapids: Brazos Press, 2005), 61.

65. Ibid., 62.

66. For more detailed description of this point, see *DKG*, 18–40.

67. Vanhoozer, "Semantics of Biblical Literature," 64.

most common objection to systematic theology."[68] The argument surfaces in a number of places. McGrath, for example, states that the evangelical preoccupation with "propositional correctness of Christian doctrine" tends to destroy the vitality of the Christian faith. The reason given is that such an emphasis views faith as "little more than intellectual assent to propositions, losing the vital and dynamic connection with the person of Jesus Christ, who, for Christians, alone *is* the truth."[69] In his survey of the rise of evangelicalism, Grenz notes that the "new evangelical theology," which was affected by the fundamentalist battle with liberalism, "oriented itself to questions of propositional truth, in contrast to the issue of one's relationship with God characteristic of classical evangelicalism."[70] Incorporating the insights of the Jewish philosopher Emmanuel Lévinas, Carl Raschke emphasizes the "priority of personal over propositional reality" and argues that a "propositional analysis" of the idea of God exhibits a trace of "heathen philosophy."[71]

But the problem with this argument is that it is characterized by reductionism and it presents a false dichotomy. Even if some theologians of the past could be charged with an overemphasis on the propositional, it does not follow that a commitment to propositional theology necessarily leads to a de-emphasis on the personal dimensions of the faith.[72] Many examples could be cited that keep both emphases in balance, but I will make reference to only one. John Frame, in *DCL*, defines *doctrine* as "teaching of the word of

68. Vanhoozer, "On the Very Idea of a Theological System: An Essay in Aid of Triangulating Scripture, Church and World," in *Always Reforming: Explorations in Systematic Theology*, ed. A. T. B. McGowan (Downers Grove, IL: InterVarsity Press, 2006), 134.

69. Alister McGrath, *A Passion for Truth: The Intellectual Coherence of Evangelicalism* (Downers Grove, IL: InterVarsity Press, 1996), 178. Nancey Murphy is critical of McGrath because despite his "critical realist" view of religious language, he emphasizes the cognitive element of theological statements (see *Beyond Liberalism*, 42–45). But from another perspective, Groothuis is critical of McGrath's point that evangelicals have been too preoccupied with propositions at the expense of personal faith. For further on this, see Groothuis, *Truth Decay*, 120–27.

70. Stanley J. Grenz, *Renewing the Center: Evangelical Theology in a Post-Theological Era* (Grand Rapids: Baker Academic, 2000), 84.

71. Carl Raschke, *The Next Reformation: Why Evangelicals Must Embrace Postmodernity* (Grand Rapids: Baker Academic, 2004), 119.

72. Not everyone accused of such overemphasis is necessarily guilty of the charge. Rodney J. Decker, for instance, points out that Carl F. H. Henry, despite some criticisms to the contrary, recognized the importance of both. See Decker's "May Evangelicals Dispense with Propositional Revelation?" In a similar vein, Paul K. Helseth defends Hodge against the charge that he was too intellectualist and rationalist in his view of the believer's knowledge of God. See Helseth, "Are Postconservative Evangelicals Fundamentalists?" in *Reclaiming the Center*, 232–35.

God that leads to spiritual health."[73] Thus, theology is defined in such a way that it incorporates the application of Scripture to life. Furthermore, Frame maintains that there is a reciprocal relationship between the propositional and the practical; you cannot have one without the other.[74]

The separation between the propositional and the personal or between the doctrinal and the practical stems from a misreading of the canon of Scripture itself. Paul, for example, speaks of "doctrine conforming to godliness" (1 Tim. 6:3b). He instructs Timothy that the goal of his instruction is "love from a pure heart and a good conscience and a sincere faith" (1 Tim. 1:5). In some cases an entire epistle, such as Ephesians, may be structured so as to emphasize the doctrinal component in one part and the practical in the other, but without separating them into watertight compartments.[75] There is no reason, then, for one's perspective in this area to be characterized by disjunctive thinking.

In summary, we have looked at four common arguments used against propositional theology and have maintained that none of them entails giving up this approach to theological methodology. In some cases legitimate concerns have been raised, such as recognizing the theological significance of the diversity of literary genres in Scripture. But these can be accommodated within a propositional approach. Can anything be said in favor of the propositional approach?

IN SUPPORT OF PROPOSITIONAL THEOLOGY

In this section we will consider three points that I believe highlight the importance of the propositional approach to theology. First, the propositional approach is sustained by the conviction that God's revelation includes the communication of cognitive truths. In saying this, the propositional approach is not claiming that this is the only thing that the Scriptures communicate, but, as Ronald Nash states, at the very least "some revelation conveys cognitive information."[76] As one author points out, Christianity is not just a faith tradition; it is also a knowledge tradition that involves not only the claim that its assertions are true but also the knowability of a

73. Frame, *DCL*, 352.
74. See ibid., 353–55; *DKG*, 154–55.
75. See Peter O'Brien, *The Letter to the Ephesians*, The Pillar New Testament Commentary (Grand Rapids: Eerdmans, 1999), 272. O'Brien speaks of the relationship between the "indicative" and the "imperative."
76. Nash, *Word of God*, 45.

variety of its assertions.[77] Because the Christian revelation does include the communication of truths, it follows that such truths can be propositionally formulated, however imperfectly. "All truth," states Stuart Hackett, "in its cognitive aspect as knowledge, is in principle propositionally expressible in linguistic statements."[78]

Second, I would argue that the reflective activities associated with propositional theology, namely, summarization and coherence, to name a few, follow from the Scriptures themselves. For example, Thiselton points out that 1 Corinthians 15:3–5 reflects a tradition or an early creed "*which declares the absolute fundamentals of Christian faith and on which Christian identity . . . is built.*"[79] He also points out that such passages make a truth claim concerning the gospel and also emphasize the dimension of "*confession* or *self-involvement.*"[80] In other words, no dichotomy is made between personal faith and propositional truth. Another example of a summary-type statement is 1 Timothy 1:15, one of the "faithful" or "trustworthy" sayings.[81] According to George Knight III, this saying "summarizes and epitomizes the gospel."[82] These kinds of summary statements in the Scriptures indicate that the activity associated with propositional theology is consistent with the identity-forming nature of the Scriptures themselves. Of course, there is always the danger of abuse. Propositional theology can fall into the trap of simplistic proof-texting or fail to take into account redemptive-historical distinctions that are found in the Scriptures.[83] But the striving toward sum-

77. James P. Moreland, "Integration and the Christian Scholar," available at http://www.leaderu.com/aip/docs/moreland2b.html.

78. Stuart C. Hackett, *The Reconstruction of the Christian Revelation Claim: A Philosophical and Critical Apologetic* (Grand Rapids: Baker Book House, 1984), 257. In an essay defending the possibility of speaking "literally" of God, Alston makes a similar point. He maintains that as long as it is possible for members of a linguistic community to form a concept of P, "it will be possible for P to become the meaning of a predicate term in the language." William Alston, *Divine Nature and Human Language* (Ithaca, NY and London: Cornell University Press, 1989), 28.

79. Anthony C. Thiselton, *The First Epistle to the Corinthians*, The New International Greek Testament Commentary (Grand Rapids: Eerdmans, 2000), 1:186 (italics his). Many other commentators concur on this point. See Thiselton for references.

80. Ibid., 1:188.

81. "Here is a trustworthy saying that deserves full acceptance: Christ Jesus came into the world to save sinners—of whom I am the worst" (NIV).

82. George W. Knight III, *The Faithful Sayings in the Pastoral Letters* (Grand Rapids: Baker, 1979), 47.

83. Carson points out, for example, that discussions about the nature of assurance can move too quickly to "atemporal questions" without taking into account such redemptive-historical matters. See D. A. Carson, "Reflections on Assurance," in *Still Sovereign: Contemporary Perspec-*

marization and coherence is not necessarily the imposition of a foreign thought structure on the text of the Bible.[84]

Third, and last, it could be argued that the tendency toward abstraction and systematization, which is characteristic of propositional theology, is a result of systematic theology's being a normative type of discourse rather than merely descriptive. Descriptive discourse, as Paul Griffiths points out, concerns itself with elucidating the practices and beliefs (including the propositional contents) of a given community.[85] Normative discourse, on the other hand, tends to be more abstract and systematic because it is concerned with "judgment and truth" and has a universal scope. Griffiths points out that the move toward the more abstract kind of discourse is a phenomenon found not only in Western cultures but as a characteristic of many other cultures as well, including the East. Such a move plays a "vital part" when communities seek to establish "non-community specific truths."[86]

In conclusion, each of the criticisms reviewed in this essay is concerned with a perspective that is important for theology. Some are concerned about how the theologian uses and interprets the Scriptures (the normative perspective), others are concerned about the context in which the theologizing is done and the kind of theology produced (the situational perspective), while others are concerned about the relationship between Christian life and dogma (the existential perspective). Yet none of these concerns entails a rejection of propositional theology. In fact, a carefully nuanced approach to propositional theology can deal adequately with all three perspectives, as noted in the response to the criticisms above, without seeking to force systematic theology to become something that it is not.[87]

---

tives on Election, Foreknowledge, and Grace, ed. Thomas S. Schreiner and Bruce A. Ware (Grand Rapids: Baker, 2000), 254.

84. Systematic theology presupposes that the basic laws of logic, which are obviously presupposed in propositional theology, are "not inventions of dubious worth but discoveries of the basic relationships that make both coherent communication and knowledge of truth possible." D. A. Carson, "Unity and Diversity in the New Testament: The Possibility of Systematic Theology," in Scripture and Truth, ed. D. A. Carson and John D. Woodbridge (Grand Rapids: Academie Books, 1983), 80.

85. Paul Griffiths, "Denaturalizing Discourse: Abhidharmikas, Propositionalists, and the Comparative Philosophy of Religion," in Myth and Philosophy, ed. Franke E. Reynolds and David Tracy (Albany: State University of New York Press, 1990), 59.

86. Ibid., 61. The specific example that Griffiths uses to illustrate this move comes from the development of Buddhism.

87. I would argue that Dr. Frame's triperspectival approach to systematic theology is a good model in this regard.

24

Neopaganism: Stepchild of Secular Humanism

Peter R. Jones

INTRODUCTION

Aravind Adiga, author of *The White Tiger*, returned to New York after living for a time in India, the land of his birth. To his surprise, he discovered that the "mystics of Brooklyn" had moved from their Greenwich Village haven into the mainstream of New York City. Incense sticks, Tibetan scrolls of the Buddha, and the many-armed gods of Hinduism had caught the imagination of Western spiritual seekers. Adiga noted with irony that during this same period, Indian intellectuals had been captivated by secular rationalism, Western science, and technology. He tells of a New York friend, once a strident atheist and rationalist, who is now absorbed in Jewish mysticism, and whose wife now takes her health concerns to a medicine man in Chinatown, who prescribes roots and crystals.[1]

As postmodern deconstruction rightly affirms, statements of faith and confessions are, by definition, nonverifiable; their ultimate truthfulness is presupposed. John Frame and his teacher, Cornelius Van Til, have always insisted that everyone lives according to presuppositions. Such "statements

---

1. Aravind Adiga, "Mystical Mischief: An Indian Marvels at the West's Embrace of Psychics, Palmists, and Other Mumbo Jumbo," *Time*, July 18, 2008, 56.

of faith" are "verified" only on a pragmatic level by their correspondence to the givens of human reality. Adiga's story of his New York City friends is an example of the tectonic shift that our North American cultural/spiritual "statement of faith" has undergone in the last generation. In a surprising social metamorphosis, many Westerners are looking not to Western rationalism but to the mystical East for spiritual wisdom.

Before responding to such a shift, we must first verify and understand it, which is the goal of this descriptive essay. Modern Christian apologists have successfully challenged secular humanism, but few have taken on neo-paganism, a movement that has taken us by surprise. One exception is James Buchanan, divinity professor in the New College, Edinburgh, who stated in 1859, with remarkable foresight:

> The grand ultimate struggle between Christianity and Atheism will resolve itself into a contest between Christianity and Pantheism. For, in the Christian sense, Pantheism is itself Atheistic, since it denies the Divine personality, and ascribes to the universe those attributes which belong only to the living God; but then it is a distinct and very peculiar form of Atheism, much more plausible in its pretensions, more fascinating to the imagination, and less revolting to the reason, than those colder and coarser theories which ascribed the origin of the world to a fortuitous concourse of atoms, or to the mere mechanical laws of matter and motion. It admits much which the Atheism of a former age would have denied; it recognizes the principle of causality, and gives a reason, such as it is, for the existing order of Nature; it adopts the very language of Theism, and speaks of the Infinite, the Eternal, the Unchangeable One; it may even generate a certain mystic piety, in which elevation of thought may be blended with sensibility of emotion, springing from a warm admiration of Nature; and it admits of being embellished with the charms of a seductive eloquence, and the graces of a sentimental poetry. It may be regarded, therefore, not indeed as the only, but as the most formidable rival of Christian Theism at the present day.[2]

I quote this lengthy portion because it contradicts other predictions about religion made in the same period of the nineteenth century and shows that our present situation is the product of a long, tortuous, often subter-

---

2. James Buchanan, *Modern Atheism under Its Forms of Pantheism, Materialism, Development and Natural Laws* (Boston: Gould and Lincoln, 1859), 146.

ranean development. Buchanan's declaration is a remarkable prediction of what is occurring now, 150 years later.

What progeny did we expect the Enlightenment to produce? Probably not the neopagan stepchild that has stepped onto the spiritual stage, claiming the inheritance.

THE LIFE AND DEATH OF SECULARISM

Life

When I first came from Europe to America in 1964, I discovered Van Til and Francis Schaeffer. (John Frame was still a youthful musical genius trying to decide whether he should become the world's greatest classical organist or its leading Reformed apologist!) The threat from the East at that time was not spiritual but material: atheistic Marxism. Communism had spread from the Soviet Union to China to Korea to Vietnam and to Cuba. Countries were falling like dominoes, and we were next! We feared not only Marxist planetary domination but the final ideological victory of atheistic humanism and the disappearance of religion altogether. This latter enemy seemed already to have invaded certain segments of the American Academy.

Humanism emerged in Europe between 1200 and 1400 as the *studia humanitatis*, or "humanistic studies," a term that eventually described an established intellectual and cultural curriculum, focused on grammar, rhetoric, history, poetry, and moral philosophy. From the eighteenth to the twentieth centuries, secular humanism triumphed. The Enlightenment project, based on faith in human reason as the norm of truth and the source of salvation, began with the *cogito* of René Descartes (1596–1650). The Enlightenment will forever be associated with the French revolution, when Paris revolutionaries in 1789 set up an altar to the "Goddess Reason" in the middle of Notre Dame Cathedral. Article 10 of the Declaration of the Rights of Man states: "No one shall be disquieted on account of his opinions, including his religious views, provided their manifestation does not disturb the public order established by law." The "law" was revealed by secularism.

Secular humanism had every reason to be self-confident. Social observers and philosophers declared its inevitable victory over religion. The philosopher Voltaire delivered a bone-chilling verdict on Christianity: "*Ecrasez l'infame*" ("crush that vile, unspeakable thing"). Ludwig Feuerbach (1804–72) called Christianity a "delusion" and God "a human projection."[3] In the middle of the nineteenth century, Karl Marx dismissed religion as the "opiate of the people," while his contemporary, the French philosopher Auguste Comte (1798–1857), argued that secularization was the inevitable result of human maturity and that mankind would progress toward a superior state of civilization by means of the science of sociology. Ivan Petrovich Pavlov (think "Pavlovian conditioned reflex") was a true son of the nineteenth century, believing in the omnicompetence of science as an expression of the truth of materialistic philosophy. Born in 1849, he trained for the priesthood but was disaffected with Christianity under the influence of Darwin. He came to believe that science would replace religion because it could answer all questions pertaining to life.[4] Sigmund Freud, in his book *The Future of an Illusion* (1927), saw in secularism the tool in the new age of scientific enquiry to bring about the demise of a primitive illusion. Freud, who referred to himself as a "Godless Jew," went on to argue that religion is a "mass delusion," which formally enshrines our "infantile" longing for an all-powerful protective (but also threatening) father figure. For Freudian psychology, religion was a pathological condition, the great obstacle to mental health, from which the future utopian world would be healed.

The fear that religion would disappear, even in "Christian" America, seemed especially valid in the 1960s. " 'Death of God' theologians" such as Thomas J. J. Altizer, Gabriel Vahanian, Paul Van Buren, David Miller, and William Hamilton, Americans all, celebrated the new-world triumph of Nietzschean deicide. Man had come of age and no longer needed "the God hypothesis." With other theological students, I studied this radical "Christian" option, convinced by my professors and by my own reading that the "death of God" movement represented the cultural triumph of secular humanism.

These predictions have come true in the demise of the Christian religion as the dominant social force in Western civilization.[5] In 1967 the sociologist Peter Berger noted the "overall decline in the plausibility of Christianity," due, in his opinion, to the rise of the "age of revolution." No longer submission to

---

3. Ludwig Feuerbach, *The Essence of Christianity* (1841), quoted in Alister McGrath, *The Twilight of Atheism: The Rise and Fall of Disbelief in the Modern World* (New York: Doubleday, 2004), 57.

4. B. P. Babkin, *Pavlov: A Biography* (Chicago: University of Chicago Press, 1971), 85.

5. See chapters 3–6 of James Herrick's *The Making of the New Spirituality: The Eclipse of the Western Religious Tradition* (Downers Grove, IL: InterVarsity Press, 2003) for a full-scale account of the effects of rationalism on Christianity from the Enlightenment to the Modern period.

the will of God but "history and human action" served to explain the great questions of theodicy.[6] He saw the great effect of secularism as creating "a crisis of credibility" for religion in general and Christianity in particular.[7] Most (including Berger)[8] failed to foresee the *demise of secular humanism*.

Berger has since changed his mind! In a 2008 article entitled "Secularization Falsified," Berger now states:

> It has been more than a century since Nietzsche proclaimed the death of God. The prophecy was widely accepted as referring to an alleged fact about increasing disbelief in religion, both by those who rejoiced in it and those who deplored it. As the twentieth century proceeded, however, the alleged fact became increasingly dubious. And it is very dubious indeed as a description of our point in time at the beginning of the twenty-first century. Religion has not been declining. On the contrary, in much of the world there has been a veritable explosion of religious faith.[9]

Death

The "inevitable" triumph of atheistic secularism and the demise of religion did not occur. Andre Malraux, in the middle of the twentieth century and at the high point of the achievements of secularism, predicted that the twenty-first century would be religious. The postmodern deconstructionist Mark C. Taylor, professor at Williams College, observes that "the twenty-first century will be dominated by religion in ways that were inconceivable just a few years ago."[10] Just a few years ago it was difficult to think that a movement whose triumphant success began with the fall of the Bastille in 1789 would effectively end two hundred years later with the fall of the Berlin Wall in 1989.

Secular humanism is dying, much to the disgust of Harvard geneticist Richard Lewontin, who states that "the reason for opposition to scientific accounts of our origins, is not that people are ignorant of facts, but that they have not learned to think from the right starting point . . . [that] science

6. Peter Berger, *The Sacred Canopy: Elements of a Sociological Theory of Religion* (New York: Doubleday, 1967), 79.

7. Ibid., 127.

8. Ibid., 171.

9. Peter L. Berger, "Secularization Falsified," *First Things* (February 2008): 1.

10. Mark C. Taylor, "The Devoted Student," *New York Times*, December 21, 2006.

[is] *the only begetter of truth.*"[11] Like it or not, the public must learn that "we exist as material beings in a material world, all of whose phenomena are the consequences of material relations among material entities."[12] British sociologist Steve Bruce also defends secularism, seeing no valid religious alternative on the horizon. He dismisses the increasing presence of Eastern religious ideas in the West as no evidence against secularization, since "most of it is shallow."[13] He believes that the New Age movement "is eclectic to an unprecedented degree . . . [Thus] I cannot see how a shared faith can be created from a . . . world of pick-and-mix religion." Another sociologist dismisses this spirituality as an exotic, egotistical focus on the spiritual well-being of the self and asks pointedly: "Where are the New Age schools, nurseries, communes, colleges, ecological housing associations, subsistence farming centers, criminal resettlement houses, women's refuges, practical anti-racism projects and urban renewal programs?"[14]

Those who still believe that secular humanism is triumphing will point to the enemies of religion, especially the New Atheists. It is important to realize, however, that much of the contemporary rejection of religion is a rejection of the *Christian* religion. Richard M. Price, who once professed to be a born-again Christian, argues that the notion of a personal God conflicts with our morally neutral universe, creating an unhealthy, superstitious approach to life. The God of the Bible, according to Price, is "a Frankenstein Monster, a divine bully, and an obsessive stalker."[15] The endorsements on the back of Price's book include those of John Shelby Spong, Don Cupitt, and Clark H. Pinnock.

Much of the new atheism attacks the God of the Bible. The well-known Oxford evolutionary biologist Richard Dawkins also has Christianity in his sights. For him, the biblical Yahweh is psychotic, Aquinas's proofs of God's existence fatuous, and religion generally nonsense. Faith is a form of irrationality, a "virus of the mind."[16] Daniel Dennett (Austin B. Fletcher professor of philosophy at Tufts University) compares belief in God to

11. Quoted in Phillip Johnson, "The Unraveling of Scientific Materialism," *First Things* 77 (November 1997): 23.

12. Quoted in ibid.

13. Steve Bruce, *God Is Dead: Secularization in the West* (Oxford: Blackwell, 2002), 156.

14. Christopher Partridge, *The Re-Enchantment of the West: Alternative Spiritualities, Sacralization, Popular Culture, and Occulture*, vol. 1 (London and New York: T&T Clark International, 2004), 35.

15. Richard M. Price, *The Reason-Driven Life: What Am I Here on Earth For?* (Amherst, NY: Prometheus Books, 2006).

16. See Richard Dawkins, *The God Delusion* (London: Houghton Mifflin, 2006).

belief in the Easter Bunny.[17] Sam Harris, author of *The End of Faith* and *Letter to a Christian Nation*, is amazed that hundreds of millions of people worldwide profess religious beliefs when there is no rational evidence for any of those beliefs.[18]

The very existence of so many tomes, however, may be an indication that "religion" is hard to take down. If religion was supposed to disappear, asks Alister McGrath, why is Richard Dawkins's four-hundred-page book *The God Delusion* still necessary?[19] Turkish philosopher Harun Yahya believes that "atheism, which people have tried for hundreds of years as 'the ways of reason and science,' is proving to be mere irrationality and ignorance."[20] Wolfhart Pannenberg states: "Atheism as a theoretical position is in decline worldwide."[21] The social commentator David Brooks has a sobering take on this: "My guess is that the atheism debate is going to be a sideshow. The cognitive revolution is not going to end up undermining faith in God, but end up challenging faith in the Bible."[22]

McGrath says that atheism is now seen by many as an embarrassing link with a largely discredited past. He believes atheism's "future seems increasingly to lie in the private beliefs of individuals rather than in the great public domain it once regarded as its habitat."[23] The foundations are cracking; one of the greatest atheists of the twentieth century, philosopher Anthony Flew, recently rejected atheism. In January 2004, Flew informed the Christian apologist Gary Habermas that he had become a theist. Although still rejecting the concept of special revelation, whether Christian, Jewish, or Islamic, he had concluded that theism was true. He embraced the notion of intelligent design, believing it impossible for evolution to account for the fact that one single cell

---

17. Daniel Dennett, *Freedom Evolves* (London: Viking Penguin, 2003). See http://www.the-brights.net (accessed July 2003).

18. Sam Harris, *The End of Faith: Religion, Terror and the Future of Reason* (New York: W. W. Norton & Co., 2004); *Letter to a Christian Nation* (New York: Knopf, 2006).

19. Alister McGrath, *The Darwin Delusion: Atheist Fundamentalism and the Denial of the Divine* (Downers Grove, IL: InterVarsity Press, 2007), 8.

20. Quoted in Uwe Siemon-Netto, "Analysis: Atheism Worldwide in Decline," United Press International (March 1, 2005).

21. Quoted in ibid.

22. David Brooks, "Connecting Science and Mysticism," *New York Times*, May 13, 2008, reprinted in *San Diego Union-Tribune*, May 14, 2008.

23. Alister McGrath, "The Twilight of Atheism," *Christianity Today* (March 2005). See also his book *Twilight of Atheism*, 230; Johnson, "The Unraveling of Scientific Materialism," 22–25; Michael Novak, "The Godlessness That Failed," *First Things* 104 (June/July 2000): 35–39; Dale Fincher, "Dying under Its Own Irrelevance," Ravi Zacharias International Ministries (April 21, 2005).

can carry more data than all the volumes of the *Encyclopedia Britannica* put together. In Flew's words, he simply "had to go where the evidence leads."[24]

Mark Driscoll (pastor of an eight-thousand-member church) tells of a church that spent a large sum of money to organize a debate on atheism. No one from the community attended. Mark suggests that this church may still be assuming that her neighbors were either atheists or Christians. The fact is that people are very spiritual, and may even spend a great amount of time praying, without having any idea to whom.

In the political realm, not only are the foundations cracked—they have collapsed. Marxism is the political form of secular humanism, and one by one, Marxist regimes have disappeared. In a 2006 campaign speech, then presidential candidate Barack Obama criticized liberals "who dismiss religion in the public square as inherently irrational or intolerant."[25]

In academia, the title of a 2006 secular literature conference suggests that something is afoot: "God Is Undead: Post-Secular Notions in Contemporary Literature and Theory." In this conference a professor of comparative religions gave a course entitled "The End of the Modern World."[26] Jacques Berlinerblau, author of *The Secular Bible*, wrote a provocative article entitled "Secularism in the Elimination Round," in which he denounces the embarrassingly offensive and simplistic arguments of the New Atheists.[27]

Factors Producing the Demise of Secular Humanism

The Critique of Secular Humanism's Failures

The optimistic belief that the world's problems could be solved simply by scientific advance and social engineering has been confounded. According to Rocco Buttiglione, a theologian close to the pope, the pontiff "does not

24. See http://www.biola.edu/philchristi.

25. E. J. Dionne Jr., "Faith & Politics: After the Religious Right," *Commonweal Magazine* (February 2008).

26. Michael C. Kalton is professor of comparative religion at the University of Washington, Tacoma. See his article "Extending the Neo-Confucian Tradition: Questions and Reconceptualizations for the Twenty-First Century," in Mary Evelyn Tucker and John Berthrong, eds., *Confucianism and Ecology: The Interrelation of Heaven, Earth and Humans* (Cambridge, MA: Harvard University Center for the Study of World Religions, 1998), 78.

27. Jacques Berlinerblau is associate professor at Georgetown University. See *The Secular Bible: Why Non-Believers Must Take Religion Seriously* (Cambridge: Cambridge University Press, 2005); "Secularism in the Elimination Round," *Chronicle of Higher Education* (June 2007).

attack Marxism or liberal secularism because they are the wave of the future," but because the "philosophies of the twentieth century have lost their appeal, their time has already passed." Although Christopher Hitchens, Dawkins, and Sam Harris try to argue that religion is the cause of violence, they fail to explain the atrocities of atheistic regimes led by the French Revolution, Josef Stalin, Pol Pot, Mao Tse Tung, and Kim Jong-il. Secularism has produced two devastating world wars; industrialization has created a series of mounting ecological disasters; and the West has begun to lose its faith, not now in religion, but in science and the autonomous human reason. The moral crisis of our time, says David Harvey, is a crisis of Enlightenment thought.[28]

A Christian philosopher, Crystal Downing, observes that "postmodernism undermined absolutist explanations of reality, like Marxism."[29] Marxism has certainly lost its luster, as seen in this quote from a lecture for tourists at the esteemed Chinese Academy of Social Sciences in Beijing:

> One of the things we were asked to look into was what accounted for the success, in fact, the pre-eminence of the West all over the world . . . but in the past twenty years, we have realized that the heart of your culture is your religion: Christianity. That is why the West has been so powerful. The Christian moral foundation of social and cultural life was what made possible the emergence of capitalism and then the successful transition to democratic politics. We don't have any doubt about this.[30]

"It is significant that Christianity is emerging in China at a time when there is a massive ideological vacuum left in society by the nationwide collapse of belief in Marxism-Leninism," wrote David Aikman in *Jesus in Beijing*.[31] He continued, "It is hard to find anyone in China today who truly believes in the theoretical truth of China's official political ideology . . . Marxism (the political form of Secular Humanism) was tried in the extreme form during Mao's nearly two decades of utopian economic and social tinkering (1958–1976) and it was found to be irremediably destructive."[32]

28. David Harvey, *The Condition of Postmodernity* (Cambridge and Oxford: Blackwell, 1990), 41.

29. Crystal L. Downing, *How Postmodernism Serves (My) Faith* (Downers Grove, IL: IVP Academic, 2006), 36.

30. Mary Kapp, "Born Again Beijing," http://www.campusreportonline.net (accessed August 10, 2007).

31. *Jesus in Beijing: How Christianity Is Transforming China and Changing the Global Balance of Power* (Washington, DC: Regnery Publishing, 2006), quoted in Kapp, "Born Again Beijing."

32. Ibid.

For some, the crisis is not only moral but ontological. Secular humanism has produced a disenchantment of the cosmos, a profound sense of ontological and epistemological alienation or separation between the self and the world, leaving the human ego isolated. Secular humanism accepts this ontological isolation as normative, and it then becomes "the legitimated interpretive principle of the modern mind, giving us the subject/object split of modern rationalism."[33]

Some believe that the most fundamental critique of secular humanism comes from the distaff side of current thinking, namely, the feminist hermeneutic, the significance and power of which "is only beginning to be realized by the contemporary mind."[34] Secularism has become identified by feminism with "a [chauvinistic and] patriarchal conception of nature—as a mindless, passive feminine object, to be penetrated, controlled, dominated, and exploited."[35] This feminist perspective, according to Richard Tarnas, "has brought forth perhaps the most . . . radically critical analysis of conventional intellectual and cultural assumptions in all of contemporary scholarship, permitting the contemporary mind to consider less-dichotomized alternative perspectives that could not have been envisioned within previous interpretive frameworks."[36]

The Anti-intellectualism of the Sixties

In the 1960s the dropouts were dropping out from both Christianity and secular humanism. Many turned to Zen Buddhism, which opposes both biblical Christianity and humanistic rationalism. The Buddhist guru Linchi Rinzai warned: "Only keep the Mind from being stirred up."[37] A Zen adept said:

> While the majority of the people living in the West do not consciously feel as if they were living through a crisis of Western culture . . . there is an agreement at least among a number of critical observers, as to the existence and the nature of the crisis. . . . Man has followed rationalism to

33. Richard Tarnas, *The Passion of the Western Mind: Understanding the Ideas That Have Shaped Our World View* (New York: Ballantine Books, 1993), 431.

34. Ibid., 407.

35. Ibid.

36. Ibid.

37. Lit-sen Chang, *Asia's Religions: Christianity's Momentous Encounter with Paganism* (Phillipsburg, NJ: P&R Publishing, 2000), 149.

the point where rationalism has transformed itself into utter irrationality. Since Descartes, man has increasingly split thought from effect.[38]

Since the sixties we have observed the intrusion of this "new" spirituality into the popular culture, especially in North America. We got used to the Moral Majority, but what is the "Religious Left"? Martha Stewart, the diva of all things practical and material, is a faithful reader of the old *New Age Journal*, now *Body and Soul*, and learned yoga during her time in jail. Al Gore's *Current TV* hires Gotham Chopra (the son of Hindu guru Deepak Chopra) to be on his staff to "bring progressive spiritual themes into the mass media."[39] In December 2006, a British Broadcasting poll of young people ages sixteen through nineteen in ten major cities in the world found that a whopping 89 percent believed in God or some higher power—not exactly a promising pool for the future of secularism. Liberal Christianity, now calling itself "progressive Christianity," is shedding its rationalistic habits. In general, this 1960s, dropout, anti-rational generation may well be the maturing stepchild of yesterday's secularist orthodoxy.

The Critique of Postmodern Deconstruction

"Postmodernism has undermined the assumptions of secular humanism."[40] The atheists and secularists should fear not the evangelicals but their own "atheistic" children. The late Jean-François Lyotard's terse definition of *postmodernism* was "incredulity toward metanarratives."[41] He referred to all metanarratives, and especially the metanarrative of secular humanism. "The irony is delicious," says theologian Don Carson. "The modernity which has arrogantly insisted that human reason is the final arbiter of truth has spawned a stepchild that has arisen to slay it."[42]

In the 1960s a number of "postmodern" philosophers began to argue that all truth and all ideologies—including atheistic secular humanism—

38. Ibid., 151.
39. "What Is Enlightenment? Redefining Spirituality for an Evolving World," *What Is Enlightenment?* 31 (December 2005–February 2006): 29.
40. Downing, *How Postmodernism Serves (My) Faith*, 26.
41. Jean-François Lyotard, *The Postmodern Condition: A Report on Knowledge* (Minneapolis: University of Minnesota Press, 1984), xxiv. I am indebted to my student Jeff Locke for this reference.
42. D. A. Carson, *The Gagging of God: Christianity Confronts Pluralism* (Grand Rapids: Zondervan, 1996), 100.

are merely subjective points of view, with no objective grounding in fact. A classic representative of recent trends in the history of philosophy is the postmodern philosopher Michel Foucault. In the 1950s he was a convinced secularist and a paying member of the French Communist Party. He left it when his suspicion grew that Marxism was just another ideology of power, having little to do with reality.

In 1959 Foucault received his doctoral degree and two years later published his thesis: "Madness and Unreason: History of Madness in the Classical Age." Foucault critiques Descartes' thesis "I think, therefore I am." Foucault accuses Descartes of doubting everything *except* his own sanity, thus holding to reason as his anchor to reality. Perhaps, argues Foucault, Descartes should have considered another possibility—his own insanity. Descartes was not as "objective" as he thought himself to be.

The destruction of all sure, safe starting points is perhaps a simple definition of the "postmodern" way of thinking. It is taught in most university philosophy departments throughout the world as "gospel truth." Atheistic secularism's complete dismissal of the value of religion is embarrassing to postmodern intellectuals who have become convinced of the subjective character of all worldviews. These non-Christian postmoderns actually speak of "the embarrassing intolerance of atheism."[43] Postmodern intellectuals find the old atheistic secularism to be embarrassingly intolerant of religion. All worldviews (including atheism) are subjective, after all. Postmoderns value tolerance, even the tolerance of religion and spirituality.

Sociologists[44] also note the same movement, identifying the 1960s as the beginning of postmodernism and the breakdown of "grand narratives." In their place is skepticism toward universal truths, a belief in relative, personal truth, and the growth of pluralism in the religious sphere. Popular novelist and Christian convert Ann Rice "lost faith in atheism" because it is "a mystical decision." A postmodern "hermeneutics of suspicion" is leveled against all proponents of worldviews or overarching descriptions of reality—including secular humanism. The postmodern laser gun was first aimed not at Christianity but at Enlightenment secularism, the belief that reason could deliver objective truth. An informed observer called this

43. Cited in McGrath, *Twilight of Atheism*, 230.
44. Robert S. Ellwood Jr., *The 60s Spiritual Awakening* (New Brunswick, NJ: Rutgers University Press, 1994), 4; Anthony Giddens, *The Consequences of Modernity* (Stanford, CA: Stanford University Press, 1990); James Beckford, "Religion, Modernity and Post-Modernity," in Bryan Wilson, ed., *Religion: Contemporary Issues* (London: Bellew, 1992).

postmodern critique "a rage against humanism and the Enlightenment legacy."[45] The passion and rage comes through with the following apology for postmodern intellectual surgery:

> Postmodernism signals the death of such "metanarratives" whose secretly terroristic function was to ground and legitimate the illusion of a "universal" human history. We are now in the process of wakening from the nightmare of modernity, with its manipulative reason and fetish of the totality, into the laid-back pluralism of the postmodern, that heterogeneous range of life-styles and language games which has renounced the nostalgic urge to totalize and legitimate itself . . . Science and philosophy must jettison their grandiose metaphysical claims and view themselves more modestly as just another set of narratives.[46]

In his new book *Reinventing the Sacred*, the renowned biologist and complexity theorist Stuart A. Kauffman, with a tip of his hat to the postmodern critique of reason, repeatedly speaks to the limitations of rationality:

> God is our chosen name for the ceaseless creativity in the natural universe, biosphere, and human cultures. Because of this ceaseless creativity, we typically do not and cannot know what will happen. We live our lives forward, as Kierkegaard said[,] . . . into mystery, and do so with faith and courage, for that is the mandate of life itself. . . . [This] means that reason alone is an insufficient guide to living our lives. Reason, the center of the Enlightenment, is but one of the evolved, fully human means we use to live our lives. Reason itself has finally led us to see the inadequacy of reason. We must therefore reunite our full humanity. We must see ourselves whole, living in a creative world we can never fully know.[47]

Postmodernism has brought an end to secularism, even for a growing number of scientists, but it raises a serious question: where does postmodernism lead us? The Reformed thinker Lydia Jaeger notes, "L'irrationalisme postmoderne est, en fait, l'ultramodernité: La modernité poussée jusqu'à ses

---

45. Richard J. Bernstein, ed., *Habermas and Modernity* (Oxford: Oxford University Press, 1985), 225.

46. T. Eagleton, "Awakening from Modernity," *Times Literary Supplement* (February 20, 1987), quoted in Harvey, *Condition of Postmodernity*, 9.

47. Quoted in "What Is Enlightenment?" (*What Is Enlightenment* teleconference, June 26, 2008).

conséquences logiques extrêmes"[48]—the ultimate contribution of autonomous reason is that reason has no reasonable grounds. There is perhaps a further level of irrationalism to discover.

What Comes after the Postmodern?

If postmodernism is really the ultimate expression of rationalistic modernity, what will be autonomous humanity's next reincarnation? Some see postmodernism as the "celebration of an ending, but not clearly the making of anything new."[49] Philosophically, we are at an impasse. Postmodernism claims to know only one thing certainly—that there is no objective truth! But this tenet must also apply to postmodernism, which thus slays itself. Carson observes that "at the moment there is no pattern on the horizon to replace postmodernism."[50] Alister McGrath, in his study on the demise of atheism, is equally nonplussed: "It is far from clear what the future of atheism will be, or what will replace it."[51]

Postmodern deconstruction has produced a precarious intellectual situation, which is, at its best, a passageway to something else. Many deconstructionists would say what Nietzsche said: "We would not let ourselves be burned to death for our opinions: we are not sure enough of them for that."[52] The postmodern buzzwords are *tolerance* and *pluralism*, but English theologian E. R. Norman once said: "Pluralism is a word society employs during the transition from one orthodoxy to another."[53] Pluralism is a socially and philosophically unstable state because people need some kind of coherent orthodoxy or worldview.

OUR RELIGIOUS FUTURE: RELIGIOUS PAGANISM

McGrath asks, "What will replace atheism?" My thesis is that *pan*theism will replace *a*theism. Forty years ago the Christian apologist Francis Schaeffer predicted the invasion of Eastern spirituality: "Pantheism will be pressed

---

48. Lydia Jaeger, "Entre modernité et postmodernité: faut-il réinventer l'église?" *La Revue Réformée* 243-2007, 4 (July 2007): 39.

49. Robert C. Solomon and Kathleen Marie Higgins, *Reading Nietzsche: A Short History of Philosophy* (New York: Oxford University Press, 1996), 173.

50. Carson, *Gagging of God*, 79.

51. McGrath, *Twilight of Atheism*, xii.

52. Cited in Ben Macintyre, *Forgotten Fatherland* (San Francisco: HarperCollins, 1992), 17.

53. Source unknown.

as the only answer to ecological problems and will be one more influence in the West's becoming increasingly Eastern in its thinking . . . The Eastern religions will be to Christianity a new, dangerous, Gnosticism."[54] Contemporary sociologist Christopher Partridge, although recognizing what he calls "the collapse of the Christian milieu," adds tellingly that such a collapse "does not mean that the West has become fundamentally secular."[55] He goes on: "The whole thrust of Enlightenment secularism, in opposition . . . to dogma and revealed religion can be considered to have acted in such a way as to prepare the ground for spiritual and mystical religion."[56] By banishing the spirituality of biblical faith as untenable for intelligent human beings, secularism prepares the ground for a nontheistic spirituality. People cannot live without some form of spirituality. The "Emergent" mystic Phyllis Tickle makes this very point in *Rediscovering the Sacred*, a book that won a 1996 Catholic Press Association Book Award in Spirituality.[57] The New Age popularizer Marianne Williamson, known as the "guru to the stars," declared that we are in the midst of a "revolution that will usher in a mystical age."[58]

According to Johannes van Oort, professor of church history and the history of dogma at the University of Utrecht, the Netherlands: "Gnosis in one form or another is expected to become the main expression of secular religion in the new millennium. In order to equip the Church for this new age, the scientific study of Gnosticism is vital."[59] Gnosticism, of course, is merely a variant form of religious paganism.

A contemporary philosopher, author of a major book on postmodernism, ends his magisterial study with the following observation: "The condition of Postmodernity is undergoing a subtle evolution, perhaps reaching a point of self-dissolution into something different. But what?"[60]

Lutheran scholar Frederic Baue asks the same question: "What comes after the Postmodern?" He answers: "A phase of Western or world civilization that is

---

54. Francis Schaeffer, *The God Who Is There* (Downers Grove, IL: InterVarsity Press, 1968), 70; *Pollution and the Death of Man* (Downers Grove, IL: InterVarsity Press, 1970). See also Os Guinness, *Dust of Death* (Downers Grove, IL: InterVarsity Press, 1973), 229, 281.

55. Partridge, *Re-Enchantment of the West*, 1:4.

56. Ibid., 53.

57. Phyllis Tickle, *Rediscovering the Sacred: Spirituality in America* (New York: Crossroad Publishing, 1995).

58. Marianne Williamson, *Healing the Soul of America: Reclaiming Our Voices as Spiritual Citizens* (New York: Simon & Schuster, 2000), 254.

59. Johannes van Oort, "New Light on Christian Gnosis," *Louvain Studies* 24 (1999): 39.

60. Harvey, *Condition of Postmodernity*, 358.

innately religious but hostile to Christianity . . . or worse, a dominant but false church that brings all of its forces to bear against the truth of God's Word."[61] Baue does not predict the further secularization of society but a spiritualization of it. In other words, a deconstructed world, dissected and left in pieces by postmodernism, will be put back together again, not by reason but by "myth" or "unreason," as the title of a recent book on modern philosophy describes it.[62] The British sociologist Christopher Partridge, in total independence from Baue, documents a most interesting phenomenon in modern culture:

> There is some evidence to suggest that "a rising tide of spirituality . . . is producing a re-enchantment of the world" . . . There seems to be a gradual, yet ubiquitous growth of "spirituality" in the West. . . . In a sense, we are witnessing a return to a form of magical culture—what I will call "occulture." Although it is perhaps a little silly to speak of an occultural reformation or revolution, there is nevertheless a significant religio-cultural shift happening in the "real world."[63]

This shift in the West means that "the centre of spiritual gravity is moving away from Judaeo-Christian theology to the eclecticism of occulture."[64] Partridge agrees with a Dutch historian of esoteric Western religion, Wouter Hanegraaff, who speaks of the "profound *transformation* of religion" in the West, away from traditional Christianity and toward what he describes as "magic."[65] Others also note this trend. Paul M. Zulehner is one of the world's most distinguished sociologists of religion and dean of Vienna University's divinity school. He notes that although atheism continues apace in the former East Germany and the Czech Republic, in the rest of Europe and in every major European city except Paris, spirituality is booming—not that of revived Christianity but the spirituality of paganism.[66] Jean Houston, a "seer," and guru to former first lady Hillary Clinton during the 1990s, noticed the change and wrote in 1995: "We are living in a state both of breakdown and

---

61. Frederic W. Baue, *The Spiritual Society: What Lurks beyond Postmodernism?* (Wheaton, IL: Crossway, 2001), 16 (emphasis mine).

62. Richard Wolin, *The Seduction of Unreason: The Intellectual Romance with Fascism from Nietzsche to Postmodernism* (Princeton, NJ: Princeton University Press, 2004). See also Susan Jacoby, *The Age of American Unreason* (New York: Pantheon, 2008).

63. Partridge, *Re-Enchantment of the West*, 1:38–40.

64. Ibid., 128.

65. Ibid.

66. Siemon-Netto, "Atheism Worldwide."

breakthrough . . . a whole system transition, . . . requir[ing] a new alignment that only myth can bring."[67] Philosopher Richard Tarnas shares this opinion. He believes that "we are living in one of those rare ages, like the end of classical antiquity or the beginning of the modern era, that bring forth, through great stress and struggle, a genuinely fundamental transformation in the underlying assumptions and principles of the cultural world view."[68] He goes on: "The Western mind . . . had largely dissolved the foundations of the modern worldview, leaving the contemporary mind increasingly bereft of established certainties, yet also fundamentally open in ways it had never been before."[69] Did the popular 1960s bards have it right?

> When the moon is in the seventh house
> And Jupiter aligns with Mars,
> Then peace will guide the planets,
> And love will steer the stars.
> This is the dawning of the Age of Aquarius.[70]

WHY RELIGIOUS PAGANISM WILL SUPERSEDE SECULAR HUMANISM

The Spiritual Hunger of the Human Soul

The neopagan accusation that secular humanism has produced a sense of human alienation and a disenchanted cosmos goes to the heart of the weakness of materialism noted throughout history. The pagan Neoplatonist Plotinus opposed the materialism of the Epicureans and Stoics by arguing that their materialism could not explain thought and thus their own true selves as thinking subjects. As Plato said, the most real beings are immaterial, including the human soul. All these objections are still true, and neopagans make them with great force. The pagan spiritualist Thomas Berry agrees. He lowers the boom on the scientific community, which has insisted "until

---

67. Jean Houston is clear about the myth we need—the myth of Isis, ancient Egyptian goddess of magic and the underworld, as her book indicates: *The Passion of Isis and Osiris: A Gateway to Transcendent Love* (New York: Ballantine, 1995), 2.

68. Richard Tarnas, *Cosmos and Psyche: Intimations of a New World* (New York: Penguin, 2006), xiii.

69. Tarnas, *Passion*, 394.

70. "Aquarius," from *Hair* (1967), lyrics by James Rado and Gerome Ragni, music by Galt MacDermot.

recently that the universe can only be understood as the random act of minute particles with neither direction nor meaning." In so doing, secular scientists have "desouled the Earth."[71] Christians would agree with much of this critique. Theologian David Wells states: "While we now bask in relative plenty, the means of amassing that plenty—the reorganization of the world by the processes of modernization—has diminished our soul."[72]

The Rational/Irrational Dance of the Autonomous Human Mind

Reformed thinkers such as Herman Dooyeweerd, Van Til, Schaeffer, and Frame have long described the odd alliance in apostate, autonomous thinking between rationalism and irrationalism. Plato incorporates rationalism and irrationalism. For him, reason is totally competent to understand the Forms but incompetent to make sense of the changing world of experience. The ancient Greeks affirmed the autonomy of their own reason, yet they knew their reason was fallible and not omnipotent. They recognized areas of reality that defy rational analysis (change for Parmenides, the world of sense for Plato, prime matter for Aristotle, etc.). The Greek response to these mysteries is to say that part of the world is essentially unknowable and irrational. We can't know it because it can't be known.[73] It is the chaos of the "shapeless stream." It is illusion (Parmenides), nonbeing, or nothingness. Aristotle endorses the mystery religions to say that ultimately *mathein* (understanding) comes through *pathein* (mystical experience).

Rationalists/secular humanists today are likewise destined to become irrationalists because they are unable to account for the totality of existence, and therefore their rationality has no ultimate basis. Equally, postmodern irrationalists, in order to affirm the "truth" of unreason, must use reason to deduce and proclaim that truth.

Pagan Evangelism: The Charm Campaign for Secular Humanists

Modern pagan thinkers address the secular humanist with flattery, charm, and utopian hope. The reassuring line goes something like this: We

71. Thomas Berry, *The Great Work: Our Way into the Future* (New York: Bell Tower, 1999), 78.

72. David Wells, *God in the Wasteland: The Reality of Truth in a World of Fading Dreams* (Grand Rapids: Eerdmans, 1994), 13.

73. We recall the slogan "What my net can't catch isn't fish." See Cornelius Van Til's pamphlet *Why I Believe in God* (Philadelphia: Orthodox Presbyterian Church, n.d.).

are brothers and fellow travelers, playing our different parts on the road to utopian human transformation. Richard Tarnas wraps his arms around the bogeyman of materialistic reason by arguing that "the Enlightenment [was] . . . a necessary stage in the evolution of the human mind."[74] This postmodern pagan reaches back to integrate the pagan rationalist/modernist in his history of human redemption—in the name of an evolving universe. As it has evolved, the universe has brought forth "new stages of human knowledge."[75] It was the birth of the new human being. "The growingly autonomous human intellect . . . has itself been an authentic expression of nature's unfolding," a "process . . . now reaching a highly critical stage of transfiguration."[76] As Alexander Pope is reputed to have observed: "God said, 'Let Newton be!' and all was light."

Tarnas does not say what authority the human mind is rejecting in its search for autonomy, but he implies a liberation from the chains of traditional theism and the notion of a creator God. Ken Wilber also sees the union of Enlightenment liberalism and spirituality. Liberalism was "a *profound* move" away from the "Mythic-Order/Theism"[77] (i.e., biblical orthodoxy). Why is the move so profound? In his nine stages of "The Human Consciousness Project," which traces the spiritual evolution of humanity, Wilber marginalizes theism by placing it fourth in his ascending order. The most advanced consciousness (within "second-tier consciousness") is level 9—Integral-Holonic. The most primitive is level 1—Archaic-Instinctual:

Second-tier Consciousness:
   9. Integral-Holonic
   8. Universal Holistic
   7. Integrative

First-tier Consciousness:
   6. The Sensitive Self (Green Egalitarianism)
   5. Scientific Achievement (Enlightenment Rationalism)
   4. Mythic Order (determined by an All-powerful Other—Theism)
   3. Power Gods (Magical-Mythical)

74. Tarnas, *Passion*, 436.
75. Ibid., 435.
76. Ibid.
77. Ken Wilber, *A Theory of Everything: An Integral Vision for Business, Politics, Science and Spirituality* (Boston: Shambhala, 2001), 80–82.

2. Magical-Animistic

1. Archaic-Instinctual

This all-inclusive, evolutionary schema attempts to put biblical theism in its place—fourth from the bottom out of nine. One of Wilber's disciples, an "integral" geopolitician named Steve McIntosh, employs Wilber's transformational scheme to make recommendations for sub-Saharan Africa. Since the sub-Saharans are still locked in level 3, Power Gods (with a dash of "tribalism"), he proposes that they use some of level 4's evangelical Christian moral teaching, before evolving to higher planes, once level 4 shows itself to be problematic.[78] He fails to see that Christianity's moral teaching derives from the theism he rejects as primitive.

In his history of Western thinking, Tarnas eliminates Christian theism as a moribund system that began withering in the early days of the Enlightenment. For him the real struggle of Western thinking in the last two centuries was between secular rationalism and spiritual Romanticism, represented by figures such as Schiller, Schelling, Hegel, Coleridge, and Steiner, for whom "the relation of the human mind to the world was ultimately not dualistic but participatory."[79] The dynamic of Western history waiting to be resolved is the integration of Romanticism, "the West's 'inner' culture—its art and literature, its religious and metaphysical vision, its moral ideals [with secular] science, its 'outer' cosmology," claiming to define "the character of nature, man's place in the universe, and the limits of his real knowledge."[80] This conflict is manageable, however, and Tarnas will seek to develop an overarching synthesis of the outer and the inner for a holistic unity.

From the Ashes of Deconstruction Comes a Rediscovery of Significance

From the ashes of secular humanism a phoenix is reborn. Enlightenment liberalism, predicts Wilber, is now ready to embrace deep spirituality.[81] The human mind is reaching that moment of transcendence. Tarnas senses a "powerful crescendo"[82] as "many movements *gather now*

---

78. Steve McIntosh, "Integral Politics Comes of Age," *What Is Enlightenment?* (October–December 2007).

79. Tarnas, *Passion*, 433.

80. Ibid., 272.

81. Wilber, *A Theory of Everything*, 80–82.

82. Tarnas, *Passion*, 411.

on the intellectual stage as if for some kind of climactic synthesis."[83] This synthesis incorporates the postmodern understanding of knowledge, yet goes beyond it.[84] It is only when "the human mind actively brings forth from within itself the full powers of a disciplined imagination and saturates its empirical observation with archetypal insight that the deeper reality of the world emerges."[85] This is a sort of conversion experience for the secular mind. "The human spirit does not merely prescribe nature's phenomenal order; rather the spirit of nature brings forth its *own* order through the human mind when that mind is employing its full complement of faculties—intellectual, volitional, emotional, sensory, imaginative, aesthetic, epiphanic."[86] Human language needs to reconceive of itself as rooted in a deeper reality, namely, that of the universe's unfolding meaning. Hence "the imaginal intuition is not a subjective distortion but is the human fulfillment of that reality's essential wholeness, which had been rent asunder by the dualistic perception."[87]

Reason's Savior: "Scientific" Unreason

The synthesis of secularism and Romanticism is brought about by the depth psychology of Sigmund Freud and Carl Jung (1875–1961). Romanticism is vindicated by the human *sciences*.[88] "Jung found evidence of a collective *unconscious* common to all human beings and structured according to powerful archetypal principles."[89] Here we see the pagan character of this philosophical synthesis, which is firmly based on irrational experience, "the subconscious."[90] Help comes not through reason but unreason. In light of the universal crisis of religious faith in a secular age, Jung's depth psychology takes on the characteristics of a redemptive religion. Jung claims that his approach is not religious but a modern "science of the soul" rooted in empiricism. Not one of his major tenets has ever been subjected to experimental scrutiny, nor could it be, yet the religious appears. The goal of Jungianism

83. Ibid., 403 (emphasis mine).
84. Ibid., 434.
85. Ibid.
86. Ibid., 435.
87. Ibid., 434.
88. Ibid., 384.
89. Ibid., 385.
90. Ibid.

is "to become the world's final, unitary religion." Like Marx, Jung never expressed this idea as a personal goal, but rather as a historical inevitability that he stumbled upon and was obliged to proclaim.[91]

The highly significant work of the Czech neo-Jungian scholar Stanislav Grof is considered by Tarnas as "the most epistemologically significant development in the recent history of depth psychology."[92] In the first place, Grof has continued to experiment with *methodologies that produce the shamanic,*[93] *unitive, and mystical experiences* of contact with the transpersonal spiritual world. In the second place, Grof's work on the *importance of the unconscious in the prebirth and birth processes* really solves the crisis that for millennia has plagued the Western mind. In his words,

> the fundamental subject-object dichotomy . . . that has *constituted* modern consciousness . . . appears to be rooted in a specific archetypal condition associated with the unresolved trauma of human birth, in which an original consciousness of undifferentiated organismic unity with the mother, a *participation mystique* with nature, had been outgrown, disrupted, and lost. Here . . . the source of the profound dualism of the modern mind. . . . Here is the painful separation from the timeless all-encompassing womb of nature . . . Here is the profound sense of ontological and epistemological separation between self and world. . . . This fundamental sense of separation is then structured into the legitimated interpretive principles of the modern mind.[94]

People initiated into unitive, mystical experiences via the age-old "sacred technologies" listed by Grof (mysticism, drugs, and various other altered states of consciousness) are "able to access memories of prenatal intra-uterine existence." Such memories "emerged in association with archetypal experiences of paradise, mystical union with nature or with the divine or with the Great Mother Goddess."[95] *Et voila!* "The individual and the universal are reconciled."[96] This is the time-honored experience of ancient pagans.[97]

91. Harvey, *Condition of Postmodernity,* 41.

92. Tarnas, *Passion,* 425.

93. For the acceptance of the specifically shamanic experiences, see Tarnas, *Cosmos and Psyche,* 31.

94. Stanislav Grof, *Psychology of the Future: Lessons from Modern Consciousness Research* (New York: State University of New York Press, 2000), 403–31.

95. Ibid., 427.

96. Ibid., 433.

97. George Otis Jr., *The Twilight Labyrinth: Why Does Spiritual Darkness Linger Where It Does?* (Grand Rapids: Chosen Books, 1997), 49–50. The builders of the ancient Maltese temple complex at

Such approaches have produced a new optimism about the future. In Delhi in 2008 the Association of Transpersonal Personal Psychology, in which Grof is a leading light, sponsored a "World Congress on Psychology and Spirituality,"[98] which seeks a global union of the insights of mystical Eastern gurus with those of scientific Western scholars in order to chart a future course for a unique marriage of worldviews. Truth is possible again!

A new "humanistic" project for the world is under construction, a worldview for the planetary era, joining the East and the West, joining "science" and (pagan) spirituality.

A Common Metanarrative: Evolution—Scientific and Spiritual

At least one metanarrative survives the postmodern deconstruction: evolution, the origins myth that will put Humpty Dumpty back together again. Biologist David Sloan Wilson of Dartmouth seeks in evolutionary theory "a common language . . . for all things human" in which biologists, psychologists, anthropologists, social scientists, and those in the arts can apply evolutionary principles across the board in an academic context. All assume that "evolution has produced a universal landscape of the human mind," thereby escaping "the dehumanizing mercies of post modern literary theory" to rediscover as a welcome relief some sort of "universal perspective."[99]

Such a metanarrative fits with the latest statement of the Council of Europe: "The Parliamentary Assembly is worried about the possible ill-effects of the spread of creationist ideas within our education systems and about the consequences for our democracies. If we are not careful, creationism could become a threat to human rights, which are a key concern of the Council of Europe."[100] "We are witnessing a growth of modes of thought which . . . are

---

Tarxien evidently saw things much the same way. In the view of feminist art historian Elinor Gadon, a labyrinthine, underground sanctuary known as the Hypogeum served as "the womb and the place of burial where the dead returned to the Mother." Similar interpretations have been found at sites from Central America to Siberia, from ancient Roman, Celtic, and Asian settings. The Hopi Indians have womblike sanctuaries that symbolize their birth through the body of the Earth Mother.

98. See the Web site for the World Congress on Psychology and Spirituality, 2008: http://www.worldcongressps2008.org.

99. Ross Robertson, "Can Darwin Save Dartmouth from Derrida?" *What Is Enlightenment?* (July–September 2007): 25.

100. From the Parliamentary Assembly's document 31175, September 17, 2007, http://assembly.coe.int/main.asp?Link=/documents/workingdocs/doc07/edoc11375.htm, quoted by Al Mohler in his blog of October 7, 2007. See http://almohler.com/blog_read.php?id=1020.

attacking the very core of the knowledge that we have patiently built up on nature, evolution, our origins and our place in the universe."[101]

Such a position hides or woefully ignores the growth of "evolutionary spirituality," and thus the radical infringement of "church" on the state. The neopagan reconstruction is thoroughly committed to evolution, but argues that it does not go far enough. The "new" origin story incorporates the biological explanation of origins, but also unites the world in a spiritual evolution. Alan Sasha Lithman states:

> Evolution proceeds simultaneously on two interwoven tracks, one of form, the other of consciousness . . . [and] progressively leads to a new terrestrial species, emerging like our amphibious ancestors into a new milieu of consciousness. We are at a transitional moment . . . sweeping us in the inrushing evolutionary tide toward a new principle of Being . . . the perilous choice of transformation or extinction.[102]

James Lovelock, the inventor of the Gaia hypothesis, speculated that humanity is the evolving nervous system and brain of the planet, the instrumentality through which Gaia becomes self-aware.[103] Lithman, the later luminary, begs to differ. As a true pagan prophet, Lithman warns that this source of revelation, evolution, "is a direct threat to all fixed forms, ideas, answers, truths . . . and the human mind,"[104] for "there is no reason to believe that evolution arbitrarily stops with us . . . It is this subversive implication, I believe, which subconsciously pricks not only the raw nerve of our biblical-based realities but of Mind itself as Reality's final arbiter . . . [Paganism's notion of the] mutation of consciousness [ultimately] threatens . . . the Empire of Mind itself as evolution's last word."[105] We have been warned!

Ultimately, Lithman's position requires no sacrifice of the intellect, since cutting-edge thinkers believe that "quantum physics may support some of the old magical and shamanistic teachings that were once dismissed as nonsense."[106]

101. Ibid.

102. Alan Sasha Lithman, *An Evolutionary Agenda for the Third Millennium: A Primer for the Mutation of Consciousness* (Ashland, OR: White Cloud Press, 2003), 5.

103. Cited in David Spangler, *Emergence: The Rebirth of the Sacred* (New York: Dell Publishing, 1984), 45.

104. Lithman, *Evolutionary Agenda*, 11.

105. Ibid., 13.

106. "Jeffrey J. Kripal: TPC Interviews," *The Progressive Christian* 181, 4 (July–August 2007): 17.

The new Christian liberalism, called "progressive Christianity," accepts the religious movement of the 1960s as a gradual turn back toward the body and the world and to a God not as outside the universe but in the universe. Just as good and evil are part of the same spiritual unity, so on the physical level there is no ultimate distinction between particles and waves. This leads Thomas Berry to conclude that science corroborates what mystics have believed for millennia, namely, that life is one.

A Strategic Alliance: Paganism and Ecology

Already in 1984, David Spangler, an ex-Pentecostal New Ager, saw the fruitful connection between concern for the earth and the worship of it. He predicted the emergence of a holistic worldview that joins a newly discovered mysticism of universal oneness with contemporary science, particularly ecology. "At its highest, ecology is a resacralization of science, a new vision of the relationship of the unique part with the Universal Whole."[107] This opportunity for the popularization—even normalization—of neopaganism has only increased since that time. Ecology has recently become the pen with which many write *theology* in our time. This is why the ex-Jesuit neopagan Thomas Berry has ditched the term *theologian* and now calls himself a *geologian*, a "student of the earth," convinced that we are living in the "ecological age" of cosmic history. That is to say, our immediate and pressing concerns can no longer be the esoteric issues about God and metaphysics, personal sin, and otherworldly salvation. Theology can be done *only* via the pressing questions concerning the meaning and survival of the planet. "[Thomas Berry's] values," says an admiring disciple, the well-known "creation spirituality" theologian Matthew Fox, "are the ecological values . . . , which give us a comprehensive cosmology for the twenty-first century."[108]

The Religious Commitment of Radical Feminism

The highly influential feminist movement has often championed a spirituality that favors the pagan worship of the Goddess, as well as some variety of paganism. A conference at Syracuse University entitled "Feminism, Sexuality and the Return of Religion" brought together a constellation of internationally prominent philosophers and theologians to ask:

107. Spangler, *Emergence*, 42–43.
108. Matthew Fox, "A Profile of Thomas Berry, Scholar and Lover of the Earth," *EarthLight Magazine* 34 (Summer 1999).

What does the return of religion mean for women and for human sexuality? What new openings for feminism and gender theory are being made by the renewed interest of intellectuals in religion? How can we re-imagine God and the divine beyond patriarchy and homophobia?[109]

A number of things stand out: intellectuals are associated with "the return of religion"; radical feminism and homosexuality occupy a dominant place in the reimagining of God; they similarly lead the way in the deconstruction of God as Father and the rejection of biblical theism; they thus lead the way in reconstructing religion in some form of monistic spirituality. The latter is explicitly proposed by a group of contemporary Dutch biblical scholars at Utrecht University in their book *Only One God?*[110] This book argues that Asherah was the consort of Yahweh. It focuses on "women's religions" in the Hebrew Bible and from there makes the case for the relevance of folk (pagan) religion for theology today. A professor of archaeology at the University of Arizona, William Denver, in his book *Did God Have a Wife?* holds that the rediscovery of the Goddess and of women's popular cults in ancient Israel is useful for our time, by "bringing the divine mystery closer to the heart of human experience."[111] He quotes a Lutheran scholar, Erhard Gerstenberger, who states: "The question of God is a problem for mankind. . . . If we want to preserve civilization on this planet, we shall have to change the way we think about God."[112]

Rethinking God in this time of renewed interest in spirituality can only mean postulating a god who is the very antithesis of the God of biblical theism. There are no other viable options.

A Seamless Integration of Homo- and Pan-Sexuality

The power of homosexuality is apparent in the West, although its connection with religious paganism is not always seen, since arguments in its favor are political and sociological. Leading gay authors, however,

109. See http://pcr.syr.edu/2007/index.htm. Attendees included Helene Cixous, Gianno Vattimo, Bell Hooks, Judith Butler, Catherine Keller, Sarah Coakley, Mark Jordan, and Saba Mahmood.

110. Bob Becking et al., *Only One God? Monotheism in Ancient Israel and the Veneration of the Goddess Asherah* (New York: Sheffield Academic Press, 2001).

111. William D. Dever, *Did God Have a Wife? Archaeology and Folk Religion in Ancient Israel* (Grand Rapids: Eerdmans, 2005), 206ff.

112. Erhard S. Gerstenburger, *Theologies in the Old Testament* (New York: T&T Clark, 2002), 331.

clearly associate homosexuality and pagan spirituality. For example, Toby Johnson says:

> Gay attraction to and development of emotional relationships with members of our same sex results in our seeing the world with the harmonious, non-dualistic vision that is the traditional goal of mystical religion. We don't see the world polarized in the "battle between the sexes" that, in turn, generates the dualistic belief in good and evil. Gay consciousness is "pre-Edenic," fundamentally innocent, free of "original sin."[113]

The Jungian Gnostic June Singer declared in 1977 that the Age of Aquarius was the Age of Androgyny.[114] "The archetype of androgyny appears in us as an innate sense of . . . and witness to . . . the primordial cosmic unity—that is, it is the sacrament of monism, functioning to erase distinction."[115]

A Revived Christian Liberal Syncretism

Theologian Al Mohler asks, "Why, then, would some argue that Evangelicalism should follow essentially the same path? Can they not see that the liberal Protestant river has run dry?"[116] He fails to see that a new stream of life is now flowing.

Paganism is popular. "Christian" liberals, once attached to rationalist nonsupernatural forms of Christianity, are now finding their spiritual home in the new or integral spirituality of neopaganism. Now called "progressive" or "evolutionary" spirituality, it advocates the mystical, suprarational state, which offers liberation from the mythological sky-God of outdated theism. The Reverend Dr. Lauren Artress, San Francisco Grace Cathedral's Canon for Special Ministry, popularized the labyrinth. She tells the story of her awakening to enlightenment: "We mistakenly thought that the intellect was the avenue to experiencing the Sacred, to nourishing the soul. We discounted the imagination and our other faculties of knowing mystery."[117]

113. See http://www.theOoze.com.
114. June Singer, *Androgyny: Towards a New Theory of Sexuality* (London: Routledge & Kegan, 1977), 18.
115. Ibid., 20.
116. Al Mohler's blog, http://almohler.com/blog.php?selectMonth=08&selectYear=2008.
117. Lauren Artress, *Walking a Sacred Path: Rediscovering the Labyrinth as a Spiritual Tool* (New York: Riverhead Books, 1995), 8.

Again, "progressive Christianity" accepts the 1960s' religious movement as "a gradual turn back towards the body and the world . . . seeing God not as outside the universe but in the universe."[118] A Progressive pastor declares: "I encourage fellow liberal Christians to cast a wider net and include non-dualistic interpretations of Jesus, the kingdom of God, incarnation, evil and salvation. . . . Religious dualism is a major root-cause of violence and war."[119]

Such nondualistic experience, found in all the religions, is leading to a religious syncretism that fits a growing interest in globalism. I have a German student who told me that the most influential theologian among German students today is Friedrich Schleiermacher. The way to God is through our "feelings"—and this is the point of contact between Schleiermacher and other world religions. My student mentioned one brilliant woman who had told him that she was a Buddhist, but also a disciple of Schleiermacher.

Such liberalism is attractive to certain Emergent evangelicals who are drinking at the source of modern paganism, including Ken Wilber. "Integral Christianity" claims to be a fresh look at the all-embracing quality of historic Christianity, beyond popular attempts to define a Christian worldview. Using the "all quadrant, all levels" model of Ken Wilber, Richard Vincent, author of *Integral Christianity*, offers an open Christian framework for personal growth, church life, and cultural influence that moves beyond the conflict of modern and postmodern views. Vincent concludes by examining the role of tradition and dogma as "a convention for the open-minded. Integral Christianity will enlarge your faith, enrich your life, and help you open the doors to pursue the common good."[120] Alas, it may well become a significant element in the deep paganization of Christianity.

Hope for a Reunited World

Belief in pagan monism is gaining ground in the once-"Christian" West. In America, Diana Chapman Walsh is the quintessential sophisticated secular humanist academic. She is the retiring president of Wellesley College, from which graduated Hillary Clinton, Madame Chiang Kai-shek, Jackie Kennedy, Margaret Mead, Katharine Hepburn, Gertrude Stein, Julia

118. "Jeffrey J. Kripal: TPC Interviews," 18.
119. Peter Schneider, "The Times Require a Non-Dualistic View of Jesus," *The Progressive Christian* 181, 4 (July–August 2007): 4.
120. Richard Vincent, *Integral Christianity* (Colorado Springs: Bimillennial, 2008).

Child, Emily Dickinson, Madeleine Albright, my wife, Rebecca, and my two daughters, Eowyn and Gabrielle! Wellesley, whose official motto is derived from Jesus' words in Mark 10:45, "not to be served but to serve,"[121] now proposes a different orientation. Walsh's retirement speech indicates how much a religiously monistic view of existence has penetrated the soul of America:

> "Opposites do not negate each other. . . . They cohere in mysterious unity at the heart of reality." If we can accept the paradox of darkness and light . . . if we can hold the polar concepts together in their tension, then we may come eventually to see that between them lies the irreducible health in all living things—the cycles, and the rhythms, and the seasons that give life its meaning and its zest—the "hidden wholeness" described by the mystic, Thomas Merton.[122]

Neopaganism is alive and well in once-"Christian" America. Nearly thirty years ago, Jacques Ellul warned us of "the error of regarding the good as unitary, of identifying all division, fracture and separation as the bad, and seeing it as a duty to seek metaphysical unity . . . in the one." Such thinking is, according to Ellul, "a complete misunderstanding of revelation and predicts its replacement . . . [by some form] of Gnosticism."[123]

But paganism is on the rise elsewhere as well. Into the spiritual black hole fostered by Marxism and deepened by its demise rushed a powerful new spirituality. The antireligious "got religion" and the materialists discovered spirituality. The new religious consciousness does not call for dramatic *metanoia*. Men and Matter, already the reigning monarchs of Marxism, do not repent. They simply accept divine epithets. Watch how they do it.

Former Marxist Vaclev Havel, president of the Czech Republic, now wants to "lift the Iron Curtain of the Spirit," by discovering what all religions have in common. In this way, through "the divine revolution," we will save the planet.[124] The same has happened to Mikhail Gorbachev, the last leader of the Soviet empire, and a pure product of the atheistic Marxist system. He now preaches a form of religious conversion:

121. All quotations from the Bible are from the ESV.

122. http://www.wellesley.edu/PublicAffairs/Commencement/2007/DCWcharge.html.

123. Jacques Ellul, *Interpretive Essays*, ed. C. G. Christians and J. M. Van Hook (Chicago: University of Illinois Press, 1981), 302.

124. Vaclav Havel, "The Divine Revolution," *Utne Reader* (July–August 1998): 56–57.

We need *a new synthesis* that incorporates ... democratic, Christian and Buddhist values, ... which affirms such moral principles as ... the sense of oneness with nature and each other ... a kind of Ten Commandments that provides a guide for human behavior ... in the next century and beyond.[125]

The materialist has become a mystic, although we must keep in mind that when Gorbachev says "democratic," he means "humanistic Marxism" (as in the old German *Democratic* Republic of Eric Honeker), and that when he says "Christian," he means Christianity reinterpreted through the grille of monistic Buddhism. The "new synthesis" is happening as spirituality-hungry secular humanists birth a child—neopaganism. Gorbachev is accomplishing his goals by helping to sponsor the Earth Charter, a pagan-inspired United Nations blueprint for regulating life on a renewed planet. Gorbachev is a Theosophist (a follower of the occultist Madame Blavatsky).[126] This and his other "achievements" were recognized when he was given America's Liberty Medal at the National Constitution Center on Independence Mall, Philadelphia, from the hand of former president George H. W. Bush.

In 1983 John Dunphy wrote in *The Humanist*, the journal of the American Humanist Association (a classic bastion of atheism):

The battle for humankind's future must be waged and won in the public school classroom by teachers who correctly perceive their role as the *proselytizers of a new faith*, a religion of humanity that recognizes and respects the spark of ... *divinity in every human being*. ... The classroom must and will become an arena of conflict between the old and the new—the rotting corpse of Christianity ... and the new faith of humanism.[127]

The humanistic prose now throbs with spirituality.

The challenge of this synthesis, although daunting, is manageable because there is every reason to think that autonomous rationalism and mystical Romanticism are different but parallel expressions of the same way of conceiving of the world.

125. Mikhail Gorbachev, *The Search for a New Beginning: Developing a New Civilization* (HarperSan Francisco, 1995), quoted on the State of the World Forum Web page, http://www.worldforum.org.

126. Sylvia Cranston, *The Extraordinary Life and Influence of Helena Petrovna Blavatsky—Founder of the Modern Theosophical Movement* (New York: Putnam and Sons, 1993).

127. John Dunphy, *The Humanist* (January–February 1983) (emphasis mine). See reference on http://www.rae.org/bits25.htm.

Pagan "theologian" Michael York argues that there are two basic kinds of religion: either *pagan* and world-affirming (Wicca and Druidism, and some expressions of eastern religion such as Confucianism and some early forms of Hinduism) or *Gnostic* and world-denying (Buddhism, Hinduism, ancient Gnosticism, Judaism, Islam, and Christianity).[128]

York's categories are confusing and do not hold up, as York himself seems to admit in other places. He must grant an oddity, namely, that "paganism and Gnosticism have become natural allies." He also notes that "Judaism, Christianity, and Islam . . . are difficult to situate accurately between the Gnostic-pagan theological divide."[129] His categories leave several major religions out in the cold. The difficulty arguably arises from the fact that these religions, Christianity, and its two heretical forms, Judaism and Islam, are in some sense "theistic"[130] in that they distinguish between the nature of God and the nature of everything else.

The weakness in classifying religions as either world-affirming or world-denying is that both these orientations firmly coexist *within* some of the great monistic religions.

- Hinduism contains the world-affirming in Vishnu (the cosmic preserver) and the world-denying in Shiva (the cosmic destroyer). Most Tantrists say there can be no enlightenment without sexual practice. Most celibates (*brahmacharya*), on the other hand, say there is no chance of enlightenment without giving up sex altogether. Is sex really a path to enlightenment? Or is it essential to renounce our sexuality to attain the highest spiritual states? This is a raging debate among Hindu monists.[131]
- Gnosticism, as is well documented, has both ascetic and libertine forms. The recognized authority on Gnosticism, Kurt Rudolf, explains this apparent contradiction. Rudolf defines Gnosticism

128. Michael York, *Pagan Theology: Paganism as a World Religion* (New York and London: New York University Press, 2003), 159.

129. Ibid., 161.

130. Inasmuch as Judaism and Islam are in different ways Christian heresies, elements of theism persist, although deeply compromised by elements of paganism. See below for an estimate of the present state of Judaism, which has, by and large, rejected biblical theism.

131. "What Is the Relationship between Sex and Spirituality?" *What Is Enlightenment?* 13 (Spring–Summer 1998): 62.

as a form of dualism on a monistic background. Its monism is clear since it eliminates the Creator/creature distinction.[132]

- Buddhism, which is atheistic, is nevertheless monistic. A Buddhist teacher explains: "Buddhism since its inception inspired . . . the most radical form of inclusivity. This is the realization that all beings in all realms . . . have a mind ground that is . . . not separate from the mind ground of any other being."[133] Thus Buddhism can be obviously "atheistic," in that it never names a god, but it is still monistic.

Worship of created reality, however one wishes to conceive it, is monistic and thus pagan. This is why even Western atheism is an equally important expression of monism. Such a view is correctly held by Surya Das, a Hindu guru and popular author, who speaks of the "monistic materialistic worldview of Western science."[134] Lewontin's description of atheism, cited above, is a perfectly self-contained monistic description of the world: "We exist as material beings in a material world, all of whose phenomena are the consequences of material relations among material entities."[135]

Although the deontology of York is inadequate, the "eschatology" of Tarnas certainly has legs, because Romanticism and Enlightenment rationalism are not, in their deepest monistic essence, contradictory. Mitchell Silver demonstrates this. Silver, who teaches philosophy at the University of Massachusetts in Boston, is a self-identified Jewish atheist who seeks to analyze the "new god" of contemporary Judaism,[136] as expressed in the writings of Michael Lerner, Arthur Green, and Mordecai Kaplan.[137] He shows that the secularists and what he calls the new-god believers are "two groups

132. Kurt Rudolf, *The Gnostic Religion* (Boston: Beacon Press, 1958).

133. Roshi Joan Halifax, "Excerpts from Buddhist Peacework: Creating Cultures of Peace," *Boston Research Center for the Twenty-First Century Newsletter* 14 (Winter 2000): 10–11.

134. Lama Surya Das, *Awakening the Buddha Within* (New York: Bantam Doubleday, 1997), 293.

135. Quoted in Johnson, "The Unraveling of Scientific Materialism," 23.

136. Mitchell Silver, *A Plausible God: Secular Reflections on Liberal Jewish Theology* (New York: Fordham University Press, 2006).

137. Michael Lerner, *Jewish Renewal* (New York: Putnam, 1994); *Spirit Matters* (Charlottesville, VA: Hampton Roads, 2000); Arthur Green, *Seek My Face: Speak My Name* (London: Aronson Press, 1992); *These Are the Words* (Woodstock, VT: Jewish Lights, 2000); Mordecai Kaplan, *Judaism without Supernaturalism* (New York: Reconstructionist Press, 1958); *Dynamic Judaism*, ed. Mel Scult and Emanuel Goldsmith (New York: Schoken, 1985).

of moderns who accept the same literal description of reality. They agree on what is known. It is a question of their different attitudes to the unknown . . . The new god believers have a taste for extreme emotions . . . The secularists have less of a thirst for heavenly joy."[138] So the real difference between atheists and pantheists has to do only with emotions. The "new godders believe that the essential work of religion is this worldly and share with moderns the notion of 'freedom,' which flows from the rejection of supernaturalism."[139] Thus both new-godders and atheists join in the common social vision of a shared notion of freedom in a this-worldly, utopian tomorrow.

Without citing him, Silver agrees with Tarnas, who passionately believes that we are about to see this synthesis occur in "the integration of Romanticism, the West's 'inner' culture—its art and literature, its religious and metaphysical vision, its moral ideals" with secular "science, its 'outer' cosmology . . . , claiming to define the character of nature, man's place in the universe, and the limits of his real knowledge."[140] At the end of five hundred pages of philosophical and religious analysis in *The Passion of the Western Mind*, he comes to his breathtaking conclusion. He sees the synthesis as a fulfillment of Jung's prophecy of the reconciliation between the two great polarities, a *hieros gamos* (sacred marriage) between the long-dominant but now-alienated masculine (rational) and the long-suppressed but now-ascending feminine (irrational). This cosmic synthesis will finally unite the East and the West. Tarnas states: "The deepest passion of the Western mind has been to reunite with the ground of its own being."[141]

Tarnas's synthesis is not reconciliation with the Creator; it is mystical, occult union with the creation. In the unforgettable words of Mitchell Silver: "when the messiah arrives (or after the revolution), there will be those singing god's praises and others whistling a secular song, and neither need be out of tune."[142]

THE REAL STRUGGLE: MONISM AND THEISM

The great "synthetic" achievement proposed by neopagan "eschatology" is less impressive than first appears, and today's Christian apologists

138. Silver, *Plausible God*, 111.
139. Ibid., 119.
140. Tarnas, *Passion*, 272.
141. Ibid., 443.
142. Silver, *Plausible God*, 105.

must realize that the real conflict is not between autonomous mysticism and autonomous rationalism but between two irreconcilable definitions of God that cannot be shoved under the rug, as do Tarnas and Wilber. Tarnas dismisses biblical faith as without interest for thinkers after the Enlightenment.[143] Wilber, in his evolutionary schema, relegates biblical faith to level 4 of a nine-stage progress of the human spirit.[144]

The real conflict is between monism and theism, or what I like to call One-ism or Two-ism, which are strictly and genuinely irreconcilable. The human being is placed presuppositionally and morally before an unavoidable choice. The neopagan dismissal of theism is mere legerdemain to avoid the real religious question. There was only one absentee at the Parliament of the World's Religions that I attended in 1993—biblical theism. The reason? Paganism usually refuses to admit that the real confrontation is between monism and theism, between the world and God, between One-ism and Two-ism, between Homocosmology and Heterocosmology.[145]

To be fair, some pagan theorists do understand the monist/theist confrontation as representing the great religious divide. For instance, the Gnostic theologian Stephan Hoeller speaks of two kinds of religion: (1) the "internalist" religion (*esoteric*, inward-reaching), which was transmitted underground in the West, was "known to the Gnostics, mystics and alchemists throughout the centuries," and was declared heretical by the other form of religion; and (2) the "externalist" religion (*exoteric*, outward-reaching), by which he means theistic biblical faith.[146]

Scholars of religion use this terminology in defining religious approaches to truth. Hoeller uses the terms to eliminate "exoteric" religion as a thoroughly unworthy and dangerous system of thought. Believing that only Gnosticism will help avert the final catastrophe, Hoeller pleads for a wholeness that

---

143. "The traditional image of the Semitic-Augustinian-Protestant God, who creates man too weak to withstand evil temptation, and who predestines the majority of his human creatures to eternal damnation with little consideration of their good works or honest attempts at virtue, ceased to be either palatable or plausible to many sensitive members of modern culture. . . . In light of psychoanalysis, the Judaeo-Christian God could be seen as a reified psychological projection based on the child's naïve view of its libidinally restrictive and seemingly omnipotent parent." Tarnas, *Passion*, 316–17.

144. See ibid., 25; Wilber, *A Theory of Everything*, 80–82.

145. See my forthcoming book, *Trouble in Neverland: Only the Truth Can Save Us*, in which these terms will be explained.

146. Stephan A. Hoeller, *Jung and the Lost Gospels: Insights into the Dead Sea Scrolls and the Nag Hammadi Library* (Wheaton, IL: Quest Books, 1989), 3, 8–9.

includes the great world religions such as Buddhism and Hinduism. His admirable desire for "wholeness," however, excludes one exoteric religious tradition. Hoeller foresees banishing the biblical spirituality that has dominated the West for the last two thousand years. At least he is honest in his desire to eliminate as toxic the biblical view of Jesus when he says:

> Our spiritual enfeeblement is *not* due to a fall from grace on the part of Adam and Eve . . . and our regeneration will not come about by accepting a personal savior [or] by a risen redeemer, but only by the reconciliation of the gods and goddesses within us.[147]

In the main, it is the orthodox theologians of the past, over against all attempts at "synthesis," that have clearly maintained the "antithesis."

Abraham Kuyper, in his Stone Lectures of 1898, said, regarding the deep antithesis within human history: "Do not forget that the fundamental contrast has always been, is still, and always will be until the end: Christianity and Paganism,[148] the idols or the living God."[149] Writing in the 1920s, J. Gresham Machen, a stalwart defender of Christian orthodoxy and a father of presuppositional apologetics, noted the beginning of this eventually radical, apostate movement. Machen identified the liberalism entering the mainline churches in his day as paganism in Christian dress,[150] and adeptly put his finger on the essence of this apostasy at a time when it was not so obvious:

> The truth is that liberalism has lost sight of the very centre and core of the Christian teaching. . . . One attribute of God is absolutely fundamental in the Bible . . . in order to render intelligible all the rest. *That attribute is the awful transcendence of God.* It is true, indeed, that not a sparrow falls to the ground without Him. But He is immanent in the world not because He is identified with the world, but because He is the free Creator and upholder of it. Between the creature and the Creator a great gulf is fixed.[151]

---

147. Ibid., 10.

148. In recent times, Carl F. H. Henry, in his *Twilight of a Great Civilization: The Drift Toward Neo-Paganism* (Wheaton, IL: Crossway, 1988), 15, used the term *paganism* as the implication of our turning away from biblical truth: "Our generation is lost to the truth of God, to the reality of divine revelation, to the content of God's will, to the power of His redemption, and to the authority of His Word. *For this loss it is paying dearly in a swift relapse to paganism.*"

149. Abraham Kuyper, *Lectures on Calvinism* (Grand Rapids: Eerdmans, 1931), 199.

150. He used the synonym *naturalism*.

151. J. Gresham Machen, *Christianity and Liberalism* (Grand Rapids: Eerdmans, 1923), 62–63.

The last word goes to the apostle Paul, who, under the inspiration of the Holy Spirit, juxtaposed the only two possible religious approaches to life, giving us the presuppositional touchstone for our apologetics, no matter how pagan our world may become:

> They exchanged the truth about God for a lie and worshiped and served the creature rather than the Creator, who is blessed forever! Amen. (Rom. 1:25)

25

SERVANT THINKING:
THE POLANYIAN WORKINGS
OF THE FRAMEAN TRIAD

ESTHER L. MEEK

I AM GRATEFUL for the opportunity to contribute a celebrative essay in honor of John Frame's retirement. It is particularly momentous for me because John's approach to a biblically shaped epistemology, in particular, his signature triad motif, has figured prominently both as a guide to my growing understanding and in my mature thought. I owe "Mr. Frame," as I knew him when I was his student, a profound debt. This essay, I trust, will show that.

All my life, it seems, I have wanted to understand human knowing in the context of submission to the Lord of Scripture. I need not cast that in a past tense; it continues! It still seems to me that I need study no other thing besides knowing! Knowing *knowing* gives me the world. A key difference between the past and the present, however, is that anxiety has turned into delightful adventure.

At a critical juncture in my young life, as I was embarking on the formal study of philosophy, God set me down in Frame's massive theology and apologetics class, one that was a prototype for his *DKG*. I had already become acquainted with a Van Tillian, Calvinian, and presuppositional approach, thanks to a most influential undergraduate philosophy professor; the approach seemed commonsensical theologically and epistemologically.[1] Soon after my initial acquaintance with Frame's work, I also encountered that of Hungarian scientist-turned-philosopher Michael Polanyi, and eventually chose to write a dissertation on his epistemic realism.[2]

These facts of the story hardly communicate the desperation I felt about knowing. On the outside, I have always been "a good little Christian girl"; on the inside, from middle school and even earlier, I have felt clueless about knowing, and I have felt that this was a terrible thing. It seems I was born a skeptic, and a Cartesian one: it just seemed obvious to me that I could be certain only of the ideas in my mind. I had no proof that a material world existed outside my mind, let alone that God existed outside my mind! Not until I had spent decades wrestling with this did I come to see that, as recently deceased philosopher Marjorie Grene put it, the *Cogito* is one of the greatest falsehoods of philosophy, and I underwent a kind of bodily "conversion" from it.[3]

In those decades of dark unknowing, I took the only orientation I could figure to take, navigating by two human lights: John Frame and Michael Polanyi. Frame gave a believable account of knowing God and of what that implies for human knowing (to the extent that I could make sense of it); Polanyi made sense of how human knowing works (to the extent that I could make sense of that). I didn't "know" that they were right—but I "hooked my dinghy to their cruise ships," figuring they knew better than I did. It

---

1. James M. Grier has been one of the most influential people in my life. He is emeritus professor and former dean of Grand Rapids Baptist Seminary, and he continues to preach around the world, and to sit on medical ethics boards. Many of us, his students, have had our lives shaped by him. In 1977, when Mr. Grier finished his orals at Westminster for his ThM (a couple of years after I had been his student), I recall that Mr. Frame came out of the room (I was waiting in the library) and told me that it had been the finest oral exam he had ever heard.

2. Esther L. Meek, *Contact with Reality: An Examination of Realism in the Thought of Michael Polanyi* (PhD diss., Temple University, 1983). Revised version forthcoming from Paternoster Press as *Contact with Reality: Polanyi's Realism and Its Value for Christian Faith*.

3. Marjorie Grene helped Polanyi prepare his Gifford Lectures for publication. As a visiting professor at Temple University, she served informally on my dissertation committee. Her books include *The Knower and the Known* (Berkeley: University of California Press, 1974; hardback ed., 1966) and *A Philosophical Testament* (Peru, IL: Open Court, 1995), as well as numerous monographs on a wide array of philosophers. Her career spanned from studying with Heidegger in the early 1930s to collaborating in philosophy of biology in the 2000s. She was the first woman to be honored with a volume in the prestigious Library of Living Philosophers—*The Philosophy of Marjorie Grene* (Peru, IL: Open Court, 2002). I fear I cannot track down the source for this quotation; however, all of these works testify to her long-standing conviction regarding the *Cogito*.

was a reasonable risk to take to make it through the dark channel to some harbor of light and peace. I continually returned to reread their work and hold it up to my own experience to see where I was and how my pondering was doing. When I was finally given a chance to voice the direction of my thought, in 2000, I found that the working hypotheses, without my conscious realization, had melded and had become mine. My guinea-pig students also reflected that back to me, and cognitive rest, a godly sense of satisfaction, settled into my life.[4]

The angst abated; the adventure continues! What Frame and Polanyi gave me is not complete information, but a "way to go on."[5] Indeed, if knowing is what I think it is, an unfolding journey, this is the finest gift. It is how one lives artfully, knowingly, *coram Deo*. What I received from each thinker is a motif or strategy; what I have done is blend them. In this essay I want to show you that blend. But these motifs remain allusively powerful strategies; they continue to be fruitful precisely because they are difficult to specify exhaustively, because they "bear indeterminately on reality," as Polanyi would say. So in preparation to write this essay, I have puzzled afresh, and fruitfully, over the Framean triad and the Polanyian structure of knowing.

My conviction that knowing knowing is the place to start, and may justifiably warrant a lifetime of preoccupation, is something that I share with Frame, Polanyi, and John Calvin. In this I see God's good providence in leading me to know these people. Frame follows Calvin in starting with the knowledge of God, and seeing that as "the same thing from a different perspective" as knowledge of self. In his foreword to the recently rereleased *Tacit Dimension*, Amartya Sen speaks of Polanyi's "extraordinarily ambitious attempt to achieve an understanding of the world—physical as well as mental—through the perspective of knowledge."[6] There is something about knowing knowing that is a natural place to start as well as a window on everything else. This obvious truism is also profound: to know any sub-

---

4. That initial synthesis is documented in Esther L. Meek, *Longing to Know: The Philosophy of Knowledge for Ordinary People* (Grand Rapids: Brazos, 2003). Frame wrote a gracious review of the book for *Presbyterion* 29:2 (Fall 2003), online at http://www.frame-poythress.org/frame_articles/2003Meek.html.

5. A common phrase of Ludwig Wittgenstein in his *Philosophical Investigations*: this is what a child says, having been taught a number series, at the unformalizable point that he "gets it." Wittgenstein was one philosopher whose work Frame appreciated and referenced often in *DKG*. In particular, Frame took to heart Wittgenstein's idea of meaning as use (97). I believe it plays somewhat into his definition of theology as application.

6. Amartya Sen, foreword to Michael Polanyi, *The Tacit Dimension* (Chicago: University Press, 1966, 2009), ix.

ject matter involves you in knowing; human action (as opposed to chance happenings) of any sort involves knowing. So knowing is a window on the world and on our relationship with God. Thus, knowing knowing naturally opens out into all of life.

At one point in *DKG*, Frame avers that epistemology, as a discipline, is not absolutely necessary to the Christian life.[7] I would agree, technically. However, Christian discipleship stands in sore need, I believe, of the ministrations of what I call "epistemological therapy." Epistemological therapy is what I see myself as committed to for a lifetime. Frame certainly shares this conviction, for his laborious triperspectival approach in *DKG* just is his own thorough effort to administer it. What Christians get wrong about knowing poisons and truncates their knowing God without their being aware of it. What we get wrong about knowing[8] comes about because our epistemological naiveté has led us to absorb biblically defective penchants of the Western philosophical tradition, which then thwart our being shaped, epistemologically and wholly, by Scripture. This situation was worth Frame's addressing it years ago, and it is worth continuing to do so.

Frame strove to develop an account of "servant thinking."[9] All of life is about knowing God as Lord. This is literally true! For everything that exists, from least to greatest, exists by virtue of being covenantally known, and thus constituted as real, by God. That is what the covenantal lordship of God entails. All that is known into existence by him is thereby dependent on him, existing for his praise, before his gaze in interpersonal relationship with one who both transcends (in authority and power) and is near (in intimate solidarity)—as the best sort of father-child relationship, the best sort of king-subject relationship.

Created reality just is this covenant relationship with the Lord. Creation knows God as Lord, or it doesn't exist! But knowing, on any reckoning of what knowing is, is only part of that reality-encompassing relationship. Submissive action (obedience) is obviously part of it, and so is interpersonal communion. In fact, what starts to appear is a triad of aspects that together constitute a dynamic interpersonal covenantal relationship. I think that the Framean triad has as its powerful, life-giving root the fact that it is the signature, "interaspectivally" allusive, multidimensionality of interpersonal

7. *DKG*, 105.
8. This is arguably one dimension of the noetic effects of sin.
9. *DKG*, 40.

relationship. The triad recurs in reality because reality is shot through with the interpersonhood of covenant relationship.

So, of course, created reality everywhere evidences those aspects—the normative (or covenantally constitutive), the existential (or interpersoned intimacy), and the situational (the real, uncreated and created). I and many others have found that the Framean triadic motif proves most apt to develop and orchestrate the fundamental dimensions of most any subject. Jesus? Prophet, Priest, and King. Ethics? Standard, motive, and goal. Philosophy? Ethics, metaphysics, and epistemology. When I wrote a book that developed Polanyi's approach to knowing, remembering Frame's triad proved a key to unpacking the account in an innovative way. Polanyian subsidiary clues (which I will explain later in this essay) fell neatly into . . . the surface features of the world, the lived body, and "the directions."[10] Every point in reality, I believe, has its normative, situational, and existential aspects.[11]

Of course, any account of human knowing that does deference to the lordship of God should be something viably named "servant thinking." If all being is servant being, we may say that all knowing, knowing God or knowing anything (they are two perspectives of the same thing), is servant knowing. Servant thinking involves, in one's account and enactment of knowing, acknowledging God as Lord in his authority, power, and covenant solidarity.

Frame indicates that triperspectivalism captures servant thinking both in its acknowledgment of the three ways we know God as Lord and also in the situatedness that is integral to being created persons: we have to

10. Meek, *Longing to Know*, chap. 13.

11. In preparing to write this essay, I have been playing mentally with a picture of tessellated (I think that word refers to a repeated pattern) overlapping equilateral triangles. The center point of each triangle is the angle point of another. You can choose to "stand" at one center point (or angle point), and from that point reckon the normative in one direction, the situational in another, and the existential in a third. On a picture diagram, I imagine you could from that chosen point make all the top points of triangles be, say, yellow, all the bottom left points be, say, red, and all the bottom right points be, say, blue. One thing this receding repetition of triangle picks up is Frame's (and Vern Poythress's, as I recall) sense that the normative perspective, for example, involves the existential and the situational, the existential perspective of the normative perspective involves its own normative and situational, etc. This quickly runs beyond at least my foggy comprehension. But I do think that this is why the triad is so rich and allusive; it's like hearing a range of overtones in a musical chord. One thing that the tessellated diagram doesn't represent, and that I think is profoundly critical, is that the perspectives do not diverge, as would the blue, red, and yellow swaths of points. I think that covenant interpersonhood binds even the receding resonances together. Interpersonal relationship, although it is ever mysterious, is nevertheless palpably concrete and, in God's lavish grace, a most common experience.

move around if we are going to see all sides of something, and we have to see from one point to another—we have to orient from something toward something else. Although human knowing has been disfigured by sin, this dancing situatedness is our glory as humans, not some sort of metaphysical and epistemological defect of finitude.

Knowing for humans involves starting from my embodied, historied, situated, divinely accompanied person, with knee bowed before my heavenly Father—a submissive heart commitment. This is what John Frame means by a presupposition. In *DKG*, he helpfully contrasts it with epistemic foundationalism, the still-popular idea that, for there to be knowledge, there must be a foundation of certain truths; and with epistemic conventionalism, the still-popular alternative idea that a presupposition or worldview is a postulate that we arbitrarily adopt.[12]

At the time, in my beginning steps as an adult Christian, although I only half understood, this rang true to my Christianity. Presuppositionalism struck me both as undeniable and as a relief: every philosophy, not just Christianity, starts from presuppositions. But it also struck me as continuing to leave me in a perilous quandary: why this presupposition rather than another? Why *God*? It seemed so arbitrary. I did not see at the time what I have only lately come to understand, that this sort of commitment is so profoundly interpersonal in character, rather than aridly arbitrary. To trust and love another person is immensely risky, but it isn't arbitrary, and it isn't a working hypothesis!

Another thing I found especially significant about the Framean triad was the presence of the normative dimension. Frame memorably said that epistemology is a subset of ethics. Anyone who is my age and who has experienced the dusty desert of objectivism, as I will a bit simplistically designate it, and of analytic philosophy in its heyday in the twentieth century, as Frame did (I surmise), and I did, will appreciate how eye-popping this claim was, and how difficult to grasp. It made sense theologically, but philosophically?

At the time, I thought that *truth*—meaning all the propositions about reality, I confess!—was the ultimate thing to seek; Frame contexted truth in *oughtness*! Over time I came to believe that where there is oughtness, there is covenant—so *covenant* is the largest "box" in which we find ourselves! But now I realize that where there is covenant, there are persons in com-

12. *DKG*, 68, 128, 125.

munion. *Persons in communion* is, indeed, the largest "box." This is what Frame was saying, Calvin too, but it has taken me some years and paths of personal inquiry to get it. For Frame's exposition in *DKG* starts with God as covenant Lord.

Now I am able to see what then I only sensed, that Frame, with his perspectival triad, was doing epistemological therapy, unpacking the implications of the lordship of God (in the Calvinian tradition), in direct challenge to objectivism—not so much in critique of philosophy as in rehabilitation of it. The normative, I believe, as with all three aspects, is a *sine qua non* of personhood and interpersonhood (my concocted term). Just as Walker Percy, following Charles Sanders Peirce, affirms that persons are triadic in contrast with even the most humanized pet, which is only dyadic, Frame's normative is that person-defining third aspect.[13] But objectivism has had no place in its epistemology for the normative; instead, it has diminished the self to a dot and, as a result, the world it exalted to a question mark.[14]

At the time, I half understood the Framean triad. But when I encountered Polanyi, I found obvious resonances as well as a much-needed "way to go on." If Frame offered the parameters of human knowing in the context of biblical lordship, then Polanyi showed me how it worked.[15] Polanyi, like Frame, was offering a frontal challenge to objectivism. He was not doing it in the name of theology; he was doing it in preservation of science.[16] His

13. Walker Percy, *Lost in the Cosmos: The Last Self-Help Book* (New York: Picadore USA, 1983).

14. The postmodern critique of modernism can be interpreted using the Framean triad. In rightly calling into question the extremely damaging arrogance of claiming to be presupposition-less, the postmodern critique shows that modernism was attempting to deny the normative and diminish the existential. The postmodern reaction has often been to deny the situational and exalt the normative (not the existential, as people mistakenly think: subjectivism is really hyper-modernism—although of course there is plenty of that around, too).

15. We may say that Polanyi offers a situational and existential perspective on Frame's normative proposals.

16. In the 1930s, Michael Polanyi encountered and was dismayed by the growing popularity of socialized science in the United Kingdom and the Soviet Union. In an effort to dispute it, he searched the history of philosophy for an account of what he knew to be operative in scientific discovery. He found that philosophy offered no rationale for scientific discovery—that if the standard epistemology of certainty were correct, no scientific discovery could ever take place. He believed that faulty epistemology had led to the destruction of his Europe at the beginning of the twentieth century. He set about to offer an alternative epistemology, to save science and culture. See William Taussig Scott and Martin X. Moleski, *Michael Polanyi: Scientist and Philosopher* (New York: Oxford University Press, 2005).

1958 publication of his Gifford Lectures, *Personal Knowledge: Towards a Post-Critical Philosophy*,[17] showcases the responsible and impassioned commitment of the knower, without which "knowledge" is not knowledge. Thus he underscores the personal presupposition and the normative dimensions of all human knowing. I felt that this radically aligned with Frame's project.

But perhaps as Aristotle must have appeared to Aquinas, so Polanyi appeared to me in my quest to justify Christianity to myself and others: he was a philosopher with no explicitly Christian agenda who was nevertheless underscoring things that the character of Scripture's God implied. What is more, he was talking about *how knowing works*, and it made sense.

Now I come to the signature Polanyian motif which, like Frame's triad, occurs throughout human knowing, and brings (me, at least) an incrementally superior insight into the triad, into servant thinking, and into life. Polanyi is known for saying, "We know more than we can tell," and setting about to argue for the existence of tacit knowledge.[18] But his most important contribution is less widely recognized. As Grene says, it is not the existence of the tacit so much as its relationship to explicit knowledge that is "grounds for a revolution in philosophy."[19] All knowing involves the active, personally responsible struggle to shape integratively a pattern, relying subsidiarily on unspecifiable clues. All knowing involves two mutually related "levels" of awareness in a vectorially oriented structure. The word *subsidiary* implies this far better than does the word *tacit*. The word *integration* has in view the fact that the focal whole transfigures the clues on which it relies: that the clues are apprehended as such within the pattern, that they take on transformative meaning and appearance, as well as unlocking vistas of the real. Subsidiary-focal, "from-to," integration characterizes all acts of coming to know as well as all truth claims that we continue to hold responsibly.

You can see the subsidiary-focal integrative structure of knowing wherever you look. Take the everyday experience of reading—something you are performing at this instant. You are attending, not exactly *to*, but rather *from*, the letters and words printed on paper in the book you hold, or appearing on the screen of the computer at which you work. You rely on them subsidiarily, such that if I suddenly wrest the book from your

17. University of Chicago Press.

18. Polanyi, *Tacit Dimension*, 4. "Tacit Knowing," the first lecture in the book, is perhaps the best entree into Polanyi's account of knowing.

19. Marjorie Grene, "Tacit Knowing: Grounds for a Revolution in Philosophy," *Journal of the British Society for Phenomenology* 8 (October 1977): 164–71.

grasp, you stop following this train of thought (and start another sort of epistemological project!). But subsidiary and focal are so integrally connected that the Times New Roman type is fraught with meaning, and the meaning is full of the type, of the manner of expression, of the language, and of me, the author.

Particulars-turned-subsidiary clues include—as I mentioned before—features of the world, but also normative and existential ones. Subsidiary clues effectively function as extensions of our lived body, much as when I wield a hammer and it extends my lived body.[20] And, Polanyi avers, normative structures such as interpretive frameworks, or even languages, work like hammers, too. I indwell them, I pour myself into them, to attend beyond me to a further focus or project. All knowing involves integrative orientation from subsidiary to focal, from *from* to *to* and beyond. Polanyi demonstrates, throughout all of science, and about even the "most precise" scientific knowledge, that the "tacit coefficient" always undergirds and outruns it.

I will return to this motif and its connection to the Framean triad presently. My first and deeply significant realization about Polanyi's work was that it gave me a way to make ordinary human sense of faith and commitment. These had been, for me, "religious" terms that I didn't know how to unpack epistemically, whose opacity threatened to render my whole Christianity suspect. Commitment figures large in Polanyi's "fiduciary programme."[21] It involves the knower's exercising responsibility to own the truth he or she claims, not as over against reality, but in deference to it. Luther's ringing "Here I stand; I cannot do otherwise" Polanyi cites as expressing the act of upholding any truth claim, exercising great personal responsibility, yet simultaneously being compelled by submission to reality. Polanyi's alternative

20. I repeatedly use the word, *lived*, appropriated from Maurice Merleau-Ponty, to mark Polanyi's claim that our body is the only thing in the world that we normally experience, not as an object, but subsidiarily, as it bears on the world to which we attend (Polanyi, "Tacit Knowing," 16; see Merleau-Ponty's *The Phenomenology of Perception*, trans. Colin Smith [New York: Routledge and Kegan Paul, 1962]). Merleau-Ponty distinguishes this body-as-subject from body-as-object. This is the very thing that makes us feel that our body is *our* body, Polanyi says. This is why, Meek says, it is so weird to go to a doctor for a physical or a surgeon for an operation: to him or her, you are a medical specimen and plumbing. But we know our own bodies as we employ them to bear on reality. I know my left pinky as the typer of a's, q's, z's, left shifts, exclamation points, etc., or as integral to making a G chord on a guitar neck, or as the tension maintainer of the yarn when I am crocheting. That is the lived body.

21. Polanyi, *Personal Knowledge*, chap. 4, sec. 8; chap 8, sec. 12, for example.

vision of knowing daringly espouses the normative and existential dimensions of knowing, thus according profoundly with Frame.

But Polanyi makes it clear that what commitment refers to is our "manner of disposing ourselves," our personal assimilation whereby we press a tool or a framework into subsidiary service, indwelling it to extend ourselves in pursuit of the yet to be known.[22] Commitment refers to the clues we indwell subsidiarily in pursuit of a focal pattern. If that is so, then something as ordinary as my keeping balance on my bike as I ride to the store is commitment, and it is a lived body feel of a tool or framework indwelt with confidence.[23] Polanyi shows how commitment always involves my lived body. Since, for Polanyi, commitment, as indwelling subsidiaries, is essential to all knowing, it is part and parcel of "reason," rather than opposed to it. My indwelling Scripture to understand God and the world certainly fits this description. If *commitment* isn't an apt term for relying on something, I don't know what is.

There's something else in Polanyi's proposal that also deserves to be called faith or commitment. He paints a graphic and indisputable picture of the scientist in pursuit of the as-yet undiscovered reality. Polanyi raises the philosophically awkward matter of the ancient Meno Dilemma. Posed millennia ago by Plato, in a dialogue by that name, it has never satisfactorily been answered in the Western tradition. How do you come to know? For either you do or you don't know something. If you don't know it, you cannot begin to move toward knowing it; and if you do know it, you don't need to move toward knowing it. Plato used this to set up his suggestion that all learning is recalling. But this did not really resolve the dilemma. Aristotle sidestepped the dilemma by concentrating, not on coming to know (discovery), but on explanation. Most of Western philosophy has tried to make do with these less-than-satisfying alternatives. Knowledge has been deemed to be about certainty, leaving the question begging desperately to be answered, How do you *come* to know? It is a wonder, really, not to mention a radical challenge to philosophy, that scientific discovery has nevertheless taken place at a great rate.

Polanyi, who as a young man was rapidly gaining notoriety for his stellar scientific research, before he felt compelled to turn aside to redo philosophy to save science, argues that the reality of scientific discovery

22. Ibid., 61.
23. Meek, *Longing to Know*, chap. 7.

shows that we know more than we can tell—that human knowledge must be more than that which is exhaustively articulable in true statements. There must be "anticipative" knowledge, as I call it. "The kind of tacit knowledge that solves the paradox of the *Meno* consists in the intimation of something hidden, which we may yet discover. . . . We can have a tacit foreknowledge of yet undiscovered things." In fact, whenever we take a claim to be true, "we commit ourselves to a belief in all these as yet undisclosed, perhaps as yet unthinkable, consequences."[24] Polanyi concludes that the paradigmatic case of scientific knowledge is the knowledge of an approaching discovery. *Approaching!* This has always astounded me! "To hold such knowledge is an act deeply committed to the conviction that there is something there to be discovered. . . . The discoverer is filled with a compelling sense of responsibility for the pursuit of a hidden truth, which demands his services for revealing it."[25] Polanyi testified that the scientist navigates by "groping or scrabbling," guided by a "sense of increasing proximity to the solution."[26]

I hope you can easily see why Polanyi's words made my Christian heart sing, and my darkened-*Cogito* mind start to yearn for the light! Commitment to a half-understood, as yet not fully discovered reality? This too makes earthy sense of what we mean by faith. For me, and for scores of my students now, Polanyi's work has helped us to align our Christian knowing with every other kind of knowing, including the most elegant scientific discovery, and the most creative artistic achievement. It brings all human knowing together.

It also helps us understand Scripture more profoundly. We are on the way to knowing. Our conversion can be a sudden epiphany, when we see the picture differently and a profound integrative pattern transforms everything including ourselves. "Did not our hearts burn within us as we talked with him on the way?"[27] Prophecies are not predictions so much as

---

24. Polanyi, *Tacit Dimension*, 22–23.

25. Ibid., 25. Polanyi's realism, expressed repeatedly in tantalizing statements such as this one, drew me, like the waters of an oasis in a dry desert, to write a dissertation on it. Only years later did Lesslie Newbigin help me make the connection that what so drew me to Polanyi was . . . God. See footnote 42.

26. Michael Polanyi, "The Creative Imagination," *Chemical and Engineering News* 44 (April 25, 1966): 85–93.

27. This is the comment of the disciples who encountered Jesus on the road to Emmaus, realizing that he was the resurrected Christ only after they saw him break bread and give thanks (Luke 24:13–35). In *Longing to Know*, I talk about this as one of Scripture's best "Oh! I see it!" moments.

promises, anticipative knowing.[28] Knowing is less about information and more about transformative encounter. Obedience is lived truth. Legalism, by contrast, is an inappropriate fixating on what should be subsidiarily lived. Knowing unfolds, I now believe, as covenantal relationship to the end of communion. Knowing always involves authoritative guides.[29] These are some of the insights I have developed over the years.

We can start to make sense of being "on the way" in our knowing. Polanyi helps me make sense of Frame's repeatedly juxtaposed claims that the unbeliever knows God, and the unbeliever does not know God. All unbelievers may be said to know God anticipatively. For all knowing, as Frame said, is knowing God, and as Simone Weil helpfully terms it, is a "form of the implicit love of God."[30] The sophistication and realism of the Polanyian account allows us to make sense of knowing what you don't know, and not knowing what you do know, or knowing that you don't know, and knowing that you almost know . . . I could go on! And so the complexities of the unbeliever's knowledge of God don't just have to do with sin; they have to do with being human and being on the way to knowing, from one juncture toward and through another. And in being on the way, humbly we must admit, unbelievers and believers are not so different, except that, for now, Christians have, in God's sovereign grace, partly understood and been embraced by Christ the Truth.

Additionally, Polanyi helps[31] my grasp of the Framean triad by giving me a little more sense of how it works. Frame calls the normative, the situational, and the existential, *perspectives*. He uses this to say the following

28. Theologian Mike Williams showed me this alignment between a proper understanding of prophecy and what Polanyi is saying. Williams says this: there is no way that Isaiah knew Jesus of Nazareth; knowing Jesus of Nazareth, there is no way we can avoid seeing him in Isaiah 53 (personal conversation).

29. All these and other insights about knowing in connection with Scripture constitute my "covenant epistemology" as developed in *Contours of Covenant Epistemology: Conversations on the Way to Knowing* (currently in draft form). See also Esther L. Meek, "Learning to See: The Role of Authoritative Guides in Knowing," *Tradition and Discovery* 23, 2 (2005–6): 38–49 (available at http://www.missouriwestern.edu/orgs/polanyi/TAD%20WEB%20ARCHIVE/TAD32-2/TAD32-2-fnl-pg38-50-pdf.pdf); also "Longing to Know and Reading the Bible," *Comment* (Publication of Work Research Foundation, Canada, March 2006) (available at http://wrf.ca/comment/article.cfm?ID=181).

30. Simone Weil, *Waiting for God* (New York: Perennial, 2001).

31. "Polanyi helps!" is a bumper-sticker-size aphorism that expresses how I believe Polanyi's work bears on just about any topic, philosophical or otherwise. I often feel that Polanyi's insights make any person's work better.

sorts of things. All knowing is knowing God's law; all knowing is knowing the world; all knowing is self-knowledge. It is the same "content," seen from a different perspective. He even says they are identical.[32] Frame wants to hold the perspectives together even as he distinguishes between them. He talks of these avenues of knowing as being "perspectivally related."[33] Perspectives on ethics, for example—the perspective of the law, of the situation, and of the person—will be perspectives on each other and on the whole. All knowledge, Frame says, involves a subject who knows an object according to some standard or criterion (law).[34] Knowledge is an ethically responsible orientation of the person to his experience.[35] So knowing, by definition, involves the three aspects.

The perspectives wonderfully align with the ways in which God is Lord, each way being the lordship of God in one of the perspectives. Thus, the perspectives are integrally connected to our covenantal status as servant. Knowledge of God is knowledge of his authority, his law, knowledge of his control and of his natural revelation, and knowledge of his presence.[36] This affords Frame a structure for his theology of lordship. However, he is explicit: it doesn't matter where you start on the triad! He maintains that the perspectives are equally ultimate, equally important, and equally mutually dependent: each needs the other two to be what it is itself.[37] He speaks of this as generic Calvinism, in that it accords to natural revelation equal authority as that of Scripture.[38]

Really, what Frame was doing here was incredibly innovative at the time, and still is. I think that is true both theologically and philosophically. Although what he was doing was taking seriously the thought of Van Til, the theology of Calvin, and the witness of Scripture, it still is breathtaking. Theologically, is he really saying that Scripture says the world and a person's internal conviction are as authoritative as the Scripture?[39] And philosophi-

---

32. *DKG*, 71.

33. Ibid., 89.

34. Ibid., 107.

35. Ibid., 149. I note here a fundamental alignment between Frame's understanding of knowing and Polanyi's.

36. Ibid., *passim*.

37. Ibid., 163.

38. Ibid., 138.

39. One thing I find helpful to say here is that the normative, specifically Scripture, is not all there is to God or God's revelation. It is not the situational, nor the existential. But of the three, obviously, it is the one that is normative and functions normatively with respect to both me and

cally, is he really saying that knowing the world is always interpretive, according to a normative standard? Apparently the triad allows him to delineate the respects in which these things are so.

I do not need to say more for the reader of Frame's work to acknowledge that the triad can be inscrutable, even as it is allusively insightful. But Polanyi helps, as I said. For all knowing is perspectival, in the sense that it involves orienting from one point in the direction of another. The nature of that orientation involves relying on a subsidiary indwelling of the proximal from which we attend to focus outward on the other.

John Frame grew up in Pittsburgh, which I am now delighted to call my home. Pittsburghers are especially proud of the view from Mt. Washington. People say it is the second most popular evening view in the United States (the most popular one being the Grand Canyon). If you stand on Mt. Washington, just south of the confluence of the Allegheny and the Monongahela, to form the Ohio River, which defines Pittsburgh's Golden Triangle,[40] you get a spectacular view of the city. You could also view the city from the North Shore, from the upper stands of PNC Park, for example. Or you can see it from the east from University of Pittsburgh's towering Cathedral of Learning. The view from the cathedral of the 1960 World Series in the old Forbes Field was famously memorialized in a *Life* magazine photograph. A perspective is a *view from a certain point*. It's not as if the view from Mt. Washington is more Pittsburgh than the view from the Cathedral of Learning. Nor is it that somehow a perspective is not the thing itself: if you come to visit me and I want to show you Pittsburgh as it really is, I am going to take you to Mt. Washington for the view!

In his intellectual autobiography, Frame notes that his perspectivalism came into incipient form as he studied with Princeton's Dennis O'Brien, as he witnessed how the professor indwelled the thought of first one philosopher and then another to see the world: the same world, from different perspectives. Studying later with Van Til, he realized that fundamentally, when it comes to humans and God and his world, there must be three views-from-which: God, humanity, and the nonhuman world.

---

the world. By contrast, the situational isn't meant to function as the normative per se, nor is the existential. What these contribute is different, distinctively their own. Yet in that contribution they nevertheless reveal something of God that is authoritative (their normative aspect) and integral.

40. Maybe triangles are a Pittsburgh thing.

So Frame thinks of perspectives as views-from-which: you stand at the one point and look toward the other. The word *perspective* can refer to the point from which you look, the act of looking, or the looked-at. The looked-at could perhaps be distinguished as *aspect*, rather than perspective: for example, the normative aspect of natural revelation or of human knowing. But the act of looking, the connecting from the one to the other—that strategy of positioning oneself at one point and looking from it toward the other—is a critical feature of what Frame has in mind by perspective as well.

Consider this comment of Polanyi's, found in his introduction to his three-lecture series, *The Tacit Dimension*: "This structure [of tacit knowing] shows that all thought contains components of which we are subsidiarily aware in the focal content of our thinking, and that all thought dwells in its subsidiaries, as if they were parts of our body. Hence thinking is not only necessarily intentional, as Brentano has taught; it is also necessarily fraught with the roots that it embodies. It has a *from-to* structure."[41] Now, I tend to revert to thinking of a perspective as a *point*, as in *point from which*, as we have been saying. This quote contains a critically important corrective. The vectorial directedness of all knowing from subsidiary to focal never leaves the subsidiary behind or minimizes it to a mathematical point. The subsidiary awareness that supports the act of knowing profoundly imbues its focus. Mt. Washington is no mathematical point. You just have to stand there to see what I mean. Traces of coal and steel industry, a legacy of devilishly hard work, life grasped tenaciously amid difficult circumstances the way the two remaining incline railways hug the hillside and steadily climb, horizons formerly aflame and smoke-filled from belching Bessemers, now green in both senses of the word, the palpable quiet of being high in the air, the closeness of the Pittsburgh clouds, memories of the sky filled with displays of Zambelli fireworks over a massive summer regatta or blazing stadiums . . . the Mt. Washington view of Pittsburgh is fraught with its foreground.[42]

41. Polanyi, *Tacit Dimension*, xviii.
42. We might say that this is an existential perspective on the situational. I can imagine another hillside view that is, for me, a normative perspective on the situational. Here in my hometown of Aliquippa, downstream on the Ohio a bit from Pittsburgh, I can stand up in Plan Six, where the Jones & Laughlin Steel upper crust had homes, and gaze down on a now-empty seven-mile stretch of shore where the mill used to be, which for decades now has been an abandoned eyesore. This *should* not be. It testifies to the abandonment of this town, which now, in God's working, is being addressed by some exciting and innovative Christian ministries of which I am a part.

In Frame's triad, we may position ourselves at the normative and view the existential.[43] Or we may position ourselves at the situational and view the normative from there. Polanyi helps us retain the important sense of how the view is fraught with the view-from-which. And he shows how we always hold the two together in subsidiary-focal integration. That this makes sense of what Frame is trying to do is corroborated by his (and Van Til's) persistent penchant to speak of revelation of God from nature, of God from man, of man from God, of man from nature, of nature from God, of nature from man: the orientation from the view-from-which in the direction of the view is perhaps the main thing. To delineate it you need an ordered pair of coordinates, so to speak. But for Polanyi, that is just how all human knowing is: from-to!

Take, for example, the interpretation humans do as part and parcel of all our knowing and living. Interpretation is the existential's perspective on the situational. Or you can be talking about interpretation as the normative aspect of the existential. Either way, it really takes specifying the two coordinates, one with respect to, or with a view to, the other, to get at what is of interest. Interpretation is an example of one or two coordinate pairs for which we actually have a term. It helps to see us as doing that from-to, relying on the one that is "near" to focus on the one that is "far."

Much of this essay has been about how Polanyi helps Frame—how the Polanyian motif of subsidiary-focal integration complements, amplifies, and renders insightful the rich complexities of the Framean triad. Does Frame return the favor? Is there any way that Polanyi's legacy profits from Frame's? Besides my little triadic grouping of the subsidiaries in my account in *Longing to Know*, there is something far more profound—implicit in Polanyi's work, I believe, but sadly only implicit. I do not doubt that Polanyi saw himself as a follower of Christ. I do believe that the misdirection of the modernist theology that he embraced hampered his following through on his own best insights. Polanyi devoted much effort to articulating a theory of reality as characterized by mutual, emergent levels that correspond to the two-leveled structure of knowing: to know the mind of a professor, for example, a student indwells the professor's bodily workings; the student thus integrates to the "comprehensive entity" that is the professor herself or himself. But what is the highest level of reality? Although so much of his writing alludes power-

43. Grene, in *A Philosophical Testament*, more than once references a helpful term from Helmuth Plessner—*eccentric positionality*. Humans are the only animals who can and do place themselves outside their bodies. I have this in mind as I talk here of using the triad.

fully beyond itself to this, Polanyi fell short of acknowledging explicitly that reality, in its ultimate "level," is the infinite Person, One by whom, in our knowing, we find ourselves fully known.[44]

But it—God—is there, in Frame. It isn't the triad that is the most stunning feature of Frame's work. It is the covenant nearness and solidarity of the authoritative and powerful heavenly Father, whose knowing us constitutes us and then redeems us. At the end of the day, there is something bigger, for me and for John Frame, than knowing. For knowing is itself one perspective of three that mutually constitute the interpersonal covenant that is reality. It is one view onto the full-orbed relationship that makes us, sustains us, redeems us, and binds us to the Lord of all.

James Loder voices the wonder of this realization: "In the end we will not be able to imagine the depth and magnitude of the reality to which even the best images of the most profound minds are pointing us. All understanding and models must finally become transparent and vanish. Then, in death to all else, each one may appear face to face before the One who always comes from the other side of ultimate human emptiness."[45]

44. Lesslie Newbigin also verbalizes this shortfall, in *Proper Confidence: Faith, Doubt and Certainty in Christian Discipleship* (Grand Rapids: Eerdmans, 1995), 63.

45. James E. Loder, *The Transforming Moment*, 2nd ed. (Colorado Springs: Helmers and Howard, 1989), 8. I have incorporated some of Loder's profound insights into my *Contours*.

PART 4

THE CHURCH

26

A Triperspectival
Model of Ministry

Dennis E. Johnson

IN THE FORTY YEARS since I first met John Frame, first as a prospective seminary student and then as his student and much later as his colleague in pastoral ministry and theological education, I have observed something surprising, even a bit unsettling, about him. By the early 1980s, when we began to serve together as fellow elders of New Life Presbyterian Church (Escondido, California) and faculty colleagues at Westminster Seminary California, my mental image of John had blended intellectual brilliance and personal shyness (as I saw him, at least)—a scholar more at home with books and ideas than with people, especially people with ugly pasts and messy problems. But then this quiet thinker opened his home to take in a man who had recently come to faith in Christ, bringing along his messy "baggage" from pre-Jesus substance abuse. Watching John pour hours of pastoral care into that newborn brother shattered the stereotype that framed my picture of Frame. Compared to the wonder of watching John, beautifully complemented by Mary, serve as a pastor-discipler in the nitty-gritty struggle for the souls of hurting people, other surprising aspects of John Frame (e.g., a classically trained organist coming to the defense of contemporary Christian music) are mild.

631

I am thankful to God for the privilege of serving with John in church and seminary. His sometimes unconventional perspectives on the status quo in Reformed churches and the institutions that serve them, in combination with his own willingness to be pulled out of his personal comfort zone for the cause of Christ and the needs of others, have stretched both my mind and my heart, making me look at my own assumptions and my self-protective complacency from new (and sometimes uncomfortable) perspectives. In particular, I am thankful that he has given us a paradigm that helps pastors maintain biblical balance in their relationship to God's Word and God's people. That paradigm is the theme of this essay.

THREE PERSPECTIVES THAT "FRAME" PASTORAL MINISTRY

In 1997, when the seminary and I sensed God's call to me to refocus from the "safely academic" discipline of New Testament studies to the scarier area of practical theology, I inherited the first-year course in pastoral ministry and homiletics, The Ministry of the Word in Worship, which lays the foundation for the rest of our offerings on the practice of ministry (preaching, counseling, evangelism, cross-cultural missions, leadership and planning, pastoral care, and so on). To structure my version of that course, I turned to a triangular template for theological reflection that I'd learned from John—a threefold way of analyzing how finite humans come to know God, ourselves, and God's world.[1] I later learned that others, too, had found this triperspectival approach, as developed by Frame and Vern Poythress, useful for analyzing the balance of points of attention and investment that maintain biblically faithful ministry in the preaching, nurture, witness, and communal life of the church.[2] In the late

---

1. I honestly cannot recall where and when I first glimpsed John's triperspectival approach to epistemology generally and theological understanding in particular—whether in a classroom as his student in the early 1970s or in conversation as his colleague in the 1980s and 1990s, or when I read its explanation in *DKG* (62–75, 89–90) after its publication in 1987.

2. Notably, see Timothy J. Keller, "A Model for Preaching," a three-part series in the *Journal of Biblical Counseling (JBC)*, vols. 12, 13: "Part One: Three Perspectives on Preaching & the Biblical Aspect," *JBC* 12, 3 (Spring 1994): 36–42; "Part Two: The Situational Aspect," *JBC* 13, 1 (Fall 1994): 39–48; "Part Three: The Personal Aspect," *JBC* 13, 2 (Winter 1995): 51–60. Dr. Keller further developed a triperspectival approach to Christ-centered preaching in a Doctor of Ministry course that he team-taught with Dr. Edmund Clowney at Reformed Theological Seminary Orlando in the late 1990s. Audio recordings of these lectures are available from RTS on iTunes at http://itunes.rts.edu/. I have also heard Dr. Richard Kaufmann, pastor of Harbor Presbyterian Church (Frame's former student and then his pastoral colleague at New

1990s, while Frame was still teaching at Westminster Seminary California, our students and I had a great advantage: in the same semester in which he was teaching them to think triperspectively about human knowledge generally and about apologetic and theological methodology specifically in The Christian Mind course, I was able to follow along the trail he had blazed, showing them in The Ministry of the Word how the same threefold taxonomy can structure our thinking about the dimensions of preaching and pastoral ministry.

We explored the pastor-preacher's responsibility to faithfully interpret and articulate the *message of the Scriptures* (normative), to be *transformed personally* by that message so that his life increasingly conforms to God's words (existential), and to express that message in a way that *takes account of his hearers' contexts*—personal, social, cultural, and intellectual (situational). So we examined, in turn, "preaching and the Word of God" (getting God's message right), "preaching and the man of God" (taking God's message in), and "preaching and the people of God"³ (getting God's message out). I even developed a preaching version of the Frame triperspectival triangle (see below) to flesh out the ministry implications of the existential and situational

---

Life Presbyterian Church in Escondido), propose a triperspectival analysis of balanced church ministries and leadership—linking normative, existential, and situational perspectives with the biblical offices of prophet (authority), priest (presence), and king (power). Note also the influence of triperspectivalism on the theology and practice of ministry of Kaleo Church in San Diego and its elders, David Fairchild and Drew Goodmanson, as exemplified in a conference that they offered at Vintage 21 Church in Raleigh-Durham, North Carolina (http://www.goodmanson.com/2008-07/15/vintage-21-triperspectival-leadership), which has been summarized in a helpful chart, available online at http://www.goodmanson.com/wp-content/uploads/2009/03/tri_pers_colors.pdf. A Doctor of Ministry thesis supervised by Dr. Frame during his years at Westminster Seminary California illustrates appreciation for his insights on the part of a Korean-American pastor/theologian: Ezra Hyun Kim, *Biblical Preaching Is Apologia: An Analysis of the Apologetic Nature of Preaching in Light of Perspectivalism* (Doctor of Ministry project report, Westminster Seminary California, 2000). No doubt other contributions to this festschrift will illustrate further applications of triperspectival analysis to the church's practice of ministry in Word, leadership, and mercy, as her members serve God, one another, and the watching world.

3. As discussed in connection with the situational perspective below, attaching the label *people of God* to the audience of our preaching is not intended to signal that preaching, particularly under the new covenant, should be thought of as addressed only to the "already found" covenant community. Rather, the centrifugal direction of expansion of Christ's kingdom in the power of the Spirit, as portrayed vividly in the book of Acts (foreshadowed in Acts 1:8), creates a situation in which the church, when it gathers to hear the Word and worship the Lord, is to anticipate the presence of unbelievers in its midst and to take their need to hear the gospel announced in intelligible language that makes clear God's truth and authoritative claim on their allegiance (1 Cor. 14:23–25; James 2:2–7; see also 2 Cor. 3:12–13; 4:1–6).

perspectives (with which Reformed students and pastors tend to have more discomfort). I still use this triperspectival paradigm in the course.

In this essay I intend to: (1) offer further comments on what it means to see the pastor's preaching task in terms of the three perspectives, (2) survey the biblical foundation for our paying attention to all three perspectives, (3) offer some historical confirmation for what Scripture has shown us concerning our obligation to attend to all three, and finally (4) conclude with observations on the errors and imbalances that a triperspectival model of ministry can, through our humble dependence on God's sovereign grace, help us to avoid.

SEEING PREACHING IN THREE PERSPECTIVES

The Normative Perspective: Preaching and the Word of God

Frame rightly insists that the written Word of God stands over all three of the perspectives through which we come to apprehend it.[4] The Word sets the norm for our faith and life. It diagnoses the preacher's subjective experience and discloses God's remedy to his fallen nature. It interprets the situation in which preachers and their hearers hear (or mishear) the Word—a situation controlled by God's royal power, though also exhibiting our fallen condition.[5] So it is perhaps an oversimplification to identify the *Word of God* (the Bible) only with the normative perspective of our triangle. In our finitude and our fallenness, even in our preliminary exegesis of a biblical text to be preached next Sunday, we must keep in view not only lexical and syntactic analysis, historical backgrounds, and theological motifs, but also the condition of our own hearts and the cultural context in which we and our listeners live. These existential and situational perspectives do contribute

4. "Certainly Scripture does have a privileged position. What Scripture says must govern our thinking about the world and the self—and about Scripture, too. The reciprocity works this way. We come to know Scripture through our senses and minds (self) and through Scripture's relations with the rest of the world. But then what we read in Scripture must be allowed to correct the ideas we have formed about these other areas. Then as we understand the other areas better, we understand Scripture better" (*DKG*, 89).

5. The helpful category of a biblical passage's Fallen Condition Focus—the particular symptoms of our condition of sin and misery resulting from the fall that confronted the text's original recipients and similarly trouble our hearers, despite the historical and cultural distance between their life situation and ours—is developed by Bryan Chapell, *Christ-Centered Preaching: Redeeming the Expository Sermon*, 2nd ed. (Grand Rapids: Baker, 2005), 50–51.

to (or detract from) our apprehension of the Bible's meaning and message—that is the point of calling them "perspectives" from which to see the other "points" of the triangle.

Fig. 26.1. Frame Perspectival Triangle

Despite these qualifications, however, there is good reason to associate the Bible *most explicitly* with the *normative* perspective, for through his written Word our covenant Lord reveals his standards for his covenant servants' thoughts, motivations, affections, and actions. And this normative perspective is at the apex atop the triangle, signifying that the Word of God *stands over* the preacher, authoritatively mandating what he believes and teaches (God's normative authority), what he values and desires (God's transformative presence), and how he conducts himself among the people of God and the watching world (God's controlling power). As we study Scripture to prepare sermons, preachers must always ask: What are God's norms, the standards of truth and holiness to which the Lord of the covenant calls his image-bearers to conform in their convictions, affections, and actions?

Likewise, the authority of the Word stands over those who hear the Word preached, whether believers or unbelievers. By means of the Word, the Spirit of Christ (whose power and presence are central to the chart because he is central to the process) transforms the faith and the life of listeners. The Spirit operates with and through the preaching of the gospel to enable those whom the Father has given to the Son to hear the latter's voice in that message, so that the spiritually dead come to life (John 5:25). The Spirit not only regenerates but also, as the Word is proclaimed, illumines their minds to catch greater glimpses of God's glory in the face of Christ and sanctifies them to respond to his grace with growing, grateful love and obedience.

The Existential Perspective: Preaching and the Man of God

As we move down the left slope of the triangle, our focus of attention is directed to the preacher as a man of God: What is happening inside me as I wrestle with the text in the presence of its Author? The Lord of the covenant is not only *over* the preacher in his sovereign authority. He is also *with*—and *in*—the preacher in his personal presence. Because he knows the preacher through and through, his Word diagnoses the preacher's deep spiritual need for transformation: first for regeneration, lest he prove to be a blind leader of the blind (Matt. 15:14; 23:16); and then for illumination to grasp the Word rightly, and for sanctification to respond to it, personally, in humility, repentance, trust, love, and hope. Anselm's well-known confession, "I believe in order to understand," captures one dimension of a broader and deeper spiritual truth: "If anyone's will is to do God's will, he will know whether the teaching is from God or whether I am speaking on my own authority" (John 7:17).[6] Getting the message of a biblical text entails so much more than linguistic, literary, historical, and theological analysis! A mind that resists the text and the authority of its divine Speaker will be thwarted in its attempt to plumb its depths. Conversely, one humbled, tender, and receptive to the text's correction will increasingly see in it new facets of Jesus' truth and mercy. So in his weekly wrestling with the Word, the preacher must constantly ask: As I am *coram Deo* ("before God's face") in my study, confronted by the personal presence of my covenant Lord even as I leaf through lexica and commentaries, confessions and theological tomes (and run Bible-search software, of course!), what sort of person must I become in order to preach the Word with integrity, with credibility, and for the glory of God? How does this text confront my own unbelief and self-centeredness, my prone-

---

6. All quotations from the Bible are from the ESV, unless otherwise indicated.

ness to idolatry, to look in all directions for alternative "saviors" to satisfy my heart's hunger and thirst?

The existential perspective also introduces a ray of hope to the preacher who is so aware of his personal weakness, or so cowed by others' opinions, that he is tempted to timidity in his ministry of the Word. The presence of the covenant Lord through his Spirit in us not only exposes our need for the transforming gaze at Christ's glory (2 Cor. 3:18) but also authorizes us to speak as ambassadors of the King of kings (2 Cor. 5:20; Eph. 6:19–20) and empowers our feeble and fallible words so that they can convey his invincible Word with heart-vivifying and life-transforming effect: "I was with you in weakness and in fear and much trembling, and my speech and my message were not in plausible words of wisdom, but in demonstration of the Spirit and of power, that your faith might not rest in the wisdom of men but in the power of God" (1 Cor. 2:3–5). Consequently, "our gospel came to you not only in word, but also in power and in the Holy Spirit and with full conviction. . . . And you became imitators of us and of the Lord, for you received the word in much affliction, with the joy of the Holy Spirit" (1 Thess. 1:5–6).

Therefore, as the preacher hears the Lord of the Word address him, first of all, in the text of Scripture, he must be searched and humbled, his sin and doubt and fears exposed to the bright light of Jesus' glory through the Word. His trust and love must be redirected from himself and all things creaturely toward the Creator, who confronts him in majesty and in mercy. And he must be galvanized, mobilized to proclaim, explain, and apply the Word to the people of God with a self-forgetting boldness.

Yet as the arrows along the bottom of the triangle show, the connection between the pastor-preacher's existential spiritual condition and the congregation to whom he is to bring God's good news is not a one-way street, as though the preacher were a uniquely positioned mediator standing between the covenant Lord and his servant people. To be sure, the preacher is God's called spokesman to announce, interpret, and apply the Word to saints and to sinners who are not yet called to be saints. But ministry between pastor and people is a two-way street. He brings God's Word to them in pulpit, pastor's study, living room, or workplace; and his words are surrounded and supported by evidence of his love in his care and prayer for them. But also, when the Word is bearing its intended fruit in individuals and families and congregations, the people of God respond to the Word of God through care and prayer for the messenger who brings it, honoring his office and recognizing his accountability for their spiritual well-being (Phil. 4:10–19; 1 Thess. 5:12–13; Heb. 13:17).

The Situational Perspective: Preaching and the People of God

Finally, the faithful preacher will seek, in dependence on Christ's Spirit, not only to do justice to the content of the biblical text—hearing its normative message as fully and faithfully as he can—and to respond to the Word's challenge to his own heart as the Lord of the Word comes to him through the Spirit, but also to "exegete" his hearers and the situation in which they will hear the Word through his lips. The people of God belong to the preacher's situation, for they stand outside him and around him. But in another sense they and he together inhabit a much larger context that he must understand as clearly as he can, both to care for them pastorally and to communicate the Word to them in preaching. The preacher dwells with God's people in a situation that is, on the one hand, controlled by the Lord's sovereign power as Creator, Ruler, and Sustainer of all his creatures and all their actions and, on the other, infected by human rebellion and its toxic by-products, the "estate of sin and misery"[7] into which our father Adam's fall has plunged us all, pastor and people alike.

Now, I have labeled this perspective *the people of God*, but it is important to clarify who are in view.[8] On the one hand, the Bible reveals that God's covenant people are distinct from "the world," set apart from among the nations as God's special treasure, marked as his property by circumcision in the Old Testament and by baptism in the New Testament, and protected by his Spirit and the shepherds he provides. As Jesus demonstrated to his disciples in the interrogation at Caesarea Philippi, a clear boundary separates the church from those outside the church, even those who have a high opinion of Jesus himself. That boundary is the apostolic foundation on which the church takes its stand, with this confession as its cornerstone: "You are the Christ, the Son of the living God" (Matt. 16:16).[9] On the other hand, the Bible also shows that in the era of God's patient grace from the fall to the consummation, the *clear* boundaries of God's covenant people

7. WSC A.17.

8. See also footnote 3 above.

9. See Edmund P. Clowney, *The Church*, Contours of Christian Theology Series (Downers Grove, IL: InterVarsity Press, 1995), 39–42.

are also *permeable* boundaries. Abraham and his descendants were called not only to inherit God's blessing but also to become the means through whom God would bless the nations (Gen. 12:1–3), and Israel was called as the Lord's servant to become "light for the nations," bringing salvation to the ends of the earth (Isa. 49:6; see Acts 13:47) through their witness to the Lord's mercy and power to save (Isa. 45:22). Now that the Messiah has come, obeyed, died, and been raised from the dead and exalted to God's right hand, the church is called to this global mission as Jesus' witnesses (Acts 1:8). In fact, the calling of the people of God to invite all of the earth's peoples into this set-apart community and to embrace outsiders who believe is even clearer under the new covenant than under the old. The ethnic, ancestral, and national dimensions that set Israel apart from the nations under the Old Testament have been transcended, and therefore erased.

As the preacher ponders the situation of his hearers and how their context—actually, their multiple contexts—may influence, for good or ill, their reception of the message that he brings them from God, he does well to envision the challenge of appropriate contextualization in terms of a series of concentric circles. The largest circle, which encompasses all human hearers of the Word anywhere and in any time, includes such features as: (1) the universe that has been created and sustained by the triune God and that therefore displays his glory, power, and divine nature (Ps. 19; Rom. 1); (2) the identity of the human race as those uniquely fashioned in the image of God, set apart from the animal world by our prophetic (speaking/hearing), kingly (dominion), and priestly (interpersonal communion) callings in relation to our Creator, each other, and the rest of the creatures;[10] and (3) the effects of the human race's fall into sin in Adam, both with respect to human nature and with respect to the outworkings of covenant curse in man's whole earthly domain.

A smaller circle can then be drawn to include those in any era who have been called by God's special redemptive revelation into covenant relationship with himself. Within this circle are the patriarchs and their families, Israel, and the church in the new covenant era. Their shared "situation," as Hebrews implies, is the voice of God that speaks good news into the fallen world and summons faith in his promises, despite the wilderness temptation

---

10. See M. G. Kline, *Images of the Spirit* (Grand Rapids: Baker, 1980); D. E. Johnson, *Him We Proclaim: Preaching Christ from All the Scriptures* (Phillipsburg, NJ: P&R Publishing, 2007), 246–70.

to turn back from our pilgrimage toward the heavenly city (Heb. 4:1–11; 11:13–16; 13:14).

Within the group of those addressed by God's Word and summoned into God's covenant, another significant circle circumscribes our situation as those who live the "last days" (Acts 2:17; Heb. 1:2), the "end of the ages" (Heb. 9:26; see 1 Cor. 10:11) that began with the incarnation of God the Son as Jesus of Nazareth, his earthly ministry, sacrificial death, resurrection and exaltation, and bestowal of the Holy Spirit. We who live on this side of that great watershed in redemptive history enjoy the privilege of having witnessed, through the apostles' and other New Testament authors' inspired testimony, the fulfillment of God's promise in the inauguration of the kingdom by Jesus. This vantage point sets our situation apart from that of Abraham, Moses, and David (Matt. 13:17).

Then the preacher must also consider the more tightly drawn circles that distinguish the vantage points of those who are contemporary in time but whose views of reality have been shaped by different trajectories of experience and networks of relationships. Missiologists think of these situational distinctions when discussing the need to contextualize the biblical message for different audiences: language, race, ethnicity, gender, age group, social class, education level, religious or worldview commitments or assumptions, and so on. Preachers, evangelists, and missionaries sometimes disagree regarding which methods are appropriate, or what degree of reformulation is warranted, in trying to convey the Bible's message to hearers who find it foreign or virtually unintelligible. Nevertheless, such situational differences exist among our hearers, and faithful preachers find ways to address those differences.[11]

The faithful preacher, then, must attend to the situational perspective, the contexts in which he finds himself and his hearers: Who are the people to whom I am called to preach the Word? What factors in their situation (life experience, cultural identity, "location" in the intellectual development of global civilization, economic and educational advantages or disadvantages, religious legacy, etc.) may either help or hinder their reception of the Word? Recognizing the limits of my own capacities and depending on God's Spirit,

11. As Frame would remind us, every aspect of our own situation and our hearers' situation is a manifestation of the powerful control of the Lord, who sovereignly ordains all events and circumstances, even those in which human (or superhuman) participants act in ways contrary to his revealed will, resisting his authority and incurring deserved judgment for violating his law. See, for example, *PWG*, 7.

how can I bring God's message across any bridges of understanding that his providential control has already built into their minds and hearts through the situation in which he has sovereignly embedded them? Knowing my limits and the Spirit's power, how can I carry God's message over, around, or through any roadblocks to understanding and conviction that the particular syndrome of sin and misery in their past and present experience has cast in the path of their coming to Jesus?

Moreover, as the double-tipped arrow along the base of the triangle signifies, the preacher engages the situation of his hearers not merely as an exercise in effective communication but as an expression of Christian love. With respect to the people of God in particular, who share his confession of faith in Christ the Redeemer, his life is bound with theirs in the unity of the body of Christ—Jesus' body of flesh sacrificed on the cross (Eph. 2:16) and therefore the church as Christ's body, its every member interdependent on all others (Rom. 12:4–5; 1 Cor. 12:27; Eph. 4:15–16). So the preacher's *existential relation* to God the Lord, as the Spirit is present in and with him to conform him to Christ and empower his service, is a vital aspect of the *situation* of the people of God, who receive their Lord's Word from his servant's lips. The more his ear is open and his heart willing to receive and respond to the Word (Isa. 50:5), the better it will be for his hearers. And, conversely, the *existential response of the members* of Christ's flock to the nearness of the Lord is a vital dimension of the *preacher's situation*. The more they drink in the refreshment of the gospel with eager faith and grateful love, the stronger the bond of mutual care and prayer between people and pastor, and the account that he must give for their welfare will be "with joy and not with groaning" (Heb. 13:17).

The Spirit of Christ at the Center

My preaching triangle morphed over the years, as I realized that it needed to make more visual Frame's pervasive emphasis that the lordship of God entails not only his authority and power, but also his *personal presence*. It is deceptively easy to turn a discussion of the process by which pastors prepare and deliver sermons into a to-do list that focuses on the steps we take and ignores the engagement of the God who spoke Scripture and speaks still in Scripture, for whom and in whose presence we speak, and whom we and our hearers are called to know through the gospel of his Son. For myself and my students, I found it necessary to insert the

Spirit of Christ at the center, in and over the preacher's interaction with the written Word, his own response to it, and his engagement with others. In this way we are forced to remember that the ministry of the Word is more than "sound exegesis + personal spiritual discipline + effective oral communication."

As faithful craftsmen carefully handling the priceless material of God's Word (2 Tim. 2:15) in the sight of God (2 Cor. 2:17) in order to present people perfect in Christ (Col. 1:28), preachers must commit themselves to hard labor: *exegeting* the text accurately in its original biblical contexts through word study, analysis of structure, examination of background, context, occasion, and purpose; *interpreting* the message of the text as it moves from its original contexts in the history of revelation, through its fulfillment in Christ, and down into our day and age, to touch our hearers; *structuring* our sermons to enable our hearers to get the message clearly (instruction), convincingly (persuasion), and convictingly (motivation). But if we have conscientiously "followed all the steps" in our responsibility while relying on our efforts and not depending on God to give the growth, we have failed in our first responsibility: to live by faith in the personal presence and power of Christ's Spirit.

Seeing the Spirit of Christ at the center keeps us mindful that the same divine person who breathed out the Word of God (2 Tim. 3:16), speaking through the prophets to predict the sufferings of Christ and the glories to follow (1 Peter 1:10–11), is still active to illumine and empower the man of God as we prepare and preach. He opens the eyes of our hearts as we study and meditate on the text, enabling us to grasp the heart of the text's message and its relevance to the spiritual issues that we and our hearers face. His wisdom leads our reflection through the circumstantial differences between the first recipients' ancient situations and ours today, enabling us to identify the spiritual issues at the core of their need and ours,[12] and to discern how the fullness of God dwelling in Christ (Col. 2:9) addresses those issues. Because he is present in and with the preacher himself not merely as a teacher but also as a transformer, relentlessly committed to our holiness in conformity with Christ, he comes to confront our unbelief and unsubmissiveness and to lead us, even by painful paths, into the liberty of Christlike loving and living.

Seeing the Spirit at the center also molds the preacher's mind-set as he moves from the study to the pulpit. On the one hand, it is profoundly

---

12. Again, Chapell's concept of a text's Fallen Condition Focus is helpful here (see footnote 5).

humbling to be reminded, again and again, that the most formidable interpretive and oratorical skills are impotent to pierce hearts of stone or turn them into hearts of flesh, responsive to God. On the other, the humbled preacher can open the Word in the confident expectation that the same Spirit who breathed out the Word once for all long ago still breathes life into the dead today through his testimony to Jesus (John 16:12–15). This sovereign Spirit also uses his words to grow newborn infants into joyful servants, equipping each with gifts that enable ministry to others and cause the body's growth in unity, truth, and love (Eph. 4:11–16).

Having presented a paradigm for thinking triperspectivally about the key factors at work in Christian preaching, I need now to sketch the case that can be made, biblically and historically, for this analysis.

BIBLICAL FOUNDATIONS

The Normative Perspective: Preaching and the Word of God

In this collection it is not necessary to marshal extensive evidence from Scripture to support the thesis that God wants his written Word to "norm" the content of our preaching. Admittedly, some influential preachers and movements seem indifferent to the idea that Christian preaching has divine authority and power *only* when it conveys not the "wisdom of men" (whether ancient philosophy or modern psychology) but the offensive "word of the cross," revealed by God himself in Old Testament promise and New Testament fulfillment. Nonetheless, the Bible itself sanctions no such confusion. Certainly no one could come away from studying Frame's extensive writings on the Bible as the Word of God[13] with the impression that Scripture allows the preacher to draw his message from any source other than itself.

Ancient Israel was commanded to assess the claims of its prophetic preachers, discerning the true from the false, not by signs and wonders but by the conformity of their message with God's previous, public revelation given through Moses (Deut. 13:1–5). The same principle held for the evaluation of prophets in the apostolic church (1 John 4:1–3).

---

13. John M. Frame, "God and Biblical Language: Transcendence and Immanence," in John W. Montgomery, ed., *God's Inerrant Word: An International Symposium on the Trustworthiness of Scripture* (Minneapolis: Bethany Fellowship, 1973), 159–77; *DKG*; *PWG*; *IDSCB*; *DWG*.

The apostle Paul was particularly persistent in insisting that his preaching, everywhere and always, adhered to a single norm, the Word of God that finds its focal point and fulfillment in the person and work of Jesus the Messiah.[14] Despite the Greeks' taste for wisdom and Jews' love of power, Paul's resolution at Corinth was to preach "nothing . . . except Jesus Christ and him crucified" (1 Cor. 2:2). Writing to the Colossians, he identified his message as "the gospel" (Col. 1:23), "the word of God" (v. 25), "the mystery . . . now revealed" (v. 26), and climactically, "Christ in you, the hope of glory" (v. 27). To the Philippians he referred to the content of his own preaching and that of others as "the gospel" (Phil. 1:7, 12, 16), "the word" (v. 14), and simply "Christ" (vv. 15, 17, 18).

The epistle to the Hebrews itself classically exemplifies both the Scripture-defined and the Christ-centered content of Christian preaching. Its self-designation, "word of exhortation" (Heb. 13:22), identified it for first-century Hellenistic Jews as a homiletical exposition of the Holy Scriptures—a sermon.[15] Its main point—explicitly identified—is Jesus' superiority as High Priest over against the priestly qualifications and ministry of Aaron and his descendants of the tribe of Levi (8:1). In fact, the movements of this sermon flow from the superiority of revelation in the Son in contrast to previous prophetic speech from God (1:1–4:13), through the Son's superior priesthood (4:14–7:28) and mediatorial role (8:1–13), then through the superiority of the sanctuary and sacrifice associated with Christ's priestly ministry (9:1–10:31), and on to the superior inheritance to which the Son now leads believers (10:32–12:28; cf. 13:14). Each of these movements is supported by the exposition of Old Testament texts (Pss. 8, 95, 110; Gen. 14:17–20; Jer. 31:31–34; Hab. 2:4). A survey of the apostles' sermons preserved in the book of Acts would yield similar results. In venues in which hearers' acquaintance with and respect for the Old Testament Scriptures could be anticipated, early Christian preachers consistently cited Old Testament passages and showed their fulfillment in Jesus and his redemptive mission (e.g., Acts 3:13–26). In pagan settings they did not cite Scripture explicitly, but the content of their message is demonstrably rooted in Israel's ancient Scriptures, supplemented

14. For a fuller development of the content of Paul's preaching, see Johnson, *Him We Proclaim*, 62–97.

15. Note the same term in Acts 13:15. See William Lane, *Hebrews 1–8*, WBC, vol. 47A (Waco, TX: Word, 1991), lxix–lxxx; followed by Johnson, *Him We Proclaim*, 171–78.

by the new covenant revelation that had recently been brought by Christ (e.g., Acts 17:22–31).[16]

God demands that his heralds and ambassadors, as stewards of his mysteries of whom he requires trustworthiness (1 Cor. 4:1–2), submit the words they speak in his name to the Word he has spoken in the Bible.

The Existential Perspective: Preaching and the Man of God

Scripture likewise teaches that preachers themselves must be transformed by the Word they are charged to deliver. This transformation takes place as they are confronted by the personal presence of the Lord of the covenant. Old Testament prophets were often called to their office of revelation and proclamation by the Lord's summons to enter, via vision, his heavenly court, there to behold his glory and to receive his message for his people. Perhaps the most dramatic was Isaiah's vision in the temple, in which he saw the Lord, high and exalted, whereupon Isaiah was overcome with shame and terror over his own defilement. After his symbolic cleansing with a burning coal from the Lord's altar, the prophet eagerly volunteered to carry God's message to Israel (Isa. 6:1–13; see Ezek.1:4–3:15). Likewise, Christ called and prepared his apostles for their ministry of the Word by his personal presence, both in his earthly ministry and in his return to them (John 14:18, 26, 28) through the power of the Spirit outpoured at Pentecost.

Yet perhaps the clearest expression of the integral bond between the transforming presence of the Lord and his servant's qualification to preach his Word is found in the experience of Saul of Tarsus, whose call from the risen Lord on the Damascus road so transformed him that he became the prime exhibit of the redemptive grace that he henceforth proclaimed: "I was a blasphemer, persecutor, and insolent opponent . . . the foremost [sinner]. But I received mercy for this reason, that in me, as the foremost, Jesus Christ might display his perfect patience as an example to those who were to believe in him for eternal life" (1 Tim. 1:13–16). Paul was profoundly aware that his own experience before the face of God demonstrated two vital truths: (1) the best that conscientious law-observance can offer is worthless and repugnant in God's sight (Phil. 3:4–8), and (2) God shows

16. See D. E. Johnson, *The Message of Acts in the History of Redemption* (Phillipsburg, NJ: P&R Publishing, 1997), 141–65.

astonishing grace to his worst human enemy, who deserved only wrath. In Paul, Christ-persecutor-turned-Christ-preacher, the medium incarnated the message.

Throughout Scripture the motif recurs: men whom God calls to proclaim his Word are men whose encounter with God through his Word transforms their lives. The postexilic priest and scribe Ezra fulfilled the priestly calling to teach the Torah (Deut. 33:10; Mal. 2:6) so faithfully because he was committed not only to understand the text (normative perspective) and to convey it to the people (situational perspective) but also to obey it himself (existential perspective): "Ezra had set his heart to study the Law of the LORD, and to do it and to teach his statutes and rules in Israel" (Ezra 7:10). Paul urged his spiritual son and ministerial apprentice Timothy, "Keep a close watch on *yourself* and on the teaching" (1 Tim. 4:16). To the ability to teach that must characterize "the Lord's servant" he conjoined such character virtues as purity, faith, patience, and gentleness (2 Tim. 2:22–26). In fact, his lists of criteria to be sought in elders/overseers are heavily weighted in the direction of virtues demonstrated in relationships (although not overlooking doctrinal soundness and aptness to teach) (1 Tim. 3:1–7; Titus 1:6–9). The preacher to the Hebrews also reminds his readers of leaders who had passed from the scene, mentioning not only their ministry of the Word but also "the outcome of their way of life [Greek: *anastrophē*]" in his challenge to "imitate their faith" (Heb. 13:7). Preachers are painfully aware, as Paul was, that we have by no means attained the perfection to which Christ has called us (Phil. 3:12). Yet as we stand before the Lord of the Word, preachers must respond to the Word of the Lord in humility, faith, repentance, and renewed love, so that we can also say with Paul, "Join in imitating me" (Phil. 3:17)—or, better yet, "Be imitators of me, as I am of Christ" (1 Cor. 11:1; see Titus 2:7).

The Situational Perspective: Preaching and the People of God

Reformed theologians and pastors are often suspicious of calls to pay attention to the experiential context and mental framework of their hearers. Some approaches to contextualization in cross-cultural missions have produced religious syncretism rather than churches that are appropriately indigenized while remaining set apart from their cultural contexts by the countercultural gospel of Christ crucified. Some approaches to church growth in North America have virtually (yet often imperceptibly) exchanged the Bible's good news of divine grace that reconciles us to God through Christ's cross for therapeutic good advice that leaves hearers' self-reliance unchallenged. Nonetheless, such abuses do not nullify the pervasive motif throughout Scripture of God's speaking sovereignly and flexibly into the changing and diverse situations of his human image-bearers as they inhabit the world he has created and as they encounter the bitter effect of their rebellion against him.

The self-evident diversity of the Bible—a collection of sixty-six documents composed over a span of roughly one and a half millennia in three languages, reflecting various literary genres, and addressed to diverse ethnic groups living in rural and urban locales, confronted by various spiritual, social, and physical threats—attests to the commitment of Scripture's divine Author to speak at every point precisely the message that his people's situation calls for, and in the medium best suited to reach their minds and hearts. In his 1894 inaugural address at Princeton Seminary, Geerhardus Vos, the "father" of Reformed biblical theology, noted how audience-sensitive God has been in the ways he has revealed himself in the Bible:

> God has interwoven the supernaturally communicated knowledge of himself with the historic life of the chosen race, so as to secure for it a practical form from the beginning. Revelation is connected throughout with the fate of Israel. Its disclosures arise from the necessities of that nation, and are adjusted to its capacities . . .[17]

Vos's observation about the engagement of Old Testament revelation with Israel's changing historical situations, and therefore with Israel's varying needs and capacities, is equally true of the New Testament revelation. Although imparted within a single generation, the twenty-seven New Testament documents were originally delivered to first-century churches taking root in urban centers from Jerusalem to Rome and confronting a variety of theological threats (pressures on Gentiles to Judaize and on Jewish Christians to return to Judaism, or invitations to compromise with pagan-

17. Geerhardus Vos, "The Idea of Biblical Theology as a Science and as a Theological Discipline," in Richard B. Gaffin Jr., ed., *Redemptive History and Biblical Interpretation: The Shorter Writings of Geerhardus Vos* (Phillipsburg, NJ: Presbyterian and Reformed, 1980), 10.

ism or urbane wisdom) and external opposition (from social ostracism up to physical violence).

The aptly contextualized character of Scripture is also true of the preaching recorded in the Bible. Two New Testament examples will have to suffice at this point: the sermons and speeches of Acts convey a consistent gospel message with a set of central themes, but they also display diverse strategies and styles depending on the audience and circumstances of each address.[18] Sermons preached in the temple or synagogues, addressed to audiences composed of Jews and Gentile God-fearers, regularly cited Old Testament texts and demonstrated their fulfillment in Jesus. Sermons delivered to pagans at Lystra and Athens began not with Scripture but with the general revelation that confronted them in the created order and in their own constitution as those made in the image of God (Acts 14:15–17; 17:22–31). From that starting point Christ's heralds led their hearers to several sobering truths: (1) their religious trust had been misplaced, (2) they were answerable to the unique Creator of the universe and the era of accountability had arrived (17:30; also implied in 14:16), and (3) God had spoken a fresh word in history, in the resurrection of Christ (17:31). Other features of the sermons of Acts fit the incidents that evoke them (the outpouring of the Spirit, the healing of a lame man, the accusations against Stephen) and specifically engage the worldview of the audience (e.g., philosophical views of the Epicureans and Stoics in Paul's Areopagus address). The apostolic preachers met their hearers where they found them intellectually, religiously, and experientially. But these preachers did not leave their hearers where they found them. They led them persuasively to the truth of the gospel.

The second example of situation-sensitive preaching is the epistle-sermon to the Hebrews. Although traditionally classified as a "general" epistle, this document is a not an encyclical like 1 Peter (addressed to Christians in five Roman provinces, 1:1) or James ("to the twelve tribes in the Dispersion," 1:1). Rather, Hebrews was written (to be spoken!) to a specific congregation with a specific history (previous joy in serving and suffering, Heb. 6:10; 10:32–34) and specific contemporary challenges (exclusion from "the camp" of Judaism and persecution on the horizon, posing tempta-

---

18. Jay E. Adams, *Audience Adaptations in the Sermons and Speeches of Acts* (Nutley, NJ: Presbyterian and Reformed, 1976); Roger Wagner, *Tongues Aflame: Learning to Preach from the Apostles* (Fearn, Ross-shire, UK: Mentor, 2004), 87–96, 119–337. See also Johnson, *Message of Acts*, 61–66, 191–201.

tions to draw back from trusting Jesus and to return to Israel's sanctuary, sacrifices, and priesthood, 13:13; 12:4; 3:12; 4:1; 6:4–6). As we have seen, the preacher to the Hebrews, knowing his readers' regard for the Hebrew Scriptures as the Word of God, builds his case for the superiority of Jesus through interpretation of one Old Testament text after another. Moreover, he intersperses comments that demonstrate his knowledge of their trials and show the relevance of his theme to the decision confronting them.

The biblical case could be made more extensively, but this sketch is sufficient, I think, to demonstrate that the Bible itself calls those who preach its life-giving message not only to submit their thoughts to its content (normative perspective) and to surrender their hearts to the Spirit's transforming power (existential perspective), but also to love so much that they take their hearers' understanding, experience, and circumstances into account in the words and the ways that they proclaim God's good news (situational perspective).

HISTORICAL CONFIRMATIONS

But someone might wonder: Is this threefold analysis of angles of vision through which preachers should view their mission simply a recent Framean innovation? Even granting that such motifs can be found in the Bible when one goes looking for them, are we the first generation of pastors to have discovered that we must not only heed the norm of the Word but also attend to the Spirit's agenda for our own hearts and to our responsibility to address God's people in the midst of their life contexts?

To begin to answer such questions, consider this sample of pastoral wisdom from those who have gone before us.

The Normative Perspective

Among those who appreciate John Frame's work I suspect that there is little controversy regarding the normative centrality of the Bible, the written Word of God, for preaching. The ways in which the Scriptures have been interpreted and applied have varied over the history of the church, as Hughes Oliphant Old's magisterial series, *The Reading and Preaching of the Scriptures in the Worship of the Christian Church*, amply illustrates.[19] Still, Old's title

19. Hughes Oliphant Old, *The Reading and Preaching of the Scriptures in the Worship of the Christian Church*, 6 vols. (Grand Rapids: Eerdmans, 1998–2007).

is accurate: throughout the church's history, its preaching has sought (or at least claimed) to be the preaching *of the Scriptures*. When the centrality of the Bible itself in preaching has been compromised and other sources of wisdom or branches of learning have displaced or overshadowed Scripture in the pulpit, the church and its witness have suffered.

Certainly the Protestant Reformation placed a great emphasis on the primacy of the written Word in the church's preaching. The Reformers affirmed, over against the accretion of ecclesiastical tradition that distorted late medieval Christianity, a *sola Scriptura* principle that had implications not only for theological method but also for the weekly (and even daily) life and worship of the church, in which the preaching of God's Word was restored to its proper place. Early English Puritan William Perkins, for example, wrote, "The Word of God alone is to be preached, in its perfection and inner consistency. Scripture is the exclusive subject of preaching, the only field in which the preacher is to labour."[20] Likewise the Swiss churches affirmed in the first chapter of their Second Helvetic Confession (1566):

> Wherefore when this [written] Word of God is now preached in the church by preachers lawfully called, we believe that the very Word of God is proclaimed, and received by the faithful; and that neither any other Word of God is to be invented nor is to be expected from heaven: and that now the Word itself which is preached is to be regarded, not the minister that preaches; for even if he be evil and a sinner, nevertheless the Word of God remains still true and good.[21]

Robert L. Dabney, American Presbyterian theologian and pastor in the nineteenth century, affirmed the centrality of the Word to preaching in his terse job description of the preacher: "The preacher's business is to take what is given him in the Scriptures, as it is given to him, and to endeavor to imprint it on the souls of men. All else is God's work."[22]

Although pastors' desires to bring sermons that are relevant to their hearers' needs may sometimes be misled by superficial perceptions of "rel-

---

20. William Perkins, *The Art of Prophesying, with the Calling of the Ministry* (1592, 1606; repr., Edinburgh: Banner of Truth, 1996), 9.

21. Quoted in Arthur C. Cochrane, ed., *Reformed Confessions of the 16th Century* (Philadelphia: Westminster, 1966), 225.

22. R. L. Dabney, *Evangelical Eloquence: A Course of Lectures on Preaching* (original title, *Sacred Rhetoric*, 1870; repr., Edinburgh: Banner of Truth, 1999), 37.

evance," resulting in the marginalization of the Bible in preaching, heirs and students of the Reformation recognize that only the exposition of the Scriptures, in the fullness of their witness to Jesus the living Word, can address the deep needs of human hearts with true relevance and divine authority.

The Existential Perspective

From the Second Helvetic Confession's assertion that the Word of God retains its authority, even if proclaimed by a preacher who is "evil and a sinner," one might infer that the preacher's "existential" response to the Lord's transformative purposes for the Word can be a matter of indifference. Yet that is not the conclusion reached by the church's great theologians over the centuries.

In *De Doctrina Christiana*, one the church's earliest handbooks on homiletics, Augustine stated: "More important than any amount of grandeur of style to those of us who seek to be listened to with obedience is *the life of the speaker*." Although "a wise and eloquent speaker who lives a wicked life certainly educates many who are eager to learn," Augustine insisted that such a preacher's resistance to the Word in his own life would inevitably have adverse effects on his pastoral ministry to others: "people do not listen with obedience to the man who does not listen to himself, and they despise the word of God preached to them as well as despising the preacher."[23]

In the tradition of Reformed theology, one of the classic manuals on pastoral ministry is Puritan Richard Baxter's *The Reformed Pastor*.[24] Baxter's charge to pastors is drawn from Paul's exhortation to the elders of the church at Ephesus: "Take heed therefore unto yourselves, and to all the flock, over the which the Holy Ghost hath made you overseers, to feed the church of God, which he hath purchased with his own blood" (Acts 20:28 KJV). The majority of the treatise elaborates the meaning, methods, and motives of caring for the flock through public and private instruction in the Word, visitation, and other aspects of pastoral care. Before addressing any of these "situ-

23. Augustine, *On Christian Teaching*, trans. R. P. H. Green (Oxford: Oxford University Press, 1997), 4.17.59, 60 (emphasis added).

24. Richard Baxter, *Gildas Salvianus: The Reformed Pastor* (1656), in Baxter, *The Practical Works of the Rev. Richard Baxter* (London: James Duncan, 1830), 14.i–ixiii, 45–400. Also available in abridged form as William Brown, ed., *The Reformed Pastor* (1829, 1862; repr., Edinburgh: Banner of Truth, 1974).

ational" themes, however, Baxter's first chapter expounds the verse and specifically applies the apostle's opening instruction, "Take heed . . . unto yourselves." Baxter writes: "Take heed to yourselves, lest you should be void of that saving grace of God which you offer to others, and be strangers to the effectual workings of that Gospel which you preach."[25] "Take heed to yourselves, lest you live in those actual sins which you preach against in others; and lest you be guilty of that which you daily condemn."[26] "Take heed also to yourselves, that you be not unfit for the great employments that you have undertaken," by which he means failing to develop the disciplines and skills to interpret and apply the Scriptures both in the pulpit and in private pastoral care.[27] "Moreover, take heed to yourselves, lest your example contradict your doctrine, and lest you lay such stumbling-blocks before the blind, as may be the occasion of their ruin; lest you may unsay that with your lives, which you say with your tongues."[28]

In a similar vein, Charles Bridges in the nineteenth century wrote in *The Christian Ministry*:

> If the ministry be a spiritual work, a corresponding *spiritual character* seems to be required in its administrators. . . . It is evident, however, that this Ministerial standard presupposes a deep tone of experimental and devotional character—habitually exercised in self-denial, prominently marked by love to the Saviour, and to the souls of sinners; and practically exhibited in a blameless consistency of conduct.[29]

Across the Atlantic, Archibald Alexander, founding professor of the Presbyterian church's theological seminary at Princeton, New Jersey, likewise stressed for his students the imperative of piety in pastors in his lectures on pastoral theology. Among the fourteen reasons that he gave in one lecture for the pastor's attention to his own heart response to the Word are these:

25. Ibid., 53 (52–61). The wording is quoted from the 1830 Duncan edition; page numbers for this edition are followed by page numbers in parentheses for the full discussion of each point in the (more readily available) Banner of Truth edition.

26. Ibid., 54 (67–68).

27. Ibid., 55 (68–71).

28. Ibid., 58 (63–67).

29. Charles Bridges, *The Christian Ministry, with an Inquiry into the Causes of Its Inefficiency* (1830; repr., London: Banner of Truth, 1967), 27–28 (emphasis in original).

(2) The work is so great and sacred, and the consequences so awful, that none will duly feel and act under the responsibilities of the office, but one whose heart is warmed with fervent love to Christ and the souls of men. (3) The duties of the ministry will never be faithfully performed by any one but he who is deeply under the influence of divine truth. He will become indolent or careless or will sink into discouragement—or will become entangled with worldly engagements.... (5) [Piety] is necessary to preserve the minister from ambition and vain glory. (6) Necessary to make him to speak with confidence of the excellency and comforts of true piety.[30]

Academic preparation for pastoral ministry often focuses students' attention on the biblical and theological information and the intellectual skills needed to interpret the Scriptures accurately. Practical preparation for ministry often focuses on the practices and skills of communicating the gospel, counseling, and leadership. A triperspectival model of ministry affirms the indispensable importance of these normative and situational dimensions in the preparation for and practice of the ministry of the Word in the church and in the world. But the teaching of Scripture and the church's shepherds who have gone before us make it clear that pastoral service flourishes only as one's understanding of biblical truth (normative) and one's engagement with people in their joys and sorrows (situational) are integrated with the pastor's own humble and grateful receptivity to the grace of God revealed in the Word and brought near by the Spirit (existential).

The Situational Perspective

Although some efforts in the realm of "seeker sensitivity" entail subtle distortions of the church's message to make it less offensive to those outside the church, the remedy for such aberrations from biblical fidelity is not to ignore the situation of those who hear us preach. The preacher is responsible to understand his hearers' mind-set and assumptions so well that he can articulate the gospel with such clarity that its bold affront

30. Archibald Alexander, "Qualifications for Pastoral Office," Lectures on Pastoral Theology 12:11 (box 12, manuscript 11, of the Alexander papers, Princeton Theological Seminary Library), quoted in James M. Garretson, *Princeton and Preaching: Archibald Alexander and the Christian Ministry* (Edinburgh: Banner of Truth, 2005), 63.

to human self-centeredness and self-reliance becomes unavoidable. The church's shepherds in previous eras knew this well.

Augustine, although trained in classical rhetoric, was so convinced of his responsibility as a Christian preacher to make the gospel clearly known to his congregants, whatever their educational level or social class, that he even advised compromising oratorical correctness for the sake of communicative effectiveness:

> We should not shirk the duty of making plain to the minds of others the truths which we have ourselves perceived, however hard they may be to comprehend, with as much effort and argument as may be necessary. . . . The careful pursuit of this clarity sometimes leads one to neglect elegant vocabulary and consider not what sounds good but what is good for putting over and making clear what one has to say. . . . What is the use of correct speech if it does not meet with the listener's understanding? There is no point in speaking at all if our words are not understood by the people to whose understanding our words are directed.[31]

The *ad fontes* ("to the source") motif that was central to the Reformation drove its leaders *back* to the Scripture in its original languages. But their conviction that God's Word belongs to all propelled their efforts *out* in a burst of Bible translation to bring God's Word within reach of average church members (even the illiterate could, once again, hear God speak their own language). In the 1640s the Westminster Assembly articulated the theological rationale for God's address to his people in their own tongues:

> The Old Testament in Hebrew (which was the native language of the people of God of old), and the New Testament in Greek (which, at the time of the writing of it, was most generally known to the nations), being immediately inspired by God, and, by His singular care and providence, kept pure in all ages, are therefore authentical; so as, in all controversies of religion, the Church is finally to appeal unto them. But, because these original tongues are not known to all the people of God, who have right unto, and interest in the Scriptures, and are commanded, in the fear of God, to read and search them, therefore they are to be translated into the vulgar language of every nation unto which they come, that, the Word of God dwelling

---

31. Augustine, *On Christian Doctrine*, 4.8.22, 4.10.24.

plentifully in all, they may worship Him in an acceptable manner; and, through patience and comfort of the Scriptures, may have hope.[32]

From the fact that God's selection of Hebrew and Greek was motivated by his sensitivity to the situation and comprehension of his audience (his ancient people spoke Hebrew; the nations to whom the New Testament was first addressed spoke Greek), the divines drew the conclusion that every national and ethnic group should be able to hear God's Word in its own language. The people of God "have interest in" the message of the Scriptures and must have access to them. The accommodation of God in stooping to speak our lisping language, an idea developed so cogently by John Calvin,[33] mandates the translation of his Word into every tongue on earth.

God's adaptability as a communicator to fit his words to his audience's capacities has implications for his preachers' practice, as the Westminster Assembly showed in the *Directory for the Publick Worship of God* that accompanied its confession and catechisms. In their preparations to preach, pastors were counseled in the *Directory* to anticipate and answer obstacles that could hinder hearers' reception of the message: "If any doubt obvious from scripture, reason, or prejudice of the hearers, seem to arise, it is very requisite to remove it, by reconciling the seeming differences, answering the reasons, and discovering and taking away the causes of prejudice and mistake." The preacher must be strategic in protecting his hearers from theological error, not "rais[ing] an old heresy from the grave" but refuting false views that actually threaten the people. "In applying comfort . . . he is carefully to answer such objections as a troubled heart and afflicted spirit may suggest to the contrary." Among the truths taught in a particular biblical text, he is to apply those that "he findeth most needful and seasonable," as he

---

32. WCF 1.8.

33. John Calvin, *Institutes of the Christian Religion*, ed. John T. McNeill, trans. Ford Lewis Battles, Library of Christian Classics, vols. 20, 21 (Philadelphia: Westminster, 1960), 1.17.13. At a later point Calvin defends God from those who would cite the expiration of the Mosaic ceremonial laws as evidence of God's instability: "God ought not to be considered changeable merely because he accommodated diverse forms to different ages, as he knew would be expedient for each. . . . If a householder instructs, rules, and guides, his children one way in infancy, another way in youth, and still another in young manhood, we shall not on this account call him fickle and say he abandons his purpose. Why, then, do we brand God with the mark of inconstancy because he has with apt and fitting marks distinguished a diversity of times? . . . He has accommodated himself to men's capacity, which is varied and changeable" (2.11.13).

has discovered the people's spiritual needs "by his residence and conversing with his flock."[34]

In the sixteenth century, William Perkins's *The Art of Prophesying* had reminded Reformed pastors that preaching involves not only drawing appropriate doctrinal truth from biblical texts but also applying it "in ways which are appropriate to the circumstances of the place and time and to the people in the congregation." Perkins argued that "this is the biblical approach to exposition," citing Old and New Testament texts that describe different pastoral strategies to meet different spiritual needs: " 'I will seek what was lost and bring back what was driven away, bind up the broken and strengthen what was sick' (*Ezek.* 34:15, 16). 'And on some have compassion, making a distinction, but others save with fear, pulling them out of the fire' (*Jude* 22, 23)." Perkins then went on to profile categories of hearers whose various spiritual states the preacher must take into account in framing and applying the message.[35]

Brief as these samples have been, they illustrate that previous generations of wise pastors have recognized that their gospel calling and love for those to whom they preach demand that they carefully discern their hearers' shared and distinctive struggles, and then that they strategically identify how best to speak God's good news into those situations.

Ministerial Applications

A triperspectival model of ministry calls pastors to bow to *Scripture* as the norm for their message and their methods, to submit to the Spirit's transformation by the Word in *their own lives*, and then to convey the Word clearly and persuasively to *their hearers*. Neglecting any of these perspectives will produce ministry that lacks biblical balance.

When preachers neglect the *normative perspective*, their perception of their own spiritual condition becomes disconnected from the reality-reflecting mirror of the Word (James 1:23–25). Self-perception that is not anchored in the truth of Scripture may drift in various currents: preoccupation with subjective experience, superficial complacency, deep discourage-

---

34. *The Directory for the Publick Worship of God* (1645), in *The Confession of Faith, the Larger and Shorter Catechisms with the Scripture Proofs, Together with the Sum of Saving Knowledge . . .* (Inverness: Publications Committee of the Free Presbyterian Church of Scotland, 1976), 380.

35. Perkins, *Art of Prophesying*, 54, 56–63.

ment, or others. Likewise, when Scripture is not the pastor's functioning authority and touchstone for faith and life, his analysis of his hearers' situation and diagnosis of the needs to be addressed in preaching may remain superficial, confusing symptoms with causes. As a result, the remedies that his preaching offers may be equally shallow, like bandages on cancer, when only the radical surgery that the Spirit performs through the message of the cross would cure.

When preachers neglect the *existential perspective*, they hold both God's Word and their people at arm's length, however rigorous their exegesis of biblical texts and however perceptive their analysis of cultural trends or others' spiritual struggles. They read the Word in order to use it in the lives of others, closing their ears against the divine Speaker, who calls the preacher himself to repentance and trust, to humble joy, to the pursuit of holiness, and to communion with God through his ever-present Spirit. When the pastor is not repeatedly, refreshingly amazed by grace, he sees hurting people as irksome chores rather than as beloved children of the Father. A formulaic procedure for moving from text to pulpit, bypassing the preacher's heart, can mask for a time the stolid independence with which a pastor fulfills his tasks and sustains his routine. Sooner or later, however, unless the Spirit's life-sustaining floodwaters break through to irrigate parched soil and withered vines, the drought of his heart will spread, subtly but surely, to others.

When preachers neglect the *situational perspective* and the experience of the people to whom they preach (professing believers and their covenant children, but also those not yet drawn to Christ in faith), preaching to the church in its worship loses its sense of calling to bear witness to the nations of the saving deeds of God in Christ. The church is then in danger of becoming ingrown, more absorbed in contesting internal disagreements than in discipling all nations. Christians who consistently hear preaching that merely *presupposes* their knowledge of the gospel and thus focuses instead on other topics, even those taught in Scripture, tend to forget the radical depth of their own guilt and the lavish mercy of God in Christ. Consequently, rather than being often surprised by the sweetness of grace, they hear mention of the cross with "Of course" complacency rather than with "And can it be?" wonder. Their hearts drift toward self-righteousness, self-pity, judgmentalism, a spirit of competition, and aloofness from those who don't "have it together."

A triperspectival model of pastoral ministry keeps us mindful of the three foci that warrant our constant attention. It also provides a diagnostic tool by which we can recognize the signs that we may be leaning "off balance" and can take corrective action. The authority of the Lord, speaking in his Word, defines the content we preach, diagnoses the condition of our own hearts, and describes the situation in which we and others meet to hear the voice of the Lord. The presence of the Lord, coming in his Spirit, illumines our understanding of the Word, implements Christlike change in us, and invades our hearers' situation in life-imparting power through the gospel. The power of the Lord, controlling all things, assures us that his Word, we ourselves, and those whom we serve are bound together in his redemptive plan that will—without doubt—arrive at his intended destination: his supreme glory and our complete rescue by the triumph of Jesus the Christ.

27

I'VE BEEN "FRAMED"!
THE INFLUENCE OF JOHN FRAME
AND HIS TEACHING ON THIS PASTOR
AND PASTORAL MINISTRY

SCOTTY SMITH

CONTRIBUTING TO the "Frame Fest" feels like being cast in the last scene of the classic Frank Capra movie *It's a Wonderful Life*. Perhaps you can visualize the cheerful parade of men and women from every segment of Bedford Falls streaming into George Bailey's home to say thanks, and to offer their gifts of gratitude for the impact of one man's life on the many. I humbly take my place in the gospel-parade of brothers and sisters from diverse backgrounds and kingdom callings to say, "Thank you, John. You've served us faithfully and with so much kindness and humility."

That John, no doubt, feels awkward in receiving such attention and appreciation only underscores why we "consider the outcome of his way of life" and want to "imitate his faith" (Heb. 13:7). It is easy to love and respect John Frame.

Among the panoply of esteemed academics and practitioners celebrating John's life and work, I have been asked to offer some thoughts about the pastoral implications of multiperspectivalism. It is a joy to take on that assignment because it involves personal narrative as much as practical application. My offering is decidedly and unashamedly testimonial—not a eulogy fit for a funeral but a thank-you fit for a servant of Jesus who continues to impact the way pastors like me heed the call to repentance and faith in Jesus. God has used John's "Frame-work" in *this* pastor's life for nearly forty years, especially in the last decade. Indeed, the wine of multiperspectivalism took quite a while to become vintage libation in my soul. That says a lot more about my sin and brokenness than John's ability as a teacher and writer.

John continues to be a very important conduit of God's Word and Spirit in my journey to gospel sanity, even though we've actually spent precious little time together face to face. Certainly one of my current joys is co-teaching a Doctor of Ministry class on The Theology of Ministry with John at RTS Orlando. I am a different *man* because of John's influence, not *just* a different thinker and practitioner. It is neither cliché nor cutesy to say, "I've been 'Framed'!" Think about it: even the man's *name* evokes multiperspectivalism!

A FRAME IS A SUPPORTING STRUCTURE—THE STRUTS AND BEAMS UPON WHICH WE CONFIDENTLY BUILD A SUPERSTRUCTURE

As I catalogue the ways John has influenced me, shaped how I do pastoral ministry, and guided how I seek to mentor other young pastors, it's a "no-brainer"—I must start with his impact on my view of the Bible. John helped me embrace the Scriptures as the quintessential frame for *everything*. He took this borderline bibliolater and led me through the abstractions of Van Tillian presuppositionalism into the land of deep conviction and humble assurance that the Bible is uniquely the Word of God.

I remain intrigued, convicted, and encouraged at John's relationship to the Word of God, which is to say, to the God of the Word. For John's care in studying and his joy in heeding the voice of the Scriptures are simply an expression of his worship of the triune God. Never testy or strident in his defense of the inspiration and authority of the Scriptures, John is an unwavering model of a scholar who trembles at the Word of the Lord and, concomitantly, a child of God who delights in the Lord of the gospel.

Because of John's influence on how I think about the Bible, I was able to navigate my way through the minefields of many "worship wars" as a young church planter. He helped me understand that *every* principle, including the regulative principle, must bow the knee to the Scripture principle. If the regulative principle takes us back only to sixteenth-century Geneva, then the journey has not taken us far enough. We are always in a "back-to-the-Bible" movement. We read the Bible because the Bible reads us.

Perhaps this also explains why John has been such a great example to all of us on how to respond to detractors and critics. His identity is not bound up with his opinions being championed. Rather, his passion is focused on simply being as faithful to the Scriptures as he can possibly be.

A FRAME IS A CONTEXT—LIKE THE HISTORICAL SETTING OF A STORY

Along with helping me center and settle into the view of the Scriptures that I still affirm, John enabled me to see the doxological dance between systematic theology and biblical theology. Although, historically, Westminster Seminary has evidenced familial tensions between the champions of systematic theology and biblical theology, John provided me with the big picture—the context in which both are celebrated as critical disciplines and interdependent friends.

John has done this by eschewing both extremes of de-contextualized proof-texting and overtheologizing of particular texts. Indeed, systematic theology is not a study of abstract data but the unfolding revelation of the creator-redeemer God in the history of redemption, centering on the person and work of Jesus. And yet, as God speaks in the totality of his revelation, he also speaks to us in the particulars of his revelation at every point in redemptive history. He reveals himself both in the macro-revelation of Scripture as a whole and in the micro-revelation of every inscripturated word.

These two building blocks of John's teaching were pretty easy for me to grasp, and I still grasp them quite gladly and tightly! However, my journey into multiperspectivalism is another story.

To "Frame" Someone Is to Set Him Up to Take a Fall

I must be careful with this next perspective! "Framing" someone is usually thought of in pejorative terms, and I certainly do not intend to charge John with *anything* unloving or unethical—*au contraire*! However, there *is* such a thing as being *redemptively* set up for "a fall"—that is, a humbling. Think of King David, and Jeremiah, and Paul. Although I certainly don't put myself in the realm of that triad of gospel heroes, God the Holy Spirit definitely used our brother John's ministry as a means of bringing me to much-needed humility and a good measure of healing through the gospel.

I first met John in January 1975 during my inaugural semester at Westminster Theological Seminary Philadelphia. Arrogant, insecure, and disconnected from my heart, I walked into the classrooms of WTS a monoperspectival, normative-loving, grade-hungry seminarian. With that profile, I really was not very notorious. It seemed like there were several of my type in the student body. Up till that point in my seven years of knowing Jesus, my spiritual formation had largely consisted of memorizing isolated Bible verses and stockpiling evidential apologetics. I certainly could have invested my time less wisely, but it seemed that my efforts generated more self-righteousness and evangelistic argumentativeness than "faith expressing itself in love."

I had no theological heritage before coming to faith in Jesus in 1968 as a senior in high school. A product of the Jesus Movement, I prided myself in being theologically eclectic. However, a couple of years before matriculating to Westminster, I got my first impactful glimpse of the sovereignty of God and a tantalizing taste of the theology of grace. This good gift was granted through studying the Greek text of Ephesians with a professor and friend of mine at the University of North Carolina—a Christian scholar who was working on his PhD in classics while I was finishing my undergraduate studies in religion.

To this day, I am thankful that I *became* Reformed internally before I was able to *speak* Reformed publicly. That makes me glad for a lot of reasons, mainly because, had I only been convinced of the dogma of grace without any real encounter with the God of grace, I would have been even more ensconced in living out of my head than I already was.

After my conversion as a senior in high school, I unwittingly exchanged the abuse of alcohol for an abuse of theology. The two essentially served the same function in my life. I started drinking as a junior in high school as a way to (1) numb the unvoiced wounds of my heart, (2) lower my fears and inhibitions, and (3) gain a sense of control over my world.

It is easy to understand how alcohol was a suitable sacrifice to this idolatrous trio. But how did a cognition cocktail serve the same purpose? I found, especially in Reformed theology, that believing you are right can lead to feeling powerful, which usually leads to the illusion of being in control. Please hear me say, loud and clear, that the problem was *not* with Reformed theology; the problem was with me and my abuse of Reformed theology. It is possible to turn *any* worldview into notionalism and a head trip. As I would later discover, there is *no* theology more calculated to humble the arrogant and gentle the madman than the theology of sovereign grace.

However, the more I grew proficient in Reformed-speak, the more exhilarating it felt, very akin to the sensation I had when being under the influence of alcohol. To have answers and categories for virtually *every* question life threw at me kept the pain in my heart at bay; I felt less the insecure introvert; and I experienced a sense of control, especially over "messy" feelings and mysteries, and, of course, over Arminians and charismatics! All you have to do in order to feel large, intact, and powerful is to equate knowledge with spirituality, *especially* if knowing is nothing more than the ability to assimilate and regurgitate information.

This is where John Frame officially enters my story. Little did I anticipate that the first class I had with John would be an introduction to God's disruptive grace. My baptism into multiperspectivalism was incredibly confusing and troubling. This was *not* because I understood what John was talking about and was rattled by the implications. I wish! Rather, my problem was that I could not make heads or tails of what he was even *talking* about. And if seminary is all about mastering the information for the purpose of making great grades and offering sacrifices to your idol structures (as it definitely was for me), that's a very disconcerting place in which to find yourself.

After John would finish lecturing on some aspect of multiperspectivalism, I'd borrow Tremper Longman's notes and Xerox a copy. Scribe Longman, we called him, for Tremper had the uncanny ability to write down, in legible block-letter form, *everything* a professor said. But even *his* notes could not help me break the "Framean code." We monoperspectival types don't get or embrace multiperspectivalism easily.

So why am I indebted to John *today* for confusing me so royally *then*? Allow me to fast-forward into the messiness of pastoral ministry and the complexities of marriage to tell more of the story.

A Frame Is a Surrounding Structure—like the Frame of a Door

Though initially I could not understand John's paradigm of multiperspectivalism, his humility and childlike wonder in class pointed me toward the door of God's grace—Jesus, *the* Door extraordinaire. I didn't see it, but my biggest crisis as a young seminarian was not to settle the issue of epistemological complexities but to deal with my harmatological deficiencies. Although the two are interrelated, they are not synonymous. In short, my need was not as much for great grades as it was for God's grace. Broken sinner trumps confused student. That's why I'm thankful that as smart as John is, he's that much nicer and kinder.

To Frame a Thought Is to Express Oneself in a Specific Way—as in, "She Framed Her Words with Culinary Imagery"

As long as I have been exposed to John, he has always sought to "frame" his teaching with a view of the triperspectival glory of Jesus—the ultimate Prophet, Priest, and King. That emphasis ultimately proved to be the portal through which multiperspectivalism became central to my hermeneutics, theology of spiritual formation, and pastoral ministry. My problem, initially, was in treating the three offices of Christ like three flavors of ice cream— Prophet = chocolate, Priest = strawberry, and King = vanilla; and I've always been a chocolate guy, not a Neapolitan guy.

In God's goodness, I came to realize, after graduating from Westminster, that I needed a whole lot more than a trustworthy prophet just to give me "normative" answers for micromanaging my life and the multitude of people challenges that emerge in pastoral ministry. Go figure! I needed a compassionate and gracious High Priest, whose mercies would be more than a match for my heart and its "existential" crisis. I also needed a mighty King to make cosmos of the chaos of my "situational" reality, and to thrust me into a larger narrative than my own navel-gazing story. In short, I needed *all* of Jesus. Even though my multiperspectival "Aha!" moment did not happen on the campus of Westminster, it did happen in the context of ministry, and through my wife's courageous growth in grace.

When I began at Westminster, I never had any intention of becoming a pastor. I assumed I would end up in a ministry like L'Abri or some Christian study center, serving the Lord with my wife in a setting free from the trappings of "institutional Christianity." But as providence would have it, we got pregnant and I needed a job, so I became the youth pastor at First Presbyterian Church in Winston-Salem, North Carolina, in 1977.

To get to know the "new guy" better, the senior staff of First Presbyterian took me on a weekend retreat to a beautiful home in the mountains of North Carolina. After a wonderful evening meal, we gathered comfortably in the den in front of a huge stone fireplace. Two searching questions were put before me. "Scotty, what are your biggest heart-struggles in life?" And, "What questions about God or mysteries of the faith are you still pondering?" I maybe paused about sixty seconds before answering with these words: "I'm not really struggling with anything because I have found great sufficiency in Jesus, and I can't think of any questions for which Reformed theology hasn't provided all the answers I need."

As soon as I finished speaking, a discernible pall fell over my circle of new colleagues. Although no one said it, I am sure they must have been thinking, "What have we done in hiring this moron? How did he get through the interview process?" Over the course of the next year and a half, I was increasingly exposed as an insecure youth pastor who loved teaching the youth more than he loved the youth, and who was fuller of himself than full of God's grace. The beckoning of brokenness began.

In 1979, I took a new position as youth pastor at First Presbyterian Church in Nashville, Tennessee. Displacing my wife, Darlene, from our beloved Tar Heel state proved to be the severe mercy through which she began her most demanding and liberating growth in grace. The wounds and pain of childhood sexual abuse could not be denied, hidden, or ignored any longer. Darlene began a healing journey that was both intimidating and inviting to me. It was intimidating because she dared to go to dark places in her story for which Jesus, as a wonderful and merciful High Priest, alone was sufficient—places that I was unwilling to go with her, into either her story, or mine.

Darlene wrestled with God in a way that was unnerving to me, confronting not only the tragedy of her abuse but also the cruel wound of her father's suicide, which occurred only four weeks after our first child was born. The healthier Darlene got, the more it disrupted the fragile equilibrium in our marriage. Her growth exposed the lockdown of my own heart, even as it revealed how intimacy-deficient I was. Although this process was not very "fun," in a profound way it was quite inviting. Darlene's willingness to accept her brokenness made it easier for me to begin discovering and dealing with mine.

Another inviting dimension of Darlene's journey was seeing how her growing experience of Jesus' high priestly ministry propelled her into Jesus' kingly commitment to make all things new. Far from throwing sequential pity parties for herself or becoming paralyzed by victimization, Darlene became an advocate for others who had been traumatized by various forms of abuse. Indeed, as the comfort of Christ came into her life she entered more willingly into the sufferings of Christ.

It's not a reach to say that the "Frame-work" of triperspectivalism came alive to me through my own wife's grueling growth in the gospel.

A Frame Is the Lens-Holding Part of a Pair of Glasses

John Frame could not give me eyes or sight, but he did help me see that the knowledge of God involves a multitude of epistemological perspectives that can be observed, understood, and experienced *only* through the lens of the gospel. Although the purpose and limits of this article do not allow for much more detail, suffice it to say that God arranged the circumstances of his choosing to bring me to near physical, emotional, and spiritual burnout at the height of my so-called success as the planting/senior pastor of Christ Community Church, in Franklin, Tennessee. I never hurt so "good" in my life.

Over the course of the past seven or eight years, I have come to know more of the glory and grace of Jesus than I could ever have hoped for. Through counseling, friendship, and a lot of hard work, I have been able to grieve the deepest wounds in my story, identify and repent of idols that robbed me and those I love, and discover that the gospel is a whole lot bigger and better than I ever imagined. I pray I will be even more engaged with these realities in the coming years.

A FRAME IS AN ARTIST'S TOOL FOR CREATING BEAUTY— LIKE A NEEDLEPOINT HOOP, OR THE FRAME TO WHICH AN ARTIST SECURES HIS CANVAS

In conclusion, my indebtedness to John Frame's hard work and heart work in the gospel can been seen in a triperspectival aesthetic of beauty—that is, in how we have developed most of our ministries in Christ Community Church (outlined below) with the intent of revealing the threefold offices of Christ, to the glory of our triune God.

Our Core Values

- Gospel Astonishment: Revealing Christ through the various ministries of the gospel.
- Gospel Culture: Adoring Christ together in covenant community.
- Gospel Movement: Applying Christ in our neighborhoods, in our culture, and among the nations.

Our Philosophy of Ministry and Spiritual Formation

Informed minds, enflamed hearts, and engaged hands—all through the gospel of God's grace.

Our Counseling Ministry

Jesus is the Prophet who speaks, the Priest who cares, and the King who transforms.

Our Services of Worship

Our entire service of worship is now built so that the ministry of the Word and sacraments unfolds in a three-part liturgy:

- We gather to listen to Jesus, our great Prophet, giving him our attention and our conscience.
- We respond by adoring Jesus, our great High Priest, by giving him our sin and our brokenness.

- We go forth to obey Jesus, our great King, by giving him our obeisance and our obedience, as his worshiping servants in the community and among the nations.

Our Church-Planting Model

Planting gospel-driven churches involves exegeting the texts of Scripture (normative), the souls of people (existential), and the culture of the community (situational).

Even Our Understanding of the Gospel Itself

The gospel is like a great song. It has an amazing lyric (normative) and a contagious melody (existential) that lead to a transforming dance (situational).

Thus, speaking for myself, but no doubt in symphony with many others, I finish this essay where I began: "I've been 'Framed'!"—and thankfully so.

28

JOHN FRAME'S MISSIONAL-
ECUMENICAL VIEW OF THE
CHURCH: UNITY IN CHRIST ALONE

JOHN H. ARMSTRONG

JOHN FRAME IS a lucid thinker who deeply cares for the church of Jesus Christ. Lucid thinkers often write things that make you say: "I wonder why I never saw that." Or, if you are a teacher or preacher, "I wonder why I never said that." Perhaps nowhere is this more self-evident than in John's doctrine of the church. John is a conservative, rigorous, and confessional Presbyterian. Make no mistake about that. But he is not prepared to allow this system of thought to limit his thinking about the church. He listens to the whole of Scripture, looks over the history of the church, and longs for what Jesus desired in the High Priestly Prayer in John's Gospel.

> My prayer is not for them alone. I pray also for those who will believe in me through their message, that all of them may be one, Father, just as you are in me and I am in you. May they also be in us so that the world may believe that you have sent me. I have given them the glory that you gave me, that they may be one as we are one—I in them and you in me—so that they may be brought to complete unity. Then the

world will know that you sent me and have loved them even as you have loved me. (John 17:20–23)[1]

The Nature of the Church

Frame's doctrine of the church is correctly built on the biblical premise that salvation is more than the rescue of individuals. Faithfully committed to a biblical theology of the covenant, Frame recognizes that God saves families, even nations. Indeed, God called the family of Abraham, through a gracious covenant, to be a holy nation. "In the New Testament that nation is the church of Jesus Christ."[2] This understanding of Israel and the church is not developed by Frame into an anti-Semitic polemic, but rather according to the inclusive and apostolic use of the term *holy nation* in a text such as 1 Peter 2:9.

My point is proved by how Frame answers the most basic question of all, at least in considering the doctrine of the church: what is the church? The lucidity of Professor Frame is again apparent when he answers: "Essentially, the church is the people of God in all ages."[3] Frame acknowledges the traditional distinction between the *visible* and *invisible* church,[4] but candidly admits that this "language is from tradition, not the Bible."[5] One senses, after reading all that Frame has written about the church, that he is a more faithful listener to the big themes of Scripture than many of his critics who also espouse a high view of the Bible.

So what is a church as we see it? Frame says it is a community of people "who credibly profess faith in Christ, with their children."[6] This community consists of all who confess Christ, everywhere and at all times. Visible churches include believers and unbelievers, but all members are members of the visible covenant community. Some keep the covenant and some break it.

Frame further says: "The word *church* in the New Testament refers to local, regional and universal bodies."[7] In the New Testament era, Christians

1. All Scripture quotations are from TNIV.
2. *SBL*, 233.
3. Ibid., 236.
4. WCF 25.1–2.
5. *SBL*, 236.
6. Ibid., 237.
7. Ibid.

met mostly in homes, as house churches. Regionally, there was a city church, such as the church of Rome. There is also a universal church, the whole body of believers throughout the world—the whole earth (*oikoumene*). Frame does not position the local/city/regional church against the universal church, but accepts both as biblical. This is a key to understanding Frame's thought about unity and reunion, which we will see in a moment.

THE UNIVERSALITY OF THE CHURCH

What distinguishes Frame's thinking from so many of his peers is his simple, humble commitment to the *oikoumene*, the whole church spread across the earth. *Oikoumene* is derived from the Greek word *oikein*, "to inhabit." In antiquity the term referred to "the inhabited earth." Politically, the term was used to designate the realm of the Greco-Roman Empire, to mark the cultural distinctions between the civilized world and the barbarian. In Psalm 24:1 (LXX) the term is used as a synonym for *earth*. In the New Testament the term is sometimes used with a political connotation (cf. Luke 4:5–7; Rev. 16:14), and in Hebrews 2:5 the word is used of the expected reign of God, called "the *oikoumene* to come."

Subsequently, the more widespread use of this term was linked to the extension of the Christian community across the entire Roman Empire. By the fourth century the term had become synonymous with "the Christian world." The adjective (Latin *universalis*) refers to everything that has universal validity. This is how the term came to be used of councils and leaders in the early centuries of Christianity. The first church councils, whose primary teaching is still highly esteemed through the whole church, were *ecumenical* councils, from *oikoumene*.

In the Reformation, Protestant churches lost their sense of this ecumenical dimension, breaking down into national entities organized around various confessions and differing traditions. By this sad division, one that Frame does not look at with delight or pleasure, we now have thousands upon thousands of "churches," regional groups or denominations.

To understand John Frame's view of these historical developments is to enter a world that many in his context are unwilling to enter. It is a world where a minister and theologian such as he can celebrate the gains of the Reformation while realizing that Jesus came to establish a church, not denominations. It is a world in which the unity of the church is spiritual but also relational—which means it ultimately must be organizational. It is this call, central to Frame's understanding of the church, that puts him at odds with so many of his peers.

THE MISSIONAL NATURE OF THE CHURCH

Some two hundred years after the Protestant Reformation, a revival of genuine piety—sometimes despised in Reformed circles by the epithet *pietism*—called on the church to see that its nature was deeply rooted in a worldwide calling to obey the mission of Jesus Christ. It is safe to say that the Protestant Reformers did not grasp this mission as deeply as their heirs would over the centuries to follow. But the Reformers' struggle was about the gospel and the faithfulness of the church, more than about its mission and growth. Frame longs to see the two brought together. He is unwilling to sacrifice the core truths of the Reformation, while at the same time he profoundly longs to see mission and growth in disciple-making at the center of Reformed life and thought.

The new sense of the worldwide calling of the church, flowing from various prayer movements and revivals, eventually reminded a growing number of Protestants (especially after the seventeenth century) that unity was a vital theme of Holy Scripture. This same sense of calling led Christians, especially beginning in the nineteenth century, to develop "ecumenical" concerns and to foster efforts that resulted in this term's being used in the modern era to embrace "a spiritual attitude manifesting the awareness of the oneness of the people of God and the longing for its restoration."[8]

More than perhaps any other conservative Reformed theologian I know, at least in the early twenty-first century, Frame has understood that the nature of the church must not be divorced from the task of the church. In his primer on systematic theology, *Salvation Belongs to the Lord*, Frame links the nature of the church with the missionary task of the church by admitting: "It is actually hard . . . to separate these two things. If the church isn't doing what it's supposed to do, we may question whether it is a church."[9] Thus Frame argues that the traditional three "marks" of the church are not

---

8. Konrad Raiser, "*Oikoumene*," in *Dictionary of the Ecumenical Movement*, ed. Nicholas Lossky et al. (Grand Rapids: Eerdmans, 1991), 741–42.

9. *SBL*, 247.

entirely adequate. Added to them must be the mark of carrying out the Great Commission.

Frame is clearly right. Yet many still argue against him, especially within the tradition and denominations in which he has been an elder over the course of his ministry. (Frame has been an elder in the Orthodox Presbyterian Church and the Presbyterian Church in America.) Some theologians will point to the early creeds of the church and suggest that mission is not set forth as part of the essence of the church. The answer to this point seems obvious to me. The church that wrote these creeds was actively engaged in the mission of Christ and did not need to confess this point, since it was neither under attack nor in serious doubt. This was the church of the martyrs and the church of early Christendom. It had not settled into the patterns it would take in the centuries that followed.

Frame believes that the nature and task of the church are so closely related that "you can't have one without the other."[10] But some of his peers have been extremely uncomfortable with this point, believing that mission is the work of the church but not part of its *essence*. Frame is extremely careful to note that he disagrees with theologians who say that "the task of the church is its nature" because they want to "de-emphasize qualities like body of Christ and bride of Christ."[11] As God calls individuals by giving them the status of sons and daughters, and then by giving them a calling to serve him and one another, so he also calls the church as a body corporate.

Frame's view of the church is also deeply sensitive to how Jesus and the apostles related the church to the kingdom of God. New Testament theologians often speak of the church as the "servant" of the kingdom. The church and kingdom are *not* the same but they cannot be separated. This understanding, as much as any single biblical insight I know, has helped serious Catholic and Protestant theological conversation to advance since Vatican II. Frame seems to accept this emphasis, although he does not develop it significantly in his written work. He says that the church should maintain a "military metaphor—the headquarters of the kingdom of God, the base from which God's dominion extends and expands."[12]

Perhaps nothing John Frame has written has caused as much angst in his own circles as his writing on unity and church reunion. Frame believes

10. Ibid.
11. Ibid.
12. Ibid., 249.

that Christians should move away from denominationalism toward unity and reunion.

In his *Evangelical Reunion*, Frame argues that the barriers we have built between various conservative/evangelical churches can be torn down. He roots this belief in several arguments but appeals practically to our missional DNA. He writes about the "environment" in other countries in which missionaries often serve, and suggests that many conservative missionaries have found the chasm between American denominations is inappropriate to their mission environment.[13] This mission environment has not led toward doctrinal indifference but rather toward "a renewed appreciation of one's doctrinal tradition, along with a greater respect for Christians outside that tradition and an ability to work together with them."[14]

He then applies this same line of missional thinking to the American church, and says we can do better by not competing with one another, but rather by cooperating in ways that show our desire for relational oneness. He even shows the reader that this can be applied personally and that "denominational chauvinism can be broken down . . . by personal evangelism."[15]

He applies this same missional perspective to the early church and concludes that we have very good reasons to "see our denominational differences in perspective."[16] Seeing and acting on this perspective are what Frame's *Evangelical Reunion* is really all about. He admits that our differences seem important from one angle, but from "other angles (which are arguably more in accord with those of the Bible) they do not seem to be so great."[17] Frankly, the first time I read this statement I said, "Of course he is right, but this is so inconsistent with what I hear from within the ecclesial tradition (denominations) that John represents!" John concludes his argument about putting denominations into this missional perspective by writing:

> I am convinced that such openness will in time be used of God to bring his church to a oneness beyond anything we have experienced in our day—a oneness not based on doctrinal indifference, but on a fuller understanding of God's word than any of our present groups can claim to have.[18]

13. *ER*, 77.
14. Ibid.
15. Ibid., 80.
16. Ibid., 82.
17. Ibid., 83.
18. Ibid.

I first read those words in 1993. I read them again in early 2009. They seem even more amazing now than sixteen years ago. Perhaps I am so amazed because I have followed Frame's hopeful missional-ecumenical perspective for these many years and discovered firsthand how right his thinking has been. I am utterly convinced that John Frame's ecclesial optimism is not misplaced. Let me explain why.

FRAME THE MISSIONAL-ECUMENIST

I have shown how Frame grounds his view of unity and reunion in the nature of the church *and* the mission of Christ. I have introduced a term of my own to describe this perspective: *missional-ecumenism*. Let me explain what I mean. *Missional-ecumenism* is a term that I have coined, so far as I can tell. I have simply taken two existing words and put them together. By this I wish to stress two truths that are bound together in Scripture: (1) God is both a unity in himself and as such is a sending God; and (2) God's revealed desire for us in John 17:20–23 is that we would be (relationally) one with him in this sending and sent (mission) process. Thus we have missional-ecumenism.

The word *missional* has been used in various ways over the past fifteen years. I want to be very clear in expressing how I am using it. Although *missional-ecumenism* is my term, I believe my friend John Frame will agree with the biblical theology that undergirds my choice of words.

Missional is a relatively recent theological word that reconceptualizes the idea inherent in *missio Dei* (mission of God). It underscores that God sends us into the world as his "sent ones" who are his mission in *both* community life and mission activity. This is what Frame actually contends for in his material on the mission and nature of the church. The key text here is John 20:21, "As the Father has sent me, I am sending you." Christopher Wright correctly notes that "mission is and always has been God's before it becomes ours. The whole Bible presents a God of missional activity, from his purposeful, goal-oriented act of creation to the completion of his cosmic mission in the redemption of the whole creation—a new heaven and a new earth."[19]

19. Christopher Wright, "An Upside-Down World," *Christianity Today* 51:1 (January 2007), http://www.ChristianityToday.com.

FRAME THE REALIST

In John Frame's prophetic call to embrace ecumenism he remains a realist. He is too deeply theological to gloss over our deep differences. But he is also too deeply theological to settle for the sectarianism that so easily defines our present church experience. Instead of surrendering one side or the other of this theological tension, Frame opts to go where few conservative Reformed theologians have been willing to go—to a healthy, vigorous, open ecumenism that is profoundly rooted in mission.

But Frame's realism still shines brightly throughout his work on the church. He knows that the total organizational union of all Christians is not practical, at least not at this time in our history. He understands the real problems we face, but never settles for a divided church as the long-term answer to these problems. He believes that unity, especially among evangelicals and Bible-believing groups, is not only possible but highly desirable. This we can pursue right now. Only our unwillingness prohibits us from acting.

Those of us who know John personally have heard him say on various occasions that we should not hold annual celebrations of the birth of our denomination. We should, instead, mourn our collective sin. The first time I heard Professor Frame say this, I laughed and said, "Sure, John, and who will take that suggestion to heart?" But he was serious. He explains this view in a footnote in the preface of his book *Evangelical Reunion*:

> Not everyone who advocates a split (or the perpetuation of a split) is guilty of sin. Sometimes those who leave a denomination and/or start a new one are in the right; sometimes it is right to turn down an opportunity for reunion. However, it is my firm conviction that wherever occurs a denominational division, and whenever an existing division is prolonged, there is sin everywhere. That sin may be in the original group, the seceding group, or both. Most often, in my judgment, the last alternative is the case.[20]

FRAME THE HUMBLE THEOLOGIAN

Many of Frame's critics do not grasp the fact that a *humble apologetics* (John Stackhouse's term) is always appropriate, now more than ever. Frame represents such a stance when it comes to his treatment

20. *ER*, 13.

of the doctrine of the church. In the preface to *Evangelical Reunion,* he confesses that his own views are limited by his position (and thus experience) within two small denominations: the Orthodox Presbyterian Church (OPC) and the Presbyterian Church in America (PCA). But he still warmly appeals to readers from beyond these two denominations, even while he acknowledges that he could not find many helpful illustrations for his argument from outside "the Presbyterian and Reformed tradition."[21]

But Frame does not stop there. He admits even more. He writes: "I am not a specialist in modern church history, and I hesitate to use examples that I have not experienced from the inside, so to speak."[22] Most theologians fall short of "humble" theology precisely because they embrace their own expertise too confidently. The tendency is then to believe that competence in one small area of thought makes you an expert in almost every other area. Professor Frame avoids this error brilliantly, choosing to remain a learner at the feet of Jesus his Lord.

The way Frame explains his treatment of church unity is a reflection of this "humble" theology. He suggests that those from beyond his own ranks might learn from him precisely because they can gain

> a [more] objective perspective on the issues discussed than if I were discussing your own denomination. If you *are* in one of these groups, you may lose the advantage of objectivity but gain the advantage of a more existential or personal involvement. Some readers will need more of the one, some more of the other; I'll trust the Spirit to sort all that out.[23]

What a brilliant and truly humble ideal—trust the Holy Spirit to sort out the details while you also suggest that there is more to be learned while we all struggle (together) within our present situation.

Finally, Frame appeals to the reader of this prophetical call for reunion by saying his book is not for everyone. He has specifically written, he informs us, for those who have a "friendship" with Jesus Christ.[24] This is where humble theology always begins.

21. Ibid.
22. Ibid.
23. Ibid.
24. Ibid., 15.

Frame the Ecclesial Revolutionary

Frame believes that denominations "are something of a sacred cow in Christian circles."[25] We look at them, in many Protestant contexts, as one would look upon a favorite team. This is our team, "our country, right or wrong." We want to see our team win where others fail. We are even pleased if we win at the expense of others. "Failure to support our team then turns out to be a kind of blasphemy, almost like renouncing Jesus himself."[26]

The problem is obvious, as Frame sees it. We are too sectarian. The word *sect*, from the Latin *secta*, which is from *sequi*, means "to follow." It is commonly used to refer to a group that has broken away from some larger religious group, and thus holds distinctive or unusual views. In this sense the earliest Christians were a sect of the Jews. In the modern sense, the term generally refers to a group that breaks away from an older, established church and follows the unique and particular teachings of a leader who forms the basis for the new group. By this understanding, sectarianism has come to refer to an excessively doctrinaire commitment to one's own view(s) or group. It usually results in a narrow-minded devotion to one's own church or group. Those who disagree are often condemned by the sectarian(s), sometimes harshly. Some sectarians disavow all relationship to any established Christian church.

I believe Frame is referring to sectarianism when he talks about the way we see our denomination as "our team." He admits that what he is asking the reader to hear may well go unheeded by many. He admits in his introduction:

> Perhaps it is foolish for me to write this book, since many will see it as an attack on their team, their country, their mother, their home. Actually, I don't think it is. I think my argument, if implemented, will produce a much stronger team and country, a far more comfortable maternal home. Indeed, rather than destroying all we love and cherish in our denominations, my proposal will preserve all that is good about them far more effectively than we seem able to preserve it today.[27]

25. Ibid., 16.
26. Ibid.
27. Ibid., 16–17.

Frame suggests that the application of his ideas will lead to loss, even sadness. But the people of Jesus ought to be willing to make this "tiny sacrifice for Jesus"[28]—"tiny" because of his sacrifice for us (1 John 4:7–11).

Frame clearly grasps that what he was doing, by calling for unity and reunion among fellow evangelical Christians, was radical. (He doesn't develop what this means for nonevangelicals, especially Roman Catholics and the Orthodox, although one can sense his reticence and caution.) Although one can fault Professor Frame for not addressing the wider issues of ecumenism (he wrote this in 1991 when the ecumenical conversation was very much alive in the broader post-Vatican II Catholic Church), I believe his core understanding is the beginning for evangelicals—especially for serious Reformed evangelicals.

One of Frame's consistent appeals, going back over the entire course of his writing on theology, has been his desire to see Christians "trust and obey God's written word, the Holy Scriptures."[29] This is what made his book so consequential for me personally. I am Reformed and I am also deeply committed to the sacred Scriptures. Before I could even begin to grasp the importance of the missional-ecumenical connection, I needed someone like John Frame to humbly take me to the Bible. He says his treatment of *Evangelical Reunion* is a "Bible study," and I profoundly agree. If his view is to be refuted, then the serious reader will have to engage him with the Bible first and foremost! Frame wants to truly allow Scripture to make "disruptive, dramatic changes."[30]

He adds: "Before you read the argument, perhaps you should ask yourself whether, if God wanted you to help him tear down all the old, familiar denominational structures, you would be willing to join the project."[31] He then makes one of the most candid admissions I have ever encountered in a modern, conservative Reformed theologian: "I am writing in this book to potential ecclesiastical revolutionaries, to those who are so sold out to Jesus that they are willing to give up many cherished things for him."[32]

I am honored to know Professor Frame personally. No one who meets him would see him as a shadowy revolutionary who wants to blow up structures or spiritually burn down institutions with his words. His revolution is

28. Ibid., 17.
29. Ibid., 16.
30. Ibid.
31. Ibid.
32. Ibid.

one that does not employ the weapons of the flesh, but rather the weapons of the Spirit. His revolution is rooted in Jesus, the one who calls us to take up our cross and die. Frame writes to "put the authority of God above the comfort of the status quo."[33] This is his revolution.

But do not miss his point here. To follow where John Frame leads you will cost you deeply. You will be called to give up cherished things. I learned this by trying, inconsistently I must admit, to follow John's basic thoughts over the past fifteen years. Some of John's peers warned me and even argued against his view of the church. The problem for me was simple—John's arguments convinced me, and I had to follow them because I believed I was following Jesus and making the "tiny" sacrifice for which he so simply appealed in *Evangelical Reunion*.

FRAME'S ARGUMENT FOR UNITY IN CHRIST ALONE

There are many ways to argue for the unity of the one, holy, catholic, (and) apostolic church. John Frame makes his case by appealing *totally* to the written Word. This is a great strength. One could argue that it is also his weakness, since he does not deal with many issues that must be addressed from the Christian tradition itself. But the strength is obvious—he takes us to the Supreme Court, the Holy Scripture, and here he leads us to Christ alone.

His argument begins in the Old Testament, by showing that Israel was called to be one people. It then reaches into the New Testament by showing that this same appeal to oneness remains. The believer in Jesus worships at one altar, as did the believer in the Old Testament. From here Frame argues that Jesus built only *one* church. His simple point is evident: "The word church is regularly used in the singular to refer to the whole New Testament people of God (Matt. 16:18; cf. Acts 5:11; 12:5; 1 Cor. 10:32; 15:9; Gal. 1:13; Eph. 1:22; etc.)." This oneness is of a "higher order" than that of Old Testament Israel.[34] Frame says the Scripture also teaches this doctrine of church unity through images such as "a temple, the body of Christ, the bride of Christ, the flock of the Good Shepherd, the branches of the vine, the people (or family) of God."[35] Furthermore, the *one* Spirit baptizes us into *one*

33. Ibid.
34. Ibid., 26.
35. Ibid.

body, and this *one* body is given the gifts of *one* Spirit. God's love, revealed in Christ, binds us as *one*; thus there is only *one* gospel, *one* baptism, and *one* Lord's Supper.[36]

On the opposite side of this unity, the New Testament "rebukes the mentalities and practices that were later to produce denominational division in the church."[37] These mentalities and practices include autonomy, factionalism, lust for power, unwillingness to seek reconciliation, failure to maintain church discipline, inattention to doctrinal and practical unity, and the failure to help believers in need.[38] Further, "When the Scripture speaks of the church as the body of Christ, it contrasts harmonious working together of the parts of the body with 'schism' or 'division.' "[39]

But the last two of Frame's biblical arguments for one church are the two that most influenced me to live out my passion for the unity of the whole church and never settle for mere intellectual agreement.

Frame believes that Jesus' prayer that *the church would be one* is vital. This is why he turns to the text with which I began this essay (John 17:20–23). Jesus clearly prayed that we would be one as he and his Father are one. Frame's clear, simple exposition of this text blows away the common misunderstanding that has been applied by Protestant polemicists who insist that there is no mandate here for visible unity. But one unsettling question remains: "Are we prepared to say that Jesus' prayer has not yet been answered?" Frame answers this question in a way that turns the whole debate back on those who insist that Jesus was *not* praying for our visible unity. He says: "I have no doubt that the prayer of Jesus will one day be fully answered, that God will unite the church in his own time and will unite it organizationally as well as in all other respects."[40] This statement undoubtedly frightens many. It thrills me. Let me explain.

JOHN 17: A TEXT BADLY INTERPRETED

I can think of no other passage of Holy Scripture for which there have been so many wrong explanations. Some teachers are quite sure they know

36. Ibid., 26–27.
37. Ibid., 27–28.
38. Ibid., 28.
39. Ibid.
40. Ibid., 29.

exactly what this text does *not* mean. In the end, most of their interpretations are nothing more than personal *reactions*.

When conservative theologians of Scripture come to these verses, they generally offer suggestions about what these words do *not* mean. Consider a few:

- We should *never* try to unite several different churches or congregations. The union of churches, or denominations, is *not* in view here.
- We should *never* engage in serious dialogue with churches that we believe unfaithful to the truth.
- There is *no common mission* that *all* churches are called to engage in; thus there is no reason to share in Christ's mission visibly.
- There is no concern in this prayer for the worldwide church, at least as seen in any *visible* form, since this would lead to *ecumenism*, one of the great enemies of the gospel.
- Whatever this prayer means, we must always keep in the forefront the serious biblical warnings about compromise and false teaching; cf. Deut. 7:1–6; 2 Cor. 6:14; Rev. 18:4.

Many seem to fear so deeply what Jesus is saying that they are intent on escaping an honest exposition. This is why they conclude that John 17 is talking about an *invisible unity* that is true regardless of what we do. They argue that the church, consisting of all true Christians, must *necessarily* be invisible. This church is the "one, holy, catholic and apostolic church" that the early Christians spoke about. Since this church is unified, and can never be anything but unified, Jesus is praying about a type of oneness that we already possess. If this is true then the prayer has nothing to do with what *we* should do now or in the future. It has been answered and is still being answered, and thus the text has no real bearing on the subject of (visible) unity between Christians right now.

I suggest that we need to read John 13–17, which is one redemptive-historical context, and let these amazing words sweep over our hearts. Then we should ask one simple question: *"Why would Jesus pray about something that is already true regardless of what we do with his words?"* It just makes no sense at all to read these words in this way, especially given the reference to our being *brought* to complete unity. How are we *brought* to something that we already possess?

Although it is true that all who believe in Christ are already *one* in him, it is *not* true that what he prayed for here has already come to pass in all our lives and churches. The truth is that the reality for which Jesus prays is not evident in most of our congregations where there is *supposedly* agreement about doctrine, i.e., in our various denominations.

How to Understand Unity

So what is Jesus *really* praying for? I suggest that he is praying for our *relational* unity. If you please, the unity that he prays for is *spiritual*, but in the sense that it is Spirit-given and Spirit-sustained. This unity is not something that we can create on our own. (I am certainly *not* using *spiritual* here as a synonym for *invisible*.) If the unity for which Jesus prays is between people in human relationships, then this unity can be lost to divisions, rivalries, factions, and church splits. This is why we need a new vision, one that Professor Frame gives in his clear biblical exposition.

Jesus is *not* addressing the issue of denominations (since they did not exist) nor universal church councils (which did not exist either). Most biblical scholars, including modern Catholic ones, agree with this point. Remember, Jesus is praying that all his followers will live as he lived. The words here have a clear reference to his personal relationship with his Father. But you say, "His oneness with the Father was eternal." Right you are, but this is not what is in view. Look more carefully at the text. The second person of the eternal Trinity, the *Logos*, was incarnate in the man Christ Jesus. Jesus lived fully and completely as a human person. In his humanity Jesus lived day to day in total dependence on his Father. This relationship, lived by the fullness of the Holy Spirit, was one of perfect unity. Thus *relational* oneness between Jesus and the Father was a perfectly expressed unity of persons. This relational aspect is what is in view in John 17.

This becomes particularly clear in verse 23 where Jesus prays that his disciples "may be *brought* to *complete* unity." We already have perfect spiritual unity in our relationship with Jesus. But we do not *experience* this unity *relationally* unless we are "brought" into it through day-to-day experience. This tells me that there is a dynamic *process* going on as we share life in the Trinity. When Christians respond to one another in the way for which Jesus prayed, then the results will be exactly what this prayer asks the Father to give to us: "Then the world will know that you sent me and have loved them even as you have loved me" (v. 23).

WHY DOES THIS REALLY MATTER?

So why is relational unity between Christians so important? In the High Priestly Prayer, Jesus says that his mission hangs on our being the answer to this prayer. Frame says, "Unity is given by divine sovereignty but requires the efforts of human beings."[41] He adds, "God's sovereignty does not entail human passivity. Scripture's emphasis on God's sovereignty in restoring unity does not undermine human efforts in that direction; rather, it encourages them."[42] Here is the point of Jesus' prayer: the mission of Christ is so closely linked with the church *relationally* that the world will *not* understand and experience God's love until we are "brought" to *experience* this unity.

Given what we have seen, I have to ask honestly, How has the church survived in the world given our egregious schisms, faithlessness, and corruption?

Historian Clyde Manschreck suggests that the message of the early Christian church has been "abused, institutionalized, abandoned, [and] rationalized."[43] But the church is still here, sometimes in poor health and occasionally pulsating with power and great blessing, as in China today. More often than not the church is truly "lukewarm"—alive but in obvious need of divine judgment (Rev. 3:16).

It is my thesis that every single church should regularly ask, What does Christ *really* think of *our* church? Such a question is genuinely troubling but truly honest. Asking it may actually prompt deep repentance and far less boasting about our importance.

The church began to express visible life through Peter's confession of faith in the divine revelation that Jesus was the Christ (Matt. 16:13–18). Then the power of the Holy Spirit was poured out on the earliest disciples (Acts 2), and the festival of Pentecost became a birthday celebration. These disciples did not bear the sword, or engage aggressively in the politics of their

41. Ibid.
42. Ibid.
43. Clyde L. Manschreck, A History of Christianity in the World (Englewood Cliffs, NJ: Prentice Hall, 1974), 20.

day. They loved all people everywhere, caring for those in need and serving the oppressed wherever possible. Congregations grew in the face of intense opposition. Not even the powers of hell could stop their mission.

From that day to the present the church has marched like a mighty army around the globe. From the martyrdom of Stephen (Acts 7), through the waves of slaughter brought about by Roman persecution, through Muslim hordes attacking Christian lands, and finally through twentieth-century communist opposition, the church has grown. This is happening today in the churches of China, India, Africa, and Latin America. The church cannot be stopped. Why? *It is God's church.* There have been times when it almost seemed like the light would go out. But God has kept his promise and his church continues to grow, even where he has administered corrective discipline to his people (cf. Rev. 2–3).

But what exactly has kept the church through all this suffering and trial? I believe the real story shows that it was not a vague belief in the concept of God, but a living, active faith in the God who *is* love (1 John 4:8, 16). The very substance and nature of God is love. If this is true, then all of his activity in this world comes out of the loving heart of God.

This "new religion" of love was not "an external system of ritual sacrifice . . . but an internal flooding of the mind and spirit with divine love and understanding."[44] The power of God's Spirit transformed these first believers, resulting in incredible joy and peace. In addition, the early church "understood itself for what it was intended to be: *a spiritual kingdom sharing spiritual truth with a troubled world.*"[45]

Conclusion

Professor Frame says: "It is when denominations are most true to their tradition, that they are most ecumenical."[46] It is apparent that I agree. Frame suggests that when we are *better* Reformed Christians, *better* Baptist Christians, *better* Lutheran Christians, *better* Pentecostal Christians, we are all *better* Christians.[47] And, he concludes, "On the day when, God willing, all

44. Warren Angel, *Yes We Can Love One Another: Catholics and Protestants Can Share a Common Faith* (Carlsbad, CA: Magnus Press, 1997), 10.
45. Ibid.
46. *ER*, 63.
47. Ibid.

denominations are re-absorbed into the one, true church, nothing of value need be destroyed."[48]

The vision behind such a statement is exceeded by that of very few modern Reformed theologians. The courage that it took to articulate such a view of the church may seem "tiny" to Professor Frame. I know that it cost him personally to articulate this prophetic stance. I am profoundly grateful that he did so, since his words penetrated my mind and heart years ago. These words were used to bring about a change that led me to embrace the missional-ecumenical stance I have articulated. It is an understanding for which I now give my life daily by ministering to churches around the world.

48. Ibid.

29

JOHN FRAME'S PASTORAL METHOD
FOR CHRISTIAN UNITY

D. CLAIR DAVIS

FOR FORTY YEARS I have delighted in John Frame and his work for Christ. His zeal for loving interaction within Christ's church has engrossed and thrilled me. He is a meticulous biblical theologian, but also one with heartfelt concern for the unity of the church of Jesus Christ. As I've asked myself where the church is going, it has seemed hard to be committed to the truth of the Bible and the gospel of Jesus as the only way of salvation without becoming very narrow on and blind to everything else. How can we tell the difference between the core of the faith and implications that are not always as clear and compelling as some believe? How can we intelligibly encourage and bless people within different theological traditions? John Frame has gone a long way in discovering how, and his method can teach us all.

This is of vital and strategic importance today. Fueled by hordes of committed godly but woefully biblically illiterate believers, with their disgust with irrelevant ingrown denominations, the "Emergent" church is growing rapidly. It seems committed to being relevant and teachable, a very good thing; but it seems unwilling to continue to learn from our Christian heritage, at least its evangelical Protestant expression. That seems very limiting to me—just another variety of narrowness! The old liberal church is dying, both here and in Europe, but at the same time the emerging church with a similar agenda may be taking its place.

That may not be the worst thing. Emergent is trying to do things better, but many have just stopped trying anything. In our jaded time, religion may still have a limited place in individual lives, yet as something for vibrant discussion and concerted action, it seems unreal. But what if today we were not content with ignoring each other because our viewpoints seem so different? What if we sought to pray, along with our Lord in John 17, that we might be one so that the world would believe? What if our prayer lives became truly "missional," going beyond personal desires? Could we understand each other and rejoice in each other in the way we use the Bible?

Bemoaning the state of the church is one thing. Advancing a viable alternative is much harder and more helpful. How will we find the place for the authority of Scripture today? How can we seriously explore our rapidly changing cultural environment without succumbing to thoroughgoing relativism? Will we be able to say more than "just go back to the Bible"?

For me, giving good answers to those questions is the meaning of the labors and heart of John Frame. He is one who has given his academic life to this enterprise. In the words of Robert Dick Wilson of the old Princeton Seminary, he has not shirked the difficult questions.

Think about how we got to the hard place where we find ourselves today. How did our churches get so confused? How did it happen that the denominational churches lost interest in their theological identity? Why was the response of those committed to that identity largely ineffectual? Why did those who left the churches find it so hard to agree among themselves? Was it possible to have done it better? Can we see a better way ahead?

Early Distractions

The earliest distraction from the heart of the gospel came through the "psychologizing" of faith in the American Awakenings. How should the church respond when membership is declining, when Christian life and growth seem pitifully weak? One answer was to call into question the conversion of people and also their pastors. If that is the problem, then the next question must be: How can true conversions be facilitated? That question can be very difficult.

But if there is a recognizable sequence within most conversions, is it not possible to make use of that sequence to aid people in accomplishing the great change of trusting in Christ? Reference to the *plan of salvation* or *ordo salutis* became common in Puritanism. Since William Perkins and his *Golden Chain*, the key text had been Romans 8:29–30, which describes the course of God's work in his people from predestination to glorification. With that clear path before us, we are indeed assured that nothing can separate us from the love of Christ. But why are we so sure that the path described lies before us *prior* to faith in Christ? Could it not rather be the hard but glorious path of the battle with sin and suffering *throughout* the believer's experience? Isn't Romans 8 just the long version of Philippians 1:6, encouraging us by reminding us that when God begins a work in your heart, he will continue it to the end? It would help if the Bible gave us more detail about the conversions it describes, but in reading the many accounts in Acts, about all we can see there is that the Holy Spirit worked through the preaching of Christ's resurrection and many, many believed. The focus is on the message, not on the shape of the response.

Nevertheless, much of the church went the way of *describing* the gospel more vigorously than proclaiming it. The church spoke of the mysterious work within the heart much more than of the triumph of the Savior in his resurrection. Certainly many took the gospel more seriously than they previously had, and there were rich "harvests." But increasingly, the parable of the Oliver Wendell Holmes *Deacon's Masterpiece* and its "One Hoss Shay," which seemed never to wear out but at the end disintegrated into a pile of dust, came to describe American religion. Taking a hard look at your heart can seem helpful—but meaningful only when you take a good look at Jesus risen from the dead at the same time. Otherwise, all that is left at the end is the collapse of the New England theology, which intended to be God-honoring but ended with the unsolved and unsolvable puzzle: how can you induce faith?

Nineteenth-Century Struggles

How could that happen—that the great insight of the Reformation that faith in Christ is always *extraspective*, never defined by its own quality but always by its object, the crucified and risen Jesus Christ, could be so easily lost? After that theological disaster, how could the church change its agenda? If looking inward were fruitless, wouldn't a flurry of outward activity be more promising? The nineteenth century became the time of tireless Christian activity, when God's people put more money toward transforming society than did the national government. Wouldn't all that activity restore the "objective" side of the faith?

To a great extent the sacrifice and dedication of believers did much for the country and the glory of Christ. But some basic issues were hard to relate to clear biblical teaching. If alcoholism were destroying the family, then how did the answer to that threat relate to the best wine provided by Jesus at the Cana wedding feast? If the evils of black slavery were obvious, then how did that relate to the faith of Abraham and other biblical slave owners? These ethical issues seemed to have no clear biblical answers. Why wasn't it possible to be clear on temperance without moving to teetotalism? Why wasn't it possible to separate biblical slavery from its obvious racist context? (No one argued for the value of incompetent whites' becoming slaves to black masters.) Instead it was easier to appeal to "the mind of Christ," and intuitively read his mind where the Bible seemed regrettably silent. By far the most adept in that exercise were the Unitarian abolitionists! Romanticism was in the air, and Christians forgot the source of their faith and life in the Bible alone.

What should have been objective—faith in the risen Jesus Christ—had been psychologized; and then obedience was no longer biblical either but had become pious guesswork. If such elementary issues were so fuzzy, then it would be strange if theology were any clearer, including the question: what good is Calvinism? Everyone knows how dangerous it is to focus on God and his grace, how that seems to inevitably lead to antinomian "easy believism." Biblical Calvinism may be the spiritual backbone of believers in the hard battle with the world, the flesh, and the devil—but it could become abstract and irrelevant. Fundamentalism had its say: when the issues of the day are the truly basic ones of the authority of the Bible and the deity of Christ, isn't it only reasonable to avoid the secondary ones, the divisive ones, which seem to make little practical difference anyway?

Although some were enthusiastic about their doctrinal heritage, they seemed unclear about how to make it relevant to their culture. So the voices for doctrinal reform, or even replacement with a "modern" theology without content, could seem very loud.

Disunity in the Early Twentieth Century

Even Princeton Theological Seminary, with its rich heritage and academic resources, was also singularly uninterested in communicating the gospel within the new culture, for its "practical" theology was just where it was weakest. Even though widespread ministry was happening, few seemed to recognize how hard it was to live for the glory of Jesus, and the great doctrines of God's grace could seem abstract and puzzling. Whenever I think of that, I remember the text of "Amazing Grace" by John Newton, who also penned the following words in a letter:

> I believe most persons who are truly alive unto God, sooner or later meet with some pinches in their experience which constrain them to flee to those doctrines for relief, which perhaps they had formerly dreaded, if not abhorred, because they knew not how to get over some harsh consequences they thought necessarily resulting from them, or because they were stumbled by the miscarriages of those who professed them. In this way I was made a Calvinist myself; and I am content to let the Lord take his own way, and his own time, with others.[1]

Without feeling the pinches, barely perceptible in the Gilded Age or the time of the flappers, people didn't feel the need to take Calvinism seriously. But still, I will always find it hard to grasp why there was no active response to the 1923 Auburn Affirmation's rejection of vital Christian doctrines on the part of twelve hundred Presbyterian ministers. Bradley Longfield's *Presbyterian Controversy* might explain it best: throughout the church there was widespread conviction, regardless of theological direction, that a narrow sectarianism would not meet the needs of the day, and that therefore utmost flexibility was necessary.

J. Gresham Machen's *Christianity and Liberalism* appeared then, at just the right time. Its thesis was very timely and clear: without a recognition of the historical basis for Christianity, there really is no Christian faith. But Machen advanced no real plan of action, except calling on those who no longer believed the Westminster Confession to withdraw from the church. But why should they, when it was clear to all that the confession no longer functioned?

1. John Newton to Mr. S., July 26, 1775.

Princeton was "reorganized" largely to express its direct relationship to the denomination, whose theological orientation was no longer the same as the seminary's. Its critics saw that disjunction in terms of the school's irrelevant curriculum. Out of that context Westminster Theological Seminary came into being in 1929. Its founding board represented a broad spectrum of seasoned leaders within the church. The intention of the new seminary was to train ministers enthusiastic for the biblical and confessional heritage of the church, to carry out a careful long-term plan for transforming the church and returning it to its roots.

But almost immediately Machen did something new and surprising, organizing an "Independent Board for Presbyterian Foreign Missions." He was convinced, correctly, that there were denominational board missionaries who were not committed to the Christian gospel, and concluded that there should be a new board that believers could support. But why? It has always been possible for churches and individuals to designate their giving directly to the missionaries of their choice. Does this free up undesignated funds for liberal missionaries that no one wishes to support directly? Perhaps that case could be made from an actuarial standpoint, but I have never seen it. Further, I am shocked by the very minimal constitutional support argued for the new board. Anyone taking the trouble to look at the index of the Digest of General Assembly minutes under "foreign missions" would immediately discover that in the 1920 union with the Calvinistic Methodist Church, the CMs had been reassured that of course they could continue their former mission board as long as they wished (which they did till about 1937), because support for missions was through "free-will offerings." But Machen made no reference at all to that clear statement, nor to the union agreement between Old School and New School in 1870. Why not? Was Machen so focused on the Christian conscience that work with the constitution seemed irrelevant? It appears that, somehow, serious effort to work for change from within the church had been left behind.

At that point Machen and Westminster lost the great conservative leadership of the church. It was not surprising that Samuel Craig wrote in an editorial in the old *Christianity Today* that everyone would pick Machen for the All-American team, but no one would choose him as quarterback. The Westminster faculty followed Machen's lead in telling the members of the Westminster board that if they wouldn't stand with the Independent Board, they shouldn't be with the seminary, so the board members left. It wasn't surprising that Professor O. T. Allis, a stalwart of the faculty who had come over from Princeton, also found it appropriate to resign.

Certainly the ecclesiastical trials leading to the expulsion of Machen and other members of the Independent Board were blatantly unfair, insofar as they were not permitted to bring evidence of liberalism within the denominational board. No doubt those so expelled from ministry were justified in beginning a new denomination, the group that became the Orthodox Presbyterian Church (OPC). But to my mind, their case could have been much stronger and clearer. It could have spelled out why direct support of evangelical missionaries was not reasonable. It should have said why the great parachurch boards should not be worked with to a greater extent. (That was when the China Inland Mission had designated a part of China as "Presbyterian"!)

Not only did non-OPC faculty leave Westminster, but faculty from other denominations, Cornelius Van Til, Ned Stonehouse, and R. B. Kuiper from the Christian Reformed Church, and John Murray from the Free Presbyterian Church of Scotland, thought it appropriate, perhaps necessary, to identify with the OPC. Even though Westminster never became a denominational seminary, it functioned as such, as faculty took major theological leadership in the new church.

But the new group found it hard to stay together. They knew what they were together against, but didn't seem to know what they had in common with each other. That story is still murky for me, but why was it that all the younger faculty were promoted except Allen MacRae, who with Carl McIntire and Francis Schaeffer then moved on to found Faith Seminary and the Bible Presbyterian Church?

Were the new seminary and church needed because Machen wanted all the power? Or because of John Murray's dispensationalism article, emphasizing weaknesses of that movement but not its strengths? Could there have been greater effort given into clarifying the issues surrounding alcohol? At any rate, whereas there had been one small seminary and denomination, now there were two of both. It began to seem to outsiders that the new church had not really been formed for religious reasons after all, but instead because of cantankerous personalities.

Previously, Presbyterians had given leadership to all the evangelical churches, with top people in all evangelical denominations attracted to Princeton. (When the General Assembly had investigated Princeton and inquired into why most of the scholarship money was going to non-Presbyterians, the faculty had an easy answer: "We can't help it that our best students aren't Presbyterians.") How should the new church work at reaching out to other evangelicals? What sort of leadership to the nation and its churches should it give? That was the vision surrounding the brief existence of the Committee of Nine within the OPC under the direction of Edwin Rian, author of the brilliant and moving *Presbyterian Conflict*, the grand apologetic for the Machen movement. But the Nine appeared to assume too much authority for themselves and were in danger of diluting the Reformed emphasis, so many thought. That endeavor was quickly aborted.

Also given to Rian was the task of beginning a Christian university, resembling the Free University of Amsterdam, where a common Reformed worldview could give direction to the larger Reformed community. But there were problems. Could its faculty include people from the Reformed Episcopal Church? Could Gordon Clark be included on the philosophy faculty? That dream also came to a speedy end, after a substantial investment in property. The Rian story is unclear, but it is not so surprising that he returned to the mother Presbyterian church, saying that by reading Calvin he had learned that the OPC was schismatic. For him and others, the new movement seemed to value its own purity over ministry to the larger evangelical world.

Further Twentieth-Century Controversy Within

After the death of Machen in 1937, theological leadership went to Van Til, Westminster's professor of apologetics, who had introduced a new direction in that discipline. The path of the Machen movement was very consistent with that viewpoint. The older Princeton apologetic had been based on Scottish commonsense realism, the assertion that because no experience could have meaning on the basis of the religious and moral skepticism of David Hume and Immanuel Kant, the old empirical case for Christianity is still compelling. Van Til and the Dutch direction he represented went further, maintaining that without consistent Christian (Reformed) commitment, nothing in the world could make sense, going beyond experience. Without commitment to the Creator, there was no meaning within the creation at all. (Van Til was seen by many as a further advance in Christian thinking, unknown within the earlier world in which the gospel was not under as severe an attack. But B. B. Warfield in his earlier review of Francis

Beattie's *Apologetics* had shown that he both understood and rejected the Dutch direction.)

How important to the new church was the Van Til direction? As modern culture removed itself further and further from Christianity, was a "transcendental" apologetic that concerned itself with the presuppositions of knowledge necessary, and was the older apologetic outdated? Would that not continue the great work begun by Machen, of recognizing that when basic Christian doctrine was rejected, Christianity itself was under attack? But was unwillingness to accept Van Til's leadership in detailed evaluation of current theology the same thing as agreeing with Machen that without Christ's resurrection, there was no Christianity? Or was it possible to regard Van Til as indeed a great Christian scholar, but also to believe that the Reformed world had room for someone holding another perspective?

The OPC struggle over the views of Gordon Clark revealed how little room there was. While at Wheaton, Clark's Creed Club had appreciated Van Til, and Clark had sent his best students to Westminster, believing that his own rejection of the older empirical apologetic worked well with Van Til's approach. But Clark's ordination was opposed by followers of Van Til, who thought Clark did not posit a sufficient distance between the knowledge that God himself has and the kind we have, i.e., the meaning of the "incomprehensibility of God." Van Til became convinced that Clark was a rationalist, and Clark that Van Til was a skeptic. Although Clark's ordination was upheld by the church (a rare instance in which Westminster and the OPC parted ways), control of the Board of Foreign Missions remained with the Van Til party as the result of John Murray's election by one vote. (Is it a reliable legend that this election would not have happened if someone had not been in the men's room?) That was the signal for Clark and his friends to withdraw from the church.

No doubt it was necessary for long-neglected questions to be thoroughly explored. But were the conclusions unnecessarily exclusive? Was there room in the new movement for breadth and flexibility? Or was it to be always "all or nothing"?

Developments in the Bible Presbyterian Church were much the same, as severe tensions arose with accompanying divisions, many revolving around the control of Carl McIntire. In the early 1950s Francis Schaeffer, once president of the Westminster student body who had led the student exodus to Faith Seminary, experienced a great crisis of faith: Was it possible that the evangelical gospel could really be true, when apparently its inevitable result was deep-seated "meanness" among its adherents? Schaeffer roamed the Swiss mountains in torment of heart, reevaluating the case for Christianity from the ground up, and becoming thoroughly convinced that it was after all totally true—and then went on to underline Paul's directive to speak the truth in love and to write *True Spirituality*, his great manifesto.

Schaeffer's torment to a great extent paralleled the insights that had been developing outside the separatist movement. With leadership from younger men, Edward Carnell and Carl Henry in particular, both former students of Clark at Wheaton, the New Evangelical movement began as an attempt to transcend the differences of the liberals and the evangelicals, featuring the ministry of Billy Graham, who worked with evangelicals and liberals and Catholics! They also began the National Association of Evangelicals, whose membership was open to evangelical denominations, or churches within liberal denominations, or individuals; the Evangelical Theological Society, whose only creed was the inerrancy of the Bible; and Fuller Seminary, today easily the largest of all evangelical seminaries in the world. Fuller had announced that its vision was to perpetuate the scholarly legacy and evangelical leadership of Princeton. What did that say about Westminster? That it was too narrow for the task? But Fuller's subsequent rejection of biblical inerrancy and its advocacy of the ordination of women encouraged the separatist movements to reinforce their strategy of keeping distance from those remaining in the liberal denominations.

By the mid-1960s the changing of the guard at Westminster was beginning. The original faculty had died or retired, to be replaced by those who had not gone through the battle with Machen. How conscious were those newcomers of the necessity to draw firm lines over against compromise in any form? In that setting the seminary chose its first president, Edmund Clowney. He had been a student and supporter of Clark. (His entering class at Westminster in 1939 totaled seven students, one from Calvin and six from Clark's Creed Club.) Clowney wrestled with the questions of funding and constituency and reached out to the conservatives in the Southern Presbyterian Church. He added many board members from the South, outside the OPC. He was active in InterVarsity, its summer camp, and the Urbana Missions Conference. Was he Reformed or merely an evangelical? Did he sell out the cause for Southern money? In my view there can be no dichotomy at all between faithfulness to the heritage and reaching out to as many as possible, but not

696

all saw it that way. For me he is the greatest saint and theologian in my life, the beating heart of my Westminster. His books are all remarkable, but I meditate especially through his sermons. Without Clowney the spectacular increase in students and impact at Westminster would not have happened. (But no one predicted or planned the "Jesus people," who came from nowhere, filling Westminster—and are hard to fit into this story.)

Within the OPC two major doctrinal controversies began. One was the view of the Sabbath held by Frank Breisch. As moderator of a church without a pastor, Breisch had approved the reception of a member who owned a delicatessen doing half its business on Sunday. (I recall detailed discussions in presbytery on whether it was necessary for people without refrigerators to buy fresh milk on Sunday.) As Breisch took a new look at the Westminster Confession's teaching on the Sabbath, he concluded that it went beyond the Bible and that he could not affirm that the Lord's Day was the Christian Sabbath. Although presbytery had room for him, a complaint went to General Assembly. As a member of his Wheaton church and his friend, I became active in his defense. We made use of the Warfield dictum that the Reformed faith was where the Reformed creeds agree, and of course Calvin's Geneva Catechism and the Heidelberg Catechism do not hold the Westminster Confession view. Yet the OPC was not ready to ask what views were vital to the Reformed faith, but only whether it regarded a view as biblical. That had a God-honoring sound to it, but followed through consistently seemed to suggest that there was no room in the church for anyone in the minority of a biblical interpretation. (The case was referred to a study committee whose report affirming the necessity of accepting the confession on the Sabbath was adopted by the Assembly ten years later.) Does my appreciation of the differing expressions of the Reformed faith make me too flexible? I did come to doubt the credibility of the OPC's understanding of its heritage.

The other controversy is better known, that of Westminster professor Norman Shepherd's view of justification. I believe he affirmed that as we relate to God covenantally, in terms of our obedience to him, the basis of our acceptance by God in our justification includes our obedience as well as our faith, expressed by speaking of our obedient faith or faithful obedience. Of course, the Bible and the confession affirm that faith never exists without obedience, or justification without sanctification. But does Shepherd's view blur the necessary distinction between the two? Does it appear to replace

697

the righteousness of Christ with our own righteousness as the ground of our acceptance with God? When Shepherd brought his views to the OPC presbytery, it as well as the Westminster community was involved. After over seven years of seminary discussion, the seminary's final action was to remove him as incompetent to teach, since his views were so unclearly expressed. But the public announcement sounded as though he were being fired without any doctrinal concerns at all. The Presbytery of Philadelphia had many long Saturday meetings, and at the end a motion to find Shepherd's views acceptable failed by one vote, and a motion to find them unacceptable failed by one vote, so presbytery took no action. Shepherd transferred to the Christian Reformed Church, just before formal charges against him would have been filed.

Shepherd and supporters maintained that his views were thoroughly Reformed and that his opponents were noncovenantal Lutheran or evangelical in their views, holding to a view of justification based on "merit," not on union with Christ. Clowney's Westminster was perceived as capitulating to its new constituency, "less Reformed" than the OPC. The OPC came to believe that it needed its own theological training for its emerging leadership. Failure to secure agreement on what seemed to be such basic gospel was disheartening to many, and cast doubt on the unity of the movement.

In the seventies and eighties there was increasing zeal for church union, with much Clowney leadership. Weren't the concerns of the new Southern PCA the same as for the Northerners? Hadn't the Reformed Presbyterian Evangelical Synod people shaken off their old Bible Presbyterian McIntire past? Wasn't there real repentance for the unloving spirit of the 1930s, and much personal reconciliation? (Could you even say this: Couldn't the spirit of the Clowney Westminster be also expressed in a united Presbyterian church?) But union with the OPC was problematic. In view of its widespread concurrence with Shepherd that an "evangelical" view of justification wasn't really "Reformed," was it really on the same page with the rest? From the OPC side, wouldn't union with a body ten times its size inevitably compromise its hard-fought distinctive Reformed testimony? The Clowney vision was to be only incompletely fulfilled. He became a PCA minister.

The story to this point has a pessimistic, even cynical cast. Is it really possible to stand vigorously for the truth of the Bible without becoming cantankerous? Had Schaeffer come down from the mountains too soon, since people proved to be a lot meaner than he thought? Sad though the

Rian story was, isn't it even sadder that his example of being both faithful and relevant is so rare? In that final battle with the opponents world, flesh, and devil, will we contend boldly with evangelicals at our side, or will we need to fight them off at the same time?

Is there really a church of Jesus Christ, or instead a variety of idiosyncratic denominations? Is the "pluriformity of the church" something to be applauded, or exposed as a weasel-word for *schism*? Is a desire for listening to and learning from each other ultimately the beginning of the slippery slope? If hope deferred for the unity of the church can make the heart sick, should we just learn to get over it?

A Unifying Vision for the Twenty-first Century and Beyond

At this hard place in our history and in our own personal disappointments, we need the hope that only the Lord can give us. We need to keep trusting him. But it is encouraging to see a place to begin, as we pray and work for the unity of Christ's church. I believe John Frame shows us a beginning. I pray that we can learn from him a way of reading the Bible with integrity but also with wisdom, confident that when we use his Word his way, his promise will be fulfilled. John gives us so much else in so many places, but for me this is the heart of our need and the heart of his ministry.

It can help to see Frame sizing up specific situations, and then to go on to his method underneath. I see too much theory out there, and not enough reality. Start with his fascinating and arresting *MWC*, a chapter in Sung Wook Chung's *Alister E. McGrath and Evangelical Theology*.[2] Here Frame surveys some twenty-one serious disputes that have divided the Machen movement. He distills their merits, concluding generally that there were great misunderstandings, that people should have listened to each other more diligently and with much more good faith. Then he concludes with nuggets of pastoral advice for doing it better from now on. *MWC* is an amazing little gem, a great antidote to all the looming cynicism I just summarized. Specifically, in all the disputes I've mentioned, as well as in many more, he concludes that they were mistaken and unnecessary. He believes the attack on dispensationalism was not helpful and that the church should have found room for Breisch

2. Sung Wook Chung, ed., *Alister E. McGrath and Evangelical Theology: A Dynamic Engagement* (Grand Rapids: Baker, 2003).

and his Sabbath view, since after all it was Calvin's view too, and different varieties of Reformed perspectives should be able to accept each other. He is convinced that it was unjust to remove Shepherd. (Well, here I just can't agree with Frame, but I value his judgment.) He is sure there should have been room in the church for both Van Til and Clark, since deep down each honored what was so precious to the other.

Frame gives here also a brief treatment of the "worship wars," which he does much more definitively in *WST*. I think that of all the issues he takes up, this is today one of the most lively and important. Not everyone gets involved in the nuances of a theological debate, but everyone finds himself "comfortable" or "uncomfortable" in a worship service. Whenever I try to learn something of the flavor of a General Assembly I can't attend, I look at the blogs. Invariably the Assembly worship services get the most attention: Did that testimony belong in worship? Was that woman up front really leading? Isn't going up front for the Lord's Supper dangerously Roman Catholic? When a few years ago a "PCA Identity Statement" was being discussed, a prominent place was given to latitude in worship styles. I think the Statement was intended both to describe the state of affairs across the PCA and also to endorse it; that is, to say that there is much diversity within the PCA on many things, and that's a good thing. Unity on the Bible and the gospel goes well with diversity in practice, is what I heard it saying.

That's the backdrop for Frame's *WST*. He's clearly committed to the Reformed "regulative principle," that God tells us how to worship him and that obedience here is at least as important as anywhere else. But he goes on to ask what it is that the Bible really says. The older language of "circumstances" of worship is not really helpful; why don't we work in terms of the "application" of biblical principle, of using the wisdom God has given us to apply his Word in worship, as we do in all the rest of life? We do not add to the Word, but we apply it, as we must. Frame deals with the biblical principles with integrity, but he always puts more of them on the table than are usually there. Especially engaging to me is his focus on boldness;[3] we come to God as mature sons and daughters with free access to our Father. The cross has taken away the distance between us. So rigid rules are out of place in worship, as they are in conversation between friends. He can even talk of the place of humor,[4] as it helps us to see ourselves in God's perspective.

3. *WST*, 81.
4. Ibid.

(For reasons unknown to me and usually unintended by me, when I preach, my choice of words or illustrations seems funny to some people. I've tried to change and be more formal, but it comes out stilted. John, here you give me a generous helping of liberty in Christ, and I'm so grateful.)

For me, the most valuable discussion in the book is Frame's treatment of how we should handle the disagreements, the ones that give us the worship wars. I'm startled and then deeply helped in that here he points us to the "weaker brother" of Romans 14. I think it fits very well. We should seek in love to help our brothers, both those musically and liturgically on the left and the right, to understand God's Word in a better way, but always in love. "We should be expecting in our churches—particularly in our worship, when God draws near to us—surprising discoveries of unity. One way God works among us, then, is when we learn one another's music."[5]

Surprising discoveries of unity indeed! In theologian talk it would go like this: *already* we are indeed one in Christ, as we recognize how imperfectly we express that truth, even while so much *not yet* is sadly still with us. This is the language of bold faith. Frame teaches us how to be firmly committed to the Bible but also to understand how we need to work in faith with ourselves and with other people to together read that Bible. This little popular book becomes for me the gateway to Frame.

With that practical application, we can work through Frame's signature triad. It involves "not only ethics (the normative perspective) but also the culture in which we live (the situational perspective) and the resources of redemption on which we draw daily (the existential perspective)."[6] As I reflect on these three, it strikes me that most people are content with only two of them. The liberal is sure that theology is about yourself and the world in which you live, and that agenda tends to swallow up listening to God in his Word. Someone working with people in Christian counseling is very much aware of the need for the individual to listen to God, but may not do much with the culture around him. The "missional" person is very much aware that without translating the gospel into the culture, the message is meaningless, but he may be so missional that he neglects pastoral care. Putting all three together is rare indeed, and gives much promise for our way ahead.

Think, then, of the triad of the three tools we need in order to respond faithfully to God's love for us, its three vital "perspectives." We need all of

5. Ibid., 142.
6. *DCL*, xxv.

them. Especially since we are committed to the unity of Christ's body, we will use all those tools all the time, and will beware of slighting any. As we keep the church's unity clearly before us, we honor the riches of these perspectives, and avoid any reductionism that would take any away.

One corner of the triangle is the normative. We learn to listen closely to God as he talks to us in his Word, the Bible. Frame takes up that listening process: what do we need to hear first that gives understanding to the rest? Is it law? Is it gospel? Is redemptive history the place to look? Ethical example? All of the above! But the main thing is to remember who God is and who you are, and to bow before him. Although we always need to pay attention to the situation and to our existential self, we must above all listen to God again and again, trusting that he has given us in his Word all that we need for life and godliness. We dare not try to be wiser than God, or more loving or more relevant; we are always in his presence as our Lord.

Yet the situational, or the cultural, is also very important. We need to respect where God in his good plan has placed us and aggressively do his will right there. This is where I am now: Carol and I worship at Cristo Rey, a Hispanic congregation. Our pastor, Josh, wears a robe and tells us that this can be very meaningful in that culture. But my culture is New Life, and I am turned off by a robe. To me it suggests distance, a lording it over the congregation. I also think of it in terms of academic regalia, which it originally was: the Geneva gown. Even though I recognize that part of church worship is instruction, the gown to me suggests too much academia. But the Cristo Rey situation is now my situation too, and God calls me to respond to the gown by loving his people in our church, and delighting in this way of ministering to them. Where God has put me is where I am called to love!

The existential is even more personal. Under God's Word, in this situation where he has placed me, how is God calling me to honor him by sizing myself up? (This suggests to me the opening pages of Calvin's *Institutes*, where knowledge of God and self-knowledge are interdependent.) Ordinarily when I consider God's Word and the place of his choosing and then look to myself, I jump immediately to asking this: As I know myself, where am I most likely to be resistant to God? Then I seek to lean against that sinful tendency. (Don't Aristotle's ethics say something about allowing for the wind when shooting at a target?) But God has given me two great mentors, John and Paul (really!), who both tell me: Clair, you're too hard on yourself. This startling counsel arouses me then to appreciate what there is in me that not only doesn't resist, but truly delights in the place where God is present to me with his Word. What is it to be self-aware? It has to be more than knowing what's evil in your heart, and goes on to recognizing also the good gifts of wisdom and love that God has already given you, shaping you for his Word in this place. You can be joyful about being joyful, not just grieved about your grief. You can live in the *already*, not just in the *not yet*.

I am moved and blessed by thinking of myself this way. My Lord has given me very clear direction in his Word. He has also in his kind sovereignty put me in this place. He has made me who I am (but he is never the author of sin). Everything comes together. Now I've been reading Paul Miller's *A Praying Life*. He pushes me to recognize that if I'm not in the presence of God praying for something, then I'm abdicating that piece of my life to the secular world where God is out of place. Frame helps me go to so many places and people, and then Paul Miller helps me to see whether I'm really there.

Then I think of the insights of Richard Baxter, author of *The Reformed Pastor*. After twenty years in his church he began to call on his people at their homes to talk with them about their faith. The downside was that even after all his preaching, they still didn't really understand anything. But the upside was truly remarkable: in two hours one on one, they could grasp so much. Doesn't Tim Keller say something like this: If you really want to be a preacher, get out of the books and spend time talking with people? That sounds like Frame's existential, doesn't it? Live in the place God has put you in, love the people where you are, delight in the work of God in your heart—that's the way you take seriously what God is saying to you.

Frame helps us with unity because we see more angles. We work to see how close others' statements are to ours, in different ways. If one way of connecting with people seems counterproductive, let's try something else, as we move around the triangle. That seems very promising to me. It is light-years away from the old liberalism, in which experience always trumped Bible. This is working hard to look at the Bible in every way there is, engaging with it and with people, working to understand each other and the Lord.

RETROSPECTIVE

Let's try again for another look at the church's track record. The first time around was accurate, I think, but without much hope for a better way. Let's do it again, praying through all the corners of the triad. Begin by asking

703

again: where did all that liberalism come from? I think it went like this: the doctrinal issues between Reformed and Lutheran had been globalized, while at the same time they were learning so much from each other "devotionally," as Puritan helps to Christian living turned into Lutheran pietism. If we can relate to each other experientially but not doctrinally, where does that leave doctrine? Isn't that a tipsy triad? Isn't it easy to go from there to this: experience trumps doctrine? What if those who came before us could have asked, if we're on the same page in prayer and Bible reading, then mustn't we be very close doctrinally? So close that we'll keep trying? If the big problem is how is Jesus present in the Supper, why don't we talk about how we know he's here the rest of the time? I think that would have gone very far. I think we would have had real credibility with each other, and would never have thought of looking somewhere else outside of the Bible.

Today, I have a soft spot in my heart for dispensationalism. I'm so into long-term planning that I need people to remind me that Jesus is likely to come back pronto (that's how we talk at Cristo Rey). It's good to follow their zeal to see the Lord's love for his people through all those ages of testing and failure and then God's enduring patience; it feels a lot like biblical theology. It's so helpful that they vigorously remind us that we're not under law but under grace, even though it can take effort to work through the implications. I wish John Murray had said something like that. Then we could have talked together with the dispensationalists about living for Christ over the long haul, I think—just in case Jesus doesn't come back pronto.

Where Do We Go from Here?

Right now the role of women in the church seems impossible to even talk about. Two PCA General Assemblies in a row didn't want to do it. But some wise people said: "We don't want to do it because that will put the churches in a box and they won't do any work themselves." Could it just be that the situation of an urban church with many single women is different from that of a church full of babies? Maybe it *would* work better to think and pray this through locally or regionally before we do it more broadly. My own situation is two strange General Assemblies—or were they, in God's kind providence, so strange after all?

If we worked our way around the triangle a few more times, what do you think we'd find? I've heard far too many sermons concluding with the deadening words: "Now may God bless his Word to your hearts." That's preacher talk for: "I haven't a clue how any of that Bible makes a difference in my own life, and I'm not going to even think about how it might matter in yours." It's easy to take our curiosity about the Bible as an excuse for not caring about what we should be doing with it. We can do much better.

We can do better because of John's triad! Isn't it appealing? It speaks not of a frustrating either/or, but rather of a joyful both/and (how do you speak of a triad in binary language?). We look seriously at the world as it is today, with its culture very different from anything that has ever come before, and with surprises in our own lives and in the lives of the people we know. There must be more than pat answers—and there are.

It always comes back to the unity of the church, though. Without that unity, we'll just keep talking to ourselves and not hear the Lord through his people as we should. As a teacher, I have wondered about the anomaly of an independent seminary not accountable to the church. Still, in Presbyterian logic there are always three values: right, wrong, and irregular (which means something like doing the best you can under the circumstances). If a seminary can minister to people from eighty denominations from forty countries—and we did—that has to be right even though irregular. But now that we think of it, isn't a denomination also irregular? Has an irregular seminary been a helpful response to all those irregular denominations?

That's a temporary answer that works for me, and it's not so bad. We can go into class and talk through very important things without ever involving our churches. Could that be an expression of "pluriformity"? But that's still only a beginning. We need to be serious about John 17. What a blend that is: that fellowship and love between Jesus and his Father, at the very cusp of the cross! All those secret nights in prayer for Jesus that have gone before, and now at the end we're invited to listen in on that fellowship. But there's much more than that: Jesus is bringing us along into that amazing fellowship of love, and tells us that's why others will believe.

Have you been reading Tim Keller's *Reason for God*? I think it has three parts. The first is looking at the problems with the gospel and the answers. Second is the case for Christianity, focusing on Jesus Christ, who he is and what he does. But I think there's then a third part, transitioning to the question: Now what about you? It's important that you understand all that, but why should you give your heart to Jesus? Keller's answer goes all the way back to the ancient church, which talked mostly about one thing, the Trinity, that the One God exists in Three. What is God like? Father, Son, and Spirit; that's who he is. You are made in that image, not to reflect a first cause, or an unmoved mover, or a ground of all being. You are made to live and flourish in that great family of love. Your life doesn't make any sense, you aren't meaningful, you don't fit unless you love and are loved, not in some trivial or passing way, but in the everlasting fellowship of God's Trinitarian family. Keller says it better.

What do you think of that? Are you still content with merely knowing that you aren't going to hell? Or that Jesus paid it all? But why? What was the point? If Jesus is praying a prayer pleasing to his Father in John 17, there's so much more to it all, isn't there? A fellowship of love, a community of love, a family of love—what would that be like? What is that like already?

It begins with the Lord's presence in your life. See Paul Miller's *A Praying Life* again. The Lord is there. He loves you. Nothing at all is boring or irrelevant to him. When you don't understand, you can pour out your heart to him. When it seems too hard to take, he is there. When the plan seems not to be working, he knows what he's doing. Looking again and again to him is not a pious platitude but reality.

But your "personal" faith isn't "individualistic." Jesus gave us all the gifts of the Holy Spirit we'll ever need—but not all to one person, not all to you all by yourself. Without the wisdom and patience and courage and joy and compassion of God's people all around us, we'll always come up short. When you've just heard a sermon that touched your heart, what do you talk about afterwards? The weather, sports, the economy? Why is that? When you pray for someone, do you tell her about it? Why not?

Have you heard David Powlison tell us that what counseling is really all about is just being a good Christian friend? Do you have friends like that? Are you a friend like that? Is the presence of the Holy Spirit something private, or something you have together?

There, I think, is where Frame's method is so valuable. You can help others to see just what piece of the situation they should look at first. You can listen to friends telling you about the gospel when you're thinking law—or the other way around. You can hear about your existential blindness, and marvel as you respond: "Really? Is that how I come over?" And then repent from the new look at yourself that the Holy Spirit through those friends just gave you. You can boldly say to someone, "There's more to you than the downside; let me tell you how you've brought Christ closer to me."

That's the unity of the church, not on paper but working out powerfully in lives. This piece is about John Frame, so once more I tell you all how blessed we are that he is present in our theology, our church, and our lives. But who is it after all who is there, whom John shows us? Whose method is it that we have been given? I'm hearing again the words of Billy Graham, when he was asked what he was doing that was so fruitful: "I was just there when it happened." John is "just there" when many grand things happen.

Tip O'Neill was on to something: all politics is local politics. Most church unity is local. Talk big about the ecumenical mandate, but never talk meaningfully to the folks in church? I don't think so. But still, the Trinitarian dance in which we whirl includes whirlers up the street, across the prairie, in the country, in the world, doesn't it?

What does that look like? How can it look better? Within my tiny Presbyterian subculture I think about old friends in the OPC, still there after I've moved on to the PCA. I think about people I hear about in the Evangelical Presbyterian Church, who have seen the need for fellowship in a Bible-believing climate, but are puzzling over the ordination of women. Oh, I must be honest: I think about people in my PCA whom I find hard to understand and even just to stand. How can the triad work with them and me?

What do you expect me to say? Will this come as an anticlimax? I think there has to be more talk—talk with honesty and love. We have to talk. (For details, see Frame's *ER*.) We need to talk about the situation, about all those without God and without hope in the world, and how we need to pray for and encourage each other. We'll have to talk existentially, encouraging each other to rejoice in Jesus and be diligent in loving him.

I remember something that happened about forty years ago, at a meeting of the Chicago Society of Biblical Research. About two-thirds of the group consisted of Roman Catholics from DePaul and Roosevelt, marked by their shiny black shoes. That day a Catholic scholar read with great enthusiasm and joy what he had just learned, what he was sure was the key to the whole Bible: it was the covenant! I'm still speechless. Of course, Catholics are much closer to us than the liberal Presbyterians; that's so obvious. Wouldn't the triad work with them, too?

Thank you again, John. Thank you that I'm not alone in the world, wondering why no one else appreciates my Gordon Clark or my Frank Breisch. Thank you for appreciating a contemporary worship style. Thank you that our friend Harvie's concern for the gospel and culture is not being lost. But thank you most of all for clear light in many dim places, for a way to go ahead with the Bible, our Father's Word.

PART 5

WORSHIP

30

WHAT JOHN FRAME
TAUGHT ME ABOUT WORSHIP

REGGIE M. KIDD

TO MITIGATE JOHN FRAME'S embarrassment at the publication of a book focused on him, I wish to preface my tribute to him by offering tribute to others. I do so largely because Frame provided the perspective that enabled me to hear these other voices. Perhaps it's a roundabout way to approach the subject of worship—but for Frame and for me, worship is life. Worship is the place where heaven and earth are reconciled. It's the place where all offerings are finally placed in grateful adoration of their source.

For years, I have been parsing the significance of one insight I gained from Edmund Clowney (1917–2005), president and professor of practical theology at Westminster Theological Seminary when I was there in the mid-1970s. Ours, Professor Clowney pointed out, is a Singing Savior.[1]

Clowney taught me that theology is not just about ideas and propositions and abstract nouns—it's about a person. Jesus didn't simply come to clear up a legal mess, or merely to settle an account in overdraft. The God-man came to be with us. As one of us, God incarnate now leads us in joyful praise to his Father and ours. Through Clowney, then, I came to realize that

---

1. Edmund P. Clowney, "The Singing Savior," *Moody Monthly* (July–August 1979): 40–41.

if I'm not resonating with the Redeemer's melody line, I'm probably not understanding redemption's propositional truths.

Before coming to teach at RTS Orlando, I had been designing and leading worship services for a good twenty years. For the longest time my chief aim was to craft a set of songs that would complement the sermon and not require me to change capo settings on my guitar (I used to use a "screw-down" type of capo that kept the guitar from going out of tune with capo changes, but that also took an eternity to adjust). It was after being asked to teach worship at RTS Orlando and lead its chapel services that I had the opportunity to explore the heritage of Reformed worship more deeply. I started to see how much bigger worship is.

It was Hughes Oliphant ("Scoti") Old who, first in his writings and eventually in his friendship, introduced me to Calvin's worship sensibility:[2]

- an aspiration to reform worship according to Scripture and according to what can be known about the practice of the ancient church;
- the place of the reading of Scripture and the reciting of creeds;
- the understanding that song is a function of prayer;
- the preeminence of the psalms in congregational song;
- a robust sacramental sense, whereby Jesus sets his lavish gifts before us—and would do so weekly, if only we would assent;
- a willingness to remain committed to working things through in community when things don't go your way;
- a desire for holy community and a zeal for evangelical ecumenicity.

Somehow Calvinists have gained a reputation for parsimonious spirits and acerbic (if any) wit. Scoti Old's sparkling wit and kindness of heart prove that it doesn't have to be that way.

Moreover, Old's friendship and writings have helped me to discern that the boring worship I grew up with in a Presbyterian church was not the fault of the Presbyterian-ness of the worship, but of the spiritual deadness and theological obliviousness of the people involved (beginning with me).

2. See esp. Hughes Oliphant Old, *Worship Reformed according to Scripture*, rev. expanded ed. (Louisville: Westminster John Knox Press, 2002).

Old's writings have helped me to understand what was so satisfying about the worship I have experienced under the guidance of Mort Whitman at Westminster Chapel, Williamsburg, Virginia (OPC); Norman Shepherd at Westminster Seminary (Shepherd made sure that the John Murray legacy of a cappella metrical psalm-singing was not ignored at WTS); James Montgomery Boice at Tenth Presbyterian, Philadelphia; Wallace Tinsley at Filbert PCA, Filbert, South Carolina; and Larry Mininger at Lake Sherwood OPC, Orlando, Florida. In each of these settings—some more "formal," others less so; some where the musical voice was "Bach," others where the musical voice was "Bubba"—a characteristically Presbyterian mix of transcendence and immanence, of awe and conviviality, were in play.

It was Robert Webber (1933–2007) who took me into the landscape that Scoti Old had mapped out in his study of Reformed worship's patristic roots: our forebears sought to reform worship not simply through bare appeal to the Bible, but also through a conscientious reading of the ancient church's attempts to be guided by the Bible.[3]

Webber noted that attention to the Bible's story line and its theology had led the ancient church to something like a consensus that worship consists in a fourfold pattern of:

- gathering in the name of the triune God: the heavenly Father, his Son our Sin-Bearer and our Christus Victor, and the Holy Spirit;
- rehearsing God's character and deeds in the reading and exposition of the Word of God;
- participating in the meal that celebrates Christ's death for our reconciliation, mediates his resurrected presence among his people, and promises his return in glory;
- sending God's people into the world in the power of the Spirit, as God's missional agents to embody God's life and tell his story.[4]

For his own part, Webber concluded that the churches most closely approximating the early church's obedience to Scripture are those that pre-

3. Hughes Oliphant Old, *The Patristic Roots of Reformed Worship*, Züricher Beiträge zur Reformationsgeschichte, Band 5 (Zürich: Theologischer Verlag, 1975).
4. Robert E. Webber, *Ancient-Future Worship: Proclaiming and Enacting God's Narrative* (Grand Rapids: Baker, 2008).

serve the shape and content of those ancient liturgies. He found himself in the Anglican communion.[5] In 2001 he and Luder Whitlock persuaded me to augment my duties at RTS Orlando by joining the peripatetic faculty of the Institute for Worship Studies (now the Robert E. Webber Institute for Worship Studies) to help teach this "ancient-future" worship sensibility from an evangelical perspective.

Ed Clowney taught me to listen for the voice of Jesus in worship, Hughes Oliphant Old taught me to honor lessons about worship from the Great Reformation, and Robert Webber taught me to take account of worship in the Great Church. In certain respects those three voices are not entirely concordant. Two are Presbyterian, one Anglican. One is musically pretty much a "Bach" and maybe a "Bubba" guy; the others have made room for the "Blues Brothers." Two are Calvinist; the other, more eclectic.

But in a more important—the most important—respect, they are concordant. And it is John Frame who taught me to see that concordance, because of the way he taught me to revere God's Word.

WHAT JOHN FRAME TAUGHT ME ABOUT THE NORMATIVITY OF THE WORD IN WORSHIP

It is John Frame who made me utterly and unapologetically determined to be shaped by the Word of the Lord, and the Lord of the Word. Over the years, his triperspectival approach to theology has helped me to bow to the authority of the Word (the Word is normative), doing so simultaneously as one who knows he is grounded in community (the Word is situational) and is being shaped by God's love for the sake of loving others (the Word is existential).

Two of my most vivid memories of my first year of seminary have to do with John Frame. The first was his course on the doctrine of the Word of God. He pressed home the Bible's claims to be God's divine-human Word, worthy of the same esteem that the people of God gave to God's law in Ezra's day when they stood in its hearing with lifted hands, shouted, "Amen! Amen!" and bowed low and worshiped the Lord with faces to the ground (Neh. 8:5–6). The course closed with a lecture on various failed attempts to synthesize the Bible—e.g., with Aristotelianism under Thomas Aquinas,

5. Robert E. Webber, *Evangelicals on the Canterbury Trail: Why Evangelicals Are Attracted to the Liturgical Church* (Waco, TX: Word, 1985).

with Romanticism under Friedrich Schleiermacher, and with existentialism under Paul Tillich. The desire to synthesize the Word of God with human wisdom is understandable, since the Word is fully divine and fully human. But the scandal of the Word, especially in our day, lies in its divinity. Thus, we need especially to assert and live its divinity.

The second was a chapel talk that Frame gave on 1 Timothy 1:5. He made a simple point: the goal of God's instructions is to promote love. We're not obeying the Word if we're not loving God and loving our neighbor. The normativity of God's Word is a relational normativity—thus, God's Word will inevitably move us toward knowing and loving himself and others.

During my time at RTS Orlando, Frame has published his two books on worship and engaged in a *WTJ* skirmish with T. David Gordon on the regulative principle.[6] Meanwhile, R. J. Gore published his *Covenantal Worship*, championing the simpler (dare I say, Framean and Oldian?) expression of the regulative principle over the more casuistic principle that came into ascendancy among many post-Calvin Calvinists.[7]

Since joining our faculty, Frame has generously shared his classically rooted organ-playing gifts in chapel. On several occasions he and I have had the opportunity to lead worship together, he at the piano, I on the guitar. Normally, the songs we play together are far beneath his talents. He has also shown that same generosity in the classroom. When my students' "Well, what would Professor Frame say about such and such?" has left me with no recourse except, "I don't know. Let's see if he's not too busy," Frame has shown himself ready with no notice at all to drop what he's doing, come into the classroom, and answer for himself. And to do so, to invoke a Framean standard, "clearly, concisely, and cogently."

Even though I'm probably supposed to, I'm not going to argue the case, but I will simply state that I think Frame, Old, and Gore offer an approach to Calvinistic worship that is true to the Bible, and in sync with the heart of what Calvin was trying to accomplish. Old contends that the Calvinistic instinct was to look to Scripture to govern, without expecting to find a spe-

---

6. *WST*; *CWM*; John Frame, "Some Questions about the Regulative Principle," *WTJ* 54 (1992): 357–66; John Frame, "Reply to T. David Gordon," *WTJ* 56, 1 (Spring 1994): 181–83; T. David Gordon, "Some Answers about the Regulative Principle," *WTJ* 55 (1993): 321–29. Frame's current thoughts appear in "A Fresh Look at the Regulative Principle" (2008), at http://www.frame-poythress.org; and may be traced in his discussion of the first four commandments in his *DCL*.

7. R. J. Gore Jr., *Covenantal Worship: Reconsidering the Puritan Regulative Principle* (Phillipsburg, NJ: P&R Publishing, 2002).

cific warrant for everything. In matters of worship it was the dispensational hermeneutic of Baptists that demanded specific warrant, e.g., "Show us where the New Testament commands us to baptize our babies the way Old Testament parents circumcised their sons." The Calvinistic hermeneutic was more covenantal, organic, and theological—more reflectively biblical than casuistically so.[8]

Frame's approach to Scripture's governance in worship is especially commendable in this respect: he recognizes that Scripture speaks in some places prescriptively and proscriptively, in other places paradigmatically and poetically and proverbially. Scripture mandates wisdom and dependence on the Holy Spirit. Scripture sets the limits of its own specificity in matters of worship, and then says in effect, "Figure it out under my aegis, out of regard for one another, in dependence on my Holy Spirit" (Rom. 14–15). Frame's approach to Scripture's governance of worship is helpful because he reminds us of the varied nature of God's speech, and thus of the varied ways in which God would shape our worship.

We violate Scripture when we make it something it is not. Scripture is not a worship manual, a worship directory, a *Book of Common Prayer*, or a *Book of Common Worship*. Scripture does speak prescriptively and proscriptively about worship—but fundamentally, God did not give us the Bible because he thought we needed a casuistry of worship. We need so much more than a worship rulebook could provide. We need redemption. We need hearts brought from death to life. We need minds made new by the regenerating work of the Holy Spirit. We need the end of Satan's dominion and the inauguration of the reign of God's beloved Son. Scripture tells us this story, calls for an obedience of faith, and promises the Lord's presence through the ministry of the Holy Spirit. Scripture tells us that we are now those who "worship in the Spirit of God and glory in Christ Jesus" (Phil. 3:3).[9] Gathered worship now has at its core the radiant presence of the One who showed up in shadows and figures in the Old Testament.

One form of divine speech that comes into its own in the light of Christ's person and work is the sapiential. The Wisdom whose personal and eternal identity old covenant revelation had but hinted at (Prov. 1–9, especially) has

---

8. Hughes Oliphant Old, *The Shaping of the Reformed Baptismal Rite in the Sixteenth Century* (Grand Rapids: Eerdmans, 1992), 119–20, 283–84.

9. All quotations from the Bible are from the NASB.

now walked the earth, and taken up residence in God's people by the Holy Spirit (Colossians, especially).

Thus, although Frame is happy to discuss at some length the sorts of things that Scripture (both Old and New Testament) calls on us to do, he is loath to say that they amount to a worship checklist.

A recurring theme is that "where specifics are lacking, we must apply the generalities by means of our sanctified wisdom, within the general principles of the word."[10] In this regard, Frame sounds rather like the Paul of Galatians: "It was for freedom that Christ set us free; therefore keep standing firm and do not be subject again to a yoke of slavery" (Gal. 5:1). What matters is "faith working through love" (v. 6). "Walk by the Spirit, and you will not carry out the desire of the flesh" (v. 16). One of the things that marks Frame's approach is that he argues that greater attention to scriptural norms leads to the granting of greater freedom in worship. He believes "Scripture leaves many questions open—questions that different churches in different situations can legitimately answer differently."[11]

It seems to me that the letter to the Romans is a case in point. All the profound theology of chapters 1–13—a rich jambalaya of *ordo salutis* and *historia salutis*, of personal salvation and cosmic renewal—leads to a singular appeal in chapters 14–15 to get along on debatable matters of fellowship and worship: to drink, or not to drink? to set aside one day as special, or to reckon all days special? We must not trivialize the matters and set them aside as nonessential—especially when we consider their implications for worship. If we are supposed to meet together for worship (and we are), how can we do so when we can't agree on when that's supposed to be? If table fellowship is vital to worship (and it is), how can we drink together if we can't agree on what we should be drinking? What's striking about the letter to the Romans is how hard Paul works to teach the Roman Christians everything they're supposed to understand about everything else, but then how nuanced he becomes on these matters: respectful of how they may continue to differ (14:4–5), but confident that they will adopt a single-minded pattern of cruciformity (15:2–3, 5) so that "with one voice" they can glorify God (15:6). His abiding desire for them is this: wisdom in the good and innocence with regard to the evil of divisiveness, stumbling blocks, and self-gratification (16:17–19).

10. *WST*, 54–55.
11. Ibid., xvi.

A regulative principle that is worth its salt affirms the Bible's teachings on love, on mutual honor and deference, on dependence on the Holy Spirit, and on the need to apply wisdom. Frame's writings and his teaching are replete with such wisdom. For instance, his demurral in accepting the distinction between "elements" and "circumstances" lies in his concern that we not short-circuit our responsibility to adhere to the scripturally revealed purpose of worship, and then to discern wisely what that calls for in a given place and time. Keep in view what the worship service is for, and questions such as drama, drums, and dance will take care of themselves.

One day I asked Frame if he'd step into my class and answer a student's question about his thoughts on the frequency of communion. His answer went something like this:

> Well, I think you could make a good case for celebrating communion weekly, allowing it to be as regular a part of people's pattern of life as the preaching of the Word. I can also understand why some churches would want to make communion a special time of celebration, and take some time to ramp up to it. Those churches may find it more satisfying to celebrate the Table quarterly or annually.
>
> What I find least satisfactory—although a lot of churches are going to it—is the compromise measure of monthly communion. To me, that seems too infrequent to feel like a part of your normal spiritual diet. And it seems not infrequent enough if you really want to build up to it—it's probably just infrequent enough to be an inconvenience to the preaching pastor, who has to figure out how to "work it in" every four or five weeks, depending.

And former RTS Orlando student Linc Ashby recounts this bit of wisdom:

> My favorite story about John occurred just as many of us were packing up our things one evening as his class, Pastoral and Social Ethics, concluded. We had spent the majority of our time discussing (or was it arguing) about the 4th commandment on the Sabbath, and what it allowed, restricted, etc. . . .
>
> A little bent out of shape I pressed deeper, with about half of the class still milling around, "John (he let us call him by his first name), what do you do on the Sabbath?" I remember having a slightly accusatory tone in my voice.

He laughed that little awkward laugh of his and said something like this: "Well, Linc, my family and I go to worship, of course. And then we come home and enjoy a meal together. And we've just moved to Orlando so we haven't started this yet, and my wife was the one responsible for this idea when we lived in California, but during the afternoon I used to teach the Bible to the homeless men who were living with us."

. . . As you might imagine the entire class, or what was left of them, stopped whatever it was they were doing and just stood there at a standstill. He went on to explain, very humbly I might add, that his wife had set up some kind of partnership with a nearby homeless shelter where, after a few of the men there had gone through the initial detox and were ready to re-enter society, the Frame family would take a few in at a time, long enough for them to get back on their feet, find a job, an apartment, etc. . . .

They lived with the Frames and on Sunday afternoons he would hang out with them teaching them the Scriptures. After finally pulling my jaw up off the floor, I said something like, "Why didn't you just tell us that? We could have just moved on to commandment number 5." I'll never forget that night.[12]

What John Frame Taught Me about Situational Responsibility in Handling the Word in Worship

I study theology already embedded in an interpretive reality. My family circle, my network of friends, my ministry environment and its heritage—they all shape me and I shape them.

But the Bible tells me that one situational reality trumps all others. "Y'all's the onliest family I got," says Denzel Washington's character Private Trip to the rest of his unit on the night before the big battle scene in the movie *Glory*. To belong to Christ's family—to be among those who have joined Abraham's tribe in quest of a city with foundations—that's the onliest family that any believer really has. If it is wrong to read Scripture unmindful of its normativity, it is also wrong to read it outside of the situational reality that it says I'm in: the body of Christ.

A seminary course I took with Frame was "Doctrine and the Christian Life." The point of the course was largely this (and I freely paraphrase):

12. Posted at http://reggiekidd.com/RK/2009/06/23/currently-pondering-frame-rouault-me-dium-message/#comments (June 23, 2009).

You are a Christian first, and a Calvinist second. Listen for the concerns that animate brothers and sisters who don't think like you. You may not be able to affirm their formulations, but you may very well be able to understand why they do things the way they do. You may come to understand what they're afraid of in your formulation. You may or may not see the need to reformulate. But you will know that only on the far side of listening. And who knows, you may win the argument simply by virtue of winning the relationship. And/or you may find you actually have something to learn from them.

I wasn't prepared for a theologian to apply such common sense in his theology, to be so measured in his judgments, or to be so willing to grant what was valid in contrary views. Frame taught us that those who differ from us often value important things, and that if there is value in our own views, it may be because, and really only because, our approach happens to better approximate those values.

John Frame taught me that theology is done in community, and involves listening. When I entered the evangelical liturgical community's universe of discourse, I was surprised to discover how passionate its members are for renewing worship along *biblical* lines. For instance, they note, appreciatively, that evangelical churches (Reformed and otherwise) distinguish themselves largely on the basis of their owning a "higher view of Scripture." But my evangelical liturgical friends wonder why evangelical churches often have little actual Scripture in our services. They wonder why we nonliturgical evangelicals read it so little, and why we put up with sermons that are often only tangentially related to what little Scripture is read.

At first, I didn't understand what they were saying. Then I began to notice how Scripture functions in evangelical liturgical circles. Typically, at the start of such services a deacon carries a copy of the Gospels into the service as a part of the procession, placing it on the altar until the time for its reading. The time for the ministry of the Word consists of an Old Testament reading by a congregant, who concludes with the dialogue:

The Word of the Lord.
Thanks be to God.

Then follows a psalm. It may be rendered in any number of ways: simplified Anglican chant, Russian chant, plainsong chant, a sung metrical paraphrase, antiphonal reading, congregational reading. More often than not, the psalm is shared musically—more in tune, I submit, with the genre itself.

But we're only getting warmed up. We've heard from the testament of promise. Now for the testament of fulfillment. In a typical liturgical service, what follows next is a New Testament epistle reading, rendered again by a congregant, who concludes:

> The Word of the Lord.
> *Thanks be to God.*

The reading of the Word is crowned with the reading of the Gospel. A deacon, as the officer of the church "closest to the people," carries the Gospel into the midst of the congregation, who themselves stand and face the Gospel and the deacon. The deacon reads the Gospel—but only after, first, censing the Gospel (symbolizing our prayer that the Lord illumine the Word for us), and second, initiating another dialogue:

> The Holy Gospel of our Lord Jesus Christ, according to [Matthew, Mark, Luke, or John].
> *Glory to you, Lord Christ.*

Following the reading, there is yet one more dialogue:

> The Gospel of the Lord.
> *Praise to you, Lord Christ.*

Now the preacher preaches. And when liturgical preachers do their job, they unpack some portion of what has been read, or show the way in which the texts together tell their part of the whole of the coherent biblical story.

Finally, there's one more piece of dialogue. The congregation adds its "Amen" to the proclaimed Word by reciting the Nicene Creed. The whole pattern recalls Exodus 24:3, where Moses recounts to the people the ordinances of the Lord and the people respond: "All the words which the LORD has spoken we will do!"

With regard to the Bible, my evangelical liturgical friends pressed the question on me: can we inculcate a high view of Scripture merely by claiming it? Or do we not need to embody that high view in sacred action and in giving opportunity for an attentive hearing of it? Now, I haven't drunk the

Kool-Aid about the normativity of the ancient church's worship. But I do believe that our communal identity with our ancient brothers and sisters means that they could be a lot more instructive for us.

Sometimes Frame is critiqued for being more evangelical than Reformed. I'm like, "So we're supposed to be Calvinists first, Christians second? For sure, that's Kool-Aid I'm not drinking." I'm proud of him for defending "something close to biblicism."[13]

Nonetheless, it is Frame's own championing of a situational perspective—of a reading of Scripture that is accountable to Christ's church—that should make us eager to learn what earlier generations have to teach us about Scripture, as well as about what members of other communions may have to teach us. Part of the situation that all believers live in is the trajectory that Christ thrust into the world—the larger family, and the concentric circles of family that extend Christ's life and work into the world, and that manifest the age to come in every age. We all have our blind spots. We all need each other.

What John Frame Taught Me about the Existential in Worship: Keeping It Real

Theologians are people too. Some of us are likable, some not. Some are worth getting to know; others are better in book form or in audio or video. Sometimes when you get to know a theologian personally, you discover a great congruity between what he teaches and who he is. (Another theologian, perhaps not so much.) Over the years, John Frame has shown me what to aspire to: humility, graciousness, guilelessness, truthfulness. In a word, Christlikeness.

"The Bible will always be full of things you cannot understand as long as you will not live according to the things you do understand," Billy Sunday is supposed to have said. I've known no one who taught and lived the converse of this truth better than John Frame. If anyone deserves a hearing for his theology of worship because of the existential, cruciform proof of its truthfulness, it is this man.

Although his delight is classical music, love leads him to lay his training and his tastes at the altar of service to Christ and his people. His theological

13. *IDSCB.*

training, expertise, and primary interests lie elsewhere, but he steps into the fray on worship because love won't let him not say "Yes" when his church asks him to share what he knows. He could write obtuse prose if he wanted, but love compels him to write theology with simple vocabulary, straightforward logic, and matter-of-fact prose. His natural reserve and almost painful shyness could leave him behind a closed study door, but love bids him to open his home and his heart to people who need help getting off the streets.

At the center of our enterprise is a Person. It is his presence that C. S. Lewis described as finally reconciling all of the church's discordant voices: "Someone, who against all divergences of belief, all differences of temperament, all memories of mutual persecution, speaks with the same voice."[14]

I have been privileged to know several theologians older than I who, despite their peculiarities and principial differences, evidence that voice. In this article I have mentioned some who especially carry that voice. I could add five RTS Orlando colleagues: Simon Kistemaker, Roger Nicole, Charles ("Sherry") MacKenzie, Bruce Waltke, and Steve Brown. What they all share is a youthfulness that Catholic Thomistic philosopher Josef Pieper says characterizes those who age well in Christ: "that strong-hearted freshness, that resilient joy, that steady perseverance in trust that so distinguish the young and make them lovable."[15]

Eminently clear is that voice, and especially vibrant is that strong-hearted freshness, that resilient joy, and that steady perseverance in my former teacher and now colleague and friend John Frame.

---

14. C. S. Lewis, *Mere Christianity* (New York: Macmillan, 1952), 9.
15. Josef Pieper, *Faith, Hope, Love* (San Francisco: Ignatius Press, 1997), 111.

31

RETHINKING, REFORMING: FRAME'S CONTRIBUTIONS TO CONTEMPORARY WORSHIP

PAXSON H. JEANCAKE

INTRODUCTION

On any given Sunday at my church in California, I will stand before my congregation with an electric guitar or an acoustic guitar strapped around me. I will lead a team of other players on electric guitar, acoustic guitar, bass, piano, drums, and auxiliary percussion. I will have several other vocalists, male and female, singing lead and harmony. From time to time I will have a saxophone player, or a brass or string ensemble. We will sing upbeat, driving modern worship songs by Chris Tomlin, Matt Redman, Lincoln Brewster, Tommy Walker, Kristian Stanfill, Kathryn Scott, Brenton Brown, Paul Baloche, Joel Houston, and Israel Houghton—to name a few. We will sing ancient and traditional hymn texts set to modern melodies from songwriters within the Indelible Grace community—people like Matthew Smith, Sandra McCracken, Kevin Twit, and Chris Miner. We will sing modern hymns by Keith and Kristyn Getty, Stuart Townend, and songwriters within the Sovereign Grace movement like Steve and Vikki Cook. From time to time we will also sing some of the older contemporary worship songs (that is meant to sound like an oxymoron) from Vineyard Music or Maranatha! Music—songs that everybody knows and can sing out strong.

We will have a female within our congregation lead us through our Community Life and Prayer time, highlighting various events and happenings within our church. She may invite people to share testimonies, she may tell a humorous story pertaining to the life of our congregation, or she may ask us to watch a video that highlights an event or ministry opportunity. At the end of this time she will pray for our morning worship.

After greeting one another we may use a call-to-worship text that is a lectionary reading from the Book of Common Prayer, or we may utilize a crafted text from one of many liturgical resources. We will pray a corporate prayer of renewal, confessing our sins and our need for the Spirit's work in our lives. We may sing a traditional hymn with a traditional melody, but with an additional chorus section. There may be a dramatic sketch before the sermon—something humorous, something serious, or both. After the sermon, we may recite an ancient creed or partake of the Lord's Supper. After a closing song we will receive a blessing before being sent out to serve our world.

All of our various texts (song lyrics, announcements, and sermon points) will be displayed on a screen and printed in our bulletin. We will use an assortment of images on our slides—everything from photographs taken by members of our congregation to fine art and classic paintings. We will have a very capable crew in the back of the room adjusting the lighting, mixing the sound, and running the multimedia from a computer. We have two identical services on Sunday morning.

My church is not a megachurch. We are not seeker-driven, non-denominational, or part of the charismatic movement. We are part of the Reformed community (Presbyterian Church in America [PCA]) that affirms the Westminster Confession of Faith, our Book of Church Order, and the regulative principle of worship. The worship I have described is representative of a large number of churches across North America that are part of the Reformed community. But it has not *always* been this way.

Throughout the ages God has raised up uniquely qualified individuals to act and to speak within a particular moment in history, leaving an indelible mark and a lasting influence on the church and culture of the time. Such is the story and influence of John Frame. In his book *CWM*, Frame writes:

We revere Luther and Calvin because they had the courage to rethink, from the ground up, the current traditions about salvation and worship. They were respectful of tradition, as all Christians should be. But they were not bound to it, only to the God of Scripture.[1]

As I began to prepare for this article, reflecting on the impact Frame has had in the area of contemporary worship, I thought of people like Luther and Calvin. I thought of these men because the combination of their gifts, courage, and unique cultural situation all worked together providentially to bring about major shifts in the history of the church. Like Luther and Calvin, Frame challenged us to rethink and reform worship in light of biblical convictions.

With regard to Frame's prominent role in the so-called worship wars, Dick Kaufmann, Frame's friend and pastor for fifteen years, had this to say: "John was one of, if not the, key player in why we're not where we were in the 1980s and 1990s." I couldn't agree more. In this article I'd like to share why.

My Journey with Frame

I still remember the first time I heard the name John Frame. I was taking Reggie Kidd's Theology of Worship course at Reformed Theological Seminary in Orlando, Florida. The course outline was broken down into three parts: cognitive, existential, and teleological. I remember resonating with Kidd's simple, yet profound triad and shared it with my pastor at the time. I'll never forget his response: "Yeah, that's Frame." That conversation began my exploration into the thought and writings of John M. Frame. I read WST in the spring of 2000 just before transitioning to a church in Atlanta, and Frame's thoughts on worship were very refreshing to me. It would be a couple of years later, however, while taking courses at Reformed Theological Seminary in Atlanta, that I would get to meet Frame in person.

At RTS Atlanta I enjoyed taking three courses under Frame: Apologetics, The Doctrine of God, and Pastoral and Social Ethics. I read his books and spent countless hours figuring out all the various triads they contained. I would often turn back and forth between different chapters and the analytical outline to see if a certain section reflected the normative, existential, or

1. *CWM*, 4.

situational perspective.[2] I also read other authors' books and noticed Frame's triperspectival influence on them.

In 2003, as I neared graduation at RTS Atlanta, I asked Frame if he would be my advisor for my integrative paper—the culmination of the master of arts in religion (MAR) degree at RTS. Frame agreed and I was elated. I then had the privilege of getting to know Frame on a bit more personal level. We would have lunch on occasion when he was in Atlanta teaching. I would send him e-mails with questions about my paper, and I was always amazed at how quickly and poignantly he responded. Once my paper was finished I had hopes of its one day being published, and I envisioned Frame writing the foreword.

In 2006 that hope became a reality as Wipf and Stock published *The Art of Worship: Opening Our Eyes to the Beauty of the Gospel.*[3] Frame wrote the foreword and the book is, of course, filled with triads. In three major sections I discuss how to cultivate gospel-centered worship leaders (existential); how to discover a gospel-centered worship theology (normative); and how to develop gospel-centered worship communities (situational). As it has for so many others, Frame's triperspectival approach has shaped the way I observe, interpret, and apply virtually everything! I have a deep admiration for John Frame as a theologian, a mentor, and a friend. It is with great pleasure that I now expound upon his contributions to contemporary worship.

Brief Sketch of the Contemporary Worship Movement

The contemporary worship phenomenon was birthed in part from the influence of the charismatic movement and the Jesus Movement of the 1970s when young students of the hippie generation were being converted through the ministry of places like Calvary Chapel on the West Coast and Belmont Church of Christ in the Southeast. Music is always an indicator of spiritual revival, and as more and more youth were becoming Christians, songs were birthed. Before long a whole new contemporary movement of worship and musical expression was growing.

One has to imagine a time in history when people like Chris Tomlin, Matt Redman, and Darlene Zschech were not household names in the world

2. Frame's triperspectivalism has been very influential for me and many others. I will not expound on this unique approach here because another article in this work covers it sufficiently.

3. Paxson H. Jeancake, *The Art of Worship: Opening Our Eyes to the Beauty of the Gospel* (Eugene, OR: Wipf and Stock, 2006).

of contemporary worship. This was a time before Hillsong, Passion, Indelible Grace, and the more recent explosion of worship music. During the 1980s the major publishing companies were Maranatha! Music and Hosanna! Integrity. The movement had not become as widespread, ecumenically, as it is today. Certainly, in most Reformed churches the phenomenon was treated with a great deal of skepticism.

During the time that this phenomenon was gaining momentum, particularly on the West Coast through people like Chuck Smith and John Wimber, John Frame moved to Escondido, California to help establish a new campus for Westminster Theological Seminary. He and other founders and early teachers at the campus went with a missionary vision, for California had very few Reformed churches, and Westminster was one of the few Reformed seminaries west of the Mississippi. These were exciting times for Frame. He was stirred by the vision of helping to establish a new campus for Westminster and by helping to establish a new church with Dick Kaufmann.

Frame's Contributions to Contemporary Worship

In the next three sections of this article I will describe Frame's contributions to contemporary worship, perspectivally. In the first section (existential) I will tell the story of Frame's early experience in music ministry, the influence of Jack Miller and Dick Kaufmann, and his fourteen years as the worship leader at New Life Presbyterian Church in Escondido. These formative events in Frame's life shaped his perspective on contemporary worship. In the second section (normative) I will recount the various ways in which Frame has fleshed out his biblical and theological convictions about contemporary worship: his books and articles on worship as well as his views on various topics related to contemporary worship. Finally, in the last section (situational) I will share Frame's indelible mark and lasting influence on former students and current worship leaders, pastors, and other leaders in the church and throughout the world.

FRAME'S FORMATIVE YEARS AS A WORSHIP LEADER

Early Background in Music and Worship

Frame has written how, as a young teenager, the music ministry of his church in Pittsburgh changed him profoundly. There he took organ lessons and sang in the choir. In Frame's own words, "The youth ministry taught me the gospel; the music ministry drove it into my heart. From that time on, I have been deeply interested in worship."[4] Frame has also had much formal training in music. He took private lessons in classical piano for eight years; organ for five; clarinet for two; and harmony, counterpoint, and improvisation for three or four. In school he played in both band and orchestra. In *CWM*, Frame notes that he loves "classical music far more than any other musical genre," although he does enjoy occasional exposure to jazz and to older pop music. Interestingly, in *CWM* he admits that he does not have much of an ear for contemporary rock, and he would not say that contemporary worship music is one of his personal musical passions.[5] Thus, an obvious question is, "How did John Frame become such a strong voice for advocating contemporary worship and contemporary worship music?"

To understand how this could be, we first have to understand two men who had a profound impact on Frame's life: C. John (Jack) Miller and Dick Kaufmann.

The Influence of Jack Miller, Dick Kaufmann, and New Life Presbyterian Church

Jack Miller taught practical theology at Westminster Theological Seminary in Philadelphia. He also founded New Life Church in that city, as well as World Harvest Mission and Sonship—a ministry of conferences and resources that articulate Miller's vision of gospel-centered Christian living. After citing Jack's "evangelistic boldness" and "humble spirit" as profound influences, Frame writes:

> I suppose that Jack's greatest influence on me was to make me willing to endure the scorn of traditionalists in the church. Jack's emphasis on evangelism led him to employ a style of worship at New Life that was far from the Presbyterian tradition. He used contemporary songs, guitars, cultivated informality. Many in our circles balked at this, even ridiculed it. But people came to Christ by God's grace, overcame besetting sins, became

4. John Frame, "Backgrounds to My Thought," in this festschrift.
5. *CTW*, 4.

zealous for Christ. Eventually, many who at first mocked New Life became enthusiastic members.[6]

Frame's bold stance on endorsing a contemporary approach to worship within the Reformed community in the 1980s and 1990s was bound to bring ridicule. However, Frame was able to persevere and stay true to his convictions partly because of the influence of Jack Miller. Frame had witnessed the worship model at New Life in Philadelphia, and he had seen the fruit of Jack's approach: people heard the gospel, came to Christ, and overcame sin patterns. Frame realized that people heard the message because it was conveyed in a musical language they could understand and in an atmosphere of grace and authenticity that was compelling. Understanding the evangelistic fervor of Jack Miller and his influence on Frame is the first key to understanding how Frame became such an advocate of contemporary worship and contemporary worship music.

Another profound influence in Frame's life was Dick Kaufmann and the ministry and vision of New Life Presbyterian Church in Escondido, California. Providence seems to have brought Dick Kaufmann and John Frame together. In fact, in a conversation with me, Dick mentioned that during their move out to California, his and Frame's belongings ended up on the same moving van!

Dick had been a ruling elder at New Life in Philadelphia and felt called to plant a church in California that would have the same ministry approach and vision: reaching the unchurched rather than merely attracting Reformed people. Frame became the elder in charge of worship at the California incarnation of New Life, and he taught an adult class on worship there, which led directly to the writing of his book *WST*. Frame was also asked to reply to letters the church received that were critical of New Life's worship. That correspondence led to the publication of his book *CWM*.

Frame cites Jack Miller as a major inspiration behind the writing of both *WST* and *CWM*. He shares how Jack "defined for me what life in the church should be like," and how Dick Kaufmann, his pastor for fourteen years, "defined . . . the model of a godly pastor." These two men and their respective ministries challenged Frame's thinking in many areas. Their attitude of love and grace to believer and unbeliever, friend and enemy alike rebuked Frame's pride and spiritual complacency.[7]

6. Frame, "Backgrounds to My Thought."
7. Ibid.

Worship at New Life Presbyterian Church in Escondido, California

In *CWM* Frame writes of how God's grace enabled him to persevere in learning and using a style of music he did not personally enjoy. He even notes how he "was dragged kicking and screaming" into the world of contemporary worship music. The main biblical considerations that motivated him through the years at New Life, however, were the Great Commission and the emphasis on intelligible worship in 1 Corinthians 14. The vision of New Life was to have a form of worship that "spoke intelligibly to the community we sought to reach: not only long-time Presbyterians, but also non-Presbyterian Christians and the unchurched."[8] Frame describes how all those involved needed to put aside, to a large extent, their own prejudices and preferences to reach that goal. They had to esteem the interests of others above their own. Frame says, "God blessed that desire, and many came to a saving knowledge of Christ through the church's ministry."[9]

In *WST*, Frame's concluding chapter is called "Putting It All Together." There he describes a typical service at New Life in Escondido. This chapter offers a very practical and insightful window into how Frame planned and led worship that was faithful to biblical mandates, particularly the Great Commission and intelligibility in worship. Frame notes how, at one point in a service,

> I led in prayer, including adoration of God's greatness and majesty and confession of our lost and guilty condition, acknowledging that we have forgiveness and access to God only through God. . . . I asked God to open our eyes to see this world as he sees it . . . to give us faithfulness to serve him single-mindedly.[10]

According to Frame, this was the invocation, but at New Life they wouldn't call it that. They tried to avoid liturgical-sounding language as much as possible. Interestingly, like Frame, I took a step of faith and moved my family to California in 2008. We felt called to a church in the Sacramento area and have been challenged in the same sensitivities to intelligibility in worship. As worship leaders and pastors, it is easy to use liturgical-sounding language—language that is likely to be unfamiliar to a portion of those in

8. *CWM*, 143.
9. Ibid.
10. *WST*, 148.

attendance. California, especially, is not as churched as other parts of the United States and requires greater sensitivity with regard to communication in worship. Thus, Frame and the leaders at New Life were very intentional in the choice of words they used in their worship services.

Frame also shares some insights into his song-selection process at New Life: sometimes he used more contemporary songs, and sometimes more traditional ones, depending on what best supported the theme of a particular service. A general pattern that he found to be edifying was to sing one or two traditional hymns (taking advantage of the greater theological richness of that genre) and then follow them with a simple contemporary praise chorus. According to Frame, "following one or two hymns with a simple chorus allows people to meditate on rich truths and gives childlike adoration to the God who has done such wonderful things."[11]

In the final chapter of *CWM*, Frame presents what he calls his "*CWM* Song Book." This is basically a list of songs used at New Life for which he could list a publisher or at least an author. In that chapter he also offers his criteria for choosing songs: "I look for songs that are consistent with Scripture and Reformed doctrine, excellent in musical and poetic quality, and singable—songs that communicate well with people today."[12]

I have previously mentioned that I was able to have a conversation with Dick Kaufmann, hoping to glean his thoughts regarding Frame's worship leadership at New Life. Dick had a number of insightful things to say. He mentioned how Frame would often use the call to worship (again, they would not call it that) to present the gospel. He shared how Frame spoke and led very naturally and in a way that was intelligible, underscoring the church's agreed-on value of speaking in the vernacular. They did not speak in religious language, but just tried "to be real." Dick added that Frame's short gospel presentations would both prepare people to sing and tie in well with the theme of the sermon for that morning.

When Frame moved to California in 1980, he could scarcely have imagined the way in which the Lord would use him in the context of the growing contemporary worship movement. It was a great step of faith to help establish a new seminary and to help plant a new church with a vision for reaching unbelievers. He would spend fourteen years developing the

11. Ibid., 149–50.
12. *CWM*, 145.

worship ministry at New Life Church, all the while being challenged and stretched theologically, musically, and liturgically.

Thus, Frame's first contribution to contemporary worship was not his books or articles, but his very life as a growing, persevering worship leader at a young church plant with a vision for carrying out the Great Commission and speaking intelligibly to those New Life was trying to reach. He learned the musical language and nuances of contemporary worship and contemporary worship music, not because it was his strength or his personal preference, but because he was compelled by God's Word and by the power of the gospel.

FRAME'S INFLUENTIAL WRITINGS ON CONTEMPORARY WORSHIP

Having looked at Frame's contributions to contemporary worship from the existential perspective, I would now like to highlight the writings that emerged from biblical and theological reflection as he was immersed in the world of contemporary worship at New Life in Escondido.

Contemporary Worship Themes in *WST*

WST was published in 1996 and was the result of Frame's teaching a class on worship as an elder at his church in California. In the preface to *WST* Frame writes,

> In a way, this volume seeks to summarize the thinking underlying the worship of "New Life" Presbyterian churches: New Life Presbyterian Church in Escondido, California, where I worship, our "mother church" of the same name in Glenside, Pennsylvania, and others.[13]

I find it interesting and worthy to note that Frame's own personal narrative underscores his triperspectival approach; one can readily see how his biblical and theological convictions (normative) emerged from his role as a worship leader (existential) in the context of a Presbyterian church in southern California (situational) with a worship style and philosophy that was quite different from many of its more traditional counterparts at the time. In this section I will highlight some of the topics and themes in *WST*

13. *WST*, xvi.

that are particularly relevant to contemporary worship: Frame's view of the regulative principle; the tone of worship; the place of drama in worship; and the role of the physical body in worship, including the clapping of hands, the lifting of hands, and dancing.

Frame's View of the Regulative Principle. As I have reflected over the years on the regulative principle of worship and its use and abuse, I have come to see that it is surrounded with irony. Interestingly, some of my observations (and Frame's) reveal a passionate *advocacy* for certain elements in worship about which Scripture does not seem to offer direct or specific commands, and a passionate *prohibition* of other elements and applications about which Scripture appears to give the most direct and specific commands. Frame writes:

> For example, there is no New Testament command to administer baptism in a Sunday meeting, and there is no historical record of that ever being done in the New Testament period. Baptisms in the New Testament are typically performed outside of formal meetings. But the nature of baptism, as a sign and seal of the covenant of grace, and as a solemn, public oath to the Lord and profession of faith in him, surely makes it appropriate.[14]

I think everyone would agree that baptism is something that should be a part of corporate worship, yet Scripture nowhere gives a direct command about it. However— and this is what I think is so ironic—Scripture does give clear and simple imperatives to clap one's hands (Pss. 47:1; 97:8), raise one's hands (Pss. 63:4; 134:2; 1 Tim. 2:8), and dance (Pss. 148:3; 150:4). The irony is that the actions these simple imperatives command are rarely seen and often ridiculed (sometimes on the basis of the regulative principle!) in the context of Reformed worship. I believe that these scriptural imperatives are readily dismissed because they are not physical expressions with which many Reformed churches feel "comfortable." Thus, these actions simply get ignored or dismissed by a kind of cultural hermeneutic that sees these postures as being meant for and applied as a part of ancient Jewish culture.

I use these examples and state this irony and discrepancy because Frame was such a fresh and affirming voice for me (and, I know, for many others)

14. Ibid., 55.

as I tried to wrestle with the role of the regulative principle—its definition and its practical application for the weekly decisions about worship.

I leave it to my friend Reggie Kidd to expound more upon this particular topic elsewhere in this volume. Here I will simply state that I wholeheartedly agree with and submit to the definition and role of the regulative principle articulated by Frame in *WST*. It was like a breath of fresh air to read Frame's view of this controversial subject. I have referred to this articulation on many occasions—either to remind myself of my own understanding or to offer as a defense when in dialogue with someone of a different persuasion. Frame writes:

> The regulative principle . . . sets us free within limits, to worship God in the language of our own time, to seek those applications of God's commandments which most edify worshipers in our contemporary cultures. We must be both more conservative and more liberal than most students of Christian worship: conservative in holding exclusively to God's commands in Scripture as our rule in worship, and liberal in defending the liberty of those who apply those commandments in legitimate, though nontraditional ways.[15]

As a young worship leader who was still in seminary, I found those words a call to freedom when I read books from or found myself face-to-face with those who could not imagine anything other than pianos and traditional hymns in worship, and who passionately argued for these things on the basis of the regulative principle. According to Frame's definition, the regulative principle would be more aptly called the "Scripture principle."

When I read Frame, I found myself in like company. I felt a kindred spirit. I felt I had found someone who had a lot of experience and knowledge about the subject and yet articulated a belief that resonated deeply with my own intuitions about God, the prescriptions and freedom of his Word, and the importance of completely appropriate, contemporary applications and expressions that most edify God's people in worship.

The Tone of Worship. Contemporary worship is generally characterized as having a healthy freedom of emotion, participation, informality, and even humor. I love the fact that Frame has a whole chapter in *WST*

15. Ibid., 46.

dealing with the tone of worship. Frankly, I had not seen a lot about such considerations (especially the emotions) in other Reformed writings on worship. Like his view of the regulative principle, Frame's thoughts on the tone of worship were very affirming and encouraging for me as a young worship leader within the PCA. I guess in some ways Frame made me feel like I wasn't an outsider within my own denomination.

I began leading worship when I was in college and then continued leading in a volunteer or interim capacity while working as a graduate student at the University of Alabama at Birmingham. I would lead for various groups and ministries on evenings throughout the week and on Sunday at my church. During this time I was influenced by the music and worship of the Vineyard, which has a much more charismatic style of worship. Over the years, I have led worship in more charismatic settings and have attended a few Vineyard conferences and worship services. Needless to say, the style is very different from most PCA worship services. In more charismatic settings, one might feel out of place *by not raising one's hands* during worship!

Personally, I love the freedom of expression in these various settings. There is a sense of expectancy in worship demonstrated by a healthy level of emotional engagement, which is completely normal. I say that because, generally, the worship in many Reformed churches is void of much emotion. Frame writes:

> Literature on worship, especially in Reformed circles, is full of condemnations of "emotionalism," especially in the charismatic movement and some other forms of evangelicalism. But there is little in this literature on the positive value of emotions in worship or the emotional content of the word of God. Reformed theology has always been rather uneasy about the emotions.[16]

Frame goes on to observe how in the Scriptures God speaks to us in a variety of ways, some intellectual and some emotional (using the letter to the Romans and the book of Psalms as examples). He also describes how Scripture has much to say about our own emotional life—how we should feel about things. He cites joy, peace, anxiety, fear, courage, and love—concepts that have an emotional character to them.

16. Ibid., 77.

Frame describes the various "attitudes" that we bring to worship and, of course, cites numerous biblical texts to support his claims. He talks about reverence (Heb. 12:28), joy (Pss. 2:11; 98:46; John 8:56; Acts 2:46; Jude 24; Rev. 19:7), sorrow for sin (Ps. 51; Isa. 6), participation (1 Cor. 14), faith (Rom. 14:23; Heb. 11:6), love (Matt. 22:37–40; John 13:34–35), boldness (Eph. 3:12; Heb. 4:16; 10:19; 13:6), and family intimacy (John 15:14–15). Frame encourages worship planners and worshipers to give thought to the subjective quality of the worship service.

Unlike many others who hold a different view of the regulative principle, Frame feels that Scripture allows a considerable amount of freedom when it comes to how formal or informal, quiet or noisy the service should be, or how friendly, chatty, solemn, or humorous the worship leader should be. He is not limited by common prejudices, but remains open to the fact that God can reveal himself in both formal and informal settings. Reverence and awe, for example, are not attitudes that come only in solemn worship services. He cites, anecdotally, being overwhelmed by the majesty of God in the midst of an informal worship service.[17]

In *WST* Frame talks about how we go to church to *do* something: to bring praise to God and to minister to one another. Frame reminds us that worship should encourage us to sing from the heart, pray fervently, and hear God's Word with the expectation that we will change our behavior in response.[18] Surely, this sense of expectancy that Frame is describing found its roots in his experiences at New Life in Philadelphia and in Escondido. Others have since been encouraged and inspired to pray for, plant, and cultivate churches with the same sense of freedom and expectancy.

Frame ends this section on the tone of worship by stating, "It is important that people of Reformed conviction give more positive attention to the emotional component of worship."[19] I believe this is one of Frame's major contributions to contemporary worship. I made a personal statement about this earlier, but I'll say it again. Frame helped those who feel completely at home with Reformed doctrine (e.g., the doctrines of grace, the authority of the Scripture, the sovereignty of God), yet who long for more freedom of expression in worship, not feel like outsiders. By offering serious, biblical reflection on the role of the emotions, Frame helped release this subject from

17. Ibid., 79–82.
18. Ibid., 80.
19. Ibid., 78.

an argument against *emotionalism* to a healthy and appropriate defense of a wide variety of expression in worship.

The Place of Drama in Worship. During the 1980s and 1990s many of the seeker-driven churches like Willow Creek Community Church in Barrington, Illinois, began to incorporate drama in their services. Often these churches would use drama to communicate biblical concepts and topics to people in a clear and fresh way. It would be common for a dramatic sketch to precede the pastor's message in a given worship service, making a natural segue into the sermon content.

Drama, a common component of contemporary worship, would typically not be an element of worship in more traditional worship settings. Frame, however, makes a good argument for the use of drama in worship by appealing to Scripture. He writes:

> God often teaches his people through drama. The book of Job, the Old Testament sacrifices and feasts, and the New Testament sacraments are reenactments of God's great works of redemption. As we have seen, the traditional liturgy has continued this process of reenactment for many centuries, so drama in worship is nothing new.[20]

Frame endorses drama on biblical grounds, yet he is honest in acknowledging that he is not a strong advocate of its use simply because of the logistical considerations (e.g., the time needed to write, plan, rehearse, etc.). In Frame's opinion dramas are most effective in worship when they pose a question to which the sermon presents a scriptural answer. I would add that drama is also effective when it raises tension for which the sermon brings resolution.

Although it is not found in *WST*, I would like to cite a concept that I feel is very pertinent to the discussion of drama. In both *DKG* and *DCL*, Frame describes the difference between "seeing" and "seeing as." I talk about this concept in my own book *The Art of Worship*. It has been a powerful concept for me, particularly as I have appropriated the role of the arts in worship.

In *DCL*, Frame describes the picture of a "duck-rabbit," a drawing in which one can see a duck or a rabbit, depending on how one looks at it. He describes how one can have 20/20 vision, seeing all the lines in the drawing,

---

20. Ibid., 93.

without being able to identify it as a picture of a duck, a rabbit, or both. Quite profoundly, Frame shows how this is also true in moral contexts. Sometimes we know all the facts, we can "see," but discernment has not reached us at a heart level—we are unable to "see as."

Frame shows as well how moral and gospel discernment can come through a Scripture text or a relevant fact, but just as often can occur in unexpected ways.[21] To illustrate this point Frame reminds us of the story of how the prophet Nathan approached David after the king had committed adultery with Bathsheba and then murdered her husband Uriah (2 Sam. 11 –12). Initially, David did not make the connection between God's law and his own actions in a way that would impress upon him his obligation to repent. What brought David to repentance was not the revelation of some fact about Scripture or the situation of which he was previously unaware, but an emotional shock.[22]

Nathan told the story of a poor man who had one ewe lamb that he raised as a family pet. A rich man, who owned many sheep, stole the poor man's lamb and killed it to feed a guest. David was outraged by the story because Nathan had drawn him in emotionally. When Nathan proclaimed to David, "You are the man!" (2 Sam. 12:5–7), it shocked David, it took him by surprise, and it allowed him to discern in his heart what he had done. He was able to "see as." "Scripture, therefore, teaches ethics in many ways: through laws and through narrative . . . but also through proverbs, parables, songs."[23] With regard to our ability to "see as," Frame notes how artistry and nuance play significant roles.

I share all of this because it is a powerful concept for understanding not only the role of drama in worship, but the role of other artistic expressions as well. Churches that incorporate drama know that story, shock, surprise, and emotional engagement play a powerful role in the lives of believers and unbelievers. Like Nathan's parable, a well-executed drama draws people in, raises questions and tensions, stirs up emotions (all characteristics of good drama), and, together with the Spirit's work, has the potential to bring about profound moral discernment in believer and unbeliever alike.

In *The Art of Worship* I describe how story, imagery, and experience and lyrical and poetic expression all have the potential to open our eyes to the

---

21. *DCL*, 357.
22. Ibid., 358.
23. Ibid., 359.

beauty of the gospel in the context of corporate worship. They are the artistic means through which God allows us to "see as." Thus, I greatly appreciate Frame's use of this concept. Coupled with an affirmation of drama and other artistic expressions, he encourages worship planners to think outside the box and brings a heightened awareness to the intersection of our creativity and the Spirit's role in worship planning.

The Role of the Physical Body in Worship. Contemporary worship is further characterized by physical expression: clapping of hands, lifting of hands, and dancing. In a chapter on music in worship, Frame describes the "music of the body." At the beginning of this section he writes:

> People communicate, not only by word, but also by body language. In this we image the God of Scripture, who communicates both through spoken word and through natural revelation. Some (especially Presbyterians like me) prefer to worship quietly in a sitting position, but to most people in the world it is natural to accompany words with physical action.[24]

I love the fact that Frame is honest about his own personal preference, yet acknowledges the legitimacy of physical expression, both culturally and biblically. In most Presbyterian churches, dance, raising one's hands, and clapping are not common expressions. Presbyterians have often been labeled as the "frozen chosen." There is a lot of truth in this statement. Generally, Reformed worship is not characterized by much physical expression, yet Frame writes, "God wants body as well as spirit to be engaged in his worship. Clapping expresses joy; lifting the hands is a way of drawing toward God as the object of our worship and the source of our blessing."[25]

As in so many other areas, Frame's endorsement of physical expression in worship was a breath of fresh air, particularly for those who had come from different cultural or denominational backgrounds in which the freedom to raise one's hands was not an issue. Contemporary worship leaders are sometimes criticized as being "worship cheerleaders," for trying to manipulate or manufacture physical expression from worshipers. Without completely denying this claim, I would contend that one's apprehension about

24. *WST*, 130–31.
25. Ibid., 131.

physical expression usually reveals one's bias toward the *cerebral* aspect of worship over and against the *physical* aspect of worship. Frame, however, recognizes the holistic nature of worship and encourages us to engage not only spiritually and intellectually, but physically as well.

Dance, as a form of physical expression and a somewhat common facet of contemporary worship, has definitely been a source of controversy. I broached this topic briefly in my discussion of Frame's view of the regulative principle. Here, I will simply make a few additional comments regarding Frame's argument for the legitimacy of dance in worship. I appreciate his perspective on this controversial topic:

> Dance in worship is first of all the simple, natural, physical dimension of the reverent joy we share in Christ. Most of us, even those who are not very demonstrative in our worship, find it natural to sway, however slightly, to the rhythm of the songs we sing. That movement itself is a simple form of dance. If that is justifiable, who is to draw the line to show precisely how much movement is permitted? And if such simple movements are justifiable, why not greater movement, especially in view of the biblical references to dance?[26]

As he does with drama, Frame acknowledges some concerns about the use of dance in worship. He describes how in our modern culture, both popular dance and classical ballet have become saturated with eroticism. He notes that many churches would rather prohibit liturgical dance altogether than allow people to move down the aisles of the church in sexually provocative clothing or with sensuous movements. For Frame, however, it would not be right to throw out the baby with the bathwater—dismissing entirely a form of worship that God commands. Frame concludes this section with a personal experience:

> Of the dances I have witnessed, those which conveyed best the joy of Jesus were dances coordinated with well-known hymn tunes on biblical themes. As the meaning of these hymns was underscored and enhanced by the dancers, I found that in watching them I became more and more a worshiper and less and less a liturgical critic.[27]

26. Ibid., 132.
27. Ibid., 132.

I can remember reading this for the first time and sharing Frame's sentiments. When I was first approached by a dancer at our church who wanted to incorporate dance into our worship, I admit I was a bit apprehensive. What would this look like? What would people think? However, I wanted to celebrate this person's gifts and could not think of any biblical reasons for not having her dance in worship. Within a few months of her initial offer, the right occasion presented itself and we had our first liturgical dance as a part of our Palm Sunday celebration. Like Frame, as I watched the dance movements coordinated with the lyrics and melody of the song we were singing, I too became more and more engaged as a worshiper and less and less a skeptic of liturgical dance. Interestingly, dance became somewhat of a regular expression in our worship at that church, occurring about every other month.

In *WST*, Frame introduced himself as a voice and an advocate for so many worship leaders and pastors planning contemporary worship. The church (especially Reformed and Presbyterian churches) needed an open, culturally aware, honest, and biblical treatment of such controversial topics as the regulative principle, our emotions, drama, and physical expression in worship. Frame provided a strong, biblically saturated articulation of these topics and gained the allegiance of many, young and old, of like mind.

Frame's Biblical and Theological Convictions in *CWM*

In his second volume, *CWM*, Frame became more involved in the "worship wars" and took on a more defensive posture, elucidating his issues with the critics of contemporary worship. By giving serious biblical reflection to these issues, Frame caused many pastors, elders, and worship leaders to rethink their own worship practices and philosophies. In this section I will summarize the various convictions that are foundational for Frame.

Sola Scriptura versus Traditionalism. One major issue that Frame realized he had to address in *CWM* was the role of *traditionalism* versus the Reformed principle of *sola Scriptura* in theological method. Frame has described this as the central burden of his theological efforts in the past, and most likely it will continue to be so in future writings. The concern for Frame is the tendency to *substitute historical and sociological research for exegesis.* As Frame began to interact more and more with the critics of contemporary worship (people like David Wells, Michael Horton, Marva

Dawn, Darryl Hart, and John Muether), he began to discern that a flawed theological method was a major underlying factor in their work.

Frame would describe this flawed method as the following: (1) offer historical and sociological sketch of all the ills of the contemporary worship movement (subjectivism, humanism, anti-intellectualism, psychologism, professionalism, consumerism, pragmatism, and temporal chauvinism);[28] (2) assume without serious study or argument that contemporary worship music arises out of that movement; (3) then present a distorted description of contemporary worship music to make it fit the critic's concept of that movement.[29] In Frame's opinion

> the critics have frequently condemned CWM [contemporary worship
> music], not on the basis of biblical principle, but because they judge it to
> be part of a historical development of which they disapprove. That kind of
> argument seems to me to be unfair to CWM. More importantly for many
> other areas of discussion, it violates *sola Scriptura*, one of the defining
> principles of Protestant theology.[30]

In addition to addressing this issue throughout *CWM*, Frame devotes an entire appendix (nearly twenty-five pages) to articulating what he refers to as *sola Scriptura* in theological method. There he acknowledges that he has "been motivated to write this book as much by concerns about the theological method lying behind criticisms of CWM as by concerns about the use of CWM itself."[31]

In Frame's opinion the historical- and sociological-oriented theologians tend to be uncritical of traditions and critical of the contemporary church, and their arguments are often based on their preferences rather than biblical principles. In one place Frame notes how one suspects that "the critics' problems with CWM are not merely theological, but personal, even emotional. It seems that they just don't like CWM, and they are searching for reasons (however inadequate those reasons may be to an objective reader)

---

28. Frame compiled this list from three major sources: David F. Wells, *God in the Wasteland: The Reality of Truth in a World of Fading Dreams* (Grand Rapids: Eerdmans, 1994), Marva J. Dawn, *Reaching Out without Dumbing Down: A Theology of Worship for This Urgent Time* (Grand Rapids: Eerdmans, 1995), and Mark Noll, *The Scandal of the Evangelical Mind* (Grand Rapids: Eerdmans, 1994).

29. This is a paraphrase of Frame's issue with Darryl Hart in *CWM*, 114.

30. Ibid., 175.

31. Ibid.

to justify that dislike."[32] Frame believes that the Reformed community needs to return to an explicitly exegetical model of theology, one based on the principle of *sola Scriptura*.

> My overall purpose in this essay is to reiterate the Reformation doctrine of *sola Scriptura*, the doctrine that Scripture alone gives us ultimate norms for doctrine and for life, and to apply that doctrine to the work of theology itself, including both historical and systematic disciplines. That point may seem obvious to many of us, but I am convinced that certain applications of this doctrine need to be re-emphasized in the present situation.[33]

Frame is not motivated by the stagnant tradition of the Reformation; he is motivated by the principle of *sola Scriptura*, which *came out of* the Reformation. This is the fundamental distinction between Frame and many of his critics. It is also a point of serious concern for Frame. Thus, *CWM* is as much a defense of the principle of *sola Scriptura* as it is a defense of contemporary worship music. Understanding the value that Frame places on exegesis rather than historical or sociological research is an important point of orientation for any reader of *CWM* as well as his approach to contemporary worship in general.

Intelligibility in Worship. Another value that Frame takes very seriously is *intelligibility in worship*. For Frame, the way we communicate in worship (e.g., the words, lyrics, and language we use) is a very important issue. In *CWM* he writes:

> Much of the worship leader's creative task is seeking effective means of communication . . . Worship ought to be edifying to the church and meaningful even to outsiders. Edification and meaningfulness require attention to language. Therefore, the apostle Paul in 1 Corinthians 14 insists that worship be intelligible.[34]

As noted earlier, intelligibility in worship was a fundamental value at New Life in Escondido. Thus, for Frame and others involved in planning and leading worship, the language they used was very important. This included

32. Ibid., 129–30.
33. Ibid., 176.
34. Ibid., 17.

the language of their prayers, their songs, and their sermons. They wanted to communicate in such a way that worship at New Life would be intelligible to visitors and unbelievers.

Some have criticized the effort within the contemporary worship movement to make language intelligible, describing this as "dumbing-down." In response to this critique Frame writes, "A good teacher is not somebody who speaks a rarefied, perhaps archaic, intellectual jargon that no student can understand. Rather, an effective teacher speaks the present language of his students."[35] Frame came to appreciate contemporary worship music, in part, because he realized that it spoke in a language that was relevant and accessible to the people he and his church were trying to reach.

To address this issue on a practical level, Frame contrasts two different songs: a traditional hymn ("Arise, My Soul, Arise," by Charles Wesley) and a contemporary worship song ("Father God, I Wonder," by Ian Smale). He demonstrates how in one verse Wesley brings out fifteen different theological points. He notes how any one of the fifteen points could constitute the subject matter of a sermon, even a series of sermons. He acknowledges, however, that although it is a good teaching hymn, "it is not easily remembered."[36] He also writes:

> I have sung it a hundred times or so, and I still have to open the hymnal to get the words right. The traditional tunes used for the hymn are not much help. None of them, in my judgment, is a very good means to impress these truths on the hearts of modern worshipers.[37]

By way of contrast, Frame demonstrates how the contemporary worship song "Father God, I Wonder" focuses on one of the fifteen points that Wesley raised (adoption), is set to a memorable tune, and gives people time to meditate on the wonder of that biblical teaching. Thus, Frame concludes that although Wesley's hymn has far more intellectual "content" and "depth" than Smale's, it is not obvious that it is a better teaching tool. According to Frame, Smale's hymn may "very well be more helpful to more people today in bringing them to a higher level of understanding." He concludes this comparison by stating that "though it may sound strange to say it, the intel-

35. Ibid., 100.
36. Ibid., 103.
37. Ibid.

lectual function of worship is one of the best arguments in favor of CWM, as long as we understand that intellectual function scripturally rather than from the standpoint of the secular academy."[38]

Frame is highly concerned with intelligibility in worship. His desire is that worshipers come to a real encounter with the Lord Jesus. For Frame, worship is not merely an educational experience, but a meeting between us and God. Furthermore, edifying believers and unbelievers alike is essential. If people cannot understand the language being used in worship, how can they be edified?

Thus, Frame believes strongly in using contemporary and not archaic language to speak into the lives of modern people. This conviction is vital for understanding Frame's motivation for embracing contemporary worship music and the impact he had in causing others to think seriously about how we communicate in worship.

The Great Commission. A third value underlying Frame's convictions about contemporary worship music is the *Great Commission.* After citing Matthew 28:18–20 and explaining how the Great Commission defines the task of the church in the world until Jesus returns, Frame writes:

> As we have seen, worship has both a vertical and a horizontal focus. It seeks to glorify God and to edify the congregation. These are not, of course, separate from one another, since God is glorified in the edification of his people, and since people are edified only in learning how better to glorify God. The horizontal focus is defined by the Great Commission. In worship, we evangelize, baptize, and teach.[39]

This conviction grew, in part, from the influence of Jack Miller, which was discussed earlier. For Frame, evangelism and nurture are not neatly separable, but can occur simultaneously in the context of corporate worship. With this conviction Frame is not saying that we must set aside all of our traditions, all the time. He is not saying that *everything we do* in worship must be simplistic and modern, or easily accessible to unbelievers. But in every service there must be "words and music that in a plain and vivid way point the visitor to the justice and the love of Christ."[40]

38. Ibid., 104.
39. Ibid., 21.
40. Ibid., 23.

For many churches in the Reformed community in the 1980s and 1990s, doxological evangelism was a new concept. Frame was able to give serious biblical reflection to the role of the emotions and physical expression in worship, thereby releasing these expressions from the "ghetto" of charismatic worship practices. In the same manner, in *CWM*, Frame articulated a solid argument for the role of evangelism in worship and lessened people's fears about congregations morphing into seeker-driven churches.

As with the issues of *sola Scripture* and intelligibility, Frame caused many to stop and think seriously about the implications of the Great Commission and the role of doxological evangelism. Because of his influence, more and more church leaders today acknowledge that although they do not need to become seeker-*driven*, every church should be seeker-*sensitive* in the context of corporate worship.

Denominationalism. A fourth and final issue underlying contemporary worship and contemporary worship music that Frame is honest in addressing is *denominational pride*. In his chapter on tradition and contemporaneity he writes:

> I believe that opponents of CWM are concerned not only with CWM's supposed departure from the traditions of the church universal but also with the fact that CWM may represent a tradition other than that of their own denominations.[41]

Frame has a strong opinion when it comes to denominations. In his book *ER*,[42] Frame argued that denominations themselves are not warranted by Scripture and that they are due to sin: sin either on the part of those who leave one denomination to start another, or on the part of those in the original body who force people to leave on account of conscience.[43] Based on that belief, Frame is more readily able to recognize the imperfections within his own denomination and the genuine blessings of God upon those other than his own. Some people find such an attitude much more difficult to attain and are unable either to see or to admit the weaknesses of their own denomina-

---

41. Ibid., 139.
42. Available online at http://www.frame-poythress.org/frame_books.htm.
43. Although the original discussion took place in *ER*, Frame refers to it as well in *CWM*, 139.

tions. Often they are equally unable to discern any of the strengths of other heritages within the body of Christ or to draw inspiration from them.

Frame states that we should not "treasure our denominational liturgical styles so highly as to make them immune to reformation."[44] Unfortunately, there are those who simply cannot embrace contemporary worship or contemporary worship music because they associate it with a certain heritage that is different from their own (e.g., the charismatic movement). These people cannot see that it is possible to glean from other movements and denominations while holding firm to one's own theological convictions.

These four major themes (*sola Scriptura* versus traditionalism, intelligibility, the Great Commission, and denominationalism) are important issues underlying Frame's thinking on contemporary worship and his motivation in writing *CWM*. Moreover, because Frame is so passionate about these values, they surface again and again in his subsequent writings and dialogues.

Of course, in *CWM* Frame not only addresses the underlying issues with his critics, but also spends a number of chapters endorsing the very positive aspects of contemporary worship music itself: its God-centeredness, its scriptural basis, its freshness and communication, its quality, its edifying character, and its authenticity.[45] By citing specific examples of each of these virtues, Frame reveals a true knowledge of the genre and elucidates a biblical basis for its endorsement.

Frame definitely has more of a defensive posture in *CWM* than *WST*. Even his dedication page has a bit of an edge to it: "To the New Life Churches, who swim against the current of Reformed opinion for the sake of the Reformed gospel."[46] One must remember that in 1997 the so-called worship wars were in full swing. There was passionate dialogue over the emotionally charged topic of worship and worship music. During this period, Frame responded to people like Marva Dawn and Darryl Hart with boldness and humility—plainly stating his thoughts and biblical convictions, while remaining balanced and acknowledging some of the valid concerns of his critics. His various writings laid out a cogent and comprehensive endorsement of the use of contemporary worship music and its ability to communicate in intelligible and fresh ways, to edify God's people, and to penetrate the culture with the message of the gospel.

44. Ibid.
45. Ibid., 31–41.
46. Ibid., dedication page.

The Role of the Visual Arts in Worship

In addition to his writings targeting issues directly related to contemporary worship, Frame has also written other books and articles that speak more indirectly to the subject. In *DCL* Frame expounds his view of the second commandment, which has profound implications for some issues related to contemporary worship, namely, the role of the visual arts in worship.

The meaning of the second commandment is a point of much debate and controversy with regard to worship practice. The first time I heard Frame's articulation of the commandment I was a student in his Pastoral and Social Ethics course in seminary. I had always heard people denounce the use of visual imagery in worship on the basis of the second commandment. This never seemed like the proper biblical interpretation for a number of reasons, but mainly because it appeared that God himself seemed to give specific instructions for a lot of visual art (images, vestments, and architecture) to be used in the spaces designated for corporate worship—the tabernacle and the temple (Ex. 25:18–20; 28:33–34).

As with his analysis of so many other areas of biblical doctrine, Frame's explanation and clarification of the second commandment was so obvious, I immediately agreed with it and wondered how others could draw such different conclusions. Here is the statement of the commandment in Exodus 20:4–6 (ESV):

> You shall not make for yourself a carved image, or any likeness of anything that is in heaven above, or that is in the earth beneath, or that is in the water under the earth. You shall not bow down to them or serve them, for I the LORD your God am a jealous God, visiting the iniquity of the fathers on the children to the third and the fourth generation of those who hate me, but showing steadfast love to thousands of those who love me and keep my commandments.

Frame's understanding and explanation of the second commandment is that we should not make images *for the purpose of bowing down to them and serving them.* He explains that what God forbids is not art in itself, or even art located in a place of worship, but art made as an object of worship. Citing numerous biblical examples from Genesis, Exodus, Numbers, 1 Kings, Ezekiel, and Hebrews, Frame draws the following important conclusion regarding visual images: nothing in the Bible suggests that making images is always wrong. Indeed, God himself requires the making of images in the very context of worship. According to Frame, "It is the misuse of an image that God condemns, not its existence or presence."[47]

This understanding of the second commandment completely changes the way one thinks about visual imagery and its use in the context of corporate worship. Rather than a fear of the imagination and skepticism of the arts, Frame's view actually encourages creativity and the use of the arts in the context of worship. Along with a revival in the *performing arts* (music, drama, dance), contemporary worship has sparked a revival in the use of *visual arts* in worship as well. Frame's view of the second commandment has been influential in the rethinking of this controversial subject, particularly within the Reformed community.

In an article entitled "A Response to 'Redeeming the Arts,'" Frame also acknowledges that the emphasis on the "primacy of the intellect" has been another reason why the church has done an injustice to the arts and the imagination. The primacy of the intellect is the view that God's revelation always addresses the intellect first, and that the intellect then processes the information and distributes it to the will and the emotions. Frame regards the Reformation as largely a "scholar's movement," and that Protestantism tended to appeal to the better educated. Frame states, "The church, especially its Reformed branch, needs to frankly admit that intellectualism is an error to be corrected. Only then will it be in a position to serve as a patron of the arts."[48] He concludes the article by saying: "The church . . . needs to quell the 'fear of imagination' by making better use of the arts in its ministry and especially in its worship."[49]

In my former church and in the church I now serve, we have issued a number of calls to artists—invitations for visual, literary, and performing artists to engage with a particular theme and/or season of the Christian year. These calls have been very successful in drawing out and celebrating the artistic gifts of our church body. In my current church, we actually have a gallery for displaying art and issue these calls to artists on a regular basis. For each new exhibit, we ask the artists to submit a reflection with their work describing the creative process—a "behind the scenes" look at how they went from a moment of inspiration to a completed work.

47. DCL, 454.
48. John M. Frame, "A Response to 'Redeeming the Arts,'" *Creative Spirit* 4, 2 (2005): 2.
49. Ibid., 3.

In both churches, celebrating the arts in a robust and integrative way has been a very positive experience. Sometimes a work of art may remain as part of the worship space. Often the art becomes integrated into the media in the worship service (e.g., as background for worship slides). Thus, as one who loves music, writing, and photography, and as one who has developed artists within the church, I greatly appreciate Frame's endorsement and encouragement of the arts, especially their use in worship. Here, as in so many other facets of contemporary worship, Frame has been one of the most significant voices advocating a revival of the arts in our present day.

FRAME'S INDELIBLE MARK ON OUR CURRENT SITUATION

As a worship leader, writer, and professor, John Frame helped navigate the church through the "growing pains" of the contemporary worship movement. He has since left a lasting influence on many and an indelible mark on our current situation.

Today we find ourselves in a situation that is somewhat "post-contemporary/traditional" and "post-blended" in its approach to and terminology of worship (though these models do still exist). The musical and liturgical landscape is drastically different from what it was twenty or thirty years ago. Today we are in a more "modern-liturgical, ancient-future" culture of worship where liturgical heritage is intersecting with modern styles and technology. Ancient prayers, creeds, and practices are merging with modern forms of communication and technology, modern styles of music and instrumentation, and current cultural values.

Today, smaller is better (to some degree) as the parish model of worship is becoming more widespread. Mercy and justice are much more on the radar, and urban centers are being more intentionally targeted than the suburbs for church planting. Ancient and obscure hymn texts are finding their way back into corporate worship, but with modern melodies; podcasts are helping to expand the ministry and outreach of the church; independent musicians and songwriters are singing their songs in church; and the work of local artists is being hung and projected—both indicators of the value of indigenous art in local communities.

In this final section I simply want to bring us to the present day, look around, and see some of the indications of Frame's influence on our current situation. To do that I want to highlight a few people who represent Frame's indelible mark on students and worship leaders, the church, and the world.

Frame's Influence on Students and Worship Leaders

Frame has had a profound impact on a large number of students—people he has taught in seminary who are now teaching, leading worship, and pastoring others. Here I want to highlight two such individuals who have appropriated Frame's influence in their own way. The first is Reggie Kidd.

Reggie is a friend and mentor to a number of worship leaders. He is a professor of New Testament at Reformed Theological Seminary in Orlando, Florida, and was a student of Frame's at Westminster Theological Seminary in Philadelphia. For years Kidd has taught a course on worship and served for fifteen years as the dean of chapel. Like Frame, he has simultaneously worn the hat of seminary professor and worship leader. He is also the author of an important book on worship[50] and teaches at the Webber Institute for Worship Studies. Thus, his influence stretches long and wide.

Kidd's unique approach to worship and theology has Frame's fingerprints all over it. I noted earlier how Kidd's course on worship was organized in a triperspectival manner (cognitive, existential, and teleological). For years *WST* and *CWM* have been on the reading list for his Theology of Worship course at RTS. Kidd alone has exposed countless students to Frame's books on worship, bringing them into an encounter with Frame's challenging thoughts and insights. As I also mentioned, I was first introduced to Frame through Kidd.

In addition to his former students at Westminster, Frame has influenced a younger generation of students at Reformed Theological Seminary. West Breedlove represents one such individual.

West is the director of music ministries at Cedar Springs Presbyterian Church in Knoxville, Tennessee. He and I were friends and fellow worship leaders in college. We were both influenced by some of the prominent worship leaders at the time, people like Kevin Prosch and Brian Doerksen, worship leaders in the Vineyard movement. And we have both been profoundly influenced by Frame. I asked West to explain how Frame has impacted his life and the church. He said:

50. Reggie M. Kidd, *With One Voice: Discovering Christ's Song in Our Worship* (Grand Rapids: Baker, 2005).

The truth is his impact has been so thorough on me and my theology of worship that I can't point a finger at anything specific. Everything has been influenced. I read *WST* a few years after college, while I was leading worship full time in a PCA church, and I realized I needed to be around that kind of thinking. I needed to be in an environment where I could learn to think like that.[51]

After reading *WST*, Breedlove was so inspired by Frame's teaching that he wrote a song called "In Spirit and Truth." Breedlove pointed out that the song is "saturated with Scripture, which my songs before reading Frame's book weren't." He says that an immediate effect of Frame's influence was letting "the Scriptures have a prominent place in my thoughts about worship."

Regarding Frame's influence on the church, Breedlove believes that Frame has made appropriating good theology to worship accessible for people. He noted how songwriters from Sovereign Grace to Indelible Grace have read Frame's books or been to a conference where he was teaching. Breedlove cites three important values that Frame has instilled in modern songwriters: musical freedom, a strong scriptural standard for lyric writing, and the acknowledgment that cultural connotations carry a lot of weight in the music we should use. Breedlove believes that these three values have given the modern Christian community some very helpful direction and parameters for worship.

In his final comments, Breedlove shared how Frame's pastoral heart has also influenced the Christian community: "How far better off we are, taking his advice to sacrifice our personal tastes for the edification of our brothers and sisters. He has shown us the importance of showing preference to one another on stylistic matters."

Frame's Influence on the Church and the World

Scotty Smith is also a former student of Frame and the founding pastor of Christ Community Church in Franklin, Tennessee. Christ Community had a profound impact on me when I was trying to discern the direction of my own life as a worship leader. The church has hosted a number of worship conferences since 1998 and has been a key player in the dialogue on

51. This and the following quotes from West Breedlove are from e-mail correspondence with the author, June 3–4, 2009.

contemporary worship. Smith and the leaders at Christ Community have encouraged, challenged, and inspired a vast number of pastors, worship leaders, and artists. I asked Scotty to describe Frame's influence in his life and how that influence has been fleshed out in the context of Christ Community Church.

Smith's journey with Frame goes back to 1975 when Scotty was a student at Westminster. He took courses from Frame, but did not fully appreciate and appropriate the treasures Frame had to offer until later decades. He joked that if it were possible to give someone a "liturgical copyright," Frame would be the recipient.

Smith described two overlapping triads that are the foundation of the liturgical framework at Christ Community: the Christological triad (Prophet, Priest, and King) and the narrative triad (historical, existential, and eschatological). Although no one would see such language printed in a bulletin or projected on a screen at the church, these concepts are the biblical and theological basis behind every aspect of the church's liturgy, and they clearly represent Frame's triperspectival influence. Each service creatively highlights Christ's role as Prophet, the normative dimension of the Word that speaks into our lives; each service brings attention to Christ's role as High Priest, as we encounter him personally in the existential dimension of our lives; and each service recognizes and celebrates Christ's role as King, commissioning us to go forth and serve the world.

All of these dimensions are appropriated within the *historical* context of the church, our *present* cultural setting, and our *future* hope. Smith described how these two triads help shape and direct not only the verbal language that is chosen (lyrics, sermon content, creeds, prayers), but also the "sonic" language of the service, i.e., "what the service sounds like this week." Clearly, Smith and others at Christ Community have reflected deeply on Frame's thoughts and insights and have uniquely interpreted and applied that influence to their own doxological context in Franklin, Tennessee.

Steve Childers is a professor of practical theology at Reformed Theological Seminary in Orlando, Florida, and the founder of Global Church Advancement (GCA). GCA hosts conferences all over the world, teaching and equipping church planters. Thus, Steve has exposed countless leaders to Frame and his thoughts on worship. The GCA manual, which contains all the material to train the church planters, is filled with triads and insights from Frame.

I partnered with GCA for several years and helped teach through the material on worship. Although the content would evolve, the organization of it remained the same: worship should be biblically based (normative), wholehearted (existential), and culturally contextualized (situational). For Childers, organizing the worship material around Frame's three perspectives made it accessible in a wide variety of contexts, including African and Asian cultures. This demonstrates the power behind Frame's triperspectival approach. Thoughts and insights are able to transcend ethnicities and cultures as they are fleshed out in the global concepts of God's Word, humanity, and culture. Thus, through Steve Childers and the ministry of GCA, Frame's thoughts on worship are quite literally touching the nations and cultures of the world.

Final Thoughts

Reggie Kidd, West Breedlove, Scotty Smith, and Steve Childers represent the students, worship leaders, churches, and leaders across North America and around the world who have been impacted by Frame. He played a key role in paving the way for modern worship leaders, young and old. His mark on our current situation is undeniable. His life, his writings, his students, and his students' students have literally changed (and are still changing) the face of worship, especially in Reformed circles. We are not where we were, in part, because of Frame.

In closing I would simply like to say, "Thank you, John." Thank you for shaping and influencing so many. Thank you for serving the church and laboring for the kingdom so steadily, so humbly. Thank you for giving individuals like me the license to be who we are, recognizing the liberating nature of God's Word. I am so grateful for your friendship and the impact you have had on my life. I will forever "think in triads."

PART 6

ETHICS

32

FRAME'S ETHICS: WORKING THE
IMPLICATIONS FOR PASTORAL CARE

DAVID POWLISON

JOHN FRAME is not a pastoral counselor, and I am not a philosopher or systematic theologian. So when the editor of this volume asked me to contribute an essay on the topic of "Frame's ethics," it presented an unusual challenge. My first response was, "Why me? Who am I that I should go to Pharaoh? I am slow of mind, speech, and tongue when it comes to Christian philosophy. Please send someone else." But this kind invitation did not come to me at random. The bent and intent of Frame's ethics is consistently pastoral and transformative, not abstract. I have often thought of the work I do as "Frame's ethics on wheels." In conversations over the years with colleagues at the Christian Counseling and Education Foundation (CCEF) and at Westminster Seminary, that phrase has often come up; it forms a significant part of our self-understanding. This invitation to contribute thus presented a wonderful opportunity to write about a subject that is near and dear to me.

Two features make Frame's approach to ethics immediately relevant to pastoral counseling. First, his triperspectival outlook heads straight in the direction of counseling. Christian ethical reflection tends to emphasize the normative. Indeed, the slant and balance of discussion in his *DCL* tilts to the normative perspective (ethics per se), as Frame acknowledges.[1] But he consistently recognizes and calls attention to the significance of situational and existential factors. By doing this, he continually keeps on the table the three variables that characterize cure of souls.

Second, Frame discusses ethics as a subset of the Christian life with all its characteristic processes, dynamics, and developments. Ethical reflection tends to be casuistic and static (I mean both words in a good sense). It begins with an ethical question and concludes with an ethical judgment. But cure of souls neither begins nor ends that way. It begins with a perplexity of problems.

The "case" is a complex person alive to a multifactored situation containing significant pressures (and often pain), significant opportunities (and perhaps felicity), significant influences for bad (and perhaps for good). The subject is always a mixed case—either a covenant-breaker bedewed with common graces, or a covenant-keeper compromised by indwelling sin and prone to suffer. This mixed case is as unpredictable as Scottish weather. The human actor may operate more or less constructively, more or less destructively, in any number of significant spheres: various relationships, work life, recreational choices, financial dealings, intellectual interests, aesthetic sensibilities and skills, sexual feelings and behavior, civic and political activities, etc. This mixed case is capable of the entire range of emotions, any of which may be good or evil—or as mixed as muddy water. Analysis is never enough to change someone—and never exhaustive, and never adequate to explain what happens next. We offer flashes of illumination. Even if a relatively clear-cut ethical judgment can be made about some feature of the total person and total life-situation, the implementation into action is never clear cut. The Redeemer's mercy and power are necessary. Other people help or hinder. There are complicating and limiting factors, simplifying and accentuating factors.

Furthermore, there is no stasis or finality. Genuine progress is partial progress, often halting progress, sometimes the arrest of regress, always just a next step in the right direction. Pastoral care, like the soul being cured, grapples amid complexities of process. Change is an untidy business. Ministry seeks to implement the reign of grace and truth in Christ's people. On the one hand, we are God's workmanship, recreated in Christ Jesus for good works that God has already prepared (Eph. 2:10). On the other hand, we are ignorant and wayward, beset with weakness, still sinning, liable to suffer (Heb. 5:2–3). There is no stasis in Jesus' dealings with his disciples;

1. See *DCL*, xxv, 853.

there is no stasis in Paul's letters; there is no stasis in the Christian life or in ministry. Each day there is a new development in the case—hence the need for relevant, daily encouragement (Heb. 3:12–14).

Frame pushes in this direction. He is not content with abstract analysis or casuistic judgment. Our need for a merciful, powerful Christ (and for other people as means of grace) always seems near at hand. He does not abstract the standard of right conduct from our standard-bearer and sin-bearer, from our outer troubles and inner struggles. Some thinkers might not like it that Frame is willing to walk close to the ragged edge of life lived and untidy historical process. Some philosophers and theologians seem to dream of life in a cool, clean empyrean where rational thought can be divested of unruly humanity and history. But it is hugely helpful for pastoral care that Frame acknowledges that the most significant "ethical cases"—i.e., people—appear as mixed and mixed-up cases, not pure cases. It is hugely helpful that Frame endorses the full range of humanness (e.g., his argument that Scripture neither teaches nor implies the "primacy of the intellect," but speaks of either fidelity or infidelity in the person as a whole). It is hugely helpful that Frame maintains the healthy tension between common grace and the antithesis, not allowing either reality to slide into relative irrelevance. It is hugely helpful that Frame emphasizes and seeks to live out the irenics that befits redemptive ministry.

Frame's ethics has *implications* for cure of souls. How do we understand the dynamics of progressive sanctification ("change process")? How do we understand the dynamics of hands-on care ("counseling process")? Frame's thought has deep-structure significance. That significance is not even hinted at by the sparse references to "counseling" in Frame's books.[2] Reciprocally, his significance could not be guessed by the few references to or contributions by Frame in, say, *The Journal of Biblical Counseling* (formerly *Journal of Pastoral Practice*).[3]

---

2. In *DCL*, *counseling* is not even an index word. There are two passing references to Jay Adams's "nouthetic counseling," both guardedly appreciative. But, significantly, Frame does choose counseling illustrations in several key places where he discusses how ethical norms come to application and realization in daily life (*DCL*, 32–33, 358–59).

3. Frame's three articles in *JPP/JBC* treat general Christian topics, not counseling: "Proposal for a New Seminary" (2, 1 [1978]: 10–17) suggests how theological education might better equip for pastoral competency; "Covering Ourselves" (7, 4 [1985]: 2–6) describes how "unhappy ministries" result when the savor of God's grace is lost; "Scripture and the Apologetic Task" (13, 2 [1995]: 9–12) notes how truth and love both shape apologetics as a ministry to persons, not a mere critique of ideas.

Furthermore—a nuance Frame himself will appreciate—his signifi-cance and influence are not direct. Care and cure of souls represents a further application, an extension, a creative outworking of his positive teaching. Here's an analogy. Frame often notes that application of Scripture always "does something" with Scripture. Theological reflection, ministry activity, and personal obedience (ὑπακοή; taking to heart; faith working through love) always go beyond simple exegesis. Application does more than reca-pitulate the timely meaning of original text to original audience in origi-nal context. The appropriation of Scripture for theological, ministerial, or personal purposes is always a "development upon" Scripture. It answers current questions, addresses current needs, illumines current problems. Wisdom watches and listens intently at *both* hermeneutical horizons, and adapts Scripture to persons and situations. By analogy, biblical counseling has developed upon Frame and adapted him. The nature of that adaptation can be captured in a nutshell. When Frame illustrates the triad of factors in ethical judgment, he says, "Imagine that you are a pastor or a counselor, and someone comes to your office with an ethical problem."[4] In the pages that follow, I will modulate that statement: "When you are a pastor or a counselor, everyone who comes into your office is an ethical problem."

In my case, Frame's influence was direct. I sat under his teaching in Doctrine of the Christian Life and Doctrine of the Word, two blockbuster courses at Westminster Theological Seminary in the late 1970s. The flex-ibility and adaptability of his triperspectivalism proved hugely provocative and helpful as I developed into a pastoral counselor. He influenced me not only as a thinker, but as a Christian man. I arrived at WTS having been a believer for less than a year. He was a model to a neophyte Christian. His manner bore the marks of Christ's goodness to him—good cheer, humility, kindness, curiosity, pervading confidence in the truth, the essential optimism of a man with a living hope. No surprise, the embodiment of those same graces is of essential significance in doing pastoral care.

This essay will neither summarize nor offer a critical analysis of Frame's ethical model. I will make no attempt to set Frame in his intellectual and historical context, comparing and contrasting his thinking with that of, say, Cornelius Van Til or other thinkers with whom he has closely interacted throughout his career. I will not trace the history of the biblical counseling movement and how Frame influenced developments there over the past thirty

4. *DCL*, 32.

years. Those are worthy tasks for others to take up. Instead, I will reflect on implications of Frame's ethics for understanding cure of souls.

Frame's significance and influence in this area has never been acknowledged or described in print. This essay seeks to give honor where honor is due, not by directly tracing intellectual debts, but by walking out one of the implications. I will describe and illustrate the significance of his triad of norm, situation, and person.

PASTORAL CARE NEEDS A MULTIPERSPECTIVAL GAZE
BECAUSE SOULS CURE TRIADICALLY

No surprise, Frame's most significant influence arises from his consistently triperspectival gaze. He makes us see what is going on in the Bible; he enables us to see what is going on in people. Scripture is the normative practical theology. As such, Scripture embodies how normative, situational, and existential factors co-inhere in the process of redemption. These same factors co-inhere in ethical judgment and decision-making. They co-inhere in every person's life, whether positively or negatively. Souls find cure at the intersection of person, situation, and Redeemer.

Let me illustrate. In the course of teaching and counseling, I have asked many people to talk or write about *how* God drew them to seek and know him, *how* he changed them. I pose a series of questions, asking them to describe, as far as it is possible, the significant and decisive factors.

> In considering your growth as a Christian, what passage of Scripture has proved most significant? Why? What does it touch? Why did this particular revelation from and about God have an impact? As our Lord has shepherded and shaped you, what passage has been most meaningful? What do these words address? How do these words make a difference?[5]

Almost invariably, people tell stories. These stories exhibit common features: (1) a challenging, troubling, disorienting situation; (2) a sense of personal struggle with sins, disturbing emotions, confusion; (3) God's intervening voice and hand, via Scripture, often mediated through a godly

---

5. As a reader, you might want to put your own life into the discussion. How do you answer these questions? Reflection on your own experience will invigorate your engagement with the discussion that follows.

person; and finally (4) the way all these come together, by the grace of God, in a qualitative change in the one who bears witness. The person changes in some significant way: a new understanding of God, self, and situation; a change of heart; a turning to God in awakened faith; a recognition of God's providence in the situation; new actions of wisdom and obedience. In other words, people answer with a Framean triad set in motion. People intuitively mention a dynamic interplay of normative, situational, and existential factors, with a *metanoia* occurring in the existential dimension. (Thankfully, no one ever uses such polysyllabic abstractions!) In unpacking this, I will first say a word about Scripture, and then will present two case studies.

Scripture per se is practical theology, and practical theology operates triperspectivally. As a redeeming Word, God's message per se is composed of those elements Frame terms normative, situational, and existential. All sound exegesis intuits this. The text contains original message, original context, and original audience. Of course, the text is a message revealing some aspect of God's person, point of view, purposes, will, promises, character, and actions. We all know this. The Word is God's normative self-revelation. But Scripture never reveals God after the manner of systematic theology or biblical theology. For example, read Ephesians and it almost seems that systematic and redemptive-historical categories have been run through a confetti machine. But that is not quite true. There is a logic to revelation, but it is a practical theological logic. Practical theology traffics in normative truth always in relation to what is true existentially and situationally.

The text always speaks pointedly to existential realities—thoughts, choices, beliefs, and emotions—both in persons portrayed in the text and to the original audience, and, by extension, to later readers whom an inscripturated text envisions. The text always speaks pointedly into some complicating or pressuring situation—whether specified in micro-stories (e.g., Ruth, 1 Samuel, Luke) or typified as an experiential pattern (e.g., Psalms, Proverbs). For example, Ruth abounds in existential and situational details. We learn names, places, events, time of day; vagaries of weather and climate change, and something of the agricultural cycle in the Levant; the emotional devastation of bereavement and poverty, nuanced by how that psychological experience was colored by the meaning of those events in that cultural context; that Ruth was a Moabite, and yet in the line of the anointed king; how covenant fidelity worked its way into everyday speech patterns; the danger of sexual harassment; what field hands ate for lunch; cultural forms regarding kinship and inheritance; the social customs making provision for the poor; the "he said, she said" of numerous conversational exchanges; a young widow's dressing up to meet an older man; the personal, cultural, and covenantal reasons that animated joyful women gathering around a new grandmother; and other bits of local color and personal story. All the existential and situational detail matters. We already know this about the Bible—sort of. But our theological habits train us to rush over the significance of existential and situational details. Systematic theology—the work of determining timeless Truths of Christian faith—excises the true details. Biblical theology—the work of determining the great Story of God's redemption—excises the particular stories. We easily forget that redemptive ministry engages the particulars. Pastoral counseling (like Scripture, like all forms of practical theology) lives in the details, because people live and die in the stories. We will be a wise people when the church's counseling ministries are as rich as Ruth or Psalms in situational and existential feel, and as rich as Romans or Colossians in normative revelation of our Redeemer and his ethical will.

When souls are being cured, people bear witness triadically: their external troubles, their internal struggles, their God of active providence and relevant speech. Almost invariably, they specify how two means of grace served as vectors of their encouragement, instruction, and transformation: the reorienting truth of a particular passage of Scripture and the trustworthy love of a person or persons who embodied Christ. This essay will consider the first of these, the effect of particular truth. I will present two stories.[6] They are "typical" in that triadic features recur in every redemption story. They are idiosyncratic in that they demonstrate the individuality and local color of any good story. The details matter. That is why "the world itself could not contain the books that would be written" (John 21:25). Yet the stories trace similar themes. That is why each story tells "things that Jesus did" (John 21:25).

6. Each is based primarily on one person's written story, slightly modified in three ways. First, identifying details have been altered. Second, I have supplemented the discussion with further knowledge gained in pastoral conversations. Third, I have woven in some particulars from other people whose experience was analogous, thus creating a composite case.

CHARLES

Charles is a single man in his early thirties, a well-taught layman, active in his Asian-American church, a computer programmer by profession. He writes:

> Recently I have returned often to Psalm 119:86: "All your commandments are faithful; they persecute me with a lie; help me!" Immediately, it says to me that there is such thing as *completely* and *always* trustworthy. Especially in recently experiencing being sinned against by broken trust, gossip, and betrayal . . . I cling to the truth that God is always trustworthy and what he says to me is trustworthy. He helps me to trust again. When I say, "Help me!" I *know* I'm talking with my Father, even in the midst of facing broken trust from people who hurt me, who don't even think there's a problem, who don't even want to try to resolve it. It's like I'm dealing with a cover-up. Everybody seems to be avoiding what happened. When I try to bring it up, *I'm* viewed as the problem because I want to name and resolve what happened, not just pretend.
>
> It's so hard to forgive in this situation. It's easy to grumble inside, to get caught up in my dark, fiery emotions, to replay the video of what happened, to get bitter and paranoid around my group of friends. Sometimes I just pack it in, and surf the Web checking out sports cars and ecotourist adventures. I have a new sympathy for why someone might just chuck the church and become a drunk. But Jesus calls me to forgive from the heart. Mark 11:25 is open and shut: one of God's faithful commands. I know that's where I need to go, if I'm to come out of this as a constructive person, not destructive or self-destructive. And I'm getting there. God is faithful. *God . . . is . . . faithful.* Jesus truly forgives me when I struggle. As I confess my bitterness and grumbling, he truly helps me. I need him to clear my head in order to sort out what I need to do next, and so I can do it in the right way and not just tangle things up more.

I think of such stories as catching the flash of a goldfinch on the wing. We are privileged to enter into a man's life as it is happening. What are we seeing and hearing?

The passage Charles cites explicitly names a common life *situation*: mistreatment by the words of another person. Notice, there is not necessarily a perfect one-to-one fit between this Scripture and Charles's life, but it is "close enough" to be relevant. "Close enough" relevance is analogical relevance. That involves hermeneutical and ethical intricacies that are far easier to illustrate than to state. A subsequent conversation with Charles revealed what had happened. A long-standing friend and trusted confidant had betrayed trust. He had gossiped about a sensitive confidence, degrading Charles in the eyes of their circle of fellowship. In the psalm, the persecutory liars are identified as enemies of both God and psalmist, people never to be trusted, who threaten literal death and destruction. In Charles's situation, the sense of threat—"death and destruction"—is metaphorical, a devastating estrangement in social relations. The pain and perplexity are aggravated because there had been real trust, and this trust was betrayed. The offense came not from an identified enemy, but from a brother in Christ who treated him in an "enemy-like" manner, and who now tries to smooth it over by acting as if nothing happened. The particular "lie" was actually a factual truth, but a "true" statement used maliciously becomes an expression of The Lie. The situational reference contained in Psalm 119:86 is appropriate and relevant, but Charles has intuitively done something quite intricate in connecting it to what happened to him.

The *existential* struggle provoked by being sinned against is only implicit in the actual words of Psalm 119:86. But a sense of personal distress, affliction, temptation to reactive sin, and need for help are "obvious," both from universal human experience and as implied in the cry for help, and as illustrated throughout Psalm 119 and the rest of Scripture. Charles legitimately reads his unhappiness and his problematic reactions back into the passage: "They persecute me with a lie [*and I feel threatened, overwhelmed, hurt, frustrated in all my efforts, and unhappy, and I am tempted to be angry, fearful, escapist, and mistrusting*]." We witness his version of the universal struggle with double evil: evils come upon us (situational) and evils come from within us (existential). Mistreatment occasions many temptations (the double sense of *peirasmos*), and Charles's story candidly expresses his experience of trial and temptation. We witness—and feel—his need for help. His Scripture passage of choice comfortably contains many variations on the human theme, including his own.

And then there is the *normative* revelation of God. The Lord never tells all in any one moment of self-revelation. Various aspects of God's person, purposes, character, will, promises, and actions come onto the table in various portions of Scripture: always timely to the complexities of a particular situation, always pointedly appropriate to the perplexities of existential

767

choice. Here in Psalm 119:86, we hear one truth and overhear another: God's directive words are true and faithful, and he is a helper on whom the needy may call. In Charles's story—again, a typical application of Scripture, generating encounter with God and ethical transformation—we hear not only the overt revelation in this one verse, but numerous echoes, conflations, and allusions arising from the biblical back story. This wider context shapes Charles's reception of Psalm 119:86. For example, the verse per se does not mention the Father, or the work of Jesus, or the forgiveness of our sins, or the command of Mark 11:25, or the goal of coming out into daylight as a constructive human being—but the verse easily bears such fine gifts to a man in his need.

All three "perspectives" come together, and Charles turns—from the world of sin and death, to the God of grace and life. An existential *change* occurs (and recurs; it is not "one and done"). Charles continues to engage his ongoing situation in the light and by the power of the normative Redeemer Lord. We hear faith working all through his story:

> I have returned often . . . Immediately, it says to me . . . I cling . . . He helps me to trust again. When I say, "Help me!" I *know* I'm talking with my Father . . . I know that's where I need to go . . . *God . . . is . . . faithful* . . . As I confess . . . he truly helps me.

Notice the active verbs, his italics, the immediacy of relationship.

This example contains all vertical ethics so far, but Charles is in motion towards horizontal ethics. He is working out the "attitudinal" forgiveness (Matt. 6:9–15; Mark 11:25) that is the precondition for constructively approaching another to work toward "transacted" forgiveness (Matt. 18:15–17; Luke 17:3–4). The last sentence in his story is homely on the surface, but it contains an entire triperspectival ethical philosophy. It is Frame's *DCL* in less than fifty words! Charles is committed to sorting out what to do next (normative standard). He is committed to going forward with the right attitude (existential motive). He is committed to seeking to disentangle knotted interpersonal relationships, rather than exacerbating estrangement (situational goal).

Note three further implications. First, Charles is changing, but there is no stasis. The story is not over. Ethical renewal is not idealized ethical perfection or moral self-improvement. There are people he must talk with. Much good has been happening, but the process is still going somewhere, and the outcome remains indeterminate. Charles is processing to the next phase of struggle. We rejoice at what we witness so far. But we sit on the edge of our chairs, waiting with eager longing to see if peacemakers will sow peace, bringing to further realization the ethical glory of the sons of God. What happens next is fraught with uncertainty. How will the former friend respond? How will the circle of friends respond? Will church leaders step in and help if the situation continues unresolved? Will Charles regress into bitterness, self-pity, and fantasizing over Corvettes, or will he go forward in the light? His life is a holy experiment. The grace and goodness of God will finally triumph. But the glory is not yet fully apparent.

John Frame delights to say, "There, we see it again! Notice the triadic pattern reappearing." Indeed, we do see it, again and again. Progressive sanctification is ethics on wheels, ethics imbued with appreciation for long, ever-evolving obediences in the right direction. This is what pastoral care is meant to facilitate.

Second, cure of souls usually involves a different sort of ethical judgment from the analyses and judgments pertaining to depersonalized ethical cases and dilemmas. It calls for more than coming to a thoughtful Christian *position*; it calls for an ethics that is on the move. Casuistic ethical discourse— e.g., abortion, just war, definition of marriage, grounds for divorce, medical decision-making—only occasionally touches down in daily pastoral care. Even casuistic analysis of matters immediately pertinent to Charles's situation—How should a Christian respond to violation of trust by a brother? When is church discipline appropriate, and how should it proceed?—does not plumb the intricacies of personal and pastoral need. Such topical ethical judgments frame the cure of souls, but do not carry it along. Luther cogently sets the Christian life in motion because of situational and existential realities:

> This life, therefore, is not righteousness but growth in righteousness, not health but healing, not being but becoming, not rest but exercise. We are not yet what we shall be, but we are growing toward it. The process is not yet finished but it is going on. This is not the end but it is the road. All does not yet gleam in glory but all is being purified.[7]

7. Martin Luther, "Defense and Explanation of All the Articles, 1521," in *Luther's Works*, vol. 32, American ed., ed. Jaroslav Pelikan and Helmut T. Lehmann (Philadelphia: Augsburg Fortress, 1958), 24.

Frame's ethics comports with Luther's vision.

The triperspectival gaze frustrates some theologians. It seems too fluid, easily morphing from one perspective to another, easily morphing from one meaning of, say, *normative* to another meaning, then on to another. They worry that it might make us relativistic. Although the pastoral situation even sets Frame's triads in motion and adds torrents of new information, Charles's story is not relativistic. Pastoral care and counseling demands just such creativity and flexibility. Keeping the triadic structure of redemption in mind keeps you oriented. You come to know what kind of thing you are hearing, wherever you happen to pick up the conversation. You develop an instinct for what you have not yet heard that is important, so you can ask the right questions.

Third, the triadic nature of change shows up the failures of much typical pastoral counseling. Churchly advice often reduces the dynamic of ethical transformation to a doctrinalistic, moralistic, or pietistic exhortation to "Just _____." Here is some of what I have witnessed or read.

- Just remember God's sovereignty.
- Just affirm that you're a child of the King.
- Just get involved in a small group.
- Just get into an accountability relationship.
- Just give your troubles to Jesus.
- Just get into counseling.
- Just attend to the means of grace: preaching, sacrament, and personal devotions.
- Just have a mountaintop experience.
- Just cast out the demon of bitterness.
- Just repent of bitterness and love your enemy.
- Just go to the person, and if he won't listen, take one or two others with you, that every charge may be established.
- Just take this key verse, Psalm 119:86, and pray the Ezer Prayer ("Help me") every day, claiming your victory. This verse is the key that opens God's storehouse of blessing. (OK, I made this one up. But its logic is for real.)

Some of this counsel contributes well when stripped of the "just" and functioning as part of a larger whole. Other bits of counsel are nonsense, mystifying and misleading to both counsel-giver and counsel-receiver. But none of these bits captures triadic reality or describes what actually helped Charles. The ethical reorientation of a human being never comes via a pat answer or a quick fix. Charles illustrates something better, something richer, more human, more humane, true to Scripture and life.

CHARLOTTE

My second example is more intricate biblically, richer experientially, and more complex situationally. Charlotte is a female seminary student in her mid-twenties, single, with intuitive counseling skills. Let me set the stage by some comparison with the previous case study.

The similarities are basic: both reveal triadic transformation. But the timeline for Charles's story was relatively short: an experience in the immediate past, still churning in the present, and calling for further action in the immediate future. Charlotte's story comes to a point in the present, but it reflects retrospectively on a long history.

Charles's story interacts with immediate situational stressors and immediate sinful responses. Charlotte wrestles with larger forces: long-standing patterns of how she comes at life; the fundamental discomfort of the human condition; contradictions operative in herself, in her experience of the church, and in relation to non-Christians.

The change process in Charles was linear: specifically sinned against, specific sinful responses, specific promise and command of God, transactions of repentance and faith—and an anticipation of specific behavioral fruit. The changes in Charlotte are more atmospheric, and she bears different varieties of fruit. We hear a particularly deep intimacy in her relationship to God. She makes one striking behavioral change. There are certain transformations that might be termed internal fruit: subtle reorientation in how she understands herself, her situation, her God; a refinement in how her conscience functions.

As you read Charlotte's story, notice particularly the organic relationship between situational, existential, and normative factors. Frame has often written that each perspective entails the others, that each is a door opening into the same room. Charlotte illustrates that this is no theory, and gives us a feel for the seamlessness of the whole fabric. Here are her words:

771

I've returned a lot to Isaiah 51:12–13a and 15–16: "I, I am he who comforts you. Who are you that you are afraid of man who dies, of the son of man who is made like grass, and have forgotten the LORD, your Maker, who stretched out the heavens and laid the foundations of the earth, and you fear continually all the day. . . . I am the LORD your God, who stirs up the sea so that its waves roar—the LORD of hosts is his name. I have put my words in your mouth and covered you in the shadow of my hand, establishing the heavens and laying the foundations of the earth, and saying to Zion, 'You are my people.' "

This reminds me that this world is not a "comfortable" one and assures me that Christ is the only true comfort (despite those things I try to fill in to comfort me instead). It lends confidence to not be afraid of what those around me are thinking about me—freedom to live transparently. The awareness that I am always forgetting about God stings my cheeks. I'm an amnesiac to his sovereignty and grace in the world and in my life.

These verses so insanely juxtapose and bind together the hugeness of Creator God and the close intimacy of Christ. He is incomprehensibly vast and powerful. He stretched out the heavens and laid the foundations of the earth; he stirs the roaring waves; he is LORD of hosts; and, again—in case I missed it the first time—he establishes the heavens and lays the foundations of the earth. In the exact same breath, he is wonderfully intimate. "I, I am he who comforts." I can't get over that double-I. He made me; he puts his very words in my mouth; his hand covers me; he says, "You are my people."

Somehow life makes the MOST sense in the middle of this tension and seeming paradox of God's identity. I feel it on the deepest level of my relationship with God. I am also comforted when I see how this parallels other tensions, confusions, and contradictions both around me and within me. God is not tidy, all black and white with straight-lines, fitting into a box—and neither am I—and knowing that is an affirmation and a comfort!

I was always intimidated by people and their possible opinions of me. Last week in a missions class, I had to hold my tongue because I was dominating the conversation for most of the three-hour discussion. It's all coming out, after being hemmed in by fear for all those years of awkward insecurity!

This is an ethical feast. My discussion will be briefer, as many of the points made about Charles are also applicable to Charlotte. But this story is worth savoring. It portrays the Christian life in ways that go "beyond ethics as ethics is usually conceived,"[8] and go beyond the cure of soul as cure of soul is usually conceived. It is Framean in its triadic lineaments, and it is in motion.

Notice the variety of situational[9] problems on the table. In the foreground: the potential disapproval of others in every social situation. In the wider context: that this is an essentially uncomfortable world; some unspecified sense of "tensions, confusions, and contradictions around me." From conversation, I learned that Charlotte is alluding to brushing up against self-righteous pettiness in an ecclesiastical conflict, and to her encounter with theological dogmatism in hard-edged people who seemed to understand neither God, nor themselves, nor others, nor life. She is also alluding to the sense of contradiction she experiences when instances of hypocrisy and inhumanity in Christian people are juxtaposed with instances of honesty, care, and humanity in non-Christians.

Notice the complex of existential[10] problems. In the foreground: Charlotte's atmospheric fear of man, shyness, social anxiety, and withdrawal. In the background: discouragement and confusion in the face of both what is around her and her inner struggles. She feels out of step with some of the comfortable verities of her evangelical subculture. She also alludes to the false comforts to which she turns as easy substitutes for Christ: self-medicating through food, exercise, friends, and novels.

Notice the complex normative revelation of the Redeemer: this most magnificent and most comforting God of Isaiah 51. He tells Charlotte not to be afraid (the one command), and gives her plenty of good reasons. Nor-

8. *DCL*, xxv.
9. I am using *situational* in a broader sense than Frame usually does. In his ethical discussion, he focuses on the cultural aspect of our overall situation (*DCL*, 853–908). Pastoral care must closely attend to the influence of cultural factors—intellectual and other products, institutional structures, social customs and assumptions—whether that culture is the secular surround, an ecclesiastical subculture, a familial microculture, etc. In our two cases we also see the significance of noncultural situational factors: e.g., being sinned against, or the threat of disapproval. A systematic theology of the situation includes *every* significant factor: weather and seasons, current political and economic conditions, Satan, physical abilities and disabilities, general life hardships such as poverty and sickness, birth order, and everything else under the sun with which human beings interact.
10. I am using *existential* in a more comprehensive way than Frame does in his ethical discussion. I include the totality of a person's experience and responses, whether problematic or redeemed. The existential factor works both with fidelity to God, faith, etc. (the "right motive" in ethics) and with the infidelities of false belief, lusts of the flesh, and idolatry. It includes all the actions, emotions, thoughts, attitudes, etc., that register either the fruit of the Spirit or the works of the flesh.

mative commands come with normative reasons. This is how redemptive process works out both in Scripture and in our lives and ministries.

I employ the *normative* category in a somewhat broader way than Frame does in his ethical discourse, where *normative* refers to the standard to which God calls us. For the purposes of pastoral care, I conflate indicatives and imperatives, as Scripture does, so I include the entire self-revelation of God as a "normative-divine" perspective, if you will. Each good command comes with good reasons. Back in Charles's story, the truths that echo in the background always tie trustworthy reasons to trustworthy commands.

- Forgive (standard), as you have been forgiven in Christ (God's person, work, promise).
- Take refuge (standard) in your Rock and Shepherd, who is a safe place for the afflicted (a train of evocative reasons).
- Be an imitator (standard) of God as a beloved child (a cornucopia of promise), and walk in love (standard) as Christ loved us and gave himself up for us, an offering and a sacrifice to God as a fragrant aroma (the propitiatory burnt offering of the Lamb, whose fragrance soothes and pleases God).

Here in Charlotte's story, the command says, "Don't be afraid." She intuitively extends this to include its positive meanings: "Enter in. Get involved. Care. Speak up." Isaiah 51 gives her a cascade of normative reasons: the reproofs of 51:12 that sting her cheeks; the many wonders and intimacies that comfort her "on the deepest level."

As in the previous case study, the passage Charlotte mentions—ported forward from a very different redemptive-historical context and individualized—seems uniquely appropriate. It is "close enough" for relevance. She reads and appropriates this passage by peopling it with her own experience and by enriching it with echoes and allusions from the person and work of Christ.

Finally, notice the dynamic of change. A new existential reality emerges. A transformative engagement occurs between strong Savior and needy child: stinging cheeks at realizing her amnesia, the experience of deep comfort. The behavioral consequences are striking: new freedom to live and speak transparently, a conscience newly sensitized to the dangers of talking too much. Her newfound voice is particularly significant. Action registers that change is real. Again, we witness a Framean triad in which redemptive movement takes place in the existential dimension.

Charlotte's story also illustrates several other features of cure of souls. First, change is a lifelong process in which we witness thematic continuities. In the classroom incident, God is rescripting patterns that go back to childhood. Sin is usually not new-hatched; righteousness does not fall like random fire from heaven. As you get to know a person, you learn to see patterns and themes in the interplay of existential and situational factors, just as students of Scripture learn to see patterns and themes in the Bible. It helps a person to know that the Vinedresser is pruning purposefully, and that God typically works on something specific, not everything at once.

Second, how is it that Charlotte and I view her "speaking up" as a fruit of the Spirit? That item is not on any list of fruits (although I think it is implicitly among the "things like these" of Galatians 5:23). We know it is good fruit because we understand her situational and existential factors in the light of normative revelation. Fear of man coached Charlotte to stay in the background, to play it safe. In social groups, she was virtually a nonparticipant, unable to bring her thoughts to the point of joining in audibly. She was self-preoccupied, not loving; she was fearful, not free. As the fruit of repentance and faith, the Spirit freed her to participate. He loosens her tongue, because that is what love and obedience now look like in Charlotte's life.

Third, Charlotte's ironic, humorous sensibility of the need to hold her tongue captures other features of the Christian life. It is evidence that her conscience is alive, sensitive, malleable. Such bursts of intuitive wisdom are unquantifiable, unscriptable, electrifying—and are one aspect of ethical transformation into wisdom.

Fourth, needing to hold her tongue also illustrates how the cure of any living soul calls for continual course corrections. She finds her voice, and immediately realizes that there are sins of the tongue, and times when love quiets down and listens. It is a new lesson.

Fifth, in this ironic need to quiet down, Charlotte is tasting the logic of Luther's curious exhortation, "Sin boldly!" The Christian life lurches forward, rather than marching in a straight line. The grace of Christ means a person can live life without paralyzing perfectionism and scrupulosity, and can cheerfully expect frequent course corrections. Charlotte has always held back in social settings. Now that she is beginning to speak up, she will probably say things she regrets, or may find herself talking too much. It is safer to hang in the background and nod agreeably (cf. Prov. 17:28 on the fool who keeps silent!). It is risky to mix it up. She will make mistakes, even sinning verbally (James 3:2). Other people will not always agree with her if Charlotte does not seem to always agree with them. She will have to learn to face and solve conflicts, rather than always avoiding conflict. She will have to ask forgiveness more often. She might sin "more," but she is actually sinning less, and growing up as a daughter of the King. She will always need course corrections.

Cure of souls puts Frame's ethics on wheels. A sin-sick soul revives and begins to live. The Christian life is organically alive, growing, interacting with what is happening in the surrounding environment, engaged in a lifelong holy experiment in redemption. I hope that I have been able to communicate something of the dynamic.

Conclusion

The goal of this essay has been to illustrate how Frame's triad illumines the change process. The way a soul is actually cured should correlate to the way pastors and other counselors set about trying to cure souls. Making disciples is the goal of all pastoral ministry. It is the particular goal of counseling ministry, which is uniquely privileged with opportunities to know people and to make God's words of life personal.

I have not spelled out the strategic and methodological correlates. I hope that some of those are obvious and irresistible. I hope that what we have considered changes the way you approach people. I hope that you will take to heart what you heard in Charles's and Charlotte's stories, and that you will work out what it means to help others join them. I will close with seven exhortations about ministry that seem fitting given where we have come.

1. Give yourself to acquiring situational and existential knowledge of people. Approach that lifelong labor with the same earnestness and gladness with which you acquire knowledge of the Bible.

2. Love the people you come to know. Where there is darkness and wrong (and there is much that is dark and wrong), you will fill up what is lacking in the sufferings of Christ. Where there is light and right (and you will be overwhelmed at how many bright things you come to know), you will feel that people are your crown of joy and exultation.

3. Don't ever give Truth without connecting it to all that is true about a person's life. Don't ever tell The Story without connecting it to the innumerable stories both then and now. Don't just do Bible exposition (which attends to people's situational and existential realities way back then and way over there), and not touch the situational and existential realities of the person or people with whom you are now speaking. I am convinced that "speaking truth in love" does not refer to normative Truth only, whether in systematic categories or biblical-theological themes or Bible exposition. It refers to telling a person (or people) the situational, existential, normative truth right now—the way the Bible tells the truth.

4. Do your topical casuistry carefully, the biblical view of ____, and then put your ethics on wheels. Casuistry keeps you oriented, but you are working with complex people in complex situations. Remember Charles, about whom you came to know so much relevant, significant detail. He *sought* God honestly. Scripture drew him to seek his God.

5. Get your doctrine straight, the biblical view of ____, and then put your doctrine on wheels. Doctrine keeps you oriented, but you are working with complex people in complex situations. Remember Charlotte, about whom you came to know so much relevant, significant detail. She *knows* so much about her God. Scripture revealed God to her.

6. You are dealing with people. Don't ever say words such as *indicative* or *imperative* or *normative, situational, existential* when you are speaking with a human being who is still breathing. Don't use shorthand—*gospel, cross, metanarrative, justification, sovereignty, redemptive-historical*, etc.—when you have an opportunity to use longhand. The Bible uses shorthand only after the meaning is crystal clear, established in some detail in the context. And biblical shorthand typically moves forward with a nuance or fresh angle, rather than simply talking in technical jargon. Most people get very little out of shorthand, but get a great deal out of details and stories.

7. Those are six ways of saying the same thing. And here is a seventh: become as Ruthian as you are Romanesque, as Psalmic as you are Colossianic. We who are Reformed by conviction have always loved Truth, and now we love The Story. But we still have a hard time paying attention to the stories and all the other things that are true.

33

WHY IT IS NEVER RIGHT TO LIE: AN EXAMPLE OF JOHN FRAME'S INFLUENCE ON MY APPROACH TO ETHICS

WAYNE GRUDEM

I COUNT IT A PRIVILEGE to contribute to this volume of essays in honor of my friend and former professor, John Frame. When I was a student at Westminster Seminary (1971–73), his classes, his evident devotion to God's Word, and the example of his life had a life-changing impact on me and significantly affected all my subsequent teaching and writing. My entire Bible-centered approach to all I have written on theology and ethics (including this essay!) owes much to his example and the convictions he instilled in me in his classes. Then nearly thirty years after I graduated from Westminster, I indirectly received another benefit from him: My son Elliot was able to take classes from John at Reformed Theological Seminary in Orlando and to understand firsthand why I appreciated his teaching so greatly.

I hope this essay will be understood as I intend it—as a genuine expression of deep gratitude for John Frame's teaching, even though I argue for a position on lying that is somewhat different from his own. When I selected the topic for this essay, I had thought (from an imperfect memory) that John's own position on lying was the same as my own: that it is never right to lie. But when I read the section on bearing false witness in his *DCL*,[1] I was surprised to find that his position differs from mine, because he thinks there are times when it is not wrong to lie, particularly in situations involving "the promotion of justice against the wicked, especially when they seek innocent life."[2]

Did my memory simply fail me? Not exactly. I dug out my class notes from 1973 (the May 14 class) and found this section:

> Problem: Nazis at door, Jews in basement
> 1. Tell truth
> 2. Lie
> 3. Say nothing; don't respond.
> Frame inclines to #1 or #3, but problems. Are there adequate linguistic conventions in war for telling truth to enemy? In some situations, you are expected to tell truth. Lift white flag, then wouldn't be right to come out shooting. What *could* you say to Nazis at door that they *would* believe? You don't want to rule out all deceptive maneuvers, etc. Certainly it's legitimate to conceal the truth.[3]

The line that said "Frame inclines to #1 or #3" seems to indicate that he thought then (with some hesitation) that a person should either tell the truth or remain silent, but not lie. That in fact is the position I myself have adopted, and will support in this essay.

But now in *DCL*, when John comes to the ninth commandment, "You shall not bear false witness against your neighbor" (Ex. 20:16),[4] he argues that it does *not* prohibit all lying:

> So we have no obligation to tell the truth to people who, for example, seek innocent life. In many volumes and essays on ethics, authors refer to perhaps the most famous of all ethical dilemmas: During World War II, a Christian is sheltering Jews in his home, protecting them from the Nazis.

---

1. *DCL*, 830–43.

2. Ibid., 839.

3. Section copied from my handwritten class notes from Systematic Theology 5323 at Westminster Seminary Philadelphia, May 14, 1973. In personal conversation by phone (July 13, 2009), I read John this section from the notes. He told me that he thought his position on this question had moved from what it had been in 1973, but he encouraged me to publish my argument anyway, saying, "Well, maybe you will convince me!" With that encouragement, and not intending any disrespect, I offer this essay for his consideration and the consideration of other readers.

4. All quotations from the Bible are from the ESV.

SS officers come to the door and ask him directly whether he is hiding Jews . . . In this case . . . I think the obligation is clearly to deceive the SS . . . If there were any chance to mislead the SS officers, as Rahab misled the officers of her own people, I think the Christian should have availed himself of that strategy.[5]

He also lists sixteen passages from Scripture "in which someone misleads an enemy, without incurring any condemnation, and sometimes even being commended."[6] He says:

In these passages, there is deceit, and that deceit brings harm. But the harm comes to an enemy, not to a neighbor . . . It does appear that the Bible passages listed above, which justify deception in certain cases, all have to do with the promotion of justice against the wicked, especially when they seek innocent life . . . We should recall that in the ninth commandment the requirement to tell the truth is conditioned on a relationship, that of "neighbor."[7]

My intention in this essay is to argue for the position of "early Frame" (1973 notes) rather than this position of "later Frame" (2008 book). And I do so with the greatest respect and appreciation for both early and later Frame, for him as a professor and a friend.

WHAT IS *LYING*?

It is important to clarify at the outset exactly what is being discussed. The question is the narrow one of verbal affirmations of something one believes to be false. In this sense, *lying* is "affirming in speech or writing something you believe to be false."

Several related acts are not included in this definition. On this narrow definition, *lying* does not include:

---

5. *DCL*, 839–40.

6. Ibid., 836. The passages are (1) Ex. 1:15–21; (2) Josh. 2:4–6; 6:17, 25; Heb. 11:31; James 2:25; (3) Josh. 8:3–8; (4) Judges 4:18–21; 5:24–27; (5) 1 Sam. 16:1–5; (6) 1 Sam. 19:12–17; (7) 1 Sam. 20:6; (8) 1 Sam. 21:13; (9) 1 Sam. 27:10; (10) 2 Sam. 5:22–25; (11) 2 Sam. 15:34; (12) 2 Sam. 17:19–20; (13) 1 Kings 22:19–23; (14) 2 Kings 6:14–20; (15) Jer. 38:24–28; (16) 2 Thess. 2:11.

7. *DCL*, 836, 839.

(1) *Silence.* This is saying nothing, so silence is not exactly an affirmation of anything; note Jesus' silence in Matthew 26:63.

(2) *Nonverbal actions intended to mislead or deceive someone.* An action is something that happens; it is neither true nor false like a verbal affirmation of something. An example is leaving a light on in our house when we are away for a weekend—an observer may rightly conclude, "The Grudems left a light on," but that may or may not mean that we are at home.

(3) *Ironic statements, especially in humor.* These are not truly affirmations when understood rightly.

(4) *Hyperbole.* These kinds of statements are not intended to be taken as literally true, but they use impossible exaggeration for rhetorical effect: "It took me forever to write this chapter"; "first take the log out of your own eye" (Matt. 7:5).

(5) *Unintentional falsehoods.* For example, you may be misinformed and then affirm something that is actually false. But because you do not believe it to be false, it does not fit the definition of *lying* given above.

I want to be clear that in this essay I am *not* making a moral judgment about these other acts. People may argue about acts (1) to (5), saying that some of them are *seldom or never wrong*, and that others are *often or perhaps always wrong* (depending on other factors). Those are interesting issues, but addressing them is not my main purpose in this essay. They are not the same as *lying* in the narrow sense of "affirming in speech or writing something you believe to be false," which is my concern here.

Of course, some may argue against this narrow definition of *lying*, saying, for example, "Deceptive actions are the *same thing* as lying." But that is not a careful statement. Deceptive actions are in *some* ways similar to lying (their goal is to persuade someone else to believe something untrue) and in *some* ways different from lying. For example, actions are ambiguous and can have various meanings, while verbal affirmations are not ordinarily ambiguous. Also, the Bible treats deceptive actions and false affirmations differently, as I will indicate below. And lying involves a contradiction between what you think to be true and what you say, which does not occur in deceptive actions (a difference that was very significant to Augustine).

781

The differences are important, and show at least that the two categories should be separately analyzed.

And Scripture itself seems to use *lie* and *lying* quite often in this narrow sense—to mean affirming in words something that one thinks to be false—in passages such as these:

> I am *speaking the truth* in Christ—I am *not lying*; my conscience bears me witness in the Holy Spirit. (Rom. 9:1)

> For this I was appointed a preacher and an apostle (*I am telling the truth, I am not lying*), a teacher of the Gentiles in faith and truth. (1 Tim. 2:7)

One further clarification is needed: I agree that a few actions are understood to be exactly equivalent to affirming something in speech or writing. In modern American society, for example, nodding the head up and down is understood as equivalent to saying "yes," and shaking the head back and forth is understood as equivalent to saying "no." Another example is that of an injured person who has lost his voice but who is able to point to the words *yes* and *no* on a board held in front of him. These might be called "verbal-equivalent actions." They are unambiguous ways to affirm or deny something, and they belong in the same category as "affirming something in speech or writing." They do not belong in my category (2) above, "nonverbal actions intended to mislead or deceive someone."

Such a restriction of *lying* to this narrow sense of speech or writing is not new with me. The respected church father Augustine (AD 354–430), the most famous defender of the view that lying is always wrong, argued only against lying in the narrow sense that I have defined above, that is, affirming in speech or writing something that one believes at the time to be untrue.[8]

---

8. See the extensive discussion in Paul J. Griffiths, *Lying: An Augustinian Theology of Duplicity* (Grand Rapids: Brazos, 2004). Griffiths represents Augustine's view as follows: "The lie is a verbal act, something we do with words" (25). And he says that for Augustine, "the lie is deliberately duplicitous speech, insincere speech that deliberately contradicts what its speaker takes to be true" (31). "Nonverbal actions cannot be lies" (33). "Silence—the refusal of speech—is also excluded" (33). "Error is excluded from the lie . . . Jokes are not lies" (34). "Augustine's definition of the lie, then, excludes in principle nonverbal communication in general and silence in particular" (38). Augustine himself says, "That man lies, who has one thing in his mind and utters another in words, or by signs of whatever kind" (*On Lying* sec. 3, NPNF First Series, 3:458). He concludes *On Lying* by saying, "It clearly appears then . . . that those testimonies of Scripture have none other meaning than that we must never at all tell a lie; seeing that not any examples of lies,

Westminster Seminary professor John Murray takes the same position in *Principles of Conduct*: after a discussion of several passages of Scripture (such as the stories of Rahab in Joshua 2 and the Egyptian midwives in Exodus 1), he concludes that "the upshot of our investigation has been that no instance demonstrates the propriety of untruthfulness under any exigency."[9] Murray defines *liar* as follows:

> the person who is to be branded as a liar is the person who affirms to be true what he knows or believes to be false or affirms to be false what he knows or believes to be true.[10]

He later says, "The injunctions of Scripture which bear directly on the demand for truthfulness have reference to speech or utterance."[11]

The Westminster Larger Catechism says that the ninth commandment prohibits "speaking untruth, lying,"[12] and requires "speaking the truth, and only the truth, in matters of judgment and justice, and in all other things whatsoever."[13]

BIBLICAL STANDARDS ABOUT TRUTHFULNESS AND LYING

Biblical Condemnations of Lying in General

The Bible has numerous commands prohibiting *lying* in the sense of "affirming in speech or writing something you believe to be false." These verses condemn false speech and see it as characteristic of sinners who are far from God, or they approve of truthfulness in speech, or they say that truthfulness is a characteristic of righteous people. What follows is a sample of such verses, but many more could be added. (These verses illustrate the *normative perspective* in John Frame's three-perspective, or *triperspectival*, system of ethics.)

---

worthy of imitation, are found in the manners and actions of the Saints" (ibid., sec. 42, NPNF First Series, 3:476).

9. John Murray, *Principles of Conduct* (Grand Rapids: Eerdmans, 1957), 146.

10. Ibid., 133.

11. Ibid., 135. As for actions intended to deceive, Murray later argues that there was no wrongdoing on the part of Joshua or the army of Israel when it retreated from the city of Ai, drawing its inhabitants into an ambush by actions intended to deceive (ibid., 144; cf. Josh. 8).

12. WLC 145.

13. Ibid. 144.

You shall not *bear false witness* against your neighbor. (Ex. 20:16)

My lips will not *speak falsehood*, and my tongue will not utter deceit. (Job 27:4)

You destroy those who *speak lies*. (Ps. 5:6)

Everyone *utters lies* to his neighbor; with flattering lips and a double heart they speak. (Ps. 12:2)

The wicked are estranged from the womb; they go astray from birth, *speaking lies*. (Ps. 58:3)

But the king shall rejoice in God; all who swear by him shall exult, for the mouths of *liars* will be stopped. (Ps. 63:11)

No one who utters lies shall continue before my eyes. (Ps. 101:7b)

I said in my alarm, "All mankind are *liars*." (Ps. 116:11)

I hate and abhor *falsehood*, but I love your law. (Ps. 119:163)

Deliver me, O LORD, from *lying lips*, from a deceitful tongue. (Ps. 120:2)

Rescue me and deliver me from the hand of foreigners, whose *mouths speak lies* and whose right hand is a right hand of falsehood. (Ps. 144:11)

Truthful lips endure forever, but a *lying tongue* is but for a moment. (Prov. 12:19)

Lying lips are an abomination to the LORD, but those who act faithfully are his delight. (Prov. 12:22)

The righteous hates *falsehood*, but the wicked brings shame and disgrace. (Prov. 13:5)

Remove far from me *falsehood and lying*; give me neither poverty nor riches; feed me with the food that is needful for me. (Prov. 30:8)

No one enters suit justly; no one goes to law honestly; they rely on empty pleas, *they speak lies*, they conceive mischief and give birth to iniquity. (Isa. 59:4)

They bend their tongue like a bow; *falsehood and not truth* has grown strong in the land; for they proceed from evil to evil, and they do not know me, declares the LORD. (Jer. 9:3)

Everyone deceives his neighbor, and *no one speaks the truth*; they have taught their tongue to *speak lies*; they weary themselves committing iniquity. (Jer. 9:5)

Your rich men are full of violence; your inhabitants *speak lies*, and their tongue is deceitful in their mouth. (Mic. 6:12)

But Peter said, "Ananias, why has Satan filled your heart to *lie* to the Holy Spirit and to keep back for yourself part of the proceeds of the land? . . . You have not *lied* to men but to God." (Acts 5:3–4)

Therefore, having *put away falsehood*, let each one of you *speak the truth* with his neighbor, for we are members one of another. (Eph. 4:25)

Do not lie to one another, seeing that you have put off the old self with its practices and have put on the new self, which is being renewed in knowledge after the image of its creator. (Col. 3:9–10)

The law is not laid down for the just but for the lawless and disobedient, for . . . the sexually immoral, men who practice homosexuality, enslavers, *liars*, perjurers, and whatever else is contrary to sound doctrine. (1 Tim. 1:9–10)

And in their mouth *no lie was found*, for they are blameless. (Rev. 14:5)

But as for the cowardly, the faithless, the detestable, as for murderers, the sexually immoral, sorcerers, idolaters, *and all liars*, their portion will be in the lake that burns with fire and sulfur, which is the second death. (Rev. 21:8)

> Outside are the dogs and sorcerers and the sexually immoral and mur-
> derers and idolaters, and everyone who loves and practices *falsehood*.
> (Rev. 22:15)

Therefore, the Bible's moral standards regarding lying include not only the ninth commandment, but an entire collection of Old Testament and New Testament verses that prohibit speaking lies or falsehood. And there are many other verses similar to those listed here, condemning things such as "lying," "falsehood," "liars," and those who "speak lies."

Does the Mention of *Neighbor* Narrow the Application of the Ninth Commandment?

But do these verses condemn all lying? They seem to, but John Frame suggests that the ninth commandment, "You shall not bear false witness against your neighbor" (Ex. 20:16), may not prohibit all affirmations of falsehood. He writes, "What then is a lie? I would say that a lie is a word or act that intentionally deceives a neighbor in order to hurt him. It is false witness *against* a neighbor."[14] Later he writes, about Bible passages that promote some deception, that they

> all have to do with the promotion of justice against the wicked, especially
> when they seek innocent life . . . The requirement to tell the truth is condi-
> tioned on a relationship, that of "neighbor" . . . I have questioned whether a
> neighborly relationship exists between a believer and someone who seeks
> to murder . . . We have no obligation to tell the truth to people who, for
> example, seek innocent life.[15]

But I am not persuaded that the wording of the ninth command-ment, "You shall not bear false witness *against your neighbor*" (Ex. 20:16), is intended to show us that there are some people to whom we are allowed to lie. Another explanation of that wording is possible.

John Calvin explained the concrete references in the Ten Command-ments by saying that God formulated the *positive* commands in a way that would be easier for us to accept. For example, "Honor your father and your mother" (Ex. 20:12) commands us to be subject to all rightful authority

---

14. *DCL*, 835 (emphasis in original).
15. Ibid., 839.

(such as the civil government), but God phrases the requirement in terms of parents, and "by that subjection which is easiest to tolerate, the Lord therefore gradually accustoms us to all lawful subjection."[16]

By contrast, Calvin says that the things prohibited in the *negative* commands put forth the most hateful examples of that whole category of wrongdoing, in order to shock us into appreciating how hateful they all are. Thus, concerning the seventh commandment, "You shall not commit adultery" (Ex. 20:14), Calvin says, "But he expressly forbids fornication, to which all lust tends, in order through the foulness of fornication . . . to lead us to abominate all lust."[17]

Therefore, Calvin realizes that "You shall not bear false witness against your neighbor" (Ex. 20:16) pictures a courtroom scene in which the "false witness" is likely to harm the neighbor by causing loss of life or property, but the wording of the commandment in this way is *not meant to narrow the application to neighbors only*, for, Calvin says, "as he forbade cruelty, shamelessness, and avarice in the preceding commandments, *here he bars falsehood* . . . For we must always come back to this: one particular vice is singled out from various kinds *as an example*, and the rest are brought under the same category, the one chosen being an especially foul vice."[18]

Therefore, there is an alternative to seeing "against your neighbor" as limiting the scope of the ninth commandment. It seems that a better understanding is that "You shall not bear false witness *against your neighbor*" is chosen as *a particularly hateful example* of lying, because it is a courtroom setting in which you intentionally speak falsely against your neighbor (whom you should love!) in a way that will cost him his goods (perhaps to your benefit) or even his life. By this God means to show us how hateful all lying is, not merely this kind of lying.

The other use of *neighbor* in the Ten Commandments confirms this understanding:

> You shall not covet *your neighbor's* house; you shall not covet *your neighbor's* wife, or his male servant, or his female servant, or his ox, or his donkey, or anything that is *your neighbor's*. (Ex. 20:17)

16. John Calvin, *Institutes of the Christian Religion*, 2 vols., ed. John T. McNeill, trans. Ford Lewis Battles, Library of Christian Classics, vols. 20–21 (Philadelphia: Westminster, 1960), 21:401 (2.8.35).

17. Ibid., 405 (2.8.41).

18. Ibid., 411–12 (2.8.47).

But surely we would not want to argue that the mention of *neighbor* narrows the application, so that it is wrong to covet your *neighbor's* house or wife but acceptable to covet your *enemy's* house or wife!

In the same way, "Honor your father and your mother" (Ex. 20:12) does not mean that we should honor *only* our parents, but also implies an obligation to honor other rightful authorities in our lives. Rightly understood, then, "You shall not covet your neighbor's house; you shall not covet your neighbor's wife" implies "You shall not covet *anybody else's* house; you shall not covet *anybody else's* wife."

Similarly, "You shall not bear false witness against your neighbor" implies "You shall not bear false witness *at all*," or, to put it in terms of lying, "You shall not *speak lies* at all." And numerous other verses of Scripture also confirm this when they condemn lying in general but make no mention of a neighbor.

The Character of God as the Basis for Not Lying

The biblical commands against lying are ultimately rooted in the character of God, who never lies.

> *God is not man, that he should lie*, or a son of man, that he should change his mind. Has he said, and will he not do it? Or has he spoken, and will he not fulfill it? (Num. 23:19)

> *Every word of God proves true*; he is a shield to those who take refuge in him. (Prov. 30:5)

> . . . in hope of eternal life, which *God, who never lies*, promised before the ages began . . . (Titus 1:2)

> By two unchangeable things, in which *it is impossible for God to lie*, we who have fled for refuge might have strong encouragement to hold fast to the hope set before us. (Heb. 6:18)

This, then, is the ultimate reason why lying is wrong: it makes us unfaithful image-bearers of God. The New Testament tells us, "Therefore *be imitators of God*, as beloved children" (Eph. 5:1), and when we speak truthfully we rightly portray our Creator as a God who speaks the truth. But if we lie, we are not rightly imitating God's own truthful speech. If we lie, we are falsely portraying our Creator as one who lies as well, and that dishonors him.

This connection between not lying and bearing God's image is seen in Paul's statement to the Colossians:

> *Do not lie to one another*, seeing that you have put off the old self with its practices and have put on the new self, which is being renewed in knowledge *after the image of its creator*. (Col. 3:9–10)

By contrast, the character of Satan is such that he lies according to his own nature:

> *You are of your father the devil*, and your will is to do your father's desires. He was a murderer from the beginning, and has nothing to do with the truth, because *there is no truth in him. When he lies, he speaks out of his own character, for he is a liar and the father of lies.* (John 8:44)

The ground for these ethical norms against lying, therefore, is found not in any human results (such as the benefit or harm that lying might do to somebody else, or whether someone might be led to think something false), but in the fact that *our lying dishonors God's own character.* God seeks creatures who rightly represent his image, whereas Satan consistently promotes all kinds of falsehood and lying speech.

Did Jesus Ever Lie?

Sometimes people will argue that there are difficult situations (such as trying to protect a person in hiding from a murderer) in which it is morally right to lie in order to protect life (see discussion below). But a strong objection to this view comes from the life of Christ. The New Testament tells us that Christ "in every respect has been tempted as we are, yet without sin" (Heb. 4:15). But that means that if people today are ever tempted to tell a lie in order to preserve someone's life, then Jesus must have also faced this same kind of temptation. And if we are required to lie in such a situation, then Jesus was required to lie as well. And this means that Jesus actually lied, actually affirmed something that he believed to be untrue. It seems necessary to conclude that, according to this position, Jesus actually affirmed a falsehood!

But this would be impossible for Jesus, who was also God, since "it is impossible for God to lie" (Heb. 6:18). Therefore, Jesus never lied. And therefore, we never have to lie either. Jesus' own moral character, and the truthfulness of all his words, provides additional evidence that Scripture prohibits us from ever telling a lie. The character of God, who never lies, is manifested to us in the life of Jesus, who never told a lie.

Do the Narrative Examples in Scripture Overturn or Modify Our Understanding of Lying?

In spite of this strong testimony of Scripture against lying, a number of ethical writers (including John Frame) have argued that specific *narrative examples* in Scripture show that God sometimes approved of human lies that were done for a good purpose, particularly to save human life. It is necessary to examine some of these passages.

Rahab's Lie. It is admitted by all that Rahab lied to the men who were looking for the Hebrew spies:

> And Joshua the son of Nun sent two men secretly from Shittim as spies, saying, "Go, view the land, especially Jericho." And they went and came into the house of a prostitute whose name was Rahab and lodged there. And it was told to the king of Jericho, "Behold, men of Israel have come here tonight to search out the land." Then the king of Jericho sent to Rahab, saying, "Bring out the men who have come to you, who entered your house, for they have come to search out all the land." But the woman had taken the two men and hidden them. And she said, "True, the men came to me, but I did not know where they were from. And when the gate was about to be closed at dark, *the men went out. I do not know where the men went.* Pursue them quickly, for you will overtake them." But she had brought them up to the roof and hid them with the stalks of flax that she had laid in order on the roof. So the men pursued after them on the way to the Jordan as far as the fords. And the gate was shut as soon as the pursuers had gone out. (Josh. 2:1–7)

The question is whether this passage or later passages (both Hebrews 11:31 and James 2:25 mention Rahab) show that God actually approved of Rahab's lie.

Here a careful examination of the context is important: It shows that Rahab was a "prostitute" (v. 1) who lived in the Canaanite city of Jericho. Nothing in the historical context indicates that she had any prior instruction in the moral standards required by the God of Israel (other than what she could know by common grace). To regard Scripture as holding up an untrained, uninformed Canaanite prostitute as a model of ethical conduct is asking too much of the text.

New Testament passages commend her faith and her receiving the spies and sending them out safely, but they conspicuously avoid mentioning her lie:

> By faith Rahab the prostitute did not perish with those who were disobedient, because she had given a friendly welcome to the spies. (Heb. 11:31)

> And in the same way was not also Rahab the prostitute justified by works when she received the messengers and sent them out by another way? (James 2:25)

These verses certainly do praise Rahab. But they are quite different from saying something like this:

> By faith Rahab the prostitute did not perish with those who were disobedient, *because she told a skillful lie* to save the spies.

Or:

> And in the same way was not also Rahab the prostitute justified by works when she received the messengers *and told a lie* to keep them safe?

Nowhere in Scripture is there any verse like this, an explicit approval of a lie, even one told to protect innocent life. The dozens of statements in Scripture about lies always condemn them.

John Calvin rightly observes:

> As to the falsehood, we must admit that *though it was done for a good purpose, it was not free from fault.* For those who hold what is called a dutiful lie to be altogether excusable, do not sufficiently consider how precious truth is in the sight of God. Therefore, although our purpose be to assist

our brethren . . . *it can never be lawful to lie*, because that cannot be right which is contrary to the nature of God. And God is truth.[19]

And Augustine takes the same position:

> Therefore, touching Rahab in Jericho, because she entertained strangers, men of God, because in entertaining of them she put herself in peril, because she believed on their God, because she diligently hid them where she could, because she gave them most faithful counsel of returning by another way, let her be praised as meet to be imitated . . . But *in that she lied* . . . yet *not as meet to be imitated* . . . albeit that *God hath* those things memorably honored, *this evil thing mercifully overlooked.*[20]

Therefore, Scripture does not hold up Rahab's lie as an example for believers to imitate.

The Hebrew Midwives in Egypt. Does this passage show that God approved of lying?

> Then the king of Egypt said to the Hebrew midwives, one of whom was named Shiphrah and the other Puah, "When you serve as midwife to the Hebrew women and see them on the birthstool, if it is a son, you shall kill him, but if it is a daughter, she shall live." But the midwives feared God and did not do as the king of Egypt commanded them, but let the male children live. So the king of Egypt called the midwives and said to them, "Why have you done this, and let the male children live?" The midwives said to Pharaoh, "Because the Hebrew women are not like the Egyptian women, for they are vigorous and give birth before the midwife comes to them." So God dealt well with the midwives. And the people multiplied and grew very strong. And because the midwives feared God, he gave them families. (Ex. 1:15–21)

At least three factors call God's supposed approval into question: (1) The statement of the midwives may in fact be largely true, or true as a generalization. It is entirely reasonable that when Pharaoh's plan became

---

19. John Calvin, *Commentaries on the Book of Joshua*, trans. Henry Beveridge (repr., Grand Rapids: Baker, 2005), 47 (emphasis added).

20. Augustine, *Against Lying*, sec. 34, NPNF First Series, 3:497 (emphasis added).

known to the Hebrew people, they often delayed calling these midwives until after they had given birth, perhaps using other midwives or perhaps assisting one another in the birth process. And the midwives themselves may have been complicit in this plan, even teaching the Hebrew women how to help one another at the time of childbirth. (2) God's favor on the midwives is due primarily or entirely to what is said in verse 17 (that they "let the male children live") and verse 21 (that they "feared God"). (3) The passage is not at all a clear commendation of lying. Augustine writes that God's favor on them "was not because they lied, but because they were merciful to God's people. That therefore which was rewarded in them was, not their deceit, but their benevolence."[21]

Elisha's Statement to the Syrian Soldiers. The king of Syria has sent a band of soldiers to capture Elisha, but God miraculously protects him in the following way:

> And when the Syrians came down against him, Elisha prayed to the LORD and said, "Please strike this people with blindness." So he struck them with blindness in accordance with the prayer of Elisha. And Elisha said to them, *"This is not the way, and this is not the city. Follow me, and I will bring you to the man whom you seek." And he led them to Samaria.*
> As soon as they entered Samaria, Elisha said, "O LORD, open the eyes of these men, that they may see." So the LORD opened their eyes and they saw, and behold, they were in the midst of Samaria. (2 Kings 6:18–20)

Then the king of Israel, who is in the city of Samaria, asks Elisha if he should kill the Syrian soldiers whom Elisha has captured (v. 21), but Elisha tells the king to feed them and send them on their way (v. 22).

Did Elisha (a prophet of God) lie to the Syrian army? He said, "This is not the way, and this is not the city" (v. 19), but the words are actually ambiguous, somewhat enigmatic. What way? What city? (The one where God wants them to go?) The Lord had blinded them (v. 18), so they decided to follow Elisha. The statement "I will bring you to the man whom you seek" (v. 19) is, again, somewhat enigmatic, but rather than leaving them, Elisha did in fact bring them to a place where they encountered him face to face. This is by no means a clear example of a

21. Ibid., sec. 32, NPNF First Series, 3:495.

clear falsehood approved by God. (And in any case, it was not told to save Elisha's life or anyone else's life, for the Syrian soldiers were already blinded and harmless.)

Other Passages. John Frame mentions several other passages "in which someone misleads an enemy, without incurring any condemnation, and sometimes even being commended"[22] (see list in footnote 6 above).

The passages fall into several categories, but none of them contains a clear lie (in the sense of a verbal affirmation of what the speaker believed to be false) that is approved by God. Some passages contain *deceptive actions*, such as a military ambush at Ai (Josh. 8:3–8), a surprise attack (2 Sam. 5:22–25), and David's pretending to be insane (1 Sam. 21:13). These deceptive actions do seem to be approved by God in these passages, but they do not fall into the category of *lying* as defined in this article.

But are such deceptive actions sufficiently different from *lying* (as defined in this article) so that we are justified in putting them into a different category? I think they are, for several reasons: (1) Scripture treats them differently, always condemning lies but not always condemning such deceptive actions. (2) Actions are not true or false (as verbal affirmations are), but they are just something that happens. (3) People instinctively treat them differently: If on a weekend I leave a light on in my house (to deter burglars by making them think I am home) and then my neighbor bumps into me while I'm staying in a hotel in Tucson (two hours away), the neighbor might have seen my light but will not think me to be a liar. But if I tell my neighbor, "I'm going to stay home this weekend" and then the neighbor bumps into me at a Tucson hotel, he will think that I lied to him. This is because (4) actions have ambiguous meanings, but propositions ordinarily do not. I am not saying that deceptive actions are never wrong (sometimes they surely are), but that they belong in a distinct category, one that I am not dealing with in this essay.

Other passages have to do with *God's sending a deceptive spirit* or a lying spirit to wicked unbelievers (1 Kings 22:19–23; 2 Thess. 2:11), and these passages raise difficult questions about God's providential use of evil agents to carry out judgment, but they do not necessarily show God's approval of the lies any more than God's ordaining that evil people would crucify Christ

22. *DCL*, 836.

(Acts 2:23; 4:27–28) shows that God approved of their evil deeds (he did not: Acts 2:23).

Other passages simply *report that someone lied* (just as Scripture narratives *report* other sins, such as murder and adultery), without indicating God's approval of the lie (these passages include Michal's lie to protect David in 1 Samuel 19:14, and her lie to protect herself in verse 17; David's counsel to Jonathan to lie in 1 Samuel 20:6; and a woman's lie to protect David's messengers in 2 Samuel 17:20).

In still other passages are cases of what we may call *deceptive speech*, but it is not clear that anyone actually told a lie in the sense of affirming something he thought to be false. These passages include Judges 4:18, where Jael invites Sisera into her tent; 2 Samuel 15:34, where David tells Hushai to say that he will be Absalom's servant (he was, but he was an unfaithful servant); and Jeremiah 38:26–27, where Jeremiah reports that he had made a request to the king (which he might actually have done).

One passage deals with *stating part of the truth*: In 1 Samuel 16:1–5, God tells Samuel to mention part of the purpose of his journey, that is, to say that he is going to Bethlehem to offer a sacrifice (which is true), but Samuel remains silent regarding the other thing he is going to do: anoint David as king. There is no affirmation of anything false, but since God commands Samuel what to say, the passage seems to approve of some cases in which a person states part of the truth and remains silent on other matters.

But in none of these passages is it clear that someone told a lie and it was approved by God. Therefore, these narrative passages should not be urged against the consistent testimony of many normative statements of Scripture that uniformly condemn lying as something that is always displeasing to God.

From the normative perspective, then, taking into account the teaching of Scripture as a whole, it is always wrong to lie.

But Do Some Circumstances Require a Person to Lie?

In this section I consider what John Frame calls the *situational perspective* on the question of lying. Are there some circumstances (some situations) in which God requires us to tell a lie to bring about a good result (such as saving a person's life)?

Lying in Order to Protect Life?

There do not seem to be any Scripture passages that lead us to the conclusion that lying is sometimes necessary to protect a human life (see the discussion of Rahab's lie above). But people have brought up other situations that seem especially difficult. One example is a Christian during World War II who is hiding some Jewish persons in the basement of his house, and some Nazi soldiers come to the door and ask him if he is hiding any Jews in the house. Isn't it better to lie to protect life than tell the truth and bring about the death of these Jews?

Interestingly, Augustine in about AD 395 treated a similar situation of a bishop named Firmus who was hiding a righteous person who was fleeing from the corrupt emperor, and the emperor's messengers came to capture the person. The bishop refused to lie, but neither would he disclose the hiding place. The emperor's messengers apparently tried to force him to disclose the hiding place, and as a result, he "suffered many torments of body" but "he stood firm in his purpose," and eventually, by his courage, he obtained a pardon from the emperor himself for the man he was protecting. Augustine said, "What conduct could be more brave and constant?"[23] Augustine thought it would have been wrong to lie, even for the purpose of protecting a human life.

Real-Life Situations Offer Many More Options

It must be said that real-life situations are always more complex, and offer more options, than a hypothetical situation sketched in a sentence or two in an ethics textbook. For example, telling the truth and lying are not the only options, since *silence* is always an option (although it may lead to suffering, as with the bishop that Augustine used as an example). A fourth option is saying any of a hundred different things that don't answer the question asked, such as, "I will not cooperate with any attempt to capture and kill Jewish people." Yes, that may mean the Nazi soldiers will force their way in and search around, but they probably would have done that anyway. Who can say that they would even believe the Christian if he denied harboring Jews?

Some would argue that in this situation, such evildoers (such as murderers) had "forfeited their right to the truth." I would probably agree with

23. Augustine, *On Lying*, sec. 23, NPNF First Series, 3:468.

this (at least the truth regarding the hidden Jews), and so I would not tell them the truth (we have no general obligation to tell everything we know). But that does not mean that I must lie to them either. A Christian in that situation should immediately pray for God's wisdom to know what to say without lying, and without disclosing where the Jews were hidden.

Does This Situation Present a "Tragic Moral Choice"?

Some ethicists would use this situation to argue for a "tragic moral choice," a case in which we must commit a lesser sin (lying) to avoid a greater sin (murder, or giving aid to a murderer, or at least not preventing a murder when we could do so). But John Frame would disagree with this viewpoint, and so would I, on the basis that *there are no such tragic moral choices*—that is, God's desiring us to disobey one of his commands in order to obey another. Frame gives several reasons for rejecting the idea that there are situations in which we have to sin, including the following (numbers in parentheses represent Frame's own numbering of his arguments, of which I have included only four in this discussion):

> (1) "In Scripture, we have a moral duty to do what is right, and never to do what is wrong." (3) This view implies that "the law of God itself is contradictory, for it requires contradictory behavior." (6) Since Jesus "in every respect has been tempted as we are" (Heb. 4:15), this view requires that Jesus himself had to sin in some situations, but Scripture repeatedly affirms that Jesus never sinned. (7) First Corinthians 10:13 guarantees that God "will not let you be tempted beyond your ability, but with the temptation he will also provide the way of escape," and this implies that no tempting situations are so hard that all the options are sinful. Frame writes, "So I must conclude that there are no tragic moral choices, no conflicts of duties."[24]

I agree with this position. I think this is significant, because I am concerned that in today's evangelical Christian world, too often such carefully constructed "hard cases" are used as a wedge to open the door a crack, to get people to admit that in some situations it is morally right (and acceptable to God!) to disobey one of God's commands in Scripture. This was essentially the position of Joseph Fletcher, whose 1966 book *Situation Eth-*

---

24. *DCL*, 233; the entire discussion on tragic moral choice is at ibid., 230–34.

ics[25] constructed all sorts of hard cases in which a person supposedly had to lie, or murder, or commit adultery, or steal, in order to follow the greater principle of "love" for others (that is, to do good for others).

But such reasoning from hard cases quickly leads to easy rationalization for many other sins. It is easy for people to progress from (1) it is *sometimes* right to lie to preserve a human life to (2) it is right to lie when it does more good than harm to (3) it is right to lie when you think it will bring a good result to (4) it is sometimes right to break *other* commands of the Bible when it will do more good than harm. The end result is a terribly weak personal ethical system that lacks any backbone, that ignores the commands of Scripture, and that simply seeks to bring about good results by whatever means (without getting caught). The whole system can quickly slide to moral relativism.

The Need to Consider All the Results of Telling a Lie

When considering this situational perspective for an ethical question, we need to ask what *results* will come from a given action. If a person lies (even to protect life), several results will follow:

(1) The other person's life might or might not be preserved. But we cannot be sure that different actions (silence, or giving other answers) would not have also preserved life (especially if we trust in God's sovereign control over situations).

(2) God will be dishonored, because a human being who is in God's image, and who represents God on the earth, has told a lie and thus represented his Creator as a liar.

(3) People will begin to think of the person who lied as (at least sometimes) a liar, someone whose words cannot always be trusted.

(4) The moral character of the person who lied will be eroded, because in a difficult situation he failed to obey the biblical commands against lying.

(5) It will become easier to lie in the future, because once a person thinks it is right to lie in some circumstances, this will seem to be an easy solution in additional circumstances, and the person's lying will become more frequent.

25. Joseph Fletcher, *Situation Ethics* (Philadelphia: Westminster Press, 1966).

(6) The act of lying may be imitated by others, multiplying these results in other situations.

But if a person remains silent or tells the truth (refusing to lie), then several good results will follow:

(1) God will be trusted to bring about the right results, including protecting the other person's life.
(2) God will be honored, because the speaker's actions portray his Creator as one who tells only the truth.
(3) People will begin to think of the person who told the truth as someone whose words can always be trusted.
(4) The moral character of the person who did not lie will be strengthened, because in a difficult situation he faithfully obeyed the biblical commands against lying.
(5) The speaker will be more likely to always tell the truth in the future, remembering that it was not necessary to lie in this difficult situation in the past.
(6) The speaker's truthfulness may be imitated by others, multiplying these results in other situations. In this way the work of the kingdom of God will be advanced.

Other Situations

Our approach to other difficult situations would be similar to the approach above, in every case maintaining the principle that it is never right to tell a lie. Therefore, for example, there is no such thing as a "little white lie" (that is, a supposedly "harmless" lie told so as to get someone to a surprise birthday party, to conceal a Christmas present, and so forth). Other means of getting the person to the surprise party should be used (many truthful things can be said that do not involve lying).

What should a husband say when his wife asks if he likes a dress she bought, or her new haircut, but he in fact does not think the dress or the haircut is attractive? Here I can give personal counsel (from forty years of marriage): It is always better to tell the truth, and to do so following Ephesians 4:15, "speaking the truth *in love*." This will mean speaking with kindness, humility, and thoughtfulness, and also speaking truthfully. ("Well, it wouldn't be my favorite . . . but the color is nice," or something like that.) The result may be momentary disappointment, but in the long term a husband and wife will trust each other always to speak truthfully, and with love and kindness, and the benefits to any marriage will be great.

What about conventional idioms or habitual greetings such as "How are you?" I think that "fine" can cover many situations (both speaker and hearer understand it to apply rather broadly), and "OK, thanks" can be a truthful answer in almost any situation. (Even in great distress, I can be "OK" because I am trusting the Lord.) Or at times a more specific answer might be appropriate. These are not really difficult situations, and creative thought will no doubt lead to opportunities for even more beneficial answers.[26]

Lying Accompanies Most Other Sins

It is significant that lying often accompanies other sins. The murderer, the adulterer, and the thief all lie to conceal their wrongdoing. And those who promote false religions often use falsehood to advance their views:

> Now the Spirit expressly says that in later times some will depart from the faith by devoting themselves to deceitful spirits and teachings of demons, through the insincerity of *liars* whose consciences are seared. (1 Tim. 4:1–2)

But if lying is often used to cover up other sins, then a society in which lying is unacceptable, and in which truthfulness is held in high regard, might expect to see a decrease in other wrongdoing as well. (Certainly parents who have raised children, or teachers who have taught elementary students, will testify that if lying can be eliminated, then much other bad conduct will be eliminated as well.)

The Moral Character of the Speaker

John Frame's understanding of ethics also requires us to look at a question from a third perspective, the *existential perspective*: what about the speaker himself?

Truthfulness and lying are often highly significant indicators of a person's inward moral character. In fact, truthfulness in speech may be the most

---

26. My friend C. J. Mahaney often answers, "I'm doing far better than I deserve," which leads to many interesting conversations!

frequent test of our integrity each day. In ordinary life, people don't often encounter opportunities to murder, commit adultery, steal, or break other laws without a high probability of being found out and suffering serious consequences. But people do have opportunities many times every day to tell a small lie (usually with little likelihood of being caught) or to speak truthfully. For example, the expressions "I don't know," "I don't remember," "I thought you said . . . ," and "I forgot" can be outright lies, but who could ever prove it? Small exaggerations of events or distortions of factual details can be spoken repeatedly in situations in which the hearers have no way of knowing that they are untrue. But in each case, God is dishonored and the liar's moral character is further eroded, his conscience is progressively hardened against God's law, and he becomes more open to committing other kinds of sin as well.

> O LORD, who shall sojourn in your tent? Who shall dwell on your holy hill? He who walks blamelessly and does what is right and speaks truth in his heart. (Ps. 15:1–2)

Each time a person speaks the truth or lies, he aligns himself either with God, "who never lies" (Titus 1:2), or with Satan, "a liar and the father of lies" (John 8:44).

A person who tells the truth (or remains silent), even in a difficult situation, faithfully represents his Creator as one who tells the truth, and therefore becomes more closely conformed to the image of God. In addition, telling the truth often requires inward trust in God to govern the circumstances and the outcome of the situation.

CONCLUSION

If lying is understood to mean "affirming in speech or writing something you believe to be false," then the overall testimony of Scripture is that lying is always wrong in every situation and every circumstance of life—and this will be true for all eternity.

34

MEDICAL ETHICS: BUILDING ON JOHN FRAME AND HIS WORK

FRANKLIN E. (ED) PAYNE, MD

TWO TRILLION DOLLARS poured into the grave, placed on the altar of false hope and possible immortality, and spent for increased suffering and injury. In 2005, spending for medical care in the United States reached $2 trillion. That amount is 16 percent of the gross domestic product. It is money spent for bodies that will eventually end up in the grave, money spent for a practice of medicine that does not match the science of medicine, money that actually causes net harm and injury to the American people, even apart from the heinous practice of abortion.

These figures have likely gotten your attention.[1] You may be asking just who this iconoclast of the "miracles of modern medicine" is. Just who is this destroyer of one of the marvels of modern science?

I am simply a Christian and physician dedicated to the truth of the Bible, the Reformed faith, and the best of modern science. The Reformed

---

1. I will deal with statistics and issues within the United States. Those of most other Western countries would be similar. The difficulties of Third World countries would be considerably different for the present and near future. Yet because the power of the United States to affect all other countries of the world is considerable, most of these issues would eventually apply to every developed nation.

faith is the best system of biblical doctrine. Dr. John Frame has contributed a great deal to that doctrine and to ethics. But he has gone on to do what few other theologians and pastors have done: he has worked to systematize Reformed ethics in general and medical ethics in particular.

Frame has addressed many areas of medical ethics in his articles and books, many of which are posted on the Frame-Poythress Web site. I do not claim to have read everything that he has written on medical ethics. Much less do I claim to have read *everything* that he has written. But I have read the whole of *ME*, read widely in a number of his books, and read many of the Frame-Poythress Web site's articles on a variety of subjects. On many issues, one of his books or his site is one of my first sources for opinion and insight. I truly believe that if all great Christian thinkers were as consistent, thoughtful, and gracious as Frame, the whole of Christendom would be the better for glorifying God and enjoying him forever. For example, Frame presses hard for the unity and love of Christians for each other in Reformed essentials, although he acknowledges differences between serious minds that should not cause the rancor and bitterness that have been seen too often in Reformed circles.[2]

How does one write on medical ethics in one chapter? Only in outline form could I even begin to address all of Frame's issues. Thus, I will have to be selective. My plan is not to touch on large areas of agreement among those who are Reformed, for example, on the issues of abortion and overt euthanasia. I will focus on areas that tend to be overlooked, yet are crucial to a biblical understanding of modern medicine. At a few points I will have to differ with Frame or suggest a more complete development of his thought. Frame's background in philosophy marks our starting point.

THE MATERIALISM OF MODERN MEDICINE

Everywhere Frame has argued and written for consistency and system in theology, ethics, and worldview. His best manifestation of these goals may be his recent *DCL*. Evangelical Christians are well aware of, and are even activists against, the evil practice of abortion and the insidious intrusion of euthanasia in "defective" infants and the "poor quality of life" in the elderly. But when they routinely go to the doctor, do they carry a tenor of caution because of these murderous practices? *Brothers and sisters, the philosophy that directs the killing of the unborn and the unfit is the same one that governs the*

2. *MWC*, http://www.frame-poythress.org/frame_articles/2003Machen.htm.

whole of the practice of medicine. That worldview is materialism or scientific realism. Simply, this belief means that a person is nothing but a chemical or biochemical process. He is the result of a blind, evolutionary process. There is no soul. There is no basis on which to determine morals or ethics.[3]

"Well," you might say, "that is obvious. So what?" *If medicine condones active killing, it is naive to think that that murderous intent or erroneous thinking does not carry over into every other area of medicine.* Admittedly, some areas are not as clearly affected as others. Emergency medicine can do amazing things to save lives and preserve function. But those same personnel are also there to find donors for heart, lung, and other transplants. There is abundant evidence that these organ donors are sometimes hurried "to donate."

Readers may be aware of the technical-ethical attitude in most areas of science: "If we can, we will."[4] This same attitude pervades modern medicine. If there is the least indication for a drug, it will be used. Thus, many thousands of children are on dangerous antipsychotics at younger and younger ages. Surgical procedures, such as tonsillectomies and hysterectomies, are notoriously performed routinely for reasons for which *medical science* has no indications. "Check your prostate" screams from the television every day, when the real scientific evidence has demonstrated for several decades that finding and treating prostate cancer neither increases life expectancy nor decreases the morbidity of old age (although the "kind" of morbidity may be altered).

Although the high-profile issues of abortion and euthanasia get more attention, the failure of Bible-believing Christians to understand that the "science" of modern medicine is based on a worldview that is totally inconsistent and at war with Christianity may be the most serious philosophical and ethical mistake they make relative to modern medicine. The same "science" that is dogmatic about evolution and that Christians are fighting in the schools and in the courts is the operating basis of modern medicine. Many, if not most, of the now-numerous tests that women are given during pregnancy are for the purpose of finding a defective baby and having it aborted. Or the physician orders these tests for the avoidance of a lawsuit

---

3. Frame equates morals and ethics, and so do I.

4. For an excellent discussion of how various technologies can affect thinking and behavior, see Neil Postman, *Technopoly: The Surrender of Culture to Technology* (New York: Vintage Books, 1993).

over a less-than-perfect baby. For sure, some of the tests may contribute to the health of the baby and mother during pregnancy, but their justification for that reason is minimal as compared to the other reasons named.

THE SCIENCE OF MODERN MEDICINE

Lately, I have become interested and have begun writing in the area of philosophy.[5] I am coming to believe that all serious Christians should understand the basics of philosophical thinking. One basic principle has direct application here: *Empirical science is based on the inductive method, which can never produce truth.* If the "hard science" of physics has experienced such great changes of theory and practice over the last two hundred years, the "soft science" of medicine can be reasonably expected to be even more tenuous and subject to change. Indeed, I have seen complete opposites in medicine. In the early 1970s, a low-fiber diet was recommended for most intestinal problems. Now, a high-fiber diet is strongly recommended for the same conditions. Treatments for cancer change as fast as the cancer centers can stock the medications or calibrate their radiation devices. Sodium bicarbonate used to be a mainstay of cardiac resuscitation, but it is now mostly avoided.

"Well," you might ask, "what about all the 'miracles of modern medicine'?" There are two problems here. The first may be considered pedantic. The second is more complicated. First, *only God performs miracles.* Man cannot perform miracles. The Roman Catholic Church requires extensive documentation of miracles, but evangelicals throw the word around as if miracles occurred every day because of, and sometimes in spite of, modern medicine. A miracle is a serious biblical issue, and we should treat it as such. In balance, let me say that I believe that God still performs miracles today, and that there are times to pray for them. But we need to be more precise in our speech and understanding about what is and is not a miracle. Modern medicine performs no miracles. God rarely performs miracles today (when one considers the billions on planet Earth with various illnesses and injuries).

Second, what about all the great achievements of modern medicine (since I will not let you call them miracles)? Well, objectively those are not easy to discern. Here is probably a good place to state emphatically that *I do believe in a* science *of medicine*, in spite of preceding comments. I even

5. http://www.biblicalphilosophy.org.

believe that in many, many instances, that particular science can tell us the best course of action for patients. The problem is that there is a serious disconnect between the *science* of medicine and the *practice* of medicine.

There are many influences on the practice of medicine other than its own science. (1) According to some "watchdog" groups, pharmaceutical companies spend almost twice as much each year on advertising as they do on research.[6] They advertise to patients on television, in newspapers, via the Internet, and in other media. They have thousands of pharmaceutical representatives ("reps") who target physicians in both academia and private practice. Published studies easily prove that physicians are more influenced by this advertising and the personal influence of reps than by medical science.[7] In general, the newer drugs are prescribed far more often than their older counterparts, usually with little or no increase in benefits to the patients, but at greatly increased cost.

(2) Physicians attend medical conferences where the "leading experts" present their newest research, usually from tightly controlled, experimental studies. Of course, physicians feel the pressure to practice the most-up-to-date medicine. So out goes the old and in comes the new, with little regard to results that may be achieved in the real world of office and hospital medical practice versus the experimental design. Of course, patients want the latest and best as well. The problem is that the latest is often not the best, but it is usually the most expensive.

(3) There are the dramatic cases that virtually every physician has experienced at least once in his career. There is the hypertensive patient whose blood pressure was markedly lowered by a new medication after "everything else" had been tried. There are the few carotid endarterectomies (removal of hardened fatty material from the large arteries in the neck) that have averted major strokes in a few patients, but those few cases have triggered thousands of similar operations that have provided no benefit to patients and have even initiated strokes by the procedures themselves. There are the few cancer "cures"[8] from heavy-duty chemotherapy or radiation therapy as contrasted with those who have had no benefit or whose deaths have been caused before the effect of the cancer would have taken their lives.

6. http://www.nakedcapitalism.com/2007/09/brazenness-of-big-pharma.html.

7. http://medicine.plosjournals.org/perlserv/?request=get-document&doi=10.1371/journal.pmed.0040150&ct=1.

8. By definition, a "cure" in cancer is a patient who survives five years after treatment is begun, regardless of whether the cancer is eradicated.

Two statements can be made about the virtual disconnect of the practice of medicine from the science of medicine. One is limited in general to the practice of medicine; the other is directed to Christians in medicine:

(1) *There is a science of medicine.* It may be difficult to see through all my criticisms of my profession, but again, I value the science of medicine. I value it highly, and I try my best to practice that science. But I have been severely chastised by several institutions, including one that is an academic center, for not prescribing antibiotics for common colds and viruses (without complications). The science of medicine is overwhelmingly clear: antibiotics are not indicated in these situations. But the practice of medicine and the science of medicine could not be further apart on this one issue.

(2) *The silence of Christians on this difference between science and practice is deafening.* The ninth commandment states, "You shall not bear false witness against your neighbor" (Ex. 20:16).[9] Frame has wonderfully exposited on this commandment in his *DCL*. Practicing medicine against its own best science is bearing false witness. As Christians, and particularly Reformed and thinking Christians, we should discern the best medical science and practice it with our patients. In the area of psychiatric "disease," for example, in schizophrenia and bipolar disorder, there is a crying need for the application of the best science and the best biblical counseling for the best results that can be achieved in this earthly existence. Yet evangelical and Reformed Christians in these areas rarely discern the issues, much less practice them.

THE GREATEST ETHICAL ISSUES IN MODERN MEDICINE

I believe *the greatest ethical issue of modern medicine is abortion.* The United States is approaching the mark of 50 million aborted babies since the *Roe v. Wade* decision of 1973.[10] The most recent statistics account for an average of 1,287,000 abortions per year for 2004–6. Although evangelicals were surprised by and were slow to respond to and develop positions against abortion after the 1973 decision, there seems to be a fairly united stance against all forms of abortion by this group today. Frame has sufficiently addressed this issue in many places, so there is no need to repeat what he has already

9. All quotations from the Bible are from the NKJV.
10. http://www.nrlc.org (Web site of National Right to Life).

said so well.[11] I will simply state that all abortions are wrong by biblical standards and that it is rare that a choice must be made between the life of the mother and that of her unborn child or children. Even in that rare instance, both Frame and John Jefferson Davis have clearly argued that a Christian is never faced with "conflicts of duty" or "tragic moral choices."[12]

I want to posit that *the second greatest ethical issue in modern medicine in the United States is idolatry*, the worship of the body within materialism. In general, this worship of materialism is almost as dominating among Christians as it is among non-Christians. I have already cited the proportion and total that is spent on medical care.[13] Brothers and sisters, the body is under God's curse (Gen. 2:16–17; 3:16–19). "It is appointed for men to die once" (Heb. 9:27). Although one can argue that one goal of medicine in its dominion task is to turn back and occasionally correct the damages of the curse, all the evidence (a very small portion of which I will present) so far is that such correction is quite limited. Furthermore, personal sins cause a great deal of direct disease and distress as well.[14]

REASONS FOR THE IDOLIZING OF MATERIALISM

Let us review what is behind this idolatry.

Medical Results

The most important stimulus of this worship is the supposed efficacy of modern medicine. Let us look at some particulars. Modern medicine is supposed to have increased life expectancy. The easiest target in this myth is to add abortions to the statistics. Since the life expectancy of aborted babies is zero, factoring in those 1.2 million abortions per year reduces life expectancy to about 50 years from the time of conception (eliminating spontaneous miscarriages).

11. E.g., *DCL*, 717–32.

12. *ME*, 8–10; *DCL*, 230–34; John Jefferson Davis, *Evangelical Ethics: Issues Facing the Church Today*, 3rd ed. (Phillipsburg, NJ: P&R Publishing, 2004), 18–22.

13. Interestingly, "medical care" is more often referred to as "health care." This shift is deliberate because modern medicine believes that it can not only provide "health," but also preserve "health" and "prevent" disease. In reality, it rarely accomplishes either.

14. This limited effect may be seen in other areas as well. Farmers continually fight weeds, soil depletion, and the like. Highway maintenance is evident by continual repairs on roadways and roadbeds.

But even leaving out abortions, the contribution of modern medicine to life expectancy is suspect. First, the most significant contribution according to most authorities is the conquering of childhood and other infectious diseases. Dr. Leonard Sagan, physician and epidemiologist, has written a book that largely refutes most common claims that modern medicine has caused this increase in life expectancy.[15] For example, he demonstrates that a decline in deaths from smallpox attributable to the smallpox vaccine is equivocal at best. He demonstrates dramatically that the decline of diphtheria and whooping cough *preceded* mass immunizations. Tuberculosis had declined to more than manageable levels *before* there were effective antibiotics for its treatment. Sagan goes on to discuss modern sanitation, levels of education, purpose in living, and many other factors that have probably had much more effect on increased life expectancy than medicine.

A more recent book by Nortin M. Hadler, MD, reviews possible positive contributions of the treatment or "prevention" of heart disease (cholesterol-lowering drugs, cardiac stents, heart artery bypass grafts, etc.), breast cancer, prostate cancer, and colorectal cancer.[16] He finds them woefully lacking in real results, compared to the hype and aggressive manner in which they are pursued.

On the opposite side, the iatrogenic[17] causes of disease and death must be subtracted from any achievements. One journal article has attributed over 100,000 deaths each year among hospitalized patients to adverse drug reactions.[18] A later study has estimated 195,000 deaths of a similar nature.[19] Almost 400,000 additional patients were injured in some way.

> The most stunning statistic, however, is that the total number of deaths caused by conventional medicine is an astounding 783,936 per year. It is now evident that the American medical system is the leading cause of death and injury in the US. (By contrast, the number of deaths attributable to heart disease in 2001 was 699,697, while the number of deaths attributable to cancer was 553,251.5.)[20]

15. Leonard A. Sagan, *The Health of Nations: True Causes of Sickness and Well-Being* (New York: Basic Books, 1987).

16. Nortin M. Hadler, *Worried Sick: A Prescription for Health in an Overtreated America* (Chapel Hill, NC: University of North Carolina Press, 2008).

17. *Iatrogenic* means "induced inadvertently by a physician or surgeon or by medical treatment or diagnostic procedures."

18. http://www.whale.to/drugs/iat.html.

19. http://www.medicalnewstoday.com/articles/11856.php.

20. http://www.lef.org/magazine/mag2004/mar2004_awsi_death_01.htm.

I don't want to be too dogmatic about these statistics. The authors have surely extrapolated a great deal of data in a manner that cannot be entirely without bias. But *such is the nature of all statistics in medicine.* So the negative side of medicine is just as "scientific" as the positive side. The primary point here is that such statistics are possible for the iatrogenic side of medicine, as well as the positive side.

Then there are the hidden statistics. Patients who die in traffic accidents on the way to the physician's office or hospital are not counted in these negative statistics. I just heard this week of another helicopter-ambulance crash that killed three, including the patient. They will not be counted as iatrogenic deaths, but they surely were. Ambulances have slowed down and are much more cautious because of their mounting toll of injuries and deaths. None of those statistics appear as iatrogenic casualties. Nor does the case of a patient I know of who died from drinking a concoction that was supposed to be administered at the other end of the body—rectally.

I have covered so much, so quickly and superficially, as to be really inadequate to the subject. But the reader can do a great deal of research on his own. All this information is on the Internet, more or less. Sometimes a primary source may be pay-for-view, but someone, somewhere, has usually written a summary that is without cost. All a reader has to do is to type in pertinent words on an Internet search engine.

I have been at this statistics game for almost thirty years. I am convinced that even apart from abortion, modern medicine is more dangerous to your health and well-being than it is of benefit. We could argue statistics forever. *But there is more.*

Modern medicine defends homosexuality, promiscuous heterosexual immorality, illicit drug abuse (including IV drug abuse), and "families" of lesbians and homosexuals. With these immoralities come hundreds of thousands of deaths from HIV/AIDS, millions of other sexually transmitted diseases, tuberculosis, and a host of other infectious diseases that are loathsome to discuss. And those tragedies do not even include the heartache and misery of soul from lifestyles that flout God's instructions.

The American Academy of Pediatrics has an official position against spanking. Too many parents have experienced firsthand the investigative and judicial power of social and legal constraints against spanking. Much of that momentum comes from this academy. And an editor of the *Journal of the Medical Association of Georgia* was fired because he took a stand *against* gun control. Another physician wrote to the *Journal of the American Medical Association* that all physicians who thought homosexuality was wrong should lose their licenses to practice medicine.

But if we are thinking consistently within a biblical worldview, are these results not expected? God's norm is sexual fidelity in marriage between a man and a woman for their lifetimes. When man or modern medicine comes up with other norms, we should expect terrible consequences. Today, as quantified in the medical literature itself, we have those terrible consequences.

Moses before the Israelites offered them a choice:

> See, I have set before you today life and good, death and evil, in that I command you today to love the LORD your God, to walk in His ways, and to keep His commandments, His statutes, and His judgments, that you may live and multiply; and the LORD your God will bless you in the land which you go to possess. But if your heart turns away so that you do not hear, and are drawn away, and worship other gods and serve them, I announce to you today that you shall surely perish; you shall not prolong your days in the land which you cross over the Jordan to go in and possess. I call heaven and earth as witnesses today against you, that I have set before you life and death, blessing and cursing; therefore choose life, that both you and your descendants may live; that you may love the LORD your God, that you may obey His voice, and that you may cling to Him, for He is your life and the length of your days; and that you may dwell in the land which the LORD swore to your fathers, to Abraham, Isaac, and Jacob, to give them. (Deut. 30:15–20)

The reader should note the association of "life," "good," "blessing," and "length of days." In another place, God says that he will put "none of the diseases" (Ex. 15:26; Deut. 7:15) on the Israelites that he had on the Egyptians.[21] Other verses note the association of God's way with life and any other way with death (Prov. 8:36; John 14:6; Rom. 6:23).

Christians are more familiar with the association of spiritual life with God and his commandments. Because of the unity of soul (spirit) and *body*, however, the health of either is dependent on the other. Although not all illness is due to personal sin (John 9:1–3), there is a clear association of

---

21. S. I. McMillen, *None of These Diseases*, 2nd ed. (Old Tappan, NJ: Fleming H. Revell, 1984). I do not agree with all the associations that Dr. McMillen makes between sin and illness, but in most instances there is sufficient correlation for serious consideration.

some sins and illnesses. As noted above, there is an epidemic of crippling and deadly sexually transmitted diseases around the world. Anyone who follows God's plan of sexuality, however, does not have to worry about any of these diseases. Furthermore, *all* sexually transmitted diseases could be wiped out in one generation, if everyone were faithful in marriage.

Unless it begins to understand and obey God's prescriptions, modern medicine will never know how to use the science that it has developed. In its attempt, based on the religion of materialism, it sows death and disease, as well as life and health. *So the efficacy of modern medicine is mostly a myth.* There are no miracles. There are a few great achievements in isolated areas, but overall modern medicine is destructive to health because it denies the God of health—of the soul as well as of the body.

Medical Care as a Right

Rights are a privilege granted by an authority. "We have a right when we have ethical and/or legal permission to do something or to possess something."[22] The Declaration of Independence states that "all men . . . are endowed by their creator with certain unalienable rights, that among these are life, liberty, and the pursuit of happiness."[23] But no right is unconditional. The most basic right—life—can be abused. Sexual immorality, overeating to gross obesity, cigarette smoking, alcoholism, and other personal sins destroy the body, and eventually life itself. So if medical care is a "right," it cannot be granted unconditionally. Thus, even if the right to life were granted, it would have to have conditions (ethical norms).

Furthermore, after a considerable review, we have seen that medical care alone offers no net benefits. So what is the use of a right to medical care, if it has no benefit?

More strongly, however, I argue that medical care is not a right because no form of welfare is a right. If it is a right, then it must be enforced with the full power of the civil magistrate, as the right to life ought to be.[24] The

22. *DCL*, 16.

23. Mostly, until this time, the right of "happiness" was actually "property." The Enlightenment was already influencing politics with a biblical base.

24. This statement shows how far the degradation of modern law has progressed. Although the state is mandated by God to provide justice for all human life, today in America not only have the unborn been denied protection, they are allowed to be targets of a godless medical profession and hedonistic society. "Those who practice such things are deserving of death [and] not only do the same but also approve of those who practice them" (Rom. 1:32).

power of the state is the sword or the death penalty. By what reasoning can the state "take life" (possessions, as means to life) and "give life," as medical care, to others?

Frame has argued for "limited government welfare."[25] I challenge that he has not thought through this matter as carefully as he has other issues. On a pragmatic level, how is welfare to be limited? His discussion of the state evolving from the family is helpful, especially in light of modern states that have destroyed tribal groups and their cultures. But the power of the sword cannot be wielded with a sword in one hand and a ladle of soup in the other. Both their means and their ends are different, especially in terms of power to harm. Also, as I have discussed, the ladle of soup comes at the price of a ladle of soup from someone else. Surely, in our reasoning, we have to be careful with absolutes. I do not see how welfare can be limited, since welfare programs were intended to be limited. Medicare cost $1 billion in its first year in 1965 but had grown to $8 billion by 1971 and to $280 billion by 2003. All state welfare is transfer of wealth by the power of the sword, taking from one person to give to another. And practically speaking, there is no way to "limit" it. The bureaucracy that grows to administer it will not seek its own destruction. Instead, that bureaucracy will seek to grow itself.

We who are Reformed must insist on finding on a biblical level what obligates us specifically, not just what is implied or permitted, as in the regulative principle for worship. On that principle, where is any specific duty placed on civil government to provide welfare of any kind? Although Scripture does not say a great deal about the responsibilities of civil government, with the exception of duties of the theocratic state of Israel and its case law, there is no mention of responsibilities for welfare in Romans 13:1–7 or elsewhere. In 1 Samuel 8:11–18, there is no mention by God that one of the king's functions would be to provide welfare. By contrast, all the exhortations are to individuals or to the church to provide for others—for example, the Good Samaritan (Luke 10:25–37), widows in the church (1 Tim. 5:3–10), and one church assisting other saints (2 Cor. 9:1–5).

Some Christians say that government welfare is simply a form of charity. Yet by definition, charity is voluntary—but the collection of gov-

---

25. *DCL*, 819, 824–25, 827; Davy Crockett and Edward Ellis, "Not Yours to Give," http://www.trinityfoundation.org/journal.php?id=23.

ernment-levied taxes that fund welfare is forced redistribution. Thus, by definition, government does not provide welfare but an arbitrary system of redistribution.

Finally, there is a personal element to charity that government cannot provide. When people are able to work, they should be expected to do so (2 Thess. 3:10). Individuals, families, and churches are far better able to provide the necessary oversight to determine who is and who is not able to work than is government. Making this determination requires multiple levels of oversight that government cannot properly supply. Therefore, government-provided welfare lacks flexibility and freedom at the level where the actual welfare is provided.

The Lure of Big Money

Medical care has become a huge commercial enterprise. From medications to bandages to appliances to operating rooms to office buildings and hospitals, virtually every industry is involved in medical care in one way or another, and each wants its share. This enterprise is entirely controlled by a few "gatekeepers": physicians and administrators. Thus, all these industries work to influence the small number of gatekeepers.

I have already reviewed how pharmaceutical companies work to sell their products. Multiply their activities many times, and one can begin to see the pressures on physicians and medical administrators. Being human, if they are offered incentives, they can be moved to select a certain product or procedure that they might not otherwise have chosen. Because the practice of medicine is a soft science, any slight variation in former practices can be changed with little justification needed. For example, coronary artery bypass surgery (CABG) has been shown to be effective for only one narrowly defined entity, yet hundreds of thousands of these continue to be performed every year as "life-saving" procedures.[26]

Physicians' Creative Diagnoses

Because of God's curse on Adam's sin, growing old is not pleasant. It involves aches and pains, deteriorating joints, clogging arteries, failing kidneys, brittle bones, and a host of other maladies. Our system has fostered

26. Hadler, *Worried Sick*, 22, 23, 25.

the idea that for every problem, medicine can find a solution. How many television commercials have you seen that advise "Consult your physician!" as if he always has the answer? I live in a town with one of the highest physician-to-patient ratios in the world, and yet there are long waiting times to get in to see almost any physician in any specialty. In our current system, based as it is on philosophical materialism, demand for medical care will always exceed supply.

As if patient expectations were not enough, the system continually creates new diagnoses. An English professor writes of how being shy has become "social anxiety disorder," the treatment for which is a medication that the pharmaceutical industry has already spent $93 million advertising.[27] Psychiatry is not alone. In virtually every other medical specialty, diagnoses have multiplied exponentially. A contributing factor is the necessity today to categorize everything according to numerical code. For an ailment to lack a code is not acceptable. A code will be found!

Medical Care as Power Politics

With Medicare and Medicaid becoming the largest item in federal and state budgets, "big bucks" means "big power plays." I do not need to reiterate here the politics of "big bucks." They are as distorted and subject to deceit as the politics surrounding roads, transportation, military contracts, and other facets of government spending. In all their activities, lobbyists have only the bottom line of their companies and their own political aspirations in mind.

Disappearance of Free-Market Medical Care

Biblical and other conservative economists have been diligent in their criticisms of the declining free market in the United States and throughout the world. But the same principles in other areas have not been readily applied to medicine. (1) On the receiving end, the patient usually pays little out of pocket relative to the cost of his or her care. Instead, there are insurance copays—or even no-pays, in the case of many government programs. So the patient has no incentive to shop around or limit what he needs or wants.

27. Judith Graham, "Shyness Shows How Drugs Seek to 'Cure' Former Virtue," *Augusta Chronicle*, May 4, 2008, 5G. The book she reviews is Christopher Lane, *Shyness: How Normal People Became a Sickness* (New Haven: Yale University Press, 2007).

(2) All the forces already named influence the physician, usually toward "the latest and the best," which are also the most expensive. (3) Politicians and big business are additional forces that demand medical services and products without cost considerations. When Bill Clinton became president, his wife, in association with huge medical corporations, almost succeeded in totally nationalizing medical care. They were blocked by a small organization known as the Association of American Physicians and Surgeons (AAPS).[28] This group is not explicitly Christian, but it has a better understanding of biblical economic principles than any other medical group, Christian or non-Christian.

An application of biblical economics to medicine alone might be sufficient to stem the rising costs of health care. I have already argued that government has no biblical warrant to provide welfare in any form, much less medical care. The application of that principle would remove what has been the greatest driving force economically since Medicare began in 1965. By feeding this tremendous amount into the medical system, costs for services, products, and research have fed an ever-increasing demand. Of course, private insurers have also had to meet the same level of provision, further increasing medical inflation.

Although it may seem heartless at first glance, many of the nationally celebrated "end-of-life" and "brain-death" cases could have been avoided simply on the basis of economics. Each case is too complex to discuss here, but limiting payment to families or nongovernment entities would have limited the notoriety of the cases and the medical options. Before you become horrified at the idea of "placing money before lives," answer this question: "Is it right to steal to provide for your family when they are starving?" The same commandment applies. "You shall not steal" includes the principle "You shall not forcibly and unrighteously take another man's possessions to give to another *for any reason.*"

The desire to have "everything" (in medical care) for "nothing" (no personal cost) has infected Christians and non-Christians alike. The insurance program of one Reformed denomination failed while trying to fulfill such desires. The simple biblical principles are that the individual and family are responsible for their own economic decisions, with help from outside by voluntary charities—the church providing for her own being primary. The answers to the questions of the Westminster Larger Catechism on the

28. http://www.aapsonline.org.

eighth commandment are enlightening on these particular responsibilities. Insurance must be for large and catastrophic illnesses and injuries, not the aches and pains common to mankind in his fallen state.[29]

Other Factors

There are other forces that drive the engine of modern medicine. (1) Families want to be sure that they have done "everything possible" for their loved ones, especially the elderly. One study showed that individuals do not necessarily want "everything" done for themselves, although they do want "everything" for people in their families.[30] (2) Formerly taboo medical advertising is growing. It extends from ads for simple aspirin to fat-lowering drugs to surgical procedures to hospitals. (3) Similar to some of the prior discussion, but slightly different, is envy. Associated with the "right" to medical care and "entitlement" is "I want what you have." If anyone is going to get the best medical care, then I should get it, too. (4) There is also the technological pressure that "if we can," then "we should." (5) Finally, there are demands from outside of medicine. Schools want treatment of "hyperactive" children. Schools and businesses want work excuses. A child needs a physical to go to camp or play a school sport. Estimates are that 25 percent of office visits in primary care are for this reason.

I trust that you can now better understand the explosive growth of modern medicine and its accompanying costs. The forces are complex but identifiable. This growth can especially be understood as a result of secular humanism, our culture's dominant religion, in its manifestation as scientific materialism. The modern man thinks: "If this biological body is all that I will ever have, I surely want it preserved and maintained for as long as possible. And if God does not exist, then I must look to the government for wants and needs that my family cannot supply." These desires have no restrictions apart from the self-governance that comes from biblical obedience and an understanding of biblical principles for life, especially those of economics. Other than an innate morality eroded by secular humanism, there are no principles to prevent my getting whatever I want, at any cost, from anyone else. Does not evolution teach survival of the fittest, which has been translated by modern America as the group with the most votes?

29. See the section "What about the Medically Uninsured?" below.
30. *American Medical News* (March 27, 1987): 31.

Therefore, the escalation of medical care can be understood as part of our secular religion. Yet Bible-believing Christians should know better. We have the hope of heaven. We have the Ten Commandments to determine how we are to live. We can have health that results from righteous living. We have the supreme source of truth in the Bible that is absolute in the face of limited and quickly changing empiricism. From the Bible, principles that are true may be deduced.[31] From experimental science, inductive reason cannot determine truth. From humanism comes only self-interest.

Christians worship at the altar of modern medicine. With few exceptions do I see any difference in the practices of Christian physicians or Christian patients. Although the institution of the hospital is largely attributable to Christians, the original emphasis on "care" has changed to the attempt to "cure." Christian physicians do not discern the extremely limited "cure" potential of what they do. They do not see through the pharmaceutical "reps" who influence what they prescribe. They do not see the virtual nonefficacy of medicine that I have discussed above. They discern abortion, and the rising death star of euthanasia, but they do not see these other biblical issues.

The same attitude is seen in Christians' prayers. Prayer for the sick tends to be the overwhelming focus in corporate prayer. In its proper perspective, prayer for the sick is proper. But do we pray for healing of the unbeliever so that he can continue to curse God, or do we pray for whatever it takes for God to humble and regenerate him? Do we pray that ninety-year-old Aunt Sally with multiple organ failure will be miraculously healed, or do we pray that she will be given a peaceful death to be with Christ? How often does God grant our prayers for miracles? Which is more important, to pray for someone's healing and return to health or to pray for that person's spiritual growth through this illness? These are just a few biblical principles that should direct our prayers, rather than simply praying for someone to be healed.

Lest someone miss it, let me reiterate my belief in modern medical science: *Within a biblical perspective, I believe modern medicine has much to offer.* It offers not so much in terms of cures as it does in terms of our ability to diagnose and understand the physiology of the body. Alternative medicine, to which many Christians seem to be drawn, has less to offer than modern medicine. In common with all other fallen human beings, Christians can be irrational. Across the theological spectrum, from theonomists

31. WCF 1.6.

to Pentecostals, at times belief in alternative medicine becomes a test of orthodoxy and fellowship.

I suspect that such confused thinking about medicine among Reformed and non-Reformed Christians reveals how little trained we are to think critically and biblically. As those with the Book of Truth and under orders to be transformed by the renewing of our minds, we should be among the leading thinkers of our age. Alas! Much more are we its followers. We have indeed become of the world and not just in the world.

We must remember that health is more closely related to spirit (mind) than to body. If a young Christian man were to ask me, "What vocation would facilitate the best health for the most people?" I would answer, "You should become a thoroughly theological and practical preacher of the Word of God." Regeneration and obedience are far and away the greatest influence on the health of the body, and they foreshadow the perfect health we will have in eternity!

Emotional Problems: A Review of and Request to Reconsider the Primacy of the Intellect

Frame's comments on "the primacy of the intellect" relate directly to some issues in modern medicine:

> Does reason have some sort of "primacy" over the other faculties? Well, all of our emotional inclinations, imaginative ideas, intuitions, experiences, and so forth must conform to reason, or they do not tell us the truth. . . . *The primacy of reason* in the above sense says very little. It does not rule out a similar primacy for the other faculties, even the emotions. Imagine someone who claims that he has come to know something through his emotions. If his claim is correct, then his emotions have led him into "conformity with truth." Given the definition above, that is the same as "conformity to reason." Emotion, in other words, as a way of attaining knowledge, is a form of reason. If his claim is not correct, one may still call his emotions a form of reason, for they are one of the capacities by which he makes judgments and inferences, even though they are not reliable in this case. In this case, we may say that his emotions are reason in a descriptive, not a normative sense.[32]

32. *DKG*, 331.

Among Reformed theologians, including J. Gresham Machen[33] and the authors of *Classical Apologetics*,[34] one often hears the view known as "the primacy of the intellect." What this seems to mean is that God's revelation addresses first of all the human intellect. The intellect, in turn, applies the truth to the will and to the emotions. At least this is what God, on this view, originally intended. One result of the fall, however, is that the hierarchy of intellect, will, and emotions was overturned, so that the intellect is now dominated by the will and the emotions. Salvation, then, returns human nature to its proper balance. The Christian life is, like the ideal life of the Greek philosophers, a life of reason, though of course it is a reason based upon God's Word rather than on autonomous philosophy.

I disagree with Machen on this point, though I do sympathize with him. . . . I offer a similar evaluation of contemporary Reformed attempts to repress the passions. Feelings do play a positive role in the Christian life, as we have seen.[35]

At this point you may be wondering what the intellect, will, and emotions have to do with medical ethics. Just this: "emotional problems" are a major part of modern medical thinking. Anxiety disorders, depression of various shades and descriptions, "affective" problems, aggressive behavior, attention-deficit hyperactivity disorder (ADHD), and a host of other diagnoses falling under "emotional problems" can be found in the *DSM-IV-TR*.[36] Although *emotional problems*, as a term, is more colloquial than technical and professional, it is accurate in terms of how these problems are addressed in medicine, psychology, and psychiatry.[37] They are treated as "emotional problems," and medications are prescribed for the "emotional" symptoms that present to the physician.

33. J. Gresham Machen, *What Is Faith?* (New York: Macmillan, 1925), 54, 57. How can anyone differ with Machen? Was he not a canonical writer? I have my tongue in my cheek, of course. Frame's *MWC* is a delightful and helpful paper that all the Reformed ought to read.

34. R. C. Sproul et al., *Classical Apologetics* (Grand Rapids: Zondervan, 1984), 228–30.

35. *DCL*, 377.

36. *Diagnostic and Statistical Manual of Mental Disorders: DSM-IV-TR*, 4th ed., text rev. (Washington, DC: American Psychiatric Publishing, 2000). This manual is the standard for psychological and psychiatric disorders and has been revised many times, not just four as the Roman numeral might suggest.

37. A psychiatrist has a medical degree with psychiatric training. A psychologist has a degree in psychology or "education." (There is little difference in study between an EdD in education and a PhD in psychology.) Psychiatrists tend to focus more on the prescription of medications than on "psychotherapy" (counseling), while psychologists focus on the latter. But they often work together. By law, psychologists may not prescribe medication in most jurisdictions.

As we have already seen, this approach is consistent with the philosophical materialism of modern medicine. If there is a problem within the complex of chemicals that is called a "human being," there must be a "chemical disorder." If one listens carefully to talk among evangelical Christians, "emotional problems" and "chemical disorder" are spoken of with virtually no recognition of this underlying philosophical framework.

Although there are "gray issues about gray matter,"[38] that is, real brain disease versus spiritual problems, the majority of "emotional problems" treated with medications are problems of sinful thought and behavior—the patient's own sin or the sins of others that affect him. At the risk of raising the tent flap and allowing the whole camel inside, I am willing to grant some organic etiologies of depression, schizophrenia, bipolar disorder, and symptoms resulting from stroke, traumatic brain injury, geriatric brain deterioration, and other clearly defined brain disorders. Collectively, however, these amount to less than 10 percent of the problems that are labeled "psychiatric." I cannot "prove" that number, which is based on my over forty years' experience in medicine and on my training in biblical counseling, but I am confident that it is accurate.

Where does Frame's disagreement on the primacy of the intellect fit in here? First, I do not believe his position is biblical or consistent with his own work. Second, his position may grant too much to theological and medical/counseling issues. (The reader should at this point reread Frame's remarks quoted as the opening paragraphs of this section.)

In 1989 I wrote a paper, "A Definition of Emotions,"[39] because of "emotional" issues in medicine. My definition of *emotion* was "the momentary (acute) and ongoing (chronic, continuous) disturbance within the mind (soul, spirit) caused by the discrepancy between perceived reality and one's desires." I found then, and still find it to be true, that writers and speakers rarely define *emotion*. Instead, they simply list emotions: anger, worry, sadness, happiness, fear, depression, and so on. Using synonyms such as *feelings* and *affections* is not sufficient. A failing of some definitions (often violated even by the standard dictionaries) is that they incorporate the defined word itself or synonyms that still do not convey a real meaning.

---

38. Franklin E. Payne, *Biblical Healing for Modern Medicine* (Augusta, GA: Covenant Books, 1993), 73–88. A word search at our Web site, http://www.bmei.org, would also be fruitful.

39. *Journal of Biblical Ethics in Medicine* 3, 4 (1989): 61–67, http://www.bmei.org.

The Glossary for this festschrift defines *emotions* as "human feelings, inclinations, dispositions." "Feelings" is not really helpful, since it is simply a synonym for *emotions* and is no more descriptive. But "inclinations" and "dispositions" are consistent with the "ongoing" component of my own definition. It is crucial to distinguish "acute" (or, perhaps better, "momentary") from "ongoing."

The key to understanding emotions comes from the word *emotion* itself. Remove the *e-* and the *-s* and you get *motion*. Change the ending to get *motive*. So emotion consists of a change in the status of one's body and soul, and in a direction determined by motive. As Machen said:

> Human affection, apparently so simple, is really just brimming with dogma. It depends upon a host of observations treasured up in the mind with regard to the character of our friends. . . . Human affection is thus really dependent upon *knowledge*. . . . The knowledge of God is the very basis of religion.
>
> . . . The human mind has a wonderful faculty for the condensation of perfectly valid arguments, and what seems like an instinctive belief may turn out to be the result of many logical steps.[40]

Thus, *motion* or the tendency toward motion is bound up with the roots and etymological history of *emotion*.[41]

For example, I am driving down the highway, peacefully contemplating complex theological ideas, when another car races by and swerves in front of me, missing me by inches, as the driver honks vigorously. Powerful, momentary emotions are triggered—fear first, then anger. What happens next is central to our concern here: revenge! I want to speed up and pass him, demonstrate my anger and frustration, and make some maneuver to "get him back."

At this point the primacy of the intellect and ongoing emotions become crucial. If anger is an ongoing problem, I will likely take some sort of revenge, thus placing myself and other drivers at risk of serious injury. But if I have cultivated the fruits of the Spirit (Gal. 5:22–23), they will calm the momentary feelings just generated. My intellect will tell me that this situation is a part of God's providence and that it is wrong and dangerous to seek revenge (Ex. 20:13; Rom. 12:17).

40. J. Gresham Machen, *Christianity and Liberalism* (Grand Rapids: Eerdmans, 1925), 54, 57.

41. http://www.etymonline.com.

As Frame has discussed for many years, we see the intricate interaction of the situation, the normative (intellect), and the emotions. But even ongoing emotions cannot give direction to the situation. I may "feel" the immediate emotions of fear and anger subside, as peace and patience take over, but these alone are incapable of directing thought, speech, or action. I become calm and controlled because of these fruits, but what is my specific action to be? I choose in my mind to make certain decisions among several options. I recognize that there are fools in this world, that revenge is wrong and dangerous, that I had another destination, and that God is sovereign.

I strongly agree with Frame's emphasis on making emotions more central to Reformed and Presbyterian thinking, and I agree that Machen's "warriors" should consider the "feelings" of others.[42] After all, part of Immanuel's introduction was that he was "full of grace and truth" (John 1:14).[43] I would, however, like Frame to reconsider his position on the primacy of the intellect. Anger alone has no direction.[44] Some thought or situation triggers this emotion, and once triggered, what am I to do with it? One response is "not [to] let the sun go down" on it (Eph. 4:26). Or suppose I feel sad. What is the thought or situation that makes me sad? What do the Scriptures say about dealing with my sadness? Suppose I am happy. What event made me happy? How do I manage happiness?

Let's consider another dimension of emotions and intellect—values. " 'Love the Lord your God with all your heart, with all your soul, with all your strength, and with all your mind,' and 'your neighbor as yourself' " is a command (Luke 10:27). At times I must go against my momentary dislike (even hatred) to become reconciled to my brother (Matt. 5:23–24) because of the scriptural command (intellectual consideration), the value that I place on obedience to the Lord, or both. My momentary emotion must be overcome by my intellect or the ongoing value of the Lord's directive.

Biblical emotions seem to have a deep, stable character. The fruits of the Spirit—love, joy, peace, patience, kindness, gentleness, goodness, grace, and others—have an "abiding" quality. Indeed, many of the verbs that illustrate

---

42. *MWC*. See also John Frame, "Hurting People's Feelings or The Pathos Game," http://www.frame-poythress.org.

43. The word *love* in such concepts as "showing love" and "doing the loving thing" has become so overused and misunderstood that I suggest *grace and kindness* as a better designation of our attitudes and actions toward one another.

44. This reality may be seen when the police are called to a domestic argument. Often, the anger of the disputants may be directed toward the police, even to the extent of bodily harm!

the walking out of the Christian life in the New Testament have that same "ongoing" quality of action, from past to present to future.

What emotions are and how they are managed is a huge issue for current medical practice. Are drugs the answer to fixing "emotional problems," to developing right values, or to following directives (the primacy of the intellect)?

If a patient comes to me with a temperature of 104 degrees and severe chest pain, barely able to breathe, I will probably diagnose bacterial pneumonia. I can treat his symptoms (emotions) by giving him an antipyretic[45] for the fever and narcotics for pain. Then he will not care as his fever subsides and his breathing becomes shallower and slower, and finally stops. He has died, but his symptoms have been treated! Yet what he needed was an antibiotic as well as treatment of the symptoms.

Sometimes emotions become so intense that medications are needed. Sometimes, as I have mentioned, true organic problems exist. But the large majority of people who are prescribed psychotropic drugs need a change in their thinking and behavior far more than they need to have their emotions quieted. Jay Adams has written numerous books that give biblical direction to these problems (that is, biblical, or "nouthetic," counseling), although he "has always admitted the importance of medical care for physical problems."[46] Recently, a psychiatrist and a nouthetic counselor have collaborated to write about many of these issues in *Will Medicine Stop the Pain?*[47]

There is some evidence that Frame is not consistent with his own position. He writes in *DCL*, "The existential perspective never permits us to transgress the normative."[48] Also, when he rejects the "subjectivism" of Friedrich Schleiermacher as "the final authority of theology," Frame is rejecting emotion without direction (control of the normative or primacy of the intellect). Additionally, he says:

> We should also counsel people not to act on momentary emotions. We should also counsel them not to act on every idea that pops into their heads

---

45. An antipyretic is a drug that reduces the body's temperature in situations such as fever.
46. *MWC*.
47. Elyse Fitzpatrick and Laura Hendricksen, *Will Medicine Stop the Pain? Finding God's Healing for Depression, Anxiety, and Other Troubling Emotions* (Chicago: Moody, 2006). Dr. Hendricksen was herself a "victim" of dependency on medications. Thus, she speaks not only as an authority but as one who has experienced the problem about which she writes.
48. *DCL*, 330.

or on every desire or impulse. But ideas that are tempered and refined and prayed over to the point of cognitive rest (an emotion!) ought to be acted on. And emotions refined by thought, maturity, and good habits of decision making may well be reliable guides also.[49]

Thus, Frame and I may be closer to each other than may appear at first glance. Because human affection is "just brimming with dogma," emotion, in and of itself, has no direction. Emotion is always tied to the existential (thoughts and situation) dimension. Thus, modern medicine's frequent mistreatment of "emotional problems" ignores the primacy of the intellect.

WHAT ABOUT THE MEDICALLY UNINSURED?

"According to the Census Bureau's 2005 Current Population Survey (CPS), there were 45.8 million uninsured individuals in 2004, or 15.7% of the civilian non-institutionalized population."[50] As Christians, we should be concerned about those who are unfortunate, including a population that is "uninsured."

More importantly, however, we should be concerned about biblical ethics. Today, perhaps the most popular attribute of God that Christians focus on is love—"God is love" (1 John 4:8). But if God is not truth before he is love, we cannot believe that he is love. Furthermore, it is readily evident that *love* in Scripture has dimensions that colloquial uses of *love* do not have (e.g., Rom. 13:8, 10; Gal. 5:14). God is also righteous. Only the Bible can truly describe God's righteousness; its full dimensions transcend human thought. All these attributes bear on the problem of the "medically uninsured" (MU).

As with much that I have already discussed, the MU are really a political, or "talking-point," category, not a social issue. Just as we have seen inflated numbers and misconceptions about the homeless,[51] so the MU are also a diverse lot. Almost a third of this group is eligible for Medicaid, but they do not bother to apply. Others have chosen not to purchase medical insurance (MI) because they are young or healthy and do not think they will need it. Generally, they are correct.

49. Ibid., 382.
50. http://aspe.hhs.gov/health/reports/05/uninsured-cps/index.htm.
51. *DCL*, 828–29.

All the MU can receive emergency care at any emergency room. Laws require all hospitals that receive government funds (that is, all hospitals!) to provide medical care to everyone with an "emergency," leaving *emergency* to be defined only by the patient or his family. Although this requirement may not provide for ongoing care, it eliminates much of the reason for insurance, that is, for hospitalization. So in a major way, the MU already have MI.

The really needy subcategory is a group of the MU with treatable problems that are not emergencies. All the plans for the MU, however, would be far more expensive than directly paying for their medical needs. Although I have already shown that government welfare is biblically indefensible, the diversity of this group illustrates practically how government intervention inflates both the issue and its cost. The larger the group (broadening the definition), the more power politicians gain and the greater appeal they can make to the vox populi as saviors of this group. Again, government cannot manage at the micro-level of individual and family. Therefore, it must broaden the category to be certain that the "needy" group is covered. A large bureaucracy is necessary, inflating the costs and perpetuating itself indefinitely.

Then there is the question of need. As we have seen, based on the best medical science available, real efficacy in medicine is difficult to prove. If billions more in coverage is generated, will that damage this group more than it will help? Should abortion fall within sound medical practice? Should treatment for any and all diseases of lifestyle and unethical behavior be included? The MU cannot be isolated from the larger ethical and efficacy issues summarized below.

(1) MI, as it currently exists, does not pass the several tests of moral hazard that have been well recognized for several centuries. For example, when your house burns down, you have a well-defined loss and a well-defined coverage. Medical care has many gray areas, efficacy problems, and perceived needs, rather than real needs.

(2) Having MI does not guarantee good medical care, which is a moral and a scientific issue. It is an amazing paradox that the American people want "womb to tomb" nationalized medical care, when the failures of other nations' systems are well known and documented. And there is Americans' own considerable dissatisfaction with their own nationalized

systems that already exist (education, Social Security, postal service, etc.). Was the truth of the "blind lead[ing] the blind" (Matt. 15:14) ever better illustrated?

(3) Medical care is almost fully nationalized now. Consider state monopoly by licensure, insane malpractice laws, state insurance laws, the Health Insurance Portability and Accountability Act (HIPAA), and the regulations of such organizations as the Food and Drug Administration (FDA), the Occupational Safety and Health Administration (OSHA), and the Joint Council for the Accreditation of Healthcare Organizations (JCAHO). All these laws greatly increase the cost of medical care. I have seen OSHA and JCAHO virtually shut down hospitals and clinics in order to meet their inspections and regulations!

(4) The true price of medical care is mostly hidden. The MU are charged as much as seven times the amount charged insured patients, even though the charges on the bills of both may initially look the same. Rates that are negotiated and copays make the difference, but it is concealed from the MU and the insured alike.

(5) The church has both allowed and blessed the welfare ministries of the civil government, including Medicare, Medicaid, and a plethora of other state and federal programs that give medical care "free" or at minimal cost (to the patient). For various historical reasons, such as the social gospel of the nineteenth century and creeping socialism by (primarily) the federal government, the church has moved out of these ministries just as the civil government has moved into them. Often, if not predominantly, Christians even defend this civil intrusion as "Christian charity." Perhaps a biblical understanding of the roles of church and state in welfare is the most basic aspect of a biblical ethic that would help us gain a systematic understanding of the more definitive roles of each.

In short, a truly free market, not extant in over a century in the United States, coupled with the church's reclaiming the true gospel would solve the cost problem as completely as is feasible. This solution would be more affordable than any other current proposal. Moving toward a biblical ethic that involves restoring a free-market approach to medical care, coupled with an increasing role for the church, is the only solution that will truly be effective in the short and long runs.

There are only two possible futures. One is reformation in the church, not only in the areas I have discussed but also in the totality of church-state relationships. As this grows, it will effect changes in the other institutions of society. Unless Christians begin to understand and apply biblical principles to the areas discussed in this article, then "judgment [must] begin at the house of God" (1 Peter 4:17). The other is an increasing statism (the "City of Man" that Augustine of Hippo described long ago) and bankruptcy (of which we are on the verge today, as I write this chapter).

A Parting Word

Readers should note that all the studies cited in this chapter are results based on groups of people. There are always individual exceptions to these group results—sometimes numerous exceptions. That is one of the major difficulties of medical science versus the practice of medicine on individual patients. If you question any study results that conflict with your personal medical situation, you should consult with your physician or do your own research.

For Further Reading

Adams, Jay E. *Christian Counselor's Manual.* Grand Rapids: Baker, 1973.

———. *Competent to Counsel.* Nutley, NJ: Presbyterian and Reformed, 1973.

———. *More than Redemption.* Phillipsburg, NJ: Presbyterian and Reformed, 1979.

Biblical Medical Ethics Library. http://www.bmei.org. The most comprehensive and biblical writings anywhere. This site consists of all past issues of *The Journal of Biblical Ethics in Medicine* and *Biblical Reflections on Modern Medicine*, neither of which is still being published. If this site cannot be accessed, http://www.biblicalworldview21.org, where all materials are being transferred, may be checked.

"Christian Worldview of Medicine" and "Christian Worldview of Psychology/Counseling." http://www.churchcouncil.org/Reformation_net/default.htm.

Davis, John Jefferson. *Evangelical Ethics: Issues Facing the Church Today*. 3rd ed. Phillipsburg, NJ: P&R Publishing, 2004.

McMillen, S. I. *None of These Diseases*. 2nd ed. Old Tappan, NJ: Fleming H. Revell, 1984.

Payne, Franklin E. *Biblical Healing for Modern Medicine*. Augusta, GA: Covenant Books, 1993.

———. *Biblical/Medical Ethics*. Milford, MI: Mott Media, 1985.

———. *God Confronts Culture: The Almost Complete Biblical and Christian Worldview*. Augusta, GA: Covenant Books, 2007.

———. *Making Biblical Decisions*. Escondido, CA: Hosanna House, 1989.

———. *What Every Christian Should Know about the AIDS Epidemic*. Augusta, GA: Covenant Books, 1991.

Ramsey, Paul. "The Indignity of 'Death with Dignity,' " *Studies Hastings Center* 2, 2 (May 1974): 47–62.

———. *The Patient as Person*. New Haven: Yale University Press, 1970.

"Report of the Heroic Measures Committee of the Presbyterian Church in America," 16th General Assembly, 1988. http://www.pcahistory.org/pca/2-378.doc.

Stob, Henry. "The Ethics of Science and Medicine." In *Ethical Reflections: Essays on Moral Themes*. Grand Rapids: Eerdmans, 1978.

Welch, Edward T. *Addictions: A Banquet in the Grave*. Phillipsburg, NJ: P&R Publishing, 2001.

———. *Blame It on the Brain? Distinguishing Chemical Imbalances, Brain Disorders, and Disobedience*. Phillipsburg, NJ: P&R Publishing, 1998.

———. *Counselor's Guide to the Brain and Its Disorders: Knowing the Difference between Disease and Sin*. Grand Rapids: Zondervan, 1991.

PART 7

CULTURE

35

FRAME'S UNIQUE CONTRIBUTIONS TO
THE CHRIST-AND-CULTURE DEBATE

P. ANDREW SANDLIN

I HAVE BEEN PRIVILEGED to introduce John Frame as a speaker on
several occasions. I always manage to tell the audience that I am never certain
which is greater: John's charity or his scholarship. In an era in which conservative Reformed scholarship seems at a nadir[1] while conservative Reformed
acrimony approaches an apex,[2] I can imagine no more apt description of
Frame's invaluable, but unfortunately rare, combination of fervent love and
stellar scholarship, nor a more needed antidote to many present dilemmas
in the Reformed theological community. I pray that this chapter, offered in
gratitude to Frame for his significant influence on and many kindnesses to
me and to countless others, will reflect that rare combination.

---

1. Frame complains in *IDSCB* that conservative Reformed theology has increasingly veered
in the direction of history and away from exegesis.

2. See *MWC* for a brief taxonomy on the many, and sometimes divisive, disputes within a
prominent wing of the conservative Reformed community in the United States. We should not
assume that all or even most in the Reformed community worldwide are theologically conservative. See the numerous nonconservative entries in David Willis and Michael Welker, eds., *Toward
the Future of Reformed Theology* (Grand Rapids: Eerdmans, 1999). For a striking example of a
boldly anti-conservative Reformed theologian, see H. M. Kuitert, *I Have My Doubts* (London:
SCM, 1992).

Frame on Culture

No one acquainted with Frame's theological corpus should be surprised that he titled his multivolume magnum opus A Theology of Lordship. Although displeased with efforts to ascertain *the* single basic motif by which to understand God, Frame argues that God's lordship over his entire creation is *a* chief motif of the Bible and, therefore, a suitable rubric under which to write a Christian theology.[3] Taking a cue from his teacher and longtime colleague Meredith Kline,[4] Frame interprets lordship as a covenantal concept by which God relates to man in both grace and law in fulfilling his purposes in the earth. Frame stands self-consciously within the Reformed tradition, and with its commitment to God's ubiquitous sovereignty, perhaps no tradition in Christendom (with the possible exception of Roman Catholicism[5]) has developed as much interest in the relationship between Christ and culture.[6] "A world and life view, a vision of the sovereignty of God and the lordship of Jesus Christ manifest in every sphere of life, a theology of the kingdom of God that transcends time and space—this is the grand design of Reformed theology at its best."[7] Frame's theology, a *reforming* Reformed program, consistently touches on cultural issues. His most sustained, explicit treatment of culture comprises part 5 of *DCL*; while scanning Frame's entire corpus, I will address this section as the major source of my assessment of his views on culture. I will first summarize Frame's views of culture. Then, in the major portion of this chapter, I will suggest three unique contributions (corresponding roughly to the normative, existential, and situational perspectives of Frame's triperspectivalism) that he makes to the Christ-and-culture debate (CCD).

Culture Defined

Culture, strictly defined, usually denotes those products of human interactivity with nature that reflect the self-conscious goal of human benefit:

3. *DKG*, 11.
4. Ibid., 11–12.
5. See the extensive works on culture by noted Roman Catholic historian Christopher Dawson. Start with *The Historic Reality of Christian Culture* (London: Routledge and Kegan Paul, 1960).
6. Ernst Troeltsch, *The Social Teaching of the Christian Churches* (New York: Harper, 1960), 2:621. Standard Reformed works include H. Henry Meeter, *The Basic Ideas of Calvinism*, 5th ed. (Grand Rapids: Kregel, 1960), and Henry Van Til, *The Calvinistic Concept of Culture*, 2nd ed. (Grand Rapids: Baker, 2001).
7. I. John Hesselink, *On Being Reformed* (Ann Arbor, MI: Servant, 1983), 111.

education, science, entertainment, technology, architecture, the arts—even such simple human products as meals, toys, and personal grooming products. Frame adds to a conventional definition a distinctly Christian element: "Creation is what God makes; culture is what we make."[8] Culture is not identical to creation; its distinctive trait is the human use of that creation for man's benefit. Culture is what we get when man intentionally employs creation for beneficial purposes. A tomato is not an aspect of culture; a pizza is. Oxygen is not an example of culture; an oxygen mask is. Creation plus man's beneficial interaction with it equals culture.

Man's preeminent, God-given task (Gen. 1:26–28) is to "turn creation into a culture, into a home for human society,"[9] under God's direction. The Reformed have traditionally labeled this task "the cultural mandate," which Frame champions. Man is God's "servant-king,"[10] ruling the earth under God's authority. The cultural mandate is, therefore, a religious task, and since "religions are totalitarian . . . govern[ing] everything,"[11] the cultural mandate is a comprehensive calling. Humanity is charged with cultivating all of life to God's glory, in harmony with God's revealed norms.

When we ponder such a comprehensive task, we might think also of the Great Commission (Matt. 28:18–20), Jesus' charge to his disciples to preach the gospel to the world, baptize converts, and disciple them for God's glory according to all that Jesus had taught. We might suppose that this Great Commission, since it contains the gospel, supersedes, or at least marginalizes, the cultural mandate; but Frame argues, perhaps surprisingly, that the Great Commission and the cultural mandate are actually two sides of the same coin.[12] Of course, the cultural mandate was established before the fall of man and the Great Commission after it; thus the Great Commission takes into account the momentous reality of man's sin, as well as his salvation from that sin by faith in Jesus Christ, but the cultural mandate persists as God's plan for humanity (especially, but not only, for godly, regenerate humanity). The massive cultural discontinuity introduced by the fall did not void the cultural mandate. It did, however, introduce the exercise of the cultural mandate by ungodly people.[13] The premier cultural conflict in history

---

8. *DCL*, 854.
9. Ibid.
10. Ibid., 856.
11. Ibid., 858.
12. Ibid., 307–11, 862.
13. Ibid., 858–59.

derives from the coexistence of two religious races, the children of Adam and the children of Jesus Christ, both of whom fulfill the cultural mandate in harmony with their own rival religious conditions, however imperfect that harmony may be. Since religions cannot be neutral with respect to culture (or anything else), Christian culture conflicts with non-Christian culture. The godly ones worship and serve the Creator; the ungodly worship and serve the creature.

This conflict does not imply that Christians have nothing to learn from unbelievers in the cultural realm or that they may never cooperate with them. Frame agrees with the Reformed tradition in affirming "common grace," God's kindness toward saved and lost irrespective of their spiritual condition.[14] God restrains evil individuals, and he grants talents and abilities—including cultural talents and abilities—to unbelievers. At times, he bestows even *greater* gifts to non-Christians, and Christians would be foolish not to avail themselves of the products of these gifts. These gifts benefit society through "scientific discoveries, produce labor-saving inventions, develop businesses that supply jobs, [and] produce works of art and entertainment."[15] The cultural antithesis is ethical and not metaphysical: it is not sinful man and his cultural activities as such that create the conflict but the activities that swerve from God-honoring purposes disclosed in the Bible. Where unbelievers' cultural activities do not violate God's Word and where they enhance the human condition, Christians may (and should) join and support those activities. The conflict emerges when both Christians and non-Christians act in the cultural realm *according to their respective spiritual conditions.* This is the inescapable conflict, not over the fact of the cultural mandate, but over the exercise of that mandate by two very different kinds of individuals.[16] Christian culture results when the Christian faith is consciously and consistently incorporated into culture by Christians.

Since, however, Christians have historically spoken with anything but consensus on the question of how they should relate to culture, it is necessary to take up how Frame plots his specific position on that dispute, before addressing his unique contributions to that debate.

14. Ibid., 859–61.
15. Ibid., 861.
16. Abraham Kuyper, *Principles of Sacred Theology,* trans. J. Hendrik De Vries (Grand Rapids: Baker, 1980), 150–54.

The Christ-and-Culture Debate

In situating his views in the CCD, Frame is content to enlist Richard Niebuhr's classic five-part classification:[17] Christ against culture; the Christ of culture; Christ above culture; Christ and culture in paradox; and Christ the transformer of culture.

The *Christ against culture* paradigm (#1) suggests that the two are antithetical; since Christians are a spiritual race ethically separate from the world, they should protect themselves from that world's culture, which stands consistently under God's judgment and is always ready to seduce them from godly submission and obedience. There is no reason to work for cultural change because, first, Christians are called to cultural separation, not engagement; second, we have no expectation of success; and finally, such engagement with the world may seduce us from following Jesus. This is the paradigm of Anabaptists and other sectors of the radical Reformation, including many evangelicals today. Frame appreciates the antithetical dimension of the *Christ against culture* paradigm (after all, there certainly is an antithesis between the godly and ungodly), but he notes that the legitimate antithesis is not between Christ and culture as such. For one thing, the world is not the culture. The term *world* in the Bible often (not always) denotes the evil system in history inspired by Satan and rebellion against God; sometimes *world* simply means the created order, whether good or bad. Culture is what man makes of the world in this latter sense. Where *world* is understood as man's rebellion (as it is frequently in 1 John, for example), Frame concludes: "Christ against the world, yes; Christ against culture, no."[18] The problem is not culture, but *sinful* culture.

The polar opposite of Christ against culture is the *Christ of culture* paradigm (#2). This paradigm is often identified with Protestant liberalism, but it has deep roots in church history, tracing back to a number of the church fathers. It is the idea that humans share in a common culture and that, since Christianity is the spiritual summit toward which the best elements in human culture point, Christians are called to find and identify with commonalities in that culture, which surrounds both believer and unbeliever. In the ancient world, this meant finding points of contact with Greek philosophy. In more recent times, the cultural commonality has included naturalism,

17. H. Richard Niebuhr, *Christ and Culture* (New York: Harper & Row, 1951).
18. *DCL*, 867.

scientism, and the inherent goodness of man. This last trait in particular, according to Frame, was implicit in the *Christ of culture* paradigm from the beginning and is its Achilles' heel: it does not take human sin into account as it should. Jesus did not come to earth chiefly to furnish an example of the best that humanity has to offer. He came to die for our sins. Culture as such is never a reliable barometer of exemplary humanity, for the simple reason that sinners tend to create sinful culture. The right kind of culture is possible when sin and its effects have been mitigated by the power of the gospel. To enmesh Christianity in culture as that culture stands, without a radical biblical critique, is to compromise God's standards for culture.

The next paradigm, *Christ above culture* (#3), which was articulated by Thomas Aquinas and is often identified with Roman Catholicism, sees both good and evil in culture but understands culture (and much else) according to a nature-grace distinction. Nature is what God gives in creation—for example, natural reason and other inherent human abilities. Grace, on the other hand, is a special *supernatural* endowment. "By our natural abilities we plow the soil, marry and raise families, achieve various kinds of earthly happiness. But to reach our highest purpose, a supernatural purpose, we need God's grace."[19] Man, the recipient of both natural and supernatural gifts, cultivates nature and in this way introduces grace into culture. Despite the fact that, Frame observes, this paradigm might be superficially appealing, it commits a serious error: it assumes that nature (natural revelation) is valid without Jesus and the Bible (special revelation). The Bible does not depict nature as essentially unspoiled and simply in need of the helping hand of grace in order to reach its highest potential. In "plow[ing] the soil, marry[ing] and rais[ing] families, [and] achiev[ing] various kinds of earthly happiness," we need God and Christ and the Bible no less than we need them in church. Grace is not a supplement to nature or to culture. All of human life must be lived to God's glory and on his explicit terms revealed in Jesus and the Bible. Christ is not to be merely the goal of culture; he must be its very foundation.

If the *Christ above culture* paradigm is standard fare among Roman Catholics, *Christ and culture in paradox* (#4) is considered a viable option among Protestants, especially Lutherans. It is often a correlate of the "Two Kingdoms" view. The two kingdoms are (in essence) the church and the world (including culture). God rules both, but he rules them in different ways. He

19. Ibid., 869.

rules the church by his Word and Spirit and gospel; he rules the world by the providence of his natural laws. The church is sacred, the sphere of the gospel; the world is secular, the sphere of the law. The world is under God's authority, but he exercises that authority in a different way than he does in the church.[20] Frame has two big problems with *Christ and culture in paradox*. First, "Scripture never speaks of natural laws in the sense of impersonal forces through which God works."[21] Although nature is not supernature, even in nature God's hand is always and directly at work. God's sovereignty exercised both inside *and* outside the church is that of continual, loving, just, and immediate care. More importantly, though, God does not establish two divergent standards of justice, one in the church and one in the world. *Christ and culture in paradox* argues that the Bible is not a standard appropriate to the world or culture, the "natural" realm. Therefore, believers should make no attempt to Christianize the culture. Christianity (the gospel and the Bible) governs the church; natural law governs the world. Frame does not object to the role of natural revelation in fashioning Christian culture, but he does object to attempts to isolate it from special revelation: "God's moral standards are one, even though they come through two media."[22] Employing special revelation as the standard for culture does not imply the coercive (political) imposition of Christianity on unbelievers. It does, however, require that Christians act culturally in a distinctively Christian way and attempt peacefully to implement the Bible's standards in the world. Frame spends considerable time critiquing the *Christ and culture in paradox* position (likely because it has recently gained an increasing foothold in the Reformed community), and in the final analysis he finds the paradigm "very confusing."[23]

The final paradigm (#5), which Niebuhr traces historically to Augustine and F. D. Maurice,[24] is *Christ the transformer of culture*, the idea, as Frame defines it, "that Christians should be seeking to transform culture according to the standards of God's Word."[25] Unlike the *Christ against culture* paradigm, it sees culture not as irremediably depraved or as irreversibly doomed, but as a legitimate object of Christianization. Unlike the *Christ of culture* view,

20. Ibid., 870–71.
21. Ibid.
22. Ibid., 872.
23. Ibid., 873.
24. Niebuhr, *Christ and Culture*, 206–29.
25. *DCL*, 873.

it posits typical ("natural") culture not as normative but as sinful and in need of redemption. Unlike *Christ above culture*, it denies the nature-grace scheme and contends that grace (the supernatural revelation of Jesus Christ and his Word) is no less necessary in the ordinary, "natural" areas of life than in the church. Unlike *Christ and culture in paradox*, it repudiates a dualism isolating gospel from law, church from world, and secular from sacred. *Christ the transformer of culture* urges Christians to labor by the power of the Holy Spirit, by the declaration of the gospel, and by fidelity to the Bible, to change gradually a sinful, rebellious culture into a righteous, submissive one, although this change will never be complete before the eternal state. In fact, Frame carefully distinguishes his views from moralism,[26] trying to save the world apart from God's grace in Jesus; from triumphalism, assuming that Christians can expect complete transformation in this life; and from pietism, believing that culture cannot be Christianized except by explicitly Christian expression: "To apply Christian standards to art . . . does not mean that we must turn our artistic works into salvation tracts." "A transformational approach does not mean that every human activity practiced by a Christian (e.g., plumbing, car repair) must be obviously, externally different from the same activities practiced by non-Christians."[27] Nor does Frame think that substandard cultural expressions by Christians (such as kitsch art and cheap music) justify adopting the world's "high" cultural standards. The cure for impoverished cultural expressions by Christians is not to adopt the more formally impressive expressions of unbelief but to improve Christian cultural expressions. Christians must transform culture, not abandon it, identify with it, or bifurcate it.

Frame's Unique Contributions

In his definition and formal treatment of the CCD, Frame operates within a standard, if older, segment of the Reformed tradition.[28] In working out the

26. The descriptive terms such as *moralism* are mine; the ideas are Frame's.
27. *DCL*, 874.
28. His formal views are not significantly different, for instance, from those of Meeter and Van Til (footnote 6). Frame is not a theonomist and does not endorse the specifics of the Christian Reconstructionist program. He supports, however, the theonomic impulse to transform culture according to biblical standards. See his "The One, the Many and Theonomy," in *Theonomy: A Reformed Critique*, ed. William S. Barker and W. Robert Godfrey (Grand Rapids: Zondervan, 1990), 89–99.

implications of his cultural views, however, he makes at least three unique, if not at all points exclusive, contributions to the CCD that warrant careful attention.

The Normative Perspective: *Sola Scriptura*, Not Repristination

The cultural counterpart to Frame's unflagging devotion to *formal* biblical inerrancy and authority[29] is his *material* opposition to theologically conservative repristination projects. Repristination derives from the primitivist impulse, coming in two varieties: (1) the belief that earlier times were superior to our own (chronological primitivism), and (2) the belief that more developed and civilized societies are inferior to less developed and civilized ones (cultural primitivism).[30] Primitivism of both varieties, and usually intertwined, has a long history. The ancient Greeks were among the early primitivists who cast their eyes backward longingly at the previous ages when, it was supposed, humanity lived together peacefully, eating honey and nuts, eschewing private property, holding everything in common, sharing sexual and sensual delights in an earthly bliss, and enjoying harmony with the animals.[31] Theology has not been exempt from this primitivist impulse. Theological primitivists today look back with wistfulness at a supposed golden age of theology—for Eastern Orthodoxy that age is the early undivided church, for the Roman Catholics the medieval era and the dominance of Thomism, for Protestants the Reformation, for Pentecostals the Azusa Street Revival of 1906–15, and so forth. When such primitivists move beyond contemplation and commit themselves to activism, they generally undertake some sort of repristination project, the attempt to recover and revive desirable elements of the bygone golden age in the hopes of reversing the apostasy of our time.

Frame offers recent examples of such repristination in the Reformed community. Although, for example, he commends Francis Schaeffer, Os Guinness, David Wells, and Kenneth Myers, all of whom have thoughtfully engaged the CCD, he disagrees with the propensity of each to look

---

29. John M. Frame, "Scripture Speaks for Itself," in *God's Inerrant Word*, ed. John Warwick Montgomery (Minneapolis: Bethany, 1973), 178–200. See also *DCL*, 156–75. Frame's full bibliology is scheduled to appear in the upcoming installment of the Theology of Lordship series, titled *The Doctrine of the Word of God*.

30. Arthur O. Lovejoy and George Boas, *Primitivism and Related Ideas in Antiquity* (Baltimore and London: Johns Hopkins, 1935), 1–22.

31. George Boas, "Primitivism," in *Dictionary of the History of Ideas*, ed. Philip P. Wiener (New York: Charles Scribner's, 1973), 3:578–85.

back to a specific earlier historical period on which to pattern present cultural projects. Schaeffer, Frame observes, sees the ancient Greek world as embracing objective standards of truth, and the modern world since the nineteenth century as eroding those standards by an increasing sub-jectivism and relativism: Hegel, Kierkegaard, and Nietzsche spoiled the golden age of objective truth. Similarly, Guinness identifies the pessi-mistic humanism of the 1960s as the pivotal apostate era, a transition from rationalism to irrationalism, a dire movement into the abyss of a post-Christian culture. Wells, on the other hand, situates the present era in its subjectivism, experientialism, professionalism, consumerism, and pragmatism as dramatically different from *all* previous eras. Finally, Myers indicts today's popular culture as a leading culprit, an apostasy from the high culture of the days of yore with its stress on transcendence and absolutes, with "roots in antiquity."[32] In each case, the Reformed cultural critic criticizes the present with a recourse to the past, depicts some period in the past as a lost golden era whose virtues we should revive, and even posits the past as to some degree a standard in assessing contemporary cultural trends.

Although not unappreciative of the gains of the past, Frame in his unflinching devotion to *sola Scriptura*, "the doctrine that Scripture, and only Scripture, has the final word on everything,"[33] will have none of this repristination. The past is not a standard, even a subordinate standard, in judging the present or planning the future. "Scripture alone" applies to cultural projects no less than the church life: tradition has no authority in the cultural mandate. Only the Bible does.[34]

This distinctively *sola Scriptura* cultural program puts Frame at odds with both cultural conservatism and cultural progressivism. Cultural conservatives, as we have seen, wish to import the past into the present. Cultural progressives deny any externally binding authority of any kind and trust inevitable historical progress to impel their direction.[35] Against cultural conservatism, Frame repudiates repristination projects; against cultural progressivism, he champions biblical authority. Frame rejects both forms of chronological snobbery—that form which dismisses the

---

32. *DCL*, 883, citing Myers.
33. *CWM*, 177.
34. *DCL*, 891.
35. Nicholas K. Kittrie, *The War against Authority* (Baltimore and London: Johns Hopkins, 1995).

past and deifies the present, as well as that form which reveres the past and reviles the present.

Following Cornelius Van Til, Frame resists the temptation to posit "major turning points" in history by which to explain the cultural depravity of the present or recent past.[36] Aside from our Lord's earthly redemptive work, the only "turning point" in history of any consequence is the fall of man. No period is culturally privileged on the ground of its placement in linear history, for the simple reason that sin is no respecter of historical periods. Even if we uphold Calvin's Geneva or Puritan New England as exemplary, if flawed, Christian culture, their shining examples derive from the fact that they were Christian, not that they are (from our standpoint) old.

For Frame, history is not (for instance) a decline from a legitimate rationalism to an illegitimate irrationalism, but a constant tension between both rationalism and irrationalism, each of which sinful man adopts at one time or another depending on the rebellious exigencies of the moment. The rationalism of ancient Greeks such as Plato is no less dangerous than the irrationalism of nineteenth-century existentialists such as Nietzsche, and Christian repristination projects reviving rationalist aspects of ancient Greece in efforts to halt the spread of recent irrationalism are akin to immunologists prescribing tuberculosis as a cure for AIDS. Both are potentially fatal, and a disease is not less pernicious simply because of its antiquity. Indeed, Frame hints that the older cultural diseases are likely more dangerous to us today: "We tend to discount older exponents of non-Christian values, viewing them with the halo that comes with long cultural acceptance. For that reason, these older thinkers are often more dangerous than those that are more contemporary and more obviously anti-Christian."[37]

Frame's *sola Scriptura* paradigm as it pertains to culture is increasingly the minority report among today's conservatives. In fact, it is hard to think of *any* major theologically conservative participants in the CCD who do not espouse some sort of repristination. Both *Touchstone* (Episcopal, Anglo-Catholic, and Roman Catholic) and *First Things* (Roman Catholic) magazines, conservative flagships in the CCD, rely heavily on tradition.[38] Numerous Reformed culturalists, in addition to those already mentioned,

36. *DCL*, 886–87.
37. Ibid., 896.
38. The cultural program of the emergent church, to the extent that it is thoughtfully articulated, repudiates repristination, but it is not theologically conservative. See Phyllis Tickle, *The Great Emergence* (Grand Rapids: Baker, 2008), and Tim Conder, "The Existing Church/Emerg-

are reviving the older natural law tradition and do not offer the Bible's standards as a source for their cultural program.[39] The problem is not natural revelation. Frame's *sola Scriptura* does not imply that he limits man's knowledge to the Bible.[40] Nonetheless, the ethics of the Bible, available, although less fully, in natural revelation, are God's standard for the world. Nor does Frame propose a repristination of his own—the Bible-based society of the American Puritans, for instance. He is not looking backward in history for usable patterns of Christian culture. He is looking all the way back—and forward—to the Bible.

Frame's normative perspective on the cultural mandate and his resultant refusal to embrace repristination projects have specific, unique implications for the CCD. One example will suffice. Liberated from the restraints of repristination, Frame employs cultural strategies inaccessible to other conservatives. Since he is no more dispositionally suspicious of the present than the past, he can assess the pros and cons of today's culture on their own merit, apart from any chronological privileging or de-privileging. A prime example is his aversion to an exclusively "high" culture and to its frequent offspring, cultural elitism.[41] High culture (classical art, music, and literature) has almost always had its counterpart in "low" culture (folk music, peasant dances, and orally transmitted morality tales). The former was usually the province of the wealthy, educated, and privileged, while the latter the monopoly of the masses. Over time, and particularly in late modernity,[42] the ubiquity of visual and audio technologies has created a much larger demand for low, or "pop," culture, which is nearly always accessible. High culture has not been replaced, but marginalized.

Frame observes that in the last century, American evangelicals reengaged culture after a twenty-year hiatus (1925–45) that coincided with a spike in conservative anti-intellectualism. This accident of history led

---

ing Church Matrix," in *An Emergent Manifesto of Hope*, ed. Doug Pagitt and Tony Jones (Grand Rapids: Baker, 2007), 98–107.

39. The conservative Reformed advocates of a social order based on natural law tend to be influenced by Meredith Kline's view of society as a common-grace phenomenon. See his *Kingdom Prologue* (Overland Park, KS: Two Age, 2000), 155–60. On the prominent role of natural law within the Reformed tradition, see Stephen J. Grabill, *Rediscovering the Natural Law in Reformed Theological Ethics* (Grand Rapids: Eerdmans, 2006).

40. *DCL*, 164–65.

41. Ibid., 889–93.

42. But see Peter Gay's thesis on the elitist roots of movies in *Modernism* (New York and London: W. W. Norton, 2008), 358–91.

culturally savvy evangelicals to crave intellectual and cultural respectability, sometimes at the expense of biblical fidelity. At the least, it stimulated them to embrace high culture and devalue folk and pop culture, which they identified with the dreaded anti-intellectualism they were trying to escape. They became cultural elitists, opting for high culture. The problem, Frame notes, is that the high culture they were trying to recover was not especially biblical and, in fact, was no more biblical than the popular culture against which they were revolting. Ironically, by craving high culture and cultural elitism, evangelicals sometimes *lowered* their biblical standards.

Frame does not, however, counter cultural elitism with cultural populism (pop culture is no more valuable, as such, than high culture) but with a program that embraces all levels of culture in conformity with biblical standards. Christians should engage all areas of culture, rock music no less than classical music, TV no less than ballet, finger painting no less than museum art. Cultural transformation means transforming *all* of culture.

It is obvious that cultural elitism, on the other hand, severely limits the range of the cultural mandate. By its very nature, elitism excludes the vast majority. Even were the repristination programs of the evangelical cultural elitists wildly successful, they would impact only a fraction of the population, the vast majority of which never has been and never will be—and probably never should be—attracted to high culture. By contrast, Frame's eagerness to embrace and transform culture at all levels and among all classes dramatically increases the possibility of Christianization.

One gets the impression that Frame would support culturally aware Christians in heavy-metal bands, martial arts, children's crafts, clothing design, stock-car racing, and even street art, all in fulfilling the cultural mandate, as long as they conformed their activity to the Bible and brought glory to God. One need not participate in classical music, sculpture, architecture, or opera to fulfill the cultural mandate. Frame's extensive interest in movies, for example, reflects his view that popular culture is a fit vehicle for cultural reclamation by Christians.[43]

---

43. *DCL*, 893–902; see also his numerous movie reviews at http://www.frame-poythress.org/frame_books.htm#theologyatthemovies.

The effect of Frame's *sola Scriptura*[44] approach is a comprehensive cultural strategy that directly touches every aspect of culture, not one that only indirectly filters down to the common dregs from the upper echelons. His is a theoretical framework(!) for simultaneous, top-to-bottom cultural interaction within the *Christ the transformer of culture* paradigm.

The Existential Perspective: Diversity, Not Uniformity

The unique cultural application of Frame's normative perspective noted above leads to its counterpart in his existential perspective. In a discussion of the individual Christian's role in cultural transformation, he writes:

> These decisions [of where and how to minister culturally] should also be based on one's gifts, calling, station in life. I do not believe, with the Christian "culturalists," that every Christian, or even every mature Christian, has an *obligation* to attend art exhibits, concerts, films, etc. Christians should seek to influence the world for Christ in *some* way: that is the Great Commission. But the precise way in which they reach out to the world may differ greatly from one believer to another. My brother-in-law is pastor of a church in the inner city of Philadelphia. He does not normally go to films, dramas, or art exhibits. But he is definitely "in" the world, the real world, and he ministers to it with all the strength God provides him. A knowledge of entertainment media would be of little use to him in his ministry, and I would be the last person to urge him to become "culturally aware."[45]

Frame takes seriously the integrity and diversity of the individual Christian's vocation or calling, but he does not directly identify the Great Commission and cultural mandate as that calling.[46] With respect to calling, the Great Commission and cultural mandate are principally aspects of the situational, not the existential, perspective. They are the collective calling of believers, the tasks of the Christian community. No single Christian can fulfill the Great Commission and cultural mandate; he is dependent on his fellow believers in the church to assist him. In other words, although each

---

44. In labeling Frame's project *sola Scriptura*, I do not imply that Reformed proponents of cultural repristination do not also affirm *sola Scriptura* but that they do not allow its full implications to shape their cultural projects as Frame does.

45. *DCL*, 894, emphases in original.

46. Ibid., 311–13.

Christian is called in some way to contribute to these missions, he was never meant to fulfill those tasks in isolation.

In the inescapable interface between the situational perspective and the existential perspective as they both relate to the CCD, this means that the church and larger Christian community should never expect or demand of individuals a uniformity of calling. Too often they do. Every church and Christian ministry devises and develops its own distinctives, and it is tempted to encourage all Christians to conform to that unique emphasis. The "Christian 'culturalists,' " as Frame calls them, are inclined to expect all Christians to participate in some specific cultural task that happens to be the cause-of-the-month. Christian political activists, educators, businesspersons, technologists, and artists may myopically suppose that theirs is the principal (or, worse yet, exclusive) sphere by which God intends to transform culture at a particular historical juncture. In the 1970s and 1980s, for example, the most visible form of Christian cultural activity was politics, notably of the conservative variety.[47] Although Christians were quietly engaged in other aspects of the cultural mandate, the great push was for transformation by politics. Real cultural action was in conservative politics, and other spheres were at the margins. This mind-set, which aped the strategy of the 1960s political Left, fostered an impoverished exercise of the cultural mandate and did not meet the goals it set for itself. The radical Left of the 1960s, conversely, had already divested its hope in politics and reinvested it in culture. This, in fact, is the root of postmodernism: radicalism by cultural rather than specifically political revolution.[48] Alternatively, we know now that Christian political victories of the 1970s and 1980s did not, for the most part, translate into cultural transformation, and we are paying a high price for our single-dimensional strategy. The redirected 1960s radicals got there before us. We have some catching up to do. Culture trumps politics.

Attention to Frame's warnings about elitism, as well as his insistence on the cultural effectiveness of fidelity to ordinary, day-to-day Christian calling, would have spared us some grief. Unfortunately, the overemphasis on political activism was accompanied by an underemphasis on the cultural implications of individual vocation. The effect of this imbalance was despair

47. Richard V. Pierard, "The New Religious Right in American Politics," in *Evangelicalism and Modern America*, ed. George Marsden (Grand Rapids: Eerdmans, 1984), 161–74.
48. Steven Best and Douglas Kellner, *The Postmodern Turn* (New York and London: Guilford, 1997), 2–37.

when it was discovered that politics is not the tail that wags the cultural dog, but the other way around.[49] Had churches complemented political action not just with recapturing the arts (both high and pop) and other highly visible areas of culture, but also with Christians conscious of the revolutionary cultural impact of their modest daily vocations, they could have avoided much of the despair over the cultural failures of their political activism—failures that could not but occur. Moreover, Christians would have been investing greater energy in Christ-honoring friendships, godly families, Christian education from preschool to graduate school, mercy ministries, and other spheres that, although generally less visible and glamorous than politics, yield more permanent cultural transformation.

Christians of all stations should be persevering, aware of their role in gospel declaration and cultural reclamation, without feeling inept because they can do little more than be faithful in the mundane, day-to-day tasks God has given them. The Christian mother rearing young children at home, for instance, is not called to engage in some additional, more explicit, cultural tasks (1 Tim. 5:14). Rearing her children *is* her cultural task, and it, no less—and sometimes much more—than Christian politics and moviemaking, contributes to cultural transformation.

Frame's warm pastoral concern for the individual is exhibited in this thesis. Far from an ivory-tower theologian, he is intent that theology passes the rubber-meets-the-road test.[50] Does our theology benefit the ordinary Christian? Frame's does, and in benefiting the ordinary Christian, the implications of Frame's existential perspective also contribute to the CCD.

The Situational Perspective: Bridges, Not Gates

From a theoretical standpoint, the aspect of Frame's theology that has generated the most controversy in the conservative Reformed community is his conviction that the situational perspective should not be overshadowed by the normative perspective. The Reformed tend to be heavy on normative standards but less occupied by their unique situational responsibilities.[51] This community stands unreservedly for the verbal inspiration and inerrancy of

---

49. Paul Weyrich, "The Moral Minority," *Christianity Today* online, http://www.ctlibrary.com/ct/1999/september6/9ta044.html, Sept. 6, 1999.

50. John M. Frame, "Reflections of a Lifetime Theologian," *Christian Culture* (May 2008): 4, 6–7, also in this festschrift.

51. *DKG*, 89–90.

the Bible—that is one of the chief traits that make it conservative.[52] The Bible is the norm for Christian life and the church.[53] This Reformed devotion to biblical authority is not unique among conservatives. What *is* unique is the extensive scope of the regulative character with which the Reformed vest the Bible.[54] The Bible was given not just to announce salvation; it is calculated also to govern every aspect of our lives.[55] The Reformed community's conviction about the covenantal unity of the ethical stipulations of the Old and New Testaments,[56] in addition to its emphasis on the Bible's regulative character, translates into prioritizing the normativity of Scripture in the Christian life. Frame in no way disputes this emphasis, but he fears that in stressing the normative side of the Christian life, many of his Reformed colleagues underemphasize the situational side: they do not spend sufficient time pondering how Scripture as norm should effectively interface with the surrounding culture. If theological liberals compromise the normative character of the faith in stressing the situational,[57] the imbalance is reversed for the theological conservatives, notably the Reformed.

This imbalance comes to the fore in the question of how the church relates to the wider culture as it constructs and conducts its own ministry.[58] Frame takes as a prominent example church music, a topic about which he is particularly interested since he is a trained, accomplished musician. Frame's (nuanced) support for contemporary worship music (CWM) has possibly elicited more criticism within the Reformed ranks than any other of his specific positions. For many of the Reformed, CWM is the province of evangelicals, charismatics, and Pentecostals, not Calvinists, yet Frame has dared to defend it!

---

52. John D. Woodbridge, *Biblical Authority: A Critique of the Rogers-McKim Proposal* (Grand Rapids: Zondervan, 1982), 49–140.

53. Frame, in fact, outstrips many of his colleagues' commitment to the scope of biblical authority by arguing that natural revelation is not sufficient to govern culture (*DCL*, 951–56). The Bible should govern culture.

54. Richard E. Muller, "A Lutheran Professor Educated at Westminster Theological Seminary Looks for Similarities and Dissimilarities," *Concordia Theological Quarterly* 61, 1–2 (1997): 85–89.

55. *DKG*, 12–18, 61–64.

56. Knox Chamblin, "The Law of Moses and the Law of Christ," in *Continuity and Discontinuity*, ed. John S. Feinberg (Westchester, IL: Crossway, 1988), 181–202. On the historical roots of this Reformed distinctive, see Jaroslav Pelikan, *Reformation of Church and Dogma (1300–1700)* (Chicago and London: University of Chicago Press, 1984), 203–17.

57. Donald E. Miller, *The Case for Liberal Christianity* (San Francisco: Harper & Row, 1981), 33.

58. *DCL*, 904–8.

He takes on all the major Reformed criticisms of CWM.[59] To the criticism that CWM assimilates the worst standards of culture, Frame counters that it is "maddeningly difficult"[60] to specify how musical standards can be stringently assessed by recourse to the Bible. Are electric guitars unsuitable for public worship? If so, why? Are folk tunes with scriptural lyrics prohibited? Why? The Bible forbids neither electric guitars nor folk tunes. To the argument that CWM is too simple or that it "dumbs down the faith," Frame documents that CWM does not necessarily "dumb down"; and even if CWM is sometimes simple, the Bible does not teach that worship music (or worship in general) should be as intellectual as possible.[61] To the charge that CWM reflects poor quality, Frame rejoins that quality must not be defined abstractly but against some standard, and if that standard is the extent to which church music faithfully communicates the Word of God, the charge of "poor quality" against CWM is often misguided.[62] And so on. When subjected to the acid test of *sola Scriptura*, most objections to CWM dissolve.

Undergirding Frame's defense of CWM, however, is his belief that cogent communication of the truth is a crucial part of what the church is all about, and the church does not communicate merely by declaring (or singing). It must account for culture, the culture of the audience and their reception of the Christian message, in its task of communicating. People need to *understand* and resonate with what is being communicated (1 Cor. 14), and CWM does help many people in our culture to understand and resonate. Moreover, what will communicate effectively in one culture or time period will not be effective in others. That is to say, modes of communication are culture-dependent.[63] This assertion may gall many of the Reformed, committed, as they tend to be, to the normative perspective above other factors, but the normative will accomplish little if it is not meshed within the situational. The Bible will not actually *function* as an authority if people do not understand what it is teaching. This implies an ironic fact, although Frame, to my knowledge, has never quite stated it this way: a refusal to take the situational perspective with utmost seriousness diminishes the normative perspective—*if we neglect to ponder the issue of communicating the truth, we subtly, if unintentionally, undermine biblical authority.* This is the last error

59. See his full treatment in *CWM*.
60. *DCL*, 905.
61. *CWM*, 99–105.
62. Ibid., 107–9.
63. *DCL*, 906.

that Bible-affirming Calvinists wish to be guilty of, but they are guilty of it if they dismiss or diminish the situational perspective.

At the root of the indispensability of communication in worship is the church's objective to edify.[64] We worship publicly not only (or even mainly) to benefit ourselves but to benefit others, although God's glory, of course, is our chief objective. In worship, neither the normative perspective nor the existential perspective may overshadow the situational perspective. Since each of us has a distinctive personality and history and viewpoint, he is bound to reflect certain preferences that he brings to public worship. This means that, if a prime goal of public worship is to edify our fellow believers (and minister to the unbelievers present), each of us is called to sacrifice his own preferences in deference to others. We are *all* obliged to bend a little bit so that *all* will hear and see the Bible's truth communicated in ways that benefit *all*. With respect to church music, this sacrifice dictates that "unless it be shown to be inappropriate for worship, everyone's music should be heard: old people's and young people's music; European, African-American, and other ethnic music; complex music and simple music. This is how we defer to one another—serve one another—in the body of Jesus Christ."[65] Diversity of church music is a critical means of edifying the body—the entire body, not just the believers who are "like us."

What is true of CWM pertains more broadly. As the church relates to society, it must find points of contact—not so much theological contact as cultural contact—which translates partly into effective communication, by which believers sacrifice their own standards and preferences to benefit their fellow Christians and the unconverted. As a result, we have no reason to assume that in *our* culture, the United States early in the twenty-first century, Frame would dismiss out of hand (for example) sermons utilizing PowerPoint and movie clips, dramatic productions visualizing the gospel and other biblical truths, and innovative liturgies that speak immediately and directly to the congregants. Frame has no interest in elevating tradition as such, no matter how sacred and beloved, and he endorses groundbreaking procedures, techniques, and media that faithfully communicate the Bible. But neither is he eager to alienate older congregants and members, so there must be diversity in public worship. He calls on all Christians to sacrifice their own preferences for the sake of the gospel (1 Cor. 9:19–23).

64. Ibid., 905.
65. *CWM*, 25.

Frame invites Christians to confront the reality that the church must relate to culture not merely "out there" in society but also within its own four walls every Sunday (and at other times). In defending the antithesis between the church and the world, conservative Christians sometimes utter slogans such as, "The church must protect itself from the culture," or, "Our apostasy is due to our inviting the culture into the church." If these sentiments are shorthand for, "The church must protect itself from depravity in the surrounding society," they are correct. But as they stand, such assertions do not account for the fact that the influence of culture on the church is inescapable—and undesirable. It is inescapable: language itself is a cultural product, and a church that employs language has already felt the impact of the wider culture (even sign language in an all-deaf church is culturally conditioned!). One hears the anecdote about churches that, in a Herculean effort to quash all but the normative perspective, do nothing in worship but read the Bible. But the Bible they are reading is a translation, a cultural product if there ever was one, and even if every congregant flawlessly read the Bible's original languages of Greek, Hebrew, and Aramaic, in hearing that Word read they would bring to it cultural assumptions by which they would mentally interpret the words they were hearing.[66] The church simply cannot escape culture.

Nor should it. The sacred task of the church is to glorify God by evangelizing and discipling the nations. Every nation, every people, every *person*, embodies a culture. To evangelize and disciple is always to assume a historical context. We are not disembodied spirits, detached from history, and we cannot speak in a de-culturated way. The church must enter intensively but judiciously into its own surrounding culture(s), pondering, scrutinizing, assessing, always considering effective cultural means by which to fulfill the Great Commission and cultural mandate. As agents of cultural transformation, Christians are charged to reclaim culture not by preaching a de-cultured message and exhorting their hearers to leave culture behind to follow Jesus (as if that option were even available to us), but, rather, by taking the eternal *and* historical *and* transcultural—and, therefore, eminently *cultural*[67]—Word of God to the heart of every culture, finding every

---

66. Gerhard Ebeling, *The Problem of Historicity* (Philadelphia: Fortress, 1967), 8–33.

67. Philip Edgcumbe Hughes, "The Truth of Scripture and the Problem of Historical Relativity," in *Scripture and Truth*, ed. D. A. Carson and John D. Woodbridge (Grand Rapids: Zondervan, 1983), 173–94.

appropriate avenue for effectively communicating the redemptive message of Jesus Christ.

Our task is not to erect iron gates at the church doors to protect against cultural influences. Rather, it is to fashion bridges by which to invite those influences *into* the church;[68] assess which of them conform to Scripture and which do not; discover which are suitable vehicles for effective biblical communication; and, in undertaking that communication and in *living* the truth both in and *as* a culture (2 Cor. 3:1–3), gradually transform culture by the power of the Holy Spirit.

Frame's situational perspective as it pertains to the CCD includes the church's dedication to deep cultural immersion by which God's people sacrificially communicate infallible biblical truth to the body of Christ and to their sinful world.

Conclusion

Missiologists (theologians of "mission") have increasingly wrestled with the complexities of the interface between church and culture.[69] Frame's principal contributions to the CCD outlined in this chapter flow from his nearly unprecedented wedding of (1) an unwavering conception of biblical authority to (2) an uncompromising insistence on cultural relevance. The most vocal proponents of verbal inspiration and inerrancy, with rare exception,[70] are not known for their passionate attempts to speak and practice the truth in culturally relevant ways. Conversely, missiologists and other disciples of a culturally sensitive Christian message are not generally among the champions of an undiluted biblical authority.[71] Frame refuses to compromise either biblical authority or cultural relevance, fusing them into a potent weapon by which to transform culture.

68. *DCL*, 907.

69. Simon Barrington-Ward, "Theology of Mission," in *Westminster Dictionary of Christian Theology*, eds., Alan Richardson and John Bowden (Philadelphia: Westminster, 1983), 372–75. For an update of this debate, see *Church between Gospel and Culture*, ed. George R. Hunsberger and Craig Van Gelder (Grand Rapids: Eerdmans, 1996), and Darrell Guder, ed., *Missional Church* (Grand Rapids: Eerdmans, 1998).

70. Examples include Carl F. H. Henry and R. J. Rushdoony. Yet neither spent much time, as Frame has, suggesting concrete, practical ways for the church to interact relevantly with culture.

71. Lesslie Newbigin, arguably the most influential missiologist in the twentieth century and a valuable contributor to the CCD, explicitly denied the Bible's infallibility. See his *Proper Confidence* (Grand Rapids: Eerdmans, 1995), 89.

Frame's triperspectivalism contributes uniquely to the CCD. His unwavering *sola Scriptura* (normative perspective) repudiates repristination projects and presses for biblical standards in all areas of culture, high, low, and in between. His commitment to the integrity of each believer's calling (existential perspective) unleashes a diversity of godly cultural effects, even if not every individual is directly engaged in cultural tasks. His accent on effective communication and edification (situational perspective) boldly champions the church's immersion in culture and the culture's immersion in the church—not ethical immersion, but pedagogical immersion.

Amid a creeping traditionalism on the one hand and a radical revisionism on the other, Frame has stressed the binding authority of the immutable Bible (normative) declared by diversely gifted Christians (existential) with an utter willingness to sacrifice themselves for the wider church and the world (situational) to transform culture for God's glory.

36

PASSIONATELY DEMONSTRATING TRUTH: TRIANGULATING CULTURAL RESTORATION

JEFFERY J. VENTRELLA

"THEOLOGY AS APPLICATION":[1] this single phrase unlocks a plethora of possibilities; it is at once liberating, motivating, and direction-al.[2] If indeed theology *is* application, reflecting the Lord and his attributes of control, authority, and presence,[3] then one application of this theology must include the public square. That inclusion must also, at multiple levels, be "triangular."[4]

Demonstrating this reality is the burden of this chapter.[5] In par-ticular, does Frame's triperspectivalism as applied to jurisprudence form

1. *DKG*, 84.
2. Note the "triangle": liberating (situational), motivating (personal), and directional (normative).
3. This triad is fundamental to Frame's theology of lordship. See, e.g., *DCL*, 21–24.
4. Throughout this chapter, the terms *triangular, triangulate, triangulating, triangle*, etc., should be taken as shorthand parlance for Frame's triperspectival approach to theology.
5. Although this chapter seeks to show the pertinence of Frame's formulations, one should not confuse extolling these theories with honoring the man. Certainly, one deliciously appro-priate way to honor this man, someone who has assiduously labored to convince the church of "theology as application," is to demonstrate that his theological formulations "have traction" in God's world. That being said, honoring the man qua man should not be overlooked. John Frame is a man of God who has consistently, compassionately, and competently (note the triangle!)

855

a conceptual and methodological foundation for restoring the public square? Moreover, do Frame's triangles—employed strategically—equip, envision, and educate[6] citizens and legal advocates to "passionately demonstrate truth"[7] in the public square? In short, can one triangulate cultural restoration?

TRIANGULATING PUBLIC ETHICS: PRELIMINARY CONSIDERATIONS

Triangulating Ethics in the Public Square: Why Bother?

At the outset, one should consider whether an exercise to triangulate public justice is simply that: a mere academic exercise devoid of real-life opportunity. Perhaps a jurisprudent with too much free time can show academically that triperspectivalism can somehow relate theoretically to the real world. Does this showing actually matter? Should it matter? Would it be meaningful? Would it be relevant?

In fact, not only is public justice amenable to triangulation, but public justice greatly benefits at multiple levels when Frame's insights are applied to it. As will be shown, this application brings clarity, balance, and progress to such efforts. And because theology is application, it is ethically essential.

As Frame notes, he began pondering and developing his scheme when he saw how his mentor, Cornelius Van Til, employed a triangle of sorts to explain ethics.[8] Van Til shows (unintentionally?) that the *ought* of theistic ethics is in fact triangular:

> The individual believer has a comprehensive task. His is the task of ex-terminating evil from the whole universe. He must begin this program in himself. As a king reinstated, it is his first battle to fight sin within his own heart. This will remain his first battle till his dying day. [person]
>
> We must go one step further. It is our duty not only to seek to destroy evil in ourselves and in our fellow Christians, but it is our further duty to seek to destroy evil in our fellow man. [situation]

---

identified, stewarded, and exercised the gifts of God in service to God for the glory of God. In so doing, as an uncommonly gracious friend and mentor, he has incarnated both love of God and love of neighbor.

6. Note the triangle: *equip* (situation), *educate* (norm), and *envision* (person).

7. Note the triangle: *passionately* (personal), *demonstrate* (situational), and *truth* (normative).

8. See, e.g., *CVT*, 203.

Still further we must note that our task with respect to the destruction of evil is not done if we have sought to fight sin itself everywhere we see it. We have the further obligation to destroy the consequences of sin in this world as far as we can.[9] [norm]

Van Til's blunt rhetoric, "destroy evil," "exterminating evil," sounds almost like swashbuckling triumphalism. Yet destroying evil, as Van Til formulated it, is a practical and necessary ethical mandate,[10] not limited to matters of the heart, interpersonal conflicts, or the local church. Rather, the lordship of Christ demands that even the structures of culture be transformed from evil to good to the extent providentially feasible. As D. A. Carson explains:

> [Yet], it is possible so to focus on the rescue and regeneration of *individuals* that we fail to see the temporally good things we can do to improve and transform some social *structures*. One does not abolish slavery by doing nothing more than helping individual slaves. Christian educational and academic *structures* may help countless thousands develop a countercultural way of looking at all reality under the Lordship of Christ. Sometimes a disease can be knocked out; sometimes sex traffic can be considerably reduced; sometimes slavery can be abolished in a region; sometimes engagement in the arts can produce wonderful work that inspires a new generation. . . . More importantly, doing good to the city [Jer. 29], doing good to all people . . . is part of our responsibility as God's redeemed people in this time of tension between the "already" and the "not yet."[11]

Again, why bother? Because Christ's lordship demands it. The question thus becomes, What hath the triangle wrought for this mandate? Much, as will be shown.

9. Cornelius Van Til, *Christian Theistic Ethics* (Phillipsburg, NJ: Presbyterian and Reformed, 1980), 86–87.

10. Indeed, the destruction of evil should be a proper focus of spiritual disciplines such as prayer. Jesus' model prayer includes this specific petition: "Deliver us from evil" (Matt. 6:13), a petition Scripture evidently anticipates being answered in history to some measure as correlative to Jesus' mission: "The reason the Son of God appeared was to destroy the works of the devil" (1 John 3:8b). Also, "The God of peace will soon crush Satan under your feet" (Rom. 16:20), and, "For he must reign until he has put all his enemies under his feet" (1 Cor. 15:25; unless otherwise indicated, all Scripture quotations are from the ESV).

11. D. A. Carson, *Christ and Culture Revisited* (Grand Rapids: Eerdmans, 2008), 217–18 (footnotes omitted; emphasis added).

Beyond Geometry: Triangles for Cultural Engagement?

By way of preface, note Paul's teaching regarding cultural engagement. Paul's teaching, particularly Romans 1:18–32, verifies that cultural engagement will involve law in its many forms. This can be seen most succinctly from his analysis of truth's encounter with the world. This encounter produces a predictable pattern in history, a pattern that expresses itself culturally, and ultimately implicates the law of the culture. Paul reasons as follows:

- Conscience: man suppresses, not obliterates, the truth in unrighteousness.[12]
- Conversion: man exchanges "the truth" for "the lie."[13]
- Communion (spiritual): man worships and serves with creation as the object, not the Creator.[14]
- Conduct (ethics):[15] man practices unrighteousness.[16]
- Culture (law): man approves of unrighteousness.[17]

This pattern culminates in the approval of unrighteous practices. This is why the culture's law is implicated and must be a concern of any Bible-believing Christian. According to Paul, paganism presses its practices seeking approval, and in doing so brings into play the cultural icons that grant approval, including the law. The question, therefore, is not whether the law will be involved; the question is whether the extant law will approve righteousness or unrighteousness. The law and the public square are inherently a Christian concern.

The question then becomes: who approves? The answer is triangular. In Western culture, approval is granted, generally speaking, by the "robes of the culture." In other words, institutions exist that are recognized as supplying that culture's approval or law. In the West, these robes include the academy (classroom), the judiciary (courtroom), and the clergy (confession

---

12. Rom. 1:18.
13. Rom. 1:25 NKJV. Note the parallel between "the truth" and "the lie" as the articular is used, which is unfortunately obscured by many English translations.
14. Rom. 1:25.
15. Ethics correlates with theology and man's response to theology, worship: man becomes like the idols he makes (Ps. 135:18).
16. Rom. 1:32.
17. Ibid.

room). Note that this triad is triperspectival. The academy supplies the culture with norms, ascribing what is "right" and "wrong." The judiciary applies those norms to particular situations. The clergy absolves or accuses the individual.

Note the following examples, which fall under the rubric: "The Approval of Evil Practices: Romans 1:32 and the Robes of Culture."

Academy-norm-orthodoxy.[18] The academy is the robe that declares what is culturally "right" and what is culturally "wrong." The "knowledge" the academy imparts is predominantly normative. However, because natural man suppresses the truth, often this robe articulates a norm that likewise inverts or perverts truth. It is "knowledge" falsely so-called.[19] The Left evidently (at least implicitly) understands the potent role this robe plays in influencing the culture. A few examples will suffice:

> Every child in America entering school at the age of five is *mentally ill* because he comes to school with certain allegiances to our Founding Fathers, toward our elected officials, toward his parents, toward a belief in a supernatural being, and toward the sovereignty of this nation as a separate entity. *It's up to you as teachers to make all these sick children well*—by creating the international child of the future.[20]

> Long before the cultural revolution broke out at street level in the 1960's, Kinsey spoke to overflow crowds in *universities* across the nation and the world, persuading them that traditional sexual norms were false

18. In an effort to better pedagogically describe and utilize triperspectivalism for equipping Christian law students, the three perspectives were labeled orthodoxy—norm, orthopraxis—situation, and orthopathos—person. This latter term, a neologism, was developed during informal discussions between Frame and the author in August 2002 in conjunction with Frame's participation as faculty for the Blackstone Legal Fellowship. This effort flowed from the conviction that cultural engagement must include passionate, heart-rooted efforts, unlike the self-righteous hypocritical actions of the ranking "legal experts" of the day, the Pharisees. See Mark 7:6b: "This people honors me with their lips, but their heart is far from me."

19. Cf. 1 Tim. 6:20: "Avoid . . . what is falsely called 'knowledge'" (*pseudo gnostes*).

20. Jim Nelson Black, *Freefall of the American University: How Our Colleges Are Corrupting the Minds and Morals of the Next Generation* (Nashville: WND Books, 2004), 87, quoting Harvard psychiatrist Chester M. Pierce, keynote speaker (1972), Association of Childhood Education (emphasis added).

and that the American male was promiscuous, self-pleasuring, and significantly homosexual.[21]

The power base of the Left is now in the universities, since the trade unions have largely been killed off. The universities have done a lot of good work by setting up, for example, African-American studies programs, Women's Studies programs, and Gay and Lesbian Studies programs. They have created power bases for these movements.[22]

We have defended *the right for individuals to engage in polygamy.* We defend freedom of choice for mature, consenting individuals.[23]

These examples illustrate ways in which the academy, as a robe of culture, trumpets norms, especially to the next generation. In this way, these declared norms are approved.

Judiciary-situation-orthopraxis. As with the robe of the academy, the robe of the judiciary or the court system also approves practices. However, with the judiciary, the practices that are approved stem from particular situations, i.e., those adjudicated in particular cases and controversies. However, with the legal doctrines of *stare decisis* and the role of precedent in the Western legal tradition, such situational decisions "approve" of particular practices and thereby prospectively impact similarly situated litigants.

Consider these examples:

The Constitution is what the judges say it is.[24]

As radical as I think people tried to characterize the [Earl] Warren court, it wasn't that radical. It didn't break free from the essential constraints that were placed by the Founding Fathers in the Constitution.[25]

---

21. Peter Jones, *The God of Sex: How Spirituality Defines Sexuality* (Colorado Springs: Victor Books, 2006), 20 (emphasis added).

22. Black, *Freefall,* 11, quoting Richard Rorty (emphasis added).

23. Nadine Strossen, law professor and ACLU past president, quoted in the *Yale Daily News,* January 19, 2005 (emphasis added).

24. New York Gov. Charles Evans Hughes, later chief justice of the United States.

25. Senior Instructor Barack Obama, WBEZ-FM, "The Court and Civil Rights," Chicago Public Radio, Odyssey series, January 18, 2001.

At the heart of liberty is the right to define one's own concept of existence, of meaning, of the universe, and of the mystery of human life.[26]

These declarations conjure fresh illustrations for David's descriptive analysis of the public square's dynamics:

Why do the nations rage
    and the peoples plot in vain?
The kings of the earth set themselves,
    and the rulers take counsel together,
    against the LORD and against his anointed, saying,
"Let us burst their bonds apart
    and cast away their cords from us."[27]

Just as David described, today we see "kings" and "rulers," those governing in the public square, seeking to rule autonomously by casting off the "bonds" and "cords," the law, of the Anointed One. An unredeemed judiciary will ultimately seek to approve practices contrary to the law of the Lord. Its very nature tends toward codifying radical autonomy, that is, "approving" man's becoming "like God, knowing [determining autonomously] good and evil."[28]

Clergy-person-orthopathos. The clergy is the robe that either excuses or accuses the individual person and his actions. The Left understands the potent role that this robe plays in matters of the public square.
    Consider these examples:

We do not want the word to go out that we want to *exterminate the Negro population*, and *the minister* is the man who can straighten out that idea if it ever occurs to any of their more rebellious members.[29]

It is the misfortune of the churches that they are too often misused by visionaries for the promotion of "reforms" in fields foreign to religion.

26. The United States Supreme Court: *Planned Parenthood v. Casey*, 505 U.S. 833, 851 (1992).
27. Ps. 2:1–3.
28. Gen. 3:5.
29. Jonah Goldberg, *Liberal Fascism: The Secret History of the American Left from Mussolini to the Politics of Meaning* (New York: Doubleday, 2007), 273, quoting Margaret Sanger to C. J. Gamble, Dec. 10, 1939, in Charles Valenza, "Was Margaret Sanger a Racist?" *Family Planning Perspectives* 17, 1 (Jan.–Feb. 1985): 46 (emphasis added).

> *The departures from Christian teachings are astounding* in many cases, leaving the beholder aghast at the unwillingness of some churches to teach "Christ and Him crucified." If the churches are to become organizations for political and scientific propaganda, they should be honest and reject the Bible, scoff at Christ as an obsolete and unscientific teacher, and strike out boldly as champions of politics and science as modern substitutes for the old time religion.
>
> Carried to its logical conclusion, the [Lambeth] committee's report [permitting the use of contraception], if carried into effect, would sound *the death knell of marriage* as a holy institution by establishing degrading practices that would encourage indiscriminate immorality.[30]

These examples demonstrate how each "robe" fulfills Paul's understanding of what occurs when truth encounters the world: following suppression, exchange, and worship—and absent redemption—unrighteousness will be practiced and then pressed for approval. This last phase implicates law and the public square.

More than this, however, Scripture discloses that triangulation can be more than descriptive; rather, by triangulating, the faithful can discern how to engage and restore this fallen culture, even as paganism presses for the approval of perverted practices. The Scripture, in commenting on the men of Issachar, contains this interesting description of them; it is overtly triangular:

> Of Issachar, men who had understanding of the times [situation], to *know* [person] what Israel ought to do [norm], 200 chiefs, and all their kinsmen under their command.[31]

Note that the action contemplated is corporate/sociopolitic: what *Israel* "ought" to do. Determining this *ought* did not stem simply from woodenly extracting a Talmudic edict, but rather it depended on the involvement of *persons* who understood the *situation*. These perspectives, person and situation, impacted the discernment process and thereby helped form the explication and application of the corporate norm. This implies that these

---

30. Charles J. Chaput, *Render unto Caesar: Serving the Nation by Living Our Catholic Beliefs in Political Life* (New York: Doubleday, 2008), 125, quoting *The Washington Post*, March 22, 1931 (emphasis added).

31. 1 Chron. 12:32.

perspectives are at least valuable to consider in contemplating ethical matters affecting the public square.

Query: can triangulation of this corporate (that is, public) type be formally and beneficially utilized prospectively, or is the Scripture's description regarding Issachar simply an aside, irrelevant to today's legal challenges? To answer this query requires analysis of the structure of law, and asking whether it too admits of triangulation.

Triangulating the Law: A Common (Law) Example—Of Musicians and Mobsters

Is everyday law amenable to triangulation? Although to many, this presents perhaps an arcane query, the reality is that even the most mundane legal notion reflects triangularity. Consider simple contacts. What is the essence of contract law? It is "vow." Contract law exists to enforce promises. Yet is every contract enforceable? Is every promise to be enforced? Why not? Here is one illustration, utilized because of Frame's penchant for film and film reviews.[32] This notable excerpt is from the 1972 movie classic, *The Godfather*:

> **Kay**: Michael, you never told me your family knew Johnny Fontane!
> **Michael**: Oh sure, you want to meet him?
> **Kay**: Yeah!
> **Michael**: You know, my father helped Johnny in his career.
> **Kay**: Really? How?
> **Michael**: Let's listen to this song.
> **Kay** [after listening to Johnny for a while]: Please, Michael. Tell me.
> **Michael**: Well when Johnny was first starting out, he was signed to this contract with a Big Band leader. And as his career got better and better he wanted to get out of it. Now, Johnny is my father's godson. My father went to see the bandleader, with a contract for $10,000 to let Johnny go, but the bandleader said no. So the next day, my father went to see the bandleader again, only this time with Luca Brasi. Within an hour, the bandleader signed the release, with a certified check of $1000.
> **Kay**: How did he do that?
> **Michael**: My father made him an offer he couldn't refuse.

---

32. *TAM*, Bibliography in this festschrift, and *DCL*, 900–902.

Kay: What was it?

Michael: Luca Brasi held a gun to his head, and my father assured the band-leader, that either his signature or his brains would be on the contract.[33]

Again, was this contract enforceable? No. Why not? Because contract law is about more than the promise given. The bandleader received an offer, made a promise, signed an agreement, and received consideration.[34] In other words, the promise—the normative component to the agreement—existed. Case closed? No, because contract law is triangular: there is a *person* and a *situation* that must be examined in addition to the promise, the operative *norm*.

In this example, the bandleader (person) was coerced by the hulking and not-so-pleasant Luca Brasi wielding his weapon (situation). Although the norm formally existed, that is, the promise had been "signed, sealed, and delivered," this contract would not technically be enforceable. Why? Because even at common law, contract law recognizes defenses to contractual performance such as duress, the lack of capacity, disability, etc. These defenses implicitly recognize the triperspectival nature of contract law.

Note carefully: these recognized defenses consider the *situational* and *personal* perspectives in evaluating the enforceability of a *norm* (a promise given). Moreover, contracts designed to further illicit purposes, i.e., improper norms such as murder, gambling, and prostitution, are likewise not enforceable, thereby completing the triangle.

Triangulating the Law: Some Structural Corporate Examples— Of Madison and Moulton

But what about the bigger picture? Specifically, what about formally instituting triangular law via a triangular legal system? As but one example, note that the framers of the U. S. Constitution, drawing on Montesquieu and Locke, crafted the structure of federal powers along triperspectival avenues: the Legislative Branch is normative, dictating the applicable norms; the Executive Branch is personal, implementing those norms; and the Judicial Branch is situational, applying those norms to particular situations arising among persons interacting with them.

---

33. Accessed from http://www.imdb.com.

34. The traditional elements leading to the formation of an enforceable contract include offer, acceptance, and the passing of consideration.

Similarly, note that Lord Moulton's *Domains*, designed for sustaining a healthy and productive society, were likewise triangular. The proper focus in his mind was to establish law (the normative); freedom (the situational); and something he deemed "Obedience to the Unenforceable" (the personal).[35]

Triangulating the Law: A Political Example—Of Commies and Containment[36]

Triangulation can also be utilized strategically when facing a particularly large problem such as the threat of communism. During the Cold War, note that the three major efforts deployed against the spread of communism were triangular: the Truman Doctrine, which supported nations to prevent them from falling into Soviet subjugation (normative); the Marshall Plan, which helped to reconstruct Europe following World War II to obviate susceptibility to communism's spread (situational); and the CIA's covert and clandestine service, which developed and deployed human intelligence to blunt Soviet infiltration, advancement, and counterintelligence (personal).[37]

Whether intentionally or not, these examples illustrate that the law—whether small and ad hoc, or structural and systemic—can be described as operating triperspectivally. The question then becomes whether triperspectivalism can be employed normatively, that is, in an intentionally strategic prospective manner for purposes seeking "the welfare [*shalom*] of the city,"[38] with an aim for restoring culture. Before addressing this crucial question, the legal culture will first be assessed in order to ascertain whether such an effort is necessary: should theology, which is application, actually be applied here with an aim toward restoring culture?

35. David Wells, *The Courage to Be Protestant: Truth Lovers, Marketers, and Emergents in the Postmodern World* (Grand Rapids: Eerdmans, 2008), 170.

36. Marxism itself is triangular: consider Marx's so-called Positive Humanism: atheism—norm; cosmopolitanism—situation; and communism, the proletariat—person. See, e.g., Henry Paolucci, *A Brief History of Political Thought and Statecraft* (Smyrna, DE: Griffon House, 2004), 50, quoting Karl Marx (without citation).

37. Tim Weiner, *Legacy of Ashes: The History of the CIA*, Sony Reader e-book version (New York: Doubleday, 2007), 90.

38. Jer. 29:7. Interestingly, this familiar passage, God's letter to his exiled people, contains a triangular message: (1) whom we shall trust, worship, serve, and obey—theology (norm); (2) how we should live—ethics (situation); and (3) in what we shall hope—eschatology (person). Jeffery J. Ventrella, *Thriving in Babylon Today* (privately available sermon and related legal lecture).

Assessing the Legal Culture: The Case of the AWOL Triangles

One need not be triperspectivally well-versed to know that public justice in America is less than ideal. What is interesting to note, however, is that American jurisprudence is crucially deficient precisely regarding the "sides" forming this jurisprudential triangle. This implies that better understanding these perspectives will aid in fashioning solutions to this jurisprudential deficit.

Assessing the Situational: The Challenge of the Judiciary

As mentioned, the judiciary in the American constitutional structure addresses the situational perspective. Courts apply stated norms to particular persons in particular discrete situations.[39] Sadly, the courts in America have departed from justice. Here are a few examples:[40] (1) Courts countenance the starvation of a woman, but not a dog;[41] (2) courts permit humans to be aborted but forbid the destruction of spotted-owl embryos; (3) courts permit colleges to consider race in law-school admission but do not allow prison wardens to consider race and gang affiliation vis-à-vis housing violent prisoners; (4) courts consider minors too immature to be executed for premeditated murder but consider them fully capable to choose abortion without consulting parents; (5) courts nullify laws banning virtual child pornography but affirm laws that criminalize the running of political ads months leading up to a federal election.

The current judicial function, as applying the situational perspective, is manifestly problematic; unrighteous practices have been approved by this robe of culture. This is not particularly newsworthy. However, what needs desperate attention is not further critique of the problem[42] but,

39. Note that in federal judicial matters, jurisdiction exists only for matters involving actual "Cases . . . and Controversies" (U.S. Const. art. III, sec. 2); abstract or advisory rulings are thereby proscribed. This confirms the "situational" function of courts under the American system.

40. Synopsis derived from Mark W. Smith, *Disrobed: The New Battle Plan to Break the Left's Stranglehold on the Courts* (New York: Crown Forum, 2006), 5–6.

41. In the matter of Terri Schiavo, an American civil court—for the first time in history—affirmatively *ordered* the death of an innocent human, not simply permitting a "pulling of the plug." Yet when football player Michael Vick mistreated dogs, he was aggressively (and rightly) prosecuted.

42. The parade of horribles is easily assembled: same-sex "marriage," abortion on demand, embryonic stem-cell experimentation, censorship of religious speech via nondiscrimination codes and political correctness agendas, etc. See, e.g., http://www.telladf.org.

rather, a strategic viable solution: theology as application.[43] This requires understanding that neither the problem nor the solution lies solely with the courts. This is why activism that focuses simply on appointing "strict constructionist"[44] judges, although necessary, will never be sufficient in restoring the legal culture.

Assessing the Personal: The Challenge for the Advocate

Perhaps a more fundamental question ought to be addressed: when justice is not manifest in court decisions such as the ones described above, why not? God's Word describes just such a circumstance and posits one factor helpful to this triangular analysis:

> Justice is turned back,
>   and righteousness stands afar off;
> for truth has stumbled in the public squares,
>   and uprightness cannot enter.
> Truth is lacking,
>   and he who departs from evil makes himself a prey.
> The LORD saw it, and it displeased him
>   that there was no justice.
> He saw that there was no man,
>   and wondered that there was no one to intercede. (Isa. 59:14–16a)

The issue seems plain: justice, which should be both public and stable, is instead teetering. This metaphor is graphic: truth is stumbling. Where? In "the public squares." Note the assumptive language: the public squares are places in which truth should be stabilized, evident, and influential. It is not.

43. Andy Crouch notes that cultural engagement can center on critiquing, condemning, copying, consuming, and/or creating. Andy Crouch, *Culture Making* (Downers Grove, IL: Inter-Varsity Press, 2008), 68–70. In conservative religious circles, a case could be made that when engagement does occur, far too much effort is spent on critique and condemnation, necessary as they may be, and far too little time is spent on creating a righteous culture, that is, seeking the good of the city, including its jurisprudential facets.

44. Technically speaking, the notion of "strict constructionism" differs from hermeneutical "originalism." This latter theory of constitutional jurisprudence focuses on the original plain public meaning of the text, and thus is broader than strict literalism. One might say the former tends toward "dispensational 'literalism' " and the latter is more Reformed. For an explication of these and other theories, such as the "living constitution," see Steven G. Calabresi, ed., *Originalism: A Quarter-Century of Debate* (Washington: Regnery Publishing, 2007).

And what is it that catches the Lord's attention? The lack of an intercessor,[45] a person, to address the fact that truth (the norm) is stumbling in the public squares (the situation).

Thus, remediating truth that has stumbled must include attention to the personal perspective: the identifying, training, and deploying of advocates and activists.[46] Restoring the legal culture must therefore be triangulated; a "two-sided triangle" consisting solely of norm (abortion is killing an innocent human being) and situation (appoint strict-constructionist judges) will not suffice. For justice to flourish there must be a norm, applied by persons, to particular situations.

Assessing the Normative: Who's Lord and Whose Law?

Jesus prays that his disciples would be sanctified "in the truth" and that the Father's "word is truth" (John 17:17). This setting apart must be according to a standard, a norm. Applied culturally, this implicates the lord of the culture, because law is an expression of lordship.[47]

As Van Til and Frame affirm, there can be no neutrality.[48] A lord will exist, and that lord will influence the public norm. The question then becomes whether the cultural lord is the true and living Lord, and thus whether the applicable standard is his norm, his revelational Word, the truth.[49]

In terms of the current legal landscape, this means restoring both the vocabulary and substance of transcendent standards, which have all but departed from American jurisprudence because of legal realism and legal positivism. This project is both delicate and difficult and cannot be achieved rapidly for several reasons.

45. The Lord notes that he will supply the intercessor: the Anointed One (Isa. 59:16). Yet, by way of creaturely analogue, the implied necessity of human intercessors who will steady truth that has stumbled is significant.

46. *DCL*, 943; Frame, *In Defense of Christian Activism*, http://www.christianculture.com (April 19, 2006).

47. As fellow Van Tillian R. J. Rushdoony noted: "Every state is a law order, and every law order represents an enacted morality . . . Every morality represents a form of theological order, i.e., is an aspect and expression of religion." R. J. Rushdoony, *Christianity and the State* (Vallecito, CA: Ross House Books, 1986), 7.

48. *CVT*, 46, 333.

49. Frame notes that revelation is itself triperspectival: special revelation (norm), general revelation (situation), and illumination in the sense of Ephesians 1:17 (person). *SBL*, 57. Each of these issues a norm in some sense.

First, identifying the locus (or loci!) of the operative norms lacks consensus, even among the faith community. Put differently, if there are *oughts*, where ought the *oughts* to be found? Does the solution involve restoring the natural-law tradition[50] or a more "specially revelational" approach[51] such as something toward biblicism?[52] More problematic: how does a legal system steeped in immanence (legal positivism), and devoid of transcendence, transition toward the transcendent?

Second, there seems to be a decided lack of tactical clarity among many interested in this project. Consider the question of abortion. Some activists, embracing functional pragmatism (hyper-situationalism), want no legal action taken until practical victory, defined as overruling *Roe v. Wade*, is assured: "The precedent is so bad that we must not litigate any abortion matter until the Court changes."[53]

50. Frame has analyzed the problematic character of uncritical reliance on natural law. *DCL*, 242–50. The Left has essentially utilized an ethically corrupted and inverted version of natural law (no doubt unrecognizable by Aquinas) via its "living constitution" hermeneutic coupled with the doctrine of "substantive due process." Many textualists and originalists understandably cringe upon hearing suggestions to restore notions of natural law or transcendent standards untethered to a particular legal text. Yet ask whether restoring the use of something toward a natural-law vocabulary could be a tactical benefit for recapturing the language of transcendence in ethics and thereby jurisprudence. This would seem to be critical for establishing a context for discussing such matters if, in the public square, Christianity is to be considered anything other "than a harmless delusion." J. Gresham Machen, *Education, Christianity, and the State*, 2nd ed. (Hobbs, NM: The Trinity Foundation, 1995), 51. Are not notions of transcendence implicit when articulating ideas of "life, liberty, and the pursuit of happiness," especially since these "unalienable rights" are purportedly "endowed by their Creator"? (Declaration of Independence, July 4, 1776). And, of course, even if the legal system recognizes a transcendent standard—as it should, and as it must at some point—the role of that transcendent standard in the legal process, that is, who stewards the transcendent, is another matter: is it the judiciary (situation), the executive (person), or the legislature (norm)? Under traditional notions of natural law, a human law that violates divine law is not bad law; it is not law at all. If this is true, the question remains as to which state agent may properly adjudicate this circumstance. At Nuremberg, the International Military Tribunal did so. But ask whether a sitting judge who believes that abortion violates the natural law—as it most surely does—should thereby refuse to follow precedent that upholds the "right" of abortion.

51. "Intrusion ethics," it should be noted, appears ultimately unworkable (see *DCL*, 838–39; Greg L. Bahnsen, *Theonomy in Christian Ethics* [Texarkana, TX: Covenant Media Press, 1998], app. 4), and yet even a moderate theonomic approach worries many for its implications and is not itself without some hermeneutical challenge. See, e.g., Vern Poythress, *The Shadow of Christ in the Law of Moses* (Phillipsburg, NJ: P&R Publishing, 1995).

52. *IDSCB*, 269–318.

53. Some well-meaning activists assert this point as if they were "protecting" against the creation of worse precedent, as if the American abortion regime could be any worse; in reality, only China's one-child policy, replete with forced abortions, is more draconian than current American jurisprudence.

Others adopt what essentially is a utopian view of law (hyper-normativity) by contending that only "pure" legal efforts ought to be utilized, and thereby these advocates enervate (if not outright condemn) jurisprudential incrementalism:[54] "Regulating abortion clinics implicitly affirms the 'right' of abortion and thereby is necessarily evil."[55]

Third, some who have correctly identified the transcendent standard in some area of law, such as affirming life (as summarized in the sixth commandment),[56] have too often failed to triangulate and thus have become hyper-normative or hyper-situational in their approach. This one- or two-sided triangle is no triangle at all, and therefore it is no wonder that jurisprudential progress stalls and cultural restoration lags. Merely hammering the applicable norm, for example, is no guarantee for actually establishing that norm in culture because culture is multiperspectival. What is needed in addition to correctly identifying the operative norm is to equip persons to apply that norm situationally. This is the burden of the next section.

REORIENTING THE LEGAL CULTURE: TRIANGULATING FOR STRATEGIC LEGAL ADVOCACY

Addressing the question posed above will not occur on a blank slate. This is because an organization, the Alliance Defense Fund (ADF), came into being in 1993. Its mission is to engage the legal culture in a way that brings the right standards to the right contexts by the right actors.[57] The goal of ADF is twofold, as noted by cofounder Bill Bright: (1) keep the door open for the spread of the gospel, and (2) transform the legal system for Jesus Christ.

54. The flaw of such purist (hyper-normative, anti-incremental) "reasoning" will be analyzed subsequently. Cf. Deut. 7:22a: "The LORD your God will clear away these nations before you little by little."

55. The surface plausibility of this assertion is illusory. The ethical demands of the sixth commandment still operate even where abortion is legally protected, meaning that regulating this evil procedure in an effort to reduce or eliminate collaterally tragic consequences such as infection, mutilation, sterility, and death from purported "safe and legal" abortions remains ethically prescribed.

56. *DCL*, 684–90.

57. Note the triangle: *right standards* (norm), *contexts* (situation), and *right actors* (person). The following exposition regarding ADF and its efforts is not the author's promotion of his nonprofit employer, but rather is a real-time illustration of how effectively Frame's triangles can be employed.

This bold mission, aimed squarely at restoring culture via legal efforts, will require full-orbed triangulation. Efforts must be directed toward the normative, situational, and personal perspectives, all as applied. After all: theology is application. Let the grand experiment begin.

Restoring the Normative: Identifying Strategic Objectives for Legal Engagement

Paul, in describing unregenerate man, notes that he is "alienated and hostile in mind, doing evil deeds" (Col. 1:21). Man, in his fallen state, is not oriented toward the true and living God; he is alienated from the authoritative one and his authoritative ways (norm). Natural man suppresses the truth, resulting in a hostility of mind, which is quite personal (person). This precipitates evil actions (situation). Absent redemption, this necessarily leads to triperspectival consequences: guilt (norm), corruption (situation), and eternal judgment in hell (very personal).

This triangulation of individual fallenness also produces cultural ramifications: normative alienation when externalized collectively produces religious censorship as truth is increasingly suppressed;[58] evil deeds (practices) occur situationally, including at the most basic societal level, the family;[59]

58. The antithetical progression of Romans 1:25–32 anticipates these phenomena: the truth is suppressed in unrighteousness; the truth is then exchanged for the lie; this results in a worship response: the creature is served, rather than the Creator; this worship results in evil practices—people become like what they worship (Ps. 135:18); and lastly, according to Paul (and here lies the key nexus for legal analysis), the unregenerate man will seek to have these practices approved, or to use legal jargon, codified (Rom. 1:32). This approval occurs culturally via the robes of culture: the academy, the judiciary, and the clergy. These robes are likewise—surprise, surprise—triperspectival: normal, situational, and personal, respectively. See Jeffery J. Ventrella, *The Cathedral Builder: Pursuing Cultural Beauty* (Powder Springs, GA: American Vision, 2007), xv–xvi.

59. The family in particular, as society's basic unit (*DCL*, 595–602), issues the fundamental coordinated relationships of the culture. Undermine the family, and over time, the entire society unravels. This is one reason that so many revolutionaries have strategically targeted the family and parent-child relationships; they often "focus on the family," but with a radically different agenda: erode and subvert the family via progressive education, sexual "liberation," egalitarianism, etc., and the civilization will be captured. See, e.g., Paula Ettlebrick, professor and advocate of homosexual behavior: "Being queer means pushing the parameters of sex, sexuality, and family, and in the process transforming the very fabric of society. . . . We must keep our eyes on the goals of providing true alternatives to marriage and of *radically reordering society's view of family*." "Since When Is Marriage a Path to Liberation?" *Out/Look* (Fall 1989), reprinted in *Lesbians, Gay Men, and the Law*, ed. Wm. Rubenstein, 402–3, 405 (emphasis added).

and the hostility of mind personally and collectively expressed wages war against those made in God's image, including promoting their very death.[60] This collective fallenness has expressed itself jurisprudentially in America as these practices are "approved" and codified.

In 1993, a number of evangelical leaders, including James Dobson, Bill Bright, Marlin Maddoux, Larry Burkett, and D. James Kennedy, spearheaded an effort to affect the American legal—not policy—landscape. They identified the law because they understood that the Left's agenda regarding religious censorship,[61] the redefinition of the family,[62] and abortion on demand[63] were products of judicial, not legislative, efforts. The judiciary was the Left's preferred means for imposing its agenda. In Paul's parlance, paganism presses for practices to be approved (Rom. 1:32).

In response, ADF was founded in 1993 and launched in 1994. This unique alliance sought to affect the legal landscape via training, strategy, and funding, and later via direct litigation. ADF's strategic objectives focused on three areas: religious liberty, the family, and life.

What is intriguing is that these strategic targets are triangular—whether intentionally chosen to be or not. Consequently, protecting religious liberty (norm), the family (situation), and life (person) represents a full-orbed triperspectival strategy of legal engagement, targeting for containment, if not redemption,[64] the collective cultural expression of fallen man in the jurisprudential realm.

Restoring the Situational: The Blackstone Legal Fellowship as a Triangular Solution

ADF, having determined these three jurisprudential goals, understood that means were necessary for effectuating these objectives. People, working in particular situations, apply norms. Because this project would necessarily

---

60. "All who hate me love death" (Prov. 8:36b).

61. The courts removed prayer and Decalogue displays from the public square.

62. Marriage, for example, has been redefined by judicial fiat in Massachusetts, Iowa, and Connecticut.

63. Starting with invalidating anti-contraception statutes in 1965 and culminating in sodomy's decriminalization in 2003, the courts have redefined human sexuality with the codification of a radical, "anything goes" sexual autonomy.

64. Law and politics are not salvific, of course, but legal efforts can be redemptive in the sense that legal reformation serves to create "prior conditions of the human mind . . . [that is,] those favorable conditions for the reception of the gospel." Machen, *Education*, 51.

be intergenerational, ADF determined to influence the next generation of jurists, scholars, attorneys, and leaders. This effort, focusing on the formation, development, and deployment of Christian law students, became known as the Blackstone Legal Fellowship.[65] This approach to situationally preparing the next generation of legal leaders is itself an exercise in applied triangulation.[66]

Blackstone's triangular curriculum: Psalm 78. In conceiving of Blackstone, ADF sought to craft a program whose graduates would, in a Van Tillian sense, do damage to evil.[67] If that was the conviction, the question became what should be studied. What should form the curriculum? Instead of training law students in nothing more than a baptized version of legal positivism, did a curriculum exist that would equip these future leaders not simply to make a living, but rather to make a difference, especially to future generations?

God's Word provides insight for answering such questions. In particular, if the intention is to impact future generations, there must be study focusing on three areas. As Psalm 78 instructs:

> He established a testimony in Jacob
> and appointed a law in Israel,
> which he commanded our fathers
> to teach to their children,
> that the next generation might know them,
> the children yet unborn,
> and arise and tell them to their children,
> so that they should set their hope in [1] God
> and not forget [2] the works of God,
> but keep [3] his commandments. (Ps. 78:5–7)

Note the textual linkage: to influence future generations requires present instruction in three areas: God, his works, and his law. This triad is triper-

---

65. This fellowship honors Sir William Blackstone, the first chair of law at Oxford. Blackstone, although an important historical figure whose writings greatly influenced America's jurisprudence, is also a metaphor for the transcendent "higher law," a precondition for restoring the rule of law. For a modern biography of Blackstone and his contribution, see Robert Stacey, *Sir William Blackstone and the Common Law* (Powder Springs, GA: American Vision, 2003, 2008).

66. Frame would no doubt contend there is no other kind!

67. Cf. footnote 8 and accompanying text.

spectival: God (person), his works (situation), and his law (norm). From this, an entire curriculum was birthed, commencing by prototype in 2000.[68]

1. Studying God: the personal perspective. During the fellowship's internship, God, his person, and his attributes are studied. In particular, the historical battles defining Christian orthodoxy focusing on the Trinity and the person of Christ are examined. Rightly understood, these truths demand, indeed provoke, a response in the student: a proper apprehension of the true and living God demands a response: worship.[69] Moreover, it is seeking God (Ps. 63) that grants an understanding of justice (Prov. 28:5). To truly promote justice and thereby restore society will require advocates who seek God; they will understand justice.[70]

2. Studying God's works: the situational perspective. God's works are situational. The fellowship focuses on two categories of his works: redemptive acts and providential acts. Redemption is important because, as Wittgenstein noted, "Only someone who can reflect on the past can repent."[71] Providence is important as well: recall that Stalin not only expelled Trotsky, his rival, and had him assassinated, but also directed that Trotsky's image be removed from all Soviet historical archives. Stalin understood that if one could control in the present what one believed about the past, one could influence, if not control, what one would think and do in the future.

68. The nine-week internship includes a substantial monetary scholarship coupled with airfare, lodging, and meals, together with a six-week field internship (theology is, after all, application). In 2009, the 10th Blackstone Class operated in eight countries and trained nearly 110 Christian law students. Frame served as Blackstone faculty for a number of years, until his writing commitments demanded less travel time. His marvelous address created for the fellowship, "Loving God with Your Mind without Becoming an Intellectual Pharisee," remains mandatory reading for Blackstone interns.

69. See, e.g., Pss. 47, 63, 150.

70. The curriculum extends well beyond citing a few proverbs; instruction is directed at demonstrating that because theology correlates with ethics, all deviations from orthodox Trinitarianism and Christology results in grave cultural idols: Docetism leads to the idol of self, and Ebionism leads to the idol of state—*Brave New World* and *1984*. Lordship and law relate: the lord of a culture is the lawgiver of that culture. A further exposition of this unique new-old curriculum, however, is beyond the purview of this chapter.

71. Ludwig Wittgenstein, *Zettle* (Berkeley: University of California Press, 1967), 519, 91e, quoted in Douglas R. Groothuis, *Truth Decay: Defending Christianity against the Challenges of Postmodernity* (Downers Grove, IL: InterVarsity Press, 2000), 225.

Accordingly, the Blackstone curriculum includes numerous sessions directed toward recapturing the religious factors and contexts that underpin the American experiment, American exceptionalism, federalism, and other historical facets "airbrushed" from modern legal instruction. This historical context—the situational perspective—is crucial for garnering the meaning and proper function of America's constitutionalism.[72]

3. Studying God's law: the normative perspective. Finally, God's law must be known and studied, both the law embedded in the created order ("written on the heart"[73]) and the law specially revealed. This law provides the normative perspective. The Blackstone curriculum includes sessions surveying "what we can't not know"[74] as well as the natural-law context of the Declaration of Independence and the Constitution.[75]

Restoring the Personal: Presenting Triangular Advocacy—Structuring, Crafting, and Advancing Strategic Legal Arguments

Applying the triangle to cultural restoration/transformation is straight-forward, if challenging: what does God's Word (norm) require me (person) to do today (situation)? This section focuses on the too-often-forgotten personal perspective. Far too often, activists become "hyper-normative" in seek-

---

72. One fall while guest-lecturing at Harvard and Stanford law schools, the author asked the students how many had had a course in constitutional law. All hands were raised. Then it was asked how many had been assigned to read *The Federalist* in conjunction with that course. Not one hand remained raised. After the guest lecture, a Stanford student asserted that the wrong question had been posed. The student stated that what should have been asked was whether, in conjunction with the constitutional law course, the *Constitution* had been assigned to be read. No one had received that assignment. The manifest absence of the document's ratification debate (the situational perspective) as well as the document itself (the normative perspective) perhaps provides a major clue as to why American constitutional jurisprudence is so crabbed: the training of future attorneys is at best a "one-sided triangle," which, like a "square circle," does not exist.

73. J. Budziszewski, *Written on the Heart: The Case for Natural Law* (Downers Grove, IL: InterVarsity Press, 1997).

74. Cf. J. Budziszewski, *What We Can't Not Know: A Guide* (Dallas: Spence, 2003).

75. The Declaration of Independence contains four explicit references to God: "Creator," "Divine Providence," "Supreme Judge of the World," and Blackstone's term, "the law of nature and nature's God." Contrary to the polemics of Isaac Kramnick and R. Laurence Moore, *The Godless Constitution: The Case against Religious Correctness* (New York: W & W Norton Co., 1996), the Constitution and its structure is hardly godless. See P. Andrew Sandlin, *Catholicity, Culture and American Exceptionalism*, private address, Blackstone Legal Fellowship; Jeffery J. Ventrella, "What's God Got to Do with It??!! The Prima Facie Propriety of Public Religious Expression," *Thomas M. Cooley Law Review* 23, 1 (2006): 77.

ing to identify and impose the "right" answer to the ethical or legal quandary by emphasizing, for example, "family values." This approach, although necessary, is not sufficient. The right standard must be applied to a particular situation *by a person*. In the legal realm, this means that attention must be directed toward understanding the advocate and advocacy. The person applying the norm matters.

1. The characteristics of a triangular advocate. Scripture discloses that the Holy Spirit is our *paraclete*, translated "comforter" or "helper."[76] Jesus is called our *paraclete* as well: 1 John 2:1. But here, the English rendering is "advocate." Just as the Creator and Redeemer is an advocate, so too the renewed man in some analogical way functions as an advocate. Jesus' work as an advocate is triperspectival: Jesus was engaged (situational), he was efficient (personal), and he was effective (normative). Or put textually: "Christ [person] died for our sins [situation] in accordance with the Scriptures [norm]" (1 Cor. 15:3b). So too, advocates for cultural restoration must manifest these characteristics.

Advocates must be *engaged*; they should not be "potted plants" for Jesus. They must be *efficient*: advocates ought to steward, not squander, their gifts for the kingdom, utilizing what the Lord has bestowed on them for his glory. Finally, advocates must be *effective*. The tactics and strategies employed must actually accomplish something righteous. Results,[77] rather than mere activity, must be the goal, and consequently the formation of strategy must keep this perspective of advocacy in mind.[78]

2. The practice of triangular advocacy. As an advocate must himself be "triangular"—engaged, efficient, and effective—the work or practice that the advocate does must also be triangular.

a. The situational perspective: general cultural strategies. An advocate engages in the culture. This is a situational endeavor. Scripture sets forth a general strategy for such engagement. This strategy, which itself is triangu-

76. See, e.g., John 16:7.
77. As the Bible makes plain: Jesus' birth, life, death, resurrection, and ascension actually accomplished redemption; they did not merely make salvation possible. See John Murray, *Redemption Accomplished and Applied* (Grand Rapids: Eerdmans, 1955).
78. ADF is sometimes described this way: "ADF is not a 'think tank'; it is a 'do tank.'"

lar, can be seen in and derived from 1 Corinthians 9, a familiar narrative of Paul's ministry:

> Although meat sacrificed to idols is nothing, he instructs the Christians to be sensitive to those who are weak, avoiding needless offense (compassion-existential-orthopathos). In a Jewish context, he becomes a Jew to the Jews, adapting his approach to the context, although he is liberated from the ceremonial law (concession-situational-orthopraxis). Yet, he remains bound under the Law of Christ, the moral imperatives of the faith (compromise-normative-orthodoxy).
>
> He employs the triangle "all for the sake of the gospel, that I may share with them in its blessings." Notice his teleological and unobstructed, yet urgent focus: His passion is to "win more," "win Jews," "win those under the law," "win those outside the law," "win the weak," becoming "all things to all people" to "save some."
>
> It is in this context that he urges Christians to run the race to win, not aimlessly.[79]

This means that the Christian advocate seeking to maximize cultural penetration must have compassion always (person) and concession where possible (situation), but should compromise never (norm). Again note Paul's goal: winning, that is, being effective. This is precisely the focus of one advocating for cultural reclamation.

b. The normative perspective: structuring strategic argument. If the situational strategy is generally to emulate Paul in 1 Corinthians 9, how is the advocate's actual normative argument to be structured? Does it exclusively focus only on the norm, or is it also triangular? Again, triperspectivalism provides an answer. Dave Harvey, explaining how to engage a culture missionally, notes:

> The best way to create a platform for truth [orthodoxy: norm] in the common culture is by authenticating our truth through our service [orthopraxis: situation], and authenticating our truth through our humility [orthopathos: person]. . . . [The unsaved] need to encounter methods [orthopraxis: situation] and motives [orthopathos: person] that are as

---

79. Ventrella, *Cathedral Builder*, 97–98.

noble as the message [orthodoxy: norm] that we're seeking to deliver to them.[80]

Presenting a normative perspective involves more than uttering norms, which is exactly what Frame teaches: each perspective includes the others.[81] When advancing truth, in the sense of the norm or standard, that effort should be triangular: Message + Method + Motive.

c. The personal perspective: delivering strategic argument. Frame's triangles also inform as to how a strategic argument ought to be delivered and structured. Again, this effort admits of many triads and triangles. Each will be briefly outlined.

(i) The advocate's utterance: the ethics of advocated speech. An advocate's speech ought to conform to Scripture's ethics. That ethic is triperspectival:

Let no corrupting talk come out of your mouths, but only such as is good for building up [norm—orthodoxy], as fits the occasion [situation—orthopraxis], that it may give grace to those who hear [person—orthopathos].[82]

An example may help illustrate this point. In advocating for marriage and against counterfeits such as same-sex "marriage," one ought not in a public setting (or anywhere else) repeatedly scream, "God hates fags!"[83] Rather, an advocate must speak that which is uncompromisingly "good" (norm), but he must also understand the situation to discern whether his message and manner cohere to the opportunity the Lord has providentially granted to him. If so, then he must fashion his remarks with an eye toward the audience, the listener (person). Not only must his words be intelligible,[84] they must also confer grace.[85]

80. Dave Harvey, *Church Planting in the Common Culture* (Gaithersburg, MD: Sovereign Grace Ministries, 2002), 6.
81. *PP*; accessed at http://www.frame-poythress.org/frame_articles/PrimerOnPerspectivalism.htm.
82. Eph. 4:29.
83. This is the warped methodology of the Fred Phelps-led group known as Westboro Baptist Church.
84. Cf. 1 Cor. 14 regarding public worship and the need for intelligibility, even (especially!) for unbelievers. Also see Frame's explication of this, *CWM*, 17–20.
85. The author has participated in approximately sixty formal debates addressing same-sex "marriage." By the Lord's grace, following a rigorous exchange, he has often been approached by practitioners of homosexual behavior who, although strongly disagreeing with the message,

(ii) The advocate's presentation: structuring effective advocacy. Substantively, the advocate's presentation must be triperspectival (Eph. 4:29). But there exists yet another triangle that informs the formality or structure of the argument. An argument's structure should also manifest a triangular structure by including/considering: (1) proof—norm; (2) protocol—situation; and (3) persuasion—person.

Certainly the advocate must present the normative truth: marriage is composed of the legal union of one man and one woman, abortion takes an innocent life, etc.[86] Identifying and presenting such a norm could be succinct and conclusory, or it could be predicated on a protracted intricate discussion.[87] Without such a norm in whatever form, however, the persons within the culture will not be sanctified by the truth (John 17:17).

In addition to setting forth the norm, i.e., proof, an advocate presents in a situation. He must therefore be cognizant of the protocol associated with this occasion (situation) for advocacy. Are there formal conventions for addressing the topic? Is the matter amenable to evidential proffers, and if so, what are the acceptable forms of promulgation? Is there an applicable etiquette? More than one legally sound argument has been rejected because of an advocate's failure to apprehend the applicable protocol.

Finally, the advocate must rightly address the particular audience, the person. Flawless logic presented according to impeccable protocol will be ineffective unless it also persuades the decision maker. As one cynical advocate recognizing this reality remarked, "I'd rather be lucky than right." Persuasion, or the competent use of rhetoric, must accompany the advocate's efforts.[88] In short, effective legal advocacy must include proof, protocol, and persuasion. It must be triangulated.

---

expressed appreciation and gratitude for the method and manner used to defend God's creational design.

86. How a particular norm is articulated by a person may depend on the situation. Paul, when speaking in court (!), chose words that were "true and rational" (Acts 26:25). This implies that one need not quote the Bible in order to make a biblical argument. Yet the operative norm must be included explicitly or implicitly in the presentation at some level, and critical thinking (rationality) is ethically required.

87. During the Blackstone internship, the students are encouraged to provide the "John 3:16 version" of a particular point, as well as the "Library of Congress version."

88. Because "brute facts" do not exist, the advocate faces a situation in which "letting the facts speak for themselves" often fails to produce a righteous result. For example, in *Stenburg v. Carhart*, 530 U.S. 914 (2000), which invalidated a ban on the barbaric procedure known as partial birth abortion, five justices looked into the abyss of hell and did not blink. Although a similar ban on this hideous practice later passed constitutional muster (*Gonzales v. Carhart*, 550 U.S. 124

Restoring the Culture: Implementing Triangular Legal Strategies—Current Issues

Developing Strategic Legal Efforts for Restoring Culture: Ending Abortion

Triangulation is also a key practical tool for fashioning full-orbed effective legal tactics. Consider abortion. What is abortion? Most pro-choice people would respond that abortion is "reproductive freedom;"[89] most pro-life people would say that abortion kills babies. But the triangular reality is this: women (personal) who are pregnant (situation) have abortions (norm). Abortion as a cultural evil is triperspectival, and therefore abortion as a legal issue requires a triperspectival remedy.

Put differently, this issue will not likely be won by simply focusing on the status of the unborn—as critical as that point is—because it is not the only point impacting abortion. What is necessary is a multifaceted informed approach for ending legal abortion. This can be, and is being, accomplished as follows:

1. As to norm/orthodoxy. With the normative perspective, the legal analysis is straightforward. This perspective focuses on the wrongness of taking innocent life: *abortion* = women who are pregnant have *abortions.* This perspective legally focuses on protecting the innocent life taken by abortion. Efforts advancing this perspective would include, but not be limited to, the following: (a) direct efforts to ban abortion: i. constitutional amendments—national, (ii) constitutional amendments—state, (iii) criminal sanctions regarding abortion or aspects of its administration; (b) efforts designed to protect speech: (i) protecting dissent, (ii) protecting interactive protest, (iii) protecting interactive counsel of women seeking abortion, (iv) protecting the promotion of speech offering abortion alternatives.

2. As to situation/orthopraxis. The situational perspective focuses on abortion from another angle: *abortion* = women *who are pregnant* have

---

[2007]), this tragic history illustrates that persuasion necessitates much more than simply presenting the facts. The person must be addressed. And to persuade one who actively suppresses the truth in unrighteousness requires dredging the conscience: see, e.g., J. Budziszewski, *The Revenge of Conscience: Politics and the Fall of Man* (Dallas: Spence, 1999).

89. A search of the Web sites of the leading abortion advocates, such as Planned Parenthood, NOW, NARAL, and the ACLU, discloses the utter absence of the word *abortion*, a telling evidence flowing from Romans 1:18—the suppression of the truth.

abortions. This situational perspective exists and must also be legally addressed. Efforts predicated on this perspective would include, but not be limited to, the following: (a) clinic regulation: licensing, health standards, medical standards, reporting standards; (b) mandatory pre-procedural ultrasound testing and disclosure; (c) informed consent that includes not only technical medical data but also an explanation of associational risks and correlations of abortion (such as breast cancer), and legal waivers, including explicit descriptions of the waiver of the mother-child parental relationship; (d) favorable statutes of repose for prosecuting malpractice claims; and (e) fetal homicide statutes.

3. As to person/orthopathos. Finally, in order to be full-orbed in addressing abortion, another perspective must be legally engaged. With this perspective, the women affected by abortion are addressed: *abortion = women* who are pregnant have abortions. Efforts directed toward advancing these legal interests as related to abortion would include: (a) protecting the operation and expressive rights of pregnancy resources centers, (b) developing mandatory post-abortion care and counsel, and (c) developing a mechanism, such as an escrowed account, funded by the abortion industry, designed to provide post-abortion legal restitution for those women who incur post-abortion syndrome, although not rising to the level of medical malpractice.

Developing Strategic Legal Efforts for Restoring Culture: Preventing the Redefinition of Marriage

This same method can operate vis-à-vis preserving marriage. First, consider this issue with triangularity. What is marriage? Marriage (norm) consists of the legal union (situation) of one man and one woman (personal). The most obvious efforts to prevent the redefinition of marriage include normative efforts to recognize[90] and preserve the definition constitutionally.[91] But other efforts of equal validity exist once the issue is "triangulated." These include the following:

90. Marriage is decidedly not a creature of the state; rather, concerning marriage, the state functions in two ways. The state (1) recognizes and (2) regulates marriage; it does not create marriage. See Jeffery J. Ventrella, "Square Circles?!! Restoring Rationality to the Same-Sex 'Marriage' Debate," *Hastings Constitutional Law Quarterly* 32, 2 (2005): 681.

91. Interestingly, the advocates of homosexual behavior utilized their own triangle in efforts aimed at defeating Proposition 8 in California: these advocates employed this triad: (1) sloganeering that "no harm" had occurred in Massachusetts (norm); (2) engaging in rigorous door-to-

1. As to orthodoxy/norm. (a) Enacting and defending "defense of marriage acts" (DOMA), (b) state constitutional amendments, (c) sodomy laws,[92] (d) marital regulation laws including (i) eligibility (consanguinity, gender/sex, monogamy), (ii) tax implications, (iii) inheritance implications, (iv) restoring fault-based divorcement, and (v) increasing covenant marriage options.

2. As to orthopraxis/situation. (a) Preserving expressive rights vis-à-vis hate-speech codes, (b) creating and defending parental opt-out rights re: education, (c) creating and defending employee opt-out re: diversity training, (d) defeating or limiting domestic partner benefit schemes, (e) invalidating governmentally coerced contracting schemes, and (f) protecting the right of conscience vis-à-vis public accommodations and nondiscrimination codes.

3. As to orthopathos/person. (a) Age of consent, (b) capacity to consent, (c) protecting liberty of conscience vis-à-vis (i) mandatory diversity training, (ii) mandatory conditioner orthodoxy for professional licensing (medical, pharmacology, legal, counseling/psychological, sociology and social work, cosmetology), (iii) mandatory condition for contracting with the state, (d) protecting faith-based efforts re: AIDS counsel and comfort (chaplaincy, etc.), and (e) preserving church autonomy, including removing the restrictions on pulpit speech directed toward moral issues and candidates affecting the public square.[93]

CONCLUSION

Frame's triangles are certainly descriptive; yet they are also prescriptive, and therefore prospective. When employed prospectively, these triangles

---

door canvassing efforts (situation); and (3) choosing photogenic "couples" from the community to tell their stories of being normal and adjusted (person). By God's grace, this triangle did not persuade the electorate.

92. Tragically, the U.S. Supreme Court, by invoking "international law" and simultaneously rejecting moral justifications for legal statutes, invalidated laws that criminalize consensual sodomy. *Lawrence v. Texas*, 539 U.S. 558 (2003). Correcting this legal error presents an enduring, yet essential challenge if loving one's neighbor means something more than being nice. *DCL*, 728–29.

93. Michael Horton's critique of this effort wholly misses the mark in two ways: (1) his analysis presupposes a "two kingdom" view of church and state, something Frame has shown to be problematic (*DCL*, Appendix E), and (2) he misconstrues ADF's initiative regarding churches and their pulpits. In other words, both facts and law are mistaken. See Michael Horton, *Christless Christianity: The Alternative Gospel of the American Church* (Grand Rapids: Baker, 2008) .

not only provide tactical insight, but identify strategic targets for cultural engagement and restoration: the robes of culture.

These robes serve as gatekeepers for cultural convention. The robes will either codify stumbled truth or steady it. Where do moral aberrations originate in the public square? Is it not from the academy (norm), the judiciary (situation), and the clergy (person)? Once detached from normative standards, these robes serve as signposts and seals for the prevailing cultural orthodoxy—and will, if left unchecked, ultimately mandate the silencing of dissent. Why? Because they will invariably tend toward approving unrighteous practices. After all, there can be only one cultural orthodoxy.

As the church seeks to take Christ, his full orthodoxy, and his lordship into the public square in an effort to steady stumbled truth, it must direct its best arguments toward the most culturally significant targets: the robes. The robes must be recaptured in message, method, and manner. The clergy must stand against unrighteous practices and thereby promote a culture of life, family, and religious liberty; the academy must teach against unrighteous practices and thereby promote a culture of life, family, and religious liberty; and the judiciary must apply the law that "we can't not know," and thereby promote a culture of life, family, and religious liberty—a culture advancing the common good for everyone: Christ transforming culture for the benefit of all.

By intentionally "triangulating," Christian citizens may more effectively be liberated, motivated, and directed toward greater ethical fidelity in applying Christ's lordship to all areas of life, including the public square where truth often stumbles. Frame's triangles call and equip the church to be engaged, efficient, and effective culturally. Accordingly, the bride must triangulate; she must passionately demonstrate truth. Christ's lordship demands nothing less.

37

JOHN FRAME'S THEOLOGY IN THE PRESENT CULTURAL CONTEXT

JOHN J. BARBER

WHAT DO DUSTIN HOFFMAN and John Frame have in common? Both play improvisational piano. And both have made statements about the lordship of God. In an interview, the actor Hoffman said, "If God was to say to me, 'You want to play really good jazz piano, you have to give up what you are doing,' I would do it in a minute."[1] Although we are not certain to what extent the actor possesses true knowledge of God, his self-reflective, hypothetical dialogue with God demonstrates, at the least, a superficial recognition of God's power to make him a better jazz pianist. John Frame wants God to help him to become a more proficient pianist as well. However, where Frame's declarations about God's lordship differ from the type stated by Hoffman is that Frame's are not of a supposed nature; they are biblically based. Moreover, Frame's thoughts on lordship have meaning for the mission of the church to transform wide-ranging areas of present-day culture. How so?

Before proceeding, I need to make a point of clarification. Although Frame has addressed the relationship of God's lordship to an array of cultural subjects including feminism, medical ethics, moviegoing, music,

1. *AARP Magazine* (March–April 2009): 42.

and more, it is not the goal of this writing to interact with his views on these issues. Rather, the purpose here is to decipher the control belief and the central themes of Frame's theology and their import for our present-day milieu. The following examination falls under three main headings that function as a breakdown of Frame's entire theological system, as this writer sees it. The headings are *perspectivalism, ethics,* and *presuppositional apologetics.* The analysis will conclude with a brief interaction with Frame's overall position on culture.

PERSPECTIVALISM

The term *perspectivalism* is not found in Frame's writings. Rather, he uses words such as *perspectives* or *perspective* when addressing a broad array of theological issues. *Perspectivalism* is another way to express the perspectives motif that is throughout his theology. For Frame, the perspectival stress of his theology is motivated by his overarching concern with God's lordship over all of life. Lordship is the defining control belief of Frame's theology. As he so divisively puts it, "The central message of Scripture is that God is Lord."[2] The theologian wants us to see God's relationship to the world from three perspectives: control, authority, and presence (hereafter referred to as CAP). At one point, Frame refers to CAP as his "lordship triad,"[3] and in another place as the "lordship attributes."[4] By these phrases he means, "The three lordship attributes are 'perspectivally related,' that is, each one is involved in the other two. None of them can be rightly understood, except as inseparably related to the others. So redemption necessarily involves God's control and authority, as well as his presence."[5] Frame is committed to seeing everything about God, from his acts, to his attributes, to the way in which creatures have knowledge of God, in mutual dependence. References to CAP, directly or indirectly, are so multitudinous in his written volumes and select treatises that space does not permit a full analysis of its reference points.[6] Perspectivalism occupies a cardinal area of importance

2. *DG*, 25.
3. *PWG*, 32.
4. *DKG*, 17.
5. *DG*, 41.
6. In the chapter titled "Images of God" in *DG*, Frame comments, "Names, images, and attributes, then, are perspectivally related: they tell us the same truths about God in different ways." *DG*, 362–64.

in Frame's theology because, according to him, CAP sums up the essence of God's lordship. "Control, authority, personal presence—remember the triad. It will appear often in this book [DKG], for I know of no better way to summarize the biblical concept of divine lordship."[7]

Frame understands lordship in the context of the covenants of Scripture, which, for him, necessarily include not only redeemed people, but all the peoples of the world.[8] It is the covenantal criterion that leads Frame to an arrangement of his theology that is seminal. He reverses many of the traditional theological categories that have marked the history of dogmatics for centuries. "Thus, I shall discuss God's acts before his attributes. . . . I will proceed from history to eternity, from the ethical to the metaphysical, from the communicable to the incommunicable."[9] Although he justifies this reversal on the grounds that it "does not make much substantive difference what doctrine comes first and what comes second," and also because the reversal serves a "pedagogical difference"[10] for students and pastors who lack philosophical training and who would thus find his order "more intelligible and interesting,"[11] I cannot help but see this reversal as the natural outcome of Frame's stress on covenantal lordship, for to begin theological reflection from the vantage point of the Lord of the covenant is to begin in the concrete, not the abstract.

Now, what can we garner from Frame's perspectivalism for our contemporary cultural environment? As noted, Frame's perspectivalism is decisive for its emphasis on the lordship of God that provides cohesion to his entire theology. Out of this cohesion emerges a specific, philosophical profile that prompts the reader to reflect culturally. It is not that the theologian keeps the issue of culture proximate to the theological challenge. It is rather that by stressing God's lordship in and over the world, the issue of culture inevitably surfaces as a *prima facie* consideration. The archetype of lordship, more specifically that God is Lord of the covenant, makes this a certainty—as, for example, his doctrine of God always begins, regardless of the subheading in view, with the covenantal criterion, the effect of which is to automatically involve the creation, and the cultural situation we forge

---

7. DKG, 17.
8. Some examples of Frame's thought regarding God's supreme covenantal authority over all people can be found in DG, 12, 34, 102, and also in DKG, 13.
9. DG, 14.
10. Ibid., 13.
11. Ibid., 14.

from the creation. The very structure of the theologian's work makes us think of culture as a central issue. He never treats culture as an area of possible choice of theological reflection, but always as an *ought* of theology and therefore of Christian participation.

More narrowly speaking, perspectivalism provides us a cogent context for discussing an important crisis in today's culture. Informed watchers of Western culture are correct that we are living in a postmodern age, heading toward the abyss of a revived nineteenth-century collision with social despair. One of the great marks of the age is fragmentation. The overt and far-reaching secularization of society has resulted in an erosion of values and has left people with a fragmented view of the world, one in which they are unable to interpret the times in which they live. Thus many people ask, "If God exists, then why were thousands of lives lost in the tsunami of 2004? Why is there Holocaust-like suffering in the Sudan?" With only a fragmented view of reality to rely on, such people are forced to conclude that either God is in control of human events, but does not care whether people suffer, or that he is not in control and is thus impotent to help. Or perhaps he does not exist at all. So they ruminate, "I must be agnostic or atheist because I cannot understand these things."[12] The result is gross confusion. Fragmentation has also left many families confused and in disarray. The average family is broken. Children are growing up with emotional problems and are turning to sex, drugs, and alcohol for relief. Many dads are given to Internet porn, marriages are dissolving, and there is abuse in the home. The tour de force of Frame's perspectivalism is to provide an answer to the fragmentation and resultant confusion that is sweeping culture and society, and that is having a direct bearing on numerous families. His claim that everything in God is mutually dependent, and that this dependence is manifestly indicated in the creation, means that all things are related and therefore find meaning in God.[13] People who view God's relationship to the world and the world's relationship to God according to CAP are but a short step from victory over confusion and disarray.

The *P* of *CAP* especially provides people a basis for meaning in life. Frame speaks of presence also as "absolute presence," by which he means "that

---

12. The leading universities and divinity schools that have abandoned any notion of the metaphysical in favor of humanistic subjectivism and doubt have nothing constructive to offer those who walk in darkness. They are like the blind leading the blind.

13. See Frame's comment on this fact in *DG*, 12.

without him [God] there could be no meaning, no significance, no purpose in anything."[14] There is hope in this statement for Dustin Hoffman. God's absolute presence in the world provides us absolute certainty (as absolute as creators can be) not only that God is "there," as Francis Schaeffer put it, but also that God is *here* in the fullest sense. When Hoffman says, "If God was to say to me . . . ," the "if" of his statement suggests wishful thinking, void of real meaning, significance, and purpose. The offhand expression, "If God was to . . . " can be the casual agnostic's way of saying, "If God." In this case, it assumes the element of indeterminate chance that is the big brother of all cultural fragmentation and confusion. But God's presence provides Hoffman assurance that God is accessible and is ready to hear his request to become a better pianist. Moreover, Hoffman can anticipate becoming a better jazz musician because God is even *in* his piano. God is in the piano not in the pantheistic sense, but in the sense that he is present in all things. So he is in the piano but is not limited to the piano. Herein lay the answers for Hoffman's aspiration. God is unavoidably approachable and unavoidably present in the very object(s) of our longing. The more important thing for the actor is to be sure he has a good relationship with God in Christ.

On another level, the believing artist can find in Frame's transposition of the usual theological flow of thought some helpful clues toward an enabling theology of the arts. To provide some background for this point, let us note the fact that Scholastic theology had a regrettable effect on the shape of medieval drawings, frescoes, and architecture: a separation between theory and practice. The idea inherent in Scholastic thought that matter is essentially inadequate, in need of divine supplementation, was echoed in the many exceptionally poor representations of natural subjects. Completely unrealistic and two-dimensional, the art creations reveal a total lack of attentiveness to robust nature.[15] The nominalist breakup of High Scholasticism also affected the shape of art, but differently. The Flemish Renaissance painter, Jan van Eyck, best captures the stress on nominal reality. His "down to earth" compositions highlighted the material qualities of his subjects. Van Eyck's exacting patience for acute detail is most apparent in *Portrait of Giovanni Arnolfini and His Wife*. It is his concentration on every microscopic detail that sets van Eyck

---

14. Ibid., 102.

15. I do not mean to suggest that all medieval art was bad. This was the age of the great cathedrals, Vintners' stained glass, and the school of music at Notre Dame. But in most of these cases there is an unnatural quality to the art, a stylization or forced value that appears at odds with nature.

apart as the "atomist" of the family of Renaissance artists. The quest for detailed perfection was a feature of Renaissance art. Now, one might argue that Renaissance art represents some of the highest quality in art history. In spite of this, the overwhelming fixation with perfection led most artists of the period to avoid "mystery" in art, something that would not be tackled in earnest until Rembrandt. Perhaps far worse was the psychological stress the pursuit of perfection inflicted on some of the more noteworthy painters and sculptors of the Renaissance period. Michelangelo was so consumed with pursuing perfection in form that he was driven nearly mad.

Frame's unique approach provides needed balance between the medieval devaluation of nature and the nerve-racking obsession with absolute form typical of the Renaissance.[16] When we think about God's lordship perspectivally, we think about it as servants within the covenant relationship. We will draw, paint, sculpt, or produce film as creatures, in creaturely ways and language, and thus by means of accommodation. Therefore, we need not be consumed with trying to capture perfection in our opus, sonata, or sketch, but are free to explore the subjective world of mystery, speculation, and imagination. Yes, we will use our God-given capacity of imagination, for God is Lord of the imagination and, as in the case of Hoffman's piano, is even in it.[17] At the same time, we will not attempt to explore the world of mystery, speculation, and imagination autonomously, for all that we do will be aided by God's revelation. This means we will create from the standpoint of his reality, his creation, as he made it, a fact that will bring realism and objectivity to our creations. So then, our art will always remain relative to our position as covenant servants: a status that reminds us *both* of our limits *and* of our freedom.

Additionally, the Christian artist who looks to Scripture as a source for inspiration, beginning with God's acting out in history, begins with the drama, color, and sound of his presence. In the mind's eye we see the sparrows, green grass, and lovely lilies. We hear the babbling brooks; we stand in awe at the wonderment of creation, recoil at the sight of a valley of dry bones,

---

16. We could continue on through art history, and the arts generally, and note the swing between emphases on abstraction—such as in the romanticized world of Friedrich—and exactness, order, and harmony found in the art of Poussin during the European Enlightenment.

17. To draw from Frame's example, we say, "God is love." We understand that phrase subjectively—in its warmth and assurance to us as creatures. But the phrase also tells us something important about the objective nature of God, apart from which we would have no real understanding of what it means that God loves us. For more on this point, see *DG*, 190.

and marvel at four horses of different colors bearing riders with messages profound. The very encounter with the Lord is one steeped in creativity.

Moving now to a different area of cultural activity, we note that the C of *CAP* offers a basis on which to remain vigilant in what has been called the "culture war." In commenting on the efficacy of God's control over his creation, Frame notes:

> To say that God's controlling power is efficacious is simply to say that it always accomplishes its purposes. God never fails to accomplish what he sets out to do. Creatures may oppose him, to be sure, but they cannot prevail. For his own reasons, he has chosen to delay the fulfillment of his intentions for the end of history, and to bring about those intentions through a complicated historical sequence of events. In that sequence, his purposes appear sometimes to suffer defeat, sometimes to achieve victory. But . . . apparent defeat actually makes his eventual victory all the more glorious. The cross of Jesus is, of course, the chief example of this principle.[18]

Elsewhere, Frame speaks in similar terms, such as his references to the new creation representing the *telos*, or the goal, of creation and thus of history,[19] and to God's plan behind all history.[20] More references are available, but essentially Frame's historical position is proleptical. By *proleptical* I do not mean to suggest that Frame is aligned with the modern historicist-idealist system of Wolfhart Pannenberg. For Pannenberg, a historical prolepsis is simply a claim staked out in history that, when history is fulfilled, will be proved or disproved. So, according to Pannenberg, the cross "anticipates" the reconciliation of the world. It is at the point of reconciliation that Christians will know whether or not their belief has been vindicated. Contra this idea, Frame believes that God is the determinate cause of all things in history, immutably in charge of all events, every nanosecond and microparticle. There is no room in Frame's theology for libertine indeterminacy. Frame's consistent obsequiousness to God's lordship in the processes of history provides us a proleptical view of history in which history is not seen as random events (libertine free will) or hopeful events (Pannenberg), but descriptive events that anticipate a coming reality.

18. Ibid., 47.
19. See ibid., 297.
20. See ibid., 313.

Now, returning to the above quote, the word *makes* is pregnant with meaning. It suggests that it is not the apparent defeat of God's purposes in the creation that makes victory all the more glorious. It is the sovereign God *working* in and through each apparent defeat that assures ultimate victory. To faithfully interpret Frame's meaning, we could say that all that happens on the stage of culture, whether good or bad, is proleptically oriented toward a final goal—the ultimate victory of God at the consummation of time. Things are this way because God is at work in each event. So even though God's children may suffer persecution and loss in this life, even though it may appear that Satan and his evil minions are gaining the upper hand on the world stage, God is in control, working all things together to serve his eternal ends. Despite the ups and downs and the victories and the defeats associated with our custodial responsibility to culture, God's sovereignty assures the church a successful outcome.

That God uses our defeats—in our attempts to affect the horizontal processes of history—to accomplish his final purposes ought to encourage Christians to live not in isolationist occupation in the world, but as a community bent on obedience to the Cultural Mandate (Gen. 1:26–28; 2:15) and Great Commission (Matt. 28:18–20) of the Bible.[21] This obedience counters the popular model that would have us wringing our hands waiting for escape from this "vale of tears." Ours is not a "polishing of the brass on the Titanic" but a living out of a tangible expression of "the conviction of things not seen" (Heb. 11:1; all Scripture quotations are from the NASB). We are always about our Father's work: on the side of justice, showing mercy to the sick of heart and body, teaching the eternal truths of knowing him and making him known at every level of culture, and humbly proclaiming the transforming message of reconciliation to all. Such a life is facilitated as we tarry in prayer and seek to model the life of Christ. Frame's proleptical emphasis means that we must interpret even our supposed failures at attempting to affect the culture for Christ as successes. In recent years, many Christians have abandoned efforts

---

21. For his views on the Cultural Mandate and the Great Commission, see chapter 17 of *DCL*. *DCL*, 855, 862, are also quite helpful. In chapter 17 of *DCL*, Frame addresses the continuity and discontinuity of the twin mandates, although he seems to lean more on the side of continuity. He also discusses in this section some of the theories on how the two commands relate biblically. I have argued in my book, *The Road from Eden* that the Cultural Mandate and the Great Commission are not separate commands but "bookends" of a single doctrine of dominion, established in Genesis 1:28 and expanded through the language of the covenants until it finds full expression in Jesus' missional command of Matthew 28. In essence, then, I hold that the Great Commission is what the Cultural Mandate looks like after the resurrection.

at direct cultural engagement out of a deep sense that their work has produced few results. But if Frame is right (and indeed he is) that God is at work in our failures, then this not only changes our definition of *success* in the struggle for cultural renewal, but also tells us we must remain vigilant in the struggle, for how will God be at work in our failures unless we are there to fail?

ETHICS

John Frame believes that all things can be reduced to ethics.[22] Anecdotally, many years ago, when I was a student of Frame, he said before our class in apologetics, "Everything can be boiled down to a matter of ethics." So it comes as little surprise when he writes of his entire system of epistemology.

> Although my epistemology was published before my ethics, I developed the threefold scheme in ethics before applying it to epistemology. Ethics is its [the threefold scheme in ethics] natural home, and I think the ethical applications of it are more easily understood than the applications to epistemological theology. Indeed the point of my epistemology is that epistemology can be fruitfully understood as a subdivision of ethics and thus can be fruitfully analyzed by the use of my meta-ethic.[23]

By *metaethic* Frame means to develop a general method for approaching ethical problems, not a mechanical system for answering all ethical questions with fixed resolution. For the purpose of this writing, however, I do not intend to draw too hard a distinction between "ethics" and "metaethics" as Frame presents the two, but simply to address the consequence of making ethics a ground from which to draw conclusions about practical issues.[24]

Frame believes that only God's Word can define the nature and scope of ethics. "A fully Christian ethic accepts only God's word as final . . ."[25] In keeping with the revelation of God's declaration in Scripture, the world, and the self, Frame presents us a view of ethics from three perspectives: the exis-

22. The following section is not a concise evaluation of *DCL* but rather provides a brief overview of ethics as a base for Frame's theology and how he sees it function in deliberations on culture. For other references on the primacy of ethics in Frame's system of thought, see *DG*, 186–87, 199, 400.

23. *PWG*, 40.

24. By adding the world and the self, Frame does not mean to set these over and against the Bible as separate authorities. He means that the biblical God is revealed to us in the world and the self, and that these forums are subservient to the interpretive key of God's special revelation.

25. *DG*, 195.

tential perspective, the situational perspective, and the normative perspective.[26] The most important thing to understand is that by boiling everything down to a matter of ethics, Frame is again not arguing from the abstract, but makes human behavior before God a door to knowledge about the world and how best to live in it. In other words, for Frame, knowledge is not only propositional in nature, although it contains propositional elements,[27] but essentially ethical, insofar as God defines all truth and *is* truth. According to Frame, even propositional truths are to be interpreted ethically, that is, in relationship to God. "Therefore, propositional knowledge is based on knowledge of a person. He supplies the norms, the justifications, that are missing in secular accounts of knowledge, as well as the truths that we are to believe and the mental capacity for us to come to knowledge. . . . He is the ultimate *truth*: the truth is what he is and what he has decreed to be."[28]

At this point, let us return to the area of the fine arts and see how Frame's reductionism of all things to ethics assists us in the process of the valuation. Pablo Picasso was not a believer, yet he is considered the greatest painter of the twentieth century. Undoubtedly, Picasso demonstrated technical brilliance and aesthetic vision in his compositions. Although from a human perspective his life productions may be considered great, sin had reduced him to a mere vestige of the image of God, meaning that his work was not sound from an ethical perspective. Just as there is no such thing as a "brute fact," as Van Til used to say, so also there is no such thing as brute art, brute music, or brute cross-stitch. All forms of art, and indeed every manner of cultural activity, summons holy judgment, for all of it is done in God's world using God's gifts and energies. We can do such things for his glory or for our own. Before John Frame, the ancient prophet Isaiah declared that the acceptability of man's work before God cannot be divorced from the matter of ethics: "For all of us have become like one who is unclean, and all our righteous deeds are like a filthy garment" (Isa. 64:6). Without a redemptive relationship between the sculptor, musician, ballet artist, candlestick maker and God, their labor, although it may reflect the interests of beauty and the design of God's creation in a broad sense, will fall short in gaining God's full approval. It is therefore not enough to seek great artistic accomplishments in color, sound, texture, proportion, movement

26. A full treatment of the three perspectives is found in *DCL*, 131–360.
27. For more on Frame's discussion on propositional truth, see *DG*, 475–79.
28. Ibid., 480–1.

on stage, or shape. Instead, *right values* must also flow from our hands, as those values flow from our redeemed hearts.

Art, music, and every other form of human creativity, once they are accomplished, are nothing more than an image of something that exists in God's universe. The painter cannot paint anything more than what his eye can see, or his imagination can take from nature and elaborate on. The composer of music cannot write using anything more than what his ear can hear, or his imagination can take from nature and elaborate on. In any case, the painter and the composer—indeed all artisans—have at their disposal the existential, situational, and normative perspective of God's Word, no more and no less. The artist can build something using these perspectives with a twisted and sinful starting point and create something of great indifference to God's lordship, and be led down what Frame calls "blind alleys." Or, as a covenant child, he can complete a meaningful image that reflects God's creation and his gift of creativity. So then, Frame encourages Dustin Hoffman, who seeks to be a better improvisational pianist, to reflect on what "better" means in God's view of things. "Better" includes more than hitting right notes at the right times, with just that perfect feel, but also includes the aspect of Hoffman's dependence on God as a saved sinner. Frame would not want Hoffman to think that his piano playing has merely an ethical *component* to it, as if that component could be defined apart from the TRUE truth of God's Word. Rather, he would want the actor to understand that the very act of piano playing is itself an intensely ethical activity. Playing jazz piano is an extension of one's spiritual values and worldview, which are based in one's relationship to God. Moreover, as Frame reminds us, God is not merely the source of values, but also the "supreme evaluator"[29] (see Gen. 1:3–4, which records that after saying, "Let there be light," he "saw that the light was good"). Hence, every touch of the piano keys must exhibit the quality of aesthetic deference to the Lord of all creativity and to his evaluation of our creativity in light of the existential, situational, and normative perspectives of God's great revelation.

A further point we can take from Frame's ethics is his belief that Christians ought to know something substantive about the culture in which they live. The existential, situational, and normative perspectives unite in his idea that none can exist without the subjects of knowledge knowing something about the objects of culture. This is especially the case respecting the

29. Ibid., 81.

normative perspective. "To know what Scripture says about abortion, we must know something about abortion. To know what Scripture says about nuclear weapons, we must know something about nuclear weapons."[30] Thus, we must not only know what Scripture says *to* cultural issues, but also be versed *in* cultural subjects so that we might understand them better and also speak authoritatively and, we hope, convincingly about them to nonbelievers. For example, since the Bible speaks *to* when life begins, we ought to be educated, to some extent, *in* biology. Frame holds that the Bible is meaningless unless we understand the culture.[31] Nevertheless, most Christians are woefully unprepared to speak with any real depth of understanding to the issues of the day: nuclear weapons, abortion, infanticide, medical ethics, the economy, the Iraq War, feminism, human cloning, the nature of great art, and more. Frame is not asking us to become experts in every field of culture, or even one for that matter. But to assent to his view that every event in life is perspectivally related, and all within an intensely ethical encounter with the living God who evaluates all of our judgments and actions, precludes us from being cultural eunuchs and instead places us under a certain obligation to "discern the signs of the times" (Matt. 16:3).

We find the same idea of immediate integration between ethics and culture in Frame's view that all theology is application.[32] It is about problem solving, something that stands at the forefront of Frame's whole system of theology. As he says, the intent of all theology "is not to reproduce the

30. Ibid., 195–6.

31. In Ibid., 197, he writes, "Yes, Scripture is meaningless unless it is applicable to situations, so we must indeed understand the times in which we are living." By this point, it is important to note what Frame does not mean. A dangerous trend is afoot, especially in the universities in which students are taught to use art, literature, poetic language, and other modes of artistic expression as interpretive *tools* to find meaning in the Bible. This is an interdisciplinary approach that seeks not merely to apply what Scripture says to painting, for example, but also to use painting as a hermeneutical key to understand the meaning of Scripture better than what Scripture alone provides. This methodology finds its roots in the nineteenth-century revolution in aesthetics, spearheaded by the *Sturm und Drang*, a small group of young intellectuals who no longer sought the meaning of poetic and artistic language in objective truths, as had the writers of the Enlightenment, but in the speaker's subjectivity and personality. For the members of the *Sturm und Drang*, the potential effects of poetry and art are connected with a complex dialectical process of cultural evolution that involves language, history, and consciousness. Frame's idea, that Scripture is meaningless unless it is applied to situations, is not dialectical at its core. In other words, he is not suggesting that the meaning of Scripture lies in the changing relationship between the biblical text and the objects of culture. Rather, his concern is practical, indeed pastoral. It is intended to relate the objective truth of the biblical texts to situations and to human subjectivity.

32. For this integration, see ibid., 379.

emphasis of Scripture . . . but to apply Scripture to the needs of people."[33] But of course how can we apply Scripture to the needs of people unless we have developed some sort of close relationship with them? Thus, to best help Dustin Hoffman break through the indeterminacy of his proposition, "If God was to . . . ," to a point at which he can come to God as his child and seek God's help in growing as a musician, requires the presence of someone in his life not merely to offer conceptual theological content, but to pastor him theologically.

In contrast with his own system of ethics, Frame has much to say about non-Christian ethical systems. A major point in his syllabus is that the main problem with non-Christian ethical systems is that nonbelief is utopian by nature. "The main problem [with secular ethics] is not conceptual confusion, a lack of logical skill, or ignorance of facts, although such problems do exist in both Christian and non-Christian ethical systems. The chief problem is rather unbelief itself."[34] He further brings out the utopian slant of secular ethics with this pithy comment: "But we cannot exist without ultimate values, so we become gods ourselves."[35] Frame says something quite similar elsewhere when he dissects secular ethics, revealing its natural propensity toward relativism and dogmatism. Abridging Frame, because secular liberalism rejects God, anything is permitted. But since such an idea can lead only to chaos, the secularist replaces God with another moral absolute: his own autonomous moral judgment. Seeing that this judgment is of the nature of a false god, it seeks to impose itself on others—hence its aggressively utopian character.[36] So when the theologian says that the basic problem with non-Christian thought is unbelief itself, he is not comparing this unbelief to a dead battery with no zip. Unbelief is a force to be reckoned with and must be understood in the context of nothing less than spiritual warfare. "There is a war, but the war is between Christ and Satan, Christ and unbelief, not Christ and culture."[37]

Frame's identification of the unbending moral relativism of secular ethics, and its proclivity to turn warlike, challenges Christians who practice self-imposed cultural abandonment. A fully lived discipleship must

33. Ibid., 7. See also *DKG*, 81–85.
34. *DG*, 194.
35. Ibid., 114.
36. For Frame's fuller discussion on this topic, see *DCL*, 899. At ibid., 858, he makes a helpful similar point regarding the totalitarian nature of world religions.
37. Ibid., 862.

assume direct confrontation with the false kingdoms of the world, for the combative nature of secular thought makes this fact unavoidable. Believers may attempt to avoid the culture war, but the culture war will find them. It remains a conflict needing much prayer and wisdom. For, on the one hand, unbelief is embodied in flesh and bone, and all too often we are called to meet unregenerate people on the stage of world affairs and in the marketplace of ideas, where we must have great resolve, forthright conviction, and the power of his might (Acts 25:13–26:32). On the other hand, our unbelieving neighbor is not our enemy (Eph. 6:12) but is one whom we are called to love (Matt. 5:43–48) and to evangelize (Matt. 28:18–20). This is not a warfare the church can expect to win wearing Saul's armor. "The gathering of people out of Satan's clutches into Christ's kingdom, is accomplished not through warfare or politics, not through the influence of money of fame, but 'through the foolishness of the message preached' (1 Cor. 1:21)."[38]

A theological handle that can help us ascertain why many Christians are all too often willing to forfeit their posts as guardians of culture is found in what Frame calls "The Square of Religious Opposition."[39] Following Frame's "Square," they hold to an *unbiblical view of God's transcendence.* This is the legacy of ancient philosophers who, with their anthropomorphic propensity to picture God as half man and half animal, stressed God's indefinable and indecipherable nature over his nearness in order to shield him from the popular religions of the day that stressed his sameness with man. As if to enlist themselves into the family tree of dualists, many modern evangelicals base their form of cultural obscurantism in the recognizable apologetic: because God is so lofty, so pure, and so far beyond us, he is to be sheltered from the polluted here and now.[40] Unbiblical transcendence always leads to an injudicious effort to remove God from the day-to-day chaos of the world. Human escape from, or at least indifference toward, the issues that constitute the sociopolitical fabric of the material world is always close behind. The result of unbiblical transcendence is the deifica-

---

38. *DG*, 527. We ought not to overstate Frame's position regarding politics. He believes that Christians ought to be active participants in politics. So when he speaks of gathering people out of Satan's clutches through the preaching of the Word of God, not politics, he is reacting against the "politicization of the gospel," not against applying the gospel to the associated realms of government and electoral politics.

39. See ibid., 107–14.

40. I also believe that, following Frame's Square, the cultural pietists' unbiblical idea of immanence reflects the subjectivism or sentimentalism of the Greek pantheists and the nineteenth-century Romanticists, but without the theology that God is in all.

tion of the sacrosanct world of exclusive religion over our duty to God's Cultural Mandate and Great Commission.

Presuppositional Apologetics

Understanding the import of Frame's presuppositional apologetics is critical for our physical stewardship of culture. Frame is highly given to the apologetic capability of the Word of God: "Legitimate apologetic argument presupposes the truth of Scripture, and it renounces the idea of human intellectual independence or autonomy."[41] As a consequence, his apologetic calls us to pistical reliance on Scripture. Nowhere is this more apparent than in his positions that the viability of the resurrection of Jesus is not predicated on the testimony of more than five hundred witnesses to the resurrection, but on its centrality to the apostolic witness,[42] and that we can rectify the matter of a loving God and the presence of evil by understanding that God does not feel he needs to explain his actions to us, but instead solves the problem of evil *in us* by giving us *new hearts* and calling us to trust him with the "why" of natural evil.[43] Frame believes that apologetics encompasses a threefold purpose: proof, a defense of the gospel, and a potent offense against the foolishness of secular thought.[44] As with everything else in Framean theology, presuppositional apologetics is perspectivally related.[45]

Much can be said regarding Frame's positions on apologetics. However, the distilled essence of his views is to take no prisoners. Once more, an anecdotal recollection serves our purposes. It was a day just before the start of classes at Westminster Theological Seminary Philadelphia when a group of us students were sitting in a circle, introducing ourselves to each other. John Frame approached us and asked, "What are you guys talking about?" A student replied, "We're discussing Van Til." To this, Frame responded, "Everything Van Til ever said can be reduced to two ideas: that all men undeniably know God, and that the only way to approach them is to pull the rug right out from under them." Frame's Van Tillian reduction takes as its cue the withstanding principle of presuppositional apologetics: "no neutrality." This principle is grounded in the divine inspiration, infallibil-

---

41. *AGG*, 86.
42. See ibid., 58.
43. Chapter 7 of *AGG* covers this issue in full.
44. He speaks to the dual nature of apologetics in ibid., 2–3.
45. The perspectival nature of apologetics is addressed in ibid., 3.

ity, and authority of Scripture. Parenthetically, many evidentialists[46] claim that Van Til was "a Thomist with a presupposition." This false evaluation is immediately challenged by the fact that when Moses asked God to reveal his name (Ex. 3:13), Yahweh did not respond, "Tell them 'I think' sent you (epistemology)." Rather, he said, "Thus you shall say to the sons of Israel, 'I AM has sent me to you'" (v. 14, ontology). It appears that God is a Thomist with a presupposition.

The applicatory force of Frame's apologetic system is seen in many ways, but especially as a powerful prescription for aiding the church in calling postmoderns to Christ. We are living in a day when many pastors have relinquished commitment to the all-sufficiency of Scripture to call people to salvation in order to embrace a new set of concerns revolving around innovation in ministry. This abandonment is based in the wrongheaded notion that to speak to a postmodern about the Bible is a cross-cultural experience. Frame seems to be unaware that the images of God in Scripture have generated controversy.[47] Yet his enabling theology of the Word of God counters the ridiculous notion that the Bible is cultural-bound language. "The unbeliever cannot (because he will not) come to faith apart from the biblical gospel of salvation. We would not know about the unbeliever's condition apart from Scripture. And we cannot address it apologetically unless we are ready to listen to Scripture's own principles of apologetics."[48] Clearly there are legitimate questions churches must ask that pertain to the contextualization of the gospel in our world, such as, "How is the gospel received by people of different subcultures?" Today, however, an increasing number of pulpits place far too much emphasis on contextualization and not enough on the apologetic power of *sola Scriptura* to minister to people of different subcultures.

Frame's point that apologetics includes a potent offensive is also much needed and lies at the heart of the Great Commission, in which Jesus commands us to "go" to the nations of the world with the good news. We are therefore not to wait for the Dustin Hoffmans of the world to walk through the doors of our churches on Sunday morning, but to engage them where they are. Indeed, the reader of Frame's works has surely noted the way in

---

46. Although John Frame is a presuppositional apologist, he is not against the use of evidence in the presentation of the gospel and its associated truths. For more on this point, see ibid., chap. 3.

47. In this regard, see his comments in DG, 363.

48. *AGG*, 8.

which he is always showing the "straw men" in non-Christian systems of thought, exposing their fallacies and inconsistencies and bringing every thought captive to the obedience of Christ. On this level, John Frame reminds us of Francis Schaeffer—a "very smart evangelist," as Frame once remarked to me of Schaeffer, who used apologetics as a means to reach a world lost in the wreckage of incredulity. I am reminded of Henry Krabbendam's comment, as well, that apologetics can quickly become an exercise in "circling the wagons" if Christians do not practice aggressive evangelism.[49]

There is also a discipleship emphasis in Frame's presuppositional apologetic. Because postmodern thought fundamentally rejects metaphysics, it cannot provide a unified explanation of the universe. In this sense, the postmodern dilemma actually predates Lyotard by centuries as it has appeared in different forms (e.g., particulars and universals). Because postmodern thought cannot provide a reasonably sufficient explanation of the universe, neither can it offer us a philosophical context by which we can substantiate our communal life. Accordingly, the philosophy runs afoul of itself: because it is unable to justify its interpretation of reality with reality itself, it produces a mental split between *individualism* and *multiculturalism*. Given that the schema of Frame's apologetics is, like everything else in his work, perspectivally related via CAP, he presents us with an organic interpretation of the universe and thus a consistent presentation of how we can learn to think about the world in which we live, i.e., worldview.[50]

In conjunction with Frame's presuppositional apologetics, let us now consider the theologian's concept of *natural law*. Some context is needed for this discussion, so let us back up and note that, because of his perspectivalism, Frame is reticent to make hard-and-fast distinctions in almost any area of theology, including his doctrine of the Word of God. Consequently, the reader of Frame's works may be tempted to think that his triperspectivalism blurs the Word of God, the world, and the self.[51] A perfect example from which this sort of opinion can be derived is found in his caution that "In

49. He made this remark when teaching on the Gospel of John during the 2008 Presbyterian Evangelistic Fellowship Annual Family Conference.

50. Space does not permit a detailed examination of Frame's thinking on worldview. However, note Frame's complete discussion of worldview, or metaphysics, as he calls it, in *AGG*, 34–50.

51. He also explains, "Someone might look at this reasoning and say that in the end it makes Scripture, the world, and the self identical. Or even God himself, the world, and the self. And I say no. These three are not identical. But the knowledge of them is identical. You can't know one apart from knowing the others." E-mail message to the author, April 2, 2009.

my triperspectivalism, you should not equate the normative perspective with Scripture. The normative perspective (like the other two perspectives) includes everything, because everything reveals God in one way or another. Scripture is not the same thing as the normative perspective, but it is one object within the normative perspective (and indeed within the other two perspectives as well). It is the norm that norms other norms, the *norma normans*, the covenant document, etc."[52] Here Frame is not saying that the normative perspective contains the Bible or that it is identical with the Bible.[53] He is saying that Scripture is *within* the normative perspective, but that there are other things in the normative perspective as well. The same can be said of the situational and the existential perspectives. But my Bible sits on my desk. How can Scripture be an object within my situational and existential perspective? Frame defends against interpretations of his perspectivalism that infer unwarranted indistinction. "Someone might look at this reasoning and say that in the end it makes Scripture, the world, and the self identical. Or even God himself, the world, and the self. And I say no. These three are not identical. But the *knowledge* of them is identical. You can't know one apart from knowing the others."[54] Since it is not the purpose of this writing to unpack fully Frame's doctrine of the Word of God, let us conclude that we should not equate the Framean normative perspective with Scripture,[55] but rather see that his perspectivalism creates broad overlap between Scripture and other areas of theology traditionally reserved for separate treatment.

This is most certainly true with respect to the conventional division between special and general revelation. Frame holds to the traditional classifications. He thinks of Romans 1 the same way Van Til did: General revelation is given to everyone through the creation and leaves everyone without excuse because it reveals God's nature and attributes, his ethical standards, and his wrath against us for violating these standards. He also agrees with

---

52. Ibid.

53. He appears to indicate in *DG*, 195–96, that the normative perspective and Scripture are the same.

54. E-mail message to the author, April 2, 2009.

55. According to Frame, the three perspectives are identical. They contain the same content. They all contain everything there is. Thus, the normative perspective contains everything, because everything reveals God. The situational perspective includes everything, because everything is part of my environment. The existential perspective includes everything, because everything is part of my experience. That means, of course, that ultimately the three perspectives are identical. This is why Frame calls them "perspectives." They are not different things, but different ways of looking at the whole universe.

Van Til that fallen man's response to general revelation is suppression of the truth, exchanging it for a lie, and violating its commands.[56] So, in general, he agrees with the traditional view that the gospel, the way of salvation, is not part of general revelation. The gospel, or "special" revelation, is through the preaching of Christ. Despite this, he does not fully agree that general revelation does not contain special revelation. He holds that there is a sense in which even Scripture is general revelation, i.e., a verbal object that reveals the existence of God and his moral demands, and that leaves people without excuse, but that they repress in unrighteousness.[57]

This brings us to his view of natural law. In concert with his triperspectival approach to special and general revelation, Frame accepts natural law, but cautions against a view of natural-law theory that teaches that within the secular sphere we are to rely on a set of self-reliant laws, without any recourse to special revelation. Frame's problem with such a theory is that Scripture does not distinguish a "secular" sphere from a "religious" one, and that we should never try to understand anything without consulting Scripture. Taking these two points together, Frame is therefore not convinced that there are natural laws, if by "natural law" one means a kind of impersonal machinery by which God governs creation.[58] Natural laws, according to this view, are a kind of medium *between* God and the creation. On the contrary, Frame thinks Scripture represents God as making things happen *in* nature by his direct personal action.[59]

Now, what can we glean from Frame's idea of natural law for our present cultural context? Frame's views on natural law find expression in the question, "What is the proper apologetic method for arguing in favor of a God-centered social ethic?" Since the 1970s (and here I am thinking mainly of the modern tug-of-war over social ethics in America), the main strategy of Christian

56. Frame offers a brief but excellent discussion on general revelation, especially as he understands its apologetic function, in *AGG*, 7–9.

57. The content of this paragraph is from an e-mail message from John Frame to the author, April 2, 2009.

58. Many experts, citing Blackstone's *Commentary on the Laws of England*, define *lex naturalis* as that which posits the existence of a law whose content is set by nature and that therefore has validity everywhere. The intersection between natural law and natural rights is a component in the United States Declaration of Independence. Frame would take issue with a law that is set by an impersonal force called "nature."

59. See Frame's explanation of natural law in *DG*, 246–51. Along these lines, Frame wrote to me, "Certainly I don't equate 'natural laws' in this sense with natural revelation. I am willing, as I state in *DG*, to accept natural laws in other senses, particularly in the sense of general regularities in God's providence. In that lesser sense, natural laws would be equivalent to natural revelation." E-mail message to the author, April 2, 2009.

social activists has been to appeal to truths associated with natural law (these would include truths associated with general revelation and providence). So we have argued against abortion by appealing mainly to an impersonal "sanctity of life," against homosexuality because it is not "natural," against same-sex marriage on the basis of poll results that show most Americans still resist the idea, against the encroachment of secular values in society according to commonsense principles, and for the right of Christians to use public facilities for Christian events based on the First Amendment to the Constitution. Apologists for the Judeo-Christian ethic in America who speak in these terms do so predominantly because they find in America's founders what they believe to be a facilitating theory—that the world and our lives are not ruled by chance, or by fate, but by the associated ideas of natural law and God's providence—and therefore appeal to it regularly as a means to counter the regress of that ethic. Certainly the founders ought to have a voice in the continuing debate over the shape of publicly held values, especially since it was their philosophy of government and public life that birthed a nation and set it on its course. Notwithstanding the founders' reliance on natural law, disputes remain over the extent to which their language emerged from a deistic context versus a fully biblical one.

Frame's presuppositional apologetics employs a central position that remands the modern debate over social ethics back to scriptural sources. His discontent with the deontological view of natural law emphasizes the interconnection between natural moral virtue and supernatural virtue as revealed in Scripture. His perspectival interpretation suggests the question, "How is natural law promulgated and embodied?" This question is indeed central for the debate on social ethics today, and Frame's perspectival view of Scripture makes a persuasive case that we dare not embrace a view of natural law that finds its content and validity set by nature alone, and that therefore focuses on the ethicalness of actions while bypassing their consequences, and that conceives of the state as an institution directed at bringing its subjects to true happiness, without reference to God's revealed laws. Hence, Frame does not believe that God intends for Christians to cultivate the world by appealing to natural law only. Rather, following Calvin, he points to our need to look at nature through the "spectacles" of Scripture. And although disputes remain over the extent to which the biblical language emerged, the Christian apologist can presuppose its divine source and wield the sword of the Spirit knowing that it will hit its mark.

The need for thoughtful dialogue with modern man continues in the search for a standard for right action in the world. The role of natural law in our public conversation will continue. It is the principle of lordship that cautions us against such dialogue *strictly* on the basis of mechanical laws or good sense, which stress the capability of autonomous human intelligence to adapt to the infinite variability of human affairs, or on the basis of our shared humanity with non-Christians. If the Christian social cause in America has stalled, it is because we were afraid that if we quoted Scripture as a means of changing secular perceptions on issues, we would be marginalized. Frame reminds us of the limitations of a deontological natural-law theory as an apologetic tool to defend ethical values and actions. His theology is at one with the biblical presupposition that all men know the truth but suppress it in unrighteousness, and that the greatest means at our disposal to disciple others is the power of the Word of God in conjunction with the Holy Spirit.

Frame's Overall Position on Culture

According to H. Richard Niebuhr's famous five-tier breakdown of the historic Christian positions on Christ and culture, Frame supports the "Christ, the Transformer of Culture" model. At the end of his solid critique of the first four models of Christ and culture, he admits, "So, by process of elimination, but not only that, I find myself supporting the fifth view, that Christians should be seeking to transform culture according to the standards of God's Word."[60] Frame succinctly clarifies what a transformer of culture does. "Similarly, the Christian should seek to bring biblical standards to bear in all areas of society and culture. Our motive is not to try to make non-Christians live the Christian life, but simply to work out the implications of our faith in all areas of life."[61] This brief statement is a rallying call to the church to change increasingly pluralist and multicultural societies for Christ. It is a call to self-reflectively appropriate and interpret current cultural norms in the scales of Scripture and also to apply the conditions of our Christian faith to all the elements that together constitute culture. Nonetheless, there are challenges for the transformer of culture.

First, there is the controversiality of the notion that the church ought to bring biblical standards to bear on all levels of society and culture. This

60. *DCL*, 874.
61. Ibid., 873.

concern is not unwarranted, for there are many who have gone about the task from wrong motives, and also from the adoption of faulty biblical principles, creating great havoc along the way. But by providing us with an integral link between the Cultural Mandate and the Great Commission of the Bible as the framework for our life of obedience, Frame maintains the priority of kingdom building in the hearts of people and avoids the scandal of advocating cultural reform apart from the grace of God.[62]

Second, we must recognize that the paradigmatic function of the twin mandates of Scripture does not discern for us the particularities from culture to culture. A goodly bit has been said in this monograph respecting the American cultural scene. However, the Lord's marching orders are to "all the nations" (Matt. 28:19). We must be sensitive to the fact that to transform world cultures is not to equalize people's everyday existence. There is a contextualization process, to be sure, one that must cause us to reflect on the transcultural significance of the gospel, and thus of the ways in which we can best articulate the implications of the gospel from culture to culture while not disrupting the unique customs of diverse people groups that are not at variance with Scripture.

Third, further complicating the quest to transform culture(s) is the fact that the cultural forms of life of modernity that developed out of the European Enlightenment—for example, science and technology—have expanded and will continue to expand globally. On the one hand, this globalization of modernity is accompanied by a heightened awareness of, and attachment to, particular cultures and culture-specific values, resulting in an increasing pluralism *between* cultures. On the other hand, the more recent advance of postmodernity has facilitated a process of homogenization among world cultures, resulting in egalitarianism and culture-nonspecific values *within* cultures. Thus, the mission of transformation is one fraught with challenges and questions. Indeed, the competing elements of thought that characterize the world stage make culture a difficult thing to define.

Fourth, an added challenge for the cultural transformationist is to reflect more critically on what makes culture "Christian." Regarding what transformation is *not*, Frame says, "To apply Christian standards to art, for example, does not mean that we must turn our artistic works into gospel tracts."[63] Also, "A transformational approach does not mean that every

---

62. Again, for Frame's views on the relationship of the Cultural Mandate and the Great Commission, see ibid., chap. 17.

63. Ibid., 874.

human activity by a Christian (e.g., plumbing, car repair) must be obviously, externally different from the same activities practiced by non-Christians."[64] So, on the one hand, our transformational efforts should aim high: to create top-quality productions, regardless of the cultural venue. On the other hand, God has made it inescapable for Christians to affirm cultural similarities with non-Christians. But even here, "there is always a difference [between Christian and non-Christian work in culture], but often the difference is that of motive, goal, and standard, rather than anything external."[65]

In conclusion, the relationship of Christianity and culture is a complicated issue with a complicated history. The nascent church grappled with how it ought to react to its Greco-Roman environment, and especially to the political situation created by its repressive landlord. Many early Christians believed martyrdom offered the best answer inasmuch as they considered dying for the crucified One a potent means to hasten the great day of the Lord when Satan and the idolatrous kingdoms of the world will be defeated forever. By the early third century, the need for Christian teachers to spend large amounts of time fashioning apologetics designed to defeat paganism cultivated a mistrustful outlook within parts of early Christendom toward *all* culture. Writing during this period, Tertullian's rhetorical query, "What does Athens have to do with Jerusalem?"[66] spoke for many who concurred that the pagan culture of Greece was of no significance to the Christian church. Van Til states that Tertullian's response contra paganism was so acute that he condemned "every form of culture simply because of its pagan origin and association."[67] Indeed, his was "a declaration of war against these very things for which the Roman administration stood, *the mos maiorum*, the rule of secular law, and the binding authority of custom."[68] Christian teachers, centered mainly in the East, had the opposite response: utter fervor for Greek thought and civilization. So whereas Tertullian looked upon the relationship between the church and Rome as an antithesis, many of the Greek fathers viewed Rome and Jerusalem as offspring of the same *logos*. To them this signified that Christians could do more for the gospel "in the world" as the empire's friends. This line of thought is seen in the *Epistle to*

64. Ibid.
65. Ibid.
66. Tertullian, *Prescription against Heretics*, 7.
67. H. R. Van Til, *The Calvinistic Concept of Culture* (Grand Rapids: Baker, 1972), 67.
68. W. H. C. Frend, *Martyrdom and Persecution in the Early Church* (Oxford: Blackwell, 1965), 366.

Diognetus (ca. 185). The letter states that the Christians' presence in the world has made the world a better place.

Some two thousand years later, not only do Christians remain split over the relationship of Christ and culture, but the passage of time has introduced a variety of new theories to the public discussion to help fill in the middle ground. So the dialogue today is quite rich. "What is the proper Christian response to culture?" "Are we to transform culture?" "If so, what are the best means for achieving this end?" "Or ought Christians to practice a Tertullian-like aloofness to culture?" These types of questions will remain a fertile source of debate within Christian communities until the end of the present age. But as this writer has argued, the study of Christianity and culture is predominantly a biblical/theological endeavor. Thus, it is proper theology that offers us the best hope in addressing these sorts of questions. Although a good many attempts have been made in print to answer "why" Christians ought to be involved in the public square, in the arts, and in related cultural fields, and some effort has been made to teach Christians "what" they can do to bring God's standards to bear on culture, it is John Frame's theology of lordship that provides contemporary Christians a most timely and salutary foundation for their abiding responsibility as God's vicegerents both to dress the garden and to disciple nations. In the very preliminary years when the shape of the Framean theology of lordship was yet in its embryonic form, the theologian likely saw himself as one committed to originating a much-needed outlook in theology with important meaning for culture. Now in its mature years, what has emerged is a body of work that truly sets John Frame apart as a theologian of culture—*par excellence*.

38

DOING THEOLOGY TODAY

CARL F. ELLIS JR.

"Theology is the application of the Word of God by persons to all areas of life."[1]
Dr. John Frame

"For the word of God is living and active. Sharper than any double-edged sword, it penetrates even to dividing soul and spirit, joints and marrow; it judges the thoughts and attitudes of the heart." (Heb. 4:12)[2]

FACETS IN THEOLOGY

Two Approaches

There are essentially two approaches to music, the formal and the dynamic. We call them *classical* and *jazz*. We know what classical music is—the little dots, circles, and lines of Beethoven and Brahms that come to life when a conductor stabs the air with a baton. These sounds that fill the air are not the conductor's or the violinists'. They belong to Beethoven and Brahms. The beauty of a classical piece is found in the mind of the composer,

---

1. *SBL*, 315.
2. All quotations of Scripture are from the NIV.

in the music as it is *written*. Thus the goal of the classical musician is to reproduce as faithfully as possible the sounds the great composers imagined. Only in rare moments and clearly marked cadenzas do classical musicians improvise. Their main task is not to improvise but to imitate.

Jazz is different. The beauty of jazz is found in the soul of the musician and in the music as it is *performed*. Jazz is improvisational. Just as classical music has developed musical composition into a fine art, jazz has cultivated musical improvisation into a fine art. The notes that fill the air do not belong to a deceased composer; they issue from the vibrant souls of great performers like "Diz,"[3] "Byrd,"[4] and "Lady Day."[5]

Theology bears analogy with music in that it too can be approached as formal or dynamic. The two modes reflect two aspects of God's nature. Like classical music, the classical approach to theology comprises the formal methods of arranging what we know about God and his world into a reasoned, cogent, and consistent system. Classical theology interacts in critical dialogue with the philosophies of the world. It investigates the attributes of God and communicates primarily through a written tradition.

The jazz approach to theology investigates God's dealing with people in the joys and trials of daily life. This improvisational approach is illustrated in the oral tradition that emerged in the African-American experience. The jazz approach is not so much concerned with the status of theological propositions as with the hurts of oppressed people. It is communicated not so much by a literary tradition as by an oral tradition. And it is not so much concerned with facts as it is with life skills: knowing *how* rather than knowing *what*.

Jazz theology is a participation in the basic patterns revealed in biblical life situations. It inquires not only *what* God did and said but *how* he said and did it. Furthermore, it expects him to do it again in a similar way in our lives: "Didn't my Lord deliver Daniel? Well, I know he'll deliver me." Effective black preachers respond to current situations by theologizing creatively on their feet, just as jazz musicians improvise new music and enliven old songs in response to the feeling and needs of the moment.

Classical theology and classical music reflect God's oneness. The unity of God's purpose and providence is reflected in the consistent explanations

3. Dizzy Gillespie.
4. Charlie Parker.
5. Billie Holliday.

and consonant harmonies of classical music and classical theology. The genius of classical theology is in theology as it was formulated.

But God is not just classical. God is jazz. Not only does he have an eternal and unchanging purpose, but he is intimately involved with the difficulties of sparrows and slaves. Within the dynamic of his eternal will, he improvises. God's providential jazz liberates slaves and weeps over cities. Jazz can be robustly exultant or blue; God has been triumphant and also sad. Jazz portrays the diversity, freedom, and eternal freshness of God. The genius of jazz theology is in the theology *as it is done.*

Soul

When the people of Judah were captured and taken from Canaan to Babylon, they were confused, to say the least. They had in their possession the Scriptures stating God's promise that the land of Canaan would be theirs forever. Yet here they were, having lost Canaan, captive minorities in the land of a foreign superpower.

The captive people constantly asked, "If God promised the land to us forever, how did we end up in this Babylonian predicament? What happened to God's covenant promises? How could God let us down?"

Someone was inspired by God to deal with these questions. He plunged into this awesome task by getting hold of three books: *The Annals of Solomon*, *The Annals of the Kings of Israel*, and *The Annals of the Kings of Judah*. He proceeded to select material out of these scrolls, analyze it, and arrange it into a theological framework. As he did this he reflected on God, who is absolutely faithful and trustworthy to keep all his promises. In his work he demonstrated that it was not God who failed the covenant, but the people. His work became the books of 1 and 2 Kings.[6]

African-Americans have essentially the same question: Why are we here? It cannot be demonstrated that their arrival in chains was a direct result of their own sin. However, the example of how 1 and 2 Kings were written serves as a paradigm for the development of African-American theology.

We must remember that because African slaves were long denied access to reading and writing, there developed among them an oral rather than

6. Ray Dillard, professor of Old Testament, Westminster Theological Seminary Philadelphia.

a literary tradition. To say that we have no theology because we have not produced it in literature is like saying that the Jews of the exodus had no revelation before Sinai. The Jews were always singing about something, and some of these songs came to be recorded in the five books of Moses. It is within our oral tradition that we find historic black theology. The rich oral tradition of the black church—its music and its preaching—is the locus of theology in African-American culture.

The power of the oral tradition was greatly multiplied by the power of God's Word, because the only indigenous channel of expression we had was the church. We learned to transform the Bible from its written form into an oral form, using soul culture. We produced a *theological dynamic* that captured nuggets of biblical truth in forceful phrases and images from life experience, and we created a *cultural dynamic* of deeply moving expressions of God-consciousness. These two merged to become the *soul dynamic* that simmered during the days of slavery and grew throughout the nineteenth century.

For African-Americans, the written Word of God was like powdered milk, having all the nutrients of whole milk yet undrinkable in its existing form. Transforming the written Word of God into an oral Word of God was like adding water.[7] Although this transformed Word of God does not have the same authoritative weight as Scripture, it made the Word of God "drinkable" and had a powerful effect on the African-American community. Viewed comparatively, this theological dynamic was to classical Christian theology as art is to science, as intuitive knowledge is to cognitive knowledge, as the concrete is to the abstract, as the multidimensional is to the linear, as a mental image is to a concept.

The Emergence of Theology

One of the main purposes of doing theology is to understand life from God's perspective. While this theology can make valuable contributions, it cannot fully address our unique challenges. We can be thankful for the insights of historical theology. However, we cannot continue our dependence on yesterday's theology because it does not adequately address the issues we face *today*. For this, we must free ourselves from "theological welfare," roll

7. An illustration often used by Dr. Henry Mitchell, author of *Black Preaching* (New York: Harper & Row, 1970) and *Black Belief* (New York: Harper & Row, 1975).

up our sleeves, and get busy doing biblically sound theology—a theology that connects with our current life context.

When life's situations and biblical truth interact with each other, they produce two things:

1. *Praxis*—the art of putting biblical truth into reality according to our life theme. All of us, whatever people group we belong to, have personal, social, and cultural issues that must be addressed by biblical truth.
2. *A biblical paradigm*—the identification of basic biblical patterns that connect with our life situation.

When praxis and the biblical paradigm interact, theology emerges.

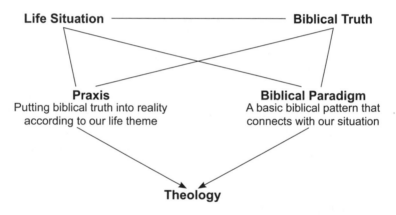

Fig. 38.1. Praxis and the Biblical Paradigm

The meaning of the Bible is found in its application to a life situation. Apart from this, the Bible does not say much to us. Of course, the Bible does apply in our context, but if we don't see it, then we do not really understand it. To apply biblical truth, we must first recognize and understand it. When we fail to apply biblical truth, it's not because the words of the Bible are not saying anything, it's just that we can't hear properly.

Not only does God reveal himself in the words of the Bible, he also is revealed in the basic patterns of the biblical life situations. This is what jazz theology gives us. For every situation we go through in life, there is a basic pattern already revealed in the Bible. In other words, whatever we experience today, someone in the Bible has already experienced its basic patterns. Solomon said it best, "What has been will be again, what has been done will be done again; there is nothing new under the sun" (Eccl. 1:9).

Basic Patterns

The biblical narratives are not just packages for God's revelation. They are also revelation itself. The Scriptures teach us what we need to know to be in covenant obedience to God. If God just wanted to give us the *principles*, the Bible could have fit on a tract. However, we can be thankful that God embedded these truths in the lives of fallen people like us. God, in the act of revelation, applied his truth to human situations. In essence, the Bible is not just a record of his revelation, it is also a record of his *application* of revelation. Thus, what we have in Scripture is a record of God doing theology.

In order to dig out the riches in the Bible, we must do the following things.

Examine basic biblical patterns. We must prayerfully look for these patterns in the biblical life situations. The key is understanding that along with the words of the Bible, the basic patterns in the life situations of biblical characters are also important.

Match biblical patterns with similar experiences in our own lives. We must prayerfully look for the basic patterns in our life situations and in the life situations of those to whom we minister. Then we must prayerfully match them with biblical situations having a similar pattern.

Take the match-ups to the Scriptures. Once we match the biblical patterns to our own situation, we can see the biblical principles revealed. For example, if I know that what I'm going through is similar to what David went through under Saul, then I can look into the Scripture to see how to deal with it. Once we have done this, we can search the Scriptures to discover essentially three things:

1. The *situational* perspective—in other words, how was God in control *then*?
2. The *normative* perspective—in other words, how was God speaking *then*?

3. The *existential* perspective—in other words, how was God present *then*?

The Bible gives all of this information away.

We may not understand our situation. We may not know why we're going through what we're going through. But when we look at someone in the Bible who's been through an experience that has a basic pattern similar to ours, we can discover the biblical principles that address our current situation. Once we understand this, we can frame our life situation correctly using the above three perspectives. Thus, we will have insight into how:

God is in control *now.*

God is speaking *now.*

God is present *now.*

Be inquisitive. Once we have developed this basic theological framework, we can begin to fill in the details. To do this, we need to go through what I call a theological process.

THE THEOLOGICAL PROCESS

Questions

The theological process is based on questions. Jesus told us that unless we come in faith, like a little child, we cannot enter the kingdom of heaven (Matt. 18:3). One thing little children do is ask questions. A lot of questions. In this way the finer details come as we begin to formulate specific questions about our situation and ask God for answers.

The development of my book *Beyond Liberation*[8] came out of this very same process. As a university student in the late 1960s, I was trying to figure out what God had to do with the black cultural revolution that was sweeping across the country. So I asked God, "Well, what do you have to do with all this?" For the answer, I went to the Word of God and I began to

8. Later reprinted as *Free at Last? The Gospel in the African-American Experience* (Downers Grove, IL: InterVarsity Press, 1996).

read it with this question in mind. In all of my biblical studies and readings, I continued to ponder this question.

To my utter surprise, I discovered the more I read Scripture, the more I understood that the question I was asking God was not really the correct one. Since the Word of God is "useful for teaching, rebuking, correcting and training in righteousness" (2 Tim. 3:16), the Word of God began to correct my question. The more I studied, the more I began to understand that the question was not "What does God have to do with the black cultural revolution?" but "What does the revolution have to do with God?"

Next, as we meditate on God's Word and the corrected question, God gives us answers. He begins to show us things we've never seen before and in doing so, he answers our questions. Then we must come back to our situation and apply those answers. As we apply God's answers to our situation, two things happen. First, we discover a theology that's appropriate for our situation and speaks to its issues. Second, we find that new questions arise. We take these new questions back to God, get them corrected, and go through the process all over again.

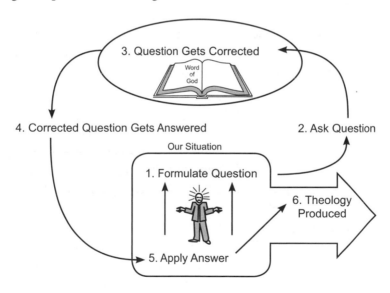

Fig. 38.2. Cycle of Questions and Answers

The Bible itself uses this technique of basic patterns. You see this in the parables and illustrations of Jesus, the apostles, and the prophets. You also see this in the books of Proverbs and Ecclesiastes. Through basic patterns of life, the Bible teaches us wisdom.

A classic example of this is found in 2 Samuel 12:1–13. After David slept with Bathsheba and had her husband Uriah killed, he thought he had everything covered up. Then the prophet Nathan confronted him in an indirect way, describing what he had done with Bathsheba using a different cast of characters. In essence, Nathan used basic patterns. As a result, David saw the horror of his sin and repented.

Often, in Bible narratives, many of the details of the original life situation are purposefully omitted. Why? Because the Bible is designed for us to get into those patterns and supply details from our life situations.

Finally, in every theological process, God himself must have final say. We should always be open for correction and rebuke, and allow God to show us that, perhaps, what we've done is not right. His ways are not our ways (Isa. 55:9). We always have to check what we've done against what God says in Scripture.

Application

The Bible can provide a basic framework for understanding our current situation. The main purpose of the theological process is to develop a framework to understand our situation by learning how to see it from God's point of view. After doing this, then we begin to fill in the details inside the frame.

Consequently, the Bible is meant to be applied to us; it's not meant to be spiritual knowledge that is disconnected from application. God wants us to get into his Word to understand our situation from his point of view and to govern our responses according to his principles. This is how we will gain wisdom. If we wisely apply the Word of God to our life situations, we will make a difference in our culture.

The African-American church today is in desperate need of a fresh approach to theology—a theology that is true to Scripture and, at the same time, speaks to our current situation. It is very important that we understand that God speaks to us in many ways in the Bible, and one important way is through its basic patterns. Now, if we approach theology this way, the Word of God will come alive and speak to us not just in the "sweet by and by," but also in the "nasty now and now."

Implications for Yesterday

> For there our captors asked us for songs, our tormentors demanded songs of joy; they said, "Sing us one of the songs of Zion!" How can we sing the songs of the LORD while in a foreign land? (Ps. 137:3–4)

Suffering in the Antebellum South

When the gospel is applied in a particular cultural context, the result is Christianity. There are many expressions of Christianity because there are many different cultures. Because of our cultural differences, it is not wrong to have a Christianity with a particular cultural application. Christianity is cross-cultural. However, these cultural expressions of Christianity should never contradict each other if they are true to God's Word. In fact, they will have a complementary relationship as they focus on God's redeeming grace through Jesus Christ. It is this shared foundation of biblical truth that anchors these cultural applications of the gospel.

In the antebellum South, for example, the institution of slavery was king. While volumes have been written about the antebellum period, we cannot find a set of volumes written by Southern antebellum African-American theologians. For this, we simply have to listen to the oral tradition of that time. In the themes of the Negro spirituals, we hear lyrics like "I've been 'buked and I've been scorned and I've been talked about sure as you're born." Or "Sometimes I feel like a motherless child a long way from home." Or "Soon I will be done with the troubles of the world; goin' home to be with God."

These themes of suffering are prevalent throughout the music that emerged from the experience of slavery in the South. Although many had become Christians, African-American slaves never would have come up with a triumphant perspective like "Onward Christian soldiers marching as to war with the cross of Jesus going on before." Why? Because the main theme in their lives was suffering. Thus, they developed a *theology of suffering*. Even today, the oral tradition still contains many of these same themes.

The Southern theology of suffering addressed the central themes of salvation by grace. The church was seen as a place where slaves did not have to deal with the suffering that so dominated their lives. That is why salvation in the African-American church in those days was seen more in collective terms. This view is very similar to the way the Israelites looked at salvation in the Old Testament (see Ex. 14:13).

The theology of suffering was presented in the paradigm of the exodus. We've heard these themes of deliverance from slavery and oppression many times: "Deep river. I want to cross over Jordan. Deep river. I want to cross over to campground." Or the classic, "Go down Moses. Way down in Egypt land. Tell ol' Pharaoh to let my people go." Obviously, they weren't just singing about an Egyptian across the Atlantic.

Core Concerns

The Southern theology of suffering also addressed cultural core concerns—cultural values and/or issues that were life-defining and life-controlling. I will focus on three of these: survival, refuge, and resistance to oppression.

The first concern was survival. Obviously, the slaves found themselves in a perilous situation. As a result, survival was a critical issue for them. Refuge was the second important issue. The church was seen as the place where they could escape, to some extent, the domination of the white slave masters.

Traces of this theme still survive in the oral tradition. The prayers uttered by the saints often include lines like, "Lord, make a place for me in your kingdom where every day will be Sunday." To some extent, church is still considered a place of refuge.

The third cultural concern was resistance to oppression. The institution of slavery was so overwhelming that it was virtually impossible to resist it completely. However, many of the slaves began to resist it verbally through the oral tradition. For example, if their masters were present and claimed to be Christians, slaves would sing songs with lyrics like, "Heaven, heaven. Everybody talking about heaven ain't going to heaven." These subtle comments empowered their resistance.

Negro spirituals were the first expression of African-American theology. These old spiritual songs contained both a theological meaning and a message of freedom. This form of oral tradition and its double meaning was an important form of communication then, and it still reveals much to us today.

Theological Power

By 1900, most African-Americans still lived in the rural South and were sharecroppers. Under the thumb of white supremacy, the African-American church continued to function on the theology of suffering. This theology was intuitive and ethical. It was a means of survival and a method of coping with the harsh realities of economic deprivation, racism, and social injustice.

Much later, in the twentieth century, the theology of suffering continued to carry the Southern church. In 1955 Dr. Martin Luther King Jr. transformed this theology from a method of coping with suffering into a powerful spiritual weapon against injustice and segregation. This happened at the beginning of the Montgomery bus boycott.

On December 1, 1955, Rosa Parks boarded a Montgomery, Alabama, city bus after work. She entered the front door, paid her fare, exited the front door, re-entered through the back door, and took a seat in the first row in the "colored" section. This demeaning procedure was dictated by the Jim Crow laws and customs of the day. After a few stops, the seats in the white section in the front of the bus became full, and the bus driver moved the sign that designated the beginning of the colored section back a few rows. Since Ms. Parks was now in the white section, the bus driver ordered her to move farther back (where there was standing room only) and let a white man have her seat. She refused, the driver called the police, and she was arrested.

In response to her arrest, community leaders organized a one-day bus boycott. The plan was to have a one-day boycott on December 5, 1955, then decide how to proceed at a rally that night at Holt Street Baptist Church. On that cold and cloudy morning, onlookers watched as the buses drove by with no black passengers onboard. The boycott was a success.

That afternoon, the leaders met and formed the Montgomery Improvement Association and chose Dr. Martin Luther King Jr. as their spokesperson. Dr. King then was scheduled to speak at the rally. His powerful message about human dignity, Christian love, and nonviolence set the tone for the Montgomery bus boycott, which lasted 381 days. Dr. King's presentation of theology as a weapon for fighting injustice was so revolutionary that by Christmas, African-Americans from one end of this country to the other were talking about the "new force" in the land.

The events in Montgomery weren't the beginning of the civil-rights struggle. For example, the NAACP was already fighting the battle in the courts. The Urban League fought in the employment bureaus. However, on that December night the civil-rights *struggle* became the civil-rights *movement*, and it was nothing less than a cultural revolution—a revolution empowered by theology.

Marginalization in the Antebellum North

The situation of African-Americans in the antebellum North was distinctly different from the South. The experience in the North was more characterized by marginalization than by suffering. To nullify the effects of daily marginalization, a *theology of empowerment* (praxis) emerged as African-Americans interacted with biblical truth. This theology was couched in the paradigm of the exile. It was in the North that African-Americans began to understand that, like the people of Judah, they were exiled from their homeland. It was in the North that people began to talk about the "African diaspora" and draw a parallel to the Jewish diaspora.

Like its Southern counterpart, the Northern theology of empowerment addressed salvation by grace through faith in Christ. It also addressed cultural core concerns such as human dignity, African identity, and the divine significance of the African-American experience.

Human dignity was important for African-Americans in both the North and the South, but it had different manifestations. In the South it included the pursuit of freedom. In the North it involved preserving a positive self-image.

Because of their subdominant cultural position, African-Americans were constantly confronted with standards of aesthetics based on the dominant culture's European ideals. Consequently, there was a cacophony of subliminal messages each day saying they were irregular and insinuating that something was wrong with them. In response, the Northern theology of empowerment emphasized the *imago Dei*. This idea that humans have inherent value because they are made in God's image was a critically important basis for the human dignity of African-Americans.

We generally associate the search for African identity with the Black Consciousness Movement of the late 1960s and early 1970s. However, this movement was based on fundamental concepts that were themselves the fruit of the Northern theology of empowerment. For example, in the eighteenth and nineteenth centuries, black people were referred to as *Negroes*. Yet most early black institutions were identified by the word *African*.

920

Among the early congregations founded under black leadership was the *African* Baptist Church in Savannah, Georgia. The first black Presbyterian church was founded in Philadelphia. It was called the First *African* Presbyterian Church. The second was called the Second *African* Presbyterian Church. The first black denomination was called the *African* Methodist Episcopal Church. The second was called the *African* Methodist Episcopal Zion Church. Among the first black parachurch organizations was the Free *Africa* Society. Others followed.

Clearly, African identity was an important issue. Why was it important? It wasn't because African-Americans thought that Africa was the perfect place. This identity was an application of Romans 12:2: "Do not conform any longer to the pattern of this world, but be transformed by the renewing of your mind. Then you will be able to test and approve what God's will is—his good, pleasing and perfect will."

The Northern antebellum thinkers never really accepted the tag of *Negro*. They knew whenever you allow others to label you, they will end up defining you. Therefore, they reasoned, "We are not going to accept the dominant culture's label. God did not create us as Negroes. He created us as Africans. And we are going to affirm what God created us to be." This was a subtle form of protest. In essence, this response was an early form of what was later called Afrocentrism. Many militants of the 1960s never realized that Afrocentrism was originally a Christian concept.

This issue of significance can be summed up in the question: "Why are we here?" It is obvious that African-Americans were not immigrants. Immigrants never ask this question because they know why they have chosen to come here.

In an attempt to discover meaning and gain understanding, black Christian thinkers asked, "Is there a divine reason why we are here?" They searched the Scriptures to see if anybody else had been through a similar experience (basic patterns). As a result, the stories of Joseph in Egypt; Daniel, Hananiah, Mishael, and Azariah in Babylon; and Queen Esther in Persia found fresh meaning and application.

As they studied these basic patterns, they began to ask, "Does our presence in America have divine and global significance?" As they wrestled with this, they began to sense a call from God to take the gospel of Jesus Christ to the rest of the African diaspora and beyond.

921

Diaspora

By 1870, the African-American church was experiencing explosive growth because core cultural concerns were being addressed theologically. In fact, this was one of the most dramatic examples of church growth in the history of the church. By the late 1800s, there was an extensive African-American missions movement. This became known as Pan-Africanism. Beginning in the mid-1700s, black people (including former slaves) from the United States, England, Nova Scotia (now part of Canada), Haiti, Cuba, other Caribbean islands, and Brazil immigrated to various parts of Africa. They went to such places as Nigeria, Sierra Leone, Liberia, and South Africa, creating a kind of transnational black community. Because of the interaction between them, a pan-African consciousness emerged. The major portion of the leadership in these communities came from the church. African-American men like Rev. Martin Robinson Delaney and Rev. Alexander Crummell were among these leaders. They traveled extensively throughout this pan-African community and spoke with authority.

This form of Pan-Africanism is in contrast to the form that later emerged during the Black Consciousness Movement. The later form had a radically different foundation and philosophy, with roots in secular humanism and Marxism. Consequently, many people today fail to realize that Pan-Africanism was originally a Christian concept, rooted in missions.

Vacuum

Great gains were made in the years immediately after the Civil War. The abolition of slavery and post–Civil War Reconstruction set the stage for astounding economic, political, and social progress by African-Americans. As the exodus paradigm was being realized, the need for the theology of suffering began to decline. African-Americans were, in fact, coming out of slavery ("Egypt"). As a result, the southern church adopted the northern church's developing theology of empowerment. However, three traumatic events occurred between 1875 and 1900 that changed the course of the African-American church: (1) the end of the post–Civil War Reconstruction of the South; (2) the industrial revolution in the North; and (3) the consolidation of European colonialism over sub-Saharan Africa.

The End of the Post–Civil War Reconstruction in the South. The final death blow to Reconstruction came in 1877, when President Rutherford B. Hayes removed federal troops that had been enforcing the Fourteenth and Fifteenth Amendments in the South. As a result, white supremacy was reestablished throughout the South through terrorism and political disenfranchisement. In the wake of these events, a new type of slavery was established—the sharecropper system.

The Industrial Revolution in the North. After the Civil War, America experienced a significant growth in jobs due to the Industrial Revolution. Looking for opportunity, former slaves were the ideal candidates to become members of the skilled labor force in the emerging industries in the North. However, many Northern industrialists did not want an African-American workforce. This period saw a wave of massive European immigration, which many industrialists encouraged. From this workforce emerged white-only labor unions.

Along with the rise in immigration came the need to Americanize all immigrants who spoke different languages and had different cultures. To encourage people to assimilate into what the dominant culture defined as American culture, "the melting pot" concept was promoted. Of course, many were unable to "melt" or blend in. Therefore, those who had greater difficulty "melting" ended up being confined to urban ghettos, e.g., "the Black belt" ("the 'hood"), Chinatown, Jew town, Little Italy, the barrio, etc.

The end result was that African-Americans in both the North and South were excluded from the skilled labor force and from mainstream American life. With the dawning of the twentieth century, African-Americans saw the development of institutional racism that was structural, systemic, and subtle.

The Consolidation of European Colonialism over Sub-Saharan Africa. As the colonial powers tightened their grip in Africa, black missionaries were persecuted, pushed out, and excluded from the colonies. As a result, the African-American missions movement was decimated and the church developed a bad case of missions amnesia.

The African-American church was caught off guard by these traumas. As concern for survival again became the overwhelming issue, the developing theology of empowerment was abandoned by 1900. The church reverted to the theology of suffering that had developed during slavery. The result was a theological vacuum pertaining to empowerment and its related concerns. By 1910, the explosive growth of the African-American church had ended.

The attempts to fill the theological vacuum can be placed into two general categories: *alternative theologies* of empowerment and *ideologies* of empowerment.

Alternative Theologies of Empowerment. Soon after the development of the theological vacuum, several attempts were made to fill it. Among them were several black Jewish sects and the United Negro Improvement Association (the Garvey Movement). The most successful of these were the Black Nationalist Islamic sects like "Nation of Islam."

Ideologies of Empowerment. Around 1900, W. E. B. DuBois proposed black solidarity through education. Next came the New Negro Movement, also known as the Harlem Renaissance. In 1965, Malcolm X proposed Black Nationalism. In 1967, two years after the death of Malcolm, Black Nationalism was popularized by the Black Consciousness Movement.

THE TWENTIETH CENTURY

Beginning early in the twentieth century and continuing through the early 1970s, large numbers of African-Americans in the rural South migrated to the urban North in search of jobs and a better way of life. By 1920, housing discrimination forced African-Americans into over-crowded ghettos. Those who were functional became the achievers. They lived by values that usually led to success. As a result they became the working and middle classes. Those who were dysfunctional became the nonachievers. Because they were without "achiever values," they were not successful, and many of them joined the ranks of the underclass and criminals.

Racial segregation facilitated the integration of the ghetto by class. From World War I through the mid-1960s the ghetto was a community. It had leaders like pastors, teachers, and businessmen, and institutions like churches, fraternities, sororities, and social clubs flourished. People partici-pated in activities representative of both value systems, such as cotillions, weddings, graduations, playing the numbers, and gangs.

Before the 1960s, the achievers had a sense of responsibility to address the issues of their nonachiever neighbors. They did not look to government programs to solve these problems because there were none. The achievers took it upon themselves to inculcate achiever values into all, especially nonachievers. Thus, almost all leaders and institutions in the ghetto spoke with one voice, from the pulpit to the barber shop. In this way a consensus developed that achiever values were superior. There was an unwritten law among African-Americans that achievers had to be ambassadors to the dominant culture for the advancement of the race. Also, they knew that the nonachievers would be used as excuses or reasons to maintain the discriminatory roadblocks to success.

Before the mid-1960s the overarching African-American strategy for success involved *assimilation* into the dominant culture in terms of values and aesthetics. Values assimilation facilitated participation in mainstream culture. However, aesthetics assimilation was problematic and even destructive, especially for people of non-European descent. The African-American assimilation strategy failed to make this all-important distinction. Thus, it was inherently flawed. If a black history course was offered at any university, there would be virtually no interest. A course in Western civilization would have provoked much more interest. We didn't want to be Negroes. We just wanted to be Americans.

In 1967, the overarching strategy shifted from assimilation to *identification*—identification with African-American culture. This was the beginning of the Black Consciousness Movement. One reason for this shift was the trauma associated with aesthetic assimilation. Although the Black Consciousness Movement was a major cultural revolution, it did not change the status of achiever values. They were still preeminent. Thus, in the early days of the "revolution," to be black was to be an achiever in pursuit of excellence. This is why the achievers continued to be the stabilizing force in the ghetto. They were like the magnesium rods in a nuclear reactor. As long as they are in place, the reactor is stable and safe. If they are removed, a meltdown will result.

A second great migration began around 1965 and ended by 1985. This was the migration of the achievers from the ghetto to other areas of the city or to the suburbs. Three major factors led to this. First, there was the dismantling of housing discrimination. Second, there was the growing hostility between achievers and nonachievers. The nonachievers saw no benefit from the great gains in civil rights. They were unable to walk through the newly opened doors of opportunity. Achievers, on the other hand, ran through those doors and experienced a dramatic improvement in quality of life. Hence, the quality-of-life gap increased significantly. Third, there was the surge in gang violence in the ghetto. When the population between the ages of five and nineteen reaches 40 percent, a "critical mass" develops for major gang formation. Because dysfunctional families were mostly headed by a single parent, these young people were easily reached. Gangs had always been part of the ghetto scene. But now gangs proliferated and terrorized the ghetto. Gang members were predominantly from nonachiever backgrounds. Therefore, their primary targets were achievers.

Nonachievers became suspicious of achievers. They began to associate achiever values with the discredited pre-black aesthetics assimilation strategy. Thus, they equated achievement with trying to be "white." In the minds of nonachievers, achiever values were discredited and achievers themselves were regarded as "sellouts."

Achievers continued to live by their values, but now they no longer attempted to instill these values into nonachievers. Eventually, the voice of the achievers was silenced in the ghetto. They were drawn out by the lure of a better quality of life and pushed out by the hostilities of resentful gangs of nonachievers.

The exodus of the achievers led to the meltdown of the ghetto into social chaos. Along with the silencing of the achievers came the amplification of the cultural influence of the nonachievers through several phenomena including "gangsta rap." This led to a devastating crisis in African-American culture—a crisis of values. Achiever values began to lose their preeminence and credibility among the youth. Eventually, nonachiever values became a dominant influence. Even though the overwhelming majority of African-Americans were achievers, nonachieverism became the new basis of African-American identity.

This is what Bill Cosby denounced in his speech before the NAACP on the fiftieth anniversary commemoration of the *Brown v. Topeka Board of Education* Supreme Court decision—a decision that declared that racial segregation was unconstitutional.[9]

9. This speech was delivered at Constitution Hall in Washington, DC, on May 17, 2005.

The "Obama phenomenon" has somewhat encouraged achievers to come out of the closet, but it remains to be seen if this will be enough to fully address the cultural crisis.

IMPLICATIONS FOR TODAY AND TOMORROW

The earth will be filled with the knowledge of the glory of the LORD, as the waters cover the sea. (Hab. 2:14)

Overdue

The African-American experience is the history of a struggle for progress and against obstacles. The arena of this struggle mostly involved four interlocking aspects of culture, values, practices, and aesthetics. Before the great civil-rights gains, most obstacles emerged from outside African-American culture. However, today most of these obstacles have emerged from within the culture.

When achievers were setting the trends, African-Americans had a strong basis for progress because achiever values were preeminent. However, the racist practices of American society did violence to these values. To remove this obstacle, American practices needed reform. This was accomplished through the civil-rights movement.

As more African-Americans entered mainstream life, those who assimilated into the dominant culture had the advantage over those who did not. However, acceptance of Eurocentric standards did violence to their sense of human aesthetics. To remove this obstacle, their sense of aesthetics needed reform. This was accomplished through the Black Consciousness Movement. Hence the mantra, "Black is beautiful."

Aesthetics reform had an empowering effect. African-Americans embraced values that seemed to affirm their sense of aesthetics and excluded those that did not. However, some thinkers were not satisfied with mere *aesthetics* blackness and began to push for *ontological* blackness. They noticed a righteousness differential between the oppressor and the oppressed. In this situation, the oppressed tend to be more righteous than the oppressor. Oppression occurs when people impose their sin on others, causing them to suffer the consequences. Because the oppressed resist oppression, they resist sin, and resisting sin is always more righteous than yielding to it.

927

As the oppressed focus on their resistance, their own sin is driven beneath the surface. When liberation comes, however, their own sin will resurface with all its negative effects. The Israelites learned this lesson under the judges. They disobeyed God in the first place by not driving out the Canaanites (Deut. 7:1–6; Judg. 1:27–2:2). The Canaanites regrouped, regained their strength, and came back to oppress the Israelites. Israel resisted. They cried out to God for help, sought God's ways, and were delivered from oppression. But each time they were liberated, their sin resurfaced, and they betrayed their call to be a light to the nations.

Because they were without a biblical worldview, those who advocated *ontological* blackness misinterpreted the righteousness differential. They did not understand that it manifested only within the oppressed/oppressor relationship. Thus, they did not see the righteousness differential for what it was, that is, relative and temporary. They saw it as ontological and permanent.

The advocates of ontological blackness assumed *all* values held by whites were hostile. They did not make the distinction between values that support Eurocentrism and achiever values that some whites happen to hold. They were right to reject the former but wrong to reject the latter. This contributed to the African-American cultural crisis.

Removing this obstacle will require value-system reform. This can be accomplished through a new movement to restore the preeminence of achiever values. This has presented Christian culture warriors with an enormous opportunity. A new cultural revolution is overdue. Why can't the next one be empowered by biblical truth? Movements are like avalanches in the mountains. They are inevitable in the winter. The only question is how they will be triggered. Are we going to wait for it to happen or are we going to trigger it?

A movement requires four things to erupt: (1) a sense of core values among the people, (2) an awareness of negative forces that are doing violence to the core values, (3) a general discontent with the direction in which things seem to be going, and (4) an accessible empowerment concept that overcomes the negative forces. The first three ingredients are in place. All that is needed is an empowerment concept. Today, African-American thinkers are searching for such a concept.

When segregation seemed insurmountable, Dr. King gave us a weap-onized application of the theology of suffering. The resulting empowerment gave rise to the civil rights movement that defeated segregation.

When Eurocentric aesthetics violated our sense of dignity, an Afro-centric sense of aesthetics emerged, giving rise to the Black Consciousness Movement. The resulting empowerment renewed our sense of dignity. Mal-colm X is often referred to as the father of this movement, but most of the concepts he used were themselves the products of Christian theology—the Northern theology of empowerment.

The most powerful aspect of a people group is its culture. When Jesus gave us the Great Commission, he commanded us to disciple the nations (Matt. 28:18–20). There are two approaches to this. First, we can impact the individual, who will in turn impact the culture. Second, we can impact the culture, which will in turn impact the individual. Both are essential if we are to be faithful to Jesus' command.

We have tended to focus on the first approach and neglect the second. A theologically powered movement can serve as a potent strategy to impact the culture by nudging the culture toward the kingdom.

Today's values confusion is a corrosive negative force. The door is wide open for the emergence of a new movement empowered by a Bible-centered value system.

> Who knows but that [we] have come to [this] position for such a time as this? (Esth. 4:14c)

The resulting empowerment will move us closer to the day when "the earth will be filled with the knowledge of the glory of the LORD, as the waters cover the sea." (Hab. 2:14)

PART 8

FUTURE RELEVANCE

39

JOHN FRAME AND THE
FUTURE OF THE CHURCH

RICHARD L. PRATT JR.

IT IS MY DELIGHT to contribute to this volume in honor of John Frame, especially because I have been asked to explore the potential of his theology for the future of the church. Speaking of Frame's influence in such broad terms may seem a bit grandiose. After all, he has spent most of his life primarily serving the interests of relatively small and isolated conservative Reformed and Presbyterian denominations in North America. In many respects, however, this is precisely where Frame stands out from his peers. Although he has selflessly devoted himself to the often idiosyncratic struggles of his own tradition, the weight of his scholarship has been felt far beyond its borders. I frequently confess that Frame has been the single most influential living theologian in my own life. My colleagues in theological education have nearly unanimously echoed similar sentiments. But more than this, I have been amazed at how many theologians across the spectrum have acknowledged his impact on their lives as well. The breadth of Frame's influence makes it appropriate to explore how his theology can, and perhaps will, have significant impact on the future of the church.

933

Background

When we consider John Frame and the future of the church, our minds naturally turn to three of his books: *Worship in Spirit and Truth*,[1] *Contemporary Worship Music: A Biblical Defense*,[2] and his earlier work titled *Evangelical Reunion: Denominations and the One Body of Christ*.[3] His books on worship and music address these subjects largely in terms of the regulative principle, which has little relevance for anyone other than Reformed theologians. The proposals of *ER*, however, have much to say to broader ecclesiastical associations, even though they grew out of discussions over the union of the Orthodox Presbyterian Church and the Presbyterian Church in America.

ER represents the application of Frame's theology to the kinds of issues we will explore in this article. Unfortunately, this book is not one of Frame's most popular or influential books, at least by comparison with the tomes *The Doctrine of the Knowledge of God*,[4] *The Doctrine of God*,[5] and *The Doctrine of the Christian Life*.[6] So we will summarize how Frame approaches this subject as a backdrop to the rest of this article.

The first part of *ER* is titled "The Road to Denominationalism."[7] It presents a biblical theology of the church, highlighting the biblical basis for seeking unity.[8] Frame concludes that denominationalism began within the Christian church after the Council of Chalcedon,[9] and he calls for movement toward "post-denominational ecclesiology."[10]

The second part is titled "Some Roads back to Unity." Here he deals with God's eschatological plan to reunite his people as an ideal toward which churches today should strive. He offers examples of situations in which stressing denominational distinctives is counterproductive. He suggests practical guidance for dealing with doctrinal differences, as well as differences in practice and priorities. Frame also addresses emotions and attitudes

---

1. Hereafter *WST*.
2. Hereafter *CWM*.
3. Hereafter *ER*.
4. Hereafter *DKG*.
5. Hereafter *DG*.
6. Hereafter *DCL*.
7. *ER*, 21–63.
8. "We must first be assured that Jesus Christ established on earth one church, not many denominations. Further, the unity of the church is not merely 'spiritual,' but also organizational." Ibid., 21.
9. Ibid., 34–35.
10. Ibid., 41–44.

that hinder the reunion of the church. He ends the book with guidelines for reunification and options short of full reunification.

Those familiar with Frame's other writings can see from this summary that he has addressed the question of denominationalism by applying some of the most pervasive themes of his theology. His concerns are based on Scripture; he presses not for perfection but for attainable goals; he offers practical solutions to differences among Christians; and he addresses the ways emotions and attitudes impinge on the process. *ER* thus provides a helpful backdrop to the concerns of this article.

The balance of this study will divide into two main parts: cultural challenges facing the church in the future and practical steps toward that future. To make our effort of manageable size, I will limit the scope of our topic in two ways. Rather than speaking of "the church" in general, I will concentrate on associations that are typically identified as conservative or evangelical branches of the Reformed tradition. It is only fitting to concentrate on the communities in and for which Frame forged his theological positions. In addition to this, rather than simply speaking of "the future," I will have in mind the *near* future, the rest of the twenty-first century. We can derive great benefit from exploring the potential impact of Frame's theology on issues that have begun to appear in our day and that portend what the next generation of conservative Reformed Christians is likely to face.

Cultural Challenges

A number of cultural challenges arose in the last decades of the twentieth century that have the potential of moving Reformed theology to the foreground, or of relegating it to the margins of Christian theology in the near future. If we engage these issues well, Reformed theology may prove to be a greater global force than ever before, but if we mishandle them, the results may be devastating.

We are reminded in this regard of Paul's example. As Paul moved from one place to another, he faced significant theological challenges from various cultures and subcultures. Paul described his strategy for dealing with these challenges in this way: "To the Jews I became like a Jew, to win the Jews. . . . To those not having the law I became like one not having the law . . . so as to win those not having the law. . . . I have become all things to all men so that by all possible means I might save some" (1 Cor. 9:20–22; Scripture references are from the NIV unless noted otherwise). Had Paul not responded in this way to the cultural challenges he faced, he would have risked irrelevance and perhaps even the failure of his entire ministry.

In our day, Reformed theologians face similar challenges not only when they go from one culture to another, but even when they stay in one place. The Reformed tradition has spread from its origins in Geneva to a variety of places on the globe. At each stage, it has sought to serve the peoples of those lands and has often significantly enriched their cultures. Yet a number of cultural challenges are now coming to the foreground that will require Reformed theologians to "make [themselves] slave[s] to everyone, to win as many as possible" (1 Cor. 9:19). Although every generation faces unique issues that require unique responses, from time to time a generation will experience dramatic cultural challenges that require daring theological responses. In my estimation, we are in such a time. Like Paul, if we fail to respond well, then we will risk irrelevance and perhaps even the virtual disappearance of the Reformed tradition.

It is difficult to distill these cultural challenges into a handful of issues, but for the sake of time I will raise three matters that will significantly test advocates of Reformed theology in the near future. We will speak of them in terms of increasing geographical scope: first, the growth of postmodern values within conservative Reformed churches in North America; second, demographic shifts in North America; and third, the blossoming of Christianity outside North America.

Postmodern Values in Reformed Churches

In our day, it is difficult to deny that postmodern values have entered the ranks of laypeople and clergy in conservative Reformed churches in North America.[11] Until twenty years ago, Reformed scholars paid little attention to what leading academic figures had announced for decades as the birth of the postmodern. Perhaps we thought that it was little more than a passing fad, or nothing new at all. Whatever the case, our theologians apparently felt it unnecessary to address the matter directly until they saw that the ideologies of postmodernism and the cultural structures of postmodernity threatened to capture the imaginations of members in our churches. Even

11. *DCL*, 88–90, 884–85.

so, when conservative Reformed theologians have addressed these matters, their assessments have been almost uniformly negative, and at times arrogantly dismissive.

Although the term *postmodern* resists succinct definition, one way to summarize what it means in many circles is to see it as a synthesis of certain premodern and modern values. In his *DCL*, Frame summarizes five characteristics of postmodern outlooks in this way, following suggestions that I had made elsewhere.[12] (1) For postmodern people, truth is no longer discovered "primarily through rational and scientific investigation under the guidance of rationalistic philosophers and scientists," but "both through [various forms of] mythology and rational-scientific means." (2) Postmodern people no longer view ultimate reality as physical, with spiritual realities (if they exist) being uninvolved. Instead, "ultimate reality is both physical and spiritual (impersonal and personal)," and these dimensions of reality "interact in countless ways." (3) For postmodern people, "the individuality of the independent objective scholar (transcendent subject) is [no longer] prized over conformity to received traditions." Instead, self-reliant "individuality is disdained as self-deceptive, [even though] individuals are encouraged to defy oppressive traditions." (4) Modes of human communication are valued differently as well. The modern period exhibited "heavy reliance on written communication . . . due to rising literacy and publishing technologies." By contrast, for postmodern people, "written communication is lowered to the level of other formats, especially the iconographic, due to widespread electronic technologies." (5) Modern people largely endorsed "rational and scientific meta-narratives" that "depict history as progressing toward [a rational, scientifically based] utopia." Yet postmodern people value "fragmented, heteromorphic multi-narratives [that] depict history as cycles and counter-cycles of cacophony and harmony."

For quite some time, postmodern values of these sorts were largely limited to a relatively small group of communities. However, in our day, popular music, movies, and other art forms exude these values so much that hardly anyone has remained unaffected. Postmodern values even reside in members and clergy of Reformed churches. Laypeople, who live with postmodernity six days a week, bring those values to their church life. As a theological professor for the past two decades, I can testify that a large portion of our young leaders are quite at home with postmodern ways of

12. *DCL*, 884–85.

believing, reasoning, feeling, and behaving. These cultural and ecclesial realities raise significant challenges for Reformed theology because our tradition was born under the influence of the Renaissance and matured in the world of the Enlightenment. Traditional Reformed theology rightly sought to express the Christian faith in ways that communicated well within modern Europe. As a result, the manner in which it has been expressed and lived—its language, subject matter, organization, and priorities—has been more attuned to modern values than to postmodern values.

Today, however, laypeople and leaders find themselves increasingly dissatisfied with significant aspects of traditional Reformed theology. Roughly corresponding to our summary of postmodern values above, we can mention a few tendencies that are not difficult to see. (1) Postmodern people within Reformed churches wed rational theological reflection with a deep appreciation for intuitions, emotions, and the like, as modes of theological validation. (2) Postmodern people in our churches long for extraordinary spiritual experiences to become regular facets of their worship and daily lives. (3) They yearn for more emphasis on community rather than the academy, deep connections of affection and service among believers, as the arena in which theology should be developed. (4) They join their appreciation of traditional preaching with an awareness of multimedia as effective ways to learn and communicate theology. (5) They not only embrace European and North American cultural narratives in their story of the kingdom of God, but want to value the cultural narratives and ideals of Latin America, Asia, the former Soviet Union, and Africa as part of the kingdom story as well.

These changes in the internal culture of Reformed churches raise crucial questions for theologians and church leaders in our day. Will we be able to reform our traditional theological expressions, priorities, and practices in ways that speak well to postmodern believers among us? Are there ways to expand our reliance on intuitive and emotional modes of theological validation? Is it possible for Reformed theologians today to enhance the experiential (or "experimental," to use older language) side of our faith? Can our church communities become more than groups that gather weekly and experience only superficial relationships? Can we follow our Reformed forebears of the last two centuries, who added hymns, pianos, organs, orchestras, and the like to the worship styles of Calvin and the Puritans, by including more variety of media in our worship and educational events? Can Reformed theology incorporate Christian stories from cultures that have not up to now come under significant influence from our branch of the church? Much is at stake in our responses to these questions.

Demography within North America

A second way in which cultural changes are challenging Reformed churches rises out of recent demographic shifts in North America. Hardly anyone living in Canada or the United States is unaware of this phenomenon. We see it as we go about our daily lives; we hear and read about it in the news. No reasonable person of forty years of age or older can doubt that our population is undergoing dramatic demographic realignments.

It is well known that the Reformed tradition played an important role in shaping the beliefs and practices of the early English-speaking colonies of the North American continent. Despite the presence of various kinds of professed non-Christians and the growth of other Christian traditions, Reformed theology continued to play a significant role for quite some time. In the nineteenth century, industrialization brought large waves of Asian immigrants to the West and surges of Roman Catholic immigrants from Europe to the East. The emancipation of African-American slaves led to the increase of their population and presence especially in Southern and Northern urban centers. Nevertheless, as these and other changes were taking place, Reformed theologians and churches generally felt little need to express Christian theology in ways that addressed the unique concerns of these communities. As a result, although America grew into a nation of exceptional ethnic variety, Reformed churches continued to consist almost entirely of people who were of non-Hispanic, Western European descent.

In the decades after World War II, even more dramatic demographic changes began to occur in North America. Continuing immigration, as well as relatively high birth rates among minorities, increased the influence of African-American, Asian-American, and Latin American communities. The initiation and enforcement of civil-rights legislation during the last decades of the twentieth century enabled these same groups to play increasingly significant roles. The recent election of the first African-American president illustrates just how much change has taken place in the nation. Yet despite even these dramatic changes, the Reformed tradition has failed to reach these populations in significant numbers.

As one example, consider the growth of the Latin American population in the United States in recent years. The United States Census Bureau reported in May 2008 that the Latino population in the United States had increased to 45.5 million, representing the largest minority group and making up 15.1 percent of the population.[13] Forecasts of continued growth point to a Hispanic population as large as 30 percent by the midpoint of this century.[14] In fact, if the growth of Latino and other minority communities continues as it has in recent decades, non-Hispanic Caucasians, the nearly exclusive demographic of Reformed churches, will become a minority population as early as 2050.[15]

Another demographic development in recent years is the increasing Muslim population in the United States. No official census data are kept of religious affiliation, but unofficial studies have sought to identify the number of adherents to Islam. Estimates vary, but all surveys agree that their numbers are growing at remarkable rates.[16] As a result of immigration, larger families, and successful conversions, the Muslim faith and its influence have grown more than ever before.

These developments ought to give us pause as we consider the future of conservative Reformed churches in North America. To put the matter boldly, Reformed churches primarily serve people of non-Hispanic, Western European descent, and this traditional constituency is shrinking in relative size and influence at an incredible rate. In the foreseeable future, our domestic fields "ripe for harvest" (John 4:35) will consist more and more of unbelievers among Latin American, African-American, Asian-American, and Muslim populations.

Unfortunately, the challenges that these emerging groups present may cause many Reformed churches to pursue the path of least resistance. We will be prone

13. http://www.census.gov/Press-Release/www/releases/archives/population/011910. html; http://www.census.gov/Press-Release/www/releases/archives/population/006808. html. The fact that not all regions of the nation will be equally affected or affected as quickly is no reason to forestall leveraging resources and aid for the sake of the gospel in those areas where the challenge is felt. The apostle Paul's repeated call for his churches to be aware of and support other churches ought to be instructive.

14. "Percent of the Projected Population by Race and Hispanic Origin for the United States: 2008 to 2050," http://www.census.gov/population/www/projections/tablesandcharts.html.

15. "The non-Hispanic, single-race white population is projected to be only slightly larger in 2050 (203.3 million) than in 2008 (199.8 million). In fact, this group is projected to lose population in the 2030s and 2040s and comprise 46 percent of the total population in 2050, down from 66 percent in 2008." http://www.census.gov/Press-Release/www/releases/archives/population/012496.html.

16. Estimates vary from 2 million to 8 million, depending on the definition of *Muslim* used or differences as a result of varied methodology. Estimates may be subject to inflation or under-estimated based on political considerations.

to isolate ourselves, to lower expectations, and to be satisfied with belonging to a branch of the church that has fewer and fewer advocates. In fact, the low numbers of conversions and overall growth of Reformed denominations in North America in the past few decades may indicate that many of us have already chosen this path. If we follow our past strategies of isolation, we will continue to fall further and further behind the general population growth of North America.

It would appear, then, that Reformed theologians face a critical choice. Will we choose a direction that may lead to the virtual disappearance of our branch of the church in this continent? Or will we choose a path that will bring our tradition into significant engagement with portions of our society that are growing in number and influence? Our Reformed forebears dealt with similar situations in Europe and faced odds much worse than our own. Yet they committed themselves to serving Christ as their new cultural conditions required. My hope is that we will learn to do the same.

Global Christian Expansion

In addition to dealing with postmodern tendencies in our churches and changes in the demography of North America, Reformed theologians must also face the challenge of the rapid growth of Christianity outside North America. We are now in an age of globalization.[17] What happens in one part of the world touches every other part of the world. Education, economics, industry, the arts, and even religion must be viewed on a global scale as never before. The earth is flat once again.[18]

We are facing global changes in the Christian faith that we could hardly have imagined just a century ago. These changes are taking place on a flat earth so that what happens to churches in Africa, Asia, and Latin America will shape the church in North America as well.[19] We will mention just two considerations: first, shifts in Christian populations, and second, the resulting changes of theological agenda.[20]

17. For a cogent presentation of current trends toward globalization, see Martin Wolf, *Why Globalization Works*, 2nd ed. (New Haven: Yale University Press, 2005).

18. See Thomas L. Friedman, *The World Is Flat: A Brief History of the Twenty-first Century*, 3rd ed. (New York: Farrar Straus & Giroux, 2007).

19. Cf. Josh Yates, "Globalization and the Gospel: Rethinking Mission in the Contemporary World," Occasional Paper No. 30, presented at the Forum for World Evangelization, Pattaya, Thailand, September 29–October 5, 2004, http://www.lausanne.org/documents/2004forum/LOP30_IG1.pdf.

20. Philip Jenkins, *The Next Christendom: The Coming of Global Christianity* (Oxford: Oxford University Press, 2002).

On the one hand, statistical data strongly suggest to many missiologists that the majority of evangelical Christians on the earth no longer live in the West.[21] Some projections indicate that the *vast* majority of evangelical Christians will soon live outside the United States.[22] This shift may be a result to some extent of stagnant or declining general population growth in the Western world; it may also be explained in part as the positive results of Protestant missionary efforts in recent centuries. Whatever the case, astounding numbers of people in Asia, Africa, and South America are professing faith in the Christian gospel.

On the other hand, as these changes in global Christian population continue, we will soon discover that Christian theology will change. As Jenkins put it:

> The types of changes of the coming decades promise to be much more sweeping. . . . If in fact the bulk of the Christian population is going to be living in Africa, Asia, or Latin America, then practices that now prevail in those areas will become ever more common across the globe.[23]

If this prediction is correct, we will soon see the concerns of Asian, Latin American, and African believers rising in prominence in our own Christian theology. Systematic theology, biblical theology, and practical theology will move in directions quite different from today.

I have found that this possibility perplexes many advocates of Reformed theology in North America. Their reasoning goes something like this: If we are right to believe that our theology faithfully reflects the teachings of Scripture, then why would responsible, faithful theologians in Africa, Asia, or Latin America have significantly different theological outlooks? Should we anticipate substantial changes to occur simply because leading theologians of the future may live outside Western Europe and North America?

21. See works such as those of Ralph Winter, David Bosch, and others. See as well Richard Tiplady, ed., *One World or Many? The Impact of Globalisation on World Mission* (Pasadena, CA: William Carey Library, 2003).

22. "The largest single bloc [of Christians], some 560 million people, is still to be found in Europe. Latin America, though, is already close behind with 480 million. Africa has 360 million, and 313 million Asians profess Christianity. . . . If we extrapolate these figures to the year 2025, and assume no great gains or losses through conversion, then there would be around 2.6 billion Christians, of whom 633 million would live in Africa, 640 million in Latin America, and 460 million in Asia. Europe, with 555 million, would have slipped to third place." Jenkins, *The Next Christendom*, 2–3.

23. Ibid., 107.

The reasons for anticipating such changes are rather straightforward. Apart from any consideration of the possibility of error, we must recognize that followers of Christ in every region of the world have unique histories and current experiences that deeply affect the ways they connect their lives to the history of the Bible. Christians throughout the world concentrate on how the Scriptures are relevant to their concerns. In this sense, different cultural backgrounds lead faithful Christians in different directions as they interpret the Scriptures.

For decades we have heard calls for Western missionaries to contextualize the gospel for other parts of the world.[24] We would be wise to continue to heed this call. Even so, if current trends continue, we will soon not be concerned so much with Westerners, contextualizing Christian theology for other parts of the world. We will begin to hear calls for Asian, African, and Latin American theologians to contextualize *their* theology for *us*. As the Christian population continues to move toward the South and East, it will not be long before the leading theologians of the Christian faith will reside in those parts of the world and set the pace for the rest of us.

Consider just one example from our own history. Reformed theologians naturally view biblical history as leading almost directly into the currents of Western culture. Yet as Reformed theologians faced different circumstances in Western culture, their approaches to theology varied. For instance, the early expression of continental Reformed theology in the Heidelberg Catechism reflects a keen awareness of the political turmoil and suffering that its advocates endured for their faith. It is not surprising that this catechism opens with the well-known question, "What is your only comfort in life and in death?" and proceeds to identify the "Triple Knowledge" that assures us of this comfort. By contrast, in the context of Puritan power in England, the Westminster Shorter Catechism begins with another well-known question: "What is the chief end of man?" It proceeds then to identify the principal teachings of Scripture as the beliefs and duties of those who wish to glorify God and enjoy him forever. The differences between these Reformed catechisms are not superficial; they reflect significantly different conceptual categories and priorities that accord with the ways Reformed theologians connected their cultural experiences to the Scriptures.

24. For example, see P. G. Hiebert, *Anthropological Insights for Missionaries* (Grand Rapids: Baker, 1985), 171–92.

For better or worse, the story of the Reformed church in North America has been one of relative security and prosperity. Professing Christian faith has not been entirely convenient at times, but it has seldom been dangerous or life-threatening for the majority of American Reformed theologians. For more than two hundred years, most of our leading theologians have experienced little persecution or suffering for the sake of the gospel. To be sure, our missionaries have experienced terrible hardships at times. Yet it is fair to say that Reformed theology in North America has not been forged in the crucible of physical deprivation, economic oppression, or persecution.

Now, by comparison, Christians in parts of Asia, Latin America, and Africa today are quite aware of the dangers associated with following Christ. The reality of injustice, tribal warfare among Christians, Muslim persecution, hunger, epidemics, and the like take a prominent role in much of their theological reflection. When theologians who have themselves endured such struggles take leading roles in dealing with theological topics, their concerns are likely to be very different from those that spring from North American soil. This will be true even among those who identify with the Reformed tradition in other parts of the world.

Discussions of the attributes of God will not remain abstractions as they often do in our circles, but will be focused on how experiences of severe suffering for Christ shape Christian understanding and belief in his attributes. We can only imagine how the love of God is formally expressed in a culture where Christians of neighboring tribes have warred with each other. We can only guess at the ways the omniscience of God is expressed in a country where prison is a common experience for followers of Christ. Although there will be similarities between the theological reflections of Christians who live in the comforts of North America and Christians who face hardships in other parts of the world, there are sure to be astounding differences as well.

All of this is to say that Reformed theologians today stand at a global crossroads. We must ascertain how much we believe our distinctively Reformed theological heritage has to offer those who are likely to become the leading theologians of the Christian world within this century. Do we believe that our orientation toward Scripture is merely appropriate for Western civilization? Or do we believe that we have something important to offer every branch of the church in every part of the world?

I do not believe that Reformed theology is perfect, but I do believe that our tradition has some important contributions to make to the church universal. For this reason, I think that it is incumbent on Reformed churches today to lead the way in serving our family in Christ where the numbers of Christians are growing so rapidly. To reach this goal, much more of our teaching, ministry, and funds must be devoted to reaching the growing Christian majority outside Europe and North America. Moreover, we must find ways that exemplify our theological interdependence with believers in other parts of the world. We cannot take ourselves out of our Western skins, but we can seek humbly to serve churches elsewhere in the world, to listen to their concerns, and to learn from them as they learn from us.

PRACTICAL GUIDANCE

Having identified some of the challenges that will test the resolve of the Reformed tradition in North America, we will now turn to some of the ways Frame's theology may help us. We will deal with four issues that have shaped my own ministry and offer us all practical guidance for the future: (1) the nature of theological convictions, (2) theology as application to life, (3) the importance of multiple perspectives, and (4) the future of theological education.

Theological Convictions

One of the most important lessons I learned from Frame as a young student was how the doctrine of *sola Scriptura* should affect my theological convictions. I attended Westminster Seminary in Philadelphia in 1978–79, and during that year I concentrated on several of his classes. Having consumed Cornelius Van Til's writings, I had already grasped that a commitment to the authority of Scripture was a basic presupposition of the Christian faith. From Frame, however, I discovered that *sola Scriptura* could be maintained only with a concomitant belief in the relative imperfection of every theological formulation.[25]

25. For instance, see *DKG*, 76–85 and 308–9. "Clearly, an extrascriptural creed is not infallible, except insofar as it accurately applies the Scriptures. But we have no way of infallibly determining when it does that." Also, see *DKG*, 378–79, Maxim 40: "Do not regard your theological system as superior in any way (materially or formally) to Scripture itself. Make sure your emotional attachments and attitudes are consistent with this resolution." Maxim 52: "Do be loyal to

I was one among many young advocates of Van Til's apologetic method who extended his presuppositional strategy inappropriately. As far as we were concerned, not only was the Bible a nonnegotiable, a basic commitment of Christian faith, but our Reformed understandings of what the Bible taught were granted nearly the same status. It wasn't long, however, before I became aware that Reformed scholars at Westminster Seminary and around the world disagreed with each other at least as much as they agreed. Their differences were not limited to a handful of insignificant matters, but included major issues such as the value of human rationality and logic, the place of Old Testament law in the Christian life, God-honoring worship, and even the *ordo salutis*.

It was here that Frame meant so much to me. At that time, Westminster Seminary was widely known for having a dogmatic student body. Frame confronted this spirit of dogmatism time and again by sharply distinguishing the authority of the Scriptures from the authority of our theological formulations drawn from the Scriptures. As I came to realize, if just one theological formulation is counted perfect, as the Scriptures, a flawless and complete theological statement, then the Scriptures are no longer "our supreme judge"[26] to which all theology must be submitted. Scriptures are no longer treated as the *only* unquestionable authority. Even if it is responsible to believe (as we should) that the Bible teaches a number of doctrines rather clearly, none of our understandings or formulations of these doctrines are perfect because they involve processing by fallible interpreters. They always remain subject to inspection and revision according to better understandings of Scripture. To be sure, Frame is not the first Reformed theologian to express this line of reasoning, but his emphasis led me to take a very different approach to the levels of conviction I attached to my beliefs.

For instance, Frame's influence is evident in my book *He Gave Us Stories*. This book is primarily devoted to interpreting Old Testament narratives, but many students and colleagues are surprised to see that the first third of the book does not address interpretive techniques specifically related to these portions of the Bible. On the contrary, it focuses on the ways the Holy Spirit uses several imperfect influences to empower our interpretive efforts. I identify these primary influences as our experiences of (1) indi-

---

your confessional tradition, being aware, however, of its fallibility. Do not, therefore, subscribe to 'every statement' in any human confession." See also *DG*, 9–15.

26. WCF 1.10, also 31.4.

vidual Christian living, (2) interaction in community, and (3) exegesis of Scripture. In this model, exegesis stands alongside individual religious intuitions, gifts, and callings, as well as interaction with our religious heritage and current sacred communities. Recognizing the influence of all these forces alerts us to the fact that unlike the object of Scripture itself, our understandings of Scripture are always affected by the foibles of finite and sinful human subjects.

This is not to say, however, that we are cast into the abyss of skepticism. On the contrary, the Holy Spirit ordinarily uses these influences to grant degrees of confidence, psychological conviction, or "cognitive rest"[27] about what we believe the Scriptures teach on particular matters. The Spirit's usual course is to correlate our levels of conviction to the strength of resonance among individual Christian living, interaction in community, and exegesis.

In this sense, responsible Christian theology involves not simply formulating what we believe, but also determining the levels of conviction we should attach to these formulations. In the normal course of things, correlations between theological formulations and convictions result from wittingly or unwittingly assessing the degree of resonance or mutual confirmation among the major influences on our interpretation of Scripture. When our experiences of faith as individual followers of Christ, the past and present witness of the church, and careful exegetical efforts lead us to the same conclusions, our level of conviction should be relatively high. When they fail to do so, our degree of confidence should be lower.

If we imagine our theological beliefs as suspended within a concentric, multilayered, gelatinous sphere, then those beliefs that we hold with the highest levels of conviction occupy the central areas of the sphere. Formulations of far less conviction are located toward the outer layers of our sphere of beliefs. We hold to those relatively few beliefs occupying the center so strongly that they are very difficult to change. To do so would have enormous effects on the entire system. Those beliefs on the periphery of the sphere are held with so little conviction that they are easy to change, and doing so has little effect on the rest of our beliefs. Between these two extremes are the theological formulations that have different degrees of systemic importance and that we

27. *DKG*, 152–53, 355. "I have spoken earlier of the mysteriousness of that 'cognitive rest' that marks the moment of persuasion. There is not a rational argument that infallibly leads to that point, which is the result of the work of God's Spirit and of many created means."

hold with various levels of conviction. This model helps us see that a system of theology is not a tightly constructed, rigid, logical system that crumbles when one portion of it is modified, removed, or replaced. On the contrary, different beliefs are more or less essential to our systems of belief.

In the classroom I often speak of these matters in terms of what I call "the cone of certainty." If we remove a cone-shaped sample of our sphere of beliefs and stand it upright, we acquire a model in which our theological beliefs are arranged from the top to the bottom of a cone depending on the level of conviction we have for each one.

I cannot stress enough that this process is the *ordinary* way the Spirit works. Following the distinction between ordinary and extraordinary providence in Westminster Confession of Faith 5.3, we should acknowledge that God is free to give us levels of theological convictions in unusual ways. The Holy Spirit sometimes brings us to higher or lower degrees of confidence apart from the relative resonance of the three major influences on our formulations. We are right to follow these extraordinary convictions in good conscience unless we learn otherwise. Under normal circumstances, however, responsible levels of conviction arise when we correlate beliefs with the relative, joint force of Christian living, interaction, and exegesis.

My way of expressing these matters is subject to criticism, but something like it will certainly help Reformed churches face the tests that we will encounter in the near future. If we hope to engage the cultural changes before us, we must find ways of differentiating levels of conviction and stop fearing that any change will disrupt the coherence of our entire theological system. Such adjudications of conviction enable us to respond to challenges with fidelity to our tradition, as well as a cautious willingness to reassess what we believe.

For instance, if we want to minister to postmodern believers within Reformed circles, we should hold doctrines taught in the ecumenical creeds, the central doctrines of our confessions, and the like, with unyielding tenacity. Yet we must also distinguish them from many other beliefs we hold. Our views on musical styles in worship, the dynamics of Christian community, and unusual experiences of the Holy Spirit are hardly as sure as other beliefs we hold. We will have to affirm them with much less tenacity if we hope to minister to postmodern Christians. If we hope to do more than simply condemn these believers and send them to other churches, we must find ways to identify what is more certain and less certain in the positions we hold.

The same is true for Reformed churches as they deal with the demographic shifts that are taking place in North America. Unless we maintain *sola Scriptura* by prioritizing what we believe the Scriptures to teach, we are likely to find that fewer and fewer of our neighbors will even understand what we have to offer, much less accept it.

The need for this kind of adjudication of convictions is even more pronounced when we consider the future of the Reformed tradition around the globe. Although I hardly hope that every Christian in every land will become like me and many other Christians in the Reformed tradition, I still hope that our theological stances will have a chance to season the burgeoning churches of Asia, Africa, parts of the former Soviet Union, and Latin America. At this time, these segments of the body of Christ largely ignore us, and they will continue to do so unless we distinguish the more peripheral elements of our belief system from its more central concerns.

Theology as Application

A closely related feature of Frame's theological method turns on his definition of theology. As he puts it, "Theology is the application of the Word of God by persons to all areas of life."[28] Of course, we see here once again that Frame emphasizes *sola Scriptura* by giving God's Word such a prominent, authoritative role in Christian theology. Yet this statement has much more to say about the process of theologizing than often meets the eye. It will help to delineate at least two senses in which theology is application of Scripture to life.

On the one side, the statement indicates what theology *ought* to be. I have found that most students understand Frame's words in this sense. They see it as an affirmation that theology should be practical or useful, as it were, for believers. This ethical sense is a vital facet of what Frame means.

For quite a while now, missiologists have employed the term *contextualization* for this process.[29] They have often insisted that Western missionaries must contextualize the gospel and other teachings of Scripture to the cultures

28. Ibid., 81. Frame goes on to define application as "teaching as the use of God's revelation to meet the spiritual needs of people, to promote godliness and spiritual health."

29. For a sampling of views on contextualization, see Bruce J. Nicholls, "Theological Education and Evangelization," in *Let the Earth Hear His Voice*, ed. J. D. Douglas (Minneapolis: World Wide, 1975); George W. Peters, "Issues Confronting Evangelical Missions," *Evangelical Missions Tomorrow*, ed. Wade T. Coggins and Edwin L. Frizen Jr. (Pasadena, CA: William Carey Library, 1977).

in which they minister. Sometimes these calls are benign, referring to cultural concerns that have little bearing on the substance of biblical teaching. At other times, missiologists have urged that biblical norms such as baptism and the Lord's Supper are to be contextualized as well.[30] In reaction to these kinds of extreme positions, conservative Reformed theologians often reject the notion of contextualization altogether, insisting that the normativity of biblical teaching is all that needs to be considered as theology is communicated across cultural lines.

Frame, however, argues that the Reformed concept of divine revelation supports the call to contextualization in theology. He acknowledges a crucial role for the interplay of special and general revelation in theological work. One implication of this interplay is that the general revelation of God in cultural and personal matters must be taken into account. As he put it:

> In the Reformed faith, the concept of application is not a threat to *sola Scriptura*, because Calvinists believe in a comprehensive revelation of God in Scripture, the world, and self. Everything reveals Him, for everything is under His control, authority and presence. . . . Reformed theology has been one of the most successfully "contextualized." . . . The progress theology makes is precisely a progress in contextualizing its message.[31]

Here we see Frame's threefold distinction of the more familiar twofold division between special and general revelation. Following Calvin's triad of revelation in Scripture, in humanity as the image of God, and in the external creation,[32] Frame speaks of revelation in terms of "Scripture, the world, and [the] self." These distinctions also correlate with Van Til's extensive discussion of special and general revelation in his *Introduction to Systematic Theology*.[33] From this point of view, situations and people as general revelation must be integrated with our understanding of the Scriptures, if we hope to apply the Scriptures well to "all areas of life."

---

30. For instance, see H. Kraft, *Communication Theory for Christian Witness* (Nashville: Abingdon, 1986) 115–19.

31. *DKG*, 307–8.

32. John Calvin, *Institutes of the Christian Religion*, Library of Christian Classics XX, ed. John T. McNeill, trans. Ford Lewis Battles, (Louisville: Westminster John Knox Press, 1960), 1.1.1–5.

33. Cornelius Van Til, *An Introduction to Systematic Theology* (self-published class syllabus, 1971), 62–158.

Naturally, for many conservative Reformed theologians such outlooks sound too relativistic and subjective, as if the Scriptures might mean radically different things for different circumstances and persons. In fact, Frame's teachings on these matters have been used by his students to support versions of relativism and subjectivism. Yet Frame's commitment to the supreme authority of Scripture stands sharply against such misuse of his views.[34] Instead, he simply argues that the authoritative teaching of Scripture must be contextualized or formulated in ways that are appropriate for the world and persons to whom it is being applied.

On the other side, the adage "theology is application" also indicates what Christian theology *always is.* That is to say, no matter how hard we try to do otherwise, all theologians who work with Scripture will always understand Scriptures in terms of some aspect of their lives. There is no theology that is simply derived from the Scripture. It is impossible to avoid the concerns of our lives when we interpret Scripture, even if those concerns are merely academic. As a result, in one way or another all theology, including Reformed theology, is by its very nature application.

Acknowledging the two senses in which theology is the application of Scripture can be very helpful to Reformed churches as they seek to minister in the near future. On the one side, to apply the riches of our heritage to postmodern people in our churches, to different American subcultures, and to the majority church outside North America, we must learn from them how general revelation has brought them to postures of Christian faith that are different from ours. Simply put, we must not assume that what has been important to us needs to be important to them. What is it about their world and the persons in it that has led them to focus on this or that in Scripture? How have their experiences brought them to awareness of biblical teaching that we have hardly considered? What legitimate concerns do they have that may seem irrelevant to us? Only when we pause long enough to learn the answers to these kinds of questions will we be able to help them apply the Scriptures and the magnificent treasures of Reformed theology to their lives.

On the other side, the fact that theology always is application should make us ready to acknowledge that Reformed theology does not account for all teachings of Scripture in perfect balance and order. To be sure,

34. For Frame's argument that his views and their underlying assumptions do not result in a relativism, see *PP*, nn7, 8.

if I did not believe that Reformed theology represents the best interpretation of Scripture on the whole, I would not be a part of it. Yet the
contents, structures, and emphases of Reformed theology have resulted
from our tradition's application or contextualization of Scripture. This
is one reason why our formal theologies look so different from the Bible
itself. We have taken portions of Scripture and drawn certain conclusions in large measure because of God's general revelation in the world
around us and in ourselves. We have learned much about the Scriptures
through this process; we have much to offer the entire body of Christ.
Yet we have much to learn and to improve. To put the matter boldly, the
ways we express and live the Scriptures are by their very nature *our* ways
to express and live them. They may have been quite appropriate for our
historical contexts, but not quite as appropriate for our current contexts.
From time to time, I put the matter this way: "To represent Reformed
theology, we must re-present it. Simply repeating Reformed theology
doesn't represent it at all."

Multiple Perspectives

Perhaps Frame is best known for championing an approach to theology
that is often called *multiperspectival* or *triperspectival.*[35] Stemming from his
own studies in philosophy and supported by the approach taken in some of
Van Til's writings, Frame convincingly advocates approaching nearly every
feature of Christian theology from multiple perspectives. At the heart of the
matter is the fact that human beings are limited in their ability to understand the revelation of God, and pursuing topics from different perspectives
will enhance our understanding much as viewing a physical object from
multiple angles often helps us understand it better. Although he broke the
pattern from time to time, Frame identified three main ways of looking at
different theological issues, using a variety of terms for each perspective as
he pursued different topics.[36] Broadly speaking, however, Frame spoke of

35. "The general concept is simply that because we are not God, because we are finite, not
infinite, we cannot know everything at a glance, and therefore our knowledge is limited to one
perspective or another. . . . There is one truth, and each perspective is merely an angle from which
that truth can be viewed. We will never achieve perfect knowledge of that one truth, but we
advance toward it step by step. That advance always involves enriching our present perspectives
by referring to those of others" (*PP*).

36. See *PWG* where Frame briefly lays out the normative, situational, and existential perspectives as interrelated with the three lordship attributes of authority, control, and presence. This

the value of exploring theological topics from normative, situational, and existential perspectives.

Like many of his other students, I hesitated to accept Frame's consistent application of these three perspectives to nearly every issue. It seemed artificial and mechanical. As time went by, however, I began to value his approach more and more. First, as young students are inclined, I enjoyed criticizing philosophers and theologians by pointing out how their analyses had not been sufficiently multidimensional. After that, I became convinced that applying different sets of criteria to the same issue nearly always enlarged and deepened my own understanding. Biblical and theological matters that I once understood only as they had been handed down to me became increasingly kaleidoscopic. Finally, I began to discover that applying Frame's threefold normative, situational, and existential perspectives provided helpful heuristic devices for my own analysis of hermeneutical issues in Old Testament studies.[37]

In 1985 I published a short article titled "Pictures, Windows and Mirrors in Old Testament Exegesis,"[38] in which I applied triperspectivalism to Old Testament interpretation.[39] This article was my attempt to reconcile a tension that I and many others have felt in recent Reformed theology: the tension between biblical theology and systematic theology.

In my estimation, the heart of the matter can be put in this way. As the influence of Geerhardus Vos on conservative Reformed theology in America grew during the mid-twentieth century, the discipline of biblical theology was thought to organize reflection on Scripture in the Scriptures' own terms. For Vos and his advocates, this meant that like the Bible itself, biblical theology was best when organized around the thread of redemptive history, the historical unfolding of salvation from Genesis to Revelation. Systematic theology, however, was an abstract, secondary theological organization of the findings of biblical theology according to a set of traditional concerns. These traditional concerns, however, were thought to be *scholastic*, *Hellenistic*, and *rationalistic*, terms designed to indicate how distant systematic theology was from the Scriptures themselves.

---

lordship triad is developed most fully in *DG*, 21–115. These triads shape Frame's approach to most other areas of systematic, biblical, and practical theology.

37. See *DG*, 15n31. There he mentions the pedagogical aspects of these triads, with his own ongoing assessment of their value and possible dangers.

38. Richard Pratt, "Pictures, Windows and Mirrors in Old Testament Exegesis," *WTJ* 45 (1983): 156–67.

39. *DKG*, 203–4.

Naturally, this dichotomy caused all kinds of problems for anyone committed both to confessional Reformed theology and to the supreme authority of Scripture. If biblical theology reflected the Bible's own theology, then it should have reached the same conclusions as traditional Reformed systematic theology. But it did not. Biblical theologians espoused viewpoints that were in tension with the concerns of traditional systematic theology. For many advocates of this way of thinking, it seemed impossible to hold a commitment to Scripture and traditional Reformed theology together.

Frankly, Frame's multiperspectivalism saved systematic theology from my rubbish bin. If I had to choose between theology that followed Scripture (i.e., biblical theology) and traditional systematic theology, the choice was simple. I would follow the Scriptures. In Frame's view, however, biblical theology was not necessarily closer to scriptural teaching than systematic theology. At a time when it was not popular to do so, he claimed that both disciplines simply represented different perspectives on the Scriptures. Biblical theology looked at Scripture through the lens of history, and systematic theology looked at Scripture through the lens of various Western philosophical and traditional theological categories. In his view, each approach had its own strengths and weaknesses. One did not necessarily reflect the teachings of Scripture better than the other.

In my article, I followed this line of reasoning by distinguishing three complementary exegetical perspectives or strategies: thematic analysis, historical analysis, and literary analysis. In the first place, using the metaphor of a mirror, I argued that systematic theology follows a thematic exegetical strategy, asking questions of Scripture that primarily reflect on issues raised by the Western church in response to its historical circumstances. The Scriptures are so rich that they are able to answer many of the questions we have, even if those questions are not emphasized in Scripture. Systematic theology brought this feature of Scripture to the foreground.

Biblical theology, however, is oriented toward historical analysis of the Scriptures. To be sure, not every part of Scripture has a historical orientation that fits well with biblical theology. Nevertheless, the Scriptures can be viewed historically. Biblical theologians recognize this historical character of Scripture by alternating between synchronic and diachronic assessments of biblical teachings. They concentrate on the distinctive teachings of each period of biblical history and the ways in which these teachings developed over the course of biblical history.

To these two exegetical strategies, I added a third perspective that I called literary analysis of Scripture. This perspective on the Bible was in its early stages in conservative Reformed circles when I entered Old Testament studies, but I thought it important to distinguish it from systematics and biblical theology as a third perspective on Scripture. Instead of looking at the Bible primarily as a mirror of our thematic concerns or a window through which we can view redemptive history, I suggested that exegesis could also view the Scriptures as pictures, by concentrating on their intended communicative impact. The Scriptures could also be viewed in this way because biblical writers integrated literary form and content to influence or impact their original readers in certain ways.

In my view, these exegetical strategies are not at odds with each other. On the contrary, they are highly interdependent, forming webs of multiple reciprocities. They simply represent various emphases that the Holy Spirit has led and probably will lead his people to have as they approach the Bible. Taken together, systematic, biblical, and "literary" theologies are perspectives that enable us to grasp the teaching of Scripture more thoroughly.

What has multiperspectivalism to do with the future of the church? It reminds us of something we encounter every time we interact with others theologically. Outlooks that are often treated as competing or mutually exclusive may not be. Although many theological differences among believers cannot be reconciled, careful perspectival assessment often shows them to be different but compatible emphases.

As Reformed churches in North America are tested by postmodern shifts among their members, growing accountability to ethnic minorities in the West, and the need to serve alongside the majority of Christians who reside in Asia, Africa, and Latin America, we will encounter multitudes of theological differences among us. Many of these differences will be substantial and irreconcilable. But more often than we may expect, they will result from one group or another emphasizing one perspective on a topic over another. When this is the case, integrating different perspectives with each other may actually prove beneficial for all believers involved. Whenever we can resolve tensions in the body of Christ by embracing the perspectives of others, we will be in a much better position to minister together.

Theological Education

In my estimation, one of the most radical positions Frame ever expressed was his "Proposal for a New Seminary."[40] Although written rather early in his career, in 1978, Frame pointed out a number of weaknesses in traditional Protestant seminary education. In response to these problems he proposed that theological education should probably look quite different than it does. In 2001, Frame qualified a number of his suggestions, saying, "The 'situation' I describe in the paper may have been a bit overdrawn then."[41] What I find to be interesting in the proposal is how it is another example of Frame's applying his theology to a particular subject. He evaluated the need for change in theological education in 1978 in ways that are not surprising for those who are familiar with his theological method. I am convinced, however, that the need for change in theological education is even more pronounced in our day.

There are many ways we could explore the future of theological education, but for our purposes here it will suffice to combine two features of Frame's theology that we have already mentioned. As we have seen, Frame has urged that "theology is the application of Scripture to all areas of life" and that life can be viewed from three main vantage points: the normative, situational, and existential perspectives. In this light, education in theology ought to amount to education in applying Scriptures to the full range of life. By and large, the goal is to prepare ministers of the gospel for service to the church and the world, but if their preparation is theological in Frame's sense of the term, then it will prepare ministers to handle the Scriptures with at least three chief concerns: norms, situations, and persons.

Without a doubt, traditional seminary education in the Reformed tradition concentrates primarily on the normative dimensions of theology. It devotes much attention to the Scriptures as the only absolute norm for theology. In a secondary sense, it also draws students toward the norms of the Reformed tradition, the ways in which this branch of the church should understand and use the Scriptures. These features of traditional seminary education are positive, and we have experienced much success in these areas.

40. See John M. Frame, "Proposal for a New Seminary" (unpublished: 1978), http://www.frame-poythress.org/frame_articles/1978Proposal.htm.
41. Ibid., Postscript 2001.

Unfortunately, however, when theological institutions spend the vast majority of students' time focusing on these normative dimensions of their education, other crucial matters hardly receive the attention they deserve. If the goal of education in theology is by definition to provide education in the application of Scripture to life, then other dimensions of life must become much more central in our educational curricula. Situational and existential concerns must play a much more significant role than we normally give them.

For example, traditionally educated ministers may be well equipped to handle Scripture in line with certain norms. Yet their ministries suffer because they have not been taught how to apply Scripture to the situations in which they will find themselves and their congregants. One or two classes on preaching, church planting, and church management are hardly adequate for preparing ministers for the array of circumstances they will face in ministry. I think it is not an overstatement to say that most theological students in the Reformed tradition are attracted to our schools because they already have propensities toward overemphasizing the more normative dimensions of seminary education. For them, the term *practical* often means "of secondary importance." Only rarely do professors of practical theology stand out as pinnacles of our educational institutions. So if we hope to prepare ministers of the gospel, we must take much more seriously the task of preparing them, developing their skills at applying the Scriptures to the practical challenges of circumstances into which their ministries will bring them.

Beyond this, traditional theological education is especially weak in preparing students to apply Scripture to the more existential dimensions of life. One way in which this is true is that students easily graduate from our seminaries without having done much self-reflection. They often begin seminary with the hope that their education will help them grow in sanctification, but it isn't long before the normative, academic demands of the seminary push these desires to the margins of their lives. No matter what terminology we use—*spirituality, piety, sanctification, character development*, etc.—Frame's definition of *theology* presses theological educators to concentrate more on personal, existential concerns. We desperately need to have the goal of developing something akin to Daniel Goldman's idea of "emotional intelligence" in our theological students.[42]

42. See Daniel Goldman, *Emotional Intelligence* (New York: Bantam Books, 1995).

I have little doubt that these aspects of theological education may be "better caught than taught," as the saying goes. Yet I am convinced that one avenue for addressing even this dimension of the problem is to transform the role of professors in theological education.[43] At this stage in history, the role of a professor is not much different from what it was during the medieval period. In those days, scholars used their lectures primarily as ways to disseminate information. They spoke and students took notes as they had opportunity. Today, in most of our seminary classrooms, professors still function in much the same way, primarily as human data transfer units. They spend their classroom time behind their lecterns and transfer data to the students, who take notes as they have opportunity.

We live in a day, however, when the basic data of theological education can be transferred to students much more effectively by other means. Although books maintain an important role in this process, electronic media have made it possible for much of the information that was once the center of a classroom experience to be communicated by other means. My own interest in these possibilities for theological education was sparked in large part by Babin's *The New Era in Religious Communication*.[44] Whatever we think of it, theological education is already impacted by multimedia communication and will almost certainly continue to be in the near future.

This shift in theological education offers us opportunities for meeting the challenges facing Reformed theology in the near future. First, we can meet the needs of students who come to us espousing postmodern values. For example, adopting effective multimedia communication of basic information to these students will give professors the opportunity to change from their traditional role. Time with professors is a scarce commodity and should not be spent on tasks that can be accomplished by other means. If we employ effective mediated data transfer, then professors will be able to present themselves as persons to students as persons. They will be able to exemplify skills and attitudes, service and love in ways that traditional classroom practices do not allow. Such exposure may be intimidating to professors of theology, but these roles

---

43. I see this transformation of the role of theological professors as a crucial dimension of my work at Third Millennium Ministries (www.thirdmill.org).

44. P. Babin, *The New Era in Religious Communication* (Minneapolis: Fortress Press, 1991).

will enable us to give more attention to the situational and existential dimensions of theological education that postmodern students typically desire so much.

Second, by employing effective mediated curricula to transfer basic data, we may also open some important avenues for Reformed theologians to serve the leadership of growing minorities in North America. One of the greatest obstacles facing many Latin American and African-American churches is the academic requirements for admission to our traditional schools. In many of these communities, church leaders serve without much formal education. If we turn our efforts toward multimedia to transfer basic theological data, then we can offer them foundational information in support of their own theological learning communities. By this means, we may be able to reach portions of the population of North America that normally have little to do with us or our theology.

Third, developing curricula in multiple languages that can be distributed at many levels of technology at very low cost will serve the cause of Christ around the world as well. In my experience, the cry of the majority church outside North America is for leadership training. Their own efforts are largely underfunded and inadequate by their own estimations. Creating a multimedia curriculum and making it available to those who lead theological education in Africa, Asia, Latin America, and the former Soviet Union will provide them with a solid theological base for their efforts and enable them to focus more on preparing students who will apply the Scriptures to situations and persons. Perhaps in this way the leading churches of the next century will be able to avoid some of the pitfalls of our traditional theological educational system.

Conclusion

The theological outlooks John Frame has taught for decades have enormously positive potential for guiding conservative Reformed churches in North America as cultural changes test our resolve in the near future. We have touched on just a few ways his insights can equip us for these challenges. Yet I would be remiss not to mention one other factor that is often overlooked about John Frame, his life. In line with his own theological principles, Frame's life has been an example of the kind of theologian our churches will need more and more in approaching years. He has exemplified the spirit of a humble servant-theologian, a man tirelessly devoted to others in service to the kingdom of God. As those who have known him personally will understand, his personal character as a follower of Christ may yet be his greatest contribution to the future of the church.

RESPONSES TO SOME ARTICLES

JOHN M. FRAME

WE HAD THOUGHT at one time that I would respond to each of the essays, briefly to some, more extensively to others, following Van Til's example in *Jerusalem and Athens*. I wrote up a few of these responses, however, and didn't like them much. How many times, and ways, can you say, "Joe has understood my thought well and has provided some good, careful analysis?" That same kind of comment would apply to each of the many essays in the volume. That would not be very helpful to readers. On the other hand, for me to respond to each substantive idea of each article could double the length of this already record-length festschrift. So I decided to drop the idea of responding to each essay. Nevertheless, there are a few essays that raise issues that seem to cry out for a response, places where a reader might well say, "I wonder what Frame thinks of this." So I will include at this juncture some comments about controversial points raised in some selected essays.

First, to **James Anderson**, who in a note to his fine essay comments, "Frame makes remarks about each perspective's 'including' the other two that seem to erode their distinctiveness." I agree with his analysis—that the three perspectives (normative, situational, and existential) have different senses, but the same referent (namely, the whole of human knowledge). That is implicit, I think, in the very idea of a "perspective." A perspective is a whole, viewed from a particular angle. So all perspectives refer to the whole, but they refer to it in different ways. And I like James's suggestion that we can call those ways "senses." But the point of my language was this: When I analyze

961

the normative perspective of something, say, the doctrine of sanctification, I realize that one of the biblical norms is that we should apply those norms to life situations and to our own experience. So the normative perspective, among other things, requires us to investigate the situational and existential in a certain way. The normative perspective, that is, requires a particular analysis of the other two. I don't think it is misleading, then, to say that the normative perspective *includes* a particular kind of situational analysis. Obviously, the situational perspective is subject to a normative analysis. But the reverse is also true: the normative must take note of the relevant facts of the situational. Same for all pairings of the perspectives. To make this point at the general level, I think the idea of mutual inclusion is appropriate.

James also questions my view of transcendental argument. I will take that up here in my response to **Don Collett**. (**Steve Scrivener** also addresses this issue.) Don continues here a discussion we have had for some years on this subject, documented in his essay. Cornelius Van Til described his distinctive apologetic method as "transcendental," also as "presuppositional." Following Immanuel Kant, who most influenced the later use of "transcendental" in philosophy, I take a transcendental argument to be any argument that seeks to establish the conditions that make knowledge possible. Van Til often interprets this to mean an argument that establishes the "possibility of predication," the possibility of attaching a predicate to a subject. And unlike Kant, Van Til finds that condition in the God of Scripture. For Van Til, further, God is the condition, not only of intellectual meaning, but also of all kinds of meaning, all coherence of mind, feeling, will, beauty, and goodness.

Now, Van Til thought that the "traditional apologetics" of Thomas Aquinas, Joseph Butler, William Paley, and others failed to show that God was the transcendental condition of predication. He even thought that their arguments led to a different god from the God of the Bible. For Van Til, these arguments presupposed that something could be understood perfectly well without God (such as being or causality or purpose) and then tried, by such autonomous reasoning, to prove the God of the Bible. But a god who can be reached by autonomous reasoning is not the God of the Bible.

I never agreed with Van Til about this. I do not believe that Aquinas, for example, thought that causality was perfectly understandable without God. Rather, I think it more likely that he was making the opposite point:

that causality is unintelligible unless there is a first cause, and the God of the Bible is the only being who can really be the first cause of everything.

And it seemed to me that if Aquinas argued correctly in showing that God is the first cause of everything, then God is the transcendental condition of everything: of meaning, coherent thought, and predication, as well as motion, causality, and contingency. On that understanding, Aquinas's argument, like Van Til's, is transcendental and presuppositional. If that is true, then Van Til's argument may not be as singular as he thought it was.

Don Collett, however, defends the uniqueness of Van Til's argument by pointing out that for Van Til it is not enough to say with Aquinas that causality proves God. For Van Til, it is important that even the *denial* of causality proves God. For if God is the transcendental ground of intelligibility, causality cannot be meaningfully affirmed *or denied* unless God exists. So Van Til argued that even atheism presupposes theism;[1] even the denial of God presupposes God.[2] This double argument, that either the affirmation or the denial of something presupposes God, fits in well with some definitions of *presupposition* in modern analytic philosophy. For P. F. Strawson, Bas van Fraassen, and others, to say that A *presupposes* B is to say not only that A implies B, but also that not-A implies B. Van Til would modify Aquinas's argument to say not only that causality implies God, but also that the *denial* of causality implies God. To construct an argument with that double premise is to argue by presupposition, to argue transcendentally.

So I told Collett in my earlier reply[3] that I was willing to use this definition of *presupposition* in describing Van Til's position, rather than describing his argument as a mere implication, a *modus ponens*. But I still wonder if Collett isn't exaggerating the difference between presupposition (Strawson's sense) and implication. Isn't it more like this, that Strawson's presupposition embraces two implications? A presupposes B = if A then B, and

---

1. Hence Van Til's famous illustration of the little girl sitting on her father's lap while slapping him on the face. He supports her, even as she is fighting him.

2. One problem here is that to say that atheism presupposes theism supposes that atheism can be stated coherently. But if atheism presupposes theism, then it bears in itself a contradiction that destroys its coherence. If it is incoherent, it is unclear how it can be said to presuppose anything. What Van Til would probably say is that atheism, stated as a philosophical position, does have some coherence—by borrowed capital from theism, or that its coherence can at least be assumed "for the sake of argument." So in what follows I will mostly assume that and ignore this particular problem. But at a later point of this discussion I will need to look at a related issue.

3. "Reply to Don Collett on Transcendental Argument," *WTJ* 65 (2003): 307–9, available at http://www.frame-poythress.org/frame_articles/2003ReplytoCollett.htm.

if not-A then B. "If A then B" is one traditional implication. "If not-A then B" is another. So why shouldn't we look at "A presupposes B" as a shorthand for talking about two traditional implications at the same time?

Collett would say that I have missed the point here. What is unique about presuppositional arguments in the Strawson/van Fraassen mode is that you can do this:

If A, then B. (Meaning that B is the presupposition of A.)

Not-A

Therefore B.[4]

Although this is "analogous" to traditional *modus ponens* and *modus tollens* arguments, it is not one of those traditional forms. In fact, most observers who are not in on the discussion of presuppositions would dismiss this argument as a formal fallacy.

I'm willing to grant that the argument above is valid, given the Strawson/Van Til understanding of presupposition. But we need to get back to basics here. A good deductive argument, in apologetics, needs to have three qualities. It needs to be *valid* (i.e., it follows the laws of logic), *sound* (its premises are true and therefore its conclusion is true), and *persuasive* (it is effective in bringing people to believe the conclusion).[5] There are many arguments that are valid and sound, but not persuasive, such as this one:

God's speech never errs.

The Bible is God's speech.

Therefore, the Bible never errs.

4. Of course, you can also do this: "If A, then B. A. Therefore B." This looks like a traditional *modus ponens*, and is not controversial. What is unique about presuppositional arguments conceived in this way is that "If A, then B" and "not-A" will together imply B, and that both this and the former argument are valid.

5. Alert readers will note my three perspectives here: validity is normative (following laws); soundness is situational (stating true facts about the world); and persuasiveness is existential (appealing to the hearts and minds of its audience).

This argument is certainly valid, and most evangelical Christians will regard it as sound, as I do. But skeptics will typically not find it persuasive. They will have many questions about and objections to the premises, and until those are dealt with they will not consider adopting the conclusion. The same may be said about the Collett version of the transcendental argument. Take this argument about causality:

> If causality exists, God exists (in the sense that God is the presupposition or transcendental ground of causality).
>
> There is no causality.
>
> Therefore God exists.

Given Collett's analysis, this is a valid argument. The truth of the premises we may assume here for the sake of argument, and on that assumption the argument is sound. But it would not be persuasive to anyone inclined to skepticism. Most would reply, I think, that the first premise needs to be argued.[6] *Why* should anyone grant that the God of the Bible is the presupposition of causality?

So the Collett argument needs many subarguments if it is to be persuasive. And I think that those subarguments will use traditional argument forms, mainly *modus ponens* and *modus tollens*. How can we prove that God is the transcendental ground of causality? Not by repeating the Collett transcendental argument again and again; for that is what is problematic. We need to establish the first premise. How do we do that? By showing that it is meaningless to speak of causality unless God exists. How do we do that? Perhaps by showing (with traditional apologists) that an infinite series of causes is unintelligible, and that to deny that infinite series is to affirm God. Or maybe there are other ways. But in any case, we are trying to prove the first premise of the transcendental argument by using traditional arguments—which was my point all along.

The next step, after we have proved that God is the transcendental ground of causality (or anything else), will be an argument like this:

---

6. The second one too, of course. But we assumed that only for the sake of argument.

> If God is the transcendental ground of x, he exists.
>
> God is the transcendental ground of x.
>
> Therefore, God exists.

That, like the supporting arguments for the second premise, is a traditional argument, in this case a *modus ponens*. So traditional arguments are legitimate and indeed necessary in these two ways: (1) the supporting arguments for God's being the transcendental ground, and (2) the argument from God's being transcendental ground to God's existing.

To look at this from another perspective: Van Til's transcendental argument seems to me to say this:

> If anything is intelligible (coherent, meaningful), God exists.
>
> Something (causality, motion, banana peels, Augustine) is intelligible (coherent, meaningful).
>
> Therefore, God exists.

But this is a traditional *modus ponens*. To put it into Collett's mode, you would have to be able to say:

> If anything is intelligible, God exists.
>
> Nothing is intelligible.
>
> Therefore, God exists.

But then God is not merely the transcendental ground of intelligibility; he is the transcendental ground of intelligibility and nonintelligibility, meaningfulness and meaninglessness. This dissolves, for me, the original meaning and attractiveness of transcendental argument. Again, I want to retreat into common sense. Do we really want to say that even a meaningless, unintelligible world would presuppose God? What would "presuppose" *mean* in a meaningless world? Indeed, if "nothing is intelligible" (the second premise above), then not even God is intelligible, not even to himself. And then what kind of God would he be? I must reluctantly conclude that at this point the transcendentalizing of apologetics implodes into nonsense.[7]

Where does this leave us? I continue to believe, on the basis of Scripture, that God is the ground of all meaning in the world. I continue to believe that even the borrowed-capital intelligibility of atheism is grounded in God. I continue to believe that God grounds the intelligibility of both true and false assertions about reality, insofar as they are intelligible. If we understand what we are talking about, we can argue that to either assert or deny the existence of a causal order proves God's existence. But I'm not willing (and I gather that Don is not willing either) to abandon traditional argument forms like *modus ponens* altogether, or to say that apologists who use these forms have somehow proved a god antithetical to the God of the Bible. Nor am I willing to say that when someone argues from finite reality (say, A) to God, they must be presupposing that A is intelligible apart from God. Showing that God exists (and I am not forgetting that the Holy Spirit has the final word here) requires many arguments. Further, I believe that the apologetic tradition has come up with some arguments that get us at least *part* of the way to our destination. And I still think that the Strawson/van Fraassen/Collett transcendental argument can be adequately formulated by two traditional arguments: "If A, then God exists. A. Therefore God exists," and "If not-A, then God exists. Not-A. Therefore God exists."

Although the Collett formulation is valid, it is not much use in practical apologetics. It may be an illustrative way to explain what it means to say that God is the transcendental ground of reality, just as "God says he exists, therefore God exists" is a way of illustrating the role of divine authority in Christian epistemology. But it is not an argument that by itself would convince any skeptic.[8] For such arguments, we need to look to traditional logic and evidence. Is it, then, possible to show by traditional argument (empowered by the Holy Spirit) that God is the *transcendental* ground of meaning? Yes; by the two argument forms I suggested at the beginning of this discussion: (1) If A, then God exists, and (2) if not-A, then God exists. If we can establish these premises, and the logic leading to their conclusions, they will justify that God

---

7. Have I just formulated a *reductio*?

8. The ontological argument is similar in this respect. To say, "God has all perfections; existence is a perfection; therefore God exists" will not convince many skeptics. But it may be a useful way of illustrating the point that God's existence is necessary, not merely contingent, given Christian presuppositions about perfections.

is transcendental ground in the Strawson/Van Til sense, and they will justify the argument "If A, then God exists; Not-A; therefore God exists."

And to tell the truth, I still believe that just one of these two traditional arguments could be adequate. I ask again, as I asked before: if Aquinas succeeds in showing that God is the first cause of everything, doesn't that argument alone show that God is the first cause of intelligibility and meaning, that he is the first cause even of the intelligibility of false statements? Aquinas's argument does not have a *distinctively* presuppositional form. But is there any reason to deny that it entails a presuppositional conclusion?

This is why I still like to speak of "presuppositionalism of the heart," of which Collett is somewhat critical. I have always thought that Van Til understood presupposition as something more than a position in a logical argument. He often linked godly presuppositions to the process of regeneration and sanctification, as basic commitments of the heart. The question I addressed in *AGG* is whether this heart-presupposition could be precisely identified by the argument forms an apologist chooses to use. In one obvious sense, it cannot be. Someone might well prove God's existence, even using the Strawson/Collett argument form, and still be unregenerate, affirming God hypocritically rather than from the heart. That person would be a presuppositionalist in apologetic method, but not a presuppositionalist of the heart.

In another sense, too, there is a disconnection between presuppositionalism of the heart and presuppositionalism in apologetic theory. Someone might use traditional arguments to show that God is the transcendental ground of meaning, as I suggested above that Aquinas did. If so, there is no distinctive argument form that necessarily identifies him as a presuppositionalist. If he is one, he is a presuppositionalist of the heart, one who subjects all his thinking to the God of Scripture.

As we move to the paper of **Paul Helm**, we move from logic and epistemology to metaphysics. In Paul's gracefully written article, he deals with questions I raised in a review about his views of "levels of causation, evil as privation, the divine permission of evil, and divine weakness." On the first and last topics, he and I are in full agreement, if I understand him rightly. His view of levels of causation is fully compatible with mine,[9] as is his view

9. See *DG*, 154–58.

of God's "power and weakness."[10] I'm less sure of our agreement in the other two areas, although he has given me a lot to chew on by going deeply into the biblical, theological, and philosophical literature.

First, privation. I must (for lack of space and expertise) bypass what Paul says about Augustine, neoplatonism, and John Calvin, largely conceding what he says about these writers. But I would make some further distinctions in regard to Genesis 1–2. I agree that in this passage "goodness" applies to the realization of God's creative purposes (cf. 1 Tim. 4:4), and that the lack of such realization (as in Gen. 2:18) is "not good," but I cannot accept the metaphysical implications sometimes derived from these facts. Is goodness here identical with being, one of the transcendental perspectives on being (along with substance, unity, truth, and beauty), as many medieval theologians believed?[11] Or is goodness a property distinct from being, that beings have in various degrees, and that some beings may not have at all? I'm inclined to think the latter view is true. For example, it would be wrong to say that because Satan is consummate evil he doesn't exist, or that he in some sense has minimum being, whatever that might mean. Rather, it seems to me that Scripture never questions the reality of evil, or of evil beings, or the degree of their reality. The reason is that for the biblical writers evil is not a metaphysical defect, nor the result of a metaphysical defect, but a personal choice.

On this basis, when God declares the creation to be good, his statement is contingently, not necessarily, true. Things are not good merely because they are, and they are not evil because they fail fully to be. Rather, "it was good" indicates the completion of God's work at the end of each creation day and then again at the end of the creation week. "Good" did not necessarily apply to each midday state of affairs. I think the "not good" of Adam's singleness in Gen. 2:18 was such a midday assessment. At that point, Adam was a created being, was real, but he was not fully formed, because his rib had not yet become a mate. So the current state of his formation was "not good."

10. Ibid., 526–28.
11. It is important in this discussion to distinguish between *teleological* goodness and *moral* goodness (see my *DCL*, 14–15). To say that something is teleologically good is to say that it can be used for a good purpose. To say that someone is morally good is to say that he or she obeys God. Everything is teleologically good (Gen. 1:31; 1 Tim. 4:4), but not all persons are morally good. Now, moral goodness is a subdivision of teleological goodness, in the sense that moral goodness has a good purpose. But even evil beings are teleologically good, since God uses them to bring about his good purposes. Since everything is teleologically good, it is plausible to say that teleological goodness is "convertible with being." But moral goodness is not, since even those who lack moral goodness are beings.

Now, it is not entirely wrong to think of evil as a "lack" or "privation." But many things can be defined as privations of their opposites. Femininity can be defined as a lack of masculinity. But that does not entail that female persons have less reality than males, or that they are real only insofar as they have masculine qualities.

Further, such definitions are often reversible. Masculinity can be defined as the lack of femininity. And good can be defined as a privation of evil. It would be hard to find fault with the latter definition if we did not believe antecedently that the world is God's good creation and that evil entered, after the creation, to be a temporary, if disastrous, scourge. So I don't believe that thinking of evil as a privation gives us any apologetic advantage. It's simply another way of stating that in the Christian worldview good is prior to evil and sovereign over it.

Paul's main point is that the idea of evil as a privation provides a "neat metaphysical response" to the question of how God can be sovereign over everything and yet not the "author of sin." But I don't understand how this response is helpful. Whether evil is a being or a privation of being, God is still sovereign over it, by his eternal plan, creation, and providence. Calling evil a privation does not entail that we should not blame him for bringing it about. I sometimes tell people that it's like a baker being accused of making the holes in his doughnuts too big. Imagine him replying: "I am responsible only for the dough, not for the holes in it." Of course, that would be silly. The baker chose to make the holes, and he determined what size they should be. He is responsible both for the dough in his doughnuts and for the lack of dough. Similarly, God is responsible for the being in his creation and also for the lacks, the privations of being.

Of course, I don't believe that God is to blame for evil. I've addressed that issue in my writings, although I don't believe that there is a fully satisfactory answer available to us now.[12] But I don't find the privation doctrine helpful.

Paul is surprised that I give so much attention at one point to Étienne Gilson's metaphysical analysis of evil as privation. One reason could be that I spent a full semester back around 1963 going through Gilson's *The Spirit of Medieval Philosophy*[13] in a seminar led by Cornelius Van Til. I did

12. *AGG*, chaps. 6–7; *DG*, chap. 9.
13. New York: Charles Scribner's Sons, 1940.

not follow Van Til at every point.[14] But I was convinced of the danger of "confusing the ethical with the metaphysical." That is to say, it is important for us to remember that sin is not a defect in being (which would actually be a defect in God's creation) but is ethical—personal rebellion by human beings against our personal God.

Now, I certainly agree with Paul (and with the Westminster Confession) that God created Adam good, but "under a possibility of transgressing."[15] The possibility must have been there, because the actuality later occurred. I could not, however, present a spiritual MRI of Adam to indicate what it was that made transgression possible. Paul thinks it makes sense to say that this possibility should be described as a defect in being. Certainly it was a defect, in that someone who is indefectibly good is better than someone who is defectibly good. But that is not a moral difference, for the defectibility of goodness does not bring any blame upon the person. And I hesitate for the above reasons to say that it is a metaphysical difference (i.e., a lack of being). So, as often in theology, I must say, "I don't know what it was."

Does consideration of these issues lead to a "free-will defense" against the problem of evil? Well, certainly Adam's sin was his choice. And Adam alone is to blame for it. But of course it was God who created him as he was and who foreordained his fall. Normally I think of a "free-will defense" as an appeal to human libertarian freedom (the ability to perform acts not caused by anything) as the sole reason for sin and evil. We don't have that, given the understanding of God's sovereignty that Paul and I share. Should we broaden the concept of a free will-defense to include the view that the sinner alone is to blame for his sins, even though they are divinely foreordained? Perhaps that is what Paul is asking us to do. But I think it's best to use "free-will defense" in a more standard way.

Howard Griffith questions my view that God's knowledge may grow in some sense when he is interacting in time with human beings. Paul also addressed this issue in his review of *DG*.[16] Certainly we should be cautious in this area, and I am more than ready to be corrected. I do believe that God exists above time, unchangeably, and that as a supratemporal being he

14. Chapter 25 of my *CVT* presents the flavor of some of the debates that took place in this seminar.

15. WCF 4.2.

16. Paul Helm, "A Good Big Book," *Modern Reformation* (March–April 2003): 51–52.

knows absolutely everything: all eternal truths, and all truths about events in time, events that are to us past, present, and future. But it does seem to me that when God enters temporal relationships with human beings (as with Abraham, Moses, et al.) he necessarily behaves in some ways as a temporal being. He does not bring every feature of his supratemporal existence into time, for that would be incompatible with the nature of time.

For example, when God comes into history, he does one thing on Monday, another thing Tuesday, and another thing Wednesday. He is pleased for a time, then wrathful. That temporal movement is a kind of change. When we speak of God doing A on Monday and B on Tuesday, that is not an anthropomorphism. That really happens. We would never say, "It *appears* that God's actions are spread out in time, but they are really simultaneous." No, they really are spread out in time. They represent a process of divine activity. That process is, of course, a process of one action after another. God sent his Son "when the fullness of time had come," the actual time of the incarnation. That event happened at one time, not at all times simultaneously. At one time Jesus' birth was future, and at another time it was past.

Is there a process of divine *knowledge* also, as there is a temporal process of divine actions? When God enters time, what he does on Tuesday is appropriate to that time period. It is an appropriate response to the events of Monday, and an appropriate anticipation to the events of Wednesday. When events take place on Monday, God knows they take place and when. Of course, he knows the whole sequence by knowing his eternal plan. But within time, he knows what has happened (temporally), what is happening, and what will happen. And as an event changes from future to past, he knows and understands that temporal transition.

So when God enters history, the temporal progression of events is part of his knowledge. His knowing is one temporal act he performs (as well as being an eternal event). As he performs one act after another, he thinks one thought after another. He knows one state of affairs after another and acts in a way appropriate to that knowledge.

Scripture explicitly tells us that Jesus "increased in wisdom and in stature and in favor with God and man" (Luke 2:52). It is hard to understand how Jesus the eternal Son of God could gain wisdom he didn't have before; but we can relate that fact to the reality of his human nature. That problem seems to me to be similar to the one above—that God-in-time gains knowledge in his involvements with creatures. Could it be that whenever

God enters time he takes on some human characteristics, foreshadowing the incarnation? In time, his actions are not simultaneous, but successive, like those of Jesus, even though God has foreordained them from all eternity. Perhaps then there is an analogy between (1) the divine and human natures of Christ, and (2) the relationship between God-above-time and God-in-time. At least I think this concept is worthy of discussion. I acknowledge, however, that the idea is somewhat speculative, and I will quickly abandon it if it ever appears to me to contradict the clear biblical teaching of God's omniscience and sovereignty over time.

Wayne Grudem's fine paper leads me from philosophy and theology to the area of ethics. He takes issue with my argument that it is sometimes right to lie. Wayne indicates that I have changed my view on this over the years. Actually, I have gone back and forth several times. I am willing to be persuaded again, and Wayne leaves me almost persuaded, but not quite. I can only skim the issues here, but some things should be noted:

1. Wayne's definition of *lying* is different from mine. He restricts *lying* to "affirming in speech or writing something you believe to be false." On this definition, misleading actions (such as intentionally deceiving an enemy in time of war) would not constitute lying. My reply: I fail to see any morally relevant difference between intentionally misleading someone with the lips and misleading him with an action. Wayne says:

> An action is something that happens; it is neither true nor false like a verbal affirmation of something. An example is leaving a light on in our house when we are away for a weekend—an observer may rightly conclude, "The Grudems left a light on," but that may or may not mean that we are at home.

I agree that actions in themselves are neither true nor false. But they do sometimes mislead people, and often they are performed intentionally to deceive. If verbal misrepresentations are wrong, they are wrong because they deceive people we should not deceive (as stated clearly in the ninth commandment). So I fail to see how actions and words are different in this respect. Wayne does offer more arguments in this connection, but I am not quite convinced by them.

2. I agree that "you shall not bear false witness against your neighbor" does not in itself limit our obligation to neighbors only. I have argued in *DCL*

that (as in the Westminster Larger Catechism) the commandments bind us beyond the specific contexts of their original statements. But it is significant that the ninth commandment bases this obligation on a *relationship* that we have with someone. That is also the case with Paul's words in Ephesians 4:25, "Therefore, having put away falsehood, let each of you speak the truth with his neighbor, for we are members one of another." Here the obligation is based on our relationship with other members of the body of Christ. Now, I agree that the ninth commandment has applications beyond our fellow believers. We should communicate truth in every situation as much as possible. But I believe Scripture does justify deception in some cases, cases where people who are not our neighbors would use the truth for evil purposes.

3. I cannot here go through all the narrative examples that I think are instances of justified lies. For that, see the discussion of the ninth commandment in *DCL*. But let me look here briefly at the case of Rahab. It seems to me that her faith, for which the New Testament commends her, was shown *entirely* through her deception. To "hide" the spies was itself to mislead those who were hunting for them. And she clearly lied (even verbally) when she told the king's men that she didn't know where the spies were from, that she didn't know where they had gone, and (contradicting her assertion of ignorance) that if the soldiers followed the spies in a particular direction they would find them. To send the spies "by another way" (James 2:25) (i.e., a different way from the way she told the king's men) was a lie. Her action in this case falsified her words.

More could be said, of course. But the general direction of my reply to Wayne would be to go over the narrative examples with some care, and the biblical evaluations of those examples.

In general, however, I must say that Wayne's article contains some very careful exegesis and analysis. It is the best argument for the position of Augustine and John Murray that I have seen.

The article by **Franklin E. ("Ed") Payne** will shock many readers. Ed has written a searing indictment of his own profession. Certainly this has taken much courage.[17] I admire him for this. He has shown a similar spirit in his *Biblical/Medical Ethics*[18] and other writings, and I have learned much

---

17. I have some very critical words to speak about my own profession as well. But I have not cut nearly as deeply into the pretensions of theology as Ed has into those of medicine.

18. Milford, MI: Mott Media, 1985.

from him. I do think, however, that his article contains some overstatements. I, for example, cannot say with him that "*the philosophy that directs the killing of the unborn and the unfit is the same one that governs the whole of the practice of medicine.*"[19] "The whole" covers a lot of territory! But I have known many doctors who, like Ed, do not at all sanction abortion or euthanasia and who seek only to treat illness and injury as best they can. I cannot say what is the percentage of doctors under the dominion of murderous ideas of unbelieving medicine. I can be persuaded that many doctors prescribe unnecessary drugs and perform unnecessary procedures. But some of these may be honestly wrong, rather than driven by a murderous impulse.

But I agree entirely with Ed that the secular, unbelieving worldview is a powerful movement in medicine as in every other field of modern thought and culture. Ed also persuades me that there has been a dangerous disconnection between the science of medicine and the practice of medicine. Much of this stems from idolatry, the divinization of human minds and actions.

Now, Ed challenges my assertion that government welfare may sometimes be legitimate. Actually, the passages he cites from *DCL* (819, 824–25, 827) are concessions, in contexts where my general burden is to *limit* government's role in providing for the poor. Clearly in these passages I favor free enterprise, capitalism rather than socialism. In fact, I can't remember ever having voted for a Democrat. But I cannot be an absolutist with regard to political theories. I have to go with Scripture. And as I understand Scripture (*DCL* 593–621), the state is the government of the family of Adam, as the church is the government of the family of Christ. Families take care of their own. In the Bible, the nuclear family has the first responsibility in welfare (1 Tim. 5:8). The second line of defense against disaster is the family of God (by tribes in the OT, the church in the NT). But what if neither the family nor the church has resources sufficient to meet a need? In such cases I do not have biblical ground to say that the state, the family of Adam, must never, ever, try to help.

Finally, Ed questions my critique of the "primacy of the intellect" and my positive view that emotions play a legitimate role in knowledge. The main problem here is that he defines *emotion* very differently from how I do. He defines it as "the momentary (acute) and ongoing (chronic, continuous) disturbance within the mind (soul, spirit) caused by the discrepancy between perceived reality and one's desires." On the contrary, I do not see

19. Emphasis his.

emotion as a disturbance, or as caused by a discrepancy between perception and desire. Ed's definition may be valuable in some medical/psychological contexts, but not in the epistemological contexts I try to explore. For me, *emotion* can apply to any or all human feelings, and those feelings, although they sometimes mislead, can sometimes lead us to truth. Usually, when we feel hot, it is hot. Often when we feel betrayed, we have been betrayed. Of course, emotions sometimes mislead us as well. But so do the intellect and the senses. So I think these classic divisions in the human mind should be considered equal, and I argue in *DKG* that in fact they are not really divisions at all, but perspectives on all human knowledge. The process of knowing is not a battle between three or more independent faculties struggling up in our heads. We gain knowledge as whole persons. Intellect is the person thinking; perception is the person perceiving; emotion is the person feeling; etc. Each of these informs the others and indeed defines the others.[20]

I have always said, however, that we should not, as a rule, follow our *momentary* emotions. Here I agree with Ed. And I would add that we should not follow our momentary ideas, or our momentary impulses, or our momentary perceptions either. Thought is a process of going around and around the data presented to us, with all of our faculties operating. I do indeed teach, as Ed says, that the existential perspective should never be allowed to transgress the normative. But of course, since these are perspectives, I have to say that the reverse is also true: the normative should not be allowed to transgress the existential either, given a right understanding of both of them. Same for the relations between the situational and the others.

I have come now to the end of my interactions with selected essays in this book. I hope that none of the other essayists will be disappointed that I have not chosen also to discuss his or her essay in this section. Of course, space permits only a certain amount of this interaction. My failure to discuss the ideas of a particular essay here does not mean at all that I think less of it, or that I haven't benefited from it. My purpose here has not been to present my reactions to all the essays, only to respond to some ideas that might be especially controversial. My overall view of this festschrift is that the papers are of exceedingly high quality. They have all given me a great deal to think about, and a great deal to be thankful for.

20. For my argument, see *DKG*, 319–46 and *DCL*, 361–82.

Appendix A: Directory of Frame's Major Ideas

John M. Frame

In this appendix I list my most important or distinctive ideas and the best places to find them discussed. Of course, the articles in this festschrift are also an important source, but in this appendix I refer mainly to my own writings. The divisions reflect the order of this volume. Within the divisions, I have placed the titles in a pedagogical order, simplest first.

INTRODUCTORY

1. The persons of the Trinity are related perspectivally, but are not *merely* perspectives on one another.
   - *PP.*

2. In their involvement with creation and history, the three persons of the Trinity are all involved with everything that happens. But Scripture does present a rough division of labor among them: the Father devises the eternal plan, the Son executes that plan, and the Spirit applies it. So emerges the pattern *authority*, *control*, and *presence*.
   - *PP.*
   - *DG*, 693–94.

3. The covenant lordship of God and specifically of Jesus Christ is central to biblical teaching.
   - *SBL*, 23–26.
   - *DKG*, 11–18.

- *DG*, 21–25.
- *DCL*, 19–21.

4. In the concept of divine covenant lordship, three ideas predominate: the Lord's *control*, *authority*, and *presence*. I call these the *lordship attributes*. They are related to the Trinitarian distinctions (2, above), and they generate, in turn, a series of threefold perspectival distinctions.

- *SBL*, 8–12.
- *DKG*, 15–18.
- *DG*, 36–102.
- *DCL*, 21–24.

5. Since we are finite, we need to look at things from many perspectives in order to get a full understanding. I call this *general perspectivalism*.

- *PP*.
- *DKG*, 191–94.
- *CVT*, 119–23.
- Vern Poythress, *Symphonic Theology* (Grand Rapids: Zondervan, 1987), and at http://www.frame-poythress.org.

6. The Trinitarian distinctions and the lordship attributes imply that there are basically three objects of human knowledge: God's revelation (law or norm), the world, and the self. None of these can be fully understood apart from the others.

- *PP*.
- *DKG*, 65–73.

7. The Trinitarian distinctions and the lordship attributes generate three perspectives under which anything can be viewed: the *normative* (showing how anything functions as divine revelation), the *situational* (showing how it functions as an object in the world), and the *existential* (showing how it functions as part of our subjective experience). I call this *special perspectivalism*.

- *PP*.
- *ME*, 1–6.
- *DKG*, 73–75.
- *DG*, 194–96.
- *PWG*, 50–54.
- *DCL*, 33–37.

8. The three perspectives indicate three ways in which we may justify our claims to knowledge.

- *DKG*, 101–64.

THEOLOGY

Nature and Method

1. Theology is the application of God's Word, by persons, to all areas of life.
   - *SBL*, 72–81.
   - *DKG*, 76–85.

2. Exegetical, biblical, and systematic theology are perspectivally related, and all three labels are misnomers.
   - *SBL*, 81–82.
   - *DKG*, 206–14.

3. Scripture warrants the use of logic in theology, but we should also take note of the limitations of logic.
   - *DKG*, 242–60.
   - *CVT*, 151–75.

4. The phrase *logical order* in theology (as in the *order of the decrees* and the *ordo salutis*) is so ambiguous as to be meaningless.
   - *SBL*, 182–83.
   - *DKG*, 260–67.
   - *DG*, 334–39.
   - "Salvation and Theological Pedagogy," in *CWT* and at http://www.frame-poythress.org.

5. Every theological doctrine may be understood as a perspective on all the others.
   - *DKG*, 267–70.

6. In theology today, too much emphasis is placed on church history and contemporary thought, and too little on Scripture itself. For this reason, contemporary liberal and evangelical theology abounds with genetic fallacies and a kind of traditionalism that supplants *sola Scriptura*.
   - "Muller on Theology," in *CWT* and at http://www.frame-poythress.org.
   - *IDSCB*.
   - *TRAD*.
   - *DKG*, 291–92, 302–14.

7. Creeds, confessions, and other human traditions have legitimate uses in theology, but too great an emphasis on them, or too high a regard for them, can compromise *sola Scriptura*.
   - *DKG*, 304–14.

- "My Use of the Reformed Confessions," in *CWT* and at http://www.frame-poythress.org.

8. Since theology is an intensely personal discipline, spiritual maturity is a qualification of the theologian.
- "Studying Theology as a Servant of Jesus" (pamphlet), in *CWT* and at http://www.frame-poythress.org.
- *DKG*, 40–49, 319–28.

9. The Reformed faith is evangelical, is predestinarian, and emphasizes the comprehensive covenant lordship of God in Christ.
- *IRF.*

Doctrine of the Word of God, Scripture

All the entries below will be further discussed in *DWG* (forthcoming).

1. The Word of God is God's power, authoritative speech, and personal presence. Indeed, it is God himself, present with us. These correspond to the lordship attributes, since God always speaks as Lord.
- *PWG*, 9–16.
- *SBL*, 43–50.
- *DG*, 470–75.
- *DCL*, 31–35.

2. God reveals himself through events, words, and persons.
- *PWG*, 19–35.
- *SBL*, 51–57.
- *DCL*, 135–43.

3. Human words are able to refer truly to God, because God has made them for that purpose, as well as for speaking about the creation.
- "God and Biblical Language," in John W. Montgomery, ed., *God's Inerrant Word* (Minneapolis: Bethany Fellowship, 1974), and at http://www.frame-poythress.org.

4. The written Word of God is just as authoritative as the divine voice from heaven and the inspired words of prophets and apostles.
- *SBL*, 53–55, 58–66.

5. Scripture is the covenant document by which the covenant Lord rules his people. It is the ultimate constitution of God's people.
- *PWG*, 24–29.
- *SBL*, 59–66.

6. Scripture is God's Word.
- *PWG*, 22–30.
- *SBL*, 55, 58–65.
- "Scripture Speaks for Itself," in John W. Montgomery, ed., *God's Inerrant Word* (Minneapolis: Bethany Fellowship, 1974), 178–200, and in *CWT* and at http://www.frame-poythress.org.
- "Antithesis and the Doctrine of Scripture," inaugural lecture on receipt of the J. D. Trimble chair of systematic theology and philosophy, at http://www.frame-poythress.org.

7. Since Scripture is God's Word, it has qualities corresponding to the attributes of lordship: power, authority, clarity.
- *DCL*, 144–50.

8. The authority of Scripture entails its inerrancy. But inerrancy is not the same thing as precision.
- *SBL*, 67–69.
- "Is the Bible Inerrant?" in *CWT* and at http://www.frame-poythress.org.

9. Scripture also bears the attribute of necessity. Without it, we have no covenant relation with God, and no salvation.
- "No Scripture, No Christ," *Synapse II* 1, 1 (January 1972): 1. Also in *Presbyterian Guardian* 48 (January 1979): 10–11, and at http://www.frame-poythress.org.
- *SBL*, 69.
- *DCL*, 153–55.

10. The message of Scripture is comprehensive, governing all of life. It is not limited to a narrowly defined "religious" sphere.
- *DCL*, 150–53.
- *CVT*, 128–30.

11. Scripture is sufficient, meaning that it contains all the words of God that we need for any area of life.
- *SBL*, 70–71.
- *DCL*, 156–75.
- *AGG*, 18–26.
- See titles listed under "Nature and Method," 6–7, where I discuss theological practices that in my judgment compromise *sola Scriptura*.

Doctrine of God

1. The biblical God differs from the supreme beings of all other religions and philosophies in that he is (1) both absolute and personal, (2) clearly distinct from creation, and (3) Lord of all.
- *AGG*, 34–50.
- *DG*, 25–35.
- *CVT*, 51–61.

2. God's *transcendence*, biblically, is not the doctrine that God is far from us, or that we cannot speak of him. It is rather that God is King over all, especially as control and authority. His *immanence* should be understood as his covenant presence.
- *SBL*, 13.
- *DKG*, 13–15.
- *DG*, 103–18.
- *DCL*, 41–43.

3. God's simplicity follows from his personhood.
- *DG*, 225–30.

4. There is biblical reason to discuss God's acts in history before his attributes.
- *DG*, 241–45.

5. Miracle is an extraordinary demonstration of God's lordship. It does not necessarily constitute an exception to natural law.
- *SBL*, 16–17.
- *DG*, 241–73.

6. There is no sharp distinction in Scripture between miracle and providence.
- *SBL*, 18.
- *DG*, 274–88.

7. God's decrees take his foreknowledge into account, and vice versa.
- *DG*, 149–52.

8. It is important to distinguish between eternal election and historical election.
- *SBL*, 177–82.
- *DG*, 317–34.

9. God's attributes are perspectives on his lordship.
- *DG*, 387–92.

10. God's attributes reflect his lordship attributes. So we may distinguish between attributes of power, authority, and goodness.
- *DG*, 388–401.

11. God's eternity, immensity, immateriality, and invisibility may be fruitfully understood as attributes of power: God's lordship over time, space, matter, and light.
- *DG*, 387–599.

12. God's *will* may be understood in three senses: decree, precept, and vocation (situational, normative, and existential, respectively).
- *DG*, 528–42.

13. God's aseity includes his epistemological self-attestation and ethical self-justification, as well as his metaphysical self-existence.
- *DG*, 600–618.

14. *Substance* and *person* had various meanings before and during the Trinitarian controversy. Neither is uniquely appropriate to describe the Trinitarian distinctions, but we are unlikely to find better terminology.
- *DG*, 696–707.

15. The doctrine of the Trinity supports the lordship of God.
- *SBL*, 41.
- *DG*, 732–35.

Doctrine of Man

1. Man, the image of God, reflects the lordship attributes. The image is physical (situational), official (normative), and ethical (existential).
- *SBL*, 88–90.
- Meredith G. Kline, *Images of the Spirit* (Eugene, OR: Wipf and Stock, 1999).

2. Human mental faculties, such as reason, will, and emotions, are not separate, competing organs. Rather, they are aspects of human personality and perspectives on one another. Reason (normative), will (situational), and emotions (existential) reflect the lordship attributes.
- *SBL*, 93–94.
- *DKG*, 319–46.

3. Although God brings all things to pass, human beings are responsible. They are also free in the sense that they act out of their own natures and desires. They are not free in the *libertarian* sense (being able to act without any cause).
- *SBL*, 94–97.
- *DG*, 119–59.
- *CVT*, 79–83.

4. Even sin reflects the lordship attributes, for in sin a creature tries to replace God as the Lord of all. So sin brings guilt (normative), pollution (existential), and punishment (situational).

- *SBL*, 102.

The Person and Work of Christ

1. Jesus is truly God and truly man.

- *SBL*, 129–45.
- *DG*, 644–87.

2. Jesus is Lord, and so reflects the three lordship attributes as Prophet (authority), Priest (presence), and King (control).

- *SBL*, 146–58.

3. Jesus' covenant lordship is the most impressive argument for his deity. As Lord, he takes the role that Yahweh took in the Old Testament.

- *SBL*, 132–34.
- *DG*, 650–57.

The Application of Redemption

1. Justification, adoption, and sanctification represent aspects of our union with Christ: normative, situational, and existential, respectively.

- *SBL*, 200–221.

2. The grounds given in the Westminster Confession of Faith by which we may be sure of our salvation (18.2) correspond to the lordship perspectives: the divine promise of salvation (normative), the fruits of salvation in our lives (situational), and the Holy Spirit's witness that we are the children of God (existential).

- *SBL*, 218–21.

Eschatology

Scripture does not present the events of the last days in an order precise enough to justify any of the standard millennial positions. The Bible invokes the return of Christ and the last judgment mainly to encourage our faithful obedience to the Lord.

- *SBL*, 300–313.
- *DCL*, 282–85.

APOLOGETICS

Biblical Epistemology

1. God is knowable, but incomprehensible.
   - *DKG*, 18–40.
   - *DG*, 200–207.

2. Gordon Clark and Cornelius Van Til, in their controversy in the 1940s, misunderstood each other, but in fact each granted the point that was most important to the other.
   - *DKG*, 37–40.
   - *CVT*, 89–113.

3. The believer's knowledge of God involves obedience to him.
   - *DKG*, 40–49.

4. All human cognitive faculties (such as reason, perception, and intuition) are perspectivally related, governing one another. None is "primary." The doctrine of the primacy of the intellect is unbiblical.
   - *SBL*, 93–94.
   - *DKG*, 319–46.
   - *CVT*, 141–50.

5. Emotion plays a positive role in human knowledge. For example, knowledge culminates in a feeling, *cognitive rest*, which indicates to us that our inquiry is over, at least for the time being.
   - *DKG*, 152–53.

6. Facts and interpretation are ultimately identical.
   - *DKG*, 99–100.

7. The unbeliever really knows God, but suppresses that knowledge. His knowledge and suppression work against each other, and it is difficult to understand when and how one of these will determine his response in a particular situation.
   - *DKG*, 49–61.
   - *CVT*, 187–230.

8. The unbeliever's approach to knowledge, following the example of Eve in the garden, is a combination of *rationalism* (belief that human reason is the ultimate standard of truth) and *irrationalism* (belief that there is no ultimate standard of truth). The history of non-Christian thought is a history of wavering between these poles.
   - *DKG*, 360–64.

985

- *AGG*, 191–202.
- *CVT*, 231–38.
- "Greeks Bearing Gifts," in W. Andrew Hoffecker, ed., *Revolutions in Worldview* (Phillipsburg, NJ: P&R Publishing, 2007).

9. Non-Christian epistemologies divide along three perspectives: rationalism (normative), empiricism (situational), and subjectivism (existential).
- *DKG*, 109–22.

10. Knowledge of the world is a knowledge of (1) divine revelation in the world (normative), (2) objects in the world (situational), and (3) ourselves (existential). We cannot fully know one of these without the other two.
- *DKG*, 62–75.

11. Human knowledge may be justified normatively (by agreement with the laws of thought, Scripture being the highest of these), situationally (by agreement with the facts), and existentially (by a godly sense of satisfaction).
- *DKG*, 101–64.

12. The Christian should always accept Scripture as his *presupposition*, that is, his ultimate standard of truth. He must do this, even when he is seeking to convince a non-Christian of the truth of Christ.
- *DKG*, 44–45, 125–26.
- *AGG*, 3–9.
- *CVT*, 131–40.

13. To argue for the truth of Scripture on the presupposition of Scripture is a form of circular argument. But it is a kind of circularity that every system relies on when it tries to argue for its ultimate standard of truth.
- *AGG*, 9–14.
- *DKG*, 130–33.
- *CVT*, 299–310.

14. The circular character of the Christian argument does not rule out the use of evidence, even though our presupposition judges the quality of the evidence. Evidence can "broaden out" the circular argument to make it more persuasive.
- *AGG*, 57–69.
- *CVT*, 177–86.

15. The Bible encourages certainty and discourages doubt in many cases. Through faith and the work of the Spirit, we can be sure of the fundamental doctrines of Scripture. Those doctrines then become our presuppositions, our fundamental tests of truth, and by them we can become certain about other matters.
- *AGG*, 77–82.

- *DKG*, 134–36.
- "Certainty," in Campbell Campbell-Jack et al., *New Dictionary of Apologetics* (Leicester, UK: IVP, 2006), 141–45, and at http://www.frame-poythress.org.

Apologetic Argument

1. Apologetics may be defined as "the application of Scripture to unbelief," or as "the discipline that teaches Christians how to give a reason for their hope."
- *DKG*, 87.
- *AGG*, 1.

2. Apologetics may helpfully be divided into *proof*, *defense*, and *offense*.
- *AGG*, 1–3.

3. An apologetic argument ought to be logically valid, sound (using true premises), and persuasive (note three perspectives).
- *AGG*, 60–64.
- *DKG*, 355–58.

4. To persuade a non-Christian is not just to make him assent to the propositions of the faith. It is, by the power of the Spirit, to bring him to repentance (including intellectual) and faith. So apologetics is evangelism and vice versa.
- *AGG*, 54, 74.

5. Our argument for the existence of the biblical God ought to be presuppositional, or transcendental. That is, we should present him as the ground of all intelligibility, so that even atheism presupposes theism. This may or may not employ a distinct argument form.
- *AGG*, 69–77.
- *CVT*, 311–22.
- See also Donald Collett, "Frame and Transcendental Argument Revisited," in this volume, and my response to him in the "Responses to Some Articles" in this festschrift.

6. Agnostics are really atheists because their behavior shows a commitment to an atheist worldview.
- *AGG*, 92–93.

7. Distinctions between right and wrong can be justified only on the presupposition of an absolute-personal supreme being.
- *AGG*, 93–102.
- "Do We Need God to Be Moral?" at http://www.frame-poythress.org.
- *DCL*, 57–63.

8. Epistemology and metaphysics depend on ethics because they require commitment to values of intellectual integrity. Since ethics presupposes God, therefore, epistemology and metaphysics do as well.
- *AGG*, 93–119.
- *DKG*, 62–64.

9. For us today, there is probably no fully satisfying solution to the problem of evil. But it is important to point out that (1) God reproves criticisms of his actions, (2) God brings good out of evil, often surprisingly, and (3) in glory our hearts will be such that we will no longer be troubled by evil.
- *AGG*, 149–90.
- *DG*, 160–82.
- *CVT*, 83–86.

10. We may respond to most non-Christian thought by pointing out how it veers between rationalism and irrationalism.
- *DKG*, 360–64.
- *AGG*, 191–202.
- *CVT*, 231–38.
- "Greeks Bearing Gifts," in W. Andrew Hoffecker, ed., *Revolutions in Worldview* (Phillipsburg, NJ: P&R Publishing, 2007).

The Church

1. To say that the Word, sacraments, and discipline are "marks" that distinguish the true church is to make a valid theological inference from Scripture, but Scripture does not explicitly state that they are marks, and they are hard to evaluate.
- *SBL*, 241–42.
- *ER*, 133–39.

2. Worship (normative), the Great Commission (situational), and love (existential) are explicitly biblical marks of the church.
- *SBL*, 241–42.

3. The Great Commission applies the cultural mandate to the situation following the fall and the work of Christ.
- *SBL*, 249–53.
- *DCL*, 307–11.

4. The tasks of the church can be summarized as worship (normative), witness (situational), and nurture (existential).
- *SBL*, 253–56.

5. The means of grace are the Word, fellowship (broader than the traditional *sacraments*), and prayer. These are normative, situational, and existential, respectively.
- *SBL*, 260–73.

6. In one sense, every church member is an officer ("general office") and thus should be engaged in teaching, rule, and ministry of mercy. In another sense, God raises up officers ("special office") who are specifically gifted to carry out leadership functions in the church.
- *SBL*, 256–59.

7. Church officer candidates should be evaluated according to their character (existential), skills (situational), and knowledge (normative).
- "Proposal for a New Seminary," in *CWT* and at http://www.frame-poythress.org.

8. To facilitate proper training of pastors and other offices by biblical criteria, it is best for them to be trained by means of an apprentice system in a church with academic supplements, rather than in an academic institution (as is usual today) with fieldwork supplements.
- "Proposal for a New Seminary," in *CWT* and at http://www.frame-poythress.org.

9. Scripture never mentions denominationalism, and it rebukes factionalism, the root of denominationalism. Denominations play no role in New Testament church government.
- *ER*, 21–34.

10. Denominations are always the result of sin.
- *ER*, 33–38.

11. We should not glorify our denominations but seek to eliminate them.
- *ER*, 155–69.

12. We should support any union between denominations that is acceptable to our consciences.
- *ER*, 132–49.

13. In evaluating other churches and denominations, we should avoid gossip and follow the rule "innocent until proven guilty."
- *ER*, 140, 142–49.

WORSHIP

1. Worship is the work of acknowledging the greatness of our covenant Lord.
- *WST*, 1.

2. Worship can be understood in narrow and broad senses. The narrow sense is our coming together in church to join others in worship. The broad sense is our living every day as living sacrifices as "our spiritual worship" (Rom. 12:1–2 ESV).

- *WST*, 9–10.

3. Worship is the ultimate goal of redemption.

- *WST*, 10–11.

4. Worship should be biblical (normative), God-centered (situational), and edifying (existential).

- *WST*, 4–9.

5. The "regulative principle of worship" means that everything we do in worship must be an application of a biblical principle. Some traditional refinements of this principle do not have a biblical basis.

- *WST*, 37–49.
- *DCL*, 450–86.

6. Worship should edify the worshipers, so we should give much thought to *communication* in worship.

- *WST*, 7–9.
- *CWM*, 17–20.

7. The "dialogue form" of worship (God speaks, man responds) is of some value, but it neglects the fact that in worship God is always speaking and we are always responding.

- *WST*, 69–71, 89–109.

8. The idea that worship should be a reenactment of redemption (reading of the law, confession of sin, assurance of pardon) is valuable, but it may obscure the fact that believers come to worship already forgiven.

- *WST*, 68–69.

9. Scripture permits drama and commends dance, hand-lifting, and clapping.

- *WST*, 92–94, 130–32.

10. Scripture does not limit worship music to the book of Psalms.

- *WST*, 123–27.

11. Contemporary music is appropriate in worship if it meets biblical criteria.

- *CWM*.

12. Preaching should not be limited to a narrative of redemptive history, and it may invoke biblical characters as moral examples.

- *DCL*, 137–38, 290–97.

ETHICS

1. Ethics is theology, viewed as a means of determining which persons, acts, and attitudes receive God's blessing and which do not.
- *DCL*, 10.

2. Ethics can be understood under three perspectives: normative, situational, and existential.
- *PP*.
- *PWG*, 37–56.
- *ME*, all.
- *DCL*, 19–382.

3. Non-Christian ethics generally divides along lines reflecting the lordship perspectives: teleological (situational), deontological (normative), and existential (existential).
- *DCL*, 41–125.

4. God governs our ethical lives by his control, authority, and presence.
- *DCL*, 24.

5. The virtues *faith*, *hope*, and *love* reflect the lordship perspectives (normative, situational, and existential, respectively).
- *DCL*, 26–27.

6. The necessary and sufficient criteria of good works in WCF 16.7 reflect the lordship perspectives: right goal (situational), right standard (normative), right motive (situational).
- *DCL*, 27–29.

7. Scripture gives us three reasons to do good works, which reflect the lordship perspectives: the commandment of God (normative), the history of redemption (situational), and the inner work of the Spirit (existential).
- *DCL*, 29–31.

8. The three lordship perspectives also justify the diversity in forms of Christian ethics: command (normative), narrative (situational), and virtue (existential).
- *DCL*, 31.

9. What really matters in the Christian life are the commandments of God (1 Cor. 7:19, normative), faith working through love (Gal. 5:6, existential), and new creation (Gal. 6:15, situational).
- *DCL*, 31–32.

10. The three perspectives dictate three things to focus on as we make ethical decisions: the problem (situational), God's Word (normative), and ourselves (existential).
- *DCL*, 32–33.

11. Non-Christian ethics, like non-Christian epistemology (above), is rationalistic and irrationalistic.
- *DCL*, 41–53.

12. Non-Christian ethics is based on a naturalistic fallacy, the attempt to derive moral norms from an impersonal reality.
- *DCL*, 57–63.

13. Christian ethics is based on divine revelation, especially in Scripture.
- *DCL*, 131–384.

14. Law and gospel are distinguishable, but in Scripture they are not to be separated. There is law in the gospel, and gospel in the law.
- *DCL*, 182–92.

15. Old Testament laws continue to bind believers in the New Testament, but their specific applications change, sometimes greatly, with the advent of the new covenant. It is important to investigate each of the Old Testament laws to see how the coming of Christ affects their application.
- *DCL*, 206–24.

16. Some ethical considerations take priority over others.
- *ME*, 10–32.
- *DCL*, 224–30.

17. There is no such thing as *tragic moral choice* or *conflict of duties*.
- *DCL*, 230–34.

18. Natural-law ethics violates the principle of the sufficiency of Scripture.
- *DCL*, 156–75, 239–50.

19. Godly subjectivity, even emotions, is an important factor in making moral decisions.
- *DCL*, 349–82.

20. The Ten Commandments present ten perspectives on the ethical life. Each views the whole Christian life from one perspective.
- *DCL*, 385–404.

21. The Sabbath continues into the new covenant as a weekly day of rest and refreshment.
- *DCL*, 513–74.

22. The state is the government of the family of Adam; the church is the government of the family of God.
   - *DCL,* 593–621.

23. Men and women are ontologically equal, but their roles are not interchangeable. Women should not be ordained to the office of teaching elder. Nevertheless, it is not wrong for a woman to speak in worship under the authority of the male elders.
   - *DCL,* 622–47.

24. Scripture teaches us to guard not only against murder, but against the *possibility* of destroying human life.
   - *DCL,* 684–90.

25. Physical death is "irreversible cessation of circulatory and respiratory functions" and/or "irreversible cessation of all functions of the entire brain, including the brain stem."
   - *ME,* 58–61, 75–82.
   - *DCL,* 732–34.

26. Abortion is the taking of innocent life and therefore murder, unless it is done to save the mother's physical life.
   - *DCL,* 717–45, 998–1000.

27. Scripture legitimizes divorce on the bases of sexual impurity and abandonment of one's marriage vows.
   - *DCL,* 769–81.

28. Evangelical and Reformed churches need to give much higher priority to the needs of the poor.
   - *DCL,* 808–29.

29. The ninth commandment's prohibition on false witness does not extend to those who are seeking to take innocent life.
   - *DCL,* 830–43.

30. Scripture calls believers to bring all aspects of culture under the dominion of Christ, transforming them to reflect the standards of God's Word.
   - *DCL,* 853–75, 943–56.

APPENDIX B: DIRECTORY OF
FRAME'S MAJOR TRIADS

JOHN M. FRAME

The doctrine of the Trinity and my understanding of God's lordship as control, authority, and presence yield a number of threefold distinctions I have found useful in explaining many doctrines in theology, apologetics, and ethics. This Appendix lists many of these and the main locations in my writings where they are discussed. The order of topics follows the structure of this book. In each triad, the first member represents the normative perspective, the second the situational, and the third the existential.

For a list of 112 unexplained triads, some serious, some bizarre, some tongue-in-cheek, see *DG*, 743–50. That list overlaps this one.

INTRODUCTORY

1. Trinity: Father, Son, Holy Spirit.
   - *PP*.
   - *DG*, 619–735.

2. Lordship: authority, control, presence.
   - *PP*.
   - *SBL*, 8–12.
   - *DKG*, 15–18.
   - *DG*, 36–102.
   - *DCL*, 21–24.

3. Covenant lordship in the suzerainty treaty: law, history, sanctions.
   - *DKG*, 40–41nn35, 36.

994

4. Objects of knowledge: God's revelation, the world, the self.
- *PP.*
- *DKG,* 65–73.

5. Perspectives under which anything can be viewed: normative, situational, existential.
- *PP.*
- *PWG,* 50–54.
- *ME,* 1–6.
- *DKG,* 73–75.
- *DG,* 194–96.
- *DCL,* 33–37.

Theology

Nature and Method

1. Nature of theology: application of the Word of God, to all areas of life, by persons.
- *SBL,* 72–81.
- *DKG,* 76–85.

2. Types of theology: exegetical, biblical, systematic.
- *SBL,* 81–82.
- *DKG,* 206–14.

3. Metaphors for the uses of Scripture in theology (Richard Pratt): pictures, windows, mirrors.
- *DKG,* 204–5.

Doctrine of the Word of God, Scripture

1. The nature of the Word of God: God's authoritative, powerful, personal speech.
- *PWG,* 9–16.
- *SBL,* 43–50.
- *DG,* 470–75.
- *DCL,* 31–35.
- *DWG* (forthcoming).

2. Media of revelation: words, events, persons.
- *PWG,* 19–35.
- *SBL,* 51–57.
- *DCL,* 135–43.
- *DWG.*

3. Forms of revelation: special, general, existential.
   - *PWG*, 31–32.
   - *DWG*.

4. Attributes of Scripture: authority, power, clarity.
   - *DCL*, 144–55.
   - *DWG*.

5. Additional attributes of Scripture: necessity, comprehensiveness, sufficiency.
   - *DCL*, 144–75.
   - *DWG*.

6. Frequent literary pattern in Scripture, the chiasm: first theme, second theme, return.
   - *DG*, 750.

Doctrine of God

1. The Trinity: Father, Son, Spirit.
   - *PP*.
   - *DG*, 619–35.

2. Lordship: authority, control, presence.
   - *PP*.
   - *SBL*, 8–12.
   - *DKG*, 15–18.
   - *DG*, 36–102.
   - *DCL*, 21–24.

3. Ways in which Scripture reveals God: descriptions, acts, intra-Trinitarian life.
   - *DG*, 241–45.

4. God's acts: creation, providence, miracle.
   - *DG*, 241–312.

5. Miracles: signs, powers, wonders.
   - *DG*, 241–73.

6. Providence: revelation, government, concurrence.
   - *DG*, 274–88.

7. God's law, redemption accomplished, redemption applied.
   - *DG*, 244n6.

8. Election, effectual calling, individual soteriology.
   - *DG*, 244n6.

9. Biblical descriptions of God: attributes, images, names.
- *DG*, 343–44.

10. Classification of divine attributes: knowledge, power, goodness.
- *DG*, 387–400.

11. Cross-classification of divine attributes: attributes of authority, control, presence.
- *DG*, 398–99.

12. Example of the attributes mentioned above: omniscience, omnipotence, omnipresence.
- *DG*, 469–599.

13. God's righteousness: standards, actions, moral excellence.
- *DG*, 446–68.

14. Senses of God's *will*: preceptive, decretive, wisdom.
- *DG*, 528–42.

15. God's spirituality: authority, control, presence.
- *DG*, 576–99.

Doctrine of Man

1. Aspects of the divine image: official, physical, ethical.
- *SBL*, 88–90.

2. Intellect, will, emotions.
- *SBL*, 93–94.
- *DKG*, 319–46.

3. Human responsibility: accountability, liability, integrity.
- *DG*, 119–59.

4. Effects of the fall: guilt, punishment, pollution.
- *SBL*, 102.

Doctrine of Christ

Offices: Prophet, King, Priest.
- *SBL*, 146–58.

The Application of Redemption

1. Justification, adoption, sanctification.
- *SBL*, 200–221.

2. Grounds for assurance of salvation: the promises of the Word, the fruits of faith, and the inner testimony of the Spirit.
  • *SBL*, 218–21.

APOLOGETICS

Biblical Epistemology

1. Objects of knowledge: God's revelation, the world, the self.
  • *PP.*
  • *DKG*, 65–73.

2. Perspectives under which anything can be viewed: normative, situational, existential.
  • *PP.*
  • *PWG*, 50–54.
  • *ME*, 1–6.
  • *DKG*, 73–75.
  • *DG*, 194–96.
  • *DCL*, 33–37.

3. Non-Christian epistemology: rationalist, empiricist, subjectivist.
  • *DKG*, 109–22.

4. Divisions of philosophy: epistemology, metaphysics, ethics.
  • *AGG*, 93–119.
  • *DKG*, 62–64.

5. Elements of knowledge: norm, object, subject.
  • *DKG*, 62–75.

6. Secular definition of *knowledge*: justified, true, belief.
  • *DKG*, 62–75.

7. Elements of justification: laws of thought, accord with facts, godly satisfaction.
  • *DKG*, 101–64.

Apologetic Argument

1. Divisions of apologetics: proof, offense, defense.
  • *AGG*, 1–3.

2. Qualities of a good argument: valid, sound, persuasive.
  • *AGG*, 60–64.
  • *DKG*, 355–58.

3. Defensive apologetic strategies: challenge non-Christian's conceptual framework, present facts, persuade him personally.

- *DKG*, 348–57.

4. Offensive apologetic strategies: attack the rationalist/irrationalist dialectic, attack errors, make point of contact with the knowledge the unbeliever has, but suppresses.

- *DKG*, 358–68.

5. Responses to the problem of evil: God reproves criticism, he brings good from evil, he changes our hearts to praise him for all he has done.

- *AGG*, 149–90.
- *DG*, 160–82.
- *CVT*, 83–86.

The Church

1. Traditional marks: Word, discipline, sacraments.

- *SBL*, 241–42.
- *ER*, 133–39.

2. Biblical marks: worship, Great Commission, love.

- *SBL*, 241–42.

3. Tasks: worship, witness, nurture.

- *SBL*, 253–56.

4. Means of grace (slightly expanded from tradition): Word, fellowship, prayer.

- *SBL*, 260–73.

5. Offices in the church: teaching, ruling, mercy.

- *SBL*, 256–59.

6. Qualifications of officers: knowledge, skills, character.

- "Proposal for a New Seminary," in *CWT* and at http://www.frame-poythress.org.

7. Parties in Reformed community: doctrinalists, Kuyperians, pietists.

- *IRF*.

Worship

Qualities of good worship: biblical, God-centered, edifying.

- *WST*, 4–9.

999

Ethics

1. God's governance of our ethical life: revelation, providence, presence.
   - *DCL*, 24.

2. Our appropriate response: faith, obedience, worship.
   - *DCL*, 25–26.

3. The three theological virtues: faith, hope, love.
   - *DCL*, 26–27.

4. Necessary and sufficient criteria of good works: standard, goal, motive.
   - *DCL*, 27–29.

5. Biblical reasons for doing good works: God's command, the history of redemption, the presence of the Spirit.
   - *DCL*, 29–31.

6. Types of Christian ethics: command, narrative, virtue.
   - *DCL*, 31.

7. What really matters: God's commands, new creation, faith working through love.
   - *DCL*, 31–32.

8. Factors in ethical judgment: Scripture, situation, moral agent.
   - *DCL*, 32–33.

9. Perspectives on the discipline of ethics: normative, situational, existential.
   - *DCL*, 33–36.

10. Three ethical principles: deontological, teleological, existential.
    - *DCL*, 50–51.

11. Types of non-Christian religious ethical approaches: law without gospel, fate, self-realization.
    - *DCL*, 57–71.

12. Types of non-Christian secular ethics: deontological, teleological, existential.
    - *DCL*, 52–53, 72–125.

13. Revelation in ethics: Word-revelation, revelation through nature and history, revelation through persons.
    - *DCL*, 135–43.

14. Attributes of Scripture, first triad: authority, power, clarity.
    - *DCL*, 144–50.

15. Attributes of Scripture, second triad of attributes: necessity, comprehensiveness, sufficiency.
- *DCL*, 150–75.

16. Major systems of the human body: nervous, respiratory, circulatory.
- *ME*, 58–62, 75–81.

GLOSSARY

JOHN M. FRAME

One of the fun things about being a theologian (or any other kind of academic) is that you get to invent new words and sometimes attach new meanings to old ones. I try not to do this too often, but over the years I have done some of it. In the Glossary below, I do not, for the most part, define standard theological terms (such as *holiness* and *justification*). These definitions can be obtained from standard theologies, theological dictionaries, and online sources. But I include terms that I have invented, or that I have attached unusual definitions to, or that have a special prominence in my writings (even though the definitions may be standard). I here use the same topical headings as in my Bibliography in this volume, but I omit the topics in which there are no distinctive terms to be defined.

I include references to places in my books and articles where I discuss these concepts. For this purpose, I use these abbreviations:

AGG: Apologetics to the Glory of God
CWM: Contemporary Worship Music: A Biblical Defense
CWT: Collected Works of John Frame, vol. 1, Theology
DCL: The Doctrine of the Christian Life
DG: The Doctrine of God
DKG: The Doctrine of the Knowledge of God
DWG: Doctrine of the Word of God (forthcoming)
ER: Evangelical Reunion
IRF: Introduction to the Reformed Faith
NOG: No Other God
PP: A Primer on Perspectivalism

PWG: Perspectives on the Word of God
SBL: Salvation Belongs to the Lord
TRAD: Traditionalism
WST: Worship in Spirit and Truth

Often, words or forms of words that are defined elsewhere in this Glossary are in bold. For more key terms, with references to my writings, see the study guides for my books, included in my *Collected Works* CD and DVD sets.

Introductory: Lordship and Perspectivalism

authority. God's right to demand unqualified obedience from his creatures. A **lordship attribute.** *DKG*, 15–18; *DG*, 80–93; *PP*.

control. God's power over the world, a **lordship attribute.** *DKG*, 15–18; *DG*, 36–79; *PP*.

covenant. Relation between the Lord and his servants. In divine-human covenants, God as covenant Lord selects a certain people from among all the nations of the earth to be his own. He rules over them by his law, in terms of which all who obey are blessed and all who disobey are cursed. But there is grace as well as law. God's grace establishes the covenant, and, since all men are sinners, it's only by grace that God sends any covenant blessing. God's creation and government of the world is analogous to covenant: he rules all things as the Lord. *DKG*, 12–13; *DG*, 21–35; *PP*.

covenant solidarity. See **presence.**

existential perspective. Dealing with a subject, emphasizing its character as a part of human experience, an aspect of human subjectivity. Derived from the **lordship attribute** of **presence,** for God is present to our innermost heart and mind. *DKG*, 62–75; *DCL*, 33–37, 131–382; *PP*; *PWG*, 50–56.

lordship. God's relation to his **covenant** people, involving his **control** and **authority** over them and his **presence** with them. Analogously, God's relationship to the whole creation. *DG*, 21–35; *PP*.

lordship attributes. Qualities that appear prominently in biblical descriptions of God's **lordship:** his **control, authority,** and **presence.** *DKG*, 15–18; *DG*, 36–115; *DCL*, 19–37; *PP*.

multiperspectival. Of or relating to an account of something that considers more than one **perspective.** *PP*.

normative perspective. Dealing with a subject, emphasizing its character as divine revelation. Derived from the **lordship attribute** of divine **authority.** *DKG*, 62–75; *DCL*, 33–37, 131–238; *PP*; *PWG*, 50–56.

perspective. A view or study of an object from a particular angle. When a tree is viewed from the north, the south, the east, and the west, these views constitute four perspectives. *DKG, 73–75; PP.*

presence. Also termed **covenant solidarity.** God's taking a people from among the other peoples to be his own exclusive possession. He commits himself to being with them ("Immanuel, God with us"), to be their God and for them to be his people. Often his presence is literal, as in the burning bush, the tabernacle, the temple, the person of Jesus (John 1:14), and the bodies of believers. A **lordship attribute.** *DKG, 15–18; DG, 94–102.*

situational perspective. Dealing with a subject, emphasizing its character as a fact of nature, history, or both. Derived from the **lordship attribute** of **control,** for God's control governs all the facts of nature and history. *DKG, 62–75; DCL, 33–37, 239–313; PP; PWG, 50–56.*

triperspectival. Considering a subject from three perspectives connected with the **lordship attributes: normative, situational,** and **existential.** *PP.*

THEOLOGY

1. Nature, Method of Theology

application. "Teaching" in the New Testament sense; using the content of Scripture to answer human questions, meet human needs, and promote spiritual health. See **theology.** *DKG, 81.*

biblical theology. Theology that seeks to apply the Bible, seen as a history of redemption. *DKG, 207–12.*

exegetical theology. Theology that seeks to apply particular passages of Scripture (of any length, including the whole Bible). *DKG, 206–7.*

historical theology. A study of the church's **theology** through history, **applying** the Word of God to the church's past for the sake of the church's present edification. *DKG, 310.*

practical theology. Part of **systematic theology** that applies what Scripture says about communicating the gospel. *DKG, 214.*

progress in theology. Application of Scripture to more and more situations as the church encounters them. *DKG, 307.*

Reformed theology. A tradition of theology that emphasizes evangelical distinctives, the sovereignty of God, and the comprehensive covenant **lordship** of Jesus Christ. *IRF.*

systematic theology. Theology that seeks to apply the Bible as a whole. *DKG*, 212–14.

theology. The **application** of the Word of God, by persons, to all areas of life. *DKG*, 81.

traditionalism. Coming to theological conclusions on the basis of human tradition, without sufficient biblical grounding. See *TRAD*.

triangulation. Coming to theological conclusions by comparing historical or contemporary views without direct reference to Scripture. Often it proceeds by comparing view A on this side and view B on that side, and formulating view C, perceived to preserve the good, but not the bad, of both extremes. See *TRAD*.

2. Doctrine of the Word of God, Scripture

I do not provide as many references in this part of the Glossary. I use these terms in my lectures in the course Scripture and God, included in my *CWT*. I expect that I will also deal with these terms in my forthcoming *DWG*. *PWG* and a few of my articles also deal with some of these concepts.

authority of the Word. The right of God's Word to be obeyed and believed without question. Corresponds to the **lordship attribute** of **authority.** *PWG*, 12–13.

bibliolatry. Giving the devotion to the Bible that is appropriate to give only to God himself.

clarity of Scripture. The view that Scripture is clear enough so that the plan of God's salvation can be understood by all persons through the use of ordinary means of grace (teaching, sacraments, prayer).

covenant document. The suzerainty treaty that served in Hittite culture as a binding attestation of the lord's words governing the covenant relationship. Parallel to God's covenant words to his people.

divine voice. God's speech without human or written mediation, as when God spoke to Israel at Mount Sinai. *PWG*, 23–24.

event media. Events of nature and history that bring God's Word to us. Corresponds to the **lordship attribute** of **control.** Sometimes called *general* or *natural revelation. PWG*, 21–22.

existential revelation. Revelation through our own nature as the image of God, and as God's writing on our heart, creating in us an obedient disposition. Correlative to the traditional concepts of general and special revelation. Roughly equivalent to the traditional concept of illumination, or the internal testimony of the Spirit.

free speech of God. Speech not essential to God's being, but expressed by his decision to speak; his speech about creatures and to them. Cf. **necessary speech of God.** *DG*, 236, 474.

general sufficiency of Scripture. The view that at all times in redemptive history, Scripture has been **sufficient** for God's people. Cf. **particular sufficiency.**

God's Word through prophets and apostles. God's speech through mediation of human speakers and writers. Has the same power and authority as the **divine voice.** *PWG*, 24.

inerrancy. Truth in the sense of correspondence to fact. To say that Scripture is inerrant is to say that everything it asserts is true. It makes good on its claims.

infallibility. A stronger term than **inerrancy.** *Inerrant* means that there are no errors; *infallible* means that there *can be* no errors, that errors are impossible. Frame rejects looser or weaker definitions of *infallible*.

inspiration. An act of God creating identity between a divine word and a human word.

linguistic model of the Trinity. The view that the Father is the speaker, the Son is his speech, and the Spirit is the breath that carries his speech to its destination.

media of the Word. Means that God uses to bring his Word to us. *PWG*, 19–35.

necessary speech of God. That speech that is essential to God's being God; the eternal communication between the persons of the Trinity. Cf. **free speech of God.** *DG*, 236, 474.

necessity of Scripture. The view that without Scripture, we have no adequate basis for faith in Christ.

particular sufficiency of Scripture. The doctrine that, following the completion of the canon, we should not expect any more divine additions to Scripture or any revelation of the same level as Scripture. Cf. **general sufficiency.**

person media. God's Word's coming to us through divine and human persons: theophany, Christ, the Spirit, prophets and apostles, church leaders, other believers, all people in the image of God. *PWG*, 30–32.

power of the Word. The capacity of the Word, through the Holy Spirit, to accomplish God's purposes in the world and in persons. Corresponds to the **lordship attribute** of **control.** *PWG*, 10–12.

precision. Stating the truth without any approximation. Scripture is true, but not always precise.

propositions. Assertions claiming to state facts. There are propositions in Scripture, but there are other kinds of language there as well. *PWG*, 11–12.

self-authenticating; self-attesting. Since God's Word is the highest authority for us, it cannot be validated by anything higher than itself. So the ultimate source of Scripture's authority is its own word, validated to our hearts and minds by the Holy Spirit.

sufficiency of Scripture. The view that Scripture contains all the divine words necessary for us to please God in any area of life.

suzerainty treaty. See **covenant document.**

Word as God's address. God's Word speaking authoritatively to rational agents. Synonym for God's *preceptive will.* Corresponds to the **lordship attribute** of **authority.**

Word as God's decree. God's Word governing all that comes to pass. Synonym for God's *decretive will* or *decree.* Corresponds to the **lordship attribute** of **control.**

Word as God's presence. God's Word conveying God to creatures. Corresponds to the **lordship attribute** of **presence.** *PWG,* 13–16.

Word as God's self-expression. The Word as God's dwelling place, so that to encounter the Word is to encounter him, and vice versa. Corresponds to the **lordship attribute** of **presence.**

Word media. God's Word's coming to us through human words, by God directly, by the prophets and apostles, and by their writings. *PWG,* 22–23.

Word of God. God's powerful, meaningful self-expression. Note correlation with the three **lordship attributes.** *DG,* 471; *PWG,* 9–16.

written Word of God. God's Word in written form. It has the same power and authority as other forms of the Word. *PWG,* 24–29.

3. Doctrine of God

attributes of authority. Divine attributes that emphasize God's constant or static character, his eternal truth: righteousness, justice, truth, aseity, simplicity, essence. Cf. the **lordship attributes** of **control, authority,** and **presence.** *DG,* 398–99.

attributes of control. Divine attributes that emphasize God's dynamic or active character: goodness, love, speech, will, power, etc. Cf. the **lordship attributes** of **control, authority,** and **presence.** *DG,* 398–99.

attributes of goodness. Divine attributes pertaining to God's moral nature: goodness, love, grace, justice, righteousness, holiness, joy. *DG,* 398, 402–68.

attributes of knowledge. Divine attributes pertaining to God's intellectual capacity: speech, incomprehensibility, truth, knowledge, wisdom, mind, knowability. *DG*, 399, 469–512.

attributes of power. Divine attributes pertaining to God's transcendence and exaltation over other things: eternity, immensity, incorporeality, will, power, existence, aseity, essence, glory, spirituality, omnipresence. *DG*, 399, 513–616.

attributes of presence. Divine attributes that emphasize God's presence to himself and to the world: integrity, involvement, blessedness, joy, beauty, perfection, holiness, knowledge, glory, spirituality, omnipresence. Cf. the **lordship attributes** of **control, authority,** and **presence.** *DG*, 398–99.

author-character model. The best illustration I know of the relation between divine sovereignty and human responsibility. Like a playwright, God controls everything that happens in the "drama" of nature and history. But as in a good play, the events of the drama also have an explanation within the world of the play itself. So, as with God's relation to the world, each event of the play has two causes: divine and creaturely. *DG*, 156–59.

covenant preservation. An aspect of providence, whereby God shows his love to his covenant people by rescuing them from danger and providing for their earthly needs. *DG*, 282–84.

creaturely otherness. God's making of creatures to be genuinely different from himself, so that their acts are not his, although he foreordains them, and his acts are not ours. This is one source of our sense of freedom and independence. *DG*, 146.

essential invisibility. God's not being limited to any particular visible form, but being able to use any visible form in revealing himself. *DG*, 590.

eternal election. God's eternal choice of a people to enjoy the full blessing of fellowship with him forever. *DG*, 325–30.

eternal preservation. An aspect of providence, the fulfillment of **covenant preservation** and of all God's promises to his people.

God in himself. An ambiguous expression that can mean (1) God as he exists apart from us, or (2) God as he is revealed to us, and therefore as he really and truly is. We cannot know God in himself in sense 1, but we can in sense 2.

historical election. God's choosing people and nations in history for specific tasks related to redemptive history. *DG*, 317–25, 329–30.

"I am he" or "ani hu" passages. Passages using these phrases or similar ones, in which God or Jesus identifies himself as the "I am" of Exodus 3:14. Deut. 32:39; Isa. 41:4; 43:10, etc.; John 8:24, 28; 9:9; 18:5–6, 8. *DG*, 22n41.

immanence (biblical). The **lordship attribute** of **covenant presence.** *DG*, 103–6.

immanence (nonbiblical). God's being so near to us that he cannot be distinguished from finite persons and objects. Thus when he draws near, he becomes a creature, or the creatures become God. In this sense modern theologians sometimes say that God is "wholly revealed." *DG*, 107–14.

incomprehensibility of God. The doctrine that although we can genuinely know God, we cannot know him exhaustively or know him as he knows himself. *DG*, 200–207.

metaphysical preservation. An aspect of providence whereby God preserves the metaphysical existence of the world, so that it is constantly dependent on him, although it has no specific tendency to fall into nonbeing. *DG*, 278–79.

miracle. An extraordinary demonstration of God's covenant lordship. *DG*, 258.

monogenes. A Greek term that Frame translates in the older way, "only-begotten," rather than (as do modern translators) "unique." *DG*, 659n21, 710–11n53.

open theism. The view that God does not know the future exhaustively, because he cannot know in advance the free choices of rational agents. *DG*, 485–86; *NOG*.

preservation. An aspect of divine providence. Frame subdivides this into **metaphysical, redemptive-historical, covenantal,** and **eternal preservation.** *DG*, 274–88.

redemptive-historical preservation. As an aspect of providence, God's preservation of the world from his own judgment of sin until redemption is complete. *DG*, 279–82.

semi-cessationist. The view that **miracles** in a broad sense continue, and that spectacular miracles may occur, but that we should not expect them as a normal part of the Christian life. Frame also calls this view *semi-continuationist.* *DG*, 264–65.

transcendence (biblical). God's exaltation as King, involving the **lordship attributes** of **control** and **authority.** *DG*, 103–6.

transcendence (nonbiblical). God's being so far from us that we cannot know him or truly speak of him. In this sense, modern theologians sometimes say that God is "wholly other" or "wholly hidden." *DG*, 107–14.

vocation; God's will of wisdom. God's knowledge of what choices will be best for individuals; his will that we make the wisest choices, by prayerfully applying Scripture to our circumstances. Adds a third concept to the traditional ones of God's "decretive" and "preceptive" wills. *DG*, 539–42.

Apologetics

1. Apologetic Method and Epistemology

apologetics. (1) The application of Scripture to unbelief (including the unbelief remaining in the Christian). *DKG*, 86–87. (2) The study of how to give to inquirers a reason for the hope that is in us (1 Peter 3:15). *AGG*, 1.

apologetics as defense. Giving answers to objections; "defending and confirming the gospel" (Phil. 1:7 NIV). *AGG*, 2, 149–90.

apologetics as offense. Attacking the foolishness of unbelieving thought (Ps. 14:1, 1 Cor. 1:18–2:16). *AGG*, 2, 191–202.

apologetics as proof. Presenting a rational basis for faith; demonstrating Christianity to be true. *AGG*, 2, 57–148.

argument by presupposition. Showing that Christianity is the necessary presupposition of meaning and rationality, and that the denial of Christianity destroys all meaning and rationality. Synonym for **transcendental argument.** *AGG*, 69–75.

autonomy. The claim that one is competent to serve as the final criterion of truth and right.

broad circularity. A **circular** argument enriched by evidence. For example: "Scripture is true because evidences X, Y, and Z imply its truth," when X, Y, and Z themselves are warranted by Scripture. *DKG*, 131.

circularity. An argument in which the conclusion **justifies** itself. All arguments seeking to prove the existence of an ultimate or final authority are circular in this sense. *DKG*, 130.

cognitive rest. A godly sense of satisfaction, which is the goal of **existential justification.** *DKG*, 152–53.

competing circularities. Arguments in which each party appeals to an authority that he considers to be self-attesting. *DKG*, 132–33.

epistemology. Theory of knowledge. One of the major divisions of **philosophy,** along with **metaphysics** and **value theory.**

existential justification. Justifying a belief according to the **existential perspective,** by showing that it brings true subjective satisfaction. *DKG*, 108, 149–62.

fact. What is the case. Inseparable from **interpretation.** *DKG*, 71.

faculties of the mind. Intellect, will, emotions, imagination, perception, intuition, etc., all perspectives on the heart, for human beings know and experience the world as whole persons. *DKG*, 319–46.

interpretation. A person's understanding of what the facts are. Inseparable from **fact.** *DKG,* 71.

irrationalism. The view that human reason has no reliable access to truth. *DKG,* 60–61.

justification (in epistemology). An account of why someone should believe a proposition to be true. *DKG,* 104–6.

knowledge of God. A relationship of friendship or enmity with God, involving a covenantal response of the whole person to God's **lordship,** in obedience or disobedience. *DKG,* 48.

metaphysics. Theory of being, dealing with the general structure of the world. One of the major divisions of **philosophy,** along with **epistemology** and **value theory.**

narrow circularity. A **circular** argument that directly asserts the self-justification of a conclusion without additional premises: for example, "God exists because God exists." *DKG,* 130–31.

neutrality. An attempt to reason without any religious **presupposition.**

normative justification. Justifying a belief according to the **normative perspective,** by showing that it conforms to the norms of thought. *DKG,* 108, 123–39.

ontology. In my work, a synonym for **metaphysics.**

person variable. The fact that a particular person's response to an apologetic argument may differ from that of another person. Because an argument that will **persuade** one person will not necessary persuade another, arguments should be formulated with a particular audience in mind. *AGG,* 64, 67–68, 89–90.

persuasion. Convincing a person that your belief is true (as a goal of apologetics). An apologetic argument, therefore, should be valid (employing right logic), sound (incorporating true premises), and persuasive. Persuasion is the **existential perspective** of apologetic argument. Synonym for **cognitive rest.** *AGG,* 60–64; *DKG,* 119, 131, 355–58.

philosophy. An attempt to understand the world in its broadest, most general features; the exposition and defense of a **worldview.** Its constituents are **metaphysics, epistemology,** and **value theory.** A subdivision of **theology.** *DKG,* 85–86.

presupposition. A belief that takes precedence over another and therefore serves as a criterion for determining the truth of another. An **ultimate** presupposition takes precedence over all other beliefs. The ultimate presupposition is the basic commitment of the heart. *DKG,* 45, 125–26.

presuppositionalism of the heart. A basic commitment of the heart to bring all reasoning under the **lordship** of Christ. In Frame's judgment, it is impossible to distinguish presuppositional from traditional apologetics merely by the form of their arguments, claims to certainty or probability, etc. *AGG*, 85–88.

rationalism. (1) The view that human reason is the final judge of truth and falsity, right and wrong. (2) The philosophical position that human reason is to be trusted above human sense experience. *DKG*, 60–61.

rationalist-irrationalist dialectic. The view that would-be autonomous thought is **rationalistic** in that it believes itself to be the final judge of truth and right; but that it is **irrationalistic** in that it believes the universe has no intrinsic order beyond the human person himself. So autonomous thought vacillates from optimistic to pessimistic views of reason, and back again. *DKG*, 360–63; *AGG*, 193–202.

situational justification. Justifying a belief according to the **situational perspective**, by showing that it is in accord with the **facts.** *DKG*, 108, 140–49.

transcendental argument. Arguing that something is a condition of meaning or rationality. Synonym for **argument by presupposition.** *AGG*, 69–75.

value theory. Chiefly ethics and aesthetics. One of the major divisions of **philosophy,** along with **metaphysics** and **epistemology.**

worldview. General understanding of the universe. The biblical worldview is unique in its view of (1) the Supreme Being as absolute personality, (2) the **lordship** of God, and (3) the Creator-creature distinction.

2. Cornelius Van Til

To my knowledge, I have not developed any distinctive terminology in my writing about Van Til. But Van Til himself developed a great deal of distinctive terminology in expounding his own position. A few years ago, I formulated "A Van Til Glossary," providing my own definitions of Van Til's distinctive terms. In my writings about Van Til (and about other subjects), I use these definitions. His technical terms are also my technical terms. So I reproduce the Glossary below. As in the original version, I refer both to my own *Cornelius Van Til: An Analysis of His Thought* (Phillipsburg, NJ: P&R Publishing, 1995) and to Greg Bahnsen, *Van Til's Apologetics: Readings and Analysis* (Phillipsburg, NJ: P&R Publishing, 1998). In the Glossary below, *CVT* refers to the former, *VTA* to the latter, and *VT* to Van Til.

absolute personality. VT's basic characterization of God. Unlike any non-Christian view, the biblical God is both absolute (a self-existent, self-sufficient, self-contained) and personal (thinking, speaking, acting, loving, judging). See *CVT*, 51ff.

ad hominem argument. Argument that exposes deficiencies in the arguer rather than deficiencies in the proposition under discussion—thus, a logical fallacy. But ad hominem argument is often appropriate. See *VTA*, 116ff., 468, 492; *CVT*, 153.

all-conditioner. VT's characterization of God in "Why I Believe in God" (see *VTA*, 121–43). God is the one who ultimately influences all reality, including our own thinking and reasoning about him.

analogy; analogical reasoning. (1) (Aquinas) Thinking in language that is neither literally true (univocal) nor unrelated to the subject matter (equivocal), but that bears a genuine resemblance to that subject matter. (2) (VT) Thinking in subjection to God's revelation and therefore thinking God's thoughts after him.

antithesis. The opposition between Christian and non-Christian thought. See *CVT*, 187ff.

apologetics. That branch of theology that gives reasons for our hope. VT saw it as involving proof, defense, and offense.

a priori knowledge. Knowledge acquired prior to experience, used to interpret and evaluate experience. Contrasted with *a posteriori knowledge*, knowledge arising out of experience. See *VTA*, 107n177.

authority of the expert. The principle that submission to the knowledge of someone better informed, rather than absolute submission to God, is the best way to truth. To VT, this is the only kind of authority the unbeliever will accept.

autonomy. The attempt to live apart from any law external to the self. To VT, this is the paradigm attitude of unbelief. See *VTA*, 109n.

blockhouse methodology. An apologetic approach that begins with beliefs supposedly held in common between believers and unbelievers, and then tries to supplement that common ground with additional truth. VT finds this methodology in Aquinas's distinction between natural reason and faith, and in other forms of "traditional apologetics." See *VTA*, 64, 535ff., 708ff.

borrowed capital. The truth known and acknowledged by the unbeliever. He has no right to believe or assert truth based on his own presuppositions, but only on Christian ones. So his assertions of truth are based on borrowed capital.

brute fact. (1) (VT) Fact that is uninterpreted (by God, man, or both) and therefore the basis of all interpretation. (2) Objective fact; fact not dependent on what man thinks about it.

certainty. (1) Assurance of one's beliefs (also termed *certitude*). (2) The impossibility of a proposition's being false. VT emphasized that Christian truth is certain and should be presented as a certainty, not a mere **probability.**

chance. The condition of events' occurring without cause or reason. See *VTA*, 728.

circular argument. (1) Argument in which the conclusion of an argument is one of its premises. (2) Argument assuming something that would ordinarily not be assumed by someone who didn't believe the conclusion. See *VTA*, 518ff.; *CVT*, 299ff.

common ground. That which believer and unbeliever have in common, making it possible for them to engage in apologetic discussion. See **point of contact.** VT sometimes denied that Christians and non-Christians had any beliefs in common. But his actual view was that they *would* not have such common beliefs if each were fully consistent with his presuppositions. See *VTA*, 276, 420–24, 730.

common notions. Beliefs that Christians and non-Christians have in common. VT sometimes denied that there were any of these. But see **common ground.**

contingency. (1) Dependence on something else for origin or continued being; the opposite of necessity. (2) **Chance.**

correlative. Mutually dependent. For VT, the unbeliever holds that God and the world are correlative.

creatively constructive. What unbelieving thought attempts to be on VT's view. It attempts to be the original standard of all truth, as opposed to Christian thought, which is "receptively reconstructive" (= **analogical** in the second sense).

deductivism. (1) Trying to deduce the whole of theology from one "master concept." (2) Drawing deductions from one biblical concept that are incompatible with other biblical concepts. See *CVT*, 166.

determinism. (1) The view that every event in the world has a cause. (2) The view that every event in the world has a *finite* cause. VT might be considered a determinist in sense 1, but not in sense 2. Determinisms of both kinds, however, often presuppose *impersonal* causation as ultimate. In that sense, VT rejected determinism and pointed out that it is equivalent to **chance.**

eminence. Way of knowing God by reasoning that he must possess the best qualities of creatures in infinite degree. One of Aquinas's three means of knowing God, the others being causality and **negation.** VT believes that this method, if not governed by Scripture, yields a finite God, only somewhat larger than creatures.

epistemology. Theory of knowledge.

ethics. Theory of behavior.

evidence. (1) The facts used in an argument to establish a conclusion. (2) Statements of such facts. See *CVT*, 177ff.

fact. A state of affairs in the real world, governed by law.

fideism. Belief that God is known by faith and not by reason. VT is sometimes accused of fideism, but he repudiated it frequently. See *VTA*, 77–82.

full-bucket difficulty. God is all-glorious, and no glory can be added to him; yet he calls on creatures to glorify him. VT said, therefore, that glorifying God was like trying to add water to a full bucket.

implication. (1) The act of drawing a conclusion from a premise or premises. (2) The conclusion derived from the premises. (3) In idealist philosophy, a method of thinking that employs logic with an understanding of the psychological workings of the mind in its situational context. VT sometimes speaks of his approach as a "method of implication" in the third sense, something more than mere deduction or induction, but including both of them. See *VTA*, 172–73.

incomprehensibility of God. (1) Our inability to know God exhaustively. (2) The lack of identity between any human thought and any divine thought. Sense 1 is the more common meaning in theology; sense 2 was the subject of the VT/Clark controversy.

indirect argument. A synonym for **reductio.**

irrationalism. Belief that human reason is inadequate to discover truth. VT believes that unbelievers are both irrationalistic and rationalistic at the same time. See *VTA*, 717ff.; *CVT*, 231ff.

limiting concept. Also termed **supplementative concept.** Concept of something (such as an actual infinity of objects) that doesn't exist (or cannot be proved to exist), but that can serve a useful purpose in thought. Kant believed that the concepts of God, freedom, and immortality were limiting concepts. On his view, we should live "as if" these existed. VT holds that some theological concepts (e.g., the idea that sin can destroy the work of God) are not literally true, but can be affirmed on a similar "as if" basis. See *CVT*, 165–69.

metaphysics; ontology. (1) A general view of the world, a world-and-life view. (2) The fundamental realities that exist.

monism. Belief that reality is all of one kind; hence, denial of the Creator-creature distinction.

negation; remotion; via negativa. Way of knowing God by ascribing to him the opposite of creaturely qualities that are perceived as limits. One of Aquinas's three means of knowing God, the others being **eminence** and causality. In VT's view, when this method is used apart from Scripture, it yields a god who is a "pure blank," a mere negation of finite reality.

neutrality. Trying to think or live without making a religious commitment or ultimate **presupposition.** In VT's view, this is impossible. Attempting it presupposes a commitment against the true God.

noetic effects of sin. The effects of sin on human thought, reasoning, knowledge. In VT, the sinner knows God, but represses that knowledge (Rom. 1).

objective knowledge; truth. Knowledge or truth whose truth does not depend on what man thinks.

one-and-many problem. Knowledge involves uniting particulars into universal categories. But if every particular is exhaustively described by universal categories, then it is no longer particular. But if some particularities cannot be described by universal categories, then they can't be known, or they have no nature. The same problem can be described in terms of the relation of logic to fact, and of that of subject to object. See *VTA*, 706; *CVT*, 63ff.

point of contact. A belief held in common between two people that enables them to reason toward further agreement. In VT, particularly the point of contact between believer and unbeliever. See **common ground.** For VT it is found not in a common **worldview**, but in the true knowledge of God that the believer has, and the unbeliever also has but suppresses. See *VTA*, 105n.

predication. Attaching a predicate to a subject; hence, making an assertion. VT says that only the Christian **worldview** makes predication possible.

presupposition. (1) A belief that precedes other beliefs. (2) A belief that governs other beliefs. (3) Ultimate presupposition: the belief that governs all other beliefs, or the most fundamental commitment of the heart.

probability. The degree to which a proposition approaches certainty. VT believed that Christianity was certain, not merely probable, and that for an apologist to claim mere probability is to deny the clarity of God's revelation.

proof. An argument that establishes the truth of a conclusion. VT believed that there was "absolutely certain proof" of Christian theism by way of his transcendental argument. See *VTA*, 78–82.

qualitative/quantitative difference. In the Clark controversy, the difference in views of God's **incomprehensibility.** Clark denied holding a "merely quantitative" view (that God knows more propositions than we), because he held that God knows the world by a different *mode* from man. VT found Clark's view of the difference to be insufficient, but he refused to state precisely the difference he referred to as "qualitative."

rationalism. (1) Belief that human reason (seen as the whole apparatus of human thought, including sensation and memory) is the ultimate arbiter of truth and falsity. (2) Belief that human reason (as opposed to sense experience) is the road to knowledge. VT believes that all unbelievers are rationalistic in the first sense—and also **irrationalistic.**

reductio ad absurdum. A form of argument in which, rather than directly proving a conclusion, the arguer reduces the contrary conclusion to an absurdity.

Hence it is also called *indirect argument* or *argument from the impossibility of the contrary.* VT believed that all transcendental arguments must take this form. Frame disagrees.

self-attestation; self-authentication. In any system of thought, that the ultimate authority justifies itself. For VT, that ultimate authority is God, especially when speaking in Scripture. See *VTA*, 209–19, 715.

sense of deity, divinity. Calvin's way of describing the knowledge that the unbeliever has but suppresses. Also termed **sensus deitatis, divinitatis, semen religionis.**

starting point. In VT, synonym for **presupposition.** Therefore, it doesn't necessarily refer to a beginning point in time, but rather to a belief that governs other beliefs.

suaviter in modo, fortiter in re. Gentle in manner, strong in substance. VT's description of an ideal apologetic presentation. See *VTA*, 441.

supplementation. In apologetics, presenting Christian truth as something merely additional to what the non-Christian believes already. See **blockhouse methodology.**

system. One's attempt to express his **worldview** in a coherent set of thoughts.

that and what. In VT, criticism of some apologists for trying to prove *that* God is, without considering *what* he is. In Frame, emphasis that one can never prove God's entire nature in one argument, so the *what* is a matter of degree. We cannot actually mention everything. But an apologetic argument must be consistent with everything the Bible says about God. See **unit.** See also *VTA*, 217, 708.

transcendental argument. An argument that seeks to show the necessary conditions for the possibility of rational thought or meaningful discourse. VT believed this was the only kind of argument appropriate to a Christian apologetic, since the biblical God is the author of all meaning and rationality.

unit, whole (defending Christianity as a). Defending the particular elements of Christianity with an awareness of the connection of each element with the overall system of truth; not proving everything at once, although VT sometimes seems almost to demand that proof from apologists he criticizes. See *VTA*, 26, 103n511.

univocal. (1) (Aquinas) Language that describes its object literally. (2) (VT) Thinking **autonomously** rather than **analogously,** as if one were divine.

worldview. Also termed **world-and-life view.** A philosophy, particularly a metaphysic; a way of understanding reality that governs all thought and life.

3. Existence of God

My versions of the traditional arguments have a **transcendental** twist.

cosmological argument. The argument that if we try to discuss "cause" without God, our reasoning degenerates into **rationalism, irrationalism,** or both. *AGG*, 109–14.

epistemological argument. The argument that human reasoning is futile without moral standards, and that those standards in turn presuppose God. See **moral argument.** *AGG*, 102–4.

moral argument. The argument that all meaning and reasoning presupposes moral principles. But moral principles in turn presuppose God as **absolute personality.** *AGG*, 93–102.

ontological argument. The argument that a definition of God (a being with all perfections) implies his existence. Works only as a **presuppositional** argument that assumes a distinctively biblical concept of perfection.

teleological argument. The argument that one cannot even speak of "purpose" or "design" apart from moral values (see **moral argument**), which in turn presuppose God. *AGG*, 105–9.

4. The Problem of Evil

This is the question of how evil can exist if God is all-good, all-powerful, and all-wise. I reject a number of traditional defenses and accept three (there's that number again).

God-is-his-own-standard defense. Because of who God is, human beings have no right to bring accusations against him (Job 38–42; Rom. 9:14–15, 19–21). Frame sometimes calls this the "shut-up defense," as in the gag line " 'Shut up,' he explained." This is the **normative perspective.** *AGG*, 171–78.

greater-good defense. God promises us that he will bring good out of evil (Rom. 8:28). This is the **situational perspective.** *AGG*, 179–87.

new-heart defense. Regeneration and our eventual glorification change our values and presuppositions so that we lose the inclination to charge God with wrongdoing. This is the **existential perspective.** *AGG*, 187–90.

THE CHURCH

1. Unity

biblical presbyterianism. Government by multiple elders in each congregation, with church courts at various regional levels to deal with matters that cannot be resolved in the local congregation. In its biblical form, these courts encompass the wisdom of *all* the churches in a region, not just the Presbyterian ones. *ER*, 29–31.

breadwinners (ecclesiastical). Frame's metaphor for those who are called to focus on evangelism and missions. Cf. **homemakers.** *DCL*, 230.

courtship metaphor. The view that church-union discussions between denominations are like courtship: trying to determine whether a union would be advantageous for both parties. Opposed to **reconciliation metaphor.** *ER*, 142–44.

denomination. A faction of the church, out of fellowship with other factions, holding to some "distinctives" of doctrine, practice, worship, ethnicity, style, history, social class, etc.

denominationalism. Attempts to justify and maintain the separate existence of denominations.

homemakers (ecclesiastical). Frame's metaphor for those who are called to focus on the church's internal condition (orthodox doctrine, proper procedures). See also **breadwinners.** *DCL*, 230.

marks of the church. Traditionally, the true preaching of the Word, the right administration of the sacraments, and church discipline. Frame would add love (John 13:34–35), the Great Commission (Matt. 28:19–20), and true worship (John 4:24). *ER*, 132–41; *SBL*, 241–42.

one, true church. The church as it existed during the apostolic period: one in spirit, fellowship, doctrine, and government. *ER*, 38–40.

post-denominational view of the church. The view that we should not take biblical promises concerning the gifts of the Spirit, divine preservation of the church, etc., to apply to **denominations.** God has promised that the gates of hell will not prevail against the church (Matt. 16:18). He has not made the same promise to any denomination, for the New Testament does not mention denominations. *ER*, 41–44.

reconciliation metaphor. Frame's view that a union between two denominations should be thought of not as a kind of **courtship,** but as reconciliation following an illegitimate divorce. *ER*, 142–44.

reunion. The restoration of the original unity of the church, breaking down current denominational divisions.

tolerance. Willingness to live within the church with those who hold different views on some matters, without seeking to impede their ministries or exercise church discipline. Paul urges toleration between meat-eaters and vegetarians in Romans 14, for example. The church should not expect uniformity in all doctrinal and practical matters. *ER*, 84–104.

2. Worship, Preaching

celebration of the resurrection. The main purpose of New Testament worship after the resurrection and ascension of Jesus. Not emphasized in *WST*, but Frame emphasizes it today.

dialogue model. Worship arranged into (1) speeches of God to us and (2) our response to him. In Frame's judgment this structure can be valuable, but Scripture doesn't require it, and it can confuse the fact that in one sense God is always speaking to us and we are always responding to him. It can also lead to rigid role distinctions (e.g., the preacher alone being permitted to speak as an individual, because he alone speaks for God) that are not biblically justified. *WST*, 69–71.

horizontal focus in worship. Seeking in worship to edify one another (1 Cor. 14; Heb. 10:24–25). *WST*, 7–8; *CWM*, 17–20, 90–97.

redemptive-historical preaching. Preaching that focuses on the historical narrative of Scripture, culminating in the atonement and resurrection of Christ. In some circles, this kind of preaching avoids reference to Bible characters as moral examples and even avoids ethical applications of texts. In Frame's opinion, the focus on redemptive history is often edifying but not biblically required. The avoidance of moral content is, in Frame's view, a distortion of biblical preaching, and such preaching is a distortion of Scripture. *DCL*, 290–97.

reenactment of redemption. An order of worship in which the congregation confesses its sins, receives absolution, and then receives instruction. This is legitimate, but it may confuse the fact that the congregation assembles as people already redeemed by Christ. *WST*, 68–69.

regulative principle of worship. The principle that everything we do in worship must be prescribed in Scripture, either as an explicit requirement or as an application of an explicit requirement. *WST*, 37–43; *DCL*, 464–86.

vertical focus in worship. Seeking above all to please God in worship. *WST*, 4–5, 7–8.

worship. Acknowledging the greatness of our covenant Lord. *WST*, 1.

worship in the broad sense. All of life carried on to God's glory; presenting our bodies as living sacrifices (Rom. 12:1). *WST*, 9–10, 29–30.

worship in the narrow sense. Special occasions at which we explicitly, publicly or privately, acknowledge the greatness of God. *WST*, 9–10, 30–35.

ETHICS

aisthesis. Our capacity for moral perception; our ability to see resemblances between our experiences and biblical descriptions of good and evil. *DCL*, 356–59.

broad meaning (of the commandments). The application of each commandment by which it can be seen as a perspective of all of life. *DCL*, 399.

ceremonial laws. (1) Laws pertaining to the ceremonies of religious worship. (2) Laws that are given for a limited time or place, rescinded upon their fulfillment by a greater reality. *DCL*, 213–17.

change in symbolic weight. The view that the change of day of the Sabbath from the seventh day to the first was mainly symbolic: looking backward to a completed redemption, rather than forward to a redemption to come. But that is a change of emphasis, not of absolute meaning. *DCL*, 567–68.

choice between two evils. Choice between two alternatives, each of which will bring some harm: for example, a surgeon's choosing between whether to operate (and bring some pain) and not to operate (and leave someone to die). *DCL*, 230–34.

choice between two wrongs. Also termed **tragic moral choice.** Choice between alternatives that are both sinful. Frame denies that these exist. *DCL*, 230–34.

Christian "irrationalism." The renunciation of rational autonomy. *DCL*, 43–45.

Christian "rationalism." The belief that divine revelation gives us access to truth. *DCL*, 43–45.

Christian teleological ethic. An ethic focused on the **situational perspective,** examining the environment in which we make ethical decisions, especially the means necessary to reach the goal of the glory of God. *DCL*, 240.

command ethics. A value system that emphasizes objective moral norms. *DCL*, 31.

covenant document. The written text setting forth the terms of a covenant. *DCL*, 20–21.

currently normative. The condition of biblical laws' governing our conduct today, rather than being restricted to a past time. *DCL*, 200.

Decalogical hermeneutics. The rules for interpreting and applying the Ten Commandments. *DCL*, 390–95.

deontological principle. A good deed is a response to duty, even at the price of self-sacrifice. Divine duties are necessary and universal. They take precedence over any other consideration. Corresponds to the **lordship attribute** of **authority.** *DCL*, 49–51.

doctrine of carefulness. That God not only forbids murder, but requires us to take special precautions against the possibility of human life being destroyed. *DCL*, 688–90, 724–25.

dokimazein. "Proof," in Romans 12:1–2 and elsewhere; knowledge that comes through the process of ethical discipline. *DCL*, 355.

duck-rabbit. Picture that can be seen either as a duck or as a rabbit, used as an illustration of the importance of comparing the patterns of our experience to those of Scripture. *DCL*, 356–59.

dying. A condition in which medical help is unable to restore circulation, respiration, and brain activity. *DCL*, 732–36.

emotions. Human feelings, inclinations, dispositions. *DCL*, 370–82.

envy. Being upset or angry at the prosperity of someone else. *DCL*, 845–46.

epistemological truth. True knowledge of facts. *DCL*, 352.

ethical analogies. Resemblances between our experiences and the biblical descriptions of good and evil. *DCL*, 356–59.

ethical conservatism. Seeking answers to ethical problems that are as rigorous/demanding as possible. *DCL*, 6–7.

ethical liberalism. Seeking answers to ethical problems that maximize liberty and minimize legalistic restrictions. *DCL*, 6–7.

ethical truth. Good behavior, as walking in God's statutes. *DCL*, 352.

ethics. Theology when viewed as a means of determining which human persons, acts, and attitudes receive God's blessing or curse. *DCL*, 10–11.

ethics based on fate. A religiously oriented value system with an impersonal, necessitarian causality and empiricist epistemology. Has a situational emphasis. *DCL*, 57–63.

ethics based on self-realization. A monistic, pantheistic value system that stresses self-discipline and personal emancipation. *DCL*, 63–66.

ethics de facto. What standards we actually have, whether right or wrong. *DCL*, 12.

ethics de jure. What moral standards we ought to have. *DCL*, 12.

existential ethics. A value system holding that a good deed is a deed that is true to you. A form of self-realization. *DCL*, 72–90.

existential principle. A good deed comes from a good motive. Corresponds to the **lordship attribute** of **presence.** *DCL*, 50–51.

existential priorities. Priorities among divine commands arising from individual callings: for example, some may be called to pray much longer than others. *DCL*, 227–30.

experience (in ethics). Ethical knowledge gained from the senses and from continual wrestling with good and evil. *DCL*, 364–66.

fate. A synonym for **chance;** whatever happens. *DCL*, 57–63.

freedom in society. In the Christian view, freedom that implies limited government. In the non-Christian view, freedom that leads to moral anarchy. *DCL*, 48–49.

general office. Authority given to all believers to teach, rule, and show mercy. *DCL*, 639.

glorifying God. Reflecting God's glory in our being and behavior. *DCL*, 302–3.

heart. The center of human existence; the whole person as God sees him. The good or evil nature, which motivates all action. *DCL*, 362.

honor. In the fifth commandment, reverence, submission, and financial support owed to a superior. *DCL*, 576–77.

immanence (biblical view). God's truly revealing himself in Word and deed. *DCL*, 41–43.

immanence (nonbiblical view). God's being indistinguishable from the world. *DCL*, 41–43.

individual vs. corporate obligations. The view that individual obligations must be carried out by an individual, by himself. Corporate obligations must be carried out by a group, with individuals playing various roles. *DCL*, 229.

inwardness. The condition of God's law being internalized. Outward conformity is necessary, but insufficient. *DCL*, 325.

justice (general and specific meanings). In general, what is morally right, in the sense of fairness or equity. With special reference to the system of justice, in the fair administration of the law. *DCL*, 18.

kingdom of God. God's acts in history to establish his rule on earth, by defeating his enemies and bringing all people to a conscious awareness of his sovereignty. *DCL*, 278.

less explicitly religious ethics. Sometimes called *secular ethics*, though these approaches have presuppositions not unlike religious ones. *DCL*, 55–57.

literally normative. The condition of biblical laws' current application being literal rather than merely symbolic. *DCL*, 200.

lust. Desire to break God's law in sexual matters. *DCL*, 766–68.

meta-ethics. A second-order discipline, a theological reflection on the nature of right and wrong, ethical methods, and ethical presuppositions. *DCL*, 11–12.

metaphysical truth. The absolute as contrasted with the relative; what is ultimate, eternal, complete, permanent, substantial. *DCL*, 352.

moral heroism. Actions that display love in extreme ways: for example, the widow who gave all she had to the Lord. *DCL*, 196–200.

morality. The view of Frame that *morality* and *ethics* are synonymous terms that can refer to the description of human customs as well as the (normative) evaluation of those customs (i.e., as right or wrong). *DCL*, 12.

moral syllogism. A syllogism in which the major premise sets forth a moral principle, the second premise sets forth a situation to which that principle needs to be applied, and the conclusion states the application of the principle to the situation. *DCL*, 166–68.

motive. An inner disposition that governs ethical action. *DCL*, 324–25.

narrative ethic. Learning our ethical responsibilities by hearing stories; trying to understand how these stories should affect our lives. *DCL*, 31.

natural-law ethics. Ethics based on natural revelation, usually thought to be knowable to man through reason and conscience alone, apart from Scripture. *DCL*, 242–50.

naturalistic fallacy. Inferring what ought to be from what is. *DCL*, 59–63.

non-Christian irrationalism. Skepticism. *DCL*, 43–45.

non-Christian rationalism. Grounding human reason in some mundane authority. *DCL*, 43–45.

normative priorities. Priorities among divine commands specified explicitly in Scripture itself. *DCL*, 225–26.

paradox of ethical decision. The paradox that when our conscience is misinformed we ought nevertheless to follow it, because it defines for us what is good. *DCL*, 363–64.

patterns. Structures of human experience reflecting those of biblical teaching, so that we are able to call things in our experience by their biblical names. *DCL*, 356–59.

permission. A good action that is not prescribed or proscribed. *DCL*, 17–18.

problem of the virtuous pagan. How can unbelievers do good works, granting that people are totally depraved apart from grace? *DCL*, 27–29.

propositional truth. Epistemological truth formulated in statements. *DCL*, 352.

punishment. The legitimate response of authority to someone's wrongdoing. *DCL*, 694–95.

rational autonomy. Reason, apart from tradition or revelation, as the final standard of knowledge. *DCL*, 43–45.

redemptive-historical invisibility. According to Deuteronomy 4:15–19, God's choice at Mount Sinai to reveal himself to Israel without a visible form.

At other times in redemptive history, he chooses to reveal himself visibly. *DCL*, 456–60.

redemptive history. (1) The historical events by which God prepares for and achieves human redemption from sin. (2) The written accounts of these events in Scripture. *DCL*, 271–97.

right. (1) Conformity to norms, laws, standards. (2) Deserved privilege; legal/ethical permission to have or do something. *DCL*, 15–16.

seeing as. Seeing the events of our experience as examples of biblical categories. *DCL*, 356–58.

situational perspective (in ethics). The perspective that focuses on the object of knowledge. Answers the question: "What are the best means to accomplish God's purpose?" *DCL*, 33.

situational priorities. Priorities among divine commands arising from situational factors: for example, the legitimacy of David's men eating the consecrated bread when they were hungry. *DCL*, 226–27.

sound doctrine. Doctrine not merely as a set of theological propositions, but as an active process of learning that leads to spiritual health. *DCL*, 9.

subjects of ethical predication. Persons, acts, and attitudes. These are the only things that Scripture regards as ethically good or bad, right or wrong. *DCL*, 11.

teleological ethics. The view that the ethical value of an action is measured by the extent to which it maximizes happiness and minimizes unhappiness. *DCL*, 91–100.

teleological principle. A good deed maximizes the happiness of living creatures. A good deed does good. Corresponds to the **lordship attribute** of **control.** *DCL*, 49–51.

theonomy. The view that the civil laws of Israel (along with the penalties for crimes given in those laws) continue to bind present-day civil governments. *DCL*, 217–24.

tragic moral choice. Also termed **choice between two wrongs.** The notion that in some situations we have no choice but to sin, as a result of the lack of nonsinful alternatives. *DCL*, 23–34.

transcendence (biblical view). God's being sovereign in his right and might. *DCL*, 41–42.

transcendence (nonbiblical view). God's being unknowable. *DCL*, 41–42.

two-age structure. The view that the old age, "this age" in the New Testament, is the period of the reign of sin; the new age is the coming of the kingdom of God, which began with Jesus' incarnation, atonement, resurrection, and ascension. Until Jesus returns, the two ages overlap. *DCL*, 276–79.

value. A quality of worth or merit. *DCL*, 13.

virtue. Ground of praise for something or someone. Subdivided into moral virtues such as love, fidelity, integrity; elements of good character and nonmoral virtues such as efficiency, skill, talent. *DCL*, 14.

virtue ethic. An ethic that focuses on the virtues, describing them and employing them as motivations for ethical behavior. *DCL*, 31.

works of mercy. Works done on the Sabbath to heal or meet other important human needs. Part of the fundamental meaning of the Sabbath. *DCL*, 550–52.

works of necessity. Works that must be done on the Sabbath to keep human life on an even keel. *DCL*, 547–50.

CULTURE

borrowed capital. Van Til's view of how unbelieving culture borrows elements of Christian theism in order to maintain stability. *DCL*, 880.

Christ, the transformer of culture. H. Richard Niebuhr's term for the common Reformed view that Christ has given his people a mission to transform every area of human life to reflect God's glory. *DCL*, 874–75.

Christ above culture. H. Richard Niebuhr's term for the view of medieval scholasticism, in which there is a synthesis between Christianity and culture, and redemption is a supplement to nature. *DCL*, 868–70.

Christ against culture. H. Richard Niebuhr's term for the view that places Christ and culture in antithesis to one another. *DCL*, 864–67.

Christ and culture in paradox. H. Richard Niebuhr's term for the Lutheran "two-kingdom" view, in which God rules the church by his law and gospel rules the state by natural law only. *DCL*, 870–73.

Christian culturalists. Those who believe that every Christian is responsible to be knowledgeable about cultural movements. *DCL*, 894.

common grace. Nonsaving grace, which leads to many good things even in fallen culture. *DCL*, 860–61.

"culchah." Refinement, education, good taste as found among the elite. *DCL*, 857.

cultural mirror. Harvie Conn's description of film as an indicator of cultural trends. *DCL*, 897.

culture. What God makes through us, as opposed to creation, which is what God makes by himself. *DCL*, 864.

dualism. Another term for **Christ and culture in paradox.**

egalitarianism. Belief that everyone is morally equal. Stems from nonbelief in God as a person who makes choices among people. *DCL*, 899.

folk culture. Ken Myers's term for culture that is less sophisticated and urban than **high culture,** but that provides meaning in traditional societies and has virtues of "honesty, integrity, commitment to tradition, and perseverance in the face of opposition." *DCL*, 883.

genetic fallacy. A cousin to the **naturalistic fallacy,** which argues that something is good because it comes from a good source, or bad because it comes from a bad source. Often found in literature dealing with Christians' use of elements of culture. *DCL*, 908.

high culture. Ken Myers's term for what has been considered the noblest kind of culture, which in his view can provide a transcendent perspective. *DCL*, 882–83.

intelligible communication. Paul's main concern about worship in 1 Corinthians 14, to which churches today need to give more attention. *DCL*, 905.

language of worship. The verbal and musical vocabulary understood by a particular body of Christians, in which they clearly hear the gospel and are motivated to praise and testify. *DCL*, 905.

modern culture. Culture as transformed by the Enlightenment and the Industrial Revolution. Emphasizes rational scientific method, physical reality, individuality, written communication, a view of history moving toward utopia. *DCL*, 884–85.

optimistic humanism. Os Guinness's term for nonbelievers who persist in affirming the meaningfulness of life, while rejecting God, who is the only basis for such meaning. *DCL*, 880.

pessimistic humanism. Os Guinness's term for nonbelievers who honestly recognize that without God there can be no meaning, and who therefore embrace meaninglessness. *DCL*, 880–81.

popular culture. Ken Myers's term for the lowest cultural denominator, encouraged by the Industrial Revolution and the increasing amount of leisure in society. Disposable entertainment, with none of the virtues of **high culture** and **folk culture.** *DCL*, 883.

postmodern culture. Development since the mid-twentieth century, calling into question the assurances of **modern culture.** Combines elements of the modern with some of those of the premodern: both mythology and science, etc. *DCL*, 884–85.

power of communication. In Frame's view, an important element in judging the quality of art and communication, more so than generally understood. *DCL*, 892–93.

premodern culture. Culture as it existed before the modern period, which persists in some parts of the world. Emphasizes spiritual reality, community, oral communication, a cyclical view of history. *DCL*, 884–85.

special grace. God's redemption of sinners, which also impacts society and culture. *DCL*, 860.

synthesis. Another term for **Christ above culture.**

the Christ of culture. H. Richard Niebuhr's term for the view that Christ affirms all that is good and right in culture. *DCL*, 867–68.

the line of despair. In Francis Schaeffer's analysis, the historical point (occurring at different times in different areas of culture) at which hope was lost for the attainment of objective truth. *DCL*, 880.

world. (1) The whole creation of God. (2) Everything opposed to God under Satan's dominion. Not identical to **culture;** rather, the bad part of culture. *DCL*, 865–67.

BIBLIOGRAPHY

JOHN M. FRAME

This list contains all the books, articles, written sermons, course materials, and audio and video materials that I have produced to date. I have arranged them into topics, so that readers might more easily make use of them. Occasionally, one title will be included under more than one topical designation.[1]

Most of the articles listed here (but only a few of the books) can be found online at http://www.frame-poythress.org or at Third Millennium Ministries' *Reformed Perspectives* site, http://www.reformedperspectives.org. These sites are noted only when readers are unlikely to be able to find the titles elsewhere.

I intend also to include all my books, articles, course materials, sermons, and interviews, together with all audio and video lectures and courses, in *The Collected Works of John M. Frame*, CD-ROM and DVD set (Phillipsburg, NJ: P&R Publishing; Whitefish, MT: Bits & Bytes, Inc., 2008). Volume 1 available; volumes 2 and 3 to follow.

INTRODUCTORY

1. The Gist of My Theological Approach

These titles present in summary form some of my more characteristic ideas. For people who are becoming acquainted with my work for the first time, I would recommend reading them in this order:

1. For a year-by-year bibliography, see the Works of John Frame and Vern Poythress Web site at http://www.frame-poythress.org and volume 1 of my *Collected Works*.

"Reflections of a Lifetime Theologian." Interview by Andrew Sandlin. *Christian Culture* (April–May 2008): 1–8, and in the present volume.

"A Primer on Perspectivalism" (2008). Available at http://www.frame-poythress.org.

"Introduction to the Reformed Faith" (1999). Available at http://www.reformed perspectives.org and http://www.frame-poythress.org.

Perspectives on the Word of God. Eugene, OR: Wipf and Stock, 1999. A rather short book about Scripture and ethics.

Salvation Belongs to the Lord. Phillipsburg, NJ: P&R Publishing, 2006. This is an introductory systematic theology, dealing with all the standard theological topics. In this book I try to show how a perspectival approach focused on God's lordship can illumine many theological discussions. Available in Chinese at http://www.thirdmill.org/chinese/books+articles.asp.

2. Popular Articles on My Fundamental Themes

"The Burden of Change: A Warning against Laziness and Shortcuts." *Christian Culture* (September 2004): 4.

"How to Be Confident Amid Millennial Frenzies." Available at http://www.reformed perspectives.org and http://www.frame-poythress.org.

"Loving God with Your Mind without Becoming an Intellectual Pharisee" (2005). Available at http://www.frame-poythress.org and http://www.frame-poythress. org. More technical than the previous title.

"A Theology of Opportunity," "A Theology of Opportunity: Breaking Through to the Foundations of Our Faith." *Equip for Ministry* 1, 2 (June–July 1995): 7–9. The first title is that given to the piece (which was also abridged somewhat) by the editors; the second is my original title. The same article, with some variation, can be found at http://www.frame-poythress.org. The emphasis is on *sola Scriptura*.

3. Interviews and Biographical Material

"Blogging in the Name of the Lord: John M. Frame." Interview by Guy Davies (October 6, 2008). Available at Exiled Preacher Web site, http://exiledpreacher.blogspot.com/.

"Dr. John Frame." Interview by Twoth (January 29, 2007). Available at http://twoth. blogspot.com/search?q=john+frame and at http://www.frame-poythress.org.

"An Interview with John Frame," by Marco Gonzalez (December 2005). On Reformation Theology Web site at http://www.reformationtheology.com/2005/12/ an_interview_with_john_frame_b_1.php#more. Also at http://www.frame-poythress.org.

"John M. Frame." Interview with Steve Hays. In *Love the Lord with Heart and Mind*, ed. Steve Hays and James Anderson (n.p., 2008, 2009), 27–32. At http://www.triapologia.com/hays/love_the_lord.pdf, and at http://www.frame-poythress.org.

"Reflections of a Lifetime Theologian." See above under section 1, "The Gist of My Theological Approach."

"Testimony" (2008). For a book of Christian testimonies by Princeton University alumni. Completed, awaiting publication.

See audio interviews listed under "Audio and Video Materials" toward the end of this bibliography.

4. People in My Life

"Remembering Donald B. Fullerton" (2005). Available at http://www.frame-poythress.org.

"Thanks for Dick Gaffin" (2007). Available at http://www.frame-poythress.org.

"Tribute to D. Clair Davis." In *The Practical Calvinist: An Introduction to the Presbyterian and Reformed Heritage. In Honor of Dr. D. Clair Davis on the Occasion of His Seventieth Birthday and to Acknowledge His More Than Thirty Years of Teaching at Westminster Theological Seminary in Philadelphia*, edited by Peter A. Lillback. Fearn, Ross-shire, UK: Christian Focus, 2002.

5. Covering a Number of Subjects

The Collected Works of John M. Frame (CD-ROM and DVD set). Phillipsburg, NJ: P&R Publishing; Whitefish, MT: Bits & Bytes, Inc., 2008. Volume 1 available; volumes 2 and 3 to follow. See introduction to this Bibliography for more information.

Spirit of the Reformation Study Bible. Grand Rapids: Zondervan, 2002. I was the theological editor for this Bible.

THEOLOGY

1. Nature, Method of Theology

To get started on my view of the nature of theology, I would recommend that you read in this order: (a) "Studying Theology as a Servant of Jesus," (b) "In Defense of Something Close to Biblicism" and the other articles I mention below in connection with that title, (c) "Machen's Warrior Children," (d) my book *The Doctrine of the Knowledge of God*.

"The Burden of Change: A Warning against Laziness and Shortcuts." *Christian Culture* (September 2004): 4.

The Doctrine of the Knowledge of God. Phillipsburg, NJ: P&R Publishing, 1987. With study guide. Translated into Indonesian in 2000. This is my first published book, in which I attempt to formulate a theory of knowledge based on Scripture and develop ideas for theological and apologetic method. This is a fundamental source for "theology as application" and for triperspectivalism. I reply to Mark Karlberg's review of this book in Appendix B of my *DG* (Phillipsburg, NJ: P&R Publishing, 2002).

"Essence of Christianity." *Christian Culture* (November 2005): 2. Posted at http://www.frame-poythress.org.

"Ethics, Preaching, and Biblical Theology" (1999). For more on my understanding of biblical and systematic theology, see *DKG* and "Salvation and Theological Pedagogy." Available at http://www.reformedperspectives.org and http://www.frame-poythress.org.

"In Defense of Something Close to Biblicism." *WTJ* 59 (1997): 269–318, with replies by David Wells and Richard Muller and a further reply by me. Also published as an appendix to *CWM*. I consider this one of my most important articles. It should be taken together with "Muller on Theology" and "Traditionalism." In these articles I set my approach over against a pervasive trend in evangelical and Reformed theology: the tendency to base theological judgments not directly on Scripture but on an analysis of historical and/or contemporary thought. On the contrary, I advocate a strong form of the principle of *sola Scriptura* (the sufficiency of Scripture), which was once common in Protestant theology, but has in the last century been eclipsed.

"Logic." In *Dictionary for the Theological Interpretation of the Bible*, edited by Kevin Vanhoozer. Grand Rapids: Baker, 2005, 462–64. Here I defend the position of the Westminster Confession of Faith (1.6) that the counsel of God is found not only in what Scripture explicitly says, but also in "good and necessary" logical deductions from Scripture. But our use of logic is fallible, and it is one source of theological error.

"Machen's Warrior Children." In *Alister E. McGrath and Evangelical Theology: A Dynamic Engagement*, edited by Sung Wook Chung. Grand Rapids: Baker, 2003. I argue here that in American Reformed circles since 1936, too much time and effort has been spent on unedifying and divisive controversies.

"Muller on Theology." *WTJ* 56 (Spring 1994): 133–51. See my comments about "In Defense of Something Close to Biblicism" above.

"My Use of the Reformed Confessions" (2005). From an earlier presentation to the Board of Trustees at Westminster Theological Seminary in California. Available at http://www.frame-poythress.org.

"Preface" to *Always Reforming: Explorations in Systematic Theology*, edited by A. T. B. McGowan. Downers Grove, IL; Leicester, England: InterVarsity Press; Apollos, 2006, 9–12.

Response to Jeremy Jones, "Renewing Theology." Available at Common Grounds Online, http://commongroundsonline.typepad.com/common_grounds_ online/2008/09/john-frame-resp.html. Posted September 22, 2008.

Review of *Evangelical Theology: A Survey and Review*, by Robert Lightner. *WTJ* 50, 1 (Spring 1988): 222–26.

Review of *The Grammar of Faith*, by Paul Holmer. *WTJ* 42, 1 (Fall 1979): 219–31.

Review of *Handmaid to Theology: An Essay in Philosophical Prolegomena*, by Winfried Corduan. *WTJ* 45, 2 (Fall 1983): 441–48.

Review of *The Nature of Doctrine: Religion and Theology in a Postliberal Age*, by George Lindbeck. *The Presbyterian Journal* 43 (February 27, 1985): 11–12. Also appears as Appendix H in *DKG* and at http://www.frame-poythress.org.

Review of *On Theology*, by Schubert Ogden. *WTJ* 50, 1 (Spring 1988): 157–65.

Review of *Systematic Theology: A Historicist Perspective*, by Gordon Kaufman. *WTJ* 32, 1 (November 1969): 119–24.

"The Road to a Generous Orthodoxy." Review of *A Generous Orthodoxy: Why I Am a Missional, Evangelical, Post/Protestant, Liberal/Conservative, Mystical/Poetic, Biblical, Charismatic/Contemplative, Fundamentalist/Calvinist, Anabaptist/ Anglican, Methodist, Catholic, Green, Incarnational, Depressed-Yet-Hopeful, Emergent, Unfinished Christian*, by Brian McLaren. *Act3 Journal* 14, 3 (2005): 97–105. McLaren is a well-known writer in the "emergent churches." His theological method is, well, historically unusual. Also posted at http://www. frame-poythress.org.

"Salvation and Theological Pedagogy." *Reformation and Revival Journal* 14, 1 (Winter 2005): 57–70. Deals with relations between *ordo salutis* (a systematic theological arrangement of doctrine), *historia salutis* ("history of redemption," a biblical theological arrangement), and some other similar categories. This supplements my discussions of exegetical, biblical, and systematic theology in *DKG* and "Ethics, Preaching, and Biblical Theology."

"Studying Theology as a Servant of Jesus." *Reformation and Revival* 11, 1 (Winter 2002): 45–69. Thoughts for people entering seminary.

"Systematic Theology and Apologetics at the Westminster Seminaries." In *The Pattern of Sound Doctrine: Systematic Theology at the Westminster Seminaries*, edited by David VanDrunen. Phillipsburg, NJ: P&R Publishing, 2004, 73–98.

"A Theology of Opportunity," "A Theology of Opportunity: Breaking Through to the Foundations of Our Faith." *Equip for Ministry* 1, 2 (June–July 1995): 7–9. The first title is that given to the piece (which was also abridged somewhat) by the editors; the second is my original title. The same article, with some variation, can be found at http://www.frame-poythress.org. The emphasis is on *sola Scriptura*.

"Traditionalism" (1999). Published in two parts in *Chalcedon Report* (October 2001): 15–19, and (November 2001): 434–35. See my comments above under "In Defense of Something Close to Biblicism." Available at http://www.reformed perspectives.org and http://www.frame-poythress.org.

2. Doctrine of the Word of God, Scripture

To get acquainted with my work in this area, start with my early article "No Scripture, No Christ," then the short book *Perspectives on the Word of God*. Then read my article "Scripture Speaks for Itself" and my 2006 lecture "Antithesis and the Doctrine of Scripture." If that whets your appetite, go to the "Course Materials" section at the end of this bibliography and look at my lecture outline for the course Doctrine of the Word of God. That will have to do until I finish the book of that title. You can also get audio recordings of my course lectures on this subject in the first volume of my *Collected Works*; see the course Scripture and God.

See also writings mentioned above under section 1, "Nature, Method of Theology," on the sufficiency of Scripture.

"Antithesis and the Doctrine of Scripture" (2006). Inaugural lecture on receipt of the J. D. Trimble Chair of Systematic Theology and Philosophy. Available at http://www.frame-poythress.org.

"Covenant and the Unity of Scripture" (1999). Available at http://www.reformed perspectives.org and http://www.frame-poythress.org.

The Doctrine of the Word of God. Phillipsburg, NJ: P&R Publishing, forthcoming. This will be a large systematic discussion of the Word of God and Scripture, from Scripture itself, and in interaction with modern theology. It will be the last volume of my Theology of Lordship series.

"God and Biblical Language: Transcendence and Immanence." In *God's Inerrant Word: An International Symposium on the Trustworthiness of Scripture*, edited by John W. Montgomery. Minneapolis Bethany Fellowship, 1974, 159–77.

Counters the idea that God's truth is too transcendent to be expressed truly in human language.

"Is the Bible Inerrant?" (1999). Available at http://www.reformedperspectives.org and http://www.frame-poythress.org. In German at http://www.bucer.de.

"No Scripture, No Christ." *Synapse II* 1, 1 (January 1972): 1. Also in *Presbyterian Guardian* 48 (January 1979): 10–11.

Perspectives on the Word of God. Phillipsburg, NJ: P&R Publishing, 1990. Reprinted by Eugene, OR: Wipf and Stock, 1999. In Russian translation by Odessa, Ukraine: Godeistvize, 2002. A short book, dealing with the Word of God, Scripture, and ethics.

"Rationality and Scripture." In *Rationality in the Calvinian Tradition*, edited by H. Hart, J. Vander Hoeven, and N. Wolterstorff. Lanham, MD: University Press of America, 1983, 293–317.

Review of *Biblical Errancy: An Analysis of its Philosophical Roots*, edited by Norman L. Geisler. *WTJ* 45, 2 (Fall 1983): 433–41.

Review of *Christ and the Bible*, by John Wenham. *Banner of Truth* 118–19 (July–August 1973): 39–41.

Review of *The Divine Spiration of Scripture: Challenging Evangelical Perspectives*, by A. T. B. McGowan (2008). To be posted at http://www.frame-poythress.org.

Review of *Inspiration and Incarnation: Evangelicals and the Problem of the Old Testament*, by Peter Enns (2008). Posted at http://www.frame-poythress.org.

Review of *The Last Word*, by N. T. Wright. *Penpoint* 17, 4 (August 2006). Available at http://www.frame-poythress.org.

Review of *The Nature and Extent of Biblical Authority*, by the Committee on Biblical Authority of the Christian Reformed Church. This volume is also known as "Report 44" of the Christian Reformed Church. Available at http://www.thirdmill.org and http://www.frame-poythress.org.

Review of *The Uses of Scripture in Recent Theology*, by David H. Kelsey. *WTJ* 39, 2 (Spring 1977): 328–53.

"Scripture Speaks for Itself." In *God's Inerrant Word: An International Symposium on the Trustworthiness of Scripture*, edited by John W. Montgomery. Minneapolis: Bethany Fellowship, 1974, 178–200. A survey of Scripture's testimony about itself.

"The Spirit and the Scriptures." In *Hermeneutics, Authority, and Canon*, edited by D. A. Carson and John Woodbridge. Grand Rapids: Zondervan, 1986, 217–35. Reprinted by Eugene, OR: Wipf and Stock, 2005. Summarizes the role of the Spirit in inspiration and illumination; critical of some recent views.

"Toronto, Reformed Orthodoxy, and the Word of God: Where Do We Go from Here?" *Vanguard* (January–February 1975): 3–4. Available at http://www.frame-poythress.org.

"What Is God's Word?" In *The Dooyeweerdian Concept of the Word of God*, edited by Robert Morey. Nutley, NJ: Presbyterian and Reformed, 1974, 32–37, and in *Presbyterian Guardian* 42 (November 1973): 142–43.

"The Word of God and the AACS: A Reply to Prof. Zylstra." *Presbyterian Guardian* 42 (April 1973): 60–61. In the early 1970s, I engaged in controversy with advocates of Herman Dooyeweerd's Philosophy of the Idea of Law. One of the main issues in that debate was the nature of the Word of God and Scripture. For that discussion, see this title, the one immediately below, and the two immediately above, all of which are posted at http://www.frame-poythress.org. See also my booklet *The Amsterdam Philosophy: A Preliminary Critique* (Phillipsburg, NJ: Harmony Press, 1972; and at http://www.frame-poythress.org). Under "Apologetics, Epistemology, Philosophy" below I mention this booklet together with other documents of the controversy.

"The Word of God in the Cosmonomic Philosophy," Parts 1 and 2. *Presbyterian Guardian* 41 (October 1972): 123–25; (November 1972): 140–42. Available at http://www.frame-poythress.org.

3. Doctrine of God

Many of the titles below are incorporated into my major work on this subject, *The Doctrine of God* (Phillipsburg, NJ: P&R Publishing, 2002). My article "God" in the *Zondervan Pictorial Bible Encyclopedia* is in effect a summary of the book, and readers may find that a useful introduction when the encyclopedia is released. The article "The Wonder of God Over Us and In Us" is a good popular introduction to my thinking in this area. The other titles speak for themselves.

"Death of God Theology." In *New Dictionary of Theology*, edited by Sinclair B. Ferguson and David F. Wright. Downers Grove, IL: InterVarsity Press, 188–89.

"Determinism, Chance, and Freedom." In *New Dictionary of Christian Apologetics*, edited by W. C. Campbell-Jack, Gavin J. McGrath, and C. Stephen Evans. Downers Grove, IL: InterVarsity Press, 2006, 218–20.

"Divine Aseity and Apologetics." In *Revelation and Reason: New Essays in Reformed Apologetics*, edited by K. Scott Oliphint and Lane G. Tipton. Phillipsburg, NJ: P&R Publishing, 2007, 115–30.

The Doctrine of God. Phillipsburg, NJ: P&R Publishing, 2002. This is the second of my Theology of Lordship series. I have tried here to present a full exposition of the Bible's teaching about God. This book contains the fullest exegetical argument for my emphasis on divine lordship.

"Does the Bible Affirm Open Theism?" In *Apologetics Study Bible*. Nashville: Broadman and Holman, 2007. Available at http://www.frame-poythress.org.

"Does God Know Everything?" *Moody Magazine* (March–April 2003): 26–30. Interview with Alan Sholes and Lisa Cockrel.

"Free Will and Moral Responsibility" (1999). Available at http://www.reformed perspectives.org and http://www.frame-poythress.org.

"God." In *Zondervan Pictorial Bible Encyclopedia*. Completed, awaiting publication. This long-delayed volume will be an updated and extensively revised version of the *Zondervan Pictorial Encyclopedia of the Bible*, edited by Merrill C. Tenney (Grand Rapids: Zondervan, 1975).

"God With Us, Here and Now" (1999). Available at http://www.reformedperspectives. org and http://www.frame-poythress.org.

"The Lord of Authority." *Northland News* 1, 5 (October 1–7, 2000): 1.

"The Lord of Power." *Northland News* 1, 4 (September 23, 2000): 1.

"The Lord of Presence." *Northland News* 1, 6 (October 8–14, 2000): 1.

No Other God. Phillipsburg, NJ: P&R Publishing, 2001. In Korean, translated by Sung-Kook Hong (Seoul: Christian Literature Crusade, 2005). Critique of open theism.

"Open Theism and Divine Foreknowledge." In *Bound Only Once: The Failure of Open Theism*, edited by Douglas Wilson. Moscow, ID: Canon Press, 2001, 83–94.

"Providence in All of Life" (2006). Available at http://www.frame-poythress.org.

Review of *God: The Contemporary Discussion*, edited by Frederick Sontag and M. Darrol Bryant. *WTJ* 46 (1984): 198–205. Also appears as Appendix F in my *DG*.

Review of *Miracles and the Critical Mind*, by Colin Brown. *WTJ* 47, 1 (Spring 1985): 140–46.

Review of *The Providence of God*, by Benjamin Farley. *WTJ* 51, 2 (Fall 1989): 397–400. Also appears as Appendix D in my *DG*.

Review of *The Providence of God*, by Paul Helm. *WTJ* 56, 2 (Fall 1994): 438–42. Also appears as Appendix E in my *DG*.

"Scientia Media." In *Evangelical Dictionary of Theology*, edited by Walter Elwell. Grand Rapids: Baker Book House, 1984, 987–88. On whether God has "middle knowledge."

"Trinitarian Analogies" (1999). Available at http://www.reformedperspectives.org and http://www.frame-poythress.org.

"The Wonder of God Over Us and With Us." *Reformed Quarterly* (Winter 2000): 12–13, 17.

4. Covenants, Justification

The issues of covenant and justification have been very controversial in American Presbyterian circles over the last thirty years. I have not taught these subjects, but I have followed the discussion. My own positions, especially on Norman Shepherd and the "Federal Vision," are best expressed in "Reflections of a Lifetime Theologian," the interview of me by Andrew Sandlin included in the present volume (see also section 1 under "Introductory" in this Bibliography). In addition, the following titles may be relevant.

"Foreword" to *Backbone of the Bible: Covenant in Contemporary Perspective*, edited by P. Andrew Sandlin. Nacogdoches, TX: Covenant Media Press, 2004.

"Galatians 3:15–29: A Dialogue" (2000). A sermon.

"Law and Gospel." Posted January 4, 2004, for The Chalcedon Foundation at http://www.chalcedon.edu/articles/0201/020104frame.php. Also available at http://www.frame-poythress.org.

5. Theological Education

I am somewhat radical on questions of how to prepare people for ministry. Essentially, I believe that the prevalent academic model is insufficient. Rather than have a fieldwork component in a program based on academics, I believe that fieldwork in a church should be the main structure of ministerial education, with academic supplements as needed. That's the thrust of my "Proposal for a New Seminary." But until that structure becomes the norm, I certainly think there is some value in the more traditional form of theological education, within which I have been laboring all my life. To support and encourage students in regard to traditional seminaries, I wrote "Learning at Jesus' Feet" and "Studying Theology as a Servant of Jesus."

"Becoming a Theology Professor" (2008). Available at http://www.frame-poythress.org.

"Case Study: Proposals for a New North American Mode." In *Missions and Theological Education in World Perspective*, edited by Harvie M. Conn and Sam Rowen. Farmington, MI: Associates of Urbansu, 1984, 369–86.

"Learning at Jesus' Feet: A Case for Seminary Education." Pamphlet published by Reformed Theological Seminary, Orlando, FL, 2003.

"Proposal for a New Seminary." *Journal of Pastoral Practice* 2, 1 (Winter 1978): 10–17. Earlier version of "Case Study" (see above). Also in *Reformed Theology* (Korean), published by Reformed Presbyterian Seminary, Gardena, CA, 1992.

"Studying Theology as a Servant of Jesus." Pamphlet published by Reformed Theological Seminary Bookstore, 2000.

6. Other Topics

"Infralapsarianism." In *Encyclopedia of the Reformed Faith*, edited by Donald K. McKim. Louisville: John Knox/Westminster, 1992, 193–94.

"Introduction" to *The Covenant Baptism of Infants*, by Jim West. Palo Cedro, CA: Christian Worldview Ministries, 1992, iii.

"Preface" to *New Flesh, New Earth: The Life-Changing Power of the Resurrection*, by P. Andrew Sandlin. Lincoln, CA: Oakdown, 2003, 9–10.

Review of *Calvinism and the Amyraut Heresy*, by Brian Armstrong. *WTJ* 34, 2 (May 1972): 186–92. "Four-point" Calvinism.

Review of *Reformed Dogmatics*, by John Beardslee. *The Presbyterian Journal* 36 (October 5, 1977): 19–20.

"Second Chance." In *Evangelical Dictionary of Theology*, edited by Walter Elwell. Grand Rapids: Baker, 991–92.

"Theology in the Age of the Internet," to be published in *The Complete Works of John M. Frame*, CD-ROM set. Phillipsburg, NJ: P&R Publishing; Whitefish, MT: Bits & Bytes, Inc. Volume 1 published in 2008; volumes 2 and 3 forthcoming.

"Virgin Birth of Jesus." In *Evangelical Dictionary of Theology*, edited by Walter Elwell. Grand Rapids: Baker, 1984, 1143–45.

"Westminster Catechisms." In *Evangelical Dictionary of Theology*, edited by Walter Elwell. Grand Rapids: Baker, 1984, 1168. See also my lecture outlines on the Shorter Catechism under "Course Materials" at the end of this Bibliography.

"Westminster Confession of Faith," in *Evangelical Dictionary of Theology*, ed. Walter Elwell. Grand Rapids: Baker, 1984, 1168–69.

APOLOGETICS

1. Apologetic Method and Epistemology

Probably the best way to get started on my approach to apologetics is to read my "Presuppositional Apologetics" in *Five Views of Apologetics*. (Read also in that book about the alternative views and the interaction between the five authors.) I have also summarized my view in the other articles dealing with "Presuppositionalism" and "Van Til" (in the next group of titles below). I am considered a presuppositionalist, but I try to find good in other methods as well. One particular attempt to bridge the apologetic divisions was my "Epistemological Perspectives and Evangelical Apologetics," which also shows how my perspectivalism applies to apologetics. Then the reader should look at my main apologetics book, *Apologetics to the Glory of God*, and also my *The Doctrine of the Knowledge of God*, which places apologetics within a biblical view of knowledge. Among the other articles, I am particularly fond of the little paper on "Certainty."

"Apologetics." In *Dictionary for the Theological Interpretation of the Bible*, edited by Kevin Vanhoozer. Grand Rapids: Baker, 2005, 57–58.

"Apologetics at Westminster." *Update* 8, 2 (1990): 2.

Apologetics to the Glory of God: An Introduction. Phillipsburg, NJ: P&R Publishing, 1994. Translated into Indonesian (2000). In Chinese (China Evangelical Seminary Press, 2003). In Japanese, translated by Kunio Sakurai of Tokyo Christian University (Publication Committee of the Presbyterian Church of Japan, 1998; also Tokyo: Word of Life Press, 2006). In Korean, translated by Ji-Hyun Jun (Seoul: Yungeum Press, 1997). This is my main formulation of my apologetic approach.

"Bahnsen at the Stein Debate" (2006). Available at http://www.frame-poythress.org.

"A Blind Beggar Becomes an Apologist." *In Covenant* 4, 3 (June 2001): 1–2. Also at http://www.frame-poythress.org.

"Certainty." In *New Dictionary of Christian Apologetics*, edited by W. C. Campbell-Jack, Gavin J. McGrath, and C. Stephen Evans. Downers Grove, IL, InterVarsity Press, 2006, 141–45.

"Christianity and Contemporary Epistemology" *WTJ* 52 (1990): 131–41.

"Divine Aseity and Apologetics." In *Revelation and Reason: New Essays in Reformed Apologetics*, edited by K. Scott Oliphint and Lane G. Tipton. Phillipsburg, NJ: P&R Publishing, 2007, 115–30.

The Doctrine of the Knowledge of God. Phillipsburg, NJ: Presbyterian and Reformed, 1987. With study guide. My first published book, in which I attempt to set forth a biblical theory of knowledge, with implications for apologetic and theological method. I reply to Mark Karlberg's review of this book in Appendix B of my *DG*.

"Epistemological Perspectives and Evangelical Apologetics." *Bulletin of the Evangelical Philosophical Society* 7 (1984): 1–7. Originally a lecture presented in 1982.

"Euthyphro, Hume, and the Biblical God" (1999). Available at http://www.reformed perspectives.org and http://www.frame-poythress.org.

"Foreword" to *Every Thought Captive*, by Richard L. Pratt Jr. Phillipsburg, NJ: Presbyterian and Reformed, 1979, vi–vii.

"Logic." in *Dictionary for the Theological Interpretation of the Bible*, edited by Kevin Vanhoozer. Grand Rapids: Baker, 2005, 462–64. Also posted at http://www.frame-poythress.org.

"Presuppositional Apologetics." In *Five Views of Apologetics*, edited by Steve Cowan. Grand Rapids: Zondervan, 2000. One major article, four replies, and a concluding article.

"Presuppositional Apologetics: An Introduction" (1999), http://www.reformed perspectives.org, http://www.frame-poythress.org.

"Presuppositionalism," in *New Dictionary of Christian Apologetics*, ed. W. C. Campbell-Jack, Gavin J. McGrath, and C. Stephen Evans. Downers Grove, IL., InterVarsity Press, 2006, 575–78.

"Reply to Don Collett on Transcendental Argument." *WTJ* 65 (2003): 307–9.

Review of *Belief Policies*, by Paul Helm. *WTJ* 57 (1995): 248–51.

Review of *A Christian Handbook for Defending the Faith*, by Robert Morey. *The Presbyterian Journal* 38 (February 20, 1980): 14–15.

Review of *Classical Apologetics*, by R. C. Sproul, John Gerstner, and Arthur Lindsley. *WTJ* 47, 2 (Fall 1986): 279–99.

Review of *Longing to Know: The Philosophy of Knowledge for Ordinary People*, by Esther Meek. *Presbyterion* 29, 2 (Fall 2003): 120–23.

Review of *Questions of Religious Truth*, by W. Cantwell Smith. *WTJ* 30, 2 (May 1968): 241–42.

"Scripture and the Apologetic Task." *The Journal of Biblical Counseling* 13, 2 (Winter 1995): 9–12. (From *AGG*, chap. 1.)

"Self-Refuting Statements." In *New Dictionary of Christian Apologetics*, edited by W. C. Campbell-Jack, Gavin J. McGrath, and C. Stephen Evans. Downers Grove, IL: InterVarsity Press, 2006, 660–62.

"Systematic Theology and Apologetics at the Westminster Seminaries." In *The Pattern of Sound Doctrine: Systematic Theology at the Westminster Seminaries*, edited by David VanDrunen. Phillipsburg, NJ: P&R Publishing, 2004, 73–98.

"Transcendental Argument." In *New Dictionary of Christian Apologetics*, edited by W. C. Campbell-Jack, Gavin J. McGrath, and C. Stephen Evans. Downers Grove, IL: InterVarsity Press, 2006, 716–17.

"Triads for Apologetics" (2002). Available at http://www.reformedperspectives.org and http://www.frame-poythress.org.

"The Ugliness of Evangelism." *Synapse III* (Fall 1974): 1, 5, 7, 11. Also at http://www.frame-poythress.org.

"Unregenerate Knowledge of God." In *New Dictionary of Christian Apologetics*, edited by W. C. Campbell-Jack, Gavin J. McGrath, and C. Stephen Evans. Downers Grove, IL: InterVarsity Press, 2006, 732–35.

2. Cornelius Van Til

I studied with the great apologist and theologian Cornelius Van Til at Westminster Seminary from 1961–64. I still consider myself his disciple, but a critical disciple. The best way to understand Van Til, of course, is to look at his own writings, perhaps "Why I Believe in God," then "The Defense of Christianity and My Credo," then *Christian Apologetics*. I have summarized Van Til's thought many times, as the list below indicates. The simplest of these is "Van Til: His Simplicity and Profundity." "Van Til Reconsidered" is a bit more complicated, in effect summarizing my larger work, *Cornelius Van Til: An Analysis of His Thought*. You can also get some help from the titles in the preceding section on "presuppositional apologetics." When I speak of "presuppositionalism," I usually mean Van Til's presuppositionalism.

"Cornelius Van Til." In *Biographical Dictionary of Evangelicals*, edited by Timothy Larsen. Leicester, England; Downers Grove, IL: InterVarsity Press, 2003, 682–84.

"Cornelius Van Til." In *Handbook of Evangelical Theologians*, edited by Walter Elwell. Grand Rapids: Baker, 1993, 156–67.

Cornelius Van Til: An Analysis of His Thought. Phillipsburg, NJ: P&R Publishing, 1995. Published in Indonesian (Surabaya: Penerbit Momentum, 2002). In this book I have tried to deal comprehensively with Van Til, both as apologist and as theologian.

"Cornelius Van Til, Apologist." In *Apologetics Study Bible*. Nashville: Broadman and Holman, 2007, 1690.

"Johnson on Van Til: A Rejoinder," with Steve Hays. *Evangelical Quarterly* 76, 3 (July 2004): 227–39. Available at http://www.vantil.info.

Letter to the Editor (on Richard Horner's review of *CVT*). *New Horizons* (July 1996): 22.

"The Problem of Theological Paradox." In *Foundations of Christian Scholarship: Essays in the Van Til Perspective*, edited by Gary North. Vallecito, CA: Ross House, 1976, 295–330. Same as "Van Til the Theologian" (below).

"Reply to Mark W. Karlberg." *Mid-America Journal of Theology* 9, 2 (Fall 1993): 297–308 (actually published in 1998). Also appears as Appendix C of my *DG*.

Review of *Van Til: Defender of the Faith*, by William White. *The Presbyterian Journal* 38 (February 13, 1980): 21–22. A shorter version of the next title.

Review of *Van Til: Defender of the Faith*, by William White. *WTJ* 42, 1 (Fall 1979): 198–203.

"Van Til and the Ligonier Apologetic." *WTJ* 47, 2 (Fall 1985): 279–99. A review article dealing with John Gerstner, R. C. Sproul, and Arthur Lindsley, *Classical Apologetics* (Grand Rapids: Zondervan, 1984). Reprinted at http://www.netopia. geocities.com/gtrammel/pages/view/index.nhtml, at http://www.reformed.org, and as appendices to my books *AGG* and *CVT*.

"Van Til, Cornelius." In *New Dictionary of Christian Apologetics*, edited by W. C. Campbell-Jack, Gavin J. McGrath, and C. Stephen Evans. Downers Grove, IL: InterVarsity Press, 2006, 739–40.

"A Van Til Glossary" (2000). Posted at http://www.reformedperspectives.org and http://www.frame-poythress.org.

"Van Til: His Simplicity and Profundity." *Update* (March 1986): 1–2.

"Van Til on Antithesis." *WTJ* 57 (1995): 81–102. Anticipates chap. 15 of my *CVT*.

"Van Til Reconsidered" (2005). Posted at http://www.frame-poythress.org.

"Van Til the Theologian." Phillipsburg, NJ: Pilgrim Publications, 1976. Same as "The Problem of Theological Paradox" above. Translated into French by André Coste, *La Revue Reformée* 167 (Janvier 1991): 7–42. This long essay deals with Van Til's use of logic and paradox: he wants theology to be a system, but he opposes what he calls "deductive systems." I try to understand here what he means by that. Also published at http://www.netopia.geocities.com/gtrammel/pages/view/index.nhtml and at http://www.reformed.org.

3. Existence of God

This is one of the major subjects of apologetic discussion. "How to Believe in God in the 2000s" is a series of three sermons that present a basic presuppositional argument. See also the material on this subject in my *Apologetics to the Glory of God*.

Debate with philosopher Michael Martin on his "Transcendental Argument for the Non-Existence of God" (1996). Available at http://www.reformed.org.

"Do We Need God to Be Moral?" Debate with Paul Kurtz in *Free Inquiry* 16, 2 (Spring 1996). Published earlier as "Who Needs God?" *Dallas Morning News*, October 28, 1995, G1, G3, G6. Also available at http://www.frame-poythress.org.

"Encounter on a Plane: Evidence for the Biblical God." Excerpt from my book *AGG*. Originally published in *Areopagus Proclamation* 5, 9, #9506 (June 1995).

"How to Believe in God in the 2000s." A series of three sermons, dealing with presuppositions, natural revelation, and Scripture. Originally done in the 1990s, adapted and revised later on. Posted in 2005 at http://www.frame-poythress.com.

"Infinite Series." In *New Dictionary of Christian Apologetics*, edited by W. C. Campbell-Jack, Gavin J. McGrath, and C. Stephen Evans. Downers Grove, IL: InterVarsity Press, 2006, 353–54. This issue arises especially in connection with cosmological arguments for God's existence. Posted at http://www.frame-poythress.org.

"Ontological Argument." In *New Dictionary of Christian Apologetics*, edited by W. C. Campbell-Jack, Gavin J. McGrath, and C. Stephen Evans. Downers Grove, IL: InterVarsity Press, 2006, 513–16. Posted at http://www.frame-poythress.org.

"Unregenerate Knowledge of God." In *New Dictionary of Christian Apologetics*, edited by W. C. Campbell-Jack, Gavin J. McGrath, and C. Stephen Evans. Downers Grove, IL: InterVarsity Press, 2006, 732–35. Posted at http://www.frame-poythress.org.

4. Deity of Christ

"The Claims of Christ" (1999). A sermon on John 5. Posted at http://www.reformed perspectives.org and http://www.frame-poythress.org. See also *DG*, chap. 28.

5. The Problem of Evil

Another issue commonly discussed in the apologetics literature is this: If God is all-good, all-wise, and all-powerful, how can there be evil in the world? Here are some responses.

Apologetics to the Glory of God. Phillipsburg, NJ: P&R Publishing, 1994, chaps, 6, 7.

"The Bible on the Problem of Evil" (1999). Posted at http://www.reformedperspec tives.org and http://www.frame-poythress.org. Formerly available in Lithuanian at http://www.prizme.It/straipsiai/straips,php?action=view&id=422.

The Doctrine of God. Phillipsburg, NJ: P&R Publishing, 2002, chap. 9.

"Interview with John Frame on the Problem of Evil," by Andy Naselli (2008). Available at Between Two Worlds Web site, http://theologica.blogspot.com/search?q=problem+of+evil+frame.

Review of *Evil Revisited: Responses and Reconsiderations*, by David Ray Griffin. *Calvin Theological Journal* 27, 2 (November 1992): 435–38.

6. Philosophy

Apologetics is in constant dialogue with philosophy, which attempts to set forth a general view of the world, knowledge, and values. Like Van Til, I have argued the importance of a *biblical* basis for philosophy, as for all other human thought. Some of the worst problems in apologetics and theology come from attempts to judge Scripture by nonbiblical philosophy. I have given a general account of the role philosophy should take in *The Doctrine of the Knowledge of God*, and the following titles deal with various philosophical issues.

The Amsterdam Philosophy: A Preliminary Critique. Phillipsburg, NJ: Harmony Press, 1972. On this movement, see also "The Word of God and the AACS: A Reply to Prof. Zylstra," "The Word of God in the Cosmonomic Philosophy," "Toronto, Reformed Orthodoxy, and the Word of God: Where Do We Go from Here?" and "What is God's Word?" under section 2 of "Theology" above. See also under section 2 of "Culture" below: "Are the Reformed Creeds Worth Keeping in Schools?" "Church Creeds and Christian Schools," "Constitutional Revision in the NUCS: Counting the Cost," "School Subscription to Church Creeds," and "The Quiet Crisis in the Christian Schools."

"God and Biblical Language: Transcendence and Immanence." In *God's Inerrant Word: An International Symposium on the Trustworthiness of Scripture,* edited by John W. Montgomery. Minneapolis: Bethany Fellowship, 1974, 159–77. Deals with the question whether God's Word is too transcendent to be expressed truly in human language. The article deals with Flew's "Gardener" parable and the logical positivist critique of religious language.

"Greeks Bearing Gifts." In *Revolutions in Worldview: Understanding the Flow of Western Thought,* edited by W. Andrew Hoffecker. Phillipsburg, NJ: P&R Publishing, 2007, 1–36. Critical survey of Greek religion and philosophy.

Review of *The Edges of Language,* by Paul Van Buren. *WTJ* 36, 1 (Fall 1973): 106–11.

Review of *Handmaid to Theology: An Essay in Philosophical Prolegomena,* by Winfried Corduan. *WTJ* 45, 2 (Fall 1983): 441–48. His handmaid is the philosophy of Thomas Aquinas.

Review of *The Legacy of Logical Positivism: Studies in the Philosophy of Science,* edited by Peter Achinstein and Stephen F. Barker. *WTJ* 34, 2 (May 1972): 199–201.

Review of *New Essays on Religious Language,* ed. Dallas M. High. *WTJ* 33, 1 (November 1970): 126–31.

7. Other Apologetic Subjects

"Greg Bahnsen: Student/Scholar." *The Counsel of Chalcedon* XVII, 11 and 12 (January–February 1996): 4–8.

"Is Intelligent Design Science?" (2006). Available at http://www.frame-poythress.org.

Review of *Alive: An Enquiry into the Origin and Meaning of Life,* by Magnus Verbrugge. *WTJ* 47, 2 (Fall 1985): 373–79.

THE CHURCH

For many years I have been concerned about the divisions in the church of Christ, among them denominational differences. Scripture makes no provision for denominations. The church as Jesus founded it was one, not only in spirit, but also in government. The apostle Paul rebuked the development of denominational attitudes (1 Cor. 1:12–13; 3:1–4). Yet today there are thousands of denominations. In my judgment this weakens the church and its testimony to the world. For a short argument on this subject, see my "Guidelines for Church Union." For a longer discussion, see my book *Evangelical Reunion*.

1. Unity

Evangelical Reunion: Denominations and the Body of Christ. Grand Rapids: Baker, 1991. Posted at http://www.reformedperspectives.org and http://www.frame-poythress.org.

"Guidelines for Church Union." *Presbyterian Journal* 42 (August 24, 1983): 8–10.

"Is Realignment a Biblical Option?" *New Horizons* 10, 6 (June–July 1989): 18.

"Only One Legitimate Issue Before Us." *New Horizons* 7, 4 (April 1986): 13.

"Reformation in Our Personal Attitudes." *Reformation Today* (July–August 1997): 21–24. Excerpt from *Evangelical Reunion*.

"Unity of Faith Inseparable from Unity of Conviction." *The Wanderer* (July 31, 1975): 5.

"Walking Together" (1999). Available at http://www.reformedperspectives.org and http://www.frame-poythress.org.

"Where Did Denominations Come From?" *Reformation Today* (July–August 1997): 11–14. Excerpt from *Evangelical Reunion*.

2. Worship, Preaching

When I moved to California in 1980, I was part of a Presbyterian church being planted in the city of Escondido. Rather than maintain traditional Presbyterian worship, we determined to use a contemporary style. The reason was not merely a desire to be different. Rather, we hoped that instead of just creating an additional option for Reformed believers, God would enable us to reach out to the unchurched and to Christians who ordinarily would not darken the door of a Presbyterian church. I believe that God blessed this decision. But some of our Reformed brethren were very critical of it. My *Worship in Spirit and Truth* is a summary of biblical teachings on worship, based on a class I taught in the church to explain why we worship as we do. *Contemporary Worship Music: A Biblical Defense* presents my arguments against those who opposed our style of worship.

1046

Often in these debates people would raise the issue of the "regulative principle," the teaching of the Westminster Standards (WCF 1.6, 20.2, 21.1; WLC 109) that all the elements of worship must be *prescribed* by Scripture. I believed, and still do, that our worship was in line with this regulative principle. But I did have to defend that view in debate, some examples of which are mentioned below. See also my *The Doctrine of the Christian Life* (Phillipsburg, NJ: P&R Publishing, 2008), in which the discussions of the first four commandments bear on worship, and in which I discuss the regulative principle under the second commandment.

"Above the Battle?" (2003). Photocopied for worship course. Reviews of books by Marva Dawn, by Michael Horton, and by John Muether and Darryl Hart. Available at http://www.reformedperspectives.org and http://www.frame-poythress.org.

"A Class in Praise." *Life at New Life* (May–June 1985): 1. On choirs.

Contemporary Worship Music: A Biblical Defense. Phillipsburg, NJ: P&R Publishing, 1997.

"Contemporary Worship Music: Quality." in *More Than a Worship Band*, edited by Tim Dearborn and Scott Coil. Calvin Institute of Christian Worship, 2002: 175–82. Reprints a chapter of my book *CWM*.

The Doctrine of the Christian Life. Phillipsburg, NJ: P&R Publishing, 2008. The discussion of the first four commandments is especially relevant to worship.

"Ethics, Preaching, and Biblical Theology" (1999). Some people think that sermons should be wholly dedicated to narrating the history of redemption. These people often believe that preaching should not set forth moral obligations, or at least that we should never use Bible characters as moral examples. I disagree with these views and explain why in this article. Available at http://www.reformedperspectives.org and http://www.frame-poythress.org.

"Foreword" to *The Art of Worship: Opening Our Eyes to the Beauty of the Gospel*, by Paxson H. Jeancake. Eugene, OR: Wipf and Stock, 2006.

"Foreword" to *Covenantal Worship: Reconsidering the Puritan Regulative Principle*, by R. J. Gore Jr. Phillipsburg, NJ: P&R Publishing, 2002, ix–x.

"A Fresh Look at the Regulative Principle" (2008). Available at http://www.frame-poythress.org.

"How Does God Regulate Worship?" *Presbyterian Network* (Spring 1999): 12–17.

"Music in Worship" *New Horizons* 7, 4 (April 1986): 1–2.

"The Regulative Principle: Scripture, Tradition, and Culture." Debate with Darryl Hart on Warfield computer list. Published in hard copy by Westminster Campus Bookstore, edited by Charles R. Biggs, 1998. See http://www.frame-poythress.org.

"Reply to T. David Gordon." *WTJ* 56, 1 (Spring 1994): 181–83. This concerns the "Some Questions" article below.

"Serving One Another in Worship." *In Covenant* 4, 3 (March 2001): 1–2.

"Some Journal Entries on Preaching" (2006). Does the Bible tell us that every worship service must contain a sermon, patterned after the apostolic preaching in the book of Acts? In my journal, I raise some of my hesitations about this idea. Available at http://www.frame-poythress.org.

"Some Questions about the Regulative Principle." *WTJ* 54 (1992): 357–66.

"We Used to Sing Only Psalms; What Happened?" *Reformed Worship* (Spring 1987): 32–34.

"Worship and the Reformation Gospel" (2005). Lectures given at a worship conference. Available at http://www.frame-poythress.org.

Worship in Spirit and Truth. Phillipsburg, NJ: P&R Publishing, 1996. In Hungarian (2002; I am unable to decipher the publication data). In Portuguese, *Em Espirito e em Verdade* (Sao Paulo: Editora Cultura Christa, 2006).

3. Other Subjects

"Is It Wrong to Market the Church?" (2006). People are always assuming that "marketing" is a clear idea, and that we must never, ever "market" the church. But what, actually, is the difference between marketing and outreach? I plead for more analysis, less rhetoric. Available at http://www.frame-poythress.org.

"Keeping Your Elders Happy" (2002). Sermon on Hebrews 13:17. Available at http://www.reformedperspectives.org.

"Lessons on Ministry from the Pharisees" (1999). Available at http://www.reformed perspectives.org and http://www.frame-poythress.org.

Ethics

1. Views

"Calvin Center Research Book Mirrors Secular Thinking." Review of *Christian Faith, Health, and Medical Practice*, by H. Bouma, D. Dickema, E. Langerak, T. Rottman, and A. Verhey. *Christian Renewal* (June 18, 1990): 16–17.

"Reformed Ethics." In *Baker's Dictionary of Christian Ethics*, edited by Carl F. H. Henry. Grand Rapids: Baker, 571–72.

"Schleiermacher and Protestant Ethics." In *Baker's Dictionary of Christian Ethics*, edited by Carl F. H. Henry. Grand Rapids: Baker, 603–4.

2. General Principles

Many of the titles below are incorporated into my major treatment of ethics, *The Doctrine of the Christian Life*. For a brief introduction to my ethical method, read *Perspectives on the Word of God* and the first part of *Medical Ethics*.

"Between the Apostles and the Parousia" (1999). Available at http://www.reformed perspectives.org and http://www.frame-poythress.org.

"Covering Ourselves." *The Journal of Pastoral Practice* 7, 4 (1985): 2–6. A sermon.

The Doctrine of the Christian Life. Phillipsburg, NJ: P&R Publishing, 2008.

"Do We Need God to Be Moral?" Debate with Paul Kurtz. *Free Inquiry* 16, 2 (Spring 1996). Published earlier as "Who Needs God?" *Dallas Morning News*, October 28, 1995, G1, G3, G6. Also available at http://www.frame-poythress.org.

"Ethics and Biblical Events." Available at http://www.frame-poythress.org.

"Ethics, Preaching, and Biblical Theology" (1999). Available at http://www.reformed perspectives.org and http://www.frame-poythress.org.

"Euthyphro, Hume, and the Biblical God" (1999). Available at http://www.reformed perspectives.org and http://www.frame-poythress.org.

"Free Will and Moral Responsibility" (1999). Available at http://www.reformed perspectives.org and http://www.frame-poythress.org.

"Grow in Grace and Knowledge" (1999). A sermon. Available at http://www. reformedperspectives.org and http://www.frame-poythress.org.

"Hurting People's Feelings; or, 'The Pathos Game'" (2003). Available at http://www. reformedperspectives.org and http://www.frame-poythress.org.

"In Defense of Christian Activism." *Christian Culture* (April 2006): 1–4. Longer version available at http://www.frame-poythress.org.

"Levels of Ethical Evaluation" (1999). Available at http://www.reformedperspectives. org and http://www.frame-poythress.org.

"Living with Ourselves" (2001). Available at http://www.reformedperspectives.org and http://www.frame-poythress.org.

Medical Ethics: Principles, Persons, and Problems. Phillipsburg, NJ: Presbyterian and Reformed, 1988.

"Moral Heroism" (2001). Available at http://www.reformedperspectives.org and http://www.frame-poythress.org.

"The Need to Postpone Obedience." *Mandate* 108 (July 21, 1975): 3–4.

Perspectives on the Word of God. Phillipsburg, NJ: Presbyterian and Reformed, 1990. Reprinted by Eugene, OR: Wipf and Stock, 1999. Part 3 is a short introduction to Christian ethics.

"Preaching Christ from the Decalogue" (1999). Available at http://www.reformed perspectives.org and http://www.frame-poythress.org.

"Reactive Ethics and *Sola Scriptura*" (2005). Available at http://www.frame-poythress.org.

Review of *Paul's Ethic of Freedom*, by Peter Richardson. In *Transformation* 1, 4 (October–December 1984): 28.

3. The Law, Theonomy

Those associated with "Theonomy" or "Christian Reconstruction" believe that the civil law of the Old Testament is normative for present-day governments. Particularly, the penalties attached to crimes in the Mosaic Law (e.g., capital punishment for homosexuality or adultery) should be attached to the same crimes today. I have never been a theonomist, but theonomist writers have given me a lot to think about. The best place to find my current position is in *The Doctrine of the Christian Life*, 217–24.

"Foreword" to *A Comprehensive Faith: An International Festschrift for Rousas John Rushdoony*, edited by Andrew Sandlin. San José: Friends of Chalcedon, 1996.

"Introduction" to *The Law of the Covenant: An Exposition of Exodus 21–23*, by James B. Jordan. Tyler, TX: Institute for Christian Economics, xvii–xx.

"The One, the Many, and Theonomy." In *Theonomy: A Reformed Critique*, edited by William S. Barker and W. Robert Godfrey. Grand Rapids: Zondervan, 1990, 89–99.

"Penultimate Thoughts on Theonomy" (2001). Available at http://www.thirdmill.org and http://www.frame-poythress.org.

Review of *The Institutes of Biblical Law: A Chalcedon Study*, by Rousas John Rushdoony. *WTJ* 38, 2 (Winter 1976): 195–217.

Review of *Theonomy in Christian Ethics*, by Greg L. Bahnsen. *The Presbyterian Journal* 36 (August 31, 1977): 18.

4. Abortion

I served on the Committee to Study the Matter of Abortion in the Orthodox Presbyterian Church back in 1972. Over the years some of my writings have supported the biblical pro-life position. The *Report of the Committee* below sets forth my position in detail, and, more recently, *The Doctrine of the Christian Life*, 717–32.

"Abortion and Some Christian Assumptions." *Cambridge Fish* 3 (1972): 6. Also in *Banner of Truth* 100 (January 1972): 29–31.

"Abortion and the Christian." *The Presbyterian Guardian* 39 (November 1970): 78–80.

"Abortion and the Lonely Modern Woman." *The New Community* 2 (January 1976): 1–5.

"Abortion from a Biblical Perspective," In *Thou Shalt Not Kill: The Christian Case against Abortion*, edited by Richard L. Ganz. New Rochelle, NY: Arlington House, 1978, 43–75. Edited version of the OPC *Report of the Committee to Study the Matter of Abortion* (below).

"The Law, Theology and Abortion." *The Christian Lawyer* 4 (Winter 1972): 24–27.

"Ministries of Mercy to the Unborn" (1999). Available at http://www.reformedper spectives.org and http://www.frame-poythress.org.

Report of the Committee to Study the Matter of Abortion. In *Minutes of the General Assembly of the Orthodox Presbyterian Church*, 1971. Also published in pamphlet form. I was principal author, with much help from other committee members.

Review of *Abortion: The Personal Dilemma*, by Rex Gardner. *Cambridge Fish* 3 (1972): 3, 6. Also in *Banner of Truth* 109 (October 1972): 31–32.

Review of *Abortion: The Personal Dilemma*, by Rex Gardner. *WTJ* 35, 2 (Winter 1973): 234–37. A longer version of the above.

Review of *Our Right to Choose: Toward a New Ethic of Abortion*, by Beverly Wildung Harrison. *Eternity* 35 (October 1984): 43–44.

5. Man and Woman

I find myself on the "left wing of the complementarian movement." To be complementarian (not egalitarian) is to believe that the sexes are not interchangeable: they have different, biblically mandated roles to play in the church and in the family. But I am on the "left wing," which means that although I do not believe that women should be elders and pastors, I do think that under the authority of elders they may teach and even preach in the church. So naturally I have opponents on all sides of these thorny issues. The best place now to find my reasoning on these issues is *The Doctrine of the Christian Life*, chap. 33. The articles below, especially "May Women Teach Adult Sunday School Classes?" will give you the gist of it. I'm not enthused now about my article "Men and Women in the Image of God." It needs simplification and a reduction of pretension. *DCL*, chap. 33, includes a substantial revision of it.

"Foreword" to *Women and the Church: A Biblical Perspective*, by Mil Am Yi. Columbus, GA: Brentwood Christian Press, 1991, 7–8.

"Marriage as Unjust Suffering" (1999). A sermon. Available at http://www.reformed perspectives.org and http://www.frame-poythress.org.

"May Women Teach Adult Sunday School Classes?" (2002). Available at http://www. reformedperspectives.org and http://www.frame-poythress.org.

"Men and Women in the Image of God." In *Recovering Biblical Manhood and Womanhood: A Response to Evangelical Feminism*, edited by John Piper and Wayne A. Grudem. Wheaton, IL: Crossway, 1991, 225–32.

"Mixed Marriages" (1999). A sermon. Available at http://www.reformedperspectives. org and http://www.frame-poythress.org.

"Spousal Abuse: Ground for Divorce?" (2002). Posted at http://www.reformed perspectives.org.

6. Other Subjects

Many of these little articles are in effect first drafts of sections of *The Doctrine of the Christian Life*, and I'd rather you read the book than the articles. But if you don't want to buy the book, you may find these articles edifying on some matters.

"Capital Punishment." *The New Community* 3 (September 1977). Available at http:// www.frame-poythress.org.

"Cloning: Maybe?" (2003). Available at http://www.reformedperspectives.org and http://www.frame-poythress.org.

"Faith and the Fight against Terrorism." *Fort Worth Star-Telegram*, January 27, 2002.

"God Made Me This Way." *Tabletalk* 21, 3 (March 1997): 8–11. Also published in *Immanuel* 107 (March 1997): 3. On homosexuality. Also posted as "But God Made Me This Way" (2002), http://www.reformedperspectives.org. "But God Made Me This Way" in Korean and English in *KAPC Bulletin* 26 (May 23, 2006): 18–24.

"Imprecations: Holy Fire" (2002). Available at http://www.reformedperspectives.org.

"John Frame on Just War Theory." Posted at http://triablogue.blogspot.com/2004/06/ john-frame-on-just-war-theory.html.

Letter on Anti-Semitism and Religious Relativism. *Biblical Archaeology Review* 17, 4 (July–August 1991): 18–19.

"Meanings of 'Racism' and Some Evaluations" (2001). Available at http://www. reformedperspectives.org and http://www.frame-poythress.org..

"The Medical Model Revisited" (1999). On counseling. Available at http://www. reformedperspectives.org and http://www.frame-poythress.org.

"Minorities and the Reformed Churches" (2003). Available at http://www.reformed perspectives.org and http://www.frame-poythress.org.

"Must We Always Tell the Truth?" *Christian Culture* (September 2005): 3–4, and at http://www.frame-poythress.org.

"No Moral Justification." Letter to *Orlando Sentinel* on Terri Schiavo case, published October 24, 2003.

"No Place to Hide Our Head: The Problem of Homelessness" (2002). Available at http://www.reformedperspectives.org.

"Nursing Homes and the Fifth Commandment." *Christian Culture* (August 2002): 2.

"Oaths and Slang" (2001). Available at http://www.reformedperspectives.org and http://www.frame-poythress.org.

"The Other Shoe: Copyright and the Responsible Use of Technology." *Antithesis* 2, 4 (July–August 1991): 10–12. Posted at http://www.reformedperspectives.org; at Applelinks, http://www.applelinks.com/articles/2002/04/20020417131622. shtml; and at http://www.frame-poythress.org.

"Pastor's Page." *Life at New Life* (September–October 1984).

"Rebellion of the Heart." *Life at New Life* (January–February 1985): 1.

Response to "What Was It Like?" *New Horizons* 10, 5 (May 1989): 2–3. Comments on a war experience.

Review of *A Serrated Edge: A Brief Defense of Biblical Satire and Trinitarian Skylark-ing*, by Douglas Wilson, with reply by Wilson (2007). On the use of satire, strong language. Available at http://www.dougwils.com/index.asp?Action=A rchivesByTopic&TopicID=75 and at http://www.frame-poythress.org.

"Toward a Theology of the State." *WTJ* 51, 2 (Fall 1989): 199–226. Like "Men and Women in the Image of God," this article had to be heavily revised. The new version is in *DCL*, 593–602. Posted at http://www.thirdmill.org.

"When in the Course of Human Events Does Civil Disobedience Become Neces-sary?" (1999). Available at http://www.reformedperspectives.org and http:// www.frame-poythress.org.

"Who Owns Palestine?" *Christian Culture* (June 2002): 2.

CULTURE

1. General

I am an amateur (classical) musician, and I love movies and plays. So I have had some interest in the "Christ and Culture" discussions, favoring Abraham Kuyper's "transformationalism" over Luther's "two kingdoms." This commitment seems to me to follow simply from 1 Corinthians 10:31, that whatever we do should be done to the glory of God. That certainly includes culture. "Is Natural Revelation Sufficient to Govern Culture?" gives you my main argument, and this is amplified at various places in my *The Doctrine of the Christian Life*, especially chaps. 45–49.

"Foreword" to *The Road from Eden: Studies in Christianity and Culture*, by John Barber. Palo Alto, CA: Academica Press, 2008, xiii–xv.

"Is Natural Revelation Sufficient to Govern Culture?" *Christian Culture* (August 2006): 1–3.

"The Local Church and Cultural Transformation." *Nine Marks Journal*, print and Web versions (November–December 2007). Available at http://www.frame-poythress.org.

"A Response to *Redeeming the Arts*." *Creative Spirit* 4, 2 (2005): 19–21. Available at http://www.frame-poythress.org.

Review of *Idols for Destruction: The Conflict of Christian Faith and American Culture*, by Herbert Schlossberg. *Presbyterian Journal* 43 (June 6, 1984): 10.

Review of *Idols for Destruction: The Conflict of Christian Faith and American Culture*, by Herbert Schlossberg. *WTJ* 46, 2 (Fall 1984): 438–44. A longer version of the above.

"Should Christians Join the Cultural Elite?" (2003). Available at http://www.reformedperspectives.org and http://www.frame-poythress.org.

2. Education, Christian Schools

Our children have been in public schools, Christian schools, and home schools. So I've had many occasions to reflect on the benefits and liabilities of each. In general, I still think that homeschooling, done right, does the best job of teaching children in a God-saturated environment (Deut. 6:6–9). But that is not for everybody, and we need to accept and help believers who are called to use the other alternatives. My basic argument is in "Christians and Education."

"Are the Reformed Creeds Worth Keeping in Schools?" *The Outlook* 32 (January 1982): 7–9, and (February 1982): 6–9. This was part of my controversy with disciples of the philosopher Herman Dooyeweerd. See "The Word of God and the AACS" above under section 2 of "Theology," and also *The Amsterdam Philosophy* under section 6 of "Apologetics." Some articles below were also part of the same discussion: "Church Creeds and Christian Schools,"

"Constitutional Revision in the NUCS," "The Quiet Crisis in the Christian Schools," and "School Subscription to Church Creeds."

"Christian Schools" (2002). Available at http://www.reformedperspectives.org and http://www.frame-poythress.org.

"Christians and Education: Are Charter Schools the Answer?" (2002). Available at http://www.reformedperspectives.org.

"Church Creeds and Christian Schools." *Calvinist Contact* 1446 (March 4, 1974): 1, 5. See comment above under "Are the Reformed Creeds Worth Keeping in Schools?"

"Constitutional Revision in the NUCS: Counting the Cost." *Christian Educators Journal* 11, 4 (May 1972): 22–23. Also published as "Will the NUCS Remain Christian?" in *Presbyterian Guardian*. See comment above under "Are the Reformed Creeds Worth Keeping in Schools?"

"The Quiet Crisis in the Christian Schools." *Presbyterian Guardian* 41 (April 1972): 56–57. See comment above under "Are the Reformed Creeds Worth Keeping in Schools?"

"School Subscription to Church Creeds." *Christian Home and School* 51 (November 1972): 9–10. See comment above under "Are the Reformed Creeds Worth Keeping in Schools?"

3. Films

I've enjoyed movies all my life. I once thought I could "moonlight" as a film reviewer, but that was not to be. In any case, some of my reviews are available (mostly from around 1993) in the titles below. I try to find theological themes in films, and usually, I think, I am successful.

Review of *The Apostle* (2002). Available at http://www.reformedperspectives.org.

Review of *Shadowlands*. *Open Book* 20 (March 1994): 1–2.

"Should Christians Go to Movies?" *Christian Culture* (May 2003): 2–3. Chapter from *Theology at the Movies*, below.

Theology at the Movies. Privately published and distributed, 1994. Posted at http://www.frame-poythress.org. Excerpts posted at http://www.reformedperspectives.org in 2002: "Moving Pictures: Theologizing at the Movies," "Should Christians Go to Movies?" and "Questions to Ask of Films."

Miscellaneous

"What's the Faculty Reading?" *BookMarks* 2, 3 (April 2005): 1.

Sermons (Written)

Many of these are available at http://www.frame-poythress.org.

"1 Corinthians 1–6." Series of 30 sermons (mostly chapel talks).

"2 Peter 3: Grow in Grace"

"The Bible on the Problem of Evil"

"Euthanasia"

"Evangelism to Muslims"

"Evil"

"The Failure of Non-Christian Ethics"

"Galatians 3: A Dialogue"

"Gentleness in the Pastorate"

"God and the War"

"The God of Thanksgiving"

"God with Us"

"God's Gift of Time"

"How to Believe in God in the 2000s." Three sermons.

"Immanuel"

"John 5"

"Keeping Your Elders Happy" (Heb. 13:17)

"Marriage as Unjust Suffering"

"Maximum Christianity" (1 Cor. 9)

"Mixed Marriages" (1 Peter 3:1–6)

"Preservation" (2 Peter 3)

"Psalm 50"

"Reformation Day"

"Savior of the Crushed" (Isa. 57:15)

"Shouting for Joy" (Ps. 98)

"Why Should I Vote?"

"Widen Your Hearts"

"Working Together"

"Worship and the Reformation Gospel"

Audio and Video Materials

1. General

"The Comprehensive Covenant Lordship of Christ" (2004). Interview by Ligon Duncan on radio program. Audiobook on tape.

2. Theology—General, Multi-Subject

Foundations of Systematic Theology. Taped course. Grand Rapids: Institute for Theological Studies, 2008.

Interview by Bill Feltner on *Salvation Belongs to the Lord* for *His People* radio program. Carson City, NV: Pilgrim Radio, 2006.

Interview by Don and Nick Wight on Apologetics, the Church, and Open Theism for *Christ the King* podcast and radio show (2008). Available at their Web site at http://cdn3.libsyn.com/christtheking/episode2_low.mp3?nvb=20080901 125951&nva=20080902125951&t=0baec7acf73ab92f988ce. Contact calvary comm@vcn.com.

Systematic Theology 1: Scripture and God. Course for RTS Virtual. Available on RTS iTunes.

Understanding Theology. Audio course. Philadelphia: Westminster Media, 1976.

3. Theological Introduction, Method, Structure

The Doctrine of the Knowledge of God. Course taught at Westminster Theological Seminary, Philadelphia. Westminster Media, 1990(?).

The Doctrine of the Knowledge of God. Chapter 1 of my book read by someone other than me. Available at http://www.monergism.com.

Lecture on "Machen's Warrior Children." Probably given at Auburn Avenue Presbyterian Church, Monroe, LA, in 2003 or 2004. Available at http://www. monergism.com.

4. Word of God, Scripture

"Antithesis and the Doctrine of Scripture." Inaugural lecture delivered on receipt of the J. D. Trimble Chair of Systematic Theology and Philosophy, 2006. Available from RTS/Orlando.

"Christ and Community: People of the Book." Philadelphia: Westminster Media, 1977. Available through Reformed Theological Seminary libraries. Cassette BS480.F72 1977. Location: Jackson.

"Inerrancy: An Unbiblical Concept?" Audiobook on tape. Philadelphia: Westminster Media, 1979. Available through Reformed Theological Seminary libraries. Cassette 4600. Location: Jackson.

"Understanding Revelation." Philadelphia: Westminster Media, 1976.

5. Doctrine of God

Interview on *No Other God*. CDR Radio Network. Call 1–800–333–0601 for information.

Interviews on *Salvation Belongs to the Lord* and *No Other God*, with Brent Siddall of Trans-World Radio. Available in *The Collected Works of John Frame* CD-ROM/DVD set, vol. 1 (2008).

"Open Theism." Charlotte, NC: RTS Virtual, 2001. Lecture on audiocassette. Available through Reformed Theological Seminary libraries. Audio BT131.F73 2001.

"Sickness, Responsibility, and Ability." Sermon. Available at http://www.sermon audio.com/search.asp?speakerOnly=true&currSection=sermonsspeaker&k eyword=Dr%2E%5EJohn%5EM%2E%5EFrame.

6. Theological Education

"Going to Seminary." Interview with W. Ryan Burns at Reformed Theological Seminary Orlando, July 25, 2008. Features me talking about the pros and cons of a seminary education—along with some organ playing. Available at the Going to Seminary Web site at http://www.goingtoseminary.com/frame/.

7. Apologetics—General

Apologetics. Course for RTS Virtual Campus. Available on RTS iTunes.

The Doctrine of the Knowledge of God. Course taught at Westminster Theological Seminary, Philadelphia, 1990(?). Deals with epistemology, apologetic method, philosophy. Available from Westminster Media.

Understanding Apologetics. Course taught at Westminster Theological Seminary. Philadelphia: Westminster Media, 1976. Including Aristotle and Plotinus; early Christian thought vs. the philosophers; Greek philosophy vs. Christianity; Origen, Athanasius, Augustine. Available through Reformed Theological Seminary libraries. Cassette BR128.G8.F73 1976. Location: Jackson.

Understanding Apologetics: Roman Catholic Theology. Course taught at Westminster Theological Seminary, with guest lecturer Robert B. Strimple. Philadelphia: Westminster Media, 1976. Available at http://www.worldcat.org/oclc/14179210&referer=b.ief_results.

8. Apologetic Method

Apologetics and You. Southern Baptist Theological Seminary: Southern Apologetics Society, 2004.

Debate between John A. [i.e., H.] Gerstner and John Frame. N.P.: 1972. Available at http://www.worldcat.org/oclc/20183200&referer=brief_results.

The Doctrine of the Knowledge of God. A chapter from my book read by someone other than me. Available at http://www.monergism.com."How Does an Unbeliever 'Know God'?" Panel discussion featuring Grady Spires, John M. Frame, and Henry Krabbendam. From Jubilee Conference 1979: Interpreting God's Infallible Word. Philadelphia: Westminster Media, 1979. Available at http://www.worldcat.org/oclc/8996459&referer=brief_results.

"Presuppositional Apologetics." Chapter from *Five Views of Apologetics*, read by someone other than me. Available at http://www.monergism.com.

"Presuppositional Apologetics." Second article. Available at http://www.monergism.com.

"Presuppositional Apologetics." Discussion for Converse with Scholars online forum. Reclaiming the Mind Ministries, 2006. Available at http://www.reclaimingthemind.org/content/files/CWS/johnframepresuppositionalapologetics.mp3.

"Presuppositions." Chapter of *CVT*, read by someone other than me. Available at http://www.monergism.com.

9. Philosophy

The Doctrine of the Knowledge of God. Course taught at Westminster Theological Seminary, Philadelphia. Westminster Media, 1990(?).

History of Philosophy and Christian Thought. Course for RTS Virtual. Available through RTS iTunes.

Understanding Apologetics. Course taught at Westminster Theological Seminary. Philadelphia: Westminster Media, 1976. Including Aristotle and Plotinus; early Christian thought vs. the philosophers; Greek philosophy vs. Christianity; Origen, Athanasius, Augustine. Available through Reformed Theological Seminary libraries.

10. Church—Unity

Lecture on Church Unity (based on *ER*). Presented at Auburn Avenue Presbyterian Church, Monroe, LA, in 2003 or 2004.

11. Worship

"Christian Worship Music: Is It Postmodern?" Lecture presented at Southern Baptist Theological Seminary Worship Conference. Audiobook on CD. Louisville, KY: SBTS, 2004. Available at http://www.monergism.com.

Interview on Worship with David Vaughn. KSIV Radio, St. Louis (February 20, 2002). Call 314–961–2915 for information.

Lectures on Worship for Servanthood Class at Northland: A Church Distributed Northland Worship School, 2002, 2003, 2008.

"Music and Salvation: Why Christians Should Sing." Audiobook on tape. Mt. Olive, MS: Mt. Olive Tape Library, 1975. Available through Reformed Theological Seminary libraries (Cassette BR115.M8.F72, Location: Jackson). Also at SermonAudio.com, http://www.sermonaudio.com/search.asp?speakerOnly=true&currSection=sermonsspeaker&keyword=Dr%2E%5EJohn%5EM%2E%5EFrame.

"Music and Worship." With Wes King. Sound recording. Available through Reformed Theological Seminary libraries. Cassette BV290.F73 2001. Location: Jackson.

Reformed Conference on Church Music. Sound recording. Philadelphia: National Christian Publishers, 1978. Available through Reformed Theological Seminary libraries. Cassette ML3001.R44 1978. Location: Jackson.

"Worshiping God's Way," Parts 1 and 2. Presented at Southern Baptist Theological Seminary Worship Conference. Available at http://www.monergism.com.

12. Other

Interview on Redemptive-Historical Preaching with Gene Cook for *The Narrow Mind* online broadcast, October 2, 2006. Available at Unchainedradio.com or contact GCJR@Verizon.Net.

13. Ethics—General, Multi-Subject

Pastoral and Social Ethics. Course for RTS Virtual.

14. Ethical Method, Structure of Decisions

Making Biblical Decisions, Parts 1 and 2. Video course for Third Millennium Ministries. Available at http://www.thirdmill.org.

Sickness, Responsibility, and Ability. Sermon. Available at http://www.sermonaudio.
com/search.asp?speakerOnly=true&currSection=sermonsspeaker&keyword
=Dr%2E%5EJohn%5EM%2E%5EFrame.

15. Ethical Issues

Sexual and Ethical Conflicts in Modern Medicine. Audio recording of Northeast
Medical Ethics Conference featuring Hilton Pack Terrell, John M. Frame,
Barrett L. Mosbacker, John Jefferson Davis, Ronald W. Reed, Lewis Hicks, and
Rev. Charles McConnell. Sponsored by Forum for Biblical Ethics in Medi-
cine. Florence, SC: Journal of Biblical Ethics in Medicine, 1990. Available
through Reformed Theological Seminary libraries. Cassette R724.N67 1990.
Location: Jackson.

Toward a Christian Politics (1982). Audiobook on tape.

What Is Holiness? Sermon. Mt. Olive Tape Library, 2005. Available at http://www.
sermonaudio.com/search.asp?speakerOnly=true&currSection=sermonsspe
aker&keyword=Dr%2E%5EJohn%5EM%2E%5EFrame.

16. Miscellaneous, Unknown

Graduate Club Forum. Southern Baptist Theological Seminary, 2004.

Course Materials: Syllabi, Lecture Outlines, Study Guides

Apologetic Method (2002). Lecture outline. Available at http://www.reformed
perspectives.org.

Apologetics. Course syllabus.

Christian Apologetics (1994). Lecture outlines for church Sunday school course.

Christianity and the Great Debates (1977). Lecture outline on history of philosophy,
apologetics.

Contemporary Apologetics (1981). Study guide and lecture outline.

Cornelius Van Til (2000). Lecture outline.

The Doctrine of the Christian Life (1979). Lecture outline with study guide. Preliminary draft of my 2008 book of the same title. After 2000, called Pastoral
and Social Ethics (see below). Latest version is an outline of my book DCL.
Available at http://www.thirdmill.org. Course syllabus also available.

The Doctrine of God. Outline of my book of this title, with study guide.

The Doctrine of the Knowledge of God (1977). Lecture outline. First draft of my 1987 book of the same title. See also "*DKG* for Apologetics," at http://www. reformedperspectives.org, which covers the apologetic sections of the book. Study guide available.

The Doctrine of the Word of God (1978). Lecture outline. Will probably be reflected in my forthcoming book of this title. Available at http://www.thirdmill.org. Study guide available.

History of Epistemology (2000). Lecture outline. Course syllabus also available.

History of Philosophy and Christian Thought (2003). Course syllabus and lecture outline.

"How to Study for My Courses." Reproduced by Westminster Theological Seminary, 1975. Revised many times after.

Integrating Theology with Life (1983). Lecture outline.

"Let's Keep the Picture Fuzzy" (1985). Addition to Thoughts on Theonomy (see below).

Modern Views of God. Lecture outline and course syllabus.

Modern Views of Revelation and Scripture. Lecture outline and course syllabus.

Old Testament Survey (1987). Lecture outlines for adult Sunday school course.

Pastoral and Social Ethics. Lecture outline, course syllabus, and study guide.

Problems of Apologetics (2002). Lecture outline. Available at http://www.reformed perspectives.org.

The Public Worship of God (1982). Lecture outlines for worship course at New Life Presbyterian Church, Escondido, CA. Anticipates my later books on worship.

Review of *Turn Back the Night*, by Stephen Lawhead (1987). Lecture outline. On culture.

Science and General Culture (1984). Lecture outline.

The Shorter Catechism (1988). Lecture outlines for adult Sunday school course.

Studies in Modern Theology (1983). Lecture outline.

Systematic Theology 1: Scripture and God. Course syllabus and study guides.

The Thought of Cornelius Van Til (2003). Basically an outline of my book *CVT*. Course syllabus also available.

Thoughts on Theonomy (1984). Lecture outline.

Topics in Apologetics (2008). Lecture outline and study guide.

Worship. For a church class on worship. Follows my *WST*.

RECOMMENDED RESOURCES

JOHN M. FRAME

In my annotated Bibliography in this volume, I have tried to give some indication of how somebody who is unfamiliar with my work might start to get acquainted with it. Here I gather those recommendations and others, suggesting a reading program. I use the same topical structure as in the Bibliography and in the festschrift itself. I place the titles in a suggested order for study, rather than alphabetically. If you're interested in starting with what is most basic and moving on from there, begin with the first title, then read the second, and so on. Unless otherwise indicated, the titles are by me.

As I mentioned in the Bibliography, I expect all my writings to be included in *The Collected Works of John M. Frame*. They can also be found in other sources; see below.

INTRODUCTORY

Torres, Joseph E. "John Frame." http://en.wikipedia.org/wiki/John_Frame. The author has also written an article for this volume.

"Reflections of a Lifetime Theologian." Interview by Andrew Sandlin. *Christian Culture* (April–May 2008): 1–8. Also in the present volume.

"A Primer on Perspectivalism" (2008). http://www.frame-poythress.org.

Torres, Joseph E. "Multiperspectivalism." http://en.wikipedia.org/wiki/Multiperspectivalism.

"Introduction to the Reformed Faith" (1999). http://www.reformedperspectives.org and http://www.frame-poythress.org.

Perspectives on the Word of God. Eugene, OR: Wipf and Stock, 1999. A rather short book about Scripture and ethics.

THEOLOGY

1. Nature and Method

"Studying Theology as a Servant of Jesus." *Reformation and Revival* 11, 1 (Winter 2002): 45–69. Thoughts for people entering seminary.

"In Defense of Something Close to Biblicism." *WTJ* 59 (1997): 269–318. With replies by David Wells and Richard Muller and a further reply by me. Also published as an appendix to *CWM*. I consider this one of my most important articles. It should be taken together with "Muller on Theology" and "Traditionalism." In these articles I set my approach over against a pervasive trend in evangelical and Reformed theology: the tendency to base theological judgments not directly on Scripture, but on an analysis of historical or contemporary thought. On the contrary, I advocate a strong form of the principle *sola Scriptura* (the sufficiency of Scripture), which was once common in Protestant theology, but has in the last century been eclipsed.

"Muller on Theology." *WTJ* 56 (Spring 1994): 133–51. See my comments about "In Defense of Something Close to Biblicism," above.

"Traditionalism" (1999). http://www.reformedperspectives.org and http://www.frame-poythress.org. Published in two parts in *Chalcedon Report* (October 2001): 15–19 and (November 2001): 434–35. See my comments above, under "In Defense of Something Close to Biblicism."

"Machen's Warrior Children." In *Alister E. McGrath and Evangelical Theology*, edited by Sung Wook Chung. Grand Rapids: Baker, 2003. I argue here that in American Reformed circles since 1936, too much time and effort has been spent on unedifying and divisive controversies.

The Doctrine of the Knowledge of God. Phillipsburg, NJ: Presbyterian and Reformed, 1987. With study guide. Translated into Indonesian (2000). This is my first published book, attempting to formulate a theory of knowledge based on Scripture, and developing ideas for theological and apologetic method. This is a fundamental source for "theology as application" and for triperspectivalism. I reply to Mark Karlberg's review of this book in Appendix B of *DG*.

2. Doctrine of the Word of God, Scripture

"No Scripture, No Christ." *Synapse II* 1, 1 (January 1972): 1. Also in *Presbyterian Guardian* 48 (January 1979): 10–11. Also at http://www.frame-poythress.org.

Perspectives on the Word of God. Phillipsburg, NJ: Presbyterian and Reformed, 1990. Reprinted by Eugene, OR: Wipf and Stock, 1999. In Russian translation by Odessa, Ukraine: Godeistvize, 2002. A short book, dealing with the Word of God, Scripture, and ethics.

"Scripture Speaks for Itself." In *God's Inerrant Word*, edited by John W. Montgomery, 178–200. Minneapolis: Bethany Fellowship, 1974. Also at http://www.frame-poythress.org.A survey of Scripture's testimony about itself.

"Antithesis and the Doctrine of Scripture." Inaugural lecture on receipt of the J. D. Trimble chair of systematic theology and philosophy. http://www.frame-poythress.org.

"Doctrine of the Word of God." Lecture outline. In *Collected Works* 1.

"Scripture and God." Audio recordings of lectures. In *Collected Works* 1.

Doctrine of the Word of God. Phillipsburg, NJ: P&R Publishing, forthcoming, probably around 2012.

3. Doctrine of God

"God." For *Zondervan Pictorial Bible Encyclopedia*. Completed, awaiting publication.

"The Wonder of God Over Us and With Us." *Reformed Quarterly* (Winter 2000): 12–13, 17. Also at http://www.frame-poythress.org.

Doctrine of God. Phillipsburg, NJ: P&R Publishing, 2002. This is the second of my Theology of Lordship series. I have tried here to present a full exposition of the Bible's teaching about God. This book contains the fullest exegetical argument for my emphasis on divine lordship.

No Other God. Phillipsburg, NJ: P&R Publishing, 2001. Translated into Korean by Sung-Kook Hong (Seoul: Christian Literature Crusade, 2005). Critique of open theism.

"Scripture and God." Audio recordings of lectures. In *Collected Works* 1.

4. Covenant and Justification

"Reflections of a Lifetime Theologian." Interview by Andrew Sandlin. Also in the present volume.

5. Theological Education

"Proposal for a New Seminary." *Journal of Pastoral Practice* 2, 1 (Winter 1978): 10–17. Earlier version of "Case Study: Proposals for a New North American

Mode." In *Missions and Theological Education in World Perspective*, edited by Harvie M. Conn and Sam Rowen, 369–86. Farmington, MI: Associates of Urbansu, 1984. The original "Proposal," with some updates, can be found at http://www.frame-poythress.org. Also in *Reformed Theology* (Korean). Gardena, CA: Reformed Presbyterian Seminary, 1992.

"Learning at Jesus' Feet: A Case for Seminary Education" (pamphlet). Orlando: RTS, 2003. Also at http://www.frame-poythress.org.

"Studying Theology as a Servant of Jesus" (pamphlet). Orlando: RTS Bookstore, 2000. Also at http://www.frame-poythress.org.

6. Other Topics

Salvation Belongs to the Lord. Phillipsburg, NJ: P&R Publishing, 2006. My mini-systematics.

APOLOGETICS

1. Apologetic Method and Epistemology

"Presuppositionalism." In Campbell-Jack, Campbell, et al. *New Dictionary of Apologetics*, 575–78. Leicester, UK: IVP, 2006. A short introduction to the subject.

"Presuppositional Apologetics." In *Five Views of Apologetics*, edited by Steve Cowan. Grand Rapids: Zondervan, 2000. One major article, four replies, and a concluding article.

"Epistemological Perspectives and Evangelical Apologetics." 1982 lecture. *Bulletin of the Evangelical Philosophical Society* 7 (1984): 1–7. Also at http://www.frame-poythress.org. Relates presuppositionalism to multiperspectivalism.

Apologetics to the Glory of God: An Introduction. Phillipsburg, NJ: P&R Publishing, 1994. Translated into Indonesian (2000). Translated into Chinese China Evangelical Seminary Press, 2003. Translated into Japanese by Kunio Sakurai, Tokyo Christian University (Publication Committee of the Presbyterian Church of Japan, 1998; also Tokyo: Word of Life Press, 2006). Translated into Korean by Ji-Hyun Jun (Seoul: Yungeum Press, 1997). This is my main formulation of my apologetic approach.

The Doctrine of the Knowledge of God. Phillipsburg, NJ: Presbyterian & Reformed, 1987. With study guide. My first published book, in which I attempt to set forth a biblical theory of knowledge, with implications for apologetic and theological method. I reply to Mark Karlberg's review of this book in Appendix B of *DG*.

2. Cornelius Van Til

I studied with the great apologist and theologian Cornelius Van Til at Westminster Seminary from 1961 to 1964. I still consider myself his disciple, but a critical disciple. I list below some of the more important works of Van Til (in pedagogical order) and then the writings of mine that introduce my own understanding and analysis of Van Til. Most of Van Til's writings, and many audio lectures, can be found on CD-ROM, *The Works of Cornelius Van Til*, available in Libronix format.

a. Van Til's Writings

"Why I Believe in God." Philadelphia: Committee on Christian Education for the Orthodox Presbyterian Church, 1948. Available today at http://www.reformed. org/apologetics/index.html?mainframe=/apologetics/why_I_believe_cvt. html. Also in Bahnsen, Greg. *Van Til's Apologetic*, 121–43. Phillipsburg, NJ: P&R Publishing, 1998. This is a pamphlet that presents Van Til's basic apologetic in a striking way, as a quasi-dialogue with a secularist. Grabs the reader, but perhaps raises more questions than it answers.

The Defense of Christianity and My Credo. Nutley, NJ: Presbyterian and Reformed, 1972. Short expositions of Van Til's main themes.

Christian Apologetics. 2nd ed. Phillipsburg, NJ: P&R Publishing, 2003. This is, I think, the most concise, well-organized, and accessible of Van Til's many books.

Bahnsen, Greg. *Van Til's Apologetic*. Phillipsburg, NJ: P&R Publishing, 1998. This book focuses on Van Til's apologetic, while my *Cornelius Van Til* looks more broadly at Van Til's whole theology. Bahnsen is less critical of Van Til than I am. This book is valuable, both for Bahnsen's analysis and for many writings of Van Til that are included.

b. Frame's Writings about Van Til

"Van Til, His Simplicity and Profundity." *Update* (March 1986): 1–2. Also at http:// www.frame-poythress.org. Probably the simplest of my descriptions of Van Til.

"Van Til, Cornelius." In Campbell-Jack, Campbell, et al. *New Dictionary of Apologetics*, 739–40. Leicester, UK: IVP, 2006. Also at http://www.frame-poythress. org. A bit longer than the first title, but also concise.

"Van Til Reconsidered" (2005). http://www.frame-poythress.org. Summarizes my big book on Van Til (below).

Cornelius Van Til: An Analysis of His Thought. Phillipsburg, NJ: P&R Publishing, 1995. Translated into Indonesian (Surabaya: Penerbit Momentum, 2002). In this book I have tried to deal comprehensively with Van Til, both as apologist and as theologian.

Van Til, The Theologian. Phillipsburg, NJ: Pilgrim Publications, 1976. Same as "The Problem of Theological Paradox." Also at http://www.netopia.geocities.com/ gtrammel/pages/view/index.nhtml, http://www.reformed.org, and http:// www.frame-poythress.org. Translated into French by André Coste, *La Revue Reformée* 167 (Janvier, 1991): 7–42. This long essay deals with Van Til's use of logic and paradox: he wants theology to be a system, but he opposes what he calls "deductive systems." I try to understand here what he means by that. In this article I also relate Van Til's thought to some of my own themes, such as theology as application.

3. Existence of God

"How to Believe in God in the 2000s." http://www.frame-poythress.org. A series of three sermons, dealing with presuppositions, natural revelation, and Scripture.

Chap. 4 of *Apologetics to the Glory of God: An Introduction.* Phillipsburg, NJ: P&R Publishing, 1995.

4. The Problem of Evil

"The Bible on the Problem of Evil" (1999). http://www.reformedperspectives.org and http://www.frame-poythress.org. Translated into Lithuanian, http://www. prizme.It/straipsiai/straips,php?action=view&id=422 (2004).

Chaps. 6, 7 of *Apologetics to the Glory of God.* Phillipsburg, NJ: P&R Publishing, 1994.

Chap. 9 of *The Doctrine of God.* Phillipsburg, NJ: P&R Publishing, 2002.

5. Philosophy

The Doctrine of the Knowledge of God. Phillipsburg, NJ: Presbyterian and Reformed, 1987. With study guide. My first published book, in which I attempt to set forth a biblical theory of knowledge, with implications for apologetic and theological method. I reply to Mark Karlberg's review of this book in Appendix B of *DG*, esp. 85–88.

"Greeks Bearing Gifts." In *Revolutions in Worldview*, edited by W. Andrew Hoffecker, 1–36. Phillipsburg, NJ: P&R Publishing, 2007. Critical survey of Greek religion and philosophy.

"History of Philosophy and Christian Thought." Audio recordings of lectures. Will be available in *Collected Works* 2, and can now be found at the iTunes University site of Reformed Theological Seminary.

The Church

1. Unity

"Guidelines for Church Union." *Presbyterian Journal* 42 (August 24, 1983): 8–10. Also at http://www.frame-poythress.org.

Evangelical Reunion: Denominations and the Body of Christ. Grand Rapids: Baker, 1991. Also at http://www.reformedperspectives.org and http://www.frame-poythress.org.

"Is Realignment a Biblical Option?" *New Horizons* 10, 6 (June–July 1989): 18. Also at http://www.frame-poythress.org.

2. Worship

Worship in Spirit and Truth. Phillipsburg, NJ: P&R Publishing, 1996. Translated into Hungarian (2002). Translated into Portuguese, *Em Espirito e em Verdade* (Sao Paulo: Editora Cultura Christa, 2006). My basic text on biblical worship.

Contemporary Worship Music: A Biblical Defense. Phillipsburg, NJ: P&R Publishing, 1997. Answering critics of the use of contemporary songs in worship.

The Doctrine of the Christian Life. Phillipsburg, NJ: P&R Publishing, 2008. The discussion of the first four commandments is especially relevant to worship.

"The Regulative Principle: Scripture, Tradition, and Culture." Debate with Darryl Hart on Warfield computer list. Published in hard copy by Westminster Campus Bookstore, 1998, edited by Charles R. Biggs. Also at http://www.frame-poythress.org. Hart and I are about as far apart as we can be on issues disputed within the Reformed community. He is a strong advocate of tradition and, I would say, traditionalism. This long debate is about worship, but also more generally about what it means to be Reformed.

"Ethics, Preaching, and Biblical Theology" (1999). http://www.reformedperspectives.org and http://www.frame-poythress.org. Some people think sermons should be wholly dedicated to narrating the history of redemption. These people often believe that preaching should not set forth moral obligations, or at least that we should never use Bible characters as moral examples. I disagree with these views and explain why in this article.

Ethics

1. General Principles

Perspectives on the Word of God. Phillipsburg, NJ: Presbyterian and Reformed, 1990. Reprinted by Eugene, OR: Wipf and Stock, 1999. Part 3 is a short introduction to Christian ethics.

Medical Ethics: Principles, Persons, and Problems. Phillipsburg, NJ: Presbyterian and Reformed, 1988. The first part of this book is a concise exposition of my perspectivalism as it applies to ethics.

"Pastoral and Social Ethics." Audio recordings of lectures. In *Collected Works* 3. Based on the book immediately below. Lecture outline also available, on the same disk.

The Doctrine of the Christian Life. Phillipsburg, NJ: P&R Publishing, 2008. This is my comprehensive account of ethics.

2. Abortion

"Ministries of Mercy to the Unborn" (1999). http://www.reformedperspectives.org and http://www.frame-poythress.org. Summary treatment.

Report of the Committee to Study the Matter of Abortion. In *Minutes of the General Assembly of the Orthodox Presbyterian Church* (1971). Also published in pamphlet form. Also at http://www.opc.org. I was principal author, with much help from other committee members.

Doctrine of the Christian Life, 717–32. Phillipsburg, NJ: P&R Publishing, 2008.

3. Other Subjects

On other ethical topics, consult *Doctrine of the Christian Life*. Phillipsburg, NJ: P&R Publishing, 2008.

Culture

"Is Natural Revelation Sufficient to Govern Culture?" *Christian Culture* (August 2006): 1–3. Also at http://www.frame-poythress.org.

Chaps. 45–49 of *Doctrine of the Christian Life*. Phillipsburg, NJ: P&R Publishing, 2008.

Index of Names

Index of Subjects

Index of Scripture

CONTRIBUTORS

James N. Anderson (BEng, PhD, PhD, University of Edinburgh) is assistant professor of theology and apologetics at Reformed Theological Seminary (RTS) in Charlotte, North Carolina, and an ordained minister, having served at Charlotte Chapel in Edinburgh, Scotland. He holds PhDs in computer simulation and philosophical theology from the University of Edinburgh.

Before joining RTS, Dr. Anderson was engaged in postdoctoral research at the University of Edinburgh for ten years. A revision of his second doctoral dissertation was published under the title *Paradox in Christian Theology: An Analysis of Its Presence, Character, and Epistemic Status* (Paternoster, 2007).

In his spare time Dr. Anderson maintains the Web site http://www.vantil.info, dedicated to the works and influence of Cornelius Van Til, which he launched in 2002. He is married to Catriona and has two young daughters, Eilidh and Erin.

John H. Armstrong (BA, Wheaton College; MA, Wheaton College Graduate School; DMin, Luther Rice Seminary) is president of ACT 3: Advancing the Christian Tradition in the Third Millennium (www.act3online.com). After serving as a pastor for twenty years, Dr. Armstrong started ACT 3 as an international itinerant ministry to leaders and churches. The ministry has produced thousands of articles and features as well as conferences on and for the missional church.

John is the author/editor of twelve books and an adjunct professor of evangelism at the Wheaton College Graduate School. His special academic interests include Christian history, ecumenism, and the mission of the church. He is particularly interested in helping Protestant churches recover their classical foundation in the ancient creeds and writings of the fathers, and their connection to the sixteenth-century Reformers, with a strong forward focus upon the globalization of the modern church.

John is a minister in the Reformed Church in America and has been married to Anita since 1970. He has two married children and two grandchildren.

John J. Barber (MAR, Westminster Theological Seminary; MDiv, Yale University; PhD, Whitefield Theological Seminary) is the pastor of Cornerstone Presbyterian Church in Palm Beach Gardens, Florida. Dr. Barber is ordained in the Presbyterian Church in America. He has served as an adjunct professor of humanities and Western European history at Palm Beach Atlantic University and taught courses in humanities and the Bible at Belhaven College. Prior to that, Dr. Barber was theological editor for Campus Crusade for Christ's New Life publications and wrote several books with Dr. Bill Bright.

Dr. Barber is the author of numerous articles on Christianity and culture, as well as several books on the topic, including *Earth Restored: Calling the Church to a New Christian Activism* (Christian Focus, 2002), *America Restored* (Coral Ridge, 2002), and *The Road from Eden: Studies in Christianity and Culture* (Academica Press, 2008). His particular scholarly interests include the Christian roots of the Italian Renaissance and the history of American evangelicalism.

When he can find time, Dr. Barber loves surfing, scuba diving, gardening, and weight lifting. He is married to Bonnie, and they have two teenage children, Paul and Haley.

Stephen W. Brown (STB, Boston University; LittD; LHD) is professor of preaching and pastoral ministry at Reformed Theological Seminary, Orlando, Florida, where he has taught for more than fifteen years. He is ordained in the Presbyterian Church in America. In addition, Steve is president and Bible teacher on the national radio program *Key Life* and host of the talk show *Steve Brown, Etc.*

Before his radio ministry and becoming part of the RTS faculty, Steve pastored churches in Massachusetts and Florida for more than twenty-five years. He has authored thirteen books, has written articles for numerous magazines, and serves on the boards of National Religious Broadcasters and Harvest USA.

Steve and his wife, Anna, have two daughters and three granddaughters.

Robert C. (Ric) Cannada Jr. (MDiv, DMin, Reformed Theological Seminary) is chancellor and CEO of the Reformed Theological Seminary system of campuses. He has served at RTS since 1993 and as chancellor since 2004. Dr. Cannada provides leadership to five residential campuses located in Jackson, Mississippi; Orlando, Florida; Charlotte, North Carolina; Washington, DC; and Atlanta, Georgia; a degree-granting Virtual Campus (distance education) based in Charlotte; and three international Doctor of Ministry degree programs in Korea, Scotland, and Brazil. He is an ordained minister in the Presbyterian Church in America and has pastored churches in South Carolina, Arkansas, and Georgia. Immediately prior to joining RTS, Dr. Cannada served as senior pastor of First Presbyterian Church in Macon, Georgia.

Dr. Cannada and his wife, Rachel, have two children and six grandchildren, all living in Jackson, Mississippi.

Donald Collett (BA, Montana State University; MDiv, Westminster Theological Seminary California; PhD, University of St. Andrews) is assistant professor of Old Testament at Trinity Episcopal School for Ministry in Ambridge, Pennsylvania. His particular interests include theological hermeneutics, biblical theology, and philosophical theology.

Dr. Collett is married to Jamie, and they have two children, Jessica and Donnie. A native of Montana, he enjoys fly-fishing, elk hunting, and reading westerns.

D. Clair Davis (MA, Wheaton College; BD, Westminster Theological Seminary; DTh, University of Goettingen) is professor of church history and chaplain at Redeemer Seminary in Dallas, Texas. Prior to this he taught theology in the Wheaton Graduate School (1963–66), and church history and systematic theology at Westminster Theological Seminary in Philadelphia (1966–2004).

Dr. Davis has been a teaching elder in the Presbyterian Church in America since 1988, serving as associate pastor of New Life Churches in Glenside and Dresher, Pennsylvania. Since 1997 he has served on the PCA General Assembly's Committee on Mission to the World. He was formerly a minister in the Orthodox Presbyterian Church (1963–88). Dr. Davis's academic interests focus on the interaction between doctrine and life, hermeneutics, American Presbyterianism and revival, and Calvin's self-knowledge and God knowledge.

Dr. Davis's first wife, Lynn, died in 2003. He is now married to Carol, and they are enjoying exploring the role of ministry in the church together. He also delights in his four children: Erik, Jessica, Emily, and Marc. Dr. Davis follows the Green Bay Packers from afar, and enjoys the music of Dave Brubeck, exploring Hispanic culture at Cristo Rey Church in Dallas, Texas, and all things TexMex in the great Southwest. He is also enjoying reading John Frame's *DCL*.

William C. Davis (MA, Westminster Theological Seminary California; PhD, University of Notre Dame) is professor of philosophy at Covenant College and an adjunct professor of systematic theology at Reformed Theological Seminary. He has been teaching philosophy since 1992. His philosophical research has focused on the moral epistemology of the eighteenth-century Scottish philosopher Thomas Reid, most recently on Reid's ability to explain moral disagreement. Dr. Davis has also contributed to works on philosophy and popular culture (*The Lord of the Rings and Philosophy* and *The Chronicles of Narnia and Philosophy*, both edited by Gregory Bassham, et al.) and on apologetics (*Reason for the Hope Within*, edited by Michael J. Murray).

Bill has been married to Lynda for twenty-five years, and they have four children: Jonathan, Amy, Rachel, and Mark. When not playing the philosopher, he likes to run—slowly, but redeeming the time (sort of) by listening to philosophy lectures or sports talk radio.

William Edgar (Honors BA, Harvard University; MDiv, Westminster Theological Seminary; DTh, Université de Genève) is professor of apologetics at Westminster Theological Seminary in Philadelphia, where he has taught for twenty years. He is president of the Gospel and Culture Project and is ordained in the Presbyterian Church in America. He also directs the gospel-jazz band Renewal. Dr. Edgar was previously Professeur d'Apologétique at la Faculté Libre de Théologie Réformée, Aix-en-Provence, where he is currently Professeur Associé.

Dr. Edgar's scholarly interests include apologetics, theology, music aesthetics, and ethics. He is head of the Arts Network for the European Leadership Forum. He visits Asia regularly. He also sits on a number of

1104

boards, including the Huguenot Fellowship, the Institutional Review Board of Chestnut Hill Hospital, and Schloss Mittersil.

Dr. Edgar and his wife, Barbara, have two children and three grandchildren.

Carl F. Ellis Jr. (MA, Westminster Theological Seminary) is a faculty member of Redeemer Seminary in Dallas, Texas; dean of AltSem in Chattanooga, Tennessee; and president of Project Joseph, a Chattanooga-based ministry that seeks to equip the church for today's challenges. He is an ordained minister in the Presbyterian Church in America.

Previously, Mr. Ellis was dean of Intercultural Studies at Westminster Theological Seminary in Philadelphia (2006–9) and an adjunct faculty member at several schools, including The Center for Urban Theological Studies in Philadelphia, Pennsylvania; Covenant Theological Seminary in St. Louis, Missouri; Reformed Theological Seminary in Charlotte, North Carolina; Northpark Seminary in Chicago, Illinois; and the Bible Institute of South Africa, Cape Town. He has lectured and taught at numerous seminars and workshops throughout the United States and around the world.

Carl has authored five books, edited one, and published several articles in various periodicals. He lives in Chattanooga, Tennessee, and has thoroughly enjoyed his role as the father of two children, Carl III and Nicole.

John M. Frame (MDiv, Westminster Theological Seminary; MPhil, Yale University; DD, Belhaven College) is professor of systematic theology and philosophy at Reformed Theological Seminary in Orlando, Florida. He is an ordained minister of the Presbyterian Church in America. Previously, he taught at Westminster Theological Seminary in Philadelphia (1968–80) and Westminster Seminary California (1980–2000).

Dr. Frame has taught in the areas of theology, philosophy, ethics, and worship, and has written thirteen books and many articles in these areas. His major doctrinal series is A Theology of Lordship, which includes *The Doctrine of the Knowledge of God* (1987), *The Doctrine of God* (2002), *The Doctrine of the Christian Life* (2008), and *The Doctrine of the Word of God* (forthcoming). His *Collected Works* are being released on CD and DVD disks by P&R Publishing and Bits & Bytes, Inc. Many of his writings are also available online at http://www.frame-poythress.org.

Dr. Frame was pianist and worship leader at New Life Presbyterian Church, Escondido, California, from 1980 to 2000. He enjoys music, especially classical, and has also written a number of film reviews.

John and his wife, Mary, have five children, three married and living in California and Oregon, and two single and attending college.

Mark A. Garcia (MAR, Westminster Theological Seminary; PhD, University of Edinburgh) is pastor of Immanuel Orthodox Presbyterian Church in West Allegheny (Oakdale), Pennsylvania, in the Pittsburgh area. He also is a senior member of Wolfson College, Cambridge University, and was recently a visiting scholar at Cambridge in the Faculty of History, working as a theological researcher on the Minutes and Papers of the Westminster Assembly. He has enjoyed research fellowships in Geneva and Grand Rapids, Michigan, and was awarded a faculty scholarship by New College, University of Edinburgh.

The author of *Life in Christ: Union with Christ and Twofold Grace in Calvin's Theology* (Paternoster, 2008) and of various journal articles and reviews, Dr. Garcia has taught in the areas of systematic and historical theology for multiple campuses of Reformed Theological Seminary and Westminster Theological Seminary, and has lectured overseas in the United Kingdom, Spain, and Mexico. He is presently working on both an academic volume on the doctrine of Scripture and a trade book relating a biblical theology of the atonement to horrendous evils. He also continues to work with the Westminster Assembly Project.

Dr. Garcia and his wife, Jill, have four children—Adriana, Elisa, M. Andrew Jr., and Thomas—and reside in Coraopolis, Pennsylvania. His interests include the arts, reading, and explaining sports rules to his hopelessly perplexed children.

James H. Grant Jr. is a graduate of Reformed Theological Seminary in Orlando, Florida, and has been the pastor of First Baptist Church in Rossville, Tennessee, since 2003. Pastor Grant serves on the board of the Uganda Bible Institute, and is the author of *1 & 2 Thessalonians* in the Preaching the Word Series (Crossway, forthcoming). He and his wife, Brandy, have two children—Macy and Trey—and are expecting their third.

Howard Griffith (BA, University of Virginia; MDiv, Gordon-Conwell Theological Seminary; PhD, Westminster Theological Seminary) is assistant professor of systematic theology at Reformed Theological Seminary in Washington, DC. He is a minister in the Presbyterian Church in America and translator of Pierre Marcel's *A L'Ecole de Dieu* (*In God's School*; Wipf and Stock, 2009). Before joining the faculty of RTS in 2007, Dr. Griffith served twenty-three years as pastor of All Saints Reformed Presbyterian Church in Richmond, Virginia.

Dr. Griffith loves to enrich Reformed theology with redemptive-historical biblical exegesis. His passion is the doctrine of Christ.

He and his wife, Jackie, have five children—Alex, Abigail, Calvin, Graham, and Samuel—who live in northern Virginia. They enjoy family laughter, the Washington Redskins, and occasional travels to Europe.

Wayne Grudem (BA, Harvard University; MDiv, Westminster Theological Seminary; PhD, University of Cambridge) is research professor of Bible and theology at Phoenix Seminary in Phoenix, Arizona. Prior to this he taught for twenty years at Trinity Evangelical Divinity School in Deerfield, Illinois, where he was chairman of the Department of Biblical and Systematic Theology. He has published sixteen books, including *Systematic Theology* (Zondervan, 1994), *Recovering Biblical Manhood and Womanhood*, coedited with John Piper (Crossway, 1991, 2006), *The TNIV and the Gender-Neutral Bible Controversy*, coauthored with Vern Poythress (Broadman and Holman, 2004), *The First Epistle of Peter* (Tyndale NT Commentary Series; Eerdmans, 1988), and *Business for the Glory of God* (Crossway, 2003). He was also the general editor for the *ESV Study Bible* (Crossway, 2008).

Dr. Grudem is a past president of the Evangelical Theological Society, a cofounder and past president of the Council on Biblical Manhood and Womanhood, and a member of the Translation Oversight Committee for the English Standard Version of the Bible.

He and his wife, Margaret, have been married since 1969 and have three adult sons. The Grudems are members of Scottsdale Bible Church in Scottsdale, Arizona.

Paul Helm (MA, Oxford University) is a Teaching Fellow of Regent College, Vancouver, BC. Previously he taught there as J. I. Packer Professor of Philosophical Theology (2001–5) and before that as professor of the history and philosophy of religion, King's College, London (1993–2000). Prior to this, Prof. Helm was for many years a member of the Department of Philosophy, University of Liverpool. His books include *Eternal God* (Clarendon Press, 1988), *The Providence of God* (InterVarsity Press, 1994), *Faith with Reason* (Oxford, 2000), and *John Calvin's Ideas* (Oxford, 2006).

Paul is married to Angela, and they have five children, six grandchildren, and three tortoises.

John J. Hughes (BA, Vanderbilt University; ThM, Westminster Theological Seminary; PhD studies, University of Cambridge) is president of Bits & Bytes, Inc., and a full-time consultant for P&R Publishing. He has authored fourteen books, including *Bits, Bytes, & Biblical Studies: A Resource Guide for the Use of Computers in Biblical and Classical Studies* (Academie, 1987), *God's Word Complete Concordance* (with William D. Mounce; World, 1995), and over a dozen Bible software user guides. Mr. Hughes has contributed articles to *Nelson's Illustrated Bible Encyclopedia*, *The International Standard Bible Encyclopedia*, *Novum Testamentum*, the *Biblical Archaeology Review*, and the *Critical Review of Books in Religion*, and has served as an advisory board member and section editor for OUP's *Humanities Computing Yearbook*.

Previously, Mr. Hughes taught theology, New Testament, and Greek at Westmont College (1977–82), served as bivocational pastor of The Father's House (1996–2006), and chaired the Cross Currents Christian School board (1983–2006) in Whitefish, Montana, where he lives. His academic interests include apologetics, theology, New Testament studies, and World War II military history. His nonacademic interests include hiking, fishing, biking, and antelope hunting. He is a member of Faith Covenant Church (PCA) in Kalispell, Montana, where he teaches Sunday school and occasionally preaches.

John and his wife, Claire, have been married since 1968 and have three married sons, John, Ryan, and Allen, and two grandsons, Jack and Ryan.

Paxson H. Jeancake (BS, Furman University; MAR, Reformed Theological Seminary) is director of worship and arts at Valley Springs Presbyterian Church in Roseville, California, and the author of *The Art of Worship: Opening Our Eyes to the Beauty of the Gospel* (Wipf and Stock, 2006). He is also the founder of Rhythm of Worship, a ministry that seeks to serve the church and cultivate the creative process by offering musical resources, foundational teaching, and practical training. He and his wife, Allison, have recorded two worship projects: *Ascension* (2007) and *The Rhythm of Worship* (2003). Each recording is a collection of psalms, hymns, and original worship songs.

Paxson has been a guest lecturer at Reformed Theological Seminary and serves on the executive committee of the Worship Reformation Network, a national community of worship leaders with a common vision for biblical, Reformed, and gospel-driven worship. He has also served as a worship leader and consultant for Global Church Advancement and has led worship for a number of national conferences, including the 2008 Worship of God Conference, the 2007 Mercy Ministries Conference, and the 2006 General Assembly of the Presbyterian Church in America.

Paxson and Allison have two daughters, Laura Camille and Mallory. Paxson's other interests include triathlons and photography.

Dennis E. Johnson (MDiv, ThM, Westminster Theological Seminary; PhD, Fuller Theological Seminary) is professor of practical theology at Westminster Seminary California. He is a teaching elder in the Presbyterian Church in America and an associate pastor of New Life Presbyterian Church in Escondido, California. Before joining the faculty of Westminster Seminary California in 1982, he pastored Orthodox Presbyterian congregations in Fair Lawn, New Jersey, and Los Angeles, California.

Dr. Johnson is the author of *The Message of Acts in the History of Redemption* (P&R, 1997), *Triumph of the Lamb: A Commentary on Revelation* (P&R, 2001), *Let's Study Acts* (Banner of Truth, 2003), the notes on Hebrews in the *Reformation Study Bible* (P&R, 2005), and *Him We Proclaim: Preaching Christ from All the Scriptures* (P&R, 2007). He has coauthored (with Elyse Fitzpatrick) *Counsel from the Cross* (Crossway, 2009) and edited and contributed to *Heralds of the King: Christ-Centered Sermons in the Tradition of Edmund P. Clowney* (Crossway, 2009).

Dennis and his wife, Jane, have been married thirty-nine years. They are blessed with four adult children, two sons and two daughters (all married), and many grandchildren.

Peter R. Jones (MDiv, Gordon-Conwell Theological Seminary; ThM, Harvard Divinity School; PhD, Princeton Theological Seminary) is director

1109

of truthXchange (www.truthXchange.com) and adjunct professor of New Testament at Westminster Seminary California.

An ordained minister in the Presbyterian Church in America, he served as a professor/missionary in France for seventeen years and as a professor at Westminster Seminary California for eleven years. He is the author of several books, including *The Gnostic Empire Strikes Back* (P&R, 1992), *Spirit Wars* (Main Entry Editions, 1997), *Cracking Da Vinci's Code*, and, most recently, *The God of Sex* (Victor, 2006) and *Stolen Identity: The Conspiracy to Reinvent Jesus* (Victor, 2006).

Peter and his wife, Rebecca, have seven children and twelve grand-children.

Reggie M. Kidd (MAR & MDiv, Westminster Theological Seminary; PhD, Duke University) is professor of New Testament at Reformed Theological Seminary Orlando, where he has taught for twenty years. He teaches Paul's letters, worship, Hellenistic Greek, introduction to pastoral and theological studies, and a senior seminar.

Before joining the faculty at RTS Orlando, Dr. Kidd was pastor of worship at the Chapel Hill Bible Church, Chapel Hill, NC, and he has served on the board of elders and on the pastoral staff at Northland, A Church Distributed, Longwood, FL. He is currently ordained in the PCA.

His writings include *Wealth and Beneficence in the Pastoral Epistles: A "Bourgeois" Form of Early Christianity?* and *With One Voice: Discovering Christ's Song in Our Worship*. He is a columnist for Worship Leader Magazine.

He and his wife, Sharon, have three grown sons, Charlie, Bob, and Randy. Dr. Kidd enjoys cutting things with his samurai sword, and pretending to be, on any given day, B. B. King, J. S. Bach, Roger McGuinn, or Leo Kottke on the guitar.

Esther L. Meek (MA, Western Kentucky University; PhD, Temple University) is associate professor of philosophy at Geneva College in Beaver Falls (western Pennsylvania). Prior to coming to Geneva in 2004, she taught at Covenant Theological Seminary in St. Louis, Missouri. Her published work includes *Longing to Know: The Philosophy of Knowledge for Ordinary People* (Brazos, 2003) and, with Donald J. MacNair, *The Practices of a Healthy Church: Biblical Strategies for Vibrant Church Life and Ministry* (P&R, 1999). Dr. Meek's current book project is *Contours of Covenant Epistemology: Con-*

1110

versations on the Way to Knowing. Her revised dissertation has been accepted by Paternoster for publication as *Contact with Reality: Polanyi's Realism and Its Value for Christian Faith.*

Dr. Meek serves on the boards of the Polanyi Society and Aliquippa Impact Ministries. She is the mother of three grown daughters.

K. Scott Oliphint (MAR, PhD, Westminster Theological Seminary) is professor of apologetics and systematic theology at Westminster Theological Seminary in Philadelphia. Before moving to Westminster in 1991, he was in pastoral ministry in Texas. He is the author of *The Battle Belongs to the Lord: The Power of Scripture for Defending Our Faith* (P&R, 2003), *Reasons for Faith: Philosophy in the Service of Theology* (P&R, 2006), and coauthor, with Rod Mays, of *Things That Cannot Be Shaken: Holding Fast to Your Faith in a Relativistic World* (Crossway, 2008).

Scott is married to Peggy and they have three children, Jared, Joel (and his wife, Kate), and Bonnie, and one grandson, Liam.

J. I. Packer (MA, DPhil, Oxford) is Board of Governors professor of theology at Regent College, Vancouver, Canada, where he has taught since 1979. Previously, he taught at Tyndale Hall, Bristol (1955–61), and Trinity College, Bristol (1970–79), England. He is an ordained Anglican minister. The author of a number of books on the Christian life, Dr. Packer currently campaigns for the restoration of catechesis as an all-age discipline for Christian churches.

Dr. Packer has a daughter and two grandsons in England, and a son and daughter who came with him and his wife to Canada.

Franklin E. (Ed) Payne, MD, served on the faculty at the Medical College of Georgia in Augusta, Georgia, for twenty-five years, retiring from there as associate professor of family medicine in 2000. He then worked for five years in the Emergency Department at Fort Gordon, Georgia, retiring from there in 2006. In 1980, he began writing in the field of medical ethics, cofounding a journal, two newsletters, and a Web site (www.bmei.org), and producing six books and numerous articles and lectures for various Christian and secular organizations. In 2007, Dr. Payne expanded the same principles of medical ethics into another Web site (www.biblicalworld view21.org) and the book *God Confronts Culture: The Almost Complete Biblical and Christian Worldview.*

Dr. Payne is married to Jeanne, and together they have four children and ten grandchildren.

Joshua Perez (MDiv, Trinity Evangelical Divinity School; PhD, Drew University) is associate professor of theology at Nyack College, New York City Campus. He previously taught at Palm Beach Atlantic University in West Palm Beach, Florida (2003–4), Biola University in La Mirada, California (2004–6) and Lynn University in Boca Raton, Florida (2006–7). He also teaches on a regular basis at Alliance Theological Seminary. His courses include the areas of systematic theology, worldview, hermeneutics, and Christian ethics.

Dr. Pérez is involved in theological education in a number of Spanish-speaking countries. He has lectured on systematic theology and related disciplines in Cuba, Colombia, and Argentina. In addition, he served as an assistant pastor for eight and a half years with the Christian & Missionary Alliance in a Spanish-speaking congregation.

Josué is married to Johanna, and they are very thankful to the Lord for the wonderful gift of their newborn son, Daniel Josué, born in August 2008.

David Powlison (MDiv, Westminster Theological Seminary; PhD, University of Pennsylvania) teaches biblical counseling at the Christian Counseling & Educational Foundation (CCEF), and serves as adjunct professor of practical theology at Westminster Theological Seminary and at Southern Baptist Theological Seminary. He has edited CCEF's *Journal of Biblical Counseling* since 1992. His writings include *Power Encounters* (Baker, 1995), *Seeing with New Eyes* (P&R, 2003), *Speaking Truth in Love* (Punch Press, 2005), and numerous articles on practical Christian living and on the relationship between Christian faith and the modern psychologies.

David and Nan married in 1977, and they enjoy three grown children, a son-in-law and daughter-in-law, and one granddaughter. Other simple pleasures include body surfing, reading Patrick O'Brian, Mark Helprin, and Marilynne Robinson, and walking in beautiful places.

Vern Sheridan Poythress (BS, California Institute of Technology; PhD, Harvard University; ThM, MDiv, Westminster Theological Seminary; MLitt, University of Cambridge; ThD, University of Stellenbosch) is professor of New Testament interpretation at Westminster Theological Seminary Philadelphia, where he has taught for thirty years. He teaches Paul's letters, the Gospels, the book of Revelation, topics of systematic theology, and hermeneutics.

Dr. Poythress has a particular interest in interpretive principles, based on his background in linguistics and apologetics. He has also taught linguistics at the University of Oklahoma, and has published books on Christian philosophy of science, theological method, dispensationalism, biblical law, hermeneutics, Bible translation, and the book of Revelation. Dr. Poythress is a minister in the Presbyterian Church in America.

Vern is married to Diane, and they have two children, Ransom and Justin. His side interests include science fiction, string figures, volleyball, and computers.

Richard L. Pratt Jr. (ThD, Harvard University) is the founder and president of Third Millennium Ministries (www.thirdmill.org), a nonprofit electronic publishing house dedicated to bringing multimedia, seminary-level education to church leaders who serve in areas of the world where such training is often not available. Third Mill, as the ministry is commonly known, publishes and distributes free multilingual, multimedia, digital seminary curriculum in a variety of languages.

Dr. Pratt chaired the Old Testament Department at Reformed Theological Seminary in Jackson, Mississippi, and Orlando, Florida, for twenty-one years. In addition, he has served as the general editor for the *Spirit of the Reformation Study Bible* (Zondervan, 2003). Dr. Pratt's books include *Every Thought Captive* (P&R, 1979), *Pray with Your Eyes Open* (P&R, 1987), *Designed for Dignity* (P&R, 1993), and *He Gave Us Stories* (P&R, 1993). In 1998, he was the Old Testament historical consultant for *The Prince of Egypt*, the Stephen Spielberg/DreamWorks animated story of Moses.

P. Andrew Sandlin (MA, University of South Africa; STD, Edinburg Theological Seminary), an ordained minister in the Fellowship of Mere Christianity, is president of the Center for Cultural Leadership, preacher at Church of the King–Santa Cruz, theological consultant for ACT 3 Ministries, and De Yong distinguished visiting professor of culture and theology for Edinburg Theological Seminary. He has written or edited several monographs and books, most recently, *Dead Orthodoxy or Living Heresy?* (Kerygma

Press, 2008) and *The Birthday of the King* (Center for Cultural Leadership, 2008). He has also written hundreds of essays and articles, both scholarly and popular.

Andrew and his wife, Sharon, have five adult children and two grandchildren. The Sandlins live in Lake Don Pedro and in Mount Hermon, California.

Steve R. Scrivener (BA, London University; DipTh, London Reformed Baptist Seminary) has been the pastor of Coley Park Baptist Church, Reading, England, since 1998. Before that he worked in the business side of the aerospace and simulation industries.

Steve and his wife, Yvette, have three children. He likes to go walking and enjoys practicing his teenage hobby—doing conjuring shows for children.

Scotty Smith (MAR, Westminster Theological Seminary) is the founding pastor of Christ Community Church in Franklin, Tennessee, which he planted in 1986. He continues to serve there as pastor of preaching, teaching, and worship. Scotty is ordained in the PCA, and also serves as an adjunct professor of practical theology at Covenant Theological Seminary in St. Louis, Missouri, and at Reformed Theological Seminary in Orlando, Florida.

He is the author of five books: *Unveiled Hope*, with Michael Card (Nelson, 1997); *Speechless*, with Steven Curtis Chapman (Zondervan, 1999); *Objects of His Affection* (Howard, 2001); *The Reign of Grace* (Howard, 2003); and *Restoring Broken Things*, also written with Steven Curtis Chapman (Integrity, 2005).

Scotty and Darlene, his wife of thirty-seven years, have two adult married children, both of whom live in the Nashville, Tennessee, area. Scotty enjoys flyfishing, cross training, all kinds of music, and cooking.

Justin Taylor is editorial director at Crossway Books & Bibles in Wheaton, Illinois, where he was managing editor of the award-winning *ESV Study Bible*. Before this, he served as director of theological education at Desiring God in Minneapolis under John Piper. He has served as a general editor for several collections of essays, including *Suffering and the Sovereignty of God*, *Reclaiming the Center*, *The Supremacy of Christ in a Postmodern World*, *Sex and the Supremacy of Christ*, *A God-Entranced Vision of All Things*,

1114

Stand, and *The Power of Words and the Wonder of God.* In addition, he has helped to edit two new editions of works by John Owen: *Overcoming Sin and Temptation* and *Communion with the Triune God.*

Mr. Taylor is an elder at Grace Community Bible Church and blogs daily at "Between Two Worlds." He and his wife have three children.

Derek Thomas (MDiv, Reformed Theological Seminary; PhD, University of Wales, Lampeter) is John E. Richards professor of systematic and practical theology at Reformed Theological Seminary, Jackson, Mississippi, and the editorial director of the Alliance of Confessing Evangelicals. He is an ordained minister in the Presbyterian Church in America and serves as the minister of teaching at historic First Presbyterian Church, Jackson. Before his move to RTS Jackson in 1996, Dr. Thomas was the pastor of Stranmillis Evangelical Presbyterian Church in Belfast, Northern Ireland, for seventeen years.

Dr. Thomas has seventeen books in print. These include commentaries on Isaiah, Ezekiel, and Job in the Evangelical Press's Made Simple Series, and a study of Calvin's theological understanding of the book of Job.

Derek and his wife, Rosemary, have two grown children, one of whom resides in Jackson and the other with her husband and daughter in Scotland. Dr. Thomas's other interests include the music of Bruckner, Mahler, Shostakovich, and Wagner.

Joseph Emmanuel Torres (MA, Reformed Theological Seminary) is adjunct professor of theology and Bible at Nyack College, New York City campus. His research interests include biblical theology, apologetics, worldview studies, and the interface between Reformed theology and postmodernism.

Currently, Joseph resides in the Bronx, in New York City, with his wife, Jessica. He loves coffeehouses, blogging, and reading the occasional comic book, and has a borderline obsession with pugs.

Tim J. R. Trumper (PhD, University of Edinburgh) is senior minister of Seventh Reformed Church, Grand Rapids, Michigan. Previously he taught systematic theology at Westminster Theological Seminary Philadelphia, and has pastored in southeast Pennsylvania.

Dr. Trumper is an author, twice-weekly radio broadcaster, and panelist for TCT Ministries' internationally broadcast *Ask the Pastor* program. His

1115

scholarly interests include the recovery of the Fatherhood of God and our adoption as sons, the renewal of Westminster Calvinism, the advocacy of expository preaching, and ministry in the postmodern era. He is a member of the Evangelical Theological Society and the World Reformed Fellowship.

Jeffery J. Ventrella (BME, University of Northern Colorado; JD, University of California, Hastings College of the Law) is senior vice president of strategic training for the Alliance Defense Fund (ADF). He has been an ordained servant in the Christian Reformed Church and the Orthodox Presbyterian Church, and has served as adjunct faculty for two Reformed seminaries, teaching ethics and apologetics. In addition to his current ADF duties, Mr. Ventrella is a Research Fellow for the Constitutional Law and Philosophy of Law Department in the University of the Free State, South Africa.

No longer litigating, Mr. Ventrella focuses his professional energies on training Christian attorneys and law students to strategically engage and transform the legal culture under the lordship of Christ. He has debated and lectured extensively throughout the U.S. as well as in Hong Kong, Europe, and South Africa. His professional writings have appeared in both scholarly and popular publications, and he has edited, contributed to, or written six books, including *The Cathedral Builder: Pursuing Cultural Beauty* (American Vision, 2007).

Mr. Ventrella is married to Heather, and together they triperspectivally enjoy their four sons, Jefferson, Chandler, Kirklan, and Jackson, and one daughter, McKenzie.

Roger Wagner (MDiv, Westminster Theological Seminary, Philadelphia; DMin, Westminster Seminary, California) is an ordained minister of the Orthodox Presbyterian Church (1973). He has been serving as pastor of Bayview Orthodox Presbyterian Church in Chula Vista, California, since 1983. He previously served a congregation of the OPC in Sonora, California.

Throughout his ministry at Bayview Church, Dr. Wagner has been active on the board and faculty of Covenant Christian School, where he has taught biblical studies, systematic theology, ethics, and apologetics. Since 2004, he and members of his congregation have conducted evangelistic outreaches to the Czech Republic in connection with a church plant in a southern suburb of Prague.

Dr. Wagner is the author of several chapters on the church in *Back to Basics: Rediscovering the Richness of the Reformed Faith* (P&R, 1996) and a study of apostolic preaching in *Acts, Tongues Aflame: Learning to Preach from the Apostles* (Christian Focus/Mentor, 2004).

He and his wife, Sherry, have three children and five grandchildren.

Bruce K. Waltke (ThD, Dallas Theological Seminary; PhD, Harvard University; DLitt, Houghton College) is a preeminent Old Testament scholar. His teaching appointments at Dallas Theological Seminary, Regent College, Westminster Theological Seminary, and currently Reformed Theological Seminary in Orlando, Florida, have earned him a reputation as a master teacher with a pastoral heart.

In addition to serving on the translation committees of the NIV and TNIV and as editor of the *Spirit of the Reformation Study Bible* (Zondervan, 2003), Dr. Waltke has written commentaries on Genesis, Proverbs, and Micah. His latest publication, *An Old Testament Theology: An Exegetical, Canonical and Thematic Approach* (Zondervan, 2007) earned the Christian Book Award in 2007.

Luder G. Whitlock Jr. is a graduate of the University of Florida, Westminster Theological Seminary, and Vanderbilt University. He currently serves as president of Excelsis (formerly the Foundation for Reformation) and Teleios, which produces state-of-the-art e-learning and distance-learning materials. In 1975, following nearly ten years in pastoral ministry, Dr. Whitlock joined the faculty of Reformed Theological Seminary (RTS), where he also served as president for twenty-three years. Under his leadership, RTS grew from a small regional school to one of the largest and most innovative seminaries in North America, with multiple campuses in the U.S. and gateway extension programs in Asia, South America, and Europe.

Dr. Whitlock's commitment to higher education, worldwide evangelism, and interdenominational cooperation is evident in his service on and leadership of the boards of numerous national and international organizations. He has also consulted with, taught at, and served in an advisory capacity for many colleges, seminaries, and other institutions. Most recently he was executive director of The Trinity Forum, for which he is now a Senior Fellow.

Dr. Whitlock served as executive director of *The New Geneva Study Bible* (Nelson, 1995) and a major revision, published as the *Spirit of the Ref-*

ormation Study Bible (Zondervan, 2003), and was on the advisory board for the English Standard Version of the Bible. He is the author of *The Spiritual Quest: Pursuing Christian Maturity* (Baker, 2000) and has contributed to many other volumes and periodicals.

Dr. Whitlock and his wife, Mary Lou, have been married for forty-nine years and have three children and eleven grandchildren.